Marc T. Pily
1994

Labor and Employment Law

The Series in Business Law

SECOND EDITION

Labor and Employment Law

Patrick J. Cihon
Syracuse University

James O. Castagnera
Saul, Ewing, Remick & Saul

Wadsworth Publishing Company
Belmont, California

A division of Wadsworth, Inc.

Sponsoring Editor: Al Bruckner
Assistant Editor: Susan Gay
Production Editor: Abigail M. Heim
Interior Designer: Julie Gecha
Cover Designer: Jean Hammond
Composition: Graphic Composition, Inc.
Manufacturing Coordinator: Marcia Locke
Cover Printer: John P. Pow Company, Inc.
Text Printer and Binder: Arcata Graphics Corporation/Halliday Lithograph

PWS-KENT Publishing Company is a division of Wadsworth, Inc.

Printed in the United States of America

2   3   4   5   6   7   8   9—97   96   95   94   93

 This book is printed on acid-free, recycled paper.

Library of Congress Cataloging-in-Publication Data

Cihon, Patrick J.
    Labor and employment law / Patrick J. Cihon, James O. Castagnera.
  —2nd ed.
      p. cm.—(The Kent series in business law)
    Includes indexes.
    ISBN 0–534–92816–1
     1. Labor laws and legislation—United States. I. Castagnera, James.
  II. Title. III. Series.
KF3319.C54 1993
344.73′01—dc20
[347.3041]   92–17500
                                            CIP

Preface

Purpose and Organization

While this book is about law, specifically about labor relations law and employment law, it is a "law book" it is designed for use by nonlawyers. Although the primary audience for this book is students in industrial relations programs or in business schools, the book also will be useful to anyone seeking to learn about labor and employment law in the United States.

The law is a dynamic phenomenon, always evolving, much like a living organism—with new cases and statutes, like living cells, replacing their older predecessors—so that the living law of today has many features similar to those of its past and yet is remarkably changed and different, too. This observation applies to no other area of the law better than it applies to labor and employment. The last few decades have witnessed the passage of Title VII of the 1964 Civil Rights Act, the Civil Rights Act of 1991, the Age Discrimination in Employment Act, the Occupation Safety and Health Act, the Americans with Disabilities Act of 1990, and a comprehensive pension law at the federal level. Most of our fifty states have responded to the Congressional invitation by passing analogous antidiscrimination and prosafety legislation. The courts, too, have joined in revolutionizing the law of the workplace by narrowing the employment-at-will doctrine and permitting employee-plaintiffs to plead heretofore unknown causes of action, such as breach of the employer's duty of good faith and fair dealing.

In contrast to the dynamic nature of the law, the available books in the labor field have been somewhat static and slow to catch up with developments in the field. When we first set out to write this book, we surveyed all the major works on the subject. While each in its present form has made room for a nodding acquaintance with Title VII, OSHA, and the like, none has given these laws the space commensurate with their significance.

One of the two authors of this text is a practicing labor lawyer. He has observed that, while thirty years ago his older colleagues devoted perhaps 90 percent of their practice to labor relations (contract negotiations, strikes, unfair labor practices, and grievance arbitrations), today these matters consume no more than half of the labor lawyer's time. The other half is taken up with discrimination charges, wrongful termination suits, and related litigation, along with healthy doses of problems involving job safety, pension, wage and hour laws, and other social legislation directed to the work environment.

This book acknowledges these changes in the labor and employment field by covering all these areas of employment law, making it a unique entrant in its field. Ten full chapters are devoted to the National Labor Relations Act and similar legislation governing the union/employer relationship, which remains the central core of labor law in this country. An additional nine chapters survey the complex terrain of intermeshing federal and state employment laws that surround this core. The result, we are convinced, is to give the reader a grasp of labor and employment law in its totality that heretofore was unavailable between the covers of any single book.

Another aspect of this book that we feel distinguishes it from its competitors is its treatment of cases. The cases are in somewhat longer edited versions than are those offered in most other books. In this sense the book emulates law school texts, although it clearly remains a business book in its presentation of substantial textual material. Our purpose is to immerse the reader in legal reasoning and analysis to a greater depth than do most books, so that a more sophisticated insight into this reasoning process can be gained. The case extracts, including dissents and/or concurring opinions, allow the reader to experience the fact that law develops from the resolution—or at least the accommodation—of differing views.

We believe that this exposure to differing opinions and positions, as well as the immersion in the legal reasoning process, will prove valuable to those who may become involved in collective bargaining, arbitration, Equal Employment Opportunity Commission conciliation, and other quasi-legal aspects of employee relations. In no other area of the law are nonlawyer professionals exposed to such legal regulation, and in no other area do these professionals experience the need for "lawyerlike" skills to the extent that personnel directors and industrial relations specialists do. The industrial relations professional is often required to represent the employer in arbitration, in the negotiation and drafting of collective bargaining agreements and other employment contracts, in drafting employee handbooks and policies, and in representing the employer before unemployment claims referees. While this book will not provide the reader with the substantive skills of negotiating, drafting, or advocacy that such situations may demand, it will develop the skills of legal reasoning and analysis which are vital for successful performance in such situations.

Changes in the Second Edition

In the time since the first edition of *Labor and Employment Law* was published, we have had the benefit of comments from colleagues who have used the book for their classes, as well as our own experience using the book. Armed with the wisdom gained from such experiences and comments, and with the insights of various reviewers and our editors, we have undertaken a second edition.

The 1980s were not the best of years for organized labor: in 1980, 20.9 percent of the nation's workforce was unionized; by 1989, only 16.4 percent was unionized. The percentage of the workforce in labor unions has continually declined since the mid-1950s, and is now lower than at any time since World War II. The increased international economic competition faced by U.S. firms, the decline of the manufacturing sector and the rise of the service economy, the indifference (or hostility) of the Reagan and Bush administrations toward organized labor, an aggressiveness on the part of management (displayed, for instance, by the willingness of Caterpillar to challenge the United Auto Workers), and other factors all contributed to the apparent decline of the labor movement. But while labor may have reached its nadir, it is not yet defunct—unions within the traditional manufacturing sector have retained their viability. In addition, unions have had several recent "victories" in highly publicized disputes such as the Pittson Coal strike. Unions will continue to play a significant role in certain segments of the American labor market, so that traditional "labor law" will continue to be a topic of importance to business and industry.

Concurrent with the decline of the labor movement, there has been a corresponding increase in legal activity in the employment area. Employment discrimination law continues to evolve, with the flurry of recent U.S. Supreme Court decisions and the Congressional attempts to restrict or reverse those decisions. The passage of the Americans with Disabilities Act adds another dimension to the law of employment discrimination; and the emphasis on drug testing in the workplace has raised various legal problems. The state courts continue to refine the law of unjust dismissal, restricting the employment-at-will principle even further. As we move through the 1990s, it is likely that the importance of employment law will continue to increase.

In revising this book for its second edition, we have been conscious of the trends of both labor law and employment law. We have maintained the focus on traditional labor relations law, which still accounts for a significant portion of this book. But we have also increased both the scope and the depth of the coverage of employment law issues to reflect their increasing importance. We have included recent court and NLRB decisions, with special emphasis on decisions of the U.S. Supreme Court; and we have attempted to include the latest legislation from Congress. We plan to include even more up-to-date cases and legislation in the *Instructor's Manual.*

A Note to the Instructor

The comprehensive coverage and treatment that this book gives labor relations and employment law enables it to be used in any of several courses. The first part, which covers the National Labor Relations Act and related labor relations statutes and issues, can form the basis for a traditional labor law course. The chapters dealing with Equal Employment Opportunity legislation and issues offer a depth of treatment and breadth of scope that can, with only minor supplementing, form the basis of a one-term course in EEO law. When the EEO chapters are coupled with the chapters on employment law issues, the resulting material provides a solid basis for an employment law course. Lastly, of course, the entire text is ideal for either a one- or a two-term course in labor and employment law.

A Note to the Student

This book is designed for use by management or industrial relations students, but it is unique in its treatment and presentation of cases. Such cases—whether National Labor Relations Board or court decisions—and the various statutes form the framework within which all labor relations and personnel management activity takes place. You need to become familiar with the provisions of relevant statues; for that reason we have included a number of important labor and employment law statutes in the appendix section, which is an integral part of the book.

Reading Cases

You will be required to read and understand cases in order to understand and analyze the legal decisions forming the basis of the law. A case is a bit like a parable or a fable. It presents a set of facts and events that led the two opposing parties into a conflict requiring resolution by the court or agency. The judge or adjudicator is guided by legal principles (which are developed from statutes or prior cases) in the resolution of the dispute between the parties. There may be two competing legal principles—such as the employer's right to manage its affairs and the union's right to bargain about changes in working conditions—that must be reconciled or accommodated. The case is a self-contained record of the resolution of the dispute between the parties, but it is also an incremental step in the process of developing legal principles for resolution of future disputes.

It is the legal principles—their reconciliation and development—and the reasoning process involved that justify the inclusion of the cases we have selected. The critical task of the reader, therefore, is to sift through the facts of a case and to identify the legal principles underlying that case.

In analyzing a case you may find it helpful to ask, after reading the case, "Why was this particular case included at this point in the chapter? What does this case add to the textual material immediately preceding it?"

For some cases, the answer will be that the case helps illustrate and explain a significant and perhaps difficult concept, such as the duty to bargain in good faith. Or perhaps the case demonstrates the limits of, or some important exception to, a general principle or rule of labor law.

In analyzing the cases, especially the longer ones, you may find it helpful to "brief" them. This simply means to make an outline. This outline can take any form that you find, with experience and experimentation, is most useful. A commonly used outline in law schools is the following:

- Case Name and Citation
  - □ Include the court or agency deciding the case.
  - □ Include the citation, which tells where to find the reported decision.
- Key Facts (in brief)
  - □ Indicate *why* the parties are before the court or agency.
  - □ Indicate *what* the parties are seeking.
  - □ Indicate the *stage* in the legal process (i.e., Trial Court, NLRB, Appeals Court, etc.).
  - □ Relate *what happened at the prior stages* (if any) in the legal process.
- Legal Issue(s)
  - □ Include the *legal problem(s)* raised by the facts of the dispute.

- Holding(s)
  - □ Record *how* the court or agency resolves the issue(s) in the dispute.
- Reasoning of the Decision-Maker
  - □ Indicate *why* the dispute was resolved the way it was.
  - □ Indicate how the decision-maker *applied* or *reconciled* the legal principles involved.

The Case Problems

One of the features that we feel distinguish this book is the set of case problems at the end of each chapter. These are real problems drawn from real cases. Sometimes our presentation of the facts is simplified to focus on a key issue or to stimulate discussion and analysis in a certain direction. Try analyzing the problems yourself; review the text if you can't identify the underlying principles and issues. Then, if the actual cases are available on campus, look them up, observe how they differ from our simplified presentation, and consider how the court, commission, or board actually ruled. This exercise, although demanding, will reinforce your understanding and round out your mastery of each chapter's subject matter.

A Note on Citations

The numbers and initials appearing after the names of cases mentioned or included within the text are called citations. The citations refer to the volume number and report series in which the decision in the case is printed. The citations tell where to find the case decision in the law library. We have attempted to provide citations for the cases included, or referred to, in the text. For the edited cases, the citation is given under the title of the case. For cases referred to in the text, the citation is given in parentheses following the case name. In editing the cases used in Chapter One, we have included the citations for cases mentioned in the court's decisions, to offer you a sense of how often and in what ways such citations are utilized; in subsequent chapters we have omitted these internal citations. If you are interested in researching those cases cited in the court opinions, use the citation for the edited court opinion to find the unedited version in a law library; from the unedited version the citations for the cases referred to in the opinion can be found.

Acknowledgments

The authors wish to thank the many people who contributed to the completion of this book, including Professor Malcolm Myers, for his contributions to early drafts; Cheryl Brown, Bette Wills, Gloria Burhyte, Sheila Forsyth, Valerie White, Peter Hunt, and Matthew McCabe, for help with the manuscript; and our wives, Joanne Castagnera-Kane and Nancy Cihon, for their support and assistance.

We also would like to thank all those who have contributed to the preparation and production of this second edition. In particular, we wish to acknowledge the contribution and assistance of our editors at PWS-KENT Publishing Company. We are also grateful to Susan (Sue Bee) Dean for her efforts in the preparation of the manuscript.

We wish to thank the following reviewers of the first edition: Dawn Alexander-Bennett (University of North Florida), Robert Allen (University of Wyoming), Curtiss Behrens (Northern Illinois University), Jan Duffy (California Polytechnic State University), Tom Gossman (Western Michigan University), Charles Hollon (Shippensburg University of Pennsylvania), Lynda Skelton (Georgia Southern College), and George Spiro (University of Massachusetts, Amherst). In addition, we would like to thank the reviewers whose helpful comments and suggestions were used during preparation of this second edition:

Curtiss K. Behrens
Northern Illinois University

Frank J. Cavaliere
Lamar University

Anne Draznin
Sangamon State University

Bruce Elder
University of Nebraska at Kearney

Lastly, the authors wish to rededicate the book to the memory of their fathers, John E. Cihon and James Ottavio Castagnera.

Patrick J. Cihon
Law and Public Policy Department
Syracuse University

James O. Castagnera
Labor Lawyer
Saul, Ewing, Remick & Saul

Brief Contents

CHAPTER **16**   Occupational Safety and Health   **441**

CHAPTER **17**   Employee Retirement Income Security Act: ERISA   **461**

CHAPTER **18**   The Fair Labor Standards Act   **487**

CHAPTER **19**   Employee Welfare Programs: Social Security, Workers' Compensation,
                   and Unemployment Compensation   **522**

APPENDIX **A**   Text of the National Labor Relations Act   **553**

APPENDIX **B**   Text of the Labor Management Relations Act   **567**

APPENDIX **C**   Text of the Labor-Management Reporting and Disclosure Act of 1959   **578**

APPENDIX **D**   Text of the Civil Rights Act of 1964   **595**

APPENDIX **E**   Text of Title 42 U.S.C. Section 1981   **611**

APPENDIX **F**   Extracts from the Age Discrimination in Employment Act   **613**

                   Glossary   **625**

                   Index of Cases   **631**

                   Index of Subjects   **635**

Contents

CHAPTER 5

The Unionization Process   87

CHAPTER 6

Unfair Labor Practices by Employers and Unions   109

CHAPTER 7

Collective Bargaining: The Duty to Bargain in Good Faith   150

CHAPTER 8

Picketing, Strikes, and Boycotts: The Legality of Pressure Tactics   181

PART THREE Employment Law Issues 439

Labor and Employment Law

Labor Relations Law

C H A P T E R 1

Common-Law Employment Issues

ON THE EUROPEAN CONTINENT codification of the law is a tradition that can be traced from the Roman emperors Julius Caesar and Justinian, through the Code of Napoleon, to the present. By contrast, in the British Isles the common law developed primarily in an ad hoc fashion, as the decisions and opinions of various judges gradually were recorded and collected together. These published precedents were then consulted by succeeding judges; the principle of *stare decisis* prescribed that the rules and holdings of the earlier cases be followed going forward. This pattern of development applied to labor and employment law, albeit some statutory labor law can be traced back to the reign of Elizabeth I or even earlier.

The common (court-created) law has been both praised and criticized across the centuries. The English philosopher Jeremy Bentham likened it to "dog law." He explained that the way you teach a dog not to soil your carpet is to wait until he does it, then hit him on the head with a newspaper. Similarly, he argued, judges announce the rule of law that will control the case after the hapless defendant has already done the deed. But Bentham not withstanding, many commentators and legal philosophers cherish the common law for its fairness and flexibility. Today much of American labor and employment law is grounded in federal and state statutes, as well as numerous local ordinances (especially in major cities). But the common law still plays an important part in our employment relations.

Despite the enactment of such linchpin labor laws as the National Labor Relations Act (NLRA, which will be the focus of Chapters 2–11), the courts continue to play a crucial role as the final interpreters of such statutes, so that it accurately may be said that the NLRA, for example, has a huge body of common law built upon it. Consequently, you will encounter many cases sprinkled throughout this text, many being the leading decisions of the U.S. Supreme Court on critical questions of statutory interpretation.

In this opening chapter your introduction to the common law of labor and employment is a survey of several major areas of the law where the court is still, by and large, king. These include employment at will and wrongful discharge, defamation, and invasion of privacy.

Employment at Will

To appreciate how far the courts have come, we need to look back at where they were only a few decades ago. A century ago virtually every state court subscribed to the doctrine of **employment at will**. That doctrine in its raw form holds that an employee who has not been hired for an express period of time (say a year) can be fired at any time for any reason—or for no reason at all.

State and federal laws have narrowed this sweeping doctrine in many ways. The NLRA forbids firing employees for engaging in protected concerted activities. Title VII forbids discharge on the basis of race, color, gender, creed, or national origin. The Age Discrimination in Employment Act (ADEA) protects older workers from discriminatory discharge. Occupational Safety and Health Act (OSHA) makes it illegal to fire an employee in retaliation for filing a safety complaint.

Although employers may complain that employment regulation is pervasive, the fact is that these laws leave broad areas of discretion for private sector employers[1] to discharge at-will employees. Except in a few states and cities that have adopted ordinances to the contrary, the law allows an employer to discharge homosexuals and transvestites if the company does not approve of such sexual preferences. Whistleblowers—employees who bring intraorganizational wrongdoing to the attention of the authorities—have often been fired for their trouble. A few states have now addressed this issue. Sometimes employees get fired simply because the boss does not like them. In such situations, none of these employees is covered by any of the federal and state labor laws previously discussed. Should they be protected? If so, how?

Advocates of the employment-at-will doctrine defend it by pointing out that (1) the employee is likewise free to sever the working relationship at any time, and (2) in a free market, the worker with sufficient bargaining power can demand an employment contract for a set period of time if so desired. The trouble with the second point, in the view of most workers, is that as individuals they lack the bargaining power to command such a deal. That is one reason why even today almost one worker in five belongs to a union.

The first of these arguments is not so easily dismissed. If the employee is free to quit at any time with or without notice, why should the employer be denied the same discretion in discharging employees? One answer to this troublesome question—an answer given by a majority of the state courts at this time—is, "The firing of an at-will employee may not be permitted if the discharge undermines an important public policy."

Wrongful Discharge Based on Public Policy

The most commonly adopted exception to the pure employment-at-will rule (the employee can be fired at any time for any reason) is the public policy exception. If a statute creates a right or a duty for the employee, he or she may not be fired for

---

[1]Bear in mind that public employees enjoy constitutional rights, such as due process of law, that the Bill of Rights and the various state constitutions generally do not extend to private sector employees.

exercising that legal right or fulfilling that legal duty. A widely adopted example is jury duty—the courts of most states agree that an employer cannot fire an employee who misses work to serve on a jury (provided, of course, that the employee gives proper notice).

Many courts accepting this exception, however, have kept it narrow by holding that the right or duty must be clearly spelled out by statute. For instance, in *Geary* v. *United States Steel* (1974), the Pennsylvania Supreme Court upheld the dismissal of a lawsuit brought by a salesman who was fired for refusing to sell what he insisted to management was an unsafe product. The court noted, "There is no suggestion that he possessed any expert qualifications or that his duties extended to making judgments in matters of product safety." Most courts applying *Geary* have required the plaintiff-employee to point to some precise statutory right or duty before ruling the discharge wrongful.

Additionally, if the statute itself provides the employee with a cause of action, the courts are reluctant to recognize an alternative remedy in the form of a lawsuit for wrongful discharge. Thus, several Pennsylvania courts agree that an employee fired on the basis of gender or race discrimination in Pennsylvania has as his or her exclusive state law remedy the Pennsylvania Human Relations Act (PHRA), which requires that the employee initially seek redress with the commission created by that act. If the employee fails to file with the commission, thus losing the right of action under the PHRA, that person cannot come into court with the same grievance claiming wrongful discharge. Since the first edition of this text was published three years ago, other states' courts have reached similar conclusions regarding their states' antidiscrimination laws.

Perhaps it is Pennsylvania that has demonstrated most recently a strong reluctance to depart from the ancient and time-tested rule of employment at will. In the 1970s the Pennsylvania Supreme Court published dicta in one or two of its decisions that seemed to suggest that the tort of wrongful discharge was about to blossom in that commonwealth's common law. Taking their lead from this dicta, the federal district courts and the U.S. Court of Appeals for the Third Circuit, sitting in Pennsylvania, took the lead in developing and shaping this cause of action. Then, perhaps to these federal judges' dismay, in 1990 the high court of Pennsylvania issued an opinion that virtually took these legal developments back to square one.

PAUL v. LANKENAU HOSPITAL

569 A.2d 346 (Supreme Court of Pennsylvania, 1990)
Pa. LEXIS 54

PAPADAKOS, J.

This case causes us to review once again our jurisprudence on the subject of employment at-will in Pennsylvania.

Appellee, Dr. Pavle Paul, is a Yugoslavian physician who emigrated to the United States where he was employed by Appellant, Lankenau Hospital, from 1962 until his resignation on August 20, 1980. Dr. Paul sued the hospital for compensatory damages based on his claims that the hospital was estopped from discharging him for removing five refrigerators, allegedly without permission, and that such discharge caused him to be defamed. In his suit before a jury against Lankenau Hospital, he claims further that he was forced to resign because of false charges stemming from his removal of the five refrigerators from Lankenau, even though he insists he had authorization to take them.

The record shows that during his length tenure at the hospital, Dr. Paul had removed numerous items from the hospital's storage, mainly discarded medical equipment, which he would sell for profit or send to Yugoslavia. It is uncontested that material taken previously was with permission, and the only concern of this case is with the taking of the five refrigerators. At all times, Dr. Paul has maintained that he was given oral approval by a storeroom manager to transport the refrigerators. On August 20, 1980, nevertheless, he was asked to sign the letter of resignation on the grounds that he had taken the refrigerators without proper authorization....

In his suit, Dr. Paul raised nine complaints in Torts and Contracts. The trial court granted a non-suit on all counts of the Complaint excepting Count IV, estoppel and detrimental reliance, which was permitted to go to the jury with four special interrogatories:

1. Do you find that plaintiff Pavle Paul had permission from David D'Urbanis to take the refrigerators from Lankenau Hospital?
2. Do you find that it was reasonable for plaintiff to rely on permission from David D'Urbanis to take the refrigerators from Lankenau Hospital and that plaintiff fully satisfied any duty that he may have had to inquire whether the refrigerators were of no further use to the hospital?
3. Do you find that defendant Lankenau Hospital acted reasonably and believed in good faith that plaintiff Pavle Paul had taken the refrigerators without permission?
4. Do you find that plaintiff Pavle Paul resigned voluntarily from his employment at Lankenau Hospital?

The jury answered all four interrogatories in favor of Dr. Paul....

Then proceeding to the damages phase of trail, the jury awarded Dr. Paul the sum of $410,000, representing loss of all future earnings. President Judge Richard S. Lowe, however, remitted the award to $128,000, the amount Appellee would have earned from the time of his resignation to the date of the jury verdict.

Both parties filled post-trial motions. Lankenau insisted that it was entitled to a judgment not withstanding the verdict or a new trial on the grounds that estoppel is not a legal exception to the power of termination under an employment-at-will status and the issue should not have

gone to the jury. Dr. Paul sought removal of the non-suits. A panel of the Superior Court affirmed the decision below, and Dr. Paul filed allocatur with this Court, while the hospital asked for reargument. When reargument was granted, Dr. Paul withdrew his allocatur petition.

The Superior Court en banc affirmed both the estoppel decision as to Count IV of the Complaint, as well as the non-suits on the remaining counts, excepting Count VIII, defamation. On the defamation claim, the Superior Court concluded that dismissal of an innocent employee on an allegation of theft can support a cause of action for defamation and on the facts of this case, the jury should have been allowed to decide the matter.

The instant appeal derives solely from Lankenau's efforts to reverse the Superior Court on those two issues. As part of its estoppel argument, Lankenau also claims that damages under an at-will employment status should be limited to one year's wages.

A. The Estoppel Issue

We are urged by Appellee and amicus to read our controlling case, *Geary* v. *United States Steel,* 456 Pa. 171, 319 A.2d 174 (1974), as a breakthrough in the recognition of some restrictions on the doctrine of employment at-will. Also see, Comment, The Role of Federal Courts in Changing State Law: The Employment At Will Doctrine in Pennsylvania, 133 U.Pa.L.Rev. 227, 249 (1984), which concluded that "*Geary* was among the first five cases in the country to admit even the possibility of an exception to the doctrine of employment at will."

Geary involved a discharge based on an employee's report to his superiors concerning the unsafe nature of the steel pipe being manufactured and sold by the company. The majority in a 4–3 decision held that while some exceptions to the at-will employment doctrine might exist, especially in public policy areas, "this case does not require us to define in comprehensive fashion the perimeters of this privilege, and we decline to do so." 319 A.2d at 180. Moreover:

> The Pennsylvania law is in accordance with the weight of authority elsewhere. Absent a statutory or contractual provision to the contrary, the law has taken for granted the power of either party to terminate an employment relationship for any or no reason. This power of termination is explicitly recognized in the Restatement of Torts, @ 762, Privilege of Selecting Persons for Business Relations. 319 A.2d at 176 [footnotes omitted]. . . .

The Court specifically answered in the negative to the

central question of "whether the time has come to impose judicial restraints on an employer's power of discharge." 319 A.2d at 176.

Our most recent reaffirmation of *Geary* is *Clay* v. *Advanced Computer Applications*, Pa., 559 A.2d 917 (1989), in which Mr. Justice Flaherty wrote:

> It should be noted that, as a general rule, there is no common law cause of action against an employer for termination of an at-will employment relationship. *Geary* v. *United States Steel Corp.*, 456 Pa. 171, 319 A.2d 174 (1974). Exceptions to this rule have been recognized in only the most limited of circumstances, where discharges of at-will employees would threaten clear mandates of public policy. 559 A.2d at 918.

Also, see Mr. Chief Justice Nix's concurring statement that "this Court did not announce a cause of action for wrongful discharge in *Geary*. Indeed the language in *Geary* clearly states that a cause of action for wrongful discharge in an at-will employment relationship does not exist." 559 A.2d at 923.

The *Geary-Clay* analysis is dispositive of the instant case. The doctrine of equitable estoppel is not an exception to the employment-at-will doctrine. An employee may be discharged with or without cause, and our law does not prohibit firing an employee for relying on an employer's promise. In the absence of a legally cognizable cause of action, the trial court erred in submitting the issue to the jury.

B. The Defamation Issue

The defamation issue is waived under Pa.R.C.P. No. 227.1 (b)(2): (b) Post-trial relief may not be granted unless the grounds therefor, (2) are specified in the motion. The motion shall state how the grounds were asserted in pre-trial proceedings or at trial. Grounds not specified are deemed waived unless leave is granted upon cause shown to specify additional grounds. . . .

We hold that the grounds for review of the defamation claim were not properly preserved, and there was no basis upon which the Superior Court could have granted review. See, Wiegand, 337 A.2d at 257–258. . . .

But other courts, in wrongful discharge cases, are becoming increasingly willing to liberally construe statutory provisions to find public policies that are violated by the challenged discharges, especially in states in which this remains the only exception to the employment-at-will doctrine. The following case illustrates the extent to which some courts have gone in identifying a relevant public policy.

WAGENSELLER v. SCOTTSDALE MEMORIAL HOSPITAL

710 P.2d 1025 (Arizona Supreme Court, 1985)

FELDMAN, J.

Catherine Sue Wagenseller petitioned this court to review a decision of the Court of Appeals affirming in part the trial court's judgment in favor of Scottsdale Memorial Hospital and certain Hospital employees (defendants). The trial court had dismissed all causes of action on defendants' motion for summary judgment. The Court of Appeals affirmed in part and remanded, ruling that the only cause of action available to plaintiff was the claim against her supervisor, Kay Smith. . . . We granted review to consider the law of this state with regard to the employment-at-will doctrine. The issues we address are:

1. Is an employer's right to terminate an at-will employee limited by any rules which, if breached, give rise to a cause of action for wrongful termination?
2. If the "public policy" doctrine or some other doctrine does form the basis for such an action, how is it determined? . . .

Catherine Wagenseller began her employment at Scottsdale Memorial Hospital as a staff nurse in March 1975, having been personally recruited by the manager of the emergency department, Kay Smith. Wagenseller was an "at-will" employee—one hired without specific contractual term. Smith was her supervisor. In August 1978, Wagenseller was assigned to the position of ambulance charge nurse, and approximately one year later was promoted to the position of paramedic coordinator, a newly approved management position in the emergency department. Three months later, on November 1, 1979, Wagenseller was terminated.

Most of the events surrounding Wagenseller's work at the Hospital and her subsequent termination are not disputed, although the parties differ in their interpretation of the inferences to be drawn from and the significance of these events. For more than four years, Smith and Wagenseller maintained a friendly, professional, working relationship. In May 1979, they joined a group consisting largely of personnel from other hospitals for an eight-day camping and rafting trip down the Colorado River. According to Wagenseller, "an uncomfortable feeling" developed between her and Smith as the trip progressed—a feeling that Wagenseller ascribed to "the behavior that Kay Smith was displaying." Wagenseller states that this included public urination, defecation and bathing, heavy drinking, and "grouping up" with other rafters. Wagenseller did not participate in any of these activities. She also refused to join in the group's staging of a parody of the song "Moon River," which allegedly concluded with members of the group "mooning" the audience. Smith and others allegedly performed the "Moon River" skit twice at the Hospital following the group's return from the river, but Wagenseller declined to participate there as well.

Wagenseller contends that her refusal to engage in these activities caused her relationship with Smith to deteriorate and was the proximate cause of her termination. She claims that following the river trip Smith began harassing her, using abusive language and embarrassing her in the company of other staff. Other emergency department staff reported a similar marked change in Smith's behavior toward Wagenseller after the trip, although Smith denied it.

Up to the time of the river trip, Wagenseller had received consistently favorable job performance evaluations. Two months before the trip, Smith completed an annual evaluation report in which she rated Wagenseller's performance as "exceed(ing) results expected," the second highest of five possible ratings. In August and October 1979, Wagenseller met first with Smith and then with Smith's successor, Jeannie Steindorff, to discuss some problems regarding her duties as paramedic coordinator and her attitude toward the job. On November 1, 1979, following an exit interview at which Wagenseller was asked to resign and refused, she was terminated.

She appealed her dismissal in letters to her supervisor and to the Hospital administrative and personnel depart-ment, answering the Hospital's stated reasons for her termination, claiming violations of the disciplinary procedure contained in the Hospital's personnel policy manual, and requesting reinstatement and other remedies. When this appeal was denied, Wagenseller brought suit against the Hospital, its personnel administrators, and her supervisor, Kay Smith.

Wagenseller, an "at-will" employee, contends that she was fired for reasons which contravene public policy and without legitimate cause related to job performance. She claims that her termination was wrongful, and that damages are recoverable under both tort and contract theories. The Hospital argues that an "at-will" employee may be fired for cause, without cause, or for "bad" cause. We hold that in the absence of contractual provision such an employee may be fired for good cause or for no cause, but not for "bad" cause. The at-will rule has been traced to an 1877 treatise by H. G. Wood, in which he wrote:

> With us the rule is inflexible, that a general or indefinite hiring is prima facie a hiring at will, and if the servant seeks to make it out as an indefinite hiring and is determinable at the will of either party . . . H. G. Wood, Law of Master and Servant Section 134 at 273 (1877). . . .

In 1932, this court first adopted the rule for Arizona: "The general rule in regard to contracts for personal services, . . . where no time limit is provided, is that they are terminable at pleasure by either party, or at most upon reasonable notice." Thus, an employer was free to fire an employee hired for an indefinite term "for good cause," for no cause, or even for cause morally wrong, without being thereby guilty of legal wrong." . . .

In recent years there has been apparent dissatisfaction with the absolutist formulation of the common law at-will rule. . . . Today, courts in three-fifths of the states have recognized some form of a cause of action wrongful discharge.

The trend has been to modify the at-will rule by creating exceptions to its operation. Three general exceptions have developed. The most widely accepted approach is the "public policy" exception, which permits recovery upon a finding that the employer's conduct undermined some important public policy. The second exception, based on contract, requires proof of an implied-in-fact promise of employment for a specific duration, as found in the circumstances surrounding the employment relationship, including assurances of job security in company personnel manuals or memoranda. Under the third approach, courts have found in the employment contract an implied-in-law covenant of "good faith and fair dealing" and have held employers liable in both contract and tort for breach of that covenant. . . .

The public policy exception to the at-will doctrine began with a narrow rule permitting employees to sue their employers when a statute expressly prohibited their discharge. This formulation was then expanded to include any discharge in violation of a statutory expression of public policy . . . Courts later allowed a cause of action for violation of public policy, even in the absence of a specific statutory prohibition. The New Hampshire Supreme Court announced perhaps the most expansive rule when it held an employer liable for discharging an employee who refused to go out with her foreman. The court concluded that termination "motivated by bad faith or malice or based on retaliation is not [in] the best interest of the economic system or the public good and constitutes a breach of the employment contract." Although no other court has gone this far, a majority of the states have now either recognized a cause of action based on the public policy exception or have indicated their willingness to consider it, given appropriate facts. The key to an employee's claim in all of these cases is the proper definition of a public policy that has been violated by the employer's actions.

Before deciding whether to adopt the public policy exception, we first consider what kind of discharge would violate the rule. The majority of courts require, as a threshold showing, a "clear mandate" of public policy. The leading case recognizing a public policy exception to the at-will doctrine is *Palmateer v. International Harvester Co.,* which holds that an employee stated a cause of action for wrongful discharge when he claimed he was fired for supplying information to police investigating alleged criminal violations by a co-employee. Addressing the issue of what constitutes "clearly mandated public policy," the court stated:

> There is no precise definition of the term. In general, it can be said that public policy concerns what is right and just and what affects the citizens of the State collectively. It is to be found in the State's constitution and statutes and, when they are silent, in its judicial decisions. Although there is no precise line of demarcation dividing matters that are the subject of public policies from matters purely personal, a survey of cases in other States involving retaliatory discharges shows that a matter must strike at the heart of a citizen's social rights, duties, and responsibilities before the tort will be allowed [citation omitted].

Other courts have allowed a cause of action where an employee was fired for refusing to violate a specific statute. . . . Similarly, courts have found terminations improper where to do otherwise would have impinged on the employee's exercise of statutory rights or duties. . . . A division of our Court of Appeals recently adopted the public policy exception, ruling that the discharge of an at-will employee who refused to conceal a violation of Arizona's theft statute was contrary to public policy. . . .

It is difficult to justify this court's further adherence to a rule which permits an employer to fire someone for "cause morally wrong." So far as we can tell, no court faced with a termination that violated a "clear mandate of public policy" has refused to adopt the public policy exception. Certainly, a court would be hard pressed to find a rationale to hold that an employer could with impunity fire an employee who refused to commit perjury. Why should the law imply an agreement which would give the employer such power? It may be argued, of course, that our economic system functions best if employers are given wide latitude in dealing with employees. We assume that it is in the public interest that employers continue to have that freedom.

We, therefore, adopt the public policy exception to the at-will termination rule. We hold that an employer may fire for good cause or for no cause. He may not fire for bad cause—that which violates public policy. . . .

We turn then to the questions of where "public policy" may be found and how it may be recognized and articulated. As the expressions of our founders and those we have elected to our legislature, our state's constitution and statutes embody the public conscience of the people of this state. It is thus in furtherance of their interests to hold that an employer may not with impunity violate the dictates of public policy found in the provisions of our statutory and constitutional law.

We do not believe, however, that expressions of public policy are contained only in the statutory and constitutional law, nor do we believe that all statements made in either a statute or the constitution are expressions of public policy. Turning first to the identification of other sources, we note our agreement with the following:

Public policy is usually defined by the political branches of government. Something "against public policy" is something that the Legislature has forbidden. But the legislature is not the only source of such policy. In common-law jurisdictions the courts too have been sources of law, always subject to legislative correction, and with progressively less freedom as legislation occupies a given field. . . . Thus, we will look to the pronouncements of our founders, our legislature, and our courts to discern the public policy of this state.

All such pronouncements, however, will not provide the basis for a claim of wrongful discharge. Only those which have a singularly public purpose will have such force. . . .

However, some legal principles, whether statutory or decisional, have a discernible, comprehensive public purpose. A state's criminal code provides clear examples of such statutes. Thus, courts in other jurisdictions have consistently recognized a cause of action for a discharge in violation of a criminal statute.

Although we do not limit our recognition of the public policy exception to cases involving a violation of a criminal statute, we do believe that our duty will seldom be clearer than when such a violation is involved. We agree with the Illinois Supreme Court that "[t]here is no public policy more basic, nothing more implicit in the concept of ordered liberty, than the enforcement of a State's criminal code." [Citations omitted.]

In the case before us, Wagenseller refused to participate in activities which arguably would have violated our indecent exposure statute, A.R.S. Section 13–1402. She claims that she was fired because of this refusal. . . .

While this statute may not embody a policy which "strikes at the heart of a citizen's social rights, duties and responsibilities" as clearly and forcefully as a statute prohibiting perjury, we believe that it was enacted to preserve and protect the commonly recognized sense of public privacy and decency. The statute does, therefore, recognize bodily privacy as a "citizen's social right." We disagree with the Court of Appeals' conclusion that a minor violation of the statute would not violate public policy. The nature of the act, and not its magnitude, is the issue. The legislature has already concluded that acts fitting the statutory description contravene the public policy of this state. We thus uphold this state's public policy by holding that termination for refusal to commit an act which might violate A.R.S. Section 13–1402 may provide the basis of a claim for wrongful discharge. The relevant inquiry here is not whether the alleged "mooning" incidents were either felonies or misdemeanors or constituted purely technical violations of the statutes, but whether they contravened the important public policy interests embodied in the law. The law enacted by the legislature establishes a clear policy that public exposure of one's anus or genitals is contrary to public standards of morality. We are compelled to conclude that termination of employment for refusal to participate in public exposure of one's buttocks is a termination contrary to the policy of this state, even if, for instance, the employer might have grounds to believe that all of the onlookers were voyeurs and would not be offended. In this situation, there might be no crime, but there would be a violation of public policy to compel the employee to do an act ordinarily proscribed by the law.

From a theoretical standpoint, we emphasize that the "public policy exception" which we adopt does not require the court to make a new contract for the parties. In an at-will situation, the parties have made no express agreement regarding the duration of employment or the grounds for discharge. The common law has presumed that in so doing the parties have intended to allow termination at any time, with or without good cause. It might be more properly argued that the law has recognized an implied covenant to that effect. Whether it be presumption or implied contractual covenant, we do not disturb it. We simply do not raise a presumption or imply a covenant that would require an employee to do that which public policy forbids or refrain from doing that which it commands.

Thus, in an at-will hiring we continue to recognize the presumption or to imply the covenant of termination at the pleasure of either party, whether with or without cause. Firing for bad cause—one against public policy articulated by constitutional, statutory, or decisional law—is not a right inherent in the at-will contract, or in any other contract, even if expressly provided. . . .

The trial court granted summary judgment against Wagenseller on the court alleging the tort of wrongful discharge in violation of public policy. [We] adopt the "public policy" exception to the at-will termination rule and hold that the trial court erred in granting judgment against plaintiff on this theory. On remand plaintiff will be entitled to a jury trial if she can make a prima facie showing that her termination was caused by her refusal to perform some act contrary to public policy, or her performance of some act which, as a matter of public policy, she had a right to do. The obverse, however, is that mere dispute over an issue involving a question of public policy is not equivalent to establishing causation as a matter of law and will not automatically entitle plaintiff to judgment. In the face of conflicting evidence or inferences as to the actual reason for termination, the question of causation will be a question of fact. . . .

The decision of the Court of Appeals is vacated and the case remanded to the trial court for proceedings not inconsistent with this opinion. So ordered.

Express and Implied Contracts of Employment

Some employees have express contracts of employment, usually for a definite duration. Others fall within the coverage of a collective bargaining agreement negotiated for them by their union. Most workers, however, either have no express agreement as to the term of their employment, or were given an oral promise of a fixed term in a state in which the statute of frauds requires that contracts for performance extending for a year or more be written. Such employees sometimes try to convince the courts that they have been given implied promises that take them outside the ranks of their at-will co-workers. An **express contract** has terms spelled out by the parties, usually in writing. **Implied contracts** are contracts that the courts infer from the behavior of the parties, or that are implied by law.

If a company provides its employees with a personnel handbook, and that handbook says that employees will be fired only for certain enumerated infractions of work rules, or that the firm will follow certain procedures in disciplining them, a worker may later argue that the manual formed part of his or her employment contract with the firm. An increasing number of state and federal courts agree.

A few courts go further and find in the common law the basis for an implied covenant of good faith and fair dealing. According to these courts, an employee at will can no longer be fired for any reason, but only for **just cause.** Presumably what constitutes "just cause" will be defined case by case. The following case involves the questions of whether a personnel handbook is enforceable as part of the employment contract, and whether the employment contract contains a covenant of good faith and fair dealing.

PINE RIVER STATE BANK v. METTILLE

115 L.R.R.M. 4493 (Minnesota Supreme Court, 1983)

SIMONETT, J.

An employee hired for an indefinite, at-will term claims his discharge was in breach of his employment contract as subsequently modified by an employee handbook. A jury awarded the employee damages and the employer appeals from a denial of its post-trial motions.

In early 1978 respondent Richard Mettille, then unemployed, nearly 48 years of age, married and living in St. Paul, sent his resume to the appellant Pine River State Bank. After an interview, the bank offered Mettille a job at a salary of $1,000 a month or $12,000 a year. Mettille accepted, moved to Pine River, and started work as a loan officer on April 10, 1978. The employment agreement was entirely oral. Nothing was said as to the position being permanent or for any specific term. Mettille conceded that he felt free

to leave the bank and to take a better job elsewhere if he wished to do so.

Mettille survived his 6-month probationary period and was shortly given the title of loan officer. His duties were to lend, procure insurance on loan collateral, file UCC financing statements, and prepare reports on student loans.

Late in 1978 the bank distributed to its employees, including Mettille, a printed Employee Handbook. The handbook had been drafted by the bank's president, E. A. Griffith, who relied heavily on a model handbook he had received at a recent seminar on employee relations sponsored by the Minnesota Bankers Association. The handbook contained information on the bank's employment policies, including such matters as working hours, time off, vacations, and sick leave. With respect to employee responsibilities, the handbook discussed such matters as punctuality, confidentiality of the work, personal appearance and conduct, and telephone courtesy. The handbook also contained sections on "job security" and "disciplinary policy." According to Griffith, the handbook was intended as a source of information for employees on bank procedures and as a guideline within the bank so that people would know when vacations would be available and how many days the employees would be allowed for vacations. Griffith testified that he never intended the handbook to become part of an employee's employment contract with the bank.

In April 1979 Mettille received his annual performance review and with it a 7 percent raise. Apparently, about this time he also took out a home improvement loan with the bank. The following September state bank officials conducted an unannounced examination of the Pine River State Bank, and after reviewing the loan portfolio, reported to Griffith that some "technical exceptions" existed, i.e., failures to comply with the applicable law and regulations. Griffith then ordered his own independent review of the 85 files noted in the examiner's report. This investigation disclosed that 58 of the 85 files contained "serious" technical exceptions and that Mettille was responsible for the serious technical exceptions in 57 of the 58 files. Characterization of these deficiencies as "serious" was made by the bank officers, because those errors created possible loss to the bank. They testified that the defective files involved loans totaling over $600,000.

Mettille was home ill at the time of the audit by the bank examiners and the subsequent review of the files by the bank. On September 28, 1979, Mettille returned to work. The president called Mettille into his office and fired him. The parties at this time did not review the list of technical exceptions. The disciplinary procedures outlined in the handbook were not followed, nor was the handbook even mentioned. Mettille was given 2 months' severance pay.

The reason for Mettille's dismissal and whether that dismissal was for good cause were sharply contested. The bank claimed that the only reason given for the dismissal was the existence of loan errors, although excessive sick leave and a reduction in force were also factors. Mettille alleged that he was fired because of a personality dispute with his superiors. He argued that no problems were discovered in the course of previous bank examinations, that the exceptions in the 1979 audit were correctable and, in fact, were corrected within a month after he was fired. He disputed that the exceptions were "serious." There was also testimony that Mettille had never received any reprimands or complaints as to his performance prior to September 1979 and that he was loyal and "tried hard." At the time of trial Mettille was still unemployed.

In November 1980 the bank sued Mettille on two notes on which he was in default. Mettille counterclaimed, alleging that the bank had breached his contract of employment by dismissing him without cause and in violation of required disciplinary procedures. The case was tried in January 1982 and the jury found: (1) that the parties had a contract under which the defendant could not be terminated without good cause; (2) that the bank terminated Mettille without good cause; and (3) that Mettille sustained damages of $27,675. The trial judge deducted from the damages award the amount owed on the notes and ordered judgment in favor of Mettille and against the bank for $24,141.07. Both parties moved for a new trial. The bank's main argument was that Mettille's employment contract was at-will and that it was free to terminate him as it did. Mettille argued that he should have been permitted to show mental anguish to recover more damages. The trial judge denied both motions. Only the bank appeals.

The issues may be broadly stated: (1) Can a personnel handbook, distributed after employment begins, become part of an employee's contract of employment? (2) If so, are job security provisions in the handbook enforceable when the contract is of indefinite duration? and (3) In this case, was the employee's summary dismissal without following the job termination procedures of the handbook a breach of contract by the employer?

Whether a handbook can become part of the employment contract raises such issues of contract formation as offer and acceptance and consideration. We need first, however, to describe the Pine River State Bank's handbook. It contains, as we have said, statements on a variety of the bank's employment practices or policies, ranging from vacations and sick leave to personal conduct and appearance. Our inquiry here, however, concerns only the job security provisions. A section entitled "Performance Review" provides for at least an annual review of the employee's work. Another section entitled "Job Security" speaks in general, laudatory terms about the stability of jobs in banking. The key section, central to this case, is entitled "Disciplinary Policy." This section provides for what appears to be a three-stage procedure consisting of reprimands for the first and second "offense" and thereafter suspension or discharge, but discharge only "for an employee whose conduct does not improve as a result of the previous action taken." The section concludes with the sentence, "In no instance will a person be discharged from employment without a review of the facts by the Executive Officer."

Generally speaking, a promise of employment on particular terms of unspecified duration, if in form an offer, and if accepted by the employee, may create a binding unilateral contract. The offer must be definite in form and must be communicated to the offeree. Whether a proposal is meant to be an offer for a unilateral contract is determined by the outward manifestations of the parties, not by their subjective intentions. An employer's general statements of policy are not more than that and do not meet the contractual requirements for an offer.

If the handbook language constitutes an offer, and the offer has been communicated by dissemination of the handbook to the employee, the next question is whether there has been an acceptance of the offer and consideration furnished for its enforceability. In the case of unilateral contracts for employment, where an at-will employee retains employment with knowledge of new or changed conditions, the new or changed conditions may become a contractual obligation. In this manner, an original employment contract may be modified or replaced by a subsequent unilateral contract. The employee's retention of employment constitutes acceptance of the offer of a unilateral contract; by continuing to stay on the job, although free to leave, the employee supplies the necessary consideration for the offer.

An employer's offer of a unilateral contract may very well appear in a personnel handbook as the employer's response to the practical problem of transactional costs. Given these costs, an employer, such as the bank here, may prefer not to write a separate contract with each individual employee. By preparing and distributing its handbook, the employer chooses, in essence, either to implement or modify its existing contracts with all employees covered by the handbook. Further, we do not think that applying the unilateral contract doctrine to personnel handbooks unduly circumscribes the employer's discretion. Unilateral contract modification of the employment contract may be a repetitive process. Language in the handbook itself may reserve discretion to the employer in certain matters or reserve the right to amend or modify the handbook provisions.

We conclude, therefore, that personnel handbook provisions, if they meet the requirements for formation of a unilateral contract, may become enforceable as part of the original employment contract.

The next issue is whether handbook provisions relating to job security require special treatment, i.e., whether they are an exception to the general rule just discussed. Put more precisely, the question is whether, in an at-will hiring, the job security provisions in a subsequently adopted employee handbook are enforceable. On this issue, the courts are split, and our own case law is unclear.

Where the hiring is for an indefinite term, as in this case, the employment is said to be "at will." This means that the employer can summarily dismiss the employee for any reason or no reason, and that the employee, on the other hand, is under no obligation to remain on the job. Nor will a claim by the employee that he or she was promised "permanent" or "lifetime" employment change the at-will nature of the hiring, at least not in the absence of some kind of additional consideration supplied by the employee which is uncharacteristic of the employment relationship itself.

Here the employee does not claim, nor could he, that he was promised "permanent" employment. The law is hesitant to impose this burdensome obligation of an employer in the absence of an explicit promise to that effect. Instead, the respondent employee is claiming that his job termination was wrongful because the job security provisions set out in the employee handbook were not followed. The appellant bank, relying on the "at-will" doctrine as expressed in our cases argues that without additional consideration, the job security provisions are not enforceable. Other cases cited by the bank hold that job termination restrictions, even if part of a contract for an indefinite duration from the outset, can never be enforceable. We need, therefore, to examine the three reasons given for the unenforceability of job termination restrictions in an employment contract of indefinite duration: (1) the at-will rule takes precedence over any such restrictions; (2) the restrictions ordinarily lack the requisite additional consideration; and (3) mutuality of obligation is missing.

The first argument, that because the contract specifies no duration the parties did not intend any job termination restrictions to be binding, is without merit. The argument misconstrues the at-will rule, which is only a rule of contract construction, as a rule imposing substantive limits to the formation of a contract. The general rule is that contracts for a specified duration can nonetheless be terminated during the period of the contract if the employer has good cause. When a contract is for an indefinite duration, the duration is not set, and a corollary is that either party may then terminate it at any time for any reason. Further, if the contract purports to establish "permanent employment," this will be interpreted as a contract for an indefinite period, and hence also at-will.

The cases which reason that the at-will rule takes precedence over even explicit job termination restraints, simply because the contract is of indefinite duration, misapply the at-will rule of construction as a rule of substantive limitation on contract formation. It should not be necessary for an employee to prove a contract is of "permanent" employment or for a specified term in order to avoid summary dismissal if the parties have agreed otherwise. There is no reason why the at-will presumption needs to be construed as a limit on the parties' freedom to contract. If the parties choose to provide in their employment contract of an indefinite duration for provisions of job security, they should be able to do so.

The second argument against enforceability is, at first glance, more troublesome in view of our case law. The argument is that a provision for job security in a contract of indefinite duration, whether initially promised or subsequently added, is not binding without additional, independent considerations other than services to be performed. Where the "permanent" employment is purchased with additional consideration, we have better reason to believe that the parties, in discussing "permanent" employment, were referring to lifetime employment and were not, instead, simply making a distinction between temporary or seasonal employment and employment which is steady or continuing although nevertheless terminable at will.

To say that job security provision in a contract of indefinite duration is never enforceable without additional consideration is to misconstrue the additional consideration exception. The requirement of additional consideration, like the at-will rule itself, is more a rule of construction than of substance, and it does not preclude the parties, if they make clear their intent to do so, from agreeing that the employment will not be terminable by the employer except pursuant to their agreement, even though no consideration other than services to be performed is expected by the employer or promised by the employee. While language in some of our cases may suggest otherwise, our discussion of additional, independent consideration . . . was primarily in the context of the employee attempting to avoid a discharge without cause by proving (albeit unsuccessfully in those cases) "lifetime" or "permanent" employment. But none of our cases purport to hold that additional, independent consideration is the exclusive means for creating an enforceable job security provision in a contract of indefinite duration. Handbook provisions relating to such matters as bonuses, severance pay and commission rates are enforced without the need for additional new consideration beyond the services to be performed. We see no reason why the same may not be true for job security provisions. Thus, the consideration here for the job security provision is Mettille's continued performance despite his freedom to leave. As such, the job security provisions are enforceable.

Finally, the third argument is that job security provisions lack enforceability because mutuality of obligation is lacking. Since under a contract of indefinite duration the employee remains free to go elsewhere, why should the employer be bound to its promise not to terminate unless for cause or unless certain procedures are followed? The demand for mutuality of obligation, although appealing in its symmetry, is simply a species of the forbidden inquiry into the adequacy of consideration an inquiry in which this court has, by and large, refused to engage. We see no merit in the lack of mutuality argument. . . . [T]he concept of mutuality in contract law has been widely discredited and the right of one party to terminate a contract at will does not invalidate the contract.

To summarize, we do not find the reasons advanced for the unenforceability of job security provisions in an at-will hiring to be persuasive. We hold, therefore, that where an employment contract is for an indefinite duration, such indefiniteness by itself does not preclude handbook provisions on job security from being enforceable, whether they are proffered at the time of the original hiring or later, when the parties have agreed to be bound thereby.

Not every utterance of an employer is binding. It remains true that "the employer's prerogative to make independent, good faith judgments about employees is important in our free enterprise system." Properly applied, we think that the unilateral contract modification analysis appropriately accommodates the interests of the employee and the employer.

We now apply the principles discussed in the first two sections to the Pine River State Bank's handbook. First of all, it should be noted that this is a breach of contract case; we are determining if there was a contract, what were its terms, and was it breached. We are not dealing with a discharge that is retaliatory, in bad faith or abusive. Nor do we have before us the question, suggested by the employee here, whether public policy should constrain an "at-will" firing.

We do not think that the language in the handbook section entitled "Job Security" constitutes any offer. It is no more than a general statement of policy. The provisions of the handbook section entitled "Disciplinary Policy" do, however, set out in definite language an offer of a unilateral contract for procedures to be followed in job termination. The handbook states that "[i]f an employee has violated a company policy, the following procedure will apply." This offer was communicated to the employees, including respondent. Mettille's continued performance of his duties despite his freedom to quit constitutes an acceptance of the bank's offer and affords the necessary consideration for that offer, with the bank gaining the advantages of a more stable and, presumably, more productive work force. Here the jury could find, as it did, that the handbook provisions on disciplinary procedures had become part of respondent Mettille's employment contract, thus restricting the bank's right to terminate Mettille at will.

But in what way do the handbook procedures restrict the bank's right to discharge Mettille at will? Although the disciplinary procedures were admittedly not followed, the trial court apparently construed the handbook to allow summary dismissal for good cause. The jury was asked, in the verdict form, to find if Mettille's dismissal had been "without good cause," and, in instructions to the jury, the jury was told (apparently without objection) that good cause consisted of a breach of the standards of job performance established and uniformly applied by the bank. Whether, assuming a good cause requirement, this was a proper definition of good cause has not been made an issue, and we need not decide it. Nor need we decide if summary dismissal for good cause can be implied or inferred in Mettille's contract or, on the other hand, if summary good cause termination is precluded by the handbook, since the

issues were not raised and, in any event, are mooted by the jury's finding of lack of good cause.

It is enough for disposition of this case that the disciplinary provision was applicable and enforceable, and that it was not followed. The bank's only excuse for not following the disciplinary procedures was that it did not have to do so, since Mettille was an "at-will" employee. This argument is without merit, since we have found the procedures to be contractually binding. Had the procedural disciplinary steps been honored, Mettille might have corrected his deficiencies to the bank's satisfaction and have kept his job. The bank did not assert otherwise and there was evidence that the loan file deficiencies were rather easily correctable and that Mettille was amenable to correction. Therefore, we hold that as a matter of law the bank breached its employment contract with Mettille by not affording him the job termination procedures of its handbook, resulting in Mettille's unemployment. . . . **Affirmed.**

But surprisingly, the state that pioneered the development of the common law of wrongful discharge—California—may now be embarking on the process of leading the American common law back from the abyss of proliferating employee lawsuits. During the late 1970s and early 1980s, the California courts were crammed with cases, as creative plaintiffs' attorneys tested the "outer envelope" of judicial tolerance for exotic theories of liability based on their clients' allegations of bad faith dealing by their former and current employers. Some juries gleefully awarded huge verdicts. Finally, an outcry from the defense bar, the business community, and members of the judicial bench led the California Supreme Court to reexamine the state's common law of wrongful discharge, paying particular attention to what damages should be available to the successful employee-litigant. The result was a retrenchment that, though not so dramatic as Pennsylvania's in *Paul* v. *Lankenau Hospital* (described earlier in the chapter), may prove to be more significant because of the California courts' historic role as a leader in setting American common-law trends.

FOLEY v. INTERACTIVE DATA CORP.

47 Cal. 3d 654; 765 P. 2d 373
(Supreme Court of California, 1988)

LUCAS, C. J.

After Interactive Data Corporation (defendant) fired plaintiff Daniel D. Foley, an executive employee, he filed this ac-

tion seeking compensatory and punitive damages for wrongful discharge. In his second amended complaint, plaintiff asserted three distinct theories: (1) a tort cause of action alleging a discharge in violation of public policy (*Tameny* v. *Atlantic Richfield Co.* (1980) 27 Cal.3d 167 [1 IER Cases 102]). (2) a contract cause of action for breach of an implied-in-fact promise to discharge for good cause only (e.g., *Pugh* v. *See's Candies, Inc.* (1981) 116 Cal.App.3d 311 [115 LRRM 4002] [all references are to this case rather than the 1988 post-trial decision appearing at 203 Cal.App.3d 743 [3 IER Cases 945]), and (3) a cause of action alleging a tortious breach of the implied covenant of good faith and fair dealing (e.g., *Cleary* v. *American Airlines, Inc.* (1980) 111 Cal.App.3d 443 [1 IER Cases 122]). The trial court sustained a demurrer without leave to amend, and entered judgment for defendant.

The Court of Appeal affirmed on the grounds (1) plaintiff alleged no statutorily based breach of public policy sufficient to state a cause of action pursuant to *Tameny;* (2) plaintiff's claim for breach of the covenant to discharge only for good cause was barred by the statute of frauds; and (3) plaintiff's cause of action based on breach of the covenant of good faith and fair dealing failed because it did not allege necessary longevity of employment or express formal procedures for termination of employees. We granted review to consider each of the Court of Appeal's conclusions.

We will hold that the Court of Appeals properly found that plaintiff's particular *Tameny* cause of action could not proceed; plaintiff failed to allege facts showing a violation of a fundamental public policy. We will also conclude, however, that plaintiff has sufficiently alleged a breach of an "oral" or "implied-in-fact" contract, and that the statute of frauds does not bar his claim so that he may pursue his action in this regard. Finally, we will hold that the covenant of good faith and fair dealing applies to employment contracts and that breach of the covenant may give rise to contract but not tort damages.

Facts

Because this appeal arose from a judgment entered after the trial court sustained defendant's demurrer, "we must, under established principles, assume the truth of all properly pleaded material allegations of the complaint in evaluating the validity" of the decision below. (*Tameny* v. *Atlantic Richfield Co.,* supra. 27 Cal.3d 167, 170 [1 IER Cases 102]; *Alcorn* v. *Anbro Engineering, Inc.* (1970) 2 Cal.3d 493, 496 [2 FEP Cases 712].)

According to the complaint, plaintiff is a former employee of defendant, a wholly owned subsidiary of Chase Manhattan Bank that markets computer-based decision-support services. Defendant hired plaintiff in June 1976 as an assistant product manager at a starting salary of $18,500. As a condition of employment defendant required plaintiff

to sign a "Confidential and Proprietary Information Agreement" whereby he promised not to engage in certain competition with defendant for one year after the termination of his employment for any reason. The agreement also contained a "Disclosure and Assignment of Information" provision that obliged plaintiff to disclose to defendant all computer-related information known to him, including any innovations, inventions or developments pertaining to the computer field for a period of one year following his termination. Finally, the agreement imposed on plaintiff a continuing obligation to assign to defendant all rights to his computer-related inventions or innovations for one year following termination. It did not state any limitation on the grounds for which plaintiff's employment could be terminated.

Over the next six years and nine months, plaintiff received a steady series of salary increases, promotions, bonuses, awards and superior performance evaluations. In 1979 defendant named him consultant manager of the year and in 1981 promoted him to branch manager of its Los Angeles office. His annual salary rose to $56,164 and he received an additional $6,762 merit bonus two days before his discharge in March 1983. He alleges defendant's officers made repeated oral assurances of job security so long as his performance remained adequate.

Plaintiff also alleged that during his employment, defendant maintained written "Termination Guidelines" that set forth express grounds for discharge and a mandatory seven-step pretermination procedure. Plaintiff understood that these guidelines applied not only to employees under plaintiff's supervision, but to him as well. On the basis of these representations, plaintiff alleged that he reasonably believed defendant would not discharge him except for good cause, and therefore he refrained from accepting or pursuing other job opportunities.

The event that led to plaintiff's discharge was a private conversation in January 1983 with his former supervisor, vice president Richard Earnest. During the previous year defendant had hired Robert Kuhne and subsequently named Kuhne to replace Earnest as plaintiff's immediate supervisor. Plaintiff learned that Kuhne was currently under investigation by the Federal Bureau of Investigation for embezzlement from his former employer, Bank of America. [Footnote omitted.] Plaintiff reported what he knew about Kuhne to Earnest, because he was "worried about working for Kuhne and having him in a supervisory position . . . , in view of Kuhne's suspected criminal conduct." Plaintiff asserted he "made this disclosure in the interest and for the benefit of his employer," allegedly because he believed that because defendant and its parent do business with the financial community on a confidential basis, the company would have a legitimate interest in knowing about a high executive's alleged prior criminal conduct.

In response, Earnest allegedly told plaintiff not to discuss "rumors" and to "forget what he heard" about Kuhne's past. In early March, Kuhne informed plaintiff that defendant had decided to replace him for "performance reasons" and that he could transfer to a position in another division in Waltham, Massachusetts. Plaintiff was told that if he did not accept a transfer, he might be demoted but not fired. One week later, in Waltham, Earnest informed plaintiff he was not doing a good job, and six days later, he notified plaintiff he could continue as branch manager if he "agreed to go on a 'performance plan.' Plaintiff asserts he agreed to consider such an arrangement." The next day, when Kuhne met with plaintiff, purportedly to present him with a written "performance plan" proposal, Kuhne instead informed plaintiff he had the choice of resigning or being fired. Kuhne offered neither a performance plan nor an option to transfer to another position. [Footnote omitted.]

Defendant demurred to all three causes of action. After plaintiff filed two amended pleadings, the trial court sustained defendant's demurrer without leave to amend and dismissed all three causes of action. The Court of Appeal affirmed the dismissal as to all three counts. We will explore each claim in turn.

I. Tortious Discharge in Contravention of Public Policy

We turn first to plaintiff's cause of action alleging he was discharged in violation of public policy. Labor Code section 2922 provides in relevant part, "An employment, having no specified term, may be terminated at the will of either party on notice to the other. . . ." This presumption may be superseded by a contract, express or implied, limiting the employer's right to discharge the employee. . . . Absent any contract, however, the employment is "at will," and the employee can be fired with or without good cause. [Footnote omitted.] But the employer's right to discharge an "at-will" employee is still subject to limits imposed by public policy, since otherwise the threat of discharge could be used to coerce employees into committing crimes, concealing wrongdoing, or taking other action harmful to the public weal. [Footnote omitted.]

Petermann v. *International Brotherhood of Teamsters*

(1959) 174 Cal.App.2d 184 [1 IER Cases 5], first stated the foregoing principle. There, the plaintiff, a union business agent, alleged he was discharged when he refused to testify falsely to a state legislative committee. The trial court granted judgment on the pleadings to defendant. The Court of Appeal found the plaintiff was an employee at will (see Lab. Code, §2922) but noted that "the right to discharge an employee under such a contract may be limited by statute [citations] or by considerations of public policy." (174 Cal.App.2d at p. 188). Overruling the trial court, the Court of Appeal declared: "It would be obnoxious to the interests of the state and contrary to public policy and sound mortality to allow an employer to discharge any employee, whether the employment be for a designated or unspecified duration, on the ground that the employee declined to commit perjury, an act specifically enjoined by statute," (Id., at pp. 188–189) [Footnote omitted].

Similarly, *Tameny* v. *Atlantic Richfield Co.,* supra. 27 Cal.3d 167, 178 [1 IER Cases 102], declared that a tort action for wrongful discharge may lie if the employer "conditions[s] employment upon required participation in unlawful conduct by the employee." In *Tameny,* the plaintiff alleged he was fired for refusing to engage in price fixing in violation of the Cartwright Act and the Sherman Antitrust Act. (Id., at p. 170.) We held the trial court erred in sustaining Atlantic Richfield's demurrer to plaintiff's tort action for wrongful discharge. Writing for the majority, Justice Tobriner concluded that "an employer's authority over its employee does not include the right to demand that the employee commit a criminal act to further its interests. . . . An employer engaging in such conduct violates a basic duty imposed by law upon all employers, and thus an employee who has suffered damages as a result of such discharge may maintain a tort action for wrongful discharge against the employer." (Id., at p. 178.) . . .

We do not decide in this case whether a tort action alleging a breach of public policy under *Tameny* may be based only on policies derived from a statute or constitutional provision or whether nonlegislative sources may provide the basis for such a claim. Even where, as here, a statutory touchstone has been asserted, we must still inquire whether the discharge is against public policy and affects a duty which inures to the benefit of the public at large rather than to a particular employer or employee. For example, many statutes simply regulate conduct between private individuals, or impose requirements whose fulfillment does not implicate fundamental public policy concerns. Regardless of whether the existence of a statutory or constitutional link is required under *Tameny,* disparagement of a basic *public* policy must be alleged, and we turn now to determining whether plaintiff has done so here.

In the present case, plaintiff alleges that defendant discharged him in "sharp derogation" of a substantial public policy that imposes a legal duty on employees to report relevant business information to management. An employee is an agent, and as such "is required to disclose to [his] principal all information he has relevant to the subject matter of the agency." (2 Witkin, Summary of Cal. Law (9th ed. 1987) Agency & Employment, §41, p. 53; see *Loughlin* v. *Idora Realty Co.* (1968) 259 Cal.App.2d 619, 629; *Jolton* v. *Minster Graf & Co.* (1942) 53 Cal.App.2d 516, 522.) Thus, plaintiff asserts, if he discovered information that might lead his employer to conclude that an employee was an embezzler, and should not be retained, plaintiff had a duty to communicate that information to his principal. [Footnote omitted.]

It is unclear whether the alleged duty is one founded in statute. No enactment expressly requires an employee to report relevant information concerning other employees to his employer, and none prohibits discharge of the employee for so doing. [Footnote omitted.] The 1872 Civil Code, however, attempted to codify the common law of master-servant relations; its provisions, now in the Labor Code, provide that "[o]ne who, for a good consideration, agrees to serve another, shall perform the service, and shall use ordinary care and diligence therein, so long as he is thus employed." (Lab. Code, §2854.) It is not clear whether the duty to communicate relevant information is subsumed under the statutory duty of ordinary care, or is a separate duty not codified by the 1872 Legislature.

Whether or not there is a statutory duty requiring an employee to report information relevant to his employer's interest, we do not find a substantial public policy prohibiting an employer from discharging an employee for performing that duty. [Footnote omitted.] Past decisions recognizing a tort action for discharge in violation of public policy seek to protect the public, by protecting the employee who refuses to commit a crime (*Tameny,* supra. 27 Cal.3d 167 [1 IER Cases 102]; *Petermann,* supra. 174 Cal.App.2d 184 [1 IER Cases 5]), who reports criminal activity to proper authorities (*Garibaldi* v. *Lucky Food Stores, Inc.* (9th Cir. 1984) 726 F.2d 1367, 1374 [1 IER Cases 354]; *Palmateer* v. *International Harvester Co.,* supra., 421 N.E.2d 876, 879–880 [115 LRRM 4165]), or who discloses other illegal, unethical, or unsafe practices (*Hentzel* v. *Singer Co.* (1982) 138 Cal. App.3d 290 [115 LRRM 4036] [working conditions hazardous to employees]). No equivalent public interest

bars the discharge or the present plaintiff. [Footnote omitted.] When the duty of an employee to disclose information to his employer serves only the private interest of the employer, the rationale underlying the *Tameny* cause of action is not implicated. [Footnote omitted.]

We concluded that the Court of Appeal properly upheld the trial court's ruling sustaining the demurrer without leave to amend to plaintiff's first cause of action.

II. Breach of Employment Contract

Plaintiff's second cause of action alleged that over the course of his nearly seven years of employment with defendant, the company's own conduct and personnel policies gave rise to an "oral contract" not to fire him without good cause. The trial court sustained a demurrer without leave to amend on two grounds: that the complaint did not state facts sufficient to give rise to such contract, and that enforcement of any such contract would be barred by the statute of frauds. The Court of Appeal affirmed, relying on the latter ground alone. We consider both grounds, discussing the statute of frauds issue first. . . .

Sufficiency of the Allegations of Oral or Implied Contract

Although plaintiff describes his cause of action as one for breach of an oral contract, he does not allege explicit words by which the parties agreed that he would not be terminated without good cause. Instead he alleges that a course of conduct, including various oral representations, created a reasonable expectation to that effect. Thus, his cause of action is more properly described as one for breach of an implied-in-fact contract. [Footnote omitted.]

As noted, the Court of Appeal did not reach the question of the sufficiency of plaintiff's allegations to state a cause of action for breach of an implied-in-fact contract term not to discharge except for good cause, because it disposed of the issue by erroneously applying the statute of frauds. Nonetheless, the court extensively criticized the reasoning of *Pugh,* supra. 116 Cal. App.3d 311 [115 LRRM 4002], stating that it "destroys the centuries-old solid and settled principle of vast and demonstrated value to employer and employee, to the world of commerce and to the public of a contract which either can terminate will." Before this court, defendant urges that we disapprove precedent permitting a cause of action for wrongful discharge founded on an implied-in-fact contract and require instead an express contract provision requiring good cause for termination, supported by independent consideration. Alternatively, defendant requests that we distinguish *Pugh* and its progeny from the present case. We conclude, however, that *Pugh* correctly applied basic contract principles in the employment context, and that these principles are applicable to plaintiff's agreement with defendant.

The plaintiff in *Pugh* had been employed by the defendant for 32 years, during which time he worked his way up the corporate ladder from dishwasher to vice president. (116 Cal.App.3d at p. 315.) When hired, he had been assured that "if you are loyal . . . and do a good job, your future is secure." (Id., at p. 317.) During his long employment, the plaintiff received numerous commendations and promotions, and no significant criticism of his work. Throughout this period the company maintained a practice of not terminating administrative personnel without good cause. On this evidence, the Court of Appeal concluded that the jury could determine the existence of an implied promise that the employer would not arbitrarily terminate the plaintiff's employment. (Id., at p. 329.) . . .

We begin by acknowledging the fundamental principle of freedom of contract: employer and employee are free to agree to a contract terminable at will or subject to limitations. Their agreement will be enforced so long as it does not violate legal strictures external to the contract, such as laws affecting union membership and activity, prohibitions on indentured servitude, or the many other legal restrictions already described which place certain restraints on the employment arrangement. As we have discussed, Labor Code section 2922 establishes a presumption of at-will employment if the parties have made no express oral or written agreement specifying the length of employment or the grounds for termination. This presumption may, however, be overcome by evidence that despite the absence of a specified term, the parties agreed that the employer's power to terminate would be limited in some way, e.g., by a requirement that termination be based only on "good cause." (*Drzewiecki* v. *H & R Block, Inc.,* supra. 24 Cal.App.3d 695, 704; *Millsap* v. *National Funding Corp.* (1943) 57 Cal.App.2d 772, 775–776.)

The absence of an express written or oral contract term concerning termination of employment does not necessarily indicate that the employment is actually intended by the parties to be "at will," because the presumption of at-will employment may be overcome by evidence of contrary intent. Generally, courts seek to enforce the actual understanding of the parties to a contract, and in so doing may inquire into the parties' conduct to determine if it demonstrates an implied contract. "It must be determined, as a

question of fact, whether the parties acted in such a manner as to provide the necessary foundation for (an implied contract), and evidence may be introduced to rebut the inferences and show that there is another explanation for the conduct." [Citation omitted.] Such implied-in-fact contract terms ordinarily stand on equal footing with express terms. (Rest.2d Contracts, supra. §§4.19.) [Footnote omitted.] At issue here is whether the foregoing principles apply to contract terms establishing employment security, so that the presumption of Labor Code section 2922 may be overcome by evidence of contrary implied terms, or whether such agreements are subject to special substantive or evidentiary limitations.

Defendant contends that courts should not enforce employment security agreements in the absence of evidence of independent consideration and an express manifestation of mutual assent. Although, as explained below, there may be some historical basis for imposing such limitations, any such basis has been eroded by the development of modern contract law and, accordingly, we conclude that defendant's suggested limitations are inappropriate in the modern employment context. We discern no basis for departing from otherwise applicable general contract principles. . . .

As the *Pugh* court explained, a rule imposing a requirement of separate consideration as a substantive limitation on an enforceable employee security agreement would be "contrary to the general contract principle that courts should not inquire into the adequacy of consideration. (See Calamari & Perillo, Contract (2d ed. 1977) §4–3, p. 136.) 'A single and undivided consideration may be bargained for and given as the agreed equivalent of one promise or of two promises or of many promises.' (1 Corbin on Contracts (1963) §125, pp. 535–536). Thus there is no analytical reason why an employee's promise to render services, or his actual rendition of services over time, may not support an employer's promise both to pay a particular wage (for example) and to refrain from arbitrary dismissal. [Citations omitted.]

The limitations on employment security terms on which defendant relies were developed during a period when courts were generally reluctant to look beyond explicit promises of the parties to a contract. "The court-imposed presumption that the employment contract is terminable at will relies upon the formalistic approach to contract interpretation predominant in late nineteenth century legal thought: manifestations of assent must be evidenced by definite, express terms if promises are to be enforceable." (Note, *Protecting At Will Employees,* supra, 93 Harv.L.Rev.

at p. 1825, fns. omitted.) In the intervening decades, however, courts increasingly demonstrated their willingness to examine the entire relationship of the parties to commercial contracts to ascertain their actual intent, and this trend has been reflected in the body of law guiding contract interpretation. [Citation omitted.] . . .

Similarly, 20 years ago, Professor Blumrosen observed that during the decades preceding his analysis, courts had demonstrated an increasing willingness to "consider the entire relationship of the parties, and to find that facts and circumstances establish a contract which cannot be terminated by the employer without cause." (Blumrosen, *Settlement of Disputes Concerning the Exercise of Employer Disciplinary Power: United States Report,* supra. 18 Rutgers L.Rev. at p. 432, fn. omitted.) "This approach has been recognized as consistent with customary interpretation techniques of commercial contracts permitting 'gap filling' by implication of reasonable terms." (Miller & Estes, *Recent Judicial Limitations on the Right to Discharge: A California Trilogy* (1982) 16 U.C. Davis L.Rev. 65. 101. fn. omitted; see also, McCarthy, Punitive Damages in Wrongful Discharge Cases (Lawpress 1985) §§3.55–3.56, pp. 206–207.)

In the employment context, factors apart from consideration and express terms may be used to ascertain the existence and content of an employment agreement, including "the personnel policies or practices of the employer, the employee's longevity of service, actions or communications by the employer reflecting assurances of continued employment, and the practices of the industry in which the employee is engaged." (*Pugh,* supra, 116 Cal.App.3d at p. 327; see Note, *Implied Contract Rights to Job Security* (1974) 26 Stan.L.Rev. 335, 350–356 [reviewing factors courts have used in implied contract analyses]). Pursuant to Labor Code section 2922, if the parties reach no express or implied agreement to the contrary, the relationship is terminable at any time without cause. But when the parties have enforceable expectations concerning either the term of employment or the grounds or manner of termination, Labor Code section 2922 does not diminish the force of such contractual or legal obligations [footnote omitted]. The presumption that an employment relationship of indefinite duration is intended to be terminable at will is therefore "subject, like any presumption, to contrary evidence. This may take the form of an agreement, express or implied, that . . . the employment relationship will continue indefinitely, pending the occurrence of some event such as the employer's dissatisfaction with the employee's services or the existence of

some 'cause' for termination." (*Pugh,* supra. 116 Cal.App.3d at pp. 324–325, fn. omitted.)

Finally, we do not agree with the Court of Appeal that employment security agreements are so inherently harmful or unfair to employers, who do not receive equivalent guarantees of continued service, as to merit treatment different from that accorded other contracts. On the contrary, employers may benefit from the increased loyalty and productivity that such agreements may inspire. (See Mauk, supra, 21 Idaho L.Rev. 201. 217.) Permitting proof of and reliance on implied-in-fact contract terms does not nullify the at-will rule, it merely treats such contracts in a manner in keeping with general contract law. (See Note, *Defining Public Policy Torts in At-Will Dismissals* (1981) 34 Stan.L.Rev. 153, 154–155 [hereafter *Defining Torts*] ["While the implied contract approach reflects a movement away from the harshness of the at-will rule, it by no means represents a rejection of the rule, since it merely allows employees to rebut more easily the presumption that their employment is terminable at will" (fn. omitted)].) We see no sound reason to exempt the employment relationship from the ordinary rules of contract interpretation which permit proof of implied terms.

Defendant's remaining argument is that even if a promise to discharge "for good cause only" could be implied in fact, the evidentiary factors outlined in *Pugh,* supra, 116 Cal.App.3d at page 329, and relied on by plaintiff, are inadequate as a matter of law. This contention fails on several grounds.

First, defendant overemphasizes the fact that plaintiff was employed for "only" six years and nine months. Length of employment is a relevant consideration but six years and nine months is sufficient time for conduct to occur on which a trier of fact could find the existence of an implied contract. [Citation omitted.] As to establishing the requisite promise, "oblique language will not, standing alone, be sufficient to establish agreement": instead, the totality of the circumstances determines the nature of the contract. Agreement may be " 'shown by the acts and conduct of the parties, interpreted in the light of the subject matter and of the surrounding circumstances.' " (*Pugh,* supra. 116 Cal.App.3d at p. 329.) Plaintiff here alleged repeated oral assurances of job security and consistent promotions, salary increases and bonuses during the term of his employment contributing to his reasonable expectation that he would not be discharged except for good cause.

Second, an allegation of breach of written "Termination Guidelines" implying self-imposed limitations on the employer's power to discharge at will may be sufficient to state a cause of action for breach of an employment contract. *Pugh,* supra, 116 Cal.App.3d 311 [115 LRRM 4002], is not alone in holding that the trier of fact can infer an agreement to limit the grounds for termination based on the employee's reasonable reliance on the company's personnel manual or policies. (See, e.g., *Robinson* v. *Hewlett-Packard Corp.* supra, 183 Cal.App.3d at 1123 [promise not to terminate without good cause demonstrated by personnel guidelines and individual performance warnings, evaluations and instructions]; *Rulon-Miller* v. *International Business Machines Corp.* (1984) 162 Cal.App.3d 241, 251 [1 IER Cases 405] [factual issue whether termination was for reasons in stated employer policies]; *Walker* vs. *Northern San Diego County Hosp. Dist.,* supra, 135 Cal.App.3d at pp. 904–905 [handbook creating right to discharge only for cause and to pretermination hearing]; *Toussaint* v. *Blue Cross & Blue Shield of Mich.,* supra, 292 N.W.2d at p. 892 [personnel manual provisions can give rise to contractual rights without showing of express mutual agreement]; *Morris* v. *Lutheran Medical Center* (Neb. 1983) 340 N.W.2d 388, 390–391 [115 LRRM 4966] [employer bound by published "Policy and Procedures"]; cf. *Hepp* v. *Lockheed-California Co.* (1978) 86 Cal.App.3d 714, 719 [unwritten but "well established" policy regulating rehiring of employees laid off for lack of work is enforceable].)

Finally, unlike the employee in *Pugh,* supra, 116 Cal.App.3d 311 [115 LRRM 4002], plaintiff alleges that he supplied the company valuable and separate consideration by signing an agreement whereby he promised not to compete or conceal any computer-related information from defendant for one year after termination. The noncompetition agreement and its attendant "Disclosure and Assignment of Proprietary Information, Inventions, etc." may be probative evidence that "it is more probable that the parties intended a continuing relationship, with limitations upon the employer's dismissal authority [because the] employee has provided some benefit to the employer, or suffers some detriment, beyond the usual rendition of service." (*Pugh,* supra, 116 Cal.App.3d at p. 326.)

In sum, plaintiff has pleaded facts which, if proved, may be sufficient for a jury to find an implied-in-fact contract limiting defendant's right to discharge him arbitrarily—facts sufficient to overcome the presumption of Labor Code section 2922. On demurrer, we must assume these facts to be true. In other words, plaintiff has pleaded an implied-in-fact contract and its breach, and is entitled to his opportunity to prove those allegations. [Footnote omitted.]

III. Breach of the Implied Covenant of Good Faith and Fair Dealing

We turn now to plaintiff's cause of action for tortious breach of the implied covenant of good faith and fair dealing. Relying on *Cleary,* supra, 111 Cal.App.3d 443 [1 IER Cases 122], and subsequent Court of Appeal cases, plaintiff asserts we should recognize tort remedies for such a breach in the context of employment termination.

The distinction between tort and contract is well grounded in common law, and divergent objectives underlie the remedies created in the two areas. Whereas contract actions are created to enforce the intentions of the parties to the agreement, tort law is primarily designed to vindicate "social policy." (Prosser, Law of Torts (4th ed. 1971) p. 613). The covenant of good faith and fair dealing was developed in the contract arena and is aimed at making effective the agreement's promises. Plaintiff asks that we find that the breach of the implied covenant in employment contracts also gives rise to an action seeking an award of tort damages.

In this instance, where an extension of tort remedies is sought for a duty whose breach previously has been compensable by contractual remedies, it is helpful to consider certain principles relevant to contract law. First, predictability about the cost of contractual relationships plays an important role in our commercial system (Putz & Klippen, *Commercial Bad Faith: Attorney Fees—Not Tort Liability—Is the Remedy for "Stonewalling"* (1987) 21 U.S.F.L.Rev. 419, 432). Moreover, "Courts traditionally have awarded damages for breach of contract to compensate the aggrieved party rather than to punish the breaching party." (Note, *"Contort": Tortious Breach of the Implied Covenant of Good Faith and Fair Dealing in Noninsurance, Commercial Contracts—Its Existence and Desirability* (1985) 60 Notre Dame L.Rev. 510, 526, & fn. 94, citing Rest. 2d Contracts, §355, com. a ["The purpose[] of awarding contract damages is to compensate the injured party"].) [Footnote omitted.] With these concepts in mind, we turn to analyze the role of the implied covenant of good faith and fair dealing and the propriety of the extension of remedies urged by plaintiff.

"Every contract imposes upon each party a duty of good faith dealing in its performance and its enforcement." [Rest.2d Contracts, §205.) This duty has been recognized in the majority of American jurisdictions, the Restatement, and the Uniform Commercial Code. (Burton, *Breach of*

Contracts and the Common Law Duty to Perform in Good Faith (1980) 94 Harv.L.Rev. 369.) Because the covenant is a contract term, however, compensation for its breach has almost always been limited to contract rather than tort remedies. As to the scope of the covenant, "[t]he precise nature and extent of the duty imposed by such an implied promise will depend on the contractual purposes." (*Egan* v. *Mutual of Omaha Ins. Co.* (1979) 24 Cal.3d 809, 818.) Initially, the concept of a duty of good faith developed in contract law as "a kind of 'safety valve' to which judges may turn to fill gaps and qualify or limit rights and duties otherwise arising under rules of law and specific contract language." (Summers, *The General Duty of Good Faith—Its Recognition and Conceptualization* (1982) 67 Cornell L.Rev. 810, 812, fn. omitted; see also Burton, supra, 94 Harv.L.Rev. 369, 371 ["the courts employ the good faith doctrine to effectuate the intentions of parties, or to protect their reasonable expectations" (fn. omitted)].) As a contract concept, breach of the duty led to imposition of contract damages determined by the nature of the breach and standard contract principles.

An exception to this general rule has developed in the context of insurance contracts where, for a variety of policy reasons, courts have held that breach of the implied covenant will provide the basis for an action in tort. California has a well-developed judicial history addressing this exception. In *Comunale* v. *Traders & General Ins. Co.* (1958) 50 Cal.2d 654, 658, we stated, "There is an implied covenant of good faith and fair dealing in every contract that neither party will do anything which will injure the right of the other to receive the benefits of the agreement." (See also *Egan* v. *Mutual of Omaha Ins. Co.,* supra, 24 Cal.3d 809, 818.) Thereafter, in *Crisci* v. *Security Ins. Co.* (1967) 66 Cal.2d 425, for the first time we permitted an insured to recover in tort for emotional damages caused by the insurer's breach of the implied covenant. We explained in *Gruenberg* v. *Aetna Ins. Co.* (1973) 9 Cal.3d 566, that "[t]he duty [to comport with the implied covenant of good faith and fair dealing] is immanent in the contract whether the company is attending [on the insured's behalf] to the claims of third persons against the insured or the claims of the insured itself. Accordingly, when the insurer unreasonably and in bad faith withholds payment of the claim of its insured, it is subject to liability in tort." (Id., at p. 575.) . . .

In our view, the underlying problem in the line of cases relied on by plaintiff lies in the decisions' uncritical incorporation of the insurance model into the employment context, without careful consideration of the fundamental poli-

cies underlying the development of tort and contract law in general or of significant differences between the insurer/insured and employer/employee relationships. [Footnote omitted.] When a court enforces the implied covenant it is in essence acting to protect "the interest in having promises performed" (Prosser, Law of Torts (4th ed. 1971), p. 613)—the traditional realm of a contract action—rather than to protect some general duty to society which the law places on an employer without regard to the substance of its contractual obligations to its employee. Thus, in *Tameny* 27 Cal.2d 167, 175–176 [1 IER Cases 102], as we have explained, the court was careful to draw a distinction between "ex delicto" and "ex contractu" obligations. (See, ante, at p.——[typed opn. at p. 11].) An allegation of breach of the implied covenant of good faith and fair dealing is an allegation of breach of an "ex contractu" obligation, namely, one arising out of the contract itself. The covenant of good faith is read into contracts in order to protect the express covenants or promises of the contract, not to protect some general public policy interest not directly tied to the contract's purposes. The insurance cases thus were a major departure from traditional principles of contract law. We must, therefore, consider with great care claims that extension of the exceptional approach taken in those cases is automatically appropriate if certain hallmarks and similarities can be adduced in another contract setting. With this emphasis on the historical purposes of the covenant of good faith and fair dealing in mind, we turn to consider the bases upon which extension of the insurance model to the employment sphere has been urged. . . .

After review of the various commentators, and independent consideration of the similarities between the two areas, we are not convinced that a "special relationship" analogous to that between insurer and insured should be deemed to exist in the usual employment relationship which would warrant recognition of a tort action for breach of the implied covenant. Even if we were to assume that the special relationship model is an appropriate one to follow in determining whether to expand tort recovery, a breach in the employment context does not place the employee in the same economic dilemma that an insured faces when an insurer in bad faith refuses to pay a claim or to accept a settlement offer within policy limits. When an insurer takes such actions, the insured cannot turn to the marketplace to find another insurance company willing to pay for the loss already incurred. The wrongfully terminated employee, on the other hand, can (and must, in order to mitigate damages [see *Parker* v. *Twentieth Century-Fox Film Corp.*

(1970) 3 Cal.3d 176, 181–182]) make reasonable efforts to seek alternative employment. (See Mauk, supra, 21 Idaho L.Rev. 201, 208.) Moreover, the role of the employer differs from that of the "quasi-public" insurance company with whom individuals contract specifically in order to obtain protection from potential specified economic harm. The employer does not similarly "sell" protection to its employees; it is not providing a public service.Nor do we find convincing the idea that the employee is necessarily seeking a different kind of financial security than those entering a typical commercial contract. If a small dealer contracts for goods from a large supplier, and those goods are vital to the small dealer's business, a breach by the supplier may have financial significance for individuals employed by the dealer or to the dealer himself. Permitting only contract damages in such a situation has ramifications no different from a similar limitation in the direct employer-employee relationship.

Finally, there is a fundamental difference between insurance and employment relationships. In the insurance relationship, the insurer's and insured's interest are financially at odds. If the insurer pays a claim, it diminishes its fiscal resources. The insured of course has paid for protection and expects to have its losses recompensed. When a claim is paid, money shifts from insurer to insured, or, if appropriate, to a third party claimant.

Putting aside already specifically barred improper motives for termination which may be based on both economic and noneconomic considerations [footnote omitted], as a general rule it is to the employer's economic benefit to retain good employees. The interests of employer and employee are most frequently in alignment. If there is a job to be done, the employer must still pay someone to do it. This is not to say that there may never be a "bad motive" for discharge not otherwise covered by law. Nevertheless, in terms of abstract employment relationships as contrasted with abstract insurance relationships, there is less inherent relevant tension between the interests of employers and employees than exists between that of insurers and insureds. Thus the need to place disincentives on an employer's conduct in addition to those already imposed by law simply does not rise to the same level as that created by the conflicting interests at stake in the insurance context. Nor is this to say that the Legislature would have no basis for affording employees additional protections. It is, however, to say that the need to extend the special relationship model in the form of judicially created relief of the kind sought here is less compelling.

We therefore conclude that the employment relationship is not sufficiently similar to that of insurer and insured to warrant judicial extension of the proposed additional tort remedies in view of the countervailing concerns about economic policy and stability, the traditional separation of tort and contract law, and finally, the numerous protections against improper terminations already afforded employees.

Our inquiry, however, does not end here. The potential effects on an individual caused by termination of employment arguably justify additional remedies for certain improper discharges. The large body of employment law restricting an employer's right to discharge based on discriminatory reasons or on the employee's exercise of legislatively conferred employee rights, indicates that the Legislature and Congress have recognized the importance of the employment relationship *and* the necessity for vindication of certain legislatively and constitutionally established public policies in the employment context. The *Tameny* cause of action likewise is responsive to similar public concerns. In the quest for expansion of remedies for discharged workers which we consider here, however, the policies sought to be vindicated have a different origin. The most frequently cited reason for the move to extend tort remedies in this context is the perception that traditional contract remedies are inadequate to compensate for certain breaches. (See, e.g., Putz & Klippen, supra. 21 U.S.F.L.Rev. at pp. 470–471; Traynor, *Bad Faith Breach of a Commercial Contract: A Comment on the Seaman's Case* (Cal. State Bar, Fall 1984) 8 Bus.L.News 1.) Others argue that the quest for additional remedies specifically for terminated workers also has its genesis in (1) comparisons drawn between the protections afforded nonunion employees and those covered by collective bargaining agreements, (2) changes in the economy which have led to displacement of middle-level management employees in "unprecedented numbers," and (3) the effect of antidiscrimination awareness and legislation that has "raised expectations and created challenges to employer decision making." [Citation omitted.]

The issue is how far courts can or should go in responding to these concerns regarding the sufficiency of compensation by departing from long established principles of contract law. Significant policy judgments affecting social policies and commercial relationships are implicated in the resolution of this question in the employment termination context. Such a determination, which has the potential to alter profoundly the nature of employment, the cost of products and services, and the availability of jobs, arguably is better suited for legislative decisionmaking. (See *Wagen-*

seller v. *Scottsdale Memorial Hospital,* supra. 710 P.2d 1025. 1040 [1 IER Cases 526]; [citation omitted]. Moreover, as we discuss, the extension of the availability of tort remedies is but one among many solutions posited to remedy the problem of adequately compensating employees for certain forms of "wrongful" termination while balancing the interests of employers in their freedom to make economically based decisions about their work force. . . . [Footnote omitted.]

As we have reiterated, the employment relationship is fundamentally contractual, and several factors combine to persuade us that in the absence of legislative direction to the contrary contractual remedies should remain the sole available relief for breaches of the implied covenant of good faith and fair dealing in the employment context. Initially, predictability of the consequences of actions related to employment contracts is important to commercial stability. [Footnote omitted.] In order to achieve such stability, it is also important that employers not be unduly deprived of discretion to dismiss an employee by the fear that doing so will give rise to potential tort recovery in every case.

Moreover, it would be difficult if not impossible to formulate a rule that would assure that only "deserving" cases give rise to tort relief. Professor Summers, in his seminal article, described the term "good faith" as used in the duty of good faith imposed in contract law and the Uniform Commercial Code [footnote omitted] as an "excluder" phrase which is "without general meaning (or meanings) of its own and serves to exclude a wide range of heterogeneous forms of bad faith. In a particular context the phrase takes on specific meaning, but usually this is only by way of contrast with the specific form of bad faith actually or hypothetically ruled out." [Citation omitted.] In a tort action based on an employee's discharge, it is highly likely that each case would involve a dispute as to material facts regarding the subjective intentions of the employer. [Footnote omitted.] As a result, these actions could rarely be disposed of at the demurrer or summary judgment stage.

Finally, and of primary significance, we believe that focus on available contract remedies offers the most appropriate method of expanding available relief for wrongful terminations. The expansion of tort remedies in the employment context has potentially enormous consequences for the stability of the business community.

We are not unmindful of the legitimate concerns of employees who fear arbitrary and improper discharges that may have a devastating effect on their economic and social status. Nor are we unaware of or unsympathetic to claims that contract remedies for breaches of contract are insuffi-

cient because they do not fully compensate due to their failure to include attorney fees and their restrictions on foreseeable damages. These defects, however, exist generally in contract situations. As discussed above, the variety of possible courses to remedy the problem is well demonstrated in the literature and include increased contract damages, provision for award of attorney fees, establishment of arbitration or other speedier and less expensive dispute resolution, or the tort remedies (the scope of which is also subject to dispute) sought by plaintiff here.

The diversity of possible solutions demonstrates the confusion that occurs when we look outside the realm of contract law in attempting to fashion remedies for a breach of a contract provision. As noted, numerous legislative provisions have imposed obligations on parties to contracts which vindicate significant social policies extraneous to the contract itself. As Justice Kaus observed in his concurring and dissenting opinion in *White* v. *Western Title Ins. Co.* (1985) 40 Cal.3d 870, 901, "our experience in *Seaman's* surely tells us that there are real problems in applying the substitute remedy of a tort recovery—with or without punitive damages—outside the insurance area. In other words, I believe that under all the circumstances, the problem is one for the Legislature."

Conclusion

Defendant may proceed with his cause of action alleging a breach of an implied-in-fact contract promise to discharge him only for good cause; his claim is not barred by the statute of frauds. His cause of action for a breach of public policy pursuant to *Tameny* was properly dismissed because the facts alleged, even if proven, would not establish a discharge in violation of public policy. Finally, as to his cause of action for tortious breach of the implied covenant of good faith and fair dealing, we hold that tort remedies are not available for breach of the implied contract to employees who allege they have been discharged in violation of the covenant. [Footnote omitted.]

Accordingly, that portion of the judgment of the Court of Appeal affirming the dismissal of plaintiff's causes of action alleging a discharge in breach of public policy and a tortious breach of the implied covenant of good faith and fair dealing is affirmed. That portion of the judgment of the Court of Appeal affirming the dismissal of the cause of action alleging an implied-in-fact contract not to discharge except for good cause is reversed, and the case is remanded for action consistent with the views expressed herein. [Footnote omitted.] **[Dissent omitted.]**

Commonly Committed Workplace Torts

Defamation and Invasion of Privacy

Legal and religious condemnations of defamation—that is, the communication of false and damaging information about someone—have been traced back at least as far as the Book of Exodus in the Bible, as well as to Roman law. By contrast, modern notions of privacy may be dated from the Industrial Revolution. In the medieval world, the dwellings of nobility and commoners alike characteristically contained a great room used for eating, sleeping, and most other domestic functions by parents, children, retainers, and guests. Marshall McLuhan, the late social critic, suggested that the proliferation of the printed word, and the creation and spread of a middle class of businesspeople and professionals, with the gift of literacy and the leisure time to enjoy it, combined to create a "consumer demand" for privacy in which to read, write, and contemplate.

Although these factors may very well have contributed to the desire for privacy, the legal argument that there existed a right of privacy that could give rise to a cause of action in a court of law can be traced to a seminal article by the future Supreme Court Justice, Brandeis, and his law partner, Warren, published in 1890. Although the law was somewhat laggard in recognizing privacy actions, today privacy and defamation actions are universally recognized.

That these torts enjoy considerable popularity in the employer-employee context is a function of our increasingly complex and heavily regulated business environment. As well, probably no technological innovation leaves many of us more nervous than the electronic computer. Computers allows firms, institutions, and agencies to amass, store, and retrieve almost unlimited amounts of data on all of us. Investigative and surveillance techniques have also become highly sophisticated. In the wake of these advances, numerous commentators have predicted the death of privacy. Particularly noteworthy is the following comment by the Privacy Protection Study Commission created by the federal Privacy Act:

> One need only glance at the dramatic changes in our country during the last hundred years to understand why the relationship between organizational record keeping and personal privacy has become an issue in almost all modern societies. The records of a hundred years ago tell us little about the average American, except when he died, perhaps when and where he was born, and if he owned land, how he got his title to it. Three quarters of the adult population worked for themselves on farms or in small towns.
> . . . Record keeping about individuals was correspondingly limited and local in nature.
> . . . The past hundred years, and particularly the last three decades, have changed all that. Three out of four Americans now live in cities or their surrounding suburbs, only one in ten of the individuals in the work force today is self-employed, and education is compulsory for every child. The yeoman farmer and small-town merchant have given way to the skilled workers and whitecollar employees who manage and staff organizations, both public and private, that keep society functioning.
> A significant consequence of this marked change in the variety and concentration of institutional relationships is that record keeping about individuals now covers almost everyone and influences everyone's life. . . .

In other words, with the great advantages that electronic technology brings to the business firm comes the necessary evil of increased likelihood and seriousness of torts of defamation and invasion of privacy, along with depersonalization and employee anxiety.

Invasion of Privacy.   An early U.S. Supreme Court case defined the right of privacy as

> [t]he right to be let alone; the right of a person to be free from unwarranted publicity.... The right of an individual (or corporation) to withhold himself and his property from public scrutiny, if he so chooses. It is said to exist only so far as its assertion is consistent with law or public policy, and in a proper case equity will interfere, if there is no remedy at law, to prevent an injury threatened by the invasion of, or infringement upon, this right from motives of curiosity, gain, or malice.

Four distinct species of the tort of invasion of privacy have emerged over the years since Brandeis and Warren set the stage for the tort's appearance:

1. intrusion upon plaintiff's seclusion or solitude or into his or her private affairs;
2. public disclosure of embarrassing private facts about the plaintiff;
3. publicity, the effect of which is to place the plaintiff in a "false light" in public;
4. appropriation of the plaintiff's name or likeness, without his or her permission, to the pecuniary advantage of the defendant.

It is important to note that although in a defamation action the publication need not be defamatory in order for liability to attach, one can readily imagine (especially in situations involving the appropriation of plaintiff's name for defendant's pecuniary gain) circumstances in which a laudatory statement is tortious.

The following case involved an alleged invasion of an employee's privacy right by an employer who had a detective agency conduct surveillance of the worker's activities at his home.

McLAIN v. BOISE CASCADE CORP.

533 P.2d 343 (Oregon Supreme Court, 1975)

McALLISTER, J.

This is a damage action in which plaintiff alleged two causes of action, one for invasion of privacy and one for civil trespass. Plaintiff demanded general and punitive damages for invasion of privacy and nominal and punitive damages for trespass. The trial court granted an involuntary nonsuit of the privacy cause of action and submitted the trespass claim to the jury after withdrawing from their consideration the claim for punitive damages. The jury returned a verdict for plaintiff for $250, being the amount prayed for as nominal damages. Plaintiff appeals.

Plaintiff was employed by Boise Cascade Corporation as a glue mixer. On May 19, 1972 he strained his back when he fell while carrying a 100 pound sack of flour to a glue machine. Plaintiff was taken to the office of Dr. D. H. Searing in Salem. Dr. Searing sent plaintiff to the hospital where he was placed in traction. On June 6, 1972, Dr. Searing wrote to Richard Cyphert, then in charge of the Boise Cascade Workmen's Compensation program, advising that plaintiff might be disabled for as much as 12 months. Dr. John D. White was called in as a consultant. He performed a myelogram on plaintiff and reported to Mr. Cyphert that he found no evidence of nerve root or lumbar disc disease and that it was possible that plaintiff was "consciously malingering." Cyphert received this letter on June 22, 1972.

On the basis of Dr. White's report Mr. Cyphert notified plaintiff his compensation payments would be terminated. At about that time Mr. Cyphert also was informed that plaintiff was performing part-time work for a mortuary while he was ostensibly disabled. On June 27, 1972 plaintiff received a written release from Dr. White permitting him to return to work with the restriction that he was not to lift more than 50 pounds. Plaintiff returned to work and was assigned an easier job, but was unable to work due to continued pain in his hip.

Plaintiff then consulted an attorney, who filed a request for a hearing with the Workmen's Compensation Board asking that plaintiff's temporary disability payments be reinstated. Mr. Cyphert received a copy of this request on July 5, 1972. On July 12, 1972 Mr. Cyphert hired the defendant United Diversified Services, Inc., to conduct a surveillance of the plaintiff to check the validity of plaintiff's claim of injury. United assigned two of its employees, Rick Oulette and Steve Collette, to conduct a surveillance. The two investigators took 18 rolls of movie film of plaintiff while he was engaged in various activities on his property outside his home. Some of the film showed plaintiff mowing his lawn, rototilling his garden and fishing from a bridge near his home.

Some of the film of plaintiff was taken from a barn behind plaintiff's house. . . . Other film was taken by Collette while plaintiff was fishing from a bridge on the Hopville Road near the northeast corner of plaintiff's property. The record is not clear as to where Mr. Collette was standing while taking that film. The remaining rolls of film were taken by Mr. Collette from a point near some walnut trees at the southeast corner of plaintiff's property.

On one occasion Collette was near the walnut trees he was seen by plaintiff. When Collette realized he had been seen he left the area. He had parked his pickup on . . . [a neighbor's] property near the southwest corner of plaintiff's tract, but abandoned the pickup when he was spotted by McLain and retrieved his truck later.

McLain did not learn about the film and picture taking until the film was shown at the Workmen's Compensation Hearing.

United's investigators did not question any of plaintiff's neighbors or friends and limited their activities to taking pictures while plaintiff was engaged in various activities outside his home. Plaintiff testified that these activities could have been viewed either by neighbors or passersby on the highway. Plaintiff further testified that he was not embarrassed or upset by anything that appeared in the films. . . .

It is now well established in Oregon that damages may be recovered for violation of privacy. . . .

The general rule permitting recovery for such intrusion is stated in Restatement of the Law of Torts 2d Section 652B (Tent. Draft No. 13, 1967) as follows:

> One who intentionally intrudes, physically or otherwise, upon the solitude or seclusion of another, or his private affairs or concerns, is subject to liability to the other for invasion of his privacy, if the intrusion would be highly offensive to a reasonable man.

It is also well established that one who seeks to recover damages for alleged injuries must expect that his claim will be investigated and he waives his right of privacy to the extent of a reasonable investigation. We quote from the Annotation, Right of Privacy—Surveillance, 13 A.L.R. 3d 1025, 1027:

> Where the surveillance, shadowing, and trailing is conducted in a reasonable manner, it has been held that owing to the social utility of exposing fraudulent claims and because of the fact that some sort of investigation is necessary to uncover fictitious injuries, an unobtrusive investigation, even though inadvertently made apparent to the person being investigated, does not constitute an actionable invasion of his privacy.

If the surveillance is conducted in a reasonable and unobtrusive manner the defendant will incur no liability for invasion of privacy.

On the other hand, if the surveillance is conducted in an unreasonable and obtrusive manner the defendant will be liable for invasion of privacy.

In this case we think the court below properly granted a nonsuit for the cause of action for invasion of privacy. In the first place, the surveillance and picture taking were done in such an unobtrusive manner that plaintiff was not aware that he was being watched and filmed. In the second place, plaintiff conceded that his activities which were filmed could have been observed by his neighbors or passersby on the road running in front of his property. Undoubtedly the investigators trespassed on plaintiff's land while watching and taking pictures of him, but it is also clear that the trespass was on the periphery of plaintiff's property and did not constitute an unreasonable surveillance "highly offensive to a reasonable man."

Plaintiff does not contend that the surveillance in this case was per se actionable. Plaintiff contends only that the surveillance became actionable when the investigators trespassed on plaintiff's property. . . . We think trespass is only one factor to be considered in determining whether the surveillance was unreasonable. . . . Trespass alone cannot automatically change an otherwise reasonable surveillance into an unreasonable one. The one trespass which was observed by plaintiff did not alert him to the fact that he was being watched or that his activities were being filmed. The record is clear that the trespass was confined to a narrow strip along the east boundary of plaintiff's property. All the surveillance in this case was done during daylight hours and when plaintiff was exposed to public view by his neighbors and passersby. . . . **The judgment is affirmed.**

Defamation.   The tort of defamation has been defined as follows:

> A communication is defamatory if it tends so to harm the reputation of another as to lower him in the estimation of the community or to deter third persons from associating or dealing with him.

Expanding on this bare-bones definition, it is said that language is defamatory

> . . . if it tends to expose another to hatred, shame, obliquy, contempt, ridicule, aversion, ostracism, degradation, or disgrace, or to induce an evil opinion of one in the minds of right-thinking persons and to deprive him of their confidence and friendly intercourse in society.

Defamation is subdivided into the torts of libel and slander, the former being defamation by writing, the latter defamation through speech. These two torts may be further divided into the libel or slander that is per se, and the libel or slander that is not per se. What makes this distinction critical in some cases is that libel/slander per se requires no showing of specific damages for the plaintiff to recover a judgment, whereas libel/slander that is not per se demands such a showing from the injured party. The term *per se* connotes that the third person to whom the defamation is communicated (and indeed the court) can recognize the damaging nature of the communication without being appraised of the contextual setting (innuendo) in which the communication was made. Professor Prosser has identified the commonly recognized forms of per se defamation as

> . . . the imputation of crime, of a loathsome disease, and those affecting the plaintiff in his business, trade, profession, office or calling. . . .

Business defamation may, thus, be defined as defamation per se having the following characteristics:

> False spoken or written words that tend to prejudice another in his business, trade, or profession are actionable without proof of special damage if they affect him in a manner that may, as a necessary consequence, or does, as a natural consequence, prevent him from deriving therefrom that pecuniary reward which probably otherwise he might have obtained.

This definition leaves the door to the courtroom wide open to the defamed employee, whose job is his or her "business, trade, or profession." Indeed, since business defamation is a per se tort, it can amount to strict liability once the plaintiff has proved that the damaging statement was published. This use of the words "strict liability" is not to say that no defenses are available. On the contrary, it is possible to identify several. First, as has already been suggested, one can dispute the contention that one published the statement, or that it is defamatory. Or one can try to prove that the statement is true. Failing these, the defendant may be able to argue successfully that the statement was made from behind the shield of a privilege.

The law recognizes some claims of absolute privilege. When Senator Proxmire made his "Golden Fleece" awards on the floor of the U.S. Senate, he was protected by an absolute privilege under the Constitution. The courts hold that remarks made during legislative proceedings enjoy absolute privilege. Other absolute privileges recognized include comments made in judicial proceedings and in communications between spouses.

The law also recognizes other, "qualified privileges." When a person is protected by qualified privilege, the remarks made will be immune from a defamation suit if the person made them in good faith. If the remarks were made with malice, or in bad faith, they will not be privileged. The law generally recognizes a qualified privilege where one person communicates with another who has a legitimate need to know the information. For example, comments concerning an employee's performance made to a supervisor, and communicated through the organizational structure, are privileged if made in good faith. As well, assessments of an employee, communicated by a former employer to a prospective employer, made in good faith, are privileged. But comments or remarks, if not made in good faith, and communicated to persons who have no legitimate need to know, are subject to a defamation action.

In the words of Professor Prosser, a defamatory statement is

> . . . in the same class with the use of explosives or the keeping of dangerous animals. If the defamatory meaning, which is false, is reasonably understood, the defendant publishes at his peril, and there is no possible defense except the narrow one of privilege.

Intentional Infliction of Emotional Distress

Under the *Restatement of Torts* (Second Edition), "one who by extreme and outrageous conduct intentionally or recklessly causes severe emotional distress to another is subject to liability for such emotional distress, and if bodily harm to the other results from it, for such bodily harm." The tort of **intentional infliction of emotional distress,** therefore, consists of four basic elements:

1. The conduct must be extreme and outrageous.
2. The conduct must be intentional, or at least, reckless.
3. It must cause emotional distress.
4. The emotional distress must be severe.

Early cases that helped develop this now widely recognized cause of action included one in which a butcher wrapped up and delivered (as a practical joke) some dead rats to a housewife, instead of the meat she had ordered! More mundane (and much more common cases) have involved bill collectors whose harassment of debtors went beyond all reasonable bounds.

The following case involves claims of both defamation and intentional infliction of emotional distress.

CHUY v. THE PHILADELPHIA EAGLES FOOTBALL CLUB

595 F.2d 1265 (U.S. Court of Appeals, 3rd Cir., 1979)

ROSENN, J.

This appeal presents several interesting questions growing out of the employment by the Philadelphia Eagles Football Club ("the Eagles") of a former professional player, Don Chuy ("Chuy"). The unexpected and unfortunate termination of Chuy's employment evoked charges by him that the Eagles had not played the game according to the rules when Chuy blew the whistle terminating his football career. . . .

Chuy joined the Eagles in 1969, having been traded from the Los Angeles Rams, another professional football club with which he had played for a half dozen years. On June 16, 1969, he met with the Eagles general manager, Palmer "Pete" Retzlaff, in Philadelphia, Pennsylvania, to negotiate a contract with the Eagles for the 1969, 1970, and 1971 football seasons. The parties concluded their negotiations by executing three National Football League (NFL) standard form player contracts on June 16, 1969, covering the 1969, 1970, and 1971 football seasons respectively at a salary of $30,000 for each season, with a $15,000 advance for the 1969 season.

The contracts each contained a standard NFL injury-benefit provision entitling a player injured in the performance of his service to his salary "for the term of his contract." Chuy sustained a serious injury to his shoulder during his first season in a game between the Eagles and the New York Giants in November, 1969. Sidelined for the remainder of the season, Chuy had to be hospitalized for most of December, 1969. During the hospitalization, his diagnosis revealed a pulmonary embolism, a blood clot in his lung, which marked the end of his professional athletic career. Following the advice of his physician, Chuy decided to retire from professional football and notified the Eagles of his intention. At the same time, Chuy requested that the Eagles pay him for the remaining two years of what he asserted was a three-year contract.

The Eagles requested that Chuy submit to a physical examination which Dr. Dick D. Harrell conducted in March, 1970. After extensive tests, Dr. Harrell concluded that Chuy suffered from an abnormal cell condition, presumably stress polycythemia, which may have predisposed him to the formation of dangerous blood clots. He therefore recommended to the Eagles that Chuy should "not be allowed to participate further in contact sports." Shortly after receiving Dr. Harrell's recommendation, General Manager Retzlaff informed Hugh Brown, a sports columnist for the Philadelphia Bulletin, that Chuy had been advised to quit football because of his blood clot condition. Brown thereupon telephoned Dr. James Nixon, the Eagles' team physician, for further information on Chuy's medical status.

On April 9, 1970, Hugh Brown's by-lined column in the *Philadelphia Bulletin* carried an account of Chuy's premature retirement. The column opened with the following:

> It's a jaw-breaker . . . Polycythemia Vera . . . and the question before the house is how Don Chuy, the Eagles' squatty guard, got hit with the jaw-breaker.
>
> "One of the consequences of Polycythemia Vera," said Dr. James Nixon, the Eagles' physician, "is that the blood cells get in each other's way. It's a definite threat to form embolisms, or emboli."

The remainder of the column quoted Retzlaff, Dr. Nixon, and Chuy's attorney concerning Chuy's medical condition and his effort to obtain compensation for the additional two years of his putative three-year contract. The Associated Press wire service picked up the story and articles appeared the next day in newspapers throughout the country, including the *Los Angeles Times*. The articles reported that Chuy had been "advised to give up football and professional wrestling because of a blood condition" and that, according to Dr. James Nixon, the Eagles' physician, "Chuy is suffering from polycythemia vera. Nixon said it is considered a threat to form blood clots."

After reading the *Los Angeles Times* article, Chuy testified that he panicked and immediately called his personal physician, Dr. John W. Perry. Dr. Perry informed Chuy that polycythemia vera was a fatal disease but that, from his records, Chuy did not have that disease. Dr. Perry added that he would run a series of tests to confirm his diagnosis. Chuy testified that he became apprehensive, despite Dr. Perry's assurances, broke down emotionally, and, frightened by the prospect of imminent death, refused to submit to any tests. Chuy stated that for the next several months, he could not cope with daily routines and he avoided people. He returned to Dr. Perry, who gave him numerous tests which disproved the presence of polycythemia vera. Nonetheless, Chuy testified that he continued to be apprehensive about death and that marital difficulties also developed.

Chuy eventually brought suit against the Eagles and the National Football League, alleging breach of contract, intentional infliction of emotional distress and defamation. . . .

The court submitted the claims to the jury by special interrogatories, and the jury returned a verdict for the plaintiff. On the basis of the jury's findings, the district court molded a damages award for breach of contract in the amount of $45,000, which reflected $60,000 salary due for the 1970 and 1971 seasons, less a $15,000 debt Chuy owed the Eagles. The jury also awarded Chuy $10,000 compensatory damages for the intentional infliction of emotional distress claim and punitive damages in the sum of $60,590.96. On the defamation claim, the jury found in its answer to the special interrogatories that Dr. Nixon's statements tended to injure Chuy's reputation, but that the columnist, Hugh Brown, did not understand that the publication of the doctor's statements would harm Chuy's reputation. The district court thereupon entered judgment against Chuy on his defamation claim.

After the entry of judgment against the Eagles in the aggregate sum of $115,590.96, both parties filed post-trial motions seeking either judgment notwithstanding the verdict (judgment n.o.v.) or a new trial. . . . The district court denied all post-trial motions and both parties have appealed.

Plaintiff's recovery of damages for emotional distress, stemming from having read Dr. Nixon's statement that Chuy was suffering from polycythemia vera, was predicated upon the principle enunciated in Section 46 of the Restatement (Second) of Torts (1965). That section provides:

> One who by extreme and outrageous conduct intentionally or recklessly causes severe emotional distress to another is subject to liability for such emotional distress, and if bodily harm to the other results from it, for such bodily harm.

Pennsylvania courts have signalled their acceptance of this evolving tort. . . . [W]e believe that the black letter rule of Section 46 of the Restatement . . . may be applied as the basis in Pennsylvania law for the tort of intentional infliction of emotional distress.

The Eagles argue that the district court should not have submitted to the jury the question whether Dr. Nixon's statements constituted "extreme and outrageous conduct"; that the court gave improper instructions concerning the intent necessary for the tort and that there was insufficient evidence for the jury to find the requisite intent; that Chuy's allegedly exaggerated and unreasonable reaction to Dr. Nixon's remarks precludes the Eagles' liability; and that the Eagles cannot be vicariously liable even if Dr. Nixon intentionally or recklessly caused Chuy severe emotional distress.

The Eagles contend first that the trial judge erred in submitting to the jury the issue whether Dr. Nixon's statements constituted "extreme and outrageous conduct." They assert that an actor's conduct must be examined as a matter of law by the court in limine. . . .

The court must determine, as a matter of law, whether there is sufficient evidence for reasonable persons to find extreme or outrageous conduct. If the plaintiff has satisfied this threshold evidentiary requirement, the jury must find the facts and make its own characterization. The district court followed precisely the Restatement's procedure.

In applying the legal standard for sufficiency of the evidence to support a finding of extreme and outrageous conduct, the district court correctly ruled that if Dr. Nixon advised sportswriter Brown that Chuy suffered from polycythemia vera, knowing that Chuy did not have the disease, such conduct could reasonably be regarded as extreme and outrageous. . . .

Liability has been found only where the conduct has been so outrageous in character, and so extreme in degree, as to go beyond all possible bounds of decency, and to be regarded as atrocious, and utterly intolerable in a civilized community.

Accepting as we must at this stage Chuy's version of the events, we have a statement to the press by a physician assumed to know the facts that a person is suffering from a potentially fatal disease, even though the physician was aware that the person was not stricken with that condition. This, of course, constituted intolerable professional conduct. Disseminating the falsehood through the national press compounded the harm. Surely Dr. Nixon's statements, as understood by the jury, went beyond the "mere insults, indignities . . . or annoyances" which people are prepared to withstand.

The Eagles next contend that the district court erred in charging the jury on intent and recklessness. Section 46 does not recognize liability for mere negligent infliction of emotional distress. However, reckless conduct causing emotional distress renders an actor as liable as if he had acted intentionally. To facilitate the jury's answer to the interrogatories, the trial judge gave instructions on the elements of the tort of infliction of emotional distress. With respect to requisite intent, he stated that the plaintiff could prevail only if the jury found (a) that Dr. Nixon's statement was intentional and (b) that the natural and probable consequences of making the statement were that it would become known to Chuy and that such awareness would cause him emotional distress.

As we understand the Eagles' argument, unless Dr. Nixon was aware that his comments were substantially certain to cause Chuy severe emotional distress, his remarks cannot be found to be "reckless." We are persuaded, however, that if Dr. Nixon's statements were intentional, he need not have been aware of the natural and probable consequences of his words. It is enough that Chuy's distress was substantially certain to follow Dr. Nixon's rash statements. Intentionally to propagate a falsehood, the natural and probable consequences of which will be to cause the plaintiff emotional distress is equivalent . . . to the "deliberate disregard of a high degree of probability that the emotional distress will follow." Thus, the district court's instruction comported with the Restatement's requirements for recklessness.

Having been properly charged, the jury reasonably could have found that the requirements of Section 46 as to intent had been met. The testimony given by Brown sufficiently supported a finding that Dr. Nixon's remarks were reckless.

Beyond the characterization of Dr. Nixon's statement as reckless and outrageous, the Eagles assert that Chuy's reaction to the statement was exaggerated and unreasonable. The Eagles point to evidence that Chuy, after reading the statement attributed to Dr. Nixon in the local newspaper, refused to undergo tests which he had been advised would disprove the presence of polycythemia vera. Nor did Chuy attempt to communicate with Dr. Nixon or Dr. Harrell to verify the newspaper account of his illness. Instead, Chuy became depressed and despondent, delaying tests for a period of six months. The Eagles assert that Chuy's failure to secure prompt medical verification of his putative illness was unjustified, precluding liability for the infliction of emotional distress. . . .

The jury in this case was asked to determine whether the "natural and probable" impact of Dr. Nixon's statements rendered the statements beyond the bounds of decency and it responded affirmatively. Thus, implicit in the jury's affirmative answer is its determination that a person of ordinary sensibility could not have withstood the distress without severe mental anguish and that Chuy did not feign his mental anxiety. . . .

The district court instructed the jury that if they found that Chuy unreasonably failed to minimize his injuries, they could accordingly reduce his damage award. We believe these instructions correctly distinguished between the severity of distress as an element of liability and the failure of the victim reasonably to mitigate damages. The jury therefore was properly instructed on the significance of Chuy's reluctance to undergo extensive medical testing after sustaining emotional distress.

Even assuming, arguendo, that Dr. Nixon committed a tort, the Eagles contend they should not have been held vicariously liable as a master responsible for the torts of a servant. . . .

The jury in this case specifically found that the Eagles had the right to control and actually did control the substance of Dr. Nixon's statements to the press concerning the physical condition of the team's players. Although the Eagles may be correct that Dr. Nixon performed his surgical duties as an independent contractor immune from team control, the jury was properly instructed to focus only on Dr. Nixon's role as press spokesman about players' medical status. There was ample evidence that in this limited function, Dr. Nixon was subject to control by team officials. Moreover, the frequency of Dr. Nixon's performance of this role established that he did it within the scope of his employment.

We conclude that the district court properly rendered a verdict against the Eagles, holding them vicariously responsible for Dr. Nixon's tortious statement to Brown. In so doing, we reject any suggestion by the Eagles that the master, to be held liable for this tort, must either participate in it or exhibit scienter.

The district court instructed the jury that it could award punitive damages as a penalty to the defendant and as a deterrent to others who might be likeminded, if the jury concluded that such damages were appropriate. . . .

Punitive damages are commonly awarded in cases of intentional torts. There is nothing peculiar about the tort of infliction of emotional distress that should limit its victims only to compensatory damages. The Restatement of Torts explicitly justifies the award of both punitive and compensatory damages for an analogous tort:

> [I]n torts which, like malicious prosecution, require a particular anti-social state of mind, the improper motive of the tortfeasor is both a necessary element in the cause of action and a reason for awarding punitive damages.

We acknowledge that not all states recognizing a tort for infliction of emotional distress allow an award of punitive damages. . . . In light of the noncompensatory purposes promoted by punitive damages in tort actions generally under Pennsylvania law, we believe Pennsylvania court would sanction an award of punitive damages in appropriate cases of tortious infliction of emotional distress. . . .

In sum, we believe that Pennsylvania courts would adopt a standard of vicarious liability for punitive damages which would encompass the conduct of Dr. Nixon found by the jury to be outrageous. The award of such damages is properly left to the jury as factfinder. The jury in this case made such an award on the basis of instructions consistent with those proposed by the defendants and in accord with governing Pennsylvania law. . . .

Plaintiff has appealed the district court's denial of his motion for a new trial on the defamation count of the complaint. On the basis of the jury's answers to pertinent interrogatories, the district court molded a verdict against plaintiff, denying him recovery for injury to his reputation caused by allegedly defamatory content of Dr. Nixon's statements recited in Brown's April 9, 1970 column.

The jury found, in answer to a specific interrogatory, that the plaintiff proved by clear and convincing evidence that Dr. Nixon intentionally told Brown that Chuy was suffering from polycythemia vera. The court also asked the jury to determine whether all of Dr. Nixon's statements mentioned in the newspaper article, when taken together, tended to injure Chuy's reputation, and the jury answered affirmatively. Finally, the jury was asked whether news columnist Brown understood that publication of Dr. Nixon's statements would tend to injure Chuy's reputation. The jury responded to this specific interrogatory in the negative. Because Pennsylvania law requires that the recipient understand the communication as defamatory for liability to exist, the response to the last interrogatory compelled the court to enter the verdict for the defendant on this issue. Although we affirm the judgment, we reach this result because we believe the remarks in question were not defamatory as a matter of law and the issue should not have gone to the jury.

To prove a case of defamation, Chuy needed first to show that Dr. Nixon's remark was capable of defamatory meaning, and whether he had made this showing was a matter for the court to decide. In reaching a decision on the question, the court, as a matter of federal constitutional law, had to apply a standard of proof based on Chuy's public status. The United States Supreme Court has established these standards of proof in response to two competing principles: the need to protect personal reputation, and the need for a vigorous and uninhibited press that will serve the strong public interest in learning about public figures. *Gertz* v. *Robert Welch, Inc.* (1976).

Beginning with *New York Times Co.* v. *Sullivan,* (1964), the United States Supreme Court has enunciated various federal constitutional rules which protect first amendment interests and which limit in several respects state causes of action for defamation. The rule to be applied depends in part upon characterization of the plaintiff as either a public official, public figure, or private person. Some individuals of "pervasive fame or notoriety" are public figures in all contexts. Alternatively, "an individual injects himself or is drawn into a public controversy and thereby becomes a public figure for a limited range of issues."

Professional athletes, at least as to their playing careers, generally assume a position of public prominence. Their contractual disputes, as well as their athletic accomplishments, command the attention of sports fans. Chuy, in particular, was a starting player for the Eagles. He had gained special prominence for being involved in a major and well-publicized trade in which his contract was assigned from the Los Angeles Rams to the Eagles. His injury was sustained on the field and led to discovery of a physical condition which forced his retirement. With all this as background, Chuy's dispute with the Eagles in the 1970 offseason concerning payment of two years' salary was no mere private contractual matter. Chuy had been thrust into public prominence long before Dr. Nixon's statements appeared in the April, 1970 *Bulletin* and we have no difficulty in concluding as a matter of law that he was a public figure. The article, which discussed Chuy's physical condition, his contractual dispute, and his retirement, clearly concerned a man who was a public figure, at least with respect to his ability to play football.

Because Chuy is a public figure, this may require that he prove by "convincing clarity" that Dr. Nixon's statement was capable of defamatory meaning. This is the standard enunciated in *New York Times Co.* v. *Sullivan,* for proof of actual malice required of a public figure. Without deciding whether the evidence of defamatory content should be measured by that standard or one less stringent, we are satisfied that Chuy failed to prove defamation.

Under Pennsylvania law, the question of whether a publication is capable of defamatory meaning is for the court in the first instance, and not for the jury. We must be governed, in ascertaining whether a particular form of words is capable of defamatory meaning by the standard announced in Restatement of Torts, Section 559 (1938), which the Pennsylvania courts have adopted. Section 559 of the Restatement provides:

> A communication is defamatory if it tends so to harm the reputation of another as to lower him in the estimation of the community or to deter third persons from associating or dealing with him.

We have carefully scrutinized the comment attributed to Dr. Nixon that Chuy suffered from polycythemia vera. We perceive no basis for Chuy's contention that it is a "loathsome disease" which should be treated as defamatory per se. Liability for imputing to another an existing loathsome disease must, according to the Restatement (Second) of Torts Section 572, "be limited to diseases that are held in some special repugnance. . . ." The decided cases concerned with loathsome disease have limited the term to sexually communicable venereal disease and leprosy. Polycythemia vera is a disease of unknown cause characterized by increased concentration of hemoglobin and a great absolute increase in red cells attended by an enlargement of the spleen. It is neither contagious nor attributed in any way to socially repugnant conduct.

We have also examined Brown's article to determine whether there is any context in which the imputation of his physical disease might be considered defamatory. Dr. Nixon's medical evaluation of Chuy's condition consists of several sentences attributed to him, the sum and substance of which is that Chuy had a blood condition known as polycythemia vera which manufactured blood cells that "get in each other's way" and form embolisms.

We perceive absolutely nothing in the statements attributed to Dr. Nixon which can be construed as defamatory. In this modern era, with its greater medical knowledge and societal concern with health and medical care, diseases and medical treatment are discussed candidly and freely in the home, in social circles, and in the media. For example, a malignancy suffered by the wife of the President of the United States, by a prominent United States senator, or by a movie star is front page public news. No one today treats such a communication as damaging to the esteem or reputation of the unfortunate victim in the community. The public's reaction today to a victim of cancer is usually one of sympathy rather than scorn, support and not rejection. Persons afflicted with cancer or other serious diseases, whether debilitating only or ultimately fatal, frequently carry on their personal or professional activities in today's enlightened world in normal fashion and without any deprecatory reflection whatsoever. Defamatory statements are those which discredit or debase a person's good name and standing or hold him up to public ridicule, hatred or contempt. The incurrence of a crippling or fatal illness is indeed unfortunate but, unless the disease is loathsome, it does not tarnish the victim's reputation or cause others to spurn him. . . .

The judgment of the district court will be affirmed. The parties to bear their own costs.

QUESTIONS

1. How have state and federal laws narrowed the sweeping doctrine of employment at will?

2. How do advocates of the employment-at-will doctrine defend it? How do you feel about this issue?

3. In the trend to modify the at-will rule, what three general exceptions have developed?

4. Is a personnel handbook enforceable as part of the employment contract? How did the case that involves this issue resolve this question? Explain.

5. Define the right of privacy. What four species of the tort of invasion of privacy have emerged?

6. Define defamation. When is language defamatory? Into what two torts is defamation divided?

7. Give some examples of absolute privilege. What is qualified privilege? Give examples.

8. The tort of intentional infliction of emotional stress consists of what four basic elements?

CASE PROBLEMS

1. Plaintiff was employed by defendant as a produce clerk at a supermarket. His duties included reducing the price of produce that was no longer first quality. He was discharged by defendant because he was improperly reducing the price of first-quality produce. The produce supervisor informed the lead produce clerk of the discharge, reviewed what plaintiff had done, and commented that reducing merchandise improperly *"is like stealing."* Plaintiff filed a grievance contending that his discharge was not for just cause. The grievance was processed, and defendant and the union worked out a settlement proposal that was presented to plaintiff. The company and union contend that plaintiff accepted it; plaintiff contends that he did not. Plaintiff brought this action against his former employer for defamation and breach of the collective bargaining agreement. Defendant moved for summary judgment.

Should the court allow this employee to sue his former employer for defamation on the basis of statements made during processing of his grievance? Why or why not? List some policy considerations pushing in each direction. See *Burns* v. *Supermarkets General Corp.,* C.A. 615 F. Supp. 154 (E.D. Pa. 1985).

2. Plaintiff Jones sustained an injury within the scope of his employment and was paid workers' compensation benefits for a short period of time. Prior to a compensation hearing on plaintiff's petition to receive additional benefits, plaintiff's counsel, in plaintiff's presence, asked the carrier's counsel whether plaintiff would be paid compensation benefits. The response allegedly was, "We would pay him if he wasn't represented by you." Jones brought an action for intentional infliction of emotional distress, claiming that he had suffered such distress as the result of the statement to his attorney.

   What defenses might the company raise to this action? How should the court rule on each of these defenses? See *Jones* v. *PMA Ins. Co.,* 495 A. 2d 203 (Pa. Super. Ct., 1985).

3. Rite-Aid of Maryland was concerned about cutting down on "inventory shrinkage" caused by employee theft. Rite-Aid supervisors Cook, Egner, and Torres were all asked to take a polygraph test pursuant to the company's policy of periodically giving such tests to detect and deter theft. When each refused, a Rite-Aid manager decided, "Well, we can't fire her outright, but what I want to do is cut her hours back until there is no longer any value for her to work here. She will become frustrated." The plaintiffs testified that "they were not fired but were simply given changes in established working hours, and/or transfers to distant stores, or other changes in working conditions." All three eventually quit.

   Maryland had a polygraph act that stated in pertinent part:

   An employer may not demand or require any applicant for employment or prospective employment or any employee to submit or to take a polygraph, lie detector, or similar test or examination as a condition of employment or continued employment.

   The Maryland courts recognized the public policy exception to the employment-at-will doctrine.

   Based on these facts, can you fashion a theory of wrongful discharge on behalf of these three supervisors? See *Moniodis* v. *Cook,* 119 L.R.R.M. 3556 (Md. Ct. Sp. App. 1985).

4. Dr. Davie L. Paice was employed by the Maryland Racing Commission as chief veterinarian since 1963. He had always been employed on a per diem basis without a written contract, although up until about 1970 he always received a letter each year from the commission. On June 18, 1981, he was fired. No reason for the termination was given to Dr. Paice, but he alleged in his complaint that "a member or members of the commission at the time and place of the meeting left one or more members of the press with the belief that there was a connection between plaintiff's firing and an alleged failure to observe working hours."

   Among other things, Dr. Paice argued he could not be discharged without a disciplinary hearing as provided in the commission's *Rules of Thoroughbred Racing.* He pointed to two provisions of the rules, which read as follows:

   . . . [W]henever it appears to the Commission that disciplinary or punitive action should be taken against any person for violation of the rules of racing . . . ," a hearing shall be conducted.

   All officials at any track shall conduct themselves at all times with complete integrity. They shall receive no remuneration, other than salary for the proper performance of their duties.

   Was Dr. Paice entitled to a hearing on the basis of these racing rules? Does your answer change if the commission is considered by the court to be a public employer? See *Paice* v. *Maryland Racing Commission,* 539 F. Supp. 458, 115 L.R.R.M. 5004 (U.S. District Ct., D. Md., 1982).

5. The supervisor of a department of a nonprofit organization received a memorandum from members of the department, concerning a high-seniority coworker. The following is an excerpt from the memorandum:

   FROM: All Professional   Feb. 8, 1971
          Staff of Community
          Activities Department

   TO: K_____

   SUBJECT: N_____

   We feel that N_____'s behavior has reached the point where it cannot be tolerated. Following our meeting with you last Thursday, we are listing the reasons:

   N_____ poses a major irritant and distraction, so that she cuts down on the productivity of both professionals and other secretaries, both in our department and in nearby departments.

   She poisons the atmosphere by constantly complaining, downgrading professionals and secretaries to other professionals and secretaries.

She constantly complains about being overworked, while spending a good amount of time wandering around the office complaining and generally wasting time.

She talks incessantly and compulsively in an extraordinarily loud voice, making it impossible for anyone not to hear her, and making it extremely difficult to concentrate. . . ."

If you were the supervisor who received this memo, would you discharge the employee? If you do so, does she have any basis for suing for wrongful discharge? In a public policy state? In an implied covenant of good faith and fair dealing state? Are there any other causes of action available to this employee? Against the employer or supervisor? Against her coworkers? Explain. See *National Council of Jewish Women, Inc.,* 57 LA 980 (Scheiber, 1971).

6. Manuel was an African-American male who was hired by International Harvester Company as its Supervisor of Equal Opportunity programs. About a year after he was hired, he was terminated during a companywide reduction in force. Believing that his discharge was racially discriminatory, Manuel pursued his administrative remedies.

Manuel subsequently brought a lawsuit against International Harvester in federal court. In his 112-count complaint, he advanced a number of legal theories, the first five alleging violation of various federal and state laws forbidding race discrimination. The twelfth count in the complaint stated that the plaintiff was discharged in violation of the company's common law duty of good faith and fair dealing. Illinois courts recognized the public policy exception to the at-will employment doctrine.

Is there a public policy argument implicit in Manuel's twelfth count? Should the court permit this count to remain in his complaint, or are there other policy considerations that might convince the court to dismiss this count? See *Manuel* v. *International Harvester Co.,* 502 F. Supp 45, 115 L.R.R.M. 4873 (N.D. Ill. 1980).

7. Margaret Rookard was the Director of Nursing at Harlem Hospital in New York City. Shortly after she began working she was asked by the acting executive director to sign permits that would authorize unlicensed nurses, employed by outside commercial agencies, to work at the hospital. Rookard believed that such permits could lawfully be issued only to nurses directly employed by the hospital. She, therefore, refused to sign.

Rookard soon found that many nurses abused the

hospital's "sign in" procedures, and either failed to sign the register, or signed for hours they had not worked; and that the hospital had not kept adequate records of its use of licensed agency nurses, and thus could not accurately evaluate bills submitted by agencies. She reported these and other discrepancies to the hospital's directors; they ignored her complaints.

After taking it upon herself to try to eliminate these problems and improve efficiency, she earned the enmity of some nurses and began receiving anonymous, threatening calls and letters. Eventually she was demoted and, finally, discharged.

Based on these facts, you can articulate a public policy exception to the at-will employment doctrine based on Rookard's "whistleblowing" with respect to the illegal use of unlicensed nurses? Does it make a difference whether her understanding of the law was correct or incorrect?

Can you make a public policy argument to support a wrongful discharge action by Rookard based on the remaining facts above? Does your answer change if Harlem Hospital was a public rather than a private hospital? See *Rookard* v. *Health and Hospital Corp.,* 710 F.2d 41, 115 L.R.R.M. 4089 (2d Cir. 1983).

8. Georgia Power Company's employment application form stated that discovery of a deliberate falsification by the applicant would result in immediate dismissal from employment. Warman was a member of the Golden Mean Society, which had as its purpose opposition to federal income taxation. Employee-members, including Warman, were engaged in a lawsuit against Georgia Power, involving a picketing of a company plant and refusing to report to work there, because the company would not acquiesce to Golden Mean demands.

During the course of discovery in the lawsuit, Warman admitted, in answer to a deposition about prior criminal convictions, that he had been convicted some years earlier in Florida of falsifying a driver's license application. Warman had not mentioned this conviction on his employment application. Georgia Power used this admission as the basis to discharge him.

Based on these facts, can you articulate a theory for a wrongful discharge action on the basis of duty of good faith and fair dealing? What about on the basis of the public policy exceptions to at-will termination? See *Burke* v. *Georgia Power Co.,* 115 L.R.R.M. 4063 (U.S. Dist. Ct., S.D. Ga., 1983).

9. Plaintiffs Janet Shawgo and Stanley Whisenhut were police officers with the Amarillo, Texas, police department. Whisenhut was a sergeant, and Shawgo was a patrolwoman. They worked different shifts, and Sergeant Whisenhut did not supervise Patrolwoman Shawgo.

   When Whisenhut and Shawgo started dating, the sergeant informed his lieutenant, who said it was all right.

   Sometime later the chief of police heard rumors that the two officers had begun living together. Instead of contacting either of the plaintiffs or their superiors, he ordered officers of the Detective Division to conduct surveillance of the plaintiffs' off-duty activities. The report of this surveillance indicated that Policewoman Shawgo was maintaining a separate residence but spending substantial time in Whisenhut's apartment.

   Based on this information, the chief had both officers disciplined. Shawgo was suspended for twelve days without pay after notification that her "cohabitation" outside marriage violated the police department's regulations. Whisenhut was also suspended for twelve days and recommended for demotion to patrolman.

   When the Civil Service Commission of Amarillo sustained the discipline, after a hearing that generated much publicity, both officers were assigned to undesirable duty and ultimately resigned. Based on these facts, discuss the possible common law causes of action that may be available to the plaintiffs: Defamation? Invasion of privacy? Constructive wrongful discharge? See *Shawgo* v. *Sprodlin,* 701 F.2d 470 (5th Cir. 1983).

10. Elizabeth A. Yoho began employment with Triangle PWC, Inc. (Triangle) on December 8, 1980, as a utility laborer. On April 2, 1981, she was assigned the task of temporary filter operator and was required to replenish manually an acid bath as part of her job. While attempting this task, she fell and spilled two gallons of acid on herself, which resulted in second- and third-degree burns over 35 percent of her body. By order dated June 1, 1981, the Workers' Compensation Commissioner awarded Elizabeth Yoho temporary total disability benefits, which she has continued to receive through the present time. On April 5, 1982, a year after her accident, Elizabeth Yoho's employment with Triangle was terminated pursuant to the provisions of a collective bargaining agreement as a result of her unavailability for work over the preceding twelve-month period.

    Based on your reading of this chapter, what arguments can you raise for and against the court entertaining Yoho's causes of action? See *Yoho* v. *Triangle PWC, Inc.,* 120 L.R.R.M. 2874 (W.Va. Supr. Ct. July 12, 1985).

C H A P T E R 2

The Development of American Labor Unions and the Legal Responses

IN 1721 AN ENGLISH court declared that a combination of journeymen-taylors [tailors], created to improve their bargaining position with the master-taylors, was a criminal conspiracy under **common law.** When that case, *King against the Journeymen-Taylors of Cambridge,* was decided, it was well-settled law that individual workers were free to make the best bargains they could with prospective employers. Individual workers were also free to withhold their services if they were dissatisfied with the bargain. Such individual freedom was known as "freedom of contract." The prosecutor in that trial argued that a combination of workers, to raise their wages, violated the Criminal Conspiracy Statute of 1720. The judges in the *Journeymen-Taylors* case held that the statute did not apply to the journeymen; nevertheless, they found the journeymen guilty of an illegal conspiracy on the basis of the common (judge-made) law. The judges held that public policy objectives recognized by the common law as being in the best interests of society required holding the combination illegal. Although freedom of contract was a laudable principle when pursued by individuals, it took on antisocial aspects when individual workers combined in order to improve their bargaining power.

The *Journeymen-Taylors* case was one example of legal restrictions placed on laborers. Such restrictions, the roots of our labor laws, go back to the fourteenth century. In 1349 an ordinance was adopted that required laborers to work for the same pay as they had received in 1347. The ordinance was an attempt to prevent laborers from demanding higher pay because of the severe shortage of workers resulting from the "Black Death" plague that devastated the country during 1348.

That ordinance was followed in 1351 by the Statute of Laborers, which provided that able-bodied persons under age sixty with no means of subsistence must work for whoever required them. The statute also prohibited giving alms to able-bodied beggars, and held that vagrant serfs could be forced to work for anyone claiming them. This statute was succeeded in 1562 by the Tudor Industrial Code, which made combinations of workers illegal.

The legal restrictions just mentioned were attempts to prevent the laborers of society from improving their lot in life at the expense of the landed class, or the employers. The Industrial Revolution brought about the rise of centralized manufacturing, with factories replacing the cottage industry in which craftsmen produced their own goods. These factories required laborers, who were subjected to harsh conditions and long hours. Despite the hardships that the new industrial age presented, it also carried the promise of a vast increase both in wealth and in mass-produced consumer goods. That increase would be sufficient to make possible a vastly improved standard of living for all classes, including the factory workers. It would be necessary, however, for laborers to join together to ensure that they would get their share of the increasing wealth of the nation. Although initial attempts at joining together were held illegal as combinations or conspiracies, the ruling class and public opinion gradually came to recognize the legitimacy of joint action by workers. This recognition was reflected in an easing of legal restrictions on such activities; the Conspiracy and Protection Act of 1875 and the Trades Disputes Act of 1906 legitimized the role of organized labor in England.

Labor Development in America

The English events chronicled above contained the seeds of the American labor relations system. Although industrialization came to America much later than to England, the craftsmen and journeymen of late eighteenth and early nineteenth century America recognized the importance of organized activity to resist employer attempts to reduce wages. The American courts reacted to such activities in much the same way as had the English courts.

One of the earliest recorded American labor cases is the *Philadelphia Cordwainers* case, decided in 1806. The cordwainers, or shoemakers, had united into a club and had presented the master-cordwainers, their employers, with a rate schedule for production of various types of shoes. The wage increases they demanded ranged from twenty-five to seventy-five cents per pair. The employers were attempting to compete with shoe producers in other cities for the expanding markets of the South and West; they sought to lower prices to compete more effectively. In response to the workers' wage demands, the employers took their complaint to the public prosecutor. The workers were charged with "contriving and intending unjustly and oppressively, to increase and augment the prices and rates usually paid to them" and with preventing, by "threats, menaces, and other unlawful means" other journeymen from working for lower wages. They were also accused of conspiring to refuse to work for any master who employed workers who did not abide by the club's rules.

In directing the jury to consider the case, the judge gave the following charge:

> What is the case now before us? . . . A combination of workmen to raise their wages may be considered in a two fold point of view: one is to benefit themselves . . . the other is to injure those who do not join their society. The rule of law condemns both. If the rule be clear, we are bound to conform to it even though we do not comprehend the principle upon which it is founded. We are not to reject it because we do not see the reason of it. It

is enough, that it is the will of the majority. It is law because it is their will—if it is law, there may be good reasons for it though we cannot find them out. But the rule in this case is pregnant with sound sense and all the authorities are clear upon the subject. Hawkins, the greatest authority on the criminal law, has laid it down, that a combination to maintaining one another, carrying a particular object, whether true or false, is criminal. . . . [T]he authority cited from *8 Mod. Rep.* does not rest merely upon the reputation of that book. He gives you other authorities to which he refers. It is adopted by Blackstone, and laid down as the law by Lord Mansfield 1793, that an act innocent in an individual, is rendered criminal by a confederacy to effect it.

. . . One man determines not to work under a certain price and it may be individually the opinion of all: in such a case it would be lawful in each to refuse to do so, for if each stands, alone, either may extract from his determination when he pleases. In the turnout of last fall, if each member of the body had stood alone, fettered by no promises to the rest, many of them might have changed their opinion as to the price of wages and gone to work; but it has been given to you in evidence, that they were bound down by their agreement, and pledged by mutual engagements, to persist in it, however contrary to their own judgment. The continuance in improper conduct may therefore well be attributed to the combination. The good sense of those individuals was prevented by this agreement, from having its free exercise.

. . . The journeymen shoemakers have not asked an increased price of work for an individual of their body; but they say that no one shall work, unless he receives the wages they have fixed. They could not go farther than saying, no one should work unless they all got the wages demanded by the majority; is this freedom? Is it not restraining, instead of promoting, the spirit of '76 when men expected to have no law but the constitution, and laws adopted by it or enacted by the legislature in conformity to it?

. . . It is not a question, whether we shall have an *imperium in imperio,* whether we shall have, besides our state legislature a new legislature consisting of journeymen shoemakers.

. . . It is now, therefore, left to you upon the law, and the evidence, to find the verdict. If you can reconcile it to your consciences, to find the defendants not guilty, you will do so; if not, the alternative that remains, is a verdict of guilty.

The jury found the defendants guilty of conspiracy to raise their wages; the judge fined each man eight dollars. The effect of the decision was to render combinations of workers for the purpose of raising wages illegal. The case produced a public outcry by the Jeffersonians and in the press.

Not all of labor's activities were held illegal; for example, in *People* v. *Melvin,* a New York cordwainers' case decided in 1809, the charge of an illegal combination to raise wages was dismissed. The court declared that the journeymen were free to join together, but they could not use means "of a nature too arbitrary and coercive, and which went to deprive their fellow citizens of rights as precious as any they contended for."

Although that language may have sounded promising, the law remained in a most unsettled state. In 1836 the New York Supreme Court in *People* v. *Fisher* found unionized workers guilty of **criminal conspiracy** under a statute that vaguely stated, "If two or more persons shall conspire . . . to commit any act injurious to the public health, to public morals, or to trade or commerce; or for the perversion or obstruction of justice or the due administration of the laws—they shall be deemed guilty of a misdemeanor." The workers—again shoemakers and again organized into a club— had struck to force the discharge of a co-worker who had accepted wages below the minimum set by the club. The defendants were guilty of conspiring to commit an act "injurious to trade or commerce," the court reasoned. Artificially high wages meant correspondingly higher prices for boots, which prevented local manufacturers from selling as cheaply as their competitors elsewhere. Furthermore, the court observed, the community was deprived of the services of the worker whose discharge was procured by the shoemakers' union.

Such decisions provoked outrage among workers in the eastern states. In the wake of such trials, mobs of workers sometimes held their own mock trials and hanged unpopular judges in effigy. Despite such popular sentiments, the courts and the law remained major obstacles to organized labor's achieving a legitimate place in society. The first step toward that achievement was the law's recognition that a labor organization was not per se an illegal conspiracy. That legal development came in the landmark decision of the Massachusetts Supreme Court in 1842 in the case of *Commonwealth* v. *Hunt.*

COMMONWEALTH v. HUNT

45 Mass. (4 Met.) 111 (Supreme Court of Massachusetts, 1842)

[Seven members of the Boston Journeymen Bootmakers' Society were convicted of criminal conspiracy for organizing a strike against an employer, Isaac B. Wait, who had hired one Jeremiah Horne, a journeyman who did not belong to the society. The indictment charged the bootmakers with having "unlawfully, perniciously, deceitfully, unjustly and corruptly" conspired to withhold their services from Master Wait until such time as he discharged Horne, and with the "wicked and unlawful intent to impoverish" Horne by keeping him from the pursuit of his trade. The trial judge had instructed the jury that if the course of conduct set forth in the indictment was found by them to be true, then it amounted to criminal conspiracy and a verdict of guilty should follow. The jury so found, and the hapless defendants appealed their conviction to the state's highest court.

Chief Justice Shaw, who wrote the court's decision, anticipated that Massachusetts workers would react violently if the high court affirmed the conviction. Some historians suggest that he also knew that the fortunes of many old Boston families

were tied to the new shoe and clothing mills and that a wave of work stoppages in the wake of an adverse ruling could jeopardize these youthful business ventures. The opinion that follows should be read with these considerations in mind.]

SHAW, C. J.

The general rule of the common law is, that it is a criminal and indictable offence, for two or more to confederate and combine together, by concerted means, to do that which is unlawful or criminal, to the injury of the public, or portions or classes of the community, or even to the rights of an individual. This rule of law may be equally in force as a rule of common law, in England and in this Commonwealth; and yet it must depend upon the local laws of each country to determine, whether the purpose to be accomplished by the combination, or the concerted means of accomplishing it, be unlawful or criminal in the respective countries.

. . . But the great difficulty is, in framing any definition or description, to be drawn from the decided cases, which shall specifically identify this offence—a description broad enough to include all cases punishable under this description, without including acts which are not punishable. Without attempting to review and reconcile all the cases, we are of opinion, that as a general description, though perhaps not a precise and accurate definition, a conspiracy must be a combination of two or more persons, by some concerted action, to accomplish some criminal or unlawful purpose, or to accomplish some purpose, not in itself criminal or unlawful, by criminal or unlawful means.

... With these general views of the law, it becomes necessary to consider the circumstances of the present case, as they appear from the indictment itself, and from the bill of exceptions filed and allowed.

... The first count set forth, that the defendants, with diverse others unknown, on the day and at the place named, being workmen, and journeymen, in the art and occupation of bootmakers, unlawfully, perniciously, and deceitfully designing and intending to continue, keep up, form, and unite themselves, into an unlawful club, society and combination, and make unlawful by-laws, rules and orders among themselves, and thereby govern themselves and other workmen, in the said art, and unlawfully and unjustly to extort great sums of money by means thereof, did unlawfully assemble and meet together, and being so assembled, did unjustly and corruptly conspire, combine, confederate and agree together, that none of them should thereafter, and that none of them would, work for any master or person whatsoever, in the said art, mystery and occupation, who should employ any workman or journeyman, or other person, in the said art, who was not a member of said club, society or combination, after notice given him to discharge such workman, from the employ of such master; to the great damage and oppression. ...

The manifest intent of the association is, to induce all those engaged in the same occupation to become members of it. Such a purpose is not unlawful. It would give them a power which might be exerted for useful and honorable purposes, or for dangerous and pernicious ones. If the latter were the real and actual object, and susceptible of proof, it should have been specially charged. Such an association might be used to afford each other assistance in times of poverty, sickness and distress; or to raise their intellectual, moral and social condition; or to make improvement in their art; or for other proper purposes. Or the association might be designed for purposes of oppression and injustice. But in order to charge all those, who become members of an association, with the guilt of a criminal conspiracy, it must be averred and proved that the actual, if not the avowed object of the association, was criminal. An association may be formed, the declared objects of which are innocent and laudable, and yet they may have secret articles, or an agreement communicated only to the members, by which they are banded together for purposes injurious to the peace of society or the rights of its members. Such would undoubtedly be a criminal conspiracy, on proof of the fact, however meritorious and praiseworthy the declared objects might be. The law is not to be hoodwinked by colorable pretences. It looks at truth and reality, through whatever disguise it may assume. ... But when an association is formed for purposes actually innocent, and afterwards its powers are abused, by those who have the control and management of it, to purposes of oppression and injustice, it will be criminal in those who thus misuse it, or give consent thereto, but not in the other members of the association. In this case, no such secret agreement, varying the objects of the association from those avowed, it set forth in this count of the indictment.

Nor can we perceive that the objects of this association, whatever they may have been, were to be attained by criminal means. The means which they proposed to employ, as averred in this count, and which, as we are now to presume, were established by the proof, were, that they would not work for a person, who, after due notice, should employ a journeyman not a member of their society. Supposing the object of the association to be laudable and lawful, or at least not unlawful, are these means criminal? The case supposes that these persons are not bound by contract, but free to work for whom they please, or not to work, if they so prefer. In this state of things, we cannot perceive, that it is criminal for men to agree together to exercise their own acknowledged rights, in such a manner as best to subserve their own interests. One way to test this is, to consider the effect of such an agreement, where the object of the association is acknowledged on all hands to be a laudable one. Suppose a class of workmen, impressed with the manifold evils of intemperance, should agree with each other not to work in a shop in which ardent spirit was furnished, or not to work in a shop with any one who used it, or not to work for an employer, who should, after notice, employ a journeyman who habitually used it. The consequences might be the same. A workman, who should still persist in the use of ardent spirit, would find it more difficult to get employment; a master employing such a one might, at times, experience inconvenience in his work, in losing the services of a skilful but intemperate workman. Still it seems to us, that as the object would be lawful, and the means not unlawful, such an agreement could not be pronounced a criminal conspiracy.

From this count in the indictment, we do not understand what the agreement was, that the defendants would refuse to work for an employer, to whom they were bound by contract for a certain time, in violation of that contract; nor that they would insist that an employer should discharge a workman engaged by contract for a certain time, in violation of such contract. It is perfectly consistent with everything stated in this count, that the effect of the agreement was, that when they were free to act, they would not engage with an employer, or continue in his employment, if such employer, when free to act, should engage with a workman, or continue a workman in his employment, not a member of the association. . . .

We think, therefore, that associations may be entered into, the object of which is to adopt measures that may have a tendency to impoverish another, that is, to diminish his gains and profits, and yet so far from being criminal or unlawful, the object may be highly meritorious and public spirited. The legality of such an association will therefore depend upon the means to be used for its accomplishment. If it is to be carried into effect by fair or honorable and lawful means, it is, to say the least, innocent; if by falsehood or force, it may be stamped with the character of conspiracy.

It follows as a necessary consequence, that if criminal and indictable, it is so by reason of the criminal means intended to be employed for its accomplishment; and as a further legal consequence, that as the criminality will depend on the means, those means must be stated in the indictment.

. . . [L]ooking solely at the indictment, disregarding the qualifying epithets, recitals and immaterial allegations, and confining ourselves to facts so averred as to be capable of being traversed and put in issue, we cannot perceive that it charges a criminal conspiracy punishable by law. The exceptions must, therefore, be sustained, and the judgment arrested.

Although *Commonwealth* v. *Hunt* did not abolish the doctrine of criminal conspiracy with regard to unions, it did make it extremely difficult to apply the doctrine to labor activities. After 1842, the legality of labor unions was accepted by mainstream judicial opinion. Furthermore, in the post–Civil War period most state appellate courts accepted the legality of peaceful strikes, *provided* that the purpose of the work stoppage was determined by the court to be legal.

The Post–Civil War Period

Although after *Commonwealth* v. *Hunt* the courts grudgingly accorded labor unions a measure of legitimacy, the labor movement was forced to struggle—sometimes violently—with employers for recognition. The years following the Civil War were a turbulent period for the American labor movement. Those years not only saw a great increase in the growth and development of unions; they were also marked by violent strikes in several industries.

The Civil War created a shortage of laborers to work in the factories producing materials for the war effort; the war years were a prosperous time for labor. After the war, however, the returning soldiers swelled the ranks of the work force, thus depressing wages. The Panic of 1873, with its widespread economic depression, also greatly weakened the labor movement, since workers desperate for employment could easily be dissuaded from union activity by their employers. Nearly fifteen years passed before labor recovered from the effects of these events.

The last decades of the nineteenth century saw three centers of labor activity: the Knights of Labor, the Socialists, and the American Federation of Labor. Each group sought to rejuvenate organized labor after the declines suffered during the 1870s.

The Knights of Labor

The Noble Order of the Knights of Labor grew out of a garment workers' local union in Philadelphia. The local had been blacklisted during the years following the Civil War. Its leaders, including Uriah Stevens, believed that the union had failed because its members were too well known and were confined to specific crafts. In

1869 they dissolved the old organization and formed Local Assembly 1 of the Noble Order of the Knights of Labor. Members were sworn to secrecy. (Such secrecy and rituals were later abolished in an attempt to attract immigrant labor into the order.)

By 1873 there were thirty-one local assemblies, all in the Philadelphia area. The Knights spread into Camden, New Jersey, and into Pittsburgh by 1875, but they still remained largely a regional organization. Not until the Railway Strike of 1877 did the Knights become a national movement.

That railway strike was a response to successive wage cuts by various railroads. It began among railway workers on the Baltimore and Ohio line at Camden on July 16, 1877, but quickly spread to workers on other lines as far west as Chicago and St. Louis. Government troops took over operation of the railroads, which resulted in numerous violent confrontations with the strikers. The strike ended in August 1877, but not before exacting a toll of hundreds of deaths and $10 million worth of property damage.

Following the strike, there was a rush of labor into the Knights. By the end of 1877, district assemblies had been established in New York, Massachusetts, Ohio, West Virginia, Illinois, and Indiana. A convention held at Reading, Pennsylvania, on January 1, 1878, officially transformed the Knights into a national organization.

From 1878 to 1884, the Order of the Knights of Labor conducted a great number of strikes as it sought to organize unskilled workers as well as skilled laborers. The Knights continued to favor industrywide organizations rather than craft unions. This attitude, however, posed problems because the unskilled workers of mixed locals (those containing both skilled and unskilled workers) could easily be replaced during a strike. Membership in the Knights grew, but turnover was high, as members were suspended for nonpayment of dues, usually in the wake of unsuccessful strikes. In 1883, for example, eighty-four thousand members were initiated but fifty-four thousand were suspended. Some locals disbanded when employers, following unsuccessful strikes, forced workers to sign **yellow-dog contracts** (contracts in which they agreed not to join any union).

The Knights suffered a number of defeats in strikes in 1886. After such setbacks they sought to form a political alliance with the agrarian reform movement and the socialists. This United Front sought to gain through political means what the Knights had failed to win through strikes, but it had only moderate success and gradually disintegrated. The Knights of Labor began to decline as the skilled trade unions pulled out; those unions believed they could more effectively achieve their goals through a more narrowly based organization that emphasized labor actions rather than political actions.

The Socialists

The establishment of the International Workingmen's Association (the First International) by Karl Marx in London in 1864 stirred interest in socialism in the United States. In 1865 the German Workingmen's Union was formed in New York City; it was later reorganized as the Social Party. In 1868, after poor electoral showings, it was reorganized as Section 2 of the First International.

The socialist movement grew during the years from 1868 to 1875, but it also experienced internal dissension and fragmentation. Although the movement had initially sought to organize unions, it turned to political activities in the aftermath of the Railway Strike of 1877. The political arm of the movement became the Socialist Labor Party, which was able to elect some local officials and state legislators in 1878. In 1880 the party aligned itself with the Greenback Party.

The Haymarket Riot of 1886 greatly injured the socialist movement. The riot erupted during a rally for a general strike over the eight-hour workday; almost three thousand people turned out to hear three anarchists speak in support of the strike at Chicago's Haymarket Square. A bomb was thrown into a group of policemen trying to disperse the crowd. Both the public outcry following the riot and the trial and conviction of the anarchist speakers and associates (who were not even present at the riot) for the bombing served to deny the socialist movement public acceptance and legitimacy.

The labor activities of the socialist movement came to be represented by the Industrial Workers of the World (the IWW, or "Wobblies") during the early decades of the twentieth century. The Wobblies were a radical union that engaged in a number of violent strikes; their counterpart in the western United States was the Western Federation of Miners, led by William "Big Bill" Haywood, a socialist labor leader.

Following the Russian Revolution in 1917, the Wobblies were eclipsed by the American Communist Party, an outgrowth of the Third International organized in Moscow in 1919. The American Communist Party, although maintaining interest in labor organizing, emphasized political activities. The influence of the Communist Party in labor activities, although important during the depression, declined during World War II and the late 1940s; the cold war and the McCarthy "red hunts" in the late 1940s and early 1950s effectively brought an end to organized labor's links to the American Communist Party.

The American Federation of Labor

The American Federation of Labor (AFL), which has become the dominant organization of the American labor movement, was the rival of both the Socialists and the Knights of Labor. The AFL emphasized union activities, in contrast to the political activities of the Knights and the Socialists. This "pure and simple" trade union movement was started by Samuel Gompers and Adolph Strasser of the Cigarmakers' Union. They pulled together a national convention in 1879, which adopted a pattern of union organization based on the British trade union system. Local unions were to be organized under the authority of a national association; dues were to be raised to create a large financial reserve; and sick and death benefits were to be provided. The national organization's focus on wages and practical, immediate goals rather than on the ideological and political aims of the Knights of Labor and the Socialists.

A federation of trade unions developed. Although the federation was open to unskilled workers, it was dominated by groups of workers from the skilled trades, or crafts. The federation's unions faced stiff rivalry from the Knights of Labor; the Knights continually "raided" the trade unions for new members. The trade unions, for their part, believed they could be more effective organizing their own crafts rather than affiliating with the unskilled workers in the Knights of Labor. The Cigar-makers chose Gompers to rally the other trade unions in opposition to the Knights of Labor. He convened a conference of trade unions in Philadelphia in 1886. The conference demanded that the Knights not interfere with the unions' activities nor compete with the unions for members. The Knights responded by affirming that they represented all workers—both skilled and unskilled. The Knights also ordered all members affiliated with the Cigarmakers' International to quit that union or forfeit membership in the Knights.

Although the struggle between the Knights of Labor and the AFL continued for a number of years, over the next decade the Knights suffered a drastic decline in membership. Employer animosity toward the Knights ran high, and a number of employers broke their contracts with the Knights. In addition, the Knights' involvement in a great many unsuccessful strikes hurt their image among workers. Skilled tradesmen, already alienated by the Knights' policy of including all workers, deserted the Knights for the AFL. From a high of seven hundred thousand members in 1886, the Knights' membership dwindled to one hundred thousand by mid-1890.

As the Knights declined, the AFL grew in size and importance. By 1900 organized labor was largely composed of the five hundred thousand skilled workers in AFL-affiliated unions. For the next few decades the AFL and its affiliated craft unions dominated the organized labor movement in America. That dominance was to be challenged by the Congress of Industrial Organizations, which developed in the late 1930s in reaction to the refusal of the AFL to sponsor a drive to organize industrial workers.

The Congress of Industrial Organizations

The Congress of Industrial Organizations (CIO) was a federation of unions that sought to organize the unskilled production workers largely ignored by the AFL. It grew out of a renewed industrywide interest in organizing activity led by the autoworkers, steel workers, and the mine workers under John L. Lewis. The AFL opposed the new organization and in 1938 expelled all unions associated with the CIO.

The CIO, which emphasized political activity as well as organizing activity, had spectacular success in organizing the workers of the steel, automobile, rubber, electrical manufacturing, and machinery industries. After years of bitter rivalry, the AFL was finally forced to recognize the success and permanency of the CIO with its 4.5 million members; the result was that the 10.5 million members of the AFL at last merged with the CIO in 1955. The resulting organization, the AFL-CIO, continues to be the dominant body in the American labor movement.

Recent Trends in the Labor Movement

The years following World War II were boom years for the labor movement. Unions grew in strength in the manufacturing industries until approximately one-third of the American labor force was unionized. Union membership in the private sector reached a peak in the early 1950s and has been slowly declining since then; by 1989 only about 16 percent of the work force was unionized. Since the 1960s, unionized employers have faced increasing competition from domestic, nonunion firms and foreign competitors. The "oil-induced" inflation of the 1970s also increased the economic pressures on manufacturers and employers, making them very sensitive to production costs—of which labor costs are a significant component. The manufacturing sector of the U.S. economy, in which the labor movement's strength was concentrated, has been hit hardest by the changing economic conditions and competition. The late 1970s and the 1980s were marked by the "restructuring" of American industry—mergers, takeovers, plant relocations to the mostly nonunion Sun Belt and overseas, and plant closings all became common occurrences. Collective bargaining, where the employer asks the union for "give backs"—reductions in wages and benefits and relaxation of restrictive work rules. The mid-1980s were characterized by the decline of the manufacturing sector and the rise of the service economy, the indifference (or hostility) of the Reagan administration toward organized labor, and an aggressiveness toward unions on the part of management. Even the owners of the football teams of the National Football League were willing to take on the union representing their employees by forcing a strike—and they succeeded; the National Football League Players Association ultimately ceased to represent the professional football players.

Although unions in the private sector have been in decline, unions in the public sector have been growing strongly since the 1960s. The increase in the number of unionized government employees at the local, state, and federal levels has somewhat offset the decline of union members in the private sector. But the 1980s were difficult for public sector unions as well. Although public sector employers do not face foreign competition, the "tax revolts" by American voters and the antigovernment attitude of the Reagan and Bush administrations put limits on the ability of government employers to improve wages and benefits for public sector employees.

As we enter the 1990s, the percentage of the American work force that is unionized is at an all-time low. But though labor may have reached its nadir, it is not yet defunct—some unions within the traditional manufacturing sector have retained their viability, and public sector unions remain strong. Unions have also had several recent "victories" in highly publicized disputes such as the Pittson Coal strike. Unions will continue to play a significant role in certain segments of the American labor market throughout the 1990s. Unions continue to serve as a "collective voice" for workers—they provide workers, as a group, a means of communicating with management about wages, benefits, and working conditions.

Legal Responses to the Labor Movement

We have seen that the courts reacted with hostility to the activities of organized labor. The common-law conspiracy doctrine was used effectively during the early and mid-nineteenth century to prohibit organized activity by workers. As judicial hostility lessened (as seen in *Commonwealth* v. *Hunt,* at page 41), organized labor grew in size and effectiveness.

Employers facing threats of strikes or boycotts by unions sought new legal weapons to use against labor activists. The development of the **labor injunction** in the late 1880s provided a powerful weapon to be used against the activities of organized labor.

The Injunction

The **injunction** was a legal device developed centuries earlier in England. As the system of law courts was established in England following the Norman Conquest, the remedies provided by such courts were limited to monetary damage awards. When legal remedies proved inadequate, plaintiffs seeking recompense petitioned the king for relief. These petitions were referred to the chancellor, the king's secretary, to be decided in the name of the king. Where appropriate, the chancellor issued a writ, or order, commanding in the name of the king that a person act, or refrain from acting, in a particular way. Over time, courts of chancery developed to provide such court orders (injunctions) when legal remedies proved inadequate; these courts, also called courts of equity, developed their own rules as to the availability of special remedies such as the injunction. The dual system of courts of law and courts of equity was carried to America with the English colonists and was preserved following the revolution.

At the present time according to the rules of equity, an injunction is available whenever monetary damages alone are inadequate and when the plaintiff's interests are facing irreparable harm from the defendant's actions. A defendant who ignores such a court order can be jailed and fined for contempt of the court.

The reputed first use of the injunction against labor activities involved a strike by employees of a railroad that had been placed under a court-appointed receiver because of financial problems. The court-appointed receiver asked the court to prohibit the union representing the employees from interfering with the receiver's court-ordered duties. The court responded by directing the union to cease the strike and by holding its leaders guilty of contempt of court when they refused. The strike ended in a matter of hours.

The Pullman Strike of 1894 clearly demonstrated the effective power of a labor injunction in preventing organized activity by labor unions. The Pullman Palace Car Company housed its workers in a "company town"; workers had to pay rent, utility bills, and even taxes to the company. When the company cut wages by 22 percent in 1893, it refused to reduce rents and service charges. The employees turned to their union for help. The American Railway Union, led by its president, Eugene Debs, commenced a boycott of all Pullman rolling stock in June 1894. Within hours, sixty thousand workers on the railways in the West ceased working; the boycott soon spread to the South and the East.

The railroad General Managers Association turned to the U.S. attorney general for help. The attorney general, Richard Olney, secured the promise of President Grover Cleveland to use federal troops, if necessary, to support the "judicial tribunes" in dealing with the strike. The attorney general then turned to the federal courts. Using the theory that railroads were, in effect, "public highways" and that any obstruction of such highways should be dealt with by the federal government as a restraint of interstate commerce, the U.S. attorney general convinced the federal district court in Chicago to issue an injunction against the strikers. The court ordered all persons "to refrain from interfering with or stopping any of the business of any of the railroads in Chicago engaged as common carriers."

Federal marshals were dispatched to enforce the writ of injunction; when they were resisted by crowds of strikers, federal troops were brought into Chicago to subdue the crowds. Eugene Debs was indicted for conspiracy in restraint of commerce and obstructing the U.S. mail. When the U.S. Supreme Court upheld the legal actions in the case of *In re Debs* (158 U.S. 164, 1895), the effectiveness of the labor injunction was convincingly established.

Throughout the last decade of the nineteenth century and the first two decades of the twentieth century, the courts willingly granted injunctions against actual or threatened strikes or boycotts by unions. The courts did not require any showing that the strike or boycott actually harmed the employer's business. The courts were also willing to assume that legal remedies such as damage awards were inadequate. Generally, the injunctions granted were written in very broad terms and directed against unnamed persons. The injunctions were often granted in *ex parte* proceedings, so-called because they occurred without any representative of the union present. Once an injunction had been granted, court officers would enforce it against the union. Union members who resisted risked jail terms and/or fines for being in contempt of the court order. In the face of such threatened sanctions, union leaders generally had to comply by stopping the strike or boycott.

The labor injunction became a potent weapon for management to use against any union pressure tactics. The unions were deprived of their chief weapons to pressure employers for economic improvements. Although the AFL emphasized union activity over political activity, it soon made the passage of anti-injunction legislation a top priority in its program.

Yellow-Dog Contracts

In addition to securing labor injunctions against union activities, employers were also able to use the courts to enforce **yellow-dog contracts,** or contracts of employment that required employees to agree not to join a union. By incorporating the anti-union promise in the contract, employers could legally make nonmembership in unions a condition of employment. Employees who joined a union could be fired for breach of their employment contract.

In the 1917 case of *Hitchman Coal Co.* v. *Mitchell* (245 U.S. 229), the Supreme

Court upheld an injunction against a strike that was intended to force the employer to abandon the yellow-dog contracts. The majority of the Court held that the union, by inducing the workers to break their contracts, was guilty of wrongly interfering with contractual relations. The Court's decision confirmed the importance of the yellow-dog contract as another weapon in the employers' legal arsenal against unions.

The Antitrust Laws

In addition to the labor injunction and the yellow-dog contract, the antitrust laws provided yet another legal weapon for employers. The Sherman Antitrust Act was passed by Congress in 1890 in response to public agitation against such giant business monopolies as the Standard Oil Company and the American Tobacco trust. The act outlawed restraints of trade and monopolozing of trade. Section 1 contained the following provision:

> Every contract, combination in the form of trust or otherwise, or conspiracy, in restraint of trade or commerce among the several states, or with foreign nations, is hereby declared to be illegal. Every person who shall make any such contract or engage in any such combination or conspiracy, shall be deemed guilty of a misdemeanor, and, on conviction thereof, shall be punished by fine not exceeding five thousand dollars, or by imprisonment not exceeding one year, or by both said punishments, in the discretion of the court.

Other provisions of the act allowed private parties to sue for damages if they were injured by restraints of trade and gave the federal courts power to issue injunctions against violators of the act. Most observers assumed the act was limited to business trusts and predatory corporate behavior. *Loewe* v. *Lawlor* (208 U.S. 274), the Danbury Hatters' case, however, made it clear that organized labor activities were also subject to the Sherman Act.

The Danbury Hatters' case grew out of an AFL boycott of the D. E. Loewe Company of Danbury, Connecticut. In order to assist efforts by the United Hatters' Union to organize the Loewe workers, the AFL called for a nationwide boycott of all Loewe products. The company responded by filing a suit under the Sherman Act in 1903. The company alleged that the boycott was a conspiracy to restrain trade, and it sought damages totaling $240,000 against the individual union members. The district court, rejecting the union's argument that the boycott did not interfere with "trade or commerce among the states," found the defendants liable for damages. The union appealed to the U.S. Supreme Court.

The Supreme Court, in this 1908 decision, held that the boycott was a combination in restraint of trade within the meaning of the Sherman Act. The Court refused to read into the act an exemption for labor activities, citing the words of Section 1 that "every . . . combination or conspiracy in restraint of trade" was illegal.

After the Supreme Court's decision in the Danbury Hatters' case, other employers also successfully attacked union boycotts under the Sherman Act. In the face of such actions, the AFL lobbied Congress for legislative relief. The passage of the Clayton Act in 1914 appeared to provide the relief sought by labor.

The key provisions of the Clayton Act, which also amended the Sherman Act, were Section 6 and Section 20. Section 6 stated

> [t]hat the labor of a human being is not a commodity or article of commerce . . . nor shall such (labor) organizations, or the members thereof, be held or construed to be illegal combinations or conspiracies in restraint of trade, under the antitrust laws.

Section 20 restricted the issuance of labor injunctions. It provided that no injunction could be issued against employees unless irreparable harm to the employer's property or property rights was threatened and the legal remedy of monetary damages would be inadequate. Samuel Gompers of the AFL declared those sections to be "labors's Magna Carta."

The effect of those sections was the subject of the 1921 Supreme Court decision of *Duplex Printing Press Company* v. *Deering* (254 U.S. 443). The case grew out of a boycott of the products of the Duplex Printing Press Company, organizied by the Machinists' Union. The union was attempting to get the employer to agree to a closed shop provision, to accept an eight-hour workday, and to adopt a union-proposed wage scale. When a strike proved unsuccessful, the union called for a national boycott of Duplex products. Duplex responded by filing suit for an injunction under the Clayton Act against the officers of the New York City Local of the Machinists' Union. The union argued that Section 6 and Section 20 of the Clayton Act prevented the issuance of an injunction against the union and its officers.

A majority of the Supreme Court held that Section 6

> assumes the normal objects of a labor organization to be legitimate, and declares that nothing in the antitrust laws shall be construed to forbid the existence and operation of such organizations or to forbid their members from lawfully carrying out their legitimate objects. . . . But there is nothing in the section to exempt such an organization or its members from accountability where it or they depart from its normal and legitimate objects and engage in actual combination of conspiracy in restraint of trade. And by no fair or permissible construction can it be taken as authorizing any activity otherwise unlawful, or enabling a normally lawful organization to become a cloak for an illegal combination or conspiracy in restraint of trade as defined by the antitrust laws.

The Court, finding no legislative intent in Section 6 or Section 20 for a general grant of immunity for conduct otherwise violative of the antitrust laws, upheld the injunction against the union and its officers. The Court's decision effectively gutted the Clayton Act provisions hailed by Gompers.

The Supreme Court did grant labor a small concession in the 1922 case of *United Mine Workers of America* v. *Coronado Coal Company* (259 U.S. 344). The mining company brought suit under the Sherman Act for damages resulting from a violent strike by the union. The Court held that whereas all strikes were not necessarily legal under the Sherman Act, the strike here had only an indirect effect on interstate commerce and was therefore not in violation of the act.

Although *Coronado Coal* provided a slight glimmer of hope for organized labor, the effects of the labor injunction and the Danbury Hatters' and *Duplex* cases continued to make things extremely difficult. Labor would have to wait for the effects of the Great Depression, as well as the accession of the Democratic Party to national power, before the legal and judicial impediments to its activities would be removed.

QUESTIONS

1. How was the criminal conspiracy doctrine used against labor union activities in the United States?

2. What were the main objectives of the Knights of Labor? What factors contributed to the decline of the Knights of Labor?

3. How did the objectives of the American Federation of Labor differ from those of the Knights of Labor? Why was the AFL more successful than the Knights of Labor?

4. Why did the CIO break away from the AFL? How did the CIO's objectives differ from those of the AFL?

5. Why was the labor injunction an effective weapon against union activities?

6. What are yellow-dog contracts? How could they be used to deter union organizing activity?

7. How were the antitrust laws used to deter union activities?

CHAPTER 3

The Development of the National Labor Relations Act

ORGANIZED LABOR REACTED TO the judicial endorsement of employer anti-union tactics by engaging in coordinated political pressure for legislative controls on judicial involvement in labor disputes. This political activity yielded results in 1932 when a federal anti-injunction act, sponsored by Senator Norris and Congressman La Guardia, was enacted. The **Norris–La Guardia Act** was reputedly drafted by Harvard law professor (and later Supreme Court Justice) Felix Frankfurter, who was a leading critic of judicial abuses of the labor injunction.

The Norris–La Guardia Act

The Norris–La Guardia Act, in effect, was a legislative reversal of the prevailing view of the judiciary that economic injury inflicted by unions pursuing their economic self-interest was unlawful both at common law and under the antitrust laws. The act created a laissez-faire environment for organized labor's self-help activities. Labor finally had its Magna Carta.

Provisions of the Norris–La Guardia Act

Section 1 of the Norris–La Guardia Act prohibited the federal courts from issuing injunctions in labor disputes except in strict conformity with the provisions set out in the act. Those provisions, contained in Section 7, required that the court hold an open-court hearing, with opportunity for cross-examination of all witnesses and participation by representatives of both sides to the controversy. The court could issue an injunction only if the hearing had established that unlawful acts had actually been threatened or committed and would be committed or continue to be committed unless restraints were ordered. The party seeking the injunction would have to establish that substantial and irreparable injury to its property would follow and that it had no adequate remedy at law. Lastly, the court would have to be convinced that the public officials charged with the duty to protect the threatened property were unable or unwilling to provide adequate protection. Only after complying with this procedure and making such findings could the court issue an injunction in a labor dispute.

Section 4 of the act set out a list of activities that were protected from injunctions, even when the foregoing safeguards might be observed. The section states that

[n]o court of the United States shall have jurisdiction to issue any restraining order or temporary or permanent injunction in any case involving or growing out of any labor dispute to prohibit any person or persons participating or interested in such dispute (as these terms are herein defined) from doing, whether singly or in concert, any of the following acts:

(a) Ceasing or refusing to perform any work or to remain in any relation of employment;

(b) Becoming or remaining a member of any labor organization or of any employer organization, regardless of any such undertaking or promise as is described in Section 3 of this act;

(c) Paying or giving to, or withholding from, any person participating or interested in such labor dispute, any strike or unemployment benefits or insurance, or other moneys or things of value;

(d) By all lawful means aiding any person participating or interested in any labor dispute who is being proceeded against in, or is prosecuting, any action or suit in any court of the United States or of any State;

(e) Giving publicity to the existence of, or the facts involved in, any labor dispute, whether by advertising, speaking, patrolling, or by any other method not involving fraud or violence;

(f) Assembling peaceably to act or to organize to act in promotion of their interests in a labor dispute;

(g) Advising or notifying any person of an intention to do any of the acts heretofore specified;

(h) Agreeing with other persons to do or not to do any of the acts heretofore specified; and

(i) advising, urging, or otherwise causing or inducing without fraud or violence the acts heretofore specified, regardless of any such undertaking or promise as is described in Section 3 of this act.

The term *labor dispute* was defined in Section 13(c) of the act, which states:

The term "labor dispute" includes any controversy concerning the terms or conditions of employment, or concerning the association or representation of persons in negotiating, fixing, maintaining, changing, or seeking to arrange terms or conditions of employment, regardless of whether or not the disputants stand in the proximate relation of employer and employee.

Finally, Section 3 of the act declared that yellow-dog contracts were contrary to public policy of the United States and were not enforceable by any federal court. Nor could the courts use such contracts as the basis for granting any legal or equitable remedies (such as injunctions).

State Anti-Injunction Laws

Although the Norris–La Guardia Act applied only to the federal courts, a number of states passed similar legislation restricting their court systems in issuing labor injunctions. Such acts are known as "little Norris–La Guardia Acts." The Supreme Court upheld the constitutionality of Wisconsin's "little Norris–La Guardia Act" in the 1937 decision of *Senn* v. *Tile Layers' Protective Union* (301 U.S. 468). Although the case did not involve the federal act, it did raise the same legal issues as would an attack on the constitutionality of the federal act; the decision in *Senn* was regarded as settling the question of the federal act's constitutionality.

Validity and Scope of the Norris–La Guardia Act

The following case illustrates the Supreme Court's approach to the validity and the broad scope of the provisions of the Norris–La Guardia Act.

NEW NEGRO ALLIANCE v. SANITARY GROCERY CO., INC.

303 U.S. 552 (Supreme Court of the United States, 1938)

ROBERTS, J.

The matter in controversy is whether the case made by the pleadings involves or grows out of a labor dispute within the meaning of Section 13 of the Norris–La Guardia Act.

The respondent sought an injunction restraining the petitioners and their agents from picketing its stores and engaging in other activities injurious to its business. The petitioners answered, the cause was heard upon bill and answer and an injunction was awarded. The United States Court of Appeals for the District of Columbia affirmed the decree. The importance of the question presented and asserted conflict with the decisions of this and other federal courts moved us to grant certiorari.

The case, then, as it stood for judgment was this: The petitioners requested the respondent to adopt a policy of employing negro clerks in certain of its stores in the course of personnel changes; the respondent ignored the request and the petitioners caused one person to patrol in front of one of the respondent's stores on one day carrying a placard which said, "Do Your Part! Buy Where You Can Work! No Negroes Employed Here!" and caused or threatened a similar patrol of two other stores of respondent. The information borne by the placard was true. The patrolling did not coerce or intimidate respondent's customers; did not physi-

cally obstruct, interfere with, or harass persons desiring to enter the store; the picket acted in an orderly manner, and his conduct did not cause crowds to gather in front of the store.

The trial judge was of the view that the laws relating to labor disputes had no application to the case. He entered a decree enjoining the petitioners and their agents and employees from picketing or patrolling any of the respondent's stores, boycotting or urging others to boycott respondent; restraining them, whether by inducements, threats, intimidation, or actual or threatened physical force, from hindering any person entering respondent's places of business, from destroying or damaging or threatening to destroy or damage respondent's property, and from aiding or abetting others in doing any of the prohibited things. The Court of Appeals thought that the dispute was not a labor dispute within the Norris–La Guardia Act because it did not involve terms and conditions of employment such as wages, hours, unionization or betterment of working conditions, and that the trial court, therefore, had jurisdiction to issue the injunction. We think the conclusion that the dispute was not a labor dispute within the meaning of the act, because it did not involve terms and conditions of employment in the sense of wages, hours, unionization or betterment of working conditions is erroneous.

Subsection (a) of Section 13 provides: "A case shall be held to involve or to grow out of a labor dispute when the case involves persons who are engaged in the same industry, trade, craft, or occupation; or have direct or indirect interests therein; . . . or when the case involves any conflicting or competing interests in a 'labor dispute' (as hereinafter defined) of 'persons participating or interested' therein (as hereinafter defined)." Subsection (b) characterizes a person or association as participating or interested in a labor dispute "if relief is sought against him or it, and if he or it . . . has a direct or indirect interest therein." Subsection (c) defines the term "labor dispute" as including "any controversy concerning terms or conditions of employment, . . . regardless of whether or not the disputants stand in the proximate relation of employer and employee." These definitions plainly embrace the controversy which gave rise to the instant suit and classify it as one arising out of a dispute defined as a labor dispute. They leave no doubt that the New Negro Alliance and the individual petitioners are, in contemplation of the act, persons interested in the dispute.

In quoting the clauses of Section 13 we have omitted those that deal with disputes between employers and employees and disputes between associations of persons engaged in a particular trade or craft, and employers in the same industry. It is to be noted, however, that the inclusion in the definitions of such disputes, and the persons interested in them, serves to emphasize the fact that the quoted portions were intended to embrace controversies other than those between employers and employees; between labor unions seeking to represent employees and employers; and between persons seeking employment and employers.

The act does not concern itself with the background or the motives of the dispute. The desire for fair and equitable conditions of employment on the part of persons of any race, color, or persuasion, and the removal of discriminations against them by reason of their race or religious beliefs is quite as important to those concerned as fairness and equity in terms and conditions of employment can be to trade or craft unions or any form of labor organization or association. Race discrimination by an employer may reasonably be deemed more unfair and less excusable than discrimination against workers on the ground of union affiliation. There is no justification in the apparent purposes or the express terms of the act for limiting its definition of labor disputes and cases arising therefrom by excluding those which arise with respect to discrimination in terms and conditions of employment based upon differences of race or color.

The purpose and policy of the act respecting the jurisdiction of the federal courts is set forth in Sections 4 and 7. The former deprives those courts of jurisdiction to issue an injunction against, inter alia, giving publicity to the existence of, or the facts involved in, any labor dispute, whether by advertising, speaking, patrolling, or by any other method not involving fraud or violence; against assembling peaceably to act or to organize to act in promotion of their interests in a labor disputes; against advising or notifying any person of an intention to do any of the acts specified; against agreeing with other persons to do any of the acts specified. Section 7 deprives the courts of jurisdiction to issue an injunction in any case involving or growing out of a labor dispute, except after hearing sworn testimony in open court in support of the allegations of the complaint, and upon findings of fact to the effect (a) that unlawful acts have been threatened and will be committed unless restrained, or have been committed and will be continued, unless restrained, and then only against the person or persons, association or organization making the threat or permitting the unlawful act or authorizing or ratifying it; (b) that substantial and irreparable injury to complainant's property will follow; (c) that, as to each item of relief granted, greater injury will be inflicted upon the complainant by denial of the relief than will be inflicted on the defendant by granting it; (d) that complainant has no adequate remedy at law; and (e) that the public officers charged with the duty to protect complainant's property are unable or unwilling to furnish adequate protection.

The legislative history of the act demonstrates that it was the purpose of the Congress further to extend the prohibitions of the Clayton Act respecting the exercise of jurisdiction by federal courts and to obviate the results of the judicial construction of the act. It was intended that peaceful and orderly dissemination of information by those defined as persons interested in a labor dispute concerning "terms and conditions of employment" in an industry or a plant or a place of business should be lawful; that, short of fraud, breach of the peace, violence, or conduct otherwise unlawful, those having a direct or indirect interest in such terms and conditions of employment should be at liberty to advertise and disseminate facts and information with respect to terms and conditions of employment, and peacefully to persuade others to concur in their views respecting an employer's practices. The District Court erred in not complying with the provisions of the act.

The decree must be reversed, and the cause remanded to the District Court for further proceedings in conformity with this opinion. [**Dissent omitted.**]

The Railway Labor Act

The **Railway Labor Act,** passed in 1926, allowed railroad employees to designate bargaining representatives of their own choosing, free from employer interference. This legislation introduced some of the ideas and approaches later incorporated in the National Labor Relations Act.

The railroads were one of the earliest industries in which the employees were unionized. As noted in Chapter 2, the railroads were the target of several violent strikes during the late nineteenth century. The importance of the railroads for the nation's economic development and the railroads' position as essentially being public utilities made them the subject of government regulation; the Interstate Commerce Commission was created in 1887 to regulate freight rates and routes. The disruptive effects of labor disputes involving the railroads were also a subject for government concern. Congress passed several laws aimed at minimizing or avoiding labor strife in the railroad industry.

Legislative Predecessors of the Railway Labor Act

In 1888 Congress enacted the Arbitration Act as a result of a bloody strike on the Chicago, Burlington and Quincy Railroad. The act provided for voluntary arbitration of disputes—the parties could voluntarily agree to submit the dispute to a three-member panel. The act also authorized the president of the United States to appoint a three-member commission to investigate the causes of any railrad labor dispute. The investigation panel could be set up at the request of either party to the dispute, at the request of the governor of any state, or at the president's own initiative.

The arbitration provisions were not used for the ten years that the unamended act existed. The investigation provision of the law was invoked by President Cleveland, at his own initiative, during the Pullman Strike of 1894; however, the strike was ended by court order and federal troops before the commission could make its report.

In 1898, in response to the inadequacies of the Arbitration Act demonstrated during the Pullman Strike, Congress passed the Erdman Act, which continued the voluntary arbitration provisions but omitted the investigatory features of its predecessor. The Erdman Act introduced the idea of mediating disputes; it provided that the U.S. commissioner of labor and the chairman of the Interstate Commerce Commission, at the request of either party to the dispute, would make every effort to settle the dispute through mediation and conciliation. If the mediation failed, the mediators were to urge the parties to arbitrate the dispute. A third feature of the act was the prohibition of employer discrimination against employees because of union membership. This prohibition, which was enforceable by prison sentences, was held unconstitutional by the Supreme Court in 1908 in the case of *Adair* v. *U.S.* (208 U.S. 161).

Although the Erdman Act was not used in a dispute until 1906, between 1906 and 1913 a total of sixty-one cases were settled under the act. In 1913 the Newlands Act amended the Erdman Act by providing a permanent board of mediation and conciliation. The board's jurisdiction covered disputes arising out of the negotiation of agreements and out of the interpretation of agreements as well. The act retained the voluntary arbitration provisions of its predecessors.

A dispute over the establishment of the eight-hour workday led to the next legislative enactment in 1916. Unions seeking the eight-hour workday refused to arbitrate or permit mediation of the dispute; they did, however, agree to call off the strike if their demand would be enacted into federal law. Congress responded by passing the Adamson Act, which provided for an eight-hour workday for the railroads.

During World War I the federal government took over operation of the nation's railroads. Upon return of the railways to their private owners following the war, Congress enacted the Transportation Act of 1920. That act revised the Newlands Act and created a Railway Labor Board. The board had three members, one each representing the carriers, the employees, and the public. The board would investigate labor disputes and publish its decisions. However, the board lacked enforcement power and had to rely on public opinion for enforcing its decisions.

Provisions of the Railway Labor Act

Finally, in 1926 Congress passed the Railway Labor Act, which established a three-step procedure for settling disputes. The first step involved using a federal mediation board to attempt to facilitate negotiation of the parties' differences. If that failed, the board would then try to induce the parties to arbitrate the dispute. Although not compelled to submit the dispute to arbitration, the parties would be legally bound by the results if they agreed to arbitration. Finally, if arbitration was refused, the board could recommend to the president that an emergency board of investigation be created. If the president created the emergency board, the parties in dispute were required to maintain the status quo for thirty days while the investigation proceeded. Even if an emergency board was not appointed, the parties were still required to maintain the status quo for thirty days. This mandatory "cooling-off" period was designed to allow the dispute to be settled through negotiation. The union retained its right to strike, and the employer could lock out once the cooling-off period expired.

The act also provided that both labor and management had the right to designate bargaining representatives without the "interference, influence or coercion" of the other party. That provision was the subject of the Supreme Court's 1930 decision of *Texas & New Orleans Railroad* v. *Brotherhood of Railway Clerks* (281 U.S. 548). The union had sought, and was granted, an injunction against employer interference with the employees' designation of bargaining representative under the act. The railroad argued that the act did not create any legally enforceable right of free choice for employees and that the act's provisions were an unconstitutional interference with management's right to operate the railroad. The Supreme Court upheld the injunction and the constitutionality of the Railway Labor Act, rejecting the railroad's challenges.

The Railway Labor Act was amended by Congress in 1934, 1936, 1951, and 1966. The act was extended to cover airline employees, and a duty to bargain with the duly designated representative of each side was spelled out. The amendments also provided that unions representing the airline or railway employees could bargain for a union shop provision. The National Railroad Adjustment Board was created to arbitrate disputes involving the railroads and unions; its awards are final and binding upon the parties. The amendments also created sanctions for enforcement of the act by declaring violations to be misdemeanors. Such violations included the interference with the designation of representatives by either party, the use of yellow-dog contracts, and the changing of any terms or conditions of employment without complying with the provisions of a collective agreement.

The amendments creating the duty to bargain with representatives of the employees were the subject of a challenge in the 1937 Supreme Court case of *Virginia Railway Co.* v. *System Federation No. 40* (300 U.S. 515). The union representing railway employees sought an injunction to force the railroad to recognize and bargain with it. The trial court ordered the railroad to "treat with" the union, and to "exert every reasonable effort to make and maintain agreements" covering conditions of employment and settling of disputes. The order was affirmed by the court of appeals, over the objections of the employer that the act imposed no legally enforceable duty to bargain. The Supreme Court, affirming the order, held that the act created a mandatory requirement of recognizing and negotiating with the bargaining representatives duly designated by the parties and that this requirement could be enforced by court order.

The National Industrial Recovery Act

The other statutory predecessor of the National Labor Relations Act was the **National Industrial Recovery Act (NIRA).** That legislation was the centerpiece of President Franklin D. Roosevelt's "New Deal." Roosevelt took office in 1933, the fourth year of the Great Depression; some fifteen million people were unemployed, and there was a widespread belief that the nation's economic growth had come to a permanent halt. Roosevelt proposed his New Deal program to pull the nation out of the depression. It involved government working closely and actively with business to revive the economy.

The NIRA set up a system in which major industries would operate under **codes of fair competition,** which would be developed by trade associations for each industry. These associations would be under the supervision and guidance of the **National Recovery Administration (NRA).** The NIRA, in Section 7(a), also provided that the codes of fair competition contain the following conditions:

> (1) That employees shall have the right to organize and bargain collectively through representatives of their own choosing, and shall be free from interference, restraint, or coercion of employers of labor, or their agents, in the designation of such representatives or in self-organization or in other concerted activities for the purpose of collective bargaining or other mutual aid or protection; (2) that no employee . . . shall be required as a condition of employment to join any company union or to refrain from joining, organizing, or assisting a labor organization of his own choosing; and (3) that employers shall

comply with the maximum hours of labor, minimum rates of pay, and other conditions of employment, approved or prescribed by the President.

The NIRA, responsible for administering the codes of fair competition under the NIRA, had to rely on voluntary cooperation from the industries being regulated. The NRA announced that codes containing provisions concerning hours, rates of pay, and other conditions of employment would be subject to NRA approval, although such conditions had not been arrived at through collective bargaining. The practical effect of this announcement was to allow industry to develop such codes unilaterally, without input from organized labor. While employees rushed to join unions, employers refused to recognize and bargain with the unions. A wave of strikes resulted, with more strikes in 1933 than in any year since 1921.

President Roosevelt issued a plea for industrial peace and created the National Labor Board to "consider, adjust and settle differences and controversies that may arise through differing interpretations" of the NIRA provisions.

The National Labor Board

The **National Labor Board (NLB)** was created in August 1933. The NLB was composed of seven members; three representative each would be chosen by the NRA's Industrial Advisory Board and Labor Advisory Board. The seventh member was Senator Robert Wagner of New York, who was chairman. The NLB initially functioned as a mediation board, seeking to persuade the parties to settle their differences peacefully. The NLB had considerable early success, relying on public sentiment and the prestige of its members. Despite its early success, however, the NLB had several serious flaws.

The partisan members of the NLB tended to vote in blocks, undermining the credibility and effectiveness of the board. The board was also inexperienced and understaffed. The most serious drawback, however, was the weakness of enforcement powers given to the NLB. The only sanctions available to the NLB were either to request that the NRA withdraw an offending company's "Blue Eagle"—a sign of compliance with the NIRA and of NRA approval (which was necessary to contract with the federal government)—or to ask the Justice Department to seek a court order to enforce a board ruling. In practice, the NLB relied mainly on the power of persuasion.

The NLB's persuasive power, however, was effective only so long as an employer was not overtly antagonistic to organized labor. In major industries such as steel and automobiles, there was a strong inclination to defy NLB orders. Several major employers refused to conduct, or to abide by the results of representation elections under Section 7(a) of the NIRA. William Green, president of the AFL, publicly lamented the destruction of the "faith that . . . workers have in . . . the National Labor Board." In March 1934 the nation's automobile manufacturers all refused to recognize the United Automobile Workers Union or to allow the board to conduct a representative election. President Roosevelt chose to have General Hugh Johnson, head of the NRA, negotiate a settlement rather than stand behind the NLB order. That decision destroyed what little effectiveness the NLB retained.

Despite its short tenure, the NLB did make several contributions to modern labor law. It evolved from a mediation service into an adjudicative body akin to the present National Labor Relations Board (NLRB). It also established the principles of majority rule and exclusive representation of the employees in a particular bargaining unit. In addition, the board developed other rules that have come to be basic principles of labor relations law, among them the following: (1) an employer was obligated to bargain with a union that had been chosen as representative by a majority of employees; (2) employers had no right to know of an employee's membership in, or vote for, a union when a secret ballot representation election was held; and (3) strikers remained employees while on strike and were entitled to displace any replacements hired if the strike was the result of employer violations of the NIRA.

The "Old" National Labor Relations Board

In June 1934 President Roosevelt formulated Public Resolution No. 44. This resolution, which was then passed by Congress, authorized the president to establish a "board or boards" empowered to investigate disputes arising under Section 7(a) of the NIRA and to conduct secret ballot representation elections among employees. Enforcement of board decisions would remain with the NRA and the Justice Department. Roosevelt then abolished the NLB and transferred its funds, personnel, and pending cases to the National Labor Relations Board (the "old" NLRB). The NLRB was denied all jurisdiction over disputes in the steel and auto industries. The NLRB reaffirmed the key rulings of the NLB; it also issued guidelines to assist regional offices in handling common types of cases and began organizing its decisions into a body of precedents guiding future action.

When the Supreme Court declared the NIRA to be unconstitutional in its 1935 decision *Schechter Poultry Corp.* v. *U.S.* (295 U.S. 495), it also destroyed the "old" NLRB.

The National Labor Relations Act

Senator Wagner introduced a proposed **National Labor Relations Act (NLRA)** in the Senate in 1935, but the bill faced stiff opposition. The National Association of Manufacturers and the general business community opposed it. Certain union leaders within the AFL, fearing the law would give equal organizing advantages to the rival CIO unions, also opposed it. Opposition to the bill lessened after the Supreme Court's *Schechter Poultry* decision; opponents were certain that the Court would also strike down the NLRA, just as it had done with the NIRA.

The NLRA was passed by Congress and enacted into law in 1935. Because of the doubts over the NLRA's constitutionality, President Roosevelt had difficulty finding qualified people willing to be appointed to the **National Labor Relations Board (NLRB)** established under the NLRA. The main concern over the constitutionality of the NLRA dealt with whether it was a valid exercise of the interstate commerce power given to Congress under the Constitution. In *Schechter Poultry* the Supreme

Court had held that the NIRA was not within the authority given the federal government under the **commerce clause** of the Constitution. In passing the NLRA, Congress had relied on the power to regulate commerce among the states given to it under the commerce clause. The findings of fact incorporated in Section 1 of the NLRA contained the following statement:

> The denial by employers of the right of employees to organize and the refusal by employers to accept the procedure of collective bargaining lead to strikes and other forms of industrial strife or unrest, which have the intent or the necessary effect of burdening or obstructing commerce. . . .

For more than a year after the passage of the NLRA there was only limited activity by the NLRB. The board set out to develop economic data supporting the findings of fact in Section 1 of the NLRA. It also sought the best possible case to take to the Supreme Court to settle the constitutionality issue.

During the same period the Supreme Court came under heavy criticism from President Roosevelt for its opposition to his New Deal initiatives. Roosevelt at one point proposed expanding the Court from nine to fifteen justices, allowing him to "pack the Court" by appointing justices sympathetic to his program. The pressure on the Court and the retirement of some of its members resulted in a dramatic shift in the Court's attitudes toward Roosevelt's New Deal. It also meant that the NLRA might get a more sympathetic reception at the Court than the NIRA had gotten.

Finally, the NLRB brought five cases to the federal courts of appeals. The cases involved an interstate bus company, the Associated Press news service, and three manufacturing firms. The board lost all three of the manufacturing company cases in the courts of appeals on the interstate commerce issue. All five of the cases were taken to the Supreme Court and were heard by the Court in February 1937. The NLRB developed its arguments in the *Jones and Laughlin Steel* case, one of the manufacturing cases, almost entirely on the interstate commerce issue. That case became the crucial litigation in the test of the NLRA's constitutionality.

The Supreme Court in its 1937 decision in *NLRB* v. *Jones & Laughlin Steel Corp.* (301 U.S. 1) upheld the constitutionality of the NLRA by a five-to-four vote. The majority opinion, by Chief Justice Hughes, held that the disruption of operations of Jones & Laughlin due to industrial strife would have a serious and direct effect on interstate commerce. In the words of the Court,

> When industries organize themselves on a national scale, making their relation to interstate commerce the dominant factor in their activities, how can it be maintained that their industrial labor relations constitute a forbidden field into which Congress may not enter when it is necessary to protect interstate commerce from the paralyzing consequences of industrial war?

By the slimmest of margins the Supreme Court had upheld the validity of the National Labor Relations Act. The decision also meant that a labor relations board effectively empowered to deal with disputes between labor and management had finally been established.

QUESTIONS

1. What were the main provisions of the Norris–La Guardia Act? How did the Norris–La Guardia Act affect labor union activities?

2. What dispute resolution procedures are available under the Railway Labor Act? Which employees are covered by the Railway Labor Act?

3. How did the National Recovery Act attempt to encourage collective bargaining? Why was the NRA unsuccessful in promoting collective bargaining?

4. What factors undermined the effectiveness of the National Labor Board?

5. What was the basis of federal jurisdiction over labor relations to support the National Labor Relations Act? What was the effect of the Supreme Court decision in the *Jones & Laughlin Steel Corp.* case?

CHAPTER 4

The National Labor Relations Act and the National Labor Relations Board: Organization, Jurisdiction, and Procedures

THE PASSAGE OF THE National Labor Relations Act, or the Wagner Act, constituted a revolutionary change in national labor policy. Workers were now to be legally protected by the federal government in their rights to organize for mutual aid and security and to bargain collectively through representatives of their own choice.

The National Labor Relations Act

The purpose of the act, as stated in Section 1, was to

> eliminate the causes of certain substantial obstructions to the free flow of commerce . . . by encouraging the practice and procedure of collective bargaining and by protecting the exercise by workers of full freedom of association, self-organization, and designation of representatives of their own choosing, for the purpose of negotiating the terms and conditions of their employment or other mutual aid or protection.

The basis of the act was the protection of the rights of employees, defined by Section 7:

> Employees shall have the right to self-organization, to form, join, or assist labor organizations, to bargain collectively through representatives of their own choosing, and to engage in concerted activities for the purpose of collective bargaining or other mutual aid or protection.

In order to protect these basic rights of employees, the act prohibited certain practices of employers that would interfere with or prevent the exercise of such rights. Those practices were designated **unfair labor practices,** and the act listed five of them:

1. interference with, or restraint or coercion of, employees in the exercise of their Section 7 rights;
2. domination of, or interference with, a labor organization (including financial or other contributions to it);
3. discrimination in terms or conditions of employment of employees for the purpose of encouraging or discouraging union membership;
4. discrimination against an employee for filing a charge or testifying in a proceeding under the act;
5. refusal to bargain collectively with the employees' legal bargaining representative.

The act reconstituted the National Labor Relations Board to enforce and administer the statute. The board created a nationwide organization, developed a body of legal precedents (drawing heavily upon decisions of its predecessors), and developed and refined its procedures. In its efforts to carry out the policies of the legislation, the board was frequently criticized for being too pro-union. Indeed, the entire orientation of the Wagner Act was pro-union in its definition of employee rights and unfair practices by employers.

Under the protection of the Wagner Act, unions were able to develop to a great extent; their powers relative to employers grew accordingly. Even during World War II, when labor and management pledged cooperation to ensure production for the war effort, some unions were accused of abusing their newly gained power under the act. A 1946 strike by the United Mine Workers, in defiance of a Supreme Court order to remain on the job, seemed to crystallize public opinion that unions had grown too powerful.

This public concern was reflected in congressional action to limit unions' abuse of their powers. Congressional critics were especially concerned over jurisdictional disputes, in which two unions claimed the right to represent the workers of an employer, leaving the employer "trapped" between them, and recognitional picketing, which was aimed at forcing an employer to recognize the union regardless of the sentiments of the employees.[1] These kinds of congressional concerns resulted in the passage of the Taft-Hartley Act in 1947. The Taft-Hartley Act outlawed the **closed shop,** a term describing an employer who agrees to hire only those employees who are already union members. It also added a list of unfair labor practices by unions and emphasized that employees had the right, under Section 7, to *refrain from* col-

---

[1]The Teamsters Union was particularly notorious for using this tactic with firms employing primarily African-American workers. The Teamsters would force the firm to recognize them as bargaining agent for the employees and collect union dues, but wages and working conditions would remain unaffected.

lective activity as well as engage in it. The purpose and effect of the Taft-Hartley Act was to balance the rights and duties of both unions and employers.

After Taft-Hartley, the National Labor Relations Act was amended several times, the most significant version being the Landrum-Griffin Act of 1959. Landrum-Griffin was passed in response to concerns about union racketeering and abusive practices aimed at union members. The act set out specific rights for individual union members against the union, and it proscribed certain kinds of conduct by union officials, such as financial abuse, racketeering, and manipulation of union-election procedures.

The National Labor Relations Board

Unless otherwise specified, the discussion throughout this and subsequent chapters will focus on the current National Labor Relations Act[2] and the present National Labor Relations Board's organization, jurisdiction, and procedure.

Organization of the NLRB

Because the Wagner Act gave little guidance concerning the administrative structure of the newly created agency, the NLRB adopted an administrative organization that made it prosecutor, judge, and jury with regard to complaints under the act. The board investigated charges of unfair labor practices, prosecuted complaints, conducted hearings, and rendered decisions. Pursuant to its statutory authority, the board did appoint a general counsel to serve as legal adviser and direct litigation, but the general counsel was subordinate to the board in virtually all matters.

The combination of prosecutorial and judicial functions was one of the major criticisms leveled by commentators and attorneys against the board in the years prior to the passage of the Taft-Hartley Act. This issue, not surprisingly, was addressed by Taft-Hartley in 1947. Although retaining the concept of a single enforcement agency, Taft-Hartley made the Office of the General Counsel an independent unit to direct the administrative and enforcement efforts of the NLRB regional offices. The board itself was expanded from three to five members. It continued to exercise the judicial function of deciding complaints filed under the act.

The newly organized NLRB represented a unique type of administrative agency structure in that it was bifurcated into two independent authorities within the single agency: the five-member board and the general counsel. Figure 4.1 depicts the organization of the two authorities of the bifurcated agency.

The Board.   The board itself is the judicial branch of the agency. The five members of the board are nominated by the president and must be confirmed by the Senate.

---

[2]The Taft-Hartley Act incorporated the National Labor Relations Act. Scholars and labor lawyers differ in whether the modern act should be referred to as the NLRA or the Labor Management Relations Act, or both. For convenience, and since the enforcing agency is still called the NLRB, we will continue to refer to the act as the National Labor Relations Act.

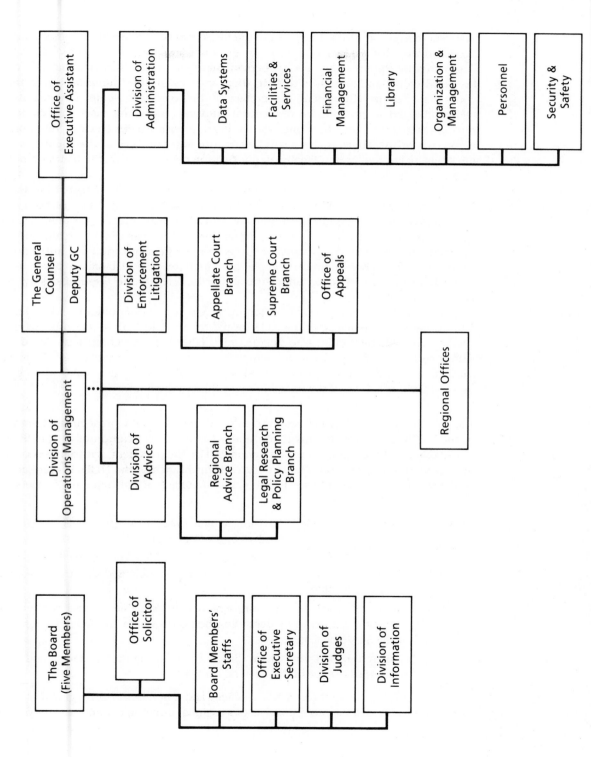

Figure 4.1   Organization chart of the National Labor Relations Board

Prepared by: Organization & Management Branch Division of Administration 7/74

They serve five-year terms. Members of the board can be removed from office by the president only for neglect of duty or malfeasance in office. One member is to be designated by the president as chairperson. Members have a staff of about twenty-five legal clerks and assistants to help them in deciding the numerous cases that come before them. The executive secretary of the board is the chief administrative officer, charged with ruling on procedural questions, assigning cases to members, setting priorities in case handling, and conferring with parties to cases that come before the board. There is also a solicitor, whose function is to advise members on questions of law and policy. Finally, an information director assists the board on public relations issues.

The NLRB also has a branch called the Division of Judges. These **Administrative Law Judges (ALJs),** formerly called Trial Examiners, are independent of both the board and the general counsel. Appointed for life, they are subject to the federal Civil Service Commission rules governing appointment and tenure. This organizational independence is necessary because the ALJs conduct hearings and issue initial decisions on unfair labor practice complaints issued by regional offices distributed throughout the United States, under the authority delegated to these offices by the general counsel.

The board is prohibited by law from reviewing an ALJ's findings or recommendations before the issuance of the ALJ's formal report. The ALJ's function is that of a specialized trial court judge—to decide unfair labor practice complaints. ALJ decisions may be appealed to the board, which functions as a specialized court of appeal. After rendering their initial decisions, ALJs (like trial court judges) have nothing to do with the disposition of the case if it is appealed to the board.

The General Counsel.   The Office of the General Counsel is the prosecutorial branch of the NLRB and is also in charge of the day-to-day administration of the NLRB regional offices. The general counsel is nominated by the president, with Senate confirmation for a four-year term. The structure of this branch of the NLRB is more complex than that of the board (see Figure 4.1). The Office of the General Counsel has four divisions:

1. the Operations-Management Division, which supervises operations of field offices and the management of all cases in the Washington, D.C., divisions;

2. the Advice Division, which oversees the function of legal advice to the regional offices, the injunction work of the district court branch, and the legal research and special projects office;

3. the Enforcement Litigation Division, which is responsible for the conduct of agency litigation enforcing or defending board orders in the federal courts of appeal or the Supreme Court;

4. the Administration Division, which directs the management, financial, and personnel work of the Office of the General Counsel.

The NLRB has thirty-three regional offices and a number of subregional offices. The staff of each regional office consists of a regional director, regional attorney, field examiners, and field attorneys. Although Section 3(d) of the act gives the general counsel "final authority, on behalf of the Board, in respect of investigation of charges and issuance of complaints . . . and in respect of the prosecution of such complaints before the Board," the Office of General Counsel has exercised its statutory right to delegate this power to the regional directors, who actually make most of the day-to-day decisions affecting enforcement of the act.

NLRB Procedures

The NLRB handles two kinds of legal questions: (1) those alleging that an unfair labor practice has taken place in violation of the act, and (2) representation questions concerning whether, and if so how, employees will be represented for collective bargaining. In either type of case, the NLRB does not initiate the proceeding; rather it responds to a complaint of unfair practice or a petition for an election filed by a party to the case. (The board refers to unfair practice cases as "C" cases and to representation cases as "R" cases.)

Unfair Labor Practice Charges   The filing of an unfair practice charge initiates NLRB proceedings in unfair labor practice cases. The act does not restrict who can file a charge; the most common charging parties are employees, unions, and employers. However, in *NLRB* v. *Indiana & Michigan Electric Co.* (318 U.S. 9, 1943), the Supreme Court held that an individual who was a "stranger" to the dispute could file an unfair labor practice charge. The NLRB has adopted a special form for the filing of unfair practice charges (see Figure 4.2).

Section 10(b) of the act requires that unfair practice charges must be filed within six months of the occurrence of the alleged unfair practice. Once a charge has been timely filed, the procedure is as follows:

- The charge is investigated by a field examiner. A charge can be resolved at this stage through mutual adjustment, voluntary withdrawal, or agency dismissal for lack of merit.

- If the charge is found to have merit, and the case has not been settled by adjustment, a formal complaint is issued by the regional director. (Between fiscal years 1966 and 1975, 33 percent of all charges filed were voluntarily withdrawn; another 33 percent were dismissed as having no merit, and the remaining 33 percent of all charges were found to have merit. Of those having merit, 60 percent were settled with no formal complaint being issued. Thus 86 percent of all charges were in fact disposed of before the hearing stage in the procedure was reached.)

- A public hearing on the complaint is held in front of an ALJ. (The Taft-Hartley amendments added the requirement that "so far as practicable" this hearing shall be conducted in accordance with the rules of evidence applicable to federal district courts. At the conclusion of the hearing, the ALJ issues a report with findings of fact and recommendations of law.

FORM EXEMPT UNDER 44 U.S.C. 3512

FORM NLRB-501 (8-83) UNITED STATES OF AMERICA NATIONAL LABOR RELATIONS BOARD **CHARGE AGAINST EMPLOYER**	**DO NOT WRITE IN THIS SPACE**	
	Case	Date Filed

INSTRUCTIONS: File an original and 4 copies of this charge with NLRB Regional Director for the region in which the alleged unfair labor practice occurred or is occurring.

1. EMPLOYER AGAINST WHOM CHARGE IS BROUGHT

a. Name of Employer		b. Number of workers employed
c. Address (street, city, state, ZIP code)	d. Employer Representative	e. Telephone No.
f. Type of Establishment (factory, mine, wholesaler, etc.)	g. Identify principal product or service	

h. The above-named employer has engaged in and is engaging in unfair labor practices within the meaning of section 8(a), subsections (1) and (list subsections) _____ of the National Labor Relations Act. and these unfair labor practices are unfair practices affecting commerce within the meaning of the Act.

2. Basis of the Charge (be specific as to facts, names, addresses, plants involved, dates, places, etc.)

By the above and other acts, the above-named employer has interfered with, restrained, and coerced employees in the exercise of the rights guaranteed in Section 7 of the Act

3. Full name of party filing charge (if labor organization, give full name, including local name and number)

4a. Address (street and number, city, state, and ZIP code)	4b. Telephone No.

5. Full name of national or international labor organization of which it is an affiliate or constituent unit (to be filled in when charge is filed by a labor organization)

6. DECLARATION

I declare that I have read the above charge and that the statements are true to the best of my knowledge and belief.

By _____　　　　_____
(signature of representative or person making charge)　　　　(title if any)

Address _____　　(Telephone No.)　　(date)

WILLFUL FALSE STATEMENTS ON THIS CHARGE CAN BE PUNISHED BY FINE AND IMPRISONMENT (U. S. CODE, TITLE 18, SECTION 1001)

Figure 4.2　　Unfair labor practice complaint form

- The ALJ's report is served on the parties and forwarded to the board in Washington, D.C. Each party then has twenty days to file exceptions to the report. These exceptions are in effect an appeal to the board. If no exceptions are taken, the ALJ's report is automatically accepted by the board as a final order.

- If exceptions have been filed to the ALJ's report by one or more parties, the board reviews the case and issues a decision and remedial order. The parties will normally have filed briefs with the board, explaining their respective positions on the exceptions. Sometimes (although rarely) a party will also request and be granted the opportunity to make oral arguments before the board. Normally a three-member panel of the board handles any single case at this stage. (In 40 percent of all the "appeals" the board approves the ALJ's report in its entirety).

See Figure 4.3 for a summary of unfair labor practice procedures.

Orders of the board are not self-enforcing; if a party against whom an order is issued refuses to comply, the NLRB must ask the appropriate federal circuit court of appeals for a judgment enforcing the order. As well, any party to the case may seek review of the board's decision in the appropriate federal court of appeal. The scope of this judicial review of the board's order is not the same as an appeal from the verdict of a federal trial court; the appeals court is required to accept the board's findings of fact provided that the findings are supported by substantial evidence in the case record. Any party to the case decided by the federal circuit court of appeals may petition the U.S. Supreme Court to grant certiorari to review the appellate court's decision. The Supreme Court generally restricts its review to cases in which a novel legal issue is raised, or in which there is a conflict among the courts of appeal. (Only a minuscule percentage of labor cases reach this final step of the procedure.)

If the regional director refuses to issue a complaint after investigating a charge, that decision can be appealed to the Office of Appeals of the General Counsel in Washington, D.C. Of 221,722 charges filed in regional offices between 1966 and 1975, 148,110 were found to be without merit and dismissed. Thirty percent of the dismissals were appealed. However, the General Counsel's Office of Appeals reversed the regional director's dismissal decision in only 6 percent of these cases. The courts have upheld the general counsel's absolute discretion in these decisions; a conclusion that the charge lacks significant merit to issue a complaint *cannot* be appealed beyond the General Counsel's Office of Appeals. As such, the charging party's statutory rights have been procedurally exhausted and terminate without any hearing or judicial review.

Representation Elections.   The other type of cases coming before the NLRB involve representation questions—employees choosing whether or not to be represented by a labor union as their exclusive bargaining agent. Although the issues and procedures involved in representation questions are discussed in detail in Chapter 5, a few points are highlighted in this discussion of NLRB procedures.

Representation proceedings are at the very heart of the National Labor Relations

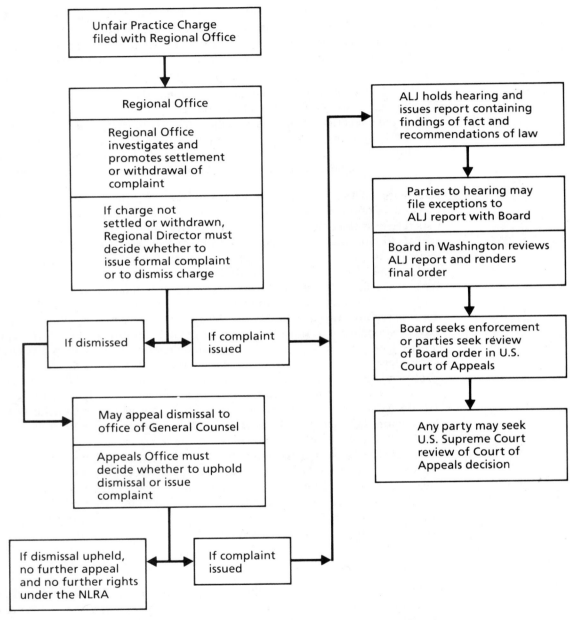

Figure 4.3   Summary of unfair labor practice procedures

Act because the acceptance or rejection of a union as bargaining agent by a group of employees is the essence of the exercise of the rights guaranteed by Section 7 of the act—to engage in, or refrain from, concerted activity for purposes of collective bargaining or mutual aid or protection. Section 9 of the act outlines the procedures available to employees for exercising their rights under Section 7.

For nearly twenty-five years the board had primary responsibility for the conduct of all representation elections. Then in 1959 Congress decided that election procedures were sufficiently settled that the board could delegate its duties in this area to the regional directors. The board did so in 1961. Specifically, the regional directors are authorized by the board to:

- decide whether a question concerning representation exists;
- determine the appropriate collective bargaining unit;
- order and conduct an election;
- certify the election's results;
- resolve challenges to ballots by making findings of fact and issuing rulings.

The board has retained limited review, as the statute suggests, to ensure uniform and consistent application of its interpretation of law and policy. There are four grounds on which the board will review an election if:

1. a significant issue of *law* or policy is raised due to an absence of or departure from reported board precedent;
2. the regional director has made a clear error regarding some *factual* issue and this error is prejudicial to the rights of one of the parties;
3. the *procedure* involved some error that prejudiced a party;
4. the board believes that one of its rules or policies is due for a *reconsideration*.

Ordinarily, once the regional director has decided that a representation election should be held involving a particular unit of employees, a Notice and a Direction of Election are issued by the regional office, even though one of the parties has appealed some aspect of the director's decision to the board in Washington. However, unless the parties have waived their right to request board review, the director will set the election date no earlier than twenty-five days from the notices. On the other hand, the date will usually not be set any later than thirty days after the director's decision to proceed.

Jurisdiction of the NLRB

Under the national Labor Relations Act, the NLRB is given authority to deal with labor disputes occurring "in commerce" or "affecting commerce" (as defined in Section 2(7) of the act). Consistent with the federal courts' traditional view of the scope of federal commerce clause powers, the Supreme Court has held that the NLRB can regulate labor disputes in virtually any company, unless the firm's contact with interstate commerce is de minimus (minuscule and merely incidental).

Rather than exercise its jurisdiction to the full extent of the federal commerce power, the NLRB has chosen to set certain minimum jurisdictional standards. These jurisdictional standards specify the limits beyond which the NLRB will decline jurisdiction over any labor dispute. The Landrum-Griffin Act recognized this policy by providing that the NLRB may decline jurisdiction over any labor dispute that would have been outside of the NLRB's minimum jurisdictional standards as of August 1, 1959. The NLRB may expand its jurisdictional standards, but it cannot contract them beyond their position as of August 1, 1959. The 1959 amendments to the act also provide that the states under certain circumstances may assert jurisdiction over labor disputes over which the NLRB declines to assert jurisdiction.

General Jurisdictional Standards.   The NLRB jurisdictional standards are set in terms of the dollar volume of business that a firm does annually. The current NLRB jurisdictional standards are as follows:

- *General Nonretail Firms.* Sales of goods to consumers in other states, directly or indirectly (termed outflow), or purchases of goods from suppliers in other states, directly or indirectly (termed inflow), of at least $50,000 per year.
- *Retail Businesses.* Annual volume of business of at least $500,000, including sales and excise taxes.
- *Combined Manufacturing and Retail Enterprises.* When an integrated enterprise manufactures a product and sells it directly to the public, *either* the retail or the nonretail standard can be applied.
- *Combined Wholesale and Retail Companies.* When a company is involved in both wholesale and retail sales, the *nonretail* standard is applicable.
- *Instrumentalities, Channels, and Links of Interstate Commerce.* Annual income of at least $50,000 from interstate transportation services, or the performing of $50,000 or more in services for firms that meet any of the other standards, *except* indirect inflow and outflow established for nonretail businesses.
- *National Defense.* Any enterprise having a substantial impact on the national defense.
- *U.S. Territories and the District of Columbia.* Same standards are applied to the territories as to enterprises operating in the fifty states; plenary (total) jurisdiction is exercised in the District of Columbia.
- *Public Utilities.* At least $250,000 total annual volume of business.
- *Newspapers.* At least $200,000 total annual volume of business.
- *Radio, Telegraph, Telephone, and Television Companies.* At least $100,000 total annual volume of business.
- *Hotels, Motels, and Residential Apartment Houses.* At least $500,000 total annual volume of business.
- *Taxicab Companies.* At least $500,000 total annual volume of business.

- *Transit Systems.* At least $250,000 total annual volume of business.

- *Privately Operated Health Care Institutions.* Nursing homes, visiting nurses' associations, and similar facilities and services, $100,000; all others, including hospitals, $250,000 total annual volume of business.

- *Nonprofit, Private Educational Institutions.* $1 million annual operating expenditures.

- *U.S. Postal Service.* The board was empowered to assert jurisdiction under the Postal Reorganization Act of 1970.

- *Multi-employer Bargaining Associations.* Regarded as a single employer for the purpose of totaling up annual business with relation to the above standards.

- *Multistate Establishments.* Annual business of all branches is totaled with regard to the board's standards.

- *Unions as Employers.* The appropriate nonretail standard.

Exempted Employers.   Not all employers—or employees of such employers—meeting the NLRB jurisdictional standards are subject to the provisions of the National Labor Relations Act. Certain kinds of employers have been excluded from the jurisdiction of the act by specific provisions in the act; other employers have been exempted as a result of judicial decisions interpreting the act.

Section 2(2) of the act defines the term *employer* as "including any person acting as an agent of an employer, directly or indirectly," but not including:

- the federal government or any wholly owned government corporation.

- any state or political subdivision thereof (country, local, or municipal governments).

- railroads, airlines, or related companies that are subject to the Railway Labor Act.

- labor organizations in their represented capacity. (Unions are covered by the act in the hiring and treatment of their own employees.)

In addition to these statutory exclusions, judicial decisions have created other exclusions. The NLRB will usually refuse to exercise jurisdiction over an employer that has a close relationship to a foreign government, even if such employers would otherwise come under its jurisdiction. The Supreme Court has held that the act does not apply to labor disputes of foreign crews on foreign flag vessels temporarily in U.S. ports, even if such ships deal primarily in American contracts (see *Incres S.S.* v. *Maritime Workers,* 372 U.S. 24, 1963). However, when the dispute involves American residents working while the vessel is in port, the dispute is subject to the act. In *Int. Longshore Assoc.* v. *Allied International, Inc.* (102 S.Ct. 1656, 1982), the Supreme Court held that a politically motivated refusal by American longshoremen to service American ships carrying Russian cargo, to protest the Soviet invasion of Afghanistan, was subject to the jurisdiction of the NLRB.

The Supreme Court has also held in *NLRB* v. *Catholic Bishop* (440 U.S. 490, 1979) that the NLRB lacked jurisdiction over a parochial high school. The Court stated that its holding was necessary in order to avoid excessive government entanglement with religion, as prohibited by the First Amendment. The NLRB has taken the position that the Court's decision only exempts from NLRB jurisdiction those organizations devoted principally to the promulgation of the faith of a religion. For example, the NLRB has refused jurisdiction over a television station owned by a church in which over 90 percent of the station's broadcasts were religious in nature. However, hospitals operated by religious organizations, or religious charity services providing aid to the elderly, have been held subject to NLRB jurisdiction because they were not principally involved with promulgating the religion's faith.

Exempted Employees.   Just as with employers, not all employees employed by employers in or affecting commerce are subject to the provisions of the National Labor Relations Act. These exclusions from coverage are the result of both statutory provisions and judicial decisions.

Statutory Exemptions.   Section 2(3) of the National Labor Relations Act, in its definition of *employee,* expressly excludes:

- individuals employed as agricultural laborers;
- individuals employed as domestics within a person's home;
- individuals employed by a parent or spouse;
- independent contractors;
- supervisors;
- individuals employed by employers subject to the Railway Labor Act.

Several of these statutory exclusions require some discussion. The NLRB holds that individuals who spend most of their time working in fields (harvesters, for example) are not covered by the act; several states have created agricultural labor relations boards to handle the labor disputes of such employees.

Independent contractors are persons working as a separate business entity; they are not subject to the direction and control of an employer. For example, a person who owns and operates a dump truck and who contracts to provide rubbish disposal service to a firm might be an independent contractor and not an employee of the firm. If the firm used its own truck and directed a worker to haul away its rubbish, the worker would be an employee and not an independent contractor. The NLRB looks to the degree of control and direction exercised by the firm over the worker to determine whether the worker is an employee or an independent contractor.

The term *supervisor* is defined in Section 2(11) of the act. The definition involves someone who, in the interest of the employer, exercises the power to direct, hire, fire, or discipline other employees. The NLRB looks to the actual nature of the duties performed and authority exercised by an individual rather than simply considering job titles or job descriptions. The following case involves the question of whether certain employees are supervisors within the meaning of Section 2(11) and thus are included or excluded from the bargaining unit.

DALE SERVICE CORP. AND UNITED FOOD & COMMERCIAL WORKERS UNION, LOCAL 400, AFL-CIO

269 N.L.R.B. 924 (National Labor Relations Board, 1984)

DONALD L. DOTSON, Chairman; DON A. ZIMMERMAN, Member; ROBERT P. HUNTER, Member

Supplemental Decision and Order

. . . . the Union was certified in a bargaining unit that included senior operators. The Regional Director for Region 5 found that senior operators exercised none of the attributes set forth in Section 2(11) of the Act and therefore concluded that they were employees within the meaning of the Act. For the following reasons, we disagree.

The record in the representation case reveals that the Respondent operates a sewage treatment plant on a 24-hour-per-day, 7-day-per-week basis. At its facility, the Respondent employs an operations manager and an assistant general manager who are admitted supervisors, four senior operators, three operators, and five maintenance employees. A normal day crew consists of one senior operator, one operator, and one to five maintenance employees; a normal night crew consists of one senior operator and one operator. The managers both work Mondays through Fridays, with their combined work hours covering the periods from 7:30 a.m. to 5 or 5:30 p.m. Thus, during the weekday night shift and on weekends, senior operators are the highest-ranking personnel at the Respondent's facility.

In the course of their jobs, senior operators and operators perform many of the same functions. Both categories of employees perform laboratory tests, inspect machinery, and operate or monitor a flock press and a biological treatment unit. Senior operators, however, have the following additional responsibility, which we find confers supervisory status: Senior operators have the authority to assign operators to specific tasks,[3] based in part on the senior operators' assessment of the employees' abilities and the expertise re-

quired. Senior operators have the authority to evaluate the work load, and, consequently, to assign overtime work to operators; to send operators home in the absence of work; and to call both operators and maintenance employees in to work, all without the managers' prior approval. In the course of their duties, senior operators must make operational decisions regarding the adjustment of equipment. These decisions are based on knowledge and experience, and require the exercise of discretion. Finally, the Respondent's assistant general manager testified that senior operators, when managers are not present, are directly responsible for the operation of the plant and the direction of the work force. This authority was acknowledged by senior operators, who testified that their duties included, "mak[ing] sure everything is running all right" and "basically run[ning] the plant." Based on all of these factors, we find that senior operators responsibly direct employees within the meaning of Section 2(11).[4]

Accordingly, we shall vacate our previous Decision and Order which granted General Counsel's Motion for Summary Judgment, and shall deny that motion; reopen the record in Case 5–RC–11694 and set aside the election conducted on 21 January 1982; and remand this proceeding to the Regional Director for Region 5 to conduct a second election in a unit consistent with this Decision.

Order

. . . . the election conducted on 21 January 1982 is set aside, and this case is remanded to the Regional Director for Region 5 for the purpose of directing a second election consistent with this Decision.

---

[3]An operations manual outlines tasks to be performed at specific times, and work varies little day to day. Within such confines, however, the senior operator determines the particular duty an operator or senior operator will perform. According to the testimony of the Respondent's assistant general manager, the tasks vary considerably in desirability.

[4]In making this finding, we note with emphasis that during the weekday night shift and on the weekends, senior operators are the highest-ranking employees present at the Respondent's facility. Both the Board and the circuit courts have noted that this factor is indicative of supervisory status.

Judicial Exemptions.   In addition to the statutory exclusions of employees under the act, the Supreme Court has also created two exemptions. These judicially created exemptions involve **managerial** and **confidential employees.** The Supreme Court, in the case of *NLRB* v. *Textron* (416 U.S. 267, 1974), held that employees in a position to formulate or effectuate management policies are excluded from NLRA coverage as managerial employees, even though they are not supervisors or persons involved with labor relations policies.

The following cases deal with the questions of whether certain employees are either managerial or confidential employees. The *Boston University* case involves the question of whether university faculty are managerial employees under the act. The *Hendricks* case addresses the question of how broad the exemption for "confidential" employees is.

BOSTON UNIVERSITY CHAPTER, AMERICAN ASSOCIATION OF UNIVERSITY PROFESSORS v. N.L.R.B.

▼

835 F.2d 399 (U.S. Court of Appeals for the First Circuit, 1987)

TORRUELLA, J.

The Boston University Chapter, American Association of University Professors (Union) has petitioned this court for review of an order of the National Labor Relations Board (Board). The Union seeks to reverse the Board's decision dismissing unfair labor practice charges filed by the Union against Boston University (University), alleging violation of Sections 8(a)(1) and (5) of the National Labor Relations Act (Act). . . .

Background

On October 18, 1974, the Union filed a petition for representation with the Board, seeking certification as the collective bargaining agent for a unit composed of all regular full-time faculty members at the University except for those in the Schools of Law, Dentistry and Medicine. The University objected to the appropriateness of the unit, alleging that the full-time faculty were excluded from coverage of the Act by virtue of either their supervisory or managerial status.[5] Notwithstanding said objections the Board ordered and held an election in which a majority of those employees presumably eligible voted in favor of being represented by the Union. After various administrative proceedings were completed the Union was certified by the Board as the bargaining representative of the unit sought.

The Union's bargaining request was rejected by the University, leading to the filing of the unfair labor practice charges presently before us. The Board's summary process was invoked and on March 22, 1977 the Board concluded that the University had violated Sections 8(a)(1) and (5) of the Act, and ordered it to bargain with the Union. The University petitioned this Court for review and the Board cross-appealed for enforcement of its order. We affirmed the Board.

On July 2, 1978, the University petitioned the Supreme Court for a writ of certiorari. On February 20, 1980, while this petition was still pending, the Supreme Court decided *N.L.R.B.* v. *Yeshiva University (1980),* a ruling which shall be discussed in further detail, but which in substance holds that under given factual circumstances university faculty members shall be considered managerial employees excluded from coverage by the Act. On March 3, 1980, the

---

[5]Supervisors, a term defined in s. 2(11), are statutorily excluded from coverage by the Act. S. 14(a). Managerial employees have been excluded by judicial interpretation. See *N.L.R.B.* v. *Bell Aerospace Co.* (1974). The term "managerial employee" has been defined to mean "those who 'formulate and effectuate managerial policies by expressing and making operative the decisions of their employer.'"

University's petition was granted and the judgment of this court recalled and remanded for further consideration in light of the ruling in *Yeshiva*.

Upon our remand to the Board, it reopened the record and in turn remanded the proceedings to the administrative law judge (ALJ) for further action. An extensive hearing was held and a comprehensive opinion issued by the ALJ on June 29, 1984. The ALJ's recommended ruling included findings to the effect that all full-time faculty in the requested unit were managerial employees as described in *Yeshiva*, and in addition, that all those above the rank of instructor were also supervisors. He thus recommended dismissal of the unfair labor practice charge against the University. The Board affirmed the ALJ's rulings and adopted the recommended order dismissing the charge against the University.

The full circle was completed to this court with the filing by the Union of the present petition seeking review of the Board's dismissal.

Standards of Review

. . . . A determination by the Board regarding supervisory or managerial status is a mixed question of law and fact. Such a ruling is nevertheless entitled to deference if it is "warrant[ed] in the record and [has] a reasonable basis in law."

Regarding the law applicable to this case, our judicial hands are tied by *Yeshiva*. The crux of that case is contained in the following passage:

> The controlling consideration in this case is that the faculty of Yeshiva University exercise authority which in any other context unquestionably would be managerial. Their authority in academic matters is absolute. They decide what courses will be offered, when they will be scheduled, and to whom they will be taught. They debate and determine teaching methods, grading policies, and matriculation standards. They effectively decide which students will be admitted, retained, and graduated. On occasion their views have determined the size of the student body, the tuition to be charged, and the location of a school. When one considers the function of a university, it is difficult to imagine decisions more managerial than these. To the extent the industrial analogy applies, the faculty determines within each school the product to be produced, the terms upon which it will be offered, and the customers who will be served.

The Court reasoned that the divided loyalty that would be present if the faculty unionized, would be "particularly acute for a university like Yeshiva, which depends on the professional judgment of its faculty to formulate and apply crucial policies constrained only by necessarily general in-

stitutional goals." The Court reemphasizes this point when it said that "Yeshiva and like universities must rely on their faculties to participate in the making and implementation of their policies."

Is Boston University a "like university"?

The Board so found, and given the limitation of Section 10(f) and *Yeshiva*, we must forcefully agree.

In adopting the ALJ's conclusion that the department chairman and full-time faculty are managerial employees pursuant to *Yeshiva*, the Board noted that:

> The faculty has absolute authority over such matters as grading, teaching methods, graduation requirements, and student discipline. Additionally, the faculty is the moving force and almost always effectively controls matriculation requirements, curriculum, academic calendars, and course schedules. The faculty also plays an effective and determinative role in recommending faculty hiring, tenure, promotions, and reappointments. (Note 3—We particularly note their authority to effectively veto curriculum and personnel decisions.) . . . That ultimate authority for decision making at the University rests with the president and board of trustees does not alter the fact that, in practice, faculty decisions on all those policy matters are effectuated in the great majority of instances. Nor does the fact that the administration occasionally has made and implemented policy decisions without faculty input detract from the collegial managerial authority consistently exercised by the faculty.

Although these findings by the Board are somewhat conclusory they track the Court's ruling in *Yeshiva*, and are fully supported by the ALJ's decision and the record. We should note that in *Yeshiva*, the various schools composing that institution were also served by a central administrative hierarchy, led by a president as chief executive officer, with the ultimate authority being vested in a board of trustees. There is no doubt, however, that here, as in *Yeshiva*, in the promulgation of the University's principal business, which is education and research, the faculty's role is predominant, and "in any other context unquestionably would be [considered] managerial." The various differences pointed to by petitioners between *Yeshiva* and the present case are minor distinctions without substance. Given the constraints of Section 10(f) and *Yeshiva*, our further consideration of this matter is an unnecessary spinning of our judicial wheels.

The decision of the Board dismissing the unfair labor charges against the University is affirmed and the petition for review is denied.

Those employees excluded from the act's coverage are not prevented from organizing and attempting to bargain collectively with their employer. There is nothing in the National Labor Relations Act to prohibit such action. Exclusion means that those employees cannot involve the act's protection for the exercise of rights to organize and bargain. There is no requirement that their employer recognize or bargain with their union or even tolerate such activity. Because those employees are denied the act's protections, the employer is free to discipline or discharge excluded employees who attempt to organize and bargain. Therefore the faculty members in *Boston University* may attempt to organize and bargain with their employer, but the university need not recognize and bargain with them.

In the following case, the Supreme Court considers the question of which employees are covered by the "confidential" employee exclusion.

NLRB v. HENDRICKS COUNTY RURAL ELECTRIC MEMBERSHIP CORP.

454 U.S. 170 (Supreme Court of the United States, 1981)

BRENNAN, J.

The question presented is whether an employee who, in the course of his employment, may have access to information considered confidential by his employer is impliedly excluded from the definition of "employee" in Section 2(3) of the National Labor Relations Act and denied all protections under the Act.

Mary Weatherman was the personal secretary to the general manager and chief executive officer of respondent Hendricks County Rural Electric Membership Corp. (Hendricks), a rural electric membership cooperative. She had been employed by the cooperative for nine years. In May 1977 she signed a petition seeking reinstatement of a close friend and fellow employee, who had lost his arm in the course of employment with Hendricks, and had been dismissed. Several days later she was discharged.

Weatherman filed an unfair labor practice charge with the National Labor Relations Board (NLRB or Board), alleging that the discharge violated Section 8(a)(1) of the National Labor Relations Act (NLRA or Act). . . .

Hendricks' defense, *inter alia,* was that Weatherman was denied the Act's protection because as a "confidential" secretary she was impliedly excluded from the Act's definition of "employee" in Section 2(3). The Administrative Law Judge (A.L.J.) rejected this argument. He noted that the Board's decisions had excluded from bargaining units only those "confidential employees . . . [']who assist and act in a

confidential capacity to persons who formulate, determine, and effectuate management policies in the field of labor relations.'" Applying this "labor nexus" test, the A.L.J. found that Weatherman was not in any event such a "confidential employee." He also determined that Hendricks had discharged Weatherman for activity—signing the petition—protected by Section 7 of the Act. . . .

Section 2(3) of the NLRA provides that the "term 'employee' shall include any employee . . ." (emphasis added), with certain stated exceptions such as "agricultural laborers," "supervisors" as defined in Section 2(11), and "independent contractors." Under a literal reading of the phrase "any employee," then, the workers in question are "employees." But for over 40 years, the NLRB, while rejecting any claim that the definition of "employee" in Section 2(3) excludes confidential employees, has excluded from the collective-bargaining units determined under the Act those confidential employees satisfying the Board's labor-nexus test. Respondents Hendricks argue that contrary to the Board's practice, all employees who may have access to confidential business information are impliedly excluded from the definition of employee in Section 2(3).

In assessing the respondents' argument, we must be mindful of the canon that "the construction of a statute by those charged with its execution should be followed unless there are compelling indications that it is wrong, especially where Congress has refused to alter the administrative construction." We therefore proceed to review the Board's determinations whether confidential employees were "employees" within Section 2(3) of the NLRA (Wagner Act), and then determine whether Congress, when it considered those determinations in enacting the Labor Management Relations Act of 1947 (Taft-Hartley Act), intended to alter the Board's practice.

In 1935 the Wagner Act became law. The employees covered by the Act were defined in Section 2(3): "The term 'employee' shall include any employee . . . but shall not include any individual employed as an agricultural laborer, or in the domestic service of any family or person at his home, or any individual employed by his parent or spouse." Although the Act's express exclusions did not embrace confidential employees, the Board was soon faced with the argument that all individuals who had access to confidential information of their employers should be excluded, as a policy matter, from the definition of "employee." The Board rejected such an implied exclusion, finding it to have "no warrant under the Act." But in fulfilling its statutory obligation to determine appropriate bargaining units under Section 9 of the Act, the Board adopted special treatment for the narrow group of employees with access to confidential, labor-relations information of the employer. The Board excluded these individuals from bargaining units composed of rank-and-file workers. The Board's rationale was that "management should not be required to handle labor relations matters through employees who are represented by the union with which the [C]ompany is required to deal and who in the normal performance of their duties may obtain advance information of the [C]ompany's position with regard to contract negotiations, the disposition of grievances, and other labor relations matters."

Following its formulation, through 1946, the Board routinely applied the labor-nexus test in numerous decisions to identify those individuals who were to be excluded from bargaining units because of their access to confidential information. And in at least one instance in which a Court of Appeals had occasion to review the Board's application of a labor-nexus test under the Wagner Act, the test was upheld.

In 1946, the Board refined slightly the labor-nexus test because in its view the "definition [was] too inclusive and needlessly preclude[d] many employees from bargaining collectively together with other workers having common interests." Henceforth, the Board announced, it intended "to limit the term 'confidential' so as to embrace only those employees who assist and act in a confidential capacity to persons who exercise 'managerial' functions in the field of labor relations." This was the state of the law in 1947 when Congress amended the NLRA through the enactment of the Taft-Hartley Act.

Although the text of the Taft-Hartley Act also makes no explicit reference to confidential employees, when Congress addressed the scope of the NLRA's coverage, the status of confidential employees was discussed. But nothing in that legislative discussion supports any inference, let alone conclusion, that Congress intended to alter the Board's pre-1947 determinations that only confidential employees with a "labor nexus" should be excluded from bargaining units. Indeed, the contrary appears. . . .

Plainly, too, nothing in the legislative history of the Taft-Hartley Act provides any support for the argument that Congress disapproved the Board's prior practice of applying a labor-nexus test to identify confidential employees whom the Board excluded from bargaining units. . . .

We also find no merit in the respondents' argument that the Board has applied the labor-nexus test inconsistently.

In sum, our review of the Board's decisions indicates that the Board has never followed a practice of depriving all employees who have access to confidential business information from the full panoply of rights afforded by the Act. Rather, for over 40 years, the Board, while declining to create any implied exclusion from the definition of "employee" for confidential employees, has applied a labor-nexus test in identifying those employees who should be excluded from bargaining units because of access to confidential business information. We cannot ignore this consistent, longstanding interpretation of the NLRA by the Board.

The Court's ultimate task here is, of course, to determine whether the Board's "labor nexus" limitation on the class of confidential employees who, although within the definition of "employee" under Section 2(3), may be denied inclusion in bargaining units has "a reasonable basis in law." Clearly the NLRB's longstanding practice of excluding from bargaining units only those confidential employees satisfying the Board's labor-nexus test, rooted firmly in the Board's understanding of the nature of the collective-bargaining process, and Congress' acceptance of that practice, fairly demonstrates that the Board's treatment of confidential employees does indeed have "a reasonable basis in law."

In *Hendricks,* the Board determined that the personal secretary, Mary Weatherman, was not a confidential secretary because she "did not act 'in a confidential capacity'" with respect to labor-relations matters. While the Court of Appeals affirmed this finding, it denied enforcement of the Board's order on the basis that the evidence failed to support the Board's additional finding, required by the Court of Appeals, that Weatherman had no access to confidential non-labor-related information. In approving the Board's limited labor-nexus exclusion, we have held that such a finding is irrelevant to the determination of whether the secretary was a confidential employee. In this Court respondent Hendricks does not argue that Weatherman came within the labor-nexus test as formulated by the Board, but rather concedes that Weatherman did not have "confidential duties 'with respect to labor policies.'" Because there is thus no dispute in this respect, and in any event no suggestion that the Board's finding regarding labor nexus was not supported by substantial evidence, we conclude that the Court of Appeals erred in holding that the record did not support the Board's determination that Weatherman was not a confidential employee with a labor nexus. We therefore reverse the judgment of the Court of Appeals in *Hendricks* insofar as enforcement of the Board's order was denied, and remand with directions to enter an order enforcing the Board's order. **So ordered.**

Although managerial employees are excluded from the act's coverage, it is not clear whether "confidential" employees are excluded from the act's coverage or are simply excluded from being included in bargaining units with other employees. If confidential employees, like managers, are excluded from the act's coverage, they are denied the protections of the act. If, however, they are excluded only from bargaining units, they remain employees under the act and are entitled to its statutory protection. The Supreme Court did not specifically address this question in *Hendricks.*

Jurisdiction over Labor Organizations.   Section 2(5) of the National Labor Relations Act defines *labor organization* as "any organization of any kind, or any agency or employee representation committee or plan, in which employees participate and which exists for the purpose, in whole or in part, of dealing with employers concerning grievances, labor disputes, wages, rates of pay, hours of employment, or conditions of work."

NLRB and Supreme Court decisions have held that the words "dealing with" are broad enough to encompass relationships that fall short of collective bargaining. For example in *NLRB v. Cabot Carbon* (360 U.S. 203, 1959), the Supreme Court held that the act encompassed employee committees that functioned merely to discuss with management, but not bargain over, such matters of mutual interest as grievances, seniority, and working conditions. There is also case law to suggest that a single individual cannot be considered a labor organization "in any literal sense." (See *Bonnaz v. NLRB,* 230 F.2d 47, D.C.Cir. 1956.)

NLRB Jurisdiction vs. State Jurisdiction.   Because of the broad reach of NLRB jurisdiction under the federal commerce power, it is important to consider whether the states have any authority to legislate regarding labor relations in the private sector. Although state laws that conflict with federal laws are void under the supremacy clause of Article VI of the Constitution, the Supreme Court has consistently held that states may regulate activities involving interstate commerce where such regulation is pursuant to a valid state purpose. In such situations, the states have concurrent jurisdiction with the federal government: The regulated firm or activity is subject to both the state and federal regulations. But where an activity is characterized by pervasive federal regulation, the Supreme Court has held that Congress has, under the supremacy clause powers, "occupied the field" so that the federal law preempts any state regulation. (One example of such preemption is the regulation of radio and TV broadcasting by the Federal Communications Commission.) Has Congress, through the enactment of the National Labor Relations Act (NLRA), preempted state regulation of private-sector labor disputes?

The Supreme Court tried to answer this question in two leading decisions. In *San Diego Building Trades Council* v. *Garmon* (359 U.S. 236, 1958), the Supreme Court held that state and federal district courts are deprived of jurisdiction over conduct that is "arguably subject" to Section 7 or Section 9 of the NLRA. More recently, in *Sears Roebuck* v. *San Diego County District Council of Carpenters* (436 U.S. 180, 1978), the Supreme Court held that state courts may deal with matters arising out of a labor dispute when the issue presented to the state court is not the same as that which would be before the NLRB. The Court said it would consider the nature of the particular state interests being asserted and the effect on national labor policies of allowing the state court to proceed. *Sears* involved a trespassing charge filed against picketing by the carpenters; no unfair practice charges were filed with the NLRB by either party to the dispute. The Court upheld the right of the state court to order the picketers to stop trespassing on Sears' property—recognizing that Congress did not preempt all state regulation of matters growing out of a labor dispute.

In *Wisconsin Dept. of Industry, Labor & Human Relations* v. *Gould* (475 U.S. 282, 1986), the U.S. Supreme Court held that the NLRA preempted a Wisconsin law that barred any firm violating the NLRA three times within five years from doing business with the state; the Court held that the law sought to supplement the sanctions for violations of the NLRA, and so was in conflict with the NLRB's comprehensive regulation of industrial relations.

In addition to the rule set out in *Sears* regarding preemption in labor relations matters, the federal legislation may also expressly preserve the right of the states to regulate activities. For example, Section 103 of the Labor-Management Reporting and Disclosure Act, dealing with internal union affairs, states that "Nothing contained in this title shall limit the rights and remedies of any member of a labor organization under any State . . . law or before any court or other tribunal. . . ." Because of this provision, states are free to legislate greater protection for union members vis-à-vis their unions, and state courts are free to hear suits that may arise under such laws.

QUESTIONS

1. What were the major provisions of the Wagner Act? What were the effects of this act?

2. What factors led to the passage of the Taft-Hartley Act? What were the effects of this act?

3. Describe the structural organization of the National Labor Relations Board. What are the functions of the board's various branches?

4. Describe the NLRB procedures for handling unfair labor practice complaints.

5. What is the effect of the NLRB jurisdictional guidelines? What role do states have in regulating labor relations?

6. Which employers are exempted from NLRA coverage? Which employers are covered by the NLRA?

7. Which employees are excluded from the coverage of the NLRA?

8. What is an independent contractor? What test does the NLRA use to determine whether employees are super-

visors? What is the test for managerial employees? For confidential employees?

9. What is the effect of the exclusion of supervisory employees? Of the exclusion of confidential employees?

CASE PROBLEMS

1. The legislature of West Virginia enacted a law in 1983 (effective July 1, 1984) requiring that at least 40 percent of the board of directors of all nonprofit and local government hospitals in the state be composed of an equal proportion of "consumer representatives" from "small businesses, organized labor, elderly persons, and persons whose income is less than the national median income." The American Hospital Association joined with a number of West Virginia hospitals in seeking an injunction against enforcement of the law and a declaratory judgment that, among other things, the law interfered with bargaining rights between the hospitals and their employees and was therefore preempted by federal law.

   If you were arguing for the plaintiff hospitals, how would you contend that this West Virginia law might interfere with the collective bargaining relationship? if you were the federal judge hearing the case, how would you rule and why? See *American Hospital Association* v. *Hansbarger,* 600 F. Supp. 465, 118 L.R.R.M. 2389 (N.D. W.Va. 1984).

2. Spring Valley Farms, Inc. supplied poultry feed to farmers who raised broiler and egg-laying poultry. Sarah F. Jones had the title of feed delivery manager with the company in Cullman, Alabama. As feed delivery manager, Jones dispatched the drivers who delivered the feed. Drivers could earn more money on "long hauls" (more than fifty miles from the mill) than on "short hauls." Therefore, Spring Valley Farms instructed Jones to "equalize" the number of long and short hauls so that all drivers would earn approximately the same wages. The company also instructed her to work the drivers as close to forty hours per week as possible and then to "knock them off" by seniority. It was left to Jones's discretion to devise methods for accomplishing these objectives.

   Does Spring Valley Farms fall under the jurisdiction of the NLRB? Is Jones as manager excluded from the

Board's jurisdiction? See *Spring Valley Farms,* 272 N.L.R.B. No. 205, 118 L.R.R.M. 1015 (1984).

3. In 1976 the citizens of New Jersey amended their state constitution to permit the legislative authorization of casino gambling in Atlantic City. Determined to prevent the infiltration of organized crime into its nascent casino industry, the New Jersey legislature enacted the Casino Control Act, which provides for the comprehensive regulation of casino gambling, including the regulation of unions representing industry employees. Sections 86 and 93 of the act specifically impose certain qualification criteria on officials of labor organizations representing casino industry employees. (Section 86, for example, contains a list of crimes, conviction of which disqualifies a union officer from representing casino employees.) A hotel employees' union challenged the state law, arguing that it was preempted by the NLRA, which gives employees the right to select collective bargaining representatives of their own choosing. The case reached the U.S. Supreme Court.

   How should the Supreme Court have ruled? Why? See *Brown* v. *Hotel Employees Local 54,* 468 U.S. 491, 116 L.R.R.M. 2921 (1984).

4. The Volunteers of America (VOA) is a religious movement founded in New York City in 1986. Its purpose is "to reach and uplift all segments of the population and to bring them to a knowledge of God." The Denver Post of the VOA, founded in 1898, is an unincorporated association operated under the direction of the national society. It maintains three chapels in the Denver area, at which it conducts regular religious services and Bible study groups. The VOA also operates a number of social programs in Denver, including temporary care, shelter, and counseling centers for women and children.

   In January 1981 the United Nurses, Professionals and Health Care Employees Union filed a petition with the NLRB to represent the counselors at these shelters.

The VOA argued it was not subject to the board's jurisdiction because (1) the First Amendment to the U.S. Constitution precludes NLRB jurisdiction over a religious organization; (2) it received partial funding from the city and county governments under contracts specifying the services it was to perform, so that the government and not VOA was the true employer. The case reached the Tenth Circuit Court of Appeals.

How should the court have ruled on these two arguments? See *Denver Post of VOA* v. *NLRB* 732 F.2d 769, 1167 L.R.R.M. 2035 (10th Cir. 1984).

5. The *Alcoa Seaprobe* was a U.S. flag, oceangoing vessel engaged in offshore geophysical and geotechnical research. While berthed in Woods Hole, Massachusetts, its owner, Alcoa Marine corporation (a Delaware corporation headquartered in Houston, Texas), had contracted with Brazil's national oil company to use *Alcoa Seaprobe* for offshore exploration of Brazil's continental shelf. When Alcoa sent the *Seaprobe* to Brazil, it did not intend to return the vessel to the United States.

The Masters, Motes & Pilots Union (International Longshoremen) filed a petition to represent the crew of *Alcoa Seaprobe*. Alcoa Marine Corporation argued that since *Seaprobe* was not expected to operate in U.S. territorial waters, the NLRA did not apply.

How should the NLRB have ruled? See *Alcoa Marine Corp.,* 240 N.L.R.B. No. 18, 100 L.R.R.M. 1433 (1979).

6. National Detective Agencies, Inc., of Washington, D.C., provided security officers to various clients in the District of Columbia. Among these clients was the Inter-American Development Bank, "an international economic organization whose purpose is to aid in the economic development and growth of its member nations, who are primarily members of the Organization of American States." The Federation of Special Police petitioned the NLRB to represent National's employees, including those who worked at the bank.

National argued that the bank could require National to issue orders and regulations to its guards, and to remove any guard the bank considered unsatisfactory. The bank had the right to interview all job applicants and to suggest wage scales. Consequently, National argued, the bank was a joint employer of the guards, and as an international organization enjoyed "sovereign immunity" from NLRA jurisdiction. Therefore, these guards should not be included in the proposed bargaining unit.

How do you think the NLRB ruled on this argument? Is this case conceptually distinguishable from the *Alcoa Seaprobe* case in problem 5? See *National Detective Agencies,* 237 N.L.R.B. No. 72, 99 L.R.R.M. 1007 (1978).

7. Burman was employed as a production supervisor at Vincow, Inc. until he was fired because his brother and cousin had led an union organizing campaign among the workers at Vincow. Burman filed an unfair labor practice complaint with the NLRB, alleging that his discharge was a violation of Section 8(a)(1). Subsequent to the firing of Burman, Vincow recognized the union as the exclusive bargaining agent of its employees. How should the NLRB rule on Burman's complaint? Explain your answer. See *Kenrich Petrochemicals* v. *NLRB,* 893 F.2d 1468 (3rd Cir. 1990).

8. The faculty at the Universidad Central de Bayamon in Puerto Rico seek to unionize in order to bargain collectively with the university over wages, working conditions, and so on. The university, which describes itself as a "Catholic-oriented civil institution," is governed by a board of trustees, of whom a majority are to be members of the Dominican religious order. Is the Universidad subject to NLRB jurisdiction, or is it exempt under the *Catholic Bishops* doctrine? See *Universidad Central de Bayamon,* 273 N.L.R.B. No. 138 (1984); 778 F.2d 906 (1st. Cir. rev'd. on rehearing, 793 F.2d 383, 1985).

9. Callaghan, an employee of Smith Transportation, is one of the leaders of an effort to unionize the Smith employees. Biggins, the personnel manager of Smith, suspects Callaghan is involved in the organizing campaign and decides to fire him. Callaghan is given notice on January 15, 1986, that his employment will be terminated on January 31, 1986. On July 20, 1986, Callaghan files a complaint with the appropriate regional office of the NLRB, alleging that he was fired in violation of Sections 8(a)1 and 3 of the NLRA. Smith Transportation argues that the complaint was not filed within the required six-month limitations period. Was the complaint filed in a timely fashion? Does the time limit run from when the employee is notified of the impending discharge or from when the discharge becomes effective? See *United States Postal Service,* 271 N.L.R.B. No. 61, 116 L.R.R.M. 1417 (1984).

10. Speedy Clean Service, Inc. provides janitorial services for office buildings; a number of its employees are His-

panics who have entered the United States illegally. When several employees try to organize a union to represent them, Speedy Clean fires all of its workers. The discharged employees file unfair labor practice charges with the NLRB; the employer argues that the illegal aliens are not entitled to protection under the act. Are illegal aliens included within the definition of "employee" under Section 2(3)? Explain your answer.

C H A P T E R 5

The Unionization Process

IN THE PRECEDING CHAPTER we discussed briefly the National Labor Relations Board's (NLRB) administrative structure and procedures in representation ("R") cases. In this chapter we will consider in greater detail the mechanisms created by the board for determining whether a company's employees will be represented by a union for purposes of collective bargaining. (The Railway Labor Act, which covers companies and employees in the railroad and airline industries, contains provisions that are analogous in many respects to the National Labor Relations Act [NLRA] procedures to be discussed in this chapter.)

Exclusive Bargaining Representative

We have seen that Section 7 of the NLRA entitles employees "to bargain collectively through representatives of their own choosing." Section 9(a) adds that

> Representatives designated or selected for the purposes of collective bargaining by the majority of the employees in a unit appropriate for such purposes, shall be the exclusive representatives of all the employees in such unit for the purposes of collective bargaining in respect to rates of pay, wages, hours of employment, or other conditions of employment.

The position of the union as exclusive bargaining agent supersedes any individual contracts of employment made between the employer and the unit employees. Any dealings with individual unit employees must be in accordance with the collective bargaining agreement.

The Taft-Hartley Act added some protection for minority factions within bargaining units by adding to Section 9(a) the stipulation that

> any individual or a group of employees shall have the right at any time to present grievances to their employer and to have such grievances adjusted, without the intervention of the bargaining representative, as long as the adjustment is not inconsistent with the terms of a collective-bargaining contract . . . then in effect.

The extent to which this proviso allows the employer to deal with individual employee grievances, and its effect on the union's position as exclusive bargaining agent, will be discussed in Chapter 7.

Employees' Choice of Bargaining Agent

Although the most common method of determining the employees' choice of a bargaining representative is to hold a secret ballot election, the NLRA does not require such procedures. Employers confronted by a union claiming to have the support of a majority of their employees may recognize the union as the exclusive bargaining agent for those employees. Section 9(a) requires only that the union, in order to become the exclusive bargaining agent, be designated or selected by a majority of the employees. It does not require that an election *must* be held to determine employee choice. The propriety of this method of recognition, called a **voluntary recognition,** is well established, provided that the employer has no reasonable doubt of the employees' preference and that recognition is not granted for the purpose of assisting one particular union at the expense of another seeking to represent the same employees.

Bargaining status achieved through a voluntary recognition imposes on the employer the duty to bargain with the union in good faith, just the same as with a union victory in a representation election conducted by the board. But the representation election method has several advantages over the voluntary recognition method. The representation election procedures involve the determination of the bargaining unit—that is, which of the employer's workers should be grouped together for purposes of representation and bargaining. Following a union victory in an election, the employer is obligated to recognize and bargain with the union for at least twelve months following the election. No petitions seeking a new representation (or **decertification**) election can be filed for that unit of employees during the twelve-month period. For a voluntary recognition, the employer is obligated to recognize and bargain with the union only for a "reasonable length" of time, unless a collective bargaining agreement is agreed upon. In the absence of an agreement, the voluntary recognition does not prevent the filing of a petition seeking a representation election for that same group of employees. In addition, an employer who voluntarily recognizes a union claiming to have majority support commits an unfair labor practice if the union does not actually have the support of a majority of the employees in the bargaining unit. Thus, a representation election conducted by the board is the method of recognition preferred by the parties in most cases.

Just as filing a charge initiates the administrative process in an unfair labor practice ("C") case, so too a petition from an interested party is needed to initiate a board-sponsored election under Section 9(c)(1)(A). Any employee, group of employees, or labor organization can file such a petition seeking a representation election or a decertification election on behalf of the employees as a whole (see Figure 5.1). An employer is entitled to file a petition only after one or more individuals or unions present that employer with a claim for recognition as the bargaining representative, according to Section 9(c)(1)(B).

Form NLRB–502
(11–59)

UNITED STATES OF AMERICA
NATIONAL LABOR RELATIONS BOARD

PETITION

Form approved.
Budget Bureau No. 64-R002 12

DO NOT WRITE IN THIS SPACE
CASE NO.
DATE FILED

INSTRUCTIONS.—Submit an original and four (4) copies of this Petition to the NLRB Regional Office in the Region in which the employer concerned is located.
If more space is required for any one item, attach additional sheets, numbering item accordingly.

The Petitioner alleges that the following circumstances exist and requests that the National Labor Relations Board proceed under its proper authority:

1. Purpose of this Petition *(Check only the one box which is appropriate)*

A. ☐ RC—CERTIFICATION OF REPRESENTATIVES (INDIVIDUAL, GROUP, LABOR ORGANIZATION).—A substantial number of employees wish to be represented for purposes of collective bargaining by Petitioner, and Petitioner desires to be certified as representative of the employees for purposes of collective bargaining, pursuant to section 9 (a) and (c) of the act. *

B. ☐ RM—REPRESENTATION (EMPLOYER).—One or more individuals or labor organizations have presented a claim to Petitioner to be recognized as the representative of employees of Petitioner as defined in section 9(a) of the act. *

C. ☐ RD—DECERTIFICATION.—A substantial number of employees assert that the certified or currently recognized bargaining representative is no longer their representative as defined in section 9(a) of the act. *

D. ☐ UD—WITHDRAWAL OF UNION SHOP AUTHORITY.—Thirty percent (30%) or more of employees in a bargaining unit covered by an agreement between their employer and a labor organization desire that such authority be rescinded.

*NOTE.—If a charge under section 8(b)(7) of the act has been filed involving the Employer named herein, the statement following the description of the type of petition shall not be deemed made.

2. NAME OF EMPLOYER	EMPLOYER REPRESENTATIVE TO CONTACT	PHONE NO.

3. ADDRESS(ES) OF ESTABLISHMENT(S) INVOLVED *(Street and number, city, zone, and State)*

4a. TYPE OF ESTABLISHMENT *(Factory, mine, wholesaler, etc.)*	4b. IDENTIFY PRINCIPAL PRODUCT OR SERVICE

5. Description of Unit Involved *(If more space is needed, continue on another sheet)*

Included

Excluded

6a. NUMBER OF EMPLOYEES IN UNIT

6b. IS THIS PETITION SUPPORTED BY 30% OR MORE OF THE EMPLOYEES IN THE UNIT?   ☐ YES ☐ NO

(If you have checked box RC in 1.A. above, check and complete EITHER item 7a or 7b, whichever is applicable)

7a. ☐ Request for recognition as Bargaining Representative was made on .... *(Month, day, year)* .... and Employer declined recognition on or about .... *(Month, day, year)* *(If no reply received, so state)*

7b. ☐ Petitioner is currently recognized as Bargaining Representative and desires certification under the act.

8. Recognized or Certified Bargaining Agent *(If there is none, so state)*

NAME	AFFILIATION
ADDRESS	DATE OF RECOGNITION OR CERTIFICATION

9. DATE OF EXPIRATION OF CURRENT CONTRACT, IF ANY *(Show month, day, and year)*	10. IF YOU HAVE CHECKED BOX UD IN 1.D. ABOVE, SHOW HERE THE DATE OF EXECUTION OF AGREEMENT GRANTING UNION SHOP *(Month, day, and year)*

11a. IS THERE NOW A STRIKE OR PICKETING AT THE EMPLOYER'S ESTABLISHMENT(S) INVOLVED? YES........ NO........	11b. IF SO, APPROXIMATELY HOW MANY EMPLOYEES ARE PARTICIPATING?

11c. THE EMPLOYER HAS BEEN PICKETED BY OR ON BEHALF OF .... *(Insert name)* .... , A LABOR

ORGANIZATION, OF .... *(Insert address)*

SINCE .... *(Show month, day, and year)*

12. ORGANIZATIONS OR INDIVIDUALS OTHER THAN PETITIONER (AND OTHER THAN THOSE NAMED IN ITEMS 8 AND 11c), WHICH HAVE CLAIMED RECOGNITION AS REPRESENTATIVES, AND OTHER ORGANIZATIONS AND INDIVIDUALS KNOWN TO HAVE A REPRESENTATIVE INTEREST IN ANY EMPLOYEES IN THE UNIT DESCRIBED IN ITEM 5 ABOVE. (IF NONE, SO STATE.)

NAME	AFFILIATION	ADDRESS	DATE OF CLAIM *(Required only if Petition is filed by Employer)*

I declare that I have read the above petition and that the statements therein are true to the best of my knowledge and belief.

....
(Petitioner and affiliation, if any)

By ....
(Signature of representative or person filing petition)   *(Title, if any)*

Address ....
(Street and number, city, zone, and State)   *(Telephone number)*

WILLFULLY FALSE STATEMENT ON THIS PETITION CAN BE PUNISHED BY FINE AND IMPRISONMENT (U.S. CODE, TITLE 18, SECTION 1001)

U S GOVERNMENT PRINTING OFFICE : 1959 OF—52985

GPO 918974

Figure 5.1   Petition to initiate NLRB election

If it is a union or employees who file a petition with the appropriate regional office of the board, the NLRB will not proceed with the election until the petitioning union or employee group presents evidence that at least 30 percent of the employee group support the election request. (If the petition is filed by an employer, under the circumstances outlined above, this rule does not apply.) Usually, this showing of support is reflected in signed and dated **authorization cards** obtained by the union from the individual employees. These cards may simply state that the signatories desire an election to be held, or they may state that the signing employee authorizes the union to be his or her bargaining representative. Other acceptable showings of employee interest can include a letter or similar informal document bearing a list of signatures and applications for union membership.

Under the board's **forty-eight-hour rule,** an employer who files a petition must submit to the regional office proof of a union's recognition demand within two days of filing the petition. Likewise, a petitioning union or employee group has forty-eight hours after filing in which to proffer authorization cards or other proof of 30 percent employee support for the requested election. Upon the docketing (logging in) of a petition, a written notification of its filing is sent by the regional director to the employer and any labor organizations claiming to represent any employees in the proposed unit or known to have an interest in the case's disposition. Employers are asked to submit a payroll list covering the proposed bargaining unit, data showing the nature and volume of the company's business for jurisdictional purposes, and a statement of company position on the appropriateness of the requested bargaining unit.

The new "R" case is then assigned to a board agent, who investigates to determine whether the following conditions exist:

1. The employer's operations affect commerce within the act's meaning.
2. A question about representation really exists (i.e., that no union already represents the employees and is shielded by the election bar rule, or some similar impediment to the election).
3. The proposed bargaining unit is appropriate.
4. The petitioning union, if any, has garnered a 30 percent showing of interest among the employees.

If the agent finds some impediment to an election, the regional director can dismiss the petition. The decision to dismiss can be appealed to the board in Washington, D.C. Conversely, the petitioning party may choose to withdraw the petition. The usual penalty for withdrawal is imposition of a six-month waiting period before the same party can petition again. (If the employer has submitted the petition, the named union may disclaim interest, also leading to dismissal.)

If the petition survives this initial investigation, the parties may still require the resolution of issues raised by the petition. Questions such as the definition of the bargaining unit, the eligibility of certain employees to participate in the election, and the number of polling places need to be settled prior to the holding of the election. The parties may agree to waive their rights to a hearing on these issues and proceed to a **consent election.** In so doing, they may either agree that all rulings of the regional director on these questions are final and binding, or they may reserve the right to appeal the regional director's decisions to the board.

If the parties fail to agree on some of these issues and have not agreed to a consent election, then a representation hearing will be held before a presiding officer, who may be a board attorney, field examiner, or ALJ. The act does not prescribe rules of evidence to be used in this proceeding (in contrast to the "C" case hearing); indeed, the board's rules and regulations state that federal court rules of evidence shall not be controlling.

A second union, with a 10 percent showing of interest from among the employees, is entitled to intervene and participate in the hearing. Such an intervention can also block a consent election and compel a hearing to take place.

Shortly after the hearing, the hearing officer will submit a report to the director, who will then render a decision either to hold an election or to dismiss the petition. This decision can be appealed by a party to the board in Washington only on the following grounds:

- A board legal precedent was not followed or should be reconsidered.

- A substantial factual issue is clearly erroneous in the record.

- The conduct of the hearing was prejudicial to the appealing party.

The board will act expeditiously on the appeal. Meanwhile, the regional director will proceed with plans for the election, which usually occurs twenty-five to thirty days after it has been ordered.

Rules Barring Holding an Election

The philosophy of the NLRB and the courts is that a board-sponsored election is a serious step, which the affected employees should not be permitted to disavow or overrule frivolously or hastily. Furthermore, the newly certified bargaining agent should be given a reasonable opportunity to fulfill its mandate by successfully negotiating a collective bargaining agreement with the company. If the board failed to protect the successfully elected bargaining representative from worker fickleness or rival union challenges, the employer would be encouraged to avoid timely and sincere bargaining in an effort to erode the union's support before an agreement is reached. The board has, therefore, fashioned several election bar rules.

Under the **contract bar rule,** a written labor contract—signed and binding on the parties and dealing with substantial terms and conditions of employment—bars an election among the affected bargaining unit during the life of that bargaining agreement. This rule has two exceptions. First, the board provides a window or **open season,** during which a rival union can offer its challenge by filing an election petition. This "window" is open between the ninetieth and sixtieth day prior to the expiration of the current collective bargaining agreement. The rationale here is that a rival union should not be completely prevented from filing an election petition;

otherwise, the employer and incumbent union could continually bargain new contracts regardless of whether the employees wished to continue to be represented by the incumbent union.

If no new petition is filed during the open-season period, then the last sixty days of the contract provide a period during which the parties can negotiate a new agreement insulated from any outside challenges. If a petition is filed during this insulated period, it will be dismissed as untimely. In the event that the employer and the incumbent union fail to reach a new agreement and the old agreement expires, then petitions may be filed any time after the expiration of the existing agreement.

The second exception to the contract bar rule is that a contract for longer than three years will operate only as a bar to an election for three years. In the *American Seating Co.* decision (106 N.L.R.B. 250, 1953), the board held that an agreement of excessive duration cannot be used to preclude challenges to the incumbent union indefinitely. Therefore, any contract longer than three years duration will be treated as if it were three years long for the purposes of filing petitions—that is, the open-season period would occur between the ninetieth and the sixtieth day prior to the end of the third year of the agreement.

Section 9(C)(3) of the NLRA provides that when a valid election has been held in a bargaining unit, no new election can be held for a twelve-month period for that unit or any subdivision of the unit. When the employees of a unit have voted not to be represented by a union, no other union may file for an election for those employees for twelve months. By the same token, when a union has been certified as the winner of the election, it is free from challenge to its status for at least twelve months. This twelve-month period usually runs from the date of certification, but when an employer refuses to bargain with the certified union, the board may extend the period to twelve months from when good-faith bargaining actually commences. The twelve-month period under Section 9(C)(3) applies only when an election has been held. When an employer has voluntarily recognized a union, the board will allow a "reasonable time" for the parties to reach an agreement before it will accept election petitions from rival unions. Although a "reasonable time" may vary depending on the circumstances of each specific case, it may well be less than twelve months.

Defining the Appropriate Bargaining Unit

The **bargaining unit** is a concept central to labor relations under both the Railway Labor Act and the National Labor Relations Act. The bargaining unit is the basic constituency of the labor union—it is the group of employees for which the union seeks to acquire recognition as bargaining agent and to negotiate regarding employment conditions. In order for collective bargaining to produce results fair to both sides, it is essential that the bargaining unit be defined appropriately. The bargaining unit should encompass all employees who share a commonality of interests regarding working conditions. It should not be so broad as to include divergent or antagonistic interests. Nor should it submerge the interests of a small, yet well-defined group of employees within the larger unit.

Section 9(b) of the NLRA provides that the definition of an appropriate bargaining unit is a matter left to the board's discretion. What constitutes an appropriate bargaining unit is the most commonly disputed issue in representative case hearings. It is also one of the most complex and difficult questions for the board and the courts to resolve. The Supreme Court in *Packard Motor Car* v. *NLRB* (330 U.S. 584, 1949) observed that "The issue as to what unit is appropriate is one for which no absolute rule of law is laid down by statute. . . . The decision of the Board, if not final, is rarely to be disturbed." This statement is a bit misleading because Section 9(b) of the NLRA does set out some guidelines for the board in determining the appropriate unit. Section 9(b) states that the goal in defining a bargaining unit is to "assure the employees the fullest freedom in exercising the rights guaranteed by this Act." Section 9(b) also contains the following five provisions:

1. The options open to the board in determining a bargaining unit include an **employerwide unit**, a **craft unit**, a **single-plant unit**, or a subdivision thereof.

2. The unit cannot contain both professional employees (as defined by Section 2(12) of the act) and nonprofessional employees, unless a majority of the professional employees have voted to be included in the unit.

3. A craft unit cannot be found to be inappropriate simply on the ground that a different unit (e.g., a plantwide unit) was established by a previous board determination, unless a majority of the employees in the proposed craft unit vote against representation in such a separate craft unit.

4. A unit including nonguard or security employees cannot include plant guards or security personnel; conversely, a union representing plant guards cannot be certified if it also includes workers other than guards as members or if it is directly or indirectly affiliated with a union representing persons other than guards.[1]

5. The extent to which employees have already been organized at the time of the filing of the election petition is not to be controlling of the board's definition of the appropriate bargaining unit.

In addition to the statutory commands, the board has also fashioned a number of other factors to be considered in determining the appropriate unit. Those factors include the following:

- the commonality of interest of included employees concerning wages, hours, working conditions, the nature of duties performed, and the skills, training or qualifications required;

- geographical and physical proximity of included workers;

- any history of prior collective bargaining tending to prove that a workable relationship exists or can exist between the employer and the proposed unit;

---

[1]By requiring that guards and security personnel be organized in a separate bargaining *and* separate unions, Congress appears to hold the view that the normal duties of plant guards can create conflicts of interest with their union loyalties.

- similarity of the unit to the employer's administrative or territorial divisions, the functional integration of the company's operations, and the frequency of employee interchange;

- the desires of the employees concerning the bargaining unit, such as might be determined through a secret ballot among workers who have the statutory prerogative of choosing between a plantwide unit or a separate craft unit. (This right to self-determination by election is referred to as the Globe doctrine, after the case in which the standards for such elections were set out, *Globe Machine and Stamping*, 3 N.L.R.B. 294, 1937, pursuant to Section 9(b)(2) of the act.)

Included in the difficult question of bargaining unit definition is the issue of craft unit severance policies; that issue has been perhaps the most difficult of all the complex matters raised by bargaining unit determination. The following case is the leading pronouncement by the board in this area. This case will also help you to understand the process of defining the appropriate bargaining unit within the context of an actual dispute between the employer and union over this issue.

MALLINCKRODT CHEMICAL WORKS

162 N.L.R.B. 387 (N.L.R.B., 1966)

[The International Brotherhood of Electrical Workers (petitioner) petitioned for a separate bargaining unit composed of certain skilled instrument mechanics, their apprentices, and helpers in the employer's instrument department. Mallinckrodt is engaged in purifying uranium ore and producing solid uranium to be used by the Atomic Energy Commission and the Defense Department.]

The Employer's uranium division [is] . . . staffed by about 560 employees. Of these, fully half are guards, supervisors, professional, technical, and clerical employees. The remaining production and maintenance unit is comprised of 130 production operators and approximately 150 maintenance employees of which 12 are instrument mechanics, the classification which Petitioner seeks to sever.

. . . It is the principal function of the instrument mechanic to make adjustments and alterations on improperly operating instruments so that the production process may continue unimpeded. Close to three-fourths of the repairs performed by the instrument mechanics occur at the place of the breakdown, that is on the production line. While the job requirements of operator and instrument mechanic are clearly defined and do not overlap, the operator is required to work with and does assist the mechanic in order to permit a speedy repair and the continuation of production. It is also necessary that the activities between the two be coordinated so that the operator may read the panel and relay the reading to the instrument mechanic. The operator also manually operates the instrument in order to see that it is functioning properly. We conclude from the foregoing that the instrument mechanic's role in the Employer's production process is uniquely and integrally a part upon which the production flow is dependent.

The instrument shop is set apart physically from other departments. . . . In charge of the 12 instrument mechanics is a foreman who reports directly to the superintendent of the instrument department. The superintendent in turn is responsible to the department manager. The instrument mechanic is identified by the blue hat which he must wear.

Instrument mechanics are classified as Trainee, Class B, A, and Special. Progression is by merit and does not occur automatically. In hiring instrument mechanics, the Employer seeks experienced mechanics so that hiring does not normally occur at the trainee or lowest level. The top graded instrument mechanic is responsible for the evaluation, installation, modification, calibration, maintenance, and dismantling of electronic, electrical pneumatic, mechanical and hydraulic instruments. . . .

At the end of their work day they return to the instrument shop. Most of the instrument mechanics spend between 50 to 60 percent of their working day away from the instrument shop, and some of them are gone as much as 80 to 90 percent of the time. . . .

Although there is no special apprenticeship program for instrument mechanics, the record shows that the Employer, when hiring instrument mechanics, seeks men with several years of industrial instrumentation background. When hired, the instrument mechanic is placed in one of the four classifications maintained by the Employer for instrumentation and, based on merit ratings, he progresses into higher rated classifications in accordance with his skill and experience. Only a top merit rated mechanic moves into the special classification. Normally it takes from 3½ to 4 years to advance from the lowest to the highest classification. At the time of the hearing, all of the instrument mechanics involved were either in the A or the special classification.

It is clear from the foregoing that the instrument mechanics are skilled workmen who work under separate supervision, and we find that the instrument mechanics constitute an identifiable group of skilled employees similar to groups we have previously found to be journeymen or craft instrument mechanics.

. . . At the outset, it is appropriate to set forth the nature of the issue confronting the Board in making unit determinations in severance cases. Underlying such determinations is the need to balance the interests of the employer and the total employee complement in maintaining the industrial stability and resulting benefits of an historical plant-wide bargaining unit as against the interest of a portion of such complement in having an opportunity to break away from the historical unit by a vote for separate representation. . . .

The cohesiveness and special interest of a craft or departmental group seeking severance may indicate the appropriateness of a bargaining unit limited to that group. However, the interests of all employees in continuing to bargain together in order to maintain their collective strength, as well as the public interest and the interests of the employer and the plant union in maintaining overall plant stability in labor relations, and uninterrupted operation of integrated industrial or commercial facilities, may favor adherence to the established patterns of bargaining.

The following areas of inquiry are illustrative of those we deem relevant:

1. Whether or not the proposed unit consists of a distinct and homogeneous group of skilled journeymen-craftsmen performing the functions of their craft on a nonrepetitive basis, or of employees constituting a functionally distinct department, working in trades or occupations for which a tradition of separate representation exists.
2. The history of collective bargaining of the employees sought and at the plant involved, and at other plants of the employer, with emphasis on whether the existing patterns of bargaining are productive of stability in labor relations, and whether such stability will be unduly disrupted by the destruction of the existing patterns of representation.
3. The extent to which the employees in the proposed unit have established and maintained their separate identity during the period of inclusion in a broader unit, and the extent of their participation or lack of participation in the establishment and maintenance of the existing pattern of representation and the prior opportunities, if any, afforded them to obtain separate representation.
4. The history and pattern of collective bargaining in the industry involved.
5. The degree of integration of the employer's production processes, including the extent to which the continued normal operation of the production processes is dependent upon the performance of the assigned functions of the employees in the proposed unit.
6. The qualifications of the union seeking to "carve out" a separate unit, including that union's experience in representing employees like those involved in the severance action. . . .

The instrument mechanics have been represented as part of a production and maintenance unit for the last 25 years. The record does not demonstrate that their interests have been neglected by their bargaining representative. In fact, the record shows that their pay rates are comparable to those received by the skilled electricians who are currently represented by the Petitioner, and that such rates are among the highest in the plant. The instrument mechanics have their own seniority system for purposes of transfer, layoff, and recall. Viewing this long lack of concern for maintaining and preserving a separate group identity for bargaining purposes, together with the fact that Petitioner has not traditionally represented the instrument mechanic craft, we find that the interests served by maintenance of stability in the existing bargaining unit of approximately 280 production and maintenance employees outweigh the interests served by affording the 12 instrument mechanics an opportunity to change their mode of representation.

We conclude that the foregoing circumstances present a compelling argument in support of the continued appropriateness of the existing production and maintenance unit for purposes of collective bargaining, and against the appropriateness of a separate unit of instrument mechanics. . . .

Bargaining Unit Definition in the Health Care Industry.   The 1974 amendments to the NLRA extended NLRB jurisdiction over nonprofit health care institutions. The congressional committee reports accompanying the amending legislation stated that "Due consideration should be given by the Board to preventing proliferation of bargaining units in the health care industry." In 1987 the board gave notice of its intention to use rule-making procedures to develop rules for bargaining unit determinations in health care institutions. The board issued its final rule for such determinations in 1989; the final rule was printed in 54 Federal Register 16336 (1989). The rule states that the board will recognize the following eight bargaining units for acute-care hospitals: physicians, registered nurses, other professional employees, medical technicians, skilled maintenance workers, clerical workers, guards, and other nonprofessional employees. No unit with fewer than six employees will be certified (except for guard units). The American Hospital Association (AHA) objected to any rules that require more than three bargaining units: professional employees, nonprofessional employees, and guards. The AHA succeeded in getting a federal district court to issue an injunction against the board's rules (718 F. Supp. 704, N.D. Ill.). On appeal, the 7th Circuit Court of Appeals vacated the injunction and remanded the case with instructions to enter judgment for the board (*American Hospital Association* v. *NLRB,* 899 F.2d 651, 1990). On appeal, the U.S. Supreme Court affirmed the court of appeals (___ U.S. ___, 111 S.Ct. 1539, 1991) and upheld the board's rules.

Voter Eligibility

Along with determining the appropriate bargaining unit, the question of which employees are actually eligible to vote in the election must also be resolved. Factors to be considered are whether an employee is within the bargaining unit and whether striking employees are able to vote.

In general, when the election has been directed (or agreed to, for consent elections), the board establishes an eligibility date—that is, the date by which an employee must be on the employer's payroll in order to be eligible to vote. The eligibility date is usually the end of the payroll period immediately preceding the direction of (or agreement to hold) the election. Employees must be on the payroll as of the eligibility date, and they must also continue to be on the payroll on the date the election is held. Employees hired after the eligibility date but before the election date are not eligible to vote.

Employees may be on strike when an election is held; this is most often the case in decertification elections, when the employees not striking seek to get rid of the union. Section 2(3) of the NLRA defines *employee* to include "any individual whose work has ceased as a consequence of . . . any current labor dispute . . . and who has not obtained any other regular and substantially equivalent employment." The board has adopted several rules clarifying the voting rights of striking employees.

The board distinguishes whether the employees are on an unfair labor practice strike or an economic strike. An **unfair labor practice strike** is a strike by employees in protest of, or precipitated by, employer unfair labor practices. The board holds that unfair labor practice strikers cannot be permanently replaced by the employer. Unfair labor practice strikers are eligible to vote in any election held during the strike; any employees hired to replace unfair labor practice strikers are not eligible to vote.

Economic strikes are strikes over economic issues, such as grievances or a new contract. Unlike unfair labor practice strikers, economic strikers may be permanently replaced by the employer. Economic strikers who have not been permanently replaced may vote in any election during the strike, but economic strikers who have been permanently replaced may vote only in elections held within twelve months after the strike begins. After twelve months, they lose their eligibility to vote. The employees hired to replace economic strikers may vote if they are permanent replacements—that is, if the employer intends to retain them after the strike is over. Replacements hired on a temporary basis, who will not be retained after the strike ends, are not eligible to vote. As a result of these rules, during the first twelve months of a strike, permanent replacements and all economic strikers may vote; after twelve months, only the permanent replacements and those economic strikers who have not been permanently replaced may vote.

Economic strikers or unfair labor practice strikers who obtain permanent employment elsewhere and who abandon their prior jobs lose their eligibility to vote. Although the board generally presumes that other employment by strikers during a strike is temporary, they will hold that a striker has lost eligibility to vote if it can be shown that he or she does not intend to return to the prior job. As well, strikers fired for wrongdoing during the strike are not eligible to vote.

When the eligibility of employees to vote is challenged, the board requires that the party challenging the eligibility must prove that the challenged employees are not eligible to vote. For example, the union would have to prove that replacements were hired only on a temporary basis, or the employer would have to show that strikers did not intend to return to their prior job. Although the board prefers that challenges to voter eligibility be resolved at a hearing prior to the election, such challenges may also be raised at the time the challenged employee votes. When an employee's right to vote is challenged, the ballot at issue is placed in a sealed envelope rather than in the ballot box. After all employees have voted, the board first counts the unchallenged ballots. If the results of the election will not be changed by the challenged ballots—because there are not enough of them to change the outcome—the board will not rule on the challenges. However, if the challenged ballots could affect the election results, the board will hold a hearing to resolve the challenges, count those ballots from the eligible voters, and then certify the election results.

Representation Election

Within seven days after the regional director approves a consent election or directs that an election be held, the employer must file an election eligibility list with the regional office. This list, called an **Excelsior list** after the decision in which the board set out this requirement (*Excelsior Underwear, Inc.,* 156 N.L.R.B. No. 111, 1966), contains the names and home addresses of all employees eligible to vote, so that the union can contact them outside their work environment, beyond the boss's observation and control. A board agent will then arrange a conference with all parties to settle the details of the election.

The election is generally held on company premises; however, if the union objects, it can be held elsewhere. The NLRB agent supervises the conduct of the election, and all parties are entitled to have observers present during the voting. All parties to the election will undoubtedly have engaged in an election campaign prior to the vote. The board regards such an election as an experiment to determine the employees' choice. The board therefore strives for **laboratory conditions** in the conduct of the election and requires that neither side engage in conduct that could unduly affect the employees' free choice.

The laboratory conditions can be violated by unfair practices committed by either side. Conduct that does not amount to an unfair practice may also violate the laboratory conditions if the board believes that wrongful misconduct will unduly affect the employees' choice. **Captive-audience speeches** given by representatives of the employee or mass meetings by the union within twenty-four hours of an election at which the union promises to waive initiation fees for members who join before the election are examples of such conduct. Actions by third parties, other than the employer and union, may also violate the laboratory conditions. In one case, the local newspaper in a small southern town printed racially inflammatory articles about the union attempting to organize the work force of a local employer. The board held that the injection of racial propaganda into the election violated the laboratory conditions and was reason to invalidate the election, which the union lost.

The board has decided that it will not monitor the truthfulness of the election propaganda of either side. Misrepresentations in campaign promises or propaganda will not, of themselves, be grounds to set aside the election results. The board's decision reversed its prior position of holding substantial misrepresentations of material facts to be grounds to set aside the election results.

The board requires that the parties in an election refrain from formal campaigning for twenty-four hours prior to the holding of the election. This **twenty-four-hour silent period** is intended to give the employees time to reflect upon their choice free from electioneering pressures. Any mass union rallies or employer captive-audience speeches during the silent period will be grounds to set aside the election results. (Figure 5.2 shows a sample ballot for a representative election.)

If either party believes the election laboratory conditions were violated, that party may file objections to the other party's conduct with the regional director within five days of the election. Postelection unfair labor practice charges could also result in the election results being set aside.

After the election is held, the parties have five days in which to file any objections with the regional director. If the director finds the objections to be valid, the election will be set aside. If the objections are found to be invalid, the results of the election will be certified. In order to be victorious, a party to the election must receive a majority of the votes cast—that is, either the union or the no-union choice

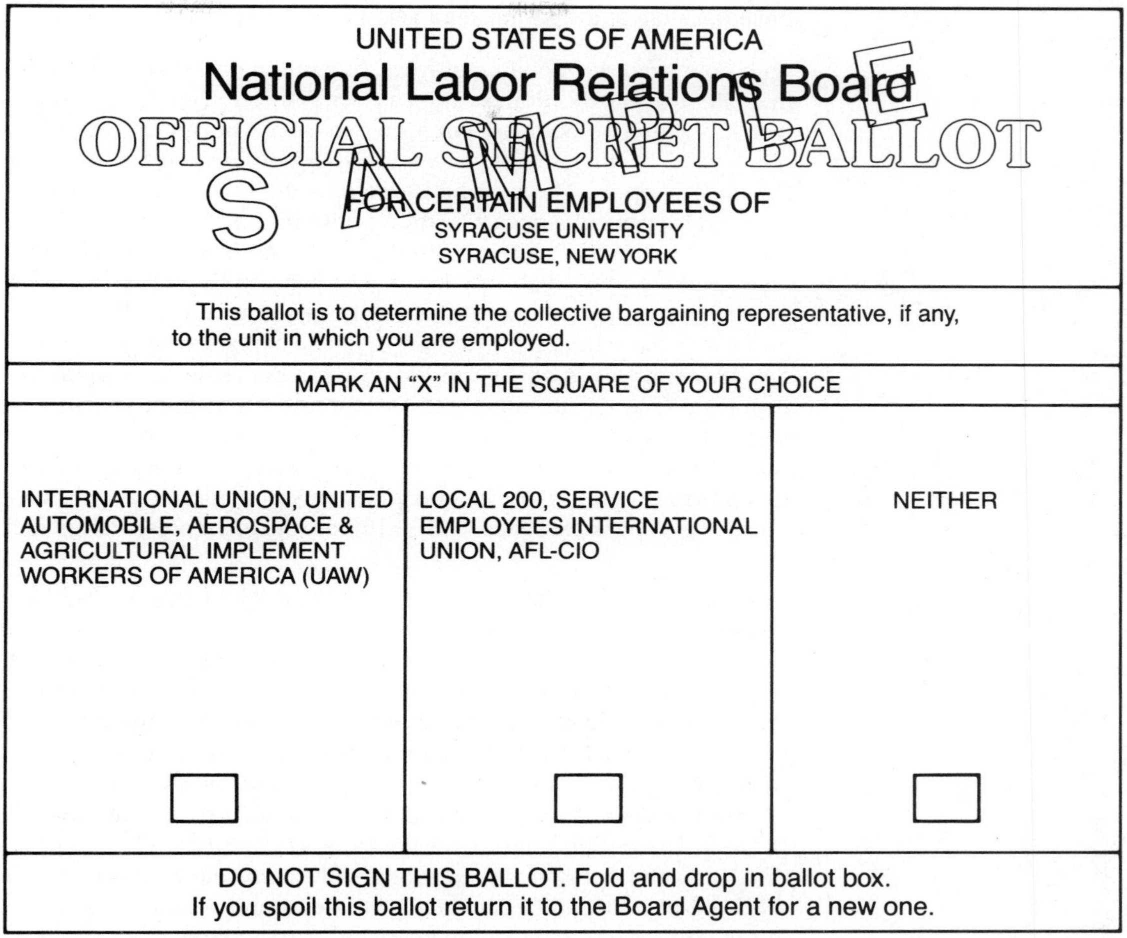

```
UNITED STATES OF AMERICA
National Labor Relations Board
OFFICIAL SECRET BALLOT
SAMPLE
FOR CERTAIN EMPLOYEES OF
SYRACUSE UNIVERSITY
SYRACUSE, NEW YORK
```

This ballot is to determine the collective bargaining representative, if any, to the unit in which you are employed.

MARK AN "X" IN THE SQUARE OF YOUR CHOICE

INTERNATIONAL UNION, UNITED AUTOMOBILE, AEROSPACE & AGRICULTURAL IMPLEMENT WORKERS OF AMERICA (UAW)	LOCAL 200, SERVICE EMPLOYEES INTERNATIONAL UNION, AFL-CIO	NEITHER
☐	☐	☐

DO NOT SIGN THIS BALLOT. Fold and drop in ballot box.
If you spoil this ballot return it to the Board Agent for a new one.

Figure 5.2 Sample NLRB representation election ballot

must garner a majority of the votes cast by the eligible employees. If the election involved more than one union, and no choice received a simple majority, the board will hold a run-off election between the two choices getting the highest number of votes. If a union wins, it will be certified as the bargaining agent for all the employees in the bargaining unit.

Because the conduct of representation elections is a matter subject to the discretion of the regional directors and the board, only limited judicial review of certification decisions is available. However, as a practical matter, an employer can obtain review of the board's certification decision by refusing to bargain with the certified union and contesting the issue in the subsequent unfair labor practice proceeding.

Decertification of the Bargaining Agent

An employee or group of employees, or a union or individual acting on their behalf, may file a decertification petition under Section 9(c)(1) of the act, asserting that "the individual or labor organization, which has been certified or is being currently recognized by their employer as the bargaining representative" no longer enjoys the unit's support. The board also requires the showing of 30 percent employee interest in support of a decertification petition in order to entertain the petition. This 30-percent rule has been criticized by some commentators in that the petition signifies nothing more than that fewer than half the employees are unhappy with their representative, yet the mere filing of the petition can totally disrupt the bargaining process because the employer may refuse to bargain while the petition is pending.

An employer is not permitted to file a decertification petition; the board will dismiss a decertification petition by employees if it discovers that the employer instigated the filing. However, a company can file an election petition if it can demonstrate by objective evidence that it has reasonable grounds for believing that the incumbent union has lost its majority status. Such petitions must be filed during the open-season periods, just as with petitions seeking representation elections.

Deauthorization Elections.   Section 9(e)(1) of the NLRA provides for the holding of a deauthorization election to rescind the **union shop clause** in a collective agreement. The union shop clause, which may be included in a collective agreement, requires that all present and future members of the bargaining unit become, and remain, union members. They typically must join the union after thirty days from the date on which they were hired. Failure to join the union or to remain a union member is grounds for discharge. The provisions of Section 9(e)(1) state that a petition for a deauthorization election may be filed by an employee or group of employees. The petition must have the support of at least 30 percent of the bargaining unit. If a valid petition is filed, along with the requisite show of support, the board will conduct a secret ballot election to determine whether a majority of employees in the unit wish to remove the union shop clause from the agreement. As is the case with representation and decertification elections, no deauthorization election can be held for a bargaining unit (or subdivision of the unit) if a valid deauthorization election has been held in the preceding twelve-month period. Unlike representation elections and decertification elections, which are determined by a majority of the votes actually cast, deauthorization elections require that a majority of the members *in the bargaining unit* vote in favor of rescinding the union shop clause in order for it to be rescinded.

Acquiring Representation Rights through Unfair Labor Practice Proceedings

Unfair labor practice charges filed with the board while representation proceedings are pending may invoke the board's **blocking charge policy.** The filing of such charges usually halts the representation case—no election will be held pending the resolution of the unfair labor practice charges. An employer may wish to forestall the election and erode the union's support by committing various unfair labor practices, thereby taking unfair advantage of this policy.

A union may wish to proceed with the pending election despite the unfair labor practice charges. It can do so by filing a request-to-proceed notice with the board. If the union proceeds and wins the election, then the effect of the unfair labor practice charges is not very important. However, if the union loses the election, it may be because of the effect of the employer's illegal actions. In that case, the union could file objections to the election and request that a new election be held—but how could the union overcome the lingering effects of the employer's unfair practices? Rather than seek a new election or proceed with the original election, the union may rely on the unfair practice charges and ask the board, as a remedy for the unfair labor practices, to order the employer to recognize and bargain with the union without its ever winning an election. The following case, *NLRB* v. *Gissel Packing Co.,* addresses the propriety of such a remedial bargaining order as a means to prevent the employer from benefiting from its illegal actions.

NLRB v. GISSEL PACKING CO.

395 U.S. 575 (Supreme Court of the United States, 1969)

[Four cases involving similar legal issues were consolidated for review by the Supreme Court. All four involved situations in which an employer was confronted by a union claiming majority support and requesting recognition. In each case the employer refused recognition and engaged in a number of unfair labor practices. In only one of the four cases did the union proceed with the election, which it lost. In the other three cases the unions chose to pursue the unfair labor practice charges rather than go through with the election. In each of the four cases the board, as a remedy for the employer's unfair practices, ordered the employer to recognize and bargain with the union. The employers sought judicial review of the board's orders in all cases. In one case the U.S. Court of Appeals for the First Circuit upheld the bargaining order, while the U.S. Court of Appeals for the Fourth Circuit refused to enforce the bargaining order in three of the cases. The losing parties then appealed to the Supreme Court.]

WARREN, C.J.

The specific questions facing us here are whether the duty to bargain can arise without a Board election under the Act; whether union authorization cards, if obtained from a majority of employees without misrepresentation or coercion, are reliable enough generally to provide a valid, alternate route to majority status; whether a bargaining order is an appropriate and authorized remedy where an employer rejects a card majority while at the same time committing unfair practices that tend to undermine the union's majority and make a fair election an unlikely possibility; . . . For reasons given below, we answer each of these questions in the affirmative.

Of the four cases before us, three —*Gissel Packing Co., Heck's, Inc.,* and *General Steel Products, Inc.*—were consolidated following separate decisions in the Court of Appeals for the Fourth Circuit and brought here by the National Labor Relations Board. All three cases present the same legal issues in similar, uncomplicated factual settings that can be briefly described together. The fourth case (*Sinclair Company*), brought here from the Court of Appeals for the First Circuit and argued separately, presents many of the same questions and will thus be disposed of in this opinion. . . .

In each case, the Board's primary response was an order to bargain directed at the employers, despite the absence of an election in *Gissel* and *Heck's* and the employer's victory in *General Steel.* More specifically, the Board found in each case (1) that the Union had obtained valid authorization cards from a majority of the employees in the bargaining unit and was thus entitled to represent the employees for collective bargaining purposes; and (2) that the employer's refusal to bargain with the Union in violation of Section 8(a)(5) was motivated, not by a "good faith" doubt of the Union's majority status, but by a desire to gain time to dissipate that status. The Board based its conclusion as to the lack of good faith doubt on the fact that the employers had committed substantial unfair labor practices during their antiunion campaign efforts to resist recognition. Thus, the Board found that all three employers had engaged in restraint and coercion of employees in violation of Section 8(a)(1)—in *Gissel,* for coercively interrogating employees about Union activities, threatening them with discharge, and promising them benefits; in *Heck's,* for coercively interrogating employees, threatening reprisals, creating the appearance of surveillance, and offering benefits for opposing the Union; and in *General Steel,* for coercive interrogation and threats of reprisals, including discharge. In addition, the Board found that the employers in *Gissel* and *Heck's* had wrongfully discharged employees for engaging in Union activities in violation of Section 8(a)(3). And, because the employers had rejected the card-based bargaining demand in bad faith, the Board found that all three had refused to recognize the Unions in violation of Section 8(a)(5).

Consequently, the Board ordered the companies to cease and desist from their unfair labor practices, to offer reinstatement and back pay to the employees who had been discriminatorily discharged, to bargain with the Unions on request and to post the appropriate notices.

On appeal, the Court of Appeals for the Fourth Circuit, in per curiam opinions in each of the three cases sustained the Board's findings as to the Section 8(a)(1) and Section 8(a)(3) violations, but rejected the Board's findings that the employers' refusal to bargain violated Section 8(a)(5) and declined to enforce those portions of the Board's orders directing the respondent companies to bargain in good faith. The court in those cases held that the 1947 Taft-Hartley amendments to the Act, which permitted the Board to resolve representation disputes by certification under Section 9(c) only by secret ballot election, withdrew from the Board the authority to order an employer to bargain under Section 8(a)(5) on the basis of cards, in the absence of NLRB certification, unless the employer knows independently of the cards that there is in fact no representation dispute. The court held that the cards themselves were so

inherently unreliable that their use gave an employer virtually an automatic, good faith claim that such a dispute existed, for which a secret election was necessary.

The first issue facing us is whether a union can establish a bargaining obligation by means other than a Board election and whether the validity of alternate routes to majority status, such as cards, was affected by the 1947 Taft-Hartley amendments. The most commonly traveled route for a union to obtain recognition as the exclusive bargaining representative of an unorganized group of employees is through the Board's election and certification procedures under Section 9(c) of the Act; it is also, from the Board's point of view, the preferred route. A union is not limited to a Board election, however, for, in addition to Section 9, the present Act provides in Section 8(a)(5) that "[i]t shall be an unfair labor practice for an employer . . . to refuse to bargain collectively with the representatives of his employees, subject to the provisions of Section 9(a)." Since Section 9(a), in both the Wagner Act and the present Act, refers to the representative as the one "designated or selected" by a majority of the employees without specifying precisely how that representative is to be chosen, it was early recognized that an employer had a duty to bargain whenever the union representative presented "convincing evidence of majority support." Almost from the inception of the Act, then, it was recognized that a union did not have to be certified as the winner of a Board election to invoke a bargaining obligation; it could establish majority status by other means under the unfair labor practice provision of Section 8(a)(5)—by showing convincing support, for instance, by a union-called strike or strike vote, or, as here, by possession of cards signed by a majority of the employees authorizing the union to represent them for collective bargaining purposes. . . .

The employers rely finally on the addition to Section 9(c) of subparagraph (B), which allows an employer to petition for an election whenever "one or more individuals or labor organizations have presented to him a claim to be recognized as the representative defined in Section 9(a)." That provision was not added, as the employers assert, to give them an absolute right to an election at any time; rather, it was intended, as the legislative history indicates, to allow them, after being asked to bargain, to test out their doubts as to a union's majority in a secret election which they would then presumably not cause to be set aside by illegal antiunion activity. We agree with the Board's assertion here that there is no suggestion that Congress intended Section 9(c)(1)(B) to relieve any employer of his Section 8(a)(5) bargaining obligation where, without good faith, he engaged in unfair labor practices disruptive of the Board's election machinery. And we agree that the policies reflected in Section 9(c)(1)(B) fully support the Board's present administration of the Act . . . ; for an employer can insist on a secret ballot election, unless in the words of the Board, he engages "in contemporaneous unfair labor practices likely to destroy the union's majority and seriously impede the election." In short, we hold that the 1947 amendments did not restrict an employer's duty to bargain under Section 8(a)(5) solely to those unions whose representative status is certified after a Board election.

We next consider the question whether authorization cards are such inherently unreliable indicators of employee desires that, whatever the validity of other alternate routes to representative status, the cards themselves may never be used to determine a union's majority and to support an order to bargain.

The objections to the use of cards voiced by the employers and the Fourth Circuit boil down to two contentions: (1) that, as contrasted with the election procedure, the cards cannot accurately reflect an employee's wishes, either because an employer has not had a chance to present his views and thus a chance to insure that the employee choice was an informed one, or because the choice was the result of group pressures and not individual decision made in the privacy of a voting booth; and (2) that quite apart from the election comparison, the cards are too often obtained through misrepresentation and coercion which compound the cards' inherent inferiority to the election process. Neither contention is persuasive, and each proves too much. The Board itself has recognized, and continues to do so here, that secret elections are generally the most satisfactory—indeed the preferred—method of ascertaining whether a union has majority support. The acknowledged superiority of the election process, however, does not mean that cards are thereby rendered totally invalid, for where an employer engages in conduct disruptive of the election process, cards may be the most effective—perhaps the only—way of assuring employee choice. As for misrepresentation, in any specific case of alleged irregularity in the solicitation of the cards, the proper course is to apply the Board's customary standards (to be discussed more fully below) and rule that there was no majority if the standards were not satisfied. It does not follow that because there are some instances of irregularity, the cards can never be used; otherwise, an employer could put off his bargaining obligation indefinitely through continuing interference with elections.

That the cards, though admittedly inferior to the election process, can adequately reflect employee sentiment when that process has been impeded, needs no extended discussion, for the employers' contentions cannot withstand close examination. The employers argue that their employees cannot make an informed choice because the card drive will be over before the employer has had a chance to present his side of the unionization issues. Normally, however, the union will inform the employer of its organization drive early in order to subject the employer to the unfair labor practice provisions of the Act; the union must be able to show the employer's awareness of the drive in order to prove that his contemporaneous conduct constituted unfair labor practices on which a bargaining order can be based if the drive is ultimately successful. Thus, in all of the cases here but the Charleston campaign in *Heck's* the employer, whether informed by the union or not, was aware of the union's organizing drive almost at the outset and began its antiunion campaign at that time; and even in the *Heck's* Charleston case, where the recognition demand came about a week after the solicitation began, the employer was able to deliver a speech before the union obtained a majority. Further, the employers argue that without a secret ballot an employee may in a card drive, succumb to group pressures or sign simply to get the union "off his back" and then be unable to change his mind as he would be free to do once inside a voting booth. But the same pressures are likely to be equally present in an election, for election cases arise most often with small bargaining units where virtually every voter's sentiments can be carefully and individually canvassed. And no voter, of course, can change his mind after casting a ballot in an election even though he may think better of his choice shortly thereafter.

The employer's second complaint, that the cards are too often obtained through misrepresentation and coercion, must be rejected also in view of the Board's present rules for controlling card solicitation, which we view as adequate to the task where the cards involved state their purpose clearly and unambiguously on their face. We would be closing our eyes to obvious difficulties, of course, if we did not recognize that there have been abuses, primarily arising out of misrepresentations by union organizers as to whether the effect of signing a card was to designate the union to represent the employee for collective bargaining purposes or merely to authorize it to seek an election to determine that issue.

In resolving the conflict among the circuits in favor of approving the Board's Cumberland rule, we think it sufficient to point out that employees should be bound by the clear language of what they sign unless that language is deliberately and clearly canceled by a union adherent with words calculated to direct the signer to disregard and forget the language above his signature. There is nothing inconsistent in handing an employee a card that says the signer authorizes the union to represent him and then telling him that the card will probably be used first to get an election. Elections have been, after all, and will continue to be, held in the vast majority of cases; the union will still have to have the signatures of 30 percent of the employees when an employer rejects a bargaining demand and insists that the union seek an election. We cannot agree with the employers here that employees as a rule are too unsophisticated to be bound by what they sign unless expressly told that their act of signing represents something else....

Remaining before us is the propriety of a bargaining order as a remedy for a Section 8(a)(5) refusal to bargain where an employer has committed independent unfair labor practices which have made the holding of a fair election unlikely or which have in fact undermined a union's majority and caused an election to be set aside. We have long held that the Board is not limited to a cease-and-desist order in such cases, but has the authority to issue a bargaining order without first requiring the union to show that it has been able to maintain its majority status.... And we have held the Board has the same authority even where it is clear that the union, which once had possession of cards from a majority of the employees, represents only a minority when the bargaining order is entered. We see no reason now to withdraw this authority from the Board. If the Board could enter only a cease-and-desist order and direct an election or rerun, it would in effect be rewarding the employer and allowing him "to profit from [his] own wrongful refusal to bargain," while at the same time severely curtailing the employees' right freely to determine whether they desire a representative. The employer could continue to delay or disrupt the election processes and put off indefinitely his obligation to bargain; and any election held under these circumstances would not be likely to demonstrate the employees' true, undistorted desires. ...

The only effect of our holding here is to approve the Board's use of the bargaining order in less extraordinary cases marked by less pervasive practices which nonetheless still have the tendency to undermine majority strength and impede the election processes. The Board's authority to issue such an order on a lesser showing of employer misconduct is appropriate, we should reemphasize, where there is also a showing that at one point the union had a majority; in such a case, of course, effectuating ascertainable employee free choice becomes as important a goal as deterring employer misbehavior. In fashioning a remedy in the exercise of its discretion, then the Board can properly take into consideration the extensiveness of an employer's unfair practices in terms of their past effect on election conditions and the likelihood of their recurrence in the future. If the Board finds that the possibility of erasing the effects of past practices and of ensuring a fair election (or a fair rerun) by the use of traditional remedies, though present, is slight and that employee sentiment once expressed through cards would, on balance be better protected by a bargaining order, then such an order should issue. ...

Given that the board has the ability, under *Gissel,* to issue a bargaining order as an appropriate remedy for unfair labor practices by an employer, a controversy arose over the propriety of the board issuing a bargaining order in a case when the union had not established evidence of majority support. In *United Dairy Farmers' Co-Op. Assoc.* v. *NLRB* (633 F.2d 1054, 1980), the 3rd Circuit Court of Appeals held that the board had the power to issue a bargaining order to counteract the effect of pervasive unfair labor practices by the employer, even where the union never established majority support. However, in *Conair Corp.* (721 F.2d 1355, 1983), *cert. denied* (467 U.S. 1241, 1984), the D.C. Circuit Court of Appeals held that it was inappropriate to issue a bargaining order where the union never established majority support. Subsequently, the NLRB itself held in *Gourmet Foods, Inc.* (270 N.L.R.B. No. 113, 1984) that it would not issue a bargaining order in cases where the union had not shown evidence of majority support during its organizing campaign.

A second controversy over the issuing of bargaining orders involves the question of whether the board, in determining if a bargaining order remedy is appropriate, should consider if the subsequent changes in the circumstances of the bargaining unit make the holding of a fair election unlikely. The board's position is that it will not consider the changed circumstances, because to do so would be to allow the employer to capitalize on its misconduct. Some of the federal courts of appeals take a different position: *NLRB* v. *Jamaica Towing, Inc.* (632 F.2d 208, 2d Cir., 1980), *NLRB* v. *Armcor Industries* (535 F.2d 239, 3rd Cir., 1976), and *NLRB* v. *Craw* (565 F.2d 1267, 3d Cir., 1977) have held that the board must consider the changed circumstances in the bargaining unit when determining whether a bargaining order is appropriate. In *Amazing Stores* v. *NLRB* (887 F.2d 328, 1989), the D.C. Circuit Court of Appeals enforced a bargaining order issued by the board even though there had been almost a complete turnover of the employees in the bargaining unit, because the employer's misconduct had been pervasive and enduring and was not dissipated by the turnover in the unit.

The *Gissel* case involved an employer who committed unfair labor practices after the union claimed majority support. But what about the situation in which an employer, after being confronted by the union claiming recognition, simply refuses to recognize the union but refrains from committing any unfair labor practices? Is the employer required to petition for an election or recognize the union? Or is it up to the union to initiate the election process? In *Linden Lumber Div., Summer & Co.* v. *NLRB* (419 U.S. 301, 1974), the U.S. Supreme Court held that an employer who receives a request for voluntary recognition from a union claiming to have the majority support of the employer's employees is not required to recognize the union, *provided* that the employer has no knowledge of the union's support (independent of the union's claim to have majority support) and does not commit any unfair labor practices. Neither is the employer required to petition the NLRB for a representation election in response to the union's request for recognition; it is then up to the union either to file a petition for an election or to institute unfair labor practice charges. Of course, if the employer does engage in unfair labor practices after receiving the union's request for recognition, the union is free to seek a *Gissel*-type bargaining order from the NLRB as a remedy. Such bargaining orders are granted infrequently, however.

QUESTIONS

1. What are the methods by which a union can acquire representation rights for a group of employees?

2. What steps are necessary in order to get the NLRB to hold a representation election? A decertification election?

3. What is the contract bar rule? What are the exceptions to it?

4. What is a bargaining unit? What factors are considered by the NLRB in determining the appropriate bargaining unit?

5. Under what conditions are economic strikers ineligible to vote in representation elections? Under what conditions are unfair labor practice strikers ineligible to vote in representation elections?

6. What is the Excelsior list? What is the significance of the twenty-four-hour silent period?

7. Under what circumstances can a union acquire representation rights through unfair labor practice proceedings?

8. When must an employer recognize a union requesting voluntary recognition?

CASE PROBLEMS

1. In 1979 employees of the Kent Corporation elected a independent union as their collective bargaining representative. A collective bargaining agreement was hammered out and ultimately ratified by the employees, effective until December 31, 1982. In November 1982 the two sides again negotiated, the result being a contract to be in effect until December 31, 1985. This agreement was signed by the Association Committee members but was never ratified by the rank and file. In fact, evidence showed there had been no association membership meetings, no election of officers, no dues ever collected, and no association treasury since 1979.

In August 1983 the Steelworkers Union filed a representation petition. The NLRB regional director ruled that the association was a defunct union and that its current contract was no bar to an election. The company filed a request for review of the decision with the NLRB in Washington, D.C. The association vice president and a member of the bargaining committee attested to their willingness to continue representing the employees. There was no evidence that the association had ever failed to act on a bargaining unit member's behalf.

How should the NLRB rule on the association's representative status? See *Kent Corporation,* 272 N.L.R.B. No. 115, 117 L.R.R.M. 1333 (1984).

2. L&J Equipment Company was engaged in the surface mining of coal, with its principal site in Hatfield, Pennsylvania, and six satellite sites in other parts of western Pennsylvania. In early 1981 the United Mine Workers of America began organizing L&J's mining employees. A few days after the first organizing meeting, a company-owned truck was destroyed by fire. Authorities determined the fire had been deliberately set. Three weeks later the United Mine Workers filed a petition for an election. The date set for the election was November 4, 1981.

During the intense election campaign, pro-management employees were threatened. A week before the election, a company-owned barn burned to the ground. The United Mine Workers won the election by a vote of thirty-nine to thirty-three.

L&J refused to bargain. The union filed a Section 8(a)(5) charge, and the board found that L&J was guilty of an unfair labor practice. L&J appealed to the U.S. Court of Appeals for the 3rd Circuit, claiming that the board abused its discretion in certifying the union in light of its pre-election improprieties.

How should the appellate court have ruled on this challenge? See *NLRB* v. *L&J Equipment Co.,* 745 F.2d 224, 117 L.R.R.M. 2592 (3d Cir. 1984).

3. Action Automotive, Inc., a retail auto parts and gasoline dealer, had stores in a number of Michigan cities. In March 1981 Local 40 of the Retail Store Employees Union filed a petition for a representation election. The union got a plurality of the unchallenged votes. But the challenged ballots could make the difference.

The union challenged the ballots of the wife of the company's co-owner/president, who worked as a general ledger clerk at the company's headquarters, and of the mother of the three owner-brothers, who worked as a cashier in one of the nine stores. The company argued that since neither received any special benefits, neither should be excluded from the employee unit or denied her vote.

The case reached the U.S. Supreme Court. What arguments could you make to the Court for the union's view? For the company? See *NLRB* v. *Action Automotive, Inc.,* 466 U.S. 970, 118 L.R.R.M. 2577 (1985).

4. Micronesian Telecommunications Corporation (MTC) had its principal office on Saipan, a Pacific Island held as a U.S. trust territory. Electrical Workers (IBEW) Local 1357 sought to represent the employees of MTC, including its employees on neighboring islands.

What jurisdictional issues should the NLRB have addressed before asserting jurisdiction of the case? What result? If the board asserted jurisdiction, what factors should it have considered with respect to whether employees on the neighboring islands belonged in the same bargaining unit with the workers on Saipan? See *Micronesian Tel. Corp.,* 273 N.L.R.B. No. 56, 118 L.R.R.M. 1067 (1984).

5. Kirksville College in Missouri was a nonprofit corporation providing health care services, medical education, and medical research. Service Employees Local 50 filed three representation petitions, seeking to represent separate units composed, respectively, of all technical, all professional, and all service/maintenance employees at the Kirksville Health Center, an unincorporated subsidiary of the college. The college also had several affiliated hospitals and rural clinics within a sixty-mile radius of the main campus.

   What factors should the NLRB consider in deciding whether technical, professional, and service employees should be in separate units? What factors must be looked at to decide whether clinic employees should properly have their own bargaining unit(s) or be part of a broader unit taking in (a) the college, (b) affiliated hospitals, and/or (c) satellite facilities? See *Kirksville College,* 274 N.L.R.B. No. 121, 118 L.R.R.M. 1443 (1985).

6. The Steelworkers Union sought to represent a unit composed of four occupational health nurses in an aluminum plant. The company argued that the nurses were managerial employees, exempt from the act, or in the alternative, professional employees who must be part of a bargaining unit of all the plant's professional employees. The nurses' primary responsibilities were treating employees' injuries and illnesses, administering routine physical examinations to applicants and employees, and maintaining logs and records.

   What additional facts did the NLRB need to decide the issues raised by the company? See *Noranda Aluminum Inc. v. NLRB,* 751 F.2d 268, 118 L.R.R.M. 2136 (8th Cir. 1984).

7. Because of the mixture of ethnic groups in the plant, the NLRB conducted the election using a ballot translated from English into Spanish, Vietnamese, and Laotian. Food & Commercial Workers Local 34 won the election 119 to 112.

   The translations were line by line. Some English-reading employees claimed this made it difficult to read. Some of the translations were later found to be somewhat inaccurate. Neither side challenged any ballots.

   How should the NLRB have ruled on the company's challenge to the election outcome, based on the flawed ballots? See *Kraft, Inc.,* 273 N.L.R.B. No. 1484, 118 L.R.R.M. 1242 (1985).

8. One employee ballot in a close election was marked with a large "X" in the "No Union" box and the word "Yes" written above the box.

   Should the NLRB count this ballot? If so, how? See *NLRB v. Newly Wed Foods Inc.,* 758 F.2d 4, 118 L.R.R.M. 3213 (1st Cir. 1985).

9. The International Brotherhood of Electrical Workers, Local Unions 605 and 985, AFL-CIO ("the union") have represented a bargaining unit comprised of MP&L's service and maintenance employees since 1938. The most recent collective bargaining agreement concerning these employees is for the term of October 15, 1983, until October 15, 1985. That agreement does not include MP&L's storeroom and warehouse employees.

   In January 1984 the union petitioned the NLRB for certification as bargaining representative of these storeroom and warehouse employees. MP&L opposed the petition, urging that the board's contract bar rule barred the election required for the union to be certified. MP&L contended that the contract bar rule must be applied to employees intentionally excluded from an existing collective bargaining agreement.

   The regional director rejected MP&L's contention. The board affirmed this decision. An election was held, and a slim majority of the storeroom and warehouse employees voted to be represented by the union. The NLRB certified the results of the election.

   To obtain judicial review of the board's decision to permit a representation election, MP&L refused to bargain with the union on behalf of the newly represented employees. The union filed an unfair labor practice charge with the board.

   How should the board have ruled on this challenge by MP&L? See *NLRB v. Mississippi Power & Light Co.,* 769 F.2d 276 (5th Cir. 1985).

10. The source of dispute was a representation election held at Kusan's Franklin, Tennessee, plant on October 19, 1979. The union won that election by a vote of 118 to 107. Kusan, however, filed objections with the board over the conduct of the election. The objections charged that the union interfered with the election by

conducting a poll of the employees and threatening and coercing employees during the course of the polling.

In December 1979 the regional director of the NLRB investigated Kusan's objections and issued a report recommending that the objections be overruled. The results of the election were certified by the board in April 1980.

Kusan's objections centered on a petition that Kusan employees who supported the union circulated among their fellow workers prior to the election. The petition, which bore approximately one hundred names, read as follows:

We, the undersigned, are voting YES for the IAM. We don't mind being on the firing line because we know it's something that has to be done. Please join with us. VOTE YES and help us to make Kusan, Inc. a better place to work and earn a living.

Kusan contends that the circulation and distribution of the petition constituted impermissible "polling" of the employees by the union.

How should the board have ruled on Kusan's objections? See *Kusan Mfg. Co.* v. *NLRB,* 749 F.2d 362, 117 L.R.R.M. 3394 (6th Cir. 1984).

C H A P T E R 6

Unfair Labor Practices by Employers and Unions

THE NATIONAL LABOR RELATIONS ACT (NLRA) defines a list of unfair labor practices by both employers and unions. Such unfair labor practices are various forms of conduct or activities that adversely affect employees in the exercise of their rights under Section 7 of the act. The unfair labor practices by employers in Section 8(a) were contained in the Wagner Act; the union unfair labor practices in Section 8(b) were added by the Taft-Hartley Act in 1947 and amended by the Landrum-Griffin Act of 1959.

Section 8(a) makes it illegal for an employer to engage in the following conduct:

- to interfere with, restrain, or coerce employees in the exercise of rights guaranteed to them by Section 7 of the act;
- to dominate, interfere with, or contribute financial or other support to a labor organization;
- to discriminate in the hiring or terms or conditions of employment of employees in order to encourage or discourage membership in any labor organization;
- to discharge or discriminate against an employee for filing charges or giving testimony under the NLRA;
- to refuse to bargain collectively with the bargaining representatives of the employees, as designated in Section 9(a).

Section 8(b) makes it illegal for unions to engage in the following kinds of conduct:

- to restrain or coerce employees in the exercise of their rights under Section 7, or to restrain or coerce an employer in the selection of a representative for collective bargaining purposes;
- to cause or attempt to cause an employer to discriminate against an employee in terms or conditions of employment in order to encourage (or discourage) union membership;

- to refuse to bargain collectively with an employer (when the union is the bargaining agent of the employees);
- to engage in secondary picketing or to encourage secondary boycotts of certain employers;
- to require employees to pay excessive or discriminatory union dues or membership fees;
- to cause an employer to pay for services that are not performed (feather bedding);
- to picket an employer in order to force the employer to recognize the union as bargaining agent when the union is not entitled to recognition under the act (**recognition picketing**).

Because both employer and union unfair practices involve, for the most part, the same kinds of conduct, we will examine them together in this chapter. The refusal to bargain by either employer or union will be discussed in Chapter 7, which deals with the duty to bargain in good faith. The union offenses of secondary picketing and recognition picketing will be discussed in Chapter 8, along with other forms of union pressure tactics.

Section 7: Rights of Employees

Because all unfair practices involve conduct that interferes with employees in the exercise of their rights under Section 7 of the NLRA, it is important to determine the exact rights granted employees by Section 7. Section 7 contains this statement:

> Employees shall have the right to self-organization, to form, join or assist labor organizations, to bargain collectively through representatives of their own choosing, and to engage in other concerted activities for the purpose of collective bargaining or other mutual aid or protection, and shall also have the right to refrain from any or all such activities. . . .

The rights under Section 7 are given to all employees covered by the NLRA; the employees need not be organized union members in order to enjoy such rights. In addition, because such rights are given to the individual employee, they may not be waived by a union purporting to act on behalf of the employees.

In order for conduct of employees to be protected under Section 7, it must be *concerted* and it must be for the purpose of collective bargaining or other mutual aid or protection. A group of employees discussing the need for a union in order to improve working conditions is obviously under the protection of Section 7, as are employees who attempt to get their fellow workers to join a union. But the protection of Section 7 also extends to activities not directly associated with formal unionization. For example, a group of nonunion employees who walked off the job to protest the extremely cold temperatures inside the shop were held to be exercising their Section 7 rights, as was an employee who circulated a petition about the management of the company's credit union. Section 7 protects employees in these situations from discipline or discharge for their conduct.

There are, of course, limits to the extent of Section 7 protection. Employees acting individually may not be protected; as well, conduct not related to collective bargaining or mutual aid or protection purposes is not protected. For example, an employee seeking to have a foreman removed because of a personal "grudge" was held not to be protected by Section 7; nor was a group of employees striking to protest company sales to South Africa protected.

Perhaps the most difficult aspect of determining whether conduct is protected under Section 7 deals with the "concerted action" requirement—when is an individual employee, acting alone, protected? The following Supreme Court decision addresses this question.

NLRB v. CITY DISPOSAL SYSTEMS

465 U.S. 822 (Supreme Court of the United States, 1984)

BRENNAN, J.

James Brown, a truck driver employed by respondent, was discharged when he refused to drive a truck that he honestly and reasonably believed to be unsafe because of faulty brakes. Article XXI of the collective-bargaining agreement between respondent and Local 247 of the International Brotherhood of Teamsters, Chauffeurs, Warehousemen and Helpers of America, which covered Brown, provides:

> [T]he Employer shall not require employees to take out on the street or highways any vehicle that is not in safe operating condition or equipped with safety appliances prescribed by law. It shall not be a violation of the Agreement where employees refuse to operate such equipment unless such refusal is unjustified.

The question to be decided is whether Brown's honest and reasonable assertion of his right to be free of the obligation to drive unsafe trucks constituted "concerted activit[y]" within the meaning of Section 7 of the National Labor Relations Act. The National Labor Relations Board (NLRB) held that Brown's refusal was concerted activity within Section 7, and that his discharge was, therefore, an unfair labor practice under Section 8(a)(1) of the Act. The Court of Appeals disagreed and declined enforcement.

James Brown was assigned to truck No. 245. On Saturday, May 12, 1979, Brown observed that a fellow driver had difficulty with the brakes of another truck, truck No. 244. As a result of the brake problem, truck No. 244 nearly collided with Brown's truck. After unloading their garbage at the landfill, Brown and the driver of truck No. 244 brought No. 244 to respondent's truck-repair facility, where they were told that the brakes would be repaired either over the weekend or in the morning of Monday, May 14.

Early in the morning of Monday, May 14, while transporting a load of garbage to the landfill, Brown experienced difficulty with one of the wheels of his own truck—No. 245—and brought that truck in for repair. At the repair facility, Brown was told that, because of a backlog at the facility, No. 245 could not be repaired that day. Brown reported the situation to his supervisor, Otto Jasmund, who ordered Brown to punch out and go home. Before Brown could leave, however, Jasmund changed his mind and asked Brown to drive truck No. 244 instead. Brown refused explaining that "there's something wrong with that truck. . . . [S]omething was wrong with the brakes . . . there was a grease seal or something leaking causing it to be affecting the brakes." Brown did not, however, explicitly refer to Article XXI of the collective-bargaining agreement or to the agreement in general. In response to Brown's refusal to drive truck No. 244, Jasmund angrily told Brown to go home. At that point, an argument ensued and Robert Madary, another supervisor, intervened, repeating Jasmund's request that Brown drive truck No. 244. Again, Brown refused, explaining that No. 244 "has got problems and I don't want to drive it." Madary replied that half the trucks had problems and that if respondent tried to fix all of them it would be unable to do business. He went on to tell Brown that "[w]e've got all this garbage out here to haul and you tell me about you don't want to drive." Brown responded,

"Bob, what you going to do, put the garbage ahead of the safety of the men?" Finally, Madary went to his office and Brown went home. Later that day, Brown received word that he had been discharged. He immediately returned to work in an attempt to gain reinstatement but was unsuccessful.

On September 7, 1979, Brown filed an unfair labor practice charge with the NLRB, challenging his discharge. The Administrative Law Judge (A.L.J.) found that Brown had been discharged for refusing to operate truck No. 244, that Brown's refusal was covered by Section 7 of the NLRA, and that respondent had therefore committed an unfair labor practice under Section 8(a)(1) of the Act. The A.L.J. held that an employee who acts alone in asserting a contractual right can nevertheless be engaged in concerted activity within the meaning of Section 7. . . .

The NLRB adopted the findings and conclusions of the A.L.J. and ordered that Brown be reinstated with back pay.

On a petition for enforcement of the Board's order, the Court of Appeals disagreed with the A.L.J. and the Board. Finding that Brown's refusal to drive truck No. 244 was an action taken solely on his own behalf, the Court of Appeals concluded that the refusal was not a concerted activity within the meaning of Section 7.

Section 7 of the NLRA provides that "[e]mployees shall have the right to . . . join or assist labor organizations, to bargain collectively through representatives of their own choosing, and to engage in other concerted activities for the purpose of collective bargaining or other mutual aid or protection." The NLRB's decision in this case applied the Board's longstanding "*Interboro* doctrine," under which an individual's assertion of a right grounded in a collective-bargaining agreement is recognized as "concerted activit[y]" and therefore accorded the protection of Section 7. [See *Interboro Contractors, Inc.,* 157 N.L.R.B. 1295, 1298 (1966), enforced 388 F.2d 495 (CA2 1967)] The Board has relied on two justifications for the doctrine: First, the assertion of a right contained in a collective-bargaining agreement is an extension of the concerted action that produced the agreement; and second, the assertion of such a right affects the rights of all employees covered by the collective-bargaining agreement.

Neither the Court of Appeals nor respondent appears to question that an employee's invocation of a right derived from a collective-bargaining agreement meets Section 7's requirement that an employee's action be taken "for purposes of collective bargaining or other mutual aid or protection." As the Board first explained in the *Interboro* case, a single employee's invocation of such rights affects all the em-

ployees that are covered by the collective-bargaining agreement. This type of generalized effect, as our cases have demonstrated, is sufficient to bring the actions of an individual employee within the "mutual aid or protection" standard, regardless of whether the employee has his own interests most immediately in mind.

The term "concerted activit[y]" is not defined in the Act but it clearly enough embraces the activities of employees who have joined together in order to achieve common goals. What is not self-evident from the language of the Act, however, and what we must elucidate, is the precise manner in which particular actions of an individual employee must be linked to the actions of fellow employees in order to permit it to be said that the individual is engaged in concerted activity. We now turn to consider the Board's analysis of that question as expressed in the *Interboro* doctrine.

Although one could interpret the phrase, "to engage in concerted activities," to refer to a situation in which two or more employees are working together at the same time and the same place toward a common goal, the language of Section 7 does not confine itself to such a narrow meaning. In fact, Section 7 itself defines both joining and assisting labor organizations—activities in which a single employee can engage—as concerted activities. Indeed, even the courts that have rejected the *Interboro* doctrine recognize the possibility that an individual employee may be engaged in concerted activity when he acts alone. They have limited their recognition of this type of concerted activity, however, to two situations: (1) that in which the lone employee intends to induce group activity, and (2) that in which the employee acts as a representative of at least one other employee. The disagreement over the *Interboro* doctrine, therefore, merely reflects differing views regarding the nature of the relationship that must exist between the action of the individual employee and the actions of the group in order for Section 7 to apply. We cannot say that the Board's view of that relationship, as applied in the *Interboro* doctrine, is unreasonable.

The invocation of a right rooted in a collective-bargaining agreement is unquestionably an integral part of the process that gave rise to the agreement. That process—beginning with the organization of a union, continuing into the negotiation of a collective-bargaining agreement, and extending through the enforcement of the agreement—is a single, collective activity. Obviously, an employee could not invoke a right grounded in a collective-bargaining agreement were it not for the prior negotiating activities of his fellow employees. Nor would it make sense for a union to negotiate a collective-bargaining agreement if individual employees could not invoke the rights thereby created against their employer. Moreover, when an employee invokes a right grounded in the collective-bargaining agreement, he does not stand alone. Instead, he brings to bear on his employer the power and resolve of all his fellow employees. When, for instance, James Brown refused to drive a truck he believed to be unsafe, he was in effect reminding his employer that he and his fellow employees, at the time their collective-bargaining agreement was signed, had extracted a promise from City Disposal that they would not be asked to drive unsafe trucks. He was also reminding his employer that if it persisted in ordering him to drive an unsafe truck, he could reharness the power of that group to ensure the enforcement of that promise. It was just as though James Brown was reassembling his fellow union members to reenact their decision not to drive unsafe trucks. A lone employee's invocation of a right grounded in his collective-bargaining agreement is, therefore, a concerted activity in a very real sense.

Furthermore, the acts of joining and assisting a labor organization, which Section 7 explicitly recognizes as concerted, are related to collective action in essentially the same way that the invocation of a collectively bargained right is related to collective action. When an employee joins or assists a labor organization, his actions may be divorced in time, and in location as well, from the actions of fellow employees. Because of the integral relationship among the employees' actions, however, Congress viewed each employee as engaged in concerted activity. The lone employee could not join or assist a labor organization were it not for the related organizing activities of his fellow employees. Conversely, there would be limited utility informing a labor organization if other employees could not join or assist the organization once it is formed. Thus, the formation of a labor organization is integrally related to the activity of joining or assisting such an organization in the same sense that the negotiation of a collective-bargaining agreement is integrally related to the invocation of a right provided for in the agreement. In each case, neither the individual activity nor the group activity would be complete without the other.

The Board's *Interboro* doctrine, based on a recognition that the potential inequality in the relationship between the employee and the employer continues beyond the point at which a collective-bargaining agreement is signed, mitigates that inequality throughout the duration of the employment relationship, and is, therefore, fully consistent with congressional intent. Moreover, by applying Section 7 to the actions of individual employees invoking their rights under a collective-bargaining agreement, the *Interboro* doctrine preserves the integrity of the entire collective-bargaining process; for by invoking a right grounded in a collective-bargaining agreement, the employee makes that right a reality, and breathes life, not only into the promises contained in the collective-bargaining agreement, but also into the entire process envisioned by Congress as the means by which to achieve industrial peace.

To be sure, the principal tool by which an employee invokes the rights granted him in a collective-bargaining agreement is the processing of a grievance according to whatever procedures his collective-bargaining agreement establishes. No one doubts that the processing of a grievance in such a manner is concerted activity within the meaning of Section 7. Indeed, it would make little sense for Section 7 to cover an employee's conduct while negotiating a collective-bargaining agreement, including a grievance mechanism by which to protect the rights created by the agreement, but not to cover an employee's attempt to utilize that mechanism to enforce the agreement.

In practice, however, there is unlikely to be a bright-line distinction between an incipient grievance, a complaint to an employer, and perhaps even an employee's initial refusal to perform a certain job that he believes he has no duty to perform. It is reasonable to expect that an employee's first response to a situation that he believes violates his collective-bargaining agreement will be a protest to his employer. Whether he files a grievance will depend in part on his employer's reaction and in part upon the nature of the right at issue. As long as the employee's statement or action is based on a reasonable and honest belief that he is being, or has been, asked to perform a task that he is not required to perform under his collective-bargaining agreement, and the statement or action is reasonably directed toward the enforcement of a collectively bargained right, there is no justification for overturning the Board's judgment that the employee is engaged in concerted activity, just as he would have been had he filed a formal grievance.

The fact that an activity is concerted, however, does not necessarily mean that an employee can engage in the activity with impunity. An employee may engage in concerted activity in such an abusive manner that he loses the protection of Section 7.

In this case, the Board found that James Brown's refusal to drive truck No. 244 was based on an honest and reasonable belief that the brakes on the truck were faulty. Brown explained to each of his supervisors his reason for refusing to drive the truck. Although he did not refer to his collective-bargaining agreement in either of these confrontations, the agreement provided not only that "[t]he Employer shall not require employees to take out on the streets or highways any vehicle that is not in safe operating condition," but also that "[i]t shall not be a violation of the Agreement where employees refuse to operate such equipment, unless such refusal is unjustified." There is no doubt, therefore, nor could there have been any doubt during Brown's confrontations with his supervisors, that by refusing to drive truck No. 244, Brown was invoking the right granted him in his collective-bargaining agreement to be free of the obligation to drive unsafe trucks. . . . Accordingly, we accept the Board's conclusion that James Brown was engaged in concerted activity when he refused to drive truck No. 244. We therefore reverse the judgment of the Court of Appeals and remand the case for further proceedings consistent with this opinion. . . . **It is so ordered.**

In a National Labor Relations Board (NLRB) decision handed down before the Supreme Court decided *City Disposal Systems,* the board held that in order for an individual employee's action to be concerted, it would require "that the conduct be engaged in with or on the authority of other employees, and not solely by and on behalf of the employee himself." (See *Meyers Industries,* 268 N.L.R.B. No 73, 1984.) The case involved an employee who was discharged after refusing to drive his truck and reporting safety problems with his truck to state transportation authorities; the employee had acted alone and the workers were not unionized. Is this holding consistent with the Supreme Court's decision in *City Disposal Systems?*

The U.S. Court of Appeals for the District of Columbia remanded the board's decision in *Meyers Industries* to the board for reconsideration (755 F.2d 941, 1985). On rehearing, the board reaffirmed its decision that the employee had not been engaged in concerted activity. When the case again came before the court of appeals, the D.C. circuit court upheld the board's decision, holding that it was a reasonable interpretation of the act (*Prill v. NLRB,* 835 F.2d 1481, 1987). In *Ewing v. NLRB* (861 F.2d 353, 2d Cir. 1988), the court of appeals upheld the board in a case similar to *Meyers Industries,* on the board's third try at justifying the conclusion that the employee did not engage in concerted activity.

Even though conduct may be concerted under Section 7, it may not be protected by the act. As noted in the *City Disposal Systems* decision, the employee may not act in an abusive manner. The board has held that illegal, destructive, or unreasonable conduct is not protected, even if such conduct was concerted and for purposes of mutual aid or protection. For example, workers who engaged in on-the-job slowdowns, by refusing to process orders, were not protected because they could not refuse to work yet continue to get paid. Threats or physical violence by employees are not protected; nor is the public disparagement of the employer's product by employees, or the referral of customers to competitors of the employer.

The rights of employees under Section 7 are at the heart of the act; they are enforced and protected through unfair labor practice proceedings under Section 8(a) and Section 8(b).

Sections 8(a)(1) and 8(b)(1): Violation of Employee Rights by Employers or Unions

Interference with, coercion, or restraint of employees in the exercise of their Section 7 rights by employers or unions is prohibited by Section 8(a)(1) and Section 8(b)(1), respectively. While violations of other specific unfair labor practice provisions may also violate Sections 8(a)(1) and 8(b)(1), certain kinds of conduct involve violations of Sections 8(a)(1) and 8(b)(1) only. This section will discuss conduct that violates those specific sections only.

The NLRB has held that any conduct that has the natural tendency to restrain or coerce employees in the exercise of their Section 7 rights is a violation; actual coercion or restraint of the employees need not be shown. Intention is not a requirement for a violation of Sections 8(a)(1) and 8(b)(1)—the employer or union need not have intended to coerce or restrain employees. All that is necessary is that they engage in conduct that the board believes has the natural tendency to restrain employees in the exercise of their Section 7 rights.

Most employer violations of Section 8(a)(1) occur in the context of union organizing campaigns. Such violations usually involve restrictions on the soliciting activities of employees or coercive or threatening remarks made by the employer. The employer's ability to make anti-union remarks will be discussed first.

Anti-union Remarks by Employer

During a union organizing campaign, the employer might attempt to persuade employees not to support the union. Such attempts may involve statements of opinion regarding the prospects of unionization and may also involve implicit promises or threats of reprisal. The extent to which the employer may communicate its position has been the subject of numerous board and court decisions. Section 8(c) of the act states that

> The expressing of any views, argument or opinion . . . shall not constitute or be evidence of an unfair labor practice under any of the provisions of this Act, if such expression contains no threat of reprisal or force or promise of benefit.

It should be clear from the wording of Section 8(c) that explicit threats to fire union sympathizers are not protected by Section 8(c) and are therefore violations of Section 8(a)(1). The board believes that because employees are economically dependent on the employer for their livelihood, they will be especially sensitive to the views explicitly or implicitly expressed by the employer. The board will therefore examine closely the "totality of circumstances" of any employer's anti-union remarks to determine if they go beyond the protections of Section 8(c) and thus violate Section 8(a)(1).

In the *Gissel Packing* decision, reprinted in Chapter 5, the Supreme Court defined the limits to which an employer may predict the consequences of unionization. The employer may make a prediction based on objective facts in order to convey the employer's reasonable belief as to demonstrably probable effects or consequences, provided that such factors are beyond the employer's control. If the employer makes predictions about matters within the control of the employer, the board is likely to view such statements as implicit threats—since the employer is in a position to make those predictions come true. Statements such as, "The union almost put us out of business last time and the new management wouldn't hesitate to close this plant," have been held to be violations of Section 8(a)(1), whereas comments such as, "If the union gets in, it will have to bargain from scratch for everything it gets," have been held to be within Section 8(c)'s protection. In *NLRB* v. *Exchange Parts* (375

U.S. 405, 1964), the Supreme Court held that the announcement of improved vacation pay and salary benefits during a union organizing campaign violated Section 8(a)(1). The Court reasoned that

> The danger inherent in the well-timed increases in benefits is the suggestion of the fist inside the velvet glove. Employees are not likely to miss the inference that the source of benefits now conferred is also the source from which future benefits must flow and which may dry up if it is not obliged.

Why is the promise of benefits not protected under Section 8(c)? How does it interfere with the employees' exercise of Section 7 rights? The following case addresses these questions.

AMERICAN SPRING WIRE CO.

237 N.L.R.B. No. 185 (N.L.R.B. 1978)

Respondent (American Spring Wire) is engaged in the manufacture of spring wire at its Bedford Heights, Ohio, plant. In October 1974 and October 1976, Board-conducted elections were held at the Bedford Heights plant in which a majority of Respondent's employees voted not to be represented by the Union. . . .

On May 27, 1977, Respondent held a meeting with its employees to explain certain operational changes that it intended to implement. Approximately 95 of Respondent's 149 employees attended, and all of the employees who attended that meeting received 2 hours' pay at their straight-time hourly rate. L. O. Selhorst, Respondent's president, conducted the meeting and spoke from a prepared text. Selhorst informed the employees that, based on recommendations from a private consulting firm, Respondent was going to implement a number of changes in job descriptions and pay rates. Under the new system, all of the employees were to receive a pay raise. Selhorst told the employees that the pay raise would make them among the best paid workers in the Nation. Selhorst also reviewed the history of the Company and its recent rapid expansion and thanked the employees for their part in helping Respondent to grow. He then told the employees that management would continue to attempt to create the "best place to work in America" and that the employees' cooperation and teamwork was needed for continued growth and improvement. Selhorst then stated that he had:

> One additional important thought. We have beaten the Union on two occasions in this plant by overwhelming majorities and I know the majority of us are tired of such activity. The

majority of us do not deserve such continuing harassment. We have set up in this Company all the means of communication possible, and to those of you who still think you can win more with the Union than you have with us in the past 9 years, well—you are dead wrong—leave us alone—get the hell out of our plant. . . .

> I want to say something to you as clearly as I possibly can. Whether or not ASW has a union is really not significant to the Corporation's future, or to myself, Dave Carruthers, or other major employees of this Company. As far as I am concerned those of us who are loyal to each other as a group can make valve spring wire, music wire, alloy wire, in Moline, Illinois; Saskatchewan, Canada; Puerto Rico; or Hawaii. We don't need Cleveland, Ohio, or all this beautiful property. Remember, nine years ago we had nothing. Today our Company has developed a certain amount of wealth and goodwill at the banks, a fantastic organization of people and many friends who supply us goods, and above all a long and growing list of customers. These people do business with us, not with this building or this land. We do not intend to have this statement appear as a threat because it is not. It is a statement of fact. Facts are that our real concern regarding a union is with the majority of you who have opposed it in the past, and who would be locked into it should it come to this plant.

> With that in mind, I want to tell you that those of us in management do not wish to become involved in another election. We need the time to do the things that will continue to promote our Company, ourselves, and hopefully, you. I am asking you as your friend not to sign union cards, as we don't have the patience to put up with it again. This next battle is yours, not ours. It is up to each one of you who is against the union to stop the card signing before it gets started. I don't care how you do it. Organize yourselves and get it done.

Based on the above speech, the General Counsel issued a complaint alleging that Respondent violated Section

8(a)(1) and (3) of the Act by: (a) threatening its employees with unspecified reprisals by telling them that, if they thought they could gain more benefits from Respondent with the Union, they could "get the hell out of our plant"; (b) threatening its employees with plant closure in order to discourage their union activity; and (c) soliciting its employees to stop employees from signing authorization cards on behalf of the Union by any means necessary. . . .

Section 8(a)(1) of the Act prohibits an employer from interfering with, threatening, or coercing employees in the exercise of their Section 7 right to support or oppose a labor organization, or to engage in or refrain from engaging in concerted activity. The issue, simply, is whether Respondent's statements complained of by the General Counsel are views or opinions, or are threatening and coercive.

We note that the first portion of the speech emphasized Respondent's commitment to its work force and the importance of employee cooperation to Respondent's growth and employee job security. The employees were also informed that they were receiving pay increases and that in the future Respondent would continue to try to improve working conditions and pay. However, immediately thereafter Selhorst changed the tone of the speech abruptly as he invited the union supporters to "get the hell out of our plant." In this context of union animus, Respondent's statement that it could produce its product elsewhere and that it did not need its Cleveland, Ohio, plant was a clear and unambiguous threat of plant closure.

In light of the threat of plant closure, Respondent's statement to union supporters to "get the hell out of our plant" and Respondent's exhortation to the assembled employees to stop the card signing by any means also were coercive and threatening. Although the major portion of Selhorst's speech was devoted to explaining legitimate business changes, conferring increased benefits, and promising further improvements in the future, we find that the speech also had an underlying message that a continuation of these benefits was conditioned on a continuation of a nonunion plant. Thus, the speech represents a classic example of "the suggestion of a fist inside the velvet glove [as] employees are not likely to miss the inference that the source of benefits now conferred is also the source from which future benefits must flow and which may dry up if it is not obliged." *NLRB* v. *Exchange Parts Co.* . . . So too, here, did Respondent unsheathe its fist from the velvet glove when Selhorst told the employees, in essence, that if they did not stop the Union management would relocate its plant, that supporters of the Union would be responsible for such relocation and should "get the hell out," and that antiunion employees should, by whatever means, stop the prounion employees, or else, in effect all would lose their jobs.

In view of the above, we find no merit to Respondent's claim that Selhorst's statements were not threatening or coercive because they did not occur within the context of a union campaign. This Board has never found that threatening or coercive conduct, such as a threat of plant closure, is unlawful only in the context of a union campaign. Moreover, we note that the Union had filed two petitions within the last 3 years and less than 6 months remained before the Union could file a new petition under Section 9(c)(3) of the Act. Thus, Respondent's unlawful statements were made in the context of recent union campaigns and possible latent or preliminary union activity. **So ordered.**

In *Heck's, Inc.* (293 N.L.R.B. No. 132, 131 L.R.R.M. 1281, 1989), the board declared that an employer did not commit an unfair labor practice by informing its unionized employees that it was opposed to their union and to unionization in general. However, the employer did commit an unfair labor practice by including its anti-union policy in its employee handbook and unilaterally requesting that all employees sign a statement agreeing to be bound by that policy.

Employer Limitations on Soliciting and Organizing

In order for employees to exercise their right, under Section 7, to choose their bargaining representative free from coercion, the employees must have access to information that will enable them to exercise this right intelligently. Such information may come from fellow employees who are active in union organizing attempts, or it may come from nonemployee union organizers. Although the union may attempt to reach the employees individually at their homes, it is more convenient and more effective to contact the employees at the work site when they are all assembled there. But organizing activities at the workplace may disrupt production and will certainly conflict with the employer's right to control and direct the work force. The employer's property rights at the workplace also include the right to control access to the premises. Clearly, then, the right of employees to organize is in conflict with the employer's property rights over the enterprise. How is such a conflict to be reconciled?

In *NLRB* v. *Babcock & Wilcox* (351 U.S. 105, 1956), the Supreme Court upheld a series of NLRB rules for employer restrictions upon nonemployee access to the premises and soliciting activity of employees. In the following case, the Supreme Court reconsidered the issues raised in *Babcock & Wilcox.*

LECHMERE, INC. v. NLRB

__ U.S. __, 60 U.S.L.W. 4145 (Supreme Court of the United States, 1992)

THOMAS, J.

. . . . This case stems from the efforts of Local 919 of the United Food and Commercial Workers Union, AFL-CIO, to organize employees at a retail store in Newington, Connecticut, owned and operated by petitioner Lechmere, Inc. The store is located in the Lechmere Shopping Plaza. . . . Lechmere's store is situated at the Plaza's south end, with the main parking lot to its north. A strip of 13 smaller "satellite stores" not owned by Lechmere runs along the west side of the Plaza, facing the parking lot. To the Plaza's east (where the main entrance is located) runs the Berlin Turnpike, a four-lane divided highway. The parking lot, however, does not abut the Turnpike; they are separated by a 46-foot-wide grassy strip, broken only by the Plaza's entrance. The parking lot is owned jointly by Lechmere and the developer of

the satellite stores. The grassy strip is public property (except for a four-foot-wide band adjoining the parking lot, which belongs to Lechmere).

The union began its campaign to organize the store's 200 employees, none of whom was represented by a union, in June 1987. After a full-page advertisement in a local newspaper drew little response, nonemployee union organizers entered Lechmere's parking lot and began placing handbills on the windshields of cars parked in a corner of the lot used mostly by employees. Lechmere's manager immediately confronted the organizers, informed them that Lechmere prohibited solicitation or handbill distribution of any kind on its property,* and asked them to leave. They did so, and Lechmere personnel removed the handbills. The union organizers renewed his handbilling effort in the parking lot on several subsequent occasions; each time they were asked to leave and the handbills were removed. The organizers then relocated to the public grassy strip, from where they attempted to pass out handbills to cars entering the lot

---

*Lechmere had established this policy several years prior to the union's organizing efforts. The store's official policy statement provided, in relevant part: "Non-associates [i.e., nonemployees] are prohibited from soliciting and distributing literature at all times anywhere on Company property, including parking lots. Non-associates have no right of access to the non-working areas and only to the public and selling areas of the store in connection with its public use."

On each door to the store Lechmere had posted a 6 in. by 8 in. sign reading: "TO THE PUBLIC. No Soliciting, Canvassing, Distribution of Literature or Trespassing by Non-Employees in or on Premises." Lechmere consistently enforced this policy inside the store as well as on the parking lot (against, among others, the Salvation Army and the Girl Scouts).

during hours (before opening and after closing) when the drivers were assumed to be primarily store employees. For one month, the union organizers returned daily to the grassy strip to picket Lechmere; after that, they picketed intermittently for another six months. They also recorded the license plate numbers of cars parked in the employee parking area; with the cooperation of the Connecticut Department of Motor Vehicles, they thus secured the names and addresses of some 41 nonsupervisory employees (roughly 20 percent of the store's total). The union sent four mailings to these employees; it also made some attempts to contact them by phone or home visits. These mailings and visits resulted in one signed union authorization card.

Alleging that Lechmere had violated the National Labor Relations Act by barring the nonemployee organizers from its property, the union filed an unfair labor practice charge with respondent National Labor Relations Board (Board).... [A]n administrative law judge (ALJ) ruled in the union's favor. He recommended that Lechmere be ordered, among other things, to cease and desist from barring the union organizers from the parking lot . . .

The Board affirmed the ALJ's judgment and adopted the recommended order, applying the analysis set forth in its opinion in *Jean Country* (1988).... A divided panel of the United States Court of Appeals for the First Circuit denied Lechmere's petition for review and enforced the Board's order. This Court granted certiorari.

Section 7 of the NLRA provides in relevant part that "employees shall have the right to self-organization, to form, join, or assist labor organizations." Section 8(a)(1) of the Act, in turn, makes it an unfair labor practice for an employer "to interfere with, restrain, or coerce employees in the exercise of rights guaranteed in [S. 7]." By its plain terms, thus, the NLRA confers rights only on employees, not on unions or their nonemployee organizers. In *NLRB* v. *Babcock & Wilcox Co.* (1956), however, we recognized that insofar as the employees' "right of self-organization depends in some measure on [their] ability . . . to learn the advantages of self-organization from others," S. 7 of the NLRA may, in certain limited circumstances, restrict an employer's right to exclude nonemployee union organizers from his property. It is the nature of those circumstances that we explore today.

Babcock arose out of union attempts to organize employees at a factory located on an isolated 100-acre tract. The company had a policy against solicitation and distribution of literature on its property, which it enforced against all groups. About 40 percent of the company's employees

lived in a town of some 21,000 persons near the factory; the remainder were scattered over a 30-mile radius. Almost all employees drove to work in private cars and parked in a company lot that adjoined the fenced-in plant area. The parking lot could be reached only by a 100-yard-long driveway connecting it to a public highway. This driveway was mostly on company-owned land, except where it crossed a 31-foot-wide public right-of-way adjoining the highway. Union organizers attempted to distribute literature from this right-of-way. The union also secured the names and addresses of some 100 employees (20 percent of the total), and sent them three mailings. Still other employees were contacted by telephone or home visit.

The union successfully challenged the company's refusal to allow nonemployee organizers onto its property before the Board. While acknowledging that there were alternative, nontrespassory means whereby the union could communicate with employees, the Board held that contact at the workplace was preferable. "The right to distribute is not absolute, but must be accommodated to the circumstances. Where it is impossible or unreasonably difficult for a union to distribute organizational literature to employees entirely off of the employer's premises, distribution on a nonworking area, such as the parking lot and the walkways between the parking lot and the gate, may be warranted." Concluding that traffic on the highway made it unsafe for the union organizers to distribute leaflets from the right-of-way, and that contacts through the mails, on the streets, at employees' homes, and over the telephone would be ineffective, the Board ordered the company to allow the organizers to distribute literature on its parking lot and exterior walkways.

The Court of Appeals for the Fifth Circuit refused to enforce the Board's order, and this Court affirmed. While recognizing that "the Board has the responsibility of applying the Act's general prohibitory language in the light of the infinite combinations of events which might be charged as violative of its terms," we explained that the Board had erred by failing to make the critical distinction between the organizing activities of employees (to whom S. 7 guarantees the right of self-organization) and non-employees (to whom S. 7 applies only derivatively). Thus, while "no restriction may be placed on the employees' right to discuss self-organization among themselves, unless the employer can demonstrate that a restriction is necessary to maintain production or discipline, . . . no such obligation is owed nonemployee organizers. . . ." As a rule, then, an employer cannot be compelled to allow distribution of union literature by nonemployee organizers on his property. As with many other rules, however, we recognized an exception. Where "the location of a plant and the living quarters of the employees place the employees beyond the reach of reasonable union efforts to communicate with them," employers' property rights may be "required to yield to the extent needed to permit communication of information on the right to organize. . . ."

Although we have not had occasion to apply Babcock's analysis in the ensuing decades, we have described it in cases arising in related contexts. Two such cases, *Central Hardware Co.* v. *NLRB* (1972), and *Hudgens* v. *NLRB* (1976), involved activity by union supporters on employer-owned property. . . . In both cases, we quoted approvingly Babcock's admonition that accommodation between employees' S. 7 rights and employers' property rights "must be obtained with as little destruction of the one as is consistent with the maintenance of the other." There is no hint in *Hudgens* and *Central Hardware,* however, that our invocation of *Babcock's* language of "accommodation" was intended to repudiate or modify *Babcock's* holding that an employer need not accommodate nonemployee organizers unless the employees are otherwise inaccessible. Indeed, in *Central Hardware* we expressly noted that nonemployee organizers cannot claim even a limited right of access to a nonconsenting employer's property until "after the requisite need for access to the employer's property has been shown."

If there was any question whether *Central Hardware* and *Hudgens* changed S. 7 law, it should have been laid to rest by *Sears, Roebuck & Co.* v. *San Diego County District Council of Carpenters* (1978). As in *Central Hardware* and *Hudgens,* the substantive S. 7 issue in *Sears* was a subsidiary one; the case's primary focus was on the circumstances under which the NLRA pre-empts state law. Among other things, we held in *Sears* that arguable S. 7 claims do not pre-empt state trespass law, in large part because the trespasses of nonemployee union organizers are "far more likely to be unprotected than protected," . . . This holding was based upon the following interpretation of *Babcock:*

> "While *Babcock* indicates that an employer may not always bar nonemployee union organizers from his property, his right to do so remains the general rule. To gain access, the union has the burden of showing that no other reasonable means of communicating its organizational message to the employees exists or that the employer's access rules discriminate against union solicitation. That the burden imposed on the union is a

heavy one is evidenced by the fact that the balance struck by the Board and the courts under the *Babcock* accommodation principle has rarely been in favor of trespassory organizational activity."

We further noted that, in practice, nonemployee organizational trespassing had generally been prohibited except where "unique obstacles" prevented nontrespassory methods of communication with the employees.

Jean Country, as noted above, represents the Board's latest attempt to implement the rights guaranteed by S. 7. It sets forth a three-factor balancing test:

> "In all access cases our essential concern will be [1] the degree of impairment of the Section 7 right if access should be denied, as it balances against [2] the degree of impairment of the private property right if access should be granted. We view the consideration of [3] the availability of reasonably effective alternative means as especially significant in this balancing process."

The Board conceded that this analysis was unlikely to foster certainty and predictability in this corner of the law, but declared that "as with other legal questions involving multiple factors, the nature of the problem, as revealed by unfolding variant situations, inevitably involves an evolutionary process for its rational response, not a quick, definitive formula as a comprehensive answer.'"

Citing its role "as the agency with responsibility for implementing national labor policy," the Board maintains in this case that *Jean Country* is a reasonable interpretation of the NLRA entitled to judicial deference. . . .

Before we reach any issue of deference to the Board, however, we must first determine whether *Jean Country*— at least as applied to nonemployee organizational trespassing—is consistent with our past interpretation of S.7. . . .

In *Babcock,* as explained above, we held that the Act drew a distinction "of substance," between the union activities of employees and nonemployees. In cases involving employee activities, we noted with approval, the Board "balanced the conflicting interests of employees to receive information on self-organization on the company's property from fellow employees during nonworking time, with the employer's right to control the use of his property." In cases involving nonemployee activities (like those at issue in *Babcock* itself), however, the Board was not permitted to engage in that same balancing (and we reversed the Board for having done so). . . . *Babcock's* teaching is straightforward: S. 7 simply does not protect nonemployee union organizers except in the rare care where "the inaccessibility of employees makes ineffective the reasonable attempts by nonemployees to communicate with them through the usual channels." Our reference to "reasonable" attempts was nothing more than a commonsense recognition that unions need not engage in extraordinary feats to communicate with inaccessible employees—not an endorsement of the view (which we expressly rejected) that the Act protects "reasonable" trespasses. Where reasonable alternative means of access exist, S. 7's guarantees do not authorize trespasses by nonemployee organizers, even . . . "under . . . reasonable regulations" established by the Board.

Jean Country, which applies broadly to "all access cases," misapprehends this critical point. Its principal inspiration derives not from *Babcock,* but from . . . *Hudgens.* . . . From [*Hudgens*] . . . the Board concluded that it was appropriate to approach every case by balancing S. 7 rights against property rights, with alternative means of access thrown in as nothing more than an "especially significant" consideration. As explained above, however, *Hudgens* did not purport to modify *Babcock,* much less to alter it fundamentally in the way *Jean Country* suggests. To say that our cases require accommodation between employees' and employers' rights is a true but incomplete statement, for the cases also go far in establishing the locus of that accommodation where nonemployee organizing is at issue. So long as nonemployee union organizers have reasonable access to employees outside an employer's property, the requisite accommodation has taken place. It is only where such access is infeasible that it becomes necessary and proper to take the accommodation inquiry to a second level, balancing the employees' and employers' rights as described in the *Hudgens* dictum. At least as applied to nonemployees, *Jean Country* impermissibly conflates these two stages of the inquiry—thereby significantly eroding *Babcock's* general rule that "an employer may validly post his property against nonemployee distribution of union literature." We reaffirm that general rule today, and reject the Board's attempt to recast it as a multifactor balancing test.

The threshold inquiry in this case, then, is whether the facts here justify application of *Babcock's* inaccessibility exception. The ALJ below observed that "the facts herein convince me that reasonable alternative means [of communicating with Lechmere's employees] were available to the Union. . . . Reviewing the ALJ's decision under *Jean Country,* however, the Board reached a different conclusion on this point, asserting that "there was no reasonable, effective alternative means available for the Union to communicate its message to [Lechmere's] employees."

We cannot accept the Board's conclusion, because it "rests on erroneous legal foundations." . . . As we have explained, the exception to *Babcock's* rule is a narrow one. It does not apply wherever nontrespassory access to employees may be cumbersome or less-than-ideally effective, but only where "the location of a plant and the living quarters of the employees place the employees beyond the reach of reasonable union efforts to communicate with them." Classic examples include logging camps . . . , mining camps . . . and mountain resort hotels. . . . *Babcock's* exception was crafted precisely to protect the S. 7 rights of those employees who, by virtue of their employment, are isolated from the ordinary flow of information that characterizes our society. The union's burden of establishing such isolation is, as we have explained, "a heavy one," and one not satisfied by mere conjecture or the expression of doubts concerning the effectiveness of nontrespassory means of communication.

The Board's conclusion in this case that the union had no reasonable means short of trespass to make Lechmere's employees aware of its organizational efforts is based on a misunderstanding of the limited scope of this exception. Because the employees do not reside on Lechmere's property, they are presumptively not "beyond the reach," of the union's message. Although the employees live in a large metropolitan area (Greater Hartford), that fact does not in itself render them "inaccessible" in the sense contemplated by *Babcock.* Their accessibility is suggested by the union's success in contacting a substantial percentage of them directly, via mailings, phone calls, and home visits. Such direct contact, of course, is not a necessary element of "reasonably effective" communication; signs or advertising also may suffice. In this case, the union tried advertising in local newspapers; the Board said that this was not reasonably effective because it was expensive and might not reach the employees. Whatever the merits of that conclusion, other alternative means of communication were readily available. Thus, signs (displayed, for example, from the public grassy strip adjoining Lechmere's parking lot) would have informed the employees about the union's organizational efforts. (Indeed, union organizers picketed the shopping center's main entrance for months as employees came and went every day.) Access to employees, not success in winning them over, is the critical issue—although success, or lack thereof, may be relevant in determining whether reasonable access exists. Because the union in this case failed to establish the existence of any "unique obstacles," that frustrated access to Lechmere's employees, the Board erred in concluding that Lechmere committed an unfair labor practice by barring the nonemployee organizers from its property.

The judgment of the First Circuit is therefore reversed, and enforcement of the Board's order denied. It is so ordered.

WHITE, J., with whom BLACKMUN, J. joins, dissenting:

. . . . For several reasons, the Court errs in this case. First, that *Babcock* stated that inaccessibility would be a reason to grant access does not indicate that there would be no other circumstance that would warrant entry to the employer's parking lot and would satisfy the Court's admonition that accommodation must be made with as little destruction of property rights as is consistent with the right of employees to learn the advantages of self-organization from others. . . . Moreover, the Court in *Babcock* recognized that actual communication with nonemployee organizers, not mere notice that an organizing campaign exists, is necessary to vindicate S. 7 rights. . . .

Second, the Court's reading of *Babcock* is not the reading of that case reflected in later opinions of the Court. We have consistently declined to define the principle of *Babcock* as a general rule subject to narrow exceptions, and have instead repeatedly reaffirmed that the standard is a neutral and flexible rule of accommodation. . . .

Third, and more fundamentally, *Babcock* is at odds with modern concepts of deference to an administrative agency charged with administering a statute. . . . [T]he Court's deci-

sion fails to recognize that *Babcock* is at odds with the current law of deference to administrative agencies and compounds that error by adopting the substantive approach *Babcock* applied lock, stock, and barrel. And unnecessarily so, for, as indicated above, *Babcock* certainly does not require the reading the Court gives it today, and in any event later cases have put a gloss on *Babcock* that the Court should recognize.

Finally, the majority commits a concluding error in its application of the outdated standard of *Babcock* to review the Board's conclusion that there were no reasonable alternative means available to the union. . . . "The judicial role is narrow: . . . the Board's application of the rule, if supported by substantial evidence on the record as a whole, must be enforced." *Ibid.* The Board's conclusion as to reasonable alternatives in this case was supported by evidence in the record. Even if the majority cannot defer to that application, because of the depth of its objections to the rule applied by the NLRB, it should remand to the Board for a decision under the rule it arrives at today, rather than sitting in the place Congress has assigned to the Board. . . .

It is evident, therefore, that, in my view, the Court should defer to the Board's decision in *Jean Country* and its application of *Jean Country* in this case. With all due respect, I dissent.

Restrictions on Employees   Although nonemployees may be barred completely, an employer may place only "reasonable restrictions" on the soliciting activities of employees. Employer rules limiting soliciting activities must have a valid workplace purpose, such as ensuring worker safety or maintaining the efficient operation of the business, and must be applied uniformly to all soliciting, not just to union activities. The employer may limit the distribution of literature where it poses a litter problem. Employee soliciting activity may be limited to nonworking areas such as cafeterias, restrooms, or parking lots. Such activities may also be restricted to "nonworking times" such as coffee breaks and lunch breaks. However, an employer may not completely prohibit such activities. In the absence of exceptional circumstances, blanket prohibitions on soliciting have been held to be unreasonable and in violation of Section 8(a)(1). "Visual-only" solicitations, such as hats, buttons, and so forth, generally may not be restricted.

When the workplace is a department store or hospital, "no-solicitation" rules may present particular problems. An employer will attempt to ensure that soliciting activity does not interfere with customer access or patient care, yet the board will ensure that the employees are still able to exercise their Section 7 rights. In *Beth Israel Hospital v. NLRB* (437 U.S. 483, 1978), the U.S. Supreme Court upheld the board order allowing a hospital to prohibit soliciting by employees in patient care areas, but prohibiting the hospital from denying employees the right to solicit in the hospital cafeteria.

Other Section 8(a)(1) Violations

Other employer practices likely to produce Section 8(a)(1) complaints may involve interrogation of employees regarding union sympathies and the denial of employee requests to have a representative present during disciplinary proceedings.

Polling and Interrogation.   An employer approached by a union claiming to have the support of a majority of employees may wish to get some independent verification of the union's claim. In *Struknes Construction* (165 N.L.R.B. 1062, 1967), the NLRB set out guidelines to reconcile the legitimate interests of an employer in polling employees regarding union support with the tendency of such a poll to restrain employees in the free exercise of their Section 7 rights. The board is willing to allow an employer to conduct a poll of employees regarding union support if it is done according to the following conditions:

1. It must be done in response to a union claim of majority support.
2. The employees must be informed of the purpose of the poll.
3. The employees must be given assurances that no reprisals will result from their choice.
4. The poll must be by secret ballot.

In addition, the employer must not have created a coercive atmosphere through unfair labor practices or other behavior; and the poll must not be taken if a representation election is pending. Why should the board preclude such a poll when an election is pending? In light of *Linden Lumber* (in Chapter 5) what happens when the poll by the employer discloses that the union has majority support?

The employer polling pursuant to the *Struknes* rules needs to be distinguished from the interrogation of employees regarding their union sympathies. Polling is to be done by secret ballot, and only in response to a union claim for voluntary recognition. Interrogation may involve confronting individual employees and questioning them about their union sympathies. Such interrogation may be in response to a union organizing campaign or a request for voluntary recognition.

The NLRB has held that interrogation of individual employees, even known union adherents, is not an unfair labor practice if it is done without threats or the promise of benefits by the employer (*Rossmore House,* 269 N.L.R.B. No. 198, 1984; affirmed sub nom *Hotel & Restaurant Employees Local 11* v. *NLRB,* 760 F.2d 1006, 9th Cir. 1985). If the interrogation is accompanied by threats against the employees or other unfair labor practices by the employer, however, it may be a violation of Section 8(a)(1).

In *Alliance Rubber* (126 L.R.R.M. 1217, 286 N.L.R.B. No. 57, 1987), the board, in a 2–1 decision, held that two polygraph examiners, hired by the employer to help in an investigation of suspected plant sabotage and drug use, were acting as agents of the employer when they interrogated employees about union activities in the course of administering polygraph exams to the employees. The board held that the questioning was made even more stressful because of its connection with the investigation into drug use and sabotage, and it implicitly gave the employees the message that engaging in union activity might result in them being suspected of engaging in unlawful activity in the plant. The company vice-president's conduct reasonably led employees to believe that the examiners asked the questions about union activities on behalf of the employer; therefore, the employer and the polygraph operators were held to have violated Section 8(a)1.

Weingarten Rights.   In *NLRB* v. *Weingarten* (420 U.S. 251, 1975), an employer refused to allow an employee to have a union representative present during the questioning of the employee about thefts from the employer. The Supreme Court upheld the NLRB ruling that such a refusal violated Section 8(a)(1). The Court reasoned that "the action of an employee in seeking to have the assistance of his union representative at a confrontation with his employer clearly falls within the literal wording of Section 7 that '[e]mployees shall have the right . . . to engage in concerted activities for the purpose of . . . mutual aid or protection.'" Previous NLRB decisions had extended the *Weingarten* rule to cover nonunion employees as well, but in *Sears, Roebuck* (274 N.L.R.B. No. 255, 1985) the NLRB held that **Weingarten rights** apply only to unionized employees. The Court of Appeals for the 3rd Circuit upheld the board's interpretation in *Slaughter* v. *NLRB* (876 F.2d 11, 3rd Cir. 1989). The *Weingarten* right to have a union representative present applies whenever the meeting with management will have the "probable" result of the imposition of discipline, or where such a result is "seriously considered."

The board has set the following two requirements on the exercise of *Weingarten* rights by unionized employees: (1) the employee must actually request the presence of a representative in order to have the right (*Montgomery Ward,* 269 N.L.R.B. No. 156, 115 L.R.R.M. 1321, 1984); and (2) an employer who violates an employee's *Weingarten* rights is not prevented from disciplining the employee, provided that the employer has independent evidence, not resulting from the "tainted" interview, to justify the discipline (*ITT Lighting Fixtures, Div. of ITT,* 261 N.L.R.B. 229, 1982).

Violence and Surveillance.   One last area of employer violations of Section 8(a)(1) involves violence and surveillance of employees. It should be clear from the wording of Section 8(a)(1) that violence or threats of violence directed against employees by the employer (or agents of the employer) violate Section 8(a)(1) because they interfere with the free exercise of the employees' Section 7 rights. Employer surveillance of employee activities, or even creating the impression that the employees are under surveillance, also violates Section 8(a)(1) since such a practice has the natural tendency to restrict the free exercise of the employees' Section 7 rights.

Union Coercion of Employees and Employers

Whereas Section 8(a)(1) prohibits employer interference with employees' Section 7 rights, Section 8(b)(1)(A) prohibits union restraint or coercion of the exercise of Section 7 rights by the employee. It is important to remember that Section 7 also gives employees the right to refrain from concerted activity. (There is an important qualification on the employees' right to refrain from union activities; Section 7 recognizes that a union shop or agency shop provision requiring employees to join the union or to pay union dues may be valid. We will discuss these provisions later in this chapter.)

Section 8(b)(1)(A).

In *Radio Officers Union* v. *NLRB* (347 U.S. 17, 1954), the Supreme Court stated that the policy behind Section 7 and Section 8(b) was "to allow employees to freely exercise their right to join unions, be good, bad or indifferent members, or to abstain from joining any union, without imperilling their livelihood."

Union threats or violence directed at employees are clear violations of Section 8(b)(1)(A)—such actions tend to coerce or interfere with the employees' free choice of whether or not to support the union. But just as with employer actions under Section 8(a)(1), less blatant conduct may also be an unfair labor practice. Where the union has waived its initiation fees for employees who join prior to a representation election, the board has found a Section 8(b)(1)(A) violation. By the same reasoning, union statements such as, "Things will be tough for employees who don't join the union before the election," were also held to violate Section 8(b)(1)(A).

Section 8(b)(1)(A) does recognize the need for unions to make rules regarding membership qualifications. A proviso to the section declares "[t]his paragraph shall not impair the right of a labor organization to prescribe its own rules with respect to the acquisition or retention of membership therein." The courts have tended to construe this provision liberally, provided that the union action does not affect the job tenure of an employee. The courts have allowed unions to fine members who refused to go on strike; they have also upheld the right of unions to file suit in state court to collect such fines. However, when a union has expelled a member for filing an unfair labor practice charge with the NLRB without exhausting available internal union remedies, the Supreme Court has found the union in violation of Section 8(b)(1)(A). The Court reasoned that "Any coercion used to discourage, retard or defeat that access [to the NLRB] is beyond the legitimate interests of a labor organization" (*NLRB* v. *Industrial Union of Marine and Shipbuilding Workers*, 391 U.S. 413, 1968).

Section 8(b)(1)(B).

Section 8(b)(1)(B) protects employers from union coercion in their choice of a representative for purposes of collective bargaining or the adjustment of grievances. The legislative history of this section suggests that it was intended to prevent unions from coercing firms into multi-employer bargaining units.

In a number of industries, employers bargain with a union on a multi-employer basis. This is particularly true in industries characterized by a number of small firms and a single, large union. Examples are coal mining, the trucking industry, construction, and the longshoring industry. In order to offset the power of the large union, the employers join together and bargain through an employers' association, or multi-employer bargaining unit. This joint bargaining by employers prevents the union from engaging in **whipsaw strikes**—that is, strikes in which the union selectively strikes one firm in the industry. Because that firm's competitors are not struck, they can continue to operate and draw business from the struck firm. The struck firm is under great pressure to concede to union demands in order to regain lost business.

When the firm capitulates, the union repeats the process against other firms. Multi-employer bargaining resists such efforts since all firms bargain together; if the union strikes one firm, the others can lock out their employees to undermine the union's pressure.

In addition to preventing whipsaw strikes, other reasons for engaging in multi-employer bargaining include the following:

- It eases each company's administrative burden by reducing the number of negotiating sessions and aiding information exchange.

- When one large company is the pacesetter in the industry and the union is likely to insist that other firms adopt approximately the same contract terms, smaller employers may have more input into the bargaining process by joining the leader in a multi-employer bargaining arrangement.

- Establishment of uniform wages, hours, and working conditions among the members of the bargaining group means firms will not have to engage in economic competition in the labor market.

Despite the legislative history of Section 8(b)(1)(B), the section does not mention multi-employer bargaining. The board and the courts have taken the position that multi-employer bargaining cannot be demanded by the interested employers, nor by the relevant union; rather, it must be consented to by both sides. The union need not agree to bargain with the employers' association; nor can it insist that any company or companies form or join such a bargaining group. However, once the parties have agreed to multi-employer bargaining and negotiations have begun, neither an employer nor the union may withdraw without the consent of the other side, except in the event of "unusual circumstances." This rule prevents one side from pulling out just because the bargaining has taken an undesirable turn. (The board has held that an impasse, or deadlock in negotiations, does not constitute "unusual circumstances.")

Unions have been found guilty of violating Section 8(b)(1)(B) when they struck to force a company to accept a multi-employer association for bargaining purposes and when they tried to force a firm to enter an individual contract in conflict with the established multi-employer unit. In addition, unions that have insisted on bargaining with company executives rather than an attorney hired by management have been held to violate Section 8(b)(1)(B).

Section 8(a)(2): Employer Domination of Labor Unions

In the years just prior to and shortly after the passage of the Wagner Act in 1935, employer-formed and dominated unions were common. Firms that decided they could no longer completely resist worker demands for collective action created **in-house unions** or **captive unions.** Such unions or employee associations created an impression of collective bargaining while allowing management to retain complete control. This type of employer domination is outlawed by Section 8(a)(2). That section also outlaws employer interference in the formation or administration of a labor organization, as well as employer support (financial or otherwise) of same.

Although in-house unions are not a common problem today, the problem of employer support is of continuing interest. Support such as secretarial help, office equipment, or financial aid is prohibited. An employer is permitted by Section 8(a)(2) to allow "employers to confer with him during working hours without loss of time or pay."

An employer who agrees to recognize a union that does not have the support of a majority of employees violates Section 8(a)(2); such recognition is a violation even if the employer acted on a good-faith belief that the union had majority support. An employer is also prohibited from recognizing one union while another union has a petition for a representation election pending before the NLRB. However, the board has held that an employer may continue negotiations with an incumbent union even though a rival union has filed a petition for a representation election (*RCA Del Caribe,* 262 N.L.R.B. No. 116, 1982). Are these two positions consistent? How can they be reconciled?

In addition to being prohibited from recognizing a nonmajority union, the employer is also forbidden from helping a union solicit membership or dues checkoff cards, or from allowing a supervisor to serve as a union officer.

One area of interest under Section 8(a)(2) has developed recently as many employers initiated innovative work arrangements among employees. In order to improve productivity and worker morale, some employers have created autonomous work groups, or quality circles, or work teams where groups of employees are given greater responsibility for determining work schedules, methods, and so forth. When such work groups or teams discuss working conditions, pay, or worker grievances with representatives of the employer, they could be classified as labor organizations under the NLRA. Section 2(5) defines a labor organization as

> any organization of any kind, or any agency or employee representation committee or plan, in which employees participate and which exists for the purpose, in whole or in part, of dealing with employers concerning grievances, labor disputes, wages, rates of pay, hours of employment, or conditions of work.

If the employer created and administers the operation of a work team or work group, and if the group or team satisfies the statutory definition of a labor organization, the employer could be faced with a violation of Section 8(a)(2).

As remedies for Section 8(a)(2) violations, the board may order the employer to cease recognizing the union, to cancel any agreements reached with the union, to cease giving support or assistance to the union, or to disband an in-house or captive union.

Sections 8(a)(3) and 8(b)(2): Discrimination in Terms or Conditions of Employment

Under Section 8(a)(3) of the NLRA, employers are forbidden to discriminate "in regard to hire or tenure of employment or any term or condition of employment to encourage or discourage membership in any labor organization." Unions, under Section 8(b)(2), are forbidden to cause or attempt to cause an employer to discriminate against an employee in violation of Subsection 8(a)(3) or to discriminate against an employee with respect to whom membership in such organization has been denied or terminated on some ground other than . . . failure to tender the periodic dues and the initiation fees uniformly required as a condition of . . . membership. . . .

The intent of these sections is to insulate an employee's employment from conditions based on his or her union sympathies, or lack thereof. If an employee is to have the free choice, under Section 7, to join or refrain from joining a union, then that employee must not be made to suffer economically for his or her choice. The wording of Sections 8(a)(3) and 8(b)(2) indicates that a violation of these sections has two elements. First, there must be some discrimination in the terms or conditions of employment—either a refusal to hire, discharge, lay off, or discipline—or a union attempt to get the employer to so discriminate. Second, the discrimination or attempt to cause discrimination must be for the purpose of encouraging or discouraging union membership.

Because the discrimination (or attempt to cause it) must be for the purpose of encouraging or discouraging union membership, intention is a necessary part of a violation of these sections. If an employer (or union) states that an employee should be fired because of participation in union activities (or lack of participation), demonstrating the requisite intention for a violation is no problem. But most complaints involving Section 8(a)(3) or Section 8(b)(2) are not as clear-cut. For example, what happens if an employee who supports the union's organizing campaign also has a poor work record? How should the board and the courts handle a case in which the employer or union has mixed motives for its actions? That is the subject of the following case.

NLRB v. TRANSPORTATION MANAGEMENT CORP.

462 U.S. 393 (Supreme Court of the United States, 1983)

WHITE, J.

The National Labor Relations Act makes unlawful the discharge of workers because of union activity, but employers retain the right to discharge workers for any number of other reasons unrelated to the employee's union activities. When the General Counsel of the National Labor Relations Board (Board) files a complaint alleging that an employee was discharged because of his union activities, the employer may assert legitimate motives for his decision. In *Wright Line.* . . . the National Labor Relations Board reformulated the allocation of the burden of proof in such cases. It determined that the General Counsel carried the burden of persuading the Board that an anti-union animus contributed to the employer's decision to discharge an employee, a

burden that does not shift, but that the employer, even if it failed to meet or neutralize the General Counsel's showing, could avoid the finding that it violated the statute by demonstrating by a preponderance of the evidence that the worker would have been fired even if he had not been involved with the Union. The question presented in this case is whether the burden placed on the employer in *Wright Line* is consistent with Sections 8(a)(1) and 8(a)(3), as well as with Section 10(c) of the NLRA, which provides that the Board must prove an unlawful labor practice by a "preponderance of the evidence."

Prior to his discharge, Sam Santillo was a bus driver for respondent Transportation Management Corporation. On March 19, 1979, Santillo talked to officials of the Teamster's Union about organizing the drivers who worked with him. Over the next four days Santillo discussed with his fellow drivers the possibility of joining the Teamsters and distributed authorization cards. On the night of March 23, George Patterson, who supervised Santillo and the other drivers, told one of the drivers that he had heard of Santillo's activities. Pattern referred to Santillo as two-faced, and promised to get even with him.

Later that evening Patterson talked to Ed West, who was also a bus driver for respondent. Patterson asked, "What's with Sam and the Union?" Patterson said that he took Santillo's actions personally, recounted several favors he had done for Santillo, and added that he would remember Santillo's activities when Santillo again asked for a favor. On Monday, March 26, Santillo was discharged. Patterson told Santillo that he was being fired for leaving his keys in the bus and taking unauthorized breaks.

Santillo filed a complaint with the Board alleging that he had been discharged because of his union activities, contrary to Sections 8(a)(1) and 8(a)(3) of the NLRA. The General Counsel issued a complaint. The administrative law judge (A.L.J.) determined by a preponderance of the evidence that Patterson clearly had an anti-union animus and that Santillo's discharge was motivated by a desire to discourage union activities. The A.L.J. also found that the asserted reasons for the discharge could not withstand scrutiny. Patterson's disapproval of Santillo's practice of leaving his keys in the bus was clearly a pretext, for Patterson had not known about Santillo's practice until after he had decided to discharge Santillo; moreover, the practice of leaving keys in buses was commonplace among respondent's employees. Respondent identified two types of unauthorized breaks, coffee breaks and stops at home. With respect to both coffee breaks and stopping at home, the A.L.J. found that Santillo was never cautioned or admonished about such behavior, and that the employer had not followed its customary practice of issuing three written warnings before discharging a driver. The A.L.J. also found that the taking of coffee breaks during working hours was normal practice, and that respondent tolerated the practice unless the breaks interfered with the driver's performance of his duties. In any event, said the A.L.J., respondent had never taken any adverse personnel action against an employee because of such behavior. While acknowledging that Santillo had engaged in some unsatisfactory conduct, the A.L.J. was not persuaded that Santillo would have been fired had it not been for his union activities.

The Board affirmed, adopting with some clarification the A.L.J.'s findings and conclusions and expressly applying its *Wright Line* decision. It stated that respondent had failed to carry its burden of persuading the Board that the discharge would have taken place had Santillo not engaged in activity protected by the Act. The First Circuit Court of Appeals, relying on its previous decision rejecting the Board's *Wright Line* test . . . refused to enforce the Board's order and remanded for consideration of whether the General Counsel had proved by a preponderance of the evidence that Santillo would not have been fired had it not been for his union activities. . . .

As we understand the Board's decisions, they have consistently held that the unfair labor practice consists of a discharge or other adverse action that is based in whole or in part on anti-union animus—or as the Board now puts it, that the employee's protected conduct was a substantial or motivating factor in the adverse action. The General Counsel has the burden of proving these elements under Section 10(c). But the Board's construction of the statute permits an employer to avoid being adjudicated a violator by showing what his actions would have been regardless of his forbidden motivation. It extends to the employer what the Board considers to be an affirmative defense but does not change or add to the elements of the unfair labor practice that the General Counsel has the burden of proving under Section 10(c). The Board has instead chosen to recognize, as it insists it has done for many years, what it designates as an affirmative defense that the employer has the burden of sustaining. We are unprepared to hold that this is an impermissible construction of the Act. "[T]he Board's construction here, while it may not be required by the Act, is at least permissible under it . . ." and in these circumstances its position is entitled to deference.

The Board's allocation of the burden of proof is clearly reasonable in this context. . . .

The employer is a wrongdoer; he has acted out of a motive that is declared illegitimate by the statute. It is fair that he bear the risk that the influence of legal and illegal motives cannot be separated, because he knowingly created the risk and because the risk was created not by innocent activity but by his own wrongdoing.

For these reasons, we conclude that the Court of Appeals erred in refusing to enforce the Board's orders, which rested on the Board's *Wright Line* decision.

The Board was justified in this case in concluding that Santillo would not have been discharged had the employer not considered his efforts to establish a establish a union. At least two of the transgressions that purportedly would have in any event prompted Santillo's discharge were commonplace, and yet no transgressor had ever before received any kind of discipline. Moreover, the employer departed from its usual practice in dealing with rules infractions; indeed, not only did the employer not warn Santillo that his actions would result in being subjected to discipline, it never even expressed its disapproval of his conduct. In addition, Patterson, the person who made the initial decision to discharge Santillo, was obviously upset with Santillo for engaging in such protected activity. It is thus clear that the Board's find-

ing that Santillo would not have been fired even if the employer had not had an anti-union animus was "supported by substantial evidence on the record considered as a whole". . . . Accordingly, the judgment is **Reversed.**

Discrimination in Employment to Encourage Union Membership

Union Security Agreements.   Although Section 8(a)(3) and Section 8(b)(2) prohibit discrimination to encourage or discourage union membership, there is an important exception regarding the "encouragement" of union membership. That exception deals with **union security agreements**—when an employer and union agree that employees must either join the union or at least pay union dues in order to remain employees. This exception requires some discussion.

Prior to the Taft-Hartley Act of 1947, unions and employers could agree that an employer would hire only employees who were already union members. These agreements, called **closed shop agreements,** had the effect of encouraging (or requiring) workers to join unions if they wished to get a job. Such agreements clearly restrict the employee's free exercise of Section 7 rights; for that reason they were prohibited. But the Taft-Hartley amendments did not completely prohibit all "union security" arrangements.

Section 8(a)(3), as amended by Taft-Hartley, contains the following provision:

> Provided, that nothing in this Act . . . shall preclude an employer from making an agreement with a labor organization . . . to require as a condition of employment membership therein on or after the thirtieth day following the beginning of such agreement, whichever is later. . . .

Section 8(a)(3) also provides that an employer can justify discrimination against an employee for nonmembership in a union only if membership was denied or terminated because of the employee's failure to pay the dues and initiation fees required of all members.

The effect of these provisions is to allow an employer and union to agree to a union shop or **agency shop** provision. A **union shop agreement** requires that all employees hired by the employer must join the union after a certain period of time, not less than thirty days. Although employees need not be union members to be hired, they must become union members if they are to remain employed past the specified time period. An **agency shop agreement** does not require that employees actually join the union, but they must at least pay the dues and fees required of union members.

Although Section 8(a)(3) states that an employer and a union can agree "to require as a condition of employment membership" in the union on or after thirty days of hiring, Section 8(b)(2) and the second proviso to Section 8(a)(3) say that a employee cannot be fired except for failure to pay dues and initiation fees. In effect, this latter language has the legal effect of reducing all union shops to the level of agency shops. Under an agency shop agreement, remember, employees need not become formal members of the union but must pay union dues. Under the language of Section 8(b)(2), formal union members cannot be fired for disobeying the union's internal rules or failing to participate in union affairs. The only difference is that they may be fined by the union for these infractions, and the fines may be enforceable in a state court. Furthermore, the law is clear that an employee who pays dues but refuses to assume full union membership cannot be held to these rules and sanctions.

Unions argue that union security provisions are needed to prevent "free riders"; since all members of the bargaining unit get the benefits of the union's agreement, whether or not they are union members, they should be required to pay the costs of negotiating and administering the agreement—union dues. Only by paying the costs of such union representation can "free riders" be prevented.

Although such agreements do prevent "free riders," they are also coercive to the extent that they may override an employee's free choice of whether or not to join a union. For that reason, the act permits states to outlaw such union security agreements. Section 14(b) states that

> Nothing in this Act shall be construed as authorizing the execution or application of agreements requiring membership in a labor organization as a condition of employment in any state or territory in which such execution or application is prohibited by State or Territorial law.

This section allows for the passage of **right-to-work laws,** which prohibit such union security agreements. In states that have passed such a law, the union shop and agency shop agreements are illegal. A number of states, mainly in the South and West (the Sun Belt) have passed such laws. It is also worth noting that Section 19 of the act was amended to allow employees with bona fide religious objections to joining unions or paying union dues to make arrangements to pay the required fees or dues to a charitable organization.

When a union security agreement is in effect, the employer must discharge an employee, upon the union's request, if the employee has been denied membership in or expelled from the union for failure to pay the required union dues or fees. Under Section 8(b)(2), the union cannot legally demand the discharge of an employee for refusing to pay "back dues" or "reinstatement fees" after a lapse of membership in a prior job. Other examples of union violations of Section 8(b)(2) are forcing an employer to agree to hire only applicants satisfactory to the union or causing an employee to be discharged for opposition to the manner in which internal union affairs are conducted, or because the worker was disliked or considered a troublemaker by the union leadership.

Hiring Halls.   In some industries employers rely on unions to refer prospective employees to the various employers. Such arrangements, known as **hiring halls,** are common in industries such as trucking, construction, and longshoring. Hiring halls and other job-referral mechanisms operated by unions may have the effect of encouraging membership in the union, since an employee must go through the union to get a job. The NLRB and the Supreme Court have held such hiring halls or referral mechanisms to be legal as long as they meet the following conditions:

1. The union must not discriminate on grounds of union membership for job referrals.
2. The employer may reject any applicant by the union.
3. A notice of the nondiscriminatory operation of the referral service must be posted in the hiring hall.

It is also legal for the union to set skill levels necessary for membership or for referral to employers through a hiring hall.

Preferential Treatment for Union Officers: Super Seniority.   In some collective agreements an employer will agree to give union officers or stewards preferential treatment in the event of layoffs or recall of employees. Such provisions, known as **super seniority** since layoff and recall are usually done on the basis of seniority, may have the effect of encouraging union membership. Yet they also serve to ensure that employees responsible for the enforcement and administration of the collective agreement remain on the job to ensure the protection of all employees' rights under the contract. However, preferential treatment that goes beyond layoff and recall rights is not so readily justified. For that reason, and because it clearly discriminates in employment conditions to encourage union activity, broad super seniority clauses may involve violations of Section 8(a)(3) and Section 8(b)(2).

Discrimination in Employment to Discourage Union Membership

Just as discrimination in terms or conditions of employment in order to encourage union membership violates Section 8(a)(3), so does discrimination that is intended to discourage union membership or activities. Most complaints alleging discrimination to discourage such activities occur in the context of union organizing campaigns or strikes.

Activity protected under Section 7 includes union organizing activity as well as strikes over economic issues or to protest unfair labor practices. The employer that refuses to hire, or discharges, lays off, or disciplines an employee for such activity, is in violation of Section 8(a)(3). Although the employer must have acted with the intention of discouraging union membership, the board has held that specific evidence of such an intention need not be shown if the employer's conduct is inherently destructive of the employees' Section 7 rights.

As noted earlier, several reasons may be behind an employer's action; anti-union motives may play a part, along with legitimate work-related reasons. Recall that in *NLRB* v. *Transportation Management,* the Supreme Court upheld the board practice of requiring the employer to show that the discipline or discharge would have occurred even without the employees' protected conduct. If the employer can meet that burden, then it is not a violation of Section 8(a)(3).

An employer who fires employees for engaging in a union organizing campaign is in violation of Section 8(a)(3). Firing employees for striking over economic demands is also a violation. Other examples of Section 8(a)(3) violations include:

- layoffs that violate seniority rules and that fall mainly upon union supporters;
- disproportionately severe discipline of union officers or supporters;

- discharging a union supporter without the customary warning prior to discharge;

- discharging a union supporter based on past misconduct that had previously been condoned;

- selective enforcement of rules against union supporters.

Strikes as Protected Activity. Strikes by employees are the essence of concerted activity; workers agree to withhold their labor from the employer in order to pressure the employer to accept their demands. A strike for collective bargaining purposes or for purposes of mutual aid and protection comes under the protection of Section 7. However, despite the purposes of the strike, if it violates the collective agreement or if workers are attempting to strike while still collecting their pay, the strike may not be protected.

When discussing the rights of strikers under the NLRA and the employer's response to the strike, the board and the courts distinguish between economic strikes and unfair labor practice strikes. As discussed in Chapter 5, an *economic strike* is a strike called to pressure the employer to accept the union's negotiating demands. It occurs after the old collective agreement has expired and negotiations for a new agreement break down. By contrast, an *unfair labor practice strike* is called to protest an employer's illegal actions. It does not involve contract demands or negotiations. The rights of strikers thus may depend on whether the strike is an unfair labor practice or economic strike.

Unfair Labor Practice Strikes. The Supreme Court has held, in *Mastro Plastics* v. *NLRB* (350 U.S. 270, 1956), that unfair labor practice strikes are protected activity under the act. That means that unfair labor practice strikers may not be fired for going on strike; nor may they be permanently replaced. Strikes that begin as economic strikes may become unfair practice strikes if the employer commits serious unfair labor practices during the strike. For example, if the employer refused to bargain with the union over a new agreement and discharged the strikers, the strike would become an unfair labor practice strike.

An employer may hire workers to replace the strikers during a unfair labor practice strike, but the strikers *must* be reinstated when the strike is over. Although misconduct on the picket line may normally be a sufficient reason for an employer to discharge a striker, the board has held in prior decisions that severe misconduct (such as physical assault) is needed to justify the discharge of an unfair labor practice striker. However, in *Clear Pine Mouldings, Inc.* (268 N.L.R.B. No. 173, 1984), the board held that the existence of an unfair labor practice strike

> does not in any way privilege those employees [on strike] to engage in other than peaceful picketing and persuasion. . . . There is nothing in the statute to support the notion that striking employees are free to engage in or escalate violence or misconduct in proportion to their estimates of the degree of seriousness of an employer's unfair labor practices.

Economic Strikes. Economic strikes, as previously noted, are work stoppages by the employees designed to force the employer to meet their bargaining demands for increased wages or other benefits. As with unfair labor practice strikes, economic strikes are protected activity; however, the protections afforded economic strikers are not as great as those given unfair labor practice strikers. As mentioned earlier in the discussion of protected activity under Section 7, on-the-job slowdowns are not protected—employees who engage in such conduct may be discharged. As well, economic strikes in violation of the collective agreement are not protected.

When the economic strike is protected, the striking employees may not be discharged for going on strike; however, the employer may hire permanent replacements for the striking employees. The right to hire permanent replacements was affirmed by the Supreme Court in 1938, in the case of *NLRB* v. *MacKay Radio & Telegraph* (304 U.S. 333). Although the striking employees may be permanently replaced, they still retain their status as "employees" under the act. (See the definition of *employee* in Section 2(3).) Because they retain their status as employees, the strikers are entitled to be reinstated if they make an unconditional application for reinstatement and if vacancies are available. If no positions are available at the time of their application, even if the lack of vacancies is due to the hiring of replacements, the employer need not reinstate the strikers. However, if the strikers continue to indicate an interest in reinstatement, the employer is required to rehire them as positions become available. That requirement was upheld by the Supreme Court in *NLRB* v. *Fleetwood Trailers Co.* (389 U.S. 375, 1967).

In *Laidlaw Corp.* (171 N.L.R.B. No. 175, 1968), the NLRB held that economic strikers who had made an unconditional application for reinstatement and who continued to make known their availability for employment were entitled to be recalled by the employer prior to the employer's hiring of new employees. The following case involves the extent of the employer's duty to reinstate unreplaced strikers.

DAVID R. WEBB CO., INC. v. NLRB

888 F.2d 502 (U.S. Court of Appeals, 7th Cir., 1990)

MANION, J.

David R. Webb Company (Webb) petitions for review of an order of the National Labor Relations Board (NLRB or the Board), in which the Board found that Webb violated Sections 8(a)(1) and (3) of the Labor-Management Relations Act (the Act), by failing to reinstate three striking employees to their pre-strike positions or the substantial equivalent of those positions. The NLRB filed a cross-application for enforcement of this order. . . .

On July 28, 1986, 246 of Webb's 260 production and maintenance employees began an economic strike. On November 3, 1986, the striking employees unconditionally offered to return to work. By then, the positions of the three employees involved in this case had been filled by permanent replacements, and therefore the employees were placed on a preferential recall list, arranged according to qualifications and seniority.

By February, these three employees had reached the top three slots on the recall list. Webb offered Alice Hill an entry-level position as a "dryer-feeder." She accepted the job but performed poorly, and Webb terminated her after one day. Rex Young replace Hill, but he lasted two days and was terminated. Eugene McGaha followed Young and two days later Webb terminated him as well. There is little dispute that the three employees failed to perform satisfactorily as dryer-feeders. Webb, however, did not return any of the three to the recall list.

The Regional Director for Region 25 of the NLRB issued a complaint against Webb, claiming it had engaged in unfair labor practices in violation of Sections 8(a)(1) and (3) of the Act by rehiring workers for positions that were not the substantial equivalent of their pre-strike positions, and then terminating them not only from that position but also from their right to recall to their original positions, or the substantial equivalent of those positions. The Board relied on *Laidlaw Corp.* v. *NLRB* for the proposition that employers violate Sections 8(a)(1) and (3) of the Act by failing to reinstate striking employees to their former or substantially equivalent positions (as they became available) after the employees have unconditionally offered to return to work following an economic strike.

Webb argued before the ALJ, as it argues on appeal, that *Laidlaw* does not require an employer to reinstate an employee to a position substantially equivalent to his pre-strike position; rather, Webb argues that any rights the employees had as economic strikers were abrogated upon *acceptance* of the lower-level dryer-feeder position. Webb contends that a striker who accepts a job other than his pre-strike position forfeits his right to future recall to that position if he is unable to perform the job he accepts and is terminated from that position. Alternatively, Webb argues that even if the employees have such a right under *Laidlaw*, Webb had offered a legitimate and substantial business justification for not reinstating these three employees to their former or substantially equivalent positions.

The ALJ held that the termination of the employees from the lower-level position and the simultaneous termination of their preferential recall rights violated Sections 8(a)(1) and (3) because Webb failed to offer a legitimate and substantial business justification for its failure to satisfy the employees' *Laidlaw* reinstatement rights. The ALJ held that those reinstatement rights included the right to eventually be recalled to their pre-strike positions or one substantially equivalent, without any impairment to the employees' previous seniority rights and other benefits. Because the pre-strike positions of two of the employees (Hill and Young) became vacant after their termination from the dryer-feeder position, the ALJ ordered Webb to reinstate the employees to their pre-strike positions. The ALJ ordered Webb to reinstate the third employee (McGaha) to his pre-strike truck driver position, if available, or to a substantially equivalent position if the truck driver position was still held by the permanent replacement who filled the position during the strike. The ALJ also ordered Webb to make the three employees whole for any loss of pay from the date they should have been reinstated to their original positions, or in McGaha's case, to a substantially equivalent position.

Webb filed exceptions to the ALJ's decision with the NLRB. After reviewing the ALJ's opinion, the NLRB issued an order adopting the ALJ's rulings, findings and conclusions. That order, however, clarified the ALJ's decision by emphasizing that because of the poor performance of the three employees in the dryer-feeder position, Webb was not required to retain them in that position; but because that position was not substantially equivalent to the employees' pre-strike positions, Webb failed to offer reinstatement sufficient to satisfy its obligations under Laidlaw.

. . . we conclude that the ALJ's relevant factual findings, as adopted by the NLRB, are supported by substantial evidence, and affirm those findings. We now review the ALJ's legal conclusions.

Section [2(3) of the Act] states that persons considered "employees" entitled to the protections of the Act include any individual "whose work has ceased as a consequence of, or in connection with, any current labor dispute . . . and who has to obtained any other regular and substantially equivalent employment." Based on this provision, the Supreme Court held in *NLRB* v. *Fleetwood Trailer Co.* that after a striker has made an unconditional offer to return to work, he is entitled to an offer of reinstatement "[i]f and when a job for which the striker is qualified becomes available." . . .

Neither . . . *Fleetwood Trailer* nor . . . *Laidlaw* defined the parameters of what action by an employer will constitute adequate reinstatement. Neither case discussed whether reinstating an employee to a different job with the company fulfilled the company's reinstatement obligation. Nor did the cases focus on whether the "substantially equivalent" language in Section 2(3) referred only to jobs at another company or whether offering a substantially equivalent job at the reinstating company met the company's obligation. A few [Courts of Appeals], however, have begun the process of establishing guidelines for reviewing the adequacy of the reinstatements of striking employees. . . .

The Eighth and Ninth Circuits have specifically stated that employees must be reinstated to their prior or substantially equivalent positions before an employer's obligation is satisfied. . . . Other Circuits have given similarly broad interpretations to the reinstatement requirement. . . .

The question before us is whether, in order to fulfill its *Laidlaw* obligation, Webb must offer an economic striker the same job, a *substantially equivalent* job, or any job for which he or she is qualified. The ALJ and the Board determined that the recall job had to be substantially equivalent, if not the same as, the employee's pre-strike position. Webb argues that the "substantially equivalent" language in Section 2(3) refers only to employment obtained elsewhere during the strike. The NLRB, in contrast, cites language from *Medallion Kitchens* that "an employer's obligation is satisfied only upon an offer to the former striker of a *substantially equivalent* job."

We are particularly deferential to the NLRB when interpreting the Labor Acts. . . . The NLRB has consistently taken the position that employers must reinstate striking employees to their former or substantially equivalent positions before the employer's *Laidlaw* obligations are satisfied. In *Providence Medical Center,* the NLRB enforced an ALJ holding that an employer must "immediately" reinstate a striking employee to his previous or a substantially equivalent position as soon as such a position becomes available, and that the striker's acceptance of an interim lower-level position does not "extinguish" the employer's duty to offer substantially equivalent employment when it later becomes available. Recently, in *Ford Bros., Inc.,* the NLRB ordered an employer to [i]mmediately reinstate all employees who were engaged in an economic strike against the Respondent . . . to their former positions, or if those positions no longer exist, to substantially equivalent positions, without prejudice to their seniority or privileges previously enjoyed, and make those employees whole for any loss of wages or benefits that they sustained. . . . This order was based on the ALJ's interpretation of the Act and the case law as placing the burden on the employer "of proving that the strikers' former positions or substantially equivalent positions, were unavailable for legitimate and substantial business reasons."

Although the application of the "substantially equivalent" language may have expanded somewhat in the evolutionary process of the case law, such an application is not unreasonable. We therefore conclude that the NLRB's interpretation of the Act, *Fleetwood Trailer* and *Laidlaw,* which requires reinstatement of a striking employee to his former or a substantially equivalent position, is consistent with the policies and the language of the Act, and with the case law thus far.

Requiring employers to reinstate striking employees to the same position they held before the strike, or a substantially equivalent position, is consistent with the policies underlying the Act. One of the policies behind the Act was to protect the rights of the employees to organize and strike. . . . We agree with the NLRB that employees will be deterred from striking if their employer can reinstate them to a lower-level position and thereby fulfill his obligations under *Laidlaw.* If lower-level positions are all that are available to an employee when he reaches the top of the recall list, he is likely to feel financial pressure (particularly after a long strike where most vacancies were filled) to take the position rather than wait until a position substantially equivalent to his pre-strike job becomes available. However, if accepting a lesser job means he may lose his right to reinstatement to his previous position if he is unable to perform satisfactorily, his options are limited. To ensure that the striker is not penalized for engaging in protected activity, we conclude that under the policies behind the Act, the process of reinstatement does not end until the employee receives his original position or one substantially equivalent to it. But the right to return is not necessarily open-ended. The Board will ultimately have to determine the obligations of the employer and the rights of the employee while waiting for a vacancy in a substantially equivalent job.

The theory behind *Fleetwood Trailer* and *Laidlaw* is that employees should not be penalized for striking, and that they remain employees regardless of such action. This logically extends to the employees' post-strike employment status, and protects the employees until they are sufficiently reinstated. . . . Likewise, a returning striker's right should not depend on the coincidence of which jobs may be open when he reaches the top of the recall list. If Webb had an opening in the employees' pre-strike jobs, or in substantially equivalent positions, when it placed the employees in the dryer-feeder position (or indeed any time before the employees were terminated from the dryer-feeder position), it would have had to offer them that position. Webb cannot now argue that because the employees chose to take the lower-level position that the company is discharged from the higher reinstatement requirement. . . .

We uphold the NLRB's determination that an employee retains his right to reinstatement until he receives the same job or one substantially equivalent to it (assuming he does not accept a substantially equivalent job elsewhere) even if in the interim he accepts a lesser or different position from his employer. . . .

Having held that striking employees must be reinstated to their former or a substantially equivalent position, we can only refuse enforcement of the NLRB order if Webb shows a legitimate and substantial business justification for removing the employees from the recall list and refusing to place them in their former or substantially equivalent positions when such became available. As the Supreme Court stated in *Fleetwood Trailer,* unless the employer who refuses to reinstate strikers can show that his action was due to "legitimate and substantial business justifications," he is guilty of unfair labor practices. . . . It is the primary responsibility of the Board and not of the courts "to strike the proper balance between the asserted business justifications and the invasion of employee rights in light of the Act and its policy.". . .

Webb argues that it has a legitimate reason for terminating employees from positions they are unable to perform. We do not take issue with that proposition. The failure to adequately perform the dryer-feeder job was cause for termination from that position, as the NLRB stated. However, it was not a sufficient reason for removing the employees from the eligibility list for their pre-strike positions or their substantial equivalent.

... because the three employees here possessed residual *Laidlaw* rights to full reinstatement, Webb could not refuse to offer them their pre-strike positions or their substantial equivalent when such vacancies arose. In sum, since all of Webb's arguments address its reasons for terminating the employees from the dryer-feeder position, and not reasons for terminating them from the recall list and their full reinstatement rights, we do not believe it has offered a valid de-

fense of a legitimate and substantial business justification for its actions. . . .

In sum, we uphold the determination of the ALJ and the NLRB that Webb violated Section 8(a)(1) and (3) of the Act by terminating the three employees from the recall list before offering them reinstatement to their pre-strike or substantially equivalent positions, and failing to offer a legitimate and substantial business reason for such termination. . . . **Enforcement granted.**

The NLRB has held that a union may waive the right of strikers to be reinstated with full seniority in exchange for an end to a strike (*Gem City Ready Mix,* 270 N.L.R.B. 191, 116 L.R.R.M. 1266, 1986; and *NLRB* v. *Harrison Ready Mix Concrete,* 770 F.2d 78, 6th Cir. 1985).

Other Strike-Related Issues. Recall that under Section 7, employees have the right to refrain from concerted activity; that includes the right to remain working rather than go on strike. As noted in our discussion of Section 8(b)(2), a union may impose some disciplinary sanctions upon union members who refuse to go on strike, but they may not cause an employer to discriminate against such employees in terms or conditions of employment. Nor may the employer offer incentives or benefits to the replacements or those employees not going on strike when such benefits are not available to the strikers. In the case of *NLRB* v. *Erie Resistor Co.* (373 U.S. 221, 1963), the Supreme Court held that the employer's granting of twenty years' seniority to all replacements violated Section 8 (a)(3). The effect of such seniority was to insulate the replacements from layoff, while exposing those employees who went on strike to layoff. This effect would continue long after the strike was over; it would place the former strikers at a disadvantage simply because they went on strike. Although *Erie Resistor* involved rather severe actions by the employer, the NLRB has held that *any* preferential treatment in terms or conditions of employment accorded to the nonstrikers or replacements, and not to the strikers, violates Section 8(a)(3).

A 1983 Supreme Court decision involved the rights of the workers hired to replace economic strikers. In *Belknap* v. *Hale* (51 U.S.L.W. 5079, 1983), the Court held that replacements hired under the promise of permanent employment could sue the employer for breach of contract if they were laid off at the end of the strike. Does *Belknap* v. *Hale* undermine the rights of strikers to be reinstated?

Employer Response to Strike Activity. Just as employees are free to go on strike to promote their economic demands, employers are free to withdraw employment from employees in order to pressure them to accept the employer's demands. This tactic, called a **lockout,** is the temporary withdrawal of employment to pressure employees to agree to the employer's bargaining proposals. A lockout needs to be distinguished from a *permanent* closure of a plant to avoid unionization.

When the employees have not gone on strike, the employer may be reluctant to "lock them out." (Why?) But when the threat of a "quickie strike" or unannounced walkout poses the prospect of damage to equipment or disruption of business, the employer may lock out to avoid such problems. The board has consistently held that such "defensive" lockouts are not unfair labor practices. Lockouts by the employers in a multi-employer bargaining unit, to avoid a whipsaw strike by the union, have been held legal by the board and the Supreme Court. What about the situation in which an employer locks out the unionized employees and hires replacements? This issue is addressed in the following Supreme Court decision.

NLRB v. BROWN

380 U.S. 300 (Supreme Court of the United States, 1965)

BRENNAN, J.

The respondents, who are members of a multi-employer bargaining group, locked out their employees in response to a whipsaw strike against another member of the group. They and the struck employer continued operations with temporary replacements. The National Labor Relations Board found that the struck employer's use of temporary replacements was lawful, but that the respondents had violated Section 8(a)(1) and (3) of the National Labor Relations Act by locking out their regular employees and using temporary replacements to carry on business. The Court of Appeals for the Tenth Circuit disagreed and refused to enforce the Board's order....

Five operators of six retail food stores in Carlsbad, New Mexico, make up the employer group. The stores had bargained successfully on a group basis for many years with Local 462 of the Retail Clerks International Association. Negotiations for a new collective agreement to replace the expiring one began in January 1960. Agreement was reached by mid-February on all terms except the amount and effective date of a wage increase. Bargaining continued without result, and on March 2 the Local informed the employers that a strike had been authorized. The employers responded that a strike against any member of the employer group would be regarded as a strike against all. On March 16, the union struck Food Jet, Inc., one of the group. The four respondents, operating five stores, immediately locked out all employees represented by the Local, telling them, and the Local that they would be recalled to work when the strike against Food Jet ended. The stores, including Food Jet, continued to carry on business by using management personnel, relatives of such personnel, and a few temporary employees; all of the temporary replacements were expressly told that the arrangement would be discontinued when the whipsaw strike ended. Bargaining continued until April 22 when an agreement was reached. The employers immediately released the temporary replacements and restored the strikers and the locked out employees to their jobs....

We begin with the proposition that the Act does not constitute the Board as an "arbiter of the sort of economic weapons the parties can use in seeking to gain acceptance of their bargaining demands." In the absence of proof of unlawful motivation, there are many economic weapons which an employer may use that either interfere in some measure with concerted employee activities, or which are in some degree discriminatory and discourage union membership, and yet the use of such economic weapons does not constitute conduct that is within the prohibition of either Sections 8(a)(1) or (3). Even the Board concedes that an employer may legitimately blunt the effectiveness of an anticipated strike by stockpiling inventories, readjusting contract schedules, or transferring work from one plant to another, even if he thereby makes himself "virtually strike-proof." ...

Specifically, he may in various circumstances use the lockout as a legitimate economic weapon....

In the circumstances of this case, we do not see how the continued operations of respondents and their use of temporary replacements any more implies hostile motivation, nor how it is inherently more destructive of employee rights, than the lockout itself. Rather, the compelling inference is that this was all part and parcel of respondents' defensive measure to preserve the multiemployer group in the face of the whipsaw strike. Since Food Jet legitimately continued business operations, it is only reasonable to regard respondents' actions as evincing concern that the integrity of the employer group was threatened unless they also managed to stay open for business during the lockout. For with Food Jet open for business and respondents' stores closed, the prospect that the whipsaw strike would succeed in breaking up the employer association was not at all fanciful. The retail food industry is very competitive and repetitive patronage is highly important. Faced with the prospect of a loss of patronage to Food Jet, it is logical that respondents should have been concerned that one or more of their number might bolt the group and come to terms with the Local, thus destroying the common front essential to multiemployer bargaining. The Court of Appeals correctly pictured the respondents' dilemma in saying, "If . . . the struck employer does choose to operate with replacements and the other employers cannot replace after lockout, the economic advantage passes to the struck member, the non-struck members are deterred in exercising the defensive lockout, and the whipsaw strike . . . enjoys and almost inescapable prospect of success." Clearly respondents' continued operations with the use of temporary replacements following the lockout was wholly consistent with a legitimate business purpose.

The Board's finding of a Section 8(a)(1) violation emphasized the impact of respondents' conduct upon the effectiveness of the whipsaw strike. It is no doubt true that the collective strength of the stores to resist that strike is maintained, and even increased, when all stores stay open with temporary replacements. The pressures on the employees are necessarily greater when none of the union employees is working and the stores remain open. But these pressures are no more than the result of the Local's inability to make effective use of the whipsaw tactic. Moreover, these effects are no different from those that result from the legitimate use of any economic weapon by an employer. Continued operations with the use of temporary replacements may result in the failure of the whipsaw strike, but this does not mean that the employers' conduct is demonstrably so destructive of employee rights or so devoid of significant service to any legitimate business end that it cannot be tolerated consistently with the Act. Certainly then, in the absence of evidentiary findings of hostile motive, there is no support for the conclusion that respondents violated Section 8(a)(1).

Nor does the record show any basis for concluding that respondents violated Section 8(a)(3). Under that section both discrimination and a resulting discouragement of union membership are necessary, but the added element of unlawful intent is also required. In *Buffalo Linen* itself the employers treated the locked-out employees less favorably because of their union membership, and this may have tended to discourage continued membership, but we rejected the notion that the use of the lockout violated the statute. The discriminatory act is not by itself unlawful unless intended to prejudice the employees' position because of their membership in the union; some element of antiunion animus is necessary.

We agree with the Court of Appeals that respondents' conduct here clearly fits into the latter category, where actual subjective intent is determinative, and where the Board must find from evidence independent of the mere conduct involved that the conduct was primarily motivated by an antiunion animus. While the use of temporary nonunion personnel in preference to the locked-out union members is discriminatory, we think that any resulting tendency to discourage union membership is comparatively remote, and that this use of temporary personnel constitutes a measure reasonably adapted to the effectuation of a legitimate business end. Here discontent on the part of the Local's membership in all likelihood is attributable largely to the fact that the membership was locked out as the result of the Local's whipsaw stratagem. But the lockout itself is concededly within the rule of *Buffalo Linen*. We think that the added dissatisfaction and resultant pressure on membership attributable to the fact that the nonstruck employers remain in business with temporary replacements is comparatively insubstantial. First, the replacements were expressly used for the duration of the labor dispute only; thus, the displaced employees could not have looked upon the replacements as threatening their jobs. At most the union would be forced to capitulate and return its members to work on terms which, while not as desirable as hoped for, were still better than under the contract. Second, the membership, through its control of union policy, could end the dispute and terminate the lockout at any time simply by agreeing to the employers' terms and returning to work on a regular basis. Third, in light of the union-shop provision that had been carried forward into the new contract from the old collective agreement, it would appear that a union member would have nothing to gain and much to lose, by quitting the union. Under all these circumstances, we cannot say that the employers' conduct had any great tendency to discourage union membership. Not only was the prospect of discouragement of membership comparatively remote, but the respondents' attempt to remain open for business with the help of temporary replacements was a measure reasonably adapted to the achievement of legitimate end—preserving the integrity of the multiemployer bargaining unit.

When the resulting harm to employee rights is thus comparatively slight, and a substantial and legitimate business end is served, the employer's conduct is *prima facie* lawful. Under these circumstances the finding of an unfair labor practice under Section 8(a)(3) requires a showing of improper subjective intent. Here, there is no assertion by either the union or the Board that the respondents were motivated by antiunion animus, nor is there any evidence that this was the case.... Thus, not only is there absent in the record any independent evidence of improper motive, but he record contains positive evidence of the employers' good faith. In sum, the Court of Appeals was required to conclude that there as not sufficient evidence gathered from the record as a whole to support the Board's finding that respondents' conduct violates Section 8(a)(3)....

Courts must, of course, set aside Board decisions which

rest on "an erroneous legal foundation." Congress has not given the Board untrammeled authority to catalogue which economic devices shall be deemed freighted with indicia of unlawful intent. In determining here that the respondents' conduct carried its own badge of improper motive, the Board's decision, for the reasons stated, supplied the criteria governing the application of Sections 8(a)(1) and (3). Since the order therefore rested on "an erroneous legal foundation," the Court of Appeals properly refused to enforce it. **Affirmed.**

Whereas *Brown* dealt with a defensive lockout in response to a strike against one employer, the Supreme Court in *American Shipbuilding Co.* v. *NLRB* (380 U.S. 300, 1965) held that an employer is free to lock out employees in anticipation of the union going on strike. That decision allows the employer to use a lockout as an offensive weapon to promote its bargaining position; the employer need not wait for the union to strike first. An employer may not engage in a lockout unless negotiations have reached an impasse, or deadlock, and exceptional circumstances are required by the board to justify lockouts prior to a bargaining impasse. A lockout accompanied by the hiring of *permanent* replacements by the employer is in violation of Section 8(a)(3). How does that situation differ from *NLRB* v. *Brown?* The NLRB upheld the use of *temporary* replacements after an offensive lockout in *Harter Equipment* (280 N.L.R.B. No. 71, 1222 L.R.R.M. 1219, 1986).

Plant Closing to Avoid Unionization.

The preceding discussion dealt with an employer's response to the economic demands of organized workers—the employer is free to lock out to avoid union bargaining demands. But what about the situation in which the employees are just in the process of forming a union—can the employer shut down the plant to avoid unionization? Recall that Section 8(a)(1) prohibits threats of closure or layoff in order to dissuade employees from joining a union. Should it make any difference whether the shutdown to avoid unionization is complete (the entire operation) or partial (only part of the operation)? The following Supreme Court decision addresses this issue.

TEXTILE WORKERS UNION v. DARLINGTON MFG. CO.

380 U.S. 263 (Supreme Court of the United States, 1965)

HARLAN, J.

Darlington Manufacturing Company was a South Carolina corporation operating one textile mill. A majority of Darlington's stock was held by Deering Milliken & Co., a New York "selling house" marketing textiles produced by others.

Deering Milliken in turn was controlled by Roger Milliken, president of Darlington, and by other members of the Milliken family. The National Labor Relations Board found that the Milliken family, through Deering Milliken, operated 17 textile manufacturers, including Darlington, whose products, manufactured in 27 different mills, were marketed through Deering Milliken.

In March 1956 petitioner Textile Workers Union initiated an organizational campaign at Darlington which the company resisted vigorously in various ways, including threats to close the mill if the union won a representation election. On September 6, 1956, the union won an election by a narrow margin. When Roger Milliken was advised of the union victory, he decided to call a meeting of the Darlington board of directors to consider closing the mill. . . . The board of directors met on September 12 and voted to liquidate the corporation, action which was approved by the stockholders on October 17. The plant ceased operations entirely in November, and all plant machinery and equipment was sold piecemeal at auction in December.

The union filed charges with the Labor Board claiming that Darlington had violated Sections 8(a)(1) and 8(a)(3) of the National Labor Relations Act by closing its plant, and Section 8(a)(5) by refusing to bargain with the union after the election. The Board, by a divided vote, found that Darlington had been closed because of the anti-union animus of Roger Milliken, and held that to be a violation of Section 8(a)(3). The Board also found Darlington to be part of a single integrated employer group controlled by the Milliken family through Deering Milliken; therefore Deering Milliken could be held liable for the unfair labor practices of Darlington. Alternatively, since Darlington was a part of the Deering Milliken enterprise, Deering Milliken had violated the Act by closing part of its business for a discriminatory purpose. The Board ordered back pay for all Darlington employees until they obtained substantially equivalent work or were put on preferential hiring lists at the other Deering Milliken mills. Respondent Deering Milliken was ordered to bargain with the union in regard to details of compliance with the Board order.

On review, the Court of Appeals . . . denied enforcement by a divided vote. The Court of Appeals held that even accepting *arguendo* the Board's determination that Deering Milliken had the status of a single employer, a company has the absolute right to close out a part or all of its business regardless of anti-union motives. The court therefore did not review the Board's finding that Deering Milliken was a single integrated employer. We hold that so far as the Labor Act is concerned, an employer has the absolute right to terminate his entire business for any reason he pleases, but disagree with the Court of Appeals that such right includes the ability to close part of a business no matter what the reason. We conclude that the case must be remanded to the Board for further proceedings.

Preliminarily it should be observed that both petitioners argue that the Darlington closing violated Section (8)(1) as well as Section 8(a)(3) of the Act. We think, however, that the Board was correct in treating the closing only under Section 8(a)(3). Section 8(a)(1) provides that it is unfair labor practices for an employer "to interfere with, restrain, or coerce employees in the exercise of" Section 7 rights. Naturally, certain business decisions will, to some degree, interfere with concerted activities by employees. . . .

. . . The AFL-CIO suggests in its *amicus* brief that Darlington's action was similar to a discriminatory lockout, which is prohibited "because [it is] designed to frustrate organizational efforts, to destroy or undermine bargaining representation, or to evade the duty to bargain." One of the purposes of the Labor Act is to prohibit the discriminatory use of economic weapons in an effort to obtain future benefits. The discriminatory lockout designed to destroy a union, like a "runaway shop," is a lever which has been used to discourage collective employee activities in the future. But a complete liquidation of a business yields no such future benefit for the employer, if the termination is bona fide. It may be motivated more by spite against the union than by business reasons, but it is not the type of discrimination which is prohibited by the Act. The personal satisfaction that such an employer may derive from standing on his beliefs or the mere possibility that other employers will follow his example are surely too remote to be considered dangers at which the labor statutes were aimed. Although employees may be prohibited from engaging in a strike under certain conditions, no one would consider it a violation of the Act for the same employees to quit their employment *en masse,* even if motivated by a desire to ruin the employer. The very permanence of such action would negate any future economic benefit to the employees. The employer's right to go out of business is no different.

We are not presented here with the case of a "runaway shop," whereby Darlington would transfer its work to another plant or open a new plant in another locality to replace its closed plant. Nor are we concerned with a shutdown where the employees, by renouncing the union, could cause the plant to reopen. Such cases would involve discriminatory employer action for the purpose of obtaining some benefit in the future from the new employees. We hold here only that when an employer closes his entire business, even if the liquidation is motivated by vindictiveness towards the union, such action is not an unfair labor practice.

While we thus agree with the Court of Appeals that viewing Darlington as an independent employer the liquidation of its business was not an unfair labor practice, we cannot accept the lower court's view that the same conclusion necessarily follows if Darlington is regarded as an integral part of the Deering Milliken enterprise.

The closing of an entire business, even though discriminatory, ends the employer-employee relationship; the force of such a closing is entirely spent as to that business when termination of the enterprise takes place. On the other hand, a discriminatory partial closing may have repercussions on what remains of the business, affording employer leverage for discouraging the free exercise of Section 7 rights among remaining employees of much the same kind as that found to exist in the "runaway shop" and "temporary closing" cases. Moreover, a possible remedy open to the Board in such a case, like the remedies available in the "runaway shop" and "temporary closing" cases, is to order reinstatement of the discharged employees in the other parts of the business. No such remedy is available when an entire business has been terminated. By analogy to those cases involving a continuing enterprise we are constrained to hold, in disagreement with the Court of Appeals, that a partial closing is an unfair labor practice under Section 8(a)(3) if motivated by a purpose to chill unionism in any of the remaining plants of the single employer and if the employer may reasonably have foreseen that such closing will likely have that effect.

. . . In these circumstances, we think the proper disposition of this case is to require that it be remanded to the Board so as to afford the Board the opportunity to make further findings on the issue of purpose and effect . . .

So ordered.

On remand, the board held that the Darlington plant was closed to deter union organizing at other plants controlled by the Millikens and therefore violated Section 8(a)(3). The decision and order were enforced by the U.S. Court of Appeals for the 4th Circuit in *Darlington Mfg. v. NLRB* (397 F.2d 760, 1968).

The Court in *Darlington* noted that a complete shutdown to avoid unionization is different from a **runaway shop,** in which the employer closes in one location and opens in another to avoid unionization. Such "runaway" conduct is in violation of Section 8(a)(3). However, the motive requirement under Section 8(a)(3) may pose a problem in determining whether the relocation of the operation violates the act. If the employer raises some legitimate business reasons for the relocation, the NLRB counsel must demonstrate that the "runaway" would not have happened except for the employees' unionizing efforts. (See the *Transportation Management* case discussed earlier in this chapter.)

As remedy for a runaway shop, the board will order that the offending employer offer the old employees positions at the new location; the employer must also pay the employees' moving or travel expenses involved. If the employer has shut down part of the operation, the board may order the employer to reopen the closed portion or to reinstate the affected employees in the remaining parts of the operation. The employees will also be awarded back pay lost because of the employer's violation. Remedies will be discussed more fully later in this chapter.

Other Unfair Labor Practices

In addition to those unfair labor practices already discussed, the NLRA prohibits several other kinds of conduct as well. Refusing to bargain in good faith, the subject of Section 8(a)(5) and Section 8(b)(3), will be discussed in Chapter 7, and union unfair practices involving picketing and secondary boycotts will be dealt with in Chapter 8. The remaining unfair labor practices are the focus of this section.

Employer Reprisals against Employees

Section 8(a)(4) prohibits an employer from discharging or otherwise discriminating against an employee who has filed charges or given testimony under the act. Because employees must be free to avail themselves of the act's procedures in order to give effect to their Section 7 rights, reprisals against employees for exercising their rights must also infringe on those rights. Violations of Section 8(a)(4) include the discharge or disciplining of an employee filling unfair practice charges and the layoff of such employees. Refusing to consider an employee for promotion because that employee filed unfair practice charges is also a violation. Section 8(a)(4) is directed only against employers; union reprisals against employees for exercising their statutory rights are dealt with under Section 8(b)(1)(a).

Excessive Union Dues or Membership Fees

Section 8(b)(5) prohibits a union from requiring excessive dues or membership fees of employees covered by a union security agreement. Because a union security agreement requires that employees join the union (or at least pay all dues and fees) in order to retain their job, some protection against union abuse or extortion must be given to the affected employees. In deciding a complaint under Section 8(b)(5), the board is directed by the act to consider "the practices and customs of labor organizations in the particular industry, and the wages currently paid to the employees affected."

Featherbedding

Section 8(b)(6) makes it unfair labor practice for a union "to cause or attempt to cause an employer to pay or deliver or agree to pay or deliver any money or other thing of value, in the nature of an extraction, for services which are not performed or not to be performed." The practice of getting paid for services *not performed* or not to be performed is known as **featherbedding.**

Although this statutory prohibition may seem straightforward, it may not be so easy to discern actual featherbedding from perfectly legal activities. For instance, a union steward may be employed to run a drill press. In reality, she may be spending much of her time assisting co-workers for the union's benefit, and may even draw additional compensation for this service from the union. If the collective bargaining agreement allows for this activity, then it is legal.

In another situation, the employer may pay for work that is not really needed—because, for instance, of technological innovations in the industry—but that through industrial custom and usage is still performed by union members. This, too, is legal under the NLRA.

In *American Newspaper Publisher's Assoc.* v. *NLRB* (345 U.S. 100, 1953), the Supreme Court held that Section 8(b)(6) is limited only to payment (or demanding of payment) for services not actually rendered. In that case, the payment by the employers for the setting of type that was not needed did not violate the act because the services, although not needed, were actually performed. Because of increasing economic competition from nonunionized firms and because of labor-saving technological developments, complaints of union featherbedding under Section 8(b)(6) are relatively rare today.

Remedies for Unfair Labor Practices

Under Section 10 of the NLRA, the NLRB is empowered to prevent any person from engaging in any unfair labor practice. Section 10(a) authorizes the board to investigate charges, issue complaints, and order hearings in unfair practice cases. If the ALJ (or the board on review) finds that an employer or union has been or is engaging in unfair labor practices, the NLRB will so state in its findings and issue a **cease and desist order** with regard to those practices. If the employer (or union) chooses not to comply with the order, the board will petition the appropriate federal court of appeals for enforcement of its order, as provided in Section 10(e).

The board may also order the offending party to take affirmative action in the wake of the unfair labor practices. For instance, when an employee has been discriminatorily discharged in violation of Section 8(a)(1), (3), or (4), the board will commonly require that the employee be reinstated, usually with back pay.

Finally, under Section 10(j) of the act, the board in its discretion may seek an injunction in a federal district court to put a halt to unfair labor practices while the parties to a dispute await its final resolution by the board. The purpose is to preserve the status quo while the adjudicative process works itself out. The board rarely uses its Section 10(j) powers. (Section 10(1) requires the board to seek a temporary restraining order from a court when a union is engaging in a secondary boycott, **hot cargo agreements,** recognitional picketing, or a jurisdictional dispute. Those unfair practices will be discussed in Chapter 8.)

When an employee has been discharged or laid off in violation of the act, the board is empowered by Section 10(c) to order reinstatement with back pay. However, Section 10(c) also states that the board shall not order reinstatement of, or back pay for, an employee who has been discharged "for cause." An employee guilty of misconduct is therefore not entitled to reinstatement. This provision is of particular interest in strike situations. Employees on an economic strike may be discharged for misconduct—violence, destruction of property, and so on. In a 1984 decision, the board held that verbal threats alone may justify discharge when they "reasonably tend to coerce or intimidate employees in the exercise of rights protected under the Act" (*Clear Pine Mouldings,* 268 N.L.R.B. No. 173, 1984). The board had held that in the case of unfair practice strikers, more severe misconduct is required to justify discharge. But in *Clear Pine Mouldings,* the board stated that unfair practice strikers are not given any privilege to engage in misconduct or violence just because they are on strike over employer unfair labor practices. In any situation physical assaults or violence will not be tolerated by the board.

When calculating back-pay awards due employees under Section 10(c), the board requires that the affected employees mitigate their damages—the board will deduct from the back-pay wages to reflect income that the employee earned or *might have* earned while the case was pending. (Welfare benefits and unemployment insurance payments are not deducted from back-pay awards by the board.) The board also requires that interest (at a rate based on the Treasury Bills index) be paid on back-pay awards under the act.

The general wording of Section 10(c) allows the board great flexibility in fashioning remedies in various unfair practice cases. Such flexibility is exemplified by the bargaining order remedy in *Gissel Packing,* considered in Chapter 5. As well, the board has required the guilty party to pay the legal fees of the complainant in cases involving severe or blatant violations. In one case involving an employer's unfair practices, which destroyed a union's majority support, the board ordered the employer to pay the union's organizing expenses for those employees.

Delay Problems in NLRB Remedies

Although the NLRB has rather broad remedial powers under the NLRA, the delays involved in pursuing the board's remedial procedures limit somewhat the effectiveness of such powers. The increasing caseload of the board has delayed the procedural process to the point at which a determined employer can dilute the effectiveness of any remedy in a particular case.

Former NLRB Chairman John Fanning, in testimony presented to the House Committee on Education and Labor in 1972, offered these projections:

> In 1957, when I was first appointed to the Board, the agency processed a total of 16,000 cases and the Board issued 353 decisions in contested unfair labor practice cases. In the current fiscal year we will receive more than 52,000 cases and we expect to issue 1,121 such decisions. In fiscal year 1978 we estimate that 57,000 cases will be filed with the agency and we expect to issue 1,242 decisions. In fiscal year 1979 the number of cases will amount to 61,000 and our published decisions will number 1,400.

Chairman Fanning's prophecies regarding the increasing workload of the board have come true. Unfortunately, for charging parties availing themselves of the NLRB's adjudicatory machinery, the board's budget and staff have not kept pace with the growth in activity. The result has been delay.

In 1976 and 1977 the lapse of time from the filing of an unfair labor practice charge in a regional office to the issuance of a complaint by the regional director was 48 to 55 days. From the issuing of the complaint to the close of the hearing consumed an additional 75 to 94 days. The ALJ typically took 89 to 111 days to announce the decision. If the ALJ's decision was challenged, the board in Washington, D.C., took from 120 to 143 days to handle the appeal. In total, a typical charge took more than a year to clear all these hurdles—and this did not include a subsequent appeal to a federal appellate court and possible Supreme Court action.

Because unfair practice cases take so long to be resolved, the affected employees are often left financially and emotionally exhausted by the process. Furthermore, the remedy, when it comes, may be too little, too late. One study found that when reinstatement was offered more than six months after the violation of the act occurred, only 5 percent of those discriminatorily discharged accepted their old jobs back.

Indeed, the final resolution of the back-pay claims of the employees in the *Darlington* case (presented earlier) did not occur until 1980—fully twenty-four years from the closing of their plant to avoid the union!

Obviously, a firm that can afford the litigation expenses may find it advantageous to delay a representation election by committing unfair practices or to refuse to bargain with a certified union in violation of Section 8(a)(5), reasoning that the lawyers' fees plus any back-pay awards will total less of a cost of doing business than will increased wages and fringes under a collective bargaining agreement.

An attempt to remedy the delay in processing unfair practice cases was made in 1978; the Labor Law Reform Bill would have expedited board review of ALJ decisions and limited judicial review. That bill was passed by the House of Representatives but was the victim of a filibuster by opponents in the Senate. Although the NLRB has attempted to reduce the backlog of cases pending (and the attendant delay in the resolution process) by increasing the workloads of ALJs and board members, the delay problem remains. That problem, with its effects upon the rights of employees under the act, poses a serious threat to the effectiveness of our national labor relations policies.

QUESTIONS

1. What is the effect of Section 7 of the NLRA? To what kinds of activity does the protection of Section 7 extend?

2. To what extent may an employer legally limit union soliciting activity by employees?

3. What constitutes a labor organization under Section 2(5) of the NLRA? To what extent may an employer offer support to a labor organization?

4. What is the relevance of motive under Section 8(a)(1)? Under Section 8(a)(3)? Explain your answer.

5. What are union security provisions? Why are closed shop agreements outlawed?

6. To what extent is an economic strike protected activity? To what extent is an unfair labor practice strike protected activity?

7. Why are employers reluctant to engage in lockouts? When may an employer use an "offensive" lockout?

8. What is featherbedding?

9. What is the effect of the delay in NLRB disposition of unfair labor practice complaints?

CASE PROBLEMS

1. The company and the union were parties to a contract that expired on October 31, 1981. Negotiations for a new contract were unsuccessful, and a strike ensued on November 2, 1981. An employee named Hudson was a member of the union at the start of the strike until November 29, when he submitted a written resignation to the union.

The union's constitution provided that union members could be disciplined for

accepting employment in any capacity in an establishment where a strike or lock-out exists as recognized under this constitution without permission. Resignation shall not relieve a member of his obligation to refrain from accepting employment at the establishment for the duration of the strike or lock-out if the resignation occurs within the period of the strike or lock-out or within fourteen days preceding its commencement.

The union notified Hudson on December 23 that he had been accused of working at the employer's facility during an authorized strike. At the trial the union found Hudson guilty as charged and imposed a $500 court-collectible fine against him. Hudson did not attend the trial and did not receive notice of the fine until the following April. In July 1983 the union filed a claim in court against Hudson to collect the fine. A trial was held in November that year, and Hudson filed an unfair labor practice charge against the union at that time.

What provision of the NLRA do you think Hudson accused the union of violating? Based on what you know concerning purposes and philosophy of the NLRA, how should the NLRB have ruled on Hudson's charge? See *IAM Local Lodge 1769,* 271 N.L.R.B. No. 146, 117 L.R.R.M. 1004 (1984).

2. The Federated Department did business under the name of Ralph's Grocery Company in California. The company entered into a collective bargaining agreement with the union. The agreement contained the following provision:

The employer agrees that any employees performing bargaining unit work set forth in this agreement, within its establishments, including employees of lessees, licensees or concessionaires shall be members of a single, overall unit, and the employer will at all times exercise and retain full control of the terms and conditions of employment within its establishments of all such employees pursuant to this agreement and shall not enter into or maintain or enforce any lease or other agreement inconsistent with the provisions hereof. Employers' obligation with respect to operators of leased departments is limited to that set forth above, provided that the employer shall furnish to the union written evidence that the operator of the leased department has assumed such obligation. Provided the employer fulfills his obligation as set forth above, employer shall not be liable for any breach of contract or failure of a leased department to abide by the wages, hours and working conditions set forth in this agreement. Seniority of employees of leased departments shall be separate from the seniority of employees of the employer and employees of other leased departments.

What is the purpose of this provision? Is it a valid "work preservation" agreement, or is it an illegal "hot cargo" agreement? If it is the latter, what provision of the NLRA might it violate? See *Food and Commercial Workers Local 1442,* 271 N.L.R.B. No. 111, 117 L.R.R.M. 1021 (1984).

3. Sandra Falcone was employed as a dental hygiene assistant. During a staff meeting Dr. Trufolo discussed some work-related problems. Falcone and a co-worker interrupted the meeting several times to disagree with Dr. Trufolo's comments. After the meeting, the office manager reprimanded Falcone and her co-worker for disrupting the meeting by questioning Dr. Trufolo and by giggling and elbowing each other. On the following Monday, Falcone presented a list of grievances to the office manager, which Falcone had discussed with co-workers. Shortly thereafter she was fired.

On these facts, did the employer commit an unfair labor practice by discharging Falcone? Upon what facts should the NLRB have determined the true motive of the discharge? See *Joseph DeRario, DMD, P.A.* 283 N.L.R.B. No. 86, 125 L.R.R.M. 1024 (1987).

4. Potter Manufacturing Co. laid off fifteen employees because of economic conditions and lack of business. The union representing the employees at Potter subsequently discovered that the employer had laid off those employees that the employer believed were most likely to honor a picket line in the event of a strike. The union filed an unfair labor practice complaint with the NLRB, alleging that the layoffs violated Sections 8(a)1 and 8(a)3. How should the NLRB rule on the complaint? See *National Fabricators,* 295 N.L.R.B. No. 126, 131 LRRM 1761 (1989).

5. Shortly after the union won a representation election in a Philadelphia-area hospital, the hospital fired the union steward, allegedly for failing to report to work. Some eighteen months after the discharge, and while the unfair labor practice charge was still in litigation, a majority of the bargaining unit presented the president of the hospital with a petition requesting that the president withdraw recognition from the union and cease bargaining with it. Pursuant to the petition, after confirming the authenticity of the signatures and that it contained a majority of the bargaining unit members, the president withdrew recognition. The union filed another unfair labor practice charge.

If the hospital was found guilty of discriminatorily discharging the union steward, can you make an argument that it committed a second unfair labor practice by withdrawing recognition from the union while the unfair labor practice charge was pending? Do you reach a different result if at the time the petition was presented the hospital had been found guilty of the discriminatory discharge but was in the process of appealing the board's decision? Any different result if the hospital had been found guilty but had immediately remedied the illegal action by reinstating the employee with back pay? See *Taylor Hospital* v. *NLRB,* unpublished opinion (3d Cir. 1985).

6. During a strike by the employees at Gillen, Inc., the picketers carried signs referring to the company and its president as "scabs." The president of Gillen, Inc., D. C. Gillen, filed a defamation suit against the union for its picketing and signs. Gillen sought $500,000 in damages, despite the fact that he could identify no business losses because of the picketing and signs. Gillen's suit was dismissed by the court as being "groundless." The union then filed an unfair labor practice complaint against Gillen, Inc., alleging that filing the suit against the picketing and signs served to coerce the employees in the exercise of their rights under Section 7. How should the NLRB rule on the complaint? Explain your answer. See *H. S. Barss Co.,* 296 N.L.R.B. No. 151, 132 LRRM 1339 (1989).

7. Rubber Workers District No. 8 began an organizing campaign at Bardcor Corporation, a small manufacturing company in Guthrie, Kentucky, during the summer of 1981. Shortly after the campaign began, the president of the corporation began taking pictures of workers in the plant. An employee named Maxine Dukes asked supervisor Mike Loreille why the pictures were being taken. Loreille responded that the president wanted something to remember the employees by after he fired them for union activity.

A majority of the company's thirty-seven employees signed union authorization cards. The next day the employer discharged eight workers, seven of whom had signed cards. After the discharge, the union filed a series of unfair labor practice charges. The company was able to justify the discharges for economic reasons and argued that the picture-taking incident and Loreille's comment were nothing but jokes.

What provision of the NLRA did the company allegedly violate by the picture-taking incident and the supervisor's comment to Ms. Dukes? Try to formulate an argument for and against finding a violation of the act by the employer in one or both of these actions. Could the picture-taking incident alone violate the act? Did the supervisor's comment alone violate the act? See *Bardcor Corporation,* 270 N.L.R.B. No. 157 (1984).

8. Employees of New Hope Industries' Donaldsonville, Louisiana, plant went on strike to protest the company's failure to pay them on time and to force assurance that they would be paid on time in the future. Emil Thiac, the sole owner of this manufacturer of children's clothing, threatened to discharge the employees in the event of a strike, and subsequently did fire them when they struck. Thiac subsequently informed an NLRB attorney investigating the situation that he would close down the plant rather than reinstate or give back pay to the discharged strikers. He also informed the attorney that efforts to obtain back pay could be futile because the company's money was tied up in trust funds for his children. Thiac ultimately closed the plant and refused to give the NLRB his home address or provide the board with any means to communicate with him.

Based on these facts, do you think the board has any way of preventing Thiac from dissipating or hiding the company's assets while the unfair labor practice charges are pending? See *Norton* v. *New Hope Industries, Inc.,* unpublished opinion (U.S. Dist. Ct., M.D. La., 1985).

9. The cases consolidated in this proceeding arose out of a strike following the 1983 expiration of the Carpenters Union and Laborers Union master labor agreements in the northern California construction industry and involved alleged illegal picketing and related acts at dozens of construction sites. Two regional offices issued complaints in 178 cases, which were consolidated for hearing. Before the hearing, the regions and the respondent unions negotiated a comprehensive settlement agreement resolving all 178 cases. The settlement agreement before us now is a formal settlement stipulation providing for judicially enforced board orders resolving ninety of these cases against ten of the respondents who were alleged to have committed the most serious and numerous violations, as well as resolving ten other board cases pending at various stages that involved common respondents and similar allegations.

The general counsel, all ten respondents, and all but one of the charging parties favor approval of this settlement. Out of forty charging parties, thirty-two have indicated in writing that they have no objections to the settlement. Only one law firm, which represented eight charging parties, has since asked to withdraw its charge. Further, the law firm has now stated that all but one of its clients are prepared to enter into this settlement agreement.

What policy considerations argue for or against board approval of a settlement in this case? See *Carpenters 46 Northern California Counties Conference Board,* 274 N.L.R.B. No. 181, 118 L.R.R.M. 1588 (1985).

10. Lawson runs 700 convenience food stores in Ohio, Indiana, Pennsylvania, and Michigan. Following the murder of an employee in a Lawson store in February 1981, the United Food & Commercial Workers Union (UFCW) began to organize Lawson sales assistants in northeastern Ohio. Some employees refused to report to work for two days after the murder as a protest against lax security measures.

In response to the complaints, Lawson installed outdoor lights at its stores, adopted a policy that no one would be required to work alone at night, and began paying overtime for work done after closing hours.

Following the initiation of the UFCW campaign, Lawson placed no-solicitation signs in all its stores and told employees that anyone violating the no-solicitation rule would be subject to discharge.

When the UFCW filed a representation petition with the NLRB on April 24, seeking an election, employees were told that the stores would close if they voted in the union. One store manager told employees not to discuss the union at work because Lawson planned to install listening devices in the stores.

What, if any, unfair labor practices has Lawson committed? See *The Lawson Co.* v. *NLRB,* 753 F.2d 471 (6th Cir. 1985).

CHAPTER 7

Collective Bargaining: The Duty to Bargain in Good Faith

EMPLOYEES JOIN UNIONS IN order to gain some influence over their working conditions and wages; that influence is achieved through the process called collective bargaining. Section 8(d) of the National Labor Relations Act (NLRA) defines collective bargaining as

> [t]he performance of the mutual obligation of the employer and the representative of the employees to meet at reasonable times and confer in good faith with respect to wages, hours, and other terms and conditions of employment, or the negotiation of an agreement or any question arising thereunder. . . .

This process of meeting and discussing working conditions is actually a highly stylized and heavily regulated form of economic conflict. Within the limits of conduct spelled out by the National Labor Relations Board (NLRB) under the NLRA, the parties exert pressure on each other in order to force some concession or agreement. The union's economic pressure comes from its ability to withhold the services of its members—a strike. The employer's bargaining pressure comes from its potential to lock out the employees or to permanently replace striking workers. The NLRB and the courts, through their interpretation and administration of the NLRA, have limited the kinds of pressure either side may exert and how such pressure may be exerted. This chapter will examine the collective bargaining process and the legal limits placed on that process.

The Duty to Bargain

An employer is required to recognize a union as the exclusive bargaining representative of its employees when a majority of those employees support the union. The union may demonstrate its majority support either through signed authorization cards or by winning a representation election. Once aware of the union's majority support, the employer must recognize and bargain with the union according to the process spelled out in Section 8(d). Section 8(a)(5) makes it an unfair labor practice for an employer to refuse to bargain with the representative of its employees, and Section 8(b)(3) makes it an unfair practice for a union representing a group of employees to refuse to bargain with their employer.

Although the NLRA imposes an obligation to bargain collectively upon both employer and union, it does not control the results of the bargaining process. Section 8(d) makes it clear that the obligation to bargain "does not compel either party to agree to a proposal or require the making of a concession." The act thus reflects an ambivalence regarding the duty to bargain in good faith. The parties, in order to promote industrial relations harmony, are required to come together and negotiate; but, in deference to the principle of freedom of contract, they are not required to reach an agreement. This tension between the goal of promoting industrial peace and the principle of freedom of contract underlies the various NLRB and court decisions dealing with the duty to bargain. The accommodation of these conflicting ideas makes the area a difficult and interesting aspect of labor relations law.

If the parties are required to negotiate, yet are not required to reach an agreement or even to make a concession, how can the board determine whether either side is bargaining in good faith? Section 8(d) requires that the parties meet at reasonable times to discuss wages, hours, and terms and conditions of employment; Section 8(d) also requires that any agreement reached must be put in writing if either party so requests. But Section 8(d) does not speak to bargaining tactics. Is either side free to insist upon its proposal as a "take-it-or-leave-it" proposition? Can either side refuse to make any proposal? These questions must be addressed in determining what constitutes bargaining in good faith.

Bargaining in Good Faith

Section 8(a)(5) requires that the employer bargain with a union that is the representative of its employees according to Section 9(a). Section 9(a) states that a union that has the support of a majority of employees in a bargaining unit becomes the exclusive bargaining representative of *all* employees in the unit. That section also states that the employer may address the grievances of individual employees as long as such adjustment is done in a manner consistent with the collective agreement and the union has been given an opportunity to be present at such adjustment. That provision raises the question of how far the employer can go in dealing with individuals rather than the union. In *J. I. Case Co. v. NLRB* (321 U.S. 332, 1944), the Supreme Court held that contracts of employment made with individual employees were not impediments to negotiating a collective agreement with the union. J. I. Case had made it a practice to sign yearly contracts of employment with its employees. When the union, which won a representation election, requested bargaining over working conditions, the company refused. The employer argued that the individual contracts covered those issues and no bargaining could take place until those individual contracts had expired. The Supreme Court held that the individual contracts must give way to allow the negotiation of a collective agreement. Once the union is certified as the exclusive bargaining representative of the employees, the employer cannot deal with the individual employees in a manner inconsistent with the union's status as exclusive representative. To allow individual contracts of employment to prevent collective bargaining would be to undercut the union's position. Therefore, the individual contracts must give way to the union's collective negotiations.

What about the situation in which individual employees attempt to discuss their grievances with the employer in a manner inconsistent with the union's role as exclusive representative? How far does the Section 9(a) proviso go to allow such discussion? That question is addressed in the following Supreme Court decision.

EMPORIUM CAPWELL CO. v. WESTERN ADDITION COMMUNITY ORGANIZATION

420 U.S. 50 (Supreme Court of the United States, 1975)

[Emporium Capwell Co. operates a department store in San Francisco; the company had a collective bargaining agreement with the Dept. Store Employees Union. The agreement, among other things, included a prohibition of employment discrimination by reason of race, color, religion, national origin, age, or sex. The agreement also set up a grievance and arbitration process to resolve any claimed violation of the agreement, including a violation of the nondiscrimination clause.]

MARSHALL, J.

This litigation presents the question whether, in light of the national policy against racial discrimination in employment, the National Labor Relations Act protects concerted activity by a group of minority employees to bargain with their employer over issues of employment discrimination. The National Labor Relations Board held that the employees could not circumvent their elected representative to engage in such bargaining. The Court of Appeals for the District of Columbia Circuit reversed, holding that in certain circumstances the activity would be protected. . . .

On April 3, 1968, a group of Company employees covered by the agreement met with the Secretary-Treasurer of the Union, Walter Johnson, to present a list of grievances including a claim that the Company was discriminating on the basis of race in making assignments and promotions. The Union official agreed to take certain of the grievances and to investigate the charge of racial discrimination. He appointed an investigating committee and prepared a report on the employees' grievances, which he submitted to the

Retailer's Council and which the Council in turn referred to the Company. The report described "the possibility of racial discrimination" as perhaps the most important issue raised by the employees and termed the situation at the Company as potentially explosive if corrective action were not taken. It offered as an example of the problem the Company's failure to promote a Negro stock employee regarded by other employees as an outstanding candidate but a victim of racial discrimination.

Shortly after receiving the report, the Company's labor relations director met with Union representatives and agreed to "look into the matter" of discrimination and see what needed to be done. Apparently unsatisfied with these representations, the Union held a meeting in September attended by Union officials, Company employees, and representatives of the California Fair Employment Practices Committee (FEPC) and the local antipoverty agency. The Secretary-Treasurer of the Union announced that the Union had concluded that the Company was discriminating, and that it would process every such grievance through to arbitration if necessary. Testimony about the Company's practices was taken and transcribed by a court reporter, and the next day the Union notified the Company of its formal charge and demanded that the joint union-management Adjustment Board be convened "to hear the entire case."

At the September meeting some of the Company's employees had expressed their view that the contract procedures were inadequate to handle a systemic grievance of this sort; they suggested that the Union instead begin picketing the store in protest. Johnson explained that the collective agreement bound the Union to its processes and expressed his view that successful grievants would be helping not only themselves but all others who might be the victims of invidious discrimination as well. The FEPC and antipoverty agency representatives offered the same advice.

Nonetheless, when the Adjustment Board meeting convened on October 16, James Joseph Hollins, Tom Hawkins, and two other employees whose testimony the Union had intended to elicit refused to participate in the grievance procedure. Instead, Hollins read a statement objecting to reliance on correction of individual inequities as an approach to the problem of discrimination at the store and demanding that the president of the Company meet with the four protestants to work out a broader agreement for dealing with the issue as they saw it. The four employees then walked out of the hearing.

Hollins attempted to discuss the question of racial discrimination with the Company president shortly after the incidents of October 16. The president refused to be drawn into such a discussion but suggested to Hollins that he see the personnel director about the matter. Hollins, who had spoken to the personnel director before, made no effort to do so again. Rather, he and Hawkins and several other dissident employees held a press conference on October 22 at which they denounced the store's employment policy as racist, reiterated their desire to deal directly with "the top management" of the Company over minority employment conditions, and announced their intention to picket and institute a boycott of the store. On Saturday, November 2, Hollins, Hawkins, and at least two other employees picketed the store throughout the day and distributed at the entrance handbills urging consumers not to patronize the store. Johnson encountered the picketing employees, again urged them to rely on the grievance process, and warned that they might be fired for their activities. The picketers, however, were not dissuaded, and they continued to press their demand to deal directly with the Company president.

On November 7, Hollins and Hawkins were given written warnings that a repetition of the picketing or public statements about the Company could lead to their discharge. When the conduct was repeated the following Saturday, the two employees were fired.

Respondent Western Addition Community Organization, a local civil rights association of which Hollins and Hawkins were members, filed a charge against the Company with the National Labor Relations Board. After a hearing the NLRB Trial Examiner found that the discharged employees had believed in good faith that the Company was discriminating against minority employees, and that they had resorted to concerted activity on the basis of that belief. He concluded, however, that their activity was not protected by Section 7 of the Act and that their discharges did not, therefore, violate Section 8(a)(1).

The Board, after oral argument, adopted the findings and conclusions of its Trial Examiner and dismissed the complaint. Among the findings adopted by the Board was that the discharged employees' course of conduct

> . . . was no mere presentation of a grievance, but nothing short of a demand that the [Company] bargain with the picketing employees for the entire group of minority employees.

Central to the policy of fostering collective bargaining, where the employees elect that course, is the principle of majority rule. If the majority of a unit chooses union representation, the NLRA permits them to bargain with their employer to make union membership a condition of employment, thereby imposing their choice upon the minority. . . . In establishing a regime of majority rule, Congress sought to secure to all members of the unit the benefits of their collective strength and bargaining power, in full awareness that the superior strength of some individuals or groups might be subordinated to the interest of the majority.

In vesting the representatives of the majority with this broad power Congress did not, of course, authorize a tyranny of the majority over minority interests. First, it confined the exercise of these powers to the context of a "unit appropriate for the purposes of collective bargaining," i.e., a group of employees with a sufficient commonality of circumstances to ensure against the submergence of a minority with distinctively different interests in the terms and conditions of their employment. Second, it undertook in the 1959 Landrum-Griffin amendments, to assure that minority voices are heard as they are in the functioning of a democratic institution. Third, we have held, by the very nature of the exclusive bargaining representative's status as representative of all unit employees, Congress implicitly imposed upon it a duty fairly and in good faith to represent the interests of minorities within the unit. And the Board has taken the position that a union's refusal to process grievances against racial discrimination, in violation of that duty, is an unfair labor practice. Indeed, the Board had ordered a union implicated by a collective bargaining agreement in discrimination with an employer to propose specific contractual provisions to prohibit racial discrimination.

Against this background of long and consistent adherence to the principle of exclusive representation tempered by safeguards for the protection of minority interests, respondent urges this Court to fashion a limited exception to that principle: employees who seek to bargain separately with their employer as to the elimination of racially discriminatory employment practices peculiarly affecting them, should be free from the constraints of the exclusivity principle of Section 9(a). Essentially because established procedures under Title VII or as in this case, a grievance machinery, are too time-consuming, the national labor policy against discrimination requires this exception, respondent argues, and its adoption would not unduly compromise the legitimate interests of either unions or employers.

Plainly, national labor policy embodies the principles of nondiscrimination as a matter of highest priority, and it is a common-place that we must construe the NLRA in light of the broad national labor policy of which it is a part. These general principles do not aid respondent, however, as it is far from clear that separate bargaining is necessary to help eliminate discrimination. Indeed, as the facts of this case demonstrate, the proposed remedy might have just the opposite effect. The collective bargaining agreement in this case prohibited without qualification all manner of invidious discrimination and made any claimed violation a grievable issue. The grievance procedure is directed precisely at determining whether discrimination has occurred. That orderly determination, if affirmative, could lead to an arbitral award enforceable in court. Nor is there any reason to believe that the processing of grievances is inherently limited to the correction of individual cases of discrimination. Quite apart from the essentially contractual question of whether the Union could grieve against a "pattern or practice" it deems inconsistent with the nondiscrimination clause of the contract, one would hardly expect an employer to continue in effect an employment practice that routinely results in adverse arbitral decisions.

The decision by a handful of employees to bypass the grievance procedure in favor of attempting to bargain with their employer, by contrast, may or may not be predicated upon the actual existence of discrimination. An employer confronted with bargaining demands from each of several minority groups would not necessarily, or even probably, be able to agree to remedial steps satisfactory to all at once. Competing claims on the employer's ability to accommodate each group's demands, e.g., for reassignments and promotions to a limited number of positions, could only set one group against the other even if it is not the employer's intention to divide and overcome them. Having divided themselves, the minority employees will not be in position to advance their cause unless it be by recourse seriatim to economic coercion, which can only have the effect of further dividing them along racial or other lines. Nor is the situation materially different where, as apparently happened here, self-designated representatives purport to speak for all groups that might consider themselves to be victims of discrimination. Even if in actual bargaining the various groups

did not perceive their interests as divergent and further subdivide themselves, the employer would be bound to bargain with them in a field largely preempted by the current collective bargaining agreement with the elected bargaining representatives. . . .

What has been said here in evaluating respondent's claim that the policy against discrimination requires Section 7 protection for concerted efforts at minority bargaining has obvious implications for the related claim that legitimate employer and union interests would not be unduly compromised thereby. The court below minimized the impact on the Union in this case by noting that it was not working at cross-purposes with the dissidents, and that indeed it could not do so consistent with its duty of fair representation and perhaps its obligations under Title VII. As to the Company, its obligations under Title VII are cited for the proposition that it could have no legitimate objection to bargaining with the dissidents in order to achieve full compliance with that law.

This argument confuses the employees' substantive right to be free of racial discrimination with the procedures available under the NLRA for securing these rights. Whether they are thought to depend upon Title VII or have an independent source in the NLRA, they cannot be pursued at the expense of the orderly collective bargaining process contemplated by the NLRA. The elimination of discrimination and its vestiges is an appropriate subject of bargaining, and an employer may have no objection to incorporating into a collective agreement the substance of his obligation not to discriminate in personnel decisions; the Company here has done as much, making any claimed dereliction a matter subject to the grievance-arbitration machinery as well as to the processes of Title VII. But that does not mean that he may not have strong and legitimate objections to bargaining on several fronts over the implementation of the right to be free of discrimination for some of the reasons set forth above. Similarly, while a union cannot lawfully bargain for the establishment or continuation of discriminatory practices, it has legitimate interest in presenting a united front on this as on other issues and in not seeing its strength dissipated and its stature denigrated by subgroups within the unit separately pursuing what they see as separate interests. When union and employer are not responsive to their legal obligations, the bargain they have struck must yield "pro tanto" to the law, whether by means of conciliation through the offices of the EEOC, or by means of federal court enforcement at the instance of either that agency or the party claiming to be aggrieved.

Accordingly, we think neither aspect of respondent's contention in support of a right to short-circuit orderly, established processes for eliminating discrimination in employment is well-founded. The policy of industrial self-determination as expressed in Section 7 does not require fragmentation of the bargaining unit along racial or other lines in order to consist with the national labor policy against discrimination. And in the face of such fragmentation, whatever its effect on discriminatory practices, the bargaining process that the principle of exclusive representation is meant to lubricate could not endure unhampered. . . .

Respondent objects that reliance on the remedies pro-

vided by Title VII is inadequate effectively to secure the rights conferred by Title VII. . . .

Whatever its factual merit, this argument is properly addressed to the Congress and not to this Court or the NLRB. In order to hold that employer conduct violates Section 8(a)(1) of the NLRA because it violates Section 704(a) of Title VII, we would have to override a host of consciously made decisions well within the exclusive competence of the Legislature. This obviously, we cannot do. **Reversed.**

Although the employer in *J.I. Case* and the employees in *Emporium Capwell* were held to have acted improperly, there is some room for individual discussions of working conditions and grievances. As well, where the collective agreement permits individual negotiation, an employer may discuss such matters with individual employees. Examples of such agreements are the collective agreements covering professional baseball and football players; the collective agreement sets minimum levels of conditions and compensation, while allowing the athletes to negotiate salary and other compensation on an individual basis.

Procedural Requirements of the Duty to Bargain in Good Faith. A union or employer seeking to bargain with the other party must notify that other party of its desire to bargain at least sixty days prior to the expiration of the existing collective agreement, or if no agreement is in effect, sixty days prior to the date it proposes the agreement to go into effect. Section 8(d) requires that such notice must be given at the proper time; failure to do so may make any strike by the union or lockout by the employer an unfair labor practice. Section 8(d) also requires that the parties must continue in effect any existing collective agreement for sixty days from the giving of the notice to bargain, or until the agreement expires, whichever occurs later. Strikes or lockouts are prohibited during this sixty-day "cooling off" period; employees who go on an economic strike during this period lose their status as "employees" and the protections of the act. Therefore, if the parties have given the notice to bargain later than sixty days prior to the expiration of the contract, they must wait the full sixty days to go on strike or lockout, even if the old agreement has already expired.

When negotiations result in matters in dispute, the party seeking contract termination must notify the Federal Mediation and Conciliation Service (FMCS) and the appropriate state mediation agency within thirty days from giving the notice to bargain. Neither side may resort to a strike or lockout until thirty days after the FMCS and state agency have been notified.

The NLRA provides for longer notice periods when the collective bargaining involves the employees of a health care institution. In that case, the parties must give notice to bargain at least ninety days prior to the expiration of the agreement; no strike or lockout can take place for at least ninety days from the giving of the notice, or the expiration of the agreement—whichever is later. As well, the FMCS and state agency must be notified sixty days prior to the termination of the agreement. Lastly, Section 8(g) requires that a labor organization seeking to picket or strike against a health care institution must give both the employer and the FMCS written notice of its intention to strike or picket at least ten days prior to taking such action. Why should a labor organization be required to give health care institutions advance notice of any strike or picketing?

As noted, Section 8(d) prohibits any strike or lockout during the notice period. Employees who go on strike during that period are deprived of the protection of the act. In *Mastro Plastics Co.* v. *NLRB* (350 U.S. 270, 1956), the Supreme Court held that the prohibition applied only to economic strikes—strikes designed to pressure the employer to "terminate or modify" the collective agreement. Unfair labor practice strikes, which are called to protest the employer's violation of the NLRA, are not covered by the Section 8(d) prohibition. Therefore the employees in *Mastro Plastics,* who went on strike during the sixty-day "cooling off" period to protest the illegal firing of an employee, were not in violation of Section 8(d) and were not deprived of the protection of the act.

Creation of the Duty to Bargain.   As discussed above, the duty to bargain arises when the union gets the support of a majority of the employees in a bargaining unit. When a union is certified as the winner of a representation election, the employer is required by Section 8(a)(5) to bargain with it. (An employer with knowledge of a union's majority support, independent of the union's claim of such support, must also recognize and bargain with the union without resort to an election.)

When an employer is approached by two unions, each claiming to represent a majority of the employees, how should the employer respond? One way would be to refuse to recognize either union (provided, of course, that the employer had no independent knowledge of either union's majority support) and to insist on an election. Could the employer recognize voluntarily one of the two unions claiming to represent the employees? That issue is dealt with in the following NLRB decision.

BRUCKNER NURSING HOME

262 N.L.R.B. 955 (N.L.R.B., 1982)

In the spring of 1974, Local 144, Hotel, Hospital, Nursing Home & Allied Health Services Union, S.E.I.U., AFL-CIO (hereinafter referred to as Local 144), and Local 1115, Joint Board, Nursing Home and Hospital Employees Division (hereinafter referred to as Local 1115), began organizational activities at Respondent Employer's nursing home facility in New York, New York. In early September 1974, Local 144 notified the Employer that it possessed a majority

of signed authorization cards, and a date was set for a card count. Shortly thereafter, Local 1115 sent a mailgram to the Employer which stated that it was engaged in organizational activity among the Employer's employees and that the Employer should not extend recognition to any other labor organization.

The card count was conducted on September 27, 1974, by an extension specialist of the New York State School of Industrial and Labor Relations. Thereafter, the extension specialist informed the Employer that Local 144 represented a majority of its employees.

Negotiations between Local 144 and the Employer commenced shortly thereafter and culminated in the execution of a collective-bargaining agreement on December 18, 1974. Local 1115 then filed, on March 7, 1975, the charges at issue in this proceeding.

On September 27, 1974, the date of the card check, Respondent Employer had approximately 125 people in its employ. At that time, Local 1115 had two authorization cards, while Local 144 possessed signed authorization cards from approximately 80 to 90 percent of the Employer's employees. No representation petition was filed on behalf of either labor organization in this proceeding.

With respect to the foregoing facts, the Administrative Law Judge found that Local 1115 possessed a "colorable claim" to representation herein based on its continuous efforts to obtain employee support during the fall of 1974, and the fact that it had actually obtained a few authorization cards. The Administrative Law Judge concluded that the Employer "by executing a collective-bargaining agreement . . . in the face of a real question concerning representation which had not been settled [by] the special procedures of the Act" had rendered unlawful assistance to Local 144 in violation of Section 8(a)(2) of the Act. In what has become a standard remedy in this type of setting, the Administrative Law Judge ordered that the Employer cease giving effect to the collective-bargaining agreement with Local 144, and further ordered the Employer to withdraw and withhold recognition from Local 144 unless and until it has been certified in a Board-conducted election.

[W]e undertake a reevaluation of what has come to be known as the *Midwest Piping* doctrine, a rule which, in one form or another, has been part of Board law for over 35 years. In this case, we will focus our attention on initial organizing situations involving two or more rival labor organizations.

As originally formulated, the "*Midwest Piping* doctrine" was an attempt by the Board to insure that, in a rival union situation, an employer would not render "aid" to one of two or more unions competing for exclusive bargaining representative status through a grant of recognition in advance of a Board-conducted election. In *Midwest Piping* itself, the Board found that an employer gave unlawful assistance to a labor organization when the employer recognized one of two competing labor organizations, both of which had filed representation petitions, and both of which had campaigned extensively for the mantle of exclusive bargaining representative. In the context of that case, we held that the employer had arrogated the resolution of the representation issue, and that a Board-conducted election was the "best" means of ascertaining the true desires of employees. We further stated that employers presented with rival claims from competing unions (in the form of representation petitions) should follow a course of strict neutrality with respect to the competing unions until such time as the "real question concerning representation" had been resolved through the mechanism of a Board-conducted election.

In cases that followed soon thereafter, we applied the principle that the duty of strict employer neutrality and the necessity of a Board-conducted election were operative only when a representation petition had been filed with the Board, and further noted that the "doctrine" should be "strictly construed" and "sparingly applied."

In subsequent decisions, the Board removed the requirement that a representation petition actually be filed, stating that a petition was not a prerequisite to the finding of a "real" or "genuine" question concerning representation. The removal of the prerequisite of a petition stemmed in part from the need to recognize the existence of a rival union contest even before formal invocation of the Board's election procedures so as to insure that those procedures would be available. If more than one union enjoyed at least some employee support, we perceived a Board-conducted election as the best way, often the only way, to guarantee employees a fair and free opportunity to make the final choice of a bargaining representative. Although often unstated, another reason for removing the petition requirement in a rival union setting was to preclude the serious possibility of employer abuse where no petition had been filed. Often we were faced with the scenario of a union presenting a substantial showing of majority support based on cards which the employer would reject while invariably professing a preference for the Board's election procedures. A short time thereafter, the employer would recognize another union and, typically, sign a contract in a remarkable accelerated bargaining process. This scenario was played once too often, so we determined that in order to protect the democratic right of employees to their own collective-bargaining representative, and to prevent employer abuse, we would require an election whenever there were two or more unions on the scene, and each had some support or organizational interest in the unit sought. We defined the "interest" that a union must have to trigger the operation of the *Midwest Piping* doctrine as a "colorable claim," a claim that was not "clearly unsupportable," or a claim that was not "naked." Thus, we held that the original *Midwest Piping* requirement of strict employer neutrality would be operative where a question concerning representation existed even though no petition had been filed unless and until a Board-conducted election had been held and the results certified. . . .

Extending the *Midwest Piping* doctrine frequently allowed a minority union possessing a few cards to forestall the recognition of a majority union in an effort either to buy time to gather more support for itself or simply to frustrate its rivals. For instance, here, where one union enjoys overwhelming support and the other has but a few cards, collective bargaining would be delayed until the 8(a)(2) charge has been resolved and the results of a later Board-conducted election have been certified. . . .

We have reviewed the Board's experience with *Midwest Piping* with a desire to accommodate the view of the courts of appeals in light of our statutory mandate to protect employees' freedom to select their bargaining representatives and in harmony with our statutory mandate to encourage collective bargaining. Having identified the difficult problems in this area, it is the Board's task to reconcile the various interests of policy and law involved in fashioning a rule which will give, as far as possible, equal consideration to each of those interests in the light of industrial reality. We have concluded that this task has not been accomplished through the modified *Midwest Piping* doctrine. Accordingly, we will no longer find 8(a)(2) violations in rival union, initial organizing situations when an employer recognizes a labor organization which represents an uncoerced, unassisted majority, before a valid petition for an election has been filed with the Board. However, once notified of a valid petition, an employer must refrain from recognizing any of the rival unions. Of course, we will continue to process timely filed petitions and to conduct elections in the most expeditious manner possible, following our normal procedures with respect to intervention and placement of parties on the ballot.

Making the filing of a valid petition the operative event for the imposition of strict employer neutrality in rival union, initial organizing situations will establish a clearly defined rule of conduct and encourage both employee free choice and industrial stability. Where one of several rival labor organizations cannot command the support of even 30 percent of the unit, it will no longer be permitted to forestall an employer's recognition of another labor organization which represents an uncoerced majority of employees and thereby frustrate the establishment of a collective-bargaining relationship. Likewise, an employer will no longer have to guess whether a real question concerning representation has been raised but will be able to recognize a labor organization unless it has received notice of a properly filed petition.

On the other hand, where a labor organization has filed a petition, both the Act and our administrative experience dictate the need for resolution of the representation issue through a Board election rather than through employer recognition. When a union has demonstrated substantial support by filing a valid petition, an active contest exists for the employees' allegiance. This contest takes on special significance where rival unions are involved since there an employer's grant of recognition may unduly influence or effectively end a contest between labor organizations. Without questioning the reliability of authorization cards or unduly exalting election procedure, we believe the proper balance will be struck by prohibiting an employer from recognizing any of the competing unions for the limited period during which a representation petition is in process even though one or more of the unions may present a valid card majority.

In addition to avoiding potential undue influence by an employer, our new approach provides a satisfactory answer to problems created by execution of dual authorization cards. It is our experience that employees confronted by solicitations from rival unions will frequently sign authorization cards for more than one union. Dual cards reflect the competing organizational campaigns. They may indicate shifting employee sentiments or employee desire to be represented by either of two rival unions. In this situation, authorization cards are less reliable as indications of employee preference. When a petition supported by a 30 percent showing of interest has been filed by one union, the reliability of a rival's expression of a card majority is sufficiently doubtful to require resolution of the competing claims through the Board's election process. . . .

The *Bruckner Nursing Home* decision dealt with a situation in which the employees were not previously represented by a union. When an incumbent union's status has been challenged by a rival union that has petitioned for a representation election, is the employer still required to negotiate with the incumbent union? In *RCA Del Caribe* (262 N.L.R.B. 963, 1983), the board held that the mere filing of a representation petition by an outside, challenging union will no longer require or permit an employer to withdraw from bargaining or executing a contract with an incumbent union. Under this rule ... an employer will violate Section 8(a)(5) by withdrawing from bargaining based solely on the fact that a petition has been filed by an outside union. . . .

If the incumbent prevails in the election held, any contract executed with the incumbent will be valid and binding. If the challenging union prevails, however, any contract executed with the incumbent will be null and void. . . .

The *Bruckner Nursing Home* and *RCA Del Caribe* decisions were departures from prior board decisions, which required that an employer stay neutral in the event of rival organizing campaigns, or when the incumbent union faced a petition filed by a challenging union. Which approach do you think is more likely to protect the desires of the individual employees? Do *Buckner Nursing Home* and *RCA Del Caribe* make it more difficult to unseat an incumbent union?

When craft employees who had previously been included in a larger bargaining unit vote to be represented by a craft union, and a smaller craft bargaining unit is severed from the larger one, what is the effect of the agreement covering the larger unit? In *American Seating Co.* (106 N.L.R.B. 250, 1953), the NLRB held that the old agreement no longer applies to the newly severed bargaining unit, and the old agreement does not prevent the employer from negotiating with the craft union on behalf of the new bargaining unit. Is this decision surprising? (Recall the *J.I. Case* decision discussed earlier and reexamine the wording of Section 8(d) in its entirety.)

Duration of the Duty to Bargain. When the union is certified as bargaining representative after winning an election, the NLRB requires that the employer recognize and bargain with the union for at least a year from certification, regardless of any doubts the employer may have about the union's continued majority support. This one-year period applies only when no collective agreement has been made. When an agreement exists, the employer must bargain with the union for the term of the agreement. Unfair labor practices committed by the employer, such as refusal to bargain in good faith, may have the effect of extending the one-year period, as the board held in *Mar-Jac Poultry* (136 N.L.R.B. 785, 1962).

When a union acquires bargaining rights by voluntary recognition rather than certification, the employer is required to recognize and bargain with the union only for "a reasonable period of time" if no agreement is in effect. What constitutes a reasonable period of time depends on the circumstances in each case. If an agreement has been reached after the voluntary recognition, then the employer must bargain with the union for the duration of the agreement.

After the one-year period or a reasonable period of time—whichever is appropriate—has expired, and no collective agreement is in effect, the employer may refuse to bargain with the union if the employer has a good-faith doubt about the union's continued majority support. This good-faith doubt must have a reasonable basis in fact. The board held in *NLRB v. Flex Plastics* (762 F.2d 272, 6th Cir. 1984) that filing a decertification petition alone does not suffice to establish a good-faith doubt about the union's majority support. When the employer can establish such a reasonable factual basis for good-faith doubts about the union's majority status, it may refuse to negotiate with the union. The board, in order to find a violation of

Section 8(a)(5), must then prove that the union in fact represented a majority of the employees on the date the employer refused to bargain.

What happens if the union employees go on strike and are permanently replaced by the employer—must the employer continue to recognize and bargain with the union? In *Pioneer Flour Mills* (174 N.L.R.B. 1209, 1969), the NLRB held that economic strikers must be considered members of the bargaining unit for the purpose of determining whether the union has majority support for the first twelve months of the strike. After twelve months, if they have been permanently replaced, the strikers need not be considered part of the bargaining unit by the employer. Unfair labor practice strikers may not be permanently replaced and must be considered members of the bargaining unit.

The following case considers the effects of the rules regarding doubts about the union's continued majority support and the status of replaced strikers.

NLRB v. CURTIN MATHESON SCIENTIFIC, INC.

494 U.S. 775 (Supreme Court of the United States, 1990)

MARSHALL, J.

This case presents the question whether the National Labor Relations Board, in evaluating an employer's claim that it had a reasonable basis for doubting a union's majority support, *must* presume that striker replacements oppose the union. . . .

Upon certification by the NLRB as the exclusive bargaining agent for a unit of employees, a union enjoys an irrebuttable presumption of majority support for one year. During that time, an employer's refusal to bargain with the union is *per se* an unfair labor practice under Sections 8(a)(1) and 8(a)(5) of the National Labor Relations Act. After the first year, the presumption continues but is rebuttable. Under the Board's longstanding approach, an employer may rebut that presumption by showing that, at the time of the refusal to bargain, either (1) the union did not in *fact* enjoy majority support, or (2) the employer had a "good faith" doubt, founded on a sufficient objective basis, of the union's majority support. The question presented in this case is whether the Board must, in determining whether an employer has presented sufficient objective evidence of a good-faith doubt, presume that striker replacements oppose the union.

The Board has long presumed that new employees hired in nonstrike circumstances support the incumbent union in the same proportion as the employees they replace. The Board's approach to evaluating the union sentiments of employees hired to replace strikers, however, has not been so consistent. Initially, the Board appeared to assume that replacements did not support the union. . . .

A 1974 decision, *Peoples Gas Systems, Inc.,* signalled a shift in the Board's approach. The Board recognized that "it is of course possible that the replacements, who had chosen not to engage in the strike activity, might nevertheless have favored union representation." Still, the Board held that "it was not unreasonable for [the employer] to infer that the degree of union support among these employees who had chosen to ignore a union-sponsored picket line might well be somewhat weaker than the support offered by those who had vigorously engaged in concerted activity on behalf o[f] union-sponsored objectives."

A year later . . . the Board reversed course completely, stating that striker replacements, like new employees generally, are presumed to *support* the union in the same ratio as the strikers they replaced. . . .

In 1987, after several Courts of Appeals rejected the Board's approach, the Board determined that no universal generalizations could be made about replacements' union sentiments that would justify a presumption either of support for or of opposition to the union. On the one hand, the Board found that the prounion presumption lacked empirical foundation because "incumbent unions and strikers sometimes have shown hostility toward the permanent replacements" and "replacements are typically aware of the union's primary concern for the striker's welfare, rather than that of the replacements." On the other hand, the Board found that an antiunion presumption was "equally unsupportable" factually. The Board observed that a striker replacement "may be forced to work for financial reasons, or may disapprove of the strike in question but still desire union representation and would support other union initiatives." Moreover, the Board found as a matter of policy that adoption of an antiunion presumption would "substantially impair the employees' right to strike by adding to the risk of replacement the risk of loss of the bargaining representative as soon as replacements equal in number to the strikers are willing to cross the picket line." Accordingly, the Board held that it would not apply any presumption regarding striker replacements' union sentiments, but would determine their views on a case-by-case basis.

We now turn to the Board's . . . no-presumption approach in this case. Respondent Curtin Matheson Scientific, Inc., buys and sells laboratory instruments and supplies. In 1970, the Board certified Teamsters Local 968, General Drivers, Warehousemen and Helpers as the collective-bargaining agent for respondent's production and maintenance employees. On May 21, 1979, the most recent bargaining agreement between respondent and the Union expired. Respondent made its final offer for a new agreement on May 25, but the Union rejected that offer. Respondent then locked out the 27 bargaining-unit employees. On June 12, respondent renewed its May 25 offer, but the Union again rejected it. The Union then commenced an economic strike. . . .

Five employees immediately crossed the picket line and reported for work. On June 25, while the strike was still in effect, respondent hired 29 permanent replacement employees to replace the 22 strikers. The Union ended its strike on July 16, offering to accept unconditionally respondent's May 25 contract offer. On July 20, respondent informed the Union that the May 25 offer was no longer available. In addition, respondent withdrew recognition from the Union and refused to bargain further, stating that it doubted that the Union was supported by a majority of the employees in the unit. Respondent subsequently refused to provide the Union with information it had requested concerning the total number of bargaining unit employees on the payroll, and the job classification and seniority of each employee. As of July 20, the bargaining unit consisted of 19 strikers, 25 permanent replacements, and the 5 employees who had crossed the picket line at the strike's inception.

On July 30, the Union filed an unfair labor practice charge with the Board. Following an investigation, the General Counsel issued a complaint, alleging that respondent's withdrawal of recognition, refusal to execute a contract embodying the terms of the May 25 offer, and failure to pro-

vide the requested information violated Sections 8(a)(1) and 8(a)(5) of the NLRA. In its defense to the charge, respondent claimed that it had a reasonably based, good-faith doubt of the Union's majority status. The Administrative Law Judge agreed with respondent and dismissed the complaint. The Board, however, reversed, holding that respondent lacked sufficient objective basis to doubt the Union's majority support.

First, the Board noted that the crossover of 5 of the original 27 employees did not in itself support an inference that the 5 had repudiated the Union, because their failure to join the strike may have "indicate[d] their economic concerns rather than a lack of support for the union." Second, the Board found that the resignation from their jobs of two of the original bargaining unit employees, including the chief shop steward, after the commencement of the strike did not indicate opposition to the Union, but merely served to reduce the size of the bargaining unit as of the date of respondent's withdrawal of recognition. Third, the Board discounted statements made by six employees to a representative of respondent [employer] during the strike. Although some of these statements may have indicated rejection of the Union as the bargaining representative, the Board noted, others "appear[ed] ambiguous at *best*." Moreover, the Board stated, "[e]ven attributing to them the meaning most favorable to the Respondent, it would merely signify that 6 employees of a total bargaining unit of approximately 50 did not desire to keep the Union as the collective-bargaining representative."

Finally, regarding respondent's hiring of striker replacements, the Board stated that . . . it would "not use any presumptions with respect to [the replacements'] union sentiments," but would instead "take a case-by-case approach [and] require additional evidence of a lack of union support on the replacements' part in evaluating the significance of this factor in the employer's showing of good-faith doubt." The Board noted that respondent's only evidence of the replacements' attitudes toward the Union was its employee relations director's account of a conversation with one of the replacements. The replacement employee reportedly told her that he had worked in union and nonunion workplaces and did not see any need for a union as long as the company treated him well; in addition, he said that he did not think the Union in this case represented the employees. The Board did not determine whether this statement indicated the replacement employee's repudiation of the Union, but found that the statement was, in any event, an insufficient basis for "inferring the union sentiments of the replacement employees as a group."

The Board therefore concluded that "the evidence [was] insufficient to rebut the presumption of the Union's continuing majority status." Accordingly, the Board held that respondent had violated Sections 8(a)(1) and 8(a)(5) by withdrawing recognition from the Union, failing to furnish the requested information, and refusing to execute a contract embodying the terms respondent had offered on May 25, 1979. The Board ordered respondent to bargain with the Union on request, provide the requisite information, execute an agreement, and make the bargaining unit employees whole for whatever losses they had suffered from respondent's failure to execute a contract.

The Court of Appeals, in a divided opinion, refused to enforce the Board's order, holding that respondent was justified in doubting the Union's majority support. Specifically, the court rejected the Board's decision not to apply any presumption in evaluating striker replacements' union sentiments and endorsed the so-called "Gorman presumption" that striker replacements oppose the union. We granted certiorari to resolve a circuit split on the question whether the Board must presume that striker replacements oppose the union.

. . . This Court . . . has accorded Board rules considerable deference. We will uphold a Board rule as long as it is rational and consistent with the Act, even if we would have formulated a different rule had we sat on the Board. Furthermore, a Board rule is entitled to deference even if it represents a departure from the Board's prior policy.

. . . the starting point for the Board's analysis is the basic presumption that the union is supported by a majority of bargaining-unit employees. The employer bears the burden of rebutting that presumption, after the certification year, either by showing that the union in fact lacks majority support or by demonstrating a sufficient objective basis for doubting the union's majority status. Respondent here urges that in evaluating an employer's claim of a good-faith doubt, the Board must adopt a second, subsidiary presumption—that replacement employees oppose the union. Under this approach, if a majority of employees in the bargaining unit were striker replacements, the employer would not need to offer *any* objective evidence of the employees' union sentiments to rebut the presumption of the union's continuing majority status. The presumption of the replacements' opposition to the union would, in effect, override the presumption of continuing majority status. In contrast, under its no-presumption approach the Board "take[s] into account the particular circumstances surrounding each strike and the hiring of replacements, while retaining the long-standing requirement that the employer must come

forth with some objective evidence to substantiate his doubt of continuing majority status."

We find the Board's no-presumption approach rational as an empirical matter. Presumptions normally arise when proof of one fact renders the existence of another fact "so probable that it is sensible and timesaving to assume the truth of [the inferred] fact . . . until the adversary disposes it." Although replacements often may not favor the incumbent union, the Board reasonably concluded, in light of its long experience in addressing these issues, that replacements may in some circumstances desire union representation despite their willingness to cross the picket line. Economic concerns, for instance, may force a replacement employee to work for a struck employer even though he otherwise supports the union and wants the benefits of union representation. In this sense the replacement worker is no different from a striker who, feeling the financial heat of the strike on herself and her family, is forced to abandon the picket line and go back to work. In addition, a replacement, like a nonstriker or a strike crossover, may disagree with the purpose or strategy of the particular strike and refuse to support that strike, while still wanting that union's representation at the bargaining table.

Respondent insists that the interests of strikers and replacements are diametrically opposed and that unions inevitably side with the strikers. . . . Respondent asserts that replacements, aware of the union's loyalty to the strikers, most likely would not support the union. . . .

These arguments do not persuade us that the Board's position is irrational. Unions do not inevitably demand displacement of all strike replacements. . . . The extent to which a union demands displacement of permanent replacement workers logically will depend on the union's bargaining power. . . . Because the circumstances of each strike and the leverage of each union will vary greatly, it was not irrational for the Board to reject the antiunion presumption and adopt a case-by-case approach in determining replacements' union sentiments.

Moreover, even if the interests of strikers and replacements conflict during the strike, those interests may converge *after* the strike, once job rights have been resolved. Thus, while the strike continues, a replacement worker whose job appears relatively secure might well want the union to continue to represent the unit regardless of the union's bargaining posture during the strike. Surely replacement workers are capable of looking past the strike in considering whether or not they desire representation by the union. For these reasons, the Board's refusal to adopt an antiunion presumption is not irreconcilable with its position . . . regarding an employer's obligation to bargain with a striking union over replacements' employment terms. . . .

In sum, the Board recognized that the circumstances surrounding each strike and replacements' reasons for crossing a picket line vary greatly. Even if replacements often do not support the union, then, it was not irrational for the Board to conclude that the probability of replacement opposition to the union is insufficient to justify an antiunion presumption. . . . The Board's no-presumption approach is rationally directed at protecting the bargaining process and preserving employees' right to engage in concerted activity. We therefore find, in light of the considerable deference we accord Board rules, that the Board's approach is consistent with the Act.

We hold that the Board's refusal to adopt a presumption that striker replacements oppose the union is rational and consistent with the Act. We therefore reverse the judgment of the Court of Appeals and remand for further proceedings consistent with this opinion. **It is so ordered.**

BLACKMUN, J. (dissenting)

. . . The Board may not assert in one line of cases that the interests of a striking union and replacement workers are ir-

reconcilably in conflict, and proclaim in a different line of decisions that no meaningful generalizations can be made about the union sentiments of the replacement employees. I therefore conclude that the judgment of the Court of Appeals should be affirmed.

SCALIA, J., with whom O'CONNOR, J., and KENNEDY, J., join (dissenting)

. . . The question presented is whether [the Board's] factual finding is supported by substantial evidence. Since the principal employment-related interest of strike replacements (to retain their jobs) is almost invariably opposed to the principal interest of the striking union (to replace them with its striking members) it seems to me impossible to conclude on this record that the employer did not have a reasonable, good-faith doubt regarding the union's majority status. The Board's factual finding being unsupported by substantial evidence, it cannot stand. I therefore dissent from the judgment reversing the Fifth Circuit's refusal to enforce the Board's order. . . .

The Nature of the Duty to Bargain in Good Faith

After having considered how the duty to bargain in good faith arises and how long it lasts, we now turn to exactly what it means—what is "good-faith" bargaining?

As we have seen, the wording of Section 8(d) states that making concessions or reaching agreement is not necessary to good-faith bargaining. Imposition of such requirements would infringe upon either party's freedom of contract and would destroy the voluntary nature of collective bargaining, which is essential to the success. What is required for good-faith bargaining, according to the NLRB, is that the parties enter negotiations with "an open and fair mind" and "a sincere purpose to find a basis of agreement."

As long as the parties bargain with an intention to find a basis of agreement, the breakdown or deadlock of negotiations is not a violation of the duty to bargain in good faith. Where talks reach a deadlock—known as an **impasse**—as a result of sincere bargaining, either side may break off talks on the deadlocked issue. In determining whether an impasse exists, the board considers the totality of circumstances—the number of times the parties have met, the likelihood of progress on the issue, the use of mediation, and so on. The board considers that a change in the position of either party or a change in the circumstances may break an impasse; in that case the parties would not be able to break off all talks on the issue.

When the impasse results from a party's rigid insistence upon a particular proposal, it is not a violation of the duty to bargain if the proposal relates to wages, hours, or terms and conditions of employment. In *NLRB* v. *American National Insurance Co.* (343 U.S. 395, 1952), the Supreme Court held that the employer's insistence upon contract language giving it discretionary control over promotions, discipline, work scheduling, and denying arbitration on such matters was not in violation of the duty to bargain in good faith. In *NLRB* v. *General Electric Co.* (418 F.2d 736, 2nd Cir. 1969, *cert. denied,* 397 U.S. 965, 1970), the Court of Appeals held that "take-it-or-leave-it" bargaining is not, by itself, in violation of the duty to bargain. But when an employer engages in other conduct indicating lack of good faith—such as refusing to sign a written agreement, attempting to deal with individual employees rather than the union, and refusing to provide the union with information regarding bargaining proposals—then the combined effect of the employer's conduct is to violate the duty to negotiate in good faith. But hard bargaining, in and of itself, is not a violation; at some point in negotiations either side may make a "final" offer and hold to it firmly.

While negotiations are being conducted, is either side free to engage in tactics designed to pressure the other into making a concession? Is such pressure during bargaining consistent with negotiating in good faith? The following case considers the questions.

NLRB v. INSURANCE AGENTS INTERNATIONAL UNION

361 U.S. 477 (Supreme Court of the United States, 1960)

BRENNAN, J.

This case presents an important issue of the scope of the National Labor Relations Board's authority under Section 8(b)(3) of the National Labor Relations Act, which provides that "It shall be an unfair labor practice for a labor organization or its agents . . . to refuse to bargain collectively with an employer, provided it is the representative of his employees . . ." The precise question is whether the Board may find that a union, which confers with an employer with the desire of reaching agreement on contract terms, has nevertheless refused to bargain collectively, thus violating that provision, solely and simply because during the negotiations it seeks to put economic pressure on the employer to yield to its bargaining demands by sponsoring on-the-job conduct designed to interfere with the carrying on of the employer's business. . . .

In January 1956 Prudential and the union began the negotiation of a new contract to replace an agreement expiring in the following March. Bargaining was carried on continuously for six months before the terms of the new contract were agreed upon on July 17, 1956. It is not questioned that, if it stood alone, the record of negotiations

would establish that the union conferred in good faith for the purpose and with the desire of reaching agreement with Prudential on a contract.

However, in April 1956, Prudential filed a Section 8(b)(3) charge of refusal to bargain collectively against the union. The charge was based upon actions of the union and its members outside the conference room, occurring after the old contract expired in March. The union had announced in February that if agreement on the terms of the new contract was not reached when the old contract expired, the union members would then participate in a "Work Without a Contract" program—which meant that they would engage in certain planned, concerted on-the-job activities designed to harass the company. It was developed in the evidence that the union's harassing tactics involved activities by the member agents such as these: refusal for a time to solicit new business, and refusal (after the writing of new business was resumed) to comply with the company's reporting procedures; refusal to participate in the company's "May Policyholders' Month Campaign"; reporting late at district offices the days the agents were scheduled to attend them, and refusing to perform customary duties at the offices, instead engaging there in "sit-in-mornings," "doing what comes naturally" and leaving at noon as a group; absenting themselves from special business conferences arranged by the company; picketing and distributing leaflets outside the various offices of the company on specified days and hours as directed by the union; distributing leaflets each day to policyholders and others and soliciting policyholders' signatures on petitions directed to the company; and presenting the signed policyholders' petitions to the company at its home office while simultaneously engaging in mass demonstrations there.

The hearing examiner filed a report recommending that the complaint be dismissed. . . .

However, the Board . . . rejected the trial examiner's recommendation, and entered a cease-and-desist order. The Court of Appeals for the District of Columbia Circuit . . . set aside the Board's order. We granted the Board's petition for certiorari to review the important question presented. . . .

. . . [T]he Board's view is that irrespective of the union's good faith in conferring with the employer at the bargaining table for the purpose and with the desire of reaching agreement on contract terms, its tactics during the course of the negotiations constituted per se a violation of Section 8(b)(3). . . .

(W)e think the Board's approach involves an intrusion into the substantive aspects of the bargaining process—again, unless there is some specific warrant for its condemnation of the precise tactics involved here. The scope of Section 8(b)(3) and the limitations on Board power which were the design of Section 8(d) are exceeded, we hold, by inferring a lack of good faith not from any deficiencies of the union's performance at the bargaining table by reason of its attempted use of economic pressure, but solely and simply because tactics designed to exert economic pressure were employed during the course of good-faith negotiations. Thus the Board in the guise of determining good or bad faith in negotiations could regulate what economic weapons a party might summon to its aid. And if the Board could regulate the choice of economic weapons that may be used as part of collective bargaining, it would be in a position to exercise considerable influence upon the substantive terms on which the parties contract. As the parties' own devices become more limited, the Government might have to enter even more directly into the negotiation of collective agreements. Our labor policy is not presently erected on a foundation of government control of the results of negotiations. Nor does it contain a charter for the National Labor Relations Board to act at large in equalizing disparities of bargaining power between employer and union.

The use of economic pressure, as we have indicated, is of itself not at all inconsistent with the duty of bargaining in

good faith. . . . The Board freely (and we think correctly) conceded here that a "total" strike called by the union would not have subjected it to sanctions under Section 8(b)(3), at least if it were called after the old contract, with its no-strike clause, had expired. . . .

The Board contends that because an orthodox "total" strike is "traditional" its use must be taken as being consistent with Section 8(b)(3); but since the tactics here are not "traditional" or "normal," they need not be so viewed. Further, the Board cites what it conceives to be the public's moral condemnation of the sort of employee tactics involved here. But again we cannot see how these distinctions can be made under a statute which simply enjoins a duty to bargain in good faith. Again, these are relevant arguments when the question is the scope of the concerted activities given affirmative protection by the Act. But as we have developed, the use of economic pressure by the parties to a labor dispute is not a grudging exception to some policy of completely academic discussion enjoined by the Act; it is part and parcel of the process of collective bargaining. On the basis, we fail to see the relevance of whether the practice in question is time-honored or whether its exercise is generally supported by public opinion. It may be that the tactics used here deserve condemnation, but this would not justify attempting to pour that condemnation into a vessel not designed to hold it.

These distinctions essayed by the Board here, and the lack of relationship to the statutory standard inherent in them, confirm us in our conclusion that the judgment of the Court of Appeals, setting aside the order of the Board, must be affirmed. For they make clear to us that when the Board moves in this area, with only Section 8(b)(3) for support, it is functioning as an arbiter of the sort of economic weapons the parties can use in seeking to gain acceptance of their bargaining demands. It has sought to introduce some standard of properly "balanced" bargaining power, or some new distinction of justifiable and unjustifiable, proper and "abusive" economic weapons into the collective bargaining duty imposed by the Act. The Board's assertion of power under Section 8(b)(3) allows it to sit in judgment upon every economic weapon the parties to a labor contract negotiation employ, judging it on the very general standard of that section, not drafted with reference to specific forms of economic pressure. We have expressed our belief that this amounts to the Board's entrance into the substantive aspects of the bargaining process to an extent Congress has not countenanced. **Affirmed.**

Subject Matter of Bargaining.   As the preceding cases indicate, the NLRB and the courts are reluctant to control the bargaining tactics available to either party. This reluctance reflects a philosophical aversion to government intrusion into the bargaining process. Yet some regulation of bargaining is necessary if the bargaining process is to be meaningful—some control is required to prevent the parties from making a charade of the process by holding firmly to arbitrary or frivolous positions. One means of control is the distinction drawn between mandatory and permissive subjects of bargaining.

Mandatory Bargaining Subjects.   **Mandatory bargaining subjects,** according to the Supreme Court decision in *Allied Chemical & Alkalai Workers* v. *PPG* (404 U.S. 157, 1971), are those subjects that "vitally affect the terms and conditions of employment" of the employees in the bargaining unit. The Supreme Court in *PPG* held that changes in medical insurance coverage of former employees who were retired were not a mandatory subject, and the company need not bargain over such changes with the union. The fact that the company had bargained over such issues in the past did not convert a permissive subject into a mandatory one; the company was free to change the insurance policy coverage unilaterally.

The NLRB and the Court have broadly interpreted the matters subject to mandatory bargaining as being related to "wages, hours, terms and conditions of employment" specified in Section 8(d) and Section 9(a). Wages have been held to include all forms of employee compensation and fringe benefits, including items such as pensions, stock options, annual bonuses, employee discounts, shift differentials, and incentive plans. Hours and terms and conditions of employment have received similar broadening. The Supreme Court, in *Ford Motor Co.* v. *NLRB* (441 U.S. 488, 1979), held that the prices of food sold in vending machines in the plant cafeteria were mandatory subjects for bargaining when the employer had some control over pricing.

The aspect of mandatory bargaining subjects that has attracted the most controversy has been the duty to bargain over management decisions to subcontract work or to close down a plant. In *Fibreboard Paper Products* v. *NLRB* (379 U.S. 203, 1964), the Supreme Court held that an employer must bargain with the union over a decision to subcontract out work previously done by bargaining unit employees. Later board and Court decisions held that subcontracting that had never been done by bargaining unit employees was not a mandatory issue; as well, decisions to change the corporate structure of a business or to terminate manufacturing operations were not mandatory subjects but rather were inherent management rights. Even the decision to go out of business entirely is not a mandatory subject of bargaining. But while the employer need not discuss such decisions with the union, the board has held that the effects of such decisions upon the employees are mandatory bargaining subjects. The employer must therefore discuss the effects of such decisions with the union—matters such as severance pay, transfer policies, retraining, and the procedure to be used for layoffs must be negotiated with the union.

The following case is a 1981 Supreme Court decision dealing with the employer's duty to bargain over a partial shutdown of its operations.

FIRST NATIONAL MAINTENANCE CORP. v. NLRB

452 U.S. 666 (Supreme Court of the United States, 1981)

BLACKMUN, J.

Must an employer, under its duty to bargain in good faith "with respect to wages, hours, and other terms and conditions of employment," Sections 8(d) and 8(a)(5) of the National Labor Labor Relations Act negotiate with the certified representative of its employees over its decision to close a part of its business? In this case, the National Labor Relations Board (Board) imposed such a duty on petitioner with respect to its decision to terminate a contract with a customer, and the United States Court of Appeals, although differing over the appropriate rationale, enforced its order.

Petitioner, First National Maintenance Corporation (FNM), is a New York corporation engaged in the business of providing housekeeping, cleaning maintenance, and related services for commercial customers in the New York City area. It contracts for and hires personnel separately for each customer, and it does not transfer employees between locations.

During the spring of 1977, petitioner was performing maintenance work for the Greenpark Care Center, a nursing home in Brooklyn. Petitioner employed approximately 35 workers in its Greenpark operation.

Petitioner's business relationship with Greenpark, seemingly, was not very remunerative or smooth. In March 1977, Greenpark gave petitioner the 30 days' written notice of cancellation specified by the contract, because of "lack of efficiency." This cancellation did not become effective, for FNM's work continued after the expiration of that 30-day period. Petitioner, however, became aware that it was losing money at Greenpark. On June 30, by telephone, it asked that its weekly fee be restored at the $500 figure, and, on July 6, it informed Greenpark in writing that it would discontinue its operations there on August 1 unless the increase were granted. By telegram on July 25, petitioner gave final notice of termination.

While FNM was experiencing these difficulties, District 1199, National Union of Hospital and Health Care Employees, Retail, Wholesale and Department Store Union, AFL-CIO (Union), was conducting an organization campaign among petitioner's Greenpark employees. On March 31, 1977, at a Board-conducted election, a majority of the employees selected the union as their bargaining agent. Petitioner neither responded nor sought to consult with the union.

On July 28, petitioner notified its Greenpark employees that they would be discharged three days later.

With nothing but perfunctory further discussion, petitioner on July 31 discontinued its Greenpark operation and discharged the employees.

The union filed an unfair labor practice charge against petitioner, alleging violations of the Act's Section 8(a)(1) and (5). After a hearing held upon the Regional Director's complaint, the Administrative Law Judge made findings in the union's favor. . . . [H]e ruled that petitioner had failed to satisfy its duty to bargain concerning both the decision to terminate the Greenpark contract and the effect of that change upon the unit employees.

The Administrative Law Judge recommended an order requiring petitioner to bargain in good faith with the union about its decision to terminate its Greenpark service operation and its consequent discharge of the employees, as well as that petitioner be ordered to pay the discharged employees back pay from the date of discharge until the parties bargained to agreement, or the bargaining reached an impasse, or the union failed timely to request bargaining or the union failed to bargain in good faith.

The National Labor Relations Board adopted the Administrative Law Judge's findings without further analysis, and additionally required petitioner, if it agreed to resume its Greenpark operations, to offer the terminated employees reinstatement to their former jobs or substantial equivalents; conversely, if agreement was not reached, petitioner was ordered to offer the employees equivalent positions, to be made available by discharge of subsequently hired employees, if necessary, at its other operations.

The United States Court of Appeals for the Second Circuit, with one judge dissenting in part, enforced the Board's order.

The Court of Appeals' decision in this case appears to be at odds with decisions of other Courts of Appeals, some of which decline to require bargaining over any management decision involving "a major commitment of capital investment" of a "basic operational change" in the scope or direction of an enterprise, and some of which indicate that bargaining is not mandated unless a violation of Section 8(a)(3) (a partial closing motivated by antiunion animus) is involved. The Board itself has not been fully consistent in its rulings applicable to this type of management decision.

A fundamental aim of the National Labor Relations Act is the establishment and maintenance of industrial peace to preserve the flow of interstate commerce. Central to achievement of this purpose is the promotion of collective bargaining as a method of defusing and channeling conflict between labor and management.

Although parties are free to bargain about any legal subject, Congress has limited the mandate or duty to bargain to matters of "wages, hours, and other terms and conditions of employment." Congress deliberately left the words "wages, hours, and other terms and conditions of employment" without further definition, for it did not intend to deprive the Board of the power further to define those terms in light of specific industrial practices.

Nonetheless, in establishing what issues must be submitted to the process of bargaining, Congress had no expectation that the elected union representative would become an equal partner in the running of the business enterprise in which the union's members are employed.

Some management decisions, such as choice of advertising and promotion, product type and design, and financing arrangements, have only an indirect and attenuated impact on the employment relationship. Other management decisions, such as the order of succession of layoffs and recalls, production quotas, and work rules, are almost exclusively "an aspect of the relationship" between employer and employee. The present case concerns a third type of management decision, one that had a direct impact on employment, since jobs were inexorably eliminated by the termination, but had as its focus only the economic profitability of the contract with Greenpark, a concern under these facts wholly apart from the employment relationship. This decision, involving a change in the scope and direction of the enterprise, is akin to the decision whether to be in business at all, "not in [itself] primarily about conditions of employment, though the effect of the decision may be necessarily to terminate employment." At the same time this decision touches on a matter of central and pressing concern to the union and its member employees: the possibility of continued employment and the retention of the employees' very jobs.

Petitioner contends it had no duty to bargain about its decision to terminate its operations at Greenpark. This contention requires that we determine whether the decision itself should be considered part of petitioner's retained freedom to manage its affairs unrelated to employment. The aim of labeling a matter a mandatory subject of bargaining, rather than simply permitting, but not requiring, bargaining, is to "promote the fundamental purpose of the Act by bringing a problem of vital concern to labor and manage-

ment within the framework established by Congress as most conducive to industrial peace." The concept of mandatory bargaining is premised on the belief that collective discussions backed by the parties' economic weapons will result in decisions that are better for both management and labor and for society as a whole. This will be true, however, only if the subject proposed for discussion is amenable to resolution through the bargaining process. Management must be free from the constraints of the bargaining process to the extent essential for the running of a profitable business. It also must have some degree of certainty beforehand as to when it may proceed to reach decisions without fear of later evaluations labeling its conduct an unfair labor practice. Congress did not explicitly state what issues of mutual concern to union and management it intended to exclude from mandatory bargaining. Nonetheless, in view of an employer's need for unencumbered decisionmaking, bargaining over management decisions that have a substantial impact on the continued availability of employment should be required only if the benefit, for labor-management relations and the collective-bargaining process, outweighs the burden placed on the conduct of the business.

Both union and management regard control of the decision to shut down an operation with the utmost seriousness. As has been noted, however, the Act is not intended to serve either party's individual interest, but to foster in a neutral manner a system in which the conflict between these interests may be resolved. It seems particularly important, therefore, to consider whether requiring bargaining over this sort of decision will advance the neutral purposes of the Act.

A union's interest in participating in the decision to close a particular facility or part of an employer's operations springs from its legitimate concern over job security. The Court has observed: "The words of [Section 8(d)] ... plainly cover termination of employment which ... necessarily results" from closing an operation. The union's practical purpose in participation, however, will be largely uniform: it will seek to delay or halt the closing. No doubt it will be impelled, in seeking these ends, to offer concessions, information, and alternatives that might be helpful to management or forestall or prevent the termination of jobs. It is unlikely, however, that requiring bargaining over the decision itself, as well as its effects, will augment this flow of information and suggestions. There is no dispute that the union must be given a significant opportunity to bargain about these matters of job security as part of the "effects" bargaining mandated by Section 8(a)(5). A union, pursuing such bargaining rights, may achieve valuable concessions from an employer engaged in a partial closing.

Moreover, the union's legitimate interest in fair dealing is protected by Section 8(a)(3), which prohibits partial closings motivated by antiunion animus, when done to gain an unfair advantage.

Thus, although the union has a natural concern that a partial closing decision not be hastily or unnecessarily entered into, it has some control over the effects of the decision and indirectly may ensure that the decision itself is deliberately considered. It also has direct protection against a partial closing decision that is motivated by an intent to harm a union.

Management's interest in whether it should discuss a decision of this kind is much more complex and varies with the particular circumstances. If labor costs are an important factor in a failing operation and the decision to close, management will have an incentive to confer voluntarily with the union to seek concessions that may make continuing the business profitable. At other times, management may have great need for speed, flexibility, and secrecy in meeting business opportunities and exigencies. It may face significant tax or securities consequences that hinge on confidentiality, the timing of a plant closing, or a reorganization of the corporate structure. The public incident to the normal process of bargaining may injure the possibility of a successful transition or increase the economic damage to the business. The employer also may have no feasible alternative to the closing, and even good-faith bargaining over it may both be futile and cause the employer additional loss.

There is an important difference, also, between permitted bargaining and mandated bargaining. Labeling this type of decision mandatory could afford a union a powerful tool for achieving delay, a power that might be used to thwart management's intentions in a manner unrelated to any feasible solution the union might propose.

While evidence of current labor practice is only an indication of what is feasible through collective bargaining, and not a binding guide, that evidence supports the apparent imbalance weighing against mandatory bargaining. We note that provisions giving unions a right to participate in the decisionmaking process concerning alteration of the scope of an enterprise appear to be relatively rare. Provisions concerning notice and "effects" bargaining are more prevalent.

Further, the presumption analysis adopted by the Court of Appeals seems ill-suited to advance harmonious relations between employer and employee. An employer would have difficulty determining beforehand whether it was faced with a situation requiring bargaining or one that involved economic necessity sufficiently compelling to obviate the duty to bargain. If it should decide to risk not bargaining, it might be faced ultimately with harsh remedies forcing it to pay large amounts of back pay to employees who likely would have been discharged regardless of bargaining, or even to consider reopening a failing operation.

We conclude that the harm likely to be done to an employer's need to operate freely in deciding whether to shut down part of its business purely for economic reasons outweighs the incremental benefit that might be gained through the union's participation in making the decision, and we hold that the decision itself is not part of Section 8(d)'s "terms and conditions," over which Congress has mandated bargaining . . .

Subsequent board decisions applying the *First National Maintenance* "balancing" test to employer decisions have held that the employer had no duty to bargain over the decision to relocate research and development operations in order to improve organizational efficiency (*United Technologies,* 169 N.L.R.B. No. 162, 1984; *Otis Elevator,* 115 L.R.R.M. 1281, 1984).

In short, when the work relocation is motivated not by a desire to cut labor costs or escape the collective bargaining agreement but by other business considerations, the employer's bargaining duty most likely is limited to negotiating about the *effects* of the move.

What is the effect of labeling a subject as a mandatory bargaining issue upon the employer's ability to make decisions necessary to the efficient operation of the enterprise? The Supreme Court opinion in *First National Maintenance* was concerned about placing burdens on the employer that would interfere with the need to act promptly. But rather than preventing employer action over mandatory subjects, the duty to bargain requires only that the employer negotiate with the union. If the union agrees or makes concessions, then the employer is free to act. If the union fails to agree and an impasse results from good-faith bargaining, the employer is then free to implement the decision. The duty to bargain over mandatory subjects requires only that the employer bargain in good faith to the point of impasse over the issue. Once impasse has been reached, the employer is free to act unilaterally. In the case of *NLRB* v. *Katz* (369 U.S. 736, 1962), the Supreme Court stated that an employer may institute unilateral changes on mandatory subjects after bargaining to impasse; however, when the impasse results from the employer's failure to bargain in good faith, any unilateral changes would be an unfair labor practice in violation of Section 8(a)(5). An employer is under no duty to bargain over changes in permissive subjects; according to the Supreme Court opinion in *Allied Chemical & Alkalai Workers* v. *PPG,* cited earlier, unilateral changes on permissive subjects are not unfair practices.

Even if an employer has bargained to impasse over a mandatory subject and is free to implement changes, the changes made must be consistent with the proposal offered to the union. To institute changes unilaterally that are more generous than the proposals the employer was willing to offer the union is a violation of Section 8(a)(5), according to the Supreme Court decision in *NLRB* v. *Crompton-Highland Mills* (337 U.S. 217, 1949). Thus the employer is not free to offer replacements wages that are higher than those offered to the union before the union went on strike. (In some very exceptional circumstances, when changes must be made out of business necessity, the employer may institute unilateral changes without reaching an impasse, but those changes must be consistent with the offers made to the union, *Raleigh Water Heating,* 136 N.L.R.B. 76, 1962.)

Permissive Bargaining Subjects.   The previous discussion dealt with mandatory bargaining subjects; the Supreme Court in *Borg-Warner* also recognized that there are permissive subjects and prohibited subjects. **Permissive bargaining subjects** are those matters not directly related to wages, hours, and terms and conditions of employment and not prohibited. Either party may raise permissive items in bargaining, but such matters cannot be insisted upon to the point of impasse. If the other party refuses the permissive-item proposal, it must be dropped. *Borg-Warner* held that insisting upon permissive items to impasse and conditioning agreement on mandatory subjects upon agreement to permissive items was a violation of the duty to bargain in good faith. Some examples of permissive items are proposals regarding union procedure for ratifying contracts, attempts to modify the union certification, strike settlement agreements, corporate social or charitable activities, and the proposal to require a transcript of all bargaining sessions. Matters that are "inherent management rights" or "inherent union rights" are also permissive subjects.

Prohibited Bargaining Subjects.   **Prohibited bargaining subjects** are those proposals that involve violations of the NLRA or other laws. Examples would be a union attempt to negotiate a closed shop provision or to require an employer to agree to a "hot cargo clause" prohibited by Section 8(e) of the act. Any attempt to bargain over a prohibited subject may violate Section 8(a)(5) or Section 8(b)(3); any agreement reached on such items is null and void. It should be clear that prohibited subjects may not be used to precipitate an impasse.

Modification of Collective Agreements.

Section 8(d) of the act prohibits any modifications or changes in a collective agreement's provisions relating to mandatory bargaining subjects during the term of the agreement unless both parties to the agreement consent to such changes. (When the agreement has expired, either party may implement changes in the mandatory subjects covered by the agreement after having first bargained, in good faith, to impasse.)

In *Milwaukee Spring Div. of Illinois Coil Spring* (268 N.L.R.B. 601, 1984), the question before the NLRB was whether the employer's action to transfer its assembly operations from its unionized Milwaukee Spring facility to its nonunion operations in Illinois during the term of a collective agreement was a violation of Sections 8(a)(1), 8(a)(3), and 8(a)(5). The transfer of operations was made because of the higher labor costs of the unionized operations; as a result of the transfer, the employees at Milwaukee Spring were laid off. Prior to the decision to relocate operations, the employer had advised the union that it needed reductions in wages and benefit costs because it had lost a major customer, but the union had rejected any concessions. The employer had also proposed terms upon which it would retain operations in Milwaukee, but again the union had rejected the proposals and declined to bargain further over alternatives to transfer. The NLRB had initially held that the actions constituted a violation of Sections 8(a)(1), 8(a)(3), and 8(a)(5); but on rehearing, the board reversed the prior decision and found no violation. The majority of the board reasoned that the decision to transfer operations did not constitute a unilateral modification of the collective agreement in violation of Section 8(d) because no term of the agreement required the operations to remain at the Milwaukee Spring facility. Had there been a work-preservation clause stating that the functions the bargaining unit employees performed must remain at the Milwaukee plant, the employer would have been guilty of a unilateral modification of the collective agreement, in violation of Section 8(d). The employer's offers to discuss concessions and the terms upon which it would retain operations in Milwaukee satisfied the employer's duty to bargain under Section 8(a)(5). The majority also held that the layoff of the unionized employees after the operations were transferred did not violate Section 8(a)(3). The effect of their decision, reasoned the majority, would be to encourage "realistic and meaningful collective bargaining that the Act contemplates." The dissent argued that the employer was prohibited from transferring operations during the term of the agreement without the consent of the union. The Court of Appeals for the D.C. Circuit affirmed the majority's decision in *U.A.W. v. NLRB* (765 F.2d 175, 1985).

Plant Closing Legislation.   Because of concerns over plant closings, Congress passed the Worker Adjustment and Retraining Act (WARN) in August 1988. The law, which went into effect February 4, 1989, requires employers with 100 or more employees to give sixty days' advance notice prior to any plant closings or "mass layoffs." The employer must give written notice of the closing or mass layoff to the employees or their representative, to the state economic development officials, and to the chief elected local government official. WARN defines a plant closing as being when fifty or more employees lose their jobs during any thirty-day period, because of a permanent plant closing, or a temporary shutdown exceeding six months. A plant closing may also occur when fifty or more employees experience more than a 50 percent reduction in the hours of work during each month of any six-month period. "Mass layoffs" are defined as layoffs creating an employment loss during any thirty-day period for 500 or more employees, or for 50 or more employees who constitute at least one-third of the full-time labor force at a unit of the facility. The act also requires a sixty- day notice when a series of employment losses adds up to the requisite levels over a ninety-day period. The notice requirement has two exceptions. One exception is the so-called failing firm exception, when the employer can demonstrate that giving the required notice would prevent the firm from obtaining capital or business necessary to maintain the operation of the firm. The other exception is when the work loss is due to "unforeseen circumstances."

Although the legislation speaks of plant closings, and Congress had industrial plant closings as a primary concern when passing WARN, the courts have held that it applies to employers such as law firms, brokerage firms, and hotels and casinos. The act imposes a penalty for failure to give the required notice—the employer is required to pay each affected employee up to sixty days' pay and benefits if the required notice is not given. The act also provides for fines of up to $500 for each day the notice is not given, up to a maximum of $30,000; however, the fines can be imposed only in suits brought by local governments against the employer. WARN does not create any separate enforcement agency, nor does it give any enforcement authority to the Department of Labor.

The act requires only that advance notice of the plant closings or mass layoffs be given; it does *not* require that the employer negotiate over the decision to close or lay off. To that extent, WARN does not affect the duty to bargain under the NLRA, or the results of the *First National Maintenance* decision.

The Duty to Furnish Information.   In *NLRB* v. *Truitt Mfg.* (351 U.S. 149, 1956), the Supreme Court held that an employer that pleads inability to pay in response to union demands must provide some financial information in an attempt to support that claim. The Court reasoned that such a duty was necessary if bargaining was to be meaningful—the employer is not allowed to "hide behind" claims that it cannot afford the union's pay demands. The rationale behind this requirement is that the union will be able to determine if the employer's claims are valid; if so, the union will moderate its demands accordingly.

The *Truitt* requirement to furnish information is not a "truth in bargaining" requirement. It relates only to claims of financial inability to meet union proposals. If the employer pleads inability to pay, the union must make a good-faith demand for financial information supporting the employer's claim. In responding to the union request, the employer need not provide all information requested by the union, but it must provide financial information in a reasonably usable and accessible form.

While the *Truitt* duty relates to financial information when the employer has pleaded inability to pay, another duty to furnish information is far greater in scope. Information relating to the enforcement and administration of the collective agreement must be provided to the union. This information is necessary for the union to perform its role as collective representative of the employees. This duty continues beyond negotiations to cover grievance arbitration during the life of the agreement as well. Such information includes wage scales, factors entering into compensation, job rates, job classifications, statistical data on the employer's minority employment practices, and a list of the names and addresses of the employees in the bargaining unit. Employers using toxic substances have been required to furnish unions with information on the generic names of substances used, their health effects, and toxicological studies. Employers are not required to turn over medical records of identified individual employees. In order to safeguard the privacy of individual employees, the courts have required that individual employees must consent to the disclosure of individual health records and scores on aptitude or psychological tests. An employer is entitled, however, to protect trade secrets and confidential information such as affirmative action plans or privately developed psychological aptitude tests.

Information provided to the union does not have to be in the exact format requested by the union, but it must be in a form that is not burdensome to use or interpret. An employer may not prohibit union photocopying of the information provided (*Communications Workers Local 1051* v. *NLRB,* 644 F.2d 923, 1st Cir. 1981).

Bargaining Remedies

We have seen that the requirements of the duty to bargain in good faith reflect a balance between promoting industrial peace and recognizing the principle of freedom of contract. In order to preserve the voluntary nature of collective bargaining, the board and the courts will not require either party to make a concession or agree to a proposal.

When the violation of Section 8(a)(5) or Section 8(b)(3) involves specific practices, such as the refusal to furnish information or the refusal to sign an already agreed-upon contract, the board orders the offending party to comply. Likewise, when an employer has illegally made unilateral changes, the board requires that the prior conditions be restored and any reduction in wages or benefits be paid back. However, if the violation of the duty to bargain in good faith involves either side's refusal to recognize or negotiate seriously with the other side, the board is limited in remedies available. In such cases the board will issue a "cease and desist" order directing the offending party to stop the illegal conduct, and a "bargaining order" directing the party to begin to negotiate in good faith. But the board cannot require that the parties make concessions or reach an agreement; it can only require that the parties return to the bargaining table and make an effort to explore the basis for an agreement. The following case deals with the limits on the board's remedial powers in bargaining order situations.

H.K. PORTER CO. v. NLRB

397 U.S. 99 (Supreme Court of the United States, 1970)

BLACK, J.

After an election, respondent United Steelworkers Union was, on October 5, 1961, certified by the National Labor Relations Board as the bargaining agent for the employees at the Danville, Virginia, plant of the H.K. Porter Co. Thereafter negotiations commenced for a collective bargaining agreement. Since that time the controversy has seesawed between the Board, the Court of Appeals for the District of Columbia Circuit, and this Court. This delay of over eight years is not because the case is exceedingly complex, but appears to have occurred chiefly because of the skill of the company's negotiators in taking advantage of every opportunity for delay in an Act more noticeable for its generality than for its precise prescriptions. The entire lengthy dispute mainly revolves around the union's desire to have the company agree to "check off" the dues owed to the union by its members, that is, to deduct those dues periodically from the company's wage payments to the employees. The record shows, as the Board found, that the company's objection to a checkoff was not due to any general principle or policy against making deductions from employees' wages. The company does deduct charges for things like insurance, taxes, and contributions to charities, and at some other plants it has a checkoff arrangement for union dues. The evidence shows, and the court below found, that the company's objection was not because of inconvenience, but solely on the ground that the company was "not going to aid and comfort the union." Based on this and other evidence the Board found, and the Court of Appeals approved the finding, that the refusal of the company to bargain about the checkoff was not made in good faith, but was done solely to frustrate the making of any collective bargaining agreement. In May 1966, the Court of Appeals upheld the Board's order requiring the company to cease and desist from refusing to bargain in good faith and directing it to engage in further collective bargaining, if requested by the union to do so, over the checkoff.

In the course of that opinion, the Court of Appeals inti-
mated that the Board conceivably might have required petitioner to agree to a checkoff provision as a remedy for the prior bad-faith bargaining, although the order enforced at that time did not contain any such provision. In the ensuing negotiations the company offered to discuss alternative arrangements for collecting the union's dues, but the union insisted that the company was required to agree to the checkoff proposal without modification. Because of this disagreement over the proper interpretation of the court's opinion, the union, in February 1967, filed a motion for clarification of the 1966 opinion. The motion was denied by the court on March 22, 1967, in an order suggesting that contempt proceedings before the Board would be the proper avenue for testing the employer's compliance with the original order. A request for the institution of such proceedings was made by the union, and in June 1967, the Regional Director of the Board declined to prosecute a contempt charge, finding that the employer had "satisfactorily complied with the affirmative requirements of the Order.". . . The union then filed in the Court of Appeals a motion for reconsideration of the earlier motion to clarify the 1966 opinion. The court granted that motion and issued a new opinion in which it held that in certain circumstances a "checkoff may be imposed as a remedy for bad-faith bargaining." The case was then remanded to the Board and on July 3, 1968, the Board issued a supplemental order requiring the petitioner to "[g]rant to the Union a contract clause providing for the checkoff of union dues." . . . The Board had found that the refusal was based on a desire to frustrate agreement and not on any legitimate business reason. On the basis of that finding the Court of Appeals approved the further finding that the employer had not bargained in good faith, and the validity of that finding is not now before us. Where the record thus revealed repeated refusals by the employer to bargain in good faith on this issue, the Court of Appeals concluded that ordering agreement to the checkoff clause "may be the only means of assuring the Board, and the court, that [the employer] no longer harbors an illegal intent."

In reaching this conclusion the Court of Appeals held that Section 8(d) did not forbid the Board from compelling agreement. That court felt that "Section 8(d) defines collective bargaining and relates to a determination of whether a ... violation has occurred and not to the scope of the remedy which may be necessary to cure violations which have already occurred." We may agree with the Court of Appeals that as a matter of strict, literal interpretation of that section it refers only to deciding when a violation has occurred, but we do not agree that that observation justifies the conclusion that the remedial powers of the Board are not also limited by the same considerations that led Congress to enact Section 8(d). It is implicit in the entire structure of the Act that the Board acts to oversee and referee the process of collective bargaining, leaving the results of the contest to the bargaining strengths of the parties. It would be anomalous indeed to hold that while Section 8(d) prohibits the Board from relying on a refusal to agree as the sole evidence of bad faith bargaining, the Act permits the Board to compel agreement in that same dispute. The Board's remedial powers under Section 10 of the Act are broad, but they are limited to carry out the policies of the Act itself. One of these fundamental policies is freedom of contract. While the parties' freedom of contract is not absolute under the Act, allowing the Board to compel agreement when the parties themselves are unable to do so would violate the fundamental premise on which the Act is based—private bargaining under governmental supervision of the procedure alone, without any official compulsion over the actual terms of the contract.

In reaching its decision, the Court of Appeals relied extensively on the equally important policy of the Act that workers' rights to collective bargaining are to be secured. In this case the Court apparently felt that the employer was trying effectively to destroy the union by refusing to agree to what the union may have considered its most important demand. Perhaps the court, fearing that the parties might resort to economic combat, was also trying to maintain the industrial peace which the Act is designed to further. But the Act, as presently drawn, does not contemplate that unions will always be secure and able to achieve agreement even when their economic position is weak, nor that strikes and lockouts will never result from a bargaining to impasse. It cannot be said that the Act forbids an employer or a union to rely ultimately on its economic strength to try to secure what it cannot obtain through bargaining. It may well be true, as the Court of Appeals felt, that the present remedial powers of the Board are insufficiently broad to cope with important labor problems. But it is the job of Congress, not the Board or the courts, to decide when and if it is necessary to allow governmental review of proposals for collective bargaining agreements and compulsory submission to one side's demands. The present Act does not envision such a process.

The judgment is reversed and the case is remanded to the Court of Appeals for further action consistent with this opinion. **Reversed and remanded.**

Because of the limitations on the NLRB's remedial powers in bargaining cases, an intransigent party can effectively frustrate the policies of the NLRA. If a union or employer is willing to incur the legal expenses and possible contempt-of-court fines, it can avoid reaching an agreement with the other side. Although unions are occasionally involved in such situations, most often employers have more to gain from refusing to bargain. The legal fees and fines may amount to less money than the employer would be required to pay in wages under a collective agreement (and the legal expenses are tax-deductible). Perhaps the most extreme example of such intransigence was the J.P. Stevens Company; in the late 1970s the company was found guilty of numerous unfair practices and was subjected to a number of bargaining orders, yet in only one case did it reach a collective agreement with the union.

Extreme cases like J.P. Stevens are the exception, however. Despite the board's remedial shortcomings, most negotiations culminate in the signing of a collective agreement. That fact is a testament to the vitality of the collective bargaining process and a vindication of a policy emphasis on the voluntary nature of the process.

Antitrust Aspects of Collective Bargaining

When a union and a group of employers agree upon specified wages and working conditions, the effect may be to reduce competition among the employers with respect to those wages or working conditions. As well, when the parties negotiate limits on subcontracting work or the use of prefabricated materials, the effect may be to reduce or prevent competition among firms producing such materials. Although the parties may be pursuing legitimate goals of collective bargaining, those goals may conflict with the policies of the antitrust laws designed to promote competition.

In the case of *U.S. v. Hutcheson* (312 U.S. 219, 1941), the Supreme Court held that a union acting in its self-interest, which does not combine with nonlabor groups, is exempt from the antitrust laws. *Hutcheson* involved union picketing of Anheuser-Busch and a call for a boycott of Anheuser-Busch products as a result of a dispute over work-assignment decisions. The Court ruled that such conduct was legal as long as it was not done in concert with nonlabor groups.

The scope of the labor relations exemption from the antitrust laws was further clarified by the Supreme Court in *Amalgamated Meat Cutters v. Jewel Tea Co.* (381 U.S. 676, 1965). In that case the union and a group of grocery stores negotiated restrictions on the hours its members would work, since the contract required the presence of union butchers for fresh meat sales. The effect of the agreement was to restrict the hours during which the grocery stores could sell fresh (rather than pre-packaged) meat. Jewel Tea argued that such a restriction of competition among the grocery stores violated the Sherman Antitrust Act. The Supreme Court held that since the union was pursuing its legitimate interests—that is, setting hours of work through a collective bargaining relationship—and did not act in concert with one group of employers to impose restrictions on another group of employers, the contract did not violate the Sherman Act.

Despite the broad scope of the antitrust exemption for labor relations activities, several cases have held unions in violation of the antitrust laws. In *United Mine Workers v. Pennington* (381 U.S. 657, 1965), the union agreed with one group of mine operators to impose wage and pension demands on a different group of mines. The union and the first group of mine owners were held by the Court to have been aware that the second group, composed of smaller mining operations, would be unable to meet the demands and could be forced to cease operations. The Supreme Court stated that if the union had agreed with the first group of employers in order to eliminate competition from the smaller mines, the union would be in violation of the antitrust laws. Although the union, acting alone, could attempt to force the smaller mines to agree to its demands, the union lost its exemption from the antitrust laws when it combined with one group of employers to force demands on the second group.

In *Connell Construction Co. v. Plumbers Local 100* (421 U.S. 616, 1975), a union attempted to force a general contractor to agree to hire only plumbing sub-contractors who had contracts with the union. The general contractor did not itself employ any plumbers, and the union did not represent the employees of the general contractor. The effect of the union demand would be to restrict competition among plumbing subcontractors. Nonunion firms, and even unionized firms that had contracts with other unions, would be denied access to plumbing jobs. The Supreme Court held that the union conduct was not exempt from the antitrust laws because the union did not have a collective bargaining relationship with Connell, the general contractor. Although a union may attempt to impose restrictions on employers with whom it has a bargaining relationship, it may not attempt to impose such restrictions on employers outside of that bargaining relationship.

In *Powell* v. *National Football League* ((888 F. 2d 559, 8th Cir 1989), the Eighth Circuit Court of Appeals held that the nonstatutory exemption from antitrust laws for collective bargaining matters extends beyond bargaining impasse and would continue to apply as long as there was a possibility that proceedings might be commenced before the NLRB, or until final resolution of the board proceedings and appeals therefrom. The court held that the exemption prevented players from bringing an antitrust challenge to the league's rule that restricted the ability of players to sign with another team, because that restriction had been conceived in an ongoing collective bargaining relationship.

In summary, then, the parties are generally exempt from the antitrust laws when they act alone to pursue legitimate concerns within the context of a collective bargaining relationship. If a union agrees with one group of employers to impose demands on another group, or if it attempts to impose work restrictions on employers outside of a collective bargaining relationship, it is subject to the antitrust laws.

QUESTIONS

1. Under what circumstances may an employer whose employees are unionized bargain legally with individual employees?

2. What procedural requirements for collective bargaining are imposed by Section 8(d)?

3. Must an employer refuse to bargain with either union when two unions are seeking to represent the employer's workers? Explain your answer.

4. When is a "take-it-or-leave-it" bargaining position legal union the NLRA? Explain your answer.

5. What are mandatory bargaining subjects? What is the significance of an item being classified as a mandatory bargaining subject?

6. Under what circumstances may an employer institute unilateral changes in matters covered by a collective agreement? Explain your answer.

7. When is an employer required to provide financial information to a union?

8. What conduct by unions is subject to the antitrust laws?

CASE PROBLEMS

1. During bargaining the employer reached an impasse on (a) a detailed "management rights" clause, (b) a broad "zipper" clause, (c) a waiver-of-past-practices provision, and (d) a no-strike provision. The employer's final economic offer consisted of an increase of ten cents per hour for seven of the nine bargaining unit

employees and a wage review for the remaining two.

Based on these facts, the NLRB concluded that the employer had engaged in mere surface bargaining and condemned the employer's final proposals as "terms which no self respecting union could be expected to accept." The company appealed the case to the Ninth Circuit.

If you had sat on the panel at the appellate court level, would you have agreed to disagreed with the board's conclusions? See *NLRB* v. *Tomco Communications, Inc.,* 567 F.2d 871, 97 L.R.R.M. 2660 (9th Cir. 1978).

2. The personnel department at an electrical utility had a policy of giving all new employees a "psychological aptitude test." The union demanded access to the test questions, answers, and individual scores for the employees in the bargaining unit. The union pointed out that among similar types of information that the NLRB had ordered disclosed in other cases were seniority lists, employees' ages, names and addresses of successful and unsuccessful job applicants, information about benefits received by retirees under employer's pension and insurance plans, information on employee grievances, and information on possible loss of work due to a proposed leasing arrangement.

The company claimed that if it released the information the union sought, its test security program would be severely compromised. Furthermore, employee confidence in the confidentiality of the testing program would be shattered. How do you think the NLRB would rule in this case? See *Detroit Edison Co.* v. *NLRB,* 440 U.S. 301, 100 L.R.R.M. 2728 (1979).

3. After collective bargaining negotiations came to an impasse, the employer locked out the bargaining unit employees. The company then hired permanent replacements without consulting or notifying the union of its actions. The end result was the virtual destruction of the bargaining unit.

In defense of its actions the company contended that the locked-out employees had engaged in a continuing pattern of in-plant sabotage and production disruptions during negotiations, which amounted to an "in-plant strike."

Did the company have the right to replace its locked-out workers? If so, did it have a duty to bargain with, or at least notify, the union before it did so? What might the union have done had the employer given it

notice and/or an opportunity to bargain about the replacement decision? See *Johns-Manville Prods. Corp.* v. *NLRB,* 557 F.2d 1126, 96 L.R.R.M. 2010 (5th Cir. 1977).

4. Sonat Marine was engaged in the business of transporting petroleum and petrochemical products. The Seafarers International Union (SIU) represented two separate bargaining units of Sonat's employees. One unit consisted of licensed employees, that is, the tugboat masters, mates, and pilots. In 1984 Sonat advised the union that it intended to withdraw recognition of the SIU as the bargaining representative of these licensed personnel at the expiration of the current collective bargaining agreement. Sonat's stated reason was that it had determined that these personnel were supervisors who were not subject to the NLRA as employees. The union demanded information on the factual basis for Sonat's position. Sonat refused to provide a response.

The union filed an unfair labor practice charge, asserting that Sonat was not bargaining in good faith. Was the union right? See *Sonat Marine, Inc.,* 279 N.L.R.B. No. 16 (1986).

5. Pratt-Farnsworth, Inc., a unionized construction contractor in New Orleans, owned a nonunion subsidiary, Halmar. During negotiations of a new collective bargaining agreement with Pratt-Farnsworth, the Carpenters' Union demanded that the company provide information concerning Halmar's business activities; the union was suspicious that the subsidiary was being used by the parent to siphon off work that could have been done by union members.

If you represented the union, what arguments would you make to support your demand for information? If you were on the company's side, how would you respond? See *Carpenters Local 1846* v. *Pratt-Farnsworth, Inc.,* 690 F.2d 489, 111 L.R.R.M. 2787 (5th Cir. 1982).

6. The company and the union commenced collective bargaining in April 1982. After four sessions the company submitted, on June 15, a contract package for union ratification. Two days later the union's membership rejected the package. No strike ensued.

Following rejection, the union's chief negotiator contacted the company and pointed out four stumbling blocks to ratification: union security, wages, overtime pay, and sickness and accident benefits. On July 7 the company resubmitted its original contract package unchanged. The union agreed to put it to a second ratification vote. However, before the vote took place, the company's president withdrew the package from the bargaining table. His reasoning was that the union's failure to strike indicated that the company had earlier overestimated the union's economic power. When in subsequent bargaining sessions the company proposed wages and benefits below those in the original package, the union charged it with bad-faith bargaining.

How should the NLRB have ruled on this complaint? See *Pennex Aluminum Corp.,* 271 N.L.R.B. No. 197, 117 L.R.R.M. 1057 (1984).

7. For more than thirty years without challenge by the union, the Brod & McClung-Pace Co.'s bargaining unit employees performed warranty work at customers' facilities. Then the international union altered its constitution to forbid its members to do such warranty work. Pursuant to this constitutional change, the local union, which was subject to the international's constitution, sought a midterm modification of its collective bargaining agreement with the company to eliminate the warranty work. When the firm refused, the union sought to achieve a unilateral change by threatening its members with court-collectible fines if they continued to perform the work.

Did the union violate the NLRA? If so, how? See *Sheet Metal Workers Int'l Ass'n, Local 16,* 271 N.L.R.B. No. 49, 117 L.R.R.M. 1085 (1984).

8. After five sessions of multi-employer bargaining, the Carpenters' Union and the Lake Charles District of the Associated General Contractors of Louisiana reached a new agreement. However, the printed contract inadvertently omitted a "weather clause," which was to state that an employee who reported for work but was sent home because of inclement weather would get four hours' pay, and an employee sent home because of weather after having started work would get paid only for hours actually worked, but not less than two hours. When the omission was discovered, the contract was already ratified and signed. The union refused to add the clause. The company then asked to reopen bargaining over the wage and reporting clauses that were affected by the omission. The union refused.

Who, if anyone, has committed an unfair labor practice? See *International Brotherhood of Carpenters Local 1476,* 270 N.L.R.B. 1432, 117 L.R.R.M. 1092 (1984).

9. The debtor, Allied Delivery System Co., filed its Chapter 11 petition on December 24, 1984. On January 16,

1985, the debtor through counsel sent a letter to Mr. Jackie Presser, President of the International Teamsters Union, seeking relief from the terms of its collective bargaining agreement with Teamsters Local 407 and seeking the designation of a representative of the union with whom the debtor could negotiate.

No response was received by the debtor or its counsel to the January 16, 1985, letter. On January 24, 1985, a second letter was sent, requesting a response to the previous letter. By letter, dated January 25, 1985, the union responded through its counsel, designating a representative of the union who was authorized to negotiate with the debtor.

A meeting was held on February 6, 1985, at which time the parties attempted to schedule another meeting. Because of scheduling conflicts on both sides, no meeting could be arranged before February 18, 1985.

On February 7, 1985, the debtor filed its motion for authority to reject the collective bargaining agreement, which was scheduled for hearing on February 19, 1985, pursuant to the requirements of 11 U.S.C. Section 113 (c)(3). Negotiations proceeded at the scheduled February 18, 1985, meeting, but no agreement was reached. The union at that time refused to accept a subsequent proposal made by the debtor in response to a proposal that had been put forth by the union.

At the hearing on February 19, the parties indicated that several additional bargaining sessions were scheduled and that they intended to continue their efforts to reach a new agreement. However, it appears that these efforts have been fruitless. The union challenges the necessity and fairness of the wage and benefit cutbacks proposed by the union and the good faith of the debtor in negotiation; the union also contends that its refusal to accept the company's proposal was for good cause.

Do you think the company fulfilled its duty to bargain in good faith? See *In re Allied Delivery System Co.,* 120 L.R.R.M. 2159 (U.S. Bankruptcy Ct., N.D. Ohio 1985).

10. Plymouth Stamping, an automotive parts company located in Michigan, decided to contract out its parts assembly operations in response to deteriorating sales and financial conditions. It notified the union on February 11, 1980, of its plans to subcontract. The notice stated that the operation would be discontinued as of February 15, that the assembly operation employees would be either laid off or transferred, and that the ac-

tion was necessary "due to economic and business reasons." The union requested a meeting, which was held on February 14, 1980. At the February 14 meeting, the company explained that the action was the result of a number of factors, including declining sales, noncompetitive wage rates, burdensome state taxes, and high workers' compensation costs. The employer, in response to a question concerning possible ways to retain the jobs, stated that the union would have to accept substantial wage cuts, a cost-of-living freeze, a reduction in some benefits, and a modification in work rules. The union requested that the employer delay any action until at least the following week; the employer, while stating that its decision was not final, requested a reply from the union by February 15 as to whether it would agree to concessions. The union failed to respond by February 15, and over the weekend (February 16 and 17) the employer moved its assembly equipment to a plant in Ohio. Meanwhile, unbeknownst to the company, the union, in a letter dated February 14, had requested information regarding the specifics of the decision; the company received the union's letter on February 20. The company responded to the union's letter on March 11; it stated that the decision was not irreversible and that it was prepared to discuss the matter with the union. The company repeated that the decision to subcontract was taken because "assembly operations are labor intensive and the costs (wages/benefits) associated with supporting this labor group have made the company noncompetitive." On March 1 the company entered into a formal leasing agreement with the subcontracting company; the lease allowed Plymouth to terminate the lease and repossess the equipment and gave the subcontractor the option to purchase the equipment. The subcontractor purchased the equipment on July 1, 1980. The union filed an unfair labor practice complaint with the NLRB, charging the employer with violations of Sections 8(a)(1) and 8(a)(5) for failing to bargain over a mandatory subject of bargaining and making a unilateral change in a mandatory subject without bargaining to impasse. How should the NLRB decide the union's complaint? See *NLRB* v. *Plymouth Stamping Division, Eltec Corp.,* 870 F.2d 1112 (6th Cir. 1989). What would have been the effect of the WARN law if it had applied to this case?

CHAPTER 8

Picketing, Strikes, and Boycotts: The Legality of Pressure Tactics

COLLECTIVE BARGAINING INVOLVES ECONOMIC conflict—each party to the negotiations seeks to protect its economic interests by extracting concessions from the other side. Both union and management back up their demands with the threat of pressure tactics that would inflict economic harm upon the other party. If the negotiations reach an impasse, the union may go on strike, or the employer may lock out to force concessions. This chapter will discuss the limitations placed on the use of such pressure tactics.

Pressure Tactics

Pressure tactics include picketing, patrolling, strikes, and boycotts by unions, and lockouts by employers. **Picketing** is the placing of persons outside the premises of an employer to convey information to the public. The information may be conveyed by words, signs, or the distribution of literature. Picketing is usually accompanied by **patrolling,** which is the movement of persons back and forth around the premises of an employer. A **strike**—the organized withholding of labor by workers—is the traditional weapon by which workers attempt to pressure employers. If the strike is successful, the economic harm resulting from the cessation of production will force the employer to accede to the union's demands. Strikes are usually accompanied by picketing and patrolling, as means of enforcing the strike. Unions may also instigate a boycott of the employer's product to increase the economic pressure upon the employer.

Employers are free to replace employees who go on strike. If the strike is an economic strike, replacement may be permanent. Employers are also free to lock out the employees—that is, to intentionally withhold work from them—to force the union to make concessions. An employer may resort to a lockout only after bargaining in good faith to an impasse; however, the bargaining dispute must be over a mandatory bargaining subject. Limitations on the right of an employer to lock out were discussed in Chapter 6 in the cases of *NLRB* v. *Brown* and *American Shipbuilding* v. *NLRB*.

Strikes may be economic strikes or unfair labor practice strikes. (The rights of the striking workers to reinstatement and their protection under the National Labor Relations Act (NLRA) were discussed in Chapter 6.) Strikes in violation of contractual no-strike clauses may give rise to union liability for damages and to judicial "back to work" orders; the enforcement of no-strike clauses is discussed in Chapter 9. The focus in this chapter will be on economic strikes and picketing. When the word *strike* is used, it refers to an economic strike unless otherwise specified.

The Legal Protection of Strikes

There is no constitutional right to strike. In fact, courts have traditionally held strikes to be criminal conspiracies (see Chapter 2). Constitutional restrictions, however, apply only to government activity; private sector strikes generally raise no constitutional issues. Strikes by private sector employees are regulated by the NLRA and are protected activity under Section 7 of the act. For public sector employees there may be no right to strike (see Chapter 11).

Although there is no recognized constitutional right to strike, there is a constitutional right to picket. The courts have held that picketing involves the expression and communication of opinions and ideas and is therefore protected under the First Amendment's freedom of speech. In *Thornhill* v. *Alabama* (310 U.S. 88, 1940), the Supreme Court held a state statute that prohibited all picketing, including even peaceful picketing, to be unconstitutional. Courts did, however, recognize that picketing involves conduct apart from speech, so that there may be some reason for limitations upon the conduct of picketing. In *Teamsters Local 695* v. *Vogt* (354 U.S. 284, 1957), the Supreme Court held that picketing, because it involves speech plus patrolling, may be regulated by the government more readily than pure speech activity.

The Norris–La Guardia Act.   As you recall from Chapter 3, the Norris–La Guardia Act, passed in 1932, severely restricted the ability of federal courts to issue injunctions in labor disputes. The act did not "protect" strikes; it simply restricted the ability of federal courts to issue injunctions. The act defines "labor dispute" very broadly, to cover disputes even when the parties are not in an employer-employee relationship. As well, the dispute need not be the result of economic concerns, as illustrated by the following case.

JACKSONVILLE BULK TERMINALS v. ILA

456 U.S. 645 (Supreme Court of the United States, 1982)

MARSHALL, J.

In this case, we consider the power of a federal court to enjoin a politically motivated work stoppage in an action brought by an employer pursuant to Section 301(a) of the Labor Management Relations Act (LMRA), 29 U.S.C., Section 185(a), to enforce a union's obligations under a collective-bargaining agreement. We first address whether the broad anti-injunction provisions of the Norris–La Guardia Act apply to politically motivated work stoppages....

On January 4, 1980, President Carter announced that, due to the Soviet Union's intervention in Afghanistan, certain trade with the Soviet Union would be restricted. Super-phosphoric acid (SPA), used in agricultural fertilizer, was not included in the Presidential embargo. On January 9, 1980, respondent International Longshoremen's Association (ILA) announced that its members would not handle any cargo bound to, or coming from, the Soviet Union or carried on Russian ships. In accordance with this resolution, respondent local union, an ILA affiliate, refused to load SPA bound for the Soviet Union aboard three ships that arrived at the shipping terminal operated by petitioner Jacksonville Bulk Terminals, Inc. (JBT) at the Port of Jacksonville, Florida during the month of January 1980.

In response to this work stoppage, petitioners JBT, Hooker Chemical Corporation, and Occidental Petroleum Company (collectively referred to as the Employer) brought this action pursuant to Section 301(a) of the LMRA, against respondents ILA, its affiliated local union, and its officers and agents (collectively referred to as the Union). The Employer alleged that the Union's work stoppage violated the collective-bargaining agreement between the Union and JBT. The Employer ... requested a temporary restraining order.... The United States District Court for the Middle District of Florida ... granted the Employer's request for a preliminary injunction ... reasoning that the political motivation behind the work stoppage rendered the Norris–La Guardia Act's anti-injunction provisions inapplicable.

The United States Court of Appeals for the Fifth Circuit ... disagreed with the District Court's conclusion that the provisions of the Norris–La Guardia Act are inapplicable to politically motivated work stoppages ...

Section 4 of the Norris–La Guardia Act provides in part:

No court of the United States shall have jurisdiction to issue any restraining order or temporary or permanent injunction in any case involving or growing out of any labor dispute to prohibit any person or persons participating or interested in such dispute ... from doing, whether singly or in concert, any of the following acts:

(a) Ceasing or refusing to perform any work or to remain in any relation of employment....

Congress adopted this broad prohibition to remedy the growing tendency of federal courts to enjoin strikes by narrowly construing the Clayton Act's labor exemption from the Sherman Act's prohibition against conspiracies to restrain trade. This Court has consistently given the anti-injunction provisions of the Norris–La Guardia Act a broad interpretation, recognizing exceptions only in limited situations where necessary to accommodate the Act to specific federal legislation or paramount congressional policy.

The Employer argues that the Norris–La Guardia Act does not apply in this case because the political motivation underlying the Union's work stoppage removes this controversy from that Act's definition of a "labor dispute." ...

At the outset, we must determine whether this is a "case involving or growing out of any labor dispute" within the meaning of Section 4 of the Norris–La Guardia Act. Section 13(c) of the Act broadly defines the term labor dispute to include "any controversy concerning terms or conditions of employment."

The Employer argues that the existence of political motives takes this work stoppage controversy outside the broad scope of this definition. This argument, however, has no basis in the plain statutory language of the Norris–La Guardia Act or in our prior interpretations of that Act. Furthermore, the argument is contradicted by the legislative history of not only the Norris–La Guardia Act but also the 1947 amendments to the National Labor Relations Act (NLRA).

An action brought by an employer against the union representing its employees to enforce a no-strike pledge generally involves two controversies. First, there is the "underlying dispute," which is the event or condition that triggers the work stoppage. This dispute may not be political, and it may or may not be arbitrable under the parties' collective-bargaining agreement. Second, there is the parties' dispute over whether the no-strike pledge prohibits the work stoppage at issue. This second dispute can always form the basis for federal court jurisdiction, because Section 301(a) gives federal courts jurisdiction over "[s]uits for violation of contracts between an employer and a labor organization."

It is beyond cavil that the second form of dispute—whether the collective-bargaining agreement either forbids or permits the union to refuse to perform certain work—is a "controversy concerning the terms or conditions of employment." This Section 301 action was brought to resolve just such a controversy. In its complaint, the Employer did not seek to enjoin the intervention of the Soviet Union in Afghanistan, nor did it ask the District Court to decide whether the Union was justified in expressing disapproval of the Soviet Union's actions. Instead, the Employer sought to enjoin the Union's decision not to provide labor, a decision which the Employer believed violated the terms of the collective-bargaining agreement. It is this contract dispute, and not the political dispute, that the arbitrator will resolve, and on which the courts are asked to rule.

The language of the Norris–La Guardia Act does not except labor disputes having their genesis in political protests. Nor is there any basis in the statutory language for the argument that the Act requires that *each* dispute relevant to the case be a labor dispute. The Act merely requires that the case involve "any" labor dispute. Therefore, the plain terms of Section 4(a) and Section 13 of the Norris–La Guardia Act deprive the federal courts of the power to enjoin the Union's work stoppage in this Section 301 action, without regard to whether the Union also has a nonlabor dispute with another entity.

The conclusion that this case involves a labor dispute within the meaning of the Norris–La Guardia Act comports with this Court's consistent interpretation of that Act. Our decisions have recognized that the term "labor dispute" must not be narrowly construed because the statutory definition itself is extremely broad and because Congress deliberately included a broad definition to overrule judicial decisions that had unduly restricted the Clayton Act's labor exemption from the antitrust laws. . . .

The critical element in determining whether the provisions of the Norris–La Guardia Act apply is whether "the employer-employee relationship [is] the matrix of the controversy." In this case, the Employer and the Union representing its employees are the disputants, and their dispute concerns the interpretation of the labor contract that defines their relationship. Thus, the employer-employee relationship is the matrix of this controversy. . . .

Even in cases where the disputants did not stand in the relationship of employer and employee, this Court had held that the existence of noneconomic motives does not make the Norris–La Guardia Act inapplicable. The Employer's argument that the Union's motivation for engaging in a work stoppage determines whether the Norris–La Guardia Act applies is also contrary to the legislative history of that Act. The Act was enacted in response to federal court intervention on behalf of employers through the use of injunctive powers against unions and other associations of employees. This intervention had caused the federal judiciary to fall into disrepute among large segments of this Nation's population. . . .

Furthermore, the question whether the Norris–La Guardia Act would apply to politically motivated strikes was brought to the attention of the 72nd Congress when it passed the Act. Opponents criticized the definition of "labor dispute" in Section 13(c) on the ground that it would cover politically motivated strikes. . . . Finally, Representative Beck offered an amendment to the Act that would have permitted federal courts to enjoin strikes called for ulterior purposes, including political motives. This amendment was defeated soundly.

Further support for our conclusion that Congress believed that the Norris–La Guardia Act applies to work stoppages instituted for political reasons can be found in the legislative history of the 1947 amendments to the NLRA. That history reveals that Congress rejected a proposal to repeal the Norris–La Guardia Act with respect to one broad category of political strikes. . . .

This case, brought by the Employer to enforce its collective-bargaining agreement with the Union, involves a "labor dispute" within any common-sense meaning of that term. Were we to ignore this plain interpretation and hold that the political motivation underlying the work stoppage removes this controversy from the prohibitions of the Norris–La Guardia Act, we would embroil federal judges in the very scrutiny of "legitimate objectives" that Congress intended to prevent when it passed that Act. The applicability not only of Section 4, but of all of the procedural protections embodied in that Act, would turn on a single federal judge's perception of the motivation underlying the concerted activity. The Employer's interpretation is simply inconsistent with the need, expressed by Congress when it enacted the Norris–La Guardia Act, for clear "mileposts for judges to follow." . . .

The Norris–La Guardia Act applied only to federal courts, but a number of states passed similar legislation restricting the issuance of labor injunctions by their courts.

Some exceptions to the Norris–La Guardia restrictions have been recognized. Sections 10(j) and 10(l) of the NLRA authorize the National Labor Relations Board (NLRB) to seek injunctions against unfair labor practices. Section 10(h) of the NLRA provides that Norris–La Guardia does not apply to actions brought under Sections 10(j) and (l), or to actions to enforce NLRB orders in the courts. The Supreme Court upheld this exemption in the case of *Bakery Sales Drivers, Local 33 v. Wagshal* (333 U.S., 347, 1948). The ability to initiate or maintain an action for an injunction under Sections 10(j) or (l) is restricted to the NLRB, *Solien v. Misc. Drivers & Helpers Union, Local 610* (440 F.2d 124, 8th Cir., *cert. denied,* 405 U.S. 996, 1972).

Another exception to the Norris–La Guardia restrictions has been recognized when a union strikes over an issue that is subject to arbitration. That exception is discussed in Chapter 9.

The NLRA.   The National Labor Relations Act, as mentioned above, makes strikes protected activity. The NLRA also contains several provisions that deal with picketing. Section 8(b)(4) outlaws secondary boycotts, and Section 8(b)(7) prohibits recognition picketing in some situations. In *NLRB v. Drivers, Chauffeurs, Helpers Local 639* (362 U.S. 274, 1960), the Supreme Court held that the NLRB may not regulate peaceful picketing that does not run afoul of Section 8(b)(4) or Section 8(b)(7). Section 8(b)(1)(A) may be used to prohibit union violence on the picket line, but it does not extend to peaceful picketing. As a result, NLRB regulation of picketing under the NLRA is limited to specific situations such as recognition picketing or secondary picketing.

State Regulation of Picketing.   Although the NLRB role in regulating picketing is limited, the states enjoy a major role in the legal regulation of picketing. *Thornhill v. Alabama,* mentioned above, prohibited the states from banning all picketing, including peaceful picketing. In *International Brotherhood of Teamsters, Local 695 v. Vogt, Inc.* (354 U.S. 284, 1957), the Supreme Court held that the states may regulate picketing when it conflicts with valid state interests. The state interest in protecting the safety of its citizens and enforcing the criminal law justifies state regulation of violent picketing. State courts may issue injunctions against acts of violence by strikers, but an outright ban on all picketing because of violence can be justified only when "the fear generated by past violence would survive even though future picketing might be wholly peaceful," according to the Supreme Court in *Milk Wagon Drivers, Local 753 v. Meadowmoor Dairies, Inc.* (312 U.S. 287, 1941).

State courts may also issue injunctions against mass picketing—picketing in which pickets march so closely together that they block access to the plant—even though it is peaceful. (See *Westinghouse Electric Co. v. U.E., Local 410,* 139 N.J. Eq. 97, 1946.) Picketing intended to force an employer to join a conspiracy in violation of state antitrust laws may be enjoined by a state court (*Giboney v. Empire Storage & Ice Co.,* 336 U.S. 490, 1949). State courts may also enjoin the use of language by pickets that constitutes fraud, misrepresentation, libel, or inciting a breach of the peace (*Linn* v. *United Plant Guard Workers Local 114,* 383 U.S. 53, 1966).

All of these cases involved picketing activity on public property. Can trespass laws be used to prohibit peaceful picketing on private property? That is the question addressed by the following case.

HUDGENS v. NLRB

424 U.S. 507 (Supreme Court of the United States, 1976)

STEWART, J.

The petitioner, Scott Hudgens, is the owner of the North DeKalb Shopping Center, located in suburban Atlanta, Ga. The center consists of a single large building with an enclosed mall. Surrounding the building is a parking area which can accommodate 2,640 automobiles. The shopping center houses 60 retail stores leased to various business. One of the lessees is the Butler Shoe Co. Most of the stores, including Butler's, can be entered only from the interior mall.

In January 1971, warehouse employees of the Butler Shoe Co. went on strike to protest the company's failure to agree to demands made by their union in contract negotiations. The strikers decided to picket not only Butler's warehouse but its nine retail stores in the Atlanta area as well, including the store in the North DeKalb Shopping Center. On January 22, 1971, four of the striking warehouse employees entered the center's enclosed mall carrying placards which read: "Butler Shoe Warehouse on Strike, AFL-CIO, Local 315." The general manager of the shopping center informed the employees that they could not picket within the mall or on the parking lot and threatened them with arrest if they did not leave. The employees departed but returned a short time later and began picketing in an area of the mall immediately adjacent to the entrances of the Butler store. After the picketing had continued for approximately 30 minutes, the shopping center manager again informed the pickets that if they did not leave they would be arrested for trespassing. The pickets departed.

The union subsequently filed with the Board an unfair labor practice charge against Hudgens, alleging interference with rights protected by Section 7 of the Act. Relying on this Court's decision in *Food Employees* v. *Logan Valley Plaza,* the Board entered a cease-and-desist order against Hudgens, reasoning that because the warehouse employees enjoyed a First Amendment right to picket on the shopping

center property, the owner's threat of arrest violated Section 8(a)(1) of the Act. Hudgens filed a petition for review in the Court of Appeals for the Fifth Circuit. Soon thereafter this Court decided *Lloyd Corp.* v. *Tanner,* and *Central Hardware Co.* v. *NLRB,* and the Court of Appeals remanded the case to the Board for reconsideration in light of those two decisions.

The Board, in turn, remanded to an Administrative Law Judge, who made findings of fact, recommendations, and conclusions to the effect that Hudgens had committed an unfair labor practice by excluding the pickets. This result was ostensibly reached under the statutory criteria set forth in *NLRB* v. *Babcock & Wilcox Co.,* a case which held that union organizers who seek to solicit for union membership may intrude on an employer's private property if no alternative means exist for communicating with the employees. But the Administrative Law Judge's opinion also relied on the Court's constitutional decision in *Logan Valley* for a "realistic view of the facts." The Board agreed with the findings and recommendations of the Administrative Law Judge, but departed somewhat from his reasoning. It concluded that the pickets were within the scope of Hudgens' invitation to members of the public to do business at the shopping center, and that it was, therefore, immaterial whether or not there existed an alternative means of communicating with the customers and employees of the Butler store.

Hudgens again petitioned for review in the Court of Appeals for the Fifth Circuit, and there the Board changed its tack and urged that the case was controlled not by *Babcock & Wilcox,* but by *Republic Aviation Corp.* v. *NLRB,* a case which held that an employer commits an unfair labor practice if he enforces a no-solicitation rule against employees on his premises who are also union organizers, unless he can prove that the rule is necessitated by special circumstances. The Court of Appeals enforced the Board's cease-and-desist order but on the basis of yet another theory. While acknowledging that the source of the pickets' rights was Section 7 of the Act, the Court of Appeals held that the competing constitutional and property right considerations discussed in *Lloyd Corp.* v. *Tanner*, "burde[n] the General Counsel with the duty to prove that other locations less intrusive upon Hudgens' property rights than picketing inside the mall were either unavailable or ineffective," and that the Board's General Counsel had met that burden in this case.

In this Court the petitioner Hudgens continues to urge that *Babcock & Wilcox Co.* is the controlling precedent, and that under the criteria of that case the judgment of the Court of Appeals should be reversed. The respondent union agrees that a statutory standard governs, but insists that, since the Section 7 activity here was not organizational as in *Babcock* but picketing in support of a lawful economic strike, an appropriate accommodation of the competing interests must lead to an affirmance of the Court of Appeals' judgment. The respondent Board now contends that the conflict between employee picketing rights and employer property rights in a case like this must be measured in accord with the commands of the First Amendment, pursuant to the Board's asserted understanding of *Lloyd Corp.* v. *Tanner*, and that the judgment of the Court of Appeals should be affirmed on the basis of that standard.

As the above recital discloses, the history of this litigation has been a history of shifting positions on the part of the litigants, the Board, and the Court of Appeals. It has been a history, in short, of considerable confusion, engendered at least in part by decisions of this Court that intervened during the course of the litigation. In the present posture of the case the most basic question is whether the respective rights and liabilities of the parties are to be decided under the criteria of the National Labor Relations Act alone, under a First Amendment standard, or under some combination of the two. It is to that question, accordingly that we now turn.

It is, of course, a commonplace that the constitutional guarantee of free speech is a guarantee only against abridgment by government, federal or state. . . . [T]he rights and liabilities of the parties in this case are dependent exclusively upon the National Labor Relations Act. Under the Act the task of the Board, subject to review by the courts, is to resolve conflicts between Section 7 rights and private property rights, "and to seek a proper accommodation between the two." What is "a proper accommodation," in any situation may largely depend upon the content and the context of the Section 7 rights being asserted. The task of the Board

and the reviewing courts under the Act, therefore, stands in conspicuous contrast to the duty of a court in applying the standards of the First Amendment, which requires "above all else" that expression must not be restricted by government "because of its message, its ideas, its subject mater, or its content."

In the *Central Hardware* case, and earlier in the case of *NLRB* v. *Babcock & Wilcox Co.,* the Court considered the nature of the Board's task in this area under the Act. Accommodation between employees' Section 7 rights and employers' property rights, the Court said in *Babcock & Wilcox,* "must be obtained with as little destruction of one as is consistent with the maintenance of the other."

Both *Central Hardware* and *Babcock & Wilcox* involved organizational activity carried on by nonemployees on the employers' property. The context of the Section 7 activity in the present case was different in several respects which may or may not be relevant in striking the proper balance. First, it involved lawful economic strike activity rather than organizational activity. Second, the Section 7 activity here was carried on by Butler's employees (albeit not employees of its shopping center store), not by outsiders. Third, the property interests impinged upon in this case were not those of the employer against whom the Section 7 activity was directed, but of another.

The *Babcock & Wilson* opinion established the basic objective under the Act: accommodation of Section 7 rights and private property rights "with as little destruction of one as is consistent with the maintenance of the other." The locus of that accommodation, however, may fall at differing points along the spectrum depending on the nature and strength of the respective Section 7 rights and private property rights asserted in any given context. In each generic situation, the primary responsibility for making this accommodation must rest with the Board in the first instance. . . .

For the reasons stated in this opinion, the judgment is vacated and the case is remanded to the Court of Appeals with directions to remand to the National Labor Relations Board, so that the case may be there considered under the statutory criteria of the National Labor Relations Act alone. **It is so ordered.**

Picketing under the NLRA

As noted above, Sections 8(b)(4) and 8(b)(7) of the NLRA prohibit certain kinds of picketing. Peaceful picketing is protected activity under the NLRA. However, violent picketing and mass picketing, as well as threatening conduct by the picketers, are not protected under Section 7. Employees who engage in such conduct may be disciplined or discharged by the employer and may also be subject to injunctions, criminal charges, and civil tort suits.

Section 8(b)(4) deals with secondary boycotts—certain union pressure tactics aimed at employers that are not involved in a labor dispute with the union. Section 8(b)(7) regulates picketing by unions for organizational or recognitional purposes.

Section 8(b)(7): Recognition and Organization Picketing.   Section 8(b)(7) was added to the NLRA by the 1959 Landrum-Griffin Act. It prohibits recognitional picketing by an uncertified union in certain situations. Section 8(b)(7) contains the following provisions:

> [It is an unfair practice for a labor organization] (7) to picket or cause to be picketed, or threaten to picket or cause to be picketed, any employer where an object thereof is forcing or requiring an employer to recognize or bargain with a labor organization as the representative of his employees, or forcing or requiring the employees of an employer to accept or select such labor organization as their collective-bargaining representative, unless such labor organization is currently certified as the representative of such employees:
>
>   (A) where the employer has lawfully recognized in accordance with this Act any other labor organization and a question concerning representation may not appropriately be raised under Section 9(c) of this Act,
>
>   (B) where within the preceding twelve months a valid election under Section 9(c) of this Act has been conducted, or
>
>   (C) where such picketing has been conducted without a petition under Section 9(c) being filed within a reasonable period of time not to exceed thirty days from the commencement of such picketing: Provided, That when such a petition has been filed the Board shall forthwith, without regard to the provisions of Section 9(c)(1) or the absence of a showing of a substantial interest on the part of the labor organization, direct an election in such unit as the Board finds to be appropriate and shall certify the results thereof: Provided further, That nothing in this subparagraph (C) shall be construed to prohibit any picketing or other publicity for the purpose of truthfully advising the public (including consumers) that an employer does not employ members of, or have a contract with, a labor organization, unless an effect of such picketing is to induce any individual employed by any other person in the course of his employment, not to pick up, deliver or transport any goods or not to perform any services.
>
>   Nothing in this paragraph (7) shall be construed to permit any act which would otherwise be an unfair labor practice under this Section 8(b).

The interpretation of Section 8(b)(7) and its application to recognitional picketing are the subjects of the following case.

SMITLEY v. NLRB

327 F.2d 351 (U.S. Court of Appeals, 9th Cir. 1964)

[After the NLRB dismissed a complaint that the union had violated Section 8(b)(7)(C), the company sought judicial review of the board's decision.]

DUNIWAY, J.

The findings of the Board as to the facts are not attached. It found, in substance, that the unions picketed the cafeteria for more than thirty days before filing a representation petition under Section 9(c) of the act, that an object of the picketing was to secure recognition, that the purpose of the picketing was truthfully to advise the public that petitioners employed nonunion employees or had no contract with the unions, and that the picketing did not have the effect of inducing any stoppage of deliveries or services to the cafeteria by employees of any other employer.... We conclude that the views of the Board, as stated after its second consideration of the matter, are correct, and that the statute has not been violated.

The Board states its interpretation of the section, including the proviso [8(b)(7)(C)] as follows;

> Congress framed a general rule covering all organizational and recognitional picketing carried on for more than 30 days without the filing of a representation petition. Then, Congress excepted from that rule picketing which, although it had an organizational or recognitional objective, was addressed primarily to the public, was truthful in nature, and did not interfere to any significant extent with deliveries or the rendition of services by the employees of any other employer.

We think that this is the correct interpretation. It will be noted that Subdivision (7) of Subsection (b), Section 8, starts with the general prohibition of picketing "where an object thereof is forcing or requiring an employer to recognize or bargain with a labor organization" (This is often called recognitional picketing) "... or forcing or requiring the employees of an employer to accept or select such labor organization...." (This is often called organizational picketing), "... unless such labor organization is currently certified as the representative of such employees:..." This is followed by three subparagraphs, (A), (B), and (C). Each begins with the same word, "where." (A) deals with the situation "where" the employer has lawfully recognized another labor organization and a question of representation

cannot be raised under Section 9(c). (B) refers to the situation "where," within the preceding 12 months, a valid election under Section 9(c) has been conducted. (C), with which we are concerned, refers to a situation "where" there has been no petition for an election under Section 9(c) filed within a reasonable period of time, not to exceed thirty days, from the commencement of the picketing. Thus, Section 8(b)(7) does not purport to prohibit all picketing having the named "object" of recognitional or organizational picketing. It limits the prohibition of such picketing to three specific situations.

There are no exceptions or provisos in subparagraphs (A) and (B), which describe two of those situations. There are, however, two provisos in subparagraph (C). The first sets up a special procedure for an expedited election under Section 9(c). The second is one with which we are concerned. It is an exception to the prohibition of "such picketing," i.e., recognitional or organizational picketing, being a proviso to a prohibition of such picketing "where" certain conditions exist. It can only mean, indeed, it says that "such picketing," which otherwise falls within subparagraph (C), is not prohibited if it falls within the terms of the proviso. That proviso says that subparagraph (C) is not to be construed to prohibit "any picketing" for "the purpose" of truthfully advising the public (including consumers) that an employer does not employ members of, or have a contract with, a labor organization. To this exception there is an exception, stated in the last "unless" clause, namely, that "such picketing," i.e., picketing where "an object" is recognitional or organizational, but which has "the" excepting "purpose," would still be illegal if an effect were to induce any individual employee of other persons not to pick up, deliver, or transport any goods, or not to perform any services. Admittedly, the picketing here does not fall within the "unless" clause in the second proviso to subparagraph (C). It does, however, fall within the proviso, since it does have "the purpose" that brings it within the proviso. It also has "an object" that brings it within the first sentence of Subsection (b) and the first clause of Subdivision (7), therefore it would not be prohibited at all. Moreover, if it did have that "object," it still would not be prohibited at all, unless it occurred in circumstances described in subparagraph (A), (B) or (C). Here, neither (A) or (B) applies; (C) does. But, unlike (A) or (B), it has an excepting proviso. Unless that proviso refers to picketing having as "an object" either recognition or organization, it can have no meaning, for it would not be an exception or proviso to anything. It would be referring to conduct not prohibited in Section 8(b) at all.

Petitioners urge that if the picketing has as "an object" recognition or organization, then it is still illegal, even though it has "the purpose" of truthfully advising the public, etc., within the meaning of the second proviso to subparagraph (C). It seems to us, as it did to the Board, that to so construe the statute would make the proviso meaningless. The hard realities of union-employer relations are such that it is difficult, indeed almost impossible, for us to conceive of picketing falling within the terms of the proviso that did not also have as "an object" obtaining a contract with the employer. This is normally the ultimate objective of any union in relation to an employer who has employees whose jobs fall within the categories of employment that are within the jurisdiction of the union, which is admittedly the situation here.

. . . We think that, in substance, the effect of the second proviso to subparagraph (C) is to allow recognitional or organizational picketing to continue if it meets two important restrictions: (1) it must be addressed to the public and be truthful and (2) it must not induce other unions to stop deliveries or services. The picketing here met those criteria. . . .

[The court affirmed the board's dismissal of the complaint.]

If a union pickets in violation of Section 8(b)(7)(C), the employer may request that the NLRB hold an expedited election. The NLRB will determine the appropriate bargaining unit and hold an election. No showing of interest on the part of the union is necessary. The NLRB will certify the results of the election; if the union is certified, the employer must bargain with it. If the union loses, continued picketing will violate Section 8(b)(7)(B). Why? Section 10(1) requires the board to seek an injunction against the picketing when it issues a complaint for an alleged Section 8(b)(7) violation.

As *Smitley* emphasizes, not all recognitional picketing violates Section 8(b)(7). The proviso in Section 8(b)(7)(C) allows recognitional picketing directed at the public to inform them that the picketed employer does not have a contract with the union. Such picketing for publicity may continue beyond thirty days, unless it causes other employees to refuse to work.

Picketing to protest substandard wages paid by an employer, as long as the union does not have a recognitional object, is not subject to Section 8(b)(7). Such picketing may continue indefinitely and is not unlawful, even if it has the effect of disrupting deliveries to the employer, according to *Houston Building & Construction Trades Council* (136 N.L.R.B. 321, 1962). Similarly, picketing to protest unfair practices by the employer, when there is no recognitional objective, is not prohibited, according to *UAW Local 259* (133 N.L.R.B. 1468, 1968).

Section 8(b)(4): Secondary Boycotts.

Section 8(b)(4), which deals with secondary boycotts, is one of the most complex provisions of the NLRA. Section 8(b)(4) contains the following provisions:

[It is an unfair practice for a labor organization] (4) (i) to engage in, or to induce or encourage any individual employed by any person engaged in commerce or in an industry affecting commerce to engage in, a strike or refusal in the course of his employment to use, manufacture, process, transport, or otherwise handle or work on any goods, articles, materials, or commodities or to perform any services; or (ii) to threaten, coerce, or restrain any person engaged in commerce or in an industry affecting commerce, where in either case an object thereof is:

(A) forcing or requiring any employer or self-employed person to join any labor or employer organization to enter into any agreement which is prohibited by Section 8(e);

(B) forcing or requiring any person to cease using, selling, handling, transporting, or otherwise dealing in the products of any other producer, processor, or manufacturer, or to cease doing business with any other person, or forcing or requiring any other employer to recognize or bargain with a labor organization as the representative of his employees unless such labor organization has been certified as the representative of such employees under the provisions of Section 9: Provided, That nothing contained in this clause (B) shall be construed to make unlawful, where not otherwise unlawful, any primary strike or primary picketing;

(C) forcing or requiring any employer to recognize or bargain with a particular labor organization as the representative of his employees if another labor organization has been certified as the representative of such employees under the provisions of Section 9;

(D) forcing or requiring any employer to assign particular work to employees in a particular labor organization or in a particular trade, craft, or class rather than to employees in another labor organization or in another trade, craft, or class, unless such employer is failing to conform to an order or certification of the Board determining the bargaining representative for employees performing such work:

Provided, That nothing contained in this Subsection (b) shall be construed to make unlawful a refusal by any person to enter upon the premises of any employer (other than his own employer), if the employees of such employer are engaged in a strike ratified or approved by a representative of such employees whom such employer is required under this Act: Provided further, That for the purposes of this paragraph (4) only, nothing contained in such paragraph shall be construed to prohibit publicity, other than picketing, for the purpose of truthfully advising the public, including consumers and members of a labor organization, that a product or products are produced by an employer with whom the labor organization has a primary dispute and are distributed by another employer, as long as such publicity does not have an effect of inducing any individual employed by any person other than the primary employer in the course of his employment to refuse to pick up, deliver, or transport any goods, or not to perform any services, at the establishment of the employer engaged in such distributions. . . .

When considering Section 8(b)(4), the courts and the board generally consider the intention behind the provisions rather than its literal wording. The intention is to protect employers who are not involved in a dispute with a union from pressure by that union. For example, if the union representing the workers of a toy manufacturing company goes on strike, it is free to picket the manufacturer (the primary employer). But if the union pickets the premises of a wholesaler who distributes the toys of the primary employer, such picketing may be secondary and prohibited by Section 8(b)(4)(B). Whether the picketing is prohibited depends on whether the union's picketing has the objective of trying to force the wholesaler to cease doing business with the manufacturer.

Most secondary picketing situations, however, are more complicated than this simple example. For example, if the primary employer's location of business is mobile, such as a cement-mix delivery truck, is the union allowed to picket a construction site where the cement truck is making a delivery? What if the union has a dispute with a subcontractor on a construction site—can it picket the entire construction site?

Primary picketing is picketing by a union against an employer with which it has a dispute. Section 8(b)(4) does not prohibit such picketing, even though the purpose of the picketing is intended to persuade customers to cease doing business with the primary employer. It is important, therefore, to identify which employer is the primary employer—the employer with whom the union has the dispute. It is helpful to consider three questions when confronting a potential secondary picketing situation. The first question is, "With whom does the union have the dispute?" That identifies the primary employer. Question two is, "Where is the union picketing? At the primary employer's premises, or at the site of a neutral employer?" Question three is, "What is the object of the union's picketing?" If the union is picketing at a secondary employer in order to force that employer to cease doing business with the primary employer, then it is illegal. But if the picketing is intended only to inform the public that the secondary employer handles the primary product, it is legal. The objective of the picketing is the key to its legality—does the picketing have an objective prohibited by Section 8(b)(4)?

Ambulatory Situs Picketing.   When the primary employer's business location is mobile, picketing by a union following that mobile location is called **ambulatory situs picketing.** The following board decision sets out the conditions under which the union may engage in ambulatory situs picketing.

SAILORS' UNION OF THE PACIFIC AND MOORE DRY DOCK CO.

92 N.L.R.B. 547 (N.L.R.B., 1950)

[Samsoc, a shipping company, contracted with Kaiser Gypsum to ship gypsum from Mexico in the ship *Phopho.* Samsoc replaced the crew of the ship with a foreign crew. The union demanded bargaining rights for the ship; Samsoc refused. The ship was in dry dock being outfitted for the voyage, and the foreign crew was on board for training. The union posted pickets at the entrances to the dry dock; the dry-dock workers refused to work on the ship but did perform other work. The dry-dock company filed an unfair practice charge with the NLRB.]

Picketing at the premises of a primary employer is traditionally recognized as primary action, even though it is

"necessarily designed to induce and encourage third persons to cease doing business with the picketed employer. . . ."

Hence, if Samsoc, the owner of the *S.S. Phopho,* had had a dock of its own in California to which the *Phopho* had been tied up while undergoing conversion by Moore Dry Dock employees, picketing by the Respondent at the dock site would unquestionably have constituted *primary* action even though the Respondent might have expected that the picketing would be more effective in persuading Moore employees not to work on the ship than to persuade the seamen aboard the *Phopho* to quit that vessel. The difficulty in the present case arises therefore, not because of any difference in picketing objectives, but from the fact that the *Phopho* was not tied up at its own dock, but at that of Moore, while the picketing was going on in front of the Moore premises.

In the usual case, the *situs* of a labor dispute is the premises of the primary employer. Picketing of the premises is also picketing of the *situs*. . . . But in some cases the *situs* of the dispute may not be limited to a fixed location; it may be ambulatory. Thus, in the *Schultz* case, a majority of the Board held that the truck upon which a truck driver worked was the *situs* of a labor dispute between him and the owner of the truck. Similarly, we hold in the present case that, as the *Phopho* was the place of employment of the seamen, it was the *situs* of the dispute between Samsoc and the Respondent over working conditions aboard the vessel.

When the *situs* is ambulatory, it may come to rest temporarily at the premises of another employer. The perplexing question is: Does the right to picket follow the *situs* while it is stationed at the premises of a secondary employer, when the only way to picket that *situs* is in front of the secondary employer's premises? . . . Essentially the problem is one of balancing the right of a union to picket at the site of its dispute as against the right of a secondary employer to be free from picketing in a controversy in which it is not directly involved.

When a secondary employer is harboring the *situs* of a dispute between a union and a primary employer, the right of neither the union to picket nor of the secondary employer to be free from picketing can be absolute. The enmeshing of premises and *situs* qualifies both rights. In the kind of situation that exists in this case, we believe that picketing of the premises of a secondary employer is primary if it meets the following conditions: (a) The picketing is strictly limited to times when the *situs* of dispute is located on the secondary employer's premises; (b) at the time of the picketing the primary employer is engaged in its normal business at the *situs*; (c) the picketing is limited to places reasonably close to the location of the *situs*; (d) the picketing discloses clearly that the dispute is with the primary employer. All these conditions were met in the present case.

(a) During the entire period of the picketing the *Phopho* was tied up at a dock in the Moore shipyard.

(b) Under its contract with Samsoc, Moore agreed to permit the former to put a crew on board the *Phopho* for training

purposes during the last two weeks before the vessel's delivery to Samsoc. . . . The various members of the crew commenced work as soon as they reported aboard the *Phopho*. Those in the deck compartment did painting and cleaning up, those in the steward's department, cooking and cleaning up; and those in the engine department, oiling and cleaning up. The crew were thus getting the ship ready for sea. They were on board to serve the purposes of Samsoc, the *Phopho's* owners, and not Moore. The normal business of a ship does not only begin with its departure on a scheduled voyage. The multitudinous steps of preparation, including hiring and training a crew and putting stores aboard, are as much a part of the normal business of a ship as the voyage itself. We find, therefore, that the *Phopho* was engaged in its normal business.

(c) Before placing its pickets outside the entrance to the Moore shipyard, the Respondent Union asked, but was refused, permission to place its pickets at the dock where the *Phopho* was tied up. The Respondent, therefore, posted its pickets at the yard entrance which, as the parties stipulated, was as close to the *Phopho* as they could get under the circumstances.

(d) Finally, by its picketing and other conduct the Respondent was scrupulously careful to indicate that its dispute was solely with the primary employer, the owners of the *Phopho*. Thus the signs carried by the pickets said only that the *Phopho* was unfair to the Respondent. The *Phopho* and not Moore was declared "hot." Similarly, in asking co-operation of other unions, the Respondent clearly revealed that its dispute was with the *Phopho*. Finally, Moore's own witnesses admitted that no attempt was made to interfere with other work in progress in the Moore yard. . . .

We are only holding that, if a shipyard permits the owner of a vessel to use its dock for the purpose of readying and training a crew and putting stores aboard a ship, a union representing seamen may then within the careful limitations laid down in this decision, lawfully picket the front of the shipyard premises to advertise its dispute with the shipowner. . . .

[The complaint was dismissed.]

Reserved Gate Picketing—Secondary Employees at the Primary Site. The *Moore Dry Dock* case deals with the legality of picketing at a secondary, or neutral, location. What about the legality of picketing that affects secondary employees at a primary site? The following case, also called the *General Electric* case, deals with that situation.

LOCAL 761, INTERNATIONAL UNION OF ELECTRICAL, RADIO & MACHINE WORKERS [GENERAL ELECTRIC] v. NLRB

366 U.S. 667 (Supreme Court of the United States, 1961)

FRANKFURTER, J.

General Corporation operates a plant outside of Louisville, Kentucky, where it manufactures washers, dryers, and other electrical household appliances. The square-shaped, thousand-acre, unfenced plant is known as Appliance Park. A large drainage ditch makes ingress and egress impossible except over five roadways across culverts, designated as gates.

Since 1954, General Electric sought to confine the employees of independent contractors, described hereafter, who work on the premises of the Park, to the use of Gate 3-A and confine its use to them. The undisputed reason for doing so was to insulate General Electric employees from the frequent labor disputes in which the contractors were involved. Gate 3-A is 550 feet away from the nearest entrance available for General Electric employees, suppliers, and deliverymen. Although anyone can pass the gate without challenge, the roadway leads to a guardhouse where identification must be presented. Vehicle stickers of various shapes and colors enable a guard to check on sight whether a vehicle is authorized to use Gate 3-A. Since January 1958, a prominent sign has been posted at the gate which states: *"Gate 3-A for Employees of Contractors Only—G.E. Employees Use Other Gates."* On rare occasions, it appears, a General Electric employee was allowed to pass the guardhouse, but such occurrence was in violation of company instructions. There was no proof of any unauthorized attempts to pass the gate during the strike in question.

The independent contractors are utilized for a great variety of tasks on the Appliance Park premises. Some do construction work on new buildings; some install and repair ventilating and heating equipment; some engage in retooling and rearranging operations necessary to the manufacture of new models; others do "general maintenance work".…

The Union, petitioner here, is the certified bargaining representative for the production and maintenance workers who constitute approximately 7,600 of the 10,500 employees of General Electric at Appliance Park. On July 27, 1958, the Union called a strike because of 24 unsettled grievances with the company. Picketing occurred at all the gates, including Gate 3-A, and continued until August 9

when an injunction was issued by a Federal District Court. The signs carried by the pickets at all gates read: *"Local 761 on Strike G.E. Unfair."* Because of the picketing, almost all of the employees of independent contractors refused to enter the company premises.

Neither the legality of the strike or of the picketing at any of the gates except 3-A nor the peaceful nature of the picketing is in dispute. The sole claim is that the picketing before the gate exclusively used by employees of independent contractors was conduct proscribed by [8(b)(4)(B)].

The Trial Examiner recommended that the Board dismiss the complaint. He concluded that the limitations on picketing which the Board had prescribed in so-called "common situs" cases were not applicable to the situation before him, in that the picketing at Gate 3-A represented traditional primary action which necessarily had a secondary effect of inconveniencing those who did business with the struck employer.…

The Board rejected the Trial Examiner's conclusion. It held that, since only the employees of the independent contractors were allowed to use Gate 3-A, the Union's object in picketing there was "to enmesh these employees of the neutral employers in its dispute with the Company," thereby constituting a violation of Section 8(b)(4)[(B)] because the independent employees were encouraged to engage in a concerted refusal to work "with an object of forcing the independent contractors to cease doing business with the Company."

The Court of Appeals for the District of Columbia granted enforcement of the Board's order. Although noting that a fine line was being drawn, it concluded that the Board was correct in finding that the objective of the Gate 3-A picketing was to encourage the independent-contractor employees to engage in a concerted refusal to perform services for their employers in order to bring pressure on General Electric. Since the incidence of the problem involved in this case is extensive and the treatment it has received calls for clarification, we brought the case here.

Section 8(b)(4)[(B)] of the National Labor Relations Act provided that it shall be an unfair labor practice for a labor organization

to engage in, or to induce or encourage the employees of any employer to engage in, a strike or a concerted refusal in the course of their employment to use, manufacture, process, transport, or otherwise handle or work on any goods, articles, materials, or commodities or to perform any services, where an object thereof is: [(B)] forcing or requiring . . . any employer or other person . . . to cease doing business with any other person. . . .

This provision could not be literally construed; otherwise it would ban most strikes historically considered to be lawful, so-called primary activity. "While Section 8(b)(4) does not expressly mention 'primary' or 'secondary' disputes, strikes or boycotts, that section often is referred to in the Act's legislative history as one of the Act's 'secondary boycott sections.'" Congress did not seek, by Section 8(b)(4), to interfere with the ordinary strike. . . ." The impact of the section was directed toward what is known as the secondary boycott whose "sanctions bear, not upon the employer who alone is a party to the dispute, but upon some third party who has no concern in it." Thus the section "left a striking labor organization free to use persuasion, including picketing, not only on the primary employer and his employees but on numerous others. Among these were secondary employers who were customers or suppliers of the primary employer and persons dealing with them . . . and even employees of secondary employers so long as the labor organization did not . . . 'induce or encourage the employees of any employer to engage in a strike or a concerted refusal in the course of their employment'. . . ."

But not all so-called secondary boycotts were outlawed in Section (b)(4)[(B)]. "The section does not speak generally of secondary boycotts. It describes and condemns specific union conduct directed to specific objectives. . . . Employees must be induced; they must be induced to engage in a strike or concerted refusal; an object must be to force or require their employer or another person to cease doing business with a third person. Thus, much that might argumentatively be found to fall within the broad and somewhat vague concept of secondary boycott is not in terms prohibited."

Important as is the distinction between legitimate "primary activity" and banned "secondary activity," it does not present a glaringly bright line. The objectives of any picketing include a desire to influence others from withholding from the employer their services or trade. . . . But picketing which induces secondary employees to respect a picket line is not the equivalent of picketing which has an object of inducing those employees to engage in concerted conduct against their employer in order to force him to refuse to deal with the struck employer.

However difficult the drawing of lines more nice than ob-

vious, the statute compels the task. Accordingly, the Board and the court have attempted to devise reasonable criteria drawing heavily upon the means to which a union resorts in promoting its cause. . . . [Discussion of cases omitted.]

From this necessary survey of the course of the Board's treatment of our problem, the precise nature of the issue before us emerges. With due regard to the relation between the Board's function and the scope of judicial review of its rulings, the question is whether the Board may apply the *Dry Dock* criteria so as to make unlawful picketing at a gate utilized exclusively by employees of independent contractors who work on the struck employer's premises. . . . The key to the problem is found in the type of work that is being performed by those who use the separate gate. It is significant that the Board has since applied its rationale, first stated in the present case, only to situations where the independent workers were performing tasks unconnected to the normal operations of the struck employer—usually construction work on his buildings. In such situations, the indicated limitations on picketing activity respect the balance of competing interests that Congress has required the Board to enforce. On the other hand, if a separate gate were devised for regular plant deliveries, the barring of picketing at that location would make a clear invasion on traditional primary activity of appealing to neutral employees whose tasks aid the employer's everyday operations. The 1959 Amendments to the National Labor Relations Act, which removed the word "concerted" from the boycott provisions, included a proviso that "nothing contained in this clause (b) shall be construed to make unlawful, where not otherwise unlawful, any primary strike or primary picketing. . . ."

In a case similar to the one now before us, the Court of Appeals of the Second Circuit sustained the Board in its application of Section 8(b)(4)(A) to a separate-gate situation. "There must be a separate gate marked and set apart from other gates; the work done by the men who use the gate must be unrelated to the normal operations of the employer and the work must be of a kind that would not, if done when the plant were engaged in its regular operations, necessitate curtailing those operations." These seem to us controlling considerations.

The foregoing course of reasoning would require that the judgment below sustaining the Board's order be affirmed but for one consideration, even though this consideration may turn out not to affect the result. The legal path by which the Board and the Court of Appeals reached their decisions did not take into account that if Gate 3-A was in fact used by employees of independent contractors who performed conventional maintenance work necessary to the normal operations of General Electric, the use of the gate would have been a mingled one outside the bar of Section 8(b)(4)[(B)]. In short, such mixed use of this portion of the struck employer's premises would not bar picketing rights of the striking employees. While the record shows some such mingled use, it sheds no light on its extent. It may well turn out to be that the instances of these mainte-nance tasks were so insubstantial as to be treated by the Board as *de minimis*. We cannot here guess at the quantita-tive aspect of this problem. It calls for Board determination. For determination of the questions thus raised, the case must be remanded by the Court of Appeals to the Board. **Reversed.**

Common Situs Picketing. The *General Electric* case made the nature of the work performed by the secondary employees at the primary site the key to whether the union may target the secondary employees with picketing. In the construction in-dustry, subcontractors and the general contractor are all working on the same proj-ect—erecting a building. Does that mean a union that has a dispute with the general contractor may picket the entire construction site (known as **common situs pick-eting**)? The following case sets out the NLRB's approach to common situs picketing.

BUILDING AND CONSTRUCTION TRADES COUNCIL OF NEW ORLEANS, AFL-CIO AND MARKWELL AND HARTZ, INC.

155 N.L.R.B. 319 (N.L.R.B., 1965)

Markwell and Hartz, Inc., is a Tennessee corporation en-gaged as a general contractor in the building and construc-tion industry. . . . At all times material herein, M & H has been engaged as general contractor on the filtration plant expansion of East Jefferson Water Works District No. 1, Jef-ferson Parish, Louisiana. . . .

Binnings Construction Company, Inc., herein called Bin-nings, and Walter J. Barnes Electrical Company, herein called Barnes, are engaged as piledriving and electrical con-tractors, respectively, in the building and construction in-dustry. . . .

M & H decided to perform about 80 percent of the proj-ect with its own employees while subcontracting the balance.

The Jefferson Water Works is surrounded by a chain-link fence, with two vehicular gates on Jefferson Highway which bounds the property on the north, and two additional gates on Arnoult Road is the principal gate insofar as the con-struction project is concerned, and is called the main gate. On Arnoult Road the northern-most gate is the warehouse gate while the southern-most shall be referred to as the rear gate.

At all times material, Respondent has been engaged in a primary labor dispute with M & H, and has had no dispute with either Binnings or Barnes.

On October 17, in connection with its dispute with M & H, Respondent commenced picketing the gates leading to the jobsite. The picketing took place during normal work-hours, with the number of pickets varying from one to three individuals. The picket sign listed both the rates that should be paid on the job and carried the following message:

MARKWELL AND HARTZ

GENERAL CONTRACTOR

DOES NOT HAVE A SIGNED AGREEMENT

WITH THE BUILDING AND

CONSTRUCTION TRADES COUNCIL

OF NEW ORLEANS AFL-CIO

The picketing continued until enjoined . . . on January 16, 1964. At no time during the picketing did employees of Binnings or Barnes cross the picket line to perform work in connection with their employer's subcontract.

The validity of Respondent's picketing prior to October 23 is not in issue. However, on that date M & H posted the two gates on Jefferson Highway and the warehouse gate on Ar-noult Road, reserving them for use of subcontractors and persons making deliveries to the project, and prohibiting their use by M & H's employees. The rear gate on Arnoult Road was designated for exclusive use of the latter.

That morning, when Respondent's picket encountered the newly marked gates, he moved to the rear gate which was reserved for M & H's employees. As a result, piledriving crews employed by Binnings entered the main gate and began working. About an hour and a half later the picket returned to the main gate, and Binnings' employees walked off. M & H then decided to remove its employees, with the exception of the superintendent and project engineer, in the hope that Binnings would then be able to complete the piledriving work. Though Respondent was notified of the absence of the primary employees, the picketing continued. When Binnings' crews again honored the picket line, M & H recalled its employees. They reported to work on October 24 at 10 A.M. to complete the piledriving work themselves. . . .

The record does not show that the gates were at any time used in a manner inconsistent with the postings. Excepting a brief period on October 23, and the period between December 16 and 20, Respondent picketed the gates which were posted for exclusive use of subcontractors and which were not used by M & H's employees and suppliers.

On these facts, we are asked to decide whether a union, in furtherance of a primary dispute with a general contractor in the construction industry, may lawfully engage in jobsite picketing at gates reserved and set apart for exclusive use of neutral subcontractors. In this connection, the General Counsel and Charging Party contend that Respondent's picketing of the subcontractor gates exceed permissible bounds of primary action and, thereby, demonstrated that Respondent unlawfully sought to enmesh secondary employers in its dispute with the general contractor. The Respondent, without denying that its conduct fell within the prohibitory terms of Section 8(b)(4)(i) and (ii)(B) of the Act, argues that the picketing was at all times in furtherance of its primary dispute with M & H and protected by the "primary strike and picketing proviso." Specifically, Respondent asserts that, as the work of the subcontractors purportedly related to the normal operations of M & H, the Supreme Court's decision in *Local 761, International Union of Electrical, Radio and Machine Workers, AFL-CIO (General Electric Co.)* v. *NLRB* and *United Steelworkers of America, AFL-CIO (Carrier Corp.)* v. *NLRB,* compel dismissal of the complaint herein. We do not agree with the Respondent's position.

In *General Electric* the Supreme Court ruled that the picketing "at a gate utilized exclusively by employees of in-

dependent contractors who work on the struck employer's premises" is lawful primary activity *unless* the following conditions exist:

> There must be a separate gate, marked and set apart from other gates; the work done by the men who use the gate must be unrelated to the normal operations of the employer, and the work must be of a kind that would not, if done when the . . . [employer] were engaged in its regular operations, necessitate curtailing those operations.

Subsequently, in *Carrier Corp.,* the Court approved the Board's application of these standards so as to permit, as legitimate primary action, picketing of a gate, owned by a railroad but cut through a fence surrounding the struck employers premises. This gate was used exclusively by neutral railroad employees entering the struck premises to perform delivery activities related to the normal operations of the struck employer.

Without passing upon whether the subcontractor gates involved herein were established and maintained in accordance with the *General Electric* requirements, we are of the opinion that the principles expressed in that case are inapposite in determining whether a union may lawfully extend its dispute with a general contractor on a construction site by picketing gates reserved for exclusive use of subcontractors also engaged on that project. Rather, we believe that this issue must be resolved in the light of the *Moore Dry Dock* standards, traditionally applied by the Board in determining whether picketing at a common situs is protected primary activity.

Unlike *General Electric* and *Carrier Corp.,* both of which involved picketing *at the premises of a struck manufacturer,* the picketing in the instant case occurred at a construction project on which M & H, the primary employer, was but one of several employers operating on premises owned and operated by a third party, the Jefferson Parish Water Works. Picketing of neutral and primary contractors under such conditions, has been traditionally viewed as presenting a "common situs" problem.

Over the years, the distinction between common situs picketing and that which occurs at premises occupied solely by the struck employer has been a guiding consideration in Board efforts to strike a balance between the competing interests underlying the boycott provisions of the Act. Mindful of the fact that "Congress did not seek, by Section 8(b)(4), to interfere with the ordinary strike," the Board has given wide latitude to picketing and related conduct confined to the sole premises of the primary employer. On the other hand, in the interest of shielding "unoffending employers" from disputes not their own, the Board has taken a more restrictive view of common situs picketing, requiring that it be conducted so as to "minimize its impact on neutral employees insofar as this can be done without substantial impairment of the effectiveness of the picketing in reaching the primary employees."

In accordance with the foregoing, the Board, in determining whether a labor organization, when picketing a common situs, has taken all reasonable precautions to prevent enmeshment of neutrals, traditionally applies the limitations set forth in the *Moore Dry Dock* case. . . .

Applying the *Moore Dry Dock* standards to the instant case requires the timing and location of the picketing and the legends on the picket signs to be tailored to reach the employees of the primary employer, rather than those of the neutral employer, and deviations from these requirements establish the secondary object of the picketing and render it unlawful. . . . Since Respondent's picketing at the neutral gates of Binnings and Barnes continued after November 16, we find, in agreement with the General Counsel, that the picketing after that date failed to comply with the *Moore Dry Dock* requirement that such action take place reasonably close to the situs of Respondent's dispute with M & H. We are completely satisfied that Respondent's picketing at the subcontractor gates was to induce strike action by employees of subcontractors with whom Respondent had no dispute. By such conduct, Respondent unlawfully sought to disrupt the operations of the neutral subcontractors and their employees and to enmesh them in the primary dispute in a manner which could not be condoned as an unavoidable by-product of legitimate primary picketing. . . .

The dissent's analysis, although well-stated and on first reading not unreasonable as an application of *General Electric* standards in a construction industry setting, nevertheless runs counter to firmly established principles governing common situs picketing in that industry. Simply because the work of the neutral subcontractors in one sense is "related to M & H's normal operations," our dissenting colleagues would exonerate the pickets' appeals to the sec-ondary employees to honor the picket line aimed at M & H. And notwithstanding their suggestion that they would apply the "related work" standard only where the dispute is with a general contractor, the plain logic of their position is equally applicable where the primary dispute is with a building construction subcontractor whose employees are working closely with employees of other subcontractors or those of the general contractors. Given the close relation—which is not only characteristic of but almost inevitable at many stages of a building construction project—of the work duties of the various other employees with those of the primary subcontractor, the principle of the dissent would also permit picket line appeals to the employees of the neutral general contractor and other subcontractors whatever the situation as to common or separate gates.

But it was precisely this claim, that the *close* working relations of various building construction contractors on a common situs involved them in a common undertaking which destroyed the neutrality and thus the immunity of secondary employers and employees to picket line appeals, that the Supreme Court rejected in *Denver Building Trades*. And there is not the slightest imitation by the Court in *General Electric* or *Carrier* that it was reversing or revising the rule in *Denver*. . . .

For the reasons stated, we conclude that Respondent violated Section 8(b)(4)(i) and (ii)(B) of the Act by inducing employees of Binnings and Barnes to engage in work stoppages, and by restraining and coercing said Employers, for an object of forcing or requiring them to cease doing business with M & H. . . .

Having found that the Respondent has engaged in certain unfair labor practices, we shall order that it cease and desist therefrom and take certain affirmative action that we find necessary to effectuate the policies of the Act. . . .

So ordered.

[The board's order in the *Markwell & Hartz* case was enforced by the Fifth Circuit Court of Appeals (387 F2d 79, 1968).]

Ally Doctrine.   Not all union picketing directed against employers other than the primary employer is prohibited. The secondary boycott prohibitions were intended to protect neutral employers from union pressure. If any employer is not neutral—because it is performing the work normally done by the workers of the primary employer, who are now on strike—may the union picket that other employer? That is the issue addressed in the following case.

NLRB v. BUSINESS MACHINE & OFFICE APPLIANCE MECHANICS CONFERENCE BOARD, IUE, LOCAL 459 [ROYAL TYPEWRITER CO.]

228 F.2d 553 (U.S. Court of Appeals, 2nd Cir. 1955), cert. denied, 351 U.S. 962 (1956)

LUMBARD, J.

This case arose out of a labor dispute between the Royal Typewriter Company and the Business Machine and Office Appliance Mechanics Conference Board, Local 459, IUE-CIO, the certified bargaining agent of the Royal's typewriter mechanics and other service personnel. The National Labor Relations Board now seeks enforcement of an order directing the Union to cease and desist from certain picketing and to post appropriate notices. . . .

On about March 23, 1954, the Union, being unable to reach agreement with Royal on the terms of a contract, called the Royal service personnel out on strike. The service employees customarily repair typewriters either at Royal's branch offices or at its customers' premises. Royal has several arrangements under which it is obligated to render service to its customers. First, Royal's warranty on each new machine obligates it to provide free inspection and repair for one year. Second, for a fixed periodic fee Royal contracts to service machines not under warranty. Finally, Royal is committed to repairing typewriters rented from it or loaned by it to replace machines undergoing repair. Of course, in addition Royal provides repair service on call by non-contract users.

During the strike Royal differentiated between calls from customers to whom it owed a repair obligation and others. Royal's office personnel were instructed to tell the latter to call some independent repair company listed in the telephone directory. Contract customers, however were advised to select such an independent from the directory to have the repair made, and to send a receipted invoice to Royal for reimbursement for reasonable repairs within their agreement with Royal. Consequently many of Royal's contract customers had repair services performed by various independent repair companies. In most instances the customer sent Royal the unpaid repair bill and Royal paid the independent company directly. Among the independent companies paid directly by Royal for repairs made for such customers were Typewriter Maintenance and Sales Company and Tytell Typewriter Company. . . .

During May, 1954, the Union picketed four independent typewriter repair companies who had been doing work covered by Royal's contracts pursuant to the arrangement described above. The Boards found this picketing unlawful with respect to Typewriter Maintenance and Tytell. Typewriter Maintenance was picketed for about three days and Tytell for several hours on one day. In each instance the picketing, which was peaceful and orderly, took place before entrances used in common by employees, deliverymen and the general public. The signs read substantially as follows (with the appropriate repair company name inserted):

NOTICE TO THE PUBLIC ONLY

EMPLOYEES OF

ROYAL TYPEWRITER COMPANY

ON STRIKE

TYTELL TYPEWRITER COMPANY EMPLOYEES

ARE BEING USED AS STRIKEBREAKERS

BUSINESS MACHINE & OFFICE APPLIANCE

MECHANICS UNION, LOCAL 459, IUE-CIO

Both before and after this picketing, which took place in mid-May, Tytell and Typewriter Maintenance did work on Royal accounts and received payment directly from Royal. Royal's records show that Typewriter Maintenance's first voucher was passed for payment by Royal on April 20, 1954, and Tytell's first voucher was passed for payment on May 3, 1954. After these dates each independent serviced various of Royal's customers on numerous occasions and received payment directly from Royal. . . .

On the above facts the Trial Examiner and the Board found that . . . the repair company picketing violated Section 8(b)(4) of the National Labor Relations Act. . . .

We are of the opinion that the Board's finding with respect to the repair company picketing cannot be sustained. The independent repair companies were so allied with Royal that the Union's picketing of their premises was not prohibited by Section 8(b)(4)(A).

We approve the "ally" doctrine which had its origin in a well reasoned opinion by Judge Rifkind in the *Ebasco* case, *Douds* v. *Architects, Engineers, Chemists & Technicians, Local 231*. Ebasco, a corporation engaged in the business of providing engineering services, had a close business relationship with Project, a firm providing similar services.

Ebasco subcontracted some of its work to Project and when it did so Ebasco supervised the work of Project's employees and paid Project for the time spent by Project's employees on Ebasco's work plus a factor for overhead and profit. When Ebasco's employees went on strike, Ebasco transferred a greater percentage of its work to Project, including some jobs that had already been started by Ebasco's employees. When Project refused to heed the Union's requests to stop doing Ebasco's work, the Union picketed Project and induced some of Project's employees to cease work. On these facts Judge Rifkind found that Project was not "doing business" with Ebasco within the meaning of Section 8(b)(4) and that the Union had therefore not committed an unfair labor practice under that Section. He reached this result by looking to the legislative history of the Taft-Harley Act and to the history of the secondary boycotts which it sought to outlaw. He determined that Project was not a person "wholly unconcerned in the disagreement between an employer and his employees" such as Section 8(b)(4) was designed to protect....

Here there was evidence of only one instance where Royal contacted an independent (Manhattan Typewriter Service, not named in the complaint) to see whether it could handle some of Royal's calls. Apart from that incident there is no evidence that Royal made any arrangement with an independent directly. It is obvious, however, that what the independents did would inevitably tend to break the strike. As Judge Rifkind pointed out in the *Ebasco* case: "The economic effect on Ebasco's employees was precisely that which would flow from Ebasco's hiring strikebreakers to work on its own premises...."

Moreover, there is evidence that the secondary strikes and boycotts sought to be outlawed by Section 8(b)(4) were only those which had been unlawful at common law. And although secondary boycotts were generally unlawful, it has been held that the common law does not proscribe union activity designed to prevent employers from doing the farmed-out work of a struck employer. Thus the picketing of the independent typewriter companies was not the

kind of a secondary activity which Section 8(b)(4)(A) of the Taft-Hartley Act was designed to outlaw. Where an employer is attempting to avoid the economic impact of a strike by securing the services of others to do his work, the striking union obviously has a great interest, and we think a proper interest in preventing those services from being rendered. This interest is more fundamental than the interest in bringing pressure on customers of the primary employer. Nor are those who render such services completely uninvolved in the primary strike. By doing the work of the primary employer they secure benefits themselves at the same time that they aid the primary employer. The ally employer may easily extricate himself from the dispute and insulate himself from picketing by refusing to do that work. A case may arise where the ally employer is unable to determine that the work he is doing is "farmed-out." We need not decide whether the picketing of such an employer would be lawful, for that is not the situation here. The existence of the strike, the receipt of checks from Royal, and the picketing itself certainly put the independents on notice that some of the work they were doing might be work farmed-out by Royal. Wherever they worked on new Royal machines they were probably aware that such machines were covered by a Royal warranty. But in any event, before working on a Royal machine they could have inquired of the customer whether it was covered by a Royal contract and refused to work on it if it was. There is no indication that they made any effort to avoid doing Royal's work. The Union was justified in picketing them in order to induce them to make such an effort. We therefore hold that an employer is not within the protection of Section 8(b)(4)(A) when he knowingly does work which would otherwise be done by the striking employees of the primary employer and where this work is paid for by the primary employer pursuant to an arrangement devised and originated by him to enable him to meet his contractual obligations.
Enforcement denied.

Publicity—"Consumer" Picketing.   The second proviso to Section 8(b)(4) allows the union to use "... publicity, *other than picketing,* for the purpose of truthfully advising the public" that the secondary employer is handling the product of the primary employer. Such publicity is legal unless it has the effect of inducing other employees to refuse to perform their services at the secondary employer's location. This proviso allows the union to distribute handbills addressed to the public, asking for the public to support the union in its strike by refusing to buy the primary product or by refraining from shopping at the secondary employer.

In the case of *NLRB* v. *Fruit and Vegetable Packers, Local 760 (Tree Fruits)* (377 U.S. 58, 1964), the Supreme Court held that the publicity proviso did not, by negative implication, prohibit peaceful picketing by a union at a supermarket that sold apples packed by the employer against whom the union was on strike. The union's picketing was directed at consumers and asked only that they refuse to buy the apples; it did not ask them to refrain from shopping at the market. The Supreme Court found that such picketing was not prohibited, since the picketing was directed at the primary product rather than the neutral supermarket.

In *Tree Fruits* the primary product, the apples, was only one of many products sold by the supermarket. May the union engage in **consumer picketing** when the secondary employer sells only one product—the primary product? In *NLRB* v. *Retail Store Employees Union, Local 1001, Retail Clerks Int. Association (Safeco)* (477 U.S. 607, 1980), the union striking against Safeco Title Insurance Co. conducted consumer picketing of local title companies, asking consumers to cancel their Safeco policies. The local title companies sold title insurance, performed escrow services, and conducted title searches; over 90 percent of their gross income was derived from the sale of Safeco title insurance. The Supreme Court held that the consumer picketing was in violation of Section 8(b)(4) because, unlike that in *Tree Fruits*, it was "reasonably calculated to induce customers not to patronize the neutral parties at all. . . . Product picketing that reasonably can be expected to threaten neutral parties with ruin or substantial loss simply does not square with the language or the purpose of Section 8(b)(4)(ii)(B)." The Court also stated that if "secondary picketing were directed against a product representing a major portion of a neutral's business, but significantly less than that represented by a single dominant product. . . . The critical question would be whether, by encouraging customers to reject the struck product, the secondary appeal is reasonably likely to threaten the neutral party with ruin or substantial loss."

The effect of the *Safeco* decision is to restrict consumer picketing (also known as product picketing) to situations in which the primary product accounts for less than a substantial portion of the business of the neutral at whose premises the picketing takes place. Other problems under consumer picketing have involved cases in which the primary product has become mixed with the product of the neutral or secondary employer. In such merged product cases, the public is unable to separate the primary product from the secondary product, so that a call to the public to avoid the primary product becomes, in effect, a call to avoid the secondary employer's product altogether. For example, if a union representing striking bakery workers pickets a fast-food restaurant urging customers not to eat the sandwich buns supplied by the struck bakery, the effect of the union's consumer picketing may be to urge consumers to boycott the restaurant totally (*Teamsters Local 327*, 170 N.L.R.B. 91, 1968, *enforced*, 411 F.2d 147, 6th Cir. 1969). In *Kroger Co.* v. *NLRB* (630, F.2d 630, 6th Cir. 1980), the union representing striking paper workers picketed grocery stores, asking consumers to refrain from using paper bags to pack their groceries. The picketing was held to violate Section 8(b)(4) because the bags had lost their separate identity and had become "merged" with the products (groceries) of the neutral grocery stores.

The Publicity Proviso.   The publicity proviso of Section 8(b)(4) purports to allow publicity, other than picketing, for the purposes of truthfully advising the public that the products of the employer against whom the union is striking are being distributed by another employer. How far does that proviso go in allowing a consumer appeals by a union? That question is addressed by the following Supreme Court decision.

EDWARD J. DeBARTOLO CORP. v. FLORIDA GULF COAST BUILDING TRADES COUNCIL

▼

485 U.S. 568 (Supreme Court of the United States, 1988)

WHITE, J.

This case centers around the respondent union's peaceful handbilling of the businesses operating in a shopping mall in Tampa, Florida, owned by petitioner, the Edward J. DeBartolo Corporation (DeBartolo). The union's primary labor dispute was with H. J. High Construction Company (High) over alleged substandard wages and fringe benefits. High was retained by the H. J. Wilson Company (Wilson) to construct a department store in the mall, and neither DeBartolo nor any of the other 85 or so mall tenants had any contractual right to influence the selection of contractors.

The union, however, sought to obtain their influence upon Wilson and High by distributing handbills asking mall customers not to shop at any of the stores in the mall "until the Mall's owner publicly promises that all construction at the Mall will be done using contractors who pay their employees fair wages and fringe benefits."* The handbills' mes-

sage was that "[t]he payment of substandard wages not only diminishes the working person's ability to purchase with earned, rather than borrowed, dollars, but it also undercuts the wage standard of the entire community." The handbills made clear that the union was seeking only a consumer boycott against the other mall tenants, not a secondary strike by their employees. At all four entrances to the mall for about three weeks in December 1979, the union peacefully distributed the handbills without any accompanying picketing or patrolling.

After DeBartolo failed to convince the union to alter the language of the handbills to state that its dispute did not involve DeBartolo or the mall lessees other than Wilson and to limit its distribution to the immediate vicinity of Wilson's construction site, it filed a complaint with the National Labor Relations Board (Board), charging the union with engaging in unfair labor practices under Section 8(b)(4) of the National Labor Relations Act. . . . The Board's General Counsel issued a complaint, but the Board eventually dismissed it, concluding that the handbilling was protected by

---

*The handbill read:

PLEASE *DON'T SHOP AT EAST LAKE SQUARE MALL* PLEASE

The FLA. GULF COAST Building TRADES COUNCIL, AFL-CIO is requesting that you do not shop at the stores in the East Lake Square Mall because of The Mall ownership's contribution to substandard wages.

The Wilson's Department Store under construction on these premises is being built by contractors who pay substandard wages and fringe benefits. In the past, the Mall's owners, The Edward J. DeBartolo Corporation, has supported labor and our local economy by insuring that the Mall and its stores be built by contractors who pay fair wages and fringe benefits. Now, however, and for no apparent reason, the Mall owners have taken a giant step backwards by permitting our standards to be torn down. The payment of substandard wages not only diminishes the working person's ability to purchase with earned, rather than borrowed, dollars, but it also undercuts the

wage standard of the entire community. Since low construction wages at this time of inflation mean decreased purchasing power, do the owners of East Lake Mall intend to compensate for the decreased purchasing power of workers of the community by encouraging the stores in East Lake Mall to cut their prices and lower their profits? CUT-RATE WAGES ARE NOT FAIR UNLESS MERCHANDISE PRICES ARE ALSO CUT-RATE.

We ask for your support in our protest against substandard wages. Please do not patronize the stores in the East Lake Square Mall until the Mall's owner publicly promises that all construction at the Mall will be done using contractors who pay their employees fair wages and fringe benefits. IF YOU MUST ENTER THE MALL TO DO BUSINESS, please express to the store managers your concern over substandard wages and your support of our efforts.

We are appealing only to the public—the consumer. We are not seeking to induce any person to cease work or to refuse to make deliveries.

the publicity proviso of Section 8(b)(4). The Court of Appeals for the Fourth Circuit affirmed the Board, but this Court reversed in *Edward J. DeBartolo Corp.* v. *NLRB.* There, we concluded that the handbilling did not fall within the proviso's limited scope of exempting "publicity intended to inform the public that the primary employer's product is 'distributed by' the secondary employer" because DeBartolo and the other tenants, as opposed to Wilson, did not distribute products of High. Since there had not been a determination below whether the union's handbilling fell within the prohibition of Section 8(b)(4), and, if so, whether it was protected by the First Amendment, we remanded the case.

On remand, the Board held that the union's handbilling was proscribed by Section 8 (b)(4)(ii)(B). It stated that under its prior cases "handbilling and other activity urging a consumer boycott constituted coercion." The Board reasoned that "[a]ppealing to the public not to patronize secondary employers is an attempt to inflict economic harm on the secondary employers by causing them to lose business," and "such appeals constitute 'economic retaliation' and are therefore a form of coercion." It viewed the object of the handbilling as attempting "to force the mall tenants to cease doing business with DeBartolo in order to force DeBartolo and/or Wilson's not to do business with High." The Board observed that it need not inquire whether the prohibition of this handbilling raised serious questions under the First Amendment, for "the statute's literal language and the applicable case law require[d]" a finding of a violation. Finally, it reiterated its longstanding position that "as a congressionally created administrative agency, we will presume the constitutionality of the Act we administer." . . .

[T]he Board's construction of the statute, as applied in this case, poses serious questions of the validity of Section 8 (b)(4) under the First Amendment. The handbills involved here truthfully revealed the existence of a labor dispute and urged potential customers of the mall to follow a wholly legal course of action, namely, not to patronize the retailers doing business in the mall. The handbilling was peaceful. No picketing or patrolling was involved. On its face, this was expressive activity arguing that substandard wages should be opposed by abstaining from shopping in a mall where such wages were paid. Had the union simply been leafletting the public generally, including those entering every shopping mall in town, pursuant to an annual educational effort against substandard pay, there is little doubt that legislative proscription of such leaflets would pose a substantial issue of validity under the First Amendment. The same may well be true in this case, although here the handbills called attention to a specific situation in the

mall allegedly involving the payment of unacceptably low wages by a construction contractor.

That a labor union is the leafletter and that a labor dispute was involved does not foreclose this analysis. We do not suggest that communications by labor unions are never of the commercial speech variety and thereby entitled to a lesser degree of constitutional protection. The handbills involved here, however, do not appear to be typical commercial speech such as advertising the price of a product or arguing its merits, for they pressed the benefits of unionism to the community and the dangers of inadequate wages to the economy and the standard of living of the populace. Of course, commercial speech itself is protected by the First Amendment . . . and however these handbills are to be classified, the Court of Appeals was plainly correct in holding that the Board's construction would require deciding serious constitutional issues. . . .

The case turns on whether handbilling such as involved here must be held to "threaten, coerce, or restrain any person" to cease doing business with another, within the meaning of Section 8(b)(4)(ii)(B). We note first that "induc[ing] or encourag[ing]" employees of the secondary employer to strike is proscribed by 8(b)(4)(i). But more than mere persuasion is necessary to prove a violation of 8(b)(4)(ii): that section requires a showing of threats, coercion, or restraints. Those words, we have said, are "nonspecific, indeed vague," and should be interpreted with "caution" and not given a "broad sweep" . . . and in applying Section 8 (b)(4)(1)(A) they were not to be construed to reach peaceful recognitional picketing. Neither is there any necessity to construe such language to reach the handbills involved in this case. There is no suggestion that the leaflets had any coercive effect on customers of the mall. There was no violence, picketing, or patrolling and only an attempt to persuade customers not to shop in the mall.

The Board nevertheless found that the handbilling "coerced" mall tenants and explained in a footnote that "[a]ppealing to the public not to patronize secondary employers is an attempt to inflict economic harm on the secondary employers by causing them to lose business. As the case law makes clear, such appeals constitute 'economic retaliation' and are therefore a form of coercion." Our decision in *Tree Fruits,* however, makes untenable the notion that *any* kind of handbilling, picketing, or other appeals to a secondary employer to cease doing business with the employer involved in the labor dispute is "coercion" within the meaning of Section 8 (b)(4)(ii)(B) if it has some economic impact on the neutral. In that case, the union picketed a secondary employer, a retailer, asking the public not to buy a product produced by the primary employer. We held that the impact of this picketing was not coercion within the meaning of Section 8(b)(4) even though, if the appeal succeeded, the retailer would lose revenue.

NLRB v. *Retail Store Employees (Safeco),* in turn, held that consumer picketing urging a general boycott of a secondary employer aimed at causing him to sever relations with the union's real antagonist was coercive and forbidden by Section 8(b)(4). It is urged that *Safeco* rules this case because the union sought a general boycott of all tenants in the mall. But "picketing is qualitatively 'different from other modes of communication,' " and *Safeco* noted that the picketing there actually threatened the neutral with ruin or substantial loss. As Justice Stevens pointed out in his concurrence in *Safeco,* picketing is "a mixture of conduct and communication" and the conduct element "often provides the most persuasive deterrent to third persons about to enter a business establishment." Handbills containing the same message, he observed, are "much less effective than labor picketing" because they "depend entirely on the persuasive force of the idea."

In *Tree Fruits,* we could not discern with the "requisite clarity" that Congress intended to proscribe all peaceful consumer picketing at secondary sites. There is even less reason to find in the language of Section 8(b)(4)(ii), standing alone, any clear indication that handbilling, without picketing, "coerces" secondary employers. The loss of customers because they read a handbill urging them not to patronize a business, and not because they are intimidated by a line of picketers, is the result of mere persuasion, and the neutral who reacts is doing no more than what its customers honestly want it to do. . . .

It is nevertheless argued that the second proviso to Section 8(b)(4) makes clear that that section, as amended in 1959, was intended to proscribe nonpicketing appeals such as handbilling urging a consumer boycott of a neutral employer. . . . By its terms, the proviso protects nonpicketing communications directed at customers of a distributor of goods produced by an employer with whom the union has a labor dispute. Because handbilling and other consumer appeals not involving such a distributor are not within the proviso, the argument goes, those appeals must be considered coercive within the meaning of Section 8(b)(4)(ii). Otherwise, it is said, the proviso is meaningless, for if handbilling and like communications are never coercive and within the reach of the section, there would have been no need whatsoever for the proviso.

This approach treats the proviso as establishing an exception to a prohibition that would otherwise reach the conduct excepted. But this proviso has a different ring to it. It

states that Section 8(b)(4) "shall not be construed" to forbid certain described nonpicketing publicity. That language need not be read as an exception. It may indicate only that without the proviso, the particular nonpicketing communication the proviso protects might have been considered to be coercive, even if other forms of publicity would not be. Section 8(b)(4), with its proviso, may thus be read as not covering nonpicketing publicity, including appeals to customers of a retailer as they approach the store, urging a complete boycott of the retailer because he handles products produced by nonunion shops.

The Board's reading of Section 8(b)(4) would make an unfair labor practice out of any kind of publicity or communication to the public urging a consumer boycott of employers other than those the proviso specifically deals with. On the facts of this case, newspaper, radio, and television appeals not to patronize the mall would be prohibited; and it would be an unfair labor practice for unions in their own meetings to urge their members not to shop in the mall. Nor could a union's handbills simply urge not shopping at a department store because it is using a nonunion contractor, although the union could safely ask the store's customers not to buy there because it is selling mattresses not carrying the union label. It is difficult, to say the least, to fathom why Congress would consider appeals urging a boycott of a distributor of a nonunion product to be more deserving of protection than nonpicketing persuasion of customers of other neutral employers such as that involved in this case.

Neither do we find any clear indication in the relevant legislative history that Congress intended Section 8(b)(4)(ii) to proscribe peaceful handbilling, unaccompanied by picketing, urging a consumer boycott of a neutral employer. That section was one of several amendments to the NLRA enacted in 1959 and aimed at closing what were thought to be loopholes in the protections to which secondary employers were entitled. We recounted the legislative history in *Tree Fruits* and *NLRB* v. *Servette,* and the Court of Appeals carefully reexamined it in this case and found "no affirmative intention of Congress clearly expressed to prohibit nonpicketing labor publicity." For the following reasons, for the most part expressed by the Court of Appeals, we agree with that conclusion.

First, among the concerns of the proponents of the provision barring threats, coercion, or restraints aimed at secondary employers was consumer boycotts of neutral employers carried out by picketing. At no time did they suggest that merely handbilling the customers of the neutral employer was one of the evils at which their proposals were aimed. Had they wanted to bar any and all nonpicketing appeals, through newspapers, radio, television, handbills or otherwise, the debates and discussions would surely have reflected this intention. Instead, when asked, Congressman Griffin, co-sponsor of the bill that passed the House, stated that the bill covered boycotts carried out by picketing neutrals but would not interfere with the constitutional right of free speech....

In our view, interpreting Section 8(b)(4) as not reaching the handbilling involved in this case is not foreclosed either by the language of the section or its legislative history. That construction makes unnecessary passing on the serious constitutional questions that would be raised by the Board's understanding of the statute. Accordingly, the judgment of the Court of Appeals is **Affirmed.**

Section 8(b)(4)(D): Jurisdictional Disputes.

Section 8(b)(4)(D) prohibits a union from picketing an employer in order to force that employer to assign work to that union. If the picketing union is not entitled to that work by reason of a certification or NLRB order, such picketing violates Section 8(b)(4)(D). For example, the union representing plasterers and the union representing stone masons on the construction site of an apartment complex both might demand the right to lay the ceramic tiles in hallways and bathrooms. If either union picketed to force such assignment of the work, it would be a violation of Section 8(b)(4)(D).

When a Section 8(b)(4)(D) complaint is filed with the board, Section 10(k) requires that the board give the parties involved ten days to settle the dispute. If the parties are unable to settle the jurisdictional dispute in ten days, the board must then make an assignment of the work in dispute. Once the board awards the work, the successful union may picket to force the employer to live up to the board order. Section 10(l) requires that the board seek an injunction against the picketing when a complaint alleging a violation of Section 8(b)(4)(D) is filed.

Section 8(e): Hot Cargo Clauses

Hot cargo clauses are provisions in collective bargaining agreements purporting to permit employees to refuse to handle the product of any employer involved in a labor dispute. Section 8(e), inserted into the NLRA as one of the 1959 Landrum-Griffin amendments, prohibits the negotiation and enforcement of such clauses:

(e) It shall be an unfair labor practice for any labor organization and any employer to enter into any contract or agreement, express or implied, whereby such employer ceases or refrains or agrees to cease or refrain from handling, using, selling, transporting or otherwise dealing in any of the products of any other employer, or to cease doing business with any other person, and any contract or agreement entered into heretofore or hereafter containing such an agreement shall be to such extent unenforcible and void: Provided, That nothing in this subsection (e) shall apply to an agreement between a labor organization and an employer in the construction industry relating to the contracting or subcontracting of work to be done at the site of the construction, alteration, painting, or repair of a building, structure, or other work: Provided further, That for the purposes of this subsection (e) and section 8(b)(4)(B) the terms "any employer," "any person engaged in commerce or an industry affecting commerce," "any person" when used in relation to the terms "any other producer, processor, or manufacturer," "any employer," or "any other person" shall not include persons in the relation of a jobber, manufacturer, contractor, or subcontractor working on the goods or premises of the jobber or manufacturer or performing parts of an integrated process of production in the apparel and clothing industry: Provided further, That nothing in this Act shall prohibit the enforcement of any agreement which is within the foregoing exception.

It can be seen that the provisos to Section 8(e) exempt the garment industry and the construction industry from its provisions. The garment industry is completely exempted; the construction industry is exempted to the extent of allowing unions to negotiate hot cargo clauses that relate to work normally done at the work site.

The objective of Section 8(e) is to prohibit language in a collective agreement that purports to authorize conduct that is prohibited by Section 8(b)(4), such as refusing to handle goods produced by a nonunion employer or by an employer who is being struck by a different union. The courts have allowed contract language that authorizes conduct that is primary, such as refusing to cross a primary picket line and refusing to perform the work normally done by the employees of an employer who is the target of a primary strike. One issue that has been problematic under Section 8(e) is whether work preservation clauses outside the construction industry are prohibited by Section 8(e). The courts have consistently held that when unions seek to retain the right to perform work that they have traditionally done or to acquire work that is similar to work they have traditionally done, and such activity to enforce the clauses is directed against the employer with the right of control over the working conditions at issue, such activity is primary. In *NLRB* v. *International Longshoremen's Association* (473 U.S. 61, 1985), the Supreme Court considered a union rule penalizing shippers who used prepacked containers to ship cargo that had traditionally been loaded and unloaded by union members at the docks. The Court held that, even though the use of containers had eliminated most of the traditional loading work done by Longshoremen, the language that sought to preserve such "unnecessary" work was a legitimate work preservation clause under Sections 8(e) and 8 (b)(4). The union's objective through the language was the preservation of work similar in nature to that traditionally performed by the Longshoremen, and the employers had the power to control the assignment of such work.

Remedies for Secondary Activity

As mentioned, the NLRB is required to seek an immediate injunction against the picketing when a complaint alleging a violation of Section 8(b)(4), Section 8(b)7, or Section 8(e) is filed. The injunction is intended to prevent the activity in question until its legality can be determined. If the board holds the conduct illegal, it will issue a cease-and-desist order against it.

Section 303 of the NLRA also provides that any person suffering harm to business or property by reason of activity that violates Section 8(b)(4) may sue in federal court to recover damages for the injuries sustained and legal fees. Either the primary or secondary employer may sue under Section 303; and they may file a suit regardless of whether an unfair labor practice charge has been filed with the NLRB.

National Emergencies

Sections 206 to 210 of the NLRA, which were added by the Taft-Hartley Act of 1947, provide for injunctions forestalling strikes when they threaten the national health or safety. When a strike, or threatened strike, poses such a threat, the president is authorized to appoint a board of inquiry to report on the issues involved in the dispute. The U.S. attorney general can secure an injunction to forestall the strike for up to eighty days, and the Federal Mediation and Conciliation Service (FMCS) attempts to resolve the dispute. The parties are not bound by the FMCS recommendations, and if no agreement is reached, the NLRB is required to poll the employees to determine if they will accept the employer's last offer. If the last offer is rejected, the injunction is dissolved, and the president may refer the issue to Congress for "appropriate action."

The emergency provisions of the Taft-Hartley Act have been invoked very few times in recent years. The provisions allow the government to delay a strike; but because the parties are free to reject attempts at settlement, the act is unable to address the causes of the dispute. The dispute remains and the strike resumes once the delay period under the injunction expires.

QUESTIONS

1. Why is the right to picket protected by the U.S. Constitution? Is the right to strike also protected by the Constitution?

2. In what situations can the states regulate picketing? Explain your answer.

3. What is recognitional or organization picketing? Under what circumstances is it prohibited by the NLRA?

4. What is primary picketing? Secondary picketing? What factors determine the legality of picketing against neutral employers?

5. Why is common situs picketing at a construction site

treated differently from picketing in a *General Electric*–type situation?

6. What is the ally doctrine? How does it affect the legality of picketing under Section 8(b)(4)?

7. When is consumer picketing prohibited by Section 8(b)(4)?

8. What is a hot cargo clause? Why are hot cargo clauses prohibited by the NLRA?

9. What are the procedures available under the Taft-Hartley Act to attempt to prevent strikes that pose a danger to the national health, safety, or security?

CASE PROBLEMS

1. Plaintiff owned and operated a supermarket in Springfield, Missouri. The defendant union neither represented, nor did it claim to want to organize, the store's clerks. Nevertheless, the union sporadically picketed the market, claiming that the impetus for its picketing was that the store paid substandard wages.

Initially, the union picketed in the public street, but subsequently moved onto the store's sidewalk. After the store filed a trespass complaint with the local police, the pickets moved back to the street, but simultaneously filed an unfair labor practice charge with the NLRB. The board issued a complaint, asserting that the store violated Section 8(a)(1) of the NLRA by ordering the pickets off the sidewalk.

The store's owners initiated a lawsuit, seeking an injunction to keep the pickets off the walkway, and also to stop other alleged picketing activities. The plaintiffs alleged that the pickets called customers "scab shoppers," took down license numbers of customers' cars, and misstated on their placards that the plaintiff was an Arizona company, coming in from out of state, when in fact it was a Missouri corporation.

In what kind of picketing was the union engaging? What was the theory on which the NLRB issued its complaint on behalf of the union, and how do you think it will fare before an Administrative Law Judge?

Does the issuance of that complaint by the board preempt the Missouri state court from enjoining any of the picketers' activities? All of their activities? Is your answer any different if the Section 8(a)(1) charge is ultimately sustained by the ALJ who hears the case? See *Smitty's Super Markets* v. *Local 322,* 116 L.R.R.M. 3392 (Missouri Ct. Apps. 1982).

2. Theater Techniques, Inc. (TTI) was a supplier of theatrical props and scenery for Broadway shows. TTI had a subcontract with Nolan Studios to paint scenery and props provided by TTI. Nolan Studios' employees were represented by Local 829, United Scenic Artists, whose collective agreement gave the union jurisdiction over the sculpting and painting of props. When some props from TTI arrived at Nolan already fabricated, the union employees refused to paint them unless Nolan paid a premium rate for the work. Nolan did not inform the union that TTI had contractual control over the disputed work; but Nolan did file a complaint with the NLRB charging the union with violating Section 8(b)(4)(B) by refusing to handle the props from TTI in order to force Nolan to stop doing business with TTI. How should the board decide the unfair labor practice complaint filed by Nolan? Explain your answer. See *United Scenic Artists, Local 829* v. *NLRB,* 762 F.2d 1027 (D.C. Cir. 1985).

3. Local 366 of the Brewery, Bottling, Can & Allied Industrial Union called a strike against the Coors bottling plant in Golden, Colorado. Local 366 was affiliated with the AFL-CIO and received nationwide union support for a boycott of Coors beer during the strike.

During the course of this protracted labor dispute, Coors made an agreement with KQED, a broadcasting station in the San Francisco Bay area, under which the brewer would provide financial support and volunteers for a "Coors Day" portion of the station's annual fund-raising telethon.

Prior to the telethon, an article appeared in the *San Francisco Bay Guardian,* which stated that Coors "is notorious for anti-union activities during a . . . strike" and had long been "the subject of a labor-backed nationwide boycott." Following the appearance of the article, the coordinator of the Northern California Chapter of the Coors Boycott Committee met with the KQED general manager to inform him of the swelling opposition to "Coors Day," allegedly warning him not to stumble into a "shooting war" and that he could not guarantee the safety of the teleauction volunteers. KQED subsequently canceled "Coors Day," and Coors sued the coordinator and other union supporters for damages.

Was the boycott group a labor organization under the jurisdiction of the NLRA? If so, did the boycott group violate the NLRA? Did it violate the federal antitrust laws? Did it violate any state laws? If so, would a state court have had jurisdiction of the case? See *Adolph Coors Co.* v. *Wallace,* 570 F. Supp. 202, 115 L.R.R.M. 3100 (N.D. Cal. 1984).

4. In 1975 Delta Air Lines subcontracted the janitorial work of its offices at the Los Angeles International Airport to the National Cleaning Company. National entered into a collective bargaining agreement with the Hospital and Service Employees Union, Local 399. In 1976 Delta lawfully terminated its contract with National and made a new contract with Statewide Maintenance company, a nonunion employer. Consequently, National fired five of the six janitors who had cleaned Delta's offices.

In furtherance of its recognitional dispute with Statewide Maintenance, the union began distributing handbills at Delta's L.A. Airport facilities in front of the downtown Los Angeles office. One or two persons usually distributed the fliers at each facility. The handbilling caused no interruptions in deliveries or refusals by Delta's employees to do their work.

There were four handbills altogether. The first stated, "Please do not fly Delta Airlines. Delta Airlines unfair. Does not provide AFL-CIO conditions of employment. (signed by union)." the other side said "It takes more than money to fly Delta. It takes nerve. Let's look at the accident record." There followed a list of fifty-five accidents involving Delta between 1963 and 1976, along with total deaths and injuries.

The second handbill, distributed a week later, contained all the information on side two of the first handbill, but not the information from side one.

The third handbill, a week after that, again consisted of two sides. Side one said

Please Do Not Fly Delta Airlines. This airline has caused members of Service Employees Union, Local 399, AFL-CIO, at Los Angeles International Airport, to become unemployed. In their place they have contracted with a maintenance company which does not provide Local 399 wages, benefits and standards. We urge all union members to protest Delta's action to the Delta office in your region. If you are concerned about the plight of fellow union members . . . Please Do Not Fly Delta Airlines.

Side two contained the same accident information as the previous two broadsides.

Handbill four contained the same accident information as the prior three, with the following prefatory statement:

As members of the public and in order to protect the wages and conditions of Local 399 members and to publicize our primary dispute with the Statewide Building Maintenance Company, we wish to call to the attention of the consuming public certain information about Delta Airlines from the official records of the Civil Aeronautics Board of the United States Government.

Simultaneous with the handbilling activities, the union published copies of fliers one and three in two union newspapers, along with an advertisement stating singly, "Do Not Fly Delta."

Analyze each of the four handbills. What if anything in each constituted an illegal secondary boycott? What if anything was protected by the NLRA's publicity proviso? Is the same true with respect to the newspaper ads? See *Service Employees Local 399* v. *NLRB,* 117 L.R.R.M. 2717, 743 F.2d 1417 (9th Cir. 1984).

5. Shortly after the Soviet invasion of Afghanistan in 1979, the United States imposed an embargo on exports to the Soviet Union. However, some grain shipments were exempted from the embargo. Nevertheless, the International Longshoremen's Association (ILA), apparently disagreeing with the exemptions, adopted a resolution that its longshoremen would not handle *any* goods being exported to or arriving from the Soviet Union.

Sovfracht Chartering Corporation, a Soviet government maritime agency, chartered a Belgian ship (*The Belgium*) to transport exempt and duly licensed grain from Houston to Russia. The Houston stevedore com-

panies had to hire all longshoremen from ILA hiring halls. When TTT Stevedores, an employer party to an ILA collective bargaining agreement, sought to load the Soviet-bound grain on board *The Belgium,* it was informed that the ILA local would not provide any of its members to do the work. When informed of this decision, Sovfracht canceled *The Belgium's* stop in Houston.

Was the ILA guilty of a secondary boycott? If so, against whom? What arguments can be made that this action was not illegal activity under the NLRA? See *ILA* v. *NLRB,* 723 F.2d 963, 115 L.R.R.M. 2093 (D.C. Cir. 1983).

6. The Ironworkers Union had been engaged in organizing the employees of Stokrr's Multi-Ton Corporation. When Stokrr's refused to recognize the union, the union called a strike of the company's employees.

Perkins Trucking Company handled and transported Stokrr's products. Three days into the strike, pickets gathered around a Perkins truck as it attempted to make a pickup at the Stokrr's facility. One of the union pickets jumped on the running board of the Perkins truck and yelled at the driver, "We're going to rape your wife. . . . I'm going to break your legs." The picket then pointed at the driver's face and stated, "Just remember what I look like, because I know who you are. I'm going to get you. . . . [W]e're going to get all your trucks, you run a lot of them." At that point the police assisted the Perkins truck through the picket line to the loading dock.

Sometime later eight to twelve strikers arrived at the Perkins terminal at 7 A.M. carrying placards. But they engaged in no picketing of the terminal facility; they stood around, five to ten feet from the terminal gate. They told the assistant shop steward of the union at Perkins that they were "individuals" trying to gain information for their "personal use," and that they wanted to know if Perkins was handling any of Stokrr's freight. They were told that Perkins had not handled any Stokrr's freight for "the last couple of weeks." At about 8 A.M. the strikers departed.

Based on these facts, could it be said that Perkins was an ally of Stokrr's? What provisions of the NLRA, if any, were violated by the union? See *Iron Workers, Local 455,* 243 N.L.R.B. No. 39, 102 L.R.R.M. 1109 (1979).

7. Caruso was the sole proprietor of Linoleum & Carpet City in Spokane, Washington. He also owned a parking

lot a quarter of a mile from his business. Periodically, delivery trucks blocked access to the lot.

On October 26, 1973, Caruso found a beer truck and a van blocking the entrance to his lot. Caruso called a tow truck to have the vehicles removed. (He had first called the owner of the truck, whose name was on the truck, and asked him to remove the truck.) The driver of the van settled his share of the tow truck costs, but Contos, the driver of the truck, refused to pay his share. Contos told Caruso he would report him to the Teamsters union and the union would "break" him.

On November 9, 1973, an article was published in the *Washington Teamster.* The article, titled "Don't Patronize Carpet City in Spokane," was printed once on the front page of the teamster paper and twice more in substantially the same form on page 5. It continued to state that the owner harassed laboring people who used his parking lot. It was signed Teamsters Union, Local 690.

Soon after publication of the first three articles, people began calling Linoleum & Carpet City and stating that they would not shop there. Sales dropped dramatically and in May 1974, Caruso relocated his business hoping to minimize his losses.

Assess the union's activities in light of the NLRA—are there any unfair labor practices? Are there any common-law counts that Caruso could pursue against the union for destroying his business? If so, does he face a preemption problem? See *Caruso* v. *Teamsters Local 690,* 120 L.R.R.M. 2233 (Wash. S.C. 1983).

8. Zellers worked as an elevator installer; he was a member of Local 123 of the Elevator Constructors. Zellers was employed by Eggers Construction Co. and was working at a neutral construction site. The elevator construction crew was directed to use a separate, neutral gate at the work site because another union had set up a picket line at a different gate at the work site. When he saw the other picket line, Zellers refused to enter the work site, even though there was no picket line at the gate that he was required to use. Because of his refusal to enter the gate, Zellers was suspended by Eggers. The Elevator Constructors Union filed a grievance protesting the suspension of Zellers. Eggers then filed an unfair labor practice complaint with the NLRB, alleging that the union filing the grievance was in violation of Section 8(b)(4) because it sought to authorize Zellers refusal to work in order to force the general contractor to get rid of the employer subject to the strike by the other union. How should the board rule on Eggers unfair labor practice complaint? Explain your answer. See *NLRB* v. *Elevator Constructors,* 134 L.R.R.M. 2137 (8th Cir. 1990).

9. The appellant, David M. Yeager, was employed as a vice-president and general manager of Browning-Ferris Industries (BFI) in Toledo, Ohio. In June 1979 a group of individuals, some of whom were former employees of BFI, decided to picket the business location of BFI in Toledo. As part of the picketing process, the picketers carried signs and distributed leaflets that referred to appellant as being a little Hitler, accused appellant of maintaining a Nazi concentration camp atmosphere at BFI, and alleged that appellant did not support the Constitution of the United States, used Gestapo tactics, and cheated employees.

For purposes of clarity, a description of the organizational defendants is appropriate. Local 20 is a local union of the International Brotherhood of Teamsters, Chauffeurs, Warehousemen and Helpers of America. Its purpose and function is to organize and represent workers through the process of collective bargaining. PROD is an organization of dissident rank and file Teamsters whose stated purpose is to reform the Teamsters Union. TAP is a local chapter of PROD. Appellant alleges that all of the individual defendants are either officers or members of one or more of the three organizations.

Should Yeager be permitted to maintain an action for defamation against these defendants, or was their activity protected, or at least preempted, by the NLRA? See *Yeager* v. *Teamsters Local 20,* 114 L.R.R.M. 3383 (Ohio Ct. Apps., Lucas Cty. 1982).

10. Rainbow, a tour bus company based in Honolulu, provides ground transportation services to various tourist agencies in the Honolulu area. In 1976 Steven Kolt became a part owner and president of the company and adopted its present name.

In 1976 Rainbow was a nonunion business. In the latter part of that year and early the next year, some employees began inquiring into joining a union. Soon thereafter, on the morning of January 29, 1977, the union picketed the Rainbow yard. Approximately thirty to forty pickets were involved. The pickets were somewhat threatening and unruly and temporarily blocked ingress and egress to the Rainbow yard. Rainbow immediately sought to enjoin the picketing in Hawaii state court. On February 2, 1977, the union agreed before the state court judge to reduce the number of pickets to two.

On February 1, 1977, Rainbow commenced the lawsuit that is the subject of this appeal. Rainbow brought two counts. The first alleged violations cognizable under Section 303 of the Labor Management Relations Act, 29 U.S.C. Section 187. The second count, a pendent state law claim, alleged the union had engaged in unlawful mass picketing that tortiously interfered with Rainbow's employment contracts and resulted in a loss of business.

On March 2, 1977, the union and two former Rainbow employees filed unfair labor practice charges with the NLRB. They alleged Rainbow had unlawfully interfered with its employees' Section 7 rights, 29 U.S.C. Section 157, by threatening and terminating several of them. Rainbow answered that the union had engaged in activity violative of 29 U.S.C. Sections 158(b)(1)(A) (coercing employees in the exercise of their Section 7 rights); (b)(4) (illegal secondary conduct); and (b)(7) (illegal recognitional picketing when no petition had been timely filed). The NLRB consolidated the complaints, and a hearing was held from July 6 to July 13, 1977.

The ALJ entered his decision on March 29, 1978. The NLRB affirmed the ALJ's findings and adopted his order with minor modifications (241 N.L.R.B. 589, 101 L.R.R.M. 1042, 1979). The NLRB rejected Rainbow's claims and found for the union.

Does the NLRB's decision in favor of the union man that the company cannot recover damages in this case? Or is there a theory of recovery on which it should be permitted to proceed? See *Rainbow Coaches* v. *Hawaii Teamsters,* 704 F.2d 1443, 113 L.R.R.M. 2383 (9th Cir. 1983).

C H A P T E R 9

The Enforcement and Administration of the Collective Agreement

THE SIGNING OF A collective agreement by a union and an employer may mark the end of the bargaining process; it is also the beginning of a continuing relationship between them. The agreement creates rights for and imposes obligations on both parties. The parties are bound to uphold the terms of the contract for its duration. How can union and management ensure that the "other side" will honor the contract? What means are available to enforce the contract in the event of a breach by either side? How can disputes over the interpretation of the agreement be resolved? This chapter will discuss the means available for the enforcement and administration of the collective agreement.

Section 301 of the National Labor Relations Act (NLRA) provides that suits for violations of contracts between an employer and a labor union may be brought in federal and state courts. Therefore, either the union or employer could bring a lawsuit over the other side's failure to live up to the contract. However, lawsuits are a cumbersome means of resolving most contract disputes; they are also expensive and time-consuming. For these reasons lawsuits are impractical for resolving disputes over how collective agreements should be interpreted or applied.

Either party to the agreement could resort to pressure tactics to try to resolve a contract dispute. The union could go on strike or the employer could lock out the employees, in order to force the other side to live up to the contract. The employer generally is not willing to lock out employees and cease production over a minor matter. Nor are union members likely to strike, lose wages, and risk being replaced over minor matters.

Arbitration

Because of the shortcomings of both lawsuits and pressure tactics as a way to resolve contract disputes, the parties usually agree, as a part of their collective agreement, to establish their own process for resolving their disputes peacefully. The peaceful settlement process usually involves the process of arbitration. **Arbitration** is the settlement of disputes by a neutral adjudicator chosen by the parties to the dispute. Arbitration provides a means to resolve contractual disputes relatively inexpensively and expeditiously. Arbitration also provides flexibility, because the parties are free to tailor the arbitration process to suit their particular situation. The parties generally incorporate arbitration as the final step of the grievance procedure. In return for the agreement by each party to arbitrate their dispute, they give up their right to strike or lock out over such issues.

Interest Arbitration versus Rights Arbitration

In a labor relations setting, arbitration may be used either to settle a dispute over the creation of a new collective agreement or over the interpretation and administration of an existing agreement. When arbitration is used to create a new agreement (or renew an existing one), it is known as **interest arbitration**—the parties seek to protect their economic interests through favorable contract terms. Interest arbitration is common in the public sector, where employees are generally prohibited from striking. Interest arbitration there replaces pressure tactics as a means to resolve the negotiating impasse. Interest arbitration is much less common in the private sector.

If the dispute involves interpreting an existing agreement rather than creating a new one, the arbitration to resolve it is known as **rights arbitration.** Rights arbitration is the means to define the rights and obligations of each party under the agreement. Rights arbitration is very common in both the public and the private sector. Even though rights arbitration is not required by the NLRA, more than 90 percent of all collective agreements provide for rights arbitration as the means to resolve disputes over the interpretation and/or application of the collective agreement. This chapter will be concerned with rights arbitration; unless otherwise specified, the term *arbitration* will refer to rights arbitration.

Rights Arbitration and the Grievance Process

Rights arbitration is generally used as the final step in the **grievance process**—a process set up to deal with complaints under the collective agreement. Like rights arbitration, the grievance procedure is created by the parties to the agreement. It is not required by statute. Because it is voluntarily created by the parties under the collective agreement, the grievance process can be tailored to fit their particular situation or desires.

A **grievance** is simply a complaint that either party to the agreement is not living up to the obligations of the agreement. Most grievances are filed by employees complaining about the actions of the employer (or its agents), but management may also file grievances under the agreement.

Grievance procedures vary widely; the parties to an agreement can devise whatever procedure is best suited to their purposes. The following is an example of a four-step grievance procedure, with arbitration as the final step:

ARTICLE XIII: GRIEVANCE PROCEDURE

Section 1. Any grievance or dispute between the Company and the Union involving the interpretation or application of any terms of this Agreement shall be adjusted according to the following procedure:

STEP ONE: The employee who believes he has suffered a grievance or been unjustly treated may raise the alleged grievance with his Foreman or Assistant Foreman in an attempt to settle the same. The said employee may be accompanied or represented if he so desires by the Steward. The Foreman shall have two (2) working days to settle the grievance.

STEP TWO: If the matter is not satisfactorily settled in STEP ONE, it may be taken to the Second Step by the Union's reducing it to writing, on a mutually agreed upon form provided by the Company. Any grievance taken to the Second Step must be signed by a Steward, a Chief Steward, or a Local Union Committee member. Two (2) copies will be delivered to the Supervisor, who will sign and date the grievance upon receipt of it. A meeting will be arranged within four (4) working days following receipt of the form, between the Supervisor, Plant Superintendent, Grievant, Steward, or in his absence, Chief Steward. A written answer shall be given within four (4) working days from the date of the meeting even though an oral decision is given at the meeting. If the answer is not received during the time period, the grievance shall be deemed settled in favor of the grievant or Union.

STEP THREE: The Steward, or Chief Steward in his absence, may appeal the Second Step decision by completing the "Appeal to Third Step" portion of the grievance form and by delivering the same to the Industrial Relations Department within five (5) working days (excluding Saturday and Sunday) after the decision in the Second Step. The Industrial Relations Department shall arrange a meeting within five (5) working days (excluding Saturday and Sunday) following receipt of the appeal, between the representative designated by the Company, the Shop Grievance Committee, and the International Representative. A written answer shall be given within five (5) working days (excluding Saturday and Sunday) from the date of the meeting even though an oral decision is given at the meeting. Any failure by either party to meet the time limits required shall deem the grievance settled in favor of the other party.

STEP FOUR: Any grievance or dispute involving the interpretation or application of this Agreement, which has not been satisfactorily settled in the foregoing steps, may, at the request of either party, be submitted to an arbitrator or arbitration board selected as hereinafter provided, by written notice delivered to the other party within four (4) calendar weeks subsequent to the decision in Step Three. Any failure, by either party, to meet such time limits shall be deemed a waiver of the grievance. Unless the parties mutually agree upon arbitration by the State Board of Mediation and Arbitration, the matter shall be referred to the American Arbitration Association for arbitration under its rules. The fees and expenses of the arbitrator thus selected shall be divided equally between the parties.

Section 2. The arbitration board or the arbitrator is not authorized to add to, modify, or take away from the express terms of this Agreement and shall be limited to the interpretation or application of the provisions of the Agreement of the determination as to whether there is a violation of it. Any decision of the arbitration board or the arbitrator within the scope of the above authority shall be final and binding on both parties.

Section 3. Time time limits above set forth must be complied with strictly.

Section 4. The Company or the Union may institute a grievance at STEP THREE on any matter concerning general application, and process it through STEP FOUR.

It can be seen that the actual grievance procedure is a series of meetings between union and management representatives. As the grievance remains unresolved and moves through the various steps of the procedure, the rank of the representatives involved increases. Either party may request that a grievance unresolved at step three be submitted to arbitration.

The Courts and Arbitration

As noted, arbitration as a means to resolve grievances is a voluntary mechanism; the parties to the contract have agreed to use it. But what happens if either party refuses to submit a dispute to arbitration—what remedies are available to the party seeking arbitration? The following case deals with an attempt to use Section 301 of the NLRA to force management to arbitrate a union grievance.

TEXTILE WORKERS UNION OF AMERICA v. LINCOLN MILLS OF ALABAMA

353 U.S. 448 (Supreme Court of the United States, 1957)

DOUGLAS, J.

Petitioner-union entered into a collective bargaining agreement in 1953 with respondent-employer, the agreement to run one year and from year to year thereafter, unless terminated on specified notices. The agreement provided that there would be no strikes or work stoppages and that grievances would be handled pursuant to a specified procedure. The last step in the grievance procedure—a step that could be taken by either party—was arbitration.

This controversy involves several grievances that concern work loads and work assignments. The grievances were processed through the various steps in the grievance procedure and were finally denied by the employer. The union requested arbitration, and the employer refused. Thereupon the union brought this suit in the District Court to compel arbitration.

The District Court concluded that it had jurisdiction and ordered the employer to comply with the grievance arbitration provisions of the collective bargaining agreement. The Court of Appeals reversed by a divided vote.

The starting point of our inquiry is Section 301 of the Labor Management Relations Act of 1947, which provides:

(a) Suits for violation of contracts between an employer and a labor organization representing employees in an industry affecting commerce as defined in this chapter, or between any such labor organizations, may be brought in any district court of the United States having jurisdiction of the parties, without respect to the amount in controversy or without regard to the citizenship of the parties.

(b) Any labor organization which represents employees in an industry affecting commerce as defined in this chapter and

any employer whose activities affect commerce as defined in this chapter shall be bound by the acts of its agents. Any such labor organization may sue or be sued as an entity and in behalf of the employees whom it represents in the courts of the United States. Any money judgment against a labor organization in a district court of the United States shall be enforceable only against the organization as an entity and against its assets, and shall not be enforceable against any individual member or his assets.

There has been considerable litigation involving Section 301.... [C]ourts—the overwhelming number of them— hold that Section 301(a) is more than jurisdictional—that it authorizes federal courts to fashion a body of federal law for the enforcement of these collective bargaining agreements and includes within that federal law specific performance of promises to arbitrate grievances under collective bargaining agreements. That is our construction of Section 301(a), which means that the agreement to arbitrate grievance disputes, contained in this collective bargaining agreement, should be specifically enforced.

From the face of the Act it is apparent that Section 301(a) and Section 301(b) supplement one another. Section 301(b) makes it possible for a labor organization, representing employees in an industry affecting commerce, to sue and be sued as an entity in the federal courts. Section 301(b) in other words provides the procedural remedy lacking at common law. Section 301(a) certainly does something more than that. Plainly, it supplies the basis upon which the federal district courts may take jurisdiction and apply the procedural rule of Section 301(b).

Plainly the agreement to arbitrate grievance disputes is the *quid pro quo* for an agreement not to strike. Viewed in this light, the legislation does more than confer jurisdiction in the federal courts over labor organizations. It expresses a federal policy that federal courts should enforce these agreements on behalf of or against labor organizations and that industrial peace can be best obtained only in that way.

It seems, therefore, clear to us that Congress adopted a policy which placed sanctions behind agreements to arbitrate grievance disputes. . . . We would undercut the Act and defeat its policy if we read Section 301(a) as only conferring jurisdiction over labor organizations. . . . The question then is, what is the substantive law to be applied in suits under Section 301(a)? We conclude that the substantive law to apply in suits under Section 301(a) is federal law, which the courts must fashion from the policy of our national labor laws. The Labor Management Relations Act expressly furnishes some substantive law. It points out what the parties may or may not do in certain situations. Other problems will lie in the penumbra of express statutory mandates. Some will lack express statutory sanction but will be solved by looking at the policy of the legislation and fashioning a remedy that will effectuate that policy. The range of judicial inventiveness will be determined by the nature of the problem. Federal interpretation of the federal law will govern, not state law. But state law, if compatible with

the purpose of Section 301, may be resorted to in order to find the rule that will best effectuate the federal policy. Any state law applied, however, will be absorbed as federal law and will not be an independent source of private rights.

The question remains whether jurisdiction to compel arbitration of grievance disputes is withdrawn by the Norris–La Guardia Act. . . . Section 7 of that Act prescribes stiff procedural requirements for issuing an injunction in a labor dispute. Though a literal reading might bring the dispute within the terms of the Act, we see no justification in policy for restricting Section 301(a) to damage suits, leaving specific performance of a contract to arbitrate grievance disputes to the inapposite procedural requirements of that Act. The congressional policy in favor of the enforcement of agreements to arbitrate grievance disputes being clear, there is no reason to submit them to the requirements of the Norris–La Guardia Act.

The judgment of the Court of Appeals is reversed and the cause is remanded to that court for proceedings in conformity with this opinion. **Reversed.**

As *Lincoln Mills* indicates, if the parties have agreed to arbitration as a means of resolving disputes, the courts will require them to use it. What is voluntary about arbitration, then, is its existence—whether the agreement provides for arbitration. Once the parties have agreed to use arbitration, the courts will enforce that agreement.

What should the role of the court be when it is asked to order that a dispute be arbitrated or when it is asked to enforce an arbitration award? Those issues were addressed by the Supreme Court in three cases that came to be known as the *Steelworkers Trilogy*. In *United Steelworkers of America v. Warrior & Gulf Navigation Co.* (363 U.S. 574, 1960), the Supreme Court held that when a court is asked to order arbitration under Section 301, an order to arbitrate the grievance should not be denied "unless it may be said with positive assurance that the arbitration clause is not susceptible of an interpretation that covers the asserted dispute. Doubts should be resolved in favor of coverage." In a more recent decision, the Supreme Court again affirmed the holding of *Warrior & Gulf Navigation;* in *AT&T Technologies v. Communications Workers of America* (475 U.S. 643, 1986), the Court held that it is the role of the courts, not that of the arbitrators, to resolve questions of whether a grievance is subject to arbitration.

The limited role of the court ordering arbitration was emphasized in *United Steelworkers v. American Mfg. Co.* (363 U.S. 564, 1960), the second case in the *Trilogy*. In that case the Supreme Court held that "[t]he function of the court . . . is confined to ascertaining whether the party seeking arbitration is making a claim which on its face is governed by the contract. Whether the moving party is right or wrong is a question of contract interpretation for the arbitrator. . . . *The courts, therefore, have no business weighing the merits of the grievance.*" (Emphasis added.)

When one of the parties refuses to comply with the arbitrator's award or decision after the grievance has been arbitrated, the other party may seek to have the award judicially enforced. What is the role of the court being asked to enforce the arbitration decision? That was the subject of the final case in the *Trilogy, United Steelworkers* v. *Enterprise Wheel & Car Co.* (363 U.S. 593, 1960). In that case, the Supreme Court held that the court is required to enforce the arbitrator's decision unless it is clear to the court that the arbitrator has exceeded the authority given to him or her by the collective agreement. The Court stated that "the question of interpretation of the collective agreement is a question for the arbitrator. It is the arbitrator's construction which was bargained for; and so far as the arbitrator's decision concerns the construction of the contract, the courts have no business overruling him because their interpretation of the contract is different from his."

Under the *Enterprise Wheel & Car* decision, the court should refuse to enforce an arbitration decision that violates the law. How should the court react when an employer claims that an arbitration decision conflicts with the "policy" behind the law? That was the subject of the following Supreme Court decision.

PAPERWORKERS v. MISCO INC.

484 U.S. 29 (Supreme Court of the United States, 1987)

WHITE, J.

Misco, Inc. (Misco, or the Company) operates a paper converting plant in Monroe, Louisiana. The Company is a party to a collective-bargaining agreement with the United Paperworkers International Union, AFL-CIO, and its union local (the Union); the agreement covers the production and maintenance employees at the plant. Under the agreement, the Company or the Union may submit to arbitration any grievance that arises from the interpretation or application of its terms, and the arbitrator's decision is final and binding upon the parties. The arbitrator's authority is limited to interpretation and application of the terms contained in the agreement itself. The agreement reserves to management the right to establish, amend, and enforce "rules and regulations regulating the discipline or discharge of employees" and the procedures for imposing discipline. Such rules were to be posted and were to be in effect "until ruled on by grievance and arbitration procedures as to fairness and necessity." For about a decade, the Company's rules had listed as causes for discharge the bringing of intoxicants, narcot-

ics, or controlled substances on to plant property or consuming any of them there, as well as reporting for work under the influence of such substances. At the time of the events involved in this case, the Company was very concerned about the use of drugs at the plant, especially among employees on the night shift.

Isiah Cooper, who worked on the night shift for Misco, was one of the employees covered by the collective-bargaining agreement. He operated a slitter rewinder machine, which uses sharp blades to cut rolling coils of paper. The arbitrator found that this machine is hazardous and had caused numerous injuries in recent years. Cooper had been reprimanded twice in a few months for deficient performance. On January 21, 1983, one day after the second reprimand, the police searched Cooper's house pursuant to a warrant, and a substantial amount of marijuana was found. Contemporaneously, a police officer was detailed to keep Cooper's car under observation at the Company's parking lot. At about 6:30 P.M., Cooper was seen walking in the parking lot during work hours with two other men. The three men entered Cooper's car momentarily, then walked to another car, a white Cutlass, and entered it. After the other two men later returned to the plant, Cooper was apprehended by police in the backseat of this car with marijuana smoke in the air and a lighted marijuana cigarette in the front-seat ashtray. The police also searched Cooper's car and found a plastic scales case and marijuana gleanings. Cooper was arrested and charged with marijuana possession.

On January 24, Cooper told the Company that he had been arrested for possession of marijuana at his home; the Company did not learn of the marijuana cigarette in the white Cutlass until January 27. It then investigated and on February 7 discharged Cooper, asserting that in the circumstances, his presence in the Cutlass violated the rule against having drugs on the plant premises. Cooper filed a grievance protesting his discharge the same day, and the matter proceeded to arbitration. The Company was not aware until September 21, five days before the hearing before the arbitrator was scheduled, that marijuana had been found in Cooper's car. That fact did not become known to the Union until the hearing began. At the hearing it was stipulated that the issue was whether the Company had "just cause to discharge the Grievant under Rule II.1" and, "[i]f not, what if any should be the remedy." . . .

The arbitrator upheld the grievance and ordered the Company to reinstate Cooper with backpay and full seniority. The arbitrator based his finding that there was not just cause for the discharge on his consideration of seven criteria. In particular, the arbitrator found that the Company failed to prove that the employee had possessed or used marijuana on company property: finding Cooper in the backseat of a car and a burning cigarette in the front-seat ashtray was insufficient proof that Cooper was using or possessed marijuana on company property. . . . The arbitrator refused to accept into evidence the fact that marijuana had been found in Cooper's car on company premises because the Company did not know of this fact when Cooper was discharged and therefore did not rely on it as a basis for the discharge.

The Company filed suit in District Court, seeking to vacate the arbitration award on several grounds, one of which was that ordering reinstatement of Cooper, who had allegedly possessed marijuana on the plant premises, was contrary to public policy. The District Court agreed that the award must be set aside as contrary to public policy because it ran counter to general safety concerns that arise from the operation of dangerous machinery while under the influence of drugs, as well as to state criminal law against drug possession. The Court of Appeals affirmed. . . .

Collective-bargaining agreements commonly provide grievance procedures to settle disputes between union and employer with respect to the interpretation and application of the agreement and require binding arbitration for unsettled grievances. In such cases, and this is such a case, the Court made clear almost 30 years ago that the courts play only a limited role when asked to review the decision of an arbitrator. The courts are not authorized to reconsider the merits of an award even though the parties may allege that the award rests on errors of fact or on misinterpretation of the contract. . . .

Because the parties have contracted to have disputes settled by an arbitrator chosen by them rather than by a judge, it is the arbitrator's view of the facts and of the meaning of the contract that they have agreed to accept. Courts thus do not sit to hear claims of factual or legal error by an arbitrator as an appellate court does in reviewing decisions of lower courts. To resolve disputes about the application of a collective-bargaining agreement, an arbitrator must find facts and a court may not reject those findings simply because it disagrees with them. The same is true of the arbitrator's interpretation of the contract. The arbitrator may not ignore the plain language of the contract; but the parties having authorized the arbitrator to give meaning to the language of the agreement, a court should not reject an award on the ground that the arbitrator misread the contract. . . . So, too, where it is contemplated that the arbitrator will determine remedies for contract violations that he finds, courts have no authority to disagree with his honest judgment in that respect. If the courts were free to intervene on these grounds, the speedy resolution of grievances by private mechanisms would be greatly undermined. Furthermore, it must be remembered that grievance and arbitration procedures are part and parcel of the ongoing process of collective bargaining. . . . Of course, decisions procured by the parties through fraud or through the arbitrator's dishonesty need not be enforced. But there is nothing of that sort involved in this case.

The Company's position, simply put, is that the arbitrator committed grievous error in finding that the evidence was insufficient to prove that Cooper had possessed or used marijuana on company property. But the Court of Appeals, although it took a distinctly jaundiced view of the arbitrator's decision in this regard, was not free to refuse enforcement because it considered Cooper's presence in the white Cutlass, in the circumstances, to be ample proof that Rule II.1 was violated. No dishonesty is alleged; only improvident, even silly, fact-finding is claimed. This is hardly sufficient basis for disregarding what the agent appointed by the parties determined to be the historical facts.

Nor was it open to the Court of Appeals to refuse to enforce the award because the arbitrator, in deciding whether there was just cause to discharge, refused to consider evidence unknown to the Company at the time Cooper was fired. The parties bargained for arbitration to settle disputes and were free to set the procedural rules for arbitrators to follow if they chose. Section VI of the agreement, entitled "Arbitration Procedure," did set some ground rules for the arbitration process. It forbade the arbitrator to consider hearsay evidence, for example, but evidentiary matters were otherwise left to the arbitrator . . . Here the arbitrator ruled that in determining whether Cooper had violated Rule II.1, he should not consider evidence not relied on by the employer in ordering the discharge, particularly in a case like this where there was no notice to the employee or the Union prior to the hearing that the Company would attempt to rely on after-discovered evidence. This, in effect, was a construction of what the contract required when deciding discharge cases: an arbitrator was to look only at the evidence before the employer at the time of discharge. As the arbitrator noted, this approach was consistent with the practice followed by other arbitrators. . . . Under the Arbitration Act, the federal courts are empowered to set aside arbitration awards on such grounds only when "the arbitrators were guilty of misconduct . . . in refusing to hear evidence pertinent and material to the controversy." If we apply that same standard here and assume that the arbitrator erred in refusing to consider the disputed evidence, his error was not in bad faith or so gross as to amount to affirmative misconduct. Finally, it is worth noting that putting aside the evidence about the marijuana found in Cooper's car during this arbitration did not forever foreclose the Company from using that evidence as the basis for a discharge.

Even if it were open to the Court of Appeals to have found a violation of Rule II.1 because of the marijuana found in Cooper's car, the question remains whether the court could properly set aside the award because in its view discharge was the correct remedy. Normally, an arbitrator is authorized to disagree with the sanction imposed for employee misconduct. . . . The parties, of course, may limit the discretion of the arbitrator in this respect; and it may be, as the Company argues, that under the contract involved here, it was within the unreviewable discretion of management to discharge an employee once a violation of Rule II.1 was found. But the parties stipulated that the issue before the arbitrator was whether there was "just" cause for the discharge, and the arbitrator, in the course of his opinion, cryptically observed that Rule II.1 merely listed causes for discharge and did not expressly provide for immediate

discharge. Before disposing of the case on the ground that Rule II.1 had been violated and discharge was therefore proper, the proper course would have been remand to the arbitrator for a definitive construction of the contract in this respect.

The Court of Appeals did not purport to take this course in any event. Rather, it held that the evidence of marijuana in Cooper's car required that the award be set aside because to reinstate a person who had brought drugs onto the property was contrary to the public policy "against the operation of dangerous machinery by persons under the influence of drugs or alcohol." We cannot affirm that judgment.

A court's refusal to enforce an arbitrator's award under a collective-bargaining agreement because it is contrary to public policy is a specific application of the more general doctrine, rooted in the common law, that a court may refuse to enforce contracts that violate law or public policy. That doctrine derives from the basic notion that no court will lend its aid to one who founds a cause of action upon an immoral or illegal act, is further justified by the observation that the public's interests in confining the scope of private agreements to which it is not a party will go unrepresented unless the judiciary takes account of those interests when it considers whether to enforce such agreements. In the common law of contracts, this doctrine has served as the foundation for occasional exercises of judicial power to abrogate private agreements.

In *W. R. Grace [& Co. v. Rubber Workers]*, we recognized that "a court may not enforce a collective-bargaining agreement that is contrary to public policy," and stated that "the question of public policy is ultimately one for resolution by the courts." We cautioned, however, that a court's refusal to enforce an arbitrator's *interpretation* of such contracts is limited to situations where the contract as interpreted would violate "some explicit public policy" that is "well defined and dominant and is to be ascertained 'by reference to the laws and legal precedents and not from general considerations of supposed public interests.'"

The Court of Appeals made no attempt to review existing laws and legal precedents in order to demonstrate that they establish a "well defined and dominant" policy against the operation of dangerous machinery while under the influence of drugs. Although certainly such a judgment is firmly rooted in common sense, we explicitly held in *W. R. Grace* that a formulation of public policy based only on "general considerations of supposed public interests" is not the sort that permits a court to set aside an arbitration award that was entered in accordance with a valid collective-bargaining agreement.

Even if the Court of Appeals' formulation of public policy is to be accepted, no violation of that policy was clearly shown in this case. In pursuing its public policy inquiry, the Court of Appeals quite properly considered the established fact that traces of marijuana had been found in Cooper's car. Yet the assumed connection between the marijuana gleanings found in Cooper's car and Cooper's actual use of drugs in the workplace is tenuous at best and provides an insufficient basis for holding that his reinstatement would actually violate the public policy identified by the Court of Appeals "against the operation of dangerous machinery by persons under the influence of drugs or alcohol." A refusal to enforce an award must rest on more than speculation or assumption.

In any event, it was inappropriate for the Court of Appeals itself to draw the necessary inference. To conclude from the fact that marijuana had been found in Cooper's car that Cooper had ever been or would be under the influence of marijuana while he was on the job and operating dangerous machinery is an exercise in fact-finding about Cooper's use of drugs and his amenability to discipline, a task that exceeds the authority of a court asked to overturn an arbitration award. The parties did not bargain for the facts to be found by a court, but by an arbitrator chosen by them who had more opportunity to observe Cooper and to be familiar with the plant and its problems. Nor does the fact that it is inquiring into a possible violation of public policy excuse a court for doing the arbitrator's task. If additional facts were to be found, the arbitrator should find them in the course of any further effort the Company might have made to discharge Cooper for having had marijuana in his car on company premises. Had the arbitrator found that Cooper had possessed drugs on the property, yet imposed discipline short of discharge because he found as a factual matter that Cooper could be trusted not to use them on the job, the Court of Appeals could not upset the award because of its own view that public policy about plant safety was threatened. In this connection it should also be noted that the award ordered Cooper to be reinstated in his old job or in an equivalent one for which he was qualified. It is by no means clear from the record that Cooper would pose a serious threat to the asserted public policy in every job for which he was qualified.

The judgment of the Court of Appeals is reversed.
So ordered.

Judicial Enforcement of No-Strike Clauses

The decisions in the *Steelworkers Trilogy* emphasized that arbitration was a substitute for industrial strife. The *Lincoln Mills* decision stated that the employer's agreement to arbitrate disputes is the quid pro quo for the union's agreement not to strike over arbitrable disputes.

Many agreements contain no-strike clauses, by which the union agrees not to strike over disputes of interpretation of the agreement. In *Teamsters Local 174* v. *Lucas Flour* (369 U.S. 95, 1962), the Supreme Court held that a no-strike clause will be implied by the court, even when the agreement itself is silent on the matter, when the agreement contains an arbitration provision. The implied no-strike clause covers any dispute that is subject to arbitration under the agreement.

If the collective agreement contains an express no-strike clause, or even an implied one under *Lucas Flour,* can a federal court enforce that clause by enjoining a strike? What about the anti-injunction provisions of the Norris–La Guardia Act? That issue was presented to the Supreme Court in the following case.

BOYS MARKETS, INC. v. RETAIL CLERKS UNION, LOCAL 770

398 U.S. 235 (Supreme Court of the United States, 1970)

BRENNAN, J.

In this case we re-examine the holding of *Sinclair Refining Co.* v. *Atkinson,* that the anti-injunction provisions of the Norris–La Guardia Act preclude a federal district court from enjoining a strike in breach of a no-strike obligation under a collective-bargaining agreement, even though that agreement contains provisions, enforceable under Section 301(a) of the [NLRA] . . . , for binding arbitration of the grievance dispute concerning which the strike was called. The Court of Appeals for the Ninth Circuit, considering itself bound by *Sinclair* reversed the grant by the District Court for the Central District of California of petitioner's prayer for injunctive relief.

In February 1969, at the time of the incidents that produced this litigation, petitioner and respondent were parties to a collective-bargaining agreement which provided, *inter alia,* that all controversies concerning its interpretation or application should be resolved by adjustment and arbitration procedures set forth therein and that, during the life of the contract, there should be "no cessation or stoppage of work, lock-out, picketing or boycotts. . . ." The dispute arose when petitioner's frozen foods supervisor and certain members of his crew who were not members of the bargaining unit began to rearrange merchandise in the frozen food cases of one of petitioner's supermarkets. A union representative insisted that the food cases be stripped of all merchandise and be restocked by union personnel. When petitioner did not accede to the union's demand, a strike was called and the union began to picket petitioner's establishment. Thereupon petitioner demanded that the union cease the work stoppage and picketing and sought to invoke the grievance and arbitration procedures specified in the contract.

The following day, since the strike had not been terminated, petitioner filed a complaint in California Superior Court seeking a temporary restraining order, a preliminary and permanent injunction and specific performance of the contractual arbitration provision. The state court issued a temporary restraining order forbidding continuation of the strike and also an order to show cause why a preliminary injunction should not be granted. Shortly thereafter, the union removed the case to the Federal District Court and there made a motion to quash the state court's temporary restraining order. In opposition, petitioner moved for an order compelling arbitration and enjoining continuation of the strike. Concluding that the dispute was subject to arbitration under the collective-bargaining agreement and that the strike was in violation of the contract, the District Court ordered the parties to arbitrate the underlying dispute and simultaneously enjoined the strike, all picketing in the vicinity of petitioner's supermarket, and any attempts by the union to induce the employees to strike or to refuse to perform their services.

At the outset, we are met with respondent's contention that *Sinclair* ought not to be disturbed because the decision turned on a question of statutory construction which Congress can alter at any time.

It is precisely because *Sinclair* stands as a significant departure from our otherwise consistent emphasis upon the congressional policy to promote the peaceful settlement of labor disputes through arbitration and our efforts to accommodate and harmonize this policy with those underlying the anti-injunction provisions of the Norris–La Guardia Act that we believe *Sinclair* should be reconsidered. . . .

Subsequent to the decision *Sinclair,* we held in *Avco Corp.* v. *Aero Lodge 735,* that Section 301(a) suits initially brought in state courts may be removed to the designated federal forum under the federal question removal jurisdiction. . . .

. . . The principal practical effect of *Avco* and *Sinclair* taken together is nothing less than to oust state courts of jurisdiction in Section 301(a) suits where injunctive relief is sought for breach of a no-strike obligation. Union defendants can, as a matter of course, obtain removal to a federal court, and there is obviously a compelling incentive for them to do so in order to gain the advantage of the strictures upon injunctive relief which *Sinclair* imposes on federal courts. . . . It is ironic indeed that the very provision that Congress clearly intended to provide additional remedies for breach of collective-bargaining agreements has been employed to displace previously existing state remedies. We are not at liberty thus to depart from the clearly expressed congressional policy to the contrary.

On the other hand, to the extent that widely disparate remedies theoretically remain available in state, as opposed to federal, courts, the federal policy of labor law uniformity elaborated in *Lucas Flour Co.,* is seriously offended. The injunction . . . is so important a remedial device, particularly in the arbitration context, that its availability or non-availability in various courts will not only produce rampant forum shopping and maneuvering from one court to another but will also greatly frustrate any relative uniformity in the enforcement of arbitration agreements.

An additional reason for not resolving the existing dilemma by extending *Sinclair* to the States is the devastating implications for the enforceability of arbitration agreements and their accompanying no-strike obligations if equitable remedies were not available. As we have previously indicated, a no-strike obligation, express or implied, is the *quid pro quo* for an undertaking by the employer to submit grievance disputes to the process of arbitration. Any incentive for employers to enter into such an arrangement is necessarily dissipated if the principal and most expeditious method by which the no-strike obligation can be enforced is eliminated. While it is of course true, as respondent contends, that other avenues of redress, such as an action for damages, would remain open to an aggrieved employer, an award of damages after a dispute has been settled is no substitute for an immediate halt to an illegal strike. Furthermore, an action for damages prosecuted during or after a labor dispute would only tend to aggravate industrial strife and delay an early resolution of the difficulties between employer and union. . . .

The *Sinclair* decision, however, seriously undermined the effectiveness of the arbitration technique as a method peacefully to resolve industrial disputes without resort to strikes, lockouts, and similar devices. Clearly employers will be wary of assuming obligations to arbitrate specifically enforceable against them when no similarly efficacious remedy is available to enforce the concomitant undertaking of the union to refrain from striking. On the other hand, the central purpose of the Norris–La Guardia Act to foster the growth and viability of labor organizations is hardly retarded—if anything, this goal is advanced—by a remedial device that merely enforces the obligation that the union freely undertook under a specifically enforceable agreement to submit disputes to arbitration. We conclude, therefore, that the unavailability of equitable relief in the arbitration context presents a serious impediment to the congressional policy favoring the voluntary establishment of a mechanism for the peaceful resolution of labor disputes, that the core purpose of the Norris–La Guardia Act is not sacrificed by the limited use of equitable remedies to further this important policy, and consequently that the Norris–La Guardia Act does not bar the granting of injunctive relief in the circumstances of the instant case.

Injunctions under the doctrine of *Boys Markets* may also be issued against employers for breaches of the collective agreement that threaten the arbitration process. In *Oil, Chemical and Atomic Workers International Union, Local 2–286* v. *Amoco Oil Co.* (885 F.2d 697, 10th Cir. 1989), the court affirmed an injunction preventing an employer's unilateral implementation of a drug-testing program, pending the outcome of arbitration to determine the employer's right to institute such a program under the collective bargaining agreement.

The decision in *Boys Markets,* allowing federal courts to enjoin strikes in violation of no-strike clauses does not mean that a union may never go on strike during the term of a collective agreement. The *Boys Markets* holding is limited to strikes over issues subject to arbitration under the agreement. In the *Jacksonville Bulk Terminals, Inc.* v. *Int. Longshoremen's Ass'n* (457 U.S. 702, 1982), the Supreme Court refused to enjoin a refusal by Longshoremen to handle cargo destined for the Soviet Union in protest over the Soviet invasion of Afghanistan. The Court held that the strike was over a political dispute that was not arbitrable under the collective agreement. The policy behind that decision was first set out in the following case.

BUFFALO FORGE CO. v. UNITED STEELWORKERS OF AMERICA

428 U.S. 397 (Supreme Court of the United States, 1975)

WHITE, J.

The issue for decision is whether a federal court may enjoin a sympathy strike pending the arbitrator's decision as to whether the strike is forbidden by the express no-strike clause contained in the collective-bargaining contract to which the striking union is a party.

The Buffalo Forge Co. (employer) operates three separate plant and office facilities in the Buffalo, N.Y., area. For some years production and maintenance (P&M) employees at the three locations have been represented by the United Steelworkers of America, AFL-CIO, and its Local Unions No. 1874 and No. 3732 (hereafter sometimes collectively the Union). The United Steelworkers is a party to the two separate collective-bargaining agreements between the locals and the employer. The contracts contain identical no-strike clauses, as well as grievance and arbitration provisions for settling disputes over the interpretation and application of each contract. The latter provide:

> 26. Should differences arise between the [employer] and any employee covered by this Agreement as to the meaning and application of the provisions of this Agreement, or should any trouble of any kind arise in the plant, there shall be no suspension of work on account of such differences, but an earnest effort shall be made to settle such differences immediately [under the six-step grievance and arbitration procedure provided in sections 27 through 32].

Shortly before this dispute arose, the United Steelworkers and two other locals not parties to this litigation were certified to represent the employer's "office clerical-technical" (O&T) employees at the same three locations. On November 16, 1974, after several months of negotiations looking toward their first collective-bargaining agreement, the O&T employees struck and established picket lines at all three locations. On November 18, P&M employees at one plant refused to cross the O&T picket line for the day. Two days later, the employer learned that the P&M employees planned to stop work at all thee plants the next morning. In telegrams to the Union, the employer stated its position that a strike by the P&M employees would violate the no-strike clause and offered to arbitrate any dispute which had led to the planned strike. The next day, at the Union's direction, the P&M employees honored the O&T picket line and stopped work at the three plants. They did not return to

work until December 16, the first regular working day after the District Court denied the employer's prayer for a preliminary injunction.

The employer's complaint under Section 301(a) of the [NLRA], filed in District Court on November 26, claimed the work stoppage was in violation of the no-strike clause. Contending in the alternative that the work strike was caused by a specific incident involving P&M truck drivers' refusal to follow a supervisor's instructions to cross the O&T picket line, and that the question whether the P&M employees' work stoppage violated the no-strike clause was itself arbitrable, the employer requested damages, a temporary order and a preliminary injunction against the strike, and an order compelling the parties to submit any "underlying dispute" to the contractual grievance and arbitration procedures. The Union's position was that the work stoppage did not violate the no-strike clause. It offered to submit that question to arbitration "on one day's notice," but opposed the prayer for injunctive relief.

After denying the temporary restraining order and finding that the P&M work stoppage was not the result of the specific refusal to cross the O&T picket line, the District Court concluded that the P&M employees were engaged in a sympathy action in support of the striking O&T employees. The District Court then held itself forbidden to issue an injunction by Section 4 of the Norris–La Guardia Act because the P&M employees' strike was not over an "arbitrable grievance" and hence was not within the "narrow" exception to the Norris–La Guardia Act established in *Boys Markets* v. *Retail Clerks Union.*

On the employer's appeal from the denial of a preliminary injunction . . . [t]he Court of Appeals affirmed. It held that enjoining this strike, which was not "over a grievance which the union has agreed to arbitrate," was not permitted by the *Boys Markets* exception to the Norris–La Guardia Act.

As a preliminary matter, certain elements in this case are not in dispute. The Union has gone on strike not by reason of any dispute it or any of its members has with the employer, but in support of other local unions of the same international organization, that were negotiating a contract with the employer and were out on strike. The parties involved here are bound by collective-bargaining contracts each containing a no-strike clause which the Union claims does not forbid sympathy strikes. The employer has the other view, its complaint in the District Court asserting that the work stoppage violated the no-strike clause. Each of the contracts between the parties also has an arbitration clause broad enough to reach not only disputes between the Union and the employer about other provisions in the contracts but also as to the meaning and application of the no-strike clause itself. Whether the sympathy strike the Union called violated the no-strike clause, and the appropriate remedies if it did are subject to the agreed-upon dispute-settlement procedures of the contracts and are ultimately issues for the arbitrator. The employer thus was entitled to invoke the arbitral process to determine the legality of the sympathy strike and to obtain a court order requiring the Union to arbitrate if the Union refused to do so. Furthermore, were the issue arbitrated and the strike found illegal, the relevant federal statutes as construed in our cases would permit an injunction to enforce the arbitral decision.

The issue in this case arises because the employer not only asked for an order directing the Union to arbitrate but prayed that the strike itself be enjoined pending arbitration and the arbitrator's decision whether the strike was permissible under the no-strike clause. . . .

Boys Markets plainly does not control this case. The District Court found and it is not now disputed that the strike was not *over* any dispute between the Union and the employer that was even remotely subject to the arbitration provisions of the contract. The strike at issue was a sympathy strike in support of sister unions negotiating with the employer; neither its causes nor the issue underlying it was subject to the settlement procedures provided by the contracts between the employer and respondents. The strike had neither the purpose nor the effect of denying or evading an obligation to arbitrate or of depriving the employer of its bargain. Thus, had the contract not contained a no-strike clause or had the clause expressly excluded sympathy strikes, there would have been no possible basis for implying from the existence of an arbitration clause a promise not to strike that could have been violated by the sympathy strike in this case.

Nor was the injunction authorized solely because it was alleged that the sympathy strike called by the Union violated the express no-strike provision of the contracts. Section 301 of the Act assigns a major role to the courts in enforcing collective-bargaining agreements, but aside from the enforcement of the arbitration provisions of such contracts, within the limits permitted by *Boys Markets,* the Court has never indicated that the courts may enjoin actual or threatened contract violations despite the Norris–La Guardia Act. . . . The allegation of the complaint that the Union was breaching its obligation not to strike did not in itself warrant an injunction.

The contracts here at issue, however, also contained grievance and arbitration provisions for settling disputes over the interpretation and application of the provisions of the contracts, including the no-strike clause. That clause, like others, was subject to enforcement in accordance with the procedures set out in the contracts. Here the Union struck, and the parties were in dispute whether the sympathy strike violated the Union's no-strike undertaking. Concededly, that issue was arbitrable. It was for the arbitrator to determine whether there was a breach, as well as the remedy for any breach, and the employer was entitled to an order requiring the Union to arbitrate if it refused to do so. But the Union does not deny its duty to arbitrate; in fact, it denies that the employer ever demanded arbitration. However that may be, it does not follow that the District Court was empowered not only to order arbitration but to enjoin the strike pending the decision of the arbitrator, despite the express prohibition of Section 4(a) of the Norris–La Guardia Act against injunctions prohibiting any person from "[c]easing or refusing to perform any work or to remain in any relation of employment."

With these considerations in mind, we are far from concluding that the arbitration process will be frustrated unless the courts have the power to issue interlocutory injunctions pending arbitration in cases such as this or in others in which an arbitrable dispute awaits decision. We agree with the Court of Appeals that there is no necessity here, such as was found to be the case in *Boys Markets,* to accommodate the policies of the Norris–La Guardia Act to the requirements of Section 301 by empowering the District Court to issue the injunction sought by the employer.

The judgment of the Court of Appeals is affirmed.

So ordered.

Remedies for Breach of No-Strike Clauses.   As the preceding cases demonstrate, an employer may enjoin strikes that violate a no-strike clause when the strike is over an arbitrable issue. But even when an injunction will not be issued, an employer may still recover damages for breach of the no-strike clause through a suit under Section 301. In the *Lucas Flour* case, the Supreme Court upheld a damage award for a strike in violation of the implied no-strike clause.

Section 301 Suits.   The Supreme Court had held that suits under Section 301 are governed by the appropriate state statutes of limitation (*UAW* v. *Hoosier Cardinal Corp.,* 383 U.S. 696, 1966). More recently, in *DelCostello* v. *Teamsters* (462 U.S. 151, 1983), the Court held that suits under Section 301 by an individual employee against the employer for breach of the collective agreement and against the union for breach of the duty of fair representation were subject to the six-month limitation period under Section 10(b) of the NLRA.

Section 301, while allowing damage suits for breach of no-strike clauses, places some limitations upon such suits. Section 301(b) specifies that "any money judgment against a labor organization in a district court of the United States shall be enforceable only against the organization as an entity and its assets, and shall not be enforceable against any individual member or his assets." In *Atkinson* v. *Sinclair Refining Co.* (370 U.S. 238, 1962), the Supreme Court held that Section 301 does not authorize damage suits against individual union officials when their union is liable for violating a no-strike clause. In *Complete Auto Transit, Inc.* v. *Reis* (451 U.S. 401, 1981), the Court held that individual employees are not liable for damages from a wildcat strike not authorized by their union in breach of the collective agreement. If the employer cannot recover damages from the individuals responsible for such a strike, what other steps can the employer take against those individuals?

In *Carbon Fuel Co.* v. *United Mine Workers* (444 U.S. 212, 1979), the Supreme Court held that an international union was not liable for damages resulting from a strike by one of its local unions when the international had neither instigated, authorized, supported, or encouraged the strike. Why would the employer seek damages from the international when the local had gone on strike?

The result of the *Complete Auto Transit* and *Carbon Fuel* cases is to deprive the employer of the right to recover damages from either the union or the individual union members when a strike by the individual union members is not authorized by the union. The remedy of damages is available to the employer only when the union has called or authorized the strike in breach of the collective agreement.

When the employer can pursue arbitration over the union violation of the agreement, the court will stay a suit for damages pending arbitration, according to the Supreme Court decision in *Drake Bakeries Inc.* v. *Bakery Workers Local 50* (370 U.S. 254, 1962). The employer's obligation to arbitrate such disputes continues despite the union's breach of its contractual obligations, *Packinghouse Workers Local 721* v. *Needham Packing Co.* (376 U.S. 247, 1964).

Section 301 and Other Remedies.   Can a court hear a suit alleging a breach of contract under Section 301 even though the contract is silent about judicial remedies? In *Groves* v. *Ring Screw Works* (111 S.Ct. 498, 1990), the collective agreement provided for arbitration in discharge cases only upon agreement of both parties; it also provided that if a grievance was not resolved through the grievance procedure, the union could go on strike over the issue. Two employees who were discharged by the employer filed suit for wrongful discharge in state court; their union joined the suits as a plaintiff. The employer argued that the union could not file suit because the contract did not require arbitration. The Supreme Court reversed the court of appeals; the Court unanimously held that a contract giving the union the right to strike or the employer the right to lock out does not automatically strip federal courts of the authority to resolve contractual disputes. The union was not precluded from filing suit against the employer to enforce the contract, even though the contract was silent about judicial remedies.

Section 301 Preemption of Other Remedies. In *Allis-Chalmers Corp.* v. *Leuck* (471 U.S. 202, 1985), the Supreme Court held that if the resolution of a state law claim depends upon the interpretation of a collective agreement, the application of the state law is preempted by federal law; a suit under state law alleging bad-faith handling of a disability benefits claim was preempted by Section 301 because the collective agreement set out provisions for handling disability claims. In *I.B.E.W.* v. *Hechler* (481 U.S. 851, 1987), the Supreme Court held that an employee's tort suit against the union for failure to provide a safe place to work was precluded by Section 301 because her claim was "nothing more than a breach of the union's federal duty of fair representation." However, where state law remedies exist independently of any collective agreement and do not require interpretation of the agreement, the state law remedy is not preempted. In *Lingle* v. *Norge Division of Magic Chef, Inc.* (486 U.S. 399, 1988), the Supreme Court held that an employee who was discharged for filing a workers' compensation claim could file suit under state law for compensation and punitive damages; her suit was not preempted by Section 301.

The NLRB and Arbitration

As the preceding cases have demonstrated, the courts favor the policy of voluntary resolution of disputes between labor and management. The courts will therefore refrain from deciding issues that are subject to arbitration, instead deferring to the arbitrator's resolution of such issues. If a grievance under an agreement involves conduct that may also be an unfair labor practice under the NLRA, what is the role of the National Labor Relations Board (NLRB)? Should the board, like the courts, defer to arbitration? Or should the board decide the issue to ensure that the parties' statutory rights are protected? The following case applies to these issues.

UNITED TECHNOLOGIES

268 N.L.R.B. No. 83 (N.L.R.B., 1984)

The complaint alleges that the Respondent (United Technologies) violated Section 8(a)(1) by threatening employee Sherfield with disciplinary action if she persisted in processing a grievance to the second step. At the hearing, the Respondent denied that it had violated Section 8(a)(1) as alleged and argued that, in any event, since the dispute was cognizable under the grievance-arbitration provisions of the parties' collective-bargaining agreement, it should be re-

solved pursuant to those provisions. Accordingly, the Respondent urged the Board to defer the exercise of its jurisdiction in this matter to the grievance-arbitration machinery. The judge, relying on *General American Transportation Corp.,* rejected the Respondent's contention because the conduct complained of constituted an alleged violation of Section 8(a)(1)....

On 6 November 1981 the Union filed a third-step grievance alleging that the Respondent, through its general foreman, Peterson, intimidated, coerced, and harassed shop steward Wilson and employee Sherfield at a first-step grievance meeting by threatening disciplinary action against Sherfield if she appealed her grievance to the second step. The remedy the Union sought was that "the Company immediately stop these contract violations and General Foreman Roger Peterson be properly reprimanded and reinstructed for his misuse, abuse, and violation of the contract." The Respondent denied the Union's grievance at the third step, and the Union withdrew it on 27 January 1982 "without prejudice." The next day, the Respondent filed its own grievance alleging that "[n]otwithstanding the union's mistake in its allegations concerning General Foreman Peterson, it has refused to withdraw, with prejudice, its grievance." The Union denied the Respondent's grievance, and the Respondent appealed to the fourth step. Following a fourth-step meeting, the Union again denied the Respondent's grievance and refused the Respondent's request the matter be submitted to arbitration. Thereafter, the Union filed the charge [with the NLRB]. . . .

The Respondent and the Union were parties to a collective-bargaining agreement which was effective from 24 April 1978 through 24 April 1983. Article VII of the contract established a grievance procedure that includes an oral step, four written steps, and an arbitration provision that calls for final and binding arbitration.

Arbitration as a means of resolving labor disputes had gained widespread acceptance over the years and now occupies a respected and firmly established place in Federal labor policy. The reason for its success is the underlying conviction that the parties to a collective-bargaining agreement are in the best position to resolve, with the help of a neutral third party if necessary, disputes concerning the correct interpretation of their contract. Congressional intent regarding the use of arbitration is abundantly clear. . . .

Similarly, the concept of judicial and administrative deference to the arbitral process and the notion that courts should support, rather than interfere with, this method of dispute resolution have become entrenched in American jurisprudence. Over the years, the Board has played a key role in fostering a climate in which arbitration could flourish.

The Board endowed this sound approach with renewed vigor in the seminal case of *Collyer Insulated Wire,* in which the Board dismissed a complaint alleging unilateral changes in wages and working conditions in violation of Section 8(a)(5) in deference to the parties' grievance-arbitration machinery. The *Collyer* majority articulated several factors favoring deferral: The dispute arose within the confines of a long and productive collective-bargaining relationship; there was no claim of employer animosity to the

employees' exercise of protected rights; the parties' contract provided for arbitration in a very broad range of disputes; the arbitration clause clearly encompassed the dispute at issue; the employer had asserted its willingness to utilize arbitration to resolve the dispute; and the dispute was eminently well suited to resolution by arbitration. In these circumstances, deferral to the arbitral process merely gave full effect to the parties' agreement to submit disputes to arbitration. In essence, the *Collyer* majority was holding the parties to their bargain by directing them to avoid substituting the Board's processes for their own mutually agreed-upon method for dispute resolution.

The experience under *Collyer* was extremely positive. . . . In *National Radio* the Board extended the deferral policy to cases involving 8(a)(3) allegations. In that case the complaint alleged, inter alia, the disciplinary suspension and discharge of an active union adherent in violation of Section 8(a)(3) as well as various changes in terms and conditions of employment in violation of Section 8(a)(5). Thus, that case presented a situation where the resolution of the unilateral change issues by an arbitrator would not necessarily have resolved the 8(a)(3) issues raised by the complaint. Nevertheless, the Board decided that deferral to the grievance procedure prior to the issuance of the arbitrator's award was warranted.

Following *National Radio,* the Board routinely dismissed complaints alleging violations of Section 8(a)(3) and (1) in deference to the arbitral forum.

Despite the universal judicial acceptance of the *Collyer* doctrine, however, the Board in *General American Transportation* abruptly changed course and adopted a different standard for arbitral deferral, one that we believe ignores the important policy considerations in favor of deferral. Indeed, by deciding to decline to defer cases alleging violations of Sections 8(a)(1) and (3) and 8(b)(1)(A) and (2), the *General American Transportation* majority essentially emasculated the Board's deferral policy, a policy that had favorably withstood the tests of judicial scrutiny and of practical application. And they did so for reasons that are largely unsupportable. Simply stated, *Collyer* worked well because it was premised on sound legal and pragmatic considerations. Accordingly, we believe it deserves to be resurrected and infused with renewed life. . . .

The facts of the instant case make it eminently well suited for deferral. The dispute centers on a statement a single foreman made to a single employee and a shop steward during the course of a routine first-step grievance meeting allegedly concerning possible adverse consequences that might flow from a decision by the employee to process her grievance to the next step. The statement is alleged to be a threat violative of Section 8(a)(1). It is also, however, clearly cognizable under the broad grievance-arbitration provision of Section VII of the collective-bargaining agree-ment. Moreover, Respondent has expressed its willingness, indeed its eagerness, to arbitrate the dispute. **So ordered.**

When the board has deferred an unfair labor practice charge to arbitration, should the board automatically uphold the arbitrator's decision? This question is addressed in the following case.

OLIN CORP.

268 N.L.R.B. No. 86 (N.L.R.B., 1984)

In brief, the Union is the exclusive collective-bargaining representative of Respondent's approximately 260 production and maintenance employees. The 1980–83 collective-bargaining agreement contained the following provision:

Article XIV—Strikes and Lockouts

During the life of the Agreement, the Company will not conduct a lockout at the Plant and neither the Local Union nor the International Union, nor any officer or representative of either, will cause or permit its members to cause any strike, slowdown or stoppage (total or partial) of work or any interference, directly or indirectly, with the full operation of the plant.

Employee Salvatore B. Spatorico was president of the Union from 1976 until his termination in December 1980. On the morning of 17 December, Respondent suspended two pipefitters for refusing to perform a job that they felt was more appropriately millwright work. A "sick out" ensued during which approximately 43 employees left work that day with medical excuses. Respondent gave formal written reprimands to 39 of the employees who had engaged in the sick out. In a letter dated 29 December, Respondent notified Spatorico that he was discharged based on his entire record and in particular for threatening the sick out, participating in the sick out, and failing to prevent it.

Spatorico's discharge was grieved and arbitrated. After a hearing, the arbitrator found that a sick out had occurred at Respondent's facility on 17 December, that Spatorico "at least partially caused or participated" in it, and that he failed to try to stop it until after it had occurred. The arbitrator concluded that Spatorico's conduct contravened his obligation under article XIV of the collective-bargaining agreement set forth above. The arbitrator also stated, "Union officers implicitly have an affirmative duty not to cause strikes which are in violation of the clause, not to participate in such strikes and to try to stop them when they occur." Accordingly, the arbitrator found that Spatorico had been appropriately discharged.

Noting that the unfair labor practice charges had been referred to arbitration . . . the arbitrator addressed these charges and found "no evidence that the company discharged the grievant for his legitimate Union activities." The arbitrator again stated his conclusion that Spatorico had been discharged for participating in and failing to stop the sick out because Spatorico "is a Union officer but the contract's no strike clause *specifically* prohibits such activity by Union officers." (Emphasis added.) [The union filed unfair labor practice charges with the NLRB.]

The judge (A.L.J.) declined to defer to the arbitration award on the grounds that although the arbitrator referred to the unfair labor practice issue he did not consider it "in any serious way." The judge determined that the arbitrator was not competent to decide the unfair labor practice issue because the award was limited to interpretation of the contract. Moreover, he determined that the arbitrator did not explicitly refer to the statutory right and the waiver questions raised by the unfair labor practice charge. On the merits, however, the judge agreed with the arbitrator's conclusion in that he found Spatorico's "participation in the strike was inconsistent with his manifest contractual obligation to attempt to stem the tide of unprotected activity." The judge concluded that article XIV of the collective-bargaining agreement was sufficiently clear and unmistakable to waive, at the least, the sort of conduct in which Spatorico engaged, that, therefore, "Spatorico exposed himself to the greater liability . . ." and that Respondent did not violate Section 8(a)(3) and (1) of the Act by discharging him while merely reprimanding other employees.

We agree with the judge that the complaint should be dismissed. We do so, however, without reaching the merits because we would defer to the arbitrator's award consistent with the standards set forth in *Spielberg Mfg. Co.* In its seminal decision in *Spielberg,* the Board held that it would defer to an arbitration award where the proceedings appear to have been fair and regular, all parties have agreed to be bound, and the decision of the arbitrator is not clearly repugnant to the purposes and policies of the Act. The Board in *Raytheon Co.,* further conditioned deferral on the arbitrator's having considered the unfair labor practice issue.

It hardly needs repeating that national policy strongly favors the voluntary arbitration of disputes. The importance of arbitration in the overall scheme of Federal labor law has been stressed in innumerable contexts and forums. . . .

Accordingly, we adopt the following standard for deferral to arbitration awards. We would find that an arbitrator has adequately considered the unfair labor practice if (1) the contractual issue is factually parallel to the unfair labor practice issue, and (2) the arbitrator was presented generally with the facts relevant to resolving the unfair labor practice. In this respect, differences, if any, between the contractual and statutory standards of review should be weighed by the Board as part of its determination under the Spielberg standards of whether an award is "clearly repugnant" to the Act. And, with regard to the inquiry into the "clearly repugnant" standard, we would not require an arbitrator's award to be totally consistent with Board precedent. Unless the award is "palpably wrong," i.e. unless the arbitrator's decision is not susceptible to an interpretation consistent with the Act, we will defer.

Finally, we would require that the party seeking to have the Board reject deferral and consider the merits of a given case show that the above standards for deferral have not been met. Thus, the party seeking to have the Board ignore the determination of an arbitrator has the burden of affirmatively demonstrating the defects in the arbitral process or award. . . .

Turning now to the case before us, we find that the arbitral proceeding has met the Spielberg standards for deferral, and that the arbitrator adequately considered the unfair labor practice issue.

Some courts of appeals have rejected the NLRB's broad deferral policy under *United Technologies* and *Olin.* In *Taylor* v. *NLRB* (786 F.2d 807, 9th Cir. 1986), the court stated that the board's deferral policy inappropriately divests the board of its unfair labor practice jurisdiction under Section 10(b) of the NLRA. The court held that the policy of presuming every arbitration proceeding addresses every possible unfair labor practice issue overlooks situations when the contractual and statutory issues may be factually parallel but involve differing elements of proof or questions of factual relevance. In *Hammondtree* v. *NLRB* (894 F.2d 438, D.C. Cir. 1990), the court held that an employee may not be forced to give up the right to have the board adjudicate an unfair labor practice claim simply because the employer and union have established parallel contractual provisions and procedures for resolving the claim; only where the employee waives unfair labor practice rights or the claim rests on otherwise arbitrable matters may the board defer to arbitration.

Changes in the Status of Employers

Successor Employers

When a new employer takes over a unionized firm, what is the obligation of the successor employer to recognize the union, to adhere to the collective agreement, and to arbitrate grievances that arose under the collective agreement?

In *John Wiley & Sons, Inc.* v. *Livingston* (376 U.S. 543, 1964), the Supreme Court held that the successor employer must arbitrate a grievance arising under the collective agreement where there was a "substantial continuity of identity in the business enterprise," and the employer retained a majority of the employees from the former unionized work force. The union in *Wiley* sought only to force the new employer to arbitrate; it did not seek to force the employer to bargain with it. In *NLRB* v. *Burns International Security Services, Inc.* (406 U.S. 272, 1972), the Supreme Court dealt with a case where the union sought to force the new employer to recognize the union and to abide by the collective agreement. The Supreme Court held that the successor employer was not bound by the prior collective agreement but was required to recognize and bargain with the union because it had retained enough employees from the prior, unionized work force to constitute a majority of the new employer's work force.

What factors should be considered when determining whether a "substantial continuity of identity" of the operation exists, and at what point in the hiring process does the presence of a union's supporters constituting a majority of the work force trigger the duty to bargain with the union? Those issues were addressed by the Supreme Court in the following case.

FALL RIVER DYEING & FINISHING CORP. v. NLRB

482 U.S. 27 (Supreme Court of the United States, 1987)

BLACKMUN, J.

In this case we are confronted with the issue whether the National Labor Relations Board's decision is consistent with *NLRB* v. *Burns International Security Services, Inc.* . . . In *Burns,* this Court ruled that the new employer, succeeding to the business of another, had an obligation to bargain with the union representing the predecessor's employees. . . . Our inquiry then proceeds to three questions. . . . First, we must determine whether there is substantial record evidence to support the Board's conclusion that petitioner was a "successor" to Sterlingwale Corp., its business predecessor. Second, we must decide whether the Board's "substantial and representative complement" rule, designed to identify the date when a successor's obligation to bargain with the predecessor's employees' union arises, is consistent with *Burns,* is reasonable, and was applied properly in this case. Finally, we must examine the Board's "continuing demand" principle to the effect that, if a union has presented to a successor a premature demand for bargaining, this demand continues in effect until the successor

acquires the "substantial and representative complement" of employees that triggers its obligation to bargain.

For over 30 years before 1982, Sterlingwale operated a textile dyeing and finishing plant in Fall River, Massachusetts. Its business consisted basically of two types of dyeing, called, respectively, "converting" and "commission." Under the converting process, which in 1981 accounted for 60 to 70 percent of its business, Sterlingwale bought unfinished fabrics for its own account, dyed and finished them, and then sold them to apparel manufacturers. In commission dyeing, which accounted for the remainder of its business, Sterlingwale dyed and finished fabrics owned by customers according to their specifications. The financing and marketing aspects of converting and commission dyeing are different. Converting requires capital to purchase fabrics and a sales force to promote the finished products. The production process, however, is the same for both converting and commission dyeing.

In the late 1970s the textile-dyeing business, including Sterlingwale's, began to suffer from adverse economic conditions and foreign competition. After 1979, business at Sterlingwale took a serious turn for the worse because of the loss of its export market, and the company reduced the number of its employees. Finally, in February 1982, Sterlingwale laid off all its production employees, primarily because it no longer had the capital to continue the converting business. It retained a skeleton crew of workers and supervisors to ship out the goods remaining on order and to maintain the corporation's building and machinery. In the months following the layoff, Leonard Ansin, Sterlingwale's president, liquidated the inventory of the corporation and, at the same time, looked for a business partner with whom he could "resurrect the business." . . .

For almost as long as Sterlingwale had been in existence, its production and maintenance employees had been represented by the United Textile Workers of America, AFL-CIO, Local 292 (Union).

In late summer 1982, however, Sterlingwale finally went out of business. It made an assignment for the benefit of its creditors [who held] . . . a first mortgage on most of Sterlingwale's real property and . . . a security interest on Sterlingwale's machinery and equipment. . . .

During this same period, a former Sterlingwale employee and officer, Herbert Chace, and Arthur Friedman, president of one of Sterlingwale's major customers, Marcamy . . . , formed petitioner Fall River Dyeing & Finishing Corp. Chace, who had resigned from Sterlingwale in February 1982, had worked there for 27 years, had been vice-president in charge of sales at the time of his departure, and had participated in collective bargaining with the Union during his tenure at Sterlingwale. Chace and Friedman formed petitioner with the intention of engaging strictly in the commission-dyeing business and of taking advantage of the availability of Sterlingwale's assets and workforce. Accordingly, Friedman had Marcamy acquire . . . Sterlingwale's plant, real property, and equipment, and convey them to petitioner. Petitioner also obtained some of Sterlingwale's remaining inventory at the liquidator's auction. Chace became petitioner's vice-president in charge of operations and Friedman became its president. In September 1982, petitioner began operating out of Sterlingwale's former facilities and began hiring employees. . . . Petitioner's initial hiring goal was to attain one full shift of workers, which meant from 55 to 60 employees. Petitioner planned to "see how business would be" after this initial goal had been met and, if business permitted, to expand to two shifts. The employees who were hired first spent approximately four to six weeks in start-up operations and an additional month in experimental production.

By letter dated October 19, 1982, the Union requested petitioner to recognize it as the bargaining agent for petitioner's employees and to begin collective bargaining. Peti-

tioner refused the request, stating that, in its view, the request had "no legal basis." At that time, 18 of petitioner's 21 employees were former employees of Sterlingwale. By November of that year, petitioner had employees in a complete range of jobs, had its production process in operation, and was handling customer orders; by mid-January 1983, it had attained its initial goal of one shift of workers. Of the 55 workers in this initial shift, a number that represented over half the workers petitioner would eventually hire, 36 were former Sterlingwale employees. Petitioner continued to expand its workforce, and by mid-April 1983 it had reached two full shifts. For the first time, ex-Sterlingwale employees were in the minority but just barely so (52 or 53 out of 107 employees).

Although petitioner engaged exclusively in commission dyeing, the employees experienced the same conditions they had when they were working for Sterlingwale. The production process was unchanged and the employees worked on the same machines, in the same building, with the same job classifications, under virtually the same supervisors. Over half the volume of petitioner's business came from former Sterlingwale customers, and, in particular, Marcamy.

On November 1, 1982, the Union filed an unfair labor practice charge with the Board, alleging that in its refusal to bargain petitioner had violated Section 8(a)(1) and (5) of the National Labor Relations Act. After a hearing, the Administrative Law Judge (ALJ) decided that, on the facts of the case, petitioner was a successor to Sterlingwale. . . . Thus, in the view of the ALJ, petitioner's duty to bargain rose in mid-January because former Sterlingwale employees then were in the majority and because the Union's October demand was still in effect. Petitioner thus committed an unfair labor practice in refusing to bargain. In a brief decision and order, the Board, with one member dissenting, affirmed this decision. The Court of Appeals for the First Circuit, also by a divided vote, enforced the order. . . .

. . . [I]n *NLRB* v. *Burns International Security Services, Inc.,* this Court first dealt with the issue of a successor employer's obligation to bargain with a union that had represented the employees of its predecessor. . . . These presumptions [of majority support developed in *Burns*] are based not so much on an absolute certainty that the union's majority status will not erode following certification, as on a particular policy decision. The overriding policy of the NLRA is "industrial peace." The presumptions of majority support further this policy by "promot[ing] stability in collective-bargaining relationships, without impairing the free choice of employees." In essence, they enable a union to concentrate on obtaining and fairly administering a collective-bargaining agreement without worrying that, unless it produces immediate results, it will lose majority support and will be decertified. . . . The presumptions also remove any temptation on the part of the employer to avoid good-faith bargaining in the hope that, by delaying, it will undermine the union's support among the employees. . . .

The rationale behind the presumptions is particularly pertinent in the successorship situation and so it is understandable that the Court in *Burns* referred to them. During a transition between employers, a union is in a peculiarly vulnerable position. It has no formal and established bargaining relationship with the new employer, is uncertain about the new employer's plans, and cannot be sure if or when the new employer must bargain with it. While being concerned with the future of its members with the new employer, the union also must protect whatever rights still exist for its members under the collective bargaining agreement with the predecessor employer. Accordingly, during this unsettling transition period, the union needs the presumptions of majority status to which it is entitled to safeguard its members' rights and to develop a relationship with the successor.

The position of the employees also supports the application of the presumptions in the successorship situation. If the employees find themselves in a new enterprise that substantially resembles the old, but without their chosen bargaining representative, they may well feel that their choice of a union is subject to the vagaries of an enterprise's transformation. . . . Without the presumptions of majority support and with the wide variety of corporate transformations possible, an employer could use a successor enterprise as a way of getting rid of a labor contract and of exploiting the employees' hesitant attitude towards the union to eliminate its continuing presence.

In addition to recognizing the traditional presumptions of union majority status, however, the Court in *Burns* was careful to safeguard "'the rightful prerogative of owners independently to rearrange their businesses.'" If the new employer makes a conscious decision to maintain generally the same business and to hire a majority of its employees from the predecessor, then the bargaining obligation of Section 8(a)(5) is activated. This makes sense when one considers that the employer *intends* to take advantage of the trained workforce of its predecessor. . . .

We now hold that a successor's obligation to bargain is not limited to a situation where the union in question has been recently certified. Where, as here, the union has a rebuttable presumption of majority status, this status contin-

ues despite the change in employers. And the new employer has an obligation to bargain with that union so long as the new employer is in fact a successor of the old employer and the majority of its employees were employed by its predecessor.

We turn now to the three rules, as well as to their application to the facts of this case, that the Board has adopted for the successorship situation.

In *Burns* we approved the approach taken by the Board and accepted by courts with respect to determining whether a new company was indeed the successor to the old. This approach, which is primarily factual in nature and is based upon the totality of the circumstances of a given situation, requires that the Board focus on whether the new company has "acquired substantial assets of its predecessor and continued, without interruption or substantial change the predecessor's business operations." Hence, the focus is on whether there is "substantial continuity" between the enterprises. Under this approach, the Board examines a number of factors: whether the business of both employers is essentially the same; whether the employees of the new company are doing the same jobs in the same working conditions under the same supervisors; and whether the new entity has the same production process, produces the same products, and basically has the same body of customers. . . . In conducting the analysis, the Board keeps in mind the question whether "those employees who have been retained will understandably view their job situations as essentially unaltered." . . .

[W]e find that the Board's determination that there was "substantial continuity" between Sterlingwale and petitioner and that petitioner was Sterlingwale's successor is supported by substantial evidence in the record. Petitioner acquired most of Sterlingwale's real property, its machinery and equipment, and much of its inventory and materials. It introduced no new product line. Of particular significance is the fact that, from the perspective of the employees, their jobs did not change. Although petitioner abandoned converting dyeing in exclusive favor of commission dyeing, this change did not alter the essential nature of the employees' jobs because both types of dyeing involved the same production process. The job classifications of petitioner were the same as those of Sterlingwale; petitioners' employees worked on the same machines under the direction of supervisors most of whom were former supervisors of Sterlingwale. The record, in fact, is clear that petitioner acquired Sterlingwale's assets with the express purpose of taking advantage of its predecessor's workforce. . . .

For the reasons given above, this is a case where the

other factors suggest "substantial continuity" between the companies despite the 7-month hiatus. Here, moreover, the extent of the hiatus between the demise of Sterlingwale and the start-up of petitioner is somewhat less than certain. After the February layoff, Sterlingwale retained a skeleton crew of supervisors and employees that continued to ship goods to customers and to maintain the plant. In addition, until the assignment for the benefit of the creditors late in the summer, Ansin was seeking to resurrect the business or to find a buyer for Sterlingwale. The Union was aware of these efforts. Viewed from the employees' perspective, therefore, the hiatus may have been much less than seven months. Although petitioner hired the employees through advertisements, it often relied on recommendations from supervisors, themselves formerly employed by Sterlingwale, and intended the advertisements to reach the former Sterlingwale workforce. Accordingly, we hold that, under settled law, petitioner was a successor to Sterlingwale. We thus must consider if and when petitioner's duty to bargain arose.

In *Burns,* the Court determined that the successor had an obligation to bargain with the union because a majority of its employees had been employed by Wackenhut. The "triggering" fact for the bargaining obligation was this composition of the successor's workforce. The Court, however, did not have to consider the question when the successor's obligation to bargain arose: Wackenhut's contract expired on June 30 and Burns began its services with a majority of former Wackenhut guards on July 1. In other situations, as in the present case, there is a start-up period by the new employer while it gradually builds its operations and hires employees. In these situations, the Board, with the approval of the Courts of Appeals, has adopted the "substantial and representative complement" rule for fixing the moment when the determination as to the composition of the successor's workforce is to be made. If, at this particular moment, a majority of the successor's employees had been employed by its predecessor, then the successor has an obligation to bargain with the union that represented these employees. In deciding when a "substantial and representative complement" exists in a particular employer transition, the Board examines a number of factors. It studies "whether the job classifications designated for the operation were filled or substantially filled and whether the operation was in normal or substantially normal production." In addition, it takes into consideration "the size of the complement on that date and the time expected to elapse before a substantially larger complement would be at work . . . as well as the relative certainty of the employer's expected expansion." . . .

We conclude, however, that in this situation the successor is in the best position to follow a rule the criteria of which are straightforward. The employer generally will know with tolerable certainty when all its job classifications have been filled or substantially filled, when it has hired a majority of the employees it intends to hire, and when it has begun normal production. Moreover, the "full complement" standard advocated by petitioner is not *necessarily* easier for a successor to apply than is the "substantial and representative complement." In fact, given the expansionist dreams of many new entrepreneurs, it might well be more difficult for a successor to identify the moment when the "full complement" has been attained, which is when the business will reach the limits of the new employer's initial hopes, than it would be for this same employer to acknowledge the time when its business has begun normal production—the moment identified by the "substantial and representative complement" rule. We therefore hold that the Board's "substantial and representative complement" rule is reasonable in the successorship context. Moreover, its application to the facts of this case is supported by substantial record evidence. The Court of Appeals observed that by mid-January petitioner "had hired employees in virtually all job classifications, had hired at least fifty percent of those it would ultimately employ in the majority of those classifications, and it employed a majority of the employees it would eventually employ when it reached full complement." At that time petitioner had begun normal production. Although petitioner intended to expand to two shifts, and, in fact, reached this goal by mid-April, that expansion was contingent expressly upon the growth of the business. Accordingly, as found by the Board and approved by the Court of Appeals, mid-January was the period when petitioner reached its "substantial and representative complement." Because at that time the majority of petitioner's employees were former Sterlingwale employees, petitioner had an obligation to bargain with the Union then.

We also hold that the Board's "continuing demand" rule is reasonable in the successorship situation. The successor's duty to bargain at the "substantial and representative complement" date is triggered only when the union has made a bargaining demand. Under the "continuing demand" rule, when a union has made a premature demand that has been rejected by the employer, this demand remains in force until the moment when the employer attains the "substantial and representative complement."

Such a rule, particularly when considered along with the "substantial and representative complement" rule, places a minimal burden on the successor and makes sense in light of the union's position. Once the employer has concluded that it has reached the appropriate complement, then, in order to determine whether its duty to bargain will be triggered, it has only to see whether the union already has made a demand for bargaining. Because the union has no established relationship with the successor and because it is unaware of the successor's plans for its operations and hiring, it is likely that, in many cases, a union's bargaining demand will be premature. It makes no sense to require the union repeatedly to renew its bargaining demand in the hope of having it correspond with the "substantial and representative complement" date, when, with little trouble, the employer can regard a previous demand as a continuing one.

The reasonableness of the "continuing demand" rule is demonstrated by the facts of this case. Although the Union had asked Ansin to inform it about his plans for Sterling-

wale so that it could become involved in the employer transition, the Union learned about this transition only after it had become a *fait accompli*. Without having any established relationship with petitioner, it therefore is not surprising that the Union's October bargaining demand was premature. The Union, however, made clear after this demand that, in its view, petitioner had a bargaining obligation: the Union filed an unfair labor practice in November. Petitioner responded by denying that it had any duty to bargain. Rather than being a successor confused about when a bargaining obligation might arise, petitioner took an initial position—and stuck with it—that it *never* would have any bargaining obligation with the Union.

The judgment of the Court of Appeals is affirmed.

It is so ordered. [Dissent omitted.]

A successor can be held liable for the remedy of an unfair labor practice committed by the old employer; in *NLRB* v. *Winco Petroleum* (668 F.2d 973, 8th Cir. 1982), a successor was held subject to a bargaining order remedy even though the successor itself was not guilty of a refusal to bargain.

Bankruptcy and the Collective Agreement

The prior cases dealt with the obligations of successor employers. When an employer experiencing financial difficulties seeks protection from creditors under the bankruptcy laws, can the employer also reject the collective agreement?

When a corporation files a petition for the protection of the bankruptcy laws, the financial obligations of the corporation are suspended pending the resolution of the issue by the bankruptcy courts. What happens when a unionized employer files a petition for bankruptcy—is the employer required to adhere to the terms and conditions of the collective agreement? In the case of *NLRB* v. *Bildisco & Bildisco* (465 U.S. 513, 1984), the Supreme Court held that an employer who files for reorganization under Chapter 11 of the Bankruptcy Act does not violate Section 8(a)5 by unilaterally changing the terms of the collective agreement after filing the bankruptcy petition. The Court also held that the bankruptcy court may allow the employer to reject the collective agreement if the court finds that the agreement "burdens the estate" of the employer, and if "the equities balance in favor of rejecting the labor contract."

Following the Supreme Court's *Bildisco* decision, Congress amended the Bankruptcy Code to deal with the rejection of a collective agreement. The changes, enacted in Public Law 98-353 (1984), 11 U.S.C. Section 1113, allow the employer petitioning for bankruptcy protection to reject the collective agreement only when the following conditions are met:

1. The employer has made a proposal for contractual modifications, necessary to permit reorganization of the employer and treating all interested parties equitably, to the union.

2. The employer must provide the union with such relevant information as is necessary to evaluate the proposal.

3. The employer must offer to "confer in good faith in attempting to reach mutually satisfactory modifications."

4. The bankruptcy court finds that the union has rejected the employer's proposal "without good cause."

5. The court concludes that "the balance of equities clearly favors rejection" of the agreement.

The bankruptcy court is required to hold a hearing on the employer's petition within fourteen days and to issue its determination on the rejection issue within thirty days after the hearing.

In *Wheeling-Pittsburgh Steel Corp.* v. *United Steelworkers* (791 F2d 1074, 1986), the Third Circuit Court of Appeals held that it was an error to allow the employer to void the collective agreement where the employer did not give any persuasive rationale for asking the unionized employees to take disproportionate cuts for a five-year period without any provision for improvement if the employer's position improved. In *Teamsters Local 807* v. *Carey Trans.* (816 F2d 82, 1987), the Second Circuit Court of Appeals upheld rejection of the agreement where unionized employees were expected to take cuts greater than those for nonunion employees, because the union wages were 60 percent higher than industry average, whereas the other employees' compensation was barely competitive.

The NLRB has made it clear that filing a petition for bankruptcy protection does not affect the employer's obligation to recognize and bargain with the union (*Airport Bus Service,* 273 N.L.R.B. 561, 1984). In *Willis Elec.* (269 N.L.R.B. 1145, 1984), the NLRB held that an employer unilaterally abrogating an agreement without obtaining bankruptcy court relief is guilty of violating Section 8(a)5; economic necessity is not a defense for such conduct.

QUESTIONS

1. What is arbitration? Why is arbitration used to resolve contract disputes between unions and employees?

2. What is rights arbitration? What is interest arbitration?

3. When will a court enforce a contractual promise to arbitrate disputes over the interpretation and application of a collective agreement?

4. When should a court refuse to enforce an arbitrator's decision?

5. What remedies are available to an employer against workers striking in violation of a no-strike clause? Against a union striking in violation of a no-strike clause?

6. When will the NLRB defer consideration of an unfair labor practice complaint to arbitration?

7. When is a successor employer obligated to recognize and bargain with the union representing the employees of the former employer?

8. What is the effect of the 1984 amendments to the Bankruptcy Code on the *Bildisco* decision? When can an employer filing under Chapter 11 of the Bankruptcy Code repudiate a collective agreement?

CASE PROBLEMS

1. An employee of the Du Pont Company's plant in East Chicago attacked his supervisor and another employee and destroyed some company equipment—all for no apparent reason. He was discharged by the company. He was subsequently arrested and spent thirty days under observation in a hospital psychiatric ward. Two psychiatrists subsequently testified in court that the employee was temporarily insane at the time of the incident, and therefore he was acquitted of the criminal charges. They also testified that the worker had recovered and was not likely to suffer another mental breakdown.

   Following his acquittal, the worker's discharge was challenged by the union on the ground that the employee was not responsible for the assaults due to temporary mental incapacity. Therefore, argued the union, he was not dismissed for "just cause" as called for under the "Security of Employment" clause in the collective bargaining agreement.

   The company refused to reinstate the employee, and the union moved the grievance to arbitration. The arbitrator ruled in the union's favor and ordered the grievant reinstated to his job. Du Pont filed suit in a federal court in Indiana to overturn the arbitrator's ruling.

   If you represented the company in front of the federal judge, what arguments would you make for overturning the arbitrator's award? If you represented the union, what counterarguments would you make in response? How should the judge have ruled? See *E.I. Du Pont De Nemours & Co.* v. *Grasselli Employees Independent Ass'n of E. Chicago,* 790 F.2d 611 (7th Cir. 1985).

2. The labor contract between the West Penn Power Company of Arnold, Pennsylvania, and System Local No. 102 of the Utility Workers of America included a provision that employees engaged in the construction or maintenance of power lines would not be required to work outdoors during "inclement weather" and that the responsible supervisor would determine when weather conditions were too severe for outdoor work.

   The no-strike clause in the labor agreement required the union and its officers to make a "sincere, active effort to have work resumed at a normal rate" if the employees engaged in a wildcat strike or refused to carry out job assignments.

   One day in November, seven employees, including the union's president and vice-president, ceased working due to weather conditions, despite their supervisor's repeated orders to keep on working. West Penn subsequently suspended the five rank-and-file employees for five days each, but discharged the two union officers for "their refusal to proceed with a work assignment and to make an active effort as (union officers) to have work resumed by other union employees."

   An arbitration panel sustained the union president's discharge, while reducing the vice-president's termination to a thirty-day suspension. Both men responded by filing unfair labor practice charges with the NLRB.

   What do you think was the basis for the unfair labor practice charges filed by the two union officials? How should the NLRB respond? Should it defer to arbitration in this case? If not, how should it rule on the unfair labor practice charges? What remedy should it impose if it finds the two men were wrongfully discharged? See *West Penn Power Co.,* 274 N.L.R.B. No. 173 (1985).

3. Safeway Stores, Inc., suspended a journeyman meat cutter for disobeying an order and threatening a supervisor with physical harm. United Food and Commercial Workers Local 400 filed a grievance on behalf of the employee, and a few days later representatives of the company and the union met to discuss the grievance. Unable to reach an informal resolution, the union submitted the grievance to arbitration.

   The arbitrator found that the grievant was guilty of disobeying a direct order and that he had compounded his offense by threatening his supervisor with bodily harm. However, the arbitrator refused to sustain the discharge, because he also found that the company had not fully disclosed to the union or the grievant all the reasons for the discharge. At the grievance meeting, the company had stated that the reason for the discharge was the incident of insubordination. But during the arbitration hearing the personnel director testified that his decision to discharge the grievant was based not only on his acts of insubordination, but also on his past disciplinary record and a newspaper clipping he had seen concerning the grievant's conviction for assault and battery of his former girlfriend.

The company refused to abide by the arbitrator's decision and sought to have it overturned in the U.S. District Court for the District of Columbia.

If you had been the federal judge sitting in this case, would you have affirmed or overturned the arbitrator's award? See *Safeway Stores, Inc.* v. *United Food and Commercial Workers Local 400,* 621 F. Supp. 1233 (D.D.C. 1985).

4. *The Cleveland Press* and *The Plain Dealer,* the two daily newspapers in Cleveland, Ohio, were part of a multi-employer bargaining group that had signed a collective bargaining agreement with the Cleveland Typographical Union, Local 53. The contract stated that each covered employee was entitled to "a regular full-time job . . . for the remainder of his working life."

When the afternoon *Cleveland Press* went out of business, eighty-nine former *Press* employees sued the parent company, E. W. Scripps Company, and *The Plain Dealer* to enforce the lifetime employment guarantee in their collective bargaining agreement. In addition to their Section 301 action, the plaintiffs also charged that the two defendants had conspired to create a daily newspaper monopoly in the city of Cleveland. The defendants replied, among other defenses, that the plaintiffs had no standing to sue on this second basis.

Should the federal judge enforce the contract guarantee of lifetime jobs? If you say yes, what kind of a remedy should the judge fashion? What evidence do you see to support the plaintiffs' antitrust allegation? If defendants violated the Sherman Act, what impact should this have on their case? See *Province* v. *Cleveland Press Publishing Co.,* 787 F.2d 1047 (6th Cir. 1985).

5. Nolde Bros. Bakery's collective-bargaining agreement with the Bakery & Confectionery Workers Union, Local 358, provided that any grievance between the parties was subject to binding arbitration. During negotia-

tions over the renewal of the agreement, the union gave notice of its intention to cancel the existing agreement. Negotiations continued for several days past the termination date, and the union threatened to strike. The employer informed the union that it was permanently closing its plant. The employer paid the employees their accrued wages and vacation pay but refused to pay severance pay as called for in the collective agreement. The employer argued that its duty to pay severance pay and its duty to arbitrate the claim for severance pay expired with the collective agreement. The union sued under Section 301 to force the employer to arbitrate the question of whether the employer was required to pay severance pay. How should the court decide the union's suit—is the employer required to arbitrate the matter? Explain your answer. See *Nolde Bros.* v. *Bakery & Confectionery Workers Local 358,* 430 U.S. 243 (1977).

6. The Grissom family owned and operated a motor lodge and restaurant franchised by the Howard Johnson Co.; they employed fifty-three employees, who were represented by the Hotel & Restaurant Employees Union. The Grissoms sold their business to the Howard Johnson Co. Howard Johnson hired forty-five employees, nine of whom were former employees of the Grissoms. The union requested that Howard Johnson recognize it and meet the obligations of the prior collective agreement, but Howard Johnson refused. The union then sought arbitration of the question of the successor's obligations under the agreement; it filed a suit under Section 301 to compel Howard Johnson to arbitrate. Is Howard Johnson required to recognize and bargain with the union? Is Howard Johnson required to arbitrate the question of the successor's obligation? Explain your answer. See *Howard Johnson Co.* v. *Hotel & Restaurant Employees Detroit Local Joint Board,* 417 U.S. 249 (1974).

7. The underlying dispute in this case arose when Waller Brothers, which operates a stone quarry engaged in removing and processing stone and packing the stone in boxes for shipment, purchased an "Instapak" machine, which sprays protective padding around the stone being packed for shipment. Before the purchase of the "Instapak," the stone was packed with strips of synthetic material as padding. Employees called "Craters" pack the stone for shipment.

The union claims that it was entitled to negotiate a new wage rate for an "Instapak" machine operator, whereas the company maintains that the operation of the machine is only a function of the "Crater" job classification, which is subject to a previously negotiated wage rate. The company takes the position that both the no-strike clause and the provision for mandatory grievance arbitration contained in the collective bargaining agreement apply to this dispute. The union for its part relies on the portion of the contract that provides that wage rates are not subject to arbitration and that the union expressly reserves the right to strike in the event of a disagreement on wages.

If the union calls a strike and the company goes into court seeking a *Boys Markets* injunction, should the court grant or deny it? See *Waller Bros. Stone Co.* v. *District 23*, 620 F.2d 132, 104 L.R.R.M. 2168 (6th Cir. 1980).

8. HMC Management Corp., an apartment rental and management company, discharged two of its employees for substandard work performance. The employees, represented by the Carpenters Union, filed grievances. The employer subsequently decided to rehire one of the employees, but not the other one. When the grievance filed by the employee who was not rehired was arbitrated, the arbitrator acknowledged that the employer had sufficient reason to discharge the two employees, but held that the employer had acted improperly when it rehired one employee but not the other. The arbitrator ordered that the employer reinstate the other employee. The employer filed suit in federal court to have the arbitration award vacated. Should the court enforce or vacate the arbitrator's decision? Explain your answer. See *HMC Mgt. Corp.* v. *Carpenters District Council*, 750 F.2d 1302 (5th Cir. 1985).

9. The appellate court judge who wrote the decision of the three-judge panel in this case began his opinion as follows:

COFFIN, Chief Judge—This tempest has been brewed in a very small teapot. The dispute which precipitated the filing in this court of more than 80 pages of briefs and an extensive appendix began on July 30, 1974, when appellee Anheuser-Busch posted a notice prohibiting employees at its Merrimack, New Hampshire brewery from wearing tank-top shirts on the job. Tank-tops are sleeveless shirts which leave exposed the shoulders, arms and underarms of the wearer. Beginning on July 31, when three employees were sent home after refusing to doff their tank-tops for other shirts, the emotional temperature

rose, with over a dozen more employees, including shop stewards, being sent home a few days later. The issue peaked by August 14, when thirteen of the eighteen employees in the Brewery Department wore tank-tops, refused to put on other shirts, and went home. Approximately thirty employees in the Maintenance Department wore tank-tops on August 15. On August 16 no maintenance employees reported for work and production at the brewery was halted.

The brewery filed a lawsuit in federal district court seeking injunctive relief and damages against the employees' union on the grounds that the collective bargaining agreement contained a no-strike clause and an arbitration clause.

The union responded that (1) the employees' actions were individual, not concerted activity; (2) the employees were entitled to wear the tank-tops pending arbitration of the controversy; and (3) the employer should not be permitted to hide behind a *Boys Market* injunction after management's overreaction had itself precipitated the crisis.

How do you think the court ruled in this dispute? See *Anheuser-Busch* v. *Teamsters Local 633*, 511 F.2d 1097, 88 L.R.R.M. 2785 (1st Cir.), *cert. den.,* 423 U.S. 875, 90 L.R.R.M. 2744 (1975).

10. Stikes, an employee of Chevron Corp., was discharged for refusing to allow the employer to search her car under a company anti-drug policy, adopted in 1984, that required workers to submit to random searches of person and property. Stikes was a member of the bargaining unit represented by the Oil, Chemical and Atomic Workers Union; the collective agreement covering the bargaining unit provided for arbitration of discharge cases. Rather than submit a grievance over her discharge, Stikes filed a suit against Chevron in the state court. The suit charged Chevron with wrongful discharge, intentional infliction of emotional distress, unfair business practice, and violation of rights to privacy under the state constitution. Chevron argued that the suit was preempted by Section 301, because it was a suit to enforce the collective agreement. Does Stikes have a right to sue under state law over her discharge, or is her suit preempted by Section 301? Explain your answer. See *Stikes* v. *Chevron USA Inc.*, 914 F.2d 1265 (9th Cir. 1990).

CHAPTER 10

The Rights of Union Members

UNIONS, AS BARGAINING AGENTS representing bargaining units of employees, have significant power and control over individual employees. Those employees are precluded from dealing with the employer on matters of wages and working conditions—the employees must go through the union in dealing with the employer. Because employees are dependent on the union, they must be protected from arbitrary or unreasonable exercise of union power. This chapter explores the legal controls of unions to protect the rights of union members.

Protection of the Rights of Union Members

The legal controls on unions are the result of actions by the courts, the National Labor Relations Board (NLRB), and Congress. The courts and the NLRB have imposed a **duty of fair representation** on the part of the union—an obligation to represent fairly all members of the bargaining unit. Congress has legislated a **union member's "bill of rights"** to guarantee that union internal procedures are fair and has prohibited certain practices by unions that interfere with employees' rights under the National Labor Relations Act (NLRA).

In 1947 the Taft-Hartley Act added a list of union unfair labor practices to the NLRA. Section 7 was amended to give employees the right to refrain from engaging in concerted activity, as well as the right to engage in such activity. Section 8(b)(1)(A) prohibits union activity that interferes with, restrains, or coerces employees in the exercise of their Section 7 rights. Section 8(b)(2) prohibits unions from causing an employer to discriminate against employees in terms of conditions of employment because they are not union members. Section 8(b)(5) protects employees from unreasonable union dues and initiation fees.

The Landrum-Griffin Act of 1959 added the union members' "bill of rights" to the NLRA. Those provisions will be discussed in detail later in this chapter.

The Union's Duty of Fair Representation

The duty of fair representation is a judicially created obligation on the part of the union to represent fairly all employees in the bargaining unit. The duty was developed by the courts because of the union's role as exclusive bargaining agent for the bargaining unit. The initial cases dealing with the duty of fair representation arose under the Railway Labor Act; subsequent cases applied the duty to unions under the NLRA as well. In the following case the Supreme Court developed the concept of the duty of fair representation.

STEELE v. LOUISVILLE & NASHVILLE R.R.

323 U.S. 192 (Supreme Court of the United States, 1944)

STONE, C. J.

The question is whether the Railway Labor Act . . . imposes on a labor organization, acting by authority of the statute as the exclusive bargaining representative of a craft or class of railway employees, the duty to represent all the employees in the craft without discrimination because of their race, and, if so, whether the courts have jurisdiction to protect the minority of the craft or class from the violation of such obligation.

. . . Petitioner, a Negro, is a locomotive fireman in the employ of respondent railroad, suing on his own behalf and that of his fellow employees who, like petitioner, are Negro firemen employed by the Railroad. Respondent Brotherhood, a labor organization, is as provided under Section 2, Fourth of the Railway Labor Act, the exclusive bargaining representative of the craft of firemen employed by the Railroad and is recognized as such by it and the members of the craft. The majority of the firemen employed by the Railroad are white and are members of the Brotherhood, but a substantial minority are Negroes who, by the constitution and ritual of the Brotherhood, are excluded from its membership. As the membership of the Brotherhood constitutes a majority of all firemen employed on respondent Railroad and as under Section 2, Fourth, the members, because they are the majority, have chosen the Brotherhood to represent the craft, petitioner and other Negro firemen on the road have been required to accept the Brotherhood as their representative for the purposes of the Act.

On March 28, 1940, the Brotherhood, purporting to act as representative of the entire craft of firemen, without informing the Negro firemen or giving them opportunity to

be heard, served a notice on respondent Railroad and on twenty other railroads operating principally in the southeastern part of the United States. The notice announced the Brotherhood's desire to amend the existing collective bargaining agreement in such a manner as ultimately to exclude all Negro firemen from the service. By established practice on the several railroads so notified only white firemen can be promoted to serve as engineers, and the notice proposed that only "promotable," i.e., white, men should be employed as firemen or assigned to new runs or jobs or permanent vacancies in established runs or jobs.

On February 18, 1941, the railroads and the Brotherhood, as representative of the craft, entered into a new agreement which provided that not more than 50 percent of the firemen in each class of service in each seniority district of a carrier should be Negroes; that until such percentage should be reached all new runs and all vacancies should be filled by white men; and that the agreement did not sanction the employment of Negroes in any seniority district in which they were not working. . . .

. . . [W]e think that Congress, in enacting the Railway Labor Act and authorizing a labor union, chosen by a majority of a craft, to represent the craft, did not intend to confer plenary power upon the union to sacrifice, for the benefit of its members, rights of the minority of the craft, without imposing on it any duty to protect the minority. Since petitioner and the other Negro members of the craft are not members of the Brotherhood or eligible for membership, the authority to act for them is derived not from their action or consent but wholly from the command of the Act. . . .

Section 2, Second, requiring carriers to bargain with the representative so chosen, operates to exclude any other from representing a craft. The minority members of a craft are thus deprived by the statute of the right, which they would otherwise possess, to choose a representative of their own, and its members cannot bargain individually on behalf of themselves as to matters which are properly the subject of collective bargaining. . . .

The fair interpretation of the statutory language is that the organization chosen to represent a craft is to represent all its members, the majority as well as the minority, and it is to act for and not against those whom it represents. It is a principle of general application that the exercise of a granted power to act in behalf of others involves the assumption toward them of a duty to exercise the power in their interest and behalf, and that such a grant of power will not be deemed to dispense with all duty toward those for whom it is exercised unless so expressed.

We think that the Railway Labor Act imposes upon the statutory representative of a craft at least as exacting a duty to protect equally the interests of the members of the craft as the Constitution imposes upon a legislature to give equal protection to the interests of those for whom it legislates. Congress has seen fit to clothe the bargaining representative with powers comparable to those possessed by a legislative body both to create and restrict the rights of those whom it represents, but it also imposed on the representative a corresponding duty. We hold that the language of the Act to which we have referred, read in the light of the purposes of the Act, expresses the aim of Congress to impose on the bargaining representative of a craft or class of employees the duty to exercise fairly the power conferred upon it in behalf of all those for whom it acts, without hostile discrimination against them.

This does not mean that the statutory representative of a craft is barred from making contracts which may have unfavorable effects on some of the members of the craft represented. Variations in terms of the contract based on differences relevant to the authorized purposes of the contract in conditions to which they are to be applied, such as differences in seniority, the type of work performed, the competence and skill with which it is performed, are within the scope of the bargaining representation of a craft, all of whose members are not identical in their interest or merit. Without attempting to mark the allowable limits of differences in the terms of contracts based on differences of conditions to which they apply, it is enough for present purposes to say that the statutory power to represent a craft and to make contracts as to wages, hours and working conditions does not include the authority to make distinction among members of the craft discriminations based on race alone are obviously irrelevant and invidious. Congress plainly did not undertake to authorize the bargaining representative to make such discriminations. . . .

The representative which thus discriminates may be enjoined from so doing, and its members may be enjoined from taking the benefit of such discriminatory action. No more is the Railroad bound by or entitled to take the benefit of a contract which the bargaining representative is prohibited by the statute from making. In both cases the right asserted, which is derived from the duty imposed by the statute on the bargaining representative, is a federal right implied from the statute and the policy which it has adopted. . . .

So long as a labor union assumes to act as the statutory representative of a craft, it cannot rightly refuse to perform the duty, which is inseparable from the power of representation conferred upon it, to represent the entire membership of the craft. While the statute does not deny to such a bargaining labor organization the right to determine eligibility to its membership, it does require the union, in collective bargaining and in making contracts with the carrier, to represent nonunion or minority union members of the craft without hostile discrimination, fairly, impartially, and in good faith. Wherever necessary to that end, the union is required to consider requests of non-union members of the craft and expressions of their views with respect to collective bargaining with the employer and to give to them notice of and opportunity for hearing upon its proposed action. . . .

We conclude that the duty which the statute imposes on a union representative of a craft to represent the interests of all its members stands on no different footing and that the statute contemplates resort to the usual judicial remedies of injunction and award of damages when appropriate for breach of that duty.

The judgment is accordingly reversed and remanded. . . .
So ordered.

The *Steele* case held that the duty of fair representation arose out of the union's exclusive bargaining agent status under Section 2, Ninth, of the Railway Labor Act.

In *Syres* v. *Oil Workers Local 23* (350 U.S. 892, 1955), the Supreme Court held that the duty of fair representation also extended to unions granted bargaining agent status under Section 9(a) of the NLRA.

Unions, in representing employees, must make decisions that affect different employees in different ways. For example, in negotiating a contract, the union must decide whether to seek increased wages or improved benefits—trade-offs must be made in fashioning contract proposals. Older employees may be more concerned with pensions, whereas younger employees may be more concerned with increased wages. Should the courts monitor the union's negotiation proposals to ensure that all workers will be fairly represented? In *Ford Motor Co.* v. *Huffman* (345 U.S. 330, 1953), the Supreme Court held that unions should be given broad discretion by the courts in negotiation practices; the courts should ensure only that the union operates "in good faith and honesty of purpose in the exercise of its discretion."

The courts also give unions some leeway in exercising their contractual duties. In *Steelworkers* v. *Rawson* (496 U.S. 362, 1990), the Supreme Court held that the allegations that the union had been negligent in its duty under the collective agreement to conduct safety inspections did not amount to a breach of the duty of fair representation because mere negligence, even in the performance of a contractual duty, does not amount to a breach of the duty of fair representation.

Although the courts allow unions broad latitude in negotiations, they may be more concerned with union decisions involving individual employee grievances. In *Vaca* v. *Sipes* (368 U.S. 171, 1967) the Supreme Court held that an individual does not have an absolute right to have a grievance taken to arbitration, but the union must make decisions about the merits of a grievance in good faith and in a nonarbitrary manner.

In *Vaca*, the union refused to arbitrate the employee's grievance. If the union decides to arbitrate the grievance but mishandles the employee's claim, does it violate the duty of fair representation? What if the union gives the grievance only perfunctory handling? The following case addresses these questions.

HINES v. ANCHOR MOTOR FREIGHT, INC.

424 U.S. 554 (Supreme Court of the United States, 1976)

WHITE, J.

The issue here is whether a suit against an employer by employees asserting breach of a collective-bargaining contract was properly dismissed where the accompanying complaint against the Union for breach of duty of fair representation has withstood the Union's motion for summary judgment and remains to be tried.

Petitioners, who were formerly employed as truck drivers by respondent Anchor Motor Freight, Inc., were discharged

on June 5, 1967. The applicable collective-bargaining contract forbade discharges without just cause. The company charged dishonesty. . . . Anchor's assertion was that petitioners had sought reimbursement for motel expenses in excess of the actual charges sustained by them. At a meeting between the company and the union, Local 377, International Brotherhood of Teamsters, which was also attended by petitioners, Anchor presented motel receipts previously submitted by petitioners which were in excess of the charges shown on the motel's registration cards; a notarized statement of the motel clerk asserting the accuracy of the registration cards; and an affidavit of the motel owner affirming that the registration cards were accurate and that inflated receipts had been furnished petitioners. The Union claimed petitioners were innocent and opposed the discharges. It was then agreed that the matter would be presented to the joint arbitration committee for the area, to which the collective-bargaining contract permitted either party to submit an unresolved grievance. Pending this hearing, petitioners were reinstated. Their suggestion that the motel be investigated was answered by the Union representatives' assurances that "there was nothing to worry about" and that they need not hire their own attorney.

A hearing before the joint area committee was held on July 26, 1967. Anchor presented its case. Both the Union and petitioners were afforded an opportunity to present their case and to be heard. Petitioners denied their dishonesty, but neither they nor the Union presented any other evidence contradicting the documents presented by the company. The committee sustained the discharges. Petitioners then retained an attorney and sought rehearing based on a statement by the motel owner that he had no personal knowledge of the events, but that the discrepancy between the receipts and the registration cards could have been attributable to the motel clerk's recording on the cards less than was actually paid and retaining for himself the difference between the amount receipted and the amount recorded. The committee, after hearing, unanimously denied rehearing "because there was no new evidence presented which would justify reopening this case."

There were later indications that the motel clerk was in fact the culprit; and the present suit was filed in June 1969, against Anchor, the Union and its International. The complaint alleged that the charges of dishonesty made against petitioners by Anchor were false, that there was no just cause for discharge and that the discharges had been in breach of contract. It was also asserted that the falsity of the charges could have been discovered with a minimum of investigation, that the Union had made no effort to ascertain the truth of the charges and that the Union had violated its duty of fair representation by arbitrarily and in bad faith depriving petitioners of their employment and permitting their discharge without sufficient proof.

The Union denied the charges and relied on the decision of the joint area committee. Anchor asserted that petitioners had been properly discharged for just cause. It also defended on the ground that petitioners, diligently and in good faith represented by the Union, had unsuccessfully resorted to the grievance and arbitration machinery provided by the contract and that the adverse decision of the joint arbitration committee was binding upon the Union and petitioners under the contractual provision. . . . Discovery followed, including a deposition of the motel clerk revealing that he has falsified the records and that it was he who had pocketed the difference between the sums shown on the receipts and the registration cards. Motions for summary judgment filed by Anchor and the Unions were granted by the District Court on the ground that the decision of the arbitration committee was final and binding on the employees and "for failure to show facts comprising bad faith, arbitrariness or perfunctoriness on the part of the Unions." Although indicating that the acts of the Union "may not meet professional standards of competency . . . ," the District Court concluded that the facts demonstrated at most bad judgment on the part of the Union, which was insufficient to prove a breach of duty or make out a prima facie case against it. . . .

After reviewing the allegations and the record before it, the Court of Appeals concluded that there were sufficient facts from which bad faith or arbitrary conduct on the part of the local Union could be inferred by the trier of fact and that petitioners should have been afforded an opportunity to prove their charges. To this extent the judgment of the District Court was reversed. The Court of Appeals affirmed the judgment in favor of Anchor and the International. . . .

It is this judgment of the Court of Appeals with respect to Anchor that is now before us. . . .

It is urged that the reversal of the Court of Appeals will undermine not only the finality rule but the entire collective-bargaining process. Employers, it is said, will be far less willing to give up their untrammeled right to discharge without cause and to agree to private settlement procedures. But the burden on employees will remain a substantial one, far too heavy in the opinion of some. To prevail against either the company or the Union, petitioners must show not only that their discharge was contrary to the contract but must also carry the burden of demonstrating breach of duty by the Union. As the District Court indicated, this involves more than demonstrating mere errors in judgment.

Petitioners are not entitled to relitigate their discharge merely because they offer newly discovered evidence that the charges against them were false and that in fact they were fired without cause. The grievance processes cannot be expected to be error-free. The finality provision has sufficient force to surmount occasional instances of mistake. But it is quite another matter to suggest that erroneous arbitration decisions must stand even though the employee's representation by the union has been dishonest, in bad faith or discriminatory; for in that event error and injustice of the grossest sort would multiply. The contractual system would then cease to qualify as an adequate mechanism to secure individual redress for damaging failure of the employer to abide by the contract. Congress has put its blessing on private dispute settlement arrangements provided in collective agreements, but it was anticipated, we are sure, that the contractual machinery would operate within some minimum levels of integrity. In our view, enforcement of the finality provision where the arbitrator has erred is conditioned upon the Union's having satisfied its statutory duty fairly to represent the employee in connection with the arbitration proceedings. . . .

Petitioners, if they prove an erroneous discharge and the Union's breach of duty tainting the decision of the joint committee, are entitled to an appropriate remedy against the employer as well as the Union. It was error to affirm the District Court's final dismissal of petitioners' action against Anchor. To this extent the judgment of the Court of Appeals is reversed. **So ordered.**

Liability for Breach of the Duty of Fair Representation.   Most cases involving the duty of fair representation arise from action by the employer; after the employee has been disciplined or discharged, the union's alleged breach of the duty compounds the problem.

How should the damages awarded in such a case be divided between the employer and the union—which party should bear primary liability? In *Vaca* v. *Sipes* (368 U.S. 171, 1967), the Supreme Court also held that an employer cannot escape liability for breach of the collective agreement just because the union has breached its duty of fair representation. Where the employee has established a breach of the collective agreement by the employer and a breach of the duty of fair representation by the union, the employer and the union must share liability. In *Bowen* v. *U.S. Postal Service* (459 U.S. 212, 1983), the Supreme Court held that the employer is liable for back pay for the discharge of an employee in breach of the collective agreement, whereas the union breaching the duty of fair representation by refusing to grieve the discharge is responsible for any increase in damages suffered by the employee as a result of the breach of the duty of fair representation. In *Chauffeurs, Teamsters and Helpers, Local No. 391* v. *Terry* (494 U.S. 538, 1990), the Supreme Court held that in order to recover damages against both the employer and the union, the employee must prove both that the employer's actions violated the collective agreement and that the union's handling of the grievance breached the duty of fair representation.

The NLRB has held that when an employee has established that the union improperly refused to process a grievance or handled it in a perfunctory manner, the board is prepared to resolve doubts about the merits of the grievance in favor of the employee (*Rubber Workers Local 250 (Mack-Wayne Enclosures*), 279 N.L.R.B. No. 165, 122 L.R.R.M. 1147, 1986).

Enforcing the Duty of Fair Representation.   In *Miranda Fuel Co.* (140 N.L.R.B. 81, 1962), the NLRB held that a breach of the duty of fair representation by a union was a violation of Section 8(b)(1)(A) of the NLRA. The board reasoned that "Section 7 . . . gives employees the right to be free from unfair or irrelevant or invidious treatment by their exclusive bargaining agent in matters affecting their employment." Although the Court of Appeals for the Second Circuit refused to enforce the board's order in *Miranda* (326 F.2d 172, 1963), other courts of appeals have affirmed NLRB findings of Section 8(b)(1)(A) violations in subsequent duty of fair representation cases. The NLRB continues to hold that breach of the duty of fair representation by a union is an unfair labor practice.

The NLRB does not have exclusive jurisdiction over claims of the breach of the duty of fair representation; federal courts also may exercise jurisdiction over such claims, according to the Supreme Court in *Breininger v. Sheet Metal Workers Local 6* (493 U.S. 67, 1989). The cases developing the duty of fair representation that we have seen so far have involved lawsuits filed against both the union and the employer. Such suits are filed under Section 301 of the NLRA and may be filed either in state or federal courts and are subject to federal labor law, not state contract law. In *Steelworkers v. Rawson* (496 U.S. 362, 1990), the Supreme Court held that a wrongful death suit brought under state law against a union by the heirs of miners killed in an underground fire was preempted by Section 301. According to the Supreme Court in *Chauffeurs, Teamsters and Helpers, Local No. 391 v. Terry* (494 U.S. 538, 1990), an employee who seeks back pay as a remedy for a union's violation of the duty of fair representation is entitled to a jury trial.

In *DelCostello v. Teamsters* (462 U.S. 151, 1983), the Supreme Court held that the time limit for bringing a suit under Section 301 alleging a breach of the duty of fair representation is six months; in cases where the employee is required to exhaust internal procedures, the six-month time limit does not begin to run until those procedures have been exhausted (*Frandsen v. BRAC,* 782 F.2d 674, 7th Cir. 1986).

Exhausting Internal Remedies.

We have seen that the duty of fair representation may be enforced by either a Section 301 suit or a Section 8(b)(1)(A) unfair labor practice proceeding. Before either action can be initiated, however, the employee alleging breach of the duty of fair representation must attempt to exhaust internal remedies that may be available.

Because most complaints of breaches of the duty of fair representation result from employer actions, such as discharge or discipline, which are then compounded by the union's breach of its duty, the affected employee may have the right to file a grievance under the collective bargaining agreement to challenge the employer's actions. When contractual remedies—the grievance procedure and arbitration—are available to the employee, he or she must first attempt to use those procedures. That means that the employee must file a grievance and attempt to have it processed through to arbitration before filing a Section 301 suit or a Section 8(b)(1)(A) complaint. The requirement of exhausting contractual remedies flows from the policy of fostering voluntary settlement of disputes. This policy is behind the court's deferral to arbitration (recall the *Steelworkers Trilogy* from Chapter 9) and the NLRB deferral to arbitration (recall the *United Technologies* and the *Olin Corp.* cases from Chapter 9).

The requirement of exhausting contractual remedies is not absolute. In *Glover v. St. Louis–San Francisco Railway* (393 U.S. 324, 1969), the Supreme Court held that employees need not exhaust contract remedies when the union and employer are cooperating in the violation of employee rights. In such cases, attempts to get the union to file a grievance or to process it through to arbitration would be an exercise in futility.

Aside from contractual remedies, an employee may have available internal union procedures to deal with complaints against the union. Some union constitutions provide for review of complaints of alleged mistreatment of union members by union leaders. For example, if local union officials refuse to submit the employee's grievance to arbitration, the employee may appeal that decision to the membership of the local. An appeal to the international union leadership may also be available. Should an employee be required to exhaust such internal union remedies before filing a suit or unfair practice complaint alleging breach of the duty of fair representation?

In *Clayton* v. *United Auto Workers* (451 U.S. 679, 1981), the Supreme Court held that an employee is not required to exhaust internal union remedies when the internal union appeals procedure cannot result in reactivation of the employee's grievance or award the complete relief sought by the employee. In such cases, the employee may file a Section 301 suit or a Section 8(b)(1)(A) complaint without exhausting the internal union remedies. If such remedies could provide the relief sought by the employee, they must be pursued before filing under Section 301 or Section 8(b)(1)(A).

If the alleged breach of the duty of fair representation involves claims of discrimination based on race, sex, religion, or national origin, the affected employees may also have legal remedies under Title VII of the Civil Rights Act of 1964. Just as in *Alexander* v. *Gardner-Denver* (see Chapter 15), the remedies under Title VII are separate from any remedies under Section 301 or Section 8(b)(1)(A). The affected employees may then file a complaint with the Equal Employment Opportunity Commission under Title VII as well as filing under Section 301 and/or Section 8(b)(1)(A).

Remedies available under an action for breach of the duty of fair representation depend upon whether the employee pursues the claim under Section 301 or Section 8(b)(1)(A). Under Section 301, an action against both the employer and the union can be brought. An employee may recover monetary damages (but not punitive damages) and legal fees and may get an injunction (such as ordering the union to arbitrate the grievance or ordering the employer to reinstate the employee). Under Section 8(b)(1)(A), the NLRB can order the union to (1) pay compensation for lost wages, benefits, and legal fees, (2) arbitrate the grievance, and (3) "cease and desist" from further violations. If the employee's complaint involves action by both the employer and the union, Section 301 would be preferable; if only the union is involved, either Section 301 or Section 8(b)(1)(A) is appropriate.

Rights of Union Members

In addition to being protected by the duty of fair representation, union members have certain rights, against the union, guaranteed by statute. The union members' "bill of rights" under the Labor Management Reporting and Disclosure Act and Section 8(b)(1) establishes those rights.

Union Discipline of Members

Section 8(b)(1)(A) prohibits union actions that restrain, coerce, or interfere with employee rights under Section 7. Section 8(b)(1)(A), however, does provide that "This paragraph shall not impair the right of a labor organization to prescribe its own rules with respect to the acquisition or retention of membership therein."

In *NLRB* v. *Allis-Chalmers Mfg. Co.* (388 U.S. 175, 1967), the Supreme Court held that a union could impose fines against members who crossed a picket line and worked during an authorized strike. In *NLRB* v. *Boeing Co.* (412 U.S. 67, 1973), the Supreme Court held that a union may file suit in a state court to enforce fines imposed against members. However, if union members legally resign from the union before crossing the picket line and return to work during a strike, the union cannot impose fines against them, as held by the Supreme Court in *NLRB* v. *Textile Workers Granite State Joint Board* (409 U.S. 213, 1972).

In light of the Supreme Court decisions on the union's ability to impose fines on its members, a number of unions adopted rules limiting the right of members to resign from the union during a strike. The following case deals with the question of whether such restrictions violate Section 8(b)(1)(A).

PATTERN MAKERS' LEAGUE OF NORTH AMERICA v. NLRB

473 U.S. 95 (Supreme Court of the United States, 1985)

POWELL, J.

The Pattern Makers' League of North America, AFL-CIO (the League), a labor union, provides in its constitution that resignations are not permitted during a strike or when a strike is imminent. The League fined 10 of its members who, in violation of this provision, resigned during a strike and returned to work. The National Labor Relations Board held that these fines were imposed in violation of Section 8(b)(1)(A) of the National Labor Relations Act. We granted a petition for a writ of certiorari in order to decide whether Section 8(b)(1)(A) reasonably may be construed by the Board as prohibiting a union from fining members who have tendered resignations invalid under the union constitution. . . .

On May 5, 1977, when a collective-bargaining agreement expired, two locals began an economic strike against several manufacturing companies in Rockford, Illinois and Beloit, Wisconsin. Forty-three of the two locals' members participated. In early September 1977, after the locals formally rejected a contract offer, a striking union member submitted a letter of resignation to the Beloit association. He returned to work the following day. During the next three months, 10 more union members resigned from the Rockford and Beloit locals and returned to work. On December 19, 1977, the strike ended when the parties signed a new collective-bargaining agreement. The locals notified 10 employees who had resigned that their resignations had been rejected as violative of League Law 13. The locals further informed the employees that, as union members, they were subject to sanctions for returning to work. Each was fined approximately the equivalent of his earnings during the strike.

The Rockford-Beloit Pattern Jobbers' Association (the Association) had represented the employers throughout the collective-bargaining process. It filed charges with the Board against the League and its two locals, the petitioners. Relying on Section 8(b)(1)(A), the Association claimed that levying fines against employees who had resigned was an unfair labor practice. Following a hearing, an Administrative Law Judge found that the petitioners had violated Section 8(b)(1)(A) by fining employees for returning to work after tendering resignations. The Board agreed that Section 8(b)(1)(A) prohibited the union from imposing sanctions on the 10 employees. . . .

Language and reasoning from other opinions of this Court confirm that the Board's construction of Section 8(b)(1)(A) is reasonable. . . .

The decision in *NLRB* v. *Textile Workers* also supports the Board's view that Section 8(b)(1)(A) prohibits unions from punishing members not free to resign. There, 31 employees resigned their union membership and resumed working during a strike. We held that fining these former members "restrained or coerced" them, within the meaning of Section 8(b)(1)(A). In reaching this conclusion, we said that "the vitality of Section 7 requires that the member be free to refrain in November from the actions he endorsed in May." Restrictions on the right to resign curtail the freedom that the *Textile Workers* Court deemed so important.

Section 8(b)(1)(A) allows unions to enforce only those rules that "impai[r] no policy Congress has imbedded in the labor laws. . . ." The Board has found union restrictions on the right to resign to be inconsistent with the policy of voluntary unionism implicit in Section 8(a)(3). We believe that the inconsistency between union restrictions on the right to resign and the policy of voluntary unionism supports the Board's conclusion that League Law 13 is invalid.

Closed shop agreements, legalized by the Wagner Act in 1935, became quite common in the early 1940s. Under these agreements, employers could hire and retain in their employ only union members in good standing. Full union membership was thus compulsory in a closed shop; in order to keep their jobs, employees were required to attend union meetings, support union leaders, and otherwise adhere to union rules. Because of mounting objections to the closed shop, in 1947—after hearings and full consideration—Congress enacted the Taft-Hartley Act. Section 8(a)(3) of that Act effectively eliminated compulsory union membership by outlawing the closed shop. The Union security agreements permitted by Section 8(a)(3) require employees to pay dues, but an employee cannot be discharged for failing to abide by union rules or policies with which he disagrees.

Full union membership thus no longer can be a requirement of employment. If a new employee refuses formally to join a union and subject himself to its discipline, he cannot be fired. Moreover, no employee can be discharged if he initially joins a union, and subsequently resigns. We think it noteworthy that Section 8(a)(3) protects the employment

rights of the dissatisfied member, as well as those of the worker who never assumed full union membership. By allowing employees to resign from a union at any time, Section 8(a)(3) protects the employee whose views come to diverge from those of his union.

League Law 13 curtails this freedom to resign from full union membership. . . . Congress in 1947 sought to eliminate completely any requirement that the employee maintain full union membership. Therefore, the Board was justified in concluding that by restricting the right of employees to resign, League Law 13 impairs the policy of voluntary unionism.

Petitioners first argue that the proviso to Section 8(b)(1)(A) expressly allows unions to place restrictions on the right to resign. The proviso states that nothing in Section 8(b)(1)(A) shall "impair the right of a labor organization to prescribe its own rules with respect to the acquisition or retention of membership therein." Petitioners contend that because League Law 13 places restrictions on the right to withdraw from the union, it is a "rul[e] with respect to the . . . retention of membership," within the meaning of the proviso.

Neither the Board nor this Court has ever interpreted the proviso as allowing unions to make rules restricting the right to resign. Rather, the Court has assumed that "rules with respect to the . . . retention of membership" are those that provide for the expulsion of employees from the union. The legislative history of the Taft-Hartley Act is consistent with this interpretation. . . . Furthermore, the legislative history of the Labor-Management Reporting and Disclosure Act of 1959 confirms that the proviso was intended to protect union rules involving admission and expulsion. Accordingly, we find no basis for refusing to defer to the Board's conclusion that League Law 13 is not a "rule with respect to the retention of membership," within the meaning of the proviso. . . .

The Board has the primary responsibility for applying "the general provisions of the Act to the complexities of industrial life." Where the Board's construction of the Act is reasonable, it should not be rejected "merely because the courts might prefer another view of the statute." In this case, two factors suggest that we should be particularly reluctant to hold that the Board's interpretation of the Act is impermissible. First, in related cases this Court invariably has yielded to Board decisions on whether fines imposed by a union "restrain or coerce" employees. Second, the Board consistently has construed Section 8(b)(1)(A) as prohibiting the imposition of fines on employees who have tendered resignations invalid under a union constitution.

Therefore, we conclude that the Board's decision here is entitled to our deference.

The Board found that by fining employees who had tendered resignations, the petitioners violated Section 8(b)(1)(A) of the Act, even though League Law 13 purported to render the resignations ineffective. We defer to the Board's interpretation of the Act and so affirm the judgment of the Court of Appeals enforcing the Board's order. **It is so ordered.**

Union Members' Bill of Rights

The Labor Management Reporting and Disclosure Act (LMRDA) seeks to ensure that union members are guaranteed certain rights when subjected to internal union proceedings. Section 101 of the LMRDA is commonly called the union members' "bill of rights."

Union Discipline. Procedural safeguards against improper disciplinary action are provided by Section 101(a)(5), which states that

> No member of any labor organization may be fined, suspended, expelled, or otherwise disciplined except for nonpayment of dues by such organization or by any officer thereof unless such member has been (A) served with written specific charges; (B) given a reasonable time to prepare his defense; (C) afforded a full and fair hearing.

Section 102 of the LMRDA allows any person whose rights under the act have been violated to bring a civil suit in the federal courts for such relief as may be appropriate. In *Wooddell v. International Brotherhood of Electrical Workers, Local 71* (__ U.S. __ , 112 S.Ct. 494, 1991), the Supreme Court held that a union member suing under the LMRDA, alleging discrimination against him by the union in job referrals through the union hiring hall, was entitled to a jury trial.

When a union member alleges that his or her rights have been violated by union disciplinary action, what standards should the court apply to determine if the union procedure was reasonable? That question was addressed by the following case.

BOILERMAKERS v. HARDEMAN

401 U.S. 233 (Supreme Court of the United States, 1971)

BRENNAN, J.

Respondent was expelled from membership in petitioner union and brought this action under Section 102 [of the LMRDA] in the District Court for the Southern District of Alabama. He alleged that in expelling him the petitioner violated Section 101(a)(5) of the Act....

A jury awarded respondent damages of $152,150. The Court of Appeals for the Fifth Circuit affirmed. We granted certiorari limited to the questions whether the subject matter of the suit was preempted because exclusively within the competence of the National Labor Relations Board and, if not preempted, whether the courts below had applied the proper standard of review to the union proceedings.... We reverse.

The case arises out of events in the early part of October 1960. Respondent, George Hardeman, is a boilermaker. He was then a member of petitioner's Local Lodge 112. On October 3, he went to the union hiring hall to see Herman Wise, business manager of the Local Lodge and the official responsible for referring workmen for jobs. Hardeman had talked to a friend of his, an employer who had promised to ask for him by name for a job in the vicinity. He sought assurance from Wise that he would be referred for the job. When Wise refused to make a definite commitment, Hardeman threatened violence if no work was forthcoming in the next few days.

On October 4, Hardeman returned to the hiring hall and waited for a referral. None was forthcoming. The next day, in his words, he "went to the hall . . . and waited from the time the hall opened until we had the trouble. I tried to make up my mind what to do, whether to sue the local or Wise or beat hell of out of Wise, and then I made up my mind." When Wise came out of his office to go to a local job-site, as required by his duties as business manager, Hardeman handed him a copy of a telegram asking for Hardeman by name. As Wise was reading the telegram, Hardeman began punching him in the face.

Hardeman was tried for this conduct on charges of creating dissension and working against the interest and harmony of the Local Lodge, and of threatening and using force to restrain an officer of the Local Lodge from properly discharging the duties of his office. The trial committee found him "guilty as charged," and the Local Lodge sustained the finding and voted his expulsion for an indefinite period. Internal union review of this action, instituted by Hardeman, modified neither the verdict nor the penalty. Five years later, Hardeman brought this suit alleging that petitioner violated Section 101(a)(5) by denying him a full and fair hearing in the union disciplinary proceedings.

We consider first the union's claim that the subject matter of this lawsuit is, in the first instance, with the exclusive competence of the National Labor Relations Board. The union argues that the gravamen of Hardeman's complaint—which did not seek reinstatement, but only damages for wrongful expulsion, consisting of loss of income, loss of pension and insurance rights, mental anguish and punitive damages—is discrimination against him in job referrals; that any such conduct on the part of the union is at the very least arguably an unfair labor practice under Sections 8(b)(1)(A) and 8(b)(2) of the National Labor Relations Act . . . ; and that in such circumstances, "the federal courts must defer to the exclusive competence of the National Labor Relations Board if the danger of . . . interference with national policy is to be averted."

We think the union's argument is misdirected. Hardeman's complaint alleged that his expulsion was unlawful under Section 101(a)(5), and sought compensation for the consequences of the claimed wrongful expulsion. The critical issue presented by Hardeman's complaint was whether the union disciplinary proceedings had denied him a full and fair hearing within the meaning of Section 101(a)(5)(c). Unless he could establish this claim, Hardeman would be out of court. We hold that this claim was not within the exclusive competence of the National Labor Relations Board. . . . Congress explicitly referred claims under Section 101(a)(5) not to the NLRB, but to the federal district courts. This is made explicit in the opening sentence of Section 102. . . .

Two charges were brought against Hardeman in the union disciplinary proceedings. He was charged with violation of Article 13, Section 1, of the Subordinate Lodge Constitution, which forbids attempting to create dissension or working against the interest and harmony of the union, and carries a penalty of expulsion. He was also charged with violations of Article 12, Section 1, of the Subordinate Lodge By-Laws, which forbids the threat or use of force against any officer of the union in order to prevent him from properly discharging the duties of his office; violation may be punished "as warranted by the offense." Hardeman's conviction on both charges was upheld in internal union procedures for review.

The trial judge instructed the jury that "whether or not he [respondent] was rightfully or wrongfully discharged or expelled is a pure question of law for me to determine." He assumed, but did not decide, that the transcript of the union disciplinary hearing contained evidence adequate to support conviction of violating Article 12. He held, however, that there was no evidence at all in the transcript of the union disciplinary proceedings to support the charge of violating Article 13. This holding appears to have been based on the Fifth Circuit's decision in *Boilermakers* v. *Braswell.* There the Court of Appeals for the Fifth Circuit had reasoned that "penal provisions in union constitutions must be strictly construed," and that as so construed Article 13 was directed only to "threats to the union as an organization and to the effective carrying out of the union's aims," not to merely personal altercations. Since the union tribunals had returned only a general verdict, and since one of the charges was thought to be supported by no evidence whatsoever, the trial judge held that Hardeman had been deprived of the full and fair hearing guaranteed by Section 101(a)(5). The Court of Appeals affirmed, simply citing *Braswell.* . . .

We find nothing in either the language or the legislative history of Section 101(a)(5) that could justify such a substitution of judicial for union authority to interpret the union's regulations in order to determine the scope of offenses warranting discipline of union members. . . .

We think that this is sufficient to indicate that Section

101(a)(5) was not intended to authorize courts to determine the scope of offenses for which a union may discipline its members. And if a union may discipline its members for offenses not proscribed by written rules at all, it is surely a futile exercise for a court to construe the written rules in order to determine whether particular conduct falls within or without their scope.

Of course, Section 101(a)(5)(A) requires that a member subject to discipline be "served with written specific charges." These charges must be, in Senator McClellan's words, "specific enough to inform the accused member of the offense that he has allegedly committed." Where, as here, the union's charges make reference to specific written provisions, Section 101(a)(5)(A) obviously empowers the federal courts to examine those provisions and determine whether the union member had been misled or otherwise prejudiced in the presentation of his defense. But it gives courts no warrant to scrutinize the union regulations in order to determine whether particular conduct may be punished at all.

Respondent does not suggest, and we cannot discern, any possibility of prejudice in the present case. Although the notice of charges with which he was served does not appear as such in the record, the transcript of the union hearing indicates that the notice did not confine itself to a mere statement or citation of the written regulations that Hardeman was said to have violated: the notice appears to have contained a detailed statement of the facts relating to the fight which formed the basis for the disciplinary action. Section 101(a)(5) requires no more.

There remains only the question whether the evidence in the union disciplinary proceeding was sufficient to support the finding of guilt. Section 101(a)(5)(C) of the LMRDA guarantees union members a "full and fair" disciplinary hearing, and the parties and the lower federal courts are in full agreement that this guarantee requires the charging party to provide some evidence at the disciplinary hearing to support the charges made. This is the proper standard of judicial review. We have repeatedly held that conviction on charges unsupported by any evidence is a denial of due process . . . and we feel that Section 101(a)(5)(C) may fairly be said to import a similar requirement into union disciplinary proceedings. . . . [A]ny lesser standard would make useless Section 101(a)(5)(A)'s requirement of written, specific charges. A stricter standard, on the other hand, would be inconsistent with the apparent congressional intent to allow unions to govern their own affairs, and would require courts to judge the credibility of witnesses on the basis of what would be at best, a cold record.

Applying this standard to the present case, we think there is no question that the charges were adequately supported. Respondent was charged with having attacked Wise without warning, and with continuing to beat him for some time. Wise so testified at the disciplinary hearing, and his testimony was fully corroborated by one other witness to the altercation. Even Hardeman, although he claimed he was thereafter held and beaten, admitted having struck the first blow. On such a record there is no question but that the charges were supported by "some evidence." **Reversed.**

In order to have a valid claim under Section 101(a)(5) and Section 102, the union member must have been subjected to discipline by the union. In *Breininger* v. *Sheet Metal Workers Local 6* (493 U.S. 67, 1989), the Supreme Court held that Breininger's suit over the union's failure to refer him under a hiring hall agreement because he supported a political rival of the union business manager did not state a claim under the LMRDA. The Court held that the failure to refer him was not "discipline" within the meaning of the act.

Free Speech and Association. Whereas Section 101(a)(5) guarantees union members' procedural rights in union disciplinary proceedings, the other provisions of Section 101(a) provide for other basic rights in participating in union activities. These rights take precedence over any provisions of union constitutions or bylaws that are inconsistent with Section 101 rights. Section 101(b) states that any such inconsistent provisions shall have no effect.

Section 101(a)(2) provides for the rights of freedom of speech and assembly for union members. Every union member has the right to meet and assemble with other members and to express any views or opinions, subject to the union's reasonable rules for the conduct of meetings. As long as any item of business is properly before a union meeting, a union member may express his or her views on that item of business. The latitude given to union members to express their opinions at union meetings is very broad. Any restrictions on such expression must be reasonable and required for the orderly conducting of such meetings. Violations of these rights give rise to civil liability. In *Hall v. Cole* (412 U.S. 1, 1973), a union member was expelled from the union after introducing a series of resolutions alleging undemocratic actions and questionable policies by union officials. The union claimed such resolutions violated a rule against "deliberate and malicious vilification with regard to the execution or duties of any office." The member filed suit under Section 102, alleging violations of his rights guaranteed by Section 101(a)(2). The Supreme Court upheld the trial decision ordering that the member be reinstated in the union and awarding him $5,500 in legal fees.

In *Sheet Metal Workers International Association v. Lynn* (488 U.S. 347, 1989), an elected business agent of the union filed suit under Section 102 over his removal from office because of statements he made at a union meeting opposing a dues increase sought by the union trustee. The Supreme Court held that his removal from office constituted a violation of the free speech provisions of Section 101(a)(2).

In *United Steelworkers of America v. Sadlowski* (457 U.S. 102, 1982), the Supreme Court held that a union rule prohibiting contributions from nonmembers in campaigns for union offices did not violate a union member's right of free speech and assembly under Section 101(a)(2), even though it had the effect of making a challenge to incumbent union officers much more difficult.

The courts have recognized some other limits on union members' rights of free speech and assembly. A union member cannot preach "dual unionism"—that is, advocate membership in another union during his union's meeting. As well, the remarks of a union member are subject to libel and slander laws. The right of free assembly does not protect a group of members who engage in a wildcat strike that violates the union's no-strike agreement with the employer.

Right to Participate in Union Affairs.   The right of union members to participate in all membership business, such as meetings, discussions, referendums, and elections, is guaranteed by Section 101(a)(1) of the LMRDA. This right to participate is subject to the reasonable rules and regulations of the union's constitution and bylaws. Any provisions that are inconsistent with these rights are of no effect, by reason of Section 101(b).

The provisions of the LMRDA allow a union to require that members exhaust internal union remedies before pursuing external action for violation of the rights granted by the LMRDA. Section 101(a)(4) does provide, however, that the internal union proceedings cannot last longer than four months. If the proceedings take longer than four months, the member is not required to pursue them before instituting external proceedings.

Election Procedures. Title IV of the LMRDA requires that union elections be conducted according to certain democratic procedures. Section 401 sets the following requirements:

1. National and international labor organizations must elect their officers at least every five years.

2. Every local union must hold elections at least every three years.

3. Elections shall be by secret ballot or at a convention of delegates chosen by secret ballot.

4. There must be advance notice of the election, freedom of choice among candidates, and publication and one year's preservation of the election results.

5. Dues and assessments cannot be used to support anyone's candidacy.

6. Every candidate has the right to inspect lists of members' names and addresses.

7. Each candidate has the right to have observers at polling places and at the counting of the ballots.

In the recent case of *International Organization for Masters, Mates & Pilots* v. *Brown* (__ U.S. __ , 111 S.Ct. 880, 1991), the Supreme Court held that labor unions must cooperate with all reasonable requests from candidates for union office to distribute campaign literature despite union rules restricting such requests. In that case, the Court decided that a union refusal to provide a membership list to a candidate because of a union rule prohibiting preconvention mailings was in violation of the LMRDA.

The election provisions of the LMRDA also prohibit unduly restrictive eligibility requirements that enable incumbents to become entrenched in office. Such eligibility requirements are the subject of the following case.

STEELWORKERS LOCAL 3489 v. USERY

429 U.S. 305 (Supreme Court of the United States, 1977)

BRENNAN, J.

The Secretary of Labor brought this action in the District Court for the Southern District of Indiana under Section 402(b) of the Labor-Management Reporting and Disclosure Act of 1959 (LMRDA) . . . to invalidate the 1970 election of officers of Local 3489, United Steelworkers of America. The Secretary alleged that a provision of the Steelworkers' International Constitution, binding the local, that limits eligibility for local union office to members who have attended at least one-half of the regular meetings of the local for three years previous to the election (unless prevented by union activities or working hours), violated Section 401(e) of the

LMRDA. . . . The District Court dismissed the complaint, finding no violation of the Act. The Court of Appeals for the Seventh Circuit reversed. . . . We affirm.

At the time of the challenged election, there were approximately 660 members in good standing of Local 3489. The Court of Appeals found that 96.5 percent of these members were ineligible to hold office, because of failure to satisfy the meeting-attendance rule. Of the 23 eligible members, nine were incumbent union officers. The Secretary argues, and the Court of Appeals held, that the failure of 96.5 percent of the local members to satisfy of the meeting-attendance requirement, and the rule's effect of requiring potential insurgent candidates to plan their candidacies as early as 18 months in advance of the election when the reasons for their opposition might not have yet emerged, established that the requirement has a substantial antidemocratic effect on local union elections. Petitioners argue that the rule is reasonable because it serves valid union purposes, imposes no very burdensome obligation on the members, and has not proved to be a device that entrenches a particular clique of incumbent officers in the local. . . .

The LMRDA does not render unions powerless to restrict candidacies for union office. The injunction in Section 401(e) that "every member in good standing shall be eligible to be a candidate and to hold office" is made expressly "subject to . . . reasonable qualifications uniformly imposed." But "Congress plainly did not intend that the authorization . . . of 'reasonable qualifications . . .' should be given a broad reach. The contrary is implicit in the legislative history of the section and in its wording. . . ." The basic objective of Title IV of the LMRDA is to guarantee "free and democratic" union elections modeled on "political elections in this country" where "the assumption is that voters will exercise common sense and judgment in casting their ballots." Thus, Title IV is not designed merely to protect the right of a union member to run for a particular office in a particular election. "Congress emphatically asserted a vital public interest in assuring free and democratic union elections that transcends the narrower interest of the complaining union member." The goal was to "protect the rights of rank-and-file members to particulate fully in the operation of their union through processes of democratic self-government, and, through the election process, to keep the union leadership responsive to the membership."

Whether a particular qualification is "reasonable" within the meaning of Section 401(e) must therefore "be measured in terms of its consistency with the Act's command to unions to conduct 'free and democratic' union elections." Congress was not concerned only with corrupt union leadership. Congress chose the goal of "free and democratic" union elections as a preventive measure to "curb the possibility of abuse by benevolent as well as malevolent entrenched leadership." *Hotel Employees* expressly held that that check was seriously impaired by candidacy qualifications which substantially deplete the ranks of those who might run in opposition to incumbents, and therefore held invalid the candidacy limitation there involved that restricted candidacies for certain positions to members who had previously held union office. "Plainly, given the objective of Title IV, a candidacy limitation which renders 93 percent of union members ineligible for office can hardly be a 'reasonable qualification.'"

Applying these principles to this case, we conclude that here too the antidemocratic effects of the meeting-attendance rule outweigh the interests urged in its support. Like the bylaw in *Hotel Employees,* an attendance requirement that results in the exclusion of 96.5 percent of the members from candidacy for union office hardly seems to be a "reasonable qualification" consistent with the goal of free and democratic elections. A requirement having that result obviously severely restricts the free choice of the membership in selecting its leaders.

Petitioners argue, however, that the bylaw held violative of Section 401(e) in *Hotel Employees* differs significantly from the attendance rule here. Under the *Hotel Employees* by-law no member could assure by his own efforts that he would be eligible for union office, since others controlled the criterion for eligibility. Here, on the other hand, a member can assure himself of eligibility for candidacy by attending some 18 brief meetings over a three-year period. In other words, the union would have its rule treated not as excluding a category of member from eligibility, but simply as mandating a procedure to be followed by any member who wishes to be a candidate.

Even examined from this perspective, however, the rule has a restrictive effect on union democracy. In the absence of a permanent "opposition party" within the union, opposition to the incumbent leadership is likely to emerge in response to particular issues at different times, and member interest in changing union leadership is therefore likely to be at its highest only shortly before elections. Thus it is probable that to require that a member decide upon a potential candidacy at least 18 months in advance of an election when no issues exist to prompt that decision may not foster but discourage candidacies and to that extent impair the general membership's freedom to oust incumbents in favor of new leadership.

Nor are we persuaded by petitioners' argument that the Secretary has failed to show an antidemocratic effect because he has not shown that the incumbent leaders of the union became "entrenched" in their offices as a consequence of the operation of the attendance rule. The reasons why leaderships become entrenched are difficult to isolate. The election of the same officers year after year may be a signal that antidemocratic election rules have prevented an effective challenge to the regime, or might well signal only that the members are satisfied with their stewardship; if elections are uncontested, opposition factions may have been denied access to the ballot, or competing interests may have compromised differences before the election to maintain a front of unit. Conversely, turnover in offices may result from an open political process, or from a competition limited to candidates who offer no real opposition to an entrenched establishment. But Congress did not saddle the courts with the duty to search out and remove improperly entrenched union leaderships. Rather, Congress chose to guarantee union democracy by regulating not the results of a union's electoral procedure, but the procedure itself. Congress decided that if the elections are "free and democratic," the members themselves are able to correct abuse of power by entrenched leadership. Procedures that unduly restrict free choice among candidates are forbidden without regard to their success or failure in maintaining corrupt leadership. . . .

As for assuring the election of knowledgeable and dedicated leaders, the election provisions of the LMRDA express a congressional determination that the best means to this end is to leave the choice of leaders to the membership in open democratic elections, unfettered by arbitrary exclusions. Pursuing this goal by excluding the bulk of the membership from eligibility for office, and thus limiting the pos-

sibility of dissident candidacies, runs directly counter to the basic premise of the statute. We therefore conclude that Congress, in guaranteeing every union member the opportunity to hold office, subject only to "reasonable qualifications," disabled unions from establishing eligibility qualifications as sharply restrictive of the openness of the union political process as is petitioners' attendance rule.

Finally, petitioners argue that the absence of a precise statement of what the Secretary of Labor and the courts will regard as reasonable prevents the drafting of a meeting-attendance rule with any assurance that it will be valid under Section 401(e). . . . On the facts of this case and in light of *Hotel Employees,* petitioners' contention that they had no way of knowing that a rule disqualifying over 90 percent of a local's members from office would be regarded as unreasonable in the absence of substantial justification is unpersuasive. **Affirmed.**

Other Restrictions on Unions

Duties of Union Officers.

The provisions of the LMRDA and the Taft-Hartley amendments to the NLRA imposed a number of duties on union officers in order to eliminate financial corruption and racketeering and to safeguard union funds. All officials handling union money must be bonded; and persons convicted of certain criminal offenses are barred from holding union office for five years.

Unions are also subjected to annual reporting requirements by the LMRDA. The union reports, filed with the Secretary of Labor, must contain the following information:

1. the name and the title of each officer;
2. the fees and dues required of members;
3. provisions for membership qualification and issuing work permits;
4. the process for electing and removing officers;
5. disciplinary standards for members;
6. details of any union benefit plans;
7. authorization rules for bargaining demands, strikes, and contract ratification.

Any changes in the union constitution, bylaws, or rules must be reported. As well, detailed financial information must be reported annually; such financial reports must contain information on the following:

1. assets and liabilities at the beginning and end of the fiscal year;
2. union receipts and their sources;
3. salaries paid by the union in excess of $10,000 total;

4. any loans by the union in excess of $250;

5. any other union disbursements.

All reports and information filed with the Secretary of Labor must also be made available to union members.

Union officials must report any security or financial interest in, or any benefit received from, any employer whose employees are represented by the union, and anything of value received from any business dealing connected with the union. Employers are required to make annual reports of any expenditures or transactions with union representatives and payments to employees or consultants for the purpose of influencing organizational or bargaining activities.

Welfare and Pension Plans.   Section 302 of the Taft-Hartley and the Employee Retirement Income Security Act (ERISA) control the operation and administration of employee welfare and pension plans. Persons administering such funds must handle them to protect the interests of all employees. Union officials serving as trustees or administrators of such funds may receive only one full-time salary. They must also be careful to keep their roles as trustee and union official separated.

Section 304 of the Taft-Hartley Act, along with the Federal Election Campaign Act of 1976, controls union political contributions and expenditures. Union dues or assessments may not be used to fund political expenditures. However, the union may establish a separate political fund if it is financed by voluntary contributions by union members. Members must be kept informed of the use of such funds and must not be subject to any reprisals in connection with the collection of contributions.

QUESTIONS

1. What is meant by the duty of fair representation? What standard of conduct by a union is required by the duty of fair representation? Who is protected by the duty of fair representation?

2. Does an employee in a bargaining unit have the right to have his or her grievance taken to arbitration? When does a union's refusal to arbitrate a grievance breach the duty of fair representation?

3. What remedies are available for a breach of the duty of fair representation? How do the remedies under Section 8(b)(1) differ from those available under Section 301?

4. When can a union enforce its disciplinary rules against employees who resign from the union? Explain your answer. When can a union restrict the right of members to resign? Explain your answer.

5. What is the union members' "bill of rights"?

6. What restrictions are placed on union officers by the Taft-Hartley Act and the Labor Management Reporting and Disclosure Act amendments to the NLRA?

CASE PROBLEMS

1. The employee joined the United States Postal Service (USPS) in 1975 as a part-time substitute rural carrier near Spokane, Washington. In 1976 the employee was given a full-time rural route. He obtained this route under a provision in the collective bargaining agreement giving senior part-timers first priority for new full-time routes.

   City delivery carriers and managers were jealous of the employee for obtaining this route, the court relates. He began to experience harassment from some of his co-workers, and in addition the route he worked was overburdened. In January 1978 the employee and another man were arrested and charged with stealing equipment from a railroad yard. He pled guilty and received a suspended sentence. The theft was reported in the local press.

   USPS fired the employee, asserting that the conviction meant he no longer was entrusted to safeguard mail or postal funds. He filed a grievance, but the shop steward declined to represent him. The union's steward fulfilled this task instead. When decisions at lower steps were negative, the union considered arbitration. However, the union's general counsel advised against arbitration on the ground that there was little likelihood of success.

   Based on these facts, do you think the union fulfilled its duty of fair representation to the discharged postal worker? See *Johnson v. U.S. Postal Service and National Rural Letter Carriers Association,* 756 F.2d 1461 (9th Cir. 1985).

2. After being on sick leave for half a year because of high blood pressure, Owens attempted to return to work. Owens' family physician had approved his return to work, but Owens' employer's company physician felt that Owens' blood pressure was too high to return to work, and the employer discharged him. Owens filed a grievance over his discharge, and the union processed the grievance through the grievance procedure. In preparation for taking Owens' grievance to arbitration, the union had Owens examined by another physician; that doctor also believed that Owens should not return to work. In light of their doctor's opinion, the union decided not to take Owens' grievance to arbitration. Owens demanded that his grievance be arbitrated, but the union refused. Owens then sued the union and the employer in state court, alleging breach of the collec-

tive agreement and of the duty of fair representation. How should the court decide Owens' claims against the union? Against the employer? Explain your answer. See *Vaca v. Sipes,* 368 U.S. 171 (1967).

3. Beginning in 1973 the employer's employees had been represented by Local P–706 of the then Amalgamated Meat Cutters Union. In December 1978 an employee filed a decertification petition in Case 11–RD–284, and the parties entered into a stipulated election agreement. Shortly thereafter a notice was posted or mailed by the Meat Cutters, announcing a meeting on December 30, 1978. Of the 176 unit employees, 16 attended the meeting and voted fifteen to one for what was orally described as a "merger." On January 11, 1979, the NLRB election was held. Local P–706 remained the sole recipient of the 158 valid ballots cast. On May 4, 1979, the board issued its Decision and Certification of Representative to Local P–706, overruling, inter alia, the employer's objection, which contended that the Meat Cutters' holding of the merger vote had interfered with the election.

   Prior to the board's decision, however, the following events had taken place. Since Local P–706 was an amalgamated local, the merger process was completed on February 17 when the employees of the other employers voted. The employer's employees were expressly excluded from this vote. The February 17 tally was in favor of merger, as of course was the combined tally of the December 30, 1978, and February 17 votes. Pursuant to these votes, sometime in March, Local P–706 surrendered its charter to the Meat Cutters and admittedly became defunct. The board, which was then considering challenges and objections in the decertification proceeding, was not informed of this action.

   On July 6, Local 525 filed a petition in Case 11–AC–14 seeking to amend Local P–706's certification to reflect its merger into Local 525. On September 18 the regional director granted the employer's motion to dismiss on the ground that the December 30, 1978, merger vote was procedurally defective because the employees had not been given adequate notice of the union meeting at which the merger vote occurred. Local 525 did not request review of the regional director's decision.

   With a view to devising the "quickest way to settle the matter" and thereby remedy the deficiency of the

December 30, 1978, vote, Local 525 sent a September 27 letter to all employees of the employer who had either been members of the then defunct Local P–706 or who had since signed membership cards for Local 525. The letter informed the recipients of an October 21 meeting whose sole purpose would be to vote again on the merger issue. This letter indicated that only "Union Members" would be eligible to vote. Of the 176 unit employees, 67 members were sent letters, of which 52 were received. The October 21 vote was fourteen to none in favor of merger. Local 525 then petitioned the NLRB to be certified as the employees' collective bargaining representative.

How should the NLRB have ruled on this petition? See *Fast Food Merchandisers and Food & Commercial Workers, Local 525,* 274 N.L.R.B. No. 25, 118 L.R.R.M. 1365 (1985).

4. The plaintiff, Joan Taschner, worked for Thrift-Rack, Inc. in its warehouse for nine years, from 1973 until September 1982. Teamsters Local Union 384 was at all times relevant to this action, the exclusive bargaining representative for certain employees, including the plaintiff of Thrift-Rack.

In September 1982 the plaintiff successfully cross-bid for an outside job of driver-salesperson. While working outside as a driver, she developed a severe neurodermatitis condition and allergic reaction, requiring a doctor's supervision and medication. As a result, she was unable to perform her outside job as a driver.

The plaintiff twice requested Thrift-Rack to transfer her to her prior warehouse position, which was still open, or to any other warehouse position. The company, however, rejected her requests on grounds that the plaintiff alleges were not provided for in the collective bargaining agreement and that were in violation of past practice.

In response to the company's refusal to transfer her, the plaintiff filed a grievance with Local 384. That grievance was denied by the union agent, James Hill, on grounds that no cross-bidding was allowed, that there were two separate seniority lists for union members who were employed by the company, and that an employee must be working in a unit to be allowed to bid for a job in that unit. Plaintiff requested to take her grievance to arbitration, but that request was denied by Hill. Subsequently, the warehouse position was awarded to another employee with less seniority, no experience, and lower qualifications than the plaintiff possessed.

On November 2, 1982, Thrift-Rack again refused the plaintiff's request to transfer to any warehouse position, although there were still warehouse jobs open, some of which may not have been bid upon by warehouse workers. The company refused to give her any work, informing her that there was no work available for her and to go home. Thereafter, the plaintiff called Thrift-Rack every day for about one week. She reported that she was still on medication and could not drive, but that she was available for any other work. She specifically requested transfer to any position in the warehouse. Thrift-Rack continued to refuse to transfer her to any position in the warehouse.

What recourse did Taschner have against her union? See *Taschner* v. *Hill,* 589 F. Supp. 127, 118 L.R.R.M. 2044 (E.D. Pa. 1984).

5. Plaintiff Feist received a Coast Guard license as a third assistant engineer in 1974 and was accepted into the applicant program of the Merchant Engineers' Beneficial Association (MEBA) in 1975. From 1975 on he served aboard vessels as a licensed third engineer, completed additional schooling, and worked the required number of days to achieve what is known as "Group I" status. The plaintiff paid all MEBA dues and had satisfied the requirement of a $2,500 initiation fee for membership. The plaintiff claims that in May 1979 he was informed that the District Investigating Committee had voted to deny him membership in the MEBA. Plaintiff's application was denied a second time on September 7, 1979, and again on February 13, 1981. Plaintiff filed suit against the MEBA, alleging that he had satisfied the requirements of membership in the MEBA and had been wrongfully denied membership status and the right to a full hearing, all in violation of the LMRDA.

Acceptance into membership of the MEBA is governed by Article 3 of the National Constitution, Articles 3 and 4 of the District Constitution, and Rules and Regulations No. 3, promulgated by the National Executive Committee. Rules and Regulations No. 3 states, in pertinent part, "The MEBA reserves the absolute right in its own discretion, for any reason whatsoever (a) at any time prior to acceptance into membership to terminate any applicant's status as such, or (b) to reject the application for membership." Feist sued the union, demanding that he be admitted to membership.

How should the federal court have ruled on Feist's demand? See *Feist* v. *Engineers' Beneficial Ass'n.* 118 L.R.R.M. 2419 (E.D. La. 1983).

6. The plaintiffs were boilermakers by trade and also were union members. When boilermakers were needed on a construction job, an agreement between the parent union and participating building contractors called "Southeastern States Articles of Agreement" provided that the contractor would request the union to provide the workers and would employ those sent by the union if they were qualified. The controversy resulted from an incident in which the plaintiff boilermakers, upon arriving at the work site, found it picketed by a large and belligerent group from another trade, the pipefitters. It was agreed, for purposes of the case, that the pipefitters' acts and presence were illegal. The referred boilermakers made no attempt to pass through the picket line, and this impasse continued unbroken for several days. After the weekend had passed, a replacement group of boilermakers appeared at the work site in a large body, led by the business agent. The newly recruited boilermakers went right through the line, but the pipefitters, along with the plaintiff boilermakers who had respected the picket lines the previous week, continued to hold off, standing apart. Soon thereafter an official of the contractor came out from the job site and handed termination notices to all in that group, asserting absenteeism as the ground.

The record reflects a fear by the union that it would be in serious trouble if it could not improve its record of complying with its agreements with employers, and this incident of course involved not honoring illegal picket lines and thereby making the boilermakers abettors of illegal conduct by others.

The preceding situation is dealt with in a series of documents that were in evidence. The Articles of Agreement already mentioned provide as follows:

1.4.4. There will be no recognition of any unauthorized or illegal picket line established by any person or organization, and the international and local officers of the Union will immediately upon being informed that such a situation exists, order all employees to cross such picket line.

The Joint Referral Committee Standards entered into by employers and union provide that a registrant is not to be referred for employment from the out-of-work list for ninety days after

4. Involvement in any unauthorized strike, work stoppage, slowdown, or any other activity having the effect of disrupting the job . . .
6. Insistence on recognizing illegal or unauthorized picket lines.

This ninety-day exclusion from referral was often called "benching" in the record of this case.

The employer demanded in writing that the rules be applied to seven men, including the plaintiffs herein, and accordingly the Union Rules Committee notified all business agents nationwide, effectively blacklisting the offenders. One of the men was obliged to quit a job he had found in Florida. At the time of trial, the three plaintiffs did not yet have work as boilermakers, though the ninety days had long since expired. They were restored to the bottom of the out-of-work list—not to their previous seniority.

Evaluate the discipline handed out to these boilermakers and the manner in which it was meted. Why were they disciplined? Were they accorded due process of law? See *Turner* v. *Boilermakers Local 455,* 755 F.2d 866, 118 L.R.R.M. 3157 (11th Cir. 1985).

7. On February 23, 1983, Gerald Forrest, a union member, addressed to Carroll Koepplinger, president of the defendant union, a letter setting forth the basis of his objections to the December 1982 election. The local received Forrest's letter and filed it. Forrest did not receive a response from the union and, pursuant to the LMRDA, he thereafter filed a timely complaint with the U.S. Department of Labor. The plaintiff conducted an investigation of the allegations of Forrest's complaint and found probable cause to believe that violations of Title IV had occurred.

At the time of the election, 378 members belonged to the local. They were employed by approximately eighteen employers spread geographically in the states of Illinois and Iowa. Eight separate nomination meetings were held and were generally conducted by Koepplinger. Following the nomination meetings, the Local 518 secretary reviewed the list of the nominees to determine the eligibility of each in accordance with the union requirements. One of those requirements was that no member could be nominated to any office unless the individual had been a member of the local or international union continuously for five years immediately preceding his or her nomination. As a result of that requirement, four nominees were ruled ineligible to run for office.

The shop stewards distributed the ballot to union members in their shops while the members were working. The instruction sheet did not contain any instructions for shop stewards with respect to the procedure to be followed in issuing ballots. At least two of the shop stewards who distributed ballots were themselves candidates for union office (one of the two was unopposed). After collecting all the voted ballots, the stewards returned the package to the secretary of the local. The voted ballots were stored in an unlocked filing cabinet in the union hall. The secretary took leave of absence from the local from approximately December 23, 1982, to January 3, 1983, during which time Koepplinger had sole responsibility for the conduct of the election.

Koepplinger selected December 30, 10:00 A.M., to tally the ballots. Koepplinger was present at the local union hall during the tally but in a different room from where the tally took place. The candidates were not affirmatively advised of the time and place of the election tally, and no observers were present. It is unclear whether any candidates had actual notice of the counting. The court requested affidavits from the parties on this question. Only the plaintiff filed affidavits. Those affidavits state that the affiants were never advised of the tally by anyone from the local. They do not answer the question of whether actual notice occurred.

The referendum committee that counted the ballots did not count or reconcile the number of unused ballots and the number of voted ballots to account for all of the official printed ballots. After the election, the local maintained all the election records except for the unvoted ballots. Koepplinger threw these away approximately three weeks after the election tally as part of an office clean-up.

According to the election records, there were 328 voted ballots. There were fifteen elected officers of which three were contested races.

Should the court overturn this election? See *Donovan* v. *Graphic Arts Union,* 118 L.R.R.M. 2093 (C.D. Ill. 1984).

8. Suit was filed as a class action by ten employees of the Kroger Company (Kroger). These employees claimed that Teamsters International and Teamsters Local 327, which represented their bargaining unit, breached the union's duty to represent all members of the collective bargaining unit fairly. The employees also charged that Kroger conspired with the union to "reduce" the conditions and benefits of their employment. More specifically, the plaintiffs claimed that Local 327 failed to represent the members of the union fairly in negotiating a collective bargaining agreement with Kroger, with the result that the union "bargained away substantial bene-

fits relating primarily to seniority." The complaint charged the International Union with failing to furnish a skilled negotiator to aid in the negotiations when requested to do so by the negotiating committee.

The complaint also alleged that the business agent and president of Local 327 conspired with Kroger in formulating an agreement that contained terms and conditions that were contrary to union policies and that diminished the rights of the plaintiffs and the class they sought to represent (all the unit members in two Kroger warehouses in the Nashville, Tennessee, area). The complaint further alleged that Local 327 and its business agent and president fraudulently changed the results of a membership vote on the proposed collective bargaining agreement to reflect ratification when in fact the proposed agreement had been rejected. Finally, the complaint asserted that the agreement negotiated by Local 327 and Kroger contained a provision that discriminated against female members of the unit by prescribing a lower wage scale for the unit employees in one of the warehouses than in the other. Virtually all employees in the warehouse with the lower wage rate were women.

Did the union breach its duty of fair representation? See *Storey* v. *Teamsters Local 327,* 759 F.2d 517, 118 L.R.R.M. 3273 (6th Cir. 1985).

9. In 1983 General Motors Corporation signed a collective bargaining agreement with the International Brotherhood of Electrical Workers, under the wage provisions of which new employees joining the bargaining unit were to be paid at a different (lower) hourly rate than current members. A so-called two-tier wage scale resulted from the arbitration of a Postal Service dispute that same year. Since then, a number of other unions have accepted two-tier systems as concessions in their collective bargaining agreements. Labor negotiators commonly refer to such two-tier wage concessions as "selling the unborn."

Can you articulate an argument on behalf of these "unborn" (new employees) that two-tier labor contracts violate the union's duty of fair representation? Do you see an Equal Employment Opportunity implication to such an agreement? See "IRRA Panelists Address Two-Tier Implications for Fair Representation and Equal Opportunity," No. 1 DLR A–5 (1985).

CHAPTER 11

Public Sector Labor Relations

THE RIGHTS OF PUBLIC sector employees to organize and bargain collectively are relatively recent legal developments. The National Labor Relations Act (NLRA) excludes employees of the federal, state, and local governments from its coverage. Only in the last few decades have Congress, the executive branch, and the states adopted legal provisions allowing public employees some rights to organize and bargain collectively. This chapter will examine those legal provisions that enable public employees to engage in labor relations activities. Labor relations legislation affecting the federal sector will be examined in some detail, and certain aspects of state legislation will also be considered.

Government as Employer

Although many labor relations issues in the public sector are similar to those in the private sector, there are also significant differences. Actions taken by government employers with regard to their employees may raise issues of the constitutional rights of those employees. Both the U.S. Constitution and the various state constitutions regulate and limit government action affecting citizens. Because public sector workers are both citizens and employees, their constitutional rights must be respected by their employers. The public sector employer may therefore be limited, in its attempts to discipline or regulate its employees, by constitutional provisions. The private sector employer faces no similar constitutional problems.

Another area in which public sector labor relations differs from that of the private sector involves the idea of sovereignty. The government, as government, is sovereign; it cannot vacate or delegate its sovereignty. The government may be obligated by law to perform certain functions and provide certain services, and government officials are given authority to take such actions and make such decisions as are necessary to perform those functions. Collective bargaining involves sharing decision-making power between the employer and the union—the employer and the union jointly determine working conditions, rates of pay, benefits, and so on. For the public sector employer, collective bargaining may involve delegating to the union the authority relating to the employer's statutory obligations. Bargaining may also affect the financial condition of the employer, requiring tax increases or cutbacks in the level of public services provided by the government employer. Because of this concern over sharing or delegating government sovereignty with the union, public sector labor relations statutes may narrowly define "terms and conditions" of employment and limit the matters that are subject to collective bargaining to avoid the government employer abdicating its legal authority. In the federal government, for example, most employees have their wages set by statute; collective bargaining in the federal service is precluded from dealing with any matter that is "provided for by Federal statute." Some state public sector labor relations statutes do not provide for collective bargaining at all, but rather for consultation or "meeting and conferring" on working conditions.

A third area in which public sector employment differs from the private sector deals with the right to strike. The right to strike is protected by Section 7 of the NLRA for private sector workers. Public sector workers, in general, do not have the right to strike. The activities of the government employer are generally vital to the public interest; disruptions of those activities because of labor disputes could imperil the welfare of the public. For that reason, the right to strike by public sector workers may be prohibited (as in the federal government and most states) or be limited to certain employees whose refusal to work would not endanger the public safety or welfare (as in several states).

The following case involves a challenge to the prohibitions of strikes by federal employees. The union representing postal clerks argues that such a prohibition violates their members' constitutional rights to strike.

POSTAL CLERKS v. BLOUNT

325 F. Supp. 879 (U.S.D.C., D.C. 1971), aff'd, 404 U.S. 802 (1971)

This action was brought by the United Federation of Postal Clerks (hereafter sometimes referred to as "Clerks"), an unincorporated public employee labor organization which consists primarily of employees of the Post Office Department, and which is the exclusive bargaining representative of approximately 305,000 members of the clerk craft employed by defendant. Defendant Blount is the Postmaster General of the United States. The Clerks seek declaratory and injunctive relief invalidating portions of 5 U.S.C. Section 7311, 18 U.S.C. Section 1918, an affidavit required by 5 U.S.C. Section 3333 to implement the above statutes, and Executive Order 11491. The Government, in response, filed a motion to dismiss or in the alternative for summary judgment, and plaintiff filed its opposition thereto and cross motion for summary judgment. . . .

5 U.S.C. Section 7311(3) prohibits an individual from accepting or holding a position in the federal government or in the District of Columbia if he

(3) participates in a strike . . . against the Government of the United States or the government of the District of Columbia. . . .

Paragraph C of the appointment affidavit required by 5 U.S.C. Section 3333, which all federal employees are required to execute under oath, states:

I am not participating in any strike against the Government of the United States or any agency thereof, and I will not so participate while an employee of the Government of the United States or any agency thereof.

18 U.S.C. Section 1918, in making a violation of 5 U.S.C. Section 7311 a crime, provides:

Whoever violates the provision of Section 7311 of Title 5 that an individual may not accept or hold a position in the Government of the United States or the government of the District of Columbia if he . . .

(3) participates in a strike, or asserts the right to strike, against the Government of the United States or the District of Columbia . . . shall be fined not more than $1,000 or imprisoned not more than one year and a day, or both.

Section 2(e)(2) of Executive Order 11491 exempts from the definition of a labor organization any group which:

asserts the right to strike against the Government of the United States or any agency thereof, or to assist or participate in such strike, or imposes a duty or obligation to conduct, assist or participate in such a strike.

Section 19(b)(4) of the same Executive Order makes it an unfair labor practice for a labor organization to:

call or engage in a strike, work stoppage, or slowdown; picket any agency in a labor-management dispute; or condone any such activity by failing to take affirmative action to prevent or stop it; . . .

Plaintiff contends that the right to strike is a fundamental right protected by the Constitution, and that the absolute prohibition of such activity by 5 U.S.C. Section 7311(3), and the other provisions set out above thus constitutes an infringement of the employees' First Amendment rights of association and free speech and operates to deny them equal protection of the law. Plaintiff also argues that the language to "strike" and "participate in a strike" is vague and overbroad and therefore violative of both the First Amendment and the Due Process Clause of the Fifth Amendment. For the purposes of this opinion, we will direct our attention to the attack on the constitutionality of 5 U.S.C. Section 7311(3), the key provision being challenged. . . .

At common law no employee, whether public or private, had a constitutional right to strike in concert with his fellow workers. Indeed, such collective action on the part of employees was often held to be a conspiracy. When the right of private employees to strike finally received full protection, it was by statute, Section 7 of the National Labor Relations Act, which "took this conspiracy weapon away from the employer in employment relations which affect interstate commerce" and guaranteed to employees in the private sector the right to engage in concerted activities for the purpose of collective bargaining. It seems clear that public employees stand on no stronger footing in this regard than private employees and that in the absence of a statute, they too do not possess the right to strike. The Supreme Court has spoken approvingly of such a restriction, and at least one federal district court has invoked the provisions of a predecessor statute, 5 U.S.C. Section 118p-r, to enjoin a strike by government employees. Likewise, scores of state cases have held that state employees do not have a right to engage in concerted work stoppages, in the absence of legislative authorization. It is fair to conclude that, irrespective of the reasons given, there is a unanimity of opinion on the part of courts and legislatures that government employees do not have the right to strike.

Congress has consistently treated public employees as being in a different category than private employees. The National Labor Relations Act and the Labor-Management Relations Act of 1947 (Taft-Hartley) both defined "employer" as not including any governmental or political subdivisions, and thereby indirectly withheld the protections of Section 7 from governmental employees. Congress originally enacted the no-strike provision separately from other restrictions on employee activity, by attaching riders to appropriations bills which prohibited strikes by government employees. . . .

Given the fact that there is no constitutional right to strike, it is not irrational or arbitrary for the Government to condition employment on a promise not to withhold labor collectively, and to prohibit strikes by those in public employment, whether because of the prerogatives of the sovereign, some sense of higher obligation associated with public service, to assure the continuing functioning of the Government without interruption, to protect public health and safety or for other reasons. Although plaintiff argues that the provisions in question are unconstitutionally broad in covering all Government employees regardless of the type or importance of the work they do, we hold that it makes no difference whether the jobs performed by certain public employees are regarded as "essential" or "nonessential," or whether similar jobs are performed by workers in private industry who do have the right to strike protected by statute. Nor is it relevant that some positions in private industry are arguably more affected with a public interest than are some positions in the Government service. . . .

Furthermore, it should be pointed out that the fact that public employees may not strike does not interfere with their rights which are fundamental and constitutionally protected. The right to organize collectively and to select representatives for the purposes of engaging in collective bargaining is such a fundamental right. But, as the Supreme Court noted in *Local 232* v. *Wisconsin Employment Relations Board*, "The right to strike, because of its more serious impact upon the public interest, is more vulnerable to regulation than the right to organize and select representatives for lawful purposes of collective bargaining which this Court has characterized as a 'fundamental right' and which, as the Court has pointed out, was recognized as such in its decisions long before it was given protection by the National Labor Relations Act."

Executive Order 11491 recognizes the right of federal employees to join labor organizations for the purpose of dealing with grievances, but that Order clearly and expressly defines strikes, work stoppages and slowdowns as unfair labor practices. As discussed above, that Order is the culmination of a longstanding policy. There certainly is no compelling reason to imply the existence of the right to strike from the right to associate and bargain collectively. In the private sphere, the strike is used to equalize bargaining power, but this has universally been held not to be appropriate when its object and purpose can only be to influence the essentially political decisions of Government in the allocation of its resources. Congress has an obligation to ensure that the machinery of the Federal Government continues to function at all times without interference. Prohibition of strikes by its employees is a reasonable implementation of that obligation.

Accordingly, we hold that the provisions of the statute, the appointment affidavit and the Executive Order, as construed above, do not violate any constitutional rights of those employees who are members of plaintiff's union. The Government's motion to dismiss the complaint is granted. Order to be presented.

Federal Government Labor Relations

Historical Background

It is not clear exactly when federal employees began negotiating over the terms of their employment, but informal bargaining began as long ago as 1883. In that year the Pendleton Act, known as the Civil Service Act, was passed. It granted Congress the sole authority to set wages, hours, and other terms and conditions of federal employment. This act led to informal bargaining and congressional lobbying by federal employees seeking higher wages and better conditions.

In 1906 President Theodore Roosevelt halted the informal bargaining by issuing an executive order forbidding federal employees or their associations from soliciting increases in pay, either before Congress, its committees, or before the heads of the executive agencies. Employees violating the order faced dismissal.

In the years following the executive order, Congress passed several laws that gave limited organization rights to some federal workers. The Lloyd–La Follette Act of 1912 gave postal workers the right to join unions. In 1920 the federal government negotiated the terms of a contract with the union representing construction workers building the government-sponsored Alaskan Railroad.

It was not until 1962, with the issuing of Executive Order 10988 by President Kennedy, that large numbers of federal employees were given the right to organize. The executive order recognized the right of federal workers to organize and to present their views on terms and conditions of employment to the agencies for which they worked.

Executive Order 10988 was supplemented by Executive Order 11491, which was issued in 1969 by President Nixon. That order placed the entire program of employee-management relations under the supervision and control of the Federal Labor Relations Council.

The Federal Service Labor-Management Relations Law of 1978, which was enacted as part of the Civil Service Reform Act of 1978, was the first comprehensive enactment covering labor relations in the federal government. The Federal Service Labor-Management Relations Act (FSLMRA) took effect in January 1979.

The Federal Service Labor-Management Relations Act

The FSLMRA, which was modeled after the NLRA, established a permanent structure for labor relations in the federal public sector. It created the Federal Labor Relations Authority (FLRA) to administer the act, and it granted federal employees the right to organize and bargain collectively. It also prohibited strikes and other defined unfair practices.

Coverage.   The FSLMRA covers federal employees who are employed by a federal agency or who have ceased to work for the agency because of an unfair labor practice. Most federal agencies are covered, but some are specifically exempted. Those agencies excluded from FSLMRA coverage are the FBI, the CIA, the National Security Agency, the General Accounting Office, the Tennessee Valley Authority, the FLRA, and the Federal Service Impasses Panel. As well, any agency that the president determines is investigative in nature or has a primary function of intelligence and would thus not be amenable to FSLMRA coverage because of national security may be excluded. The FSLMRA also excludes certain employees from coverage. Noncitizens working outside the United States for federal agencies, supervisory and management employees, and certain foreign service officers are exempted. In addition, the act excludes any federal employee participating in an illegal strike.

The Thurmond Act of 1969 prohibits military personnel from belonging to a union. That act makes it a felony for enlisted personnel to join a union or for military officers or their representatives to recognize or bargain with a union. The Thurmond Act does not apply to civilian employees of the military.

Those employees covered by the FSLMRA are granted the right to form, join, or assist any labor organization or to refrain from such activity, freely and without reprisal. Employees may act as representatives of a labor organization and present views of the organization to the heads of agencies, the executive branch, and Congress.

Postal Service Employees.   The employees of the U.S. Postal Service are not subject to the FSLMRA. The Postal Service Reorganization Act, which created the U.S. Postal Service as an independent agency, provides that postal service employees are subject to the NLRA, with some limitations. The National Labor Relations Board (NLRB) is authorized to determine appropriate bargaining units, hold representation elections, and enforce the unfair labor practice provision of the NLRA for postal service employees. The postal service unions bargain with the U.S. Postal Service over wages, hours, and conditions of employment, but postal service workers are not permitted to strike. Instead, the Postal Service Reorganization Act provides for fact-finding and binding arbitration if an impasse exists after 180 days from the start of bargaining. Supervisory and managerial employees of the Postal Service are not subject to the NLRA provisions.

Administration of the FSLMRA.   The FSLMRA created the Federal Labor Relations Authority (FLRA), which assumed the duties of the Federal Labor Relations Council created by Executive Order 11491. The FLRA is the central authority responsible for the administration of the FSLMRA.

The FLRA is composed of three members who are nominated by the president and confirmed by the Senate. The members serve five-year terms. The FLRA is empowered to determine the appropriateness of units for representation, to supervise or conduct elections to determine if a labor organization has been selected as the exclusive representative by majority of the employees in the appropriate unit, to resolve issues relating to the duty to bargain in good faith, and to resolve complaints of unfair labor practices.

The FLRA has the authority to hold hearings and issue subpoenas. It may order any agency or union to cease and desist from violating the provisions of the FSLMRA, and it can enlist the federal courts in proceedings against unions that strike illegally. The FLRA may take any remedial actions it deems appropriate in carrying out the policies of the act.

Representation Issues.   Under the FSLMRA a union becomes the exclusive representative of an appropriate unit of employees when it has been selected by a majority of votes cast in a representation election. When selected, the union becomes the sole representative of the employees in the unit and is authorized to negotiate the terms and conditions of employment of the employees in the unit. The union must fairly represent all employees in the unit, without discrimination or regard to union membership. The FLRA is authorized to settle questions relating to issues of representation, such as the determination of the appropriate unit and the holding of representation elections.

Appropriate Representation Units.   The FLRA is empowered to determine the appropriateness of a representation unit of federal employees. The FLRA ensures the employees the fullest possible freedom in exercising their rights under the FSLMRA in determining the unit, and ensures a clear and identifiable community of interest among the employees in the unit in order to promote effective dealing with the agency involved. The FLRA may determine the appropriateness of a unit on an agency, plant, installation, functional, or other basis.

Units may not include any management or supervisory employees, confidential employees, employees engaged in personnel work except those in a purely clerical capacity, employees doing investigative work that directly affects national security, employees administering the FSLMRA, or employees primarily engaged in investigation or audit functions relating to the work of individuals whose duties affect the internal security of an agency. Any employees engaged in administering any provision of law relating to labor-management relations may not be represented by a labor organization that is affiliated with an organization representing other individuals under the act. An appropriate unit may include professional and nonprofessional employees only if the professional employees, by majority vote, approve their inclusion.

Representation Election. The procedures for representation elections under the FSLMRA closely resemble those for elections under the NLRA. The act allows for the holding of consent elections to determine the exclusive representative of a bargaining unit. It also provides that the FLRA may investigate the question of representation, including holding an election, if a petition is filed by any person alleging that 30 percent of the employees in a unit wish to be represented by a union for the purpose of collective bargaining. As well, when a petition alleging that 30 percent of the members of a bargaining unit no longer wish to be represented by their exclusive representative union, the FLRA will investigate the representation question.

If the FLRA finds reasonable cause to believe that a representation question exists, it will provide, upon reasonable notice, an opportunity for a hearing. If, on the basis of the hearing, the FLRA finds that a question of representation does exist, it will conduct a representation election by secret ballot. An election will not be held if the unit has held a valid election within the preceding twelve months.

When an election is scheduled, a union may intervene and be placed on the ballot if it can show that it is already the unit's exclusive representative or that it has the support of at least 10 percent of the employees in the unit. The election is by secret ballot, with the employees choosing between the union(s) and "no representation." If no choice receives a majority of votes cast, a runoff election is held between the two choices receiving the highest number of votes. The results of the election are certified; if a union receives a majority of votes cast, it becomes the exclusive representative of the employees in the unit.

A union that has obtained exclusive representation status is entitled to be present at any formal discussions between the agency and unit employees concerning grievances, personnel policies and practices, or other conditions of employment. The exclusive representative must also be given the opportunity to be present at any examination of an employee in the unit in connection with an agency investigation that the employee reasonably believes may result in disciplinary action against the employee, provided that the employee involved has requested such representation. (This right is the equivalent of the *Weingarten* rights established by the NLRB for organized employees in the private sector.)

Consultation Rights. If the employees of an agency have not designated any union as their exclusive representative on an agencywide basis, a union that represents a substantial number of agency employees may be granted consultation rights. Consultation rights entitle the union to be informed of any substantive change in employment conditions proposed by the agency. The union is to be permitted reasonable time to present its views and recommendations regarding the proposed changes. The agency must consider the union recommendations before taking final action, and it must provide the union with written reasons for taking the final action.

Collective Bargaining. The FSLMRA requires that agencies and exclusive representatives of agency employees meet and negotiate in good faith. Good faith is defined as approaching the negotiations with a sincere resolve to reach a collective bargaining agreement, meeting at reasonable times and convenient places as frequently as may be necessary, and being represented at negotiations by duly authorized representatives prepared to discuss and negotiate on any condition of employment.

Conditions of Employment.   The act defines "conditions of employment" as including personnel policies, practices, and matters—whether established by rule, regulation, or otherwise—that affect working conditions. However, the act excludes the following from being defined as conditions of employment: policies relating to prohibited political activity, matters relating to the classification of any position, and policies or matters that are provided for by federal statute.

Wages.   Wages for most federal employees are not subject to collective bargaining because they are determined by statute. Federal "blue-collar" employees are paid under the coordinated Federal Wage System, which provides for pay comparable to pay for similar jobs in the private sector; federal "white-collar" employees are paid under the General Schedule (GS), and increases and changes in GS pay scales are made by presidential order. However, in *Fort Stewart Schools* v. *Federal Labor Relations Authority* (495 U.S. 641, 1990), the Supreme Court considered the question of whether schools owned and operated by the U.S. Army were required to negotiate with the union representing school employees over mileage reimbursement, paid leave, and a salary increase. The school declined to negotiate, claiming that the proposals were not subject to bargaining under the FSLMRA. The school claimed that "conditions of employment" under the FSLMRA included any matter insisted upon as a prerequisite to accepting employment, but did not include wages. The Supreme Court upheld an order of the FLRA that the school was required to bargain over wages and fringe benefits. Whereas the wages of most federal employees are set by law under the GSs of the Civil Service Act, the school employees wages are exempted from the GS. Wages for the school employees, therefore, were within the conditions of employment over which the school was required to bargain. Section 7106 of FSLMRA, which provides that "nothing in this chapter shall affect the authority of any management official of any agency to determine the . . . budget . . . of the agency. . . ." did not exempt wages and fringe benefits from the duty to bargain; agency management seeking to avail themselves of that provision to avoid bargaining over a proposal must demonstrate that the proposal would result in significant and unavoidable increases in costs.

Management Rights.   The FSLMRA contains a very strong management-rights clause, which also restricts the scope of collective bargaining. According to that clause, collective bargaining is not to affect the authority of any management official or any agency to determine the mission, budget, organization, number of employees, or the internal security practices of the agency. As well, management's right to hire, assign, direct, lay off, retain or suspend, reduce in grade or pay, or take disciplinary action against any employee is not subject to negotiation. Decisions to assign work, contract out work, or select candidates to fill positions are not subject to negotiation.

The act also precludes bargaining over any actions necessary to carry out the mission of the agency during emergencies.

The duty to bargain extends to matters that are the subject of any rule or regulation, as long as the particular rule or regulation is not governmentwide. However, if the agency determines there is a compelling need for such a regulation, it can refuse to bargain over that regulation. The exclusive representative must be given an opportunity to show that no compelling need exists for the regulation: disputes over the existence of a compelling need are to be resolved by the FLRA.

The agency's duty to bargain includes the obligation to furnish, upon request by the exclusive representative, data and information normally maintained by the agency. Such data must be reasonably available and necessary for full and proper discussion of subjects within the scope of bargaining. Data related to the guidance, training, advice, or counsel of management or supervisors relating to collective bargaining are excluded from the obligation to provide information. The duty to bargain in good faith also includes the duty to execute a written document embodying the terms of agreement, if either party so requests.

Impasse Settlement. The FSLMRA created the Federal Service Impasse Panel, which is authorized to take any actions necessary to resolve an impasse in negotiations. The Federal Mediation and Conciliation Service, created by the Taft-Hartley Act, also assists in the resolution of impasses by providing mediation services for the parties. If the mediation efforts fail to lead to an agreement, either party may request that the Federal Service Impasse Panel consider the dispute. The panel may either recommend procedures for resolving the impasse or assist the parties in any other way it deems appropriate. The formal impasse resolution procedures may include hearings, fact-finding, recommendations for settlement, or directed settlement. The parties may also seek binding arbitration of the impasse, with the approval of the panel.

Grievance Arbitration. The FSLMRA provides that all collective agreements under it must contain a grievance procedure: the grievance procedure must provide for binding arbitration as the final step in resolving grievances. If arbitration is invoked, either party may appeal the arbitrator's decision to the FLRA for review, within thirty days of the granting of the award. Upon review, the FLRA may overturn the arbitrator's award only if it is contrary to a law, rule, or regulation, or is inconsistent with the standards for review of private sector awards by the federal courts (see Chapter 9). If no appeal is taken from the arbitrator's award within thirty days of the award, the arbitrator's award is final and binding.

When a grievance involves matters that are subject to a statutory review procedure, the employee may choose to pursue the complaint through the statutory procedure or through the negotiated grievance procedure. Examples would be grievances alleging discrimination in violation of Title VII of the Civil Rights Act of 1964; the grievor can elect to pursue the complaint through the grievance process or through the procedure under Title VII. Performance ratings, demotions, and suspensions or removals that are subject to civil service review procedures may be pursued either through the civil service procedures or the grievance procedure.

Unfair Labor Practices.   The FSLMRA prohibits unfair labor practices by agencies and unions; the unfair labor practices defined in the act are similar to those defined by Sections 8(a) and 8(b) of the NLRA.

Agency Unfair Practices.   Unfair labor practices by agencies under the FSLMRA include interfering with or restraining the exercise of employees' rights under the act, encouraging or discouraging union membership by discrimination in conditions of employment, sponsoring or controlling a union, disciplining or discriminating against an employee for filing a complaint under the act, refusing to negotiate in good faith, and refusing to cooperate in impasse procedures. It is also an unfair labor practice for an agency to enforce any rule or regulation that conflicts with a preexisting collective bargaining agreement.

Union Unfair Practices.   Union unfair labor practices under the FSLMRA include interfering with or restraining the exercise of employees' rights under the act; coercing or fining a member for the purpose of impeding job performance; discriminating against an employee on the basis of race, color, creed, national origin, sex, age, civil service status, political affiliation, marital status, or handicap; refusing to negotiate in good faith; and refusing to cooperate in impasse procedures. It is also an unfair labor practice for a union to call or condone a strike, work slowdown, or stoppage, or to picket the agency if the picketing interferes with the agency's operations. Informational picketing that does not interfere with agency operations is allowed.

Unfair Labor Practice Procedures.   Upon the filing of a complaint alleging unfair labor practices with the FLRA, the General Counsel's Office of the FLRA investigates the complaint and attempts to reach a voluntary settlement. If no settlement is reached and the investigation uncovers evidence that the act has been violated, a complaint will be issued. The complaint contains a notice of the charge and sets a date for a hearing before the FLRA. The party against whom the complaint is filed has the opportunity to file an answer to the complaint and to appear at the hearing to contest the charges.

   If the FLRA finds, by a preponderance of evidence, that a violation has occurred, it will issue written findings and an appropriate remedial order. FLRA decisions are subject to judicial review by the federal courts of appeals.

Unfair Labor Practice Remedies.   The FLRA has broad authority for fashioning remedial orders for unfair labor practices. Remedial orders may include cease-and-desist orders, reinstatement with back pay, renegotiation of the agreement between the parties with retroactive effect, or any other actions deemed necessary to carry out the purposes of the act.

   When a union has been found by the FLRA to have intentionally engaged in a strike or work stoppage in violation of the act, the FLRA may revoke the exclusive representation status of the union or take any other disciplinary action deemed appropriate. Employees engaging in illegal strikes are subject to dismissal. The FLRA may also seek injunctions, restraining orders, or contempt citations in the federal courts against striking unions.

The following case involves the review of an FLRA order revoking the exclusive representation status of the air traffic controllers' union because of its involvement in an illegal strike.

PROFESSIONAL AIR TRAFFIC CONTROLLERS ORG. v. FLRA

685 F.2d 547 (U.S.C.A., D.C., 1982)

EDWARDS, J.

Federal employees have long been forbidden from striking against their employer, the federal government, and thereby denying their services to the public at large. The United States Code presently prohibits a person who "participates in a strike . . . against the Government of the United States" from accepting or holding a position in the federal government, and violation of this section is a criminal offense. Newly hired federal employees are required to execute an affidavit attesting that they have not struck and will not strike against the government. In addition, since the inception of formal collective bargaining between federal employee unions and the federal government, unions have been required to disavow the strike as an economic weapon. Since 1969, striking has been expressly designated a union unfair labor practice.

In 1978, Congress enacted the Civil Service Reform Act, Title VII of which provides the first statutory basis for collective bargaining between the federal government and employee unions. Title VII in no way reduced the existing legal proscriptions against strikes by federal employees and unions representing employees in the federal service. Rather, the Act added a new provision applicable to federal employee unions that strike against the government. Under Section 7120(f) of Title VII, Congress provided that the Federal Labor Relations Authority ("FLRA" or "Authority") shall "revoke the exclusive recognition status" of a recognized union, or "take any other appropriate disciplinary action" against any labor organization, where it is found that the union has called, participated in or condoned a strike, work stoppage or slowdown against a federal agency in a labor-management dispute.

In this case we review the first application of Section 7120(f) by the FLRA. After the Professional Air Traffic Con-

trollers Organization ("PATCO") called a nationwide strike of air traffic controllers against the Federal Aviation Administration ("FAA") in the summer of 1981, the Authority revoked PATCO's status as exclusive bargaining representative for the controllers. . . .

The Professional Air Traffic Controllers Organization has been the recognized exclusive bargaining representative for air traffic controllers employed by the Federal Aviation Administration since the early 1970s. Faced with the expiration of an existing collective bargaining agreement, PATCO and the FAA began negotiations for a new contract in early 1981. A tentative agreement was reached in June, but was overwhelmingly rejected by the PATCO rank and file. Following this rejection, negotiations began again in late July. PATCO announced a strike deadline of Monday, August 3, 1981.

Failing to reach a satisfactory accord, PATCO struck the FAA on the morning of August 3. Over seventy percent of the nation's federally employed air traffic controllers walked off the job, significantly reducing the number of private and commercial flights in the United States.

In prompt response to the PATCO job actions, the Government obtained restraining orders against the strike, and then civil and criminal contempt citations when the restraining orders were not heeded. The Government also fired some 11,000 striking air traffic controllers who did not return to work by 11:00 a.m. on August 5, 1981. In addition, on August 3, 1981, the FAA filed an unfair labor practice charge against PATCO with the Federal Labor Relations Authority. On that same day, an FLRA Regional Director issued a complaint on the unfair labor practice charge, alleging strike activity prohibited by 5 U.S.C. Section 7116(b)(7) and seeking revocation of PATCO's certification under the Civil Service Reform Act. . . .

On the merits of this case, PATCO presents the court with two questions for review. The first question . . . is whether the FLRA's finding that PATCO called, participated in, and condoned a strike is supported by substantial evidence. The second question . . . is whether the FLRA properly exercised its discretion under the Act in revoking the exclusive recognition status of PATCO.

Section 7123(c) of the Civil Service Reform Act declares that "[t]he findings of the Authority with respect to questions of fact, if supported by substantial evidence on the record considered as a whole, shall be conclusive." 5 U.S.C. Section 7123(c). This language is identical to that governing judicial review of the decisions of the National Labor Relations Board . . . and Congress clearly intended the scope of review of FLRA factual findings to be identical to that of NLRB findings. . . . The judicial function is merely to review the substantiality of the evidence underlying the agency decision, not to "displace the [agency's] choice between two fairly conflicting views." That test of substantiality is met when the record before the court does not "preclude[ ] the [agency's] decision from being justified by a fair estimate of the worth of the testimony of the witnesses or its informed judgment on matters within its special competence or both." . . .

[T]he record contained evidence of simultaneous picketing by striking air traffic controllers at five separate FAA facilities. In each case the picketers carried signs indicating that they were on strike and that they belonged to a particular PATCO Local. In several cases FAA officials, viewing photographs taken during the strike, identified individual picketers as air traffic controllers (including certain PATCO Local officers); many of the persons identified were controllers who were scheduled for work at the times when the photographs were taken. In addition, FAA records also established massive absenteeism on August 3 and thereafter by air traffic controllers nationwide.

PATCO objects to the adequacy of this evidence, contending that it establishes only that strikes were conducted by certain PATCO Local unions, while the Respondent before the FLRA was the PATCO National union. Whatever weight PATCO's contention might otherwise have is seriously diminished by the evidence of the *simultaneous* picketing at numerous work locations and by the evidence of the *nationwide* scope of absenteeism by controllers on and after August 3. However the evidence is interpreted, it certainly cannot be characterized as a "wildcat strike on the part of one of [PATCO's] Locals." The weight of PATCO's contention is even further diminished by the fact that the PATCO National union was the exclusive bargaining agent for all bargaining unit members. For several months prior to August 3, the PATCO National union, and not the Locals,

had engaged in collective bargaining with the FAA for a national agreement. The FLRA was entitled to draw a reasonable inference from the national bargaining unit and from the nationwide picketing and absenteeism—*viz.*, that the PATCO National union, and not merely a collection of PATCO Locals, was on strike.

Moreover, the FAA introduced into evidence two videotapes of PATCO National union President Robert Poli making statements regarding the strike at news conferences. In the first videotape, Poli is recorded as announcing that the strike would begin on the morning of August 3 if no satisfactory settlement proposal was reached and if tallying of a strike vote revealed the necessary support. PATCO notes that this statement was not an actual strike call, but at most a prediction or a suggestion of conditions precedent to a strike. While what PATCO notes is indeed true, the statement nonetheless carries significant weight in light of the fact that Poli's "predicted" time of the strike exactly coincided with the extensive picketing and massive absenteeism. In the second videotape, Poli was recorded as making the simple statement: "The question is will the strike continue. The answer is yes." PATCO again contends that the statement is "no more than a prediction—a speculation about future events." While the characterization given Poli's statement by PATCO is not totally inaccurate, it does not undercut the FLRA's finding. Poli's acknowledgement of the strike and his quite certain "prediction" that it would continue negate any attempt by PATCO to disassociate the PATCO National union from the widespread and simultaneous strike activity by PATCO members nationwide.

In these circumstances—simultaneous and widespread absenteeism by union members, picketing announcing various union locals as being on strike, and accurate statements by the union president that a strike would take place under certain conditions and then that that strike would continue—we have no difficulty concluding that the FLRA's finding was supported by substantial evidence on the record as a whole. Our conclusion is made more certain by the total absence of record evidence offered by PATCO in refutation. Thus, we affirm that FLRA's finding that PATCO "call[ed], or participate[d] in, a strike" in violation of 5 U.S.C. Section 7116(b)(7)(A).

PATCO also objects to the conclusion of the FLRA that PATCO committed a separate unfair practice of condoning a strike "by failing to take action to prevent or stop such activity," a violation of 5 U.S.C. Section 7116(b)(7)(B). After finding that the evidence presented was sufficient to establish the prima facie existence of a strike, Chief A. L. J. Fenton ruled that the burden shifted to PATCO to produce evidence showing that it had taken some action to prevent or to stop the strike. PATCO offered no such evidence....

Given our affirmance of the unfair labor practice finding under Section 7116(b)(7)(A), it necessarily follows that the FLRA could conclude that the PATCO National union was aware of the strike and, as a consequence, had a statutory obligation to attempt to stop the strike activity. In addition, we believe that the FLRA was fully justified in taking official notice of proceedings in the District Court for the District of Columbia. During the early morning of August 3, 1981, the District Court issued a restraining order against the PATCO strike. During the evening of that same day, the District Court found both the PATCO National union and its President, Robert Poli, in civil contempt for violation of the restraining order. In these circumstances, PATCO certainly cannot claim lack of knowledge of the strike. On these bases, and because PATCO offered no evidence to indicate that it even attempted to end the strike, we also affirm the FLRA's unfair labor practice finding under 5 U.S.C. Section 7116(b)(7)(B).

Having determined that the FLRA properly found PATCO in violation of the no-strike provisions of the Civil Service Reform Act, we turn to the second question presented for our review: whether the FLRA properly exercised its discretion under the Act to revoke the exclusive recognition status of PATCO. This inquiry requires us to ascertain: (1) what degree of discretion Congress granted to the FLRA when it enacted Section 7120(f); (2) whether the FLRA's exercise of its discretion in this case was proper....

We have concluded that the FLRA has substantial discretion under Section 7120(f) to decide whether or not to revoke the exclusive recognition status of a union found guilty by the FLRA of striking or condoning a strike against the government. A concomitant of this conclusion is that the courts have only a limited role in reviewing the FLRA's exercise of its remedial discretion.... As with judicial review of remedial orders of the NLRB, we will uphold the remedial orders of the FLRA "unless it can be shown that the order is a patent attempt to achieve ends other than those which can fairly be said to effectuate the policies of the Act."

We have little trouble deciding that the FLRA did not abuse its discretion in this case. First, the FLRA could take official notice that PATCO has repeatedly violated legal prohibitions against striking and other job actions. In 1970, PATCO called a "sickout" of the air traffic controllers subject to its exclusive representation. "Extensive disruptions

in air service resulted as approximately one quarter of the nation's air controllers reported in sick each day between March 24 and April 14 ..." In 1978, PATCO threatened a nationwide air traffic slowdown. Based on a stipulated record, the union was held in contempt for its actions. In 1980, PATCO controllers engaged in a work slowdown at Chicago's O'Hare Airport. In August 1981, PATCO called the nationwide strike that gives rise to the present action.

Second, all of PATCO's job actions after 1970 occurred while the union was subject to an injunction resulting from its 1970 strike that prohibited such actions. Nor could PATCO have had any doubt about the continued validity of that injunction before it commenced its 1981 strike. After the effective date of the Civil Service Reform Act, PATCO petitioned the District Court for the Eastern District of New York for vacatur of its 1970 injunction on the ground that Title VII of the Act had deprived the District Court of jurisdiction to enjoin federal employee strikes. In June 1981, before the most recent strike began, the District Court reaffirmed the validity of its 1970 injunction and denied PATCO's motion.

Third, after PATCO struck on August 3, 1981, additional restraining orders and injunctions directed only at this strike issued. PATCO openly defied these injunctions as well.

Finally, PATCO's actions before and after August 3, 1981, can only be characterized as defiant. The union threatened its strike, then willfully and intentionally called and participated in it. After the strike commenced, PATCO made no attempt to end it; indeed, PATCO condoned and encouraged it. Even after the striking controllers had been terminated and a majority of the Authority had ordered revocation of its exclusive recognition status, PATCO failed to satisfy Chairman Haughton's request that it end the strike and promise to abide by the no-strike provisions of the Civil Service Reform Act.

In these circumstances the FLRA's decision to revoke PATCO's exclusive recognition status was not an abuse of discretion. The union is a repeat offender that has willfully ignored statutory proscriptions and judicial injunctions. It has shown little or no likelihood of abiding by the legal requirements of labor-management relations in the federal sector. If the extreme remedy that Congress enacted cannot properly be applied to this case, we doubt that it could ever properly be invoked.

Judicial Review of FLRA Decisions

As the *PATCO* case illustrates, final orders, other than bargaining unit determinations and arbitration awards, are subject to review in the federal courts of appeals. The party seeking review has ten days from the issuance of the FLRA decision to file a petition for review with the court of appeals for the appropriate circuit. Unless specifically authorized by the appeals court, the filing of a petition for review does not operate to stay the FLRA order.

Upon review, the court may affirm, enforce, modify, or set aside the FLRA order. Findings of fact by the FLRA are deemed conclusive if they are supported by substantial evidence. The order of the court of appeals is subject to discretionary review by the Supreme Court.

Union Security Provisions

A union granted exclusive representation rights under the FSLMRA must accept, as a member, any unit employee who seeks membership. A union may not require union membership as a condition of employment; that means that the collective agreement may not contain a closed shop or union shop provision. For the government employer to require that employees join a union in order to retain their job would violate the employees' constitutional rights of association protected by the First Amendment (or Fourteenth Amendment if the employer is a state or local government agency).

Agency shop provisions, which require that an employee pay union dues or fees but do not require union membership, do not raise the same constitutional problems. However, if the employee's dues money is spent by the union on matters other than those relating to collective bargaining or representation issues, the employee is, in effect, forced to contribute to causes and for purposes that he or she may oppose. Does this "forced contribution" violate the employee's constitutional rights?

In *Abood* v. *Detroit Board of Education* (431 U.S. 209, 1977), the Supreme Court held that union expenditures for expression of political views, in support of political candidates, or for advancement of ideological causes not related to its duties as bargaining agent can be financed only from dues or assessments paid by employees who do not object to advancing such ideas and who are not coerced into doing so. To do otherwise violates the First Amendment rights of those employees who object to such expenditures. The Court held that employees who object to political expenditures by the union are entitled to a refund of that portion of their dues payments that represents the proportion that union political expenditures bear to the total union expenditures.

In *Chicago Teachers Union, Local No. 1* v. *Hudson* (466 U.S. 435, 1986), the Supreme Court addressed the procedures that the union must make available for employees who object to union expenditures of their dues or fees. The Court held that the union is required to provide objecting members with information relating to the union expenditures on collective bargaining and political activities, and must include an adequate explanation of the basis of dues and fees. The members must also be provided a reasonably prompt opportunity to challenge, before an impartial decision maker, the amount of the dues or fees; and the union must hold in escrow the amounts in dispute pending the resolution of the challenges by the members.

The *Abood* and *Chicago Teachers Union* cases hold that individuals who object to a union's political activities are not required to pay that portion of union dues and fees that fund such non-bargaining activities. What standards is a court to use to determine which union expenditures are related to its collective bargaining activities? The Supreme Court considered that question in the case of *Lehnert* v. *Ferris Faculty Association* (__ U.S. __ , 111 S.Ct. 1950, 1991). The court set out three criteria for determining which activities can be funded by dues and fees of objecting individuals:

1. The activity must be germane to collective bargaining.

2. It must be justified by the government's interest in promoting labor peace and avoiding "free riders" who benefit from union activities without paying for union services.

3. It must not significantly add to the burdening of free speech inherent in allowing a union shop or agency shop provision.

Using those criteria, the *Lehnert* court held that the teachers' union could not charge objecting individuals for lobbying, electoral activities, or political activities beyond the limited context of contract implementation or negotiation. As well, the union could not charge for expenses incurred in conducting an illegal work stoppage, or for litigation expenses unless the litigation concerned the individual's own bargaining unit. The union could charge objecting individuals for national union programs and publications designed to disseminate information germane to collective bargaining; information services concerning professional development, job opportunities and miscellaneous matters that benefitted all teachers, even though they may not directly concern members of the individual's bargaining unit; participation by local delegates at state or national union meetings at which representation policies and bargaining strategies are developed; and expenses related to preparation for a strike. The court also held that the union could not charge the objecting individuals for public relations efforts designed to enhance the reputation of the teaching profession generally, because such efforts were not directly connected to the union's collective bargaining function.

It should be noted that private sector employees have the same right to object to political expenditures by their unions; in *Communications Workers of America* v. *Beck* (487 U.S. 735, 1988), the Supreme Court stated that "We conclude that Section 8(a)(3) . . . authorizes the exaction [from nonmembers or objecting employees] of only those fees and dues necessary to 'performing the duties of an exclusive representative of the employees in dealing with the employer on labor-management issues.'"

The FSLMRA provides that union dues may be deducted from an employee's pay only if authorized by the employee. The employer may not charge a service fee for deductions to either the employee or the union. Employee authorizations for dues deduction may not be revoked for a period of one year from their making.

State Public Sector Labor Relations Legislation

In 1954 Wisconsin adopted a public employee labor relations law covering state, county, and municipal employees. Since that first legal provision for state public sector labor relations, approximately forty states have adopted provisions relating to public sector labor relations. The various state laws differ widely in their treatment of issues such as employee coverage, impasse resolution procedures, and restrictions on the scope of bargaining. Because of the diversity of statutes, it is not possible to discuss them in detail; the remaining portion of this chapter will discuss certain general features of state public sector labor relations statutes.

Coverage of State Laws

As noted, approximately forty states have provisions for some labor relations activity by state or local employees. Most of those states have adopted statutes that provide for organizing rights and for collective bargaining by public employees. Some states that have no statutes dealing with public sector labor relations allow voluntary collective bargaining by public employees based on court decisions. Other states, while not restricting the rights of public employees to join unions, prohibit collective bargaining by public employees, based on statutory prohibitions or court decisions.

In those states have public sector labor relations statutes, the pattern of coverage of those statutes varies. Some statutes cover all state and local employees. Others may cover only local or only state employees. Some states have several statutes, with separate statutes covering teachers, police, and firefighters. Some states also allow for the enactment of municipal labor relations legislation. New York City, for example, has established an Office of Collective Bargaining by passage of a city ordinance.

The courts have generally held that there is no constitutionally protected right to bargain collectively. For that reason, the courts have upheld restrictions or prohibitions on the right to bargain. The right to join unions or to organize, however, has been held to be protected by the constitutional freedom of association under the First and Fourteenth Amendments. Because the right to organize is constitutionally protected, restrictions on that right of public employees have consistently been struck down by the courts.

But while public employees in general may have the right to organize, many states exclude supervisors and managerial or confidential employees from unionizing. Other states may allow those employees to organize, but provide for bargaining units separate from other employees. The courts have generally upheld exclusions of managerial, supervisory, and confidential employees from organizing and bargaining.

Representation Issues

Most of the state statutes authorizing public sector labor relations provide for exclusive bargaining representatives of the employees. The statutes generally create a Public Employee Relations Board (PERB) to administer the act and to determine representation issues and unfair labor practice complaints.

Bargaining Units.   Determining appropriate bargaining units is generally the function of the PERB agency created by the particular statute. Some statutes provide for bargaining by all categories of public employees, whereas other statutes may specifically define appropriate units, such as teachers within a particular school district. When the PERB is entrusted with determining the appropriate unit, it generally considers community interest factors such as the nature of work, similarity of working conditions, efficiency of administration, and the desires of the employees. Some statutes require determination based on efficiency of administration. Police and law enforcement officers and firefighters are generally in separate districtwide units (or statewide units for state law enforcement officers). Faculty at public universities may be organized in statewide units or may bargain on an institution unit basis. In general, PERB agencies seek to avoid a proliferation of small units.

Representation Elections.   The procedures for holding representation elections for units of public employees generally resemble those under the FSLMRA and the NLRA. The union seeking representation rights petitions the PERB requesting an election. The union must demonstrate some minimum level of employee support within the unit. If the parties fail to reach agreement on the bargaining unit definition, the eligibility of employees to vote, and the date and other details of the election, the PERB settles such issues after holding hearings on them.

The elections are by secret ballot, and the results are certified by the PERB. Either party may file objections to the election, with the PERB reviewing the challenges and possibly ordering a new election when the challenges are upheld.

Bargaining

As noted, a majority of states have provisions requiring, or at least permitting, some form of collective bargaining. Some statutes may use the term "meet and confer" rather than collective bargaining, but in actual operation the process is not substantially different from collective bargaining.

The scope of bargaining subjects may be restricted in order to protect the statutory authority of, or to ensure the provision of essential functions by, the public employer. As well, the public employer may be legally prohibited from agreeing with the union on particular subjects. For example, state law may require a minimum number of evaluations of employees annually, and the employer may not agree to a lesser number of evaluations.

Public sector labor relations statutes generally have broad management-rights clauses. As a result, the subjects of "wages, hours and other terms and conditions" of employment may be defined more narrowly than is the case in the private sector under the NLRA.

The state PERBs generally classify subjects for bargaining into mandatory, permissive, and illegal subjects. Mandatory topics involve the narrowly defined matters relating to wages, hours, and other terms and conditions of employment. Permissive subjects generally are those related to government policy, the employer's function, or matters of management rights. Illegal subjects may include those matters to which the employer is precluded by law from agreeing. Some states may prohibit bargaining over certain items that may be classified as permissive in other states.

PENNSYLVANIA LABOR RELATIONS BOARD v. STATE COLLEGE AREA SCHOOL DISTRICT

337 A.2d 262 (Supreme Court of Pennsylvania, 1975)

[The State College Area Education Association (the teacher's union) filed an unfair labor practice complaint with the Pennsylvania Labor Relations Board (PLRB) alleging that the Board of Directors of the State College Area School District (School District) refused to bargain over twenty-one different items. The PLRB held that five of the twenty-one items were mandatory bargaining items and that the remaining sixteen items were not subject to negotiation. Both sides appealed the PLRB ruling to the Court of Common Pleas, which held that all twenty-one items were matters of inherent managerial policy and were not subject to negotiation. Upon appeal, the Commonwealth Court affirmed the Court of Common Pleas decision. The Association appealed to the Supreme Court of Pennsylvania.

The twenty-one items in dispute included the following:

■ The provision of time during the school day for team planning of required innovative programs;

■ Timely notice of teaching assignments for the coming year;

■ The provision of separate desks and lockable drawer space for each teacher;

■ Elimination of the requirement that teachers teach or supervise two consecutive periods in separate buildings;

■ Elimination of the requirement that teachers chaperone athletic activities;

■ Elimination of the requirement that teachers unpack, store, and handle supplies;

■ Allowing a teacher to have free access, without prior notice, to his or her personal file;

■ Provision of maximum class sizes;

■ Provision that secondary teachers not be required to teach more than twenty-five periods a week and have at least one planning period per day; and

■ Provision that elementary teachers have at least one period per day for planning purposes.]

NIX, J.

The subject of this appeal is the relatively recent enactment of the Public Employe Relations Act. The dispute centers upon the tension evoked between what the legislature has specifically made bargainable and what the legislature has also specifically allowed management to reserve to its unilateral decision-making. In this instance we are required to interpret Section 701 and determine its scope in light of Sections 702 and 703. . . .

Section 701 provides:

> Collective bargaining is the performance of the mutual obligation of the public employer and the representative of the public employes to meet at reasonable times and confer in good faith with respect to wages, hours and other terms and conditions of employment, or the negotiation of an agreement or any question arising thereunder and the execution of a written contract incorporating any agreement reached but such obligation does not compel either party to agree to a proposal or require the making of a concession.

That the right to collective bargaining as to "wages, hours and other terms and conditions of employment" is not unlimited, is made clear by the two succeeding sections. Section 702 states:

> Public employers shall not be required to bargain over matters of inherent managerial policy, which shall include but shall not be limited to such areas of discretion or policy as the

functions and programs of the public employer, standards of services, its overall budget, utilization of technology, the organizational structure and selection and direction of personnel. Public employers, however, shall be required to meet and discuss on policy matters affecting wages, hours and terms and conditions of employment as well as the impact thereon upon request by public employe representatives.

Section 703 states:

The parties to the collective bargaining process shall not effect or implement a provision in a collective bargaining agreement if the implementation of that provision would be in violation of, or inconsistent with, or in conflict with any statute or statutes enacted by the General Assembly of the Commonwealth of Pennsylvania or the provisions of municipal home rule charters.

The conflict in the Commonwealth Court centered upon the extent the legislature intended to limit the scope of negotiation made mandatory under Section 701 by its inclusion of Sections 702 and 703 within this act. The majority of that court concluded that any item of wages, hours, and other terms and conditions of employment affecting policy determinations or the impairment of other performance of the duties and responsibilities imposed upon public employers by statute are not bargainable. Judge Kramer, in a dissent joined by two other members of the court, took a different view. Judge Kramer wrote:

My reading of the statute (Act 195) leads me to find a legislative intent to provide for good faith collective bargaining wherever the teachers' employment rights are directly affected by "wages, hours and other terms and conditions of employment."

Where provisions of a statute appear to be ambiguous or inconsistent, the intention of the legislature may be determined by examining the occasion, reason or necessity for the law. Thus, we should look to the circumstances that existed at the time of the enactment and determine the mischief sought to be remedied or the object to be obtained in its passage.... Prior to the passage of Act 195 the prior law prohibited all strikes by public employes and did not require collective bargaining by public employers. The chaotic climate that resulted from this obviously intolerable situation occasioned the creation of a Governor's Commission to Revise the Public Employe Law of Pennsylvania. This commission, which is commonly referred to as the Hickman Commission, issued a report recommending the repeal of the then existing law and the passage of new law which would permit the right of all public employes to bargain collectively. In recommending this change the commission suggested the need for collective bargaining to restore harmony in the public sector and to eliminate the numerous illegal strikes and the widespread labor unrest....

The declaration of policy contained in Act 195, Section 101 clearly establishes that the legislature concurred with the commission's belief that the right to collective bargaining was necessary to promote orderly and constructive relationships between public employers and employes.

In this setting we are forced to conclude that the legislature at the time of the passage of Act 195 fully recognized that the right of collective bargaining was crucial to any attempt to restore harmony in the public sector. It would be absurd to suggest that the legislature deliberately intended to meet this pressing need by providing an illusory right of collective bargaining....

Section 702, when read in conjunction with Section 701, requires us to distinguish between the area of managerial prerogative and the areas of vital concern to employes. The Commonwealth Court's premise that any interpretation of Sections 701 and 702 must recognize the dominance of a legislature intention to preserve the traditional concept of inherent managerial policy emasculates Section 701 and thwarts the fulfillment of the legislative policy sought to be achieved by the passage of the Act. Further, such a view ignores the fact that the acceptance of the Hickman Commission's recommendation and the passage of Act 195 was a repudiation of the traditional concept of the sanctity of managerial prerogatives in the public sector. The introduction of a concept of mandatory collective bargaining, regardless of how narrowly the scope of negotiation is defined, necessarily represents an encroachment upon the former autonomous position of management. Further, the Hickman Commission's recognition of the need for collective bargaining to produce stability in the public sector argues against an inference that they intended their recommendation to be construed as suggesting something less than a viable bargaining process in the public sector ...

We recognize the principle that a statute is never presumed to deprive the State of any prerogative or right unless the intention to do so is clearly manifest.... However, the passage of Act 195, in our view, expresses a manifest intention to create a sufficiently vital collective bargaining process capable of meeting the need to restore harmony within the public sector....

A determination of the interrelationship between Sections 701 and 702 calls upon us to strike a balance wherein those matters relating directly to "wages, hours and other terms and conditions of employment" are made mandatory subjects of bargaining and reserving to management those areas that the public sector necessarily requires to be managerial functions. In striking this balance the paramount concern must be the public interest in providing for the effective and efficient performance of the public service in question. . . . Thus we hold that where an item of dispute is a matter of fundamental concern to the employes' interest in wages, hours and other terms and conditions of employment, it is not removed as a matter subject to good faith bargaining under Section 701 simply because it may touch upon basic policy. It is the duty of the Board in the first instance and the courts thereafter to determine whether the impact of the issue on the interest of the employe in wages, hours and terms and conditions of employment outweighs its probable effect on the basic policy of the system as a whole. If it is determined that the matter is one of inherent managerial policy but does affect wages, hours and terms and conditions of employment, the public employer shall be required to meet and discuss such subjects upon request by the public employe's representative pursuant to Section 702.

The relationship between Sections 701 and 703 is particularly significant in a highly regulated area such as public education. . . . The majority of the Commonwealth Court reasoned that the duties and prerogatives imposed upon and granted to school boards under the Public School Code of 1949, and other pieces of legislation could not be the subject of collective bargaining under the terms of Section 703. We cannot agree.

The mere fact that a particular subject matter may be covered by legislation does not remove it from collective bargaining under Section 701 if it bears on the question of wages, hours and conditions of employment. We believe that Section 703 only prevents the agreement to and implementation of any term which would be in violation of or inconsistent with any statutory directive. The distinction between this view and that expressed by the majority of the Commonwealth Court (as we understand it) is best illustrated by an example. Under Section 1142 of the Public School Code, a minimum salary scale is set forth. Section 1151 provides that school boards may pay salaries in excess of the minimum salary. Framing the issue in accordance with the formulation suggested by the majority in the Commonwealth Court, Section 1142 created a duty not to pay below the minimum scale and Section 1151 granted the employer the prerogative to pay more than the minimum rate. Clearly, the parties are precluded from agreeing to a rate lower than the minimum scale but even though the statute vested in the public employer the prerogative to pay a higher rate, to do so as a result of collective bargaining is not "in violation of, or inconsistent with, or in conflict with" the statute in question. The mere fact that the General Assembly granted the prerogative to the employer does not exclude the possibility that the decision to exercise that prerogative was influenced by the collective bargaining process. . . .

If, however, the General Assembly mandates a particular responsibility to be discharged by the board and the board alone, then the matter is removed from bargaining under Section 701 even if it has direct impact upon "wages, hours and other terms or conditions of employment." The removal from collective bargaining results not because it necessarily falls within the purview of Section 702 (in fact it may clearly be within the scope of Section 701), but rather because to do otherwise would be in direct violation of a statutory mandate and thus excluded under Section 703. . . .

We therefore conclude that items bargainable under Section 701 are only excluded under Section 703 where other applicable statutory provisions explicitly and definitively prohibit the public employer from making an agreement as to that specific term or condition of employment. . . .

We therefore remand the case to the Pennsylvania Labor Relations Board for further proceedings consistent herewith, granting leave to each party to modify and amend their position as they may wish. **So ordered.**

Bargaining and Open-Meeting Laws. Some states have adopted open-meeting, or "sunshine," laws that require meetings of public bodies be open to the public. Such laws may present a problem for collective bargaining by public employers, because they may allow members of the general public to take part in the bargaining process. In some states, such as Ohio, collective bargaining is exempted from the open-meeting law. In other states, however, the right of the public to participate in the bargaining is legally protected.

The following case involves the question of whether or not a school board can allow a teacher to comment, at a public meeting, on matters currently being negotiated with the teachers' union.

CITY OF MADISON JOINT SCHOOL DISTRICT NO. 8 v. WISCONSIN EMPLOYMENT RELATIONS COMM'N

429 U.S. 167 (Supreme Court of the United States, 1976)

BURGER, C. J.

The question presented on this appeal from the Supreme Court of Wisconsin is whether a State may constitutionally require that an elected board of education prohibit teachers, other than union representatives, to speak at open meetings, at which public participation is permitted, if such speech is addressed to the subject of pending collective-bargaining negotiations.

The Madison Board of Education and Madison Teachers, Inc. (MTI), a labor union, were parties to a collective-bargaining agreement during the calendar year of 1971. In January 1971 negotiations commenced for renewal of the agreement and MTI submitted a number of proposals. One among them called for the inclusion of a so-called "fair-share" clause, which would require all teachers, whether members of MTI or not, to pay union dues to defray the costs of collective bargaining. Wisconsin law expressly permits inclusion of "fair share" provisions in municipal employee collective-bargaining agreements. Another proposal presented by the union was a provision for binding arbitration of teacher dismissals. Both of these provisions were resisted by the school board. The negotiations deadlocked in November 1971 with a number of issues still unresolved, among them "fair share" and arbitration.

During the same month, two teachers, Holmquist and Reed, who were members of the bargaining unit, but not members of the union, mailed a letter to all teachers in the district expressing opposition to the "fair share" proposal. Two hundred teachers replied, most commenting favorably on Holmquist and Reed's position. Thereupon a petition was drafted calling for a one-year delay in the implementation of "fair share" while the proposal was more closely analyzed by an impartial committee. The petition was circulated to teachers in the district on December 6, 1971. Holmquist and Reed intended to present the results of their petition effort to the school board and the MTI at the school board's public meeting that same evening.

Because of the stalemate in the negotiations, MTI arranged to have pickets present at the school board meeting. In addition, 300 to 400 teachers attended in support of the union's position. During a portion of the meeting devoted to expression of opinion by the public, the president of MTI took the floor and spoke on the subject of the ongoing negotiations. He concluded his remarks by presenting to the board a petition signed by 1,300–1,400 teachers calling for the expeditious resolution of the negotiations. Holmquist was next given the floor, after John Matthews, the business representative of MTI, unsuccessfully attempted to dissuade him from speaking. Matthews had also spoken to a member of the school board before the meeting and requested that the board refuse to permit Holmquist to speak. Holmquist stated that he represented "an informal committee of 72 teachers in 49 schools" and that he desired to inform the board of education, as he had already informed the union, of the results of an informational survey concerning the "fair share" clause. He then read the petition which had been circulated to the teachers in the district that morning and stated that in the 31 schools from which reports have been received, 53 percent of the teachers had already signed the petition.

Holmquist stated that neither side had adequately addressed the issue of "fair share" and that teachers were confused about the meaning of the proposal. He concluded by saying: "Due to this confusion, we wish to take no stand on the proposal itself, but ask only that all alternatives be presented clearly to all teachers and more importantly to the general public to whom we are all responsible. We ask simply for communication, not confrontation." The sole response from the school board was a question by the president inquiring whether Holmquist intended to present the board with the petition. Holmquist answered that he would. Holmquist's presentation had lasted approximately 2½ minutes.

Later that evening, the board met in executive session and voted a proposal acceding to all of the union's demands with the exception of "fair share." During a negotiating session the following morning, MTI accepted the proposal and a contract was signed on December 14, 1971.

In January 1972, MTI filed a complaint with the Wisconsin Employment Relations Commission (WERC) claiming that the board had committed a prohibited labor practice by permitting Holmquist to speak at the Democratic 6 meeting. MTI claimed that in so doing the board had engaged in negotiations with a member of the bargaining unit other than the exclusive collective-bargaining representative, in violation of Wis. Stat. Sections 111.70(3)(a)(1),(4) (1973). Following a hearing the Commission concluded that the board was guilty of the prohibited labor practice and ordered that it "immediately cease and desist from permitting employees, other than representatives of Madison Teachers Inc., to appear and speak at meetings of the Board of Education, on matters subject to collective bargaining between it and Madison Teachers Inc." The Commission's action was affirmed by the Circuit Court of Dane County.

The Supreme Court of Wisconsin affirmed. The court recognized that both the Federal and State Constitutions protect freedom of speech and the right to petition the government, but noted that these rights may be abridged in the face of "a clear and present danger that [the speech] will bring about the substantive evils that [the legislature] has a right to prevent." The court held that abridgment of the speech in this case was justified in order "to avoid the dangers attendant upon relative chaos in labor management relations."

The Wisconsin court perceived "clear and present danger" based upon its conclusion that Holmquist's speech before the school board constituted "negotiation" with the board. Permitting such "negotiation," the court reasoned, would undermine the bargaining exclusivity guaranteed the majority union under Wis. Stat. Section 111.70(3)(a)(4) (1973). From that premise it concluded that teachers' First Amendment rights could be limited. Assuming, *arguendo,* that such a "danger" might in some circumstances justify some limitation of First Amendment rights, we are unable to read this record as presenting such danger as would justify curtailing speech.

The Wisconsin Supreme Court's conclusion that Holmquist's terse statement during the public meeting constituted negotiation with the board was based upon its adoption of the lower court's determination that, "[e]ven though Holmquist's statement superficially appears to be merely a "position statement," the court deems from the total circumstances that it constituted "'negotiating.'" This cryptic conclusion seems to ignore the ancient wisdom that calling a thing by a name does not make it so. Holmquist did not seek to bargain or offer to enter into any bargain with the board, nor does it appear that he was authorized by any other teachers to enter into any agreement on their behalf. Although his views were not consistent with those of MTI, communicating such views to the employer could not change the fact that MTI alone was authorized to negotiate and to enter into a contract with the board.

Moreover the school board meeting at which Holmquist was permitted to speak was open to the public. He addressed the school board not merely as one of its employees but also as a concerned citizen, seeking to express his views on an important decision of his government. We have held that teachers may not be "compelled to relinquish the First Amendment rights they would otherwise enjoy as citizens to comment on matters of public interest in connection with the operation of the public schools in which they work." . . . Where the State has opened a forum for direct citizen involvement, it is difficult to find justification for excluding teachers who make up the overwhelming proportion of school employees and who are most vitally concerned with the proceedings. It is conceded that any citizen could have presented precisely the same points and provided the board with the same information as did Holmquist.

Regardless of the extent to which true contract negotiations between a public body and its employees may be regulated—an issue we need not consider at this time—the participation in public discussion of public business cannot be confined to one category of interested individuals. To permit one side of a debatable public question to have a monopoly in expressing its views to the government is the antithesis of constitutional guarantees. Whatever its duties as an employer, when the board sits in public meetings to conduct public business and hear the views of citizens, it may not be required to discriminate between speakers on the basis of their employment, or the content of their speech. . . .

The WERC's order is not limited to a determination that a prohibited labor practice had taken place in the past; it also restrains future conduct. By prohibiting the school board from "permitting employees . . . to appear and speak at meetings of the Board of Education" the order constitutes an indirect, but effective, prohibition on persons such as Holmquist from communicating with their government. The order would have a substantial impact upon virtually all communication between teachers and the school board. The order prohibits speech by teachers "on matters subject to collective bargaining." As the dissenting opinion below noted, however, there is virtually no subject concerning the operation of the school system that could not also be characterized as a potential subject of collective bargaining.

Teachers not only constitute the overwhelming bulk of employees of the school system, but they are the very core of that system; restraining teachers' expressions to the board on matters involving the operation of the schools would seriously impair the board's ability to govern the district. . . .

The judgment of the Wisconsin Supreme Court is reversed, and the case is remanded to that court for further proceedings not inconsistent with this opinion. **Reversed and remanded.**

Impasse Resolution Procedure.

Because most state laws restrict or prohibit strikes by public employees, they must provide some alternative means for resolving bargaining impasses. Most statutes provide for a process that includes fact-finding, mediation, and ultimately, interest arbitration.

Mediation is generally the first step in the impasse resolution process; the mediator may be appointed by the PERB at the request of either party. The mediator attempts to offer suggestions and to reduce the number of issues in dispute.

If the mediation is unsuccessful, fact-finding is the second step. Each party presents its case to the fact-finder, who will issue a report defining the issues in dispute and establishing the reasonableness of the positions of each side. The fact-finder's report may be released to the public in an attempt to bring the pressure of public opinion upon the parties to force a settlement.

If no resolution is reached after mediation and fact-finding, the statutes generally provide for interest arbitration. The arbitration may be either voluntary or compulsory, and may be binding or nonbinding. Compulsory, binding arbitration is generally found in statutes dealing with employees who provide essential services, such as firefighters and police. Nonbinding arbitration awards may be disregarded by the public employer if it so chooses; binding arbitration awards bind both parties to the arbitrator's settlement of the dispute.

In several states, the arbitration of bargaining disputes has been challenged as being an illegal delegation of the public employer's legal authority to the arbitrator. Most state courts have upheld the legality of arbitration; examples are New York, Michigan, Minnesota, Maine, Washington, and Pennsylvania. In some states, however, courts have held compulsory arbitration to be illegal. Such was the case in Texas, South Dakota, Colorado, and Utah.

Some statutes allow for judicial review of arbitration awards, generally on grounds of whether the award is unreasonable, arbitrary, or capricious.

Strikes by State Workers.

Most state public sector labor relations statutes prohibit strikes by public employees. Other states, such as Pennsylvania, Michigan, Vermont, and Hawaii, allow strikes by employees whose jobs do not immediately affect the public health, safety, and welfare. Still other states allow for strikes in situations in which the public employer refuses to negotiate or to abide by an arbitration award.

Penalties for illegal strikes vary from state to state. New York's Taylor Law, which prohibits all strikes by public employees, provides for fines and loss of dues check-off provisions for unions involved in illegal strikes. Employees who participate in illegal strikes in New York may face probation, loss of job, and loss of pay. The court may issue injunctions or restraining orders against illegal strikes.

Disciplining public sector employees, even those who have taken part in illegal strikes, may pose constitutional problems for the public sector employer. The employer must ensure that any disciplinary procedure ensures the employees "due process," including adequate notice of and an opportunity to participate in a hearing on the proposed penalty.

QUESTIONS

1. In what ways does the role of government as employer raise constitutional issues not found in the private sector?

2. Which federal employees are covered by the FSLMRA? Which federal agencies are excluded from the act's coverage?

3. Which statutes govern labor relations of U.S. Postal Service employees?

4. How do union "consultation rights" under the FSLMRA differ from collective bargaining rights under the act?

5. What restrictions are placed on the scope of collective bargaining under the FSLMRA?

6. Which procedures are available for impasse settlement under the FSLMRA?

7. What sanctions are available against unions found to have committed unfair labor practices under the FSLMRA?

8. What legal issues are raised by union security clauses in the public sector? Explain why these issues arise.

9. To what extent may states restrict the right of state public employees to join unions? To what extent may the right of state public sector employees to bargain collectively be restricted?

CASE PROBLEMS

1. In April 1978 public employee Dorothea Yoggerst heard an unconfirmed report that her boss, the director of the Illinois Governor's Office of Management and Human Development, had been discharged. While still at work, she asked a co-worker, "Did you hear the good news?"

Yoggerst was orally reprimanded by her supervisor. Subsequently, a written memorandum of the reprimand was placed in her personnel file. Two months later she resigned her job, citing this alleged infringement of her First Amendment right of free speech as her reason for leaving. Yoggerst sued four defendants, including the supervisor who reprimanded her and the personnel director.

An earlier case heard by the Supreme Court, *Connick v. Myers,* involved the firing of a public employee for distributing to her co-workers a questionnaire that challenged the trustworthiness of her superiors. In that case, the high court enunciated a two-prong test: (1) Did the speech in question address a matter of

public concern? (2) How did the employee's right to speak her mind compare to the government's interest in efficient operations? The U.S. Court of Appeals applied this same test in the Yoggerst case.

How do you think the courts ruled in these two cases? See *Yoggerst* v. *Hedges and McDonough,* 739 F.2d 293 (7th Cir. 1984); *Connick* v. *Myers,* 461 U.S. 138 (1983).

2. The Toledo Police Patrolman's Association is the union representing the employees of the Toledo, Ohio, police department. Several police department employees objected to the amount of agency fees that they were required to pay because they reflected union political expenditures. The union had charged to objectors an agency fee that was equal to 100 percent of the regular union dues. The union claimed that its collective bargaining expenditures were $166,020 annually, whereas the dues collected amounted to only $162,138 annually; but the union refused to make its financial re-

cords available to the objecting employees. The employees filed suit in federal court, asking the court to order the union to provide financial information and to submit to an audit to verify the procedure used to determine the agency fees. How should the court rule on the employees' suit? See *Tierney v. City of Toledo*, 917 F.2d 927 (6th Cir. 1990).

3. The federal Department of Health and Human Services (H&HS) decided to institute a total ban on smoking in all of its facilities. The National Treasury Employees Union, which represents the H&HS employees, demands that the agency bargain with it over the decision. The agency refuses, arguing that the decision is not subject to bargaining under the FSLMRA. How should the Federal Labor Relations Authority rule on the union's claim? See *Dept. of Health and Human Services Family Support Admin. v. Federal Labor Relations Authority*, 920 F.2d 45 (D.C. Cir. 1990).

4. A group of twenty community college faculty instructors in Minnesota refused to join the Minnesota Community College Faculty Association. Under state law, faculty unions were given the *exclusive* right to engage in discussions with administrators about matters of academic policy. The twenty nonjoiners argued that this exclusive representation scheme violated principles of free speech and academic freedom enshrined in the First Amendment.

    How did the Supreme Court respond? See *Minn. State Bd. for Community Colleges v. Knight*, 465 U.S. 271 (1984).

5. Marjorie Rowland began working at Stebbins High School in Yellow Springs, Ohio, in August 1974. The school principal subsequently asked her to resign when it was learned that she had stated she was bisexual. When she refused, the school suspended her but was forced to rehire her by a preliminary injunction issued by a federal district judge. The administration assigned her to a job with no student contact, and when her contract expired, refused to renew it. Rowland sued.

    How do you think the court ruled in this case? See *Rowland v. Mad River Local School District*, 730 F.2d 444 (6th Cir. 1984).

6. On September 22, 1978, all eighteen employees of the public works, fire, and finance departments of the city of Gridley, California, went on strike, following the breakdown in negotiations over a new collective bargaining agreement. The city notified the union that it regarded the strike as illegal and immediately revoked the union's certification as collective bargaining representative. The city's labor relations officer notified the employees that they would be fired if they did not return to work at their next regular shift. The city council met in emergency session on a Saturday and voted to terminate the employees. On Sunday the union notified the city that all employees would return to their jobs on Monday. The city refused to reinstate them.

    Although the city council had earlier declared that "participation by any employee in a strike . . . is unlawful and shall subject the employee to disciplinary action, up to and including discharge," the union challenged Gridley's actions on the basis that (1) the discharged employees had been entitled to a hearing, and (2) the sanction of revoking recognition was noncontrary to the purpose of California's public employee relations laws, that is, to permit the employees to have responsibilities of their own choosing.

    The case reached the California Supreme Court. How do you think the court ruled? See *IBEW Local 1245 v. City of Gridley*, 34 Cal. 3d 191 (Supr. Ct. Cal. 1983).

7. Student Services Inc. was a nonprofit organization that operated a bookstore, bowling alley, vending machines, and other services at Edinboro State College in Pennsylvania. The Retail Clerks Union filed a petition with the Pennsylvania Labor Relations Board, seeking a Public Employees Relations Act. After several hearings, an election was held and the union won. The board subsequently certified the union.

    The company challenged the board's jurisdiction, stating that it was not a part of the state college and therefore was a private employer covered by the NLRA. The bookstore, bowling alley, and other services were housed rent-free in a building owned by the Commonwealth of Pennsylvania and situated on the college campus. Pennsylvania law defines a "public employer" in pertinent part as "any nonprofit organization or institution and any charitable, religious, scientific, literary, recreational, health, educational or welfare institution receiving grants or appropriations from local, State or Federal governments."

    How should the court have ruled on Student Services' status? See *In the Matter of Employees of Student Services, Inc.*, 411 A.2d 569 (Pa. Super. 1980).

8. The CFC is an annual charitable fund-raising drive conducted in the federal workplace during working hours largely through the voluntary efforts of federal em-

ployees. Participating organizations confine their fund-raising activities to a thirty-word statement submitted by them for inclusion in the campaign literature.

Volunteer federal employees distribute to their co-workers literature describing the campaign and the participants, along with pledge cards. Designated funds are paid directly to the specified recipient.

The CFC is a relatively recent idea. Prior to 1957, charitable solicitation in the federal workplace occurred on an ad hoc basis. Federal managers received requests from dozens of organizations seeking endorsements and the right to solicit contributions from federal employees at their work sites. In facilities where solicitation was permitted, weekly campaigns were commonplace.

In 1957 President Eisenhower established the forerunner of the Combined Federal Campaign to bring order to the solicitation process and to ensure truly voluntary giving by federal employees. The order established an advisory committee and set forth general procedures and standards for a uniform fund-raising program. It permitted no more than three charitable solicitations annually and established a system requiring prior approval by a committee on fund-raising for participation by "voluntary health and welfare" agencies.

A number of organizations joined in challenging these criteria, including the NAACP Legal Defense and Educational Fund, Inc., the Sierra Club Legal Defense Fund, the Puerto Rican Legal Defense and Education Fund, the Federally Employed Women Legal Defense and Education Fund, the Indian Law Resource Center, the Lawyers Committee for Civil Rights under Law, and the Natural Resources Defense Council. Each of the groups attempts to influence public policy through one or more of the following means: political activity, advocacy, lobbying, and litigation on behalf of others.

On what grounds did these organizations challenge the regulations? How do you think the Supreme Court ruled? See *Cornelius* v. *NAACP Legal Defense and Educational Fund,* 473 U.S. 788 (1985).

9. The Indianapolis city government pressed theft charges against a former employee, Michael McGraw, when his supervisor discovered that he had used the computer to keep customers' lists and payment records for his private business—the sale to co-workers and others of "Nature-Slim," a liquid diet supplement for people who want to lose weight.

The city decided to press charges for theft after it was unsuccessful in blocking McGraw's application for unemployment compensation benefits. The discharge of McGraw was not related to the alleged misuse of the computer. A jury convicted McGraw on two counts of theft.

The state criminal code defines a thief in the following terms: "A person who knowingly or intentionally exerts unauthorized control over property of another person with intent to deprive the other of any part of its value, or use, commits theft, a class D felony."

Should McGraw's conviction be permitted to stand? Suppose the conviction is overturned? Should he be reinstated? See *Indiana* v. *McGraw,* 480 N.E. 2d 552 (Indiana Supr. Ct. 1985).

10. The legislature of the state of Iowa, concerned about the proliferation of drugs in American society and their alleged availability even inside the nation's prisons, passed a law allowing prison officials to conduct random blood and urinalysis tests on state correction officers. The law allowed testing without any reasonable suspicion that the officers to be tested were in fact users or under the influence of any controlled substance. A total of 1,750 officers filed a class action suit, challenging the law as a search and seizure without a warrant and as a violation of their due process rights.

How should the federal court rule? See *McDonell* v. *Hunter,* 809 F.2d 1302 (8th Cir. 1987).

Equal
Employment
Opportunity

C H A P T E R 12

Equal Employment Opportunity: Title VII of the Civil Rights Act and Race Discrimination

IDEALLY, EMPLOYERS SHOULD HIRE those employees best qualified for the particular job being filled; an employee should be selected because of his or her ability to perform the job. Determining the qualifications required for the job, however, may be difficult. In fact, required qualifications that have no relationship to job performance may disqualify prospective employees who are capable of performing satisfactorily. As well, some employers may be influenced in their selection of employees by their biases—conscious or unconscious—regarding certain groups of people. All of these factors are part of the problem of discrimination in employment.

Discrimination in employment, whether intentional or unintentional, has been a major concern of many people who believe that our society has not lived up to its ideals of equality of opportunity for all people. The glaring inequities in our society sparked violent protests during the civil rights movement of the 1960s. African Americans, Hispanic Americans, and Native Americans constituted a disproportionate share of those living in poverty. Women of all races and colors found their access to challenging and well-paying jobs limited; they were frequently channeled into lower-paying occupations traditionally viewed as "women's work."

To help remedy these problems of discrimination, Congress passed the Civil Rights Act of 1964, which was signed into law by President Johnson on July 2, 1964. The Civil Rights Act was aimed at discrimination in a number of areas of our society—housing, public accommodation, education, and employment. Title VII of the Civil Rights Act deals with discrimination in employment. It became the foundation of modern federal equal employment opportunity (EEO) law.

Title VII was amended in 1968, 1972, and 1991. The most recent amendments, made by the Civil Rights Act of 1991, were substantial, and were intended to reverse several Supreme Court decisions that were perceived as making it more difficult for plaintiffs to bring suit under Title VII. The amendments, signed into law by President Bush in November 1991, had been the subject of a bitter political dispute between President Bush and the Democrat-controlled Congress. An earlier version of the amendments, passed by Congress in 1990, had been vetoed by President Bush. The political pressures of the upcoming 1992 election and the wish to dissociate himself from the extreme conservative and former Ku Klux Klan member, David Duke, forced President Bush to approve the 1991 amendments.

This section of the book will focus on the statutory provisions requiring equal opportunity in employment. Chapter 12 ideals with the provisions of Title VII, as amended, prohibiting employment discrimination based on race. Chapter 13 will discuss the Title VII provisions regarding employment discrimination based on sex, religion, and national origin. Chapter 14 will discuss the procedures involved in Title VII enforcement actions. Lastly, Chapter 15 will discuss other EEO legislation such as the Equal Pay Act, the Age Discrimination in Employment Act, and state EEO laws.

Coverage of Title VII

Title VII of the Civil Rights Act of 1964 took effect on July 2, 1965. It prohibits the refusal or failure to hire, the discharge of any individual, or the discrimination against any individual with respect to compensation, terms, conditions, or privileges of employment because of that individual's race, color, religion, sex, or national origin.

Title VII, as amended, applies to employers, labor unions, and employment agencies. An employer under Title VII is defined as being a person, partnership, corporation, or other entity engaged in an industry affecting commerce that has fifteen or more employees. State and local governments are also covered by Title VII, but the federal government and wholly owned U.S. government corporations are not. (They are covered under separate provisions of Title VII and federal Civil Service Regulations.) Title VII does not apply to tax-exempt bona fide private membership clubs. The 1991 amendments to Title VII extended the coverage of the act to American employers that employ U.S. citizens abroad; foreign corporations that are controlled by American employers are also covered with regard to employment of U.S. citizens. For such employers, compliance with Title VII is not required if such compliance would force the employer to violate the law of the country where the workplace is located. The effect of this amendment is to overturn the Supreme Court decision in *EEOC* v. *Arabian American Oil Co.* (__U.S.__ , 111 S. Ct. 1227, 1991).

Labor unions with at least fifteen members, or that operate a hiring hall, are subject to Title VII. Unions are prohibited from discriminating in employment opportunities or status against their members or applicants on the basis of race, color, religion, sex, or national origin. Employment agencies violate Title VII by discriminating in announcing openings, interviewing applicants, or in referring applicants to employers.

Administration of Title VII

Title VII is administered by the Equal Employment Opportunity Commission (EEOC), a five-member commission appointed by the president, along with the commission's Office of General Counsel. The EEOC is empowered to issue binding regulations and nonbinding guidelines in its responsibility for administering and enforcing the act. Although the EEOC generally responds to complaints of discrimination filed by individuals, it can also initiate an action on its own if it finds a "pattern or practice" of discrimination in employment.

The regulations and guidelines under Title VII require that employers, unions, and employment agencies post EEOC notices summarizing the act's requirements. Failure to display such notices is punishable by a fine of not more than $100 per violation. The act further requires that those covered keep records relevant to the determination of whether unlawful employment practices have been, or are being, committed. Covered employers must maintain payroll records and other records relating to applicants and to employee promotion, demotion, transfer, and discharge.

The act does allow an employer to select employees on the basis of sex, religion, or national origin when the employer can establish that being of a particular sex, religion, or national origin is a **bona fide occupational qualification (BFOQ)**. In order to establish that a particular characteristic is a BFOQ, the employer must demonstrate that business necessity—the safe and efficient operation of the business—requires that employees be of a particular sex, religion, or national origin. (BFOQs will be discussed in more detail later in the next chapter.) The act recognizes BFOQs only on the basis of sex, religion, and national origin; race and color can never be used as BFOQs.

Discrimination under Title VII

It should be clear from the provisions of Section 703 that Title VII prohibits intentional discrimination in employment on the basis of race, color, religion, sex, or national origin. An employer who refuses to hire African Americans, or who will only hire women for particular positions rather than all production jobs, is in violation of Title VII. Likewise, a union that will not accept Hispanic Americans as members, or that maintains separate seniority lists for male and female members, violates the act. Such intentional discrimination is also called **disparate treatment**—that is, the particular employee is subject to different treatment because of that employee's race, sex, or national origin.

In the years immediately following the passage of Title VII, some people believed that the act was intended to protect only minority or female employees. This issue came before the Supreme Court in the 1976 case of *McDonald* v. *Santa Fe Trail Transportation Co.* (427 U.S. 273). Three employees of a trucking company were caught stealing cargo from the company. Two of the employees, who were white, were discharged; the third, an African American, was given a suspension but was not discharged. The employer justified the difference in disciplinary penalties on the ground that Title VII protected the African American employee. The white employees filed suit under Title VII. The Supreme Court emphasized that Title VII protects all employees; every individual employee is to be protected from any discrimination in employment because of race, color, sex, religion, and national origin. The employer had treated the white employees differently because of their race, and the employer was therefore in violation of Title VII.

Unintentional Discrimination—Disparate Impact

Although it should be clear that intentional discrimination in employment on the basis of race, religion, sex, color, or national origin (the "prohibited grounds") is prohibited, what about unintentional discrimination? An employer may specify certain requirements for a job that operates to disqualify otherwise capable prospective employees. Although the employer is allowed to hire those employees best able to do the job, what happens if the specified requirements do not actually relate to the employee's ability to perform the job but do have the effect of disqualifying a large proportion of minority applicants? Such a discriminatory effect of apparently neutral requirements is known as a **disparate impact.** Should the disparate impact of such neutral job requirements be prohibited under Title VII?

Frequently, the neutral requirement at issue may be a test used by the employer to screen applicants for a job. Title VII does allow the use of employment testing. Section 703(h) provides, in part,

> ... [i]t shall not be an unlawful employment practice for an employer to give and act upon the results of any professionally developed ability test provided that such test, its administration or action upon the results is not designed, intended or is used to discriminate because of race, color, religion, sex, or national origin.

The effect of that provision and the legality of job requirements that have a disparate impact were considered by the Supreme Court in the following case.

GRIGGS v. DUKE POWER COMPANY

401 U.S. 424 (Supreme Court of the United States, 1971)

BURGER, C. J.

We granted the writ in this case to resolve the question whether an employer is prohibited by the Civil Rights Act, Title VII, from requiring a high school education or passing of a standardized general intelligence test as a condition of employment in or transfer to jobs when (a) neither standard is shown to be significantly related to successful job performance, (b) both requirements operate to disqualify

Negroes at a substantially higher rate than white applicants, and (c) the jobs in question formerly had been filled only by white employees as part of a long-standing practice of giving preference to whites.

... The District Court found that prior to July 2, 1965, the effective date of the Civil Rights Act of 1964, the Company openly discriminated on the basis of race in the hiring and assigning of employees at its Dan River plant. The plant was organized into five operating departments: (1) Labor, (2) Coal Handling, (3) Operations, (4) Maintenance, and (5) Laboratory and Test. Negroes were employed only in the Labor Department where the highest paying jobs paid less than the lowest paying jobs in the other four "operating" departments in which only whites were employed. Promotions were normally made within each department on the basis of job seniority. Transferees into a department usually began in the lowest position.

In 1955 the Company instituted a policy of requiring a high school education for initial assignment to any department except Labor, and for transfer from the Coal Handling to any "inside" department (Operations, Maintenance, or Laboratory). When the company abandoned its policy of restricting Negroes to the Labor Department in 1965, completion of high school was also made a prerequisite to transfer from Labor to any other department. From the time the high school requirement was instituted to the time of trial, however, white employees hired before the time of the high school education requirement continued to perform satisfactorily and achieve promotions in the "operating" departments. Findings on this score are not challenged.

The Company added a further requirement for new employees on July 2, 1965, the date on which Title VII became effective. To qualify for placement in any but the Labor Department it became necessary to register satisfactory scores on two professionally prepared aptitude tests, as well as to have a high school education. Completion of high school alone continued to render employees eligible for transfer to the four desirable departments from which Negroes had been excluded if the incumbent had been employed prior to the time of the new requirement. In September 1965 the Company began to permit incumbent employees who lacked a high school education to qualify for transfer from Labor or Coal Handling to an "inside" job by passing two tests—the Wonderlic Personnel Test which purports to measure general intelligence, and the Bennett Mechanical Aptitude Test. Neither was directed or intended to measure the ability to learn to perform a particular job or category of jobs. The requisite scores used for both initial hiring and transfer approximated the national median for high school graduates.

The District Court had found that while the Company previously followed a policy of overt racial discrimination in a period prior to the Act, such conduct had ceased. The District Court also concluded that Title VII was intended to be prospective only and, consequently, the impact of prior inequities was beyond the reach of corrective action authorized by the Act.

The Court of Appeals was confronted with a question of first impression, as are we, concerning the meaning of Title VII. After careful analysis a majority of that court concluded

that a subjective test of the employer's intent should govern, particularly in a close case, and that in this case there was no showing of a discriminatory purpose in the adoption of the diploma and test requirements. On this basis, the Court of Appeals concluded that was no violation of the Act.

The Court of Appeals reversed the District Court in part, rejecting the holding that residual discrimination arising from prior employment practices was insulated from remedial action. The Court of Appeals noted, however, that the District Court was correct in its conclusion that there was no finding of a racial purpose of invidious intent in the adoption of the high school diploma requirement or general intelligence test and that these standards had been applied fairly to whites and Negroes alike. It held that, in the absence of a discriminatory purpose, use of such requirements was permitted by the Act. In so doing, the Court of Appeals rejected the claim that because these two requirements operated to render ineligible a markedly disproportionate number of Negroes, they were unlawful under Title VII unless shown to be job-related.

. . . The objective of Congress in the enactment of Title VII is plain from the language of the statute. It was to achieve equality of employment opportunities and remove barriers that have operated in the past to favor an identifiable group of white employees over other employees. Under the Act, practices, procedures, or tests neutral on their face, and even neutral in terms of intent, cannot be maintained if they operate to "freeze" the status quo of prior discriminatory employment practices.

The Court of Appeals' opinion, and the partial dissent, agreed that, on the record in the present case, "whites fare far better on the Company's alternative requirements" than Negroes. This consequence would appear to be directly traceable to race. Basic intelligence must have the means of articulation to manifest itself fairly in a testing process. Because they are Negroes, petitioners have long received inferior education in segregated schools and this Court expressly recognized these differences in *Gaston County* v. *United States* (1969). There, because of the inferior education received by Negroes in North Carolina, this Court barred the institution of a literary test for voter registration on the ground that the test would abridge the right to vote indirectly on account of race. Congress did not intend by Title VII, however, to guarantee a job to every person regardless of qualifications. In short, the Act does not command that any person be hired simply because he was formerly the subject of discrimination, or because he is a member of a minority group. Discriminatory preference for any group, minority or majority, is precisely and only what Congress had proscribed. What is required by Congress is the removal of artificial, arbitrary, and unnecessary barriers to employment when the barriers operate invidiously to discriminate on the basis of racial or other impermissible classification.

Congress has now provided that tests or criteria for employment or promotion may not provide equality of opportunity only in the sense of the fabled offer of milk to the stork and the fox. On the contrary, Congress has now required that the posture and condition of the job seeker be taken into account. It has—to resort again to the fable—provided that the vessel in which the milk is proffered be one all seekers can use. The Act proscribes not only overt discrimination but also practices that are fair in form, but discriminatory in operation. The touchstone is business necessity. If an employment practice which operates to exclude Negroes cannot be shown to be related to the job performance, the practice is prohibited.

On the record before us, neither the high school completion requirement nor the general intelligence test is shown to bear a demonstrable relationship to successful performance of the jobs for which it was used. Both were adopted, as the Court of Appeals noted, without meaningful study of their relationship to job-performance ability. Rather, a vice president of the Company testified, the requirements were instituted on the Company's judgment that they generally would improve the overall quality of the work force.

The evidence, however, shows that employees who have not completed high school or taken the tests have continued to perform satisfactorily and make progress in departments for which the high school and test criteria are now used. The promotion record of present employees who would not be able to meet the new criteria thus suggests the possibility that the requirements may not be needed even for the limited purpose of preserving the avowed policy of advancement within the Company. In the context of this case, it is unnecessary to reach the question whether testing requirements that take into account capability for the next succeeding position or related future promotion might be utilized upon a showing that such long range requirements fulfill a genuine business need. In the present case the Company has made no such showing.

The Court of Appeals held that the Company had adopted the diploma and test requirements without any "intention to discriminate against Negro employees." We do not suggest that either the District Court or the Court of Appeals erred in examining the employer's intent; but good intent or absence of discriminatory intent does not redeem employment procedures or testing mechanisms that operate as "built-in headwinds" for minority groups and are unrelated to measuring job capability.

The Company's lack of discriminatory intent is suggested by special efforts to help the under-educated employees through Company financing of two-thirds the cost of tuition for high school training. But Congress directed the thrust of the Act to the *consequences* of employment practices, not simply the motivation. More than that, Congress has placed on the employer the burden of showing that any given requirement must have a manifest relationship to the employment in question.

The facts of this case demonstrate the inadequacy of broad and general testing devices as well as the infirmity of using diplomas or degrees as fixed measures of capability. History is filled with examples of men and women who rendered highly effective performance without the conventional badges of accomplishment in terms of certificates, diplomas, or degrees. Diplomas and tests are useful servants, but Congress had mandated the common-sense proposition that they are not to become masters of reality.

. . . Nothing in the Act precludes the use of testing or measuring procedures; obviously they are useful. What Congress has forbidden is giving these devices and mechanisms controlling force unless they are demonstrably a reasonable measure of job performance. Congress has not commanded that the less qualified be preferred over the better qualified simply because of minority origins. Far from disparaging job qualifications as such, Congress has made such qualifications the controlling factor, so that race, religion, nationality, and sex become irrelevant. What Congress has commanded is that any test used must measure the person for the job and not the person in the abstract.

The judgment of the Court of Appeals is, as to that portion of the judgment appealed from, reversed. **So ordered.**

As *Griggs* held, the use of apparently neutral job requirements that have a disparate impact on applicants or employees of a particular race, color, sex, religion, or national origin (a "protected group" under Title VII) is prohibited by Title VII unless those requirements are job-related. The job requirements in *Griggs* were both objective criteria: having a high school diploma or getting a passing score on a particular test. *Griggs* did not consider whether an employment-selection process that relied on subjective criteria, such as the judgment of supervisors after interviewing job candidates, could be challenged using disparate impact analysis. In *Watson* v. *Fort Worth Bank & Trust* (487 U.S. 977, 1988), the Supreme Court held that subjective employment-selection practices were also subject to disparate impact analysis.

In *Wards Cove Packing Co.* v. *Antonio* (490 U.S. 642, 1989), the Supreme Court held that the plaintiff is responsible for identifying the specific employment practice allegedly causing the disparate impact. The 1991 amendments to Title VII added Section 703(k), which deals with disparate impact claims. Section 703(k) requires that the plaintiff demonstrate that the employer uses a particular employment practice that causes a disparate impact on one of the bases prohibited by Title VII. If such a showing is made, the employer must then demonstrate that the practice is job-related for the position in question, and is consistent with business necessity. Even if the employer makes such a showing, if the plaintiff can demonstrate that an alternative employment practice—one without a disparate impact—is available, and the employer refuses to adopt it, the employer is still in violation of the act. Section 703(k) states that a plaintiff shall demonstrate that each particular employment practice that is challenged causes a disparate impact, unless the plaintiff can demonstrate that the elements of the decision-making process are not capable of separation for analysis. If the employer demonstrates that the challenged practice does not have a disparate impact, then there is no need to show that the practice is required by business necessity. Work rules that bar the employment of individuals using or possessing illegal drugs are exempt from disparate impact analysis; such rules violate Title VII only when they are adopted or applied with an intention to discriminate on grounds prohibited by Title VII.

If the employment practice at issue is shown to be sufficiently job-related, and the plaintiff has not shown that alternative practices without a disparate impact are available, then the employer may continue to use the challenged employment practice because it is necessary to perform the job. Nothing in Title VII prohibits an employer from hiring only those persons who are capable of doing the job. The 1991 amendments to Title VII added a provision (Section 703(k)(2)) stating that a demonstration that an employment practice is required by business necessity may not be used as a defense to a claim of intentional discrimination under Title VII.

The Uniform Guidelines on Employee Selection

How can a plaintiff demonstrate a claim of disparate impact? How can an employer demonstrate that a requirement is job-related? The **Uniform Guidelines on Employee Selection Procedures,** a series of regulations adopted by the EEOC and other federal agencies, provide some answers to those questions.

Showing a Disparate Impact

The Supreme Court held in *Watson* v. *Fort Worth Bank & Trust* that a plaintiff must "offer statistical evidence of a kind and degree sufficient to show that the practice in question has caused the exclusion of applicants for jobs or promotions because of their membership in a protected group. In *Wards Cove Packing Co. v. Antonio* (490 U.S. 642, 1989), the Supreme Court described one way to demonstrate that hiring practices had a disparate impact on non-whites by comparing the employer's work force with the labor market from which applicants are drawn:

> The "proper comparison [is] between the racial composition of [the at-issue jobs] and the racial composition of the qualified . . . population in the relevant labor market." It is such a comparison—between the racial composition of the qualified persons in the labor market and the persons holding at-issue jobs—that generally forms the proper basis for the initial inquiry in a disparate impact case. Alternatively, in cases where such labor market statistics will be difficult if not impossible to ascertain, we have recognized that certain other statistics—such as measures indicating the racial composition of "otherwise-qualified applicants" for at-issue jobs—are equally probative for this purpose.

The Uniform Guidelines, adopted before the *Watson* and *Wards Cove* decisions, set out another way to demonstrate the disparate impact of a job requirement.

That procedure, known as the **Four-Fifths Rule**, compares the selection rates (the rates at which applicants meet the requirements or pass the test) for the various protected groups under Title VII. The Four-Fifths Rule states that a disparate impact will be demonstrated when the proportion of applicants from the protected group with the lowest selection rate (or pass rate) is less that 80 percent of the selection rate (pass rate) of the group with the highest selection rate.

For example, a municipal fire department requires that applicants for firefighter positions be at least five feet, six inches tall and weigh at least 130 pounds. Of the applicants for the positions, five of twenty (25 percent) of the Hispanic applicants meet the requirement, while thirty of forty (75 percent) of the white applicants meet the requirements. To determine whether the height and weight requirements have a disparate impact on Hispanics, the pass rate for Hispanics is divided by the pass rate for whites. Since .25/.75 = .33, or 33 percent, a disparate impact according to the Four-Fifths Rule exists. Stating the rule in equation form, disparate impact exists when:

$$\frac{\text{Pass rate for group with lowest pass rate}}{\text{Pass rate for group with highest pass rate}} < .80$$

Using the numbers from our example:

$$\frac{.25 \ (\text{Hispanic pass rate})}{.75 \ (\text{White pass rate})} = .33; \ .33 < .80$$

Therefore, a disparate impact exists, establishing a prima facie case of employment discrimination. To continue using such a test, the employer must satisfy the court that the test is sufficiently job-related.

Validating Job Requirements

The fire department must demonstrate that the height and weight requirements are job-related in order to continue using them in selecting employees. The Uniform

Guidelines provide several methods to show that the height and weight requirements are job-related. The Uniform Guidelines also require a showing of a statistical correlation demonstrating that the requirements are necessary for successful job performance. In our example, the fire department would have to show that the minimum height and weight requirements screen out those applicants who would be unable to perform safely and efficiently the tasks or duties of a firefighter.

When the job requirements involve passing an examination, it must be shown that a passing score on the exam has a high statistical correlation with successful job performance. The Uniform Guidelines set out standards for demonstrating such a correlation (known as test validity) developed by the American Psychological Association. The standards may be classified into three types: content validity, construct validity, and criterion-related validity.

Content Validity.
Content validity is a means of measuring whether the requirement or test actually evaluates abilities required on the job. The fire department using the height and weight requirements would have to show that the requirements actually determine abilities needed to do the job—that anyone shorter than five feet, six inches or weighing less than 130 pounds would be unable to do the job. That would be difficult to do; but in order to validate the requirements as job-related, such a showing is required by the Uniform Guidelines. If the job of firefighter requires physical strength, then using a strength test as a selection device would be valid. (Height and weight requirements are sometimes used instead of a physical strength test, but they are much more difficult to validate than strength tests.) For the job of a typist, a spelling and typing test would likely have a high content validity, since those tests measure abilities actually needed on the job. A strength test for typists, on the other hand, would have a low content validity rating since physical strength has little relationship to typing performance. The Uniform Guidelines set out statistical methods to demonstrate the relationship (if any) of the requirements to job performance. An employer seeking to validate such requirements must follow the procedures and conditions in the Uniform Guidelines.

Construct Validity.
Construct validity is a means of isolating and testing for specific traits or characteristics that are deemed essential for job performance. Such traits, or constructs, may be based on observations but cannot be measured directly. For example, a teacher may be required to possess the construct "patience," or an executive may be required to possess "judgment." Such traits or constructs cannot be measured directly, but they may be observed based on simulations of actual job situations. The Uniform Guidelines set out procedures and methods for demonstrating that certain constructs are really necessary to the job, and that means used to test for or identify these constructs actually do measure them.

Criterion-Related Validity.
Criterion-related validity is concerned with the statistical correlation between scores received on tests ("paper-and-pencil" tests) and job performance. An employer who administers an IQ test to prospective employees must establish that there is a high statistical correlation between successful perform-

ance on the test and successful performance on the job. That correlation may be established by giving the test to current employees and comparing their test scores with their job performance; the correlation coefficient so produced is then used to predict the job performance of other current or prospective employees taking the same test. The Uniform Guidelines provide specific procedures and requirements for demonstrating the criterion-related validity of tests used for employment selection. Failure to comply with the requirements of the Uniform Guidelines will prevent an employer from establishing that a test is job-related. If the test has not been validated, its use for employment purposes will violate Title VII, if such a test has a disparate impact. Furthermore, a test validated for one group, such as Hispanic Americans, may have to be separately validated for one or more other groups—for example, African Americans or Asian Americans.

The "Bottom Line" and Discrimination

Does the fact that an employer's work force contains a higher percentage of minority employees than does the general population of the surrounding area serve to insulate the employer from claims of discrimination in employment? The following case involves a similar issue—should the fact that an employer has promoted a greater percentage of minority employees than nonminorities constitute a defense to the claim of discrimination by minority employees? The employer argues that the "bottom line"—the number of minority employees promoted—disproves any claim of discrimination. The claimants argue that the employer used a discriminatory exam (one with a disparate impact on minorities) to select those eligible for promotion. Was Title VII violated?

CONNECTICUT v. TEAL

457 U.S. 440 (Supreme Court of the United States, 1982)

BRENNAN, J.

We consider here whether an employer sued for violation of Title VII of the Civil Rights Act of 1964 may assert a "bottom line" theory of defense. Under that theory, as asserted in this case, an employer's acts of racial discrimination in promotions—effected by an examination having disparate impact—would not render the employer liable for the racial discrimination suffered by employees barred from promotion if the "bottom line" result of the promotional process was an appropriate racial balance. . . .

Four of the respondents, Winnie Teal, Rose Walker, Edith Latney, and Grace Clark, are black employees of the Department of Income Maintenance of the State of Connecticut. Each was promoted provisionally to the position of Welfare

Eligibility Supervisor and served in that capacity for almost two years. To attain permanent status as supervisors, however, respondents had to participate in a selection process that required, as the first step, a passing score on a written examination. This written test was administered on December 2, 1978, to 329 candidates. Of these candidates, 48 identified themselves as black and 259 identified themselves as white. The results of the examination were announced in March 1979. With the passing score set at 65, 54.17 percent of the identified black candidates passed. This was approximately 68 percent of the passing rate for the identified white candidates. The four respondents were among the blacks who failed the examination, and they were thus excluded from further consideration for permanent supervisory positions. In April 1979, respondents instituted this action in the United States District Court for the District of Connecticut against petitioners, the State of Connecticut, two state agencies, and two state officials. Respondents alleged, *inter alia,* that petitioners violated Title VII by imposing, as an absolute condition for consideration for promotion, that applicants pass a written test that excluded blacks in disproportionate numbers and that was not job related.

More than a year after this action was instituted, and approximately one month before trial, petitioners made promotions from the eligibility list generated by the written examination. In choosing persons from that list, petitioners considered past work performance, recommendations of the candidates' supervisors and, to a lesser extent, seniority. Petitioners then applied what the Court of Appeals characterized as an affirmative action program in order to ensure a significant number of minority supervisors. Forty-six persons were promoted to permanent supervisory positions, 11 of whom were black and 35 of whom were white. The overall result of the selection process was that, of the 48 identified black candidates who participated in the selection process, 22.9 percent were promoted and of the 259 identified white candidates, 13.5 percent were promoted. It is this "bottom-line" result, more favorable to blacks than to whites, that petitioners urge should be adjudged to be a complete defense to respondents' suit.

After trial, the District Court entered judgment for petitioners. The court treated respondents' claim as one of disparate impact under *Griggs* v. *Duke Power Co.* However, the court found that, although the comparative passing rates for the examination indicated a prima facie case of adverse impact upon minorities, the result of the entire hiring process reflected no such adverse impact. Holding that these "bottom-line" percentages precluded the finding of a Title VII violation, the court held that the employer was not required to demonstrate that the promotional examination was job related. The United States Court of Appeals for the Second Circuit reversed, holding that the District Court erred in ruling that the results of the written examination alone were insufficient to support a prima facie case of disparate impact in violation of Title VII. The Court of Appeals stated that where "an identifiable pass-fail barrier denies an employment opportunity to a disproportionately large number of minorities and prevents them from proceeding to the next step in the selection process," that barrier must be shown to be job related. We granted certiorari. . . .

We must first decide whether an examination that bars a disparate number of black employees from consideration for promotion, and that has not been shown to be job related, presents a claim cognizable under Title VII. Section 703(a)(2) of Title VII provides in pertinent part:

It shall be an unlawful employment practice for an employer—. . .

(2) to limit, segregate, or classify his employees or applicants for employment in any way which would deprive or tend to deprive any individual of employment opportunities or otherwise adversely affect his status as an employee, because of such individual's race, color, religion, sex, or national origin.

Respondents base their claim on our construction of this provision in *Griggs* v. *Duke Power Co.*

Griggs and its progeny have established a three-part analysis of disparate impact claims. To establish a prima facie case of discrimination, a plaintiff must show that the facially neutral employment practice had a significantly discriminatory impact. If that showing is made, the employer must then demonstrate that "any given requirement [has] a manifest relationship to the employment in question," in order to avoid a finding of discrimination. Even in such a case, however, the plaintiff may prevail, if he shows that employer was using the practice as a mere pretext for discrimination.

Petitioners' examination, which barred promotion and had a discriminatory impact on black employees, clearly falls within the literal language of Section 703(a)(2), as interpreted by *Griggs.* The statute speaks, not in terms of jobs and promotions, but in terms of *limitations* and *classifications* that would deprive any individual of employment *opportunities.* A disparate impact claim reflects the language of Section 703(a)(2) and Congress' basic objectives in enacting that statute: "to achieve equality of employment *opportunities* and remove barriers that have operated in the past to favor an identifiable group of white employees over other employees." When an employer uses a nonjob-related barrier in order to deny a minority or woman applicant employment or promotion, and that barrier has a significant adverse effect on minorities or women, then the applicant has been deprived of an employment *opportunity* "because of . . . race, color, religion, sex, or national origin." In other words, Section 703(a)(2) prohibits discriminatory "artificial, arbitrary, and unnecessary barriers to employment," that "limit . . . or classify . . . applicants for employment . . . in any way which would deprive or tend to deprive any individual of employment *opportunities.*"

Relying on Section 703(a)(2), *Griggs* explicitly focused on employment "practices, procedures, or tests," that deny equal employment "opportunity." We concluded that Title VII prohibits "procedures or testing mechanisms that operate as 'built-in headwinds' for minority groups." We found that Congress' primary purpose was the prophylactic one of achieving equality of employment "opportunities" and removing "barriers" to such equality. The examination given to respondents in this case surely constituted such a practice and created such a barrier.

Our conclusion that Section 703(a)(2) encompasses respondents' claim is reinforced by the terms of Congress' 1972 extension of the protections of Title VII to state and municipal employees. Although Congress did not explicitly consider the viability of the defense offered by the state employer in this case, the 1972 amendments to Title VII do reflect Congress' intent to provide state and municipal employees with the protection that Title VII, as interpreted by *Griggs,* had provided to employees in the private sector: equality of *opportunity* and the elimination of discriminatory *barriers* to professional development. The committee reports and the floor debates stressed the need for equality of opportunity for minority applicants seeking to obtain governmental positions. Congress voiced its concern about the widespread use by state and local governmental agencies of "invalid selection techniques" that had a discriminatory impact.

The decisions of this Court following *Griggs* also support respondents' claim. In considering claims of disparate impact under Section 703(a)(2) this Court has consistently focused on employment and promotion requirements that create a discriminatory bar to *opportunities.* This Court has never read Section 703(a)(2) as requiring the focus to be placed instead on the overall number of minority or female applicants actually hired or promoted. . . .

In short, the District Court's dismissal of respondents' claim cannot be supported on the basis that respondents failed to establish a prima facie case of employment discrimination under the terms of Section 703(a)(2). The suggestion that disparate impact should be measured only at the bottom line ignores the fact that Title VII guarantees these individual respondents the *opportunity* to compete equally with white workers on the basis of job-related criteria. Title VII strives to achieve equality of opportunity by rooting out "artificial, arbitrary and unnecessary" employer-created barriers to professional development that have a discriminatory impact upon individuals. Therefore, respondents' rights under Section 703(a)(2) have been violated, unless petitioners can demonstrate that the examination given was not an artificial, arbitrary, or unnecessary barrier, because it measured skills related to effective performance in the role of Welfare Eligibility Supervisor . . .

In sum, respondents' claim of disparate impact from the examination, a pass-fail barrier to employment opportunity, states a prima facie case of employment discrimination under Section 703(a)(2), despite their employer's nondis-criminatory "bottom line," and that "bottom line" is no defense to this prima facie case under Section 703(h).

Having determined that respondents' claim comes within the terms of Title VII, we must address the suggestion of petitioners and some *amici curiae* that we recognize an exception, either in the nature of an additional burden on plaintiffs seeking to establish a prima facie case or in the nature of an affirmative defense, for cases in which an employer has compensated for a discriminatory pass-fail barrier by hiring or promoting a sufficient number of black employees to reach a nondiscriminatory "bottom line." We reject this suggestion, which is in essence nothing more than a request that we redefine the protections guaranteed by Title VII.

Section 703(a)(2) prohibits practices that would deprive or tend to deprive "*any individual* of employment opportunities." The principal focus of the statute is the protection of the individual employee, rather than the protection of the minority group as a whole. Indeed, the entire statute and its legislative history are replete with references to protection for the individual employee.

In suggesting that the "bottom line" may be a defense to a claim of discrimination against an individual employee, petitioners and *amici* appear to confuse unlawful discrimination with discriminatory intent. The Court has stated that a nondiscriminatory "bottom line" and an employer's good faith efforts to achieve a non-discriminatory work force, might in some cases assist an employer in rebutting the inference that particular action had been intentionally discriminatory: "Proof that [a] work force was racially balanced or that it contained a disproportionately high percentage of minority employees is not wholly irrelevant on the issue of intent when that issue is yet to be decided." *Furnco Construction Corp.* v. *Waters* (1978). But resolution of the factual question of intent is not what is at issue in this case. Rather, petitioners seek simply to justify discrimination against respondents, on the basis of their favorable treatment of other members of respondents' racial group. Under Title VII, "A racially balanced work force cannot immunize an employer from liability for specific acts of discrimination." *Furnco Construction Corp.*

It is clear beyond cavil that the obligation imposed by Title VII is to provide an equal opportunity for *each* applicant regardless of race, without regard to whether members of the applicant's race are already proportionately represented in the work force (emphasis in original).

It is clear that Congress never intended to give an employer license to discriminate against some employees on the basis of race or sex merely because he favorably treats other members of the employees' group . . .

The fact remains, however, that irrespective of the form taken by the discriminatory practice, an employer's treatment of other members of the plaintiffs' group can be "of little comfort to the victims of . . . discrimination." Title VII does not permit the victim of a facially discriminatory policy to be told that he has not been wronged because other persons of his or her race or sex were hired. That answer is no more satisfactory when it is given to victims of a policy that is facially neutral but practically discriminatory. Every *individual* employee is protected against both discriminatory treatment and against "practices that are fair in form, but discriminatory in operation." Requirements and tests

that have a discriminatory impact are merely some of the more subtle, but also the more pervasive, of the "practices and devices which have fostered racially stratified job environments to the disadvantage of minority citizens."

In sum, petitioners' nondiscriminatory "bottom line" is no answer, under the terms of Title VII, to respondents' prima facie claim of employment discrimination. Accordingly, the judgment of the Court of Appeals for the Second Circuit is affirmed, and this case is remanded to the District Court for further proceedings consistent with this opinion. **It is so ordered.**

Seniority and Title VII

The use of seniority, or length of service on the job, is frequently used to determine entitlement to employment benefits, promotions, or transfers, and even job security itself. Seniority systems usually provide that layoffs of workers be conducted on the basis of inverse seniority—those with the least length of service, or seniority, are laid off before those with greater seniority. Seniority within a department may also be used to determine eligibility to transfer to a different department.

Seniority may have a discriminatory effect when an employer, prior to the adoption of Title VII, refused to hire women or minority workers. If, after Title VII's adoption, the employer does hire them, those workers will have the least seniority. In the event of a layoff, the workers who lose their jobs will be women and minorities, whereas white males will retain their jobs. The layoffs by inverse seniority have a disparate impact on women and minorities. Does that mean the seniority system is in violation of Title VII, as in *Griggs?*

Section 703(h) of Title VII contains an exemption for bona fide seniority systems. That section states, in part,

> Notwithstanding any other provision of this title, it shall not be an unlawful employment practice for an employer to apply different standards of compensation or different terms, conditions, or privileges of employment pursuant to a bona fide seniority or merit system provided that such differences are not the result of an intention to discriminate because of race, color, religion, sex or national origin.

What is the effect of Section 703(h) on a seniority system that has a disparate impact or that operates to perpetuate the effects of prior discrimination? In several cases decided shortly after the adoption of Title VII, courts held that departmental seniority systems that operated to deter minority employees from transferring out of low-paying and inferior jobs were in violation of Title VII because they perpetuated prior discrimination. The issue reached the Supreme Court in the case of *International Brotherhood of Teamsters* v. *United States.* The Court had to address the question of whether a seniority system that perpetuated the effects of prior discrimination was bona fide under Section 703(h).

INTERNATIONAL BROTHERHOOD OF TEAMSTERS v. UNITED STATES

431 U.S. 324 (Supreme Court of the United States, 1977)

STEWART, J.

This litigation brings here several important questions under Title VII of the Civil Rights Act of 1964.... The issues grow out of alleged unlawful employment practices engaged in by an employer and a union. The employer is a common carrier of motor freight with nationwide operations, and the union represents a large group of its employees. The district court and the court of appeals held that the employer had violated Title VII by engaging in a pattern and practice of employment discrimination against Negroes and Spanish-surnamed Americans, and that the union had violated the Act by agreeing with the employer to create and maintain a seniority system that perpetuated the effects of past racial and ethnic discrimination ...

... The central claim ... was that the company had engaged in a pattern or practice of discriminating against minorities in hiring so-called line drivers. Those Negroes and Spanish-surnamed persons who had been hired, the Government alleged, were given lower paying, less desirable jobs as servicemen or local city drivers, and were thereafter discriminated against with respect to promotions and transfers. In this connection the complaint also challenged the seniority system established by the collective-bargaining agreements between the employer and the union. The Government sought a general injunctive remedy and specific "make whole" relief for all individual discriminatees, which would allow them an opportunity to transfer to line-driver jobs with full company seniority for all purposes.

The cases went to trial and the district court found that the Government had shown "by a preponderance of the evidence that T.I.M.E.-D.C. and its predecessor companies were engaged in a plan and practice of discrimination in violation of Title VII...." The court further found that the seniority system contained in the collective-bargaining contracts between the company and the union violated Title VII because it "operate[d] to impede the free transfer of minority groups into and within the company." Both the company and the union were enjoined from committing further violations of Title VII....

In this Court the company and the union contend that their conduct did not violate Title VII in any respect, asserting first that the evidence introduced at trial was insufficient to show that the company engaged in a "pattern or practice" of employment discrimination. The union further contends that the seniority system contained in the collective-bargaining agreements in no way violated Title VII. If these contentions are correct, it is unnecessary, of course, to reach any of the issues concerning remedies that so occupied the attention of the court of appeals.

Consideration of the question whether the company engaged in a pattern or practice of discriminatory hiring practices involves controlling legal principles that are relatively clear. The Government's theory of discrimination was simply that the company, in violation of Section 703(a) of Title VII, regularly and purposefully treated Negroes and Spanish-surnamed Americans less favorably than white persons. The disparity in treatment allegedly involved the refusal to recruit, hire, transfer, or promote minority group members on an equal basis with white people, particularly with respect to line-driving positions. The ultimate factional issues are thus simply whether there was a pattern or practice of such disparate treatment and, if so, whether the differences were "racially premised."

As the plaintiff, the Government bore the initial burden of making out a prima facie case of discrimination. And, because it alleged a system-wide pattern or practice of resistance to the full enjoyment of Title VII rights, the Government ultimately had to prove more than the mere occurrence of isolated or "accidental" or sporadic discriminatory acts. It had to establish by a preponderance of the evidence that racial discrimination was the company's standard operating procedure—the regular rather than the unusual practice.

We agree with the district court and the court of appeals that the Government carried its burden of proof....

The district court and the court of appeals, on the basis of substantial evidence, held that the Government had proved a prima facie case of systematic and purposeful employment discrimination, continuing well beyond the effective date of Title VII. The company's attempts to rebut that conclusion were held to be inadequate. For the reasons we have summarized, there is no warrant for this Court to disturb the findings of the district court and the court of appeals on this basic issue....

The district court and the court of appeals also found that the seniority system contained in the collective-bargaining agreements between the company and the union operated to violate Title VII of the Act.

For purposes of calculating benefits, such as vacations,

pensions, and other fringe benefits, an employee's seniority under this system runs from the date he joins the company, and takes into account his total service in all jobs and bargaining units. For competitive purposes, however, such as determining the order in which employees may bid for particular jobs, are laid off, or are recalled from layoff, it is bargaining-unit seniority that controls. Thus, a line driver's seniority, for purposes of bidding for particular runs and protection against layoff, takes into account only the length of time he has been a line driver at a particular terminal. The practical effect is that a city driver or serviceman who transfers to a line-driver job must forfeit all the competitive seniority he has accumulated in his previous bargaining unit and start at the bottom of the line drivers' "board."

The vice of this arrangement, as found by the district court and the court of appeals, was that it "locked" minority workers into inferior jobs and perpetuated prior discrimination by discouraging transfers to jobs as line drivers. While the disincentive applied to all workers, including whites, it was Negroes and Spanish-surnamed persons who, those courts found, suffered the most because many of them had been denied the equal opportunity to become line drivers when they were initially hired, whereas whites either had not sought or were refused line-driver positions for reasons unrelated to their race or national origin.

The linchpin of the theory embraced by the district court and the court of appeals was that a discriminatee who must forfeit his competitive seniority in order finally to obtain a line-driver job will never be able to "catch up" to the seniority level of his contemporary who was not subject to discrimination. Accordingly, this continued, built-in disadvantage to the prior discriminatee who transfers to a line-driver job was held to constitute a continuing violation of Title VII, for which both the employer and the union who jointly created and maintained the seniority system were liable.

The union, while acknowledging that the seniority system may in some sense perpetuate the effects of prior discrimination, asserts that the system is immunized from a finding of illegality by reason of Section 703(h) of Title VII . . .

It argues that the seniority system in this case is "bona fide" within the meaning of Section 703(h) when judged in light of its history, intent, application, and all of the circumstances under which it was created and is maintained. More specifically, the union claims that the central purpose of Section 703(h), is to ensure that mere perpetuation of *pre-Act* discrimination is not unlawful under Title VII. And, whether or not Section 703(h) immunizes the perpetuation

of *post-Act* discrimination, the union claims that the seniority system in this case has no such effect. Its position in this Court, as has been its position throughout this litigation, is that the seniority system presents no hurdles to post-Act discriminatees who seek retroactive seniority to the date they would have become line drivers but for the company's discrimination. Indeed, the union asserts that under its collective-bargaining agreements the union will itself take up the cause of the post-Act victim and attempt, through grievance procedures, to gain for him full "make whole" relief, including appropriate seniority.

The Government responds that a seniority system that perpetuates the effects of prior discrimination—pre- or post-Act—can never be "bona fide" under Section 703(h); at a minimum Title VII prohibits those applications of a seniority system that perpetuate the effects on incumbent employees of prior discriminatory job assignments.

The issues thus joined are open ones in this Court . . .

(1) Because the company discriminated both before and after the enactment of Title VII, the seniority system is said to have operated to perpetuate the effects of both pre- and post-Act discrimination. Post-Act discriminatees, however, may obtain full "make whole" relief, including retroactive seniority under *Franks* v. *Bowman*, without attacking the legality of the seniority system as applied to them. *Franks* made clear and the union acknowledges that retroactive seniority may be awarded as relief from an employer's discriminatory hiring and assignment policies even if the seniority system agreement itself makes no provision for such relief. Here the Government has proved that the company engaged in a post-Act pattern of discriminatory hiring, assignment, transfer, and promotion policies. Any Negro or Spanish-surnamed American injured by those policies may receive all appropriate relief as a direct remedy for this discrimination.

(2) What remains for review is the judgment that the seniority system unlawfully perpetuated the effects of *pre-Act* discrimination. We must decide, in short, whether Section 703(h) validates otherwise bona fide seniority systems that afford no constructive seniority to victims discriminated against prior to the effective date of Title VII, and it is to that issue that we now turn.

The primary purpose of Title VII was "to assure equality of employment opportunities and to eliminate those discriminatory practices and devices which have fostered racially stratified job environments to the disadvantage of minority citizens." . . . To achieve this purpose, Congress "proscribe[d] not only overt discrimination but also practices that are fair in form, but discriminatory in operation."

. . . Thus, the Court has repeatedly held that a prima facie Title VII violation may be established by policies or practices that are neutral on their face and in intent but that nonetheless discriminate in effect against a particular group. . . .

One kind of practice "fair in form, but discriminatory in operation" is that which perpetuates the effects of prior discrimination. As the Court held in *Griggs,* "Under the Act, practices, procedures, or tests neutral on their face, and even neutral in terms of intent, cannot be maintained if they operate to 'freeze' the status quo of prior discriminatory employment practices."

Were it not for Section 703(h), the seniority system in this case would seem to fall under the *Griggs* rationale. The heart of the system is its allocation of the choicest jobs, the greatest protection against layoffs, and other advantages to those employees who have been line drivers for the longest time. Where, because of the employer's prior intentional discrimination, the line drivers with the longest tenure are without exception white, the advantages of the seniority system flow disproportionately to them and away from Negro and Spanish-surnamed employees who might by now have enjoyed those advantages had not the employer discriminated before the passage of the Act. This disproportionate distribution of advantages does in a very real sense "operate to 'freeze' the status quo of prior discriminatory employment practices." But both the literal terms of Section 703(h) and the legislative history of Title VII demonstrate that Congress considered this very effect of many seniority systems and extended a measure of immunity to them. . . .

In sum, the unmistakable purpose of Section 703(h) was to make clear that the routine application of a bona fide seniority system would not be unlawful under Title VII. This was the intended result even where the employer's pre-Act discrimination resulted in whites having greater existing seniority rights than Negroes. Although a seniority system inevitably tends to perpetuate the effects of pre-Act discrimination in such cases, the congressional judgment was that Title VII should not outlaw the use of existing seniority lists and thereby destroy or water down the vested seniority rights of employees simply because their employer had engaged in discrimination prior to the passage of the Act.

To be sure, Section 703(h) does not immunize all seniority systems. It refers only to "bona fide" systems, and a proviso requires that any differences in treatment not be "the result of an intention to discriminate because of race . . . or national origin. . . ." But our reading of the legislative history

compels us to reject the Government's broad argument that no seniority system that tends to perpetuate pre-Act discrimination can be "bona fide." To accept the argument would require us to hold that a seniority system becomes illegal simply because it allows the full exercise of the pre-Act seniority rights of employees of a company that discriminated before Title VII was enacted. It would place an affirmative obligation on the parties to the seniority agreement to subordinate those rights in favor of the claims of pre-Act discriminatees without seniority. The consequence would be a perversion of the congressional purpose. We cannot accept the invitation to disembowel Section 703(h) by reading the words "bona fide" as the Government would have us do. Accordingly, we hold that an otherwise neutral, legitimate seniority system does not become unlawful under Title VII simply because it may perpetuate pre-Act discrimination. Congress did not intend to make it illegal for employees with vested seniority rights to continue to exercise those rights, even at the expense of pre-Act discriminatees.

That conclusion is inescapable even in a case, such as this one, where the pre-Act discriminatees are incumbent employees who accumulated seniority in other bargaining units. Although there seems to be no explicit reference in the legislative history to pre-Act discriminatees already employed in less desirable jobs, there can be no rational basis for distinguishing their claims from those of persons initially denied *any* job but hired later with less seniority than they might have had in the absence of pre-Act discrimination. As discussed above, Congress in 1964 made clear that a seniority system is not unlawful because it honors employees' existing rights, even where the employer has engaged in pre-Act discriminatory hiring or promotion practices. It would be as contrary to that mandate to forbid the exercise of seniority rights with respect to discriminatees who held inferior jobs as with respect to later-hired minority employees who previously were denied any job. If anything, the latter group is the more disadvantaged. . . .

(3) The seniority system in this case is entirely bona fide. It applies equally to all races and ethnic groups. To the extent that it "locks" employees into nonline-driver jobs, it does so for all. The city drivers and servicemen who are discouraged from transferring to line-driver jobs are not all Negroes or Spanish-surnamed Americans; to the contrary, the overwhelming majority are white. The placing of line drivers in a separate bargaining unit from other employees is rational, in accord with the industry practice, and consistent with NLRB precedents. It is conceded that the seniority system did not have its genesis in racial discrimina-

tion, and that it was negotiated and has been maintained free from any illegal purpose. In these circumstances, the single fact that the system extends no retroactive seniority to pre-Act discriminatees does not make it unlawful.

Because the seniority system was protected by Section 703(h), the union's conduct in agreeing to and maintaining the system did not violate Title VII. On remand, the district court's injunction against the union must be vacated....
So ordered.

In *American Tobacco Co.* v. *Patterson* (456 U.S. 63, 1982), the Supreme Court ruled that Section 703(h) applies to seniority systems that were adopted after the passage of Title VII as well as to those in operation at the time Title VII was adopted. The protection of Section 703(h) extends to rules that determine entry into seniority classifications, according to the 1980 Supreme Court decision in *California Brewers Association* v. *Bryant* (444 U.S. 598). That case involved the rule that an employee had to have worked at least forty-five weeks in a calendar year in order to be classified a "permanent employee." Permanent employees were given preference in layoffs and transfers over temporary employees (those not meeting the forty-five-week rule). An African American employee claimed that the forty-five-week rule had a disparate impact on minority workers. The Court, rejecting the claim, held that the forty-five-week rule was within the Section 703(h) exemption for bona fide seniority systems.

According to *Teamsters,* a seniority system is bona fide within the meaning of Section 703(h) when it is neutral on its face (it applies equally to all employees) and it is not intentionally used to discriminate. As well, the court will consider whether the system had its origin in discrimination, whether it has been negotiated and maintained free from discriminatory intent, and whether the basis of the seniority system is reasonable in light of industry practice.

Section 706(e)(2), added to Title VII by the 1991 amendments, addresses the time limits for a challenge to a seniority system that allegedly are used intentionally to discriminate, in violation of Title VII. According to that section, a claim may be filed after the allegedly discriminatory seniority system is adopted, after the plaintiff becomes subject to the seniority system, or after the plaintiff is injured by the application of the seniority system. Section 706(e)(2) was intended to reverse the Supreme Court decision in *Lorance* v. *AT&T Technologies, Inc.* (490 U.S. 900, 1989), which held that the time limit for challenging a seniority system ran from the date on which the system was adopted, even if the plaintiff was not subjected to the system until five years later.

Affirmative Action and Title VII

Affirmative action programs usually involve giving preference in hiring or promotion to qualified female or minority employees. Employees who are not members of the group being accorded the preference (usually white males) may be at a disadvantage for hiring or promotion. Recall that *McDonald* v. *Santa Fe Trail* held that Title VII protected every individual employee from discrimination because of race, sex, color, religion, or national origin. Is the denial of preferential treatment to employees not within the preferred group (defined by race or sex) a violation of Title VII?

Title VII does not require employers to enact affirmative action plans; however, the courts have often ordered affirmative action when the employer has been found in violation of Title VII. The courts have consistently held that remedial affirmative action plans—plans set up to remedy prior illegal discrimination—are permissible under Title VII, because such plans may be necessary to overcome the effects of the employer's prior illegal discrimination. But if the plan is a voluntary one and the employer has not been found guilty of prior discrimination, does it violate Title VII by discriminating on the basis of race or sex? That question was addressed by the Supreme Court in the following case.

UNITED STEELWORKERS OF AMERICA v. WEBER

443 U.S. 193 (Supreme Court of the United States, 1979)

BRENNAN, J.

Challenged here is the legality of an affirmative action plan—collectively bargained by an employer and a union—that reserves for black employees 50 percent of the openings in an in-plant craft-training program until the percentage of black craftworkers in the plant is commensurate with the percentage of blacks in the local labor force. The question for decision is whether Congress, in Title VII of the Civil Rights Act of 1964, left employers and unions in the private sector free to take such race-conscious steps to eliminate manifest racial imbalances in traditionally segregated job categories.

In 1974, petitioner United Steelworkers of America (USWA) and petitioner Kaiser Aluminum & Chemical Corp. (Kaiser) entered into a master collective-bargaining agreement covering terms and conditions of employment at 15 Kaiser plants. The agreement contained, *inter alia,* an affirmative action plan designed to eliminate conspicuous racial imbalances in Kaiser's then almost exclusively white craft-work forces. Black craft-hiring goals were set for each Kaiser plant equal to the percentage of blacks in the respective local labor forces. To enable plants to meet these goals, on-the-job training programs were established to teach un-skilled production workers—black and white—the skills necessary to become craftworkers. The plan reserved for black employees 50 percent of the openings in these newly created in-plant training programs.

This case arose from the operation of the plan at Kaiser's plant in Gramercy, La. Until 1974, Kaiser hired as craftworkers for that plant only persons who had had prior craft experience. Because blacks had long been excluded from craft unions, few were able to present such credentials. As a consequence, prior to 1974 only 1.83 percent (5 out of 273) of the skilled craftworkers at the Gramercy plant were black, even though the work force in the Gramercy area was approximately 39 percent black.

Pursuant to the national agreement Kaiser altered its craft-hiring practice in the Gramercy plant. Rather than hiring already trained outsiders, Kaiser established a training program to train its production workers to fill craft openings. Selection of craft trainees was made on the basis of seniority, with the proviso that at least 50 percent of the new trainees were to be black until the percentage of black skilled craftworkers in the Gramercy plant approximated the percentage of blacks in the local labor force.

During 1974, the first year of the operation of the Kaiser-USWA affirmative action plan, 13 craft trainees were selected from Gramercy's production work force. Of these, seven were black and six white. The most senior black selected into the program had less seniority than several white production workers whose bids for admission were rejected. Thereafter one of those white production workers, respondent Brian Weber (hereafter respondent), instituted this class action in the United States District Court for the Eastern District of Louisiana.

The complaint alleged that the filling of craft trainee positions at the Gramercy plant pursuant to the affirmative action program had resulted in junior black employees' receiving training in preference to senior white employees, thus discriminating against respondent and other similarly situated white employees in violation of Sections 703(a) and (d) of Title VII. The District Court held that the plan violated Title VII. . . . A divided panel of the Court of Appeals for the Fifth Circuit affirmed, holding that all employment preferences based upon race, including those preferences incidental to bona fide affirmative action plans, violated Title VII's prohibition against racial discrimination in employment. . . .

We emphasize at the outset the narrowness of our inquiry. Since the Kaiser-USWA plan does not involve state action, this case does not present an alleged violation of the Equal Protection Clause of the Fourteenth Amendment. Further, since the Kaiser-USWA plan was adopted voluntarily, we are not concerned with what Title VII requires or with what a court might order to remedy a past proved violation of the Act. The only question before us is the narrow statutory issue of whether Title VII *forbids* private employers and unions from voluntarily agreeing upon bona fide affirmative action plans that accord racial preferences in the manner and for the purpose provided in the Kaiser-USWA plan. . . .

Respondent argues that Congress intended in Title VII to prohibit all race-conscious affirmative action plans. Respondent's argument rests upon a literal interpretation of Sections 703(a) and (d) of the Act. Those sections make it unlawful to "discriminate . . . because of . . . race" in hiring and in the selection of apprentices for training programs. Since, the argument runs, *McDonald* v. *Santa Fe Trail Transp. Co.* . . . settled that Title VII forbids discrimination against whites as well as blacks, and since the Kaiser-USWA affirmative action plan operates to discriminate against white employees solely because they are white, it follows that the Kaiser-USWA plan violates Title VII.

Respondent's argument is not without force. But it overlooks the significance of the fact that the Kaiser-USWA plan is an affirmative action plan voluntarily adopted by private parties to eliminate traditional patterns of racial segregation. In this context respondent's reliance upon a literal construction of Sections 703(a) and (d) and upon *McDonald* is misplaced. It is a "familiar rule, that a thing may be within the letter of the statute and yet not within the statute, because not within its spirit, nor within the intention of its makers." The prohibition against racial discrimination in Sections 703(a) and (d) of Title VII must therefore be read against the background of the legislative history of Title VII and the historical context from which the act arose. Examination of those sources makes clear that an interpretation of the sections that forbade all race-

conscious affirmative action would "bring about an end completely at variance with the purpose of the statute" and must be rejected.

Congress' primary concern in enacting the prohibition against racial discrimination in Title VII of the Civil Rights Act of 1964 was with "the plight of the Negro in our economy." Before 1964, blacks were largely relegated to "unskilled and semi-skilled jobs." Because of automation the number of such jobs was rapidly decreasing. As a consequence, "the relative position of the Negro worker [was] steadily worsening. . . ."

Congress feared that the goals of the Civil Rights Act—the integration of blacks into the mainstream of American society—could not be achieved unless this trend were reversed. And Congress recognized that that would not be possible unless blacks were able to secure jobs "which have a future." . . . Accordingly, it was clear to Congress that "[t]he crux of the problem [was] to open employment opportunities for Negroes in occupations which have been traditionally closed to them," and it was to this problem that Title VII's prohibition against racial discrimination in employment was primarily addressed.

It plainly appears from the House Report accompanying the Civil Rights Act that Congress did not intend wholly to prohibit private and voluntary affirmative action efforts as one method of solving this problem. . . .

Given [the] legislative history, we cannot agree with respondent that Congress intended to prohibit the private sector from taking effective steps to accomplish the goal that Congress designed Title VII to achieve. The very statutory words intended as a spur or catalyst to cause "employers and unions to self-examine and to self-evaluate their employment practices and to endeavor to eliminate, so far as possible, the last vestiges of an unfortunate and ignominious page in this country's history," cannot be interpreted as an absolute prohibition against all private, voluntary, race-conscious affirmative action efforts to hasten the elimination of such vestiges. It would be ironic indeed if a law triggered by a Nation's concern over centuries of racial injustice and intended to improve the lot of those who had "been excluded from the American dream for so long," constituted the first legislative prohibition of all voluntary, private, race-conscious efforts to abolish traditional patterns of racial segregation and hierarchy.

Our conclusion is further reinforced by examination of the language and legislative history of Section 703(j) of Title VII. Opponents of Title VII raised two related arguments against the bill. First, they argued that the Act would be interpreted to *require* employers with racially imbalanced work forces to grant preferential treatment to racial minorities in order to integrate. Second, they argued that employers with racially imbalanced work forces would grant preferential treatment to racial minorities, even if not required to do so by the Act. Had Congress meant to prohibit all race-conscious affirmative action, as respondent urges, it easily could have answered both objections by providing that Title VII would not require or *permit* racially preferential integration efforts. But Congress did not choose such a course. Rather Congress added Section 703(j) which addresses only the first objection. The section provides that nothing contained in Title VII "shall be interpreted to *require* any employer . . . to grant preferential treatment . . . to any group because of the race . . . of such . . . group on account of" a *de facto* racial imbalance in the employer's work force. The section does *not* state that "nothing in Title VII shall be interpreted to *permit*" voluntary affirmative efforts to correct racial imbalances. The natural inference is that Congress chose not to forbid all voluntary race-conscious affirmative action. . . .

In view of this legislative history and in view of Congress' desire to avoid undue federal regulation of private businesses, use of the word "require" rather than the phrase "require or permit" in Section 703(j) fortifies the conclusion that Congress did not intend to limit traditional business freedom to such a degree as to prohibit all voluntary, race-conscious affirmative action.

We therefore hold that Title VII's prohibition in Sections 703(a) and (d) against racial discrimination does not condemn all private, voluntary, race-conscious affirmative action plans.

We need not today define in detail the line of demarcation between permissible and impermissible affirmative action plans. It suffices to hold that the challenged Kaiser-USWA affirmative action plans falls on the permissible side of the line. The purposes of the plan mirror those of the statute. Both were designed to break down old patterns of racial segregation and hierarchy. Both were structured to "open employment opportunities for Negroes in occupations which have been traditionally closed to them."

At the same time, the plan does not unnecessarily trammel the interests of the white employees. The plan does not require the discharge of white workers and their replacement with new black hires. Nor does the plan create an absolute bar to the advancement of white employees; half of those trained in the program will be white. Moreover, the plan is a temporary measure; it is not intended to maintain racial balance, but simply to eliminate a manifest racial imbalance. Preferential selection of craft trainees at the Gra-

mercy plant will end as soon as the percentage of black skilled craftworkers in the Gramercy plant approximates the percentage of blacks in the local labor force.

We conclude, therefore, that the adoption of the Kaiser-USWA plan for the Gramercy plant falls within the area of discretion left by Title VII to the private sector voluntarily to adopt affirmative action plans designed to eliminate conspicuous racial imbalance in traditionally segregated job categories. Accordingly, the judgment of the Court of Appeals for the Fifth Circuit is **Reversed.**

BLACKMUN, J. (concurring)

. . . In his dissent from the decision of the United States Court of Appeals for the Fifth Circuit, Judge Wisdom pointed out that this case arises from a practical problem in the administration of Title VII. The broad prohibition against discrimination places the employer and the union on what he accurately described as a "high tightrope without a net beneath them." If Title VII is read literally, on the one hand they face liability for past discrimination against blacks, and on the other they face liability to whites for any voluntary preferences adopted to mitigate the effects of prior discrimination against blacks.

In this litigation, Kaiser denied prior discrimination but concedes that its past hiring practices may be subject to question. Although the labor force in the Gramercy area was approximately 39 percent black, Kaiser's work force was less than 15 percent black, and its craftwork force was less than 2 percent black. Kaiser had made some effort to recruit black painters, carpenters, insulators, and other craftsmen, but it continued to insist that those hired have five years prior industrial experience, a requirement that arguably was not sufficiently job related to justify under Title VII any discriminatory impact it may have had. The parties dispute the extent to which black craftsmen were available in the local labor market. They agree, however, that after critical reviews from the Office of Federal Contract Compliance, Kaiser and the Steelworkers established the training program in question here and modeled it along the lines of a Title VII consent decree later entered for the steel industry. Yet when they did this, respondent Weber sued, alleging that Title VII prohibited the program because it discriminated against him as a white person and it was not supported by a prior judicial finding of discrimination against blacks.

Respondent Weber's reading of Title VII, endorsed by the Court of Appeals, places voluntary compliance with Title VII in profound jeopardy. The only way for the employer and the union to keep their footing on the "tightrope" it creates would be to eschew all forms of voluntary affirmative action. Even a whisper of emphasis on minority recruiting would be forbidden. Because Congress intended to encourage private efforts to come into compliance with Title VII, Judge Wisdom concluded that employers and unions who had committed "arguable violations" of Title VII should be free to make reasonable responses without fear of liability to whites. Preferential hiring along the lines of the Kaiser program is a reasonable response for the employer, whether or not a court, on these facts, could order the same step as a remedy. The company is able to avoid identifying victims of past discrimination, and so avoids claims for backpay that could inevitably follow a response limited to such victims. If past victims should be benefited by the program, however, the company mitigates its liability to those persons. Also, to the extent that Title VII liability is predicated on the "disparate effect" of an employer's past hiring practices, the program makes it less likely that such an effect could be demonstrated.

The "arguable violation" theory has a number of advantages. It responds to a practical problem in the administration of Title VII not anticipated by Congress. It draws predictability from the outline of present law and closely effectuates the purpose of the Act. Both Kaiser and the United States urge its adoption here. Because I agree that it is the soundest way to approach this case, my preference would be to resolve this litigation by applying it and holding that Kaiser's craft training program meets the requirement that voluntary affirmative action be a reasonable response to an "arguable violation" of Title VII. . . .

BURGER, C. J. (dissenting)

The Court reaches a result I would be inclined to vote for were I a Member of Congress considering a proposed amendment of Title VII. I cannot join the Court's judgment, however, because it is contrary to the explicit language of the statute and arrived at by means wholly incompatible with long-established principles of separation of powers. Under the guise of statutory "construction," the Court effectively rewrites Title VII to achieve what it regards as a desirable result. It "amends" the statute to do precisely what both its sponsors and its opponents agreed the statute was *not* intended to do. . . .

REHNQUIST, J. (dissenting)

. . . It may be that one or more of the principal sponsors of Title VII would have preferred to see a provision allowing preferential treatment of minorities written into the bill. Such a provision, however, would have to have been expressly or impliedly excepted from Title VII's explicit prohibition on all racial discrimination in employment. There is no such exception in the Act. And a reading of the legislative debates concerning Title VII, in which proponents and opponents alike uniformly denounced discrimination in favor of, as well as discrimination against, Negroes, demonstrates clearly that any legislator harboring an unspoken desire for such a provision could not possibly have succeeded in enacting it into law. . . .

In light of the background and purpose of Section 703(j), the irony of invoking the section to justify the result in this case is obvious. The Court's frequent references to the "voluntary" nature of Kaiser's racially discriminatory admission quota bear no relationship to the facts of this case. Kaiser and the Steelworkers acted under pressure from an agency of the Federal Government, the Office of Federal Contract Compliance, which found that minorities were being "underutilized" at Kaiser's plants. That is, Kaiser's work force was racially imbalanced. Bowing to that pressure, Kaiser instituted an admissions quota preferring blacks over whites, thus confirming that the fears of Title VII's opponents were well founded. Today, Section 703(j), adopted to allay those fears, is invoked by the Court to uphold imposition of a racial quota under the very circumstances that the section was intended to prevent. . . .

Reading the language of Title VII, as the Court purports to do," . . . against the background of [its] legislative history . . . and the historical context from which the Act arose," one is led inescapably to the conclusion that Congress fully understood what it was saying and meant precisely what it said. Opponents of the civil rights bill did not argue that employers would be permitted under Title VII voluntarily to grant preferential treatment to minorities to correct racial imbalance. The plain language of the statute too clearly prohibited such racial discrimination to admit of any doubt. They argued, tirelessly, that Title VII would be interpreted by federal agencies and their agents to require unwilling employers to racially balance their work forces by granting preferential treatment to minorities. Supporters of H.R. 7152 responded, equally tirelessly, that the act would not be so interpreted because not only does it not require preferential treatment of minorities, it does not *permit* preferential treatment of any race for any reason. . . .

To put an end to the dispute, supporters of the civil rights bill drafted and introduced Section 703(j). Specifically addressed to the opposition's charge, Section 703(j) simply enjoins federal agencies and courts from interpreting Title VII to require an employer to prefer certain racial groups to correct imbalances in his work force. The section says nothing about voluntary preferential treatment of minorities because such racial discrimination is plainly proscribed by Sections 703(a) and (d). Indeed, had Congress intended to except voluntary, race-conscious preferential treatment from the blanket prohibition of racial discrimination in Sections 703(a) and (d), it surely could have drafted language better suited to the task than Section 703(j). It knew how. Section 703(i) provides:

Nothing contained in [Title VII] shall apply to any business or enterprise on or near an Indian reservation with respect to any publicly announced employment practice of such business or enterprise under which a preferential treatment is given to any individual because he is an Indian living on or near a reservation. . . .

The Court in *Weber* upheld the legality of a voluntarily adopted affirmative action program by an employer who had not been found guilty of prior discrimination. When is an employer justified in initiating a voluntary affirmative action program—what kind of evidence must the employer demonstrate to support the adoption of the affirmative action plan? What evidence must an individual who alleges discriminatory treatment by an employer acting pursuant to an affirmative action program demonstrate in order to establish a claim under Title VII? Those questions were addressed by the Supreme Court in the following case.

PAUL E. JOHNSON v. TRANSPORTATION AGENCY, SANTA CLARA COUNTY, CALIFORNIA

480 U.S. 616 (Supreme Court of the United States, 1987)

BRENNAN, J.

Respondent, Transportation Agency of Santa Clara County, California, unilaterally promulgated an Affirmative Action Plan applicable, *inter alia,* to promotions of employees. In selecting applicants for the promotional position of road dispatcher, the Agency, pursuant to the Plan, passed over petitioner Paul Johnson, a male employee, and promoted a female employee applicant, Diane Joyce. The question for decision is whether in making the promotion the Agency impermissibly took into account the sex of the applicant in violation of Title VII of the Civil Rights Act of 1964. The District Court for the Northern District of California, in an action filed by petitioner following receipt of a right-to-sue letter from the Equal Employment Opportunity Commission (EEOC), held that respondent had violated Title VII. The Court of Appeals for the Ninth Circuit reversed. We granted certiorari . . .

In December 1978, the Santa Clara County Transit District Board of Supervisors adopted an Affirmative Action

Plan (Plan) for the County Transportation Agency. The Plan implemented a County Affirmative Action Plan, which had been adopted, declared the County, because "mere prohibition of discriminatory practices is not enough to remedy the effects of past practices and to permit attainment of an equitable representation of minorities, women and handicapped persons." Relevant to this case, the Agency Plan provides that, in making promotions to positions within a traditionally segregated job classification in which women have been significantly underrepresented, the Agency is authorized to consider as one factor the sex of a qualified applicant.

In reviewing the composition of its work force, the Agency noted in its Plan that women were represented in numbers far less than their proportion of the county labor force in both the Agency as a whole and in five of seven job categories. Specifically, while women constituted 36.4 percent of the area labor market, they composed only 22.4 percent of Agency employees. Furthermore, women working at the Agency were concentrated largely in EEOC job categories traditionally held by women: women made up 76 percent of Office and Clerical Workers, but only 7.1 percent of Agency Officials and Administrators, 8.6 percent of Professionals, 9.7 percent of Technicians, and 22 percent of Service and Maintenance workers. As for the job classification relevant to this case, none of the 238 Skilled Craft Worker positions was held by a woman. The Plan noted that this underrepresentation of women in part reflected the fact that women had not traditionally been employed in these positions, and that they had not been strongly motivated to seek training or employment in them "because of the limited opportunities that have existed in the past for them to work in such classifications." The Plan also observed that, while the proportion of ethnic minorities in the Agency as a whole exceeded the proportion of such minorities in the county work force, a smaller percentage of minority employees held management, professional, and technical positions.

The Agency stated that its Plan was intended to achieve "a statistically measurable yearly improvement in hiring, training and promotion of minorities and women throughout the Agency in all major job classifications where they are underrepresented." . . . [T]he Agency stated that its long-term goal was to attain a work force whose composition reflected the proportion of minorities and women in the area labor force. Thus, for the Skilled Craft category in which the road dispatcher position at issue here was classified, the Agency's aspiration was that eventually about 36 percent of the jobs would be occupied by women.

The Plan acknowledged that a number of factors might make it unrealistic to rely on the Agency's long-term goals in evaluating the Agency's progress in expanding job opportunities for minorities and women. . . .

The Agency's Plan thus set aside no specific number of positions for minorities or women, but authorized the consideration of ethnicity or sex as a factor when evaluating qualified candidates for jobs in which members of such groups were poorly represented. One such job was the road dispatcher position that is the subject of the dispute in this case.

On December 12, 1979, the Agency announced a vacancy for the promotional position of road dispatcher in the Agency's Roads Division. . . . The position requires at minimum four years of dispatch or road maintenance work experience for Santa Clara County. The EEOC job classification scheme designates a road dispatcher as a Skilled Craft worker.

Twelve County employees applied for the promotion, including Joyce and Johnson. Joyce had worked for the County since 1970, serving as an account clerk until 1975. She had applied for a road dispatcher position in 1974, but was deemed ineligible because she had not served as a road maintenance worker. In 1975, Joyce transferred from a senior account clerk position to a road maintenance worker position, becoming the first woman to fill such a job. During her four years in that position, she occasionally worked out of class as a road dispatcher.

Petitioner Johnson began with the county in 1967 as a road yard clerk, after private employment that included working as a supervisor and dispatcher. He had also unsuccessfully applied for the road dispatcher opening in 1974. In 1977, his clerical position was downgraded, and he sought and received a transfer to the position of road maintenance worker. He also occasionally worked out of class as a dispatcher while performing that job.

Nine of the applicants, including Joyce and Johnson, were deemed qualified for the job, and were interviewed by a two-person board. Seven of the applicants scored above 70 on this interview, which meant that they were certified as eligible for selection by the appointing authority. The scores awarded ranged from 70 to 80. Johnson was tied for second with a score of 75, while Joyce ranked next with a score of 73. A second interview was conducted by three Agency supervisors, who ultimately recommended that Johnson be promoted. Prior to the second interview, Joyce had contacted the County's Affirmative Action Office because she feared that her application might not receive disinterested review. The Office in turn contacted the Agency's Affirmative Action Coordinator, whom the Agency's Plan makes responsible for, *inter alia* keeping the Director informed of opportunities for the Agency to accomplish its objectives under the Plan. At the time, the Agency employed no women in any Skilled Craft position, and had never employed a woman as a road dispatcher. The Coordinator recommended to the Director of the Agency, James Graebner, that Joyce be promoted.

Graebner, authorized to choose any of the seven persons deemed eligible, thus had the benefit of suggestions by the second interview panel and by the Agency Coordinator in arriving at his decision. After deliberation, Graebner concluded that the promotion should be given to Joyce. As he testified, "I tried to look at the whole picture, the combination of her qualifications and Mr. Johnson's qualifications, their test scores, their expertise, their background, affirmative action matters, things like that . . . I believe it was a combination of all those."

The certification form naming Joyce as the person promoted to the dispatcher position stated that both she and Johnson were rated as well-qualified for the job. . . . Graebner testified that he did not regard as significant the fact that Johnson scored 75 and Joyce 73 when interviewed by the two-person board.

Petitioner Johnson filed a complaint with the EEOC alleging that he had been denied promotion on the basis of sex in violation of Title VII. He received a right-to-sue letter from the agency on March 10, 1981, and on March 20, 1981, filed suit in the United States District Court for the Northern District of California. The District Court found that Johnson was more qualified for the dispatcher position than Joyce, and that the sex of Joyce was the *determining factor* in her selection." The court acknowledged that, since the Agency justified its decision on the basis of its Affirmative Action Plan, the criteria announced in *Steelworkers* v. *Weber*, should be applied in evaluating the validity of the plan. It then found the Agency's Plan invalid on the ground that the evidence did not satisfy Weber's criterion that the Plan be temporary. The Court of Appeals for the Ninth Circuit reversed, holding that the absence of an express termination date in the Plan was not dispositive, since the Plan repeatedly expressed its objective as the attainment, rather than the maintenance, of a work force mirroring the labor force in the county. The Court of Appeals added that the fact that the Plan established no fixed percentage of positions for minorities or women made it less essential that the Plan contain a relatively explicit deadline. The Court held further that the Agency's consideration of Joyce's sex in filling the road dispatcher position was lawful. The Agency Plan had been adopted, the court said, to address a conspicuous imbalance in the Agency's work force, and neither unnecessarily trammeled the rights of other employees, nor created an absolute bar to their advancement.

As a preliminary matter, we note that petitioner bears the burden of establishing the invalidity of the Agency's Plan. Once a plaintiff establishes a prima facie case that race or sex has been taken into account in an employer's employment decision, the burden shifts to the employer to articulate a nondiscriminatory rationale for its decision. The existence of an affirmative action plan provides such a rationale. If such a plan is articulated as the basis for the employer's decision, the burden shifts to the plaintiff to prove that the employer's justification is pretextual and the plan is invalid. . . . That does not mean, however, as petitioner suggests, that reliance on an affirmative action plan is to be treated as an affirmative defense requiring the employer to carry the burden of proving the validity of the plan. The burden of proving its invalidity remains on the plaintiff.

The assessment of the legality of the Agency Plan must be guided by our decision in *Weber*. In that case, the Court addressed the question whether the employer violated Title VII by adopting a voluntary affirmative action plan designed to "eliminate manifest racial imbalances in traditionally segregated job categories."

We upheld the employer's decision to select less senior black applicants over the white respondent, for we found that taking race into account was consistent with Title VII's objective of "break[ing] down old patterns of racial segregation and hierarchy."

We noted that the plan did not "unnecessarily trammel the interests of the white employees," since it did not require "the discharge of white workers and their replacement with new black hirees." Nor did the plan create "an absolute bar to the advancement of white employees," since half of those trained in the new program were to be white. Finally, we observed that the plan was a temporary measure, not designed to maintain racial balance, but to "eliminate a manifest racial imbalance." . . . *Weber* held that an employer seeking to justify the adoption of a plan need not point to its own prior discriminatory practices, nor even to evidence of an "arguable violation" on its part. Rather, it need point only to a "conspicuous . . . imbalance in traditionally segregated job categories."

. . . In reviewing the employment decision at issue in this case, we must first examine whether that decision was made pursuant to a plan prompted by concerns similar to those of the employer in *Weber*. Next, we must determine whether the effect of the plan on males and non-minorities is comparable to the effect of the plan in that case.

The first issue is therefore whether consideration of the sex of applicants for skilled craft jobs was justified by the existence of a "manifest imbalance" that reflected underrepresentation of women in "traditionally segregated job categories." In determining whether an imbalance exists that would justify taking sex or race into account, a comparison of the percentage of minorities or women in the employer's work force with the percentage in the area labor market or general population is appropriate in analyzing jobs that require no special expertise. . . . Where a job requires special training, however, the comparison should be with those in the labor force who possess the relevant qualifications. . . . The requirement that the "manifest imbalance" relate to a "traditionally segregated job category" provides assurance both that sex or race will be taken into account in a manner consistent with Title VII's purpose of eliminating the effects of employment discrimination, and that the interest of those employees not benefiting from the plan will not be unduly infringed.

A manifest imbalance need not be such that it would support a prima facie case against the employer, as suggested in

Justice O'Connor's concurrence, since we do not regard as identical the constraints of Title VII and the federal constitution on voluntarily adopted affirmative action plans. Application of the "prima facie" standard in Title VII cases would be inconsistent with *Weber*'s focus on statistical imbalance, and could inappropriately create a significant disincentive for employers to adopt an affirmative action plan.

It is clear that the decision to hire Joyce was made pursuant to an Agency plan that directed that sex or race be taken into account for the purpose of remedying underrepresentation. The Agency Plan acknowledged the "limited opportunities that have existed in the past," for women to find employment in certain job classifications "where women have not been traditionally employed in significant numbers." . . . Specifically, 9 of the 10 ParaProfessionals and 110 of the 145 Office and Clerical Workers were women. By contrast, women were only 2 of the 28 Officials and Administrators, 5 of the 58 Professionals, 12 of the 124 Technicians, none of the Skilled Craft Workers, and 1— who was Joyce—of the 110 Road Maintenance Workers. The Plan sought to remedy these imbalances through "hiring, training and promotion of . . . women throughout the Agency in all major job classifications where they are underrepresented."

. . . For positions requiring specialized training and experience, the Plan observed that the number of minorities and women "who possess the qualifications required for entry into such job classifications is limited." The Plan therefore directed that annual short-term goals be formulated that would provide a more realistic indication of the degree to which sex should be taken into account in filling particular positions. The Plan stressed that such goals "should not be construed as 'quotas' that must be met, but as reasonable aspirations in correcting the imbalance in the Agency's work force. These goals were to take into account factors such as "turnover, layoffs, lateral transfers, new job openings, retirements and availability of minorities, women and handicapped persons in the area work force who possess the desired qualifications or potential for placement." The Plan specifically directed that, in establishing such goals, the Agency work with the County Planning Department and other sources in attempting to compile data on the percentage of minorities and women in the local labor force that were actually working in the job classifications comprising the Agency work force. From the outset, therefore, the Plan sought annually to develop even more refined measures of the underrepresentation in each job category that required attention.

As the Agency Plan recognized, women were most egregiously underrepresented in the Skilled Craft job category, since *none* of the 238 positions was occupied by a woman. In mid-1980, when Joyce was selected for the road dispatcher position, the Agency was still in the process of refining its short-term goals for Skilled Craft Workers in accordance with the directive of the Plan. . . .

We reject petitioner's argument that, since only the long-term goal was in place for Skilled Craft positions at the time of Joyce's promotion, it was inappropriate for the Director to take into account affirmative action considerations in filling the road dispatcher position. The Agency's Plan emphasized that the long-term goals were not to be taken as guides for actual hiring decisions, but that supervisors were to consider a host of practical factors in seeking to meet affirmative action objectives, including the fact that in some job categories women were not qualified in numbers comparable to their representation in the labor force.

. . . analysis of a more specialized labor pool normally is necessary in determining underrepresentation in some positions. If a plan failed to take distinctions in qualifications into account in providing guidance for actual employment decisions, it would dictate mere blind hiring by the numbers, for it would hold supervisors to "achievement of a particular percentage of minority employment or membership . . . regardless of circumstances such as economic conditions or the number of qualified minority applicants . . ."

The Agency's Plan emphatically did *not* authorize such blind hiring. It expressly directed that numerous factors be taken into account in making hiring decisions, including specifically the qualifications of female applicants for particular jobs. Thus, despite the fact that no precise short-term goal was yet in place for the Skilled Craft category in mid-1980, the Agency's management nevertheless had been clearly instructed that they were not to hire solely by reference to statistics.

. . . Given the obvious imbalance in the Skilled Craft category, and given the Agency's commitment to eliminating such imbalances, it was plainly not unreasonable for the Agency to determine that it was appropriate to consider as one factor the sex of Ms. Joyce in making its decision. The promotion of Joyce thus satisfies the first requirement enunciated in *Weber,* since it was undertaken to further an affirmative action plan designed to eliminate Agency work force imbalances in traditionally segregated job categories.

We next consider whether the Agency Plan unnecessarily trammeled the rights of male employees or created an absolute bar to their advancement. In contrast to the plan in *Weber,* which provided that 50 percent of the positions in the craft training program were exclusively for blacks, the Plan sets aside no positions for women. The Plan expressly states that "[t]he 'goals' established for each Division should not be construed as 'quotas' that must be met." Rather, the Plan merely authorizes that consideration be given to affirmative action concerns when evaluating qualified applicants. As the Agency Director testified, the sex of Joyce was but one of numerous factors he took into account in arriving at his decision.... the Agency Plan requires women to compete with all other qualified applicants. *No* persons are automatically excluded from consideration; *all* are able to have their qualifications weighed against those of other applicants.

In addition, petitioner had no absolute entitlement to the road dispatcher position. Seven of the applicants were classified as qualified and eligible, and the Agency Director was authorized to promote any of the seven. Thus, denial of the promotion unsettled no legitimate firmly rooted expectation on the part of the petitioner. Furthermore, while the petitioner in this case was denied a promotion, he retained his employment with the Agency, at the same salary and with the same seniority, and remained eligible for other promotions.

Finally, the Agency's Plan was intended to *attain* a balanced work force, not to maintain one. The Plan contains ten references to the Agency's desire to "attain" such a balance, but no reference whatsoever to a goal of maintaining it.... The Agency acknowledged the difficulties that it would confront in remedying the imbalance in its work force, and it anticipated only gradual increases in the representation of minorities and women. It is thus unsurprising that the Plan contains no explicit end date, for the Agency's flexible, case-by-case approach was not expected to yield success in a brief period of time. Express assurance that a program is only temporary may be necessary if the program actually sets aside positions according to specific numbers. This is necessary both to minimize the effect of the program on other employees, and to ensure that the plan's goals "[are] not being used simply to achieve and maintain ... balance, but rather as a benchmark against which the employer may measure its progress in eliminating the underrepresentation of minorities and women. In this case, however, substantial evidence shows that the Agency has sought to take a moderate, gradual approach to eliminating the imbalance in its work force, one which establishes realistic guidance for employment decisions, and which visits minimal intrusion on the legitimate expectations of other employees. Given this fact as well as the Agency's express commitment to "attain" a balanced work force, there is ample assurance that the Agency does not seek to use its Plan to maintain a permanent racial and sexual balance....

We therefore hold that the Agency appropriately took into account as one factor the sex of Diane Joyce in determining that she should be promoted to the road dispatcher position. The decision to do so was made pursuant to an affirmative action plan that represents a moderate, flexible, case-by-case approach to effecting a gradual improvement in the representation of minorities and women in the Agency's work force. Such a plan is fully consistent with Title VII, for it embodies the contribution that voluntary employer action can make in eliminating the vestiges of discrimination in the workplace. Accordingly, the judgment of the Court of Appeals is **Affirmed.**

O'CONNOR, J. (concurring)

... I concur in the judgment of the Court in light of our precedents. I write separately, however, because the Court has chosen to follow an expansive and ill-defined approach to voluntary affirmative action by public employers despite the limitations imposed by the Constitution and by the provisions of Title VII, and because the dissent rejects the Court's precedents and addresses the question of how Title VII should be interpreted as if the Court were writing on a clean slate....

In my view, the proper initial inquiry in evaluating the legality of an affirmative action plan by a public employer under Title VII is no different from that required by the Equal Protection Clause. In either case ... the employer must have had a firm basis for believing that remedial action was required. An employer would have such a firm basis if it can point to a statistical disparity sufficient to support a prima facie claim under Title VII by the employee beneficiaries of the affirmative action plan of a pattern or practice claim of discrimination....

Unfortunately, the Court today gives little guidance for what statistical imbalance is sufficient to support an affirmative action plan. Although the Court denies that the statistical imbalance need be sufficient to make out a prima facie case of discrimination against women, the Court fails to suggest an alternative standard.... I see little justification for the adoption of different standards for affirmative action under Title VII and the Equal Protection Clause.

While employers must have a firm basis for concluding that remedial action is necessary, neither *Wygant* nor *Weber* places a burden on employers to prove that they actually discriminated against women or minorities.

... While I agree with the dissent that an affirmative action program that automatically and blindly promotes those marginally qualified candidates falling within a preferred race or gender category, or that can be equated with a permanent plan of "proportionate representation by race and sex" would violate Title VII, I cannot agree that this is such a case. Rather, as the Court demonstrates, Joyce's sex was simply used as a "plus" factor.

In this case, I am also satisfied that the respondent had a firm basis for adopting an affirmative action program. Although the District Court found no discrimination against women in fact, at the time the affirmative action plan was adopted, there were *no* women in its skilled craft positions. The petitioner concedes that women constituted approximately 5 percent of the local labor pool of skilled craft workers in 1970. Thus, when compared to the percentage of women in the qualified work force, the statistical disparity would have been sufficient for a prima facie Title VII case brought by unsuccessful women job applicants. . . .

WHITE, J. (dissenting)

. . . My understanding of *Weber* was, and is, that the employer's plan did not violate Title VII because it was designed to remedy intentional and systematic exclusion of blacks by the employer and the unions from certain job categories. That is how I understood the phrase "traditionally segregated jobs" we used in that case. The Court now interprets it to mean nothing more than a manifest imbalance between one identifiable group and another in an employer's labor force. As so interpreted, that case, as well as today's decision . . . is a perversion of Title VII. I would overrule *Weber* and reverse the judgment below.

In *Firefighters Local Union No. 1784* v. *Stotts* (467 U.S. 561, 104. S.Ct. 2576, 1984), the Supreme Court was faced with the question of whether a trial court could unilaterally modify an agreement (known as a "consent decree"), settling a discrimination suit to override seniority-based layoffs. The Supreme Court held that the trial court could not make such a unilateral modification, overriding a bona fide seniority system, when the consent decree was silent as to seniority and the employer had never been found guilty of discrimination.

In *Stotts,* Justice White's opinion raised, but did not answer, the question of whether affirmative action could be used to benefit minority employees who were not themselves actual victims of discrimination. This question was addressed two years later by the Court in the case of *Local 28, Sheet Metal Workers Int'l. Ass'n.* v. *EEOC* (478 U.S. 421, 1986). In that case, the Supreme Court held that a court may impose an affirmative action program in order to remedy "persistent or egregious discrimination," even if the affirmative action program has the effect of benefitting individuals who were not themselves victims of discrimination. The Court emphasized that affirmative action programs should be imposed by a court only as a last resort, and such programs should be "tailor[ed] . . . to fit the nature of the violation" the court seeks to correct.

In another case decided the same day as *Local 28,* the Court held that a consent decree may require an affirmative action plan after the employer has been found guilty of discrimination. *Local 93, International Ass'n of Firefighters* v. *Cleveland* (478 U.S. 501, 1986). The Court also held, as in *Local 28,* that the affirmative action relief can benefit minority employees who were not personally victims of the employer's past discrimination.

Other Provisions of Title VII

The 1991 amendments to Title VII added two other provisions to the act. One addresses the ability to challenge affirmative action programs and other employment practices that implement judicial decisions or result from consent decrees. Section

703(n) now provides that such practice may not be challenged by any person who had notice of such decision or decree and had an opportunity to present objections, or by any person whose interests were adequately represented by another person who had previously challenged the judgment or decree on the same legal ground and with a similar factual situation. Challenges based on claims that the order or decree was obtained through fraud or collusion, is "transparently invalid," or was entered by a court lacking jurisdiction, are not prevented by Section 703(n).

The other added provision deals with the practice known as "race norming." Race norming refers to the practice of using different cutoff scores for different racial, gender, or ethnic groups of applicants, or adjusting test scores or otherwise altering test results of employment-related tests on the basis of race, color, religion, sex, or natural origin. Section 703(l) makes race norming an unlawful employment practice under Title VII.

QUESTIONS

1. What are the main provisions of Title VII of the Civil Rights Act? Which employers are subject to Title VII?

2. What is meant by a bona fide occupational qualification (BFOQ)? What must be shown to establish that job-selection requirements are BFOQ?

3. What is meant by disparate treatment? What is meant by disparate impact? How can a claim of disparate impact be demonstrated?

4. Can an employer use employment testing to select employees? Explain your answer. What must an employer show to continue to use job requirements held to have a disparate impact on a protected group of employees or applicants?

5. What is meant by the bottom line defense? Is it a sufficient answer to a claim of employment discrimination? Explain your answer.

6. When is a seniority system protected against challenge under Title VII? When is a seniority system bona fide under Title VII?

7. When are affirmative action programs legal under Title VII? Explain your answer.

8. What is the difference, if any, between the "job-related" test for a selection device with a disparate impact and the "business necessity" test for BFOQ?

CASE PROBLEMS

1. More than forty years ago the Philadelphia Electric Company recognized the Independent Group Association (IGA) as the representative of its employee-members for the presentation of grievances to management. Several employees formed the Black Grievance Committee (BGC) in response to their perception that IGA was unresponsive to the employer's alleged discriminatory practices. The employer refused to recognize or deal with the BGC, insisting that the IGA was to have exclusive recognition for grievance purposes.

Is Philadelphia Electric Company guilty of race discrimination in refusing to recognize the BGC? Is this refusal an unfair labor practice under the National Labor Relations Act? See *Black Grievance Committee* v. *N.L.R.B.,* 749 F.2d 1072 (3d Cir. 1984), *cert. denied,* 105 S.Ct. 565 (1985).

2. The city of Montgomery, Alabama, had a policy for its fire department that any firefighter convicted of a felony would be discharged. In August 1976 two white

firefighters were fired after being convicted of felonies. However, on appealing their discharges to the Montgomery City-County Personnel Board, they were reinstated. In November 1979 Tate Williams, an African-American man, was discharged, and on appeal, the National Labor Relations Board refused reinstatement.

Was this refusal race discrimination? Does your answer depend on whether the white firefighters had committed less serious felonies than Williams? Should the board have considered each man's overall record in rendering its decisions? Are there any other factors the board should have taken into account? See *Williams* v. *City of Montgomery,* 742 F.2d 586, 37 F.E.P. Cases 52 (11th Cir. 1984).

3. In November 1979 a supervisor saw white employee Bill Peterson accept from an employee of another company on the same construction site what appeared to be a marijuana cigarette. Peterson subsequently confessed to taking a few puffs from the "joint," and he was fired. A day later the company put out a general hiring call; Peterson applied and was rehired. In August 1980 the company promulgated a new rule that anyone fired could not be rehired for at least thirty days. In October 1980, Albert Leonard, an African-American man, was hired as a laborer. During a routine lunch-box check by a security guard at the gate that very day, Leonard was found to be in possession of marijuana. He was fired the next day, and his termination notice contained a notation "not for rehire." Leonard was never rehired, either within or after thirty days from his discharge.

Is he a victim of race discrimination? Explain your answer. See *Leonard* v. *Walsh Construction Co.,* 37 F.E.P. Cases 60 (U.S. Dist. Ct. S.D. Ga. 1985).

4. Sue Bedean, an engineer, was hired by the Tennessee Valley Authority under a voluntarily adopted affirmative action plan designed to bring females into traditionally male technical jobs. After a few months on the job, Bedean was laid off because of economic conditions; the other two engineers in her department, who were both male, were not laid off. The employer asserted that the two male engineers were more qualified than Bedean. Bedean filed suit under Title VII, arguing that the employer's failure to give her preference on layoff was a violation of the affirmative action program and of Title VII. Is the employer required by Title VII to continue to give preference to Bedean, after hiring her under an affirmative action program? Is a violation of the affirmative action program a violation of Title

VII? Explain your answer. See *Liao* v. *TVA,* 867 F.2d 1366 (11th Cir. 1989).

5. Chaline, a white male, was employed as a production manager at an African-American-oriented radio station in Houston. Chaline had previously worked as a disc jockey at other radio stations. The radio station manager, for financial reasons, decided to combine the production manager position with that of a part-time disc jockey. Chaline desired to remain as production manager and to assume the disc jockey duties. However, the station manager told him that he lacked the proper "voice" to serve as disc jockey on the station and that he was not sensitive to the listening tastes of the African-American audience. The radio station had never had a white disc jockey. The station manager asked Chaline to transfer to a position in the sales department; Chaline refused and was discharged. Chaline filed a complaint with the EEOC challenging his discharge on grounds of race discrimination.

If the complaint results in a suit in federal court, will Chaline be successful? Explain your answer. See *Chaline* v. *KCOH, Inc.,* 693 F.2d 477 (5th Cir. 1982).

6. The City of South Bend, Indiana, adopted an affirmative action plan to give preference to minorities in hiring and promotion for police and firefighter positions. The affirmative action plan was adopted voluntarily by the city in response to the marked disparity between the percentage of African-American employees in the police and fire departments with the percentage of African Americans in the general population of the city. Janowiak, a white, filed suit challenging the affirmative action plan; he argued that the city should have compared the percentage of African-American employees in the police and fire departments with the percentage of African Americans in the qualified area labor pool in order to determine whether the affirmative action plan was necessary. How will the court rule on his challenge—what is the proper comparison to determine whether the affirmative plan is justified? See *Janowiak* v. *Corporate City of South Bend,* 836 F.2d 1034 (7th Cir. 1989), *cert. denied,* 489 U.S. 1051 (1989).

7. Crystal Chambers, a twenty-two-year-old unmarried African-American woman, was employed by the Girls Club of Omaha, Nebraska. The club, whose membership was more than half African American, had as its stated goal to "provide a safe alternative from the streets and to help girls take care of themselves."

Because of two incidents of unwed motherhood

among staff members, the club's directors passed a Negative Role Model Policy, which stated that any unwed employee who became pregnant would be terminated. Pursuant to this policy, Chambers was fired when she became pregnant.

Can you suggest a theory under which Chambers could challenge her discharge based on race discrimination? Can the girls club articulate a bona fide business reason sufficient to overcome a finding of race discrimination? See *Chambers* v. *Omaha Girls Club,* 834 F.2d 697 (8th Cir. 1987).

8. King was hired by the University of Minnesota as a full, tenured professor in 1970. He was appointed to the Afro-American Studies Department and later became chairman. Four years later he was asked to step down as chairman. The University alleged it had received many complaints from King's students and colleagues concerning poor teaching, absence from class, low enrollment, and undocumented research. Consequently, the University repeatedly denied King salary increases and ultimately approved a nine-to-two vote in his department to fire him, pursuant to the complex procedures in the school's tenure code.

Assuming that King was guilty as charged, what arguments, if any, remain available to him if he tries to challenge his dismissal on the basis of race discrimination? Recall some of the issues discussed in Chapter 11; does King have any other legal theories available under which to attack his dismissal that are not available to faculty at private universities? See *King* v. *University of Minnesota,* 774 F.2d. 224 (8th Cir. 1985), *cert. denied,* 475 U.S. 1095 (1986).

9. Since his childhood, Dennis Walters, a white man, had dreamed of becoming director of the Atlanta Cyclor-

ama, a gigantic display depicting a famous Civil War battle. Before ever applying for this position, Walters gained experience in historical preservation with the Georgia Historical Commission and the North Carolina Museum of History. Despite this experience, every time he applied for the post (which became available in 1981), he was rejected. First an African-American female who had been a campaign aide to Atlanta's mayor was selected. When she left the job a year later, Walters reapplied. He was judged qualified, but when an African-American applicant was ruled unqualified, the position was reannounced rather than being offered to Walters or any other white candidate. Next, an African-American male was hired. When he was fired a short time later, Walters again applied. This time a white female was hired. Walters filed a reverse race discrimination charge with the EEOC.

Was Walters a victim of race discrimination? Does it matter whether the white female who ultimately got the job was better qualified than Walters? If Walters wins, what remedy should he receive? See *Walters* v. *City of Atlanta,* 803 F.2d 1135 (11th Cir. 1986).

10. A group of African-American steelworkers employed by the Lukens Steel Company alleged that they were victims of racial discrimination in their treatment by the company. At the same time they charged their union with illegal discrimination in violation of Title VII, asserting that the union failed to vigorously pursue their grievances against the company.

Should the courts entertain this claim against the union? Is there a possible preemption problem? If allowed to sue their union, what remedy should the African-American employees seek against the labor organization? See *United Steelworkers* v. *Goodman,* 479 U.S. 982 (1986).

C H A P T E R 13

Equal Employment Legislation: Title VII and Discrimination Based on Sex, Religion, and National Origin

THE PRECEDING CHAPTER DEALT with Title VII of the Civil Rights Act of 1964 and its prohibitions on employment discrimination based on race. This chapter will deal with the Title VII provisions regarding discrimination based on sex, religion, and national origin.

Sex Discrimination

Title VII prohibits any discrimination in terms or conditions of employment because of an employee's sex. Employers who refuse to hire women for particular jobs are in violation of the act unless they can demonstrate that being male is a bona fide occupational qualification (BFOQ) for those jobs. The act prohibits advertising for male or female employees in help-wanted notices (unless it is a BFOQ), or maintaining separate seniority lists for male and female employees. Unions that negotiate such separate seniority lists or refuse to admit female members also violate Title VII.

BFOQ—Bona Fide Occupational Qualification

As mentioned in Chapter 12, the act does allow employers to hire only employees of one sex, or of a particular religion or national origin, if that trait is a BFOQ. Section 703(e)(1), which defines the BFOQ exemption, states that

> ... it shall not be an unlawful employment practice for an employer to hire and employ employees, for an employment agency to classify, or refer for employment any individual,

for a labor organization to classify its membership or to classify or refer for employment any individual ... on the basis of his religion, sex, or national origin in those certain instances where religion, sex, or national origin is a bona fide occupational qualification reasonably necessary to the normal operation of that particular business or enterprise. ...

Notice that an employer must justify a BFOQ on the basis of business necessity. (The statutory provision also says race or color can never be used as BFOQs; in other words, there can never be a valid business necessity for selecting employees based on their race or color.) What must be demonstrated to establish a claim of business necessity by an employer? The following cases illustrate the approach taken by the courts when an employer claims a BFOQ based on sex.

DIAZ v. PAN AMERICAN WORLD AIRWAYS

442 F.2d 385 (U.S. Court of Appeals for the Fifth Circuit, 1971)

TUTTLE, J.

The facts in this case are not in dispute. Celio Diaz applied for a job as flight cabin attendant with Pan American Airlines in 1967. He was rejected because Pan Am had a policy of restricting its hiring for that position to females. He then filed charges with the Equal Employment Opportunity Commission (EEOC) alleging that Pan Am had unlawfully discriminated against him on the grounds of sex. The Commission found probable cause to believe his charge, but was unable to resolve the matter through conciliation with Pan Am. Diaz next filed a class action in the United States District Court for the Southern District of Florida on behalf of himself and others similarly situated, alleging that Pan Am had violated Section 703 of the 1964 Civil Rights Act by refusing to employ him on the basis of his sex; he sought an injunction and damages.

Pan Am admitted that it had a policy of restricting its hiring for the cabin attendant position to females. Thus, both parties stipulated that the primary issue for the District Court was whether, for the job of flight cabin attendant, being a female is a "bona fide occupational qualification (hereafter BFOQ) reasonably necessary to the normal operation" of Pan American's business. ...

We note, at the outset, that there is little legislative history to guide our interpretation. The amendment adding the word "sex" to "race, color, religion and national origin" was adopted one day before House passage of the Civil Rights Act. It was added on the floor and engendered little relevant debate. In attempting to read Congress' intent in

these circumstances, however, it is reasonable to assume, for a reading of the statute itself, that one of Congress' main goals was to provide equal access to the job market for both men and women. Indeed ... the purpose of the Act was to provide a foundation in the law for the principle of nondiscrimination. Construing the statute as embodying such a principle is based on the assumption that Congress sought a formula that would not only achieve the optimum use of our labor resources but, and more importantly, would enable individuals to develop as individuals.

Attainment of this goal, however, is, as stated above, limited by the bona fide occupational qualification exception in Section 703(e). In construing this provision, we feel, that it would be totally anomalous to do so in a manner that would, in effect, permit the exception to swallow the rule. Thus, we adopt the EEOC guidelines which state that "the Commission believes that the bona fide occupational qualification as to sex should be interpreted narrowly." Indeed, close scrutiny of the language of the exception compels this result. ...

Thus, it is with this orientation that we now examine the trial court's decision. Its conclusion was based upon (1) its view of Pan Am's history of the use of flight attendants; (2) passenger preference; (3) basic psychological reasons for the preference; and (4) the actualities of the hiring process.

Having reviewed the evidence submitted by Pan American regarding its own experience with both female and male cabin attendants it had hired over the years, the trial court found that Pan Am's current hiring policy was the result of a pragmatic process, "representing a judgment made upon adequate evidence acquired through Pan Am's considerable experience, and designed to yield under Pan Am's current operating conditions better *average* performance for its passengers than would a policy of mixed male and female hiring." (emphasis added) The performance of female attendants was *better* in the sense that they were *superior* in such non-mechanical aspects of the job as "providing reassurance to anxious passengers, giving courteous personalized service and, in general, making flights as pleasurable as possible within the limitations imposed by aircraft operations."

The trial court also found that Pan Am's passengers overwhelmingly preferred to be served by female stewardesses. Moreover, on the basis of the expert testimony of a psychiatrist, the court found that an airplane cabin represents a unique environment in which an air carrier is required to take account of the special psychological needs of its passengers. These psychological needs are better attended to by females. This is not to say that there are no males who would not [sic] have the necessary qualities to perform these non-mechanical functions, but the trial court found that the actualities of the hiring process would make it more difficult to find these few males. Indeed, "the admission of men to the hiring process, in the present state of the art of employment selection, would have increased the number of unsatisfactory employees hired, and reduced the average levels of performance of Pan Am's complement of flight attendants . . ." In what appears to be a summation of the difficulties which the trial court found would follow from admitting males to this job the court said "that to eliminate the female sex qualification would simply eliminate the best available tool for screening out applicants *likely* to be unsatisfactory and thus reduce the *average* level of performance." (emphasis added)

Because of the narrow reading we give to Section 703(e), we do not feel that these findings justify the discrimination practiced by Pan Am.

We begin with the proposition that the use of the word "necessary" in Section 703(e) requires that we apply a business *necessity* test, not a business *convenience* test. That is to say, discrimination based on sex is valid only when the *essence* of the business operation would be undermined by not hiring members of one sex exclusively.

The primary function of an airline is to transport passengers safely from one point to another. While a pleasant environment, enhanced by the obvious cosmetic effect that female stewardesses provide as well as, according to the finding of the trial court, their apparent ability to perform the non-mechanical functions of the job in a more effective manner than most men, may all be important, they are tangential to the essence of the business involved. No one has suggested that having male stewards will so seriously affect

the operation of an airline as to jeopardize or even minimize its ability to provide safe transportation from one place to another. Indeed the record discloses that many airlines including Pan Am have utilized both men and women flight cabin attendants in the past and Pan Am, even at the time of this suit, has 283 male stewards employed on some of its foreign flights.

We do not mean to imply, of course, that Pan Am cannot take into consideration the ability of *individuals* to perform the non-mechanical functions of the job. What we hold is that because the non-mechanical aspects of the job of flight cabin attendant are not "reasonably necessary to the normal operation" of Pan Am's business, Pan Am cannot exclude *all* males simply because *most* males may not perform adequately. . . .

We do not agree that in this case "all or substantially all men" have been shown to be inadequate. . . .

Appellees also argue, and the trial court found, that because of the actualities of the hiring process, "the *best* available initial test for determining whether a particular applicant for employment is likely to have the personality characteristics conducive to high-level performance of the flight attendant's job as currently defined is consequently that applicant's biological sex." Indeed, the trial court found that it was simply not practicable to find the few males that would perform properly.

We do not feel that this alone justifies discriminating against all males. Since, as stated above, the basis of exclusion is the ability to perform non-mechanical functions which we find to be tangential to what is "reasonably *necessary*" for the business involved, the exclusion of *all* males because this is the *best* way to select the kind of personnel Pan Am desires simply cannot be justified. Before sex discrimination can be practiced, it must not only be shown that it is impracticable to find the men that possess the abilities that most women possess, but that the abilities are *necessary* to the business, not merely tangential.

Similarly, we do not feel that the fact that Pan Am's passengers prefer female stewardesses should alter our judgment. On this subject, EEOC guidelines state that a BFOQ ought not to be based on "the refusal to hire an individual because of the preferences of co-workers, the employer, clients or customers. . . ."

. . . While we recognize that the public's expectation of finding one sex in a particular role may cause some initial difficulty, it would be totally anomalous if we were to allow the preferences and prejudices of the customers to determine whether the sex discrimination was valid. Indeed, it was, to a large extent, these very prejudices the Act was meant to overcome. Thus, we feel that customer preference may be taken into account only when it is based on the company's inability to perform the primary function or service it offers.

Of course, Pan Am argues that the customers' preferences are not based on "stereotyped thinking," but the ability of women stewardesses to better provide the non-mechanical aspects of the job. Again, as stated above, since these aspects are tangential to the business, the fact that customers prefer them cannot justify sex discrimination.

The judgment is reversed and the case remanded for proceedings not inconsistent with this opinion. **So ordered.**

DOTHARD v. RAWLINSON

433 U.S. 321 (Supreme Court of the United States, 1977)

STEWART, J.

The appellee, Dianne Rawlinson, sought employment with the Alabama Board of Corrections as a prison guard, called in Alabama a "correctional counselor." After her application was rejected, she brought this class suit under Title VII of the Civil Rights Act of 1964 . . . alleging that she had been denied employment because of her sex in violation of federal law. A three-judge Federal District Court for the Middle District of Alabama decided in her favor. We noted probable jurisdiction of this appeal from the District Court's judgment. . . .

At the time she applied for a position as a correctional counselor trainee, Rawlinson was a 22-year-old college graduate whose major course of study had been correctional psychology.

After her application was rejected because of her weight, Rawlinson filed a charge with the Equal Employment Opportunity Commission, and ultimately received a right to sue letter. She then filed a complaint in the District Court on behalf of herself and other similarly situated women, challenging their statutory height and weight minima as violative of Title VII and the Equal Protection Clause of the Fourteenth Amendment. A three-judge court was convened. While the suit was pending, the Alabama Board of Corrections adopted Administrative Regulation 204, establishing gender criteria for assigning correctional counselors to maximum security institutions for "contact positions," that is, positions requiring continual close physical proximity to inmates of the institution. Rawlinson amended her class-action complaint by adding a challenge to Regulation 204 as also violative of Title VII and the Fourteenth Amendment. . . .

A correctional counselor's primary duty within these institutions is to maintain security and control of the inmates by continually supervising and observing their activities. . . .

At the time this litigation was in the District Court, the Board of Corrections employed a total of 435 people in various correctional counselor positions, 56 of whom were women. Of those 56 women, 21 were employed at the Julia Tutwiler Prison for Women, 13 were employed in noncontact positions at the four male maximum security institutions, and the remaining 22 were employed at the other institutions operated by the Alabama Board of Corrections. Because most of Alabama's prisoners are held at the four maximum security male penitentiaries, 336 of the 435 correctional counselor jobs were in those institutions, a majority of them concededly in the "contact" classification. Thus . . . women applicants could under Regulation 204 compete equally with men for only about 25 percent of the correctional counselor jobs available in the Alabama prison system. . . .

. . . In *Diaz* v. *Pan American Airways,* the Court of Appeals for the Fifth Circuit held that "discrimination based on sex is valid only when the *essence* of the business operation would be undermined by not hiring members of one sex exclusively." (Emphasis in original.) In an earlier case, *Weeks* v. *Southern Bell Telephone and Telegraph Co.,* the same court said that an employer could rely on the BFOQ exception only by proving "that he had reasonable cause to believe, that is, a factual basis for believing, that all or substantially all women would be unable to perform safely and efficiently the duties of the job involved." But whatever the verbal formulation, the federal courts have agreed that it is impermissible under Title VII to refuse to hire an individual woman or man on the basis of stereotyped characterizations of the sexes, and the District Court in the present case held in effect that Regulation 204 is based on just such stereotypical assumptions.

We are persuaded—by the restrictive language of Section

703(e), the relevant legislative history, and the consistent interpretation of the Equal Employment Opportunity Commission—that the BFOQ exception was in fact meant to be an extremely narrow exception to the general prohibition of discrimination on the basis of sex. In the particular factual circumstances of this case, however, we conclude that the District Court erred in rejecting the State's contention that Regulation 204 falls within the narrow ambit of the BFOQ exception.

The environment in Alabama's penitentiaries is a peculiarly inhospitable one for human beings of whatever sex. Indeed, a federal district court has held that the conditions of confinement in the prisons of the State, characterized by "rampant violence" and a "jungle atmosphere," are constitutionally intolerable. The record in the present case shows that because of inadequate staff and facilities, no attempt is made for the four maximum security male penitentiaries to classify or segregate inmates according to their offense or level of dangerousness—a procedure that, according to expert testimony, is essential to effective penalogical administration. Consequently, the estimated 20 percent of the male prisoners who are sex offenders are scattered throughout the penitentiaries' dormitory facilities.

In this environment of violence and disorganization, it would be an oversimplification to characterize Regulation 204 as an exercise in "romantic paternalism." In the usual case, the argument that a particular job is too dangerous for women may appropriately be met by the rejoinder that it is the purpose of Title VII to allow the individual woman to make that choice for herself. More is at stake in this case, however, than an individual woman's decision to weigh and accept the risks of employment in a "contact" position in a maximum security male prison.

The essence of a correctional counselor's job is to maintain prison security. A woman's relative ability to maintain order in a male, maximum security, unclassified penitentiary of the type Alabama now runs could be directly reduced by her womanhood. There is a basis in fact of expecting that sex offenders who have criminally assaulted women in the past would be moved to do so again if access to women were established within the prison. There would also be a real risk that other inmates, deprived of a normal heterosexual environment, would assault women guards because they were women. In a prison system where violence is the order of the day, where inmate access to guards is facilitated by dormitory living arrangements, where every institution is understaffed, and where a substantial portion of the inmate population is composed of sex offenders mixed at random with other prisoners, there are few visible deterrents to inmate assaults on women custodians.

The plaintiffs' own expert testified that dormitory housing for aggressive inmates poses a greater security problem than single-cell lockups, and further testified that it would be unwise to use women as guards in a prison where even 10 percent of the inmates had been convicted of sex crimes and were not segregated from other prisoners. The likelihood that inmates would assault a woman because she was a woman would pose a real threat not only to the victim of the assault but also the basic control of the penitentiary and protection of its inmates and the other security personnel. The employee's very womanhood would thus directly undermine her capacity to provide the security that is the essence of a correctional counselor's responsibility.

There was substantial testimony from experts on both sides of this litigation that the use of women as guards in "contact" positions under the existing conditions in Alabama maximum security male penitentiaries would pose a substantial security problem, directly linked to the sex of the prison guard. On the basis of that evidence, we conclude that the District Court was in error in ruling that being male is not a bona fide occupational qualification for the job of correctional counselor in a "contact" position in an Alabama male maximum security penitentiary.

The judgment is accordingly affirmed in part and reversed in part, and the case is remanded to the District Court for further proceedings consistent with this opinion. **It is so ordered.**

The courts will also allow claims of a BFOQ based on sex when community standards of morality or propriety require that employees be of a particular sex; for example, hiring females only to work as attendants in the fitting rooms of a woman's dress shop, or hiring males as locker-room attendants for the men's locker rooms in an athletic club.

Sex Stereotyping

If an employer refuses to promote a female employee because, despite her excellent performance, she is perceived as being too aggressive and unfeminine, has the employer engaged in sex discrimination in violation of Title VII? That question was addressed by the Supreme Court in the following case.

PRICE WATERHOUSE v. ANN B. HOPKINS

490 U.S. 228 (Supreme Court of the United States, 1989)

BRENNAN, J.

Ann Hopkins was a senior manager in an office of Price Waterhouse when she was proposed for partnership in 1982. She was neither offered nor denied admission to the partnership; instead, her candidacy was held for reconsideration the following year. When the partners in her office later refused to repropose her for partnership, she sued Price Waterhouse under Title VII of the Civil Rights Act of 1964, charging that the firm had discriminated against her on the basis of sex in its decisions regarding partnership. Judge Gesell in the District Court for the District of Columbia ruled in her favor on the question of liability and the Court of Appeals for the District of Columbia Circuit affirmed. We granted certiorari . . .

At Price Waterhouse, a nationwide professional accounting partnership, a senior manager becomes a candidate for partnership when the partners in her local office submit her name as a candidate. All the other partners in the firm are then invited to submit written comments on each candidate—either on a "long" or a "short" form, depending on the partner's degree of exposure to the candidate. Not every partner in the firm submits comments on every candidate. After reviewing the comments and interviewing the partners who submitted them, the firm's Admission Committee makes a recommendation to the Policy Board. This recommendation will be either that the firm accept the candidate for partnership, put her application on "hold," or deny her the promotion outright. The Policy Board then decides whether to submit the candidate's name to the entire partnership for a vote, to "hold" her candidacy, or to reject her. The recommendation of the Admissions Committee, and the decision of the Policy Board, are not controlled by fixed guidelines: a certain number of positive comments from partners will not guarantee a candidate's admission to

the partnership, nor will a specific quantity of negative comments necessarily defeat her application. . . .

Ann Hopkins had worked at Price Waterhouse's Office of Government Services in Washington, D.C., for five years when the partners in that office proposed her as a candidate for partnership. Of the 662 partners at the firm at that time, 7 were women. Of the 88 persons proposed for partnership that year, only 1—Hopkins—was a woman. Forty-seven of these candidates were admitted to the partnership, 21 were rejected, and 20—including Hopkins—were "held" for reconsideration the following year. Thirteen of the 32 partners who had submitted comments on Hopkins supported her bid for partnership. Three partners recommended that her candidacy be placed on hold, eight stated that they did not have an informed opinion about her, and eight recommended that she be denied partnership.

In a jointly prepared statement supporting her candidacy, the partners in Hopkins' office showcased her successful 2-year effort to secure a $25 million contract with the Department of State, labeling it "an outstanding performance" and one that Hopkins carried out "virtually at the partner level." Despite Price Waterhouse's attempt at trial to minimize her contribution to this project, Judge Gesell specifically found that Hopkins had "played a key role in Price Waterhouse's successful effort to win a multi-million dollar contract with the Department of State." Indeed, he went on, "[n]one of the other partnership candidates at Price Waterhouse that year had a comparable record in terms of successfully securing major contracts for the partnership." The partners in Hopkins' office praised her character as well as her accomplishments, describing her in their joint statement as "an outstanding professional" who had a "deft touch," a "strong character, independence and integrity." Clients appear to have agreed with these assessments. . . . Evaluations such as these led Judge Gesell to conclude that Hopkins "had no difficulty dealing with clients and her clients appear to have been very pleased with her work" and that she "was generally viewed as a highly competent project leader who worked long hours, pushed vigorously to meet deadlines and demanded much from the multidisciplinary staffs with which she worked."

On too many occasions, however, Hopkins' aggressiveness apparently spilled over into abrasiveness. Staff members seem to have borne the brunt of Hopkins' brusqueness. Long before her bid for partnership, partners evaluating her work had counseled her to improve her relations with staff members. Although later evaluations indicate an improvement, Hopkins' perceived shortcomings in this important area eventually doomed her bid for partnership. Virtually all of the partners' negative remarks about Hopkins—even those of partners supporting her—had to do with her "interpersonal skills." Both "[s]upporters and opponents of her candidacy," stressed Judge Gesell, "indicated that she was sometimes overly aggressive, unduly harsh, difficult to work with and impatient with staff."

There were clear signs, though, that some of the partners reacted negatively to Hopkins' personality because she was a woman. One partner described her as "macho"; another suggested that she "overcompensated for being a woman"; a third advised her to take "a course at charm school." Several partners criticized her use of profanity; in response, one partner suggested that those partners objected to her swearing only "because it[']s a lady using foul language." Another supporter explained that Hopkins 'ha[d] matured from a tough-talking somewhat masculine hard-nosed mgr to an authoritative, formidable, but much more appealing lady ptr candidate." But it was the man who, as Judge Gesell found, bore responsibility for explaining to Hopkins the reasons for the Policy Board's decision to place her candidacy on hold who delivered the *coup de grace*: in order to improve her chances for partnership, Thomas Beyer advised, Hopkins should "walk more femininely, talk more femininely, dress more femininely, wear make-up, have her hair styled, and wear jewelry."

Dr. Susan Fiske, a social psychologist and Associate Professor of Psychology at Carnegie-Mellon University, testified at trial that the partnership selection process at Price Waterhouse was likely influenced by sex stereotyping. Her testimony focused not only on the overtly sex-based comments of partners but also on gender-neutral remarks, made by partners who knew Hopkins only slightly, that were intensely critical of her. One partner, for example, baldly stated that Hopkins was "universally disliked" by staff, and

another described her as "consistently annoying and irritating"; yet these were people who had had very little contact with Hopkins. According to Fiske, Hopkins' uniqueness (as the only woman in the pool of candidates) and the subjectivity of the evaluations made it likely that sharply critical remarks such as these were the product of sex stereotyping. . . . Fiske based her opinion on a review of the submitted comments, explaining that it was commonly accepted practice for social psychologists to reach this kind of conclusion without having met any of the people involved in the decisionmaking process.

In previous years, other female candidates for partnership also had been evaluated in sex-based terms. As a general matter, Judge Gesell concluded "[c]andidates were viewed favorably if partners believed they maintained their femin[in]ity while becoming effective professional managers"; in this environment, "[t]o be identified as a 'women's lib[b]er' was regarded as [a] negative comment." In fact, the judge found that in previous years "[o]ne partner repeatedly commented that he could not consider any woman seriously as a partnership candidate and believed that women were not even capable of functioning as senior managers— yet the firm took no action to discourage his comments and recorded his vote in the overall summary of the evaluations."

Judge Gesell found that Price Waterhouse legitimately emphasized interpersonal skills in its partnership decisions, and also found that the firm had not fabricated its complaints about Hopkins' interpersonal skills as a pretext for discrimination. Moreover, he concluded, the firm did not give decisive emphasis to such traits only because Hopkins was a woman; although there were male candidates who lacked these skills but who were admitted to partnership, the judge found that these candidates possessed other, positive traits that Hopkins lacked.

The judge went on to decide, however, that some of the partners' remarks about Hopkins stemmed from an impermissibly cabined view of the proper behavior of women, and that Price Waterhouse had done nothing to disavow reliance on such comments. He held that Price Waterhouse had unlawfully discriminated against Hopkins on the basis of sex by consciously giving credence and effect to partners' comments that resulted from sex stereotyping. Noting that Price Waterhouse could avoid equitable relief by proving by clear and convincing evidence that it would have placed Hopkins' candidacy on hold even absent this discrimination, the judge decided that the firm had not carried this heavy burden.

The Court of Appeals affirmed the District Court's ultimate conclusion, but departed from its analysis in one particular: it held that even if a plaintiff proves that discrimination played a role in an employment decision, the defendant will not be found liable if it proves, by clear and convincing evidence, that it would have made the same decision in the absence of discrimination. Under this approach, an employer is not deemed to have violated Title VII if it proves that it would have made the same decision in the absence of an impermissible motive, whereas under the District Court's approach, the employer's proof in that respect only avoids equitable relief. We decide today that the Court of Appeals had the better approach, but that both courts erred in requiring the employer to make its proof by clear and convincing evidence. . . .

In passing Title VII, Congress made the simple but momentous announcement that sex, race, religion, and national origin are not relevant to the selection, evaluation, or compensation of employees. Yet, the statute does not purport to limit the other qualities and characteristics that employers may take into account in making employment decisions. . . . Title VII eliminates certain bases for distinguishing among employees while otherwise preserving employers' freedom of choice. This balance between employee rights and employer prerogatives turns out to be decisive in the case before us.

Congress' intent to forbid employers to take gender into account in making employment decisions appears on the face of the statute. . . . We take these words [of Title VII] to mean that gender must be irrelevant to employment decisions. . . . The critical inquiry, the one commanded by the words of Section 703(a)(1), is whether gender was a factor in the employment decision *at the moment it was made.* Moreover, since we know that the words "because of" do not mean "*solely* because of," we also know that Title VII meant to condemn even those decisions based on a mixture of legitimate and illegitimate considerations. When, therefore, an employer considers both gender and legitimate factors at the time of making a decision, that decision was "because of" sex and the other, legitimate considerations— even if we may say later, in the context of litigation, that the decision would have been the same if gender had not been taken into account.

To attribute this meaning to the words "because of" does not, as the dissent asserts, divest them of causal significance. . . . It is difficult for us to imagine that, in the simple words "because of," Congress meant to obligate a plaintiff to identify the precise causal role played by legitimate and illegitimate motivations in the employment decision she challenges. We conclude, instead, that Congress meant to obligate her to prove that the employer relied upon sex-based considerations in coming to its decision. . . .

To say that an employer may not take gender into account is not, however, the end of the matter, for that describes only one aspect of Title VII. The other important aspect of the statute is its preservation of an employer's remaining freedom of choice. We conclude that the preservation of this freedom means that an employer shall not be liable if it can prove that, even if it had not taken gender into account, it would have come to the same decision regarding a particular person. . . .

. . . The central point is this: while an employer may not take gender into account in making an employment decision (except in those very narrow circumstances in which gender is a BFOQ), it it is free to decide against a woman for other reasons. . . . the employer's burden is most appropriately deemed an affirmative defense: the plaintiff must persuade the factfinder on one point, and then the employer, if it wishes to prevail, must persuade it on another.

. . . our assumption always has been that if an employer allows gender to affect its decisionmaking process, then it must carry the burden of justifying its ultimate decision. We have not in the past required women whose gender has proved relevant to an employment decision to establish the negative proposition that they would not have been subject to that decision had they been men, and we do not do so today.

We have . . . been here before. Each time, we have concluded that the plaintiff who shows that an impermissible motive played a motivating part in an adverse employment decision has thereby placed upon the defendant the burden to show that it would have made the same decision in the absence of the unlawful motive. Our decision today treads this well-worn path.

In saying that gender played a motivating part in an employment decision, we mean that, if we asked the employer at the moment of the decision what its reasons were and if we received a truthful response, one of those reasons would be that the applicant or employee was a woman. In the specific context of sex stereotyping, an employer who acts on the basis of a belief that a woman cannot be aggressive, or that she must not be, has acted on the basis of gender.

Although the parties do not overtly dispute this last proposition, the placement by Price Waterhouse of "sex stereotyping" in quotation marks throughout its brief seems to us an insinuation either that such stereotyping was not present in this case or that it lacks legal relevance. We reject both possibilities. As to the existence of sex stereotyping in this case, we are not inclined to quarrel with the District Court's conclusion that a number of the partners' comments showed sex stereotyping at work. As for the legal relevance of sex stereotyping, we are beyond the day when an employer could evaluate employees by assuming or insisting that they matched the stereotype associated with their group, for "'[i]n forbidding employers to discriminate against individuals because of their sex, Congress intended to strike at the entire spectrum of disparate treatment of men and women resulting from sex stereotypes.'" An employer who objects to aggressiveness in women but whose positions require this trait places women in an intolerable and impermissible Catch-22: out of a job if they behave aggressively and out of a job if they don't. Title VII lifts women out of this bind.

Remarks at work that are based on sex stereotypes do not inevitably prove that gender played a part in a particular employment decision. The plaintiff must show that the employer actually relied on her gender in making its decision. In making this showing, stereotyped remarks can certainly be *evidence* that gender played a part. In any event, the stereotyping in this case did not simply consist of stray remarks. On the contrary, Hopkins proved that Price Waterhouse invited partners to submit comments; that some of the comments stemmed from sex stereotyping; that an important part of the Policy Board's decision on Hopkins was an assessment of the submitted comments; and that Price Waterhouse in no way disclaimed reliance on the sex-linked evaluations. This is not, as Price Waterhouse suggests, "discrimination in the air"; rather, it is, as Hopkins puts it, "discrimination brought to ground and visited upon" an employee. . . .

As to the employer's proof, in most cases, the employer should be able to present some objective evidence as to its probable decision in the absence of an impermissible motive." Moreover, proving "that the same decision would have been justified. . . . is not the same as proving that the same decision would have been made." An employer may not, in other words, prevail in a mixed-motives case by offering a legitimate and sufficient reason for its decision if that reason did not motivate it at the time of the decision. Finally, an employer may not meet its burden in such a case by merely showing that at the time of the decision it was motivated only in part by a legitimate reason. The very premise of a mixed-motives case is that a legitimate reason was present, and indeed, in this case, Price Waterhouse already has made this showing by convincing Judge Gesell that Hopkins' interpersonal problems were a legitimate concern. The employer instead must show that its legitimate reason, standing alone, would have induced it to make the same decision.

The courts below held that an employer who has allowed a discriminatory impulse to play a motivating part in an employment decision must prove by clear and convincing evidence that it would have made the same decision in the absence of discrimination. We are persuaded that the better rule is that the employer must make this showing by a preponderance of the evidence. . . .

Since the lower courts required Price Waterhouse to make its proof by clear and convincing evidence, they did not determine whether Price Waterhouse had proved by *a preponderance of the evidence* that it would have placed Hopkins' candidacy on hold even if it had not permitted sex-linked evaluations to play a part in the decisionmaking process. Thus, we shall remand this case so that the determination can be made. . . .

In finding that some of the partners' comments reflected sex stereotyping, the District Court relied in part on Dr. Fiske's expert testimony. . . .

Indeed, we are tempted to say that Dr. Fiske's expert testimony was merely icing on Hopkins' cake. It takes no special training to discern sex stereotyping in a description of an aggressive female employee as requiring "a course at charm school." Nor, turning to Thomas Beyer's memorable advice to Hopkins, does it require expertise in psychology to know that, if an employee's flawed "interpersonal skills" can be corrected by a soft-hued suit or a new shade of lipstick, perhaps it is the employee's sex and not her interpersonal skills that has drawn the criticism.

Price Waterhouse also charges that Hopkins produced no evidence that sex stereotyping played a role in the decision to place her candidacy on hold. As we have stressed, however, Hopkins showed that the partnership solicited evaluations from all of the firm's partners; that it generally relied very heavily on such evaluations in making its decision; that some of the partners' comments were the product of stereotyping; and that the firm in no way disclaimed reliance on those particular comments, either in Hopkins' case or in the past. Certainly a plausible—and, one might say, inevitable—conclusion to draw from this set of circumstances is that the Policy Board in making its decision did in fact take into account all of the partners' comments, including the comments that were motivated by stereotypical notions about women's proper deportment. . . .

Nor is the finding that sex stereotyping played a part in the Policy Board's decision undermined by the fact that many of the suspect comments were made by supporters rather than detractors of Hopkins. A negative comment, even when made in the context of a generally favorable review, nevertheless may influence the decisionmaker to think less highly of the candidate; the Policy Board, in fact, did not simply tally the "yes's" and "no's" regarding a candidate, but carefully reviewed the content of the submitted comments. The additional suggestion that the comments were made by "persons outside the decisionmaking chain"—and therefore could not have harmed Hopkins—simply ignores the critical role that partners' comments played in the Policy Board's partnership decisions.

. . . The District Judge acknowledged that Hopkins' conduct justified complaints about her behavior as a senior manager. But he also concluded that the reactions of at least some of the partners were reactions to her as a *woman* manager. Where an evaluation is based on a subjective assessment of a person's strengths and weaknesses, it is

simply not true that each evaluator will focus on, or even mention, the same weaknesses. Thus, even if we knew that Hopkins had "personality problems," this would not tell us that the partners who cast their evaluations of Hopkins in sex-based terms would have criticized her as sharply (or criticized her at all) if she had been a man. It is not our job to review the evidence and decide that the negative reactions to Hopkins were based on reality; our perception of Hopkins' character is irrelevant. We sit not to determine whether Ms. Hopkins is nice, but to decide whether the partners reacted negatively to her personality because she is a woman.

. . . we reverse the Court of Appeals' judgment against Price Waterhouse on liability and remand the case to that court for further proceedings. **It is so ordered.**

On remand from the Supreme Court, the District Court in *Hopkins* found that Ann Hopkins had been a victim of sex discrimination and ordered that Price Waterhouse make her a partner (*Hopkins* v. *Price Waterhouse,* 737 F. Supp. 1202, D.D.C. 1990; aff'd., 970 F.2d 967, D.C. Cir. 1990).

Mixed Motive Cases under Title VII

In *Price Waterhouse* v. *Hopkins,* the Supreme Court held that when a plaintiff shows that the employer has considered an illegal factor under Title VII (race, sex, color, religion or national origin) in making an employment decision, the employer must demonstrate that it would have reached the same decision if it had not considered the illegal factor. According to the Supreme Court, if the employer can show this, the employer can escape liability under Title VII—that is, it will not have violated the statute.

The 1991 amendments to Title VII also addressed this "mixed motive" situation. Section 703(m) states that "an unlawful employment practice is established when the complaining party demonstrates that race, color, religion, sex, or national origin was a motivating factor for any employment practice, even though other factors also motivated the practice." That is, the employer violates Title VII when an illegal factor is considered, even though there may have been other factors motivating the decision or practice as well. If the employer is able to show that it would have reached the same decision in the absence of the illegal factor, then the employer's liability for remedy under Title VII is reduced under Section 706(g)(2)(B). Section 706(g)(2)(B), added by the 1991 amendments, states that the employer is subject to a court order to cease violating Title VII and is liable for the plaintiff's legal fees, but is not required to pay damages or to reinstate or hire the plaintiff.

"Sex-Plus" Discrimination

An employer who places additional requirements on employees of a certain sex violates Title VII. For example, an employer who refuses to hire females having preschool-aged children but who does hire males with preschool-aged children is guilty of a prohibited employment practice under Title VII. Such discrimination is known as **sex-plus discrimination;** the additional requirement (no preschool-aged children) becomes an issue only for employees of a certain sex (female). Because similarly situated employees (men and women both with preschool-aged children) are treated differently because of their sex, the employer is guilty of sex discrimination. The Supreme Court held that an employer hiring men with preschool-aged children, who refuses to hire women with preschool-aged children, violates Title VII in the case of *Phillips* v. *Martin Marietta Corp.* (400 U.S. 542, 1971).

Sex-Based Pay Differentials

An employer paying different wages to men and women doing the same job is violating the law unless the pay differentials are due to a bona fide seniority system, a merit pay system, a productivity-pay system, or a "factor other than sex." The Equal Pay Act prohibits paying men and women different rates of pay if they are performing substantially equivalent work, unless the difference in pay is due to one of the factors listed above. (The Equal Pay Act will be discussed more fully in Chapter 15.) Section 703(h) also allows pay differentials between employees of different sexes when the differential is due to seniority, merit or productivity-pay systems, or a factor other than sex. (That provision of Section 703(h) is known as the Bennett Amendment.)

The Equal Pay Act applies only when male and female employees are performing substantially equivalent work. Can Title VII be used to challenge pay differentials between men and women when they are not performing equal work? What is the effect of the Bennett Amendment? These issues are addressed in the following case.

COUNTY OF WASHINGTON v. GUNTHER

452 U.S. 161 (Supreme Court of the United States, 1981)

BRENNAN, J.

The question presented is whether Section 703(h) of Title VII of the Civil Rights Act of 1964, restricts Title VII's prohibition of sex-based wage discrimination to claims of equal pay for equal work.

This case arises over the payment by petitioner, the County of Washington, Ore., of substantially lower wages to female guards in the female section of the county jail than it paid to male guards in the male section of the jail. Re-

spondents are four women who were employed to guard female prisoners and to carry out certain other functions in the jail. In January 1974, the county eliminated the female section of the jail, transferred the female prisoners to the jail of a nearby county, and discharged respondents.

Respondents filed suit against petitioner in Federal District Court under Title VII, seeking backpay and other relief. They alleged that they were paid unequal wages for work substantially equal to that performed by male guards, and in the alternative, that part of the pay differential was attributable to intentional sex discrimination. The latter allegation was based on a claim that, because of intentional discrimination, the county set the pay scale for female guards, but not for male guards, at a level lower than that warranted by its own survey of outside markets and the worth of the jobs.

After trial, the District Court found that the male guards supervised more than 10 times as many prisoners per guard as did the female guards, and that the females devoted much of their time to less-valuable clerical duties. It therefore held that respondents' jobs were not substantially equal to those of the male guards, and that respondents were thus not entitled to equal pay. The Court of Appeals affirmed on that issue, and respondents do not seek review of the ruling.

The District Court also dismissed respondents' claim that the discrepancy in pay between the male and female guards was attributable in part to intentional sex discrimination. It held as a matter of law that a sex-based wage discrimination claim cannot be brought under Title VII unless it would satisfy the equal work standard of the Equal Pay Act. The Court therefore permitted no additional evidence on this claim, and made no findings on whether petitioner's pay scales for female guards resulted from intentional sex discrimination.

The Court of Appeals reversed, holding that persons alleging sex discrimination "are not precluded from suing under Title VII to protest . . . discriminatory compensation practices" merely because their jobs were not equal to higher paying jobs held by members of the opposite sex. The Court remanded to the District Court with instructions to take evidence on respondents' claim that part of the difference between their rate of pay and that of the male guards is attributable to sex discrimination. We granted certiorari. . . .

We emphasize at the outset the narrowness of the question before us in this case. Respondents' claim is not based on the controversial concept of "comparable worth," under which plaintiffs might claim increased compensation on the basis of a comparison of the intrinsic worth or difficulty of their job with that of other jobs in the same organization or community. Rather, respondents seek to prove, by direct evidence, that their wages were depressed because of intentional sex discrimination, consisting of setting the wage scale for female guards, but not for male guards, at a level lower than its own survey of outside markets and the worth of the jobs warranted. The narrow question in this case is whether such a claim is precluded by the last sentence of Section 703(h) of Title VII, called the "Bennett Amendment."

Title VII makes it an unlawful employment practice for an employer "to discriminate against any individual with respect to his compensation, terms, conditions, or privileges of employment because of such individual's . . . sex." The Bennett Amendment to Title VII, however, provides:

> It shall not be an unlawful employment practice under this subchapter for any employer to differentiate upon the basis of sex in determining the amount of the wages or compensation paid or to be paid to employees of such employer if such differentiation is authorized by the provisions of Section 206(d) of Title 29.

To discover what practices are exempted from Title VII's prohibitions by the Bennett Amendment, we must turn to Section 206(d) of Title 29—the Equal Pay Act—which provides in relevant part:

> No employer having employees subject to any provisions of this section shall discriminate, within any establishment in which such employees are employed, between employees on the basis of sex by paying wages to employees in such establishment at a rate less than the rate at which he pays wages to employees of the opposite sex in such establishment for equal work on jobs the performance of which requires equal skill, effort, and responsibility, and which are performed under similar working conditions, except where such payment is made pursuant to (i) a seniority system; (ii) a merit system; (iii) a system which measures earnings by quantity or quality of production; or (iv) a differential based on any other factor other than sex.

On its face, the Equal Pay Act contains . . . restrictions pertinent to this case. . . . The Act is restricted to cases involving "equal work on jobs the performance of which requires equal skill, effort, and responsibility, and which are performed under similar working conditions" [and] . . . the Act's four affirmative defenses exempt any wage differentials attributable to seniority, merit, quantity or quality of production, or "any other factor other than sex."

Petitioner argues that the purpose of the Bennett Amendment was to restrict Title VII sex-based wage discrimination claims to those that could also be brought under the Equal Pay Act, and thus that claims not arising from "equal work" are precluded. Respondents, in contrast, argue that the Bennett Amendment was designed merely to incorporate the four affirmative defenses of the Equal Pay Act into Title VII for sex-based wage discrimination claims. Respondents thus contend that claims for sex-based wage discrimination can be brought under Title VII even though no member of the opposite sex holds an equal but higher-paying job, provided that the challenged wage rate is not based on seniority, merit, quantity or quality of production, or "any other factor other than sex." The Court of Appeals found respondents' interpretation the "more persuasive." While recognizing that the language and legislative history of the provision are not unambiguous, we conclude that the Court of Appeals was correct.

The language of the Bennett Amendment suggests an intention to incorporate only the affirmative defenses of the Equal Pay Act into Title VII. The Amendment bars sex-based wage discrimination claims under Title VII where the pay differential is "authorized" by the Equal Pay Act. Although the word "authorize" sometimes means simply "to permit," it ordinarily denotes affirmative enabling action. Black's Law Dictionary (5th ed. 1979) defines "authorize" as "[t]o empower: to give a right or authority to act." The question, then, is what wage practices have been affirmatively authorized by the Equal Pay Act.

The Equal Pay Act is divided into two parts: a definition of the violation, followed by four affirmative defenses. The first part can hardly be said to "authorize" anything at all: it is purely prohibitory. The second part, however, in essence "authorizes" employers to differentiate in pay on the basis of seniority, merit, quantity or quality of production, or any other factor other than sex, even though such differentiation might otherwise violate the Act. It is to these provisions, therefore, that the Bennett Amendment must refer.

Petitioner argues that this construction of the Bennett Amendment would render it superfluous. Petitioner claims that the first three affirmative defenses are simply redundant of the provisions elsewhere in Section 703(h) of Title VII that already exempt bona fide seniority and merit systems and systems measuring earnings by quantity or quality of production, and that the fourth defense—"any other factor other than sex"—is implicit in Title VII's general prohibition of sex-based discrimination.

We cannot agree. The Bennett Amendment was offered as a "technical amendment" designed to resolve any potential conflicts between Title VII and the Equal Pay Act. Thus, with respect to the first three defenses, the Bennett Amendment has the effect of guaranteeing that courts and administrative agencies adopt a consistent interpretation of like provisions in both statutes. Otherwise, they might develop inconsistent bodies of case law interpreting two sets of nearly identical language.

More importantly, incorporation of the fourth affirmative defense could have significant consequences for Title VII litigation. Title VII's prohibition of discriminatory employment practices was intended to be broadly inclusive, proscribing "not only overt discrimination but also practices that are fair in form, but discriminatory in operation." The

structure of Title VII litigation, including presumptions, burdens of proof, and defenses, has been designed to reflect this approach. The fourth affirmative defense of the Equal Pay Act, however, was designed differently, to confine the application of the Act to wage differentials attributable to sex discrimination. Equal Pay Act litigation, therefore, has been structured to permit employers to defend against charges of discrimination where their pay differentials are based on a bona fide use of "other factors other than sex." Under the Equal Pay Act, the courts and administrative agencies are not permitted "to substitute their judgment for the judgment of the employer . . . who [has] established and employed a bona fide job rating system," so long as it does not discriminate on the basis of sex. Although we do not decide in this case how sex-based wage discrimination litigation under Title VII should be structured to accommodate the fourth affirmative defense of the Equal Pay Act, we consider it clear that the Bennett Amendment under this interpretation, is not rendered superfluous.

We therefore conclude that only differentials attributable to the four affirmative defenses of the Equal Pay Act are "authorized" by that Act within the meaning of Section 703(h) of Title VII.

The legislative background of the Bennett Amendment is fully consistent with this interpretation. . . .

Our interpretation of the Bennett Amendment draws additional support from the remedial purposes of Title VII and the Equal Pay Act. Section 703(a) of Title VII makes it unlawful for an employer "to fail or refuse to hire or discharge any individual, or *otherwise to discriminate against* any individual with respect to his compensation, terms, conditions, or privileges of employment" because of such individual's sex. As Congress itself has indicated, a "broad approach" to the definition of equal employment opportunity is essential to overcoming and undoing the effect of discrimination. We must therefore avoid interpretations of Title VII that deprive victims of discrimination of a remedy, without clear congressional mandate.

Under petitioner's reading of the Bennett Amendment, only those sex-based wage discrimination claims that satisfy the "equal work" standard of Equal Pay Act could be brought under Title VII. In practical terms, this means that a woman who is discriminatorily underpaid could obtain no relief—no matter how egregious the discrimination might be—unless her employer also employed a man in an equal job in the same establishment, at a higher rate of pay. Thus, if an employer hired a woman for a unique position in the company and then admitted that her salary would have been higher had she been male, the woman would be unable to obtain legal redress under petitioner's interpretation. Similarly, if an employer used a transparently sex-biased system for wage determination, women holding jobs not equal to those held by men would be denied the right to prove that the system is a pretext for discrimination. . . . Congress surely did not intend the Bennett Amendment to insulate such blatantly discriminatory practices from judicial redress under Title VII.

Moreover, petitioner's interpretation would have other far-reaching consequences. Since it rests on the proposition that any wage differentials not prohibited by the Equal Pay Act are "authorized" by it, petitioner's interpretation would lead to the conclusion that discriminatory compensation by employers not covered by the Fair Labor Standards Act is "authorized"—since not prohibited—by the Equal Pay Act. Thus it would deny Title VII protection against sex-based wage discrimination by those employers not subject to the Fair Labor Standards Act but covered by Title VII. There is no persuasive evidence that Congress intended such a result, and the EEOC has rejected it since at least 1965. Indeed, petitioner itself apparently acknowledges that Congress intended Title VII's broader coverage to apply to equal pay claims under Title VII, thus impliedly admitting the fallacy in its own argument.

Petitioner's reading is thus flatly inconsistent with our past interpretations of Title VII as "prohibit[ing] all practices in whatever form which create inequality in employment opportunity due to discrimination on the basis of race, religion, sex or national origin." . . . We must therefore reject petitioner's interpretation of the Bennett Amendment.

Petitioner argues strenuously that the approach of the Court of Appeals places "the pay structure of virtually every employer and the entire economy . . . at risk and subject to scrutiny by the federal courts." It raises the spectre that "Title VII plaintiffs could draw any type of comparison imaginable concerning job duties and pay between any job predominantly performed by women and any job predominantly performed by men." But whatever the merit of petitioner's arguments in other contexts, they are inapplicable here, for claims based on the type of job comparisons petitioner describes are manifestly different from respondents' claim. Respondents contend that the County of Washington evaluated the worth of their jobs; that the county determined that they should be paid approximately 95 percent as much as the male correctional officers; that it paid them only about 70 percent as much, while paying the male officers the full evaluated worth of their jobs; and that the failure of the county to pay respondents the full evaluated worth of their jobs can be proven to be attributable to intentional sex discrimination. Thus, respondents' suit does not require a court to make its own subjective assessment of the value of the male and female guard jobs, or to attempt by statistical technique or other method to quantify the effect of sex discrimination on the wage rates.

We do not decide in this case the precise contours of lawsuits challenging sex discrimination in compensation under Title VII. It is sufficient to note that respondents' claims of discriminatory undercompensation are not barred by Section 703(h) of Title VII merely because respondents do not perform work equal to that of male jail guards. The judgment of the Court of Appeals is therefore **Affirmed.**

The *Gunther* case held that Title VII prohibits intentional sex discrimination in pay even when the male and female employees are not performing equivalent work. In *Gunther,* the plaintiffs were able to establish a prima facie case of intentional discrimination by the employer in setting pay scales for female employees. In *Spalding v. University of Washington* (740 F.2d 686, 1984), the U.S. Court of Appeals for the Ninth Circuit held that a plaintiff bringing a *Gunther*-type claim under Title VII must establish evidence of intentional discrimination (known as disparate treatment); the court held that statistical evidence purporting to show sex-based disparate salary levels for female professors, standing alone, was not sufficient to establish intentional discrimination as required by *Gunther.*

Comparable Worth.   Some commentators felt that the *Gunther* decision was, in effect, an endorsement of the idea of **comparable worth**—that is, that employees should receive equal pay for jobs of equal value. Notice that comparable worth is different from the equal-pay-for-equal-work requirements of the Equal Pay Act. The Supreme Court in *Gunther* emphasized that it was not endorsing comparable worth; it held simply that Title VII prohibited intentional discrimination on the basis of sex for setting pay scales. The courts of appeals have consistently maintained that Title VII does not require comparable worth standards—an employer need not pay equal wages for work of equal value as long as the pay differential is not due to intentional sex discrimination by the employer. In *Lemons v. Denver* (620 F2d 228, 1980), the U.S. Court of Appeals for the Tenth Circuit held that Title VII did not prohibit a public employer from paying public health nurses salaries based on the private sector wage rates for nurses, even though the public health nurses were paid less than the predominantly male jobs of garbage collector or tree-trimmer. The employer was not guilty of sex discrimination simply by following the "market," even if the "market" wages for nurses reflected the effects of historical discrimination against women. Several states, however, have adopted laws requiring comparable worth pay for public sector employees.

Sex-Based Pension Benefits

Women, on the average, live longer than men. Such differences in life expectancy are used by actuaries in determining the premium and benefit levels for annuities purchased by individuals. Sex-based actuarial tables used to determine premiums and benefits for pensions may require that women pay higher premiums in order to receive the same levels of benefits as men of the same age. Does an employer who uses sex-based actuarial tables to determine entitlement to pensions offered as an employment benefit violate Title VII? That question was addressed by the Supreme Court in the following case.

CITY OF LOS ANGELES v. MANHART

435 U.S. 702 (Supreme Court of the United States, 1978)

STEVENS, J.

As a class, women live longer than men. For this reason, the Los Angeles Department of Water and Power required its female employees to make larger contributions to its pension fund than its male employees. We granted certiorari to decide whether this practice discriminated against individual female employees because of their sex in violation of Section 703(a)(1) of the Civil Rights Act of 1964, as amended.

For many years the Department has administered retirement, disability, and death benefit programs for its employees. Upon retirement each employee is eligible for a monthly retirement benefit computed as a fraction of his or her salary multiplied by years of service. The monthly benefits for men and women of the same age, seniority, and salary are equal. Benefits are funded entirely by contributions from the employees and the Department, augmented by the income earned on those contributions. No private insurance company is involved in the administration or payment of benefits.

Based on a study of mortality tables and its own experience, the Department determined that its 2,000 female employees, on the average, will live a few years longer than its 10,000 male employees. The cost of a pension for the average retired female is greater than for the average male retiree because more monthly payments must be made to the average woman. The Department therefore required female employees to make monthly contributions to the fund which were 14.84 percent higher than the contributions required of comparable male employees. Because employee contributions were withheld from paychecks, a female employee took home less pay than a male employee earning the same salary. . . .

The Department . . . [contends] that . . . the differential in take-home pay between men and women was not discrimination within the meaning of Section 703(a)(1) because it was offset by a difference in the value of the pension benefits provided to the two classes of employees . . . [and] in any event, the retroactive monetary recovery is unjustified. We consider these contentions in turn. . . .

It is true that the average man is taller than the average woman; it is not true that the average woman driver is more accident prone than the average man. Before the Civil Rights Act of 1964 was enacted, an employer could fashion his personnel policies on the basis of assumptions about the differences between men and women, whether or not the assumptions were valid.

It is now well recognized that employment decisions cannot be predicated on mere "stereotyped" impressions about the characteristics of males or females. Myths and purely habitual assumptions about a woman's inability to perform certain kinds of work are no longer acceptable reasons for refusing to employ qualified individuals, or for paying them less. This case does not, however, involve a fictional difference between men and women. It involves a generalization that the parties accept as unquestionably true: women, as a class, do live longer than men. The Department treated its women employees differently from its men employees because the two classes are in fact different. It is equally true, however, that all individuals in the respective classes do not share the characteristic which differentiates the average class representatives. Many women do not live as long as the average man and many men outlive the average woman. The question, therefore, is whether the existence or nonexistence of "discrimination" is to be determined by comparison of class characteristics or individual characteristics. A "stereotyped" answer to that question may not be the same as the answer which the language and purpose of the statute command.

The statute makes it unlawful "to discriminate against any *individual* with respect to his compensation, terms, conditions, or privileges of employment, because of such *individual's* race, color, religion, sex, or national origin" (emphasis added). The statute's focus on the individual is unambiguous. It precludes treatment of individuals as simply components of [a] racial, religious, sexual, or national class. If height is required for a job, a tall woman may not be refused employment merely because, on the average,

women are too short. Even a true generalization about the class is an insufficient reason for disqualifying an individual to whom the generalization does not apply.

That proposition is of critical importance in this case because there is no assurance that any individual woman working for the Department will actually fit the generalization on which the Department's policy is based. Many of those individuals will not live as long as the average man. While they were working, those individuals received smaller paychecks because of their sex, but they will receive no compensating advantage when they retire.

It is true, of course, that while contributions are being collected from the employees, the Department cannot know which individuals will predecease the average woman. Therefore, unless women as a class are assessed an extra charge, they will be subsidized, to some extent, by the class of male employees. It follows, according to the Department, that fairness to its class of male employees justifies the extra assessment against all of its female employees.

But the question of fairness to various classes affected by the statute is essentially a matter of policy for the legislature to address. Congress has decided that classifications based on sex, like those based on national origin or race, are unlawful. Actuarial studies could unquestionably identify differences in life expectancy based on race or national origin, as well as sex. But a statute which was designed to make race irrelevant in the employment market, . . . could not reasonably be construed to permit a take-home pay differential based on a racial classification.

Even if the statutory language were less clear, the basic policy of the statute requires that we focus on fairness to individuals rather than fairness to classes. Practices which classify employees in terms of religion, race, or sex tend to preserve traditional assumptions about groups rather than thoughtful scrutiny of individuals. The generalization involved in this case illustrates the point. Separate mortality tables are easily interpreted as reflecting innate differences between the sexes; but a significant part of the longevity differential may be explained by the social fact that men are heavier smokers than women.

Finally, there is no reason to believe that Congress intended a special definition of discrimination in the context of employee group insurance coverage. It is true that insurance is concerned with events that are individually unpredictable, but that is characteristic of many employment decisions. Individual risks, like individual performance, may not be predicted by resort to classifications proscribed by Title VII. Indeed, the fact that this case involves a group insurance program highlights a basic flaw in the Department's fairness argument. For when insurance risks are grouped, the better risks always subsidize the poorer risks. Healthy persons subsidize medical benefits for the less healthy; unmarried workers subsidize the pensions of married workers; persons who eat, drink, or smoke to excess may subsidize pension benefits for persons whose habits are more temperate. Treating different classes of risks as though they were the same for purposes of group insurance is a common practice which has never been considered inherently unfair. To insure the flabby and the fit as though they were equivalent risks may be more common than treating men and women alike; but nothing more than habit makes one "subsidy" seem less fair than the other.

An employment practice which requires 2,000 individuals to contribute more money into a fund than 10,000 other employees simply because each of them is a woman, rather than a man, is in direct conflict with both the language and the policy of the Act. Such a practice does not pass the simple test of whether the evidence shows "treatment of a person in a manner which but for the person's sex would be different." It constitutes discrimination and is unlawful unless exempted by the Equal Pay Act or some other affirmative justification. . . .

The Department argues that the different contributions exacted from men and women were based on the factor of longevity rather than sex. It is plain, however, that any individual's life expectancy is based on a number of factors, of which sex is only one. The record contains no evidence that any factor other than the employee's sex was taken into account in calculating the 14.84 percent differential between the respective contributions by men and women. We agree with Judge Duniway's observation that one cannot "say that an actuarial distinction based entirely on sex is 'based on any other factor other than sex.' Sex is exactly what it is based on."

In this case . . . the Department argues that the absence of a discriminatory effect on women as a class justifies an employment practice which, on its face, discriminated against individual employees because of their sex. But even if the Department's actuarial evidence is sufficient to prevent plaintiffs from establishing a prima facie case on the theory that the effect of the practice on women as a class was discriminatory, that evidence does not defeat the claim that the practice, on its face, discriminated against every individual woman employed by the Department.

In essence, the Department is arguing that the prima facie showing of discrimination based on evidence of different contributions for the respective sexes is rebutted by its demonstration that there is a like difference in the cost of providing benefits for the respective classes. That argument

might prevail if Title VII contained a cost justification defense comparable to the affirmative defense available in a price discrimination suit. But neither Congress nor the courts have recognized such a defense under Title VII.

Although we conclude that the Department's practice violated Title VII, we do not suggest that the statute was intended to revolutionize the insurance and pension industries. All that is at issue today is a requirement that men and women make unequal contributions to an employer-operated pension fund. Nothing in our holding implies that it would be unlawful for an employer to set aside equal retirement contributions for each employee and let each retiree purchase the largest benefit which his or her accumulated contributions could command in the open market. Nor does it call into question the insurance industry practice of considering the composition of an employer's work force in determining the probable cost of a retirement or death benefit plan. Finally, we recognize that in a case of this kind it may be necessary to take special care in fashioning appropriate relief.

The Department challenges the district court's award of retroactive relief to the entire class of female employees and retirees. Title VII does not require a district court to grant any retroactive relief. A court that finds unlawful discrimination "may enjoin [the discrimination] and order such affirmative action as may be appropriate, which may include, but is not limited to, reinstatement . . . with or without back pay . . . or any other equitable relief as the court deems appropriate." To the point of redundancy, the statute stresses that retroactive relief "may" be awarded if it is "appropriate." . . .

There can be no doubt that the prohibition against sex-differentiated employee contributions represents a marked departure from past practice. Although Title VII was enacted in 1964, this is apparently the first litigation challenging contribution differences based on valid actuarial tables. Retroactive liability could be devastating for a pension fund. The harm would fall in large part on innocent third parties. If, as the courts below apparently contemplated, the plaintiffs' contributions are recovered from the pension fund, the administrators of the fund will be forced to meet unchanged obligations with diminished assets. If the reserve proves inadequate, either the expectations of all retired employees will be disappointed or current employees will be forced to pay not only for their own future security but also for the unanticipated reduction in the contributions of past employees. . . . **So ordered.**

The Supreme Court noted in *Manhart* that it did not want to revolutionize the insurance industry. In the subsequent case of *Arizona Governing Committee* v. *Norris* (463 U.S. 1073, 1983), the Supreme Court held that a deferring compensation plan for state employees, administered by a private insurance company, that used sex-based actuarial tables to determine monthly benefit payments violated Title VII. The Court held that its ruling would apply prospectively only, not retroactively.

Pregnancy and Discrimination

In the 1976 case of *General Electric* v. *Gilbert* (429 U.S. 125), the Supreme Court held that General Electric's refusal to cover pregnancy or related conditions under its sick-pay plan, even though male-specific disabilities such as vasectomies were covered, did not violate Title VII. In response to the *General Electric* v. *Gilbert* decision, Congress passed the Pregnancy Discrimination Act of 1978, which added Section 701(k) to Title VII. Section 701(k) provides:

> The terms "because of sex" or "on the basis of sex" include, but are not limited to, because of or on the basis of pregnancy, childbirth, or related medical conditions; and women affected by pregnancy, childbirth, or related medical conditions shall be treated the same for all employment-related purposes, including receipt of benefits under fringe benefit programs, as other persons not so affected but similar to their ability or inability to work. . . .

Simply stated, the amendment to Title VII requires that an employer treat a pregnant employee the same as any employee suffering a nonpregnancy-related, temporary disability (unless in a relatively rare instance, the employer can establish a BFOQ for pregnancy-related discrimination). If the employer's sick-leave pay benefits cover temporary disabilities, they must also provide coverage for pregnancy-related leaves. The following case involves a challenge to a benefit plan that placed a limitation on coverage for pregnancy, while not placing a limit on other disabilities.

NEWPORT NEWS SHIPBUILDING AND DRY DOCK CO. v. EEOC

462 U.S. 669 (Supreme Court of the United States, 1983)

STEVENS, J.

In 1978 Congress decided to overrule our decision in *General Electric Co.* v. *Gilbert* (1976), by amending Title VII of the Civil Rights Act of 1964 "to prohibit sex discrimination on the basis of pregnancy." On the effective date of the act, petitioner amended its health insurance plan to provide its female employees with hospitalization benefits for pregnancy-related conditions to the same extent as for other medical conditions. The plan continued, however, to provide less favorable pregnancy benefits for spouses of

male employees. The question presented is whether the amended plan complies with the amended statute.

Petitioner's plan provides hospitalization and medical-surgical coverage for a defined category of employees and a defined category of dependents. Dependents covered by the plan include employees' spouses, unmarried children between 14 days and 19 years of age, and some older dependent children. Prior to April 29, 1979, the scope of the plan's coverage for eligible dependents was identical to its coverage for employees. All covered males, whether employees or dependents, were treated alike for purposes of hospitalization coverage. All covered females, whether employees or dependents, also were treated alike. Moreover, with one relevant exception, the coverage for males and females was identical. The exception was a limitation on hospital coverage for pregnancy that did not apply to any other hospital confinement.

After the plan was amended in 1979, it provided the same hospitalization coverage for male and female employees themselves for all medical conditions, but it differentiated between female employees and spouses of male employees in its provision of pregnancy-related benefits. In a booklet describing the plan, petitioner explained the amendment that gave rise to this litigation in this way:

> B. Effective April 29, 1979, maternity benefits for female employees will be paid the same as any other hospital confinement as described in question 16. This applies only to deliveries beginning on April 29, 1979 and thereafter.
>
> C. Maternity benefits for the wife of a male employee will continue to be paid as described in part "A" of this question.

In turn, Part A stated, "The Basic Plan pays up to $500 of the hospital charges and 100 percent of reasonable and customary for delivery and anaesthesiologist charges." As the Court of Appeals observed, "To the extent that the hospital charges in connection with an uncomplicated delivery may exceed $500, therefore, a male employee receives less complete coverage of spousal disabilities than does a female employee."

After the passage of the Pregnancy Discrimination Act, and before the amendment to petitioner's plan became effective, the Equal Opportunity Employment Commission issued "interpretive guidelines" in the form of questions and answers. Two of those questions, numbers 21 and 22, made it clear that the EEOC would consider petitioner's amended plan unlawful. Number 21 read as follows:

> 21. Q. Must an employer provide health insurance coverage for the medical expenses of pregnancy-related conditions for the spouses of male employees? Of the dependents of all employees?
>
> A. Where an employer provides no coverage for dependents, the employer is not required to institute such coverage. However, if an employer's insurance program covers the medical expenses of spouses of female employees, then it must equally cover the medical expenses of spouses of male employees, including those arising from pregnancy-related conditions.
>
> But the insurance does not have to cover the pregnancy-related conditions of non-spouse dependents as long as it excludes the pregnancy-related conditions of such non-spouse dependents of male and female employees equally.

On September 20, 1979, one of petitioner's male employees filed a charge with the EEOC alleging that petitioner had unlawfully refused to provide full insurance coverage for his wife's hospitalization caused by pregnancy; a month later the United Steelworkers filed a similar charge on behalf of other individuals. Petitioner then commenced an action in the United States District Court for the Eastern District of Virginia, challenging the Commission's guidelines and seeking both declaratory and injunctive relief. The complaint named the EEOC, the male employee, and the United Steelworkers of America as defendants. Later the EEOC filed a civil action against petitioner alleging discrimination on the basis of sex against male employees in the company's provision of hospitalization benefits. Concluding that the benefits of the new Act extended only to female employees, and not to spouses of male employees, the District Court held that petitioner's plan was lawful and enjoined enforcement of the EEOC guidelines relating to pregnancy benefits for employees' spouses. It also dismissed the EEOC's complaint. The two cases were consolidated on appeal.

A divided panel of the United States Court of Appeals for the Fourth Circuit reversed, reasoning that since "the company's health insurance plan contains a distinction based on pregnancy that results in less complete medical coverage for male employees with spouses than for female employees with spouses, it is impermissible under the statute." After rehearing the case en banc, the court reaffirmed the conclusion of the panel over the dissent of three judges who believed the statute was intended to protect female employees "in their ability or inability to work," and not to protect spouses of male employees. Because the important question presented by the case had been decided differently by the United States Court of Appeals for the Ninth Circuit, we granted certiorari.

Ultimately the question we must decide is whether petitioner has discriminated against its male employees with respect to their compensation, terms, conditions, or privileges of employment because of their sex within the meaning of Section 703(a)(1) of Title VII. Although the Pregnancy Discrimination Act has clarified the meaning of certain terms in this section, neither that Act nor the underlying statute contains a definition of the word "discriminate." In order to decide whether a petitioner's plan discriminated against male employees because of *their* sex, we must therefore go beyond the bare statutory language. Accordingly, we shall consider whether Congress, by enacting the Pregnancy Discrimination Act, not only overturned the specific holding in *General Electric* v. *Gilbert,* but also rejected the test of discrimination employed by the Court in that case. We believe it did. Under the proper test petitioner's plan is unlawful, because the protection it affords to married male employees is less comprehensive than the protection it affords to married female employees.

At issue in *General Electric* v. *Gilbert,* was the legality of a disability plan that provided the company's employees with weekly compensation during periods of disability resulting from nonoccupational causes. Because the plan excluded disabilities arising from pregnancy, the District Court and the Court of Appeals concluded that it discriminated against female employees because of their sex. The court reversed....

The dissenters in *Gilbert* took issue with the majority's assumption "that the Fourteenth Amendment standard of discrimination is conterminous with that applicable to Title VII." As a matter of statutory interpretation, the dissenters rejected the Court's holding that the plan's exclusion of disabilities caused by pregnancy did not constitute discrimination based on sex. As Justice Brennan explained, it was facially discriminatory for the company to devise "a policy that, but for pregnancy, offers protection for all risks, even those that are 'unique to' men or heavily male dominated." It was inaccurate to describe the program as dividing potential recipients into two groups, pregnant women and nonpregnant persons, because insurance programs "deal with future *risks* rather than historic facts." Rather, the appropriate classification was "between persons who face a risk of pregnancy and those who do not." The company's plan, which was intended to provide employees with protection against the risk of uncompensated unemployment caused by physical disability, discriminated on the basis of sex by giving men protection for all categories of risk but giving women only partial protection. Thus, the dissenters asserted that the statute had been violated because conditions of employment for females were less favorable than for similarly situated males.

When Congress amended Title VII in 1978, it unambiguously expressed its disapproval of both the holding and the reasoning of the Court in the *Gilbert* decision. It incorporated a new subsection in the "definitions" applicable "[f]or the purposes of this subchapter." The first clause of the Act states, quite simply: "The terms 'because of sex' or 'on the basis of sex' include, but are not limited to, because of or on the basis of pregnancy, childbirth, or related medical conditions." The House Report stated, "It is the Committee's view that the dissenting Justices correctly interpreted the Act." Similarly, the Senate Report quoted passages from the two dissenting opinions, stating that they "correctly ex-

press both the principle and the meaning of title VII." Proponents of the bill repeatedly emphasized that the Supreme Court had erroneously interpreted Congressional intent and that amending legislation was necessary to reestablish the principles of Title VII law as they had been understood prior to the *Gilbert* decision. Many of them expressly agree with the views of the dissenting Justices.

As petitioner argues, congressional discussion focused on the needs of female members of the work force rather than spouses of male employees.... When the question of differential coverage for dependents was addressed in the Senate Report, the Committee indicated that it should be resolved "on the basis of existing title VII principles." The legislative context makes it clear that Congress was not thereby referring to the view of Title VII reflected in this Court's *Gilbert* opinion. Proponents of the legislation stressed throughout the debates that Congress had always intended to protect *all* individuals from sex discrimination in employment—including but not limited to pregnant women workers. Against this background we review the terms of the amended statute to decide whether petitioner has unlawfully discriminated against its male employees.

Section 703(a) makes it an unlawful employment practice for an employer to "discriminate against any individual with respect to his compensation, terms, conditions, or privileges of employment, because of such individual's race, color, religion, sex, or national origin...." Health insurance and other fringe benefits are "compensation, terms, conditions, or privileges of employment." Male as well as female employees are protected against discrimination. Thus, if a private employer were to provide complete health insurance coverage for the dependents of its female employees, and no coverage at all for the dependents of its male employees, it would violate Title VII. Such a practice would not pass the simple test of Title VII discrimination that we enunciated in *Los Angeles Department of Water & Power* v. *Manhart* (1978), for it would treat a male employee with dependents "in a manner which but for that person's sex would be different." The same result would be reached even if the magnitude of the discrimination were smaller. For example, a plan that provided complete hospitalization coverage for the spouses of female employees but did not cover spouses of male employees when they had broken bones would violate Title VII by discriminating against male employees.

Petitioner's practice is just as unlawful. Its plan provides limited pregnancy-related benefits for employees' wives, and affords more extensive coverage for employees' spouses for all other medical conditions requiring hospitalization.

Thus the husbands of female employees receive a specified level of hospitalization coverage for all conditions; the wives of male employees receive such coverage except for pregnancy-related conditions. Although *Gilbert* concluded that an otherwise inclusive plan that singled out pregnancy-related benefits for exclusion was nondiscriminatory on its face, because only women can become pregnant, Congress has unequivocally rejected that reasoning. The 1978 Act makes clear that it is discriminatory to treat pregnancy-related conditions less favorably than other medical conditions. Thus petitioner's plan unlawfully gives married male employees a benefit package for their dependents that is less inclusive than the dependency coverage provided to married female employees.

There is no merit to petition's argument that the prohibitions of Title VII do not extend to discrimination against pregnant spouses because the statute applies only to discrimination in employment. A two-step analysis demonstrates the fallacy in this contention. The Pregnancy Discrimination Act has now made clear that, for all Title VII purposes, discrimination based on a woman's pregnancy is,

on its face, discrimination because of her sex. And since the sex of the spouse is always the opposite of the sex of the employee, it follows inexorably that discrimination against female spouses in the provision of fringe benefits is also discrimination against male employees. By making clear that an employer could not discriminate on the basis of an employee's pregnancy, Congress did not erase the original prohibition against discrimination on the basis of an employee's sex.

In short, Congress' rejection of the premises of *General Electric* v. *Gilbert,* forecloses any claim that an insurance program excluding pregnancy coverage for female beneficiaries and providing complete coverage to similarly situated male beneficiaries does not discriminate on the basis of sex. Petitioner's plan is the mirror image of the plan at issue in *Gilbert.* The pregnancy limitation in this case violates Title VII by discriminating against male employees.

The judgment of the Court of Appeals is **Affirmed.**

State Legislation.   The California Fair Employment Practices Law requires employers to provide pregnant employees up to four months of unpaid pregnancy leave, and to reinstate female employees returning from pregnancy leave to the job they held prior to the leave, unless the job is unavailable due to business necessity, in which case the employer is required to make a good-faith effort to provide a substantially similar job. The California law does not require the employer to offer such treatment to employees returning from other temporary disability leaves. California Federal Savings and Loan, a California bank, alleged that the California law violated the Pregnancy Discrimination Act because it required the employer to treat pregnant employees differently than other temporarily disabled employees. In *California Federal Savings and Loan* v. *Guerra* (479 U.S. 272, 1987), the Supreme Court upheld the California law. The majority reasoned that the Pregnancy Discrimination Act amendments to Title VII were intended merely to create a minimum level of protection for pregnant employees that could be supplemented by state legislation as long as the state laws did not conflict with the terms or policies of Title VII. The Court also noted that the California law did not prevent employers from extending the right of reinstatement to employees on other temporary disability leaves, so that the law did not require that pregnant employees be treated more generously than nonpregnant employees on temporary disability leave.

Pregnancy and Hazardous Working Conditions.   On-the-job exposure to harsh substances or potentially toxic chemicals may pose a hazard to the health of employees. The risk of such hazards may be greatly increased when pregnant employees are exposed to them; the hazards may also affect the health of the fetus carried by the pregnant employee. An employer wishing to avoid potential health problems for female employees and their offspring may prohibit women of childbearing age from working in jobs that involve exposure to hazardous substances. Do such restrictions violate Title VII, or may they be justified as BFOQs? That is the question involved in the following case.

UAW v. JOHNSON CONTROLS, INC.

__U.S.__, 111 S.Ct. 1196 (Supreme Court of the United States, 1991)_

BLACKMUN, J.

In this case we are concerned with an employer's gender-based fetal-protection policy. May an employer exclude a fertile female employee from certain jobs because of its concern for the health of the fetus the woman might conceive?

Respondent Johnson Controls, Inc., manufactures batteries. In the manufacturing process, the element lead is a primary ingredient. Occupational exposure to lead entails health risks, including the risk of harm to any fetus carried by a female employee. Before the Civil Rights Act of 1964 became law, Johnson Controls did not employ any woman in a battery-manufacturing job. . . .

. . . in 1982, Johnson Controls shifted from a policy of warning to a policy of exclusion. Between 1979 and 1983, eight employees became pregnant while maintaining blood lead levels in excess of 30 micrograms per deciliter. This appeared to be the critical level noted by the Occupational Health and Safety Administration (OSHA) for a worker who was planning to have a family. The company responded by announcing a broad exclusion of women from jobs that exposed them to lead:

"... It is [Johnson Controls'] policy that women who are pregnant or who are capable of bearing children will not be placed into jobs involving lead exposure or which could expose them to lead through the exercise of job bidding, bumping, transfer or promotion rights."

The policy defined "women . . . capable of bearing children" as "all women except those whose inability to bear children is medically documented." It further stated that an unacceptable work station was one where, "over the past year," an employee had recorded a blood lead level of more than 30 micrograms per deciliter or the work site had yielded an air sample containing a lead level in excess of 30 micrograms per cubic meter.

In April 1984, petitioners filed . . . a class action challenging Johnson Controls' fetal-protection policy as sex discrimination that violated Title VII of the Civil Rights Act of 1964.

The District Court granted summary judgment for Johnson Controls. Applying a three-part business necessity defense derived from fetal-protection cases in the Courts of Appeals for the Fourth and Eleventh Circuits, the District Court concluded that while "there is a disagreement among the experts regarding the effect of lead on the fetus," the hazard to the fetus through exposure to lead was established by "a considerable body of opinion"; that although "expert opinion has been provided which holds that lead also affects the reproductive abilities of men and women . . . [and] that these effects are as great as the effects of exposure of the fetus . . . a great body of experts are of the opinion that the fetus is more vulnerable to levels of lead that would not affect adults"; and that petitioners had "failed to establish that there is an acceptable alternative policy which would protect the fetus." The Court stated that, in view of this disposition of the business necessity defense, it did not "have to undertake a bona fide occupational qualification's (BFOQ) analysis."

The Court of Appeals for the Seventh Circuit, sitting en banc, affirmed the summary judgment by a 7-to-4 vote. The majority held that the proper standard for evaluating the fetal-protection policy was the defense of business necessity; that Johnson Controls was entitled to summary judgment under that defense; and that even if the proper standard was a BFOQ, Johnson Controls still was entitled to summary judgment. . . .

With its ruling, the Seventh Circuit became the first Court of Appeals to hold that a fetal-protection policy directed exclusively at women could qualify as a BFOQ. We granted certiorari . . . to address the important and difficult question whether an employer, seeking to protect potential fetuses, may discriminate against women just because of their ability to become pregnant.

The bias in Johnson Controls' policy is obvious. Fertile

men, but not fertile women, are given a choice as to whether they wish to risk their reproductive health for a particular job.... Respondent's fetal-protection policy explicitly discriminates against women on the basis of their sex. The policy excludes women with childbearing capacity from lead-exposed jobs and so creates a facial classification based on gender....

Nevertheless, the Court of Appeals assumed, as did the two appellate courts who already had confronted the issue, that sex-specific fetal-protection policies do not involve facial discrimination. These courts analyzed the policies as though they were facially neutral, and had only a discriminatory effect upon the employment opportunities of women. Consequently, the courts looked to see if each employer in question had established that its policy was justified as a business necessity. The business necessity standard is more lenient for the employer than the statutory BFOQ defense.... The court assumed that because the asserted reason for the sex-based exclusion (protecting women's unconceived offspring) was ostensibly benign, the policy was not sex-based discrimination. That assumption, however, was incorrect. First, Johnson Controls' policy classifies on the basis of gender and childbearing capacity, rather than fertility alone. Respondent does not seek to protect the unconceived children of all its employees. Despite evidence in the record about the debilitating effect of lead exposure on the male reproductive system, Johnson Controls is concerned only with the harms that may befall the unborn offspring of its female employees.... This Court faced a conceptually similar situation in *Phillips* v. *Martin Marietta Corp.,* and found sex discrimination because the policy established "one hiring policy for women and another for men—each having pre-school-age children." Johnson Controls' policy is facially discriminatory because it requires only a female employee to produce proof that she is not capable of reproducing.

Our conclusion is bolstered by the Pregnancy Discrimination Act of 1978 (PDA), in which Congress explicitly provided that, for purposes of Title VII, discrimination "on the basis of sex" includes discrimination "because of or on the basis of pregnancy, childbirth, or related medical conditions."... In its use of the words "capable of bearing children" in the 1982 policy statement as the criterion for exclusion, Johnson Controls explicitly classifies on the basis of potential for pregnancy. Under the PDA, such a classification must be regarded, for Title VII purposes, in the same light as explicit sex discrimination. Respondent has chosen to treat all its female employees as potentially pregnant; that choice evinces discrimination on the basis of sex.

We concluded above that Johnson Controls' policy is not neutral because it does not apply to the reproductive capacity of the company's male employees in the same way as it applies to that of the females. Moreover, the absence of a malevolent motive does not convert a facially discriminatory policy into a neutral policy with a discriminatory effect. Whether an employment practice involves disparate treatment through explicit facial discrimination does not depend on why the employer discriminates but rather on the explicit terms of the discrimination....

... We hold that Johnson Controls' fetal-protection policy is sex discrimination forbidden under Title VII unless respondent can establish that sex is a "bona fide occupational qualification."

Under Section 703(e)(1) of Title VII, an employer may discriminate on the basis of "religion, sex, or national origin in those certain instances where religion, sex, or national origin is a bona fide occupational qualification reasonably necessary to the normal operation of that particular business or enterprise." We therefore turn to the question whether Johnson Controls' fetal-protection policy is one of those "certain instances" that come within the BFOQ exception. The BFOQ defense is written narrowly, and this Court has read it narrowly....

The wording of the BFOQ defense contains several terms of restriction that indicate that the exception reaches only special situations. The statute thus limits the situations in which discrimination is permissible to "certain instances" where sex discrimination is "reasonably necessary" to the "normal operation" of the "particular" business. Each one of these terms—certain, normal, particular—prevents the use of general subjective standards and favors an objective, verifiable requirement. But the most telling term is "occupational"; this indicates that these objective, verifiable requirements must concern job-related skills and aptitudes.... By modifying "qualification" with "occupational," Congress narrowed the term to qualifications that affect an employee's ability to do the job.

Johnson Controls argues that its fetal-protection policy falls within the so-called safety exception to the BFOQ. Our cases have stressed that discrimination on the basis of sex because of safety concerns is allowed only in narrow circumstances. In *Dothard* v. *Rawlinson,* this Court indicated that danger to a woman herself does not justify discrimination. We there allowed the employer to hire only male guards in contact areas of maximum-security male penitentiaries only because more was at stake than the "individual woman's decision to weigh and accept the risks of employment." We found sex to be a BFOQ inasmuch as the employment of a female guard would create real risks of safety to others if violence broke out because the guard was a woman. . . .

Similarly, some courts have approved airlines' layoffs of pregnant flight attendants at different points during the first five months of pregnancy on the ground that the employer's policy was necessary to ensure the safety of passengers. We considered safety to third parties in *Western Airlines, Inc.* v. *Criswell,* in the context of the ADEA. We focused upon "the nature of the flight engineer's tasks," and the "actual capabilities of persons over age 60" in relation to those tasks. Our safety concerns were not independent of the individual's ability to perform the assigned tasks, but rather involved the possibility that, because of age-connected debility, a flight engineer might not properly assist the pilot, and might thereby cause a safety emergency. Furthermore, although we considered the safety of third parties in *Dothard* and *Criswell,* those third parties were indispensable to the particular business at issue. In *Dothard,* the third parties were the inmates; in *Criswell,* the third parties were the passengers on the plane. . . .

. . . The unconceived fetuses of Johnson Controls' female employees, however, are neither customers nor third parties whose safety is essential to the business of battery manufacturing. No one can disregard the possibility of injury to future children; the BFOQ, however, is not so broad that it transforms this deep social concern into an essential aspect of batterymaking.

Our case law, therefore, makes clear that the safety exception is limited to instances in which sex or pregnancy actually interferes with the employee's ability to perform the job . . .

The PDA's amendment to Title VII contains a BFOQ standard of its own: unless pregnant employees differ from others "in their ability or inability to work," they must be "treated the same" as other employees "for all employment-related purposes." This language clearly sets forth Congress' remedy for discrimination on the basis of pregnancy and potential pregnancy. Women who are either pregnant or potentially pregnant must be treated like others "similar in their ability . . . to work." In other words, women as capable of doing their jobs as their male counterparts may not be forced to choose between having a child and having a job.

. . . With the PDA, Congress made clear that the decision to become pregnant or to work while being either pregnant or capable of becoming pregnant was reserved for each individual woman to make for herself. We conclude that the language of both the BFOQ provision and the PDA which amended it, as well as the legislative history and the case law, prohibit an employer from discriminating against a woman because of her capacity to become pregnant unless her reproductive potential prevents her from performing the duties of her job. We reiterate our holdings in *Criswell* and *Dothard* that an employer must direct its concerns about a woman's ability to perform her job safely and efficiently to those aspects of the woman's job-related activities that fall within the "essence" of the particular business.

We have no difficulty concluding that Johnson Controls cannot establish a BFOQ. Fertile women, as far as appears in the record, participate in the manufacture of batteries as efficiently as anyone else. Johnson Controls' professed moral and ethical concerns about the welfare of the next generation do not suffice to establish a BFOQ of female sterility. Decisions about the welfare of future children must be left to the parents who conceive, bear, support, and raise them rather than to the employers who hire those parents. Congress has mandated this choice through Title VII, as amended by the Pregnancy Discrimination Act. Johnson Controls has attempted to exclude women because of their reproductive capacity. Title VII and the PDA simply do not allow a woman's dismissal because of her failure to submit to sterilization.

Nor can concerns about the welfare of the next generation be considered a part of the "essence" of Johnson Controls' business.

. . . Johnson Controls argues that it must exclude all fertile women because it is impossible to tell which women will become pregnant while working with lead. This argument is somewhat academic in light of our conclusion that the company may not exclude fertile women at all; it perhaps is worth noting, however, that Johnson Controls has shown no "factual basis for believing that all or substantially all women would be unable to perform safely and efficiently the duties of the job involved." Even on this sparse record, it is apparent that Johnson Controls is concerned about only a small minority of women. Of the eight pregnancies reported among the female employees, it has not been shown that any of the babies have birth defects or other abnormalities. The record does not reveal the birth rate for Johnson Controls' female workers but national statistics show that approximately nine percent of all fertile women become pregnant each year. . . . Johnson Controls' fear of prenatal injury, no matter how sincere, does not begin to show that substantially all of its fertile women employees are incapable of doing their jobs. . . .

Our holding today that Title VII, as so amended, forbids sex-specific fetal-protection policies is neither remarkable nor unprecedented. Concern for a woman's existing or potential offspring historically has been the excuse for denying women equal employment opportunities. Congress in the PDA prohibited discrimination on the basis of a woman's ability to become pregnant. We do no more than hold that the Pregnancy Discrimination Act means what it says.

It is no more appropriate for the courts than it is for individual employers to decide whether a woman's reproductive role is more important to herself and her family than her economic role. Congress has left this choice to the woman as hers to make.

The judgment of the Court of Appeals is reversed and the case is remanded for further proceedings consistent with this opinion. **It is so ordered.**

Sexual Harassment

Employees on the job may be subjected to unwelcome sexual remarks, advances, or requests for sexual favors by co-workers or by supervisors. Such conduct is known as **sexual harassment.** Although the wording of Title VII does not explicitly include sexual harassment as sex discrimination, numerous court decisions have held that sexual harassment on the job constitutes sex discrimination and is prohibited by Title VII. The issue of sexual harassment was brought into the national spotlight during the 1991 Senate hearings on the nomination of Clarence Thomas to the Supreme Court. The emotional confrontation between Anita Hill, who accused Thomas of sexual harassment, and Thomas, who denied Hill's allegations, was in many ways typical of sexual harassment cases.

It should be clear that requiring an employee to submit to a request for sexual favors in order to retain his or her job, or to get promoted, is sex discrimination in employment. But what about sexual harassment that is not specifically linked to maintaining a job or getting promoted—is it also in violation of Title VII simply because it occurs on the job? The following case involves such a situation, it also considers the EEOC Guidelines on Sexual Harassment.

MERITOR SAVINGS BANK v. MECHELLE VINSON

477 U.S. 57 (Supreme Court of the United States, 1986)

REHNQUIST, J.

This case presents important questions concerning claims of workplace "sexual harassment" brought under Title VII of the Civil Rights Act of 1964.

In 1974, respondent Mechelle Vinson met Sidney Taylor, a vice president of what is now petitioner Meritor Savings Bank (the bank) and manager of one of its branch offices. When respondent asked whether she might obtain employment at the bank, Taylor gave her an application, which she completed and returned the next day; later that same day Taylor called her to say that she had been hired. With Taylor as her supervisor, respondent started as a teller-trainee,

and thereafter was promoted to teller, head teller, and assistant branch manager. She worked at the same branch for four years, and it is undisputed that her advancement there was based on merit alone. In September 1978, respondent notified Taylor that she was taking sick leave for an indefinite period. On November 1, 1978, the bank discharged her for excessive use of that leave.

Respondent brought this action against Taylor and the bank, claiming that during her four years at the bank she had "constantly been subjected to sexual harassment" by Taylor in violation of Title VII. She sought injunctive relief, compensatory and punitive damages against Taylor and the bank, and attorney's fees.

At the 11-day bench trial, the parties presented conflicting testimony about Taylor's behavior during respondent's employment. Respondent testified that during her probationary period as a teller-trainee, Taylor treated her in a fatherly way and made no sexual advances. Shortly thereafter, however, he invited her out to dinner and, during the course of the meal, suggested that they go to a motel to have sexual relations. At first she refused, but out of what she described as fear of losing her job she eventually agreed. According to respondent, Taylor thereafter made repeated demands upon her for sexual favors, usually at the branch, both during and after business hours; she estimated that over the next several years she had intercourse with him some 40 or 50 times. In addition, respondent testified that Taylor fondled her in front of other employees, followed her into the women's restroom when she went there alone, exposed himself to her, and even forcibly raped her on several occasions. These activities ceased after 1977, respondent stated, when she started going with a steady boyfriend.

Respondent also testified that Taylor touched and fondled other women employees of the bank, and she attempted to call witnesses to support this charge. But while some supporting testimony apparently was admitted without objection, the District Court did not allow her "to present wholesale evidence of a pattern and practice relating to sexual advances to other female employees in her case in chief, but advised her that she might well be able to present such evidence in rebuttal to the defendants' cases." Respondent did not offer such evidence in rebuttal. Finally, respondent testified that because she was afraid of Taylor she never reported his harassment to any of his supervisors and never attempted to use the bank's complaint procedure.

Taylor denied respondent's allegations of sexual activity, testifying that he never fondled her, never made suggestive remarks to her, never engaged in sexual intercourse with her and never asked her to do so. He contended instead that respondent made her accusations in response to a business-related dispute. The bank also denied respondent's allegations and asserted that any sexual harassment by Taylor was unknown to the bank and engaged in without its consent or approval.

The District Court denied relief, but did not resolve the conflicting testimony about the existence of a sexual relationship between respondent and Taylor. It found instead that

> If [respondent] and Taylor did engage in an intimate or sexual relationship during the time of [respondent's] employment with [the bank], that relationship was a voluntary one having

nothing to do with her continued employment at [the bank] or her advancement or promotions at that institution.

The court ultimately found that respondent "was not the victim of sexual harassment and was not the victim of sexual discrimination" while employed at the bank.

Although it concluded that respondent had not proved a violation of Title VII, the District Court nevertheless went on to address the bank's liability. After noting the bank's express policy against discrimination, and finding that neither respondent nor any other employee had ever lodged a complaint about sexual harassment by Taylor, the court ultimately concluded that "the bank was without notice and cannot be held liable for the alleged actions of Taylor."

The Court of Appeals for the District of Columbia Circuit reversed. Relying on its earlier holding in *Bundy* v. *Jackson,* decided after the trial in this case, the court stated that a violation of Title VII may be predicated on either of two types of sexual harassment: harassment that involves the conditioning of concrete employment benefits on sexual favors, and harassment that, while not affecting economic benefits, creates a hostile or offensive working environment. The court drew additional support for this position from the Equal Employment Opportunity Commission's Guidelines on Discrimination Because of Sex, which set out these two types of sexual harassment claims. Believing that "Vinson's grievance was clearly of the [hostile environment] type," and that the District Court had not considered whether a violation of this type had occurred, the court concluded that a remand was necessary.

The court further concluded that the District Court's finding that any sexual relationship between respondent and Taylor "was a voluntary one" did not obviate the need for a remand. "[U]ncertain as to precisely what the [district] court meant" by this finding, the Court of Appeals held that if the evidence otherwise showed that "Taylor made Vinson's toleration of sexual harassment a condition of her employment," her voluntariness "had no materiality whatsoever." The court then surmised that the District Court's finding of voluntariness might have been based on "the voluminous testimony regarding respondent's dress and personal fantasies," testimony that the Court of Appeals believed "had no place in this litigation."

As to the bank's liability, the Court of Appeals held that an employer is absolutely liable for sexual harassment practiced by supervisory personnel, whether or not the employer knew or should have known about the misconduct. The court relied chiefly on Title VII's definition of "employer" to include "any agent of such a person," as well as on the EEOC guidelines. The court held that a supervisor is an "agent" of his employer for Title VII purposes, even if he lacks authority to hire, fire, or promote, since "the mere existence—or even the appearance—of a significant degree of influence in vital job decisions gives any supervisor the opportunity to impose on employees."

In accordance with the foregoing, the Court of Appeals reversed the judgment of the District Court and remanded the case for further proceedings. A subsequent suggestion for rehearing en banc was denied, with three judges dissenting. We granted certiorari. . . .

Respondent argues, and the Court of Appeals held, that unwelcome sexual advances that create an offensive or hostile working environment violate Title VII. Without question, when a supervisor sexually harasses a subordinate because of the subordinate's sex, that supervisor "discriminate[s]" on the basis of sex. Petitioner apparently does not challenge this proposition. It contends instead that in prohibiting discrimination with respect to "compensation, terms, conditions, or privileges" of employment, Congress was concerned with what petitioner describes as "tangible loss" of "an economic character," not "purely psychological aspects of the workplace environment." In support of this claim petitioner observes that in both the legislative history of Title VII and this Court's Title VII decisions, the focus has been on tangible, economic barriers erected by discrimination.

We reject petitioner's view. First, the language of Title VII is not limited to "economic" or "tangible" discrimination. The phrase "terms, conditions, or privileges of employment" evinces a congressional intent " 'to strike at the entire spectrum of disparate treatment of men and women' " in employment. Petitioner has pointed to nothing in the Act to suggest that Congress contemplated the limitation urged here.

Second, in 1980 the EEOC issued guidelines specifying that "sexual harassment," as there defined, is a form of sex discrimination prohibited by Title VII. As an "administrative interpretation of the Act by the enforcing agency," . . . these guidelines, " 'while not controlling upon the courts by reason of their authority, do constitute a body of experience and informed judgment to which courts and litigants may properly resort for guidance.' " . . . The EEOC guidelines fully support the view that harassment leading to noneconomic injury can violate Title VII.

In defining "sexual harassment," the guidelines first describe the kinds of workplace conduct that may be action-able under Title VII. These include "[u]nwelcome sexual advances, requests for sexual favors, and other verbal or physical conduct of a sexual nature." Relevant to the charges at issue in this case, the guidelines provide that such sexual misconduct constitutes prohibited "sexual harassment," whether or not it is directly linked to the grant or denial of an economic *quid pro quo,* where "such conduct has the purpose or effect of unreasonably interfering with an individual's work performance or creating an intimidating, hostile, or offensive working environment."

In concluding that so-called "hostile environment" (i.e., non *quid pro quo*) harassment violates Title VII, the EEOC drew upon a substantial body of judicial decisions and EEOC precedent holding that Title VII affords employees the right to work in an environment free from discriminatory intimidation, ridicule, and insult. . . .

Since the guidelines were issued, courts have uniformly held, and we agree, that a plaintiff may establish a violation of Title VII by proving that discrimination based on sex has created a hostile or abusive work environment. . . .

Of course, . . . not all workplace conduct that may be described as "harassment" affects a "term, condition, or privilege" of employment within the meaning of Title VII. . . . For sexual harassment to be actionable, it must be sufficiently severe or pervasive "to alter the conditions of [the victim's] employment and create an abusive working environment." Respondent's allegations in this case—which include not only pervasive harassment but also criminal conduct of the most serious nature—are plainly sufficient to state a claim for "hostile environment" sexual harassment. . . .

The question remains, however, whether the District Court's ultimate finding that respondent "was not the victim of sexual harassment," effectively disposed of respondent's claim. The Court of Appeals recognized, we think correctly, that this ultimate finding was likely based on one or both of two erroneous views of the law. First, the District Court apparently believed that a claim for sexual harassment will not lie absent an *economic* effect on the complainant's employment. ("It is without question that sexual harassment of female employees in which they are asked or required to submit to sexual demands as a *condition to obtain employment or to maintain employment or to obtain promotions* falls within protection of Title VII.") (emphasis added). Since it appears that the District Court made its findings without ever considering the "hostile environment" theory of sexual harassment, the Court of Appeals' decision to remand was correct.

Second, the District Court's conclusion that no actionable harassment occurred might have rested on its earlier "finding" that "[i]f [respondent] and Taylor did engage in an intimate or sexual relationship . . . , that relationship was a voluntary one." But the fact that sex-related conduct was "voluntary," in the sense that the complainant was not forced to participate against her will, is not a defense to a sexual harassment suit brought under Title VII. The gravamen of any sexual harassment claim is that the alleged sexual advances were "unwelcome." While the question whether particular conduct was indeed unwelcome presents difficult problems of proof and turns largely on credibility determinations committed to the trier of fact, the District Court in this case erroneously focused on the "voluntariness" of respondent's participation in the claimed sexual episodes. The correct inquiry is whether respondent by her conduct indicated that the alleged sexual advances were unwelcome, not whether her actual participation in sexual intercourse was voluntary.

Petitioner contends that even if this case must be remanded to the District Court, the Court of Appeals erred in one of the terms of its remand. Specifically, the Court of Appeals stated that testimony about respondent's "dress and personal fantasies," which the District Court apparently admitted into evidence, "had no place in this litigation." The apparent ground for this conclusion was that respondent's voluntariness *vel non* in submitting to Taylor's advances was immaterial to her sexual harassment claim. While "voluntariness" in the sense of consent is not a defense to such a claim, it does not follow that a complainant's sexually provocative speech or dress is irrelevant as a matter of law in determining whether he or she found particular sexual advances unwelcome. To the contrary, such evidence is obviously relevant. The EEOC guidelines emphasize that the trier of fact must determine the existence of sexual harassment in light of "the record as a whole" and "the totality of circumstances, such as the nature of the sexual advances and the context in which the alleged incidents occurred." Respondent's claim that any marginal relevance of the evidence in question was outweighed by the potential for unfair prejudice is the sort of argument properly addressed to the District Court. In this case the District Court concluded that the evidence should be admitted, and the Court of Appeals' contrary conclusion was based upon the erroneous, categorical view that testimony about provocative dress and publicly expressed sexual fantasies "had no place in this litigation." While the District Court must carefully weigh the applicable considerations in deciding whether to admit evidence of this kind, there is no *per se* rule against its admissibility.

Although the District Court concluded that respondent had not proved a violation of Title VII, it nevertheless went on to consider the question of the bank's liability. Finding that "the bank was without notice" of Taylor's alleged conduct, and that notice to Taylor was not the equivalent of notice to the bank, the court concluded that the bank therefore could not be held liable for Taylor's alleged actions. The Court of Appeals took the opposite view, holding that an employer is strictly liable for a hostile environment created by a supervisor's sexual advances, even though the employer neither knew nor reasonably could have known of the alleged misconduct. The court held that a supervisor, whether or not he possesses the authority to hire, fire, or promote, is necessarily an "agent" of his employer for all Title VII purposes, since "even the appearance" of such authority may enable him to impose himself on his subordinates. . . .

This debate over the appropriate standard for employer liability has a rather abstract quality about it given the state of the record in this case. We do not know at this stage whether Taylor made any sexual advances toward respondent at all, let alone whether those advances were unwelcome, whether they were sufficiently pervasive to constitute a condition of employment, or whether they were "so pervasive and so long continuing . . . that the employer must have become conscious of [them]." . . .

We therefore decline the parties' invitation to issue a definitive rule on employer liability, but we do agree with the EEOC that Congress wanted courts to look to agency principles for guidance in this area. While such common-law principles may not be transferable in all their particulars to Title VII, Congress' decision to define "employer" to include any "agent" of an employer, surely evinces an intent to place some limits on the acts of employees for which employers under Title VII are to be held responsible. For this reason, we hold that the Court of Appeals erred in concluding that employers are always automatically liable for sexual harassment by their supervisors. For the same reason, absence of notice to an employer does not necessarily insulate that employer from liability.

Finally, we reject petitioner's view that the mere existence of a grievance procedure and a policy against discrimination, coupled with respondent's failure to invoke that procedure, must insulate petitioner from liability. While those facts are plainly relevant, the situation before us demonstrates why they are not necessarily dispositive.

Petitioner's general nondiscrimination policy did not address sexual harassment in particular, and thus did not alert employees to their employer's interest in correcting that form of discrimination. Moreover, the bank's grievance procedure apparently required an employee to complain first to her supervisor, in this case Taylor. Since Taylor was the alleged perpetrator, it is not altogether surprising that respondent failed to invoke the procedure and report her grievance to him. Petitioner's contention that respondent's failure should insulate it from liability might be substantially stronger if its procedures were better calculated to encourage victims of harassment to come forward.

In sum, we hold that a claim of "hostile environment" sex discrimination is actionable under Title VII, that the District Court's findings were insufficient to dispose of respondent's hostile environment claim, and that the District Court did not err in admitting testimony about respondent's sexually provocative speech and dress. As to employer liability, we conclude that the Court of Appeals was wrong to entirely disregard agency principles and impose absolute liability on employers for the acts of their supervisors, regardless of the circumstances of a particular case.

Accordingly, the judgment of the Court of Appeals reversing the judgment of the District Court is affirmed, and the case is remanded for further proceedings consistent with this opinion. **It is so ordered.**

In *Ellison* v. *Brady* (924 F.2d 872, 9th Cir. 1991), the Ninth Circuit Court of Appeals held that the standard for evaluating hostile environment sexual harassment claims by female plaintiffs is the "reasonable woman" standard—would a reasonable woman be offended by the conduct in question? The court stated that a reasonable person standard tends to systematically ignore experiences of women; men tend to view some forms of sexual harassment as "harmless social interactions," whereas women may tend to find such conduct offensive and unwelcome. The *Ellison* case involved a female Internal Revenue Service employee who was pressured for dates and received "bizarre" love letters from a male co-worker; the court of appeals concluded that a reasonable woman could find such conduct offensive and harassing.

The EEOC Guidelines on Sexual Harassment, mentioned in *Meritor,* also provide that when an employer rewards one employee for entering a sexual relationship, other employees denied the same reward or benefit may have a valid harassment complaint. In *King* v. *Palmer* (778 F.2d 878, D.C. Cir. 1985) a supervisor promoted a nurse with whom he was having an affair rather than one of several more qualified nurses. The court held that the employer was guilty of sex discrimination against the superior nurses who were denied the promotion.

Other Sex-Discrimination Issues

Section 712 of Title VII states that

> [n]othing contained in this title shall be construed to repeal or modify any Federal, State, territorial, or local law creating special rights or preference for veterans.

Because most veterans are male, any preference in employment according to veterans will have a disparate impact on women. The effect of Section 712 is to allow such preference regardless of its disparate impact. In *Personnel Administrator of Massachusetts* v. *Feeney* (442 U.S. 256, 1979), the Supreme Court held that Section 712 was permissible under the Constitution because it was not specifically aimed at discriminating against women and did not involve intentional sex discrimination. Feeney had challenged a Massachusetts law that gave combat-era veterans an absolute preference over nonveterans for state civil service jobs. Feeney alleged that the preference and Section 712, which allowed it, violated the equal protection clause of the Constitution.

The Title VII prohibition on sex discrimination in employment does not protect transsexuals, as held in the case of *Sommers* v. *Budget Marketing Inc.* (667 F.2d 748, 8th Cir. 1982). Title VII does not prohibit discrimination against homosexuals or lesbians, the courts have consistently held that the word "sex" used in Title VII does not include sexual orientation or sexual preference.

Discrimination on the Basis of Religion or National Origin

Discrimination Based on Religion

Although Title VII prohibits discrimination in employment on the basis of religion, the prohibition is not absolute. Religion, as with sex or national origin, may be used as a BFOQ when the employer establishes that business necessity requires hiring individuals of a particular religion. For example, an employer who is providing helicopter pilots under contract to the Saudi Arabian government to fly Muslim pilgrims to Mecca may require that all pilots be of the Muslim religion because Islamic law prohibits non-Muslims from entering the holy areas of the city of Mecca. The penalty for violating the prohibition is beheading; the employer could therefore refuse to hire non-Muslims, or require all pilots to convert to Islamism. (See the case of *Kern* v. *Dynalectron Corp.,* 577 F. Supp. 1196, N. Dist. Texas 1983.)

In addition to the BFOQ provisions, Title VII allows religious corporations or educational institutions to give preference to hiring employees who are members of that religion. Section 702(a) states that

> This Title shall not apply to . . . a religious corporation, association, educational institution, or society with respect to the employment of individuals of a particular religion to perform work connected with the carrying on by such corporation, association, educational institution or society of its activities.

Because of Section 702(a), a Hebrew day school may require that all teachers be Jewish; as well, a Catholic university such as Notre Dame may require that the university president be Catholic.

But how broad is the scope of the exemption under Section 702 (a)—does it extend to all activities of a religious corporation, even those activities that are not really religious in character? The Supreme Court considered that question in the next case.

CORPORATION OF THE PRESIDING BISHOP OF THE CHURCH OF JESUS CHRIST OF LATTER-DAY SAINTS v. AMOS

483 U.S. 327 (Supreme Court of the United States, 1987)

[Note that this case was decided prior to the 1991 amendments to Title VII, when Section 702(a) was simply Section 702.]

WHITE, J.

Section 702 of the Civil Rights Act of 1964, as amended, exempts religious organizations from Title VII's prohibition against discrimination in employment on the basis of religion. The question presented is whether applying the Section 702 exemption to the secular nonprofit activities religious organizations violates the Establishment Clause of the First Amendment. The District Court held that it does, and the case is here on direct appeal.

The Deseret Gymnasium (Gymnasium) in Salt Lake City, Utah, is a nonprofit facility, open to the public, run by the Corporation of the Presiding Bishop of The Church of Jesus Christ of Latter-day Saints (CPB), and the Corporation of the President of The Church of Jesus Christ of Latter-day Saints (COP). The CPB and the COP are religious entities associated with The Church of Jesus Christ of Latter-day Saints (Church), an unincorporated religious association sometimes called the Mormon or LDS Church.

Appellee Mayson worked at the Gymnasium for some 16 years as an assistant building engineer and then building engineer. He was discharged in 1981 because he failed to qualify for a temple recommend, that is, a certificate that he is a member of the Church and eligible to attend its temples.

Mayson and others purporting to represent a class of plaintiffs brought an action against the CPB and the COP alleging among other things, discrimination on the basis of religion in violation . . . of the Civil Rights Act of 1964 . . . The defendants moved to dismiss this claim on the ground that Section 702 shields them from liability. The plaintiffs contended that if construed to allow religious employers to discriminate on religious grounds in hiring for nonreligious jobs, Section 702 violates the Establishment Clause [of the First Amendment].

The District Court first considered whether the facts of this case require a decision on the plaintiffs' constitutional argument. Starting from the premise that the religious activities of religious employers can permissibly be exempted under Section 702, the court developed a three-part test to determine whether an activity is religious. Applying this

test to Mayson's situation, the court found: first, that the Gymnasium is intimately connected to the Church financially and in matters of management; second, that there is no clear connection between the primary function which the Gymnasium performs and the religious beliefs and tenets of the Mormon Church or church administration; and third, that none of Mayson's duties at the Gymnasium are "even tangentially related to any conceivable religious belief or ritual of the Mormon Church or church administration," . . . The court concluded that Mayson's case involves nonreligious activity.

The court next considered the plaintiffs' constitutional challenge to Section 702. Applying the three-part test set out in *Lemon* v. *Kurtzman,* the court first held that Section 702 has the permissible secular purpose of "assuring that the government remains neutral and does not meddle in religious affairs by interfering with the decision-making process in religions. . . ." The court concluded, however, that Section 702 fails the second part of the Lemon test because the provision has the primary effect of advancing religion. Among the considerations mentioned by the court were: that Section 702 singles out religious entities for a benefit, rather than benefiting a broad grouping of which religious organizations are only a part; that Section 702 is not supported by long historical tradition; and that Section 702 burdens the free exercise rights of employees of religious institutions who work in nonreligious jobs. Finding that Section 702 impermissibly sponsors religious organizations by granting them "an exclusive authorization to engage in conduct which can directly and immediately advance religious tenets and practices," the court declared the statute unconstitutional as applied to secular activity. The court entered summary judgment in favor of Mayson and ordered him reinstated with backpay. Subsequently, the court vacated its judgment so that the United States could intervene to defend the constitutionality of Section 702. After further briefing and argument the court affirmed its prior determination and reentered a final judgment for Mayson. . . .

We find unpersuasive the District Court's reliance on the fact that Section 702 singles out religious entities for a benefit. Although the Court has given weight to this consideration in its past decisions, it has never indicated that statutes that give special consideration to religious groups are *per se* invalid. That would run contrary to the teaching of our cases that there is ample room for accommodation of religion under the Establishment Clause.

Where, as here, government acts with the proper purpose of lifting a regulation that burdens the exercise of religion, we see no reason to require that the exemption come packaged with benefits to secular entities. We are also unpersuaded by the District Court's reliance on the argument that Section 702 is unsupported by long historical tradition. There was simply no need to consider the scope of the Section 702 exemption until the 1964 Civil Rights Act was passed, and the fact that Congress concluded after eight years that the original exemption was unnecessarily narrow is a decision entitled to deference, not suspicion.

Appellees argue that Section 702 offends equal protection principles by giving less protection to the employees of religious employers than to the employees of secular employers. . . . In a case such as this, where a statute is neutral on its face and motivated by a permissible purpose of limiting governmental interference with the exercise of religion, we see no justification for applying strict scrutiny to a statute that passes the *Lemon* test. The proper inquiry is whether Congress has chosen a rational classification to further a legitimate end. We have already indicated that Congress acted with a legitimate purpose in expanding the Section 702 exemption to cover all activities of religious employers. To dispose of appellees' Equal Protection argument, it suffices to hold—as we now do—that as applied to the nonprofit activities of religious employers, Section 702 is rationally related to the legitimate purpose of alleviating significant governmental interference with the ability of religious organizations to define and carry out their religious missions.

It cannot be seriously contended that Section 702 imper-missibly entangles church and state; the statute effectuates a more complete separation of the two and avoids the kind of intrusive inquiry into religious belief that the District Court engaged in in this case. The statute easily passes muster under the third part of the *Lemon* test.

The judgment of the District Court is reversed, and the case is remanded for further proceedings consistent with this opinion. **It is so ordered.**

BRENNAN, J., with whom MARSHALL, J. joins (concurring)

. . . my concurrence in the judgment rests on the fact that this case involves a challenge to the application of Section 702's categorical exemption to the activities of a *nonprofit* organization. I believe that the particular character of nonprofit activity makes inappropriate a case-by-case determination whether its nature is religious or secular. . . .

. . . I concur in the Court's judgment that the nonprofit Deseret Gymnasium may avail itself of an automatic exemption from Title VII's proscription on religious discrimination.

O'CONNOR, J. (concurring)

. . . I emphasize that under the holding of the Court, and under my view of the appropriate Establishment Clause analysis, the question of the constitutionality of the Section 702 exemption as applied to for-profit activities of religious organizations remains open.

Reasonable Accommodation.   Even when religion is not a BFOQ and the employer is not within the Section 702 exemption, the prohibition against discrimination on the basis of religion is not absolute. Section 701(j) defines religion as

> includ[ing] all aspects of religious observance and practice, as well as belief, unless an employer demonstrates that he is unable to reasonably accommodate to an employee's religious observance or practice without undue hardship on the conduct of the employer's business.

An employer must make reasonable attempts to accommodate an employee's religious beliefs or practices, but if such attempts are not successful or involve undue hardship, the employer may discharge the employee. The following case explores the extent to which an employer is required to accommodate an employee's beliefs.

TRANS WORLD AIRLINES v. HARDISON

432 U.S. 63 (Supreme Court of the United States, 1977)

WHITE, J.

Petitioner Trans World Airlines (TWA) operates a large maintenance and overhaul base in Kansas City, Mo. On June 5, 1967, respondent Larry G. Hardison was hired by TWA to work as a clerk in the Stores Department at its Kansas City base. Because of its essential role in the Kansas City operation, the Stores Department must operate 24 hours per day, 365 days per year, and whenever an employee's job in that department is not filled, an employee must be shifted from another department, or a supervisor must cover the job, even if the work in other areas may suffer.

Hardison, like other employees at the Kansas City base, was subject to a seniority system contained in a collective-bargaining agreement with TWA maintains with petitioner International Association of Machinists and Aerospace Workers (IAM). The seniority system is implemented by the union steward through a system of bidding by employees for particular shift assignments as they become available. The most senior employees have first choice for job and shift assignments, and the most junior employees are required to work when the union steward is unable to find enough people willing to work at a particular time or in a particular job to fill TWA's needs.

In the spring of 1968 Hardison began to study the religion known as the Worldwide Church of God. One of the tenets of that religion is that one must observe the Sabbath by refraining from performing any work from sunset on Friday until sunset on Saturday. The religion also proscribes work on certain specified religious holidays.

When Hardison informed Everett Kussman, the manager of the Stores Department, of his religious conviction regarding observance of the Sabbath, Kussman agreed that the union steward should seek a job swap for Hardison or a change of days off; that Hardison would have his religious holidays off whenever possible if Hardison agreed to work the traditional holidays when asked; and that Kussman would try to find Hardison another job that would be more compatible with his religious beliefs. The problem was temporarily solved when Hardison transferred to the 11 p.m.–7 a.m. shift. Working this shift permitted Hardison to observe his Sabbath.

The problem soon reappeared when Hardison bid for and received a transfer from Building 1, where he had been employed, to Building 2, where he would work the day shift.

The two buildings had entirely separate seniority lists; and while in Building 1 Hardison had sufficient seniority to observe the Sabbath regularly, he was second from the bottom on the Building 2 seniority list.

In Building 2 Hardison was asked to work Saturdays when a fellow employee went on vacation. TWA agreed to permit the union to seek a change of work assignments for Hardison, but the union was not willing to violate the seniority provisions set out in the collective-bargaining contract, and Hardison had insufficient seniority to bid for a shift having Saturdays off.

A proposal that Hardison work only four days a week was rejected by the company. Hardison's job was essential, and on weekends he was the only available person on his shift to perform it. To leave the position empty would have impaired Supply Shop functions, which were critical to airline operations; to fill Hardison's position with a supervisor or an employee from another area would simply have undermanned another operation; and to employ someone not regularly assigned to work Saturdays would have required TWA to pay premium wages.

When an accommodation was not reached, Hardison refused to report for work on Saturdays. . . . [Hardison was fired by TWA.]

The Court of Appeals found that TWA had committed an unlawful employment practice under Section 703(a)(1) of the Act. . . .

In 1967 the EEOC amended its guidelines to require employers "to make reasonable accommodations to the religious needs of employees and prospective employees where such accommodations can be made without undue hardship on the conduct of the employer's business." The Commission did not suggest what sort of accommodations are "reasonable" or when hardship to an employer becomes "undue."

This question—the extent of the required accommodation—remained unsettled when this Court affirmed by an equally divided Court the Sixth Circuit's decision in *Dewey* v. *Reynolds Metals Co.*

In part "to resolve by legislation" some of the issues raised in *Dewey,* Congress included the following definition of religion in its 1972 amendments to Title VII:

> The term "religion" includes all aspects of religious observance and practice, as well as belief, unless an employer demonstrates that he is unable to reasonably accommodate to an employee's or prospective employee's religious observance or

practice without undue hardship on the conduct of the employer's business. [Section 701(j)] . . .

. . . The proponent of the measure, Senator Jennings Randolph, . . . made no attempt to define the precise circumstances under which the "reasonable accommodation" requirement would be applied.

The Court of Appeals held that TWA had not made reasonable efforts to accommodate Hardison's religious needs. . . .

We disagree. . . .

The Court of Appeals observed . . . that the possibility of a variance from the seniority system was never really posed to the union. This is contrary to the District Court's findings and to the record. . . . As the record shows, Hardison himself testified that Kussman was willing, but the union was not, to work out a shift or job trade with another employee.

We shall say more about the seniority system, but at this juncture it appears to us that the system itself represented a significant accommodation to the needs, both religious and secular, of all of TWA's employees. As will become apparent, the seniority system represents a neutral way of minimizing the number of occasions when an employee must work on a day that he would prefer to have off. . . .

We are also convinced, contrary to the Court of Appeals, that TWA cannot be faulted for having failed itself to work out a shift or job swap for Hardison. Both the union and TWA had agreed to the seniority system; the union was unwilling to entertain a variance over the objections of men senior to Hardison. . . .

Had TWA nevertheless circumvented the seniority system by relieving Hardison of Saturday work and ordering a senior employee to replace him, it would have denied the latter his shift preference so that Hardison could be given his. The senior employee would also have been deprived of his contractual rights under the collective-bargaining agreement.

Title VII does not contemplate such unequal treatment. . . . It would be anomalous to conclude that by "reasonable accommodation" Congress meant that an employer must deny the shift and job preference of some employees, as well as deprive them of their contractual rights, in order to accommodate or prefer the religious needs of others, and we conclude that Title VII does not require an employer to go that far.

Our conclusion is supported by the fact that seniority systems are afforded special treatment under Title VII itself. Section 703(h) provides in pertinent part:

> Notwithstanding any other provision of this subchapter, it shall not be an unlawful employment practice for an employer to apply different standards of compensation, or different terms, conditions, or privileges of employment pursuant to a bona fide seniority or merit system . . . provided that such differences are not the result of an intention to discriminate because of race, color, religion, sex or national origin. . . .

. . . [T]he Court of Appeals suggested that TWA could have replaced Hardison on his Saturday shift with other available employees through the payment of premium wages. Both of these alternatives would involve costs to TWA, either in the form of lost efficiency in other jobs or as higher wages.

To require TWA to bear more than a *de minimis* cost in order to give Hardison Saturdays off is an undue hardship. . . .

As we have seen, the paramount concern of Congress in enacting Title VII was the elimination of discrimination in employment. In the absence of clear statutory language or legislative history to the contrary, we will not readily construe the statute to require an employer to discriminate against some employees in order to enable others to observe their Sabbath. **Reversed.**

It should be clear from Section 701(j) that Title VII protects an employee from discrimination based on an employee's religious beliefs or practices (within the limits of reasonable accommodation). Title VII has also been held to protect atheists. The EEOC takes the position that Title VII also protects an individual's personal moral or philosophical beliefs when held with the strength or conviction of traditional religious beliefs.

If there are several ways to accommodate the employee's religious beliefs, is the employer required to provide the accommodation that is preferred by the employee? In *Ansonia Board of Education* v. *Philbrook* (479 U.S. 60, 1986), the Supreme Court held the following:

. . . We find no basis in either the statute or its legislative history for requiring an employer to choose any particular reasonable accommodation. By its very terms the statute directs that any reasonable accommodation by the employer is sufficient to meet its accommodation obligation. The employer violates the statute unless it "demonstrates that [it] is unable to reasonably accommodate . . . an employee's . . . religious observance or practice without undue hardship on the conduct of the employer's business." Thus, where the employer has already reasonably accommodated the employee's religious needs, the statutory inquiry is at an end. The employer need not further show that each of the employee's alternative accommodations would result in undue hardship. As *Hardison* illustrates, the extent of undue hardship on the employer's business is at issue only where the employer claims that it is unable to offer any reasonable accommodation without such hardship. Once the Court of Appeals assumed that the school board had offered to Philbrook a reasonable alternative, it erred by requiring the board to nonetheless demonstrate the hardship of Philbrook's alternatives. . . . We accordingly hold that an employer has met its obligation under Section 701(j) when it demonstrates that it has offered a reasonable accommodation to the employee.

Discrimination Based on National Origin

The prohibitions against employment discrimination under Title VII also extend to discrimination based on national origin. As noted, national origin may be the basis of a BFOQ under Section 703(e)(1).

Examples of discrimination on the basis of national origin include the use of English language tests when the individual being tested comes from circumstances in which English is not the primary language and English language skill is not a requirement of the work to be performed, or the refusal to hire persons associated with a specific nationality or ethnic group. The requirement that all employees speak only English while on the job may be discriminatory if English language proficiency is not required for the performance of job duties; however, an employer may require that employees who work in public-contact positions (such as sales clerks or receptionists) speak English on the job.

Title VII protects all individuals, both citizen and noncitizen, who reside in or are employed in the United States, from employment discrimination based on race, color, religion, sex, or national origin. However, the prohibition against discrimination on the basis of national origin does not include discrimination on the basis of citizenship. According to the Supreme Court decision in *Espinoza* v. *Farah Mfg. Co.* (414 U.S. 86, 1973), an employer may refuse to hire employees who are not U.S. citizens.

QUESTIONS

1. What is meant by sex-plus discrimination?

2. When can Title VII be used to challenge sex-based pay differentials for jobs that are not equivalent? Explain.

3. What is the effect of the Pregnancy Discrimination Act of 1978 on employment benefits? Must an employer offer paid pregnancy leave under Title VII?

4. What must be demonstrated to support an employer's claim that potential exposure to hazardous conditions requires restricting the employment of female employees?

5. When can an employer be held liable for sexual harassment by an employee?

6. Is the prohibition against discrimination based on religion under Title VII an absolute prohibition? Explain your answer.

7. What is meant by "national origin" under Title VII? Can an employer, under Title VII, require that employees be U.S. citizens?

CASE PROBLEMS

1. Anderson, a female attorney, was hired as an associate in a large law firm in 1978. She had accepted the position based on the firm's representations that associates would advance to partnership after five or six years, and that being promoted to partner "was a matter of course" for associates who received satisfactory evaluations. The firm also maintained that promotions were made on a "fair and equal basis." Anderson consistently received satisfactory evaluations, yet her promotion to partnership was rejected in 1984. She again was considered and rejected in 1985. The firm's rules state that an associate passed over for promotion must seek employment elsewhere. Anderson was therefore terminated by the firm on December 31, 1985. The firm, with more than fifty partners, has never had a female partner.

   Anderson filed a complaint alleging sex discrimination against the firm. The firm replied that the selection of partners is not subject to Title VII because it entails a change in status "from employee to employer."

   Does Title VII apply to such partnership selection decisions? Does Anderson's complaint state a claim under Title VII? See *Hishon* v. *King & Spaulding,* 467 U.S. 69 (U.S. Sup. Ct. 1984).

2. Cohen, a college graduate with a degree in journalism, applied for a position with *The Christian Science Monitor,* a daily newspaper published by the Christian Science Publishing Society, a branch of the Christian Science Church. The church board of directors elects the editors and managers of the *Monitor* and is responsible for the editorial content of the *Monitor.* The church subsidizes the *Monitor,* which otherwise would run at a significant loss. The application for employment at the *Monitor* is the same one used for general positions with the church. It contains many questions relating to membership in the Christian Science Church and to its religious affiliation.

   Cohen, who is not a member of the Christian Science Church, was rejected for employment with the *Monitor.* He filed a complaint with the EEOC alleging that his application was not given full consideration by the *Monitor* because he is not a member of the Christian Science Church. The *Monitor* claimed that it can apply a test of religious qualifications to its employment practices.

   Is the *Monitor* in violation of Title VII? Explain your answer. See *Feldstein* v. *Christian Science Monitor,* 555 F. Supp. 974 (D.C. Mass. 1983).

3. A group of nurses employed by the state of Illinois filed a complaint charging the state with sex discrimination in classification and compensation of employees. The nurses alleged that the state had refused to implement the changes in job classifications and wage rates recommended by an evaluation study conducted by the state. That study suggested that changes in pay and classification for some female-dominated job classes should be more equitable.

   Does the nurses' complaint state a claim under Title VII? Explain your answer. See *American Nurses Association* v. *Illinois,* 783 F.2d 716 (7th Cir. 1986).

4. Baker, a female, was employed as a history teacher by More Science High School for three years. Although she received good evaluation reviews for her first two years, her third-year review gave her a poor evaluation. Her contract of employment was not renewed after the end of her third year. During Baker's third year, the coach of the boys basketball team had given notice of his resignation, which was effective at the end of that school year. Baker was replaced as a history teacher by Dan Roundball, who was also hired as coach of the boys basketball team. Baker filed a complaint with the EEOC alleging that her contract was not renewed because the school wanted to replace her with a man who would also coach the basketball team.

   Is More Science High School guilty of violating Title VII's prohibition on sex discrimination? Explain your answer. See *Carlile* v. *South Routt School Dist.,* 739 F.2d 1496 (10th Cir. 1984).

5. Walker is a clerk with the U.S. Postal Service. The Postal Service distributes the materials for the draft

registration required of young men. Walker, although not a formal member of the Society of Friends (known as Quakers), had a long history of involvement with the Quakers. She therefore refused to distribute draft registration materials when she was working. The Postal Service fired her.

Is Walker's refusal to distribute the draft registration materials protected by Title VII? Explain your answer. See *McGinnis* v. *U.S. Postal Service,* 24 F.E.P. Cases 999 (U.S. Dist. Ct., N.D. Cal. 1980).

6. In October 1981 Rebecca Thomas was hired as a personnel assistant by Cooper Industries, a plant that manufactures hammers and axes. In February 1982 Thomas was promoted to personnel supervisor. Her boss, the plant's employee relations manager, was fired in March 1983, whereupon she filled his job in an acting capacity. The plant manager gave her the highest possible rating on her performance evaluation, but corporate officials repeatedly refused to interview her for permanent award of the position. According to testimony, the plant manager was told by the company vice-president that there was "no way" a woman could stand up to the union in the capacity of employee relations manager. A male was ultimately hired to fill the job on a permanent basis.

Is this an example of sex discrimination? Explain your answer. See *Thomas* v. *Cooper Industries, Inc.,* 627 F. Supp. 655 (W.D. N.C. 1986).

7. Alvie Thompkins was employed as a full-time instructor of mathematics at the Morris Brown College. Her classes were scheduled in academic year 1979–1980 in such a way that she was able to hold down a second full-time post as a math instructor at Douglas High School. Only one other faculty member, Thompkins' predecessor at Morris Brown College, ever held down two concurrent full-time jobs, and the college's vice-president for academic affairs testified that he had never been aware of this earlier situation. Some male, "part-time" faculty of the college were employed full-time elsewhere. Although labeled "part-timers," some of these faculty sometimes worked nine to twelve hours per semester, which was about the same as many "full-time" faculty. Thompkins was told to choose between her two full-time jobs; when she refused to make a choice, she was fired.

Is this a case of sex discrimination? Explain your answer. See *Thompkins* v. *Morris Brown College,* 752 F.2d 558 37 F.E.P. Cases 24 (11th Cir. 1985).

8. Diane L. Matthews served in the U.S. Army for four years as a field communication equipment mechanic. She received numerous awards and high performance ratings and ultimately was promoted to sergeant. She was honorably discharged in 1980. She enrolled in the University of Maine and joined the Reserve Officer Training Corps program on campus. Her ROTC instructor learned that she had attended a student senate meeting, which had been called to discuss the budget for the "Wilde-Stein Club." Upon inquiring as to the nature of the club, he was told by Matthews that it was the campus homosexual organization. On further inquiry she told the officer she was a lesbian. Although her commander did not attempt to interfere with Matthew's continued membership in the club, he reported Matthew's disclosure to his supervisor. An investigation was conducted and she was disenrolled from the ROTC program. Was Matthews a victim of sex discrimination? Explain your answer. See *Matthews* v. *Marsh,* 755 F.2d 182, 37 F.E.P. Cases 126 (1st Cir. 1985).

9. Wilson, a male, applied for a job as a flight attendant with Southwest Airlines. Southwest refused to hire him because the airline hires only females for those positions. Southwest, a small commuter airline in the southwestern United States, must compete against larger, more established airlines for passengers. Southwest, which has its headquarters at Love Field in Dallas, decided that the best way to compete with those larger airlines was to establish a distinctive image. Southwest decided to base its marketing image as the "love airline"; its slogan is, "We're spreading love all over Texas."

Southwest requires its flight attendants and ticket clerks, all female, to wear a uniform consisting of a brief halter top, hot pants, and high boots. Its quick ticketing and check-in flight counters are called "quickie machines," and the in-flight snacks and drinks are referred to as "love bites" and "love potions." Southwest claims that it is identified with the public through its "youthful, feminine" image; it cites surveys of its passengers to support its claim that business necessity requires it to hire only females for all public contact positions. The surveys asked passengers the reasons that they chose to fly with Southwest; the reason labeled "courteous and attentive hostesses" was ranked fifth in importance, after reasons relating to lower fares, frequency of flights, on-time departures, and helpful reservations personnel.

Has Southwest established that its policy of hiring

only females in flight attendant and ticket clerk positions is a bona fide occupational qualification? See *Wilson* v. *Southwest Airlines Co.,* 517 F. Supp. 292 (N.D. Texas 1981).

10. Marjorie Reiley Maguire was a professor in the theology department at Marquette University, a Roman Catholic institution. Half of the twenty-seven members of the department were Jesuits, and only one other member was female at the time Maguire came up for tenure. The school denied her tenure because of her pro-choice view on the abortion issue, that is, because she favored personal choice rather than the Church's strict ban on abortions. Was she a victim of sex discrimination? See *Maguire* v. *Marquette University,* 814 F. 2d 1213 (7th Cir. 1987).

Procedures under Title VII

THE PROVISIONS OF TITLE VII of the Civil Rights Act of 1964 (Title VII) were discussed in detail in the preceding chapters; this chapter will focus on the procedures for filing and resolving complaints of employment discrimination that arise under Title VII.

The Equal Employment Opportunity Commission

Title VII is administered and enforced by the Equal Employment Opportunity Commission (EEOC). The EEOC is headed by a five-member commission; the commissioners are appointed by the president with Senate confirmation. The general counsel of the EEOC is also appointed by the president, also with Senate confirmation.

Unlike the National Labor Relations Board (NLRB), the EEOC does not adjudicate, or decide, complaints alleging violations of Title VII; nor is it the exclusive enforcement agency for discrimination complaints. The EEOC staff investigates complaints filed with it and attempts to settle such complaints voluntarily. If a settlement is not reached voluntarily, the EEOC may file suit against the alleged discriminator in the federal courts.

The EEOC also differs from the NLRB in that the EEOC may initiate complaints on its own when it believes a party is involved in a "pattern or practice" of discrimination. In such cases the EEOC need not wait for an individual to file a complaint with it. When a complaint alleges discrimination by a state or local government, Title VII requires that the Justice Department initiate any court action against the public sector employer.

Procedure under Title VII

Filing a Complaint

Title VII, unlike the National Labor Relations Act, does not give the federal government exclusive authority over employment discrimination issues. Section 706(c) of Title VII requires that an individual filing a complaint of illegal employment discrimination must first file with a state or local agency authorized to deal with the issue, if such an agency exists. The EEOC may consider the complaint only after the state or local agency has had the complaint for sixty days or ceased processing the complaint, whichever occurs first.

State Agency Role.   A number of states and municipalities have created equal employment opportunity agencies—also known as "fair employment" or "human rights" commissions. Some state agencies have powers and jurisdiction beyond that given to the EEOC. The New York State Human Rights Division enforces the New York State Human Rights Law; in addition to prohibiting discrimination in employment on the basis of race, color, religion, sex, and national origin, the New York legislation also prohibits employment discrimination on the basis of age, marital status, disability, and criminal record. The Pennsylvania Human Relations Act established the Human Rights Commission, which is empowered to hold hearings before Administrative Law Judges to determine whether the act has been violated. The Pennsylvania legislation goes beyond Title VII's prohibitions by forbidding employment discrimination on the basis of disability.

Filing with the EEOC.   When the complaint must first be filed with a state or local agency, Section 706(e) requires that it be filed with the EEOC within 300 days of the act of alleged discrimination. If there is no state or local agency, the complaint must be filed with the EEOC within 180 days of the alleged violation. By contrast, the limitation for filing a complaint under the New York State Human Rights Law is one year, the limitations period under the Pennsylvania Human Relations act is ninety days.

As noted above, an individual alleging employment discrimination must first file a complaint with the appropriate state or local agency, if such an agency exists. Once the complaint is filed with the state or local agency, the complainant must wait sixty days before filing the complaint with the EEOC; if the state or local agency terminates proceedings on the complaint prior to the passage of sixty days, the complaint may then be filed with the EEOC. That means that the individual filing the complaint with the state or local agency must wait for that agency to terminate proceedings, or for sixty days, whichever comes first. *Mohasco Corp.* v. *Silver* (447 U.S. 807, 1980) involved a situation in which an individual filed a complaint alleging that he was discharged because of religious discrimination with the New York Division of Human Rights 291 days after the discharge. The state agency began to process and investigate the complaint; the EEOC began to process the complaint some 357 days after the discharge. The Supreme Court held that the complaint had not been properly filed with the EEOC within the 300-day limit; the Court held that the EEOC has a duty, under the statute, to begin processing a complaint within 300 days of the alleged violation. In order to allow the state agency the required sixty days for processing, the complaint must have been filed with the state agency within 240 days, so that when the EEOC began to process the complaint, it would be within the 300-day limit. However, as noted above, when the state or local agency terminates proceedings on the complaint before sixty days have passed, the EEOC may begin to process the complaint upon the other agency's termination.

EEOC Procedure and Its Relation to State Proceedings

The EEOC has entered into "work sharing" agreements with most state equal employment opportunity agencies to deal with the situation that arose in the *Mohasco* decision. Under such agreements, the agency that initially receives the complaint will process it. When the EEOC receives the complaint first, it refers the complaint to the appropriate state agency. The state agency then waives its right to process the complaint and refers it back to the EEOC; the state agency does retain jurisdiction to proceed on the complaint in the future, after the EEOC has completed its processing of the complaint. The EEOC treats the referral of the complaint to the state agency as the filing of the complaint with the state agency, and the state's waiver of the right to process the complaint is treated as termination of state proceedings, allowing the filing of the complaint with the EEOC under Section 706(c) of Title VII. In *EEOC* v. *Commercial Office Products Co.* (486 U.S. 107, 1988), the complainant filed a sex discrimination complaint with the EEOC on the 289th day after her discharge. The EEOC, under a work-sharing agreement, sent the complaint to the state agency, which returned the complaint to the EEOC after indicating that it waived its right to proceed on the complaint. The EEOC then began its investigation into the complaint and ultimately brought suit against the employer. The trial court and the court of appeals held that Section 706(c) required that either sixty days must elapse from the filing of the complaint with the state agency, or the state agency must both commence and terminate its proceedings, before the complaint could be deemed to have been filed with the EEOC. The Supreme Court, on appeal, reversed the court of appeals; the Supreme Court held that the state agency's waiver of its right to proceed on the complaint constituted a termination of the state proceedings under Section 706(c), allowing the EEOC to proceed with the complaint. As a result of this decision, in states where the EEOC and the state agency have work-sharing agreements, a complaint filed with the EEOC anytime within the 300-day time limit will be considered properly filed, and the EEOC can proceed with its processing of the complaint.

When Does the Violation Occur?   Because the time for filing a complaint under Title VII is limited, it is important to determine when the alleged violation occurred. In most situations it will not be difficult to determine the date of the violation, from which the time limit begins to run; but in some instances it may present a problem. The Supreme Court, in *Delaware State College* v. *Ricks* (449 U.S. 250, 1982), held that the time limit for a Title VII violation begins to run on the date that the individual is aware, or should be aware, of the alleged violation—not on the date that the alleged violation has an effect on the individual.

In *Lorance* v. *AT&T Technologies, Inc.* (490 U.S. 900, 1989; see Chapter 12), the Supreme Court ruled that the time limit for filing a complaint against an allegedly discriminatory change to a seniority system begins to run at the time the actual change is made. However, the effect of the decision in *Lorance* was reversed by the 1991 amendments to Title VII. Section 706(e)(2) now provides that for claims involving the adoption of a seniority system for allegedly discriminatory reasons, the violation can occur when the seniority system is adopted, when the complainant becomes subject to the seniority system, or when the complainant is injured by the application of the seniority system.

In *Bazemore* v. *Friday* (478 U.S. 385, 1986), the plaintiffs challenged a pay policy that allegedly discriminated against African-American employees. The pay policy had its origins prior to the date that Title VII applied to the employer, but the Supreme Court held that the violation was a continuing one—a new violation occurred every time the employees received a paycheck based on the racially discriminatory policy.

EEOC Procedure for Handling Complaints.   Upon receipt of a properly filed complaint, the EEOC has ten days to serve a notice of the complaint with the employer, union, or agency alleged to have discriminated (the respondent). Following service upon the respondent, the EEOC staff conducts an investigation into the complaint to determine whether reasonable cause exists to believe it is true. If no reasonable cause is found, the charge is dismissed. If reasonable cause to believe the complaint is found, the commission will attempt to settle the complaint through voluntary conciliation, persuasion, and negotiation. If the voluntary procedures are unsuccessful in resolving the complaint after thirty days from its filing, the EEOC may file suit in a federal district court.

If the EEOC dismisses the complaint or decides not to file suit, it notifies the complainant that he or she may file suit on his or her own. The complainant must file suit within ninety days of receiving the right-to-sue notice.

When the EEOC has not dismissed the complaint but has also not filed suit or acted upon the complaint within 180 days of its filing, the complainant may request a right-to-sue letter. Again, the complainant has ninety days from the notification to file suit. The suit may be filed in the district court in the district where the alleged unlawful employment practice occurred, where the relevant employment records are kept, or where the complainant would have been employed.

In *Yellow Freight System, Inc.* v. *Donnelly* (494 U.S. 820, 1990), the Supreme Court held that the federal courts do not have exclusive jurisdiction over Title VII claims; state courts are competent to adjudicate claims based on federal law such as Title VII. That means that the individual may file suit in either the federal or appropriate state court.

Because the complainant may be required to file first with a state or local agency, and may file his or her own suit if the EEOC has not acted within 180 days, several legal proceedings involving the complaint may occur at the same time. What is the effect of a state court decision dismissing the complaint on a subsequent suit filed in federal court? That issue was addressed in the next case.

KREMER v. CHEMICAL CONSTRUCTION CO.

456 U.S. 461 (Supreme Court of the United States, 1982)

WHITE, J.

As one of its first acts, Congress directed that all United States courts afford the same full-faith-and-credit to state court judgments that would apply in the state's own courts. Act of May 26, 1790, [28 U.S.C. Section 1738]. More recently, Congress implemented the national policy against employment discrimination by creating an array of substantive protections and remedies which generally allows federal courts to determine the merits of a discrimination claim. Title VII of the Civil Rights Act of 1964. The principal question presented by this case is whether Congress intended Title VII to supersede the principles of comity and repose embodied in Section 1738. Specifically, we decide whether a federal court in a Title VII case should give preclusive effect to a decision of a state court upholding a state administrative agency's rejection of an employment discrimination claim as meritless when the state court's decision would be res judicata in the state's own courts.

Petitioner Rubin Kremer emigrated from Poland in 1970 and was hired in 1973 by respondent Chemical Corporation ("Chemico") as an engineer. Two years later he was laid off, along with a number of other employees. Some of these employees were later rehired, but Kremer was not although he made several applications. In May 1976, Kremer filed a discrimination charge with the Equal Employment Opportunity Commission (EEOC), asserting that his discharge and failure to be rehired was due to his national origin and Jewish faith. Because the EEOC may not consider a claim until a state agency having jurisdiction over employment discrimination complaints has had at least 60 days to resolve the matter, the Commission referred Kremer's charge to the New York State Division of Human Rights ("NYHRD"), the agency charged with enforcing the New York law prohibiting employment discrimination.

After investigating Kremer's complaint, the Department concluded that there was no probable cause to believe that Chemico had engaged in the discriminatory practices complained of. The Department explicitly based its determination on the finding that Kremer was not rehired because one employee who was rehired had greater seniority, that another employee who was rehired filled a lesser position than that previously held by Kremer, and that neither Kre-

mer's creed nor age was a factor considered in Chemico's failure to rehire him. The NYHRD's determination was upheld by its Appeal Board as "not arbitrary, capricious, or an abuse of discretion." Kremer again brought his complaint to the attention of the EEOC and also filed, on December 6, 1977, a petition with the Appellate Division of the New York Supreme Court to set aside the adverse administrative determination. On February 27, 1978, five justices of the Appellate Division unanimously affirmed the Appeal Board's order. Kremer could have, but did not seek review by the New York Court of Appeals.

Subsequently, a District Director of the EEOC ruled that there was no reasonable cause to believe that the charge of discrimination was true and issued a right-to-sue notice. The District Director refused a request for reconsideration, noting that he had reviewed the case files and considered the EEOC's disposition as "appropriate and correct in all respects."

Kremer then brought this Title VII action in District Court, claiming discrimination on the basis of national origin and religion. Chemico argued from the outset that Kremer's Title VII action was barred by the doctrine of res judicata. The District Court initially denied Chemico's motion to dismiss. The court noted that the Court of Appeals for the Second Circuit had recently found such state determinations res judicata in an action under 42 U.S.C. Section 1981, *Mitchell* v. *National Broadcasting Co.,* but distinguished Title VII cases because of the statutory grant of the de novo federal review. Several months later the Second Circuit extended the *Mitchell* rule to Title VII cases. *Sinicropi* v. *Nassau County.* The District Court then dismissed the complaint on grounds of res judicata. The Court of Appeals refused to depart from the *Sinicropi* precedent and rejected petitioner's claim that *Sinicropi* should not be applied retroactively.

A motion for rehearing *en banc* was denied, a petitioner filed for a writ of certiorari. We issued the writ, to resolve this important issue of federal employment discrimination law over which the Courts of Appeals are divided.

Section 1738 requires federal courts to give the same preclusive effect to state court judgments that those judgments would be given in the courts of the state from which the judgments emerged. Here the Appellate Division of the New York Supreme Court had issued a judgment affirming the decision of the NYHRD Appeals Board that the discharge and failure to rehire Kremer were not the product of the discrimination that he had alleged. There is no question that this judicial determination precludes Kremer from bringing "any other action, civil or criminal, based upon the same grievance" in the New York courts. By its terms, therefore, Section 1738 would appear to preclude Kremer from relitigating the same question in federal court.

Kremer offers two principal reasons why Section 1738 does not bar this action. First, he suggests that in Title VII cases Congress intended that federal courts be relieved of their usual obligation to grant finality to state court decisions. Second, he urges that the New York administrative and judicial proceedings in this case were so deficient that they are not entitled to preclusive effect in federal courts and, in any event, the rejection of a state employment discrimination claim cannot by definition bar a Title VII action.

There is no claim here that Title VII expressly repealed Section 1738; if there has been a partial repeal, it must be implied. "It is, of course, a cardinal principle of statutory construction that repeals by implication are not favored," and whenever possible, statutes should be read consistently. There are, however,

> two well-settled categories of repeals by implication—(1) where provisions in the two acts are irreconcilable conflict, the later act to the extent of the conflict constitutes an implied repeal of the earlier one; and (2) if the later act covers the whole subject of the earlier one and is clearly intended as a substitute, it will operate similarly as a repeal of the earlier act. But, in either case, the intention of the legislature to repeal must be clear and manifest . . .

The relationship of Title VII to Section 1738 does not fall within either of these categories. Congress enacted Title VII to assure equality of employment opportunities without distinction with respect to race, color, religion, sex or national origin. To this end the EEOC was created and the federal courts were entrusted with ultimate enforcement responsibility. State anti-discrimination laws, however, play an integral role in the Congressional scheme.

No provision of Title VII requires claimants to pursue in state court an unfavorable state administrative action, nor does the Act specify the weight a federal court should afford a final judgment by a state court if such a remedy is sought. While we have interpreted the "civil action" authorized to follow consideration by federal and state administrative *agencies* to be a "trial de novo," neither the statute nor our decisions indicate that the final judgment of a state *court* is subject to redetermination at such a trial. Similarly,

the Congressional directive that the EEOC should give "substantial weight" to findings made in state proceedings, Section 706(b), indicates only the minimum level of deference the EEOC must afford all state determinations; it does not bar affording the greater preclusive effect which may be required by Section 1738 if judicial action is involved. To suggest otherwise, to say that either the opportunity to bring a "civil action" or the "substantial weight" requirement implicitly repeals Section 1738, is to prove far too much. For if that is so, even a full trial on the merits in state court would not bar a trial de novo in federal court and would not be entitled to more than "substantial weight," before the EEOC. The state courts would be placed on a one-way street; the finality of their decisions would depend on which side prevailed in a given case.

Since an implied repeat must ordinarily be evident from the language or operation of a statute, the lack of such manifest incompatibility between Title VII and Section 1738 is enough to answer our inquiry.

Nothing in the legislative history of the 1964 Act suggests that Congress considered it necessary or desirable to provide an absolute right to relitigate in federal court an issue resolved by a state court. While striving to craft an optimal niche for the states in the overall enforcement scheme, the legislators did not envision full litigation of a single claim in both state and federal forums. . . .

It is sufficiently clear that Congress, both in 1964 and 1972, though wary of assuming the adequacy of state employment discrimination remedies, did not intend to supplant such laws. We conclude that neither the statutory language nor the Congressional debates suffice to repeal Section 1738's longstanding directive to federal courts. . . .

The petitioner nevertheless contends that the judgment should not bar his Title VII action because the New York courts did not resolve the issue that the District Court must hear under Title VII—whether Kremer had suffered discriminatory treatment—and because the procedures provided were inadequate. Neither contention is persuasive. Although the claims presented to the NYHRD and subsequently reviewed by the Appellate Division were necessarily based on New York law, the alleged discriminatory acts are prohibited by both federal and state laws. The elements of a successful employment discrimination claim are virtually identical; petitioner could not succeed on a Title VII claim consistently with the judgment of the NYHRD that there is no reason to believe he was terminated or not rehired because of national origin or religion. The Appellate Division's affirmance NYHRD's dismissal necessarily decided that petitioner's claim under New York law was meritless, and thus it also decided that a Title VII claim arising from the same events would be equally meritless.

The more serious contention is that even though administrative proceedings and judicial review are legally sufficient to be given preclusive effect in New York, they should be deemed so fundamentally flawed as to be denied recognition under Section 1738. We have previously recognized that the judicially created doctrine of collateral estoppel does not apply when the party against whom the earlier decision is asserted did not have a "full and fair opportunity" to litigate the claim or issue. "Redetermination of issues is warranted if there is reason to doubt the quality, extensiveness, or fairness of the procedures followed in the prior litigation."

Our previous decisions have not specified the source or defined the content of the requirement that the first adjudication offer a full and fair opportunity to litigate. But for present purposes, where we are bound by the statutory directive of Section 1738, state proceedings need do no more than satisfy the minimum procedural requirements of the Fourteenth Amendment's Due Process Clause in order to qualify for the full-faith-and-credit guaranteed by federal law. It has long been established that Section 1738 does not allow federal courts to employ their own rules of res judicata in determining the effect of state judgments. Rather, it goes beyond the common law and commands a federal court to accept the rules chosen by the state from which the judgment is taken. . . .

The state must, however, satisfy the applicable requirements of the Due Process Clause. A state may not grant preclusive effect in its own courts to a constitutionally infirm judgment and other state and federal courts are not required to accord full-faith-and-credit to such a judgment. Section 1738 does not suggest otherwise; other state and federal courts would still be providing a state court judgment with the "same" preclusive effect as the courts of the state from which the judgment emerged. In such a case, there could be no constitutionally recognizable preclusion at all.

We have little doubt that Kremer received all the process that was constitutionally required in rejecting his claim that he had been discriminatorily discharged contrary to the statute. We must bear in mind that no single model of procedural fairness, let alone a particular form of procedure, is dictated by the Due Process Clause. "The very nature of due process negates any concept of inflexible procedures universally applicable to every imaginable situation." Under New York law, a claim of employment discrimination requires the NYHRD to investigate whether there is "probable cause" to believe that the complaint is true. Before this determination of probable cause is made, the claimant is entitled to a "full opportunity to present on the record, though informally, his charges against his employer or other respondent, including the right to submit all exhibits which he wishes to present and testimony of witnesses in addition to his own testimony." The complainant also is entitled to an opportunity "to rebut evidence submitted by or obtained from the respondent." He may have an attorney assist him and may ask the division to issue subpoenas.

If the investigation discloses probable cause and efforts at conciliation fail, the NYHRD must conduct a public hearing to determine the merits of the complaint. A public hearing must also be held if the Human Rights Appeal Board finds "there has not been a full investigation and opportunity for the complainant to present his contentions and evidence, with a full record." Finally, judicial review in the Appellate Division is available to assure that a claimant is not denied any of the procedural rights to which he was entitled and that the NYHRD's determination was not arbitrary and capricious.

We have no hesitation in concluding that this panoply of procedures, complemented by administrative as well as judicial review, is sufficient under the Due Process Clause. Only where the evidence submitted by the claimant fails, as a matter of law, to reveal any merit to the complaint may the Department make a determination of no probable cause without holding a hearing. Before that determination may be reached, New York requires the Commission to make a full investigation, wherein the complainant has full opportunity to present his evidence, under oath if he so requests. The fact that Mr. Kremer failed to avail himself of the full procedures provided by state law does not constitute a sign of their inadequacy.

In our system of jurisprudence the usual rule is that merits of a legal claim once decided in a court of competent jurisdiction are not subject to redetermination in another forum. Such a fundamental departure from traditional rules of preclusion, enacted into federal law, can be justified only if plainly stated by Congress. Because there is no "affirmative showing" of a "clear and manifest" legislative purpose in Title VII to deny res judicata or collateral estoppel effect to a state court judgment affirming that a claim of employment discrimination is unproven, and because the procedures provided in New York for the determination of such claims offer a full and fair opportunity to litigate the merits, the judgment of the Court of Appeals is **Affirmed.**

According to *Kremer,* the complainant who is unsuccessful in the state courts does not get a second chance to file a suit based on the same facts in federal court because of the full-faith-and-credit doctrine. However, the holding in *Kremer* was limited only to the effect of a state court decision. What is the effect of a negative determination by a state administrative agency on the complainant's right to sue in federal court? In *University of Tennessee* v. *Elliot* (106 S.Ct. 3220), the Supreme Court held that the full-faith-and-credit doctrine did not apply to state administrative agency decisions, so that a negative determination by the state agency would not preclude the complainant from suing in federal court under Title VII. (The Court in *Elliot* did hold that the findings of fact made by the state agency should be given preclusive effect by the federal courts in suits filed under 42 U.S. 1981 and 1983.)

In *Alexander* v. *Gardner-Denver Co.* (415 U.S. 147, 1974), the Supreme Court held that an employee was not precluded from filing suit under Title VII to challenge his discharge allegedly due to racial discrimination by an arbitrator's decision denying any discrimination and upholding the discharge. The Court reasoned that the arbitrator's decision dealt with the employee's rights under the collective agreement and had no bearing on the employee's statutory rights under Title VII. Consistent with *Alexander,* the U.S. Court of Appeals for the Sixth Circuit held that the NLRB's rejection of an unfair labor practice charge alleging racial discrimination does not preclude the filing of a Title VII suit growing out of the same situation (*Tipler* v. *E. I. du Pont de Nemours,* 433 F.2d 125, 1971). However, if an employee had voluntarily accepted reinstatement with back pay in settlement of his or her grievance against the employer, the U.S. Court of Appeals for the Fifth Circuit held that the employee had waived his or her right to sue under Title VII on the same facts (*Strozier* v. *General Motors,* 635 F.2d 424, 1981).

In the case of *Johnson* v. *Railway Express Agency* (421 U.S. 454, 1975), the Supreme Court held that an action under Title VII is separate and distinct from an action alleging race discrimination under the Civil Rights Act of 1866, 42 U.S.C., Section 1981. (That legislation will be discussed in the next chapter.)

Burdens of Proof—Establishing a Case

Once the complaint of an unlawful employment practice under Title VII has become the subject of a suit in a federal district court, the question of the burden of proof arises. What must the plaintiff show to establish a valid claim of discrimination? What must the defendant show to defeat a claim of discrimination?

The plaintiff in a suit under Title VII always carries the burden of proof; that is, the plaintiff must persuade the judge (or trier of fact) that there has been a violation of Title VII. In order to do this, the plaintiff must establish a **prima facie case** of discrimination—enough evidence to raise a presumption of discrimination. If the plaintiff is unable to establish a prima facie case of discrimination, then the case will be dismissed. The specific elements of a prima facie case, or the means to establish it, will vary depending on whether the complaint involves disparate treatment (intentional discrimination) or disparate impact (the discriminatory effects of apparently neutral criteria).

The plaintiff may use either anecdotal evidence or statistical evidence to establish the prima facie case. In *Bazemore v. Friday* (478 U.S. 385, 1986), the plaintiffs offered a statistical multiple-regression analysis to demonstrate that pay policies discriminated against African-American employees. The employer argued that the multiple-regression analysis did not consider several variables that were important in determining employees' pay. The trial court and the court of appeal refused to admit the multiple-regression analysis as evidence because it did not include all relevant variables. On appeal, however, the Supreme Court held that the multiple-regression analysis evidence should have been admitted; the failure of the analysis to include all relevant variables affects its probative value (the weight to be given to it by the trier of fact), not its admissibility.

Disparate Treatment

Claims of disparate treatment involve allegations of intentional discrimination in employment. An individual is treated differently by the employer because of that individual's race, color, religion, sex, or national origin. A plaintiff alleging disparate treatment must establish that he or she was subjected to less favorable treatment because of his or her race, color, religion, sex, or national origin. The specific elements of a prima facie case of disparate treatment under Title VII are discussed in the following case.

McDONNELL DOUGLAS CORP. v. GREEN

411 U.S. 792 (Supreme Court of the United States, 1973)

POWELL, J.

The case before us raises significant questions as to the proper order and nature of proof in actions under Title VII of the Civil Rights Act of 1964.

Petitioner, McDonnell Douglas Corporation, is an aerospace and aircraft manufacturer headquartered in St. Louis, Missouri, where it employs over 30,000 people. Respondent, a black citizen of St. Louis, worked for petitioner as a mechanic and laboratory technician from 1956 until August 28, 1964 when he was laid off in the course of a general reduction in petitioner's work force.

Respondent, a long-time activist in the civil rights movement, protested vigorously that his discharge and the general hiring practices of petitioner were racially motivated. As part of this protest, respondent and other members of

the Congress on Racial Equality illegally stalled their cars on the main roads leading to petitioner's plant for the purpose of blocking access to it at the time of the morning shift change. The District Judge described the plan for, and respondent's participation in, the "stall-in" as follows:

> . . . five teams, each consisting of four cars would "tie-up" five main access roads into McDonnell at the time of the morning rush hour. The drivers of the cars were instructed to line up next to each other completely blocking the intersections or roads. The drivers were also instructed to stop their cars, turn off the engines, pull the emergency brake, raise all windows, lock the doors, and remain in their cars until the police arrived. The plan was to have the cars remain in position for one hour. . . .

> . . . On July 2, 1965, a "lock-in" took place wherein a chain and padlock were placed on the front door of a building to prevent the occupants, certain of petitioner's employees, from leaving. Though respondent apparently knew

beforehand of the "lock-in," the full extent of his involvement remains uncertain.

Some three weeks following the "lock-in," on July 25, 1965, petitioner publicly advertised for qualified mechanics, respondent's trade, and respondent promptly applied for reemployment. Petitioner turned down respondent, basing its rejection on respondent's participation in the "stall-in" and "lock-in." Shortly thereafter, respondent filed a formal complaint with the Equal Employment Opportunity Commission, claiming that petitioner had refused to rehire him because of his race and persistent involvement in the civil rights movement in violation of Sections 703(a)(1) and 704(a). . . . The former section generally prohibits racial discrimination in any employment decision while the latter forbids discrimination against applicants or employees for attempting to protest or correct allegedly discriminatory conditions of employment.

The Commission made no finding on respondent's allegation of racial bias under Section 703(a)(1), but it did find reasonable cause to believe petitioner had violated Section 704(a) by refusing to rehire respondent because of his civil rights activity. After the Commission unsuccessfully attempted to conciliate the dispute, it advised respondent in March 1968, of his right to institute a civil action in federal court within 30 days.

On April 15, 1968, respondent brought the present action, claiming initially a violation of Section 704(a) and, in an amended complaint, a violation of Section 703(a)(1) as well. The District Court dismissed the latter claim of racial discrimination in petitioner's hiring procedures on the ground that the Commission had failed to make a determination of reasonable cause to believe that a violation of that section had been committed. The District Court also found that petitioner's refusal to rehire respondent was based solely on his participation in the illegal demonstrations and not on his legitimate civil rights activities. The court concluded that nothing in Title VII or Section 704 protected "such activity as employed by the plaintiff in the 'stall-in' and 'lock-in' demonstrations."

. . . On appeal, the Eighth Circuit affirmed that unlawful protests were not protected activities under section 704(a), but reversed the dismissal of respondent's Section 703(a)(1) claim relating to racially discriminatory hiring practices, holding that a prior Commission determination of reasonable cause was not a jurisdictional prerequisite to raising a claim under that section in federal court. The court ordered the case remanded for trial of respondent's claim under Section 703(a)(1).

. . . The critical issue before us concerns the order and allocation of proof in a private, single-plaintiff action challenging employment discrimination. The language of Title VII makes plain the purpose of Congress to assure equality of employment opportunities and to eliminate those discriminatory practices and devices which have fostered racially stratified job environments to the disadvantage of minority citizens.

As noted in [*Griggs* v. *Duke Power Co.*]:

> Congress did not intend Title VII, however, to guarantee a job to every person regardless of qualifications. In short, the Act does not command that any person be hired simply because he was formerly the subject of discrimination, or because he is a member of a minority group. Discriminatory preference for any group, minority or majority, is precisely and only what Congress has prescribed. What is required by Congress is the removal of artificial, arbitrary, and unnecessary barriers to employment when the barriers operate invidiously to discriminate on the basis of racial or other impermissible classification. . . .

There are societal as well as personal interests on both sides of this equation. The broad, overriding interest shared by employer, employee, and consumer, is efficient and trustworthy workmanship assured through fair and racially neutral employment and personnel decisions. In the implementation of such decisions, it is abundantly clear that Title VII tolerates no racial discrimination, subtle or otherwise.

In this case respondent, the complainant below, charges that he was denied employment "because of his involvement in civil rights activities" and "because of his race and color." Petitioner denied discrimination of any kind, asserting that its failure to re-employ respondent was based upon and justified by his participation in the unlawful conduct against it. Thus, the issue at the trial on remand is framed by those opposing factual contentions. The two opinions of the Court of Appeals and the several opinions of the three judges of the court attempted, with a notable lack of harmony, to state the applicable rules as to burden of proof and how this shifts upon the making of a prima facie case. We now address this problem.

The complainant in a Title VII trial must carry the initial burden under the statute of establishing a prima facie case of racial discrimination. This may be done by showing (i) that he belongs to a racial minority; (ii) that he had applied and was qualified for a job for which the employer was seeking applicants; (iii) that, despite his qualifications, he was rejected; and (iv) that, after his rejection, the position remained open and the employer continued to seek applicants from persons of complainant's qualifications. In the instant case, we agree with the Court of Appeals that respondent proved a prima facie case. . . . Petitioner sought mechanics, respondent's trade, and continued to do so after respondent's rejection. Petitioner, moreover does not dispute respondent's qualifications and acknowledges that his past work performance in petitioner's employ was "satisfactory."

The burden then must shift to the employer to articulate some legitimate, nondiscriminatory reason for respondent's rejection. We need not attempt in the instant case to detail every matter which fairly could be recognized as a reasonable basis for a refusal to hire. Here petitioner has assigned respondent's participation in unlawful conduct against it as the cause for his rejection. We think that this suffices to discharge petitioner's burden of proof at this stage and to meet respondent's prima facie case of discrimination.

The Court of Appeals intimated, however, that petitioner's stated reason for refusing to rehire respondent was a "subjective" rather than objective criterion which "carries little weight in rebutting charges of discrimination." Regardless of whether this was the intended import of the opinion, we think the court below seriously under-estimated the rebuttal weight to which petitioner's reasons were entitled. Respondent admittedly had taken part in a carefully planned "stall-in," designed to tie up access and egress to petitioner's plant at a peak traffic hour. Nothing in Title VII compels an employer to absolve and rehire one who has engaged in such deliberate, unlawful activity against it. . . .

. . . Petitioner's reason for rejection thus suffices to meet the prima facie case, but the inquiry must not end here.

While Title VII does not, without more, compel rehiring of respondent, neither does it permit petitioner to use respondent's conduct as a pretext for the sort of discrimination prohibited by Section 703(a)(1). On remand, respondent must, as the Court of Appeals recognized, be afforded a fair opportunity to show that petitioner's stated reason for respondent's rejection was in fact pretextual. Especially relevant to such a showing would be evidence that white employees involved in acts against petitioner of comparable seriousness to the "stall-in" were nevertheless retained or rehired. Petitioner may justifiably refuse to rehire one who was engaged in unlawful, disruptive acts against it, but only if this criterion is applied alike to members of all races.

Other evidence that may be relevant to any showing of pretextuality includes facts as to the petitioner's treatment of respondent during his prior term of employment, petitioner's reaction, if any, to respondent's legitimate civil rights activities, and petitioner's general policy and practice with respect to minority employment. On the latter point, statistics as to petitioner's employment policy and practice may be helpful to a determination of whether petitioner's refusal to rehire respondent in this case conformed to a general pattern of discrimination against blacks. In short, on the retrial respondent must be given a full and fair opportunity to demonstrate by competent evidence that the presumptively valid reasons for his rejection were in fact a coverup for a racially discriminatory decision. . . .

Defendant's Burden. If the plaintiff is successful in establishing a prima facie case of disparate treatment, the defendant must then try to overcome the plaintiff's claims. Is the defendant required to *disprove* those claims, prove that there was no discrimination, or merely explain the apparent discrimination? What is the nature of the defendant's burden in a disparate treatment case? That is the subject of the following case.

TEXAS DEPARTMENT OF COMMUNITY AFFAIRS v. BURDINE

450 U.S. 248 (Supreme Court of the United States, 1979)

POWELL, J.

This case requires us to address again the nature of the evidentiary burden placed upon the defendant in an employment discrimination suit brought under Title VII of the

Civil Rights Act of 1964. The narrow question presented is whether, after the plaintiff has proved a prima facie case of discriminatory treatment, the burden shifts to the defendant to persuade the court by a preponderance of the evidence that legitimate, nondiscriminatory reasons for the challenged employment action existed.

Petitioner, the Texas Department of Community Affairs (TDCA), hired respondent, a female, in January 1972, for the position of accounting clerk in the Public Service Careers Division (PSC). PSC provided training and employment opportunities in the public sector for unskilled workers. When hired, respondent possessed several years' experience in employment training. She was promoted to Field Services Coordinator in July 1972. Her supervisor resigned in November of that year, and respondent was assigned additional duties. Although she applied for the supervisor's position of Project Director, the position remained vacant for six months.

PSC was funded completely by the United States Department of Labor. The Department was seriously concerned about inefficiencies at PSC. In February, 1973, the Department notified the Executive Director of TDCA, B. R. Fuller, that it would terminate PSC the following month. TDCA officials, assisted by respondent, persuaded the Department to continue funding the program, conditioned upon PSC reforming its operations. Among the agreed conditions were the appointment of a permanent Project Director and a complete reorganization of the PSC staff.

After consulting with personnel within TDCA, Fuller hired a male from another division of the agency as Project Director. In reducing the PSC staff, he fired respondent along with two other employees, and retained another male, Walz, as the only professional employee in the division. It is undisputed that respondent had maintained her application for the position of Project Director and had requested to remain with TDCA. Respondent soon was rehired by TDCA and assigned to another division of the agency. She received the exact salary paid to the Project Director at PSC, and subsequent promotions she has received have kept her salary and responsibility commensurate with what she would have received had she been appointed Project Director.

Respondent filed this suit in the United States District Court for the Western District of Texas. She alleged that the failure to promote and the subsequent decision to terminate her had been predicated on gender discrimination in violation of Title VII. After a bench trial, the District Court held that neither decision was based on gender discrimination. The court relied on the testimony of Fuller that the employment decisions necessitated by the commands of the Department of Labor were based on consultation among trusted advisors and a nondiscriminatory evaluation of the relative qualifications of the individuals involved. He testified that the three individuals terminated did not work well together, and that TDCA thought that eliminating this

problem would improve PSC's efficiency. The court accepted this explanation as rational and, in effect, found no evidence that the decisions not to promote and to terminate respondent were prompted by gender discrimination.

The Court of Appeals for the Fifth Circuit reversed in part. The court held that the District Court's "implicit evidentiary finding" that the male hired as Project Director was better qualified for that position than respondent was not clearly erroneous. Accordingly, the court affirmed the District Court's finding that respondent was not discriminated against when she was not promoted. The Court of Appeals, however, reversed the District Court's finding that Fuller's testimony sufficiently had rebutted respondent's prima facie case of gender discrimination in the decision to terminate her employment at PSC. The court reaffirmed its previously announced views that the defendant in a Title VII case bears the burden of proving by a preponderance of the evidence the existence of legitimate nondiscriminatory reasons for the employment action and that the defendant also must prove by objective evidence that those hired or promoted were better qualified than the plaintiff. The court found that Fuller's testimony did not carry either of these evidentiary burdens. It, therefore, reversed the judgment of the District Court and remanded the case for computation of backpay. Because the decision of the Court of Appeals as to the burden of proof borne by the defendant conflicts with interpretations of our precedents adopted by other courts of appeals, we granted certiorari. . . .

In *McDonnell Douglas Corp.* v. *Green,* we set forth the basic allocation of burdens and order of presentation of proof in a Title VII case alleging discriminatory treatment. First, the plaintiff has the burden of proving by the preponderance of the evidence of a prima facie case of discrimination. Second, if the plaintiff succeeds in proving the prima facie case, the burden shifts to the defendant "to articulate some legitimate, nondiscriminatory reason for the employee's rejection." Third, should the defendant carry this burden, the plaintiff must then have an opportunity to prove by a preponderance of the evidence that the legitimate reasons offered by the defendant were not its true reasons, but were a pretext for discrimination.

The nature of the burden that shifts to the defendant should be understood in light of the plaintiff's ultimate and intermediate burdens. The ultimate burden of persuading the trier of fact that the defendant intentionally discriminated against the plaintiff remains at all time with the plaintiff. The *McDonnell Douglas* division of intermediate evidentiary burdens serves to bring the litigants and the court expeditiously and fairly to this ultimate question.

The burden of establishing a prima facie case of disparate treatment is not onerous. The plaintiff must prove by a preponderance of the evidence that she applied for an available position, for which she was qualified, but was rejected under circumstances which give rise to an inference of unlawful discrimination. The prima facie case serves an important function in the litigation: it eliminates the most common nondiscriminatory reasons for the plaintiff's rejection. As the Court explained in *Furnco Construction Co.* v. *Waters,* the prima facie case "raises an inference of discrimination only because we presume these acts, if otherwise unexplained, are most likely than not based on the consideration of impermissible factors." Establishment of the prima facie case in effect creates a presumption that the employer unlawfully discriminated against the employee. If the trier of fact believes the plaintiff's evidence, and if the employer is silent in the face of the presumption, the court must enter judgment for the plaintiff because no issue of fact remains in the case.

The burden that shifts to the defendant, therefore, is to rebut the presumption of discrimination by producing evidence that the plaintiff was rejected, or someone else was preferred, for a legitimate, nondiscriminatory reason. The defendant need not persuade the court that it was actually motivated by the proffered reasons. It is sufficient if the defendant's evidence raises a genuine issue of fact as to whether it discriminated against the plaintiff. To accomplish this, the defendant must clearly set forth, through the introduction of admissible evidence, the reasons for the plaintiff's rejection. The explanation provided must be legally sufficient to justify a judgment for the defendant. If the defendant carries this burden of production, the presumption raised by the prima facie case is rebutted, and the factual inquiry proceeds to a new level of specificity. Placing this burden of production on the defendant thus serves simultaneously to meet the plaintiff's prima facie case by presenting a legitimate reason for the action and to frame the factual issue with sufficient clarity so that the plaintiff will have a full and fair opportunity to demonstrate pretext. The sufficiency of the defendant's evidence should be evaluated by the extent to which it fulfills these functions.

The plaintiff retains the burden of persuasion. She now must have the opportunity to demonstrate that the proffered reason was not the true reason for the employment decision. This burden now merges with the ultimate burden of persuading the court that she has been the victim of intentional discrimination. She may succeed in this either directly by persuading the court that a discriminatory reason more likely motivated the employer or indirectly by

showing that the employer's proffered explanation is unworthy of credence.

In reversing the judgment of the District Court that the discharge of respondent from PSC was unrelated to her sex, the Court of Appeals adhered to two rules it had developed to elaborate the defendant's burden of proof. First, the defendant must prove by a preponderance of the evidence that legitimate, nondiscriminatory reasons for the discharge existed. Second, to satisfy this burden, the defendant "must prove that those he hired . . . were somehow *better* qualified than was plaintiff; in other words, comparative evidence is needed."

The Court of Appeals has misconstrued the nature of the burden that *McDonnell Douglas* and its progeny place on the defendant. We stated in *Sweeney* that "the employer's burden is satisfied if he simply 'explains what he has done' or 'produc[es] evidence of legitimate nondiscriminatory reasons.'" It is plain that the Court of Appeals required much more: it placed on the defendant the burden of persuading the court that it had convincing, objective reasons for preferring the chosen applicant above the plaintiff.

We have stated consistently that the employee's prima facie case of discrimination will be rebutted if the employer articulates lawful reasons for the action; that is, to satisfy this intermediate burden, the employer need only produce admissible evidence which would allow the trier of fact rationally to conclude that the employment decision had not been motivated by discriminatory animus. The Court of Appeals would require the defendant to introduce evidence which, in the absence of any evidence of pretext, would *persuade* the trier of fact that the employment action was lawful. This exceeds what properly can be demanded to satisfy a burden of production.

. . . We do not believe, however, that limiting the defendant's evidentiary obligation to a burden of production will unduly hinder the plaintiff. First, as noted above, the defendant's explanation of its legitimate reasons must be clear and reasonably specific. This obligation arises both from the necessity of rebutting the inference of discrimination arising from the prima facie case and from the requirement that the plaintiff be afforded "a full and fair opportunity" to demonstrate pretext. Second, although the defendant does not bear a formal burden of persuasion, the defendant nevertheless retains an incentive to persuade the trier of fact that the employment decision was lawful. Thus, the defendant normally will attempt to prove the factual basis for its explanation. Third, the liberal discovery rules applicable to any civil suit in federal court are supplemented in a Title VII suit by the plaintiff's access to the Equal Employment

Opportunity Commission's investigatory files concerning her complaint. Given these factors, we are unpersuaded that the plaintiff will find it particularly difficult to prove that a proffered explanation lacking a factual basis is a pretext. We remain confident that the *McDonnell Douglas* framework permits the plaintiff meriting relief to demonstrate intentional discrimination.

The Court of Appeals also erred in requiring the defendant to prove by objective evidence that the person hired or promoted was more qualified than the plaintiff. *McDonnell Douglas* teaches that it is the plaintiff's task to demonstrate that similarly situated employees were not treated equally. The Court of Appeals' rule would require the employer to show that the plaintiff's objective qualifications were inferior to those of the person selected. If it cannot, a court would, in effect, conclude that it has discriminated.

The court's procedural rule harbors a substantive error. Title VII prohibits all discrimination in employment based upon race, sex and national origin. . . . Title VII, however, does not demand that an employer give preferential treatment to minorities or women. The statute was not intended to "diminish traditional management prerogatives." It does not require the employer to restructure his employment practices to maximize the number of minorities and women hired. . . .

In summary, the Court of Appeals erred by requiring the defendant to prove by a preponderance of the evidence the existence of nondiscriminatory reasons for terminating the respondent and that the person retained in her stead had superior objective qualifications for the position. When the plaintiff has proved a prima facie case of discrimination, the defendant hears only the burden of explaining clearly the nondiscriminatory reasons for its actions. The judgment of the Court of Appeals is vacated and the case is remanded for further proceedings consistent with this opinion. **It is so ordered.**

According to *Burdine*, the defendant need only "articulate" some legitimate justification for its actions; the burden of proof—of persuading the trier of fact—remains with the plaintiff. Although the defendant need not *prove* that there was no discrimination, the nondiscriminatory justification or explanation offered by the defendant must be believable. Obviously, if the defendant's justification is not credible, then the plaintiff's prima facie case will not be rebutted, and the plaintiff will prevail.

Plaintiff's Burden of Showing Pretext.   After the defendant has advanced a legitimate justification to counter, or rebut, the plaintiff's prima facie case, the focus of the proceeding shifts back to the plaintiff. The plaintiff, as was discussed in the *McDonnell Douglas* case, must be afforded an opportunity to show that the employer's justification is a mere pretext, or cover-up. This can be shown either directly, by persuading the court that a discriminatory reason likely motivated the defendant; or indirectly, by showing that the offered justification is not worthy of credence. The burden of showing that the defendant's offered justification is a pretext for discrimination is a very difficult one—the plaintiff must convince the court that the employer intentionally acted to discriminate.

Disparate Impact

Unlike a disparate treatment claim, a claim of disparate impact does not involve an allegation of intentional discrimination. Rather, as in *Griggs* v. *Duke Power Co.,* it involves a claim that neutral job requirements have a discriminatory effect. The plaintiff, in order to establish a prima facie case, must show that the apparently neutral employment requirements or practices have a disproportionate impact upon a class protected by Title VII. (A protected class under Title VII is a group of individuals defined on the basis of race, color, religion, sex, or national origin.)

The Supreme Court in the *Wards Cove Packing Co.* v. *Antonio* and *Watson* v. *Fort Worth Bank & Trust* decisions (discussed in Chapter 12) held that a plaintiff alleging a disparate impact claim must "offer statistical evidence of a kind and degree sufficient to show that the practice in question has caused the exclusion of applicants for jobs or promotions because of their membership in a protected group."

Four-Fifths Rule. As discussed in Chapter 12, one way to establish proof of a disproportionate impact is by using the Four-Fifths Rule from the EEOC Guidelines. That rule states that a disparate impact will be presumed to exist when the selection or pass rate for the protected class with the lowest selection rate is less than 80 percent of the selection or pass rate of the protected class with the highest rate. The Four-Fifths Rule is used primarily when challenging employment tests or requirements such as a high school diploma, or minimum height and weight requirements.

Using Statistics. Another method of establishing a disparate impact may be by making a statistical comparison of the minority representation in the employers' work force and the minority representation in the population as a whole (or in the relevant area or labor market). When a job requires specific skills and training, the population used for comparison with the work force may be limited to available qualified individuals within the relevant area or labor market. The court may require specific demographic and geographic comparisons when using statistical evidence, as demonstrated in the following case.

HAZELWOOD SCHOOL DIST. v. U.S.

433 U.S. 299 (Supreme Court of the United States, 1977)

STEWART, J.

The petitioner Hazelwood School District covers 78 square miles in the northern part of St. Louis County, Mo. In 1973 the Attorney General brought this lawsuit against Hazelwood and various of its officials, alleging that they were engaged in a "pattern or practice" of employment discrimination in violation of Title VII. The complainant asked for an injunction requiring Hazelwood to cease its discriminatory practices, to take affirmative steps to obtain qualified Negro faculty members, and to offer employment and give backpay to victims of past illegal discrimination.

Hazelwood was formed from 13 rural school districts between 1949 and 1951 by a process of annexation. By the 1967–1968 school year, 17,550 students were enrolled in the district, of whom only 59 were Negro; the number of

Negro pupils increased to 576 of 25,166 in 1972–1973, a total just over 2 percent.

From the beginning, Hazelwood followed relatively unstructured procedures in hiring its teachers. Every person requesting an application for a teaching position was sent one, and completed applications were submitted to a central personnel office, where they were kept on file. During the early 1960s the personnel office notified all applicants whenever a teaching position became available, but as the number of applications on file increased in the late 1960s and early 1970s, this practice was no longer considered feasible. The personnel office thus began the practice of selecting anywhere from three to 10 applicants for interviews at the school where the vacancy existed. The personnel office did not substantively screen the applicants in determining which of them to send for interviews, other than to ascertain that each applicant, if selected, would be eligible for state certification by the time he began the job. Generally, those who had most recently submitted applications were most likely to be chosen for interviews.

Interviews were conducted by a department chairman, program coordinator, or the principal at the school where the teaching vacancy existed. Although those conducting the interviews did fill out forms rating the applicants in a number of respects, it is undisputed that each school principal possessed virtually unlimited discretion in hiring teachers for his school. The only general guidance given to the principals was to hire the "most competent" person available, and such intangibles as "personality, disposition, appearance, poise, voice, articulation, and ability to deal with people" counted heavily. The principal's choice was routinely honored by Hazelwood's superintendent and Board of Education.

In the early 1960s Hazelwood found it necessary to recruit new teachers, and for that purpose members of its staff visited a number of colleges and universities in Missouri and bordering States. All the institutions visited were predominantly white, and Hazelwood did not seriously recruit at either of the two predominantly Negro four-year colleges in Missouri. As a buyer's market began to develop for public school teachers, Hazelwood curtailed its recruiting efforts. For the 1971–1972 school year, 3,127 persons applied for only 234 teaching vacancies; for the 1972–1973 school year, there were 2,373 applications for 282 vacancies. A number of the applicants who were not hired were Negroes.

Hazelwood hired its first Negro teacher in 1969. The number of Negro faculty members gradually increased in successive years: six of 957 in the 1970 school year; 16 of 1,107 by the end of the 1972 school year; 22 of 1,231 in the 1973 school year. By comparison, according to 1970 census figures, of more than 19,000 teachers employed in that year in the St. Louis area, 15.4 percent were Negro. That percentage figure included the St. Louis City School District, which in recent years has followed a policy of attempting to maintain a 50 percent Negro teaching staff. Apart from that school district, 5.7 percent of the teachers in the county were Negro in 1970.

Drawing upon these historic facts, the Government mounted its "pattern or practice" attack in the District Court upon four different fronts. It adduced evidence of (1) a history of alleged racially discriminatory practices, (2) statistical disparities in hiring, (3) the standardless and largely subjective hiring procedures, and (4) specific instances of alleged discrimination against 55 unsuccessful Negro applicants for teaching jobs. Hazelwood offered virtually no additional evidence in response, relying instead on

evidence introduced by the Government, perceived deficiencies in the Government's case, and its own officially promulgated policy "to hire all teachers on the basis of training, preparation and recommendations, regardless of race, color or creed."

The District Court ruled that the Government had failed to establish a pattern or practice of discrimination. The court was unpersuaded by the alleged history of discrimination, noting that no dual school system had ever existed in Hazelwood. The statistics showing that relatively small numbers of Negroes were employed as teachers were found nonprobative, on the ground that the percentage of Negro pupils in Hazelwood was similarly small. The court found nothing illegal or suspect in the teacher hiring procedures that Hazelwood had followed. Finally, the court reviewed the evidence in the 55 cases of alleged individual discrimination, and after stating that the burden of proving intentional discrimination was on the Government, it found that this burden had not been sustained in a single instance. Hence, the court entered judgment for the defendants.

. . . The Court of Appeals for the Eighth Circuit reversed. After suggesting that the District Court had assigned inadequate weight to evidence of discriminatory conduct on the part of Hazelwood before the effective date of Title VII, the Court of Appeals rejected the trial court's analysis of the statistical data as resting on an irrelevant comparison of Negro teachers to Negro pupils in Hazelwood. The proper comparison, in the appellate court's view, was one between Negro teachers in Hazelwood and Negro teachers in the relevant labor market area. Selecting St. Louis County and St. Louis City, as the relevant area, the Court of Appeals compared the 1970 census figures, showing that 15.4 percent of teachers in that area were Negro, to the racial composition of Hazelwood's teaching staff. In the 1972–1973 and 1973–1974 school years, only 1.4 percent and 1.8 percent, respectively, of Hazelwood's teachers were Negroes. This statistical disparity, particularly when viewed against the background of the teacher hiring procedures that Hazelwood had followed, was held to constitute a prima facie case of a pattern or practice of racial discrimination.

In addition, the Court of Appeals reasoned that the trial court had erred in failing to measure the 55 instances in which Negro applicants were denied jobs against the four-part standard for establishing a prima facie case of individual discrimination set out in this Court's opinion in *McDonnell Douglas Corp.* v. *Green.* . . . Applying that standard, the appellate court found 16 cases of individual discrimination, which "buttressed" the statistical proof. Because Hazelwood had not rebutted the Government's prima facie case of a pattern or practice of racial discrimination, the Court of Appeals directed judgment for the Government and prescribed the remedial order to be entered.

... The petitioners primarily attack the judgment of the Court of Appeals for its reliance on "undifferentiated work force statistics to find an unrebutted prima facie case of employment discrimination." The question they raise, in short, is whether a basic component in the Court of Appeals' finding a pattern or practice of discrimination—the comparatively small percentage of Negro employees on Hazelwood's teaching staff—was lacking in probative force.

This Court's recent consideration in *International Brotherhood of Teamsters* v. *United States,* ... of the role of statistics in pattern or practice suits under Title VII provides substantial guidance in evaluating the arguments advanced by the petitioners. In that case we stated that it is the Government's burden to "establish by a preponderance of the evidence that racial discrimination was the [employer's] standard operating procedure—the regular rather than the unusual practice." We also noted that statistics can be an important source of proof in employment discrimination cases, since

> absent explanation, it is ordinarily to be expected that nondiscriminatory hiring practices will in time result in a work force more or less representative of the racial and ethnic composition of the population in the community from which employees are hired. Evidence of long-lasting and gross disparity between the composition of a work force and that of the general population thus may be significant even though Section 703(j) makes clear that Title VII imposes no requirement that a work force mirror the general population....

... There can be no doubt, in light of the *Teamsters* case, that the District Court's comparison of Hazelwood's teacher work force to its student population fundamentally misconceived the role of statistics in employment discrimination cases. The Court of Appeals was correct in the view that a proper comparison was between the racial composition of Hazelwood's teaching staff and the racial composition of the qualified public school teacher population in the relevant labor market. The percentage of Negroes on Hazelwood's teaching staff in 1972–1973 was 1.4 percent, and in 1973–1974 it was 1.8 percent. By contrast, the percentage of qualified Negro teachers in the area was, according to the 1970 census, at least 5.7 percent. Although these differences were on their face substantial, the Court of Appeals erred in substituting its judgment for that of the District Court and holding that the Government had conclusively proved its "pattern or practice" lawsuit.

The Court of Appeals totally disregarded the possibility that this prima facie statistical proof in the record might at the trial court level be rebutted by statistics dealing with Hazelwood's hiring after it became subject to Title VII. Racial discrimination by public employers was not made illegal under Title VII until March 24, 1972. A public employer who from that date forward made all its employment decisions in a wholly nondiscriminatory way would not violate Title VII even if it had formerly maintained an all-white work force by purposefully excluding Negroes. For this reason, the Court cautioned in the *Teamsters* opinion that once a prima facie case has been established by statistical work force disparities, the employer must be given an opportunity to show "that the claimed discriminatory pattern is a product of pre-Act hiring rather than unlawful post-Act discrimination."

... The record in this case showed that for the 1972–1973 school year, Hazelwood hired 282 new teachers, 10 of whom (3.5 percent) were Negroes; for the following school year it hired 123 new teachers, five of whom (4.1 percent) were Negroes. Over the two-year period, Negroes constituted a total of 15 of the 405 new teachers hired (3.7 percent). Although the Court of Appeals briefly mentioned these data in reciting the facts, it wholly ignored them in discussing whether the Government had shown a pattern or practice of discrimination. And it gave no consideration at all to the possibility that post-Act data as to the number of Negroes hired compared to the total number of Negro applicants might tell a totally different story.

What the hiring figures prove obviously depends upon the figures to which they are compared. The Court of Appeals accepted the Government's argument that the relevant comparison was to the labor market area of St. Louis County and St. Louis City, in which, according to the 1970 census, 15.4 percent of all teachers were Negro. The propriety of that comparison was vigorously disputed by the petitioners, who urged that because the City of St. Louis has made special attempts to maintain a 50 percent Negro teaching staff, inclusion of that school district in the relevant market area distorts the comparison. Were that argument accepted, the percentage of Negro teachers in the relevant labor market area (St. Louis County alone) as shown in the 1970 census would be 5.7 percent rather than 15.4 percent.

The difference between these figures may well be important; the disparity between 3.7 percent (the percentage of Negro teachers hired by Hazelwood in 1972–1973 and 1973–1974) and 5.7 percent may be sufficiently small to weaken the Government's other proof, while the disparity between 3.7 percent and 15.4 percent may be sufficiently large to reinforce it. In determining which of the two figures—or very possibly, what immediate figure—provides the most accurate basis for comparison to the hiring figures at Hazelwood, it will be necessary to evaluate such considerations as (i) whether the racially based hiring policies of the St. Louis City School District were in effect as far back as 1970, the year in which the census figures were taken; (ii) to what extent those policies have changed the racial composition of that district's teaching staff from what it would otherwise have been; (iii) to what extent St. Louis' recruitment policies have diverted to the city teachers who might otherwise have applied to Hazelwood; (iv) to what extent Negro teachers employed by the city would prefer employment in other districts such as Hazelwood; and (v) what the experience in other school districts in St. Louis County indicates about the validity of excluding the City School District from the relevant labor market.

It is thus clear that a determination of the appropriate comparative figures in this case will depend upon further evaluation by the trial court. As this Court admonished in *Teamsters,* "statistics . . . come in infinite variety. . . . [T]heir usefulness depends on all of the surrounding facts and circumstances." Only the trial court is in a position to make the appropriate determination after further findings. And only after such a determination is made can a foundation be established for deciding whether or not Hazelwood engaged in a pattern or practice of racial discrimination in its employment practices in violation of the law.

We hold, therefore, that the Court of Appeals erred in disregarding the post-Act hiring statistics in the record, and that it should have remanded the case to the District Court for further findings as to the relevant labor market area and for an ultimate determination of whether Hazelwood engaged in a pattern or practice of employment discrimination after March 24, 1972. Accordingly, the judgment is vacated, and the case is remanded to the District Court for further proceedings consistent with this opinion. **So ordered.**

Defendant's Burden. When the plaintiff has established a prima facie case of disparate impact, the defendant has two methods of responding. The defendant may challenge the statistical analysis, the methods of data collection, or the significance of the plaintiff's evidence. The defendant may also submit alternative statistical proof that leads to conclusions opposite those of the plaintiff's evidence.

Rather than attacking the plaintiff's statistical evidence, the defendant alternatively may show that the employment practice, test, or requirement having the disparate impact is job-related.

Although the Supreme Court decisions in *Watson* v. *Fort Worth Bank & Trust* and *Wards Cove Packing Co.* v. *Antonio* both held that the employer need only show some business justification for the challenged practice, and the plaintiff has the burden of persuasion for showing that the challenged practice is not job-related, the 1991 amendments to Title VII overruled those cases. Section 703(k) requires that, once the plaintiff has demonstrated that the challenged practice has a disparate impact, the employer has the burden of persuasion for convincing the court that the practice is job-related.

A defense of job-relatedness can be established by using the methods of demonstrating validity set out in the Uniform Guidelines for Employee Selection. (The methods of demonstrating that a test or requirement is content-valid, construct-valid, or criterion-valid are described in Chapter 12.)

If the defendant establishes that the practice, requirement, or test is job-related, the plaintiff may still prevail by showing that other tests, practices, or requirements that do not have disparate impacts on protected classes are available and would satisfy the defendant's legitimate business concerns. The plaintiff may also try to show that the job-related justification is really just a pretext for intentional discrimination.

Remedies under Title VII

The remedies available to a successful plaintiff under Title VII are spelled out in Section 706(g). Those remedies include judicial orders requiring hiring or reinstatement of employees, awarding of back pay and seniority, injunctions against unlawful employment practices, and "such affirmative action as may be appropriate." Section 706(k) provides that the court, in its discretion, may award legal fees to a prevailing party other than the EEOC or the United States. The Civil Rights Act of 1991 added the right to recover damages, including punitive damages for intentional violations of Title VII.

Damages

The right to recover damages for intentional violations of Title VII was created by the Civil Rights Act of 1991, which amended Title VII. The 1991 act allows claims for compensatory and punitive damages, in addition to any remedies recoverable under Section 706(g) of Title VII, to be brought under 42 U.S.C. Section 1981, as amended by the 1991 act. Section 1981 (discussed in detail in the next chapter) allows recovery of damages for intentional race discrimination. The Civil Rights Act of 1991 added an additional section to 42 U.S.C. Section 1981 that allows damages suits for intentional discrimination in violation of Title VII, for which the plaintiff could not recover under Section 1981 (that is, discrimination because of sex, religion, or national origin).

If the plaintiff can demonstrate that the defendant, excluding a governmental unit, agency, or other public sector entity, has engaged "in a discriminatory practice or discriminatory practices with malice or with reckless indifference to the federally protected rights of an aggrieved individual," the plaintiff can recover compensatory and punitive damages. Punitive damages are not recoverable against public sector defendants. The compensatory and punitive damages are in addition to any back pay, interest, or other remedies recovered under Section 706(g) of Title VII.

The damages recoverable under the newly amended Section 1981 are subject to limits, depending on the number of employees of the employer-defendant. For employers with more than 14, but fewer than 101 employees, the damages recoverable are limited to $50,000; for defendants with more than 100 but fewer than 201 employees, $100,000; for more than 200 but fewer than 501 employees, $200,000; and for employers with more than 500 employees, the limit is $300,000. The number of people employed by a defendant-employer is determined by considering the number employed in each week of 20 or more calendar weeks in the current or preceding year.

Although suits under Title VII are heard by a judge sitting without a jury, plaintiffs bringing a claim for damages under the amended Section 1981 have the right to a jury trial. As noted, damages are not recoverable against a public sector employer; as well, damages are not recoverable for disparate impact claims—in other words, the discrimination must be intentional. In mixed motive cases (see the *Hopkins* case in Chapter 12), Section 706(g)(2)(B) provides that an employer will not be liable for damages when the employer can demonstrate that it would have reached the same decision even without consideration of the illegal factor. Damages under the amended Section 1981 are also recoverable for intentional violations of the Americans with Disabilities Act of 1990 (discussed in the next chapter).

Back Pay

Section 706(g) states that the court may award back pay to a successful plaintiff. Back-pay orders spelled out by that section have some limitations, however. Section 706(g) provides that no back-pay order shall extend to a period prior to two years before the date of the filing of a complaint with the EEOC. It also provides that "Interim earnings or amounts earnable with reasonable diligence by the person or persons discriminated against shall operate to reduce the back pay otherwise allowable." That section imposes a duty to mitigate damages upon the plaintiff.

Although Section 706(g) states that a court may award back pay, it does not require that such an award always be made. What principles should guide the court on the issue of whether to award back pay? That question is the subject of the following case.

ALBEMARLE PAPER CO. v. MOODY

422 U.S. 405 (Supreme Court of the United States, 1975)

STEWART, J.

These consolidated cases raise ... important questions under Title VII.... When employees or applicants for employment have lost the opportunity to earn wages because an employer has engaged in an unlawful discriminatory employment practice, what standards should a federal district court follow in deciding whether to award or deny backpay?

... The respondents—plaintiffs in the District Court—are a certified class of present and former Negro employees at a paper mill in Roanoke Rapids, North Carolina; the petitioners—defendants in the District Court—are the plant's owner, the Albemarle Paper Company, and the plant employees' labor union, Halifax Local No. 425.

... Whether a particular member of the plaintiff class should have been awarded any backpay and, if so, how much, are questions not involved in this review. The equities of individual cases were never reached. Though at least some of the members of the plaintiff class obviously suffered a loss of wage opportunities on account of Albemarle's unlawfully discriminatory system of job seniority,

the District Court decided that *no* backpay should be awarded to *anyone* in the class. The court declined to make such an award on two stated grounds: the lack of "evidence of bad faith non-compliance with the Act," and the fact that "the defendants would be substantially prejudiced" by an award of backpay that was demanded contrary to an earlier representation and late in the progress of the litigation. Relying directly on *Newman* v. *Piggie Park Enterprises,* the Court of Appeals reversed, holding that backpay could be denied only in "special circumstances."

... The petitioners contend that the statutory scheme provides no guidance, beyond indicating that backpay awards are within the District Court's discretion. We disagree. It is true that backpay is not an automatic or mandatory remedy; like all other remedies under the Act, it is one which the courts "may" invoke. The scheme implicitly recognizes that there may be cases calling for one remedy but not another, and—owing to the structure of the federal judiciary—these choices are of course left in the first instance to the district courts. But such discretionary choices are not left to a court's "inclination, but to its judgment; and its judgment is to be guided by sound legal principles."

... The power to award backpay was bestowed by Congress, as part of a complex legislative design directed at an historic evil of national proportions. A court must exercise this power "in light of the large objectives of the Act," . . . That the court's discretion is equitable in nature, . . . hardly means that it is unfettered by meaningful standards or shielded from thorough appellate review. . . .

. . . The District Court's decision must therefore be measured against the purposes which inform Title VII. As the Court observed in *Griggs* v. *Duke Power Co.,* the primary objective was a prophylactic one:

> It was to achieve equality of employment opportunities and remove barriers that have operated in the past to favor an identifiable group of white employees over other employees.

Backpay has an obvious connection with this purpose. If employers faced only the prospect of an injunctive order, they would have little incentive to shun practices of dubious legality. It is the reasonably certain prospect of a backpay award that "provide[s] the spur or catalyst which causes employers and unions to self-examine and to self-evaluate their employment practices and to endeavor to eliminate, so far as possible, the last vestiges of an unfortunate and ignominious page in this country's history." . . .

It is also the purpose of Title VII to make persons whole for injuries suffered on account of unlawful employment discrimination. This is shown by the very fact that Congress took care to arm the courts with full equitable powers. For it is the historic purpose of equity to "secur[e] complete justice." . . . "[W]here federally protected rights have been invaded, it has been the rule from the beginning that courts will be alert to adjust their remedies so as to grant the necessary relief." Title VII deals with legal injuries of an economic character occasioned by racial or other antiminority discrimination. The terms "complete justice" and "necessary relief" have acquired a clear meaning in such circumstances. Where racial discrimination is concerned, "the [district] court has not merely the power but the duty to render a decree which will so far as possible eliminate the discriminatory effects of the past as well as bar like discrimination in the future." . . . And where a legal injury is of an economic character, "[t]he general rule is, that when a wrong has been done, and the law gives a remedy, the compensation shall be equal to the injury. The latter is the standard by which the former is to be measured. The injured party is to be placed as near as may be, in the situation he would have occupied if the wrong had not been committed."

The "make whole" purpose of Title VII is made evident by the legislative history. The backpay provision was expressly modeled on the backpay provision of the National Labor Relations Act. Under that Act, "[m]aking the workers whole for losses suffered on account of an unfair labor practice is part of the vindication of the public policy which the Board enforces."

. . . We may assume that Congress was aware that the Board, since its inception, has awarded backpay as a matter of course—not randomly or in the exercise of a standardless discretion, and not merely where employer violations are peculiarly deliberate, egregious or inexcusable. Furthermore, in passing the Equal Employment Opportunity Act of 1972, Congress considered several bills to limit the judicial power to award backpay. These limiting efforts were rejected, and the backpay provision was reenacted substantially in its original form. A Section-by-Section Analysis introduced by Senator Williams to accompany the Conference Committee Report on the 1972 Act strongly reaffirmed the "make whole" purpose of Title VII:

> The provisions of this subsection are intended to give the courts wide discretion exercising their equitable powers to fashion the most complete relief possible. In dealing with the present Section 706(g) the courts have stressed that the scope of relief under that section of the Act is intended to make the victims of unlawful discrimination whole, and that the attainment of this objective rests not only upon the elimination of the particular unlawful employment practice complained of, but also requires that persons aggrieved by the consequences and effects of the unlawful employment practice be, so far as possible, restored to a position where they would have been were it not for the unlawful discrimination.

As this makes clear, Congress' purpose in vesting a variety of "discretionary" powers in the courts was not to limit appellate review of trial courts, or to invite inconsistency and caprice, but rather to make possible the "fashion[ing] [of] the most complete relief possible."

It follows that, given a finding of unlawful discrimination, backpay should be denied only for reasons which, if applied generally, would not frustrate the central statutory purposes of eradicating discrimination throughout the economy and making persons whole for injuries suffered through past discrimination. The courts of appeals must maintain a consistent and principled application of the backpay provision, consonant with the twin statutory objectives, while at the same time recognizing that the trial court will often have the keener appreciation of those facts and circumstances peculiar to particular cases. . . .

So ordered.

In *Ford Motor Co.* v. *EEOC* (456 U.S. 923, 1982), the Supreme Court held that an employer's back-pay liability may be limited to the period prior to the date of an unconditional offer of a job to the plaintiff, even though the offer did not include seniority retroactive to the date of the alleged discrimination. The plaintiff's rejection of the offer, in the absence of special circumstances, would end the accrual of back-pay liability of the employer.

In addition, Section 706(g)(2)(B), added by the 1991 amendments to Title VII, limits an employer's liability in mixed motive cases, provided that the employer can demonstrate that it would have reached the same decision even without consideration of the illegal factor. In such situations, the employer is subject to the court's injunctive or declaratory remedies and is liable for legal fees, but is not liable for back pay or other damages, nor is the employer required to hire or reinstate the complainant.

Remedial Seniority

The *Teamsters* case, discussed in Chapter 12, held that a bona fide seniority system is protected by Section 703(h), even when it perpetuates the effects of prior discrimination. If the court is prevented from restructuring the bona fide seniority system, how can the court remedy the prior discrimination suffered by the plaintiffs? In *Franks* v. *Bowman Transportation Co.* (427 U.S. 747, 1976), the Supreme Court held that remedial seniority may be awarded to the victims of prior discrimination to overcome the effects of discrimination perpetuated by the bona fide seniority system. The Court stated that "the denial of seniority relief to victims of illegal . . . discrimination in hiring is permissible 'only for reasons which, if applied generally, would not frustrate the central statutory purposes of eradicating discrimination . . . and making persons whole for injuries suffered through past discrimination.' . . ."

The granting of remedial seniority is necessary to place the victims of discrimination in the position they would have been in had no illegal discrimination occurred.

Legal Fees

Section 706(k) provides that the court, in its discretion, may award "reasonable attorney's fees" under Title VII. The section also states that the United States or the EEOC may not recover legal fees if they prevail, but shall be liable for costs "the same as a private person" if they do not prevail.

In *New York Gaslight Club* v. *Carey* (447 U.S. 54, 1980), the Supreme Court held that an award of attorney's fees under Section 706(k) can include fees for the legal proceedings before the state or local agency when the complainant is required to file with that agency by Section 706(c).

Section 706(k) does not require that attorney's fees be awarded a prevailing party; the award is at the court's discretion. The following case discusses the principles to be followed in awarding attorney's fees.

CHRISTIANSBURG GARMENT CO. v. EEOC

434 U.S. 412 (Supreme Court of the United States, 1978)

STEWART, J.

Section 706(k) of Title VII of the Civil Rights Act of 1964 provides:

> In any action or proceeding under this title the court, in its discretion, may allow the prevailing party . . . a reasonable attorney's fee. . . ."

The question in this case is under what circumstances an attorney's fee should be allowed when the defendant is the prevailing party in a Title VII action—a question about which the federal courts have expressed divergent views.

Two years after Rosa Helm had filed a Title VII charge of racial discrimination against the petitioner Christiansburg Garment Co. (company), the Equal Employment Opportunity Commission notified her that its conciliation efforts had failed and that she had the right to sue the company in federal court. She did not do so. Almost two years later, in 1972, Congress enacted amendments to Title VII. Section 14 of these amendments authorized the Commission to sue in its own name to prosecute "charges pending with the Commission" on the effective date of the amendments. Proceeding under this section, the Commission sued the company, alleging that it had engaged in unlawful employment practices in violation of the amended Act. The company moved for summary judgment on the ground, inter alia, that the Rosa Helm charge had not been "pending" before the Commission when the 1972 amendments took effect. The District Court agreed, and granted summary judgment in favor of the company.

The company then petitioned for the allowance of attorney's fees against the Commission pursuant to Section 706(k) of Title VII. Finding that "the Commission's action in bringing the suit cannot be characterized as unreasonable or meritless," the District Court concluded that "an award of attorney's fees to petitioner is not justified in this case." A divided Court of Appeals affirmed, and we granted certiorari to consider an important question of federal law.

It is the general rule in the United States that in the absence of legislation providing otherwise, litigants must pay their own attorney's fees. Congress has provided only limited exceptions to this rule "under selected statutes granting or protecting various federal rights." Some of these statutes make fee awards mandatory for prevailing plaintiffs; others make awards permissive but limit them to certain parties, usually prevailing plaintiffs. But many of the statutes are more flexible, authorizing the award of attorney's fees to either plaintiffs or defendants, and entrusting the effectuation of the statutory policy to the discretion of the district courts. Section 706(k) of Title VII of the Civil Rights Act of 1964 falls into this last category. . . .

In *Newman* v. *Piggie Park Enterprises,* the court considered a substantially identical statute authorizing the award of attorney's fees under Title II of the Civil Rights Act of 1964. In that case the plaintiffs had prevailed, and the Court of Appeals had held that they should be awarded their attorney's fees "only to the extent that the respondents' defenses had been advanced 'for purposes of delay and not in good faith.'" We ruled that this "subjective standard" did not properly effectuate the purposes of the counsel-fee provision of Title II. Relying primarily on the intent of Congress to cast a Title II plaintiff in the role of "a 'private attorney general' vindicating a policy that Congress considered of the highest priority," we held that a prevailing plaintiff under Title II "should ordinarily recover an attorney's fee unless special circumstances would render such an award unjust." We noted in passing that if the objective of Congress had been to permit the award of attorney's fees only against defendants who had acted in bad faith, "no new statutory provision would have been necessary," since even the American common-law rule allows the award of attorney's fees in those exceptional circumstances.

In *Albemarle Paper Co.* v. *Moody,* the Court made clear that the *Piggie Park* standard of awarding attorney's fees to a successful plaintiff is equally applicable in an action under Title VII of the Civil Rights Act. . . . It can thus be taken as established, as the parties in this case both acknowledge, that under Section 706(k) of Title VII a prevailing *plaintiff* ordinarily is to be awarded attorney's fees in all but special circumstances.

The question in the case before us is what standard should inform a district court's discretion in deciding whether to award attorney's fees to a successful *defendant* in a Title VII action. . . .

. . . The terms of Section 706(k) provide no indication whatever of the circumstances under which either a plaintiff *or* a defendant should be entitled to attorney's fees. And a moment's reflection reveals that there are at least two strong equitable considerations counseling an attorney's fee award to a prevailing Title VII plaintiff that are wholly absent in the case of a prevailing Title VII defendant.

First, as emphasized so forcefully in *Piggie Park,* the plaintiff is the chosen instrument of Congress to vindicate "a policy that Congress considered of the highest priority." Second, when a district court awards counsel fees to a prevailing plaintiff, it is awarding them against a violator of federal law. As the Court of Appeals clearly perceived, "these policy considerations which support the award of fees to a prevailing plaintiff are not present in the case of a prevailing defendant." A successful defendant seeking counsel fees under Section 706(k) must rely on quite different equitable considerations. . . .

It cannot be lightly assumed that in enacting Section 706(k), Congress intended to distort that process by giving the private plaintiff substantial incentives to sue, while foreclosing to the defendant the possibility of recovering his expenses in resisting even a groundless action unless he can show that it was brought in bad faith. . . .

The first federal appellate court to consider what criteria should govern the award of attorney's fees to a prevailing Title VII defendant was the Court of Appeals for the Third Circuit in *United States Steel Corp.* v. *United States.* There a District Court had denied a fee awarded to a defendant that had successfully resisted a Commission demand for documents, the court finding that the Commission's action had not been "unfounded, meritless, frivolous or vexatiously brought." The Court of Appeals concluded that the District Court had not abused its discretion in denying the award. A similar standard was adopted by the Court of Appeals for the Second Circuit in *Carrion* v. *Yeshiva University.* In upholding an attorney's fee award to a successful defendant, that court stated that such awards should be permitted "not routinely, not simply because he succeeds, but only where the action brought is found to be unreasonable, frivolous, meritless or vexatious."

To the extent that abstract words can deal with concrete cases, we think that the concept embodied in the language adopted by these two Courts of Appeals is correct. We would qualify their words only by pointing out that the term "meritless" is to be understood as meaning groundless or without foundation, rather than simply that the plaintiff has ultimately lost his case, and that the term "vexatious" in no way implies that the plaintiff's subjective bad faith is a necessary prerequisite to a fee award against him. In sum, a District Court may in its discretion award attorney's fees to a prevailing defendant in a Title VII case upon a finding that

the plaintiff's action was frivolous, unreasonable, or without foundation, even though not brought in subjective bad faith.

In applying these criteria, it is important that a district court resist the understandable temptation to engage in post hoc reasoning by concluding that because a plaintiff did not ultimately prevail, his action must have been unreasonable or without foundation. This kind of hindsight logic could discourage all but the most airtight claims, for seldom can a prospective plaintiff be sure of ultimate success. No matter how honest one's belief that he has been the victim of discrimination, no matter how meritorious one's claim may appear at the outset, the course of litigation is rarely predictable. Decisive facts may not emerge until discovery or trial. The law may change or clarify in the midst of litigation. Even when the law or the facts appear questionable or unfavorable at the outset, a party may have an entirely reasonable ground for bringing suit.

That Section 706(k) allows fee awards only to *prevailing* private plaintiffs should assure that this statutory provision will not in itself operate as an incentive to the bringing of claims that have little chance of success. To take the further step of assessing attorney's fees against plaintiffs simply because they do not finally prevail would substantially add to the risks inhering in most litigation and would undercut the efforts of Congress to promote the vigorous enforcement of the provisions of Title VII. Hence, a plaintiff should not be assessed his opponent's attorney's fees unless a court finds that his claim was frivolous, unreasonable, or groundless, or that the plaintiff continued to litigate after it clearly became so. And, needless to say, if a plaintiff is found to have brought or continued such a claim in *bad faith,* there will be an even stronger basis for charging him with the attorney's fees incurred by the defense.

In denying attorney's fees to the company in this case, the District Court focused on the standards we have discussed. The court found that "the Commission's action in bringing the suit cannot be characterized as unreasonable or meritless" because "the basis upon which petitioner prevailed was an issue of first impression requiring judicial resolution" and because the "Commission's statutory interpretation of Section 14 of the 1972 amendments was not frivolous." The court thus exercised its discretion squarely within the permissible bounds of Section 706(k). Accordingly, the judgment of the Court of Appeals upholding the decision of the District Court is affirmed. **It is so ordered.**

Class Actions

The rules of procedure for the federal courts allow an individual plaintiff to sue on behalf of a whole class of individuals allegedly suffering the same harm. Rule 23 of the Federal Rules of Civil Procedure allows such suits, known as class actions, when several conditions are met. First, the number of members of the class is so numerous that it would be "impracticable" to have them individually join the suit. Second, there must be issues of fact or law common to the claims of all members. Third, the claims of the individual seeking to represent the entire class must be typical of the claims of the members of the class. Last, the individual representative must fairly and adequately protect the interests of the class.

When such conditions are met, the court may certify the suit as a class action suit on behalf of all members of the class. Individuals challenging employment discrimination under Title VII may sue in behalf of all individuals affected by the alleged discrimination by complying with the requirements of Rule 23. In *General Telephone Co. of the Southwest* v. *Falcon* (457 U.S. 147, 1982), the Supreme Court held that an employee alleging that he was denied promotion due to national origin discrimination is not a proper representative of the class of individuals denied hiring by the employer due to discrimination. The plaintiff had not suffered the same injuries allegedly suffered by the class members.

The EEOC need not seek certification as a class representative under Rule 23 in order to seek classwide remedies under Title VII, according to the Supreme Court decision in *General Telephone* v. *EEOC* (446 U.S. 318, 1980). The EEOC, said the Court, acts to vindicate public policy and not just to protect personal interests.

Remedies in Class Actions

Classwide remedies are appropriate under Title VII, according to the Supreme Court's holding in *Franks* v. *Bowman Transportation Co.* (424 U.S. 747, 1976), which authorized such classwide "make whole" orders. In *Local 28, Sheet Metal Workers* v. *EEOC* (see Chapter 12), the Supreme Court upheld court-ordered affirmative action to remedy prior employment discrimination. The Court specifically said affirmative relief may be available to minority group members who were not personally victimized by the employer's prior discrimination. Additionally, in *Local 93, Int'l Ass'n of Firefighters* v. *Cleveland,* the Supreme Court approved a consent decree that imposed affirmative action to remedy prior discrimination, again upholding the right of nonvictims to benefit from the affirmative remedy.

Public Employees under Title VII

Title VII was amended in 1972 to cover the employees of state and local employers; these employees are subject to the same procedural requirements as private employees. However, Section 706(f)(1) authorizes the U.S. Attorney General, rather than the EEOC, to file suit under Title VII against a state or local public employer.

Most federal employees are covered by Title VII but are subject to different procedural requirements. Section 701(b) excludes the United States, wholly owned federal government corporations, and any department or agency of the District of Columbia subject to civil service regulations from the definition of "employer" under Title VII. Section 717 of the act does provide, however, that "All personnel actions affecting employees or applicants for employment . . . in positions under the federal civil service, the D.C. Civil Service and the U.S. Postal Service . . . shall be made free from any discrimination based on race, color, religion, sex or national origin."

Section 717 also designated the federal Civil Service Commission as the agency having jurisdiction over complaints of discrimination by federal employees. However, in 1978 that authority was transferred to the EEOC under Reorganization Plan No. 1 of 1978. The EEOC adopted procedural regulations regarding Title VII complaints by federal employees. A federal employee alleging employment discrimination must first consult with an Equal Employment Opportunity (EEO) counselor within the employee's own agency. If the employee is not satisfied with the counselor's resolution of the complaint, the employee can file a formal complaint with the agency's designated EEO official. The EEO official, after investigating and holding a hearing, renders a decision; that decision can be appealed to the head of the agency. If the employee is not satisfied with that decision, he or she can either seek judicial review of it or file an appeal with the EEOC. If the employee chooses to file with the EEOC, the complaint is subject to the general EEOC procedures. The employee has ninety days from receiving notice of the EEOC taking final action on the complaint to file suit. The employee may file suit, as well, when the EEOC has not made a decision on the complaint after 180 days from its filing with the EEOC.

The Civil Rights Act of 1991 extended the coverage of Title VII to employees of Congress. The House of Representatives is directed to develop procedures for the enforcement of the rights and procedures of Title VII under the Fair Employment Practices Resolution of the House of Representatives. The act created the Office of Senate Fair Employment Practices to enforce and administer the provisions of Title VII with regard to the Senate. "Instrumentalities of the Congress," defined as including the Congressional Budget Office, the Government Printing Office, the General Accounting Office, the Architect of the Capitol, the U.S. Botanic Garden, and the Office of Technology Assessment, are directed to establish remedies and procedures for the rights protected in Title VII.

QUESTIONS

1. What are the time limits for filing a complaint alleging a violation of Title VII? Where must such a complaint be filed?

2. Describe the steps in the EEOC procedure for handling complaints alleging a violation of Title VII.

3. How does a state court's dismissal of a discrimination complaint affect the complainant's right to file suit in federal court under Title VII? What is the effect of an adverse decision in arbitration on the complainant's right to sue under Title VII? Why are the effects different?

4. What must a plaintiff show to establish a case of disparate treatment? What must the defendant show to rebut a claim of disparate treatment?

5. What must a plaintiff show to establish a complaint of disparate impact? How can a defendant rebut such a claim?

6. What remedies are available to a successful plaintiff under Title VII?

7. What procedures must be followed by federal employees in filing a complaint under Title VII?

CASE PROBLEMS

1. Morgan was an untenured faculty member at Ivy University. In February 1982 he was informed that the Faculty Tenure Committee recommended that he not be offered a tenured position with the university. Failure to achieve tenure requires that the faculty member seek employment elsewhere; the university offers such faculty members a one-year contract following denial of tenure. At the expiration of the one-year contract, the faculty member's employment is terminated.

   Morgan appealed to the tenure committee for a reconsideration. The committee granted him a one-year extension for a reconsideration. In February 1983 the committee again denied Morgan tenure at Ivy University. The university board of trustees affirmed the committee's decision. Morgan was informed of the trustees' decision and offered a one-year contract on June 26, 1983.

   Morgan accepted the one-year contract, which would expire on June 30, 1984. On June 1, 1984, Morgan filed charges with the EEOC alleging race and sex discrimination by Ivy University in denying him tenure. The one-year contract expired on June 30, 1984, and Morgan's employment was terminated.

   Assuming no state or local EEOC agency is involved, is Morgan's complaint validly filed with the EEOC? What employment practice is he challenging? When did it occur? See *Delaware State College* v. *Ricks,* 449 U.S. 250 (1982).

2. Crews was an employee of Machine Manufacturing Co. (MM); MM's work force is unionized. Crews was fired by MM on March 1, 1984, for poor work performance. Crews filed a grievance under the collective agreement, challenging the discharge. The grievance was not resolved by negotiation and was submitted to arbitration.

   The arbitrator issued her decision upholding Crews's discharge on December 15, 1984. Crews filed a complaint alleging that the discharge was in violation of Title VII with the Pennsylvania Human Rights Commission on January 1, 1985, and with the EEOC on March 1, 1985.

   Is the complaint validly filed with the EEOC? What is the effect of filing the grievance on the time limitation for filing with the EEOC? See *Int. Union of Electrical, Radio & Machine Workers, Local 790* v. *Robbins & Myers, Inc.,* 429 U.S. 229 (1976).

3. Dewhurst was a female flight attendant with Sub-Central airlines. Sub-Central's employment policies prohibited female attendants from being married, but married male employees were employed by Sub-Central. Dewhurst was married on June 15, 1980; she was discharged by Sub-Central the next day. Sub-Central, under pressure from the EEOC, eliminated the "no-married females" rule in March 1982.

   Dewhurst was rehired by Sub-Central on February 1, 1983. Sub-Central refused to recognize her seniority for her past employment with Sub-Central; the company's policy is to refuse to recognize prior service for all former employees who are rehired. Dewhurst filed a complaint with the EEOC on March 1, 1983, alleging that Sub-Central's refusal to credit her with prior seniority violated Title VII.

   Is her complaint validly filed with EEOC? See *United Airlines* v. *Evans,* 431 U.S. 553 (1977).

4. Smith, Washington, and Bailey are African-American bricklayers. They had applied for work with Constructo Co., a brick and mason contractor. Constructo refused their applications for the reason that company policy is to hire only bricklayers referred by Constructo employees. The three filed charges with EEOC, which decided not to file suit against Constructo. The bricklayers then filed suit in federal court against Constructo, alleging race discrimination in hiring.

At the trial, the three presented evidence of their rejection by Constructo. Constructo denied any racial discrimination in hiring and introduced evidence showing that African Americans make up 13 percent of its work force. Only 5.7 percent of all certified bricklayers in the greater metropolitan area are African American.

Has Constructo met its burden under Title VII? Have the three African Americans met their burden under Title VII? See *Furnco Construction Co.* v. *Waters,* 438 U.S. 567 (1978).

5. After receiving his right-to-sue letter from the EEOC, Cox contacted the local chapter of the National Association for the Advancement of Colored People for help in filing his lawsuit. The NAACP drafted his complaint and filed it on the eighty-eighth day after he received his letter. Unfortunately, it was filed with a check that was insufficient to cover the filing fees. The clerk of the court returned the complaint, and it was not filed until the ninety-sixth day. How should the court respond to the defendant's motion to dismiss Cox's suit as untimely filed? See *Cox* v. *Conrail,* 557 F.Supp. 1261 (D.D.C. 1983).

6. Uviedo sued her former employer for four claims based upon disparate payment of wages, the four claims totaled $48,000 in damages, plus two counts of discriminatory denials of promotions and a claim of constructive discharge. She lost three of the four wage claims, one of the two promotion counts, and the discharge claim.

When a plaintiff is the prevailing party in a discrimination suit, the court has the power to award her attorney's fees. What, if any, fees should Uviedo's attorney be awarded? See *Uviedo* v. *Steves Sash & Door Co.,* 753 F.2d 639, 37 F.E.P. Cases 82 (5th Cir. 1985).

7. Elizabeth Westman was employed by Valley Technologies as an engineering technician. On June 15, 1989, she was terminated after being informed by her supervisor that the company was experiencing financial difficulties and could no longer afford to employ her. Westman subsequently learned, on May 15, 1990, that she was terminated so that her supervisor could hire a less qualified male technician in her place. Upon learning of the real reason for her discharge, Westman immediately filed a complaint with the EEOC; the employer argued that her complaint should be dismissed because it was not filed within the time limit required under

Title VII. Will her complaint be dismissed, or was it properly filed? Explain your answer. See *Reeb* v. *Economic Opportunity Atlanta, Inc.,* 516 F.2d 924 (5th Cir. 1975).

8. S. A. Bouzoukis was employed as a member of the faculty of Enormous State University; she was denied tenure and offered a one-year terminal contract. Bouzoukis alleged that she was denied tenure because of sex discrimination, and retained an attorney to pursue her claim against the university. Her attorney met with university officials to discuss the complaint, and the university requested that Bouzoukis allow the university time to conduct an investigation into her complaint. The university officials stated that if Bouzoukis agreed to delay filing her complaint with the EEOC, they would not raise the issue of time limits as a defense if the complaint could not be settled through negotiations. The university's investigation and subsequent negotiations dragged on for ten months; no settlement was reached. Bouzoukis then filed the complaint with the EEOC; she later filed suit in federal court. The university argued in court that the suit should be dismissed because the complaint was not filed with the EEOC within 300 days of the alleged violation. How should the court rule on the time limit issue? Explain your answer. See *Leake* v. *University of Cincinnati,* 605 F.2d 255 (6th Cir. 1979).

9. Bernardo Huerta, an employee of the Adams Corp., was transferred to a position that prevented him from being eligible for overtime work. Huerta filed a complaint with the EEOC alleging that he had been discriminated against because of his national origin. After negotiations subsequent to the filing of the complaint, Huerta and the Adams Corp. reached a settlement agreement on his complaint. A year later, Huerta claimed that Adams had broken the settlement agreement, and filed suit in federal court. The court granted judgment for Huerta, and he asked the court to award him legal fees; Adams Corp. argued that the action to enforce the settlement agreement was not the same as an action under Title VII, and therefore Huerta should not be awarded legal fees as a prevailing party under Title VII. Should the court award Huerta legal fees? Explain your answer. See *Robles* v. *United States,* 54 Emp. Prac. Dec. (CCH) P 40, 193 (D.D.C. 1990).

10. Five individuals who had fulfilled all the administrative preconditions and received letters to sue from the

EEOC found that they were unable to obtain attorneys to assist them in prosecuting their lawsuits. Therefore, they petitioned the court to appoint attorneys to represent them. The federal judge in charge of these cases denied all these petitions on the ground that such forced appointments would constitute involuntary servitude in violation of the Thirteenth Amendment of the Constitution.

Do you think the judge ruled correctly? Explain your answer. See *In re Five Applications,* 646 F.2d 303, 25 F.E.P. Cases 1541 (5th Cir. 1981).

CHAPTER 15

Other EEO Legislation

IN ADDITION TO TITLE VII of the Civil Rights Act of 1964, as amended, a number of other legal provisions can be used to attack discrimination in employment. Some of those provisions include the Civil Rights Act of 1866 and 1870, the Equal Pay Act, the Age Discrimination in Employment Act, the Vocational Rehabilitation Act, Executive Order 11246, the Veterans' Reemployment Act, the Americans with Disabilities Act, the National Labor Relations Act, the Constitution, and the various state EEO laws. The various provisions of those statutes will be the focus of this chapter.

The Civil Rights Acts of 1866 and 1870

The Civil Rights Acts of 1866 and 1870 were passed during the Reconstruction era immediately following the Civil War. They were intended to ensure that the newly freed slaves were granted the full legal rights of U.S. citizens. The acts are presently codified in Sections 1981, 1983, and 1985 of Chapter 42 of the U.S. Code (referred to as 42 U.S.C. Sections 1981, 1983, 1985).

Section 1981

Section 1981 provides, in part, that

> All persons within the jurisdiction of the United States shall have the same right in every State and Territory to make and enforce contracts . . . as is enjoyed by white citizens. . . .

The Supreme Court held in *Jones* v. *Alfred H. Mayer Co.* (392 U.S. 409, 1968) that the acts could be used to attack discrimination in private employment. Following *Jones,* Section 1981 was increasingly used, in addition to Title VII, to challenge employment discrimination. In *Johnson* v. *Railway Express Agency* (421 U.S. 454, 1975), the Supreme Court held that Section 1981 provided for an independent cause of action (right to sue) against employment discrimination. A suit under Section 1981 was separate and distinct from a suit under Title VII.

In the 1989 decision of *Patterson* v. *McLean Credit Union* (491 U.S. 164), the Supreme Court held that Section 1981 only covered those aspects of racial discrimination in employment that related to the formation and enforcement of contracts, and did not cover harassment based on race. The Civil Rights Act of 1991 amended

Section 1981 and overturned the *Patterson* decision by adding Section 1981(b), which states:

> For the purposes of this section, the term "make and enforce contracts" includes the making, performance, modification, and termination of contracts, and the enjoyment of all benefits, privileges, terms and conditions of the contractual relationship.

The 1991 act also added Section 1981A, which gives the right to sue for compensatory and punitive damages to victims of intentional discrimination in violation of Title VII, the Americans with Disabilities Act of 1990, and the Vocational Rehabilitation Act.

The wording of Section 1981 ("... as is enjoyed by white citizens ...") seems to indicate a concern with racial discrimination. In *Saint Francis College* v. *Al-Khazraji* (481 U.S. 604, 1987), a college professor alleged that he was denied tenure because he was an Arab. The college argued that Arabs are members of the Caucasian (white) race and that the professor was therefore not a victim of race discrimination subject to Section 1981. In determining whether Section 1981 applied to the professor's claim, the Supreme Court held that

> Based on the history of Section 1981, we have little trouble in concluding that Congress intended to protect from discrimination identifiable classes of persons who are subjected to intentional discrimination solely because of their ancestry or ethnic characteristics. Such discrimination is racial discrimination that Congress intended Section 1981 to forbid, whether or not it would be classified as racial in terms of modern scientific theory. The Court of Appeals was thus quite right in holding that Section 1981, "at a minimum," reaches discrimination against an individual "because he or she is genetically part of an ethnically and physiognomically distinctive sub-grouping of *homo sapiens.*" It is clear from our holding, however, that a distinctive physiognomy is not essential to qualify for Section 1981 protection. If respondent on remand can prove that he was subjected to intentional discrimination based on the fact that he was born an Arab, rather than solely on the place or nation of his origin, or his religion, he will have made out a case under Section 1981.

Section 1983

Section 1983 of 42 U.S.C. provides that

> Every person who, under the color of any statute, ordinance, regulation, custom or usage, of any State or Territory, subjects, or causes to be subjected, any citizen of the United States or other person written the jurisdiction thereof to the deprivation of any rights, privileges, or immunities secured by the Constitution and laws, shall be liable to the party injured in an action at law, suit in equity, or other proper proceeding for redress.

As with Section 1981, Section 1983 is restricted to claims of intentional discrimination. But unlike Section 1981, the prohibitions of Section 1983 extend to the deprivation of any rights guaranteed by the Constitution or by law. In *Maine* v. *Thiboutot* (448 U.S. 1, 1980), the Supreme Court held that Section 1983 encompasses claims based on deprivation of rights granted under federal statutory law. That means that claims alleging discrimination on grounds prohibited by federal law, such as sex, age, religion, national origin, and so forth, can be brought under Section 1983. But, because of the wording of Section 1983 ("... under the color of any statute, ...

of any state), claims under Section 1983 are restricted to those cases in which the alleged discrimination is by someone acting (or claiming to act) under government authority. That means employment discrimination by public employers is subject to challenge because such employers act under specific legal authority. In general, claims against private sector employers can rarely be filed under Section 1983. Any claims against private employers under Section 1983 must establish that the employer acted pursuant to some specific government authority, this is the "state action" requirement.

Section 1985(c)

Section 1985(c) of 42 U.S.C. prohibits two or more persons from conspiring to deprive a person or class of persons "of the equal protection of the laws, or of equal privileges and immunities under the law." The provision was enacted in 1871 to protect blacks from the violent activities of the Ku Klux Klan.

In *Griffin* v. *Breckenridge* (403 U.S. 88, 1971), the Supreme Court held that a group of African Americans alleging that they were attacked and beaten by a group of whites could bring suit under Section 1985(c). It appeared that the provision could be used to attack intentional discrimination in private employment when two or more persons were involved in the discrimination. But in 1979 the Supreme Court held in *Great American Federal Savings & Loan Ass'n* v. *Novotny* (442 U.S. 366) that Section 1985(c) could not be used to sue for violation of a right created by Title VII. Relying on *Novotny,* lower courts have held that Section 1985(c) cannot be used to challenge violations of the Equal Pay Act or the Age Discrimination in Employment Act.

Procedure under Sections 1981 and 1983

A suit under Section 1981 is not subject to the same procedural requirements as a suit under Title VII. There is no requirement to file a claim with any administrative agency, such as the Equal Employment Opportunity Commission, before filing suit under Section 1981 or Section 1983. The plaintiff may file suit in federal district court and is entitled to a jury trial; a successful plaintiff may recover punitive damages in addition to compensatory damages such as back pay, benefits, and legal fees.

The right to sue under Section 1981A for compensatory and punitive damages for intentional violations of Title VII and the Americans with Disabilities Act of 1990 was added by the Civil Rights Act of 1991. The act also set upper limits on the amount of damages recoverable, based on the size of the employer (as specified in Chapter 14). Punitive damages are not recoverable against public sector employers.

The Equal Pay Act

The Equal Pay Act of 1963 prohibits sex discrimination in rates of pay. It requires that men and women performing substantially equal work be paid equally. The act does not reach other forms of sex discrimination or discrimination on grounds other than gender.

Coverage

The Equal Pay Act of 1963 was enacted as an amendment to the Fair Labor Standards Act, which regulates minimum wages and maximum hours of employment. The Equal Pay Act's coverage is therefore similar to that of the Fair Labor Standards Act. The act applies to all employers "engaged in commerce (interstate commerce)," and applies to all employees of an "enterprise engaged in commerce." Virtually all substantial business operations are covered. The Equal Pay Act coverage does not depend on a minimum number of employees, so that the act may apply to firms having fewer than the fifteen employees required for Title VII coverage.

There are some exceptions to the coverage of the Equal Pay Act. These exceptions deal with operations that are exempted from the Fair Labor Standards Act. For example, certain small retail operations and small agricultural operations are excluded. Seasonal amusement operations and the fishing industry are also exempted from the act. Although the act does cover state and local government employees, it does not cover federal employees.

Provisions

The Equal Pay Act prohibits discrimination by an employer

> between employees on the basis of sex by paying wages to employees in such establishment at a rate less than the rate at which he pays wages to employees of the opposite sex . . . for equal work on jobs the performance of which requires equal skill, effort, and responsibility, and which are performed under similar working conditions.

A plaintiff claiming violation of the Equal Pay Act must demonstrate that the employer is paying lower wages to employees of the opposite sex who are performing equal work in the same establishment. Note that the act does not require paying equal wages for work of equal value, known as comparable worth (see Chapter 13). The act requires only "equal pay for equal work." Work that is equal, or substantially equivalent, involves equal skills, effort, and responsibilities and is performed under similar working conditions.

Equal Work.   When considering whether jobs involve substantially equivalent work under the Equal Pay Act, the courts do not consider job titles, job descriptions, or job classifications to be controlling. Rather, they evaluate each job on a case-by-case basis, making a detailed inquiry into the substantial duties and facts of each position.

Effort.   Equal effort involves substantially equivalent physical or mental exertion needed for performance of the job. If an employer pays male employees more than female employees because of additional duties performed by the males, the employer must establish that the extra duties are a regular and recurring requirement and that they consume a substantial amount of time. Occasional or infrequent assignments of extra duties do not warrant additional pay for periods when no extra duties are performed. The employer must also show that the extra duties are commensurate with the extra pay. The employer who assigns extra duties only to male employees may face problems under Title VII unless the employer can demonstrate that being male is a bona fide occupational qualification (BFOQ) for performing the extra duties. Unless the employer can make the requisite showing of business necessity to justify a BFOQ, the extra duties must be available to both male and female employees.

Skill.
Equal skill includes substantially equivalent experience, training, education, and ability. The skill, however, must relate to the performance of actual job duties. The employer cannot pay males more for possessing additional skills that are not used on the job. The act requires equal or substantially equivalent skills—not identical skills. Differences in the kinds of skills involved will not justify differentials in pay when the degree of skills required is substantially equal. For example, male hospital orderlies and female practical nurses may perform different duties requiring different skills, but if the general nature of their jobs is equivalent, the degree of skills required by each is substantially equal, according to *Hodgson* v. *Brookhaven General Hospital* (436 F.2d 719, 5th Cir. 1972).

Responsibility.
Equal responsibility includes a substantially equivalent degree of accountability required in the performance of a job, with emphasis on the importance of the job's obligations. When work of males and females is subject to similar supervisory review, the responsibility of males and females is equal. But when females work without supervision whereas males are subject to supervision, the responsibility involved is not equal.

When considering the responsibility involved in jobs, the courts focus on the economic or social consequences of the employee's actions or decisions. Minor responsibility such as making coffee or answering telephones may not be an indication of different responsibility. The act does not require identical responsibility, only substantially equivalent responsibility. For instance, if a male employee is required to compile payroll lists and a female employee must make and deliver the payroll, the responsibilities may be substantially equivalent.

Working Conditions.
The act requires that the substantially equivalent work be performed under similar working conditions. According to the 1974 Supreme Court decision in *Corning Glass Works* v. *Brennan* (417 U.S. 188), working conditions include the physical surroundings and hazards involved in a job. Exposure to heat, cold, noise, fumes, dust, risk of injury, or poor ventilation are examples of working conditions. Work performed outside involves different working conditions from work performed inside. Work performed during the night shift, however, is not under different working conditions from the performance of the same work during the day.

The Equal Pay Act does not reach pay differentials for work that is not substantially equal in skill, effort, responsibility, and working conditions. However, recall that in the *Gunther* case (see Chapter 13) the Supreme Court held that Title VII prohibits intentional sex discrimination in pay, even when the jobs involved are not equivalent.

Defenses under the Equal Pay Act

Although a plaintiff may establish that an employer is paying different wages for men and women performing work involving equivalent effort, skills, responsibility, and working conditions, the employer may not be in violation of the Equal Pay Act, because the act provides several defenses to claims of unequal pay for equal work. When the pay differentials between the male and female employees are due to a seniority system, a merit pay system, a productivity-based pay system, or "a factor other than sex," the pay differentials do not violate the act.

Employers justifying pay differentials on seniority systems, merit pay systems, or production-based pay systems must demonstrate that the system is bona fide and applies equally to all employees. A merit pay system must be more than an ad hoc subjective determination of employees' merit—especially if there is no listing of criteria considered in establishing an employee's merit. Any such systems should be formal and objective in order to justify pay differentials.

The "factor other than sex" defense covers a wide variety of situations. A "shift differential," for example, involves paying a premium to employees who work during the afternoon or night shift. If the differential is uniformly available to all employees who work a particular shift, it qualifies as a "factor other than sex." But if female are precluded from working the night shift, a night-shift pay differential is not defensible under the act. A training program may be the basis of a pay differential if the program is bona fide; employees who perform similar work but are in training for higher positions may be paid more than those not in the training program. The training program should be open to both male and female employees, unless the employer can establish that gender is a BFOQ for admission to the program. In *Kouba* v. *Allstate Insurance Co.* (691 F.2d 873, 1982), the U.S. Court of Appeals for the Ninth Circuit held that using an employee's prior salary to determine pay for employees in a training program was not precluded by the Equal Pay Act. In the *Manhart* case (see Chapter 13), the Supreme Court held that an employer could not use sex-based actuarial tables to justify differential pension benefits between male and female employees. The actuarial tables purported to measure life expectancy, but since the tables were based on an employee's sex, they could not be considered a "factor other than sex."

The following case is a good illustration of the court's inquiry into the alleged equality of jobs involved in an Equal Pay Act complaint.

LAFFEY v. NORTHWEST AIRLINES

567 F.2d 429 (U.S. Court of Appeals, District of Columbia Circuit, 1976)

ROBINSON, J.

Northwest Airlines (NWA) appeals from a judgment of the District Court declaring certain of its personnel policies violative of the Equal Pay Act of 1963 and Title VII of the Civil Rights Act of 1964, and granting injunctive and monetary relief. The principal practice in issue here is the payment to women employed as stewardesses of salaries lower than those paid to men serving as pursers for work found by the court to be substantially equal. Others are the provision to stewardesses of less desirable layover accommodations and allowances for maintenance of uniforms, and the imposition of weight restrictions upon stewardesses only. In varying respects and degrees NWA challenges findings of fact and conclusions of law on these matters, as well as the propriety of the remedial measures adopted. . . .

Between 1927 and 1947, all cabin attendants employed on NWA's aircraft were women, whom NWA classified as "stewardesses." In 1947, when the company initiated international service, it established a new cabin-attendant position of "purser," and for two decades thereafter adhered to an undeviating practice of restricting purser jobs to men alone. In implementation of this policy, NWA created another strictly all-male cabin-attendant classification—"flight service attendant"—to serve as a training and probationary position for future pursers. NWA has maintained a combined seniority list for pursers and flight service attendants, on which seniority as pursers accrued to flight service attendants immediately upon assumption of their duties as such, and a separate seniority list for stewardesses. From 1951 until 1967, flight service attendants had a contractual right to automatic promotion to purser vacancies in the order of their seniority.

It was not until 1967, when a new collective bargaining agreement was negotiated, that stewardesses first became contractually eligible to apply for purser positions. During negotiations on the issue, NWA, for both the 1967 agreement and another in 1970, rejected an additional union proposal that stewardesses, like flight service attendants, be allowed to progress to purser slots according to seniority, stating that the company "prefers males and intends to have them." The company has also insisted upon the right of "selectivity" in choosing which stewardesses might become pursers, and has imposed other restrictions on stewardesses seeking purser vacancies which had not previously been laid on flight service attendants.

Company policy had been to fill purser openings by hiring "men off the street" and training them for a short time, after which notices of purser vacancies would be posted. Following the 1967 collective bargaining agreement affording stewardesses access to these jobs, however, NWA hired five male purser-applicants without ever posting notices of the vacancies. In 1970, after three years of ostensibly open admission to purser status, NWA had 137 male cabin attendants—all as pursers—and 1,747 female cabin attendants—all but one as stewardesses.

The sole female purser at that time was Mary P. Laffey, who bid for a purser vacancy in 1967, after nine years' service as a stewardess. Although that purser position was scheduled to be filled in November, 1967, processing of her application was delayed assertedly for the reason that NWA needed to administer new tests to purser applicants. These tests had never previously been used in selecting pursers, and during the interim between Ms. Laffey's application and her appointment NWA hired two male pursers without benefit of any tests. Finally, in June, 1968, Ms. Laffey became a purser, but was placed on the bottom rung of the purser-salary schedule and received less than her income as a senior stewardess.

On this appeal, NWA does not challenge holdings by the District Court that Title VII was violated by NWA's refusal to hire female pursers. Rather, the appeal focuses primarily on whether the payment of unequal salaries to stewardesses and pursers, while occupying positions as such, implicates . . . the Equal Pay Act. The purser wage scale ranges from 20 to 55 percent higher than salaries paid to stewardesses of equivalent seniority. The Equal Pay Act forbids this pay differential unless greater skill, effort or responsibility is required to perform purser duties. . . .

In gauging whether NWA's pursers and stewardesses performed equal work, the District Court analyzed in great detail NWA's flight operations and its usage of the three different categories of cabin attendants. . . .

Pure domestic commercial flights are, with some exceptions, served exclusively by stewardesses and flight service attendants. Pursers are ordinarily utilized on interport flights, transpacific commercial flights, domestic segments of international flights, and on all types of charters, military or otherwise, including pure domestic flights. Since 1967, the company has also maintained a crew of stewardesses with proficiency in one or more foreign languages, who are assigned to certain international flights.

NWA schedules a different cabin-attendant crew on each flight segment; one crew will fly the domestic segment, another will take over for the transpacific link, and still a third is used on the interport portion. Pursers and stewardesses bid separately, according to seniority, for monthly schedules.

Probing beneath the different titles, bidding schedules and salaries, the District Court made extensive factual findings comparing the work actually done by pursers and stewardesses, and held it to be essentially equal when considered as a whole. For example, pursers are assigned to the first-class section of the aircraft, which has a smaller passenger load per cabin attendant and a correspondingly more leisurely work pace as compared with the chores inherited by stewardesses assigned to the tourist-class section. The hourly workload also tends to be greater on the "short hop" domestic schedules than on the longer international flights.

Duties performed do not differ significantly in nature as between pursers and stewardesses. All must check cabins before departure, greet and seat passengers, prepare for take-off, and provide in-flight food, beverage and general services. All must complete required documentation, maintain cabin cleanliness, see that passengers comply with regulations and deplane passengers. The premier responsibility of any cabin attendant is to insure the safety of passengers during an emergency, and cabin attendants all must possess a thorough knowledge of emergency equipment and procedures on all aircraft. All attendants also must be knowledgeable in first aid techniques and must be able to handle the myriad of medical problems that arise in flight. Food service varies greatly between flights, but pursers engage in no duties that are not also performed on the same or another flight by the stewardesses. Another important duty—building goodwill between NWA and its passengers—depends on the poise, tact, friendliness, good judgment and adaptability of every cabin attendant, male or female.

The District Court found that when pursers are scheduled on pure domestic flights, their duties are identical to those of stewardesses functioning as "senior cabin attendants"—the most senior purser, or the most senior stewardesses on flights with no purser. A substantial percentage of NWA's overall utilization of pursers is on pure domestic flights and domestic segments of international flights. Similarly, a substantial percentage of the company's use of pursers is their assignment to military air charter flights. Many pursers fly flights of these types exclusively for months or years at a time. . . .

With respect to documentation responsibilities, the District Court found that pursers and stewardesses have different, but comparable, duties. Stewardesses alone sell liquor, and are alone required to complete inventory and sales records, and beverage usage reports. On flights carrying tax-free liquor, customs inventory forms must be completed by both stewardesses and pursers, and all cabin attendants are subject to discipline for error. On all flights, the senior cabin attendant and the senior in tourist—the senior stewardess in the tourist class—must make appropriate entries in the log book, and also prepare an inflight-service report, seating charts, accident reports and other diverse documents.

Pursers are responsible for administering international quarantine procedures for passengers, crew and cargo. As the requirements vary from port to port, pursers must keep their knowledge current in order to comply with applicable regulations. These duties, however, are not required on all flights to which pursers are assigned, such as on pure domestic flights on which pursers perform no documentation duties, and on certain domestic segments on which such

purser duties are minimal. To boot, pursers are instructed to carry out their international documentation responsibilities at times when no significant passenger service is required, and other cabin attendants perform all other necessary services during those times. The District Court found that "the documentary duties described which are . . . assigned only to pursers involved no greater skill, effort or responsibility than the stewardess job."

The District Court also examined another general, more intangible, duty advanced by NWA as a factor rendering the purser job different in kind from the stewardess position. The company's cabin service manual states that the senior purser on a flight will always be considered the senior cabin attendant and as such must coordinate the activities of the other attendants, and is to be held "responsible and accountable" for the proper rendering of service on that flight. But the manual further provides that if no purser is scheduled, the most senior stewardess will serve as senior flight attendant and will similarly be charged with coordination of cabin service, although she is accountable only for the conduct of service in the section of the aircraft in which she works, responsibility for the remainder being placed on the senior attendant in the other section of the aircraft.

Senior cabin attendants, be they purser or stewardess, have a number of supervisory duties. These include monitoring and, where necessary, correcting the work of other cabin attendants; determining the times of meals and movie showings; shifting cabin attendants from section to section to balance workloads; and giving pre-departure briefings on emergency equipment and procedures. On large planes, even if a purser in the first-class section is designated the senior cabin attendant, the senior in tourist shoulders these same burdens in her section of the aircraft—overseeing the great majority of passengers and cabin attendants. Stewardesses and pursers alike are subject to disciplinary action if they fail to carry out their "supervisory responsibilities."

There is, however, no merit system maintained to reward those who "supervise" better than others; all pursers and all stewardesses are on uniform, separate wage scales, regardless of whether—or how well—an individual performs. . . .

Careful evaluation of the facts comprehensively found led the District Court to conclude that NWA had discriminated against women cabin attendants on the basis of sex, in violation of Title VII and the Equal Pay Act, by compensating stewardesses and pursers unequally for equal work on "jobs the performance of which requires equal skill, effort and responsibility and which are performed under similar working conditions." More specifically the court found that NWA had discriminated in "willful violation" of the Equal Pay Act (a) by paying female stewardesses lower salaries and pensions than male pursers; (b) by providing female cabin attendants less expensive and less desirable layover accommodations than male cabin attendants; (c) by providing to male but not to female cabin attendants a uniform-cleaning allowance; and (d) "by paying Mary P. Laffey a lower salary as a purser than it pays to male pursers with equivalent length of cabin attendant service. . . ."

An Equal Pay Act claimant must show that her salary was lower than that paid by the employer to "employees of the opposite sex . . . for equal work on jobs the performance of which requires equal skill, effort, and responsibility, and which are performed under similar working conditions." The claimant bears the onus of demonstrating that the work unequally recompensed was "equal" within the meaning of the Act. Once this has been done, the claimant will prevail unless the employer asserts an affirmative defense that the wage differential is justified under one of the four exceptions enumerated in the Act—"(i) a seniority system; (ii) a merit system; (iii) a system which measures earnings by quantity or quality of production; or (iv) a differential based on any other factor other than sex." If one or more of these defenses is invoked, the employer bears the burden of proving that his policies fall within an exempted area. This interpretation of the procedural mechanics of the Equal Pay Act comports with the construction of other provisions of the Fair Labor Standards Act, of which the Equal Pay Act is a part, by which statutory exceptions and exemptions are considered matters of affirmative defense to be proven by the employer.

One of the more frequent controversies aroused by the Equal Pay Act has involved litigants' attempts to demonstrate that jobs with different titles and descriptions are in reality equal in their calls upon the job-holders. The contest often necessitates an assessment of the significance of differences in job demands advanced by the employer to show that the jobs are not equal. For "[it] is now well settled that the jobs need not be identical in every respect before the Equal Pay Act is applicable"; the phrase "equal work" does not mean that the jobs must be identical, but merely that they must be "substantially equal." A wage differential is justified only if it compensates for an appreciable variation in skill, effort or responsibility between otherwise comparable job work activities. . . .

Courts have consistently held that differences in the duties respectively assigned male and female employees must be "evaluated as part of the entire job." Thus, if in the aggregate the jobs require substantially similar skills, efforts and

responsibilities, the work will be adjudged equal despite minor variations.

When there is a disparity between salaries paid men and women for similar positions bearing different titles—such as pursers and stewardesses—the courts have scrutinized the evidence to discern whether the salary differential is justified by heterogeneous duties. . . .

An employer must show a consistent pattern of performance of additional duties in order to demonstrate that added duties are genuinely the motivating factor for the substantially higher pay. It is not sufficient that an increased workload might hypothetically have commanded a higher salary if it not in fact the basis for a significantly greater wage. The employer may not fabricate an after-the-fact rationalization for a sex-based pay difference. "[T]he semblance of [a] valid job classification system may not be allowed to mask the existence of wage discrimination based on sex."

Often, evidence superficially purporting to justify greater pay as compensation for added work is found upon close examination to have inconsistencies which render its evidentiary value weaker. Where, for example, all male employees receive greater pay but only some perform the extra tasks allegedly justifying that pay, a reasonable inference is that maleness—not the added chores—is the basis for the higher wage. This is particularly true if the duties are of peripheral importance and the increase in pay is substantial. Moreover, if some women without added compensation render the same extra performance that purportedly justified the pay differential favoring men, the inference becomes even stronger that the duties are irrelevant to the wage setting. Similar evidence of discriminatory wage patterns is to be found where women are paid only for the amount of time actually spent on the extra work, but men are uniformly paid at the higher rate regardless of whether or not they are doing the work. . . .

Applying these principles to the instant case, we perceive no error in the District Court's conclusion that the alleged differences in occupational duties proffered by NWA to justify the higher wage paid to pursers do not demonstrate that the stewardess and purser jobs are disparate. The court found that there is a uniform pay-scale for pursers which exceeds the pay-scale for stewardesses; and that these contrasting schemes are uncorrelated with pursers' and stewardesses' respective employment burdens. Pursers flying exclusively on domestic routes with no international documentation obligations are compensated evenly with pursers on international flights, despite the company's insistence that the onus of international flying is one of the explanations of the greater purser salary. To be sure, stewardesses who staff international flights do receive a foreign-flying supplement, but pursers' pay remains 20 to 35 percent larger than that of stewardesses of comparable seniority engaging solely in international travel.

Pursers consistently assigned to flights on which they do not function as the senior cabin attendant receive the same salary as those flying constantly in that capacity, while stewardesses rendering like service derive no supplemental income. A greater mantel of supervisory responsibility supposedly inherent in the position of senior cabin attendant thus does not exonerate the extra compensation awarded pursers. In fact, stewardesses' supervisory labors may exceed those of pursers. The more junior cabin attendants who need more supervision are relegated by the seniority flight-bidding system to the tourist-class section of the least desirable domestic flights, and the probability is that a stewardess acting as senior cabin attendant or senior-in-tourist will be charged with training as well as normal supervision. Pursers, possessing the more popular flights, are positioned in the first-class section with the more senior stewardesses, who require little or no supervision. The District Court further found that "a substantial percentage of the Company's overall utilization of pursers consisted of their assignment . . . exclusively, for months or years at a time," to flights on which their functions are "identical" to or "less demanding" than stewardesses' tasks.

In sum, stewardesses are confined to the same lower salaries whether or not flying as the senior cabin attendant, regardless of how taxing the service on their flights may be, and irrespective of the performance of documentation work. Pursers, at all times and under all conditions, received substantially superior salaries. This evidence leads convincingly to the conclusion that the contrast in pay is a consequence of the historical willingness of women to accept inferior financial rewards for equivalent work—precisely the out-moded practice which the Equal Pay Act sought to eradicate. . . .

It is not legally appropriate to accord stewardesses salary increments only when they serve as the senior cabin attendant. We have pointed to the inconsistencies between

occupational tasks and rewards to underscore our conviction that the District Court properly concluded that any greater duties demanded of pursers is not the foundation for their higher pay. In no way does this detract from the court's finding that the senior-cabin-attendant function was a mission that did not alter the basic equality of all cabin attendant jobs;

> The "supervisory" functions of Senior cabin attendants—whether purser or stewardess—are less important than, and require no greater skill, effort or responsibility, than the other functions assigned to all cabin attendants.

We cannot say that this finding is clearly erroneous, and it follows that all cabin attendants perform equal work and are legally entitled to places on equal salary scales. Although the senior cabin attendant is "responsible" for the cabin crew during the flight, the Secretary of Labor's regulations define job responsibility in terms of the degree of employee accountability for job performance. At the trial of this case, witnesses testified that both pursers and stewardesses are disciplined substantially less for unsatisfactory performance as senior cabin attendant than for subpar passenger service. And although the company imposes rigorous sanctions on cabin attendants charged with misconduct affecting customer relations, its records disclose only one instance of disciplinary action against a purser for failure to adequately monitor the work of other cabin attendants. This strongly suggests that the provision of high quality service to passengers—exacted of all cabin attendants—is the most important undertaking for which the company compensates pursers and stewardesses. The increased responsibility borne by the more senior personnel in both classifications is rewarded by larger salaries given to those on the upper rungs of the pay ladder, and this will continue with a combined stewardess-purser salary scale. . . .

We affirm the District Court's findings that NWA purser and stewardess positions are substantially equal within the intent of the Equal Pay Act and demand financial response at the purser-level of recompense. . . . **So ordered.**

Procedure under the Equal Pay Act

The Equal Pay Act is administered by the Equal Employment Opportunity Commission (EEOC). Prior to 1979, it was under the Department of Labor. In July 1979 the EEOC became the enforcement agency. The act provides for enforcement actions by individual employees (Section 16), or by the Secretary of Labor (Section 17), who has transferred that power to the EEOC.

There is no requirement that an individual filing a suit must file first with the EEOC. If the EEOC has filed a suit, it precludes individual suits on the same complaint. An individual suit must be filed within two years of the alleged violation. A violation will be held to be continuing for each payday in which unequal pay is received for equal work.

Remedies

An individual plaintiff's suit under Section 16 may recover the unpaid back wages due and may also receive an amount equal to the back wages as liquidated damages under the act. The trial court has discretion to deny recovery of the liquidated damages if it finds that the employer acted in good faith. An employer claiming to act in good faith must show some objective reason why it believed it was acting legally.

The back pay recovered by a private plaintiff can be awarded for the period from two years prior to the suit; however, if the court finds the violation was "willful," it may allow recovery of back pay for three years prior to filing suit. According to *Laffey*, a violation is willful when the employer was aware of the appreciable possibility that its actions might violate the act. A successful private plaintiff also is awarded legal fees and court costs.

The remedies available under a government suit include injunctions and back pay with interest. The act does not provide for the recovery of liquidated damages in a government suit.

The Age Discrimination in Employment Act

Discrimination in terms or conditions of employment based on age is prohibited by the Age Discrimination in Employment Act of 1967 (ADEA). The act's prohibitions, however, are limited to age discrimination against employees aged forty and over. It was intended to protect older workers who were more likely to be subjected to age discrimination in employment. (Although the ADEA's protection is limited to older workers, state equal employment opportunity laws may provide greater protection against age discrimination; the New York Human Rights Law, for example, prohibits age discrimination against employees eighteen and over.)

Coverage

The ADEA applies to employers, labor unions, and employment agencies. Employers involved in an industry affecting commerce, with twenty or more employees, are covered by the act. State and local governments are also included as employers; the Supreme Court upheld the inclusion of state and local governments in *EEOC* v. *Wyoming* (460 U.S. 226, 1983). Labor unions are covered if they operate a hiring hall or if they have twenty-five or more members and represent the employees of an employer covered by the act.

Provisions

The ADEA prohibits the refusal or failure to hire, the discharge, or any discrimination in compensation, terms, conditions, or privileges of employment because of an individual's age (forty and over). The act applies to employers, labor unions, and employment agencies. The main effect of the act is to prohibit mandatory retirement of employees. The act does not affect voluntary retirement by employees. It does provide for some limited exceptions and recognizes that age may be a BFOQ.

A plaintiff alleging a violation of the ADEA must establish a prima facie case that the employer has discriminated against the employee because of age. The employee must demonstrate that age was "*a* determining factor" in the employer's decision; it need not be the *only* determining factor.

The courts have adopted the Title VII procedures for establishing a claim under the ADEA; that is, the plaintiff must establish a prima facie case of age discrimination. The employer defendant must then offer a legitimate justification for the challenged action. If the defendant offers such a justification, the plaintiff can still show that the offered justification is a pretext for age discrimination.

Examples of violations of the ADEA include the mandatory retirement of workers over age fifty-five while allowing workers under fifty-five to transfer to another plant location, or the denial of a promotion to a qualified worker because the employee is over fifty.

Defenses.   When the plaintiff has established a prima facie case of age discrimination, the defendant must articulate some legitimate justification for the challenged action. The ADEA provides some specific exemptions and defenses on which the defendant may rely. The act recognizes that age may be a BFOQ and exempts executive employees from the prohibition on mandatory retirement. The act also provides that actions pursuant to a bona fide seniority system, retirement, pension or benefit system, or for good cause, or for a "reasonable factor other than age" are not violations.

The ADEA was amended in 1990 to provide an additional defense for employers—where the employer employs American workers in a foreign country and compliance with the ADEA would cause the employer to violate foreign law, the employer is excused from complying with the ADEA. The recent amendments also allow the employer to follow an early retirement incentive plan; the employer can subsidize early retirement benefits for employees or can supplement Social Security benefits to the level that the employees taking early retirement would have received at their regular retirement age.

Waivers.   The amendments also included a lengthy section dealing with waivers of ADEA claims by employees taking early retirement. An employer may ask that an employee receiving some special benefit upon early retirement waive any possible claims under the ADEA. The act requires that any such waivers must be voluntary and knowing, must be in writing, and must specifically refer to rights under the ADEA. Such waivers do not operate to waive any rights of the employee that arise after the waiver was executed. The employee waiving rights under the ADEA must receive some additional compensation for the waiver, above that to which he or she was already entitled. The employee must be advised, in writing, to consult an attorney about the waiver and must be given at least twenty-one days to consider the matter before deciding whether to execute the waiver; the employee must also be allowed to revoke the waiver up to seven days after signing it. If the waiver is part of a termination incentive program, the employer must give the employee forty-five days to consider the waiver. If the early retirement and waiver are offered to a class of employees, the employer must provide employees with the following information: a list of the class eligible for early retirement, the factors to determine eligibility for early retirement, the time limits for deciding upon early retirement, any possible adverse action if the employee declines to accept early retirement, and the date of such possible action. The employer must also pay 80 percent of the cost for the employee to consult an attorney about the waiver. For any waiver involving a claim that is already before the EEOC or a court, the employee must be given a "reasonable time" to consider the waiver.

In any suit involving a waiver of ADEA rights, the burden of proving that the waiver complies with the ADEA requirements is on the person asserting that the waiver is valid. Any waiver does not affect an employee's right to contact the EEOC or the EEOC's right to pursue any claim.

Executive Exemption. The ADEA allows the mandatory retirement of executive employees who are over the age of sixty-five. To qualify under this exemption, the employee must be in a bona fide executive or high policy-making position and, upon retirement, must be entitled to nonforfeitable retirement benefits of at least $44,000 annually. An employee who is within the executive exemption can be required to retire upon reaching age sixty-five; mandatory retirement prior to sixty-five is still prohibited.

Tenured Professors. The ADEA also allows "institutions of higher education" to set a mandatory retirement age of seventy for any employee "who is serving under a contract of unlimited tenure (or similar arrangement providing for unlimited tenure)." This exception is set to expire after December 31, 1993; the amendments inserting this exception in the ADEA also directed the EEOC to undertake a study to analyze the consequences of eliminating mandatory retirement at institutions of higher education.

Bona Fide Seniority or Benefit Plan. The ADEA allows an employer to observe the terms of a bona fide seniority system or employee benefit plan such as a retirement or pension plan as long as such plan or system is not "subterfuge to evade the purpose of this Act." The ADEA provides, however, that no seniority system or benefit plan "shall require or permit the involuntary retirement of any individual."

In *Public Employees' Retirement System of Ohio v. Betts* (492 U.S. 158, 1989), a majority of the Supreme Court held that the ADEA exception protected any age-based decisions taken pursuant to a bona fide benefit plan as long as the plan did not require mandatory retirement. In response to that decision, Congress passed the Older Workers Benefit Protection Act, which was signed into law by President Bush in October 1990. The law amends the ADEA to require that any differential treatment of older employees under benefit plans must be "cost-justified"—that is, the employer must demonstrate that the reduction in benefits is only to the extent required to achieve approximate cost equivalency of providing benefits to older and younger employees. General claims that the cost of insuring individuals increases with age are not sufficient; the employer must show that the specific level of reductions for older workers in a particular benefit program is no greater than necessary to compensate for the higher cost of providing such benefits for older workers.

Factor Other than Age.

The ADEA allows employers to differentiate between employees when the differentiation is based on a reasonable factor other than age. For example, an employer may use a productivity-based pay system, even if older employees earn less than younger employees because they do not produce as much as younger employees. The basis for determining pay would be the employees' production, not their age. Similarly, when a work-force reduction is carried out pursuant to an objective evaluation of all employees, it does not violate the act simply because a greater number of older workers than younger workers were laid off, according to *Mastie* v. *Great Lakes Steel Co.* (424 F. Supp. 1299, E.D. Mich. 1976). However, when an employer's policy is to hire workers with five years or less experience, the policy discriminates against older workers and violates the ADEA, according to *Geller* v. *Markham* (635 F.2d 1027, *cert. denied,* 451 U.S. 945, 2d Cir. 1980).

The employer is permitted to discharge or discipline employees for good cause. Such disciplining of a worker aged fifty would not violate the ADEA.

Bona Fide Occupational Qualification.

The ADEA does recognize that age may be a BFOQ for some jobs. The act states that a BFOQ must be reasonably necessary to the normal operation of the employer's business. In *Hodgson* v. *Greyhound Lines, Inc.* (499 F.2d 859, 7th Cir. 1977), the court held that Greyhound could refuse to hire applicants for bus driver positions if the candidates were over thirty-five years old, because of passenger safety considerations; a test pilot could not be mandatorily retired at age fifty-two, according to *Houghton* v. *McDonnell Douglas Corp.* (552 F.2d 561, 8th Cir. 1977).

The ADEA was amended in 1987 to permit state or local laws that set a mandatory retirement age less than seventy for firefighters or law enforcement officers, as long as such laws were in effect as of March 3, 1983. This provision will expire after December 31, 1993.

The Supreme Court considered the question of what is required to qualify as a BFOQ under the ADEA in the following case. (Note that the case was decided prior to the 1987 amendment to the ADEA that removed the age seventy upper limit on the act's protection.)

WESTERN AIR LINES, INC. v. CRISWELL

472 U.S. 400 (Supreme Court of the United States, 1985)

STEVENS, J.

The petitioner, Western Air Lines, Inc. requires that its flight engineers retire at age 60. Although the Age Discrimination in Employment Act of 1967 (ADEA) generally prohibits mandatory retirement before age 70, the Act provides an exception "where age is a bona fide occupational qualification [BFOQ] reasonably necessary to the normal operation of the particular business." A jury concluded that Western's mandatory retirement rule did not qualify as a BFOQ even though it purportedly was adopted for safety reasons. The question here is whether the jury was properly instructed on the elements of the BFOQ defense.

In its commercial airline operations, Western operates a variety of aircraft, including the Boeing 727 and the McDonnell-Douglas DC-10. These aircraft require three crew members in the cockpit: a captain, a first officer, and a flight engineer. "The 'captain' is the pilot and controls the aircraft. He is responsible for all phases of its operation. The 'first officer' is the copilot and assists the captain. The 'flight engineer' usually monitors a side-facing instrument panel. He does not operate the flight controls unless the captain and the first officer become incapacitated."

A regulation of the Federal Aviation Administration prohibits any person from serving as a pilot or first officer on a commercial flight "if that person has reached his 60th birthday." The FAA has justified the retention of mandatory retirement for the pilots on the theory that "incapacitating medical events" and "adverse psychological, emotional and physical changes" occur as a consequence of aging. "The inability to detect or predict with precision an individual's risk of sudden or subtle incapacitation, in the face of known age-related risks counsels against relaxation of the rule."

At the same time, the FAA has refused to establish a mandatory retirement age for flight engineers. "While a flight engineer has important duties which contribute to the safe operation of the airplane, he or she may not assume the responsibilities of the pilot in command." Moreover, available statistics establish that flight engineers have rarely been a contributing cause or factor in commercial aircraft "accidents" or "incidents."

In 1978, respondents Criswell and Starley were Captains operating DC-10s for Western. Both men celebrated their 60th birthdays in July 1978. Under the collective-bargaining agreement in effect between Western and the union, cockpit crew members could obtain open positions by bidding in order of seniority. In order to avoid mandatory retirement under the FAA's under-age-60 rule for pilots, Criswell and Starley applied for reassignment as flight engineers. Western denied both requests, ostensibly on the ground that both employees were members of the company's retirement plan which required all crew members to retire at age 60. For the same reason, respondent Ron, a career flight engineer, was also retired in 1978 after his 60th birthday. . . .

Criswell, Starley, and Ron brought this action against Western contending that the under-age-60 qualification for the position of flight engineer violated the ADEA. In the District Court, Western defended, in part, on the theory that the age-60 rule is a BFOQ "reasonable necessary" to the safe operation of the airline. All parties submitted evidence concerning the nature of the flight engineer's tasks, the physiological and psychological traits required to perform them, and the availability of those traits among persons over age 60.

As the District Court summarized, the evidence at trial established that the flight engineer's "normal duties are less critical to the safety of flight than those of a pilot." The flight engineer, however, does have critical functions in emergency situations and, of course, might cause considerable disruption in the event of his own medical emergency.

The actual capabilities of persons over age 60, and the ability to detect disease or a precipitous decline in their faculties, were the subject of conflicting medical testimony. Western's expert witness, a former FAA Deputy Federal Air Surgeon, was especially concerned about the possibility of a "cardiovascular event" such as a heart attack. He testified that "with advancing age the likelihood of onset of disease increases and that in persons over age 60 it could not be predicted whether and when such diseases would occur."

The plaintiff's experts, on the other hand, testified that physiological deterioration is caused by disease, not aging, and that "it was feasible to determine on the basis of individual medical examinations whether flight deck crew members, including those over age 60, were physically qualified to continue to fly." These conclusions were corroborated by the nonmedical evidence:

> The record also reveals that both the FAA and the airlines have been able to deal with the health problems of pilots on an individualized basis. Pilots who have been grounded because of alcoholism or cardiovascular disease have been recertified by

the FAA and allowed to resume flying. Pilots who were unable to pass the necessary examination to maintain their FAA first class medical certificates, but who continued to qualify for second class medical certificates were allowed to "downgrade" from pilot to [flight engineer]. There is nothing in the record to indicate that these flight deck crew members are physically better able to perform their duties than flight engineers over age of 60 who have not experienced such events or that they are less likely to become incapacitated.

Moreover, several large commercial airlines have flight engineers over age 60 "flying the line" without any reduction in their safety record.

The jury was instructed that the "BFOQ defense is available only if it is reasonably necessary to the normal operation or essence of defendant's business." The jury was informed that the "essence of Western's business is the safe transportation of their passengers." The jury was also instructed:

> One method by which defendant Western may establish a BFOQ in this case is to prove:
> (1) That in 1978, when these plaintiffs were retired, it was highly impractical for Western to deal with each second officer over age 60 on an individualized basis to determine his particular ability to perform his job safely; and
> (2) That some second officers over age 60 possess traits of a physiological, psychological or other nature which preclude safe and efficient job performance that cannot be ascertained by means other than knowing their age.
> In evaluating the practicability to defendant Western of dealing with second officers over age 60 on an individualized basis, with respect to the medical testimony, you should consider the state of the medical art as it existed in July 1978.

The jury rendered a verdict for the plaintiffs and awarded damages. After trial, the District Court granted equitable relief, explaining in a written opinion why he found no merit in Western's BFOQ defense to the mandatory retirement rule.

On appeal, Western made various arguments attacking the verdict and judgment below, but the Court of Appeals affirmed in all respects. In particular, the Court of Appeals rejected Western's contention that the instruction on the BFOQ defense was insufficiently deferential to the airline's legitimate concern for the safety of its passengers. We granted certiorari to consider the merits of this question.

Throughout the legislative history of the ADEA, one empirical fact is repeatedly emphasized: the process of psychological and physiological degeneration caused by aging varies with each individual. "The basic research in the field of aging has established that there is a wide range of individual

physical ability regardless of age." As a result, many older American workers perform at levels equal or superior to their younger colleagues....

... Congress responded with the enactment of the ADEA. The preamble declares that the purpose of the ADEA is "to promote employment of older persons based on their ability rather than age [and] to prohibit arbitrary age discrimination in employment." Section 4(a)(1) makes it "unlawful for an employer ... to fail or refuse to hire or to discharge any individual or otherwise discriminate against any individual with respect to his compensation, terms, conditions, or privileges of employment, because of such individual's age." ...

... Congress recognized that classifications based on age, like classifications based on religion, sex, or national origin, may sometimes serve as a necessary proxy for neutral employment qualifications essential to the employer's business. The diverse employment situations in various industries, however, forced Congress to adopt a "case-by-case basis ... as the underlying rule in the administration of the legislation." Congress offered only general guidance on when an age classification might be permissible by borrowing a concept and statutory language from Title VII of the Civil Rights Act of 1964 and providing that such a classification is lawful "where age is a bona fide occupational qualification reasonably necessary to the normal operation of the particular business."

Shortly after the passage of the Act, the Secretary of Labor, who was at that time charged with its enforcement, adopted regulations declaring that the BFOQ exception to ADEA has only "limited scope and application" and "must be construed narrowly." The EEOC adopted the same narrow construction of the BFOQ exception after it was assigned authority for enforcing the statute. The restrictive language of the statute, and the consistent interpretation of the administrative agencies charged with enforcing the statute, convince us that, like its Title VII counterpart, the BFOQ exception "was in fact meant to be an extremely narrow exception to the general prohibition" of age discrimination contained in the ADEA.

In *Usery* v. *Tamiami Trail Tours, Inc.,* the Court of Appeals for the Fifth Circuit was called upon to evaluate the merits of a BFOQ defense to a claim of age discrimination. Tamiami Trail Tours, Inc., had a policy of refusing to hire persons over-age-40 as intercity bus drivers. At trial, the bus company introduced testimony supporting its theory that the hiring policy was a BFOQ based upon safety considerations—the need to employ persons who have a low risk of accidents. In evaluating this contention, the Court of Appeals drew on its Title VII precedents, and concluded that two inquiries were relevant.

First, the court recognized that some job qualifications may be so peripheral to the central mission of the employer's business that *no* age discrimination can be "reasonably *necessary* to the normal operation of the particular business." The bus company justified the age qualification for hiring its drivers on safety considerations, but the court concluded that this claim was to be evaluated under an objective standard:

> [T]he job qualifications which the employer invokes to justify his discrimination must be *reasonably necessary* to the essence of his business—here the *safe* transportation of bus passengers from one point to another. The greater the safety factor, measured by the likelihood of harm and the probable severity of that harm in case of an accident, the more stringent may be the job qualifications designed to insure safe driving.

This inquiry "adjusts to the safety factor" by ensuring that the employer's restrictive job qualifications are "reasonably necessary" to further the overriding interest in public safety. In *Tamiami,* the court noted that no one had seriously challenged the bus company's safety justification for hiring drivers with a low risk of having accidents.

Second, the court recognized that the ADEA requires that age qualifications be something more than "convenient" or "reasonable"; they must be "reasonably necessary . . . to the particular business," and this is only so when the employer is compelled to rely on age as a proxy for the safety-related job qualifications validated in the first inquiry. This showing could be made in two ways. The employer could establish that it "had reasonable cause to believe, that is, a factual basis for believing, that all or substantially all [persons over the age qualifications] would be unable to perform safely and efficiently the duties of the job involved.'" In *Tamiami,* the employer did not seek to justify its hiring qualification under this standard.

Alternatively, the employer could establish that age was a legitimate proxy for the safety-related job qualifications by proving that it is "impossible or highly impractical" to deal with the older employees on an individualized basis. "One method by which the employer can carry this burden is to establish that some members of the discriminated-against class possess a trait precluding safe and efficient job performance that cannot be ascertained by means other than knowledge of the applicant's membership in the class." In *Tamiami,* the medical evidence on this point was conflicting, but the District Court had found that individual exami-

nations could not determine which individuals over the age of 40 would be unable to operate the buses safely. The Court of Appeals found that this finding of fact was not "clearly erroneous," and affirmed the District Court's judgment for the bus company on the BFOQ defense. . . .

Every Court of Appeals that has confronted a BFOQ defense based on safety considerations has analyzed the problem consistently with the *Tamiami* standard. An EEOC regulation embraces the same criteria. Considering the narrow language of the BFOQ exception, the parallel treatment of such questions under Title VII, and the uniform application of the standard by the federal courts, the EEOC and Congress, we conclude that this two-part inquiry properly identifies the relevant considerations for resolving a BFOQ defense to an age-based qualification purportedly justified by considerations of safety.

In the trial court, Western preserved an objection to any instruction in the *Tamiami* mold, claiming that "any instruction pertaining to the statutory phrase 'reasonably necessary to the normal operation of [defendant's] business' . . . is irrelevant to and confusing for the deliberations of the jury." . . . In this Court, Western slightly changes it course. The airline now acknowledges that the *Tamiami* standard identifies the relevant general inquiries that must be made in evaluating the BFOQ defense. However, Western claims that in several respects the instructions given below were insufficiently protective of public safety. Western urges that we interpret or modify the *Tamiami* standard to weigh these concerns in the balance.

Western relied on two different kinds of job qualifications to justify its mandatory retirement policy. First, it argued that flight engineers should have a low risk of incapacitation or psychological and physiological deterioration. At this vague level of analysis the plaintiffs have not seriously disputed—nor could they—that the qualification of good health for a vital crew member is reasonably necessary to the essence of the airline's operations. Instead, they have argued that age is not a necessary proxy for that qualification.

On a more specific level, Western argues that flight engineers must meet the same stringent qualifications as pilots, and that it was therefore quite logical to extend to flight engineers the FAA's age-60 retirement rule for pilots. Although the FAA's rule for pilots, adopted for safety reasons, is relevant evidence in the airline's BFOQ defense, it is not to be accorded conclusive weight. The extent to which the rule is probative varies with the weight of the evidence supporting its safety rationale and "the congruity between the . . . occupations at issue." In this case, the evidence clearly established that the FAA, Western, and other airlines all recognized that the qualifications for a flight engineer were less rigorous than those required for a pilot.

In the absence of persuasive evidence supporting its position, Western nevertheless argues that the jury should have been instructed to defer to "Westerns selection of job qualifications for the position of [flight engineer] that are reasonable in light of the safety risks." This proposal is plainly at odds with Congress' decision, in adopting the ADEA, to subject such management decisions to a test of objective justification in a court of law. The BFOQ standard adopted in the statute is one of "reasonable necessity," not reasonableness.

In adopting that standard, Congress did not ignore the public interest in safety. That interest is adequately reflected in instructions that track the language of the statute. When an employer establishes that a job qualification has been carefully formulated to respond to documented concerns for public safety, it will not be overly burdensome to persuade a trier of fact that the qualification is "reasonably necessary" to safe operation of the business. The uncertainty implicit in the concept of managing safety risks always makes it "reasonably necessary" to err on the side of caution in a close case. The employer cannot be expected to establish the risk of an airline accident "to a certainty, for certainty would require running the risk until a tragic accident would prove that the judgment was sound." When the employer's argument has a credible basis in the record, it is difficult to believe that a jury of lay persons—many of whom no doubt have flown or could expect to fly on commercial air carriers—would not defer in a close case to the airline's judgment. Since the instructions in this case would not have prevented the airline from raising this contention to the jury in closing argument, we are satisfied that the verdict is a consequence of a defect in Western's proof rather than a defect in the trial court's instructions. . . .

Western contended below that the ADEA only requires that the employer establish "a rational basis in fact" for believing that identification of those persons lacking suitable qualifications cannot occur on an individualized basis. This "rational basis in fact" standard would have been tantamount to an instruction to return a verdict in the defendant's favor. Because that standard conveys a meaning that is significantly different from that conveyed by the statutory phrase "reasonably necessary," it was correctly rejected by the trial court.

Western argues that a "rational basis" standard should be adopted because medical disputes can never be proved "to a certainty" and because juries should not be permitted "to resolve bona fide conflicts among medical experts respecting the adequacy of individualized testing." The jury, however, need not be convinced beyond all doubt that medical testing is impossible, but only that the proposition is true "on a preponderance of the evidence." Moreover, Western's attack on the wisdom of assigning the resolution of complex questions to 12 lay persons is inconsistent with the structure of the ADEA. Congress expressly decided that problems involving age discrimination in employment should be resolved on a "case-by-case basis" by proof to a jury.

The "rational basis" standard is also inconsistent with the preference for individual evaluation expressed in the language and legislative history of the ADEA. Under the Act, employers are to evaluate employees . . . on their merits and not their age. In the BFOQ defense, Congress provided a limited exception to this general principle, but required that employers validate any discrimination as "reasonably necessary to the normal operation of the particular business." It might well be "rational" to require mandatory retirement at *any* age less than 70, but that result would not comply with Congress' direction that employers must justify the rationale for the age chosen. Unless an employer can establish a substantial basis for believing that all or nearly all employees above an age lack the qualifications required for the position, the age selected for mandatory retirement less than 70 must be an age at which it is highly impractical for the employer to insure by individual testing that its employees will have the necessary qualifications for the job.

Western argues that its lenient standard is necessary because "where qualified experts disagree as to whether persons over a certain age can be dealt with on an individual basis, an employer must be allowed to resolve that controversy in a conservative manner." This argument incorrectly assumes that all expert opinion is entitled to equal weight, and virtually ignores the function of the trier of fact in evaluating conflicting testimony. In this case, the jury may well have attached little weight to the testimony of Western's expert witness. A rule that would require the jury to defer to the judgment of any expert witness testifying for the employer, no matter how unpersuasive, would allow some employers to give free reign to the stereotype of older workers that congress decried in the legislative history of the ADEA.

When an employee covered by the Act is able to point to reputable businesses in the same industry that choose to eschew reliance on mandatory retirement earlier than age 70, when the employer itself relies on individualized testing in similar circumstances, and when the administrative agency with primary responsibility for maintaining airline safety has determined that individualized testing is not impractical for the relevant position, the employer's attempt to justify its decision on the basis of the contrary opinion of experts—solicited for the purposes of litigation—is hardly convincing on any objective standard short of complete deference. Even in cases involving public safety, the ADEA plainly does not permit the trier of fact to give complete deference to the employer's decision.

The judgment of the Court of Appeals is **Affirmed.**

Procedures under the ADEA

The ADEA is enforced and administered by the EEOC. The EEOC acquired the enforcement responsibility from the Department of Labor pursuant to a reorganization in 1978. The ADEA allows suits by private individuals as well as by the EEOC.

An individual alleging a violation of the ADEA must file a written complaint with the EEOC and with the state or local equal employment opportunity (EEO) agency, if one exists. Unlike Title VII, however, the individual may file simultaneously with both the EEOC and the state or local agency, there is no need to go to the state or local agency prior to filing with the EEOC. The complaint must be filed with the EEOC within 180 days of the alleged violation, if no state or local agency exists. If such an agency exists, the complaint must be filed with the EEOC within 30 days of the termination of proceedings by the state or local agency, and it must be filed not later than 300 days from the alleged violation.

After filing with the EEOC and the state or local EEO agency, the individual must wait sixty days before filing suit in federal court. Although there is no requirement that the individual wait for a right-to-sue notice from the EEOC, the sixty-day period is to allow time for a voluntary settlement of the complaint. If the EEOC dismisses the complaint, or otherwise terminates proceedings on the complaint, it is required to notify the individual filing the complaint. The individual then has ninety days from receipt of the notice to file suit. Even though the individual must wait *at least* sixty days from filing with the agencies before bringing suit in court, the court suit may be filed any time up to two years from the alleged violation. When the violation is "willful," the individual has until three years from the alleged violation to file suit. An individual can file an age discrimination suit in federal court even if the state or local EEO agency has ruled that the employee was not the victim of age discrimination, according to the Supreme Court decision in *Astoria Federal Savings & Loan* v. *Solimino* (___ U.S. ___, 111 S.Ct. 2166, 1991). If the EEOC files suit under the ADEA, the EEOC suit supersedes any ADEA suit filed by the individual or any state agency. Unlike Title VII, which provides for a trial before a judge only, the ADEA allows for a jury trial.

The Supreme Court recently held that agreements to arbitrate employment disputes may require that ADEA claims be submitted to arbitration rather than be the subject of a court suit. In *Gilmer* v. *Interstate/Johnson Lane Corp.* (___ U.S.___, 111 S.Ct. 1647, 1991), the Court decided that a stockbroker was bound by his pledge to arbitrate any dispute arising from his employment, even if it involved allegations of age discrimination.

Suits by Federal Employees.   Despite the fact that the federal government is not included in the ADEA's definition of employer, Section 15 of the act provides that personnel actions in most federal government positions shall be made free from discrimination based on age. The ADEA protects federal workers "who are at least 40 years of age."

Complaints of age discrimination involving federal employees are now handled by the EEOC. A federal employee agency must file the complaint with the EEOC within 180 days of the alleged violation; the employee may file suit in federal court after 30 days from filing with the EEOC. The ADEA provides only for private suits in cases involving complaints by federal employees. No provision is made for suits by the EEOC.

Government Suits.   In addition to private suits, the ADEA provides for suits by the responsible government agency (now the EEOC, formerly the Secretary of Labor) against nonfederal employers. The EEOC must attempt to settle the complaint voluntarily before filing suit; there is no specific time limitation for this required conciliation effort. Once conciliation has been attempted, the EEOC may file suit anytime up to two years from the date of the alleged violation. The limitation period is extended to three years for "willful" violations.

Remedies under the ADEA

The remedies available under the ADEA are similar to those available under the Equal Pay Act. Successful private plaintiffs can recover any back wages owing; they may also recover an equal amount as liquidated damages if the employer acted "willfully." The Supreme Court, in the 1985 case of *Trans World Airlines, Inc.* v. *Thurston* (469 U.S. 111, 105 S.Ct. 613), held that an employer acts willfully when "the employer either knew or showed reckless disregard for the matter of whether its conduct was prohibited by the ADEA." Injunctive relief is also available, and legal fees and costs are recoverable by the successful private plaintiff.

Remedies in suits by the EEOC may include injunctions and back pay. Liquidated damages, however, are not available in such suits.

Executive Order No. 11246

Executive Order No. 11246, signed by President Johnson in 1965, provides the basis for the federal government contract compliance program. Under that executive order, as amended, firms doing business with the federal government must agree not to discriminate in employment on the basis of race, color, religion, national origin, or sex.

Equal Employment Requirements

The **contract compliance program** is administered by the Secretary of Labor through the Office of Federal Contract Compliance Programs (OFCCP). The OFCCP has issued extensive regulations spelling out the requirements and procedures under the contract compliance programs. The regulations provide that all firms having contracts or subcontracts exceeding $10,000 with the federal government must agree to include a no-discrimination clause in the contract. The clause, which is binding on the firm for the duration of the contract, requires the contractor to agree not to discriminate in employment on the basis of race, color, religion, sex, or national origin. The contractor also agrees to state in all employment advertisements that all qualified applicants will be considered without regard to race, color, religion, sex, or national origin and to inform each labor union representing its employees of its obligations under the program. The contracting firm is also required to include the same type of no-discrimination clause in every subcontract or purchase order pursuant to the federal contract.

The Secretary of Labor, through the OFCCP, may investigate any allegations of violations by contracting firms. Penalties for violation include the suspension or cancellation of the firm's government contract and the disbarment of the firm from future government contracts.

Affirmative Action Requirements

In addition to requiring the no-discrimination clause, the OFCCP regulations may require that a contracting firm develop a written plan regarding its employees. Firms with contracts of services or supply for over $50,000 and having fifty or more employees are required to maintain formal written programs, called **affirmative action plans,** for the utilization of women and minorities in their work force. Affirmative action plans, which must be updated annually, must contain an analysis of the employer's use of women and minorities for each job category in the work force. When job categories reveal an underutilization of women and minorities—that is, fewer women or minorities employed than would reasonably be expected based on their availability in the relevant labor market—then the plan must set out specific hiring goals and timetables for improving the employment of women and minorities. The firm is expected to make a good-faith effort to reach those goals; the goals set are more in the nature of targets than hard-and-fast "quotas." The firms must submit annual reports of the results of their efforts to meet the goals set out in the affirmative action plan.

Firms holding federal or federally assisted construction contracts or subcontracts over $10,000 are also subject to affirmative action requirements. The contracting firm must comply with the goals and timetables for employment of women and minorities set periodically by the OFCCP. Those construction industry goals are set for "covered geographic areas" of the country, based on census data for the areas. The "goals and timetables" approach to affirmative action for construction industry employees was held to be constitutional and legal under Title VII, in *Contractors Ass'n of Eastern Pennsylvania* v. *Shultz* (442 F.2d 159, 3rd Cir. 1971).

Procedure under Executive Order No. 11246

Individuals alleging a violation of a firm's obligations under Executive Order No. 11246 may file complaints with the OFCCP within 180 days of the alleged violation. The OFCCP may refer the complaint to the EEOC for investigation, or it may make its own investigation. If it makes its own investigation, it must report to the director of the OFCCP within sixty days.

If there is reason to believe that a violation has occurred, the firm is issued a show-cause notice, directing it to show why enforcement proceedings should not be instituted; the firm has thirty days to provide such evidence. During this thirty-day period the OFCCP is also required to make efforts to resolve the violation through mediation and conciliation.

If the firm fails to show cause or if the conciliation is unsuccessful, the director of the OFCCP may refer the complaint to the Secretary of Labor for administrative enforcement proceedings, or to the Justice Department for judicial enforcement proceedings. The individual filing the complaint may not file suit privately against the firm alleged to be in violation, but the individual may bring suit to force the OFCCP to enforce the regulations and requirements under the Executive Order (see *Legal Aid Society* v. *Brennan,* 608 F.2d 1319, 9th Cir. 1979).

Administrative enforcement proceedings involve a hearing before an Administrative Law Judge (ALJ). The ALJ's decision is subject to review by the Secretary of Labor; the secretary's decision may be subjected to judicial review in the federal courts (see *Firestone Co.* v. *Marshall,* 507 F. Supp. 1330, E.D. Texas 1981).

Firms found to be in violation of the obligations under the executive order, either through the courts or the administrative proceedings, may be subject to injunctions and required to pay back pay and grant retroactive seniority to affected employees. The firm may also have its government contract suspended or canceled and may be declared ineligible for future government contracts. Firms declared ineligible must demonstrate compliance with the executive order's requirements in order to be reinstated by the director of the OFCCP.

The Veterans' Reemployment Rights Act

During Operation Desert Storm, the military operation against Iraq in 1991, the U.S. military forces called a huge number of reservists to active military duty. If a member of the reserves is called to active military duty, does the employer of that person have an obligation to guarantee the job of that person when she or he is discharged from active duty? The Veterans' Reemployment Rights Act, 38 U.S.C. Section 2024(d), states that an employee called to active duty or training

"... shall upon request be granted a leave of absence by such person's employer for the period required to perform active duty for training or inactive duty training in the Armed Forces of the United States. Upon such employee's release from a period of such ... [duty,] ... such employee shall be permitted to return to such employee's position with such seniority, status, pay, and vacation as such employee would have had if such employee had not been absent for such purposes."

The Veterans' Reemployment Rights Act guarantees the returning employee's job, but the act does not state for how long a period the guarantee lasts. In *King* v. *St. Vincent's Hospital* (__ U.S. __, 112 S.Ct. 570, 1991), the Supreme Court held that the reemployment right lasts as long as the employee is in the armed forces. King had requested a leave of absence to serve a three-year tour of duty in the army. The employer refused, on the grounds that the request for a three-year leave was unreasonable, and therefore was not protected under the act. The Supreme Court's decision states that there is no limit to how long the employer must guarantee the employee's job; the Court refused to imply a limit that the length of the leave be "reasonable."

The Vocational Rehabilitation Act

The Vocational Rehabilitation Act of 1973 protects the employment rights of handicapped persons; the act's provisions prohibit discrimination against otherwise qualified handicapped persons. The act defines "handicapped individual" as

> any person who (A) has a physical or mental impairment, which substantially limits one or more of such person's major life activities, (B) has a record of such an impairment, or (C) is regarded as having such an impairment.

The act imposes obligations not to discriminate against otherwise qualified handicapped individuals. According to the Supreme Court decision in *Southeastern Community College* v. *Davis* (442 U.S. 397, 1979), a person is a qualified handicapped individual if the person "is able to meet all . . . requirements in spite of his handicap." The individual claiming to be qualified has the burden of demonstrating his or her ability to meet all physical requirements legitimately necessary for the performance of duties. An employer is not required to hire a handicapped person who is not capable of performing the duties of the job, however, the regulations under the act require the employer to make "reasonable accommodation" to the disabilities of individuals.

Reasonable accommodations required under the Rehabilitation Act are similar in concept to the accommodations required under Title VII to the religious beliefs of employees (see the *Hardison* case in Chapter 13). Reasonable accommodations include the minimal realignment or assignment of job duties, or the provision of certain assistance devices. For example, an employer could reassign certain filing or reception duties from the requirements of a typist position in order to accommodate an individual confined to a wheelchair. An employer could also be required to equip telephones with amplifiers to accommodate an employee's hearing disability. Although the extent of accommodation required must be determined case by case, drastic realignment of work assignments or the undertaking of severe financial costs by an employer would be considered "unreasonable" and would not be required.

Two main provisions of the Vocational Rehabilitation Act deal with discrimination against the handicapped. Section 503 prohibits such discrimination by employers with federal contracts, and Section 504 prohibits the denial of participation in or the benefits of any federally funded activity to an otherwise qualified handicapped individual.

Section 503

Section 503 uses an approach similar to that under Executive Order No. 11246 to enforce a nondiscrimination obligation for federal contractors. Firms having contracts or subcontracts with the federal government for more than $2,500 are required to include in the contract a clause requiring them to undertake affirmative action to employ and advance qualified handicapped individuals. Enforcement of this obligation is by the OFCCP. Contracting firms are also subject to the requirements for written affirmative action plans if their contracts meet the specified OFCCP limits.

The procedures and sanctions applicable to complaints under Executive Order No. 11246 are used for enforcement of Section 503 obligations. There is no private right for individuals to sue under Section 503.

Section 504

Section 504 imposes obligations of nondiscrimination against qualified handicapped individuals on anyone administering a program receiving federal funding. Federal agencies administering such funding are also under the no-discrimination obligation.

Section 504 applies to any person receiving *any* federal funding; no minimum amount or threshold is specified. Therefore, any amount of federal funding received by a group or organization, no matter how small, carries with it the no-discrimination requirement.

Section 504 prohibits the denial of a qualified handicapped person to participate in the activity, or receive the benefits of such activity, when the activity is federally funded. In *Southeastern Community College v. Davis* (442 U.S. 397, 1979), the Supreme Court upheld a college's refusal to admit a woman with a severe hearing disability into the registered nursing program. The woman's disability, which was not correctable by a hearing aid, would create problems in carrying out her duties during the clinical portions of her training. The college was not required to redesign the program to accommodate her disability.

From the general wording of Section 504, it appears that its prohibition reaches discrimination in employment by organizations receiving federal funding. However, courts that have considered this issue generally have held that Section 504 reached discrimination in employment only when the federal funding was specifically granted for employment purposes. The question reached the Supreme Court in the following case.

CONSOLIDATED RAIL CORP. v. DARRONE

465 U.S. 624 (Supreme Court of the United States, 1984)

POWELL, J.

This case requires us to clarify the scope of the private right of action to enforce Section 504 of the Rehabilitation Act of 1973, that prohibits discrimination against the handicapped by federal grant receipts. . . .

The Rehabilitation Act of 1973 establishes a comprehensive federal program aimed at improving the lot of the handicapped. Among its purposes are to "promote and expand employment opportunities in the public and private sectors for handicapped individuals and place such individuals in employment." To further these purposes, Congress enacted Section 504 of the Act. That section provides that:

> No otherwise qualified handicapped individual . . . shall, solely by reason of his handicap, be excluded from the participation in, be denied the benefits of, or be subjected to discrimination under any program or activity receiving Federal financial assistance.

The language of the section is virtually identical to that of Section 601 of Title VI of the Civil Rights Act of 1964, that similarly bars discrimination (on the ground of race, color, or national origin) in federally-assisted programs.

In 1978, Congress amended the Rehabilitation Act to specify the means of enforcing its ban on discrimination. In particular, Section 505(a)(2), made available the "remedies, procedure, and rights set forth in Title VI of the Civil Rights Act of 1964" to victims of discrimination in violation of Section 504 of the Act.

Petitioner, Consolidated Rail Corporation ("Conrail"), was formed pursuant to Subchapter III of the Regional Rail Reorganization Act. . . . The Act, passed in response to the insolvency of a number of railroads in the Northeast and Midwest, established Conrail to acquire and operate the rail properties of the insolvent railroads and to integrate these properties into an efficient national rail transportation system. Under Section 216 of the Act, the United States, acting through the United States Railway Association, purchases debentures and series A preferred stock of the corporation "at such times and in such amounts as may be required and

requested by the corporation," but "in accordance with the terms and conditions . . . prescribed by the Association. . . ." The statute permits the proceeds from these sales to be devoted to maintenance of rail properties, capital needs, refinancing of indebtedness, or working capital. Under this statutory authorization, Conrail has sold the United States $3.28 billion in securities.

Conrail also received federal funds under subchapter V of the Act, now repealed, to provide for reassignment and retraining of railroad workers whose jobs were affected by the reorganization. And Conrail now receives federal funds under Section 1143(a) of the Northeast Rail Service Act, that provides termination allowances of up to $25,000 to workers who lose their jobs as a result of reorganization.

In 1979, Thomas LeStrange filed suit against petitioner for violation of rights conferred by Section 504 of the Rehabilitation Act.* The complaint alleged that the Erie Lackawanna Railroad, to which Conrail is the successor in interest, had employed the plaintiff as a locomotive engineer; that an accident had required amputation of plaintiff's left hand and forearm in 1971; and that, after LeStrange was disabled, the Erie Lackawanna Railroad, and then Conrail, had refused to employ him although it had no justification for finding him unfit to work.

The District Court, following the decision of *Trageser* v. *Libbie Rehabilitation Center, Inc.,* granted petitioner's motion for summary judgment on the ground that the plaintiff did not have "standing" to bring a private action under Section 504. In *Trageser,* the Fourth Circuit had held that Section 505(a)(2) of the Rehabilitation Act incorporated into that act the limitation found in Section 604 of Title VI, which provides that employment discrimination is actionable only when the employer receives federal financial assistance the "primary objective" of which is "to provide employment." The District Court concluded that the aid provided to petitioner did not satisfy the "primary objective" test.

The Court of Appeals reversed and remanded to the District Court. There was no opinion for the court, but all three judges of the panel agreed that the cause of action for employment discrimination under Section 504 was not properly limited to situations "where a primary objective

---

*Respondent, the administratrix of LeStrange's estate, was substituted as a party before his Court upon the death of LeStrange.

of the federal financial assistance is to provide employment." ...

We granted certiorari to resolve the conflict among the circuits and to consider other questions under the Rehabilitation Act. ...

We are met initially by petitioner's contention that the death of the plaintiff LeStrange has mooted the case and deprives the Court of jurisdiction for that reason. Petitioner concedes, however, that there remains a case or controversy if LeStrange's estate may recover money that would have been owed to LeStrange. Without determining the extent to which money damages are available under Section 504, we think it clear that Section 504 authorizes a plaintiff who alleges intentional discrimination to bring an equitable action for backpay. The case therefore is not moot. ...

The Court of Appeals rejected the argument that petitioner may be sued under Section 504 only if the primary objective of the federal aid that it receives is to promote employment. Conrail relies particularly on Section 604 of Title VI. This section limits the applicability of Title VI to "employment practice[s] ... where a *primary objective* of the federal financial assistance is to provide employment" (emphasis added). As noted above, Section 505(a)(2) of the Rehabilitation Act, as amended in 1978, adopted the remedies and rights provided in Title VI. Accordingly, Conrail's basic position in this case is that Section 604's limitation was incorporated expressly into the Rehabilitation Act. The decision of the Court of Appeals therefore should be reversed, Conrail contends, as the primary objective of the federal assistance received by Conrail was not to promote employment.

It is clear that Section 504 itself contains no such limitation. Section 504 neither refers explicitly to Section 604 nor contains analogous limiting language; rather, that section prohibits discrimination against the handicapped under "*any* program or activity receiving Federal financial assistance." And it is unquestionable that the section was intended to reach employment discrimination. Indeed, enhancing employment of the handicapped was so much the focus of the 1973 legislation that Congress the next year felt it necessary to amend the statute to clarify whether Section 504 was intended to prohibit other types of discrimination as well. ... Thus, the language of Section 504 suggests that its bar on employment discrimination should not be limited to programs that receive federal aid the primary purpose of which is to promote employment.

The legislative history, executive interpretation, and purpose of the 1973 enactment all are consistent with this construction. The legislative history contains no mention of a "primary objective" limitation, although the legislators on numerous occasions adverted to Section 504's prohibition against discrimination in employment by programs assisted with federal funds. ... Moreover, the Department of Health, Education and Welfare, the agency designated by the President to be responsible for coordinating enforcement of Section 504, ... from the outset has interpreted that section to prohibit employment discrimination by all recipients of federal financial aid, regardless of the primary objective of that aid. This Court generally has deferred to contemporaneous regulations issued by the agency responsible for implementing a congressional enactment. ... Finally, application of Section 504 to all programs receiving federal financial assistance fits the remedial purpose of the Rehabilitation Act "to promote and expand employment opportunities" for the handicapped. 29 U.S.C. Section 701(8).

Nor did Congress intend to enact the "primary objective" requirement of Section 604 into the Rehabilitation Act when it amended that Act in 1978. The amendments, as we have noted, make "available" the remedies, procedures and rights of Title VI for suits under Section 504 against "any recipient of federal assistance." These terms do not incorporate Section 604's "primary objective" limitation. Rather, the legislative history reveals that this section was intended to codify the regulations of the Department of Health, Education and Welfare governing enforcement of Section 504, that prohibited employment discrimination regardless of the purpose of federal financial assistance. And it would be anomalous to conclude that the section, "designed to enhance the ability of handicapped individuals to assure compliance with [Section 504]," silently adopted a drastic limitation on the handicapped individual's right to sue federal grant recipients for employment discrimination.

Section 504, by its terms, prohibits discrimination only by a "program or activity receiving federal financial assistance." ... The District Court granted a motion for summary judgment on grounds unrelated to the issue of "program specificity." That judgment was reversed by the Court of Appeals and the case remanded for further proceedings. Thus, neither the District Court nor the Court of Appeals below considered the question whether respondent's decedent had sought and been denied employment in a "program ... receiving federal financial assistance." Nor did the District Court develop the record or make the factual findings that would be required to define the relevant "program." We therefore do not consider whether federal financial assistance was received by the "program or activity" that discriminated against LeStrange.*

We conclude that respondent may recover backpay due to her decedent under Section 504 and that this suit for employment discrimination may be maintained even if petitioner receives no federal aid the primary purpose of which is to promote employment. The judgment of the Court of Appeals is therefore affirmed. **It is so ordered.**

Contagious Diseases and the Vocational Rehabilitation Act

Does the Vocational Rehabilitation Act protect individuals with infectious diseases such as tuberculosis or AIDS—are those individuals "handicapped individuals" within the meaning of the act? That question was addressed in the following case.

SCHOOL BOARD OF NASSAU COUNTY, FLORIDA v. ARLINE

480 U.S. 273 (Supreme Court of the United States, 1987)

BRENNAN, J.

Section 504 of the Rehabilitation Act of 1973, . . . prohibits a federally funded state program from discriminating against a handicapped individual solely by reason of his or her handicap. This case presents the questions whether a person afflicted with tuberculosis, a contagious disease, may be considered a "handicapped individual" within the meaning of Section 504 of the Act, and, if so, whether such an individual is "otherwise qualified" to teach elementary school.

From 1966 until 1979, respondent Gene Arline taught elementary school in Nassau County, Florida. She was discharged in 1979 after suffering a third relapse of tuberculosis within two years. After she was denied relief in state administrative proceedings, she brought suit in federal court, alleging that the School Board's decision to dismiss her because of her tuberculosis violated Section 504 of the Act. . . . According to the medical records reviewed by Dr. McEuen, Arline was hospitalized for tuberculosis in 1957. For the next twenty years, Arline's disease was in remission. Then, in 1977, a culture revealed that tuberculosis was again active in her system; cultures taken in March 1978 and in November 1978 were also positive.

The superintendent of schools for Nassau County, Craig Marsh, then testified as to the School Board's response to Arline's medical reports. After both her second relapse, in the Spring of 1978, and her third relapse in November 1978, the School Board suspended Arline with pay for the remainder of the school year. At the end of the 1978–1979 school year, the School Board held a hearing, after which it discharged Arline, "not because she had done anything wrong," but because of the "continued reoccurence [sic] of tuberculosis." . . . The District Court held . . . that although there was "[n]o question that she suffers a handicap," Arline was nevertheless not "a handicapped person under the terms of that statute."

The court found it "difficult . . . to conceive that Congress intended contagious diseases to be included within the definition of a handicapped person." The court then went on to state that, "even assuming" that a person with a contagious disease could be deemed a handicapped person, Arline was not "qualified" to teach elementary school.

The Court of Appeals reversed, holding that "persons with contagious diseases are within the coverage of Section 504," and that Arline's condition "falls . . . neatly within the statutory and regulatory framework" of the Act. . . . The court remanded the case "for further findings as to whether the risks of infection precluded Mrs. Arline from being 'otherwise qualified' for her job and, if so, whether it was possible to make some reasonable accommodation for her in that teaching position" or in some other position. We granted certiorari. . . .

In enacting and amending the Act, Congress enlisted all

---

*Conrail does not contest that it receives federal financial assistance within the meaning of Section 504. Apparently, the government's payments to Conrail exceed the fair market value of the securities issued by Conrail to the government.

programs receiving federal funds in an effort "to share with handicapped Americans the opportunities for an education, transportation, housing, health care, and jobs that other Americans take for granted." To that end, Congress not only increased federal support for vocational rehabilitation, but also addressed the broader problem of discrimination against the handicapped by including Section 504, an anti-discrimination provision patterned after Title VI of the Civil Rights of 1964. Section 504 of the Rehabilitation Act reads in pertinent part:

> "No otherwise qualified handicapped individual in the United States, as defined in section 706(7) of this title, shall, solely by reason of his handicap, be excluded from participation in, be denied the benefits of, or be subjected to discrimination under any program or activity receiving Federal financial assistance. . . ."

In 1974 Congress expanded the definition of "handicapped individual" for use in Section 504 to read as follows:

> "[A]ny person who (i) has a physical or mental impairment which substantially limits one or more of such person's major life activities, (ii) has a record of such an impairment, or (iii) is regarded as having such an impairment."

The amended definition reflected Congress' concern with protecting the handicapped against discrimination stemming not only from simple prejudice, but from "archaic attitudes and laws" and from "the fact that the American people are simply unfamiliar with and insensitive to the difficulties confront[ing] individuals with handicaps."

. . . To combat the effects of erroneous but nevertheless prevalent perceptions about the handicapped, Congress expanded the definition of "handicapped individual" so as to preclude discrimination against "[a] person who has a record of, or is regarded as having, an impairment [but who] may at present have no actual incapacity at all."

In determining whether a particular individual is handicapped as defined by the Act, the regulations promulgated by the Department of Health and Human Services are of significant assistance. . . . The regulations are particularly significant here because they define two critical terms used in the statutory definition of handicapped individual. "Physical impairment" is defined as follows:

> "[A]ny physiological disorder or condition, cosmetic disfigurement, or anatomical loss affecting one or more of the follow-

ing body systems: neurological; musculoskeletal; special sense organs; respiratory, including speech organs; cardiovascular; reproductive, digestive, genitourinary; hemic and lymphatic; skin; and endocrine."

In addition, the regulations define "major life activities" as:

> "functions such as caring for one's self, performing manual tasks, walking, seeing, hearing, speaking, breathing, learning, and working."

Within this statutory and regulatory framework, then, we must consider whether Arline can be considered a handicapped individual. According to the testimony of Dr. McEuen, Arline suffered tuberculosis "in an acute form in such a degree that it affected her respiratory system," and was hospitalized for this condition. . . . Arline thus had a physical impairment as that term is defined by the regulations, since she had a "physiological disorder or condition . . . affecting [her] . . . respiratory [system]."

. . . This impairment was serious enough to require hospitalization, a fact more than sufficient to establish that one or more of her major life activities were substantially limited by her impairment. Thus, Arline's hospitalization for tuberculosis in 1957 suffices to establish that she has a "record of . . . impairment" . . . and is therefore a handicapped individual.

Petitioners concede that a contagious disease may constitute a handicapping condition to the extent that it leaves a person with "diminished physical or mental capabilities," . . . and concede that Arline's hospitalization for tuberculosis in 1957 demonstrates that she has a record of a physical impairment. . . . Petitioners maintain, however, Arline's record of impairment is irrelevant in this case, since the School Board dismissed Arline not because of her diminished physical capabilities, but because of the threat that her relapses of tuberculosis posed to the health of others.

We do not agree with petitioners that, in defining a handicapped individual under Section 504, the contagious effects of a disease can be meaningfully distinguished from the disease's physical effects on a claimant in a case such as this. Arline's contagiousness and her physical impairment each resulted from the same underlying condition, tuberculosis. It would be unfair to allow an employer to seize upon the distinction between the effects of a disease on others and the effects of a disease on a patient and use that distinction to justify discriminatory treatment.*

---

*The United States argues that it is possible for a person to be simply a carrier of a disease, that is, to be capable of spreading a disease without having a "physical impairment" or suffering from any other symp-

Nothing in the legislative history of Section 504 suggests that Congress intended such a result. . . .

Allowing discrimination based on the contagious effects of a physical impairment would be inconsistent with the basic purpose of Section 504, which is to ensure that handicapped individuals are not denied jobs or other benefits because of the prejudiced attitudes or the ignorance of others. By amending the definition of "handicapped individual" to include not only those who are actually physically impaired, but also those who are regarded as impaired and who, as a result, are substantially limited in a major life activity. Congress acknowledged that society's accumulated myths and fears about disability and disease are as handicapping as are the physical limitations that flow from actual impairment. Few aspects of a handicap give rise to the same level of public fear and misapprehension as contagiousness. Even those who suffer or have recovered from such non-infectious diseases as epilepsy or cancer have faced discrimination based on the irrational fear that they might be contagious. The Act is carefully structured to replace such reflexive reactions to actual or perceived handicaps with actions based on reasoned and medically sound judgments: the definition of "handicapped individual" is broad, but only those individuals who are both handicapped *and* otherwise qualified are eligible for relief. The fact that *some* persons who have contagious diseases may pose a serious health threat to others under certain circumstances does not justify excluding from the coverage of the Act *all* persons with actual or perceived contagious diseases. Such exclusion would mean that those accused of being contagious would never have the opportunity to have their condition evaluated in light of medical evidence and a determination made as to whether they were "otherwise qualified." Rather, they would be vulnerable to discrimination on the basis of mythology—precisely the type of injury Congress sought to prevent. We conclude that the fact that a person with a record of physical impairment is also contagious does not suffice to remove that person from coverage under Section 504.

The remaining question is whether Arline is otherwise qualified for the job of elementary school teacher. To answer this question in most cases, the District Court will need to conduct an individualized inquiry and make appropriate findings of fact. Such an inquiry is essential if Section 504 is to achieve its goal of protecting handicapped individuals from deprivations based on prejudice, stereotypes, or unfounded fear, while giving appropriate weight to such legitimate concerns of grantees as avoiding exposing others to significant health and safety risks. The basic factors to be considered in conducting this inquiry are well established. In the context of the employment of a person handicapped with a contagious disease, we agree with *amicus* American Medical Association that this inquiry should include:

> "[findings of] facts, based on reasonable medical judgments given the state of medical knowledge, about (a) the nature of the risk (how the disease is transmitted), (b) the duration of the risk (how long is the carrier infectious), (c) the severity of the risk (what is the potential harm to third parties) and (d) the probabilities the disease will be transmitted and will cause varying degrees of harm."

In making these findings, courts normally should defer to the reasonable medical judgments of public health officials. The next step in the "otherwise-qualified" inquiry is for the court to evaluate, in light of these medical findings, whether the employer could reasonably accommodate the employee under the established standards for that inquiry. . . .

We hold that a person suffering from the contagious disease of tuberculosis can be a handicapped person within the meaning of the Section 504 of the Rehabilitation Act of 1973, and that respondent Arline is such a person. We remand the case to the District Court to determine whether Arline is otherwise qualified for her position. The judgment of the Court of Appeals is **Affirmed.**

REHNQUIST, C.J., with whom SCALIA, J., joins (dissenting)

. . . I conclude that the Rehabilitation Act cannot be read to support the result reached by the Court. The record in this case leaves no doubt that Arline was discharged because of

---

toms associated with the disease. The United States contends that this is true in the case of some carriers of the acquired immune deficiency syndrome (AIDS) virus. From this premise the United States concludes that discrimination solely on the basis of contagiousness is never discrimination on the basis of a handicap. The argument is misplaced in this case, because the handicap here, tuberculosis, gave rise both to a physical impairment *and* to contagiousness. This case does not present, and we therefore do not reach, the questions whether a carrier of a contagious disease such as AIDS could be considered to have a physical impairment, or whether such a person could be considered, solely on the basis of contagiousness, a handicapped person as defined by the Act.

the contagious nature of tuberculosis, and not because of any diminished physical or mental capabilities resulting from her condition. Thus, in the language of Section 504, the central question here is whether discrimination on the basis of contagiousness constitutes discrimination "by reason of . . . handicap." Because the language of the Act, regulations, and legislative history are silent on this issue, the principles outlined above compel the conclusion that contagiousness is not a handicap within the meaning of Section 504. It is therefore clear that the protections of the Act do not extend to individuals such as Arline. . . .

On remand, the trial court awarded Arline back pay and ordered the school board either to reinstate her or to pay her "front pay" amounting to the present value of the amount she would have earned from the 1988–1989 school year until her projected retirement at age sixty-five (692 F. Supp. 1286, M.D. Fla. 1988).

The Civil Rights Restoration Act of 1988, passed by Congress over President Reagan's veto, amended the definition of "individual with a handicap" under the Rehabilitation Act to exclude a person with

> a currently contagious disease or infection and who, by reason of such disease or infection, would constitute a direct threat to the health or safety of other individuals or who, by reason of the currently contagious disease or infection, is unable to perform the duties of the job.

The amended language codifies the holding of the *Arline* case.

Enforcing Section 504. The Department of Health, Education and Welfare (now Health and Human Services) was initially responsible for enforcing Section 504; when the Department of Education was created, enforcement authority was transferred to that department. The regulations developed under Section 504 make the agency or department administering the funding the primary enforcement agency for complaints against the recipients of such funding. The Department of Education coordinates and oversees all such enforcement.

An individual alleging a violation of Section 504 must file a complaint with the agency administering the federal funding. That agency may use judicial proceedings or administrative proceedings similar to those used under Executive Order No. 11246. After a hearing, the agency may suspend, terminate, or refuse to grant federal assistance to a recipient found in violation of Section 504. An individual may, after processing a complaint through the administrative proceedings, institute a private suit to challenge the alleged violation of Section 504 (see *Consolidated Rail Corp.* v. *Darrone* earlier in this chapter).

AIDS and the Rehabilitation Act. Although *Arline* dealt with tuberculosis, the case was viewed with great interest because of concern over treatment of employees with AIDS. Although AIDS is contagious, medical authorities agree that it cannot be transmitted through causal contact likely to occur in the workplace. In *Chalk* v. *U.S. District Court* (840 F.2d 701, 9th Cir. 1987), the court of appeals held that a teacher with AIDS was protected by the Rehabilitation Act. The Court of Appeals for the Fifth Circuit in *Leckelt* v. *Board of Commissioners of Hospital District No. 1* (909 F.2d

820, 1990) affirmed a district court decision (13 O.S.H.C., BNA, 2086, E.D.La. 1989) that the discharge of a nurse for refusing to disclose results of his HIV test was not in violation of Section 504 of the Rehabilitation Act; hospital policy required staff to report any infectious diseases in order to protect patients, co-workers, and affected workers themselves. The trial court and the appeals court both held that the nurse was fired for failure to follow hospital policy, not solely because he was perceived to be HIV positive.

State Handicap Protection Laws.   All fifty states have laws prohibiting discrimination against the handicapped. Although the coverage of those laws varies, most of the state laws include AIDS in the definition of a handicap, so that employment discrimination against a person with AIDS is illegal in those states. The handicap discrimination laws of Kentucky and Georgia expressly exclude persons with communicable diseases from the protections of such laws, so a person with a disease such as tuberculosis or AIDS would not be protected under their laws. However, the recently enacted federal law, the Americans with Disabilities Act (ADA), which went into effect in July 1992, provides broad protection from discrimination for handicapped individuals, including persons with infectious or contagious diseases, unless such a condition presents a direct threat to the safety or health of others. The ADA would supersede state laws that conflict with it, so the provisions of the Kentucky and Georgia laws excluding contagious diseases may become invalid when the ADA takes effect. (The ADA is discussed in detail in the following section.)

The Americans with Disabilities Act

The Americans with Disabilities Act (ADA) is a comprehensive piece of civil rights legislation for individuals with disabilities; Title I of the act, which applies to employment, prohibits discrimination against individuals who are otherwise qualified for employment. The ADA applies to both private and public sector employers, but does not apply to the federal government. The act became law on July 26, 1990, effective two years after that date for employers with twenty-five or more employees, and three years from that date for employers with fifteen or more employees.

The ADA prohibits employers from discriminating on the grounds of disability against an otherwise qualified individual with a disability in regards to all aspects of employment: application procedures, hiring, terms and conditions of employment, promotion, compensation, training, and termination. The ADA defines "qualified individual with a disability" as "an individual with a disability who, with or without reasonable accommodation, can perform the essential functions of the employment position that such individual holds or desires." When determining the essential functions of a job, the court or the EEOC, which administers and enforces the ADA, is to consider the employer's judgment as to what is essential; if a written job description is used for advertising the position or interviewing job applicants, that description is to be considered evidence of the essential functions of the job.

Definition of Disability

The ADA defines "individual with a disability" very broadly: Disability means, with respect to an individual—

(a) a physical or mental impairment that substantially limits one or more of the major life activities of such individual;

(b) a record of such an impairment; or

(c) being regarded as having such an impairment.

Employees who use illegal drugs are not protected by the ADA, nor are alcoholics who use alcohol at the workplace or who are under the influence of alcohol at the workplace. Individuals who are former drug users or recovering drug users, including those persons participating in a supervised rehabilitation program and individuals "erroneously regarded" as using drugs but who do not use drugs, are under the ADA's protection.

Medical Exams and Tests

The ADA also limits the ability of an employer to test for or inquire into the disabilities of job applicants and employees. Employers are prohibited from asking about the existence, nature, or severity of a disability; however, an employer may ask about the individual's ability to perform the functions and requirements of the job. Employers are likewise not permitted to require pre-employment medical examinations of applicants; but once an offer of a job has been extended to an applicant, they can require a medical exam, provided that such an exam is required of all entering employees. Current employees are similarly protected from inquiries or exams, unless those requirements can be shown to be "job-related and consistent with business necessity." The act does not consider a drug test to be a medical examination, and it does not prohibit an employer from administering drug tests to its employees or from making employment decisions based on the results of such tests.

Reasonable Accommodation

The definition of a "qualified individual with a disability" includes the individual who is capable of performing the essential functions of a job, with reasonable accommodation on the part of the employer. The ADA imposes on employers the obligation to make reasonable accommodations for such individuals or employees, unless such accommodation would impose "undue hardship" on the employer. Examples of accommodations listed in the ADA include making facilities accessible to disabled individuals; restructuring jobs; providing part-time or modified work schedules; acquiring or modifying equipment; adjusting or modifying examinations, training materials, or policies; and providing qualified readers or interpreters. Failure to make such reasonable accommodation (which would not impose an undue hardship), or failure to hire an individual because of the need to make accommodation for that individual, is included in the definition of illegal discrimination under the act. Employers are not required to create a new position for the disabled applicant or employee, nor are they required to offer the individual the most expensive means of accommodation.

Undue Hardship.   An employer is not required to make accommodation for an individual if that accommodation would impose "undue hardship on the operation of the business of the covered entity." The ADA provides a complex definition of what constitutes an "undue hardship," including a list of factors to be considered in determining the impact of the accommodation on the employer. An accommodation imposes an "undue hardship" if it requires significant difficulty or expense when considered in light of the following factors:

> (i) the nature and cost of the accommodation needed under this act;

> (ii) the overall financial resources of the facility or facilities involved in the provision of the reasonable accommodation; the number of persons employed at such facility; the effect on expenses and resources, or the impact otherwise of such accommodation upon the operation of the facility;

> (iii) the overall financial resources of the covered entity; the overall size of the business of a covered entity with respect to the number of its employees; the number, type, and location of its facilities; and

> (iv) the type of operation or operations of the covered entity, including the composition, structure, and functions of the workforce of such entity; the geographic separateness, administrative, or fiscal relationship of the facility or facilities in question to the covered entity.

It should be obvious that the definition of "undue hardship" is intended to be flexible—what would be a reasonable accommodation for General Motors or IBM could be a significant expense or difficulty for a much smaller employer.

Defenses under the ADA

In addition to the defense of "undue hardship," the ADA sets out four other possible defense for employers.

Direct Threat to Safety or Health of Others.   Employers may refuse to hire or accommodate an individual where that individual's condition poses a "direct threat" to the health or safety of others in the workplace. "Direct threat" is defined as a "significant risk to the health or safety of others that cannot be eliminated by reasonable accommodation." The definition of disability under the act includes infectious or contagious diseases; in determining if such a disease presents a direct threat to others, the employer's considerations must be based on objective and accepted public health guidelines, not on stereotypes or public attitudes or fears. (See the *School Board of Nassau County, Florida* v. *Arline* case in the preceding section.) An employer would probably not be required to hire an individual with an active case of hepatitis or tuberculosis, but could not discriminate against an individual who has been treated for cancer, exposed to the HIV virus (associated with AIDS), or has had a history of mental illness.

Job-Related Criteria. Employers may hire, select, or promote individuals based on tests, standards, or criteria that are job-related or are consistent with business necessity. Employers could refuse to hire or promote individuals with a disability who are unable to meet such standards, tests, or criteria, or when performance of the job cannot be accomplished by reasonable accommodation. For example, an employer would be justified in refusing to hire a blind person for a bus driver position.

Food Handler Defense. An employer in the food service industry may refuse to assign or transfer to a job involving food handling any individual who has an infectious or communicable disease that can be transmitted to others through the handling of food, when the risk of infection cannot be eliminated by reasonable accommodation. The ADA requires the Secretary of Health and Human Services to develop a list of diseases that can be transmitted through food handling; only the diseases on that list (which is to be updated annually) may be used as a basis for refusal under this defense. The Secretary of Health and Human Services has stated that HIV infection (associated with AIDS) cannot be transmitted through food handling.

Religious Entities. Title I of the ADA does not prohibit a religious corporation, association, educational institution, or society from giving preference in employment to individuals of a particular religion to perform work connected with the carrying on by such corporation, association, educational institution, or society of its activities. Thus, as in the *Amos* case (see Chapter 13), a gymnasium operated by The Church of Jesus Christ of Latter-day Saints may refuse to hire an individual with a disability who is not a member of that church.

Enforcement of the ADA

The ADA is to be enforced by the EEOC. The act specifically provides that the procedures and remedies under Title VII of the Civil Rights Act of 1964 shall be those used or available under the ADA. That means that an individual must first file a complaint with a state or local agency, where appropriate, and then with the EEOC; the EEOC, or the individual if the EEOC declines, may file suit against an employer. Remedies available include injunctions, hiring or reinstatement order (with or without back pay), and attorney fees. The Civil Rights Act of 1991 amended Section 1981 to allow suits for compensatory and punitive damages against parties accused of intentional discrimination in violation of the Americans with Disabilities Act. Such damages are not available where the alleged discrimination involves provision of a reasonable accommodation of an individual's disability and the employer demonstrates that it made a good-faith effort to accommodate the individual's disability. Punitive damages are not available against public sector employers. The ADA also directs the EEOC to develop and issue regulations to enforce the act within one year of its enactment.

Drug Abuse and Drug Testing

Drug Abuse and the Rehabilitation Act.   Can an employer, under the Rehabilitation Act, legally refuse to hire persons who use or abuse drugs? In *Davis* v. *Bucher* (451 F. Supp. 791, E.D.Pa. 1978), the court held that drug addiction and alcoholism were "physical or mental impairments" within the meaning of the Rehabilitation Act. Shortly after that case was decided, Congress amended the definition of "handicapped individual" under the Rehabilitation Act to provide:

> For purposes of Sections 503 and 504, as such sections relate to employment, such term does not include any individual who is an alcoholic or drug abuser whose current use of alcohol or drugs prevents such individual from performing the duties of the job in question or whose employment, by reason of such current alcohol or drug abuse, would constitute a direct threat to the property or safety of others.

Notice that the amended Rehabilitation Act refers to current use of drugs or alcohol, and that such drug use or alcoholism must pose a danger to the property or safety of others or prevent the person from performing the duties of the job. A person who had been addicted to drugs in the past but who no longer suffers from such addiction is within the definition of "handicapped individual" of the Rehabilitation Act. An employer who institutes a policy of testing all employees or applicants for employment for drug use or alcoholism and who discharges or refuses to hire those who test positive must be prepared to demonstrate that such drug use or alcoholism would prevent the performance of job duties or pose a direct threat to the property or safety of others in order to comply with the Rehabilitation Act. A policy of testing employees for drug use only when there is some reason to suspect that an employee may be using drugs, such as erratic behavior or inconsistent work performance, would generally be acceptable providing that the employer could show the employee's drug use presented a threat to the safety or property of others.

Drug Abuse and the ADA.   As noted earlier, the ADA excludes from its protection employees who use illegal drugs, and alcoholics who use alcohol at the workplace or who are under the influence of alcohol at the workplace. Individuals who had formerly used drugs, recovering drug users (including those persons participating in a supervised rehabilitation program), and individuals who are "erroneously regarded" as using drugs but who do not actually use drugs, are all under the ADA's protection.

Drug Testing by Public Sector Employers.   Drug testing of all employees or applicants by a public sector employer would raise questions of its legality under the Constitution as well as under the Rehabilitation Act and the ADA. In the case that arose before the Rehabilitation Act was passed and therefore did not involve any question under it, the Supreme Court upheld the constitutionality of a New York City Transit Authority rule prohibiting the employment of persons using methadone (*New York City Transit Authority* v. *Beazer,* (438 U.S. 904, 1979). The Court in the *Beazer* case held that the rule served the purposes of safety and efficiency and was a policy choice that the public sector employer was empowered to make.

The constitutional challenges to public sector drug testing are based on the Fourth Amendment, which forbids unreasonable searches or seizures by the government. Drug testing is considered a search; the general requirement under the Fourth Amendment is that the government must show some reasonable cause to justify the drug testing. In *Skinner* v. *Railway Labor Executives Association* (489 U.S. 602, 1989), the Supreme Court upheld the constitutionality of Federal Railroad Administration regulations that required drug tests of all railroad employees involved in accidents, regardless of whether there was any reason to suspect individual employees of drug use. The Supreme Court held that the testing program served a compelling government interest by regulating conduct of railroad employees to ensure public safety, and that interest outweighed the privacy concerns of the employees.

In *Skinner* the fact that the employees had been involved in an accident was sufficient reason to subject them to drug testing. Would a public sector employer's requirement that all employees seeking a promotion be subject to drug tests be constitutional? The Supreme Court considered the legality of such testing in the following case.

NATIONAL TREASURY EMPLOYEES UNION v. VON RAAB

489 U.S. 656 (Supreme Court of the United States, 1989)

KENNEDY, J.

We granted certiorari to decide whether it violates the Fourth Amendment for the United States Customs Service to require a urinalysis test from employees who seek transfer or promotion to certain positions.

The United States Customs Service, a bureau of the Department of the Treasury, is the federal agency responsible for processing persons, carriers, cargo, and mail into the United States, collecting revenue from imports, and enforcing customs and related laws. An important responsibility of the Service is the interdiction and seizure of contraband, including illegal drugs. In 1987 alone, Customs agents seized drugs with a retail value of nearly 9 billion dollars. In the routine discharge of their duties, many Customs employees have direct contact with those who traffic in drugs for profit. . . . As a necessary response, many Customs operatives carry and use firearms in connection with their official duties. . . .

In May 1986, the Commissioner announced implementation of the drug-testing program. Drug tests were made a condition of placement or employment for positions that meet one or more of three criteria. The first is direct involvement in drug interdiction or enforcement of related laws, an activity the Commissioner deemed fraught with

obvious dangers to the mission of the agency and the lives of customs agents. The second criterion is a requirement that the incumbent carry firearms, as the Commissioner concluded that "[p]ublic safety demands that employees who carry deadly arms and are prepared to make instant life or death decisions be drug free." The third criterion is a requirement for the incumbent to handle "classified" material, which the Commissioner determined might fall into the hands of smugglers if accessible to employees who, by reason of their own illegal drug use, are susceptible to bribery or blackmail.

After an employee qualifies for a position covered by the Customs testing program, the Service advises him by letter that his final selection is contingent upon successful completion of drug screening. . . .

Customs employees who test positive for drugs and who can offer no satisfactory explanation are subject to dismissal from the Service. Test results may not, however, be turned over to any other agency, including criminal prosecutors, without the employee's written consent.

Petitioners, a union of federal employees and a union official, commenced this suit in the United States District Court for the Eastern District of Louisiana on behalf of current Customs Service employees who seek covered positions. Petitioners alleged that the Custom Service drug-testing program violated . . . the Fourth Amendment. The District Court agreed. The court acknowledged "the legitimate governmental interest in a drug-free work place and work force," but concluded that "the drug testing plan constitutes an overly intrusive policy of searches and seizures without probable cause or reasonable suspicion, in violation of legitimate expectations of privacy." The court enjoined the drug-testing program, and ordered the Customs Service not to require drug tests of any applicants for covered positions.

A divided panel of the United States Court of Appeals for the Fifth Circuit vacated the injunction. The court agreed with petitioners that the drug-screening program, by requiring an employee to produce a urine sample for chemical testing, effects a search within the meaning of the Fourth Amendment. The court held further that the searches required by the Commissioner's directive are reasonable under the Fourth Amendment. It first noted that "[t]he Service has attempted to minimize the intrusiveness of the search" by not requiring visual observation of the act of urination and by affording notice to the employee that he will be tested. The court also considered it significant that the program limits discretion in determining which employees are to be tested, and noted that the tests are an aspect of the employment relationship.

The court further found that the Government has a strong interest in detecting drug use among employees who meet the criteria of the Customs program. It reasoned that drug use by covered employees casts substantial doubt on their ability to discharge their duties honestly and vigorously, undermining public confidence in the integrity of the Service and concomitantly impairing the Service's efforts to enforce the drug laws. Illicit drug users, the court found, are susceptible to bribery and blackmail, may be tempted to divert for their own use portions of any drug shipments they interdict, and may, if required to carry firearms, "endanger the safety of their fellow agents, as well as their own, when their performance is impaired by drug use." "Considering the nature and responsibilities of the jobs for which applicants are being considered at Customs and the limited scope of the search," the court stated, "the exaction of consent as a condition of assignment to the new job is not unreasonable."

The dissenting judge concluded that the Customs program is not an effective method for achieving the Service's goals. He argued principally that an employee "given a five-day notification of a test date need only abstain from drug use to prevent being identified as a user." He noted also that persons already employed in sensitive positions are not subject to the test. Because he did not believe the Customs program can achieve its purposes, the dis-

senting judge found it unreasonable under the Fourth Amendment.

We granted certiorari. . . .

In *Skinner* v. *Railway Labor Executives Assn.,* decided today, we hold that federal regulations requiring employees of private railroads to produce urine samples for chemical testing implicate the Fourth Amendment, as those tests invade reasonable expectations of privacy. Our earlier cases have settled that the Fourth Amendment protects individuals from unreasonable searches conducted by the Government, even when the Government acts as an employer, and, in view of our holding in *Railway Labor Executives* that urine tests are searches, it follows that the Customs Service's drug-testing program must meet the reasonableness requirement of the Fourth Amendment.

While we have often emphasized, and reiterate today, that a search must be supported, as a general matter, by a warrant issued upon probable cause, our decision in *Railway Labor Executives* reaffirms the longstanding principle that neither a warrant nor probable cause, nor, indeed, any measure of individualized suspicion, is an indispensable component of reasonableness in every circumstance. As we note in *Railway Labor Executives,* our cases establish that where a Fourth Amendment intrusion serves special governmental needs, beyond the normal need for law enforcement, it is necessary to balance the individual's privacy expectations against the Government's interests to determine whether it is impractical to require a warrant or some level of individualized suspicion in the particular context.

It is clear that the Customs Service's drug-testing program is not designed to serve the ordinary needs of law enforcement. Test results may not be used in a criminal prosecution of the employee without the employee's consent. The purposes of the program are to deter drug use among those eligible for promotion to sensitive positions within the Service and to prevent the promotion of drug users to those positions. These substantial interests, no less than the Government's concern for safe rail transportation at issue in *Railway Labor Executives,* present a special need that may justify departure from the ordinary warrant and probable cause requirements.

. . . We have recognized before that requiring the Government to procure a warrant for every work-related intrusion "would conflict with 'the commonsense realization that government offices could not function if every employment decision became a constitutional matter.'"

. . . Under the Customs program, every employee who seeks a transfer to a covered position knows that he must take a drug test, and is likewise aware of the procedures the

Service must follow in administering the test. A covered employee is simply not subject "to the discretion of the official in the field." The process becomes automatic when the employee elects to apply for, and thereafter pursue, a covered position. Because the Service does not make a discretionary determination to search based on a judgment that certain conditions are present, there are simply "no special facts for a neutral magistrate to evaluate."

Even where it is reasonable to dispense with the warrant requirement in the particular circumstances, a search ordinarily must be based on probable cause. Our cases teach, however, that the probable-cause standard "'is peculiarly related to criminal investigations.'" In particular, the traditional probable-cause standard may be unhelpful in analyzing the reasonableness of routine administrative functions, especially where the Government seeks to *prevent* the development of hazardous conditions or to detect violations that rarely generate articulable grounds for searching any particular place or person. Our precedents have settled that, in certain limited circumstances, the Government's need to discover such latent or hidden conditions, or to prevent their development, is sufficiently compelling to justify the intrusion on privacy entailed by conducting such searches without any measure of individualized suspicion. We think the Government's need to conduct the suspicion-less searches required by the Customs program outweighs the privacy interests of employees engaged directly in drug interdiction, and of those who otherwise are required to carry firearms.

. . . Many of the Service's employees are often exposed to . . . [drug smugglers] and to the controlled substances they seek to smuggle into the country. The physical safety of these employees may be threatened, and many may be tempted not only by bribes from the traffickers with whom they deal, but also by their own access to vast sources of valuable contraband seized and controlled by the Service. The Commissioner indicated below that "Customs [o]fficers have been shot, stabbed, run over, dragged by automobiles, and assaulted with blunt objects while performing their duties." At least nine officers have died in the line of duty since 1974. He also noted that Customs officers have been the targets of bribery by drug smugglers on numerous occasions, and several have been removed from the Service for accepting bribes and other integrity violations.

It is readily apparent that the Government has a compelling interest in ensuring that front-line interdiction personnel are physically fit, and have unimpeachable integrity and judgment. Indeed, the Government's interest here is at least as important as its interest in searching travelers entering the country. We have long held that travelers seeking to enter the country may be stopped and required to submit to a routine search without probable cause, or even founded suspicion, "because of national self protection reasonably requiring one entering the country to identify himself as entitled to come in, and his belongings as effects which may be lawfully, brought in." This national interest in self protection could be irreparably damaged if those charged with safeguarding it were, because of their own drug use, unsympathetic to their mission of interdicting narcotics. A drug user's indifference to the Service's basic mission or, even worse, his active complicity with the malefactors, can facilitate importation of sizable drug shipments or block apprehension of dangerous criminals. The public interest demands effective measures to bar drug users from positions directly involving the interdiction of illegal drugs.

The public interest likewise demands effective measures to prevent the promotion of drug users to positions that require the incumbent to carry a firearm, even if the incumbent is not engaged directly in the interdiction of drugs. Customs employees who may use deadly force plainly "discharge duties fraught with such risks of injury to others that even a momentary lapse of attention can have disastrous consequences." We agree with the Government that the public should not bear the risk that employees who may suffer from impaired perception and judgment will be promoted to positions where they may need to employ deadly force. . . .

Against these valid public interests we must weigh the interference with individual liberty that results from requiring these classes of employees to undergo a urine test. The interference with individual privacy that results from the collection of a urine sample for subsequent chemical analysis could be substantial in some circumstances. We have recognized, however, that the "operational realities of the workplace" may render entirely reasonable certain work-related intrusions by supervisors and co-workers that might be viewed as unreasonable in other contexts. While these operational realities will rarely affect an employee's expectations of privacy with respect to searches of his person, or of personal effects that the employee may bring to the workplace, it is plain that certain forms of public employment may diminish privacy expectations even with respect to such personal searches. . . .

We think Customs employees who are directly involved in the interdiction of illegal drugs or who are required to carry firearms in the line of duty likewise have a diminished expectation of privacy in respect to the intrusions occasioned by a urine test. Unlike most private citizens or government employees in general, employees involved in drug interdiction reasonably should expect effective inquiry into their fitness and probity. Much the same is true of employees who are required to carry firearms. Because successful performance of their duties depends uniquely on their judgment and dexterity, these employees cannot reasonably expect to keep from the Service personal information that bears directly on their fitness. While reasonable tests designed to elicit this information doubtless infringe some privacy expectations, we do not believe these expectations outweigh the Government's compelling interests in safety and in the integrity of our borders.

Without disparaging the importance of the governmental interests that support the suspicionless searches of these employees, petitioners nevertheless contend that the Service's drug-testing program is unreasonable in two particulars. First, petitioners argue that the program is unjustified because it is not based on a belief that testing will reveal any drug use by covered employees. In pressing this argument, petitioners point out that the Service's testing scheme was not implemented in response to any perceived drug problem among Customs employees, and that the program actually has not led to the discovery of a significant number of drug users. Counsel for petitioners informed us at oral argument that no more than 5 employees out of 3,600 have tested positive for drugs. Second, petitioners contend that the Service's scheme is not a "sufficiently productive mechanism to justify [its] intrusion upon Fourth Amendment interests," because illegal drug users can avoid detection with ease by temporary abstinence or by surreptitious adulteration of their urine specimens. These contentions are unpersuasive.

Petitioners' first contention evinces an unduly narrow view of the context in which the Service's testing program was implemented. Petitioners do not dispute, nor can there be doubt, that drug abuse is one of the most serious problems confronting our society today. There is little reason to believe that American workplaces are immune from this pervasive social problem ... Detecting drug impairment on the part of employees can be a difficult task, especially where, as here, it is not feasible to subject employees and their work-product to the kind of day-to-day scrutiny that is the norm in more traditional office environments. Indeed, the almost unique mission of the Service gives the Government a compelling interest in ensuring that many of these covered employees do not use drugs even off-duty, for such use creates risks of bribery and blackmail against which the Government is entitled to guard. In light of the extraordinary safety and national security hazards that would attend the promotion of drug users to positions that require the carrying of firearms or the interdiction of controlled substances, the Service's policy of deterring drug users from seeking such promotions cannot be deemed unreasonable.

The mere circumstance that all but a few of the employees tested are entirely innocent of wrongdoing does not impugn the program's validity.... The Service's program is designed to prevent the promotion of drug users to sensitive positions as much as it is designed to detect those employees who use drugs. Where, as here, the possible harm against which the Government seeks to guard is substantial, the need to prevent its occurrence furnishes an ample justification for reasonable searches calculated to advance the Government's goal.

We think petitioners' second argument—that the Service's testing program is ineffective because employees may attempt to deceive the test by a brief abstention before the test date, or by adulterating their urine specimens—overstates the case. As the Court of Appeals noted, addicts may be unable to abstain even for a limited period of time, or may be unaware of the "fadeaway effect" of certain drugs. More importantly, the avoidance techniques suggested by petitioners are fraught with uncertainty and risks for those employees who venture to attempt them.... Petitioners' own expert indicated below that the time it takes for particular drugs to become undetectable in urine can vary widely depending on the individual, and may extend for as long as 22 days. Thus, contrary to petitioners' suggestion, no employee reasonably can expect to deceive the test by the simple expedient of abstaining after the test date is assigned. Nor can he expect attempts at adulteration to succeed, in view of the precautions taken by the sample collector to ensure the integrity of the sample. In all the circumstances, we are persuaded that the program bears a close and substantial relation to the Service's goal of deterring drug users from seeking promotion to sensitive positions.

In sum, we believe the Government has demonstrated that its compelling interests in safeguarding our borders and the public safety outweigh the privacy expectations of employees who seek to be promoted to positions that directly involve the interdiction of illegal drugs or that require the incumbent to carry a firearm. We hold that the testing of these employees is reasonable under the Fourth Amendment....

We hold that the suspicionless testing of employees who apply for promotion to positions directly involving the interdiction of illegal drugs, or to positions which require the incumbent to carry a firearm, is reasonable. The Government's compelling interests in preventing the promotion of drug users to positions where they might endanger the integrity of our Nation's borders or the life of the citizenry outweigh the privacy interests of those who seek promotion to these positions, who enjoy a diminished expectation of privacy by virtue of the special, and obvious, physical and ethical demands of those positions. We do not decide whether testing those who apply for promotion to positions where they would handle "classified" information is reasonable because we find the record inadequate for this purpose.

The judgment of the Court of Appeals for the Fifth Circuit is affirmed in part and vacated in part, and the case is remanded for further proceedings consistent with this opinion. **It is so ordered.**

SCALIA, J., with whom STEVENS, J., joins (dissenting)

. . . The issue here is what steps can constitutionally be taken to *detect* such drug use. The Government asserts it can demand that employees perform "an excretory function traditionally shielded by great privacy," while "a monitor of the same sex . . . remains close at hand to listen for the normal sounds," and that the excretion thus produced be turned over to the Government for chemical analysis. The Court agrees that this constitutes a search for purposes of the Fourth Amendment—and I think it obvious that it is a type of search particularly destructive of privacy and offensive to personal dignity.

Until today this Court had upheld a bodily search separate from arrest and without individualized suspicion of wrongdoing only with respect to prison inmates, relying upon the uniquely dangerous nature of that environment. Today, in *Skinner,* we allow a less intrusive bodily search of railroad employees involved in train accidents. I joined the Court's opinion there because the demonstrated frequency of drug and alcohol use by the targeted class of employees, and the demonstrated connection between such use and grave harm, rendered the search a reasonable means of protecting society. I decline to join the Court's opinion in the present case because neither frequency of use nor connection to harm is demonstrated or even likely. In my view the Customs Service rules are a kind of immolation of privacy and human dignity in symbolic opposition to drug use.

The Fourth Amendment protects the "right of the people to be secure in their persons, houses, papers, and effects, against unreasonable searches and seizures." While there are some absolutes in Fourth Amendment law, as soon as those have been left behind and the question comes down to

whether a particular search has been "reasonable," the answer depends largely upon the social necessity that prompts the search. . . .

The Court's opinion in the present case, however, will be searched in vain for real evidence of a real problem that will be solved by urine testing of Customs Service employees. . . . The only pertinent points, it seems to me, are supported by nothing but speculation, and not very plausible speculation at that. It is not apparent to me that a Customs Service employee who uses drugs is significantly more likely to be bribed by a drug smuggler, any more than a Customs Service employee who wears diamonds is significantly more likely to be bribed by a diamond smuggler—unless, perhaps, the addiction to drugs is so severe, and requires so much money to maintain, that it would be detectable even without benefit of a urine test. Nor is it apparent to me that Customs officers who use drugs will be appreciably less "sympathetic" to their drug-interdiction mission, any more than police officers who exceed the speed limit in their private cars are appreciably less sympathetic to their mission of enforcing the traffic laws. . . . Nor, finally, is it apparent to me that urine tests will be even marginally more effective in preventing gun-carrying agents from risking "impaired perception and judgment" than is their current knowledge that, if impaired, they may be shot dead in unequal combat with unimpaired smugglers—unless, again, their addiction is so severe that no urine test is needed for detection.

What is absent in the Government's justifications—notably absent, revealingly absent, and as far as I am concerned dispositively absent—is the recitation of *even a single instance* in which any of the speculated horribles actually occurred. . . . In *Skinner* . . . we took pains to establish the existence of special need for the search or seizure. . . . In the present case, by contrast, not only is the Customs Service thought to be "largely drug-free," but the connection between whatever drug use may exist and serious social harm is entirely speculative. . . .

Those who lose because of the lack of understanding that begot the present exercise in symbolism are not just the Customs Service employees, whose dignity is thus offended, but all of us—who suffer a coarsening of our national manners that ultimately give the Fourth Amendment its content, and who become subject to the administration of federal officials whose respect for our privacy can hardly be greater than the small respect they have been taught to have for their own.

Subsequent to the Supreme Court decisions in *Skinner* and *Von Raab,* a number of federal courts have considered the legality of public employer drug-testing programs. In *American Fed. of Govt. Employees* v. *Thornburgh (INS)* (713 F. Supp. 359, N.D.Cal. 1989), the court confined drug testing by the Immigration and Naturalization Service to the job classes specified in *Von Raab:* those employees involved directly in drug interdiction, carrying firearms, and with access to classified information. In *AFGE* v. *Thornburgh (Bureau of Prisons)* (720 F. Supp. 154, N.D.Cal. 1989), the court enjoined the Bureau of Prisons' program of mandatory, random testing of all employees, regardless of their job function, because the employer had failed to demonstrate a special need for the testing, as required by the Supreme Court decisions. *NTEU* v. *Watkins* (722 F. Supp. 766, D.D.C. 1989) upheld the Department of Energy drug testing of employees in "sensitive" positions: those with access to sensitive information; presidential appointees; law enforcement officers; those whose duties pertain to law enforcement or national security, or to protection of lives or property; those occupied with public health or safety; and those positions involved with a high degree of trust. The court in *Watkins* also held that testing employees carrying firearms was not justified unless they also had law enforcement duties, and merely holding a security clearance does not decrease one's privacy expectation to justify testing with no other justification present.

In *Harmon* v. *Thornburgh* (878 F.2d 484, D.C. Cir. 1989), the federal court of appeals held that the *Von Raab* and *Skinner* public safety rationale justifying testing focuses on the immediacy of the threat posed, and therefore the Department of Justice program of random drug testing of prosecutors, those with access to grand jury proceedings, and those with top-secret security clearances was not justified here; the court did allow testing of those employees with access to top-secret national security information. In *AFGE* v. *Skinner* (885 F.2d 884, D.C. Cir. 1989), Department of Transportation drug testing of employees in jobs with a direct impact on public health, safety, or national security, such as air traffic controllers, safety inspectors, aircraft mechanics, and motor vehicle operators, was upheld by the court of appeals.

In the case of *Georgia Association of Educators* v. *Harris* (749 F. Supp. 1110, N.D.Ga., 1990), a federal court in Georgia issued an injunction against the enforcement of Georgia legislation requiring drug tests of all applicants for state employment. The court held that the testing requirement could not stand under the standards set out in *Von Raab.*

Drug Testing by Private Employers.   Private sector employers who institute drug-testing programs for their employees or applicants are not subject to the constitutional restrictions that apply to public sector employers. Private employers who do business with the federal government or who receive federal funding are subject to the provisions of the Vocational Rehabilitation Act. The federal Drug-Free Workplace Act, passed by Congress in 1988, requires that all employers doing more than $25,000 of business per year with the federal government must have a written drug-free workplace policy and must establish a drug-free awareness program. As of July 26, 1992, private sector employers are subject to the Americans with Disabilities

Act. Neither of those acts prohibit drug testing by private sector employers, nor does any other federal employment discrimination legislation. Relevant state laws may regulate or limit drug testing by private sector employers, and if the employer is unionized, the employer may have to bargain in good faith with the union representing its employees before instituting drug-testing programs.

Drug Testing and the NLRB.   A number of National Labor Relations Board (NLRB) decisions have dealt with drug testing. An employer's mandatory drug-testing program for all employees who suffered work-related injuries was held to be a mandatory bargaining subject in *Johnson–Bateman Co.* (295 N.L.R.B. No. 26, 131 L.R.R.M. 1393, 1989); but drug testing of job applicants is not a mandatory bargaining subject, according to *Star Tribune* (295 N.L.R.B. No. 63, 131 L.R.R.M. 1404, 1989). In *Oil, Chemical and Atomic Workers Int. Union, Local 2-286* v. *Amoco Oil Co.* (885 F.2d 697, 10th Cir. 1989), the federal court of appeals issued an injunction under the *Boys Markets* doctrine (see Chapter 8) to prevent an employer from unilaterally implementing a drug-testing program, pending the outcome of arbitration over whether the collective agreement gave the employer the right to institute such a program.

The National Labor Relations Act

The unfair labor practice prohibitions of the National Labor Relations Act (NLRA) may be used to attack discrimination in employment in some instances. In *United Packinghouse Workers Union* v. *NLRB* (416 F.2d 1126, D.C. Cir. 1969), the court held that race discrimination by an employer was an unfair labor practice in violation of Section 8(a)(1) of the NLRA. Retaliation against employees who filed charges with the EEOC, by refusing to recall them from layoff, was held to violate Section 8(a)(1) in *Frank Briscoe Inc.* v. *NLRB* (637 F.2d 946, 3rd Cir. 1981).

Unions that discriminate against African Americans in membership or in conditions of employment are in violation of Section 8(b)(1)(A) and their duty of fair representation of all employees in the bargaining unit, according to the Supreme Court decision of *Syres* v. *Oil Workers* (350 U.S. 892, 1955). (See the *Steele* v. *Louisville & Nashville R.R.* case in Chapter 10.) In *Hughes Tool Co.* (56 L.R.R.M. 1289, 1964), the NLRB held that a union's refusal to represent African-American workers violated Section 8(b)(1)(A) and was grounds to rescind the union's certification as bargaining agent. Discrimination against female employees by a union also violates Section 8(b)(1)(A), as held in *NLRB* v. *Glass Bottle Blowers Local 106* (520 F.2d 693, 6th Cir. 1975). (See Chapter 10 for a discussion of the duty of fair representation.)

Employers and unions that negotiate, or attempt to negotiate, discriminatory provisions in seniority systems, pay scales, or promotion policies may commit unfair labor practices in violation of Section 8(a)(5) or Section 8(b)(3) by refusing to bargain in good faith.

Constitutional Prohibitions against Discrimination

Certain provisions of the U.S. Constitution may be used by public sector employees to challenge discrimination in their employment. The Constitution regulates the relationship between the government and individuals; therefore, the Constitution's prohibitions against discrimination apply only to government employers and to private employers acting under government support or compulsion (state action).

Due Process and Equal Protection

The primary constitutional provisions used to attack discrimination are the guarantees of **due process of law** and **equal protection** found in the Fifth and Fourteenth Amendments. The Fifth Amendment applies to the federal government, and the Fourteenth Amendment applies to state and local governments. In addition, specific enactments such as the First Amendment guarantee of freedom of religion may also be used to challenge discrimination. In *Brown* v. *GSA* (425 U.S. 820, 1976), the Supreme Court held that the only remedy available to persons complaining of race discrimination in federal government employment is provided by Section 717 of Title VII. However, not all federal employees are covered by Title VII. For example, members of the armed forces or the personal staff members of elected officials, who are not covered by Title VII, could file constitutional challenges to alleged discrimination.

In the case of *Davis* v. *Passman* (442 U.S. 228, 1979), the Supreme Court held that a member of a congressman's staff, who was not covered by Title VII, could bring a suit under the Fifth Amendment against her employer for discharging her because of intentional sex discrimination.

Challenges to employment discrimination under the due process and equal protection guarantees involve claims that the discriminatory practices deny the victims of the discrimination rights equal, or treatment equal, to those who are not targets of the discrimination. Blanket prohibitions on employment of females, or of members of a minority group, deny those employees due process of law by presuming that all women, or members of the minority group, are unable to perform the requirements of a particular job.

In *Washington* v. *Davis* (426 U.S. 229, 1976), the Supreme Court held that the constitutional prohibitions applied only to invidious, or intentional, discrimination; claims alleging disparate impact (as in *Griggs* v. *Duke Power* in Chapter 12) could not be brought under the constitutional provisions.

Not all intentional discrimination on the basis of race, sex, and so on is unconstitutional, however. In considering claims of discrimination under the Constitution, the court will first consider the basis of discrimination. Some bases of discrimination, or "classifications" by government action, will be considered "suspect classes"—that is, there is little justification for treating persons differently because they fall within a particular class. For example, racial discrimination involves classifying, and treating differently, employees by race. Such conduct can rarely ever be justified. The court will strictly scrutinize any offered justification for such conduct. The government must show that such classification, or treatment, is required because of a compelling government interest, and no less discriminatory alternatives exist. For example, classifying employees by race, while discriminatory, may be justified if it is in order to compensate employees who had been victims of prior racial discrimination.

Affirmative Action and the Constitution

This issue's most bitter battles of recent years have been fought over preferential treatment of minorities by government agencies. The following case illustrates the Court's consideration of the legality of affirmative action under the Fourteenth Amendment.

WYGANT v. JACKSON BOARD OF EDUCATION

476 U.S. 267 (Supreme Court of the United States, 1986)

POWELL, J.

This case presents the question whether a school board, consistent with the Equal Protection Clause, may extend preferential protection against layoffs to some of its employees because of their race or national origin.

In 1972 the Jackson Board of Education, because of racial tension in the community that extended to its schools, considered adding a layoff provision to the Collective Bargaining Agreement (CBA) between the Board and the Jackson Education Association (the Union) that would protect employees who were members of certain minority groups against layoffs. The Board and the Union eventually approved a new provision, Article XII of the CBA, covering layoffs. It stated:

> In the event that it becomes necessary to reduce the number of teachers through layoff from employment by the Board, teachers with the most seniority in the district shall be retained, except that at no time will there be a greater percentage of minority personnel laid off than the current percentage of minority personnel employed at the time of the layoff. In no event will the number given notice of possible layoff be greater than the number of positions to be eliminated. Each teacher so affected will be called back in reverse order for positions for which he is certificated maintaining the above minority balance.

When layoffs became necessary in 1974, it was evident that adherence to the CBA would result in the layoff of tenured nonminority teachers while minority teachers on probationary status were retained. Rather than complying with Article XII, the Board retained the tenured teachers and laid off probationary minority teachers, thus failing to maintain the percentage of minority personnel that existed at the time of the layoff. The Union, together with two minority

teachers who had been laid off, brought suit in federal court, claiming that the Board's failure to adhere to the layoff provision violated the Equal Protection Clause of the Fourteenth Amendment and Title VII of the Civil Rights Act of 1964. They also urged the District Court to take pendent jurisdiction over state law contract claims. In its answer the Board denied any prior employment discrimination and argued that the layoff provision conflicted with the Michigan Teacher Tenure Act. Following trial, the District Court *sua sponte* concluded that it lacked jurisdiction over the case, in part because there was insufficient evidence to support the plaintiff's claim that the Board had engaged in discriminatory hiring practices prior to 1972, and in part because the plaintiffs had not fulfilled the jurisdictional prerequisite to a Title VII claim by filing discrimination charges with the Equal Employment Opportunity Commission. After dismissing the federal claims, the District Court declined to exercise pendent jurisdiction over the state law contract claims.

Rather than taking an appeal, the plaintiffs instituted a suit in state court raising in essence the same claims. In entering judgment for the plaintiffs, the state court found that the Board had breached its contract with the plaintiffs, and that Article XII did not violate the Michigan Teacher Tenure Act. In rejecting the Board's argument that the layoff provision violated the Civil Rights Act of 1964, the state court found that it "ha[d] not been established that the board had discriminated against minorities in its hiring practices. The minority representation on the faculty was the result of societal racial discrimination." The state court also found that "[t]here is no history of overt past discrimination by the parties to this contract." Nevertheless, the court held that Article XII was permissible, despite its discriminatory effect on nonminority teachers, as an attempt to remedy the effects of societal discrimination. . . .

[After that decision] the Board adhered to Article XII. As a result, during the 1976–1977 and 1981–1982 school years, nonminority teachers were laid off, while minority teachers with less seniority were retained. The displaced nonminority teachers, petitioners here, brought suit in Federal District Court, alleging violations of the Equal Protection Clause, Title VII, 42 U.S.C. Section 1983, and other federal and state statutes. On cross motions for summary judgment, the District Court dismissed all of petitioners' claims. With respect to the equal protection claim, the District Court held that the racial preferences granted by the Board need not be grounded on a finding of prior discrimination. Instead, the court decided that the racial preferences were permissible under the Equal Protection Clause as an attempt to remedy societal discrimination by providing "role models" for minority schoolchildren, and upheld the constitutionality of the layoff provision.

The Court of Appeals for the Sixth Circuit affirmed, largely adopting the reasoning and language of the District Court. We granted certiorari [on the Equal Protection Clause question] to resolve the important issue of the constitutionality of race-based layoffs by public employers....

Petitioners' central claim is that they were laid off because of their race in violation of the Equal Protection Clause of the Fourteenth Amendment.... This Court has "consistently repudiated '[d]istinctions between citizens solely because of their ancestry' as being 'odious to a free people whose institutions are founded upon the doctrine of equality.' "Racial and ethnic distinctions of any sort are inherently suspect and thus call for the most exacting judicial examination."

The Court has recognized that the level of scrutiny does not change merely because the challenged classification operates against a group that historically has not been subject to governmental discrimination.

In this case, Article XII of the CBA operates against whites and in favor of certain minorities, and therefore constitutes a classification based on race. "Any preference based on racial or ethnic criteria must necessarily receive a most searching examination to make sure that it does not conflict with constitutional guarantees." There are two prongs to this examination. First, any racial classification "must be justified by a compelling governmental interest." Second, the means chosen by the State to effectuate its purpose must be "narrowly tailored to the achievement of that goal." We must decide whether the layoff provision is supported by a compelling state purpose and whether the means chosen to accomplish that purpose are narrowly tailored.

The Court of Appeals, relying on the reasoning and language of the District Court's opinion, held that the Board's interest in providing minority role models for its minority students, as an attempt to alleviate the effects of societal discrimination, was sufficiently important to justify the racial classification embodied in the layoff provision. The court discerned a need for more minority faculty role models by finding that the percentage of minority teachers was less than the percentage of minority students.

This Court never has held that societal discrimination alone is sufficient to justify a racial classification. Rather, the Court has insisted upon some showing of prior discrimination by the governmental unit involved before allowing limited use of racial classifications in order to remedy such discrimination. This Court's reasoning in *Hazelwood School District* v. *United States,* (1977), illustrates that the relevant analysis in cases involving proof of discrimination by statistical disparity focuses on those disparities that demonstrate such prior governmental discrimination. In *Hazelwood* the Court concluded that, absent employment discrimination by the school board, "nondiscriminatory hiring practices will in time result in a work force more or less representative of the racial and ethnic composition of the population in the community from which the employees are hired.'" Based on that reasoning, the Court in *Hazelwood* held that the proper comparison for determining the existence of actual discrimination by the school board was "between the racial composition of [the school's] teaching staff and the racial composition of the qualified public school teacher population in the relevant labor market." *Hazelwood* demonstrates this Court's focus on prior discrimination as the justification for, and the limitation on, a State's adoption of race-based remedies.

Unlike the analysis in *Hazelwood,* the role model theory employed by the District Court has no logical stopping point. The role model theory allows the Board to engage in discriminatory hiring and layoff practices long past the point required by any legitimate remedial purpose....

Moreover, because the role model theory does not necessarily bear a relationship to the harm caused by prior discriminatory hiring practices, it actually could be used to escape the obligation to remedy such practices by justifying the small percentage of black teachers by reference to the small percentage of black students. Carried to its logical extreme, the idea that black students are better off with black teachers could lead to the very system the Court rejected in *Brown* v. *Board of Education,* (1954).

Societal discrimination, without more, is too amorphous a basis for imposing a racially classified remedy. The role model theory announced by the District Court and the resultant holding typify this indefiniteness. There are numerous explanations for a disparity between the percentage of minority students and the percentage of minority faculty, many of them completely unrelated to discrimination of any kind. In fact, there is no apparent connection between the two groups. Nevertheless, the District Court combined irrelevant comparisons between these two groups with an indisputable statement that there has been societal discrimination, and upheld state action predicated upon racial classifications. No one doubts that there has been serious racial discrimination in this country. But as the basis for imposing discriminatory *legal* remedies that work against innocent people, societal discrimination is insufficient and over expansive. In the absence of particularized findings, a court could uphold remedies that are ageless in their reach into the past, and timeless in their ability to affect the future.

Respondents also now argue that their purpose in adopting the layoff provision was to remedy prior discrimination against minorities by the Jackson School District in hiring teachers. Public schools, like other public employers, operate under two interrelated constitutional duties. They are under a clear command from this Court . . . to eliminate every vestige of racial segregation and discrimination in the schools. Pursuant to that goal, race-conscious remedial action may be necessary. On the other hand, public employers, including public schools, also must act in accordance with a "core purpose of the Fourteenth Amendment" which is to "do away with all governmentally imposed distinctions based on race." These related constitutional duties are not always harmonious; reconciling them requires public employers to act with extraordinary care. In particular, a public employer like the Board must ensure that, before it embarks on an affirmative action program, it has convincing evidence that remedial action is warranted. That is, it must have sufficient evidence to justify the conclusion that there has been prior discrimination.

Evidentiary support for the conclusion that remedial action is warranted becomes crucial when the remedial program is challenged in court by nonminority employees. In this case, for example, petitioners contended at trial that the remedial program—Article XII—had the purpose and effect of instituting a racial classification that was not justified by a remedial purpose. In such a case, the trial court must make a factual determination that the employer had a strong basis in evidence for its conclusion that remedial action was necessary. The ultimate burden remains with the employees to demonstrate the unconstitutionality of an affirmative action program. But unless such a determination is made, an appellate court reviewing a challenge to remedial action by nonminority employees cannot determine

whether the race-based action is justified as a remedy for prior discrimination.

Despite the fact that Article XII has spawned years of litigation and three separate lawsuits, no such determination ever has been made. Although its litigation position was different, the Board [in the prior suits] denied the existence of prior discriminatory hiring practices. This precise issue was litigated in both those suits. Both courts concluded that any statistical disparities were the result of general societal discrimination, not of prior discrimination by the Board. The Board now contends that, given another opportunity, it could establish the existence of prior discrimination. Although this argument seems belated at this point in the proceedings, we need not consider the question since we conclude below that the layoff provision was not a legally appropriate means of achieving even a compelling purpose.

The Court of Appeals examined the means chosen to accomplish the Board's race-conscious purposes under a test of "reasonableness." That standard has no support in the decisions of this Court. As demonstrated in Part II above, our decisions always have employed a more stringent standard—however articulated—to test the validity of the means chosen by a state to accomplish its race-conscious purposes. . . . Under strict scrutiny the means chosen to accomplish the State's asserted purpose must be specifically and narrowly framed to accomplish that purpose. "Racial classifications are simply too pernicious to permit any but the most exact connection between justification and classification."

We have recognized, however, that in order to remedy the effects of prior discrimination, it may be necessary to take race into account. As part of this Nation's dedication to eradicating racial discrimination, innocent persons may be called upon to bear some of the burden of the remedy. "When effectuating a limited and properly tailored remedy to cure the effects of prior discrimination, such a 'sharing of the burden' by innocent parties is not impermissible."

Significantly, none of the cases [in which race-conscious classifications have been approved] involved layoffs. Here, by contrast, the means chosen to achieve the Board's asserted purposes is that of laying off nonminority teachers with greater seniority in order to retain minority teachers with less seniority. We have previously expressed concern over the burden that a preferential layoffs scheme imposes on innocent parties. In cases involving valid *hiring* goals, the burden to be borne by innocent individuals is diffused to a considerable extent among society generally. Though hiring goals may burden some innocent individuals, they simply do not impose the same kind of injury that layoffs impose. Denial of a future employment opportunity is not as intrusive as loss of an existing job.

Many of our cases involve union seniority plans with employees who are typically heavily dependent on wages for their day-to-day living. Even a temporary layoff may have adverse financial as well as psychological effects. A worker may invest many productive years in one job and one city with the expectation of earning the stability and security of seniority. "At that point, the rights and expectations surrounding seniority make up what is probably the most valuable capital asset that the worker 'owns,' worth even more than the current equity in his home." Layoffs disrupt these settled expectations in a way that general hiring goals do not.

While hiring goals impose a diffuse burden, often foreclosing only one of several opportunities, layoffs impose the entire burden of achieving racial equality on particular individuals, often resulting in serious disruption of their lives. That burden is too intrusive. We therefore hold that, as a means of accomplishing purposes that otherwise may be legitimate, the Board's layoff plan is not sufficiently narrowly tailored. Other, less intrusive means of accomplishing similar purposes—such as the adoption of hiring goals—are available. For these reasons, the Board's selection of layoffs as the means to accomplish even a valid purpose cannot satisfy the demands of the Equal Protection Clause.

We accordingly reverse the judgment of the Court of Appeals for the Sixth Circuit. **It is so ordered.**

O'CONNOR, J. (concurring in part and concurring in the judgment)

... The Equal Protection Clause standard applicable to racial classifications that work to the disadvantage of "nonminorities" has been articulated in various ways. JUSTICE POWELL now would require that: (1) the racial classification be justified by a "'compelling governmental interest,'" and (2) the means chosen by the State to effectuate its purpose be "narrowly tailored." This standard reflects the belief, apparently held by all members of this Court, that racial classifications of any sort must be subjected to "strict scrutiny," however defined. . . . JUSTICES MARSHALL, BRENNAN, and BLACKMUN, however, seem to adhere to the formulation of the "strict" standard that they authored, with JUSTICE WHITE, in *Bakke:* "remedial use of race is permissible if it serves 'important governmental objectives' and is 'substantially related to achievement of those objectives.'"

I subscribe to JUSTICE POWELL's formulation because it

mirrors the standard we have consistently applied in examining racial classifications in other contexts. . . .

Although JUSTICE POWELL's formulation may be viewed as more stringent than that suggested by JUSTICES BRENNAN, WHITE, MARSHALL, and BLACKMUN, the disparities between the two tests do not preclude a fair measure of consensus. In particular, as regards certain state interests commonly relied upon in formulating affirmative action programs, the distinction between a "compelling" and an "important" governmental purpose may be a negligible one. The Court is in agreement that, whatever the formulation employed, remedying past or present racial discrimination by a state actor is a sufficiently weighty state interest to warrant the remedial use of a carefully constructed affirmative action program. This remedial purpose need not be accompanied by contemporaneous findings of actual discrimination to be accepted as legitimate as long as the public actor has a firm basis for believing that remedial action is required. Additionally, although its precise contours are uncertain, a state interest in the promotion of racial diversity has been found sufficiently "compelling," at least in the context of higher education, to support the use of racial considerations in furthering that interest. And certainly nothing the Court has said today necessarily forecloses the possibility that the Court will find other governmental interests which have been relied upon in the lower courts but which have not been passed on here to be sufficiently "important" or "compelling" to sustain the use of affirmative action policies.

It appears, then, that the true source of disagreement on the Court lies not so much in defining the state interests which may support affirmative action efforts as in defining the degree to which the means employed must "fit" the ends pursued to meet constitutional standards. Yet even here the Court has forged a degree of unanimity; it is agreed that a plan need not be limited to the remedying of specific instances of identified discrimination for it to be deemed sufficiently "narrowly tailored," or "substantially related," to the correction of prior discrimination by the state actor.

In the final analysis, the diverse formulations and the number of separate writings put forth by various members of the Court in these difficult cases do not necessarily reflect an intractable fragmentation in opinion with respect to certain core principles. Ultimately, the Court is at least in accord in believing that a public employer, consistent with the Constitution, may undertake an affirmative action program which is designed to further a legitimate remedial purpose and which implements that purpose by means that do not impose disproportionate harm on the interests, or unnecessarily trammel the rights, of innocent individuals directly and adversely affected by a plan's racial preference. . . .

MARSHALL J., with whom BRENNAN, J., and BLACKMUN, J., join (dissenting)

When this Court seeks to resolve far-ranging constitutional issues, it must be especially careful to ground its analysis firmly in the facts of the particular controversy before it. Yet in this significant case, we are hindered by a record that is informal and incomplete. Both parties now appear to realize that the record is inadequate to inform the Court's decision. Both have lodged with the Court voluminous "submissions" containing factual material that was not considered by the District Court or the Court of Appeals. . . . No race-conscious provision that purports to serve a remedial purpose can be fairly assessed in a vacuum.

The haste with which the District Court granted summary judgment to respondents, without seeking to develop the factual allegations contained in respondents' brief, prevented the full exploration of the facts that are now critical to resolution of the important issue before us. Respondents' acquiescence in a premature victory in the District Court should not now be used as an instrument of their defeat. Rather, the District Court should have the opportunity to develop a factual record adequate to resolve the serious issue raised by the case. I believe, therefore, that it is improper for this Court to resolve the constitutional issue in its current posture. But, because I feel that the plurality has also erred seriously in its legal analysis of the merits of this case, I write further to express my disagreement with the conclusions that it has reached.

I, too, believe that layoffs are unfair. But unfairness ought not be confused with constitutional injury. Paying no heed to the true circumstances of petitioners' plight, the plurality would nullify years of negotiation and compromise designed to solve serious educational problems in the public schools of Jackson, Michigan. Because I believed that a public employer, with the full agreement of its employees, should be permitted to preserve the benefits of a legitimate and constitutional affirmative-action hiring plan even while reducing its work force, I dissent. . . .

STEVENS, J. (dissenting)

In my opinion, it is not necessary to find that the Board of Education has been guilty of racial discrimination in the past to support the conclusion that it has a legitimate interest in employing more black teachers in the future. Rather than analyzing a case of this kind by asking whether minority teachers have some sort of special entitlement to jobs as a remedy for sins that were committed in the past, I believe that we should first ask whether the Board's action advances the public interest in educating children for the future. If so, I believe we should consider whether that public interest, and the manner in which it is pursued, justifies any adverse effects on the disadvantaged group. . . .

In *U.S.* v. *Paradise* (480 U.S. 149, 1987), the Supreme Court, in a 5-4 decision, upheld a court-ordered affirmative action plan that required the Alabama Public Safety Department to promote to corporal one African-American state trooper for every white trooper promoted, until either African Americans occupied 25 percent of the corporal positions or until the department instituted a promotion policy that did not have an adverse impact on African-American troopers. The majority held that the order was necessary to remedy past "pervasive, systematic and obstinate" discrimination by the department.

Preferences for Minority Businesses. In *Fullilove* v. *Klutznick* (448 U.S. 448, 1980), the Supreme Court upheld a federal law that required that at least 10 percent of the funds under any federally funded construction contract be awarded to minority contractors. The Court held that the requirement served important government objectives in eliminating discrimination by contractors in federally funded construction projects, and that the set-aside requirement was sufficiently related to the achievement of those objectives.

In *City of Richmond* v. *J. A. Croson* (488 U.S. 469, 1989), the Supreme Court considered a minority set-aside program that required contractors with city-awarded construction contracts to subcontract at least 30 percent of the dollar amount of the contract to minority owned or controlled businesses. The Court, by a vote of 6-3, held that the set-aside requirement was unconstitutional because the city had failed to identify clearly that there was discrimination in the construction industry in Richmond, because there was no clear evidence that the remedial requirement was necessary, and because there was no relationship between the 30 percent requirement and the representation of minority businesses in the city's expenditures for construction. The Court distinguished *Fullilove* on the ground that the federal government, under its remedial powers pursuant to the Fourteenth Amendment, may act to redress the effects of societywide discrimination, but that states or municipalities must specifically identify private discrimination and their connection to it in order to undertake remedial actions involving racial preferences.

Other Constitutional Issues

Some forms of discrimination involve classifications that may be more neutral than racial classifications. The courts refer to such classifications as "nonsuspect" classes. When discrimination is based on such nonsuspect classes, the court will consider whether the discriminatory classification bears a reasonable relationship to a valid state interest. For example, in *Personnel Administrator of Massachusetts* v. *Feeney* (442 U.S. 256, 1979), the Supreme Court upheld a Massachusetts law that required all veterans to be given preference for state civil service positions over nonveterans, even though the law had the effect of discriminating against women because veterans were overwhelmingly male. The classification of applicants on the basis of veteran status was reasonably necessary for the valid government objective of rewarding veterans for the sacrifices of military service.

In *Cleveland Board of Education* v. *LaFleur* (414 U.S. 632, 1974), the Supreme Court struck down a rule imposing a mandatory maternity leave on teachers reaching the fifth month of pregnancy, on grounds that it violated the due process rights of the teachers. The rule denied the teachers the freedom of personal choice over matters of family life, and it was not shown to be sufficiently related to the school board interests of administrative scheduling and protecting the health of teachers. The rule had the effect of classifying every teacher reaching the fifth month of pregnancy as being physically incapable of performing the duties of the job, when such teacher's ability or inability to perform during pregnancy is an individual matter.

Personal grooming requirements and restrictions on hair length and facial hair for police officers were upheld by the Supreme Court in *Kelley* v. *Johnson* (425 U.S. 238, 1976) because they were reasonably related to the maintenance of discipline among members of the police force. In *Goldman* v. *Weinberger* (475 U.S. 503, 1976) the Supreme Court dismissed a challenge under the First Amendment to an Air Force uniform regulation that prevented an Orthodox Jew from wearing his yarmulke, or skullcap, while on duty. Despite the fact that the yarmulke was unobtrusive, the regulations were justified by the Air Force interest in maintaining morale and discipline, which were held to be legitimate military ends.

State EEO Laws

The discussion of employment discrimination prohibitions here has focused primarily on federal legislation. However, a number of states and cities have their own equal employment opportunity (EEO) laws or regulations. Recall that under Title VII, persons complaining of discrimination must first file their complaint with the state or local EEO agency, if one exists. (See Chapter 14.)

Many state or local EEO laws go beyond Title VII provisions. The New York Human Rights Law, for example, prohibits discrimination in employment on the bases of race, color, religion, sex, national origin, age (18 and older), marital status, disability, or criminal record. The EEO regulations enforced by the Philadelphia Human Relations Commission prohibit discrimination based on sexual preference. West Virginia prohibits discrimination on the basis of family status, and Utah prohibits discrimination on the basis of pregnancy, childbirth, or pregnancy-related conditions. Colorado now prohibits discrimination on the basis of marriage between co-workers, and includes mental impairment in the definition of protected handicaps. California, Connecticut, Michigan, Montana, New York, and North Dakota require the informed consent of the individual before testing for AIDS, and require that the test results be kept confidential. Connecticut, Wisconsin, Massachusetts, and Hawaii prohibit discrimination against persons on the basis of sexual preference.

The specific procedures and requirements involved vary from state to state. Most involve some sort of administrative procedures by an enforcement agency before the individual may file suit in the state courts. The time limits for filing claims under the various laws also vary. The Pennsylvania Human Relations Act requires that complaints be filed with the Pennsylvania Human Relations Commission within ninety days of the alleged violation, while the time limit for filing complaints with the New York State Human Rights Division is one year from the alleged violation. For a discussion of the relationship between the procedure under Title VII and state EEO provisions, see the *Mohasco* case and surrounding text in Chapter 14.

QUESTIONS

1. Against what kind of discrimination can 42 U.S.C. Section 1981 be used? What remedies are available under 42 U.S.C. Section 1981? Against what kind of discrimination can 42 U.S.C. Section 1983 be used? What action can be challenged under 42 U.S.C. Section 1985(c)?

2. What is the effect of the Equal Pay Act? How is the equivalency of work determined under the Equal Pay Act?

3. What must be established to support a claim of age discrimination under the Age Discrimination in Employ-

ment Act? What defenses are available to an employer under the ADEA?

4. What obligations are imposed on government contractors by Executive Order No. 11246?

5. Which employers are covered by Section 503 of the Vocational Rehabilitation Act? By Section 504 of the

act? What are the differences in procedures for filing complaints under Section 503 and Section 504?

6. Does the U.S. Constitution prohibit all employment discrimination based on race? All employment discrimination based on sex? Explain.

CASE PROBLEMS

1. Keller worked for the Department of Social Services. She sued both the department and the state after she was denied promotion to case worker associate III. She argued that the state had violated Title VII and Section 1983 by refusing to promote her because she was African American. The state moved for dismissal of Keller's Section 1983 count, arguing that Title VII provides a concurrent and more comprehensive remedy, and therefore, preempts Keller from coming under Section 1983.

   How should the court rule? See *Keller* v. *Prince George's County Department of Social Services,* 616 F. Supp. 540 (D. Md. 1985).

2. Marta Davis sued her employer under Section 1981 of the 1866 Civil Rights Act, claiming she was discriminated against because of her Hispanic ancestry. The company contended that Section 1981 was passed in 1866 in response to the enactment of "black codes" in several states, which prevented African Americans from exercising fundamental rights to which they were entitled as part of their newly acquired citizenship. The company asserts that because this was the clear congressional purpose for passing Section 1981, it cannot be stretched to cover national origin discrimination.

   Do you agree? See *Davis* v. *Boyle-Midway, Inc.,* 615 F. Supp. 560 (N.D. Ga. 1985).

3. The faculty of the school of nursing sued the university under the Equal Pay Act on the grounds that faculties elsewhere in the university, which were male-dominated, received substantially higher salaries than those paid to the female-dominated nursing school faculty. The university contended that it recruited its faculty nationwide and that each discipline commanded its own salary levels in the national marketplace. Therefore, said the university, the court could not

properly base its decision in this case on whether nursing faculty performed substantially the same duties as faculty in other schools and departments.

   Do you agree? Explain your answer. See *Spaulding* v. *University of Washington,* 740 F.2d 686 (9th Cir. 1984).

4. True was a female cook employed by the New York State Department of Correctional Services. She sued the department under the Equal Pay Act because, she said, although she was paid the same wage as male cooks, she earned less money because she was denied overtime work.

   Is this a proper claim under the Equal Pay Act? See *True* v. *N.Y. Dept. of Correctional Services,* 36 F.E.P. Cases 1048 (U.S. Dist. Ct., W.D. New York 1985).

5. The El Paso Natural Gas Company had a rule that pilots of the company's private planes must either accept ground jobs or retire at age sixty. Pilots' duties included night flying, visual flying, and instrument flying. Transfer to a ground job at age sixty was permitted if one was available. Otherwise, the pilot was forced to retire. El Paso argued that it was impractical for the company to try to monitor the health of a pilot after age sixty, and that the FAA regulation requiring retirement of commercial pilots after age sixty was prima facie proof of the legality of the company's rule under the ADEA BFOQ provisions.

   Do you agree? Explain your answer. See *EEOC* v. *El Paso Natural Gas Co.,* 626 F. Supp. 182 (W.D. Tex. 1985).

6. Rotert had been working as a mortgage processing officer when the company told her that her duties were being changed to those of a loan consultant and that she would be transferred to another branch. The company told the fifty-nine-year-old Rotert her salary would be the same. Rotert protested the new work as-

signment and resigned. She filed a claim for unemployment benefits, which was denied on the basis that she was not "constructively discharged" due to the new assignment. Rather, the state agency held, she had voluntarily quit. When Rotert filed an ADEA complaint, saying again that she was constructively discharged in favor of a younger employee who took her former job as mortgage processing officer, the company argued for dismissal because the issue of "constructive discharge" had already been decided against her by the state agency.

How should the court rule? See *Rotert* v. *Jefferson Federal Savings & Loan Ass'n,* 623 F. Supp. 1114 (D. Conn. 1985).

7. John Hand was an attorney for Dayton-Hudson in Detroit from 1967 to 1982. In February 1982 he lost his job as part of a corporate restructuring. The company offered Hand $38,000 in severance pay if he signed a release of all legal claims he might have against the company. Hand asserted that company policy already required the firm to pay the severance. Nevertheless, he signed the release. However, unknown to the company, he first altered it to reserve his right to file an ADEA action. The company's representative, Harms, accepted the altered release without reviewing it. Later, Hand filed an age complaint.

Should the court allow him to pursue this action or not? See *Hand* v. *Dayton-Hudson Corp.,* 775 F.2d 757 (6th Cir. 1985).

8. Neves sued the United States Department of Housing and Urban Development (HUD), alleging employment discrimination in violation of Title VII, and also in the alternative, violation of her rights under the U.S. Constitution. HUD argues that Neves's exclusive remedy is under Title VII, and therefore the constitutional count should be dismissed.

Is HUD correct? Explain your answer. See *Neves* v. *Kolaski,* 602 F. Supp. 645 (D. Rhode Is. 1985).

9. A major manufacturer of paper and pulp products decided that it wished to decrease its top-heavy management at several of its plants, mostly located on the West Coast. It therefore devised a pension plan permitting early retirement to employees in management, aged fifty-five or older, at these plants. A group of over-fifty-five managers at several of the company's other plants, who were ineligible for the new plan, sued, claiming that the plan violated the ADEA.

Are these employees correct in this assertion? (This problem is based on one of the author's experiences in legal practice.)

10. A New York State constitutional provision and a civil service statute required that military veterans with wartime service be granted extra points on competitive exams for state civil service jobs. Wartime vets received a five-point bonus on the exam, and disabled vets received an extra ten points. However, this bonus was limited to veterans who were New York residents at the time they entered military service.

Is this affirmative action program permissible under the Constitution and federal statutory law? See *Attorney General of the State of New York* v. *Soto-Lopez,* 106 S. Ct. 2317 (1986).

Employment
Law
Issues

Occupational Safety and Health

DURING THE LATE 1960S, approximately 14,500 persons were killed each year as the result of occupational or industrial accidents. Countless others were exposed to hazardous substances or contracted occupationally related illnesses because of their working conditions. In response to these problems, Congress enacted the Occupational Safety and Health Act in 1970.

How successful has the act—and related state occupational safety and health acts—been in reducing industrial accidents and deaths? Not very, the statistics suggest! A 1990 report issued by the Chicago-based National Safe Workplace Institute (NSWI) found that in 1987 (some seventeen years after the federal Occupational Safety and Health Act was passed) on-the-job injuries killed about 11,100 workers and disabled another 1.8 million in the United States.

Worse still, a 1985 study by the congressional Office of Technology Assessment estimated that every year 390,000 American workers contract job-related illnesses, and 100,000 die from them. According to the NSWI report, "Even though it is not recognized as such, occupational disease is clearly one of the most significant causes of premature death in the U.S. today." Why is this so? One reason may be that occupational health and safety was poorly funded and enforcement deemphasized during the Reagan administration. Another may be the decline in labor unions, historically a force favoring workplace safety.

The Occupational Safety and Health Act

The act has two broad goals: (1) to assure safe and healthful working conditions for working men and women; and (2) to provide a framework for research, education, training, and information in the field of occupational safety and health. The act requires employers to furnish their employees a workplace that is free from recognized hazards that cause, or are likely to cause, serious injury or death. A recognized hazard is one that is known to be hazardous, taking into account the standard of knowledge of the industry. It need not necessarily be hazardous to each and every individual employee. Nor is it necessary to show that an employer had actual knowledge of the existence of a hazard in order to find a violation of the act. It is sufficient to show that through the exercise of reasonable diligence the employer could have discovered the hazard.

In addition to the general duty of employers to furnish a workplace free from hazards, the act requires that employers meet the various health and safety standards set under the act and keep records of injuries, deaths, accidents, illnesses, and particular hazards.

The Occupational Safety and Health Act applies to all employees who work for an employer that is engaged in a business affecting interstate commerce. This broad coverage reaches almost all employers and employees in the United States and its territories, with some exceptions. The act does not apply to the federal and state governments in their capacity as employers; nor does it apply to domestic servants or self-employed persons.

The act contains no specific industrywide exemptions. However, if other federal agencies exercise statutory authority to prescribe or enforce standards or regulations affecting occupational safety or health, the Occupational Safety and Health Act does not apply. For this exemption to operate, it must be shown that the working conditions of the affected employees are covered by another federal statute that has the protection of employees as one of its purposes. As well, the other agency must have exercised its jurisdiction to make regulations or standards applying to specific working conditions that would otherwise be covered by the act. An example of such a situation involves the workers on offshore oil platforms. Their working conditions were governed by health and safety regulations enacted and enforced by both the U.S. Coast Guard and the U.S. Geological Survey. In *Marshall* v. *Nichols* (486 F. Supp. 615, E.D. Texas 1980), the court held that the Occupational Safety and Health Administration was precluded from exerting its jurisdiction over offshore oil platforms because of the coverage by the Coast Guard and the Geological Survey.

Administration and Enforcement

The Occupational Safety and Health Act created three federal agencies for administration and enforcement. The **Occupational Safety and Health Administration (OSHA)** is the primary agency created for enforcement of the act. An independent agency within the Department of Labor, it has the authority to promulgate standards, conduct inspections of workplaces, issue **citations** for violations, and recommend penalties. OSHA acts on behalf of the Secretary of Labor.

The **National Institute of Occupational Safety and Health (NIOSH)** is an agency created to conduct research and promote the application of the research results to ensure that no worker will suffer diminished health, reduced functional capacity, or decreased life expectancy as a result of his or her work experience. NIOSH also provides technical assistance to OSHA in investigations and recommends standards for adoption by OSHA.

The **Occupational Safety and Health Review Commission (OSHRC)** is a quasijudicial agency created to adjudicate contested enforcement actions of OSHA.

Whereas OSHA may issue citations and recommend penalties for violations of the act, only OSHRC can actually assess and enforce the penalties. The decisions of OSHRC can be appealed to the U.S. courts of appeals. OSHRC has three members appointed by the president for overlapping six-year terms and a number of Administrative Law Judges who have career tenure.

Standards, Feasibility, and Variances

In order to reach the goal of providing hazard-free workplaces for all employees, the act provides for the setting of standards regulating the health and safety of working conditions. The Secretary of Labor is granted authority under the act to promulgate occupational safety and health standards through OSHA. The act provides for the issuance of three kinds of standards: interim standards, permanent standards, and emergency standards.

Interim Standards

Interim standards are those that the Secretary of Labor had power to issue for the first two years following the effective date of the act. These standards were generally modeled on various preexisting industry consensus standards. The secretary, in adopting previously accepted national consensus standards, was not required to hold public hearings or any other formal proceedings. Once adopted, these standards did not have to be repromulgated under notice and comment rule-making procedures, but, rather, remain in effect until they are modified or revoked.

Permanent Standards

Permanent standards are both newly created standards and revised interim standards. These standards are developed by OSHA and NIOSH and are frequently based on suggestions made by interested parties, such as employers, employees, states and other political subdivisions, and labor unions. The Secretary of Labor is also empowered to appoint an advisory committee to assist in the promulgation of permanent standards. This committee has ninety days from its date of appointment, unless a longer or shorter period is prescribed by the secretary, to make its recommendations regarding a proposed rule.

After OSHA has developed a proposed rule that promulgates, modifies, or revokes an occupational safety or health standard, the secretary must publish a notice in the *Federal Register*. Included in this notice must be a statement of the reasons for either adopting a new, changing an existing, or revoking a prior standard. Interested parties are then allowed thirty days after publication to submit written data, objections, or comments relating to the proposed standards. If the interested party files written objections and requests a public hearing concerning these objections, the secretary must publish a notice in the *Federal Register* specifying the time and place of the hearing and the standard to which the objection has been filed.

Within sixty days after the expiration of the period for comment, or after the completion of any hearing, the secretary must issue a rule promulgating, modifying, or revoking the standard, or make a determination that the rule should not be issued. If adopted, the rule must state its effective date. This date must ensure a sufficient period for affected employers and employees to be informed of the existence of the standard and of its terms.

Emergency Standards

The Secretary of Labor may, under special circumstances, avoid the procedures described above by issuing temporary emergency standards. These standards are issued when the secretary believes that employees are exposed to grave dangers from substances or agents determined to be toxic or physically harmful. Actual injury does not have to occur before a temporary emergency standard can be promulgated, although there must be a genuinely serious emergency.

Emergency standards take effect immediately upon publication in the *Federal Register.* After publication, the secretary must then follow the procedure for formally adopting a permanent standard in order to make the emergency standard into a permanent standard. That new permanent standard must be issued within six months after its publication as an emergency standard.

Appeals of Standards

After a standard has been promulgated by the secretary, any person adversely affected by it can file a challenge to the validity of the standard. Such challenges must be filed with the appropriate federal court of appeals before the sixtieth day after the issuance of the standard.

Upon reviewing the standard, the court of appeals will uphold the standard if it is supported by substantial evidence. The secretary must demonstrate that the standard was in response to a significant risk of material health impairment. In the case of *Industrial Union Department* v. *American Petroleum Institute* (448 U.S. 607, 1980), the Supreme Court held that the secretary is required under the act to find that a proposed standard is appropriate or reasonably necessary to protect workers against a significant risk of material health impairment before the secretary may adopt the standard.

Feasibility

The act grants the secretary authority to issue standards dealing with toxic materials or harmful physical agents. A standard must be one that most adequately assures, *to the extent feasible,* on the basis of the best available evidence, that no employee will suffer material impairment of health or functional capacity, even if the employee has regular exposure to the hazard. The **feasibility** of a standard must be examined from two perspectives: technological feasibility and economic feasibility. In *United Steelworkers of America* v. *Marshall* (647 F.2d 1189, *cert. denied,* 453 U.S. 913, 1980), the D.C. Court of Appeals held that technological feasibility under the act is a "technology-forcing" concept, meaning that OSHA can impose a standard that only the most technologically advanced plants in an industry have been able to achieve. Further, OSHA can force an industry to develop and diffuse new technology to satisfy precise permissible exposure limits to toxic materials or harmful physical agents that have never before been attained, if OSHA can present substantial evidence showing that companies acting vigorously and in good faith can develop the technology.

The standard also must satisfy the requirement of economic feasibility. In the *United Steelworkers* case, the court ruled that a standard is not economically unfeasible simply because it threatens the survival of some companies within an industry; nor must the standard be drafted in such a way as to guarantee the continued operation of individual employers.

The secretary must carry the burden of proving both technological and economic feasibility when promulgating and enforcing standards governing toxic materials and harmful physical agents. However, the secretary does not have to establish that the cost of a standard bears a reasonable relationship to its benefits, as the following case demonstrates.

AMERICAN TEXTILE MFR.'S INST. v. DONOVAN

101 S. Ct. 2478 (Supreme Court of the United States, 1981)

BRENNAN, J.

The principal question presented in this case is whether the Occupational Safety and Health Act requires the Secretary, in promulgating a standard ... to determine that the costs of the standard bear a reasonable relationship to its benefits.... [P]etitioners urge not only that OSHA must show that a standard addresses a significant risk of material health impairment, ... but also that OSHA must demonstrate that the reduction in risk of material health impairment is significant in light of the costs of attaining that reduction. Respondents on the other hand contend that the Act requires OSHA to promulgate standards that eliminate or reduce such risks "to the extent such protection is technologically and economically feasible." ...

... The starting point of our analysis is the language of the statute itself:

> ... The Secretary, in promulgating standards dealing with toxic materials or harmful physical agents under this subsection, shall set the standard which most adequately assures, *to the extent feasible,* on the basis of the best available evidence, that no employee will suffer material impairment of health or functional capacity even if such employee has regular expo-

sure to the hazard dealt with by such standard for the period of his working life. [Section 6(b)(5)]

Although their interpretations differ, all parties agree that the phrase "to the extent feasible" contains the critical language ... for purposes of this case.

The plain meaning of the word "feasible" supports respondents' interpretation of the statute. According to Webster's *Third New International Dictionary of the English Language,* "feasible" means "capable of being done, executed, or effected." Accord, *The Oxford English Dictionary* 116 (1933) ("Capable of being done, accomplished or carried out"); Funk & Wagnalls *New "Standard" Dictionary of the English Language* 903 (1957) ("That may be done, performed or effected"). Thus, Section 6(b)(5) directs the Secretary to issue the standard that "most adequately assures ... that no employee will suffer material impairment of health," limited only by the extent to which this is "capable of being done." In effect then, as the Court of Appeals held, Congress itself defined the basic relationship between costs and benefits, by placing the "benefit" of worker health above all other considerations save those making attainment of this "benefit" unachievable. Any standard based on a balancing of costs and benefits by the Secretary that strikes a different balance than that struck by Congress would be inconsistent with the command set forth in Section 6(b)(5). Thus, cost-benefit analysis by OSHA is not required by the statute because feasibility analysis is.

When Congress has intended that an agency engage in cost-benefit analysis, it has clearly indicated such intent on the face of the statute. One early example is the Flood Control Act of 1936:

> [T]he Federal Government should improve or participate in the improvement of navigable waters or their tributaries, including watersheds thereof, for floodcontrol purposes if the *benefits to whomsoever they may accrue are in excess of the estimated costs,* and if the lives and social security of people are otherwise adversely affected.

A more recent example is the Outer Continental Shelf Lands Act Amendments of 1978, providing that offshore drilling operations shall use

> the best available and safest technologies which the Secretary determines to be economically *feasible,* wherever failure of equipment would have significant effect on safety, health, or the environment, except where the Secretary determines that the *incremental benefits are clearly insufficient to justify the incremental costs of using such technologies.*

These and other statutes demonstrate that Congress uses specific language when intending that an agency engage in cost-benefit analysis. . . . Certainly in light of its ordinary meaning, the word "feasible" cannot be construed to articulate such congressional intent. We therefore reject the argument that Congress required cost-benefit analysis in Section 6(b)(5).

Even though the plain language of Section 6(b)(5) supports this construction, we must still decide whether the general definition of an occupational safety and health standard, either alone or in tandem with Section 6(b)(5), incorporates a cost-benefit requirement for standards dealing with toxic materials or harmful physical agents. Section 3(8) of the Act, (emphasis added), provides:

> The term "occupational safety and health standard" means a standard which requires conditions, or the adoption or use of one or more practices, means, methods, operations, or processes, *reasonably necessary or appropriate* to provide safe or healthful employment and places of employment.

Taken alone, the phrase "reasonably necessary or appropriate" might be construed to contemplate some balancing of the costs and benefits of a standard. Petitioners urge that, so construed, Section 3(8) engrafts a cost-benefit analysis requirement on the issuance of Section 6(b)(5) itself does not authorize such analysis. We need not decide whether Section 3(8), standing alone, would contemplate some form of cost-benefit analysis. For even if it does, Congress specifically chose in Section 6(b)(5) to impose separate and additional requirements for issuance of a subcategory of occupational safety and health standards dealing with toxic materials and harmful physical agents: it required that those standards be issued to prevent material impairment of health *to the extent feasible.* Congress could reasonably have concluded that *health* standards should be subject to different criteria than *safety* standards because of the special problems presented in regulating them. . . .

. . . Agreement with petitioners' argument that Section 3(8) imposes an additional and overriding requirement of cost-benefit analysis on the issuance of Section 6(b)(5) standards would eviscerate the "to the extent feasible" requirement. Standards would inevitably be set at the level indicated by cost-benefit analysis, and not at the level specified by Section 6(b)(5).

. . . We cannot believe that Congress intended the general terms of Section 3(8) to countermand the specific feasibility requirement of Section 6(b)(5). Adoption of petitioners' interpretation would effectively write Section 6(b)(5) out of the Act. We decline to render Congress' decision to include a feasibility requirement nugatory, thereby offending the well-settled rule that all parts of a statute, if possible, are to be given effect. . . .

. . . Congress did not contemplate any further balancing by the agency for toxic material and harmful physical agents standards, and we should not "impute to Congress a purpose to paralyze with one hand what it sought to promote with the other."

The legislative history of the Act, while concededly not crystal clear, provides general support for respondents' interpretation of the Act. The congressional reports and debates certainly confirm that Congress meant "feasible" and nothing else in that term. Congress was concerned that the Act might be thought to require achievement of absolute safety, an impossible standard, and therefore insisted that health and safety goals be capable of economic and technological accomplishment. Perhaps most telling is the absence of any indication whatsoever that Congress intended OSHA to conduct its own cost-benefit analysis before promulgating a toxic material or harmful physical agent standard. The legislative history demonstrates conclusively that Congress was fully aware that the Act would impose real and substantial costs of compliance on industry, and believed that such costs were part of the cost of doing business. . . .

Variances

If an employer, or a class of employers, believes that the OSHA standard is inappropriate to its particular situation, an exemption, or variance, may be sought. This variance may be either temporary or permanent.

A temporary variance may be granted when the employer is unable to comply with a standard by its effective date because of the unavailability of professional or technological personnel or of materials or equipment necessary to come into compliance with the standard. The employer must show that all possible actions have been taken to protect employees and that all actions necessary for compliance are being undertaken. A temporary variance can be granted only after the affected employees have been given notice of the request and an opportunity for a hearing. Temporary variances can be granted for a one-year period, and may then be renewed for two six-month periods.

Permanent variances are granted when the employer establishes by a preponderance of the evidence that its particular procedures provide as safe and healthful a workplace as the OSHA standard would provide. The affected employees must be informed of the request for the permanent variance and may request a hearing. If the variance is granted, either the employees or OSHA may petition to modify or revoke the variance.

The Secretary of Labor also has authority to issue experimental variances involving new or improved techniques to safeguard worker safety or health.

Employee Rights

In addition to being granted the right to a workplace free from recognized hazards, employees under the Occupational Safety and Health Act are protected from retaliation or discrimination by their employer because they have exercised any rights granted by the act. Section 11(c)(1) of the act provides that

> No person shall discharge or in any manner discriminate against any employee because such employee has filed any complaint or instituted or caused to be instituted any proceeding under or related to this Act or has testified or is about to testify in any such proceeding or because of the exercise by such employee on behalf of himself or others of any right afforded by this Act.

Pursuant to Section 11(c)(1), the Secretary of Labor has adopted a regulation that protects employees from discrimination because they refuse to work in the face of a dangerous condition. The right to refuse can be exercised when employees are exposed to a dangerous condition posing the risk of serious injury or death, and when there is insufficient time, due to the nature of the hazard, to resort to the regular statutory procedures for enforcement. When possible, the employees should attempt to have the employer correct the hazardous condition before exercising their right to refuse. The dangerous condition triggering the employees' refusal must be of such a nature that a reasonable person, under the circumstances facing the employees, would conclude that there is a real danger of death or serious injury.

The following case involves a challenge to the right-to-refuse regulation adopted by the Secretary of Labor under Section 11(c)(1).

WHIRLPOOL CORP. v. MARSHALL

445 U.S. 1 (Supreme Court of the United States, 1980)

STEWART, J.

The Occupational Safety and Health Act of 1970 (Act) prohibits an employer from discharging or discriminating against any employee who exercises "any right afforded by" the Act. The Secretary of Labor (Secretary) has promulgated a regulation providing that, among the rights that the Act so protects, is the right of an employee to choose not to perform his assigned task because of a reasonable apprehension of death or serious injury coupled with a reasonable belief that no less drastic alternative is available. The question presented in the case before us is whether this regulation is consistent with the Act.

The petitioner company maintains a manufacturing plant in Marion, Ohio, for the production of household appliances. Overhead conveyors transport appliance components throughout the plant. To protect employees from objects that occasionally fall from these conveyors, the petitioner has installed a horizontal wire-mesh guard screen approximately 20 feet above the plant floor. This mesh screen is welded to angle-iron frames suspended from the building's structural steel skeleton.

Maintenance employees of the petitioner spend several hours each week removing objects from the screen, replacing paper spread on the screen to catch grease drippings from the material on the conveyors, and performing occasional maintenance work on the conveyors themselves. To perform these duties, maintenance employees usually are able to stand on the iron frames, but sometimes find it necessary to step onto the steel mesh screen itself.

In 1973, the company began to install heavier wire in the screen because its safety had been drawn into question. Several employees had fallen partly through the old screen, and on one occasion an employee had fallen completely through to the plant floor below but had survived. A number of maintenance employees had reacted to these incidents by bringing the unsafe screen conditions to the attention of their foremen. The petitioner company's contemporaneous safety instructions admonished employees to step only on the angle-iron frames.

On June 28, 1974, a maintenance employee fell to his death through the guard screen in an area where the newer, stronger mesh had not yet been installed. Following this incident, the petitioner effectuated some repairs and issued an order strictly forbidding maintenance employees from stepping on either the screens or the angle-iron supporting structure. An alternative but somewhat more cumbersome and less satisfactory method was developed for removing objects from the screen. This procedure required employees to stand on power-raised mobile platforms and use hooks to recover the material.

On July 7, 1974, two of the petitioner's maintenance employees, Virgil Deemer and Thomas Cornwell, met with the plant maintenance superintendent to voice their concern about the safety of the screen. The superintendent disagreed with their view, but permitted the two men to inspect the screen with their foreman and to point out dangerous areas needing repair. Unsatisfied with the petitioner's response to the results of this inspection, Deemer and Cornwell met on July 9 with the plant safety director. At that meeting, they requested the name, address, and telephone number of a representative of the local office of the Occupational Safety and Health Administration (OSHA). Although the safety director told the men that they "had better stop and think about what [they] were doing," he furnished the men with the information they requested. Later that same day, Deemer contacted an official of the regional OSHA office and discussed the guard screen.

The next day, Deemer and Cornwell reported for the night shift at 10:45 p.m. Their foreman, after himself walking on some of the angle-iron frames, directed the two men to perform their usual maintenance duties on a section of the old screen. Claiming that the screen was unsafe, they refused to carry out this directive. The foreman then sent them to the personnel office, where they were ordered to punch out without working or being paid for the remaining six hours of the shift. The two men subsequently received written reprimands, which were placed in their employment files.

A little over a month later, the Secretary filed suit in the United States District Court for the Northern District of Ohio, alleging that the petitioner's actions against Deemer and Cornwell constituted discrimination in violation of Section 11(c)(1) of the Act. As relief, the complaint prayed, *inter alia,* that the petitioner be ordered to expunge from its personnel files all references to the reprimands issued to the two employees, and for a permanent injunction requiring the petitioner to compensate the two employees for the six hours of pay they had lost by reason of their disciplinary suspensions.

Following a bench trial, the District Court found that the regulation in question justified Deemer's and Cornwell's refusals to obey their foreman's order on July 10, 1974. The court found that the two employees had "refused to perform the cleaning operation because of a genuine fear of death or serious bodily harm," that the danger presented had been "real and not something which [had] existed only in the minds of the employees," that the employees had acted in good faith and that no reasonable alternative had realistically been open to them other than to refuse to work. The District Court nevertheless denied relief, holding that the Secretary's regulation was inconsistent with the Act and therefore invalid.

The Court of Appeals for the Sixth Circuit reversed the District Court's judgment. Finding ample support in the record for the District Court's factual determination that the actions of Deemer and Cornwell had been justified under the Secretary's regulation, the appellate court disagreed with the District Court's conclusion that the regulation is invalid. We granted certiorari because the decision of the Court of Appeals in this case conflicts with those of two other Courts of Appeals on the important question in issue. That question, as stated at the outset of this opinion, is whether the Secretary's regulation authorizing employee "self-help" in some circumstances is permissible under the Act.

The Act itself creates an express mechanism for protecting workers from employment conditions believed to pose an emergent threat of death or serious injury. Upon receipt of an employee inspection request stating reasonable grounds to believe that an imminent danger is present in a workplace, OSHA must conduct an inspection. In the event this inspection reveals workplace conditions or practices that "could reasonably be expected to cause death or serious physical harm immediately or before the imminence of such danger can be eliminated through the enforcement procedures otherwise provided by" the Act, the OSHA inspector must inform the affected employees and the employer of the danger and notify them that he is recommending to the Secretary that injunctive relief be sought. At this juncture, the Secretary can petition a federal court to restrain the conditions or practices giving rise to the imminent danger. By means of a temporary restraining order or preliminary injunction, the court may then require the employer to avoid, correct, or remove the danger or to prohibit employees from working in the area.

To ensure that this process functions effectively, the Act expressly accords to every employee several rights, the exercise of which may not subject him to discharge or discrimination. An employee is given the right to inform OSHA of an imminently dangerous workplace condition or practice and request that OSHA inspect that condition or practice. He is given a limited right to assist the OSHA inspector in inspecting the workplace, and the right to aid a court in determining whether or not a risk of imminent danger in fact exists. Finally, an affected employee is given the right to bring an action to compel the Secretary to seek injunctive relief if he believes the Secretary has wrongfully declined to do so.

In the light of this detailed statutory scheme, the Secretary is obviously correct when he acknowledges in his regulation that, "as a general matter, there is no right afforded by the Act which would entitle employees to walk off the job because of potential unsafe conditions at the workplace." By providing for prompt notice to the employer of an inspector's intention to seek an injunction against an imminently dangerous condition, the legislation obviously contemplates that the employer will normally respond by voluntarily and speedily eliminating the danger. And in the few instances where this does not occur, the legislative provisions authorizing prompt judicial action are designed to give employees full protection in most situations from the risk of injury or death resulting from an imminently dangerous condition at the worksite.

As this case illustrates, however, circumstances may sometimes exist in which the employee justifiably believes that the express statutory arrangement does not sufficiently protect him from death or serious injury. Such circumstances will probably not often occur, but such a situation may arise when (1) the employee is ordered by his employer to work under conditions that the employee reasonably believes pose an imminent risk of death or serious bodily injury, and (2) the employee has reason to believe that there is not sufficient time or opportunity either to seek effective redress from his employer or to apprise OSHA of the danger.

Nothing in the Act suggests that those few employees who have to face this dilemma must rely exclusively on the remedies expressly set forth in the Act at the risk of their own safety. But nothing in the Act explicitly provides otherwise. Against this background of legislative silence, the Secretary has exercised his rulemaking power and has determined that, when an employee in good faith finds himself in such a predicament, he may refuse to expose himself to the dangerous condition, without being subjected to "subsequent discrimination" by the employer.

The question before us is whether this interpretative regulation constitutes a permissible gloss on the Act by the Secretary, in light of the Act's language, structure, and legislative history. Our inquiry is informed by an awareness that the regulation is entitled to deference unless it can be said not to be a reasoned and supportable interpretation of the Act.

The regulation clearly conforms to the fundamental objective of the Act—to prevent occupational deaths and serious injuries. The Act, in its preamble, declares that its purpose and policy is "to assure so far as possible every working man and woman in the Nation safe and healthful working conditions and to *preserve* our human resources. . . ."

To accomplish this basic purpose, the Act does not wait for an employee to die or become injured. It authorizes the promulgation of health and safety standards and the issuance of citations in the hope that these will act to prevent deaths or injuries from ever occurring. It would seem anomalous to construe an Act so directed and constructed as prohibiting an employee, with no other reasonable alternative, the freedom to withdraw from a workplace environment that he reasonably believes is highly dangerous.

Moreover, the Secretary's regulation can be viewed as an appropriate aid to the full effectuation of the Act's "general duty" clause. That clause provides that "[e]ach employer . . . shall furnish to each of his employees employment and a place of employment which are free from recognized hazards that are causing or are likely to cause death or serious physical harm to his employees." As the legislative history of this provision reflects, it was intended itself to deter the occurrence of occupational deaths and serious injuries by placing on employers a mandatory obligation independent of the specific health and safety standards to be promulgated by the Secretary. Since OSHA inspectors cannot be present around the clock in every workplace, the Secretary's regulation ensures that employees will in all circumstances enjoy the rights afforded them by the "general duty" clause.

The regulation thus on its face appears to further the overriding purpose of the Act, and rationally to complement its remedial scheme. In the absence of some contrary indication in the legislative history, the Secretary's regula-

tion must, therefore, be upheld, particularly when it is remembered that safety legislation is to be liberally construed to effectuate the congressional purpose.

In urging reversal of the judgment before us, the petitioner relies primarily on . . . the Act's legislative history.

Representative Daniels of New Jersey sponsored one of several House bills that led ultimately to the passage of the Act. As reported to the House by the Committee on Education and Labor, the Daniels bill contained a section that was soon dubbed the "strike with pay" provision. This section provided that employees could request an examination by the Department of Health, Education, and Welfare (HEW) of the toxicity of any materials in their workplace. If that examination revealed a workplace substance that had "potentially toxic or harmful effects in such concentration as used or found," the employer was given 60 days to correct the potentially dangerous condition. Following the expiration of that period, the employer could not require that an employee be exposed to toxic concentrations of the substance unless the employee was informed of the hazards and symptoms associated with the substance, the employee was instructed in the proper precautions for dealing with the substance, and the employee was furnished with personal protective equipment. If these conditions were not met, an employee could "absent himself from such risk of harm for the period necessary to avoid such danger without loss of regular compensation for such period."

This provision encountered stiff opposition in the House. Representative Steiger of Wisconsin introduced a substitute bill containing no "strike with pay" provision . . . The House ultimately adopted the Steiger bill.

The bill that was reported to and, with a few amendments, passed by the Senate never contained a "strike with pay" provision. It did, however, give employees the means by which they could request immediate Labor Department inspections. . . .

The petitioner reads into this legislative history a congressional intent incompatible with an administrative interpretation of the Act such as is embodied in the regulation at issue in this case. The petitioner argues that Congress' overriding concern in rejecting the "strike with pay" provision was to avoid giving employees a unilateral authority to walk off the job which they might abuse in order to intimidate or harass their employer. Congress deliberately chose instead, the petitioner maintains, to grant employees the power to request immediate administrative inspections of the workplace which could in appropriate cases lead to coercive judicial remedies. . . .

We read the legislative history differently. Congress rejected a provision that did not concern itself at all with conditions posing real and immediate threats of death or severe injury. The remedy which the rejected provision furnished employees could have been invoked only after 60 days had passed following HEW's inspection and notification that improperly high levels of toxic substances were present in the workplace. Had that inspection revealed employment conditions posing a threat of imminent and grave harm, the Secretary of Labor would presumably have requested, long before expiration of the 60-day period, a court injunction pursuant to other provisions of the Daniels bill. Consequently, in rejecting the Daniels bill's "strike with pay" provision, Congress was not rejecting a legislative provision dealing with the highly perilous and fast-moving situations covered by the regulation now before us.

It is also important to emphasize that what primarily troubled Congress about the Daniels bill's "strike with pay" provision was its requirement that employees be paid their regular salary after having properly invoked their right to refuse to work under the section. It is instructive that virtually every time the issue of an employee's right to absent himself from hazardous work was discussed in the legislative debates, it was in the context of the employee's right to continue to receive his usual compensation.

When it rejected the "strike with pay" concept, therefore, Congress very clearly meant to reject a law unconditionally imposing upon employers an obligation to continue to pay their employees their regular paychecks when they absented themselves from work for reasons of safety. But the regulation at issue here does not require employers to pay workers who refuse to perform their assigned tasks in the face of imminent danger. It simply provides that in such cases the employer may not "discriminate" against the employees involved. An employer "discriminates" against an employee only when he treats that employee less favorably than he treats others similarly situated. . . .

For these reasons we conclude that 29 CFR Section 1977.12(b)(2) (1979) was promulgated by the Secretary in the valid exercise of his authority under the Act. Accordingly, the judgment of the Court of Appeals is affirmed. **It is so ordered.**

[On remand, the district court ordered that the two men be paid for the remainder of their shift.]

Inspections, Investigations, and Recordkeeping

OSHA's occupational safety and health standards are enforced through physical inspections of workplaces. Practical realities in enforcing the act have forced OSHA to prioritize the inspection process. Thus, inspections are targeted first to the investigation of complaints of imminent danger, then to investigation of fatal and catastrophic accidents, investigation of complaints filed by employees alleging hazardous working conditions, investigation of high-hazard industries, and last, random general investigations.

Recordkeeping Requirements

OSHA relies on several sources of information to determine when and where inspections will occur. First, employers with eight or more employees are required under the act to keep records of and to make periodic reports to OSHA on occupational injuries and illnesses. Occupational injuries must be recorded if they involve or result in death, loss of consciousness, medical treatment other than minor first aid, one or more lost work days, the restriction of work or motion, or transfer to another job. Second, the employer is required to maintain accurate records of employee exposures to potentially toxic materials or harmful physical agents required to be monitored under the act. Third, any employee or representative of an employee who believes that a violation of a safety or health standard exists that threatens physical harm, or believes that an imminent danger exists, may request an inspection.

Inspections

The compliance officer conducting the inspection may enter without delay and at reasonable times any factory, business establishment, construction site, or workplace covered by the act. This inspection may include all pertinent conditions, structures, machines, apparatus, devices, equipment, and materials on the inspection site. The office is also given authority to question privately any employer, owner, operator, agent, or employee.

The act allows the employer and a representative authorized by the employees to accompany the inspector during the physical inspection of the work site. In *Chicago Bridge* v. *OSHRC* (535 F.2d 371, 7th Cir. 1976), the court ruled that this right is absolute and not within the discretionary judgment of the compliance officer.

The language of the act appears to allow searches to be conducted without a search warrant. The following case involves a challenge to the constitutionality of the provisions of the act that implicitly authorize warrantless searches by OSHA inspectors.

MARSHALL v. BARLOW'S, INC.

436 U.S. 307 (Supreme Court of the United States, 1978)

WHITE, J.

Section 8(a) of the Occupational Safety and Health Act of 1970 (OSHA or Act) empowers agents of the Secretary of Labor (Secretary) to search the work area of any employment facility within the Act's jurisdiction. The purpose of the search is to inspect for safety hazards and violations of OSHA regulations. No search warrant or other process is expressly required under the Act.

On the morning of September 11, 1975, an OSHA inspector entered the customer service area of Barlow's, Inc., an electrical and plumbing installation business located in Pocatello, Idaho. The president and general manager, Ferrol G. "Bill" Barlow, was on hand; and the OSHA inspector, after showing his credentials, informed Mr. Barlow that he wished to conduct a search of the working areas of the business. Mr. Barlow inquired whether any complaint had been received about his company. The inspector answered no, but that Barlow's, Inc., had simply turned up in the agency's selection process. The inspector again asked to enter the nonpublic area of the business; Mr. Barlow's response was to inquire whether the inspector had a

search warrant. The inspector had none. Thereupon, Mr. Barlow refused the inspector admission to the employee area of his business. He said he was relying on his rights as guaranteed by the Fourth Amendment of the United States Constitution.

Three months later, the Secretary petitioned the United States District Court for the District of Idaho to issue an order compelling Mr. Barlow to admit the inspector. The requested order was issued on December 30, 1975, and was presented to Mr. Barlow on January 5, 1976. Mr. Barlow again refused admission, and he sought his own injunctive relief against the warrantless searches assertedly permitted by OSHA. A three-judge court was convened. On December 30, 1976, it ruled in Mr. Barlow's favor. Concluding that *Camara* v. *Municipal Court* and *See* v. *Seattle* controlled this case, the court held that the Fourth Amendment required a warrant for the type of search involved here and that the statutory authorization for warrantless inspections was unconstitutional. An injunction against searches or inspections pursuant to Section 8(a) was entered. The Secretary appealed, challenging the judgment. . . .

The Secretary urges that warrantless inspections to enforce OSHA are reasonable within the meaning of the Fourth Amendment. Among other things, he relies on Section 8(a) of the Act, which authorizes inspection of business premises without a warrant and which the Secretary urges represents a congressional construction of the Fourth Amendment that the courts should not reject. Regrettably, we are unable to agree.

The Warrant Clause of the Fourth Amendment protects commercial buildings as well as private homes. To hold otherwise would belie the origin of that Amendment, and the American colonial experience. An important forerunner of the first 10 Amendments to the United States Constitution, the Virginia Bill of Rights, specifically opposed "general warrants, whereby an officer or messenger may be commanded to search suspected places without evidence of a fact committed." The general warrant was a recurring point of contention in the Colonies immediately preceding the Revolution. The particular offensiveness it engendered was acutely felt by the merchants and businessmen whose premises and products were inspected for compliance with the several parliamentary revenue measures that most irritated the colonists. "[T]he Fourth Amendment's commands grew in large measure out of the colonists' experience with the writs of assistance . . . [that] granted sweeping power to customs officials and other agents of the King to search at large for smuggled goods." . . . Against this background, it is untenable that the ban on warrantless searches was not intended to shield places of business as well as of residence.

This Court has already held that warrantless searches are generally unreasonable, and that this rule applies to commercial premises as well as homes. In *Camara* v. *Municipal Court,* we held:

> [E]xcept in certain carefully defined classes of cases, a search of private property without proper consent is "unreasonable" unless it has been authorized by a valid search warrant.

On the same day, we also ruled:

> As we explained in *Camara,* a search of private houses is presumptively unreasonable if conducted without a warrant. The businessman, like the occupant of a residence, has a constitutional right to go about his business free from unreasonable official entries upon his private commercial property. The businessman, too, has that right placed in jeopardy if the decision to enter and inspect for violation of regulatory laws can be made and enforced by the inspector in the field without official authority evidenced by a warrant.

These same cases also held that the Fourth Amendment prohibition against unreasonable searches protects against warrantless intrusions during civil as well as criminal investigations. The reason is found in the "basic purpose of this

Amendment . . . [which] is to safeguard the privacy and security of individuals against arbitrary invasions by government officials." If the government intrudes on a person's property, the privacy interest suffers whether the government's motivation is to investigate violations of criminal laws or breaches of other statutory or regulatory standards. It therefore appears that unless some recognized exception to the warrant requirement applies, *See* v. *Seattle* would require a warrant to conduct the inspection sought in this case.

The Secretary urges that an exception from the search warrant requirement has been recognized for "pervasively regulated business[es]," and for "closely regulated" industries "long subject to close supervision and inspection." These cases are indeed exceptions, but they represent responses to relatively unique circumstances. Certain industries have such a history of government oversight that no reasonable expectation of privacy . . . could exist for a proprietor over the stock of such an enterprise. Liquor and firearms are industries of this type; when an entrepreneur embarks upon such a business, he has voluntarily chosen to subject himself to a full arsenal of governmental regulation.

Industries such as these fall within the "certain carefully defined classes of cases," . . . The element that distinguishes these enterprises from ordinary businesses is a long tradition of close government supervision, of which any person who chooses to enter such a business must already be aware. "A central difference between those cases and this one is that businessmen engaged in such federally licensed and regulated enterprises accept the burdens as well as the benefits of their trade, whereas the petitioner here was not engaged in any regulated or licensed business. The businessman in a regulated industry in effect consents to the restrictions placed upon him."

The clear import of our cases is that the closely regulated industry . . . is the exception. The Secretary would make it the rule. Invoking the Walsh-Healey Act of 1936, the Secretary attempts to support a conclusion that all businesses involved in interstate commerce have long been subjected to close supervision of employee safety and health conditions. But the degree of federal involvement in employee working circumstances has never been of the order of specificity and pervasiveness that OSHA mandates. It is quite unconvincing to argue that the imposition of minimum wages and maximum hours on employers who contracted with the Government under the Walsh-Healey Act prepared the entirety of American interstate commerce for regulation of working conditions to the minutest detail. Nor can any but the most fictional sense of voluntary consent to later searches be found in the single fact that one conducts a business affecting interstate commerce; under current practice and law, few businesses can be conducted without having some effect on interstate commerce.

The Secretary also attempts to derive support for . . . [an] exception by drawing analogies from the field of labor law. In *Republic Aviation Corp.* v. *NLRB*, (1945), this Court upheld the rights of employees to solicit for a union during nonworking time where efficiency was not compromised. By opening up his property to employees, the employer had yielded so much of his private property rights as to allow those employees to exercise Section 7 rights under the National Labor Relations Act. But this Court also held that the private property rights of an owner prevailed over the intrusion of nonemployee organizers, even in nonworking areas of the plant and during nonworking hours.

The critical fact in this case is that entry over Mr. Barlow's objection is being sought by a Government agent. Employees are not being prohibited from reporting OSHA violations. What they observe in their daily functions is undoubtedly beyond the employer's reasonable expectation of privacy. The Government inspector, however, is not an employee. Without a warrant he stands in no better position than a member of the public. What is observable by the public is observable, without a warrant, by the Government inspector as well. The owner of a business has not, by the necessary utilization of employees in his operation, thrown open the areas where employees alone are permitted to the warrantless scrutiny of Government agents. That an employee is free to report, and the Government is free to use, any evidence of noncompliance with OSHA that the employee observes furnished no justification for federal agents to enter a place of business from which the public is restricted and to conduct their own warrantless search.

The Secretary nevertheless stoutly argues that the enforcement scheme of the Act requires warrantless searches, and that the restrictions on search discretion contained in the Act and its regulations already protect as much privacy as a warrant would. The Secretary thereby asserts the actual reasonableness of OSHA searches, whatever the general rule against warrantless searches might be. Because "reasonableness is still the ultimate standard," the Secretary suggests that the Court decide whether a warrant is needed by arriving at a sensible balance between the administrative necessities of OSHA inspections and the incremental protection of privacy of business owners a warrant would afford. He suggests that only a decision exempting OSHA inspections from the Warrant Clause would give "full recognition

to the competing public and private interests here at stake."

The Secretary submits that warrantless inspections are essential to the proper enforcement of OSHA because they afford the opportunity to inspect without prior notice and hence to preserve the advantages of surprise. While the dangerous conditions outlawed by the Act include structural defects that cannot be quickly hidden or remedied, the Act also regulates a myriad of safety details that may be amenable to speedy alteration or disguise. The risk is that during the interval between an inspector's initial request to search a plant and his procuring a warrant following the owner's refusal of permission, violations of this latter type could be corrected and thus escape the inspector's notice. To the suggestion that warrants may be issued *ex parte* and executed without delay and without prior notice, thereby preserving the element of surprise, the Secretary expresses concern for the administrative strain that would be experienced by the inspection system, and by the courts, should *ex parte* warrants issued in advance become standard practice.

We are unconvinced, however, that requiring warrants to inspect will impose serious burdens on the inspection system or the courts, will prevent inspections necessary to enforce the statute, or will make them less effective. In the first place, the great majority of businessmen can be expected in normal course to consent to inspection without warrant; the Secretary has not brought to this Court's attention any widespread pattern of refusal. In those cases where an owner does insist on a warrant, the Secretary argues that inspection efficiency will be impeded by the advance notice and delay. The Act's penalty provisions for giving advance notice of a search, and the Secretary's own regulations, indicate that surprise searches are indeed contemplated. However, the Secretary has also promulgated a regulation providing that upon refusal to permit an inspector to enter the property or to complete his inspection, the inspector shall attempt to ascertain the reasons for the refusal and report to his superior, who shall "promptly take appropriate action, including compulsory process, if necessary." The regulation represents a choice to proceed by process where entry is refused; and on the basis of evidence available from present practice, the Act's effectiveness has not been crippled by providing those owners who wish to refuse an initial requested entry with a time lapse while the inspector obtains the necessary process. Indeed, the kind of process sought in this case and apparently anticipated by the regulation provides notice to the business operator. If this safeguard endangers the efficient administration of OSHA, the Secretary should never have adopted it, particularly when the Act does not require it. Nor is it immediately apparent why the advantages of surprise would be lost if, after being refused entry, procedures were available for the Secretary to seek an *ex parte* warrant and to reappear at the premises without further notice to the establishment being inspected.

Whether the Secretary proceeds to secure a warrant or other process, with or without prior notice, his entitlement to inspect will not depend on his demonstrating probable cause to believe that conditions in violation of OSHA exist on the premises. Probable cause in the criminal law sense is not required. For purposes of an administrative search such as this, probable cause justifying the issuance of a warrant may be based not only on specific evidence of an existing violation but also on a showing that "reasonable legislative or administrative standards for conducting an . . . inspection are satisfied with respect to a particular [establishment]."

A warrant showing that a specific business has been chosen for an OSHA search on the basis of a general administrative plan for the enforcement of the Act derived from neutral sources such as, for example, dispersion of employees in various types of industries across a given area, and the desired frequency of searches in any of the lesser divisions of the area, would protect an employer's Fourth Amendment rights. We doubt that the consumption of enforcement energies in the obtaining of such warrants will exceed manageable proportions.

Finally, the Secretary urges that requiring a warrant for OSHA inspectors will mean that, as a practical matter, warrantless-search provisions in other regulatory statutes are also constitutionally infirm. The reasonableness of a warrantless search, however, will depend upon the specific enforcement needs and privacy guarantees of each statute. Some of the statutes cited apply only to a single industry, where regulations might already be so pervasive that . . .

[an] exception to the warrant requirement could apply. Some statutes already envision resort to federal-court enforcement when entry is refused, employing specific language in some cases and general language in others. In short, we base today's opinion on the facts and law concerned with OSHA and do not retreat from a holding appropriate to that statute because of its real or imagined effect on other, different administrative schemes.

Nor do we agree that the incremental protections afforded the employer's privacy by a warrant are so marginal that they fail to justify the administrative burdens that may be entailed. The authority to make warrantless searches devolves almost unbridled discretion upon executive and administrative officers, particularly those in the field, as to when to search and whom to search. A warrant, by contrast, would provide assurances from a neutral officer that the inspection is reasonable under the Constitution, is authorized by statute, and is pursuant to an administrative plan containing specific neutral criteria. Also, a warrant would then and there advise the owner of the scope and objects of the search, beyond which limits the inspector is not expected to proceed. These are important functions for a warrant to perform, functions which underlie the Court's prior decisions that the Warrant Clause applies to inspections for compliance with regulatory statutes. We conclude that the concerns expressed by the Secretary do not suffice to justify warrantless inspections under OSHA or vitiate the general constitutional requirement that for a search to be reasonable a warrant must be obtained.

We hold that Barlow's was entitled to a declaratory judgment that the Act is unconstitutional insofar as it purports to authorize inspections without warrant or its equivalent and to an injunction enjoining the Act's enforcement to that extent. The judgment of the District Court is therefore affirmed. **So ordered.**

As a result of *Marshall* v. *Barlow's,* the compliance officer now must request permission to enter the workplace or other area that is to be the subject of the search. If the employer refuses entry or forbids the continuation of an inspection, the compliance officer must terminate the inspection or confine it to those areas where no objection has been raised. Following such a refusal, an ex parte application for an inspection warrant can be obtained from either a U.S. district judge or a U.S. magistrate.

Citations, Penalties, Abatement, and Appeal

When an inspection leads to the discovery of a violation of a standard under the act, the employer is issued either a written citation describing the particular nature of the violation or a notice of de minimis violations. A de minimis violation is one that has no direct or immediate relationship to the health or safety of the workers or the workplace affected; for de minimis violations, no citations or proposed penalties are issued.

If a citation is issued, the employer must be notified by certified mail within a reasonable time, but in no event longer than six months after the identification of the violation, of any proposed penalty to be assessed. The employer then has fifteen working days within which to notify OSHA that it intends to contest the citation or the proposed penalty. If the employer does not contest, the citation becomes final and is not subject to appeal or review.

The citation must set a reasonable time for the abatement of the violation, usually not to exceed thirty days. The employer is required to post the citation, or a copy, prominently, at or near each place where the violation occurred. The employees or representatives of the employees may file a notice challenging the period of time set in the citation for the abatement.

If the employer challenges the citation, the penalty assessed, or the period for abatement, a hearing is held before an Administrative Law Judge, who makes findings of fact and conclusions of law that either affirm, modify, or vacate the citation. This order becomes final thirty days after it is filed with OSHA unless, within that time, a member of OSHRC exercises the statutory right to direct review by the full commission. Any party to the proceeding may file a petition requesting this discretionary review. A final order of the commission may be appealed to the appropriate U.S. court of appeals.

The penalty and citation may be separately challenged by the employer. However, if only the penalty is contested, the violation is not subject to review.

When the citation and proposed penalty are contested, the employer has an absolute defense to the citation if it can prove that compliance to the standard is impossible. A showing that the standards are merely impractical or difficult to meet will not excuse performance.

In the event the violation is not corrected within the allowed time, the employer is notified by certified mail of the failure to abate and of the proposed penalty. This notice and proposed penalty are final unless, here again, the employer files a notice of contest within fifteen working days. If the order is not contested, it is deemed a final order and is not subject to judicial review.

If the employer has made a good-faith effort to comply with the abatement requirements of the initial citation but the abatement has not occurred because of factors beyond the reasonable control of the employer, a petition for modification of abatement can be filed. If OSHA or an employee objects to the requested extension or modification, a hearing is held before OSHRC.

If the employer files a petition for modification, the petition must state in detail the steps taken by the employer to abate the hazard, the additional time necessary to abate, the reasons additional time is necessary, including unavailability of technical or professional personnel or equipment, and interim steps being taken to protect employees.

If the employer fails to correct a cited violation after it has become final, a fine may be imposed of not more than $1,000 per day. If the violation is found to be willful, or a repeat violation, or results in the death of an employee, OSHA can impose fines of up to $70,000. In the past, OSHA had a practice of imposing a large fine, and then allowing the offender to negotiate a reduction in the fine. In 1990, Congress amended the act to prohibit OSHA from reducing a fine for a willful violation below $7,000. The act also provides for criminal penalties of up to six months imprisonment, with the maximum increased to twelve months for a repeat violation. In the past, OSHA had been reluctant to seek prison terms for violations, but that attitude changed in 1990; in one case, a contractor found guilty of violations in a fatal trench cave-in was sentenced to 45 days in jail.

State Plans

The Occupational Safety and Health Act requires that OSHA encourage the states to develop and operate their own workplace safety and health programs, which must be "at least as effective as" the federal programs. When a state plan has been accepted by OSHA, it is monitored immediately after its approval to determine its compliance, and OSHA retains discretionary enforcement authority for three years. The state agency must file quarterly and semiannual reports with OSHA. Once the effectiveness of the state program is determined, OSHA determines whether federal enforcement will be reinstituted or fully delegated to the state. If the state plan is fully certified, it still is required to change its standards to conform to any changes made in the federal standards, unless it can show a compelling local reason against making the change.

Some states, such as California, have detailed and well-developed enforcement programs that are fully certified by OSHA. At present, nearly half of the states have plans at some level of the implementation process.

Some states have also adopted right-to-know laws, which grant employees the right to know if hazardous or toxic substances are used in their workplace. Employers may be required to label containers of toxic substances, to inform employees of toxic substances in the workplace, to train employees in the proper handling of such substances, and to inform the employee's physician of the chemical composition of substances in the workplace in connection with the physician's diagnosis or treatment of the employee.

QUESTIONS

1. What are the goals of the Occupational Safety and Health Act? How does the act attempt to meet those goals?

2. What agencies are created by the Occupational Safety and Health Act, and what are the roles of those agencies?

3. Describe the procedures used to create permanent standards under OSHA.

4. When can employees exercise the right to refuse under OSHA without fear of reprisal?

5. What is the purpose of workplace inspections under OSHA? What is the effect of the *Barlow's* case on that purpose?

6. What procedures must be followed in issuing a citation under OSHA? What penalties may be imposed for violations of OSHA?

7. What is the effect of state right-to-know laws?

CASE PROBLEMS

1. A unionized paper company had been using a system of three flagmen for moving railroad locomotives around its yard. It sought a variance to allow it to replace the flagmen with a two-way radio system. The union opposed the application for the variance, asserting that a breakdown in radio communication could result in an accident.

   Do you think the union opposed the variance for any other reasons? What should be the firm's response to the union's objection? Are there any measures the company can take to obviate the danger identified by the union? See *Hammermill Papers Group,* CCH Occupational Safety and Health Decisions 26,597 (1983).

2. The general contractor on a construction site gave an OSHA inspector permission to inspect the site. The inspector found that the masonry subcontractor was guilty of a serious violation by exposing employees to an eight-foot-high, unguarded wall opening. The subcontractor challenged the finding on the basis of an illegal search in contravention of his Fourth Amendment rights.

   Who do you think won the decision? See *J. L. Foti Construction Co., Inc.,* CCH Occupational Safety and Health Decisions 26,776 (1983).

3. An employee who was hypersensitive to tobacco smoke (tearing, scratchy eyes, difficulty breathing, chest pains, irritated throat and nasal passages) requested that his employer take steps to create a smoke-free environment in which he could work.

   Does OSHA's general duty clause require the employer to comply? Should this employee be treated as handicapped? If so, assume the applicable state discrimination law states that "a reasonable accommodation be made to a person's handicap or disability." How much accommodation is reasonable? If OSHA's general duty clause *does* apply, does it preempt the state law? See *Vickers* v. *Veterans Administration,* CCH Occupational Safety and Health Decisions 26,558 (1983).

4. A wrecking and heavy moving firm was moving a barn. As the barn was being towed across a field, it came close to three 7,200-volt power lines. A ball of fire was observed where the barn's lightning rod either came too close to, or actually touched, one of the power lines. Two employees were electrocuted and three more were injured.

   Did the company violate OSHA's general duty clause, or was this merely an unfortunate accident? Assuming that passing close to the wires was unavoidable, what steps might the company have taken to avoid the tragedy? What possible mitigating factors might there have been? See *Clyde Dingey and Sons, House Movers,* CCH Occupational Safety and Health Decisions 26,501 (1983).

5. A worker in a lead-smelting plant was reassigned from weighman to a clean-up position after he was found to have excessive blood-lead levels. He received a weighman's base pay rate for hours worked during the removal period, but did not get the shift differential and scheduled overtime earnings that would have accrued to him if he had not been removed. The OSHA stan-

dard requires workers to receive *all ascertainable amounts* they would have received had they not been removed.

If the company argues that (1) back pay is not a proper abatement expense and (2) overtime is not ascertainable, what recourse does the worker have? See *St. Joe Resources Co.*, CCH Occupational Safety and Health Decisions 26,448 (1983).

6. An electrical contractor required electricians and apprentices to wear hard hats and respirators when he felt job safety required them. An apprentice who was a member of the Sikh Aharma Brother, which requires members to wear a beard and turban, refused to comply.

   If the contractor does not require the apprentice to wear a hard hat and to shave, so that his respirator fits properly, will the contractor breach OSHA's general duty clause? If the contractor does require the apprentice to remove his turban and shave, so that he can properly use the safety equipment, is this religious discrimination in violation of Title VII? Which agency should exercise jurisdiction of this case: OSHA, EEOC, or both? What do you think the decision will be? See EEOC Decision 82–1, 28 F.E.P. Cases 1840 (January 18, 1982).

7. New Jersey passed a Worker and Community Right to Know Act in 1984. The law was passed in response to widely publicized problems of chemical exposure and dumping, which affected workers and communities at large. The law required the state's Department of Environmental Protection to develop an environmental hazardous substance list. It required employers to maintain detailed records and to label substances on the list. It also required employee education and training programs.

   OSHA had previously promulgated a hazard communication rule, which applied to manufacturers. Employers attacked the New Jersey law on grounds of federal preemption and violation of their due process rights in that requiring labeling was in some cases a "taking" of their trade secrets. New Jersey argued that there was no preemption because the state law was broader than the federal law, both in coverage of all employers and in protecting not only workers, but the general public; there was no "taking" because trade secrets are not property rights.

   How do you think the court ruled in this dispute? See *N.J. State Chamber of Commerce* v. *Hughey,* 774 F.2d 587 (3d Cir. 1985).

8. OSHA's hearing-conservation amendment to its workplace noise standard required employers to monitor workplace noise levels and, at least annually, test the hearing of employees exposed to a noise level greater than 85 dB, averaged over an eight-hour period. If an employee suffered an average hearing loss of 10 dB, *regardless of the cause,* the employer was required to provide hearing protectors, reduce the worker's exposure to noise, institute a training program, and keep records. Estimated annual compliance by covered employers was estimated by OSHA to be $254.3 million.

   If you were a covered employer, on what basis would you have challenged this amendment? See *Forging Ind. Ass'n* v. *Sec. of Labor,* 748 F.2d 210 (4th Cir., 1984).

9. Because the availability of new plots was becoming very limited, a cemetery company in a major metropolitan area began selling single plots wherein a husband and wife ultimately would be interred one on top of the other. When the first spouse died, a grave was excavated to a depth sufficient to leave room for the future interment of the surviving spouse. To "square off" the corners of the grave, a member of the cemetery's grounds crew would enter the newly dug grave with a spade or trowel to perform the task.

   One of the grounds keepers filed a complaint with OSHA claiming that it was unsafe to work in the graves without shoring. An inspector from OSHA decided that the double graves were deep enough to require proper shoring before a gravedigger enters them to square them off. The cemetery's general manager replied that no other cemetery's procedure included shoring and that if required to do so, his company would become uncompetitive.

   What recourse does the general manager have? (This case problem is drawn from the experience of one of the authors in legal practice.)

10. Karen Silkwood was a laboratory analyst for Kerr-McGee at its Cimarron plant near Crescent, Oklahoma. The plant fabricated plutonium fuel pins for use as reactor fuel in nuclear power plants. The plant was subject to licensing and regulation by the Nuclear Regulatory Commission (NRC) pursuant to the Atomic Energy Act, 42 U.S.C. Sections 2011–2284 (1976 ed. and Supp. V).

    During a three-day period in November 1974, Silkwood was contaminated by plutonium from the Cimarron plant. On November 5, Silkwood was grinding and polishing plutonium samples, utilizing glove boxes designed for that purpose. In accordance with established procedures, she checked her hands for contamination when she withdrew them from the glove box. When some contamination was detected, a more extensive check was performed. She was immediately decontaminated, and at the end of her shift the monitors detected no contamination. However, she was given urine and fecal kits and was instructed to collect samples in order to check for plutonium discharge.

The next day, upon leaving the laboratory, Silkwood monitored herself and again discovered surface contamination. Once again, she was decontaminated. On the third day, November 7, Silkwood was monitored upon her arrival at the plant. High levels of contamination were detected. Four urine samples and one fecal sample submitted that morning were also highly contaminated. Suspecting that the contamination had spread to areas outside the plant, the company directed a decontamination squad to accompany Silkwood to her apartment. The squad then monitored the apartment, finding contamination in several rooms, with especially high levels in the bathroom, the kitchen, and Silkwood's bedroom.

The contamination level in Silkwood's apartment was such that many of her personal belongings had to be destroyed. Silkwood herself was sent to the Los Alamos Scientific Laboratory to determine the extent of contamination in her vital body organs. She returned to work on November 13. That night she was killed in an unrelated automobile accident.

Bill Silkwood, Karen's father, brought a diversity action in his capacity as administrator of her estate. The action was based on common law tort principles under Oklahoma law and was designed to recover for the contamination injuries to Karen's person and property. Kerr-McGee stipulated that the plutonium that caused the contamination came from its plant, and the jury expressly rejected Kerr-McGee's allegation that Silkwood had intentionally removed the plutonium from the plant in an effort to embarrass the company. There were no other specific findings of fact with respect to the cause of the contamination.

One argument raised by the company to get the case dismissed was that because of the heavily regulated nature of the industry, Silkwood's state common law causes of action were preempted by federal law.

Should federal preemption control here? What remedy would be available under federal law? See *Silkwood* v. *Kerr-McGee Corp.,* 464 U.S. 238 (1984).

Employee Retirement Income Security Act: ERISA

THE PROVISION OF PENSION plans as part of an employee's compensation did not become widespread until the late 1940s and early 1950s. The increasing use of pensions was, in part, the result of changes to the federal tax laws that encouraged the creation of retirement income programs by allowing tax deferral of payments to such plans. Apart from the tax law provisions, however, there was little federal regulation of pension plans; and state regulation of such plans was relatively ineffective.

ERISA

In 1974 Congress enacted the **Employee Retirement Income Security Act,** known as **ERISA.** The act was passed in response to numerous instances of pension fund mismanagement and abuse. Retired employees had their pension benefits reduced or terminated because their pension plan had been inadequately funded or depleted through mismanagement. In other instances, employees retiring after twenty years or more of service with an employer were ineligible for pensions because of complex and strict eligibility requirements.

ERISA was intended to prevent such abuses and to protect the interests of employees and their beneficiaries in employee benefit plans. The act imposes standards of conduct and responsibility upon pension fund fiduciaries (persons having authority or control over the management of pension fund assets). The act also requires that pension plan administrators disclose relevant financial information to employees and the government. The act sets certain minimum standards that pension plans must meet in order to qualify for preferential tax treatment, and it provides legal remedies to employees and their beneficiaries in the event of violations. The provisions of ERISA apply to employee benefit plans established by employers. The act recognizes two types of benefit plans: welfare plans and pension plans. Welfare plans usually provide participating employees and their beneficiaries with medical coverage, disability benefits, death benefits, vacation pay, and/or unemployment benefits. Welfare plans may also include apprenticeship programs, prepaid legal services, daycare centers, and scholarship funds. Pension plans are defined as including any plan intended to provide retirement income to employees and that results in deferral of income for such employees.

ERISA's main focus is on pension plans. It seeks to ensure that all employees covered by pension plans receive the benefits due them under those plans. ERISA does *not* require an employer to provide a pension plan for its employees. However, if a pension plan is offered, ERISA will set certain minimum standards and requirements that the pension plan must meet.

Coverage

The provisions of ERISA do not apply to employee benefit plans that are established by federal, state, or local government employers. Nor does the act apply to plans covering employees of tax-exempt churches or to plans maintained solely for the purpose of complying with applicable workers' compensation, unemployment compensation, or disability insurance laws. Neither does ERISA apply to plans maintained outside the United States primarily for the benefit of nonresident aliens. But these exemptions are relatively narrow; ERISA's reach is very broad.

The two main features of ERISA—the imposition of standards for fiduciary conduct and responsibility and the setting of minimum standards for pension plan requirements—have different bases for their coverage. The fiduciary duties and conduct standards apply to any employee benefit plan established or maintained by an employer engaged in interstate commerce, or in an industry or activity affecting such commerce. They also apply to plans established and maintained by unions representing employees engaged in an industry or activity affecting interstate commerce.

The minimum standards for plan requirements must be met in order for the employee benefit plans to qualify for preferential tax treatment. Because such tax treatment enables an employer to deduct contributions to qualified benefit plans immediately but does not consider such payments as income to participating employees until they actually receive the payments after retirement, most employers seek to "qualify" their benefit plans by complying with ERISA's minimum standards. Such compliance, however, is not required. Some employers who view the ERISA requirements as being too stringent have chosen not to "qualify" their benefit plans for such preferential tax treatment. Those employers are still subject to the fiduciary duties of ERISA if they are engaged in, or affect, interstate commerce (which today includes most enterprises).

Fiduciary Responsibility

As noted, ERISA imposes standards of conduct and responsibility on fiduciaries of benefit plans established or maintained by employers and unions in or affecting interstate commerce. The act requires that all such plans must be in writing and must designate at least one named fiduciary who has the authority to manage and control the plan's operation and management. The plan must also provide a written procedure for establishing and carrying out a funding policy that is consistent with the plan's objectives and with ERISA's requirements. The written provisions must also specify the basis on which contributions to the fund and payments from the fund will be made. Last, the written plan must describe the procedure for allocation of responsibility for administering and operating the benefit plan.

ERISA requires that all assets of the benefit plan must be held in trust for the benefit of participating employees and their beneficiaries. The plan must establish a procedure for handling claims on the fund by participants and their beneficiaries. Any individual with a claim against the fund must exhaust these internal procedures before seeking legal remedies from the courts.

Fiduciary.

ERISA defines a **fiduciary** as including any person exercising discretionary authority or control respecting the management of the benefit plan, or disposition of plan assets; or who renders, or has authority or responsibility to render, investment advice (for which he or she is compensated) with respect to any money or property of the plan; or, last, who has *any* discretionary authority or responsibility in the administration of the plan. Persons not normally considered fiduciaries, such as consultants or advisers, may be found to be fiduciaries when their expertise is used in a managerial, administrative, or advisory capacity by the plan.

Fiduciary Duties.

ERISA generally codifies and expands the common-law concepts defining the role of a fiduciary. Under ERISA, fiduciaries must discharge their duties *solely* in the interest of the participants and their beneficiaries for the exclusive purpose of providing them with benefits for the participants and defraying the reasonable expenses of administering the plan.

Fiduciaries under ERISA are held to the common-law "prudent man rule"—that is, the fiduciary must act "with the care, skill, prudence and diligence that a prudent man acting in a like capacity and familiar with such matters would use in the conduct of an enterprise of like character and with like aims." For instance, the fiduciary must diversify the investments of the plan to minimize the risk of large losses, unless under the particular circumstances it would be prudent not to diversify.

Prohibited Transactions.

The act prohibits certain transactions by fiduciaries or persons "with an interest" in the benefit plan. The act defines a person "with an interest" as including a fiduciary, a person providing services to the plan, an employer whose employees are covered by the plan, or an owner having 50 percent or more interest in such an employer. The **prohibited transactions** between the plan and the person with an interest include the sale or lease of property, the extension of credit, and the furnishing of goods, services, or facilities. Also prohibited is the transfer of plan assets to, or for the use of, a person with an interest.

Fiduciaries are forbidden to engage in self-dealing with the plan—that is, dealing with the assets of the plan for their own interests. Fiduciaries are also prohibited from receiving any consideration or benefit personally from persons dealing with the plan in connection with a transaction involving the assets of the plan. The act prohibits the plan from investing more than 10 percent of its assets in the securities or property of an employer of employees participating in the plan. (Investments in such employer securities or property involving less than 10 percent of the plan's assets must still meet the prudent person test.)

Liability for Breach of Fiduciary Duty.   A fiduciary is liable to the plan for any losses resulting from the breach of any of his or her duties, responsibilities, or obligations. The fiduciary must also refund any personal profits made through personal use of the plan's assets. The fiduciary may also be subject to any other equitable or remedial measures that the court may deem appropriate, including his or her removal.

A fiduciary may also be liable for the breach of duty by a co-fiduciary under the following circumstances:

1. knowingly participating in, or undertaking to conceal, an act or omission of another fiduciary;

2. enabling another fiduciary to commit a breach by failing to comply with his or her own fiduciary responsibility;

3. failing to make reasonable efforts to remedy a breach by another fiduciary of which he or she has knowledge.

Exculpatory provisions, which seek to protect fiduciaries from liability for the breach of their duties, are generally held to be void as against public policy. The fiduciary may insure against liability for breach of duty; however, if the benefit plan provides such insurance for the fiduciary, the insurance company must be allowed to recover from the fiduciary any amounts paid out under the policy.

Fiduciaries are not liable for any breaches that occur either before they become fiduciaries or after they cease to be fiduciaries of the plan.

Bonding.   The act requires every fiduciary of an employee pension plan and every person who handles funds or property of a plan to be bonded in an amount equal to at least 10 percent of the funds handled, but not less than $1,000 and not more than $500,000. The form of the bond must be approved by the Secretary of Labor and must provide protection to the plan against any loss caused by fraud or dishonesty of the plan official.

No bonding is required for the administrator, officers, or employees of a plan under which only the general assets of a union are used to pay benefits. In addition, no bond is required of a fiduciary that is a U.S. corporation exercising trust powers or conducting an insurance business if it is subject to supervision or examination by federal or state authorities and, at all times, has a combined capital and surplus in excess of a minimum amount set by regulation, not less than $1 million.

ERISA also authorizes a plan administrator to apply to the Secretary of Labor for exemption from the bonding requirements on the ground that the overall financial condition of the plan is sound enough to provide protection for participants and their beneficiaries.

Enforcement of Fiduciary Duties

The fiduciary duty and responsibility provisions of ERISA are enforced by the Department of Labor and by plan participants and their beneficiaries. The Department of Labor is authorized by the act to bring suit against a fiduciary who breaches any duties, obligations, or responsibilities under the act. Such suits may also be brought by plan participants or the beneficiaries, who may, if successful, also recover their legal fees and costs.

If an employee benefit plan has engaged in certain prohibited transactions, the Secretary of Labor may assess a civil penalty to be paid by the plan. If the plan engaging in the prohibited transactions is qualified for preferential tax treatment, the Internal Revenue Service may impose and collect an excise tax against the plan, rather than having the Secretary of Labor levy a civil penalty.

Minimum Requirements for Qualified Pension Plans

In addition to imposing standards of conduct for benefit plan fiduciaries, ERISA sets certain minimum requirements that plans must meet in order to qualify for preferential tax treatment. The act also requires plan administrators to disclose certain relevant financial information, and it provides an insurance fund for benefits payable under certain pensions.

Types of Pension Plans

The act recognizes two types of pension plans: defined-benefit plans and defined-contribution plans.

Defined-Benefit Plan.   A **defined-benefit plan** is a pension plan that ensures eligible employees and their beneficiaries a specified monthly income for life. ERISA provides an insurance scheme to guarantee the benefits under defined-benefit plans. The insurance scheme is administered by the Pension Benefit Guaranty Corporation (PBGC), set up under the act. The PBGC collects a premium from employers offering such pensions, to provide an insurance fund. If an employer is unable to meet the payment requirements of a defined-benefit plan, the PBGC will pay monthly benefits to the participating employees, up to a maximum monthly amount. [Despite the substantial sums raised by the PBGC through employer premiums, the insurance fund is inadequate to cover all potential liability under defined-benefit pension plans.]

Defined-Contribution Plans.   **Defined-contribution plans** are plans under which an employer makes a fixed-share contribution into a retirement account each year. These funds are invested on behalf of the participating employee, who receives the proceeds upon retirement. The pension benefits under a defined-contribution plan are not insured against failure of the company and are not covered by the PBGC.

Plans Qualifying for Preferential Tax Treatment

ERISA sets certain minimum requirements that pension plans must meet in order to qualify for preferential tax treatment. Such requirements involve participation of employees, and **vesting,** that is, entitlement to nonforfeitable benefits under the plan. The requirements specified under ERISA are minimum requirements; the employer may offer more generous provisions in a pension plan. However, if the plan's requirements are more stringent than ERISA's minimum provisions, the pension plan will not qualify for preferential tax treatment.

Participation and Coverage Requirements.   Although a company's tax-qualified retirement plan need not cover all its employees, certain minimal coverage and participation requirements must be met. In reviewing these requirements, keep in mind that they constitute the "floor" below which coverage and participation cannot be permitted to drop; a company can be more liberal with the participation rules in its particular plan if it wishes.

The Internal Revenue Code permits a qualified retirement plan to require an employee to reach the age of twenty-one and to complete a year of service before being eligible to participate. If a plan provides for full and immediate vesting of company contributions into it, then participation can be conditioned upon up to two years of service. (This exception does not apply to 401(K) plans, for which the maximum period before participation remains one year of service regardless of the vesting schedule.) A plan is no longer permitted to set a maximum age for an employee's participation. (Although the law once was that new hires who were less than five years away from the plan's specified normal retirement age could be excluded, this is no longer the case.)

Plans that are permitted to require two years of service prior to plan participation cannot demand that the two years be consecutive. But employees who incur a one-year break in service can be required to start the qualification process over again when they resume employment with the sponsoring company.

A plan can exclude specified classes of employees from participation based on factors other than failure to meet minimum age and length-of-service requirements. The most common exclusion is of unionized employees subject to a collective bargaining agreement, which may very well include a provision for participation in a multi-employer plan sponsored by the union.

The "year of service" requirement (i.e., the eligibility computation period) is defined as any consecutive twelve months, whether specified in the plan as a calendar year or plan year, during which the employee puts in at least 1,000 hours. If the employee falls short of the 1,000-hour requirement during the initial computation period, the next computation period commences on the anniversary of employment, or the first day of the plan year in which that anniversary falls, if the plan so specifies. For purposes of computing the 1,000 hours, the law calls for including all hours for which the employee is paid or is entitled to be paid. Hours of service thus include paid vacation, sick days, holidays, days missed because of disability, and the like. Back pay, for example, awarded under one of the federal labor or employment laws, is also included if relevant.

A one-year break in service similarly means a calendar year, plan year, or any other consecutive twelve months designated by the plan, during which for whatever reason the employee fails to complete more than 500 hours of service. (One significant exception is parenting leave, which does not constitute such a break in service.)

In addition to participation requirements, the law also imposes coverage requirements as a condition of tax qualification. A pension plan must satisfy one of two coverage tests: either the ratio percentage test or the average benefit test. (A plan having no non–highly compensated employees will automatically meet the Internal Revenue Code's coverage requirements.)

Using the ratio percentage test, the number of non–highly compensated active employees participating must equal at least 70 percent of the highly ($75,000-plus per year, or owners, officers, and best-paid employees even if earning as little as $45,000 to $50,000) compensated, active employees.

If the average benefit test is used, the plan must not discriminate in favor of the company's highly compensated employees. The non–highly compensated workers once again must receive at least 70 percent of the highly compensated participants' average benefits.

Vesting Requirements.   Vesting means that a plan participant has gained a nonforfeitable right to some plan benefit. In the case of a defined-contribution plan, the right is to the employee's accrued account balance. If the plan is of the defined-benefit variety, the nonforfeitable right is to the accrued benefit. Vesting turns upon length of service. Until a participant's length of service compels vesting, that participant can be accruing benefits, but will not have a nonforfeitable right to those benefits. In other words, if an employee quits or is fired before vesting begins, his or her accrued benefits will be lost (unless the employee moves to a related company in the same corporation or is rehired by the same company before a one-year break in service has occurred).

Not long ago it was not unusual for plans to require ten years of service for full vesting. Recent changes to federal law have liberalized that requirement, plans must now choose between two minimum vesting schedules. Under a five-year vesting schedule, no vesting occurs until the participant completes five years of service, when 100 percent occurs. Under seven-year graded vesting, the minimum acceptable schedule is as follows:

Years of Service	Vested Percentage
Less than 3	0
3	20
4	40
5	60
6	80
7 or more	100

Two important points should be kept in mind. First, as with participation and coverage requirements, the above schedules are minimums; a particular employer's plan(s) can permit faster vesting, if the employer desires. Second, these schedules count years of service, not years of participation. Thus, in the five-year vesting option, for example, a plan that called for a year of service in order to participate, plus five years of participation, would not meet the minimum vesting schedule.

Interruptions in Service.   All vesting schedules require some period of continuous employment, and breaks in service become important in computing the time at which benefits become vested. In computing an employee's years of service, any years of service completed prior to any one-year break in service are not required to be taken into account until the employee has completed a year of service after returning to employment. Thereafter, if the number of consecutive one-year breaks totals five or more or exceeds the employee's prebreak years of service (regardless of number) and no vesting had occurred before the break in service, then the prebreak service can be ignored for vesting purposes. Additionally, years of service before the employee turned eighteen, years of service before the plan was put into effect, and—if the plan is contributory—years in which the participant declined to contribute can be disregarded.

Integration of Benefits.   Although an employee has a vested right to participate in pension plan benefits after the requisite time period, in some circumstances the amounts the employer must pay out to the employee under the plan may be reduced by the amount of payments the employee receives from some other program. For example, some pension plans may take into account the Social Security payments received by employees in calculating the monthly pension benefits to be paid to such employees. ERISA provides that a qualified plan may offset 83⅓ percent of the Social Security payments received by an employee—that is, the monthly pension benefits paid to the employee under the plan may be reduced by the amount equal to 83⅓ percent of the monthly Social Security benefits received by the employee. But after benefits to a participant have commenced, they cannot later be reduced by an increase in Social Security.

This right of offsetting benefits against those paid by other sources is known as integration. Integration is an extraordinarily complex area, even by ERISA's intricate standards. A detailed discussion of it is beyond the scope of this book.

ALESSI v. RAYBESTOS-MANHATTAN

451 U.S. 504, 101 S. Ct. 1898 (Supreme Court of the United States, 1981)

MARSHALL, J.

Some private pension plans reduce a retiree's pension benefits by the amount of workers' compensation awards re-

ceived subsequent to retirement. In these cases we consider whether two such offset provisions are lawful under the Employment Retirement Income Security Act of 1974 (ERISA), and whether they may be prohibited by state law.

Raybestos-Manhattan, Inc., and General Motors Corp. maintain employee pension plans that are subject to federal regulation under ERISA. Both plans provide that an employee's retirement benefits shall be reduced, or offset, by an amount equal to workers' compensation awards for which the individual is eligible. In 1977, the New Jersey Legislature amended its Workers' Compensation Act to expressly prohibit such offsets. The amendment states that "[t]he right of compensation granted in this chapter may be set off against disability pension benefits or payments but shall not be set off against employees' retirement pension benefits or payments."

. . . There, both District Court Judges ruled that the pension offset provisions were invalid under New Jersey law, and concluded that Congress had not intended ERISA to pre-empt state laws of this sort. The District Court Judges also held that the offsets were prohibited by Section 203(a) of ERISA. This section prohibits forfeitures of vested pension rights except under four specific conditions inapplicable to these cases. The judges concluded that offsets based on workers' compensation awards would be forbidden forfeitures, and struck down a contrary federal Treasury Regulation authorizing such offsets.

The United States Court of Appeals for the Third Circuit consolidated the appeals from these two decisions and reversed. It rejected the District Court Judges' view that the offset provisions caused a forfeiture of vested pension rights forbidden by Section 203. Instead, the Court of Appeals reasoned, such offsets merely reduce pension benefits in a fashion expressly approved by ERISA for employees receiving Social Security benefits. Accordingly, the Court of Appeals found no conflict between ERISA and the Treasury Regulation approving reductions based on workers' compensation awards and ERISA. Finally, the court concluded that the New Jersey statute forbidding offsets of pension benefits by the amount of workers' compensation awards could not withstand ERISA's general pre-emption provision. . . .

As we recently observed, ERISA is a "comprehensive and reticulated statute," which Congress adopted after careful study of private retirement pension plans. . . . Congress through ERISA wanted to ensure that "if a worker has been promised a defined pension benefit upon retirement—and if he has fulfilled whatever conditions are required to obtain a vested benefit—. . . he actually receives it." For this reason, the concepts of vested rights and nonforfeitable rights are critical to the ERISA scheme.

. . . Retirees rely on this sweeping assurance that pension rights become nonforfeitable in claiming that offsetting those benefits with workers' compensation awards violates ERISA. Retirees argue first that no vested benefits may be forfeited except as expressly provided in Section 203. Sec-

ond, retirees assert that offsets based on workers' compensation fall into none of those express exceptions. Both claims are correct; Section 203(a) prohibits forfeitures of vested rights except as expressly provided in Section 203(a)(3), and the challenged workers' compensation offsets are not among those permitted in that section.

Despite this facial accuracy, retirees' argument overlooks a threshold issue: what defines the content of the benefit that, once vested, cannot be forfeited? ERISA leaves this question largely to the private parties creating the plan. That the private parties, not the Government, control the level of benefits is clear from the statutory language defining nonforfeitable rights as well as from other portions of ERISA. ERISA defines a "nonforfeitable" pension benefit or right as "a claim obtained by a participant or his beneficiary to that part of an immediate or deferred benefit under a pension plan which arises from the participant's service, which is unconditional, and which is legally enforceable against the plan." In construing this definition last Term, we observed:

> [T]he term "forfeiture" normally connotes a total loss in consequence of some event rather than a limit on the value of a person's rights. Each of the examples of a plan provision that is expressly described as not causing a forfeiture listed in [Section 203(a)(3)] describes an event—such as death or temporary re-employment—that might otherwise be construed as causing a forfeiture of the entire benefit. It is therefore surely consistent with the statutory definition of "nonforfeitable" to view it as describing the quality of the participant's right to a pension rather than a limit on the amount he may collect.

Similarly, the statutory definition of "nonforfeitable" assures that an employee's claim to the protected benefit is legally enforceable, but it does not guarantee a particular amount or a method for calculating the benefit. As we explained last Term, "it is the claim to the benefit, rather than the benefit itself, that must be 'unconditional' and 'legally enforceable against the plan.'" . . .

It is particularly pertinent for our purposes that Congress did not prohibit "integration," a calculation practice under which benefit levels are determined by combining pension funds with other income streams available to the retired employees. Through integration, each income stream contributes for calculation purposes to the total benefit pool to be distributed to all the retired employees, even if the nonpension funds are available only to a subgroup of the employees. The pension funds are thus integrated with the funds from other income maintenance programs, such as Social Security, and the pension benefit level is determined on the basis of the entire pool of funds. Under this practice, an individual employee's eligibility for Social Security would advantage all participants in his private pension plan, for the addition of his anticipated Social Security payments to the total benefit pool would permit a higher average pension payout for each participant. The employees as a group profit from that higher pension level, although an individual employee may reach that level by a combination of payments from the pension fund and payments from the other income maintenance source. In addition, integration allows the employer to attain the selected pension level by drawing on the other resources, which, like Social Security, also depend on employer contributions.

Following its extensive study of private pension plans before the adoption of ERISA, Congress expressly preserved the option of pension fund integration with benefits available under . . . the Social Security Act and the Railroad Retirement Act of 1974. Congress was well aware that pooling of nonpension retirement benefits and pension funds would limit the total income maintenance payments received by individual employees and reduce the cost of pension plans to employers. Indeed, in considering this integration option, the House Ways and Means Committee expressly acknowledged the tension between the primary goal of benefiting employees and the subsidiary goal of containing pension costs. The Committee Report noted that the proposed bill would

> not affect the ability of plans to use the integration procedures to reduce the benefits that they pay to individuals who are currently covered when social security benefits are liberalized. Your committee, however, believes that such practices raise important issues. On the one hand, the objective of the Congress in increasing social security benefits might be considered to be frustrated to the extent that individuals with low and moderate incomes have their private retirement benefits reduced as a result of the integration procedures. On the other hand, your committee is very much aware that many present plans are fully or partly integrated and that elimination of the integration procedures could substantially increase the cost of financing private plans. Employees, as a whole, might be injured rather than aided if such cost increases resulted in slowing down the growth or perhaps even eliminat[ing] private retirement plans.

. . . In setting this limitation on integration with Social Security and Railroad Retirement benefits, Congress acknowledged and accepted this practice, rather than prohibiting it. Moreover, in permitting integration at least with these federal benefits, Congress did not find it necessary to add an exemption for this purpose to its stringent nonforfeiture

protections in [Section 203]. Under these circumstances, we are unpersuaded by retirees' claim that the nonforfeiture provisions by their own force prohibit any offset of pension benefits by workers' compensation awards. Such offsets work much like the integration of pension benefits with Social Security or Railroad Retirement payments. The individual employee remains entitled to the established pension level, but the payments received from the pension fund are reduced by the amount received through workers' compensation. The nonforfeiture provision of Section 203(a) has no more applicability to this kind of integration than it does to the analogous reduction permitted for Social Security or Railroad Retirement payments. Indeed, the same congressional purpose—promoting a system of private pensions by giving employers avenues for cutting the cost of their pension obligations—underlies all such offset possibilities.

Nonetheless, ERISA does not mention integration with workers' compensation, and the legislative history is equally silent on this point. An argument could be advanced that Congress approved integration of pension funds only with the federal benefits expressly mentioned in the Act. A current regulation issued by the Internal Revenue Service, however, goes further, and permits integration with other benefits provided by federal or state law. We now must consider whether this regulation is itself consistent with ERISA.

Codified at 26 CFR Section 1.411(a)-(4)(a) (1980), the Treasury Regulation provides that "nonforfeitable rights are not considered to be forfeitable by reason of the fact that they may be reduced to take into account benefits which are provided under the Social Security Act or under any other Federal or State law and which are taken into account in determining plan benefits." The Regulation interprets 26 U.S.C. Section 411, the section of the Internal Revenue Code which replicates for IRS purposes ERISA's nonforfeiture provision, [Section 203]. The Regulation plainly encompasses awards under state workers' compensation laws. In addition, in Revenue Rulings issued prior to ERISA, the IRS expressly had approved reductions in pension benefits corresponding to workers' compensation awards.

Retirees contend that the Treasury Regulation and IRS rulings to this effect contravene ERISA. They object first that ERISA's approval of integration was limited to Social Security and Railroad Retirement payments. This objection is precluded by our conclusion that reduction of pension benefits based on the integration procedure are not *per se* prohibited by Section 203(a), for the level of pension benefits is not prescribed by ERISA. Retirees' only remaining objection is that workers' compensation awards are so different in kind from Social Security and Railroad Retirement payments that their integration could not be authorized under the same rubric.

Developing this argument, retirees claim that workers' compensation provides payments for work-related injuries, while Social Security and Railroad Retirement supply payments solely for wages lost due to retirement. Because of this distinction, retirees conclude that integration of pension funds with workers' compensation awards lacks the rationale behind integration of pension funds with Social Security and Railroad Retirement. Retirees' claim presumes that ERISA permits integration with Social Security or Railroad Retirement only where there is an identity between the purposes of pension payments and the purposes of the other integrated benefits. But not even the funds that the Congress clearly has approved for integration purposes share the identity of purpose ascribed to them by petitioners. Both the Social Security and Railroad Retirement Acts provide payments for disability as well as for wages lost due to retirement, and ERISA permits pension integration without distinguishing these different kinds of benefits.

Furthermore, when it enacted ERISA, Congress knew of the IRS rulings permitting integration and left them in effect. These rulings do not draw the line between permissible and impermissible integration where retirees would prefer them to, and instead they include workers' compensation offsets within the ambit of permissible integration. The IRS rulings base their allowance of pension payment integration on three factors: the employer must contribute to the other benefit funds, these other funds must be designed for general public use, and the benefits they supply must correspond to benefits available under the pension plan. The IRS employed these considerations in approving integration with workers' compensation benefits. In contrast, the IRS has disallowed offsets of pension benefits with damages recovered by an employee through a common-law action against the employer. IRS also has not permitted integration with reimbursement for medical expenses or with fixed sums made for bodily impairment because such payments do not match up with any benefits available under a pension plan qualified under the Internal Revenue Code and ERISA.

. . . Similarly, the IRS has disapproved integration with unemployment compensation, for, as payment for temporary layoffs, it too is a kind of benefit not comparable to any permitted in a qualified pension plan.

Without speaking directly of its own rationale, Congress embraced such IRS rulings. Congress thereby permitted integration along the lines already approved by the IRS which had specifically allowed pension benefit offsets based on workers' compensation. Our judicial function is not to second-guess the policy decisions of the legislature, no matter how appealing we may find contrary rationales. . . .

We conclude that N. J. Stat. Ann. Section 34:15–29 is preempted by federal law insofar as it bears on pension plans governed by ERISA. We find further that Congress contemplated and approved the kind of pension provisions challenged here, which permit offsets of pension benefits based on workers' compensation awards. The decision of the Court of Appeals is **Affirmed.**

Minimum Funding Requirements

Employers with pension plans are required by ERISA to set aside a sufficient amount of funds each year to cover the benefit liabilities that accrued under the plan during that year. These funds are maintained in a funding standard account. The act also requires that past-service costs (costs for earned benefits that had been unfunded prior to the passage of ERISA) must be paid each year. The plan must pay the normal cost of the plan for that year, plus the amount necessary to amortize (in equal installments until fully amortized) those earned benefits that had been unfunded prior to ERISA's passage. The rate at which these past-service costs are amortized depends on the time at which the pension plan came into existence.

Liability due to experience gains and deficiencies of the plan must be amortized in equal installments over a maximum fifteen-year period. The determination of experience gains or losses, and a valuation of the plan's liabilities must be made at least every three years. Net amounts lost due to changes in actuarial assumptions used under the plan must be amortized over a thirty-year period.

Waivers.   The funding requirements of a plan for any given year may be waived by the IRS upon the plan's showing of hardship. It must be shown that the waiver will not be adverse to the plan's participants as a group. Any amounts waived must be amortized over a maximum fifteen-year period. A plan may not be granted more than five waivers during a fifteen-year period.

Funding Penalties.   If the required funding standards are not met by the employer, a 5 percent excise tax may be imposed by the IRS against the accumulated funding deficiency. If the deficiency is not corrected within a specified time, a penalty of up to 100 percent of the deficiency may be levied by the IRS.

PENSION BENEFIT GUARANTY CORP. v. LTV CORP.

496 U.S. 633 (Supreme Court of the United States, 1990)

BLACKMUN, J.

In this case we must determine whether the decision of the Pension Benefit Guaranty Corporation (PBGC) to restore certain pension plans under section 4047 of the Employee Retirement Income Security Act of 1974 (ERISA) was, as the Court of Appeals concluded, arbitrary and capricious or contrary to law, within the meaning of Section 706 of the Administrative Procedure Act (APA).

Petitioner PBGC is a wholly owned United States Government corporation, modeled after the Federal Deposit Insurance Corporation. . . . The PBGC administers and enforces Title IV of ERISA. Title IV includes a mandatory Government insurance program that protects the pension benefits of over 30 million private-sector American workers who participate in plans covered by the Title.* In enacting Title IV, Congress sought to ensure that employees and their beneficiaries would not be completely "deprived of anticipated retirement benefits by the termination of pension plans before sufficient funds have been accumulated in the plans.

When a plan covered under Title IV terminates with insufficient assets to satisfy its pension obligations to the employees, the PBGC becomes trustee of the plan, taking over the plan's assets and liabilities. The PBGC then uses the plan's assets to cover what it can of the benefit obligations. The PBGC then must add its own funds to ensure payment of most of the remaining "nonforfeitable" benefits, i.e., those benefits to which participants have earned entitlement under the plan terms as of the date of termination. ERISA does place limits on the benefits PBGC may guarantee upon plan termination, however, even if an employee is entitled to greater benefits under the terms of the plan. In addition, benefit increases resulting from plan amendments adopted within five years of the termination are not paid in full. Finally, active plan participants (current employees) cease to earn additional benefits under the plan upon its termination, and lose entitlement to most benefits not yet fully earned as of the date of plan termination.

The cost of the PBGC insurance is borne primarily by employers that maintain ongoing pension plans. Sections 4006 and 4007 of ERISA require these employers to pay annual premiums. The insurance program is also financed by

---

*Title IV covers virtually all "defined benefit" pension plans sponsored by private employers. A defined benefit plan is one that promises to pay employees, upon retirement, a fixed benefit under a formula that takes into account factors such as final salary and years of service with the employer. It is distinguished from a "defined contribution" plan (also known as an "individual account" plan), under which the employer typically contributes a percentage of an employee's compensation to an account, and the employee is entitled to the account upon retirement. ERISA insurance does not cover defined contribution plans because employees are not promised any particular level of benefits; instead, they are promised only that they will receive the balances in their individual accounts.

statutory liability imposed on employers who terminate underfunded pension plans. Upon termination, the employer becomes liable to the PBGC for the benefits that the PBGC will pay out. Because the PBGC historically has recovered only a small portion of that liability, Congress repeatedly has been forced to increase the annual premiums. Even with these increases, the PBGC in its most recent Annual Report noted liabilities of $4 billion and assets of only $2.4 billion, leaving a deficit of over $1.5 billion.

As noted above, plan termination is the insurable event under Title IV. Plans may be terminated "voluntarily" by an employer or "involuntarily" by the PBGC. An employer may terminate a plan voluntarily in one of two ways. It may proceed with a "standard termination" only if it has sufficient assets to pay all benefit commitments. A standard termination thus does not implicate PBGC insurance responsibilities. If an employer wishes to terminate a plan whose assets are insufficient to pay all benefits, the employer must demonstrate that it is in financial "distress" as defined in [ERISA]. Neither a standard nor a distress termination by the employer, however, is permitted if termination would violate the terms of an existing collective-bargaining agreement.

The PBGC, though, may terminate a plan "involuntarily," notwithstanding the existence of a collective-bargaining agreement. Section 4042 of ERISA provides that the PBGC may terminate a plan whenever it determines that:

> (1) the plan has not met the minimum funding standard required under Section 412 of title 26, or has been notified by the Secretary of the Treasury that a notice of deficiency under section 6212 of title 26 has been mailed with respect to the tax imposed under section 4791(a) of title 26,
> (2) the plan will be unable to pay benefits when due,
> (3) the reportable event described in section 1343(b)(7) of this title has occurred, or
> (4) the possible long-run loss of the [PBGC] with respect to the plan may reasonably be expected to increase unreasonably if the plan is not terminated.

Termination can be undone by PBGC. Section 4047 of ERISA provides:

> In the case of a plan which has been terminated under section 1341 or 1342 of this title the [PBGC] is authorized in any such case in which [it] determines such action to be appropriate and consistent with its duties under this subchapter, to take such action as may be necessary to restore the plan to its pretermination status, including, but not limited to, the transfer to the employer or a plan administrator of control of part or all of the remaining assets and liabilities of the plan.

When a plan is restored, full benefits are reinstated, and the employer, rather than the PBGC, again is responsible for the plan's unfunded liabilities.

This case arose after respondent The LTV Corporation (LTV Corp.) . . . in July 1986 filed petitions for reorganization under Chapter 11 of the Bankruptcy Code. At that time, LTV Steel was the sponsor of three defined benefit pension plans (the Plans) covered by Title IV of ERISA. Two of the Plans were the products of collective-bargaining negotiations with the United Steelworkers of America. The third was for nonunion salaried employees. Chronically underfunded, the Plans, by late 1986, had unfunded liabilities for promised benefits of almost $2.3 billion. Approximately $2.1 billion of this amount was covered by PBGC insurance.

It is undisputed that one of LTV Corp's principal goals in filing the Chapter 11 petitions was the restructuring of LTV Steel's pension obligations, a goal which could be accomplished if the Plans were terminated and responsibility for the unfunded liabilities was placed on the PBGC. LTV Steel then could negotiate with its employees for new pension arrangements. LTV, however, could not voluntarily terminate the Plans because two of them had been negotiated in collective bargaining. LTV therefore sought to have the PBGC terminate the Plans.

To that end, LTV advised the PBGC in 1986 that it could not continue to provide complete funding for the Plans. PBGC estimated that, without continued funding, the Plans' $2.1 billion underfunding could increase by as much as $65 million by December 1987 and by another $63 million by December 1988, unless the Plans were terminated. Moreover, extensive plant shutdowns were anticipated. These shutdowns, if they occurred before the Plans were terminated, would have required the payment of significant "shutdown benefits." The PBGC estimated that such benefits could increase the Plans' liabilities by as much as $300 million to $700 million, of which up to $500 million was covered by PBGC insurance. Confronted with this information, the PBGC, invoking Section 4042(a)(4) of ERISA, determined that the Plans should be terminated in order to protect the insurance program from the unreasonable risk of large losses, and commenced termination proceedings in the District Court. With LTV's consent, the Plans were terminated effective January 13, 1987.

Because the Plans' participants lost some benefits as a result of the termination, the Steelworkers filed an adversary action against LTV in the Bankruptcy Court, challenging the termination and seeking an order directing LTV to make up the lost benefits. This action was settled, with LTV and the Steelworkers negotiating an interim collective-bargaining agreement that included new pension arrangements intended to make up benefits that plan participants lost as a result of the termination. New payments to retirees were based explicitly upon "a percentage" of the difference between the benefit that was being paid under the Prior Plans and the amount paid by the PBGC." Retired participants were thereby placed in substantially the same positions they would have occupied had the old Plans never been terminated. The new agreements respecting active participants were also designed to replace benefits under the old Plans that were not insured by the PBGC, such as early-retirement benefits and shutdown benefits. With respect to shutdown benefits, LTV stated in Bankruptcy Court that the new benefits totaled "75% of benefits lost as a result of plan termination." With respect to some other kinds of benefits for active participants, the new arrangements provided 100% or more of the lost benefits.

The PBGC objected to these new pension agreements, characterizing them as "follow-on" plans. It defines a follow-on plan as a new benefit arrangement designed to wrap around the insurance benefits provided by the PBGC in such a way as to provide both retirees and active participants substantially the same benefits as they would have received had no termination occurred. The PBGC's policy against follow-on plans stems from the agency's belief that such plans are "abusive" of the insurance program and result in the PBGC's subsidizing an employer's ongoing pension program in a way not contemplated by Title IV. The PBGC consistently has made clear its policy of using its restoration powers under Section 4047 if an employer institutes an abusive follow-on plan. . . . Accordingly, the PBGC has indicated that if an employer adopts a new plan that, "together with the guaranteed benefits paid by the PBGC under the terminated plan, provide[s] for the payment of, accrual of, or eligibility for benefits that are substantially the same as those provided under the terminated plan," the PBGC will view the plan as an attempt to shift liability to the termination insurance program while continuing to operate the plan.

LTV ignored the PBGC's objections to the new pension arrangements and asked the Bankruptcy Court for permission to fund the follow-on plans. The Bankruptcy Court granted LTV's request. In doing so, however, it noted that the PBGC "may have legal options or avenues that it can assert administratively . . . to implement its policy goals. Nothing done here tonight precludes the PBGC from pursuing these options. . . ."

In early August 1987, the PBGC determined that the financial factors on which it had relied in terminating the Plans had changed significantly. Of particular significance to the PBGC was its belief that the steel industry, including LTV Steel, was experiencing a dramatic turnaround. As a result, the PBGC concluded it no longer faced the imminent risk, central to its original termination decision, of large unfunded liabilities stemming from plant shutdowns. Later that month, the PBGC's internal working group made a recommendation, based upon LTV's improved financial circumstances and its follow-on plans, to the PBGC's Executive Director to restore the Plans under the PBGC's Section 4047 powers. After consulting the PBGC's Board of Directors, which agreed with the working group that restoration was appropriate, the Executive Director decided to restore the Plans.

The Director issued a Notice of Restoration on September 22, 1987, indicating the PBGC's intent to restore the terminated Plans. The PBGC Notice explained that the restoration decision was based on (1) LTV's establishment of "a retirement program that results in an abuse of the pension plan termination insurance system established by Title IV of ERISA," and (2) LTV's "improved financial circumstances." Restoration meant that the Plans were ongoing, and that LTV again would be responsible for administering and funding them.

LTV refused to comply with the restoration decision. This prompted the PBGC to initiate an enforcement action in the District Court. The court vacated the PBGC's restoration decision, finding, among other things, that the PBGC had exceeded its authority under Section 4047.

The Court of Appeals for the Second Circuit affirmed, holding that the PBGC's restoration decision was "arbitrary and capricious" or contrary to law under Section 706(2)(A) of the APA, in various ways. . . .

Because of the significant administrative law questions raised by this case, and the importance of the PBGC's insurance program, we granted certiorari.

The Court of Appeals first held that the restoration decision was arbitrary and capricious under Section 706(2)(A) because the PBGC did not take account of all the areas of law the court deemed relevant to the restoration decision. . . . Rather, the court held that because labor law and bankruptcy law are "involved in the case at hand," the PBGC had an affirmative obligation, which had not been met, to address them.

The PBGC contends that the Court of Appeals misapplied the general rule that an agency must take into consideration all relevant factors, by requiring the agency explicitly to consider and discuss labor and bankruptcy law. We agree.

First, and most important, we do not think that the requirement imposed by the Court of Appeals upon the PBGC can be reconciled with the plain language of Section 4047, under which the PBGC is operating in this case. This section gives the PBGC the power to restore terminated plans in any case in which the PBGC determines such action to be "appropriate and consistent with its duties *under this title*, [i.e., Title IV of ERISA]" (emphasis added). The statute does not direct the PBGC to make restoration decisions that further the "public interest" generally, but rather empowers the agency to restore when restoration would further the interests that Title IV of ERISA is designed to protect. Given this specific and unambiguous statutory mandate, we do not think that the PBGC did or could focus "inordinately" on ERISA in making its restoration decision.... For these reasons, we believe the Court of Appeals erred in holding that the PBGC's restoration decision was arbitrary and capricious because the agency failed adequately to consider principles and policies of bankruptcy law and labor law.

The Court of Appeals also rejected the grounds for restoration that the PBGC *did* assert and discuss. The court found that the first ground the PBGC proffered to support the restoration—its policy against follow-on plans—was contrary to law because there was no indication in the text of the restoration provision, Section 4047, or its legislative history that Congress intended the PBGC to use successive benefit plans as a basis for restoration. The PBGC argues that in reaching this conclusion the Court of Appeals departed from traditional principles of statutory interpretation and judicial review of agency construction of statutes. Again, we must agree.

Here, the PBGC has interpreted Section 4047 as giving it the power to base restoration decisions on the existence of follow-on plans. Our task, then, is to determine whether any clear congressional desire to avoid restoration decisions based on successive pension plans exists, and, if the answer is in the negative, whether the PBGC's policy is based upon a permissible construction of the statute.

Turning to the first half of the inquiry, we observe that the text of Section 4047 does not evince a clear congressional intent to deprive the PBGC of the ability to base restoration decisions on the existence of follow-on plans. To the contrary, the textual grant of authority to the PBGC embodied in this section is broad. As noted above, the section authorizes the PBGC to restore terminated plans "in any such case in which [the PBGC] determines such action to be appropriate and consistent with its duties under [Title IV of ERISA]." The PBGC's duties consist primarily of furthering the statutory purposes of Title IV identified by Congress. These are:

> (1) to encourage the continuation and maintenance of voluntary private pension plans for the benefit of their participants;

> (2) to provide for the timely and uninterrupted payment of pension benefits to participants and beneficiaries under plans to which this subchapter applies; and

> (3) to maintain premiums established by [the PBGC] under section 1306 of this title at the lowest level consistent with carrying out the obligations of this subchapter.

On their face, of course, none of these statutorily identified purposes has anything to say about the precise question at issue—the use of follow-on plans as a basis for restoration decisions.

... The Court of Appeals relied extensively on passages in the legislative history of the 1974 enactment of ERISA which suggest that Congress considered financial recovery a valid basis for restoration, but which make no mention of follow-on plans. The court reasoned that because follow-ons were not among the bases for restoration discussed by Members of Congress, that body must have intended that the existence of follow-ons *not* be a reason for restoring pension plans.

We do not agree with this conclusion. We first note that the discussion in the legislative history concerning grounds for restoration was not limited to the financial-recovery example. The House Conference Report indicated that restoration was appropriate if financial recovery or "some other factor made termination no longer advisable." ... We see no suggestion in the legislative history that Congress intended its list of examples to be exhaustive. Under these circumstances, we conclude that ERISA's legislative history does not suggest "clear congressional intent" on the question of follow-on plans....

Having determined that the PBGC's construction is not contrary to clear congressional intent, we still must ascertain whether the agency's policy is based upon a "permissible" construction of the statute, that is, a construction that is "rational and consistent with the statute." Respondents argue that the PBGC's anti-follow-on plan policy is irrational because, as a practical matter, no purpose is served when the PBGC bases a restoration decision on something other than the improved financial health of the employer. According to respondents, "financial improvement [is] both a necessary and a sufficient condition for restoration. The agency's asserted abuse policy ... is *logically irrelevant* to the restoration decision." We think not. The PBGC's anti-follow-on policy is premised on the belief, which we find eminently reasonable, that employees will object more strenuously to a company's original decision to terminate a plan (or to take financial steps that make termination likely) if the company cannot use a follow-on plan to put the employees in the same (or a similar) position after termination as they were in before. The availability of a follow-on plan thus would remove a significant check—employee resistance—against termination of a pension plan.

Consequently, follow-on plans may tend to frustrate one of the objectives of ERISA that the PBGC is supposed to accomplish—the "continuation and maintenance of voluntary private pension plans." In addition, follow-on plans have a tendency to increase the PBGC's deficit and increase the insurance premiums all employers must pay, thereby frustrating another related statutory objective—the maintenance of low premiums. In short, the PBGC's construction based upon its conclusion that the existence of follow-on plans will lead to more plan terminations and increased PBGC liabilities is "assuredly a permissible one." Indeed, the judgments about the way the real world works that have gone into the PBGC's anti-follow-on policy are precisely the kind that agencies are better equipped to make than are courts.

None of this is to say that financial improvement will never be relevant to a restoration decision. Indeed, if an employer's financial situation remains so dire that restoration would lead inevitably to immediate retermination, the PBGC may decide not to restore a terminated plan even where the employer has instituted a follow-on plan. For present purposes, however, it is enough for us to decide that where, as here, there is no suggestion that immediate retermination of the plans will be necessary, it is rational for the PBGC to disfavor follow-on plans. . . .

We conclude that the PBGC's failure to consider all potentially relevant areas of law did not render its restoration decision arbitrary and capricious. We also conclude that the PBGC's anti-follow-on policy, an asserted basis for the resto-

ration decision, is not contrary to clear congressional intent and is based on a permissible construction of Section 4047. Finally, we find the procedures employed by the PBGC to be consistent with the APA. Accordingly, the judgment of the Court of Appeals is reversed and the case is remanded for further proceedings consistent with this opinion.
It is so ordered.

STEVENS, J. (dissenting)

In my opinion, at least with respect to ERISA plans that the PBGC has terminated involuntarily, the use of its restoration power under Section 4047 to prohibit "follow-on" plans is contrary to the agency's statutory mandate. Unless there was a sufficient improvement in LTV's financial condition to justify the restoration order, I believe it should be set aside. I, therefore, would remand the case for a determination of whether that ground for the agency decision is adequately supported by the record. . . .

In the case of an involuntary termination, if a mistake in the financial analysis is made, or if there is a sufficient change in the financial condition of the company to justify a reinstatement of the company's obligation, the PBGC should use its restoration powers. Without such a financial justification, however, there is nothing in the statute to authorize the PBGC's use of that power to prevent a company from creating or maintaining the kind of employee benefit program that the statute was enacted to encourage.

Accordingly, I respectfully dissent.

The final chapter in the LTV saga was closed on July 15, 1991, when LTV agreed with the PBGC to work out a payment schedule to resolve the underfunding of its pension plans. LTV agreed to make an initial payment of $950 million, and then annual payments to satisfy the rest of the $3.1 billion shortfall, as reported in the July 16, 1991 *Wall Street Journal.*

Discrimination

Pension plans qualifying for preferential tax treatment under ERISA must not, either by design or operation, discriminate in favor of officers, shareholders, or highly compensated employees. The act prohibits discrimination in benefits, contributions, and coverage of employee classifications under a plan. A plan may be limited to only salaried or clerical workers: employees earning *only wages* may be excluded from the plan. The key factor is that contributions and benefits of employees bear a uniform relationship to total compensation. Any variation in treatment under the plan must be applied consistently and may not discriminate in favor of the "prohibited class" of employees (officers, shareholders, and those who are highly compensated).

Reporting and Disclosure Requirements

ERISA imposes a series of reporting and disclosure requirements on the administrators of pension plans. These requirements are designed to provide the government and plan participants with the information necessary to enforce and protect participants' rights, to assure nondiscriminatory operation of the plan, to disclose prohibited transactions, and to give advance warnings of possible plan failures.

The plan must furnish plan participants and beneficiaries with a summary plan description, which must provide the name and address of the plan, its administrator and trustees, the requirements for participation, vesting and disqualification under the plan, procedures for presenting claims, and procedures for appealing denials of claims. The plan must also provide participants and beneficiaries with a summary of material modifications to the plan and with a summary annual report of the plan.

The plan must file, with the Department of Labor, a summary description of the plan (similar to that given to participants) and a summary of material modifications to the plan. The plan must file, with the Pension Benefit Guaranty Corporation (PBGC), a detailed annual premium filing form and a notice of any "reportable event," such as changes reducing benefits payable, inability to pay benefits due, failure to meet minimum funding standards, or transactions with owners. As well, the plan must file a notice of intention to terminate the plan with the PBGC at least ten days prior to the termination. Lastly, the plan must file extremely detailed financial disclosure forms with the IRS annually.

Termination of a Plan

ERISA allows the termination of any existing pension plan, subject to provisions intended to protect those persons receiving benefits and to guarantee the continuance of the benefits vested before the plan is terminated. As just mentioned, a notice of the intention to terminate the plan must be filed with the PBGC at least ten days prior to the termination. ERISA created the PBGC, financed by a premium levied against employers, to insure employees against the loss of their benefits when a defined-benefit plan is terminated. If the plan is unable to meet its obligations, PBGC will pay minimum monthly benefits to those receiving benefits under the plan.

Upon termination of a plan, the plan's assets are allocated pursuant to the following priorities: voluntary employee contributions, required employee contributions, benefits to participants receiving benefits for at least three years based on plan provisions in effect for five years, all other insured benefits, all other nonforfeitable benefits, and all other benefits. If the assets are insufficient to cover all claims within one of the described classes, then the assets will be allocated pro rata within the last subclass to receive benefits under the allocation.

When the assets of a plan are insufficient to satisfy benefit claims, the employer is liable to PBGC for 100 percent of the underfunding, subject to a limit of 30 percent of the net worth of the employer. This liability is a government lien against the property of the employer and is treated as a federal tax lien.

If there are surplus funds in the pension fund upon its termination, the employer may recover those surplus funds under certain circumstances. Section 4044(d)(1) of ERISA provides that the employer may recover any surplus assets remaining in the pension fund if (1) all liabilities to participating employees and beneficiaries for benefits under the pension plan have been satisfied, (2) the recovery of surplus assets by the employer does not violate any section of ERISA, and (3) the pension plan provides that the employer may recover any surplus funds in these circumstances. The employer is also subject to an excise tax on the amount of the surplus funds.

Multi-employer Plan Terminations or Withdrawals. When ERISA was enacted, the PBGC insurance provisions applied only to pension plans operated by single employers. PBGC coverage was not extended to multi-employer pension plans until 1980. The Multi-employer Pension Plan Amendments Act of 1980 extended PBGC coverage to multi-employers withdrawing from a multi-employer pension plan. Employers must pay a fixed amount into the fund. The amount, to be paid upon withdrawal, is the withdrawing employer's proportionate share of the plan's unfunded vested benefits. Unfunded vested benefits are defined as the difference between the present value of the plan's vested benefits and the current value of the plan's assets.

The following case involves a challenge to the employer liability provisions of the 1980 amendments to ERISA.

CONNOLLY v. PENSION BENEFIT GUARANTY CORP.

106 S. Ct. 1018 (Supreme Court of the United States, 1986)

WHITE, J.

In *Pension Benefit Guaranty Corporation* v. *R. A. Gray & Co.,* (1984) the Court held that retroactive application of the withdrawal liability provisions of the Multiemployer Pension Plan Amendments Act of 1980 did not violate the Due Process Clause of the Fifth Amendment. In these cases, we address the question whether the withdrawal liability provisions of the Act are valid under the Clause of the Fifth Amendment that forbids the taking of private property for public use without just compensation. . . .

Congress enacted ERISA in 1974 to provide comprehensive regulation for private pension plans. In addition to prescribing standards for the funding, management, and benefit provisions of these plans, ERISA also established a system of pension benefit insurance. This "comprehensive and reticulated statute" was designed "to ensure that employees and their beneficiaries would not be deprived of anticipated retirement benefits by the termination of pension plans before sufficient funds have been accumulated in the plans. . . . Congress wanted to guarantee that "if a worker has been promised a defined pension benefit upon retirement—and if he has fulfilled whatever conditions are required to obtain a vested benefit—he will actual receive it."

To achieve this goal of protecting "anticipated retirement benefits," Congress created the Pension Benefit Guaranty Corporation (PBGC), a wholly owned Government corporation, to administer an insurance program for participants in both single-employer and multiemployer pension plans. For single-employer plans that were in default, ERISA immediately obligated the PBGC to pay benefits. With respect to multiemployer plans, ERISA delayed mandatory payment of guaranteed benefits until January 1, 1978. Until that date, Congress gave the PBGC discretionary authority to pay benefits upon the termination of multiemployer pension plans. As with single-employer plans, all contributors to covered multiemployer plans were assessed insurance premiums payable to the PBGC. If the PBGC exercised its discretion to pay benefits upon a plan's termination, all employers that had contributed to the plan during the five years preceding its termination were liable to the PBGC in amounts proportional to their shares of the plan's contribution during that period, subject to the limitation that any individual employer's liability could not exceed 30 percent of the employer's net worth.

During the period between the enactment of ERISA and 1978, when mandatory multiemployer guarantees were due to go into effect, the PBGC extended coverage to numerous plans. "Congress became concerned that a significant number of plans were experiencing extreme financial hardship," and that implementation of mandatory guarantees for multiemployer plans might induce several large plans to terminate, thus subjecting the insurance system to liability beyond its means. As a result, Congress delayed the effective date for the mandatory guarantees for 18 months, and directed the PBGC to prepare a report analyzing the problems of multiemployer plans and recommending possible solutions.

The PBGC's report found, *inter alia,* "that ERISA did not adequately protect plans from the adverse consequences that resulted when individual employers terminate their participation in, or withdraw from, multiemployer plans." The "basic problem," the report found, was the threat to the solvency and stability of multiemployer plans caused by employer withdrawals, which existing law actually encouraged. As the PBGC's Executive Director explained:

> A key problem of ongoing multiemployer plans, especially in declining industries, is the problem of employer withdrawal. Employer withdrawals reduce a plan's contribution base. This pushes the contribution rate for remaining employers to higher and higher levels in order to fund past service liabilities, including liabilities generated by employers no longer participating in the plan, so-called inherited liabilities. The rising costs may encourage—or force—further withdrawals, thereby increasing the inherited liabilities to be funded by an ever decreasing contribution base. This vicious downward spiral may continue until it is no longer reasonable or possible for the pension plan to continue.

"To alleviate the problem of employer withdrawals, the PBGC suggested new rules under which a withdrawing employer would be required to pay whatever share of the plan's unfunded liabilities was attributable to that employer's participation." Again, the PBGC Executive Director explained:

> To deal with this problem, our report considers an approach under which an employer withdrawing from a multiemployer plan would be required to complete funding its fair share of the plan's unfunded liabilities. In other words, the plan would

have a claim against the employer for the inherited liabilities which would otherwise fall upon the remaining employers as a result of the withdrawal. . . .

> We think that such withdrawal liability would, first of all, discourage voluntary withdrawals and curtail the current incentives to flee the plan. Where such withdrawals nonetheless occur, we think that withdrawal liability would cushion the financial impact on the plan.

After 17 months of discussion, Congress agreed with the analysis put forward in the PBGC Report, and drafted legislation which implemented the Report's recommendations. "As enacted, the Act requires that an employer withdrawing from a multiemployer pension plan pay a fixed and certain debt to the pension plan. This withdrawal liability is the employer's proportionate share of the plan's 'unfunded vested benefits,' calculated as the difference between the present value of the vested benefits and the current value of the plan's assets."

Appellant Trustees administer the Operating Engineers Pension Plan according to a written Agreement Establishing the Operating Engineers Pension Trust, executed in 1960, pursuant to Section 302(c)(5) of the Labor Management Relations Act. The Trust receives contributions from several thousand employers under written collective-bargaining agreements covering employees in the construction industry throughout southern California and southern Nevada. Under these collective-bargaining agreements, the employers agree to contribute a certain amount to the Pension Plan, with the actual amount contributed by each employer determined by multiplying their employees' hours of service by a rate specified in the current agreement.

By the express terms of the Trust Agreement and the Plan, the employer's sole obligation to the Pension Trust is to pay the contributions required by the collective-bargaining agreement. The Trust Agreement clearly states that the employer's obligation for pension benefits to the employee is ended when the employer pays the appropriate contribution to the Pension Trust. This is true even though the contributions agreed upon are insufficient to pay the benefits under the Plan.

In 1975, the Trustees filed suit, seeking declaratory and injunctive relief, claiming that the Pension Plan is a "defined contribution plan" as defined by ERISA, and thus not subject to the jurisdiction of the PBGC. Alternatively, the Trustees argued that if the Plan was subject to the provisions of ERISA requiring premium payments and imposing contingent termination liability, the statute was unconstitutional, as it deprived the Trustees, the employers, and the plan participants of property without due process and without proper compensation.

The District Court granted summary judgment to the Trustees, finding that the Plan was a "defined contribution plan," and enjoining the PBGC from treating it in any other manner. The Ninth Circuit reversed and remanded for consideration of the constitutional issues. On remand, the District Court denied that Trustees' motion to convene a three-judge court on the ground that the Trustees' constitutional challenges were insubstantial. . . .

On the merits, the District Court granted summary judgment to the PBGC, but the Ninth Circuit reversed. The court could not agree with the District Court that the constitutional claims raised by the Trustees were so "insubstantial" that a three-judge panel could be summarily denied. The Ninth Circuit remanded the case with directions to convene a three-judge court.

During the course of the litigation to convene the three-judge court, Congress enacted the MPPAA. The District Court permitted the Trustees to file an amended complaint to include a challenge to the constitutionality of the new Act. . . .

After oral argument, the three-judge panel granted summary judgment in favor of the PBGC. The court rejected the appellants' argument that the Act violated the Taking Clause of the Fifth Amendment, holding that "the contractual right which insulates employers from further liability to the pensions plans in which they participate is not 'property' within the meaning of the takings clause." Because the court resolved this issue "on the basis that no 'property' is affected by the MPPAA," it did not discuss whether a "taking" had occurred, or whether the taking would have been for "public purpose."

. . . [T]he Trustees and Woodward Sand Co. invoked the appellate jurisdiction of this Court. . . .

Appellants challenge the District Court's conclusion that the Act does not effect a taking of "property" within the meaning of the Fifth Amendment. Rather than specifically asserting that the contractual limitation of liability is property, however, appellants argue that the imposition of noncontractual withdrawal liability violates the Taking Clause of the Fifth Amendment by requiring employers to transfer their assets for the private use of pension trusts and, in any event, by requiring an uncompensated transfer.

We agree that an employer subject to withdrawal liability is permanently deprived of those assets necessary to satisfy its statutory obligation, not to the Government, but to a pension trust. If liability is assessed under the Act, it constitutes a real debt that the employer must satisfy, and it is not an obligation which can be considered insubstantial. In the present litigation, for example, Woodward Sand Co.'s with-drawal liability, after the PBGC assessment was reduced by an arbitrator, was approximately $200,000, or nearly 25 percent of the firm's net worth.

But appellants' submission—that such a statutory liability to a private party always constitutes an uncompensated taking prohibited by the Fifth Amendment—if accepted, would prove too much. In the course of regulating commercial and other human affairs, Congress routinely creates burdens for some that directly benefit others. . . . Given the propriety of the governmental power to regulate, it cannot be said that the Taking clause is violated whenever legislation requires one person to use his or her assets for the benefit of another. . . .

Appellants' claim of an illegal taking gains nothing from the fact that the employer in the present litigation was protected by the terms of its contract from any liability beyond the specified contributions to which it had agreed. "Contracts, however express, cannot fetter the constitutional authority of Congress. Contracts may create rights of property, but when contracts deal with a subject matter which lies within the control of Congress, they have a congenital infirmity. Parties cannot remove their transactions from the reach of dominant constitutional power by making contracts about them."

If the regulatory statute is otherwise within the powers of Congress, therefore, its application may not be defeated by private contractual provisions. For the same reason, the fact that legislation disregards or destroys existing contractual rights does not always transform the regulation into an illegal taking. This is not to say that contractual rights are never property rights or that the Government may always take them for its own benefit without compensation. But here, the United States has taken nothing for its own use, and only has nullified a contractual provision limiting liability by imposing an additional obligation that is otherwise within the power of Congress to impose. That the statutory withdrawal liability will operate in this manner and will redound to the benefit of pension trusts does not justify a holding that the provision violates the Taking Clause and is invalid on its face.

This conclusion is not inconsistent with our prior Taking Clause cases. Examining the MPPAA in light of these factors reinforces our belief that the imposition of withdrawal liability does not constitute a compensable taking under the Fifth Amendment.

First, with respect to the nature of the governmental action, we already have noted that, under the Act, the Government does not physically invade or permanently appropriate any of the employer's assets for its own use. Instead, the Act safeguards the participants in multiemployer pension plans by requiring a withdrawing employer to fund its share of the plan obligations incurred during its association with the plan. This interference with the property rights of an employer arises from a public program that adjusts the benefits and burdens of economic life to promote the common good and, under our cases, does not constitute a taking requiring Government compensation.

Next, as to the severity of the economic impact of the MPPAA, there is no doubt that the Act completely deprives an employer of whatever amount of money it is obligated to pay to fulfill its statutory liability. The assessment of withdrawal liability is not made in a vacuum, however, but directly depends on the relationship between the employer and the plan to which it had made contributions. Moreover, there are a significant number of provisions in the Act that moderate and mitigate the economic impact of an individual employer's liability. There is nothing to show that the withdrawal liability actually imposed on an employer will always be out of proportion to its experience with the plan, and the mere fact that the employer must pay money to comply with the Act is but a necessary consequence of the MPPAA's regulatory scheme.

The final inquiry suggested for determining whether the Act constitutes a "taking" under the Fifth Amendment is whether the MPPAA has interfered with reasonable investment-backed expectations. Appellants argue that the only monetary obligations incurred by each employer involved in the Operating Engineers Pension Plan arose from the specific terms of the Plan and Trust Agreement between the employers and the union, and that the imposition of withdrawal liability upsets those reasonable expectations. Pension plans, however, were the objects of legislative concern long before the passage of ERISA in 1974, and surely as of that time, it was clear that if the PBGC exercised its discretion to pay benefits upon the termination of a multiem-

ployer pension plan, employers who had contributed to the plan during the preceding five years were liable for their proportionate share of the plan's contributions during that period. It was also plain enough that the purpose of imposing withdrawal liability was to ensure that employees would receive the benefits promised them. When it became evident that ERISA fell short of achieving this end, Congress adopted the 1980 amendments. Prudent employers then had more than sufficient notice not only that pension plans were currently regulated, but also that withdrawal itself might trigger additional financial obligations. . . .

The purpose of forbidding uncompensated takings of private property for public use is "to bar Government from forcing some people alone to bear public burdens which, in all fairness and justice, should be borne by the public as a whole." We are far from persuaded that fairness and justice require the public, rather than the withdrawing employers and other parties to pension plan agreements, to shoulder the responsibility for rescuing plans that are in financial trouble. The employers in the present litigation voluntarily negotiated and maintained a pension plan which was determined to be within the strictures of ERISA. We do not know, as a fact, whether this plan was underfunded, but Congress determined that unregulated withdrawals from multiemployer plans could endanger their financial vitality and deprive workers of the vested rights they were entitled to anticipate would be theirs upon retirement. For this reason, Congress imposed withdrawal liability as one part of an overall statutory scheme to safeguard the solvency of private pension plans. We see no constitutionally compelled reason to require the Treasury to assume the financial burden of attaining this goal.

The judgment of the three-judge court is **Affirmed.**

Administration and Enforcement

ERISA's provisions and requirements are enforced by the Department of Labor, the Internal Revenue Service, and individual participants and beneficiaries. The fiduciary duties and the reporting and disclosure provisions are enforced by the Labor Department; the IRS enforces the minimum vesting and participation requirements and levies tax penalties for funding violations or prohibited transactions. Individual participants and beneficiaries may bring suit to enforce their rights under the act.

The act provides criminal penalties for willful violations of the reporting and disclosure requirements. Persons willfully violating those requirements are subject to a fine of not more than $5,000, a prison term of up to one year, or both. Violations by corporate or union fiduciaries may be subject to a fine of up to $100,000.

Civil actions may be brought by a participant or beneficiary if the plan administrator fails to furnish requested materials on the plan. Civil suits may also be brought to recover benefits due under the plan. Participants may also collect penalties of up to $100 per day from an administrator who fails to provide, upon request, information to which the participant is entitled. Participants and beneficiaries, and the Secretary of Labor, may bring actions to clarify rights to future benefits, to enjoin any violation of the act or terms of the plan, and to obtain relief from a breach of fiduciary responsibilities.

The federal courts have exclusive jurisdiction over all actions brought under ERISA, except for actions by participants to recover benefits due them, to enforce their rights, or to clarify their rights to future benefits. State courts have concurrent jurisdiction with federal courts over these actions. Participants and beneficiaries are required to exhaust plan procedures and remedies before pursuing legal actions.

While state courts have concurrent jurisdiction over suits to enforce ERISA's provisions, state laws that relate to benefit plans covered by ERISA are preempted by the federal legislation. Section 514 of ERISA states ". . . the provisions of this subchapter and subchapter III of this chapter shall supersede any and all State laws insofar as they may now or hereafter relate to any employee benefit plan described in section 1003(a) of this title . . ." In *Ingersoll–Rand Co.* v. *McClendon* (—— U.S. ——, 111 S. Ct. 478, 1990), the Supreme Court held that the effect of Section 514 was to preclude the application of any state laws relating to benefit plans covered by ERISA, even when the purpose and effects of the state law were consistent with those of ERISA. This means that the provisions of ERISA provide the sole legal remedy for complaints relating to pensions or employee benefit plans covered by the statute.

QUESTIONS

1. What problems led to the passage of ERISA? How does the act attempt to correct those problems?

2. What are the bases of coverage for the dual obligations ERISA places upon pension and benefit plans?

3. What is a fiduciary? What obligations does ERISA impose upon fiduciaries?

4. What is a defined-contribution pension plan? What is a defined-benefit pension plan? Why are defined-benefit plans subject to more requirements and regulations than defined-contribution plans?

5. What is vesting? What alternative minimum requirements for vesting are imposed by ERISA?

6. What are the minimum funding requirements ERISA imposes on qualified pension plans? When may a waiver from such requirements be granted?

7. What is the role of the Pension Benefit Guaranty Corporation under ERISA? What obligations apply in the event of an employer's withdrawal from a multi-employer defined-benefit pension plan?

8. What are the enforcement procedures for ERISA's fiduciary obligations? For the minimum standards required of qualified plans under ERISA?

CASE PROBLEMS

1. The retirees were employed by White Farms while the company was an affiliate of the White Motor Corporation. The dispute concerned the White Motor Corporation Insurance Plan for Salary Employees, a nonfunded, noncontributory benefit plan that provided life, health, and welfare insurance, prescription drugs, hearing aid benefits, and dental care to retirees and their eligible dependents. White Motor employees periodically received booklets describing their benefits under these plans.

   The 1970 booklet described insurance provided and carried the explicit disclaimer that it was "not the contract of insurance." The booklet differentiated between different categories of salaried employees and appeared to have been prepared for distribution to both active and retired employees.

   The 1978 booklet was addressed specifically to retired employees. Much of the information in the booklet made no distinction between the Welfare Benefit Plan and the Pension Plan, and its summary of an alleged cancellation clause referred to both plans:

   The Company fully intends to continue your plans indefinitely. However, the Company does reserve the right to change the Plans, and, if necessary to discontinue them. If it is necessary to discontinue the Pension Plan, the assets of the Pension Fund will be used to provide benefits according to the Plan document.

   No similar clause appeared in the 1970 booklet.

   While the company was undergoing a court-supervised reorganization under Chapter 11 of the Bankruptcy Code, it decided to discontinue its noncontributory insurance coverages for its retired employees.

   On the basis of the facts presented, was the company free to discontinue its noncontributory insurance coverage for its retired employees? See *White Farm Equipment Co.* v. *Hansen,* 42 B.R. 1005 (N.D. Ohio 1984); rev'd. by 788 F.2d 1186 (6th Cir. 1986).

2. The defendant Buha obtained a state court judgment against Walter D. Kinsky and his wife in a tort action. When the judgment was not paid, Buha instituted post-judgment garnishment procedures. A writ of garnishment was served on the National Bank of Detroit in its capacity as trustee of a General Motors (GM) pension fund. When the trustee filed a disclosure indicating no liability to Kinsky, Buha demanded an examination of the garnishee.

   On November 2, 1977, GM filed the present action in the district court seeking to restrain enforcement of the writ of garnishment. The district court entered a temporary restraining order (TRO) pending hearing on GM's motion for a preliminary injunction. The TRO was entered at 5:40 P.M. on November 2, without notice to the defendants. In granting the TRO, the district court found that GM, as fiduciary of the pension plan, would be prevented from carrying out its lawful duties and responsibilities and "thereby be irreparably damaged and harmed" unless the defendants were immediately restrained.

   Garnishment is not mentioned in ERISA. However, both ERISA and the section of the Internal Revenue Code (IRC) that deals with "qualified" pension profit-sharing and stock bonus plans contain provisions against assignment or alienation of plan benefits. Nearly identical language in 29 U.S.C. Section 1056(d)(1) (ERISA) and 26 U.S.C. Section 401(a)(13)(IRC) requires plans to contain a provision that "benefits provided under the plan may not be assigned or alienated." The GM plan that was the object of the writ of garnishment contains this provision. ERISA contains one exception to the requirement of nonassignability, which permits a "voluntary and revocable assignment of not to exceed 10 percent of any benefit payment. . . ." 29 U.S.C. Section 1056(d)(2). A similar exception is contained in 26 U.S.C. Section 401(a)(13).

   Based on these facts, should Buha be allowed to garnish Kinsky's pension benefits? See *General Motors Corp.* v. *Buha,* 623 F.2d 455 (1980).

   Suppose that Kinsky and his wife got a divorce, and she sought to attach his pension because he had failed to make alimony payments? Does this hypothetical situation present any different policy issues for a court to decide? See *Carpenters Pension Trust Fund for Southern Calif.* v. *Kronschnable,* 632 F.2d 745 (9th Cir. 1980) *cert. den.,* 453 U.S. 922.

3. On December 31, 1980, defendant closed its Harrison plant, resulting in a significant reduction in its work force. A plan was formulated, known as the Har-

rison Special Supplemental Retirement Plan, under which managerial employees with a minimum of twenty-five years of service who were over fifty-five years of age could elect early retirement with substantial supplemental benefits. The plaintiffs who also had a minimum of twenty-five years of service but who were under fifty-five years of age were awarded severance pay amounting to one week's salary for each year of service in accordance with defendant's usual severance policy. Because these individuals were denied the benefits of the Harrison Special Supplemental Retirement Plan, they brought an action under the New Jersey Law Against Discrimination, N.J.S.A. 10:5–1 et seq. for relief in the form of termination benefits equal to those received by former employees who were over fifty-five.

The relevant portion of the New Jersey antidiscrimination law stated in pertinent part, "It shall be an unlawful employment practice. . . . [f]or an employer, because of the . . . age . . . of any individual, . . . to refuse to hire or employ or to bar or to discharge from employment such individual or to discriminate against such individual in compensation or in terms, conditions or privileges of employment. . . ."

Does this New Jersey law provide a remedy to these plaintiffs? If so, does the defendant have an argument available that this state law is preempted by ERISA? See *Nolan* v. *Otis Elevator Company*, 197 N.J. Super. 468, 485 A.2d 312, 36 F.E.P. Cases 1109 (1984).

4. UIT was a group insurance trust, commonly known as a multiple employer trust, the purpose of which was to allow employers with a small number of employees to secure group health insurance coverage for their employees at rates more favorable than offered directly by the insurance companies. UIT obtained a group health insurance policy from Occidental Life Insurance Company of California to furnish specified insurance benefits. Subscribers to UIT included single-employer collectively bargained programs, multi-employer health and welfare funds, and union-sponsored funds. Many of these subscriptions were the subscriber's method of fulfilling collective bargaining agreements and union agreements to furnish health insurance benefits to employees. In these situations the employer or union, or both, were committed to providing benefits to employees or members through the purchase of health insurance on a continuing basis.

Is this UIT subscription program a welfare benefit plan subject to the jurisdiction of ERISA? See *Donovan* v. *Dillingham,* 688 F.2d 1367 (11th Cir. 1982).

5. More than a half-century ago, Emil R. Ouimet purchased the Brockton, Massachusetts, shoe-trim manufacturing concern for which he had worked for several years. In 1940 he changed its name to Ouimet Leather Company. He renamed it Ouimet Stay & Leather Company when production expanded to include shoe upper strippings. In 1950 he founded Ouimet Corporation, a Delaware corporation with its principal place of business in Nashville, Tennessee. In 1968 Ouimet purchased the Avon Sole Company, located in Holbrook, Massachusetts. In 1972 Avon formed a wholly owned subsidiary, Tenn-ERO, to operate a plant in Lawrenceburg, Tennessee.

The Avon Sole Company, pursuant to collective bargaining agreements with the Rubber Workers Union and the International Brotherhood of Firemen and Oilers, instituted a pension plan for its hourly employees in 1959. The plan provided for full vesting after ten years of service. The plan was at all times underfunded, and when Avon closed its doors in 1975, its unfunded vested liability was $552,339.

Under ERISA, can either Emil Ouimet or any or all of his other enterprises be held liable for this unfunded pension liability? See *Pension Benefit Guaranty Corp.* v. *Ouimet Corp.,* 630 F.2d 4 (1st Cir. 1980).

6. Jose Abella sued his employer, Foote Memorial Hospital, for $596.59 in accumulated sick leave hours. He had worked at the hospital from 1965 until he retired in 1980. From 1965 to 1975 the hospital was owned by the Mercy Corporation, which had a policy entitling employees to be paid for accumulated sick leave upon termination of employment. When the hospital was sold by Mercy in 1975, the new owner froze the employees' accumulated sick leave entitlements and agreed in its collective bargaining agreement with the International Union of Operating Engineers in 1978 that the frozen benefits would be paid out to the employees over ten years at 10 percent per year. Section 4 of Article XIX of the labor contract said that retired employees would be paid 50 percent of their frozen entitlements. Under this scheme, Abella was paid 10 percent of his entitlement in 1979 and 50 percent of the remainder in 1980. His claim was for the accumulated hours not paid. He argued that

the new owner of the hospital had assumed Mercy's obligation and that his claim came under ERISA because it was an "employee benefit plan."

How should the court respond to Abella' arguments? See *Abella* v. *W. A. Foote Memorial Hospital, Inc.,* 557 F. Supp. 482(E.D. Mi. 1983).

7. Wesley was employed by Monsanto as a telecommunications clerk from 1977 to 1981. Her duties included delivering messages from building to building. In October 1980, she began complaining of chest pains, which ultimately were diagnosed as a heart problem. She was placed on light duty and later went out on medical leave.

Under Monsanto's disability plan, after thirty days of absence, a written claim and proof of disability had to be filed. The company did not consider Wesley's proof of disability to be adequate, and so sent her to the company doctor. The doctor found her to be only partially disabled and recommended that she return to work with light duties. She refused and was fired. She then requested copies of Monsanto's "insurance policy" and "medical benefits plan." In response to this request, Monsanto failed to provide Wesley with a copy of the disability plan.

What remedies, if any, does Wesley have under ERISA on the basis of these facts? See *Wesley* v. *Monsanto Company,* 710 F.2d 490 (8th Cir. 1983).

8. Ellis Hurn began receiving his early retirement pension benefits in June 1975. In November 1975 he accepted nomination to the office of president of the local union. As a consequence, his benefits were suspended from February 1976 until September 1976. During this period of time he was 58 and 59 years old. Hurn sued for his lost pension benefits on two grounds.

Hurn's first argument was that he had a nonforfeitable right to receive these benefits. Do you agree with this contention? Second, he asserted that the provision in the fund plan, permitting the fund trustees at their discretion to exclude from eligibility employee-beneficiaries who hold union office, was arbitrary and capricious.

Do you agree or disagree with this argument? To what provisions of ERISA can you point in support of your conclusions concerning Hurn's claims? See *Hurn* v. *Retirement Fund Trust of the Plumbing, Heating and Piping Industry of Southern California,* 648 F.2d 1252 (9th Cir. 1981).

9. Edward Shaw retired as a business agent of a District Lodge of the International Association of Machinists (IAM) on January 1, 1975. In September 1976, delegates to the IAM convention voted to amend the pension plan provisions of the union's constitution so as to phase out all cost-of-living adjustments by 1984. Shaw sued, arguing that (1) the phase-out would decrease the accrued benefits of plan participants, (2) the phase-out was a breach of fiduciary duty of the trustees and administrators, and (3) the phase-out also violated established principles of contract law.

Shaw named, as individual defendants, five union officials who were not trustees, but who administered the plan. The IAM's pension plan read as follows:

COMPUTATION OF PENSION

Pensions being paid to previously retired officers and employees shall be adjusted by applying the appropriate foregoing percentage to the straight-time compensation for the classifications or positions corresponding to those in which they were employed immediately prior to their retirement, provided, however, that in no case shall any such adjustment be made on a retroactive basis, nor increase any benefit to a survivor or beneficiary then being paid. Effective January 1, 1973, neither shall any such adjustment result in a pension payment which is less than the amount paid to the retiree at the time of retirement.

On the basis of these facts, how should the court respond to each of Shaw's three arguments? See *Shaw* v. *International Association of Machinists and Aerospace Workers Pension Plan,* 563 F. Supp. 653 (C.D. Cal. 1983).

10. Watts started working for Wikoff in September 1971 and worked there continuously until July 1979 when he was discharged by the company. At the time of his official termination in August 1979, Watts was a participant in the Wikoff Central Bank Master Profit Sharing Plan and Trust (Plan) and had accumulated a vested interest in the balance of his employer contribution account. Sometime subsequent to July 1979, Watts made two requests to the Profit Sharing Committee, which administered the plan, for immediate payment of his pension benefits. After the filing of the plaintiff's application, the committee received information that he had accepted employment with a company in competition with Wikoff, a fact not disputed by the plaintiff. Phillip Lambert, Wikoff's treasurer and a member of the committee, then notified Watts that his pension benefits

would be paid in the form of an annuity payable at the normal retirement age of sixty-five. Plaintiff then instituted this suit pursuant to 29 U.S.C. Section 1132(e) to obtain immediate payment of the nonforfeitable percentage of his benefits.

What is in dispute is the validity of a key provision of the Plan, Schedule II, as it has been applied in the context of this case. Schedule II was adopted by the committee as an amendment to the Plan in February 1977 and afforded the committee discretionary authority to disallow cash payment of vested funds in four instances. In particular, Schedule II provides:

Withdrawal Benefits: Upon withdrawal from the plan, the vested portion of a participant's account shall be distributed in either of the following methods that he may choose:

Option A: An annuity contract payable to the participant at normal retirement age.

Option B: Cash in a lump sum after a waiting period of not less than two years or more than twenty-six months. The vested portion of the participant's account shall be placed in a bank savings certificate account to earn interest for him up to the time of the lump sum distribution.

The right to receive benefits under option B may be disallowed by the Profit Sharing Committee to any withdrawn employee determined to be in competition with the Company, or by any employee terminated for dishonesty, disclosing trade secrets or conviction of a felony or crime involving moral turpitude.

Do you think this proviso is legal under ERISA? See *Watts* v. *Wikoff Color Corp. of S.C.,* 543 F. Supp. 493 (E.D. Texas 1981).

CHAPTER 18

The Fair Labor Standards Act

ALTHOUGH FEDERAL REGULATION OF the hours worked by employees, the wages they are paid, and limitations on child labor are so thoroughly entrenched in our society that they are generally taken for granted, they are a fairly recent legal development. Prior to the passage of the Fair Labor Standards Act (FLSA) in 1938, the only other federal attempt to provide such regulation in general was under the National Industrial Recovery Act of 1933. That legislation was declared unconstitutional by the Supreme Court in the 1935 case of *Schecter Poultry* v. *U.S.* (295 U.S. 495). This chapter will explore the development and operation of federal legislation regulating the hours worked by employees, the wages they are paid, and labor by children.

Background to FLSA

Early Attempts at Hours Regulation

Early federal legislation regulating the hours worked by employees dealt with work under government contracts or in specific industries. The earliest federal law governing hours of work was passed in 1892. It established the eight-hour day for "mechanics" (craftsmen) and laborers engaged in public works, whether they were employed directly by the federal government or by contractors. Similar legislation passed in 1911 provided that contracts for construction of naval ships could be awarded only to employers observing the eight-hour day for their employees. In 1912 the eight-hour day requirement was extended to contractors doing river and harbor dredging. These laws, as supplemented in 1913 and 1917, were known collectively as the Eight-Hour Law. The Eight-Hour Law remained the general standard covering government work until 1940. At that time some variance was permitted as long as the employer paid time-and-a-half for work over eight hours per day.

In addition to regulating the hours of work for government contractors, Congress also set hours limitations for specific industries. The 1907 Hours of Service Act established a maximum sixteen-hour day for railroad workers. Employees directly involved in the movement of trains were limited to thirteen hours a day, while other rail workers in facilities open around the clock were limited to nine-hour days. In 1916 Congress passed the Adamson Act to head off a threatened nationwide rail strike; the act established the eight-hour day for railroad workers. The Supreme Court upheld the Adamson Act as constitutional in the 1917 case of *Wilson* v. *New* (243 U.S. 332).

The hours worked by merchant seamen were also subjected to federal regulation. The Seamen's Act of 1915 provided for twelve-hour limits for sailors at sea ("twelve on and twelve off"), while those working in the engine room were limited to eight-hour days. (Most ships were powered by coal, which was manually shoveled by stokers.) While in port, all hands could be worked up to nine hours per day. The Merchant Marine Act of 1936 established a uniform eight-hour day for seamen.

Early Attempts at Wage Regulation

In 1931 Congress passed the Davis-Bacon Act, which provides that contractors working on government construction projects must pay the prevailing wage rates in the area. The Secretary of Labor must determine the prevailing wage rates in a geographic area. These rates must be paid by contractors working government contracts in the area. The Davis-Bacon Act is still in force.

The federal government attempted the general regulation of wages and hours through the National Industrial Recovery Act (NIRA). The NIRA, passed in 1933, was an attempt to improve general conditions during the Great Depression. The NIRA provided for the development of "codes of fair competition" for various industries. The codes, to be developed by trade associations within each industry, would specify the minimum wages to be paid, the maximum hours to be worked, and limitations on child labor. When approved by the president, the codes would have the force of law. The Supreme Court held that the NIRA was an unconstitutional delegation of congressional power in the 1935 case of *Schecter Poultry Corp.* v. *U.S.*

In 1936 the Walsh-Healy Act was passed. Like the Davis-Bacon Act, it regulates working conditions for government contractors. The Walsh-Healy Act sets minimum standards for wages for contractors providing at least $10,000 worth of goods to the federal government. It also requires that hours worked in excess of forty per week be paid at time-and-a-half the regular rate of pay. The Walsh-Healy Act is also still in force.

In 1937 the Supreme Court was presented with a case that challenged the legality of a Washington State law that set a minimum wage for women. In several prior cases, the Court had held minimum wage laws to be unconstitutional, as it had done with the NIRA.

WEST COAST HOTEL CO. v. PARRISH

300 U.S. 379 (Supreme Court of the United States, 1937)

HUGHES, C. J.

This case presents the question of the constitutional validity of the minimum wage law of the State of Washington.

The Act, entitled "Minimum Wages for Women," autho-

rizes the fixing of minimum wages for women and minors. It provides:

SECTION 1. The welfare of the State of Washington demands that women and minors be protected from conditions of labor which have a pernicious effect on their health and morals. The State of Washington, therefore, exercising herein its police and sovereign power declares that inadequate wages and unsanitary conditions of labor exert such pernicious effect.

SEC. 2. It shall be unlawful to employ women or minors in any industry or occupation within the State of Washington under conditions of labor detrimental to their health or morals; and it shall be unlawful to employ women workers in any industry within the State of Washington at wages which are not adequate for their maintenance.

SEC. 3. There is hereby created a commission to be known as the "Industrial Welfare Commission" for the State of Washington, to establish such standards of wages and conditions of labor for women and minors employed within the State of Washington, as shall be held hereunder to be reasonable and not detrimental to health and morals, and which shall be sufficient for the decent maintenance of women.

Further provisions required the Commission to ascertain the wages and conditions of labor of women and minors within the State. Public hearings were to be held. If after investigation the Commission found that in any occupation, trade or industry the wages paid to women were "inadequate to supply them necessary cost of living and to maintain the workers in health," the commission was empowered to call a conference of representatives of employers and employees together with disinterested persons representing the public. The conference was to recommend to the Commission, on its request, an estimate of a minimum wage adequate for the purpose above stated, and on the approval of such a recommendation it became the duty of the Commission to issue an obligatory order fixing minimum wages. Any such order might be reopened and the question reconsidered with the aid of the former conference or a new one. Special licenses were authorized for the employment of women who were "physically defective or crippled by age or otherwise," and also for apprentices, at less than the prescribed minimum wage.

By a later Act the Industrial Welfare Commission was abolished and its duties were assigned to the Industrial Welfare Commission consisting of the Director of Labor and Industries, the Supervisor of Industrial Insurance, the Supervisor of Industrial Relations, the Industrial Statistician and the Supervisor of Women in Industry.

The appellant conducts a hotel. The appellee Elsie Parrish was employed as a chambermaid and (with her husband) brought this suit to recover the difference between the wages paid her and the minimum wage fixed pursuant to the state law. The minimum wage of $14.50 per week of 48 hours. The appellant challenged the act as repugnant to the due process clause of the Fourteenth Amendment of the Constitution of the United States. The Supreme Court of the State, reversing the trial court, sustained the statute

and directed judgment for the plaintiffs. The case is here on appeal.

The appellant relies upon the decision of this Court in *Adkins* v. *Children's Hospital,* which held invalid the District of Columbia Minimum Wage Act, which was attacked under the due process clause of the Fifth Amendment. . . .

The recent case of *Morehead* v. *New York ex rel. Tipaldo,* came here on certiorari to the New York court, which had held the New York minimum wage act for women to be invalid. A minority of this Court thought that the New York statute was distinguishable in a material feature from that involved in the *Adkins* case, and that for that and other reasons the New York statute should be sustained. But the Court of Appeals of New York had said that it found no material difference between the two statutes, and this Court held that the "meaning of the statute" as fixed by the decision of the state court "must be accepted here as if the meaning had been specifically expressed in the enactment." That view led to the affirmance by this Court of the judgment in the *Morehead* case, as the Court considered that the only question before it was whether the *Adkins* case was distinguishable and that reconsideration of that decision had not been sought. . . .

We think that the question which was not deemed to be open in the *Morehead* case is open and is necessarily presented here. The Supreme Court of Washington has upheld the minimum wage statute of that State. It has decided that the statute is a reasonable exercise of the police power of the State. In reaching that conclusion the state court has invoked principles long established by the Court in the application of the Fourteenth Amendment. The state court has refused to regard the decision in the *Adkins* case as determinative and has pointed to our decisions both before and since that case as justifying its position. We are of the opinion that this ruling of the state court demands on our reexamination of the *Adkins* case. The importan question, in which many States having simil cerned, the close division by which the *Adkins* case was reached, and the e which have supervened, and in sonableness of the exercise of the State must be con priate, but we think i case the subject s'

The principl doubt. The const cess clause of the F States, as the due pro governed Congress. In those attacking minimum deprivation of freedom of contract. What is this freedom? The Constitution does not speak of freedom of contract. It speaks of liberty and prohibits the deprivation of liberty without due process of law. In prohibiting that deprivation the Constitution does not recognize an absolute and uncontrollable liberty. Liberty in each of its phases has its history and connotation. But the liberty safeguarded is liberty in a social organization which requires the protection of law against the evils which menace the health, safety, morals, and welfare of the people. Liberty under the Constitution is thus necessarily subject to the restraints of due process, and regulation which is reasonable in relation to its subject and is adopted in the interests of the community is due process.

This essential limitation of liberty in general governs freedom of contract in particular. More than twenty-five years ago we set forth the applicable principle in these words, after referring to the cases where the liberty guaranteed by the Fourteenth Amendment had been broadly described:

> But it was recognized in the cases cited, as in many others, that freedom of contract is a qualified and not an absolute right. There is no absolute freedom to do as one wills or to contract as one chooses. The guaranty of liberty does not withdraw from legislative supervision that wide department of activity which consists of the making of contracts, or deny to government the power to provide restrictive safeguards. Liberty implies the absence of arbitrary restraint, not immunity from reasonable regulations and prohibitions imposed in the interests of the community.

This power under the Constitution to restrict freedom of contract has had many illustrations. That it may be exercised in the public interest with respect to contracts between employer and employee is undeniable. . . . In dealing with the relation of employer and employed, the legislature has necessarily a wide field of discretion in order that there may be suitable protection of health and safety, and that peace and good order may be promoted through regulations designed to insure wholesome conditions of work and freedom from oppression.

The point that has been strongly stressed that adult employees should be deemed competent to make their own contracts was decisively met nearly forty years ago in *Holden* v. *Hardy,* where we pointed out the inequality in the position of the parties. We said:

> The legislature has also recognized the fact, which the experience of legislators in many States has corroborated, that the proprietors of these establishments and their operatives do not stand upon an equality, and that their interests are, to a certain extent, conflicting. The former naturally desire to obtain as much labor as possible from their employes, while the latter are often induced by the fear of discharge to conform to regulations which their judgment, fairly exercised, would pronounce to be detrimental to their health or strength. In other words, the proprietors lay down the rules and the laborers are practically constrained to obey them. In such cases self-interest is often an unsafe guide, and the legislature may properly interpose its authority.

And we added that the fact "that both parties are of full age and competent to contract does not necessarily deprive the State of the powers to interfere where the parties do not stand upon an equality, or where the public health demands that one party to the contract shall be protected against himself." "The State still retains an interest in his welfare, however reckless he may be. The whole is no greater than the sum of all the parts, and when the individual health, safety and welfare are sacrificed or neglected, the State must suffer."

It is manifest that this established principle is peculiarly applicable in relation to the employment of women in whose protection the State has a special interest. That phase of the subject received elaborate consideration in *Muller* v. *Oregon,* where the constitutional authority of the State to limit the working hours of women was sustained. We emphasized the consideration that "woman's physical structure and the performance of maternal functions place her at a disadvantage in the struggle for subsistence" and that her physical well-being "becomes an object of public interest and care in order to preserve the strength and vigor of the race." We emphasized the need of protecting women against oppression despite her possession of contractual rights. We said that "though limitations upon personal and contractual rights may be removed by legislation, there is that in her disposition and habits of life which will operate against a full assertion of those rights. She will still be where some legislation to protect her seems necessary to secure a real equality of right." Hence she was "properly placed in a class by herself, and legislation designed for her protection may be sustained even when like legislation is not necessary for men and could not be sustained." We concluded that the limitations which the statute there in question "placed upon her contractual powers, upon her right to agree with her employer as to the time she shall labor" were "not imposed solely for her benefit, but also largely for the benefit of all." . . .

This array of precedents and the principles they applied were thought by the dissenting Justices in the *Adkins* case to demand that the minimum wage statute be sustained.

The validity of the distinction made by the Court between a minimum wage and a maximum of hours in limiting liberty of contract was especially challenged. . . .

One of the points which was pressed by the Court in supporting its ruling in the *Adkins* case was that the standard set up by the District of Columbia Act did not take appropriate account of the value of the services rendered. In the *Morehead* case, the minority thought that the New York statute had met that point in its definition of a "fair wage" and that it accordingly presented a distinguishable feature which the Court could recognize within the limits which the *Morehead* petition for certiorari was deemed to present. The Court, however, did not take that view and the New York Act was held to be essentially the same as that for the District of Columbia. The statute now before us is like the latter, but we are unable to conclude that in its minimum wage requirement the State has passed beyond the boundary of its broad protective power.

The minimum wage to be paid under the Washington statute is fixed after full consideration by representatives of employers, employees and the public. It may be assumed that the minimum wage is fixed in consideration of the services that are performed in the particular occupations under normal conditions. Provision is made for special licenses at less wages in the case of women who are incapable of full service. The statement of Mr. Justice Holmes in the *Adkins* case is pertinent: "This statute does not compel anybody to pay anything. It simply forbids employment at rates below those fixed as the minimum requirement of health and right living. It is safe to assume that women will not be employed at even the lowest wages allowed unless they earn them, or unless the employer's business can sustain the burden. In short the law in its character and operation is like hundreds of so-called police laws that have been upheld." And Chief Justice Taft forcibly pointed out the consideration which is basic in a statute of this character: "Legislatures which adopt a requirement of maximum hours or minimum wages may be presumed to believe that when sweating employers are prevented from paying unduly low wages by positive law they will continue their business, abating that part of their profits, which were wrung from the necessities of their employees, and will concede the better terms required by the law; and that while in individual cases hardship may result, the restriction will enure to the benefit of the general class of employees in whose interest the law is passed and so to that of the community at large."

We think that the views thus expressed are sound and that the decision in the *Adkins* case was a departure from the true application of the principles governing the regulation by the State of the relation of employer and employed. . . .

With full recognition of the earnestness and vigor which characterize the prevailing opinion in the *Adkins* case we find it impossible to reconcile that ruling with these well-considered declarations. What can be closer to the public interest than the health of women and their protection from unscrupulous and overreaching employers? And if the protection of women is a legitimate end of the exercise of state power, how can it be said that the requirement of the payment of a minimum wage fairly fixed in order to meet the very necessities of existence is not an admissible means to that end? The legislature of the State was clearly entitled to consider the situation of women in employment, the fact that they are in the class receiving the least pay, that their bargaining power is relatively weak, and that they are the ready victims of those who would take advantage of their necessitous circumstances. The legislature was entitled to adopt measures to reduce the evils of the "sweating system," the exploiting of workers at wages so low as to be insufficient to meet the bare cost of living, thus making their very helplessness the occasion of a most injurious competition. The legislature had the right to consider that its minimum wage requirements would be an important aid in carrying out its policy of protection. The adoption of similar requirements by many States evidences a deep-seated conviction both as to the presence of the evil and as to the means adopted to check it. Legislative response to that conviction cannot be regarded as arbitrary or capricious, and that is all we have to decide. Even if the wisdom of the policy be regarded as debatable and its effects uncertain, still the legislature is entitled to its judgment.

There is an additional and compelling consideration which recent economic experience has brought into a strong light. The exploitation of a class of workers who are in an unequal position with respect to bargaining power and are thus relatively defenceless against the denial of a living wage is not only detrimental to their health and well-being but casts a direct burden for their support upon the community. What these workers lose in wages the taxpayers are called upon to pay. The bare cost of living must be met. We may take judicial notice of the unparalleled demands for relief which arose during the recent period of depression and still continue to an alarming extent despite the degree of economic recovery which has been achieved. It is unnecessary to cite official statistics to establish what is of common knowledge through the length and breadth of the land. While in the instant case no factual brief has been presented, there is no reason to doubt that the State of Washington has encountered the same social problem that is present elsewhere. The community is not bound to provide what is in effect a subsidy for unconscionable employers. The community may direct its law-making power to correct the abuse which springs from their selfish disregard of the public interest. The argument that the legislation in question constitutes an arbitrary discrimination, because it does not extend to men, is unavailing. This Court has frequently held that the legislative authority, acting within its proper field, is not bound to extend its regulation to all cases which it might possibly reach. The legislature "is free to recognize degrees of harm and it may confine its restrictions to those classes of cases where the need is deemed to be clearest." If "the law presumably hits the evil where it is most felt, it is not to be overthrown because there are other instances to which it might have been applied." There is no "doctrinaire requirement" that the legislation should be couched in all embracing terms. This familiar principle has repeatedly been applied to legislation which singles out women, and particular classes of women, in the exercise of the State's protective power. Their relative need in the presence of the evil, no less than the existence of the evil itself, is a matter for the legislative judgment.

Our conclusion is that the case of *Adkins* v. *Children's Hospital,* should be, and it is, overruled. The judgment of the Supreme Court of the State of Washington is **Affirmed.**

The Fair Labor Standards Act

The *Schecter Poultry* decision and the *West Coast Hotel* case were the main factors behind the **Fair Labor Standards Act (FLSA).** The *Schecter* case, which struck down the National Industrial Recovery Act, forced the federal government to attempt direct regulation of hours and wages in general. The *West Coast Hotel* case demonstrated that some regulation of working conditions was viewed by the Supreme Court as a valid exercise of government power.

After the *West Coast Hotel* decision, President Roosevelt told Congress

All but the hopelessly reactionary will agree that to conserve our primary resources of manpower, Government must have some control over maximum hours, minimum wages, the evil of child labor, and the exploitation of unorganized labor.

The FLSA was passed by Congress and signed into law on June 25, 1938. The Supreme Court held the FLSA to be constitutional in the 1941 case of *U.S.* v. *Darby Lumber Co.* (312 U.S. 100). The FLSA, as amended over the years, continues in force today. It is the essential, although unglamorous, foundation for more recent federal regulation of working conditions through OSHA, ERISA, and even ADEA. The FLSA deals with four areas: minimum wages, overtime pay provisions, child labor, and equal pay for equal work. (The Equal Pay Act is an amendment to the FLSA. See Chapter 15 for a discussion of the provisions of the Equal Pay Act.)

Coverage of the FLSA

The FLSA, as amended, provides for three bases of coverage. Employees who are engaged in interstate commerce, including both import and export, are covered. As well, employees who are engaged in the production of goods for interstate commerce are subject to the FLSA. The "production" of goods includes "any closely related process or occupation directly essential" to the production of goods for interstate commerce. Last, all employees employed in an "enterprise engaged in" interstate commerce are subject to the FLSA, regardless of the relationship of their duties to commerce or the production of goods for commerce. This basis, the "enterprise" test, is subject to minimum dollar-volume limits for certain types of businesses. Employees of small employers in such businesses would have to qualify for FLSA coverage under one of the other two bases of coverage. Employers and employees not covered by FLSA are generally subject to state laws, similar to FLSA, which regulate minimum wages and maximum hours of work.

The FLSA was extended to cover some federal employees and to include state and local hospitals and educational institutions in 1966. In 1974, FLSA coverage was extended to most federal employees, to state and local government employees, and to private household domestic workers.

The extension of FLSA coverage to state and local government employees has been legally controversial. In the 1976 decision of *National League of Cities* v. *Usery* (426 U.S. 833), the Supreme Court held that federal regulation of the working conditions of state and local government employees infringed upon state sovereignty. The question was addressed again, in 1985, by the Supreme Court in the following case.

GARCIA v.SAN ANTONIO METROPOLITAN TRANSIT AUTHORITY

469 U.S. 528 (Supreme Court of the United States, 1985)

BLACKMUN, J.

We revisit in these cases an issue raised in *National League of Cities* v. *Usery* (1976). In that litigation, this Court, by a sharply divided vote, ruled that the Commerce Clause does not empower Congress to enforce the minimum-wage and overtime provisions of the Fair Labor Standards Act (FLSA) against the States "in areas of traditional governmental functions." Although *National League of Cities* supplied some examples of "traditional governmental functions," it did not offer a general explanation of how a "traditional" function is to be distinguished from a "nontraditional" one. Since then, federal and state courts have struggled with the task, thus imposed, of identifying a traditional function for purposes of state immunity under the Commerce Clause.

In the present cases, a Federal District Court concluded that municipal ownership and operation of a mass-transit system is a traditional governmental function and thus, under *National League of Cities,* is exempt from the obligations imposed by the FLSA. Faced with the identical question, three Federal Courts of Appeals and one state appellate court have reached the opposite conclusion.

Our examination of this "function" standard applied in

these and other cases over the last eight years now persuades us that the attempt to draw the boundaries of state regulatory immunity in terms of "traditional governmental function" is not only unworkable but is inconsistent with established principles of federalism and, indeed, with those very federalism principles on which *National League of Cities* purported to rest. That case, accordingly, is overruled.

The history of public transportation in San Antonio, Tex., is characteristic of the history of local mass transit in the United States generally. Passenger transportation for hire within San Antonio originally was provided on a private basis by a local transportation company. In 1913, the Texas Legislature authorized the State's municipalities to regulate vehicles providing carriage for hire. Two years later, San Antonio enacted an ordinance setting forth franchising, insurance, and safety requirements for passenger vehicles operated for hire. The city continued to rely on such publicly regulated private mass transit until 1959, when it purchased the privately owned San Antonio Transit Company and replaced it with a public authority known as the San Antonio Transit System (SATS). SATS operated until 1978, when the city transferred its facilities and equipment to appellee San Antonio Metropolitan Transit Authority (SAMTA), a public mass-transit authority organized on a countrywide basis. SAMTA currently is the major provider of transportation in the San Antonio metropolitan area; between 1978 and 1980 alone, its vehicles traveled over 26 million route miles and carried over 63 million passengers.

As did other localities, San Antonio reached the point where it came to look to the Federal Government for financial assistance in maintaining its public mass transit. SATS managed to meet its operating expenses and bond obligations for the first decade of its existence without federal or local financial aid. By 1970, however, its financial position had deteriorated to the point where federal subsidies were vital for its continued operation. SATS' general manager that year testified before Congress that "if we do not receive substantial help from the Federal Government, San Antonio may . . . join the governing ranks of cities that have inferior [public] transportation or may end up with no [public] transportation at all."

The principal federal program to which SATS and other mass-transit systems looked for relief was the Urban Mass Transportation Act of 1964 (UMTA), which provides substantial federal assistance to urban mass-transit programs. UMTA now authorizes the Department of Transportation to fund 75 percent of the capital outlays and up to 50 percent of the operating expenses of qualifying mass-transit programs. SATS received its first UMTA subsidy, a $4.1 million capital grant, in December 1970. From then until February 1980, SATS and SAMTA received over $51 million in UMTA grants—more than $31 million in capital grants, over $20 million in operating assistance, and a minor amount in technical assistance. During SAMTA's first two fiscal years, it received $12.5 million in UMTA operating grants, $26.8 million from sales taxes, and only $10.1 million from fares. Federal subsidies and local sales taxes currently account for about 75 percent of SAMTA's operating expenses.

The present controversy concerns the extent to which SAMTA may be subjected to the minimum-wage and overtime requirements of the FLSA. When the FLSA was enacted in 1938, its wages and overtime provisions did not apply to local mass-transit employees or, indeed, to employees of state and local governments. In 1961, Congress extended minimum-wage coverage to employees of any private mass-transit carrier whose annual gross revenue was not less than $1 million. Five years later, Congress extended FLSA coverage to state and local-government employees for the first time by withdrawing the minimum-wage and overtime exemptions from public hospitals, schools, and mass-transit carriers whose rates and services were subject to state regulation. At the same time, Congress eliminated the overtime

exemption for all mass-transit employees other than drivers, operators, and conductors. The application of the FLSA to public schools and hospitals was ruled to be within Congress' power under the Commerce Clause. *Maryland* v. *Wirtz* (1968).

The FLSA obligations of public mass-transit systems like SATS were expanded in 1974 when Congress provided for the progressive repeal of the surviving overtime exemption for mass-transit employees. Congress simultaneously brought the States and their subdivisions further within the ambit of the FLSA by extending FLSA coverage to virtually all state and local-government employees. SATS complied with the FLSA's overtime requirements until 1976, when this Court, in *National League of Cities,* overruled *Maryland* v. *Wirtz,* and held that the FLSA could not be applied constitutionally to the "traditional governmental functions" of state and local governments. Four months after *National League of Cities* was handed down, SATS informed its employees that the decision relieved SATS of its overtime obligations under the FLSA.

Matters rested there until September 17, 1979, when the Wage and Hour Administration of the Department of Labor issued an opinion that SAMTA's operations "are not constitutionally immune from the application of the Fair Labor Standards Act" under *National League of Cities.* On November 21 of that year, SAMTA filed this action against the Secretary of Labor in the United States District Court for the Western District of Texas. It sought a declaratory judgment that, contrary to the Wage and Hour Administration's determination, *National League of Cities* precluded the application of the FLSA's overtime requirements to SAMTA's operations. The Secretary counterclaimed for enforcement of the overtime and recordkeeping requirements of the FLSA. On the same day that SAMTA filed its action, appellant Garcia and several other SAMTA employees brought suit against SAMTA in the same District Court for overtime pay under the FLSA. The District Court has stayed that action pending the outcome of these cases, but it allowed Garcia to intervene in the present ligation as a defendant in support of the Secretary. One month after SAMTA brought suit, the Department of Labor formally amended its FLSA interpretive regulations to provide that publicly owned local mass-transit systems are not entitled to immunity under *National League of Cities.*

On November 17, 1981, the District Court granted SAMTA's motion for summary judgment and denied the Secretary's and Garcia's cross-motion for partial summary judgment. Without further explanation, the District Court ruled that "local public mass transit systems (including [SAMTA]) constitute integral operations in areas of traditional governmental functions" under *National League of Cities.*

The Secretary and Garcia both appealed directly to this Court. During the pendency of those appeals, *Transportation Union v. Long Island R. Co.* was decided. In that case, the Court ruled that commuter rail service provided by the state-owned Long Island Rail Road did not constitute a "traditional governmental function" and hence did not enjoy constitutional immunity, under *National League of Cities,* from the requirements of the Railway Labor Act. Thereafter, it vacated the District Court's judgment in the present cases and remanded them for further consideration in the light of *Long Island.*

On remand, the District Court adhered to its original view and again entered judgment for SAMTA. The court looked first to what it regarded as the "historical reality" of state involvement in mass transit. It recognized that States not always had owned and operated mass-transit systems, but concluded that they had engaged in a longstanding pattern of public regulation, and that this regulatory tradition gave rise to an "inference of sovereignty." The court next looked to the record of federal involvement in the field and concluded that constitutional immunity would not result in an erosion of federal authority with respect to state-owned mass-transit systems, because many federal statutes themselves contain exemptions for States and thus make the withdrawal of federal regulatory power over public mass-transit systems a supervening federal policy. Although the Federal Government's authority over employee wages under the FLSA obviously would be eroded, Congress had not asserted any interest in the wages of public mass-transit employees until 1966 and hence had not established a longstanding federal interest in the field, in contrast to the century-old federal regulatory presence in the railroad industry found significant for the decision in *Long Island.* Finally, the court compared mass transit to the list of functions identified as constitutionally immune in *National League of Cities* and concluded that it did not differ from those functions in any material respect. The court stated: "If transit is to be distinguished from the exempt [*National League of Cities*] functions it will have to be by identifying a traditional state function in the same way pornography is sometimes identified: someone knows it when they see it, but they can't describe it."

The Secretary and Garcia again took direct appeals from the District Court's judgment...

Appellees have not argued that SAMTA is immune from regulation under the FLSA on the ground that it is a local transit system engaged in intrastate commercial activity. In a practical sense, SAMTA's operations might well be characterized as "local." Nonetheless, it long has been settled that Congress' authority under the Commerce Clause extends to intrastate economic activities that affect interstate commerce. Were SAMTA a privately owned and operated enterprise, it could not credibly argue that Congress exceeded the bounds of its Commerce Clause powers in prescribing minimum wages and overtime rates for SAMTA's employees. Any constitutional exemption from the requirements of the FLSA therefore must rest on SAMTA's status as a governmental entity rather than on the "local" nature of its operations.

The prerequisites for governmental immunity under *National League of Cities* were summarized by this Court.... Under that summary, four conditions must be satisfied before a state activity may be deemed immune from a particular federal regulation under the Commerce Clause. First, it is said that the federal statute at issue must regulate "the States as States." Second, the statute must "address matters that are indisputably 'attribute[s] of state sovereignty.'" Third, state compliance with the federal obligation must "directly impair [the States'] ability to structure integral operations in areas of traditional governmental functions." Finally, the relation of state and federal interests must not be such that "the nature of the federal interest . . . justifies state submission."

The controversy in the present cases has focused on the third requirement—that the challenged federal statute trench on "traditional governmental functions." The District Court voiced a common concern: "Despite the abundance of adjectives, identifying which particular state functions are immune remains difficult." Just how troublesome the task has been is revealed by the results reached in other federal cases. . . .

Thus far, this Court itself has made little headway in defining the scope of the governmental functions deemed protected under *National League of Cities.* In that case the Court set forth examples of protected and unprotected functions, but provided no explanation of how those examples were identified. The only other case in which the Court has had occasion to address the problem is *Long Island.* We there observed: "The determination of whether a federal law impairs a state's authority with respect to 'areas of traditional [state] functions' may at times be a difficult one." The accuracy of that statement is demonstrated by this Court's own difficulties in *Long Island* in developing a workable standard for "traditional governmental functions."

We relied in large part there on "the *historical reality* that the operation of railroads is not among the functions *traditionally* performed by state and local governments," but we simultaneously disavowed "a static historical view of state functions generally immune from federal regulation." We held that the inquiry into a particular function's "traditional" nature was merely a means of determining whether the federal statute at issue unduly handicaps "basic state prerogatives," but we did not offer an explanation of what makes one state function a "basic prerogative" and another function not basic. Finally, having disclaimed a rigid reliance on the historical pedigree of state involvement in a particular area, we nonetheless found it appropriate to emphasize the extended historical record of *federal* involvement in the field of rail transportation....

We rejected the possibility of making immunity turn on a purely historical standard of "tradition" in *Long Island,* and properly so. The most obvious defect of a historical approach to state immunity is that it prevents a court from accommodating changes in the historical functions of States, changes that have resulted in a number of once-private functions like education being assumed by the States and their subdivisions. At the same time, the only apparent virtue of a vigorous historical standard, namely, its promise of a reasonably objective measure for state immunity, is illusory. Reliance on history as an organizing principle results in line-drawing of the most arbitrary sort; the genesis of state governmental function stretches over a historical continuum from before the Revolution to the present, and courts would have to decide by fiat precisely how longstanding a pattern of state involvement had to be for federal regulatory authority to be defeated.

A nonhistorical standard for selecting immune governmental functions is likely to be just as unworkable as is a historical standard. The goal of identifying "uniquely" governmental functions, for example, has been rejected by the Court in the field of government tort liability in part because the notion of a "uniquely" governmental function is unmanageable. Another possibility would be to confine immunity to "necessary" governmental services, that is, services that would be provided inadequately or not at all unless the government provided them. The set of services that fits into this category, however, may well be negligible. The fact that an unregulated market produces less of some service than a State deems desirable does not mean that the State itself must provide the service; in most if not all cases, the State can "contract out" by hiring private firms to provide the service or simply by providing subsidies to existing suppliers. It also is open to question how well equipped

courts are to make this kind of determination about the workings of economic markets.

We believe, however, that there is a more fundamental problem at work here, a problem that explains why the Court was never able to provide a basis for the governmental/proprietary distinction in the intergovernmental tax immunity cases and why an attempt to draw similar distinctions with respect to federal regulatory authority under *National League of Cities* is unlikely to succeed regardless of how the distinctions are phrased. The problem is that neither the governmental/proprietary distinction nor any other that purports to separate out important governmental functions can be faithful to the role of federalism in a democratic society. The essence of our federal system is that within the realm of authority left open to them under the Constitution, the States must be equally free to engage in any activity that their citizens choose for the common weal, no matter how unorthodox or unnecessary anyone else—including the judiciary—deems state involvement to be. Any rule of state immunity that looks to the "traditional," "integral," or "necessary" nature of governmental functions inevitably invites an unelected federal judiciary to make decisions about which state policies it favors and which ones it dislikes....

We therefore now reject, as unsound in principle and unworkable in practice, a rule of state immunity from federal regulation that turns on a judicial appraisal of whether a particular governmental function is "integral" or "traditional." Any such rule leads to inconsistent results at the same time that it disserves principles of democratic self-governance, and it breeds inconsistency precisely because it is divorced from those principles. If there are to be limits on the Federal Government's power to interfere with state functions—as undoubtedly there are—we must look elsewhere to find them. We accordingly return to the underlying issue that confronted this Court in *National League of Cities*—the manner in which the Constitution insulates States from the reach of Congress' power under the Commerce Clause.

The central theme of *National League of Cities* was that the States occupy a special position in our constitutional system and that the scope of Congress' authority under the Commerce Clause must reflect that position. Of course, the Commerce Clause by its specific language does not provide any special limitation on Congress' actions with respect to the States....

What has proved problematic is not the perception that the Constitution's federal structure imposes limitations on the Commerce Clause, but rather the nature and content of those limitations. One approach to defining the limits on Congress' authority to regulate the States under the Commerce Clause is to identify certain underlying elements of political sovereignty that are deemed essential to the States' "separate and independent existence." This approach obviously underlay the Court's use of the "traditional governmental function" concept in *National League of Cities.* It also has led to the separate requirement that the challenged federal statute "address matters that are indisputably 'attribute[s] of state sovereignty.'" In *National League of Cities* itself, for example, the Court concluded that decisions by a State concerning the wages and hours of its employees are an "undoubted attribute of state sovereignty." The opinion did not explain what aspects of such decisions made them such an "undoubted attribute," and the Court since then has remarked on the uncertain scope of the concept. The point of the inquiry, however, has remained to single out particular features of a State's internal governance that are deemed to be intrinsic parts of state sovereignty.

We doubt that courts ultimately can identify principled constitutional limitations on the scope of Congress' Commerce Clause powers over the States merely by relying on *a priori* definitions of state sovereignty. In part, this is because of the elusiveness of objective criteria for "fundamental" elements of state sovereignty, a problem we have witnessed in the search for "traditional governmental functions." There is, however, a more fundamental reason: the sovereignty of the States is limited by the Constitution itself. A variety of sovereign powers, for example, are withdrawn from the States by Article I. Section 10. Section 8 of the same Article works an equally sharp contraction of state sovereignty by authorizing Congress to exercise a wide range of legislative powers and (in conjunction with the Supremacy Clause of Article VI) to displace contrary state legislation. By providing for final review of questions of federal law in this Court, Article III curtails the sovereign power of the States' judiciaries to make authoritative determinations of law. Finally, the developed application, through the Fourteenth Amendment, of the greater part of the Bill of Rights to the States limits the sovereign authority that States otherwise would possess to legislate with respect to their citizens and to conduct their own affairs.

The States unquestionably do "retai[n] a significant measure of sovereign authority." They do so, however, only to the extent that the Constitution has not divested them of their original powers and transferred those powers to the Federal Government. In the words of James Madison to the Members of the First Congress: "Interference with the power of the States was no constitutional criterion of the power of Congress. If the power was not given, Congress could not exercise it; if given, they might exercise it, although it should not interfere with the laws, or even the Constitution of the States." . . .

As a result, to say that the Constitution assumes the continued role of the States is to say little about the nature of that role. Only recently, this court recognized that the purpose of the constitutional immunity recognized in *National League of Cities* is not to preserve "a sacred province of state autonomy." With rare exceptions, like the guarantee, in Article IV, Section 3, of state territorial integrity, the Constitution does not carve out express elements of state sovereignty that Congress may not employ its delegated powers to displace. . . .

The power of the Federal Government is a "power to be respected" as well, and the fact that the States remain sovereign as to all powers not vested in Congress or denied them by the Constitution offers no guidance about where the frontier between state and federal power lies. In short, we have no license to employ freestanding conceptions of state sovereignty when measuring congressional authority under the Commerce Clause. . . . Apart from the limitation on federal authority inherent in the delegated nature of Congress' Article I powers, the principal means chosen by the Framers to ensure the role of the States in the federal system lies in the structure of the Federal Government itself. It is no novelty to observe that the composition of the Federal Government was designed in large part to protect the States from overreaching by Congress. . . . [T]he Framers chose to rely on a federal system in which special restraints on federal power over the States inhered principally in the workings of the National Government itself, rather than in discrete limitations on the objects of federal authority. State sovereign interests, then, are more properly protected by procedural safeguards inherent in the structure of the federal system than by judicially created limitations on federal power.

The effectiveness of the federal political process in preserving the States' interests is apparent even today in the course of federal legislation. On the one hand, the States have been able to direct a substantial proportion of federal revenues into their own treasuries in the form of general and program-specific grants in aid. The federal role in assisting state and local governments is a longstanding one; Congress provided federal land grants to finance state governments from the beginning of the Republic, and direct cash grants were awarded as early as 1887. . . . [A]gainst this background, we are convinced that the fundamental limitation that the constitutional scheme imposes on the Commerce Clause to protect the "States as States" is one of process rather than one of result. Any substantive restraint on the exercise of Commerce Clause powers must find its justification in the procedural nature of this basic limitation, and it must be tailored to compensate for possible failings in the national political process rather than to dictate a "sacred province of state autonomy."

Insofar as the present cases are concerned, then, we need go no further than to state that we perceive nothing in the overtime and minimum-wage requirements of the FLSA, as applied to SAMTA, that is destructive of state sovereignty or violative of any constitutional provision. SAMTA faces nothing more than the same minimum-wage and overtime obligations that hundreds of thousands of other employers, public as well as private, have to meet. . . .

This analysis makes clear that Congress' action in affording SAMTA employees the protections of the wage and hour provisions of the FLSA contravened no affirmative limit on Congress' power under the Commerce Clause. The judgment of the District Court therefore must be reversed.

Of course, we continue to recognize that the States oc-cupy a special and specific position in our constitutional system and that the scope of Congress' authority under the Commerce Clause must reflect that position. But the principal and basic limit on the federal commerce power is that inherent in all congressional action—the built-in restraints that our system provides through state participation in federal governmental action. The political process ensures that laws that unduly burden the States will not be promulgated. In the factual setting of these cases the internal safeguards of the political process have performed as intended. . . .

We do not lightly overrule recent precedent. We have not hesitated, however, when it has become apparent that a prior decision has departed from a proper understanding of congressional power under the Commerce Clause. . . .

National League of Cities v. *Usery* is overruled. The judgment of the District Court is reversed, and these cases are remanded to that court for further proceedings consistent with this opinion. **It is so ordered.**

Minimum Wages

The government regulation of **minimum wages** is an attempt to reduce poverty and bring the earnings of workers closer to the cost of living. The setting of the minimum wage was also an attempt to maintain the purchasing power of the public in order to lift the country out of the economic depths of the Great Depression.

The concept of a minimum wage may seem simple: The employer may not pay employees less than the minimum wage per hour. In 1938 the minimum wage was set at $0.25 per hour, to be raised to $0.40 per hour through the next seven years. The present wage rate is $4.25 per hour.

Although the concept of the minimum wage seems simple, administering it may present some problems because of the wide variation in methods of compensating employees. For example, many employees are paid on an hourly basis, whereas others receive a weekly or monthly salary. Waiters and waitresses often rely on tips from customers for a large percentage of their earnings. Machinists and sewing machine operators are usually paid on a "piece rate" basis—that is, they earn so much money for each piece completed. Salespeople usually earn a commission, which may or may not be supplemented by a base salary. Musicians may be paid a flat rate per engagement, and umpires or referees may be paid by the game.

Such atypical compensation methods are subject to regulations developed by the Administrator of the Wage and Hour Division of the Department of Labor. Those regulations are designed to ensure that all workers receive at least the minimum wage. If a worker is a "tipped worker," that is, one who receives tips from customers, the employer is allowed to reduce the minimum wage paid to that worker by up to

40 percent, with the difference to be made up by tips received. The earnings of workers who are paid on a piece-rate basis must average out to at least the minimum wage; the time period over which the earnings are averaged cannot be longer than a single workweek. That means that the earnings of such an employee may be less than the minimum wage for any single hour, as long as the total earnings for the week average out to the minimum wage.

Employers may require that employees be present at the workplace at certain times when they are not performing their normal duties. Should the employees be paid for those periods? Employers may also make deductions from employees' earnings for room, board, tools, work clothes, and so on. What happens when the deductions have the effect of reducing the employee's pay below the minimum wage? The following cases consider these questions. *Brennan* v. *De Laney* deals with the requirement that employees furnish their own uniforms and the issue of nonpaid break time. *Davis Brothers* v. *Marshall* is a challenge to the regulations under FLSA over deductions for meals.

BRENNAN v. DE LANEY

22 Wage & Hour Cases (U.S.D.C., M.D. Tenn. 1974)

MORTON, J.

This action was brought by the Secretary of Labor, United States Department of Labor, under Section 17 of the Fair Labor Standards Act of 1938, as amended, hereinafter referred to as the Act. Plaintiff alleges that defendant, Mrs. Blanche De Laney, has violated various provisions of the Act.

The alleged violations occurred in the period from October 1, 1970, to September 30, 1973, in connection with Mrs. De Laney's operation of Sunny View Rest Home in Nashville, Tennessee. Sunny View Rest Home is a nursing home which was owned and operated by Mrs. De Laney during the period of the alleged violations. Mrs. De Laney has subsequently leased the said nursing home to her grandson, William H. Marsh. The effective date of the lease was October 1, 1973; Mrs. De Laney's current connection with the nursing home is that of consultant.

Plaintiff has charged that, in the period from October 1, 1970, through September 30, 1973, the defendant failed to pay her employees the minimum wage required by 29 U.S.C. Section 206, and failed to keep accurate records of the hours worked by her employees, in violation of 29 U.S.C. Section 211(c).

Two specific practices by defendant are involved in these charges: (1) certain employees who did not take their

breaks as scheduled were on record as having taken them; these employees were not paid for the times they actually worked during their scheduled breaks, resulting in minimum wage and record keeping violations by defendant; and (2) the nurses aides who wore uniforms paid for these uniforms at their own expense when their hourly rate of pay was only $1.60, resulting in reducing their wage below the minimum rate required by law.

At the outset, it is clear that Sunny View Rest Home comes within the purview of the Act. It was stipulated at trial by counsel for defendant that at all times pertinent to this lawsuit, the rest home was an enterprise engaged in commerce within the meaning of the Act. Since defendant has so stipulated, the court finds further discussion on this point unnecessary.

Defendant maintains that the employees in question actually took their scheduled breaks, and in the isolated incidents when they did not take them as scheduled, they either rescheduled them or were paid for the time worked. Defendant further maintains that the nurses and aides were not required to wear uniforms in the course of their employment and therefore, the defendant should not be liable for the cost of such uniforms.

In light of the evidence developed at the trial of this cause, this court finds that plaintiff's allegations are true with regard to the lack of adequate compensation to employees who worked during their break time. Defendant would attack the credibility of plaintiff's witnesses who were or had been employees of Sunny View, because "they knowingly falsified their time cards." However, it appeared at trial that the reason the employees signed their cards indicating that they had taken their schedule break times was that they were told by Mr. Charles Bozeman, brother of defendant, that they would not get their checks unless they did so. Additionally, the testimony of the Compliance Officers involved in the investigations of the home corroborated that of the employees. The evidence in this matter clearly preponderates in favor of the plaintiff, and the court so holds.

The court also determines that the plaintiff's allegations are true with respect to the required wearing of uniforms by the nurses aides at the rest home. While there was some contradiction in the testimony at trial, the evidence preponderates in favor of the plaintiff on this matter. It is traditional for aides in nursing homes to wear uniforms, and all of the nurses aides who worked for defendant did in fact wear uniforms. There appears to have been a tacit understanding among the aides that uniforms were required, and defendant herself informed Compliance Officer Paul D. Goodwin during the April, 1971 investigation that she required aides to wear uniforms. Additionally, after the 1971 investigation, Mrs. De Laney agreed to raise wages of the aides in the amount of five cents per hour in order to compensate them for their uniforms. . . .

Having determined that defendant violated the Act, we turn now to the question of relief to be granted. . . .

Considering defendant's past history of investigations and warnings by compliance officers, this court had determined that the violations by Mrs. De Laney were willful within the meaning of Section 206. In light of the past investigations and warnings, it is difficult, if not impossible, to believe that Mrs. De Laney was not aware that she was violating the Act. Thus, the court finds the applicable statute of limitations in this case to be three (3) years.

From the period from October 1, 1970 to September 30, 1973, the court finds that the following employees and former employees of Sunny View Rest Home are due the amounts listed after the names for unpaid minimum wages:

Nurses Aides

Name	Amount
Bettye Allen	$ 162.80
Olean Baugh	323.84
Beverly Moore Gilbert	80.38
Lucy Gooch	138.35
Nancy Lindsey	78.60
Bessie Lloyd	29.60
Mary L. Rucker	77.40
Evelyn Scott	96.26
Mary Watkins	122.60
Gracie Williamson	102.45
Mary Willis	161.21
	$1,373.49

Cooks

Elizabeth Harris	112.80
Gwendolyn Jakaway	82.40
Tiny P. Jenkins	290.80
Pauline Jones	2,509.38
	$2,995.38

Kitchen Helpers & Laundry Workers

Mildred Belcher	106.40
Igesther Fields	168.00
Essie Gibson	13.40
Alice James Hunter	249.60
Shirley Robbins	2,382.40
Mildred Wiseman	28.80
	2,948.60
TOTAL	$7,317.47

Defendant shall pay the employees and former employees listed above the amounts due as listed above, plus interest at six per cent (6%) from the date such wages become due until paid. Defendant shall be enjoined from withholding payment of the unpaid back wages in an order filed contemporaneously with this Memorandum. . . . **So ordered.**

DAVIS BROTHERS v. MARSHALL

25 Wage & Hour Cases (U.S.D.C., N.D. Georgia 1981)

EVANS, J.

In this case, Plaintiff Davis Brothers, Inc. ("Davis") asks the Court to strike down 29 C.F.R. Section 531.30 as inconsistent with Section 3(m) of the Fair Labor Standards Act, 29 U.S.C. Section 203(m). Davis also seeks an injunction preventing the Secretary of Labor (the "Secretary") from any enforcement actions against Davis on the basis of 29 C.F.R. Section 531.30. In a counterclaim the Secretary requests that the Court find Davis in civil contempt for violation of a Judgment entered against Davis in *Marshall* v. *Davis Brothers, Inc.* . . . The parties have filed a Stipulation of Facts, and have agreed to proceed by way of summary judgment. Both parties have now filed motions for summary judgment.

The Fair Labor Standards Act ("FLSA") requires employers to pay a minimum wage, currently fixed at $3.35 per hour. 29 U.S.C. Section 206. Section 3(m) of the FLSA provides that in determining the amount of the "wage" paid to an employee, an employer is permitted to take a credit in the amount of the "reasonable cost" of meals provided to the employee, if the employer "customarily furnishes" such meals to his employees.* In 29 C.F.R. Section 531.30, the Secretary interprets the word "furnished" in Section 3(m) to permit an employer to take a credit only for those meals and other facilities whose acceptance and utilization by the employee is "voluntary and uncoerced."** Davis contends that in adding the requirement that acceptance of meals as part of an employee's wages be "voluntary and uncoerced," the Secretary has exceeded his authority and done violence to the language and legislative history of the FLSA.

The facts of this case are undisputed. The Court will briefly recite the facts necessary to a determination of this case.

Davis operates motels, cafeterias and restaurants in Georgia, Florida and Tennessee. It is an employer within the meaning of the FLSA. On May 23, 1978, Davis was permanently enjoined from violating the minimum wage and other provisions of the FLSA. . . .

Prior to January 1, 1980, Davis paid at least the full minimum wage in cash to all hourly food service employees (the "employees"), and permitted them to purchase meals for one half of the retail price. On January 1, 1980, Davis instituted a new policy. Employees were permitted to select food from a limited portion of the regular menu but no longer directly paid for their meals. Instead, Davis deducted $.25 or $.35 per hour from their wages as the reasonable cost of the meals it provided them. This deduction resulted in some employees receiving less than the minimum wage in cash wages. The deductions are made as a condition of employment regardless of the wishes and eating habits of the employee, and the only exceptions have been for six employees who have presented statements from their physicians that they cannot eat the food prepared by Davis. A few employees eat little or no food, and many employees would prefer the option of receiving the full minimum wage in cash.

Davis now seeks to have the Court declare 29 C.F.R. Section 531.30 (the "regulation") invalid. . . .

The more serious arguments raised by Davis concern the language and the legislative history of the FLSA. The terms of Section 3(m) explicitly grant the Secretary only the authority to determine the employer's "reasonable cost." Davis concedes that the Secretary has the additional implicit authority to decide whether an item qualifies as "board, lodging, or other facilities," to determine whether the employer "customarily furnishes" the items to his employees, and to decide whether they are furnished for the benefit of the employer. Nonetheless, Davis argues that the statute does

---

*Section 3(m) of the FLSA, 29 U.S.C. Section 203(m), provides in relevant part:
"Wage" paid to any employee includes the reasonable cost, as determined by the Administrator, to the employer of furnishing such employee with Board, lodging, or other facilities, if such board, lodging, or other facilities are customarily furnished by such employer to his employees. . . .

**29 C.F.R. Section 531.30 provides:
Section 531.30 "Furnished" to the employee:
The reasonable cost of board, lodging, or other facilities may be considered as part of the wage paid to an employee only where customarily "furnished" to the employee. Not only must the employee receive the benefits of the facility for which he is charged, but it is essential that his acceptance of the facility be voluntary and uncoerced.

not grant the Secretary the right to redefine the word "furnished." The "voluntary and uncoerced" requirement of 29 C.F.R. Section 531.30, Davis argues, in effect constitutes an administrative amendment to the statute.

However, the legislative history cited in Davis' own brief indicates that Congress intended to leave the determination of a "fair" charge entirely to the Secretary. The "fairness" of a charge involves more than just its amount; Congress must have intended to grant the Secretary the authority to determine whether the meals were properly "furnished" at all within the meaning of Section 3(m).

In enacting the FLSA, Congress wished to protect the employees from the superior bargaining position of the employer. By preventing employers from forcing employees to accept unwanted meals and lodging as part of their wages, the regulation serves this Congressional goal. Congress expressed concern that Section 3(m) might permit employers to overcharge their employees for food and lodging and so explicitly granted the Secretary the right to determine "reasonable cost." The Secretary's interpretation of "furnished" is merely his method of dealing with employers who escape the "reasonable cost" sanctions by charging their employees the reasonable cost of meals they never eat.

The Fifth Circuit has said, in a case in a related area, that "Congress has determined that the individual worker should have both the freedom and the responsibility to allocate his minimum wage among competing economic and personal interests." *Brennan* v. *Heard* (5th Cir. 1974). The regulation at issue here is not inconsistent with Section 3(m), and furthers this Congressional purpose. In the last decade, five district courts have applied the regulation without questioning the Secretary's authority to issue and enforce it. . . .

Finally, despite Davis' arguments to the contrary, the principle that receipt of meals and lodging must be voluntary to be credited as "wages" is also contained in the case of which the Secretary based 29 C.F.R. Section 531.30. *Williams* v. *Atlantic Coast Line Railroad Co.* (E.D.N.C. 1940).

The Supreme Court has stated that courts should not apply the provisions of the FLSA "in a narrow, grudging manner." . . . The Court therefore holds 29 C.F.R. Section 531.30 to be a valid exercise of the Secretary's authority under the FLSA.

It is undisputed that some Davis employees receive less than the minimum wage in cash wages. Under 29 C.F.R. Section 531.30, Davis cannot claim a meal credit of \$.25 or \$.35 per hour, because its employees' acceptance of the meals furnished by Davis is not "voluntary and uncoerced." Therefore, the Court finds that since January 1, 1980, Davis has been in violation of 29 U.S.C. Section 206, the minimum wage provision of the FLSA. . . .

Davis' Motion for Summary Judgment is DENIED in all respects. The Secretary's Motion for Summary Judgment that 29 C.F.R. Section 531.30 is lawful and that Davis is in violation of the minimum wage provisions of Fair Labor Standards Act is GRANTED. Davis is hereby ORDERED to compute the amounts due to its employees as a result of its violation, subject to verification by the Secretary.

So ordered.

As *Brennan* v. *De Laney* suggests, the law is strict as to what deductions can be taken from an employee's paycheck. Employers must also maintain accurate records reflecting the hours worked, tips received, meals eaten by employees, and so on. Failure to maintain records may mean that no deductions will be allowed, as in *De Laney*.

The law does allow for voluntary deductions, such as union dues, from an employee's pay. Some retail employers have required salespeople to sign an agreement permitting the deduction from their pay of any shortages in their cash registers. The following case deals with such "voluntary" agreements.

MAYHUE'S STORES v. HODGSON

464 F.2d 1196 (5th Cir. 1972)

RONEY, J.

An agreement that an employee will repay to his employer any shortages in money entrusted to him, when shortages occur through misappropriation, theft, or otherwise, violates the minimum wage requirements of the Fair Labor Standards Act to the extent that such required payments reduce below the minimum wage the amount of money and compensation which the employee receives. The district court held otherwise. We reverse.

Mayhue's Super Liquor Stores, Inc., a Florida corporation, owns and operates a chain of six retail liquor stores in Broward County, Florida, and is admittedly subject to the requirements of the Fair Labor Standards Act. Carl L. Mayhue, its president and sole stockholder, actively manages the affairs of the corporation, including the hiring and firing of employees and the setting of wage policies. The employees involved in this litigation are cashiers who worked for various periods of time at one or more of the six liquor stores.

This action was initiated by the corporation and Mayhue for a declaratory judgment as to the legality under the Fair Labor Standards Act of requiring employees, as a condition of employment, to sign agreements providing that the employees would make "voluntary" repayments of cash register shortages. The Secretary counterclaimed under Section 17 for an order restraining the continued withholding of unpaid minimum wages and overtime compensation resulting from two practices: (1) the voluntary repayment of shortages pursuant to the agreement, and (2) the performance of work which was required but not recorded on Mayhue's time records. He also sought an injunction against further violations on both scores.

The district court declared Mayhue's employment agreements to be valid under the Act. However, the court held that the employer had otherwise willfully violated the Act's minimum wage, overtime, and record-keeping provisions, enjoined such violations, and required restitution to certain named employees. Both parties appeal the judgment.

We reverse the judgment only with respect to the validity of that part of the employment agreement requiring repayment of cash register shortages.

The right to a minimum wage under the Fair Labor Standards Act cannot be waived by agreement between the employee and his employer. The critical question in this case is whether this agreement works such a waiver. The employer concedes that the wages paid to many employees would be below the minimum if the repayments made or required were deducted from the amount of the compensation.

The controlling provision of the agreement provides:

> It is understood that the employee is responsible for any money entrusted to him. Any shortages that occur through misappropriation, theft, or otherwise, shall be voluntarily repaid by the employee to the employer. In executing this contract at the time of employment, it is understood by both parties that the employee is the sole and only person using or entering into the safe, cash deposit box, or sole operator of a cash register.
>
> The employee agrees to voluntarily repay said missing funds to the employer within a reasonable period of time. The employer shall not deduct said shortages from the paycheck of the employee. It is understood that said shortages are considered to be a valid debt owed to the employer.
>
> Any repaid debts caused by such shortages shall not be considered as part of the calculation of basic rates of employees and shall not be used to determine whether the employee has received pay amounting to less than the Federal minimum wage.
>
> Basic rates, used for calculation of overtime pay, shall not be reduced as a result of repayment of such debts. Said debt repayment is, for all purposes, unconnected with payroll procedures and are not to be considered as payroll deductions.

In holding that this agreement in no way violates the provisions of the Fair Labor Standards Act, the district court said that a contrary holding

> would amount to a "judicial invitation" to such employees to steal. Certainly the Act is not intended to prevent an employer from protecting his property, including assets in the form of cash. Such losses, however, should not be deducted from the employees pay whether wages are being paid in cash or by check. The agreement being approved by the court contemplates "voluntary" repayment by employees. Any contrary action by the employer would, in the court's opinion, violate the provisions of the Act.

The "judicial invitation" to steal argument is not persuasive. There is no evidence that Mayhue's shortages were the result of theft on the part of the cashiers or were in any way different from the usual losses which are to be expected where cashier employees handle a large number of transactions. The agreement required repayment regardless of the reason for the shortages. If the agreement required only repayment of money that the employee himself took or mis-appropriated it obviously would not collide with the Act. As a matter of law the employee would owe such amounts to the employer, and as a matter of fact, the repayment of moneys taken in excess of the money paid to the employee in wages would not reduce the amount of his wages. This case is distinguishable from the situation where an employee has taken some money, has had the use of it, and is required to return it. In such a case there would be no violation of the Act because the employee has taken more than the amount of his wage and the return could in no way reduce his wage below the minimum.

The "voluntary-involuntary' dichotomy is meaningless for two reasons. First, if the intent of the parties were to make repayment purely voluntary on the part of the employee, an agreement would not be necessary. The agreement would be pointless. Yet the employer requires the execution of the agreement as a condition of employment. Second, the provision in the agreement that the "shortages are considered to be a valid debt owed to the employer" obviously controls the matter and expresses the intent of the parties. It overrides any argument that the repayments are voluntary on the part of the employee.

With the employee's financial picture burdened with the "valid debt" of the shortages, he is receiving less for his services than the wage that is paid to him. Whether he pays the "valid debt" out of his wages or other resources, his ef-

fective rate of pay is reduced by the amount of such debts. When it is reduced below the required minimum wage, the law is violated. Of particular relevance in this regard are the Regulations which provide:

> *"Free and clear" payment: "kick-backs."* Whether in cash or in facilities, "wages" cannot be considered to have been paid by the employer and received by the employee unless they are paid finally and unconditionally or "free and clear." The wage requirements of the Act will not be met where the employee "kicks-back" directly or indirectly to the employer or to another person for the employer's benefit the whole or part of the wage delivered to the employee. This is true whether the "kick-back" is made in cash or in other than cash. . . .

We agree with the Secretary that this agreement tended to shift part of the employer's business expense to the employees and was illegal to the extent that it reduced an employee's wage below the statutory minimum. This amounts to nothing more than an agreement to waive the minimum wage requirements of the Fair Labor Standards Act. Such an agreement is invalid. The case must be remanded to the district court for further proceedings in connection with all matters in which the agreement for repayment of shortages was involved. . . . **So ordered.**

Overtime Pay

In addition to being entitled to earn the minimum wage, employees covered by the FLSA are entitled to **overtime pay,** at one-and-a-half times their regular pay rate, for hours worked in excess of forty hours per workweek.

The term **workweek** has special significance under the FLSA. It is a "term of art" with a fairly precise meaning. A workweek consists of seven consecutive days, but the law does not require that the workweek start or end on any particular day of the calendar week. For instance, a workweek may run from Tuesday to Monday, or from Friday until Thursday. The starting day of the workweek may be changed from time to time, provided that the purpose of the change is not to avoid the requirements of the law (such as avoiding the payment of overtime to a group of workers).

As with the minimum wage, regulations have been developed to compute the hourly wages of workers paid by commission, piece-rate, and so forth for the purpose of calculating overtime pay. A more difficult question is deciding whether certain hours, not strictly part of working hours, should be included in working time for the calculation of wages and overtime. The Portal to Portal Act of 1947, which amended the FLSA, provides that preliminary or postwork activities are to be included in compensable time only if they are called for under contract or industry custom or practice. A number of cases involving the question of inclusion of non-working time come from the health care industry and deal with waiting, or "on call" time. Ambulance drivers or surgical nurses must be available for work if an emergency arises, but those employees may not be required to be at the workplace while they are waiting for such an emergency call. Does the waiting time, or "on call" time count as part of their workweek? That issue is addressed in the following case.

USERY v. SUBRIAR

22 W & H Cases 1263 (E.D. Cal. 1976)

CROCKER, J.

The Court, having heard the testimony and having examined the proofs offered by the respective parties, including post-trial briefs, the cause having been deemed submitted for decision and the Court fully advised in the premises, makes its Findings of Fact as follows:

Findings of Fact

1. This matter is before the Court upon a complaint filed by the Plaintiff, Secretary of Labor, pursuant to Section 17 of the Fair Labor Standards Act of 1938, as amended, referred to herein as the Act.

2. From 1968 until March 1974, Defendant operated places of business at Bakersfield, California and in Lamont, California, within the jurisdiction of this Court.

3. At certain times material herein, Defendant was engaged in providing ambulance service calls in an area of 400 to 450 square miles in the Eastern Bakersfield, Arvin and Lamont, California areas. Thereafter, Defendant provided said services in an area of approximately 50 square miles in Bakersfield and 50 square miles in Lamont. Defendant employed ambulance driver and ambulance attendant employees in and about his places of business in Lamont and Bakersfield, California in receiving calls and in dispatching ambulance vehicles to highways, streets and roads for the purpose of removing dead or injured persons from such highways, streets or roads. Said highways, streets or roads connect directly or indirectly to interstate highways or freeways. Approximately 20 percent of Defendant's total calls were calls made to such highways, streets or roads.

4. All parties agreed that the sole remaining issue was whether Defendant required its employees to be on call for 24 hours or only available for call.

5. At the time of their first employment, all of Defendant's employees were told and they understood that their work shift was from 8:00 a.m. until 8:00 a.m. the following day and that they would receive an hourly rate in excess of the minimum rate for all time actually worked plus time and one-half for all hours over 40 hours per week; also, that they would be paid for 10 hours per 24-hour shift, even if there were no ambulance calls. Defendant paid his employees in accordance with said understanding.

6. Defendant furnished living quarters for employees at both Lamont and Bakersfield and said employees had a choice of staying there or anywhere else that would permit them to make the ambulance calls within a reasonable time.

7. The weight of the credible evidence established that during their work shift employees were free to leave Defendant's premises at Bakersfield and Lamont on personal business and were free to follow personal pursuits while on the premises and, in fact, did so. It was only necessary for employees to advise the telephone answering service where they could be reached by telephone. This Court specifically rejects the testimony of Plaintiff's witnesses that they were required to remain on duty the entire 24 hours and could not attend to personal business and/or pursuits.

8. The Court finds that the agreement between Defendant and his employees to pay for 10 hours for being on call 24 hours is reasonable under the circumstances of this case.

9. The undisputed evidence in this case is that Defendant maintained records with respect to his employees which indicated the following:

   a. the employee's hourly rate of pay;

   b. the days assigned to 24-hour duty shifts and that such employee was paid a guaranteed 10 hours of pay for each 24-hour duty shift regardless of actual number of hours worked each 24-hour duty shift;

c. the amount of time each employee spent going out on ambulance calls each day but not including the amount of time spent by the employee in related duties such as cleaning the ambulance, putting gas in the ambulance, washing ambulance laundry, cleaning the office or office paperwork;

d. that time and one-half the employee's designated hourly rate of pay was paid for all hours worked in excess of 40 per week computed on the basis of 10 hours of work per 24-hours shift. Defendant's record keeping is adequate to comply with the Act. . . .

11. In view of this Court's findings noted above, there has been no cause shown by Plaintiff which would warrant injunctive relief.

Conclusions of Law

1. Jurisdiction is conferred on this Court by Section 17 of the Fair Labor Standards Act of 1938, as amended, 29 U.S.C. 217.

2. At all times herein, Defendant maintained a business within the jurisdiction of the Court and employed employees who were engaged in interstate commerce within the meaning of 29 U.S.C. Sections 203, 206 and 207, thereby satisfying jurisdiction and venue requirements.

3. Plaintiff has failed to present credible testimony to meet its burden of proof that Defendant violated the Fair Labor Standards Act of 1938, as amended.

4. Defendant's record keeping is adequate to comply with the Fair Labor Standards Act of 1938, as amended.

5. Defendant has not violated the Fair Labor Standards Act of 1938, as amended (29 U.S.C. 201, et seq.), and is exonerated from any liability for minimum and/or overtime payments under said Act.

6. Plaintiff's request for injunctive relief is denied.

Exemptions from Overtime and Minimum Wage Provisions

Not all employees under the FLSA are entitled to overtime pay or subject to the minimum wage. The FLSA sets out four general categories of **exempt employees:** executives, administrators, professionals, and outside salespeople.

Executive Employees. The regulations under the FLSA spell out two different tests for determining whether employees are executives and exempt. The first test, known as the *short test,* applies to employees earning more than $250 per week. Those employees must meet two requirements: (1) their primary duty must be management, and (2) they must regularly direct the work of at least two other employees. For workers earning more than $155 per week but less than $250 per week to be exempted as executives, they must meet the requirements of the *long test.* The long test includes the two requirements of the short test, and in addition, the employees must (1) have the authority to hire or fire employees or to make recommendations, which are given "particular weight," as to hiring, firing, or disciplining other workers; (2) customarily and regularly exercise discretionary powers in their work; and (3) not spend more than 20 percent (40 percent for employees of retail establishments) of their time in any week on activities that are not directly and closely related to their management duties.

Administrative Employees. The regulations under the FLSA set out two tests (a "short" test and a "long" test) for determining whether employees in administrative positions are exempt from the overtime and minimum wage provisions of the FLSA. Those employees earning more than $250 per week are exempt under the *short test* if their primary duty consists of either (1) the performance of office or nonmanual work directly related to management policies or general business operations of their employer or their employer's customers, or (2) the performance of administrative functions of a school system or educational institution in work directly related to the instruction or training carried on in them. Employees earning more than $155 per week but less than $250 per week are exempted if they meet the requirements of the *long test*. The long test includes the requirements of the short test, and in addition, the following other requirements must be met: (1) the employee must customarily and regularly exercise discretion and independent judgment; (2) the employee must regularly perform, under general supervision only, specialized or technical work requiring special training or experience, or perform special assignments, or regularly assist a proprietor or person in an executive or administrative capacity; and (3) the employee must not devote more than 20 percent (40 percent for employees of retail establishments) of time in a workweek to activities not directly and closely related to the performance of administrative duties.

Professional Employees. Employees in bona fide professional positions are exempted from the FLSA's overtime and minimum wage provisions if they meet one of several tests set out in the regulations. Persons engaged in the practice of law or medicine, and persons employed as teachers in a school system or educational institution are exempt regardless of salary level. Persons employed in professional positions and earning more than $250 per week must meet the *short test* requirements. Their primary duty must consist of (1) work requiring advanced knowledge in a field of science or acquired customarily through a prolonged course of specialized instruction; (2) work original and creative in character in a recognized field of artistic endeavor; or (3) teaching, tutoring, or lecturing as a certified or recognized teacher in a school system or educational institution. Persons in professional positions who earn between $170 and $250 must meet the *long test* requirements to be exempted. The long test requirements include the requirements of the short test, and in addition, these other requirements: (1) the person's work must require the consistent exercise of discretion and judgment in its performance; (2) the work must be predominantly intellectual and varied in character and its output cannot be standardized in relation to a given period of time; and (3) the person must not devote more than 20 percent of time in a workweek to activities not an essential part of, or incident to, his or her professional duties.

Outside Salespeople. The regulations under the FLSA exempt outside salespeople from both the overtime and minimum wage provisions. To be exempt, the following requirements must be met: (1) the person must be employed in, and regularly engage in, making sales or obtaining orders or contracts, away from his or her employer's place of business; and (2) the person must not spend more than 20 percent of the hours in a workweek in duties other than sales duties.

The following case involves the question of whether assistant managers of fast-food restaurants are exempt from the overtime and minimum wage provisions because they are employed in an executive capacity.

DONOVAN v. BURGER KING

672 F.2d 221 (U.S. Court of Appeals, 1st Circuit, 1982)

CAMPBELL, J.

Burger King appeals from a judgment of the district court enjoining it from violating provisions of the Fair Labor Standards Act ("FLSA" or "the Act"), and from withholding back pay for overtime due certain of its assistant managers. After a bench trial, the district court concluded that the assistant managers were covered by the Act, and therefore entitled to be paid at one and one-half times their regular rate for overtime hours. Burger King argued that its assistant managers were "employed in a bona fide executive . . . capacity," and therefore exempt from the pay requirements of the Act. On appeal, it repeats this argument. . . .

Burger King fast-food restaurants are operated nationwide. Some of the restaurants are company-owned, others are franchises. At issue in this case are 44 company-owned restaurants in Massachusetts and Connecticut. The restaurants are each staffed by a salaried manager, two salaried assistant managers, and a large crew of hourly employees. Except for brief periods of overlap and Fridays and Saturdays, only one of the three salaried persons is on duty at any one time. The manager usually works day shifts, while the assistant managers normally work swing and night shifts. The manager or assistant manager on duty supervises the hourly employees, up to 25 of whom may be working at any one time.

While on duty, the assistant manager enjoys decisionmaking authority roughly commensurate with that of the manager. He schedules employees, assigns work, oversees product quality, and speaks with customers. Assistant managers also train employees, determine the quantity of food to be produced at any given time, and perform various recordkeeping, inventory, and cash reconciliation duties. Many of these tasks are governed by highly detailed, step-by-step instructions contained in Burger King's "Manual of Operating Data," and admit of little or no variation. Assistant managers also spend a portion of their time performing many of the same tasks as hourly employees, such as taking orders, preparing food, and "expediting" orders, that is, filling the orders and handing them to the customers. These tasks are also spelled out in great detail in the Manual of Operating Data.

The crux of Burger King's case was its affirmative defense that the assistant managers were employed in a "bona fide executive . . . capacity" as that term is used in Section 13(a)(1), and thus exempt from the Act. Regulations promulgated by the Secretary of Labor under authority of Section 13(a)(1) specify the requirements for this exemption. In the case of employees earning at least $250 per week, two requirements only must be met: the employees' "primary duty" must be management, and they must regularly direct the work of at least two other employees. This is known as the "short test." In the case of employees earning more than $155, but less than $250, per week, there is a "long test." This includes three requirements *in addition* to the two contained in the short test: the employees must have authority to hire or fire, or at least their recommendations must be given "particular weight"; they must "customarily and regularly exercise discretionary powers"; and they must not devote more than 40 percent of their time to activities not "closely related" to their management duties. The district court found that the assistant managers here failed to meet the "primary duty" requirement common to both tests. And in the case of assistant managers whose pay scale made them subject to the "long test," it found they lacked, in addition, the authority to hire and fire and the necessary discretionary powers, and also that they devoted more than 40 percent of their time to non-managerial duties. It therefore ruled that neither those assistant managers to whom the short test applied, nor those to whom the long test applied, were exempt from the Act. The court ordered Burger King to pay back wages to 246 assistant managers in Massachusetts and Connecticut for past overtime hours, and also enjoined Burger King from violating the Act in its company-owned restaurants without limitation as to their location.

We turn . . . to the question of whether the short test assistant managers (i.e., those earning at least $250 per week) were properly held by the district court to be non-exempt and hence within the coverage of the Act. This turns on whether they have management as their "primary duty." We hold that the district court erred in concluding that the assistant managers did not meet this requirement.

The district court found that in the absence of the manager, the assistant manager on duty was "*de facto* in charge of the store." Burger King contends vigorously that this finding should be sufficient to demonstrate that the assistant managers satisfy the primary duty requirement. Under the regulations, a determination of whether an employee has management as his primary duty must be based on all the facts of a particular case. . . . Time alone . . . is not the sole test. . . . [Other] pertinent factors are the relative importance of the managerial duties as compared with other types of duties, the frequency with which the employee exercises discretionary powers, his relative freedom from supervision, and the wages paid other employees for the kind of non-exempt work performed by the supervisor.

Some of these factors quite clearly cut in favor of Burger King's contention, especially those related to freedom from supervision and a comparison of wages with other employees. The district court gave no explicit reason for its conclusion that the assistant managers did not have management as their primary duty, but in light of this regulation, two main explanations are possible. One is that it concluded that they do not exercise sufficient discretionary powers to be "managing"; the other is that they spend too much time on non-management tasks. Each of these is unpersuasive.

The supervision of other employees is clearly a management duty. The fact that Burger King has well-defined policies, and that tasks are spelled out in great detail, is insufficient to negate this conclusion. Ensuring that company policies are carried out constitutes the "very essence of supervisory work." While it may be that the assistant managers do not exercise sufficient discretionary powers to satisfy the long test requirement, that requirement is not part of the short test. It cannot be denied that the supervisory work of the assistant managers qualifies as management under the regulations.

The more difficult question is whether such work is their "primary duty." The regulation states that "[i]n the ordinary case it may be taken as a good rule of thumb that primary duty means the major part, or over 50 percent, of the employee's time." There are two problems with this guideline. First, the more natural reading of "primary" is "principal" or "chief," not "over one-half." Second, a strict time division is somewhat misleading here: one can still be "managing" if one is in charge, even while physically doing something else. The 50 percent rule seems better directed at situations where the employee's management and non-management functions are more clearly severable than they are here.

Indeed, the regulations recognize that the 50 percent rule is not conclusive. One of the examples given . . . corresponds quite closely to the picture we see of the Burger King assistant managers:

> For example, in some departments, of subdivisions of an establishment, an employee has broad responsibilities similar to those of the owner or manager of the establishment, but generally spends more than 50 percent of this time in production or sales work. While engaged in such work he supervises other employees, directs the work of warehouse and delivery men, approves advertising, orders merchandise, handles customer complaints, authorizes payment of bills, or performs other management duties as the day-to-day operations require. He will be considered to have management as his primary duty.

This example makes it quite clear that an employee can manage while performing other work, and that this other work does not negate the conclusion that his primary duty is management. If an employee is spending too great a portion of his time performing non-exempt tasks, then the 40 percent limitation of the long test, if applicable, may come into play. But as with the discretionary powers requirement, this is not an element of the short test.

Finally, the case law strongly supports the conclusion that the Burger King assistant managers have management as their primary duty. In *Rau* v. *Darling's Drug Store, Inc.,* for example, the court held that an employee who was "in charge" of a drug store (excepting the prescription department) had management as her primary duty. This was so in spite of the fact that she was also the sole sales clerk in two departments, and did a considerable amount of routine, non-exempt work ("more than fifty percent of her time was taken up with sales clerk work"). Moreover, she was unable to make any significant or substantial decisions on her own: the owner of the store made them all, including setting prices and wages. This case is well-reasoned support for the proposition that the person "in charge" of a store has management as his primary duty, even though he spends the majority of his time on non-exempt work and makes few significant decisions. In light of the district court's finding here that the assistant managers were "in charge" of the restaurant during their shifts, its conclusion that they do not have management as their primary duty cannot stand. . . .

Our conclusion that the assistant managers do have management as their primary duty is in accord with a similar case concerning Burger King restaurants in New York.

We turn next to those assistant managers earning under $250 who must meet the additional requirements of the long test if Burger King's exemption claim is to be upheld. We affirm the district courts' conclusion that these employees were not shown to have met all the requirements of the long test, and hence are non-exempt. The elements of the test are stated in the conjunctive, and therefore each element must be met to qualify for the exemption.

We conclude that the district court was not clearly erroneous in finding that assistant managers spent more than 40 percent of their time on activities not "closely related" to management, and therefore uphold the district court on this basis, without reaching its other grounds of decision.

Burger King argues only briefly that the court was clearly erroneous in its factual conclusion. We think the court's conclusion is supportable. There was considerable testimony from assistant managers that the great majority of their time was spent on menial tasks. Burger King's primary argument is that the court erred in including certain tasks in the non-exempt (not closely related to management) category. This argument in turn is broken into two branches: first, that certain tasks not performed by the hourly crew, such as cash reconciliation, were improperly classified as non-exempt, and second, that tasks performed by the crew as well as by the assistant managers, such as taking orders, were similarly improperly classified.

The first contention may be dealt with briefly. Even if it is true that those tasks performed only by the assistant managers are properly classified as exempt—a question we do not decide—it is clear from the court's opinion that it did not include time spent on these tasks in concluding that the 40 percent limit was surpassed:

> I find, despite testimony to the contrary, which I do not believe, that assistant managers do in fact in most of the Burger King Stores spend more than 40 percent of their working time in routine production tasks which are not of a managerial nature or caliber. I find those tasks are mundane and *exactly the same as those performed by concededly hourly employees.*

(Emphasis added.) The court thus found the 40 percent limit was broken even when considering only the time spent by the assistant managers on the same tasks as performed by the hourly crew. We thus turn to the question of whether that work was properly classified as non-exempt.

Burger King argues that this work cannot count as non-exempt because the assistant managers are still managing the restaurant and supervising the crews, even while performing those tasks. This line of reasoning has merit for purposes of deciding whether they meet the primary duty requirement, but misses the point as to the different, 40 percent limitation requirement. The latter measures the amount of time which one who may otherwise have management as his primary duty devotes to non-management tasks. Someone whose primary duty is management may still fail to qualify under the long test if his managerial status coexists with the performance of a significant amount of menial work, as in the case of a working supervisor or "strawboss." The Secretary's regulations make this plain. They provide that the "primary purpose" of the time percentage limitation (applicable, it will be remembered, to lower paid, long test personnel only) is to distinguish between bona fide executives and those working foremen and supervisors "who regularly perform[] 'production' work or other work which is unrelated or only remotely related to [their] supervisory activities." The regulation continues,

> (b) *One type of working foreman or working supervisor most commonly found in industry works alongside his subordinates. Such employees, sometimes known as strawbosses, or gang or group leaders perform the same kind of work as that performed by their subordinates, and also carry on supervisory functions.* Clearly, the work of the same nature as that performed by the employees' subordinates must be counted as nonexempt work and if the amount of such work performed is substantial the exemption does not apply. ("Substantial," as used in this section, means more than 20 percent. . . . *A foreman in a dress shop, for example, who operates a sewing machine to produce the product is performing clearly non-exempt work.* However, this should not be confused with the operation of a sewing machine by a foreman to instruct his subordinates in the making of a new product, such as a garment, before it goes into production.

(Emphasis added.) The regulation thus recognizes that some supervisors work alongside their crews, doing the same work as the crews, while supervising them as well. It nonetheless counts the time spent on non-exempt work toward the 40 percent limitation. This seems to describe the position of the Burger King assistant managers as found by the district court, although, of course, the concept is relevant only in those individual cases where because of weekly earnings under $250, the long rather than short test must be applied.

It needs to be emphasized that the primary duty and 40 percent requirements satisfy entirely separate if complementary concerns. The former requirement is aimed at distinguishing those whose principal responsibility is management from others. The latter requirement, which under the long test must independently be satisfied, ensures that even those who pass the primary duty test are subject to the protections of the Act if more than a certain portion of their time is devoted to performing the same tasks as those performed by no-exempt subordinates. The interpretation proposed by Burger King would eviscerate this distinction, and in effect merge the time limitation into the primary duty requirement, making it surplusage. In the face of the clear language to the contrary, we decline to adopt such a reading of the regulation, and therefore uphold the district court with respect to those assistant managers covered by the long test. . . .

The injunction is accordingly vacated insofar as it applies to assistant managers earning at least $250 per week. . . . In all other respects, the judgment of the district court is affirmed. **So ordered.**

Limitations on Child Labor

The problems of child labor are graphically demonstrated by photographs from the late nineteenth and early twentieth century showing children who had spent their youth toiling in coal mines or factories. The children, often immigrants, were subjected to the same hazardous conditions and occupational diseases as were their parents. The children received little or no formal education. The wages they received were usually meager, and their low pay had the effect of depressing the wages paid to adult workers in the same jobs.

The social and economic problems of child labor were recognized by government; many states passed legislation attempting to limit child labor. Those early laws were limited in their effectiveness, though, and the number of children employed continued to rise until about 1910. Congress made several attempts to enact federal limitations on child labor. In 1916 a law prohibiting the shipment in interstate commerce of goods produced by factories or mines employing child labor was passed. The Supreme Court, however, in the 1918 case of *Hammer* v. *Dagenhart* (247 U.S. 1), held that the law was unconstitutional because it exceeded the limited power granted to the federal government under the commerce clause of the Constitution.

The National Industrial Recovery Act (NIRA) provided that the codes of fair competition for each industry could limit child labor, but in 1935 the NIRA was held unconstitutional by the Supreme Court in *Schecter Poultry* v. *U.S.* In 1936 the Walsh-Healy Act prohibited contractors under government contracts from using child labor to produce, manufacture, or furnish materials for the contract. The Fair Labor Standards Act of 1938 at last provided for general federal regulation of child labor. In 1941 it was upheld by the Supreme Court in *U.S.* v. *Darby Lumber Co.*

The FLSA and Child Labor.   The FLSA does not prohibit all child labor; rather it proscribes only "oppressive" child labor. The act prohibits the interstate shipment of goods from establishments employing oppressive child labor. It also prohibits "oppressive" child labor in any enterprise with two or more employees engaged in the production of goods for interstate commerce. The definition of "oppressive child labor" is crucial to the administration of the act. The act defines oppressive child labor by using age restrictions and identifying hazardous occupations.

Employing minors under age eighteen in any occupation identified as hazardous by the Secretary of Labor is prohibited. Minors aged sixteen to eighteen may work in certain nonhazardous occupations, and minors aged fourteen to sixteen may be employed in nonmanufacturing or nonmining occupations for limited hours outside of school hours. Minors under age fourteen can be employed only in agriculture under specific limitations and with parental consent.

The regulations limiting work by minors aged fourteen to sixteen further specify that the minors' hours between 7 A.M. and 7 P.M. may not exceed eighteen hours per week when school is in session, or forty hours per week when school is not in session; nor may they exceed three hours per day when school is in session, or eight hours per day when school is not in session.

Specific exemptions from the category of oppressive child labor include the employment of newspaper carriers who are engaged in delivering papers to consumers; minors who are hired as actors or performers in movies, radio, television, or theatrical productions; and minors who are employed by their parents, or persons standing in the place of parents, in occupations other than manufacturing, mining, or others identified as hazardous by the Secretary of Labor.

At present, a number of occupations have been identified as hazardous by the Secretary of Labor, among them the following:

- coal mining or mining other than coal;
- occupations in or about plants manufacturing explosives or articles containing explosive components;
- occupations involving operation of motor-driven hoisting apparatus;
- logging or sawmilling occupations;
- occupations involving exposure to radioactive substances;
- occupations of motor-vehicle operator or helper;
- occupations involving operation of power-driven woodworking machines;
- occupations involving operation of power-driven metal working, forming, punching, or shearing machines;
- occupations in or about slaughtering or meatpacking plants or rendering plants;
- occupations involving the manufacture of brick, tile, or related products;
- occupations involving the operation of circular saws, handsaws, and guillotine shears;
- occupations involving wrecking, demolition, and shipbreaking.

Although child labor cases have become relatively rare in recent years, the Department of Labor strictly enforces the FLSA provision. The following case is an administrative enforcement proceeding with the Department of Labor. It illustrates the strict enforcement of the child labor prohibitions.

MARSHALL v. GENERAL MOTORS CORP.

23 Wage & Hour Cases 1134 (U.S. Department of Labor)

STERNBURG, A.L.J.

This case arises under Sections 12(c) and 16(e) of the Fair Labor Standards Act of 1938, as amended, hereinafter called the Act, and the Regulations issued thereunder.

A civil money penalty, in the amount of $1,000 was assessed against the Respondent (General Motors Corporation, Frigidaire Division) pursuant to Section 16(e) of the Act and Parts 579 and 580 of the Regulations for allegedly

employing a minor (LaVera Palice Holmes) under the age of 18 contrary to Hazardous Occupation Order No. 8. The Respondent filed a timely exception to the determination that it had committed such violation, and the Administrator referred this matter to the Chief Administrative Law Judge for hearing and final determination. Following the issuance of a Notice of Hearing, the parties to the proceeding executed and submitted to the undersigned a stipulation of facts "in lieu of a factual hearing." The parties reserved the right to submit briefs to the undersigned. Respondent chose to submit a brief which has been duly considered.

Findings of Fact

Based upon the aforementioned stipulation I find the facts to be as follows:

1. Respondent's business activities constitute an enterprise within the meaning of Section 3(r) of the Fair Labor Standards Act.
2. Respondent is subject to the Fair Labor Standards Act having been and being an enterprise engaged in commerce or in the production of goods for commerce within the meaning of Section 3(s)(1) of the Act as amended in 1966.
3. LaVera Palice Holmes, the minor involved herein, was born on March 2, 1959.
4. On February 9, 1976, LaVera Palice Holmes made and signed an Application for Employment at Frigidaire Division, General Motors Corporation, consisting of three (3) sheets. LaVera Palice Holmes listed her date of birth on the application as being March 2, 1957. Her application further reflected that she was the mother of an 8 month old daughter and had attended one semester of college.
5. On February 25, 1976, the minor signed an Application for Benefits under the Surgical and Medical Expense Plan for General Motors employees, underwritten by Metropolitan Life Insurance Company, and for benefits under Blue Cross-Blue Shield coverage. The minor listed her date of birth on the application as being March 2, 1957.
6. After the minor passed a physical examination, her application for employment was approved. Her starting date was March 1, 1976.
7. Respondent relied on the representation of the minor's age made by her. Respondent took no action to verify the age of the minor.
8. On March 9, 1976, while in the employ of Respondents, the minor was engaged in the operation of a punch press. The minor suffered an industrial injury that resulted in the amputation of her lower left arm below the elbow. Immediately following her injury, she was admitted to Kettering Medical Center (Kettering Memorial Hospital) where she was taken to surgery and operated on by D. L. Reveal, M.D., an Orthopedist.
9. On April 6, 1976, the minor filed an Application for Benefits under General Motors Group Insurance Plan, underwritten by Metropolitan Life Insurance Company containing provisions for sickness and accident benefits. The minor listed her date of birth on the application as being March 2, 1958.
10. During the period of her hospital confinement, supervisory personnel at Frigidaire began an effort to determine the true age of the minor.

    In order to ascertain the date of her birth, telephone calls were made to Fairview High School and to Sinclair Community College, to determine if the records of either showed her date of birth. The calls were made by Judy Davis, Hourly Employment Section, Personnel Department of Frigidaire Division, on March 11, 1976, who made a memorandum of the information received. The memorandum indicates that both educational school's records bear March 2, 1959 as her birth date.
11. A request was also made to the Abbeville County Health Department, Abbeville, South Carolina, for a copy of the birth certificate of the minor, LaVera Palice Holmes. The request was honored, and a copy of the birth certificate, issued March 16, 1976, was received. The birth certificate reflects March 2, 1959 as LaVera P. Holmes' birth date.
12. That employment of the minor in the operation of a punch press constituted a violation of Hazardous Order No. 8 and Section 12 of the Act.
13. That the minor suffered a serious permanent injury while operating the punch press. . . .

Discussion and Conclusions

Respondent admits, and I so find, that it violated both the Act and Regulations by employing LaVera Palice Holmes as a punch press operator prior to her having reached her eighteenth birthday. Accordingly, the sole issue remaining is the amount of the assessment.

Respondent takes the position that under all the circumstances, particularly, the fact that the minor deliberately falsified her birth date on two separate occasions, the absence of any past history of violations of the child labor provisions of the Act, and the fact that both her appearance and personal history indicated that she was at least eighteen years old at the time of her hire, no assessment should be made and the case should be dismissed.

Both the Act and the Regulations set forth the general criteria for determining the amount, if any, of the assessment due for violations of the child labor provisions of the Act. According to such criteria, past history of violations, willfulness, resultant injury, gravity of violation, etc., shall be considered. But for the fact that the minor in the instant case suffered a permanent disability while working as a punch press operator, I would have no hesitancy under all the circumstances present herein, in sustaining Respondent's position and dismissing the case without an assessment. However, such is not the case, the minor did sustain a permanent disability. Accordingly, while I do not condone the minor's actions in falsifying her birth date and I am sympathetic to Respondent's plight, I am constrained to find that an assessment is in order. Respondent can, and should, in the future escape liability for such unintentional violations as disclosed herein by requiring the presentation of certificates of age as provided for in Section 570.36 of the Regulations.

Considering the size of Respondent's business and the

type of disability suffered, I find that the civil money penalty in the amount of $1,000 is reasonable and appropriate under all the circumstances of this case.

Order

I affirm the determination of the Assistant Regional Administrator, Wage and Hour Division, U.S. Department of Labor, that the violation for which the penalty was assessed did occur.

General Motors Corporation, Frigidaire Division, shall pay forthwith, in accordance with the Act and applicable Regulations thereunder, a penalty in the amount of $1,000.

Enforcement and Remedies under FLSA

The FLSA is enforced by the Department of Labor. The Wage and Hour Division of the Labor Department performs inspections and investigations and issues rules and regulations. The Secretary of Labor is authorized to file suit on behalf of employees seeking to collect wages and overtime, and may also recover liquidated damages in an amount equal to the amount of wages owed. The secretary may also seek injunctions against violations of the act. Criminal proceedings for willful violations may be instituted by the Justice Department.

Employees may file suit to recover back wages and overtime plus liquidated damages in an equal amount. They may also seek reinstatement and may recover legal fees. The statute of limitations for violations is two years; for willful violations it is extended to three years. The Supreme Court discussed the definition of "willful" in *McLaughlin* v. *Richland Shoe Co.* (486 U.S. 128, 1988); the court defined "willful' as "that the employer either knew or showed reckless disregard as to whether its conduct was prohibited by the FLSA." Employees generally may not release employers for less than the full amount owing, nor may employees waive their rights to compensation under the act.

The child labor prohibitions are enforced by the prohibition of interstate shipment of goods produced by child labor and by fines, as demonstrated by the *Marshall* v. *GM* case. Fines may also be levied against employers who keep inadequate wage and hour records.

The following case involves a discussion of the standard used by the court in determining whether to award liquidated damages in addition to back pay.

MARSHALL v. BRUNNER

668 F.2d 748 (3rd Cir. 1982)

GARTH, J.

The Secretary of Labor, in a complaint that charged Brunner with violations of the Fair Labor Standards Act of 1938, sought an injunction against future violations of the Act, back pay for Brunner's employees, and the imposition of liquidated damages in an amount equal to the back pay. After a trial on the merits, the district court entered judgment granting the Secretary's request for an injunction against future violations of the Act and for recovery of back wages totalling $112,437.05. The court declined to award any liquidated damages. Both Brunner and the Secretary appeal.

While these appeals present questions involving the coverage of Brunner's enterprise within the ambit of 29 U.S.C. Section 203(s), the issue with which we are most concerned is whether the district court committed legal error when it concluded that an award of liquidated damages in favor of the Secretary was not justified.

We affirm all rulings of the district court, except its decision refusing to award liquidated damages.

Brunner was engaged in the business of collecting garbage, trash, and scrap metal from homes and a number of commercial enterprises in thirteen municipalities in Allegheny County. The Wage and Hour Division of the Department of Labor conducted an investigation of Brunner's business through January of 1977. The investigation uncovered evidence of extensive violations of the minimum wage, maximum hours, child labor, and record keeping provisions of the FLSA. During the investigation, officials of the Wage and Hour Division and Brunner's own counsel specifically warned Brunner about the importance of complying with the Act's record keeping requirements and its prohibitions against child labor. Despite this advice, the time cards which Brunner then began keeping were inaccurate and Brunner also employed other measures to conceal the lengthy hours that the employees actually worked. In addition, Brunner continued to employ minors in violation of the Act. On May 27, 1977 the Secretary filed this suit.

At trial, Brunner maintained that the Company was not required to comply with provisions of the FLSA because it was a local enterprise whose employees were not engaged in commerce, did not produce goods for commerce, and did not handle goods that had been moved in, or produced

for, commerce. The district court rejected this argument, and concluded that the Company was subject to the FLSA and that it had violated the minimum wage, maximum hours, child labor, and record keeping provisions of the Act. From the evidence, the district court concluded that Brunner's employees worked an average of 56 hours during a five-day workweek and were not paid the applicable minimum wage or time-and-one half for hours worked in excess of forty hours per week.

As a consequence, the district court enjoined Brunner from violating the Act, and awarded $112,437.05 in back pay to the affected employees. The district court, however, refused to assess Brunner with liquidated damages in the same amount. These appeals followed.

The coverage of the Fair Labor Standards Act extends to employees employed in "an enterprise engaged in commerce or in the production of goods for commerce." Section 203(s) of the Act provides that such an enterprise is one

> which has employees engaged in commerce or in the production of goods for commerce, or employees handling, selling, or otherwise working on goods or *materials* that have been moved in or produced for commerce by any person, . . . (emphasis added).

The parties' stipulations reveal that Brunner used "trucks, truck bodies, tires, batteries, and accessories, sixty-gallon containers, shovels, brooms, oil and gas" that had been manufactured out of state and had moved in interstate commerce. The district court thus concluded that Brunner is subject to the Act, since its employees "handl[ed] . . . goods or materials that have been moved or produced in commerce."

Brunner, however, argues that there is an exception provided in Section 203(s) for firms that are the ultimate consumers of goods that have been moved or produced in commerce. Although Brunner concedes that Congress has the power to subject Brunner to FLSA coverage, Brunner argues that Congress did not intend the Act to apply to a firm merely because the business uses motor vehicles, gas, oil and other manufactured goods in its operations.

The "ultimate consumer" exception is found in Section 203(i) of the Act, which provides in relevant part "Goods means goods . . . commodities, merchandise, or articles or subjects of commerce of any character, . . . but does not include goods after their delivery into the actual physical possession of the ultimate consumer thereof. . . ." Thus, Section 203(i) excludes from the definition of goods those goods that have been delivered into the physical possession of an ultimate consumer for its own use. Brunner's "ultimate consumer" argument proceeds on the assumption that if Brunner's employees only use products which the Company itself consumes, then Brunner's employees have not handled "goods" that have been moved or produced in commerce within the meaning of Section 203(s). Brunner further asserts that the phrase "or materials" added by Congress in the 1974 amendment did not affect the "ultimate consumer" exception.

Just as the district court rejected this argument, so do we. When the 1974 amendment to Section 203(s) added the words "or materials" to that statute, it clarified the meaning of the Act with respect to those businesses, which in the course of their own operations, use materials which have been moved in or produced for commerce. Indeed, the Senate report fully explains the purpose of the amendment:

> The bill also adds the words "or materials" after the word "goods" to make clear the Congressional intent to include within this additional basis of coverage the handling of goods consumed in the employer's business, as, e.g., the soap used by a laundry. . . . Although a few district courts have erroneously construed the "handling" clause as being inapplicable to employees who handle goods used in their employer's own commercial operations, the only court of appeals to decide this question and the majority of the district courts have held otherwise and the addition of the words "and materials" will clarify this point (citations omitted).

We are satisfied that the legislative history demonstrates that Congress intended to extend the coverage of the Act to firms, like Brunner's which use materials that have been moved in or produced in, commerce. Indeed, Brunner has cited to no authority that would justify a different interpretation of the 1974 amendment. . . .

We thus conclude that Brunner is subject to the provisions of the FLSA.

Section 216(b) of the Fair Labor Standards Act provides that any employer who violates the minimum wage or maximum hour provisions of the Act, "shall be liable to the employee or employees affected in the amount of their unpaid minimum wages or their unpaid overtime compensation, as the case may be, *and in an additional equal amount as liquidated damages*." (emphasis added). Under the Act, liquidated damages are compensatory, not punitive in nature. Congress provided for liquidated damages to compensate

employees for losses they might suffer by reason of not receiving their lawful wage at the time it was due.

In 1947 . . . Congress provided employers with a defense to the mandatory liquidated damage provision. Essentially, the defense provides that the district court has discretion to award no liquidated damages, or to award an amount of liquidated damages less than the amount provided by Section 216(b) of the FLSA, *if, and only if,* the employer shows that he acted in good faith and that he had reasonable grounds for believing that he was not violating the Act. Thus, before the district court's discretion may be invoked, the employer has the "plain and substantial burden of persuading the court by proof that his failure to obey the statute was both in good faith and predicated upon such reasonable grounds that it would be unfair to impose upon him more than a compensatory verdict." In the absence of such a showing, the district court has no discretion to mitigate an employer's statutory liability for liquidated damages.

The good faith requirement of the defense requires that the employer have an honest intention to ascertain and follow the dictates of the Act. The additional requirement that the employer have reasonable grounds for believing that his conduct complies with the Act imposes an objective standard by which to judge the employer's behavior. Moreover, an employer may not rely on ignorance alone in meeting the objective test.

Here the district court explained its refusal to award liquidated damages by "the factual circumstances surrounding the quantity and quality of the plaintiff's proof in this case." In its opinion the district court also stated "that the defendant has sustained its burden of proving that liquidated damages should not be awarded."

At no time, however, did the district court make the findings that were a prerequisite to the invocation of its discretion—that Brunner had acted in good faith and that there were reasonable grounds for believing that the Brunner business was in compliance with the Act. Furthermore, the district court's conclusion that Brunner had met its statutory burden is contradicted by the court's own findings of fact which establish conclusively that Brunner had acted in bad faith and had knowingly made deliberate attempts to circumvent the Act. The district court's findings may be summarized as follows:

(1) Brunner knew that its employees worked more than forty hours per week, but did not pay any of its employees time-and-one-half their regular rate of pay for hours over forty, as the Act requires.

(2) Prior to the Secretary's investigation Brunner kept no records of the hours worked by any employees.

(3) Following an investigation by the Wage and Hour Division, Brunner began to keep a series of inaccurate time cards which failed to reflect the actual hours worked by the employees, even though Brunner had been explicitly advised by Wage and Hour officials, as well as its own counsel, of the importance of complying with the record keeping requirements of the Act.

(4) Employees were instructed that if they did not sign the inaccurate time cards, they would not be paid.

(5) Brunner continued to employ minors in the operation of its business even after Department of Labor officials, and its own counsel, advised Brunner that the Act prohibited that practice.

(6) During and after the investigation by the Wage and Hour Division, Brunner instructed employees not to talk to the Secretary's representatives and threatened to discharge the employees if they did.

(7) Finally, three weeks prior to trial, Brunner instructed all of his employees to sign statements that they had never worked more than forty hours per week, even though Brunner knew the employees regularly worked longer hours than that.

Not only are these affirmative findings fully supported by the record, but the record discloses no evidence whatsoever upon which a finding of "good faith" or a finding of "reasonable grounds" could have been made. Indeed, based on this record, any such findings, if made, would necessarily have had to be overturned on review. It is thus apparent that the district court erred in holding that Brunner had "sustained its burden of proving that liquidated damages should not be awarded."

Counsel for Brunner, recognizing the absence of any evidence in the record which could call into play the exercise of the district court's discretion to deny liquidated damages, argues that we should remand this issue to the district court so that proof may now be provided of Brunner's "good faith" and of reasonable grounds for believing that Brunner did not violate the Act. However, the Secretary's complaint, as well as the record, disclose that the Secretary at all times had sought the imposition of liquidated damages. Indeed, at oral argument Brunner's counsel conceded that the Secretary had put liquidated damages in issue throughout the proceedings below. Brunner, however, did not respond to this claim by producing the proofs necessary under Section 260. Moreover, the very findings of fact made by the district court demonstrate convincingly that Brunner acted in bad faith and had deliberately sought to circumvent the provisions of the FLSA. On the basis of such findings and this record no remand is indicated. Thus, the Secretary is entitled to recover on behalf of the employees the full amount of liquidated damages under Section 216(b), or $112,437.05.

Having concluded that the district court did not err in holding that Brunner came within the coverage of [FLSA] . . . , we will affirm so much of the district court's judgment which is the subject of Brunner's appeal. . . .

Because we have also concluded that the district court erred in refusing to assess liquidated damages as mandated by Section 216(b), we will reverse so much of the district court's judgment as is the subject of the Secretary's appeal, and we will remand to the district court with the direction that it enter judgment against Brunner for liquidated damages in an amount equal to the back pay judgment which we have affirmed.

QUESTIONS

1. What are the main provisions of the Fair Labor Standards Act? What are the bases of coverage for the FLSA?

2. What deductions may be made from an employee's wages under the FLSA? Explain your answer.

3. Does the FLSA require the payment of overtime? Under what circumstances?

4. What are the major exceptions from the overtime and minimum wage requirements of the FLSA? What are the tests used to determine whether an employee falls under one of those exemptions?

5. What is meant by "oppressive child labor"? What is the significance of oppressive child labor under the FLSA?

6. What remedies are available for violations of the minimum wage and overtime provisions of the FLSA? What penalties may be imposed for violations of the child labor prohibitions?

CASE PROBLEMS

1. Among the limited number of employees specifically exempted from the jurisdiction of the FLSA are seamen. In 1985 the Supreme Court agreed to review a case that concerned this exemption. The case involved a group of maintenance employees working aboard a fish-processing barge, called the *Arctic Star.* It was a sort of mobile factory, towed from job site to site in the waters of Alaska, British Columbia, and Washington. The barge lacked any means of self-propulsion. Nevertheless, Icicle Seafoods, Inc. argued that the 160 crew members were not subject to the overtime and minimum wage provisions of the FLSA because they were "seamen." The Department of Labor took the position that the crew were actually "industrial maintenance employees" who monitored, maintained, and repaired the processing machinery and, consequently, were clearly within the coverage of the act.

How should the Supreme Court rule on this issue? (In attempting to answer this question, ask yourself what may have been the policy consideration(s) behind Congress' decision to create the exemption for sailors in the first place.) See *Icicle Seafoods, Inc.* v. *Worthington,* 474 U.S. 1080 (1986).

2. DialAmerica Marketing, Inc. is a telephone marketing firm that operates in twenty states and maintains its principal place of business in Teaneck, New Jersey. A major aspect of DialAmerica's business is the sale of magazine renewal subscriptions by telephone to persons whose subscriptions have expired or are near expiration. Under this "expire" program, publishers supply DialAmerica with the names and addresses of subscribers, and DialAmerica locates phone numbers for these subscribers and telephones them in an effort to sell renewal subscriptions.

Initially, DialAmerica located subscribers' phone numbers by employing in-house researchers who would find numbers by consulting telephone books and calling direction-assistance operators. In 1976 DialAmerica initiated its home researcher program as a method of increasing its capacity to locate needed telephone numbers. Under the program, persons would travel to DialAmerica's office in Teaneck and pick up cards, each of which contained the name and address of a subscriber whose telephone number was needed. They would then take these cards home, use

telephone books or operators to locate the telephone numbers of the persons listed, write the numbers on the cards in a specified manner, and then return the completed cards to DialAmerica's office.

Upon deciding to begin the home research program, DialAmerica sought researchers by placing a total of five newspaper advertisements, the last of which ran in May 1979. After that date, prospective home researchers approached DialAmerica after learning about the program from others. Those desiring such work met with an officer of the company. During the meeting, they were instructed how properly to complete the magazine expire cards, and they were asked to sign a document labeled an "Independent Contractor's Agreement." DialAmerica never rejected anyone who applied for such work, although it did subsequently discharge some home researchers who performed their work inadequately.

Upon signing the agreement to do home research work, a worker was given an initial box of five hundred cards to be researched. The worker was expected to set up an appointment to return the cards one week later. Appointments were designed to prevent too many of the home researchers (generally women, some of whom brought their small children along) from being present in the office at one time.

Home researchers were free to choose the weeks and hours they wanted to work and the number of cards they wished to research (subject to a five-hundred-card minimum per batch and to the sometimes limited availability of cards). DialAmerica instructed the researchers not to look for the phone numbers of schools, libraries, government installations, or hospitals. The researchers were instructed to keep all duplicate cards separate. DialAmerica required the use of a black ink or Flair pen and sold such pens to the researchers. The researchers were required to place their initials and the letter "H" (for home researcher) on each card they completed. When DialAmerica installed a machine to read and process the completed cards automatically, DialAmerica required that the home researchers place numbers on the cards by writing them in ink around dots preprinted on the cards. Finally, the home researchers were instructed not to wear shorts when they came to the office to pick up or deliver cards. DialAmerica did not, however, require the home researchers to keep records of the hours that they worked.

Based on these facts, do you think the "home researchers" were independent contractors exempt from the minimum wage and overtime provisions of the FLSA? Or were they really employees of DialAmerica and therefore entitled to the act's protection? See *Donovan* v. *DialAmerica Marketing, Inc.,* 757 F.2d 1376, 27 W & H Cases 113 (3d Cir. 1985).

3. In the period at issue, 1979–1981, drivers Dove and Pinner were expected to report to the premises of their employer, Admiral Limousine Service, at 8:30 A.M. and to wait there until they received a driving assignment. They were not permitted to conduct personal business while waiting, but they were allowed half an hour off for lunch. Admiral maintained this waiting time arrangement so that it would have a pool of ready drivers on its premises to meet the unpredictable number of calls it received for service. If Dove and Pinner did not receive a driving assignment by 5:00 P.M., as sometimes occurred, they were then allowed to end their workday.

Dove and Pinner were compensated in three ways. First, if they arrived by 8:30 A.M. and received no assignment or an assignment that began after 5:00 P.M., they were paid a "guarantee." The guarantee was $20 a day until September 1981, when it was raised to $30 a day. Second, if they received an assignment, they were paid a "driver's share" of the fare. The driver's share was one-third of the hourly rate paid by the customer until September 1981, when it became a flat hourly rate. If the driver's share was less than the guarantee, the drivers were paid the guarantee. Finally, tips paid by the customers were added to the drivers' paychecks. Typically, the tips were 15 percent of the fare; tips were received on 70 percent of the assignments.

Most days, Dove and Pinner received a driving assignment before 5:00 P.M., and their driver's share exceeded the guarantee. On such days, their pay was calculated solely on the basis of driving time. If a six-hour driving assignment yielded a $45 driver's share, plus tip, the driver earned this same amount whether the assignment began at 9:00 A.M. or at 4:00 P.M. To secure eligibility for the guarantee, however, in the event that no or only brief assignments came in, Dove and Pinner had to arrive at Admiral's premises by 8:30 A.M.

Dove and Pinner, on days when they received no driving assignment, waited eight hours. When they ob-

tained a driving assignment, their workday—waiting period plus driving period—often exceeded eight hours. Both worked on weekends. Their workweek, according to their estimates, generally ran well above forty hours.

On the basis of these facts, were Dove and Pinner receiving adequate compensation from Admiral? If not, where was Admiral falling short and how would you go about calculating the damages? See *Dove* v. *Coupe,* 759 F.2d 167, 27 W & H Cases 185 (D.C. Cir. 1985).

4. Plaintiffs were 163 present or former members of the Special Police Force of the Library of Congress. They received a lunch period of thirty minutes, during which they were relived from their posts but were officially on duty and subject to call. They could take their lunch break in any appropriate eating area, but had to remain on library premises, in uniform, and in possession of their firearms. While on duty, plaintiffs generally carried two-way radios. The radios were kept on during lunch, and any calls from supervisors, either in person or over the radio, had to be answered. Otherwise, plaintiffs could use their lunch period as they chose.

Before July 22, 1983, plaintiffs worked a watch of eight consecutive hours; their thirty-minute lunch break took place during the eight-hour watch. But on that date, a new collective bargaining agreement that went into effect changed the duty hours. The new agreement required plaintiffs to be present for an eight-and-one-half-hour tour of duty, only eight hours of which were paid. Twenty minutes were added to the beginning and ten minutes to the end of the shift for such activities as drawing and turning in weapons and radios and receiving duty assignments. The lunch period remained compensated time, but the pre- and postshift periods were not.

Plaintiffs claim their lunch period was not duty free, could not be offset against the uncompensated time spent before and after the shift on employer-required activities, and must be included in "hours worked" in determining entitlement to overtime pay.

How should the court respond to these claims of the library guards? See *Agner* v. *U.S.,* 27 W & H Cases 515 (U.S. Claims Ct. 1985).

5. The Global Home Products Enterprise (Global) oversaw the manufacturing of cookies and candy and sold them to local groups, retail stores, and door-to-door salespeople such as Charles Thomas. Thomas first be-

came connected with Global in California. Global asked Charles Thomas to move to Charlotte, North Carolina, in early 1983 to sell Global products from this location.

At the beginning of his work in Charlotte, Thomas advertised that he wanted to hire children between the ages of twelve and sixteen. After learning of state laws, he later advertised for children only between the ages of fourteen and eighteen. Thomas routinely attempted to talk with the parents of his crew members before they began work with him. He spoke with most of the parents and had them sign a parent permission form that told the parents of some of the working conditions. However, he had not spoken with all parents or received parent permission forms from parents of all the children.

Thomas instructed his sales force on their responsibility to be ready to work and gave them speech cards to practice their sales pitch to customers. One of the documents given to the children stated that "I have too much homework" is not an acceptable excuse for missing work.

Thomas drove a van to pick up the children at their homes. He took them to a neighborhood and assigned them streets on which they were to sell the cookies and candy. The children went door-to-door selling the cookies. They then gave Mr. Thomas the checks and cash they received for the products. The children were paid $0.60 per box sold, out of the purchase price of $3.00 per box.

During periods in which school was in session, Charles Thomas had frequently kept children away from home past 7:00 P.M. during the week, often as late as 9:00 P.M. On weekends, he usually took the Charlotte children out of the Charlotte area and often did not return them to their homes until 11:30 P.M. or 12:00 midnight. Parents of the children testified that their children would return home tired and hungry. Charles Thomas testified that he would often drive the children to a fast-food restaurant when working late.

Based on these facts, did Thomas violate the child labor provisions of the FLSA? Did Global? See *Thomas v. Brock,* 615 F. Supp. 553, 27 W & H Cases 535 (W.D.N.C. 1985)

6. The grievants were employed as meat inspectors. Their duty was to ensure the wholesomeness of meat products slaughtered, processed, or sold in Vermont. They performed these functions in slaughterhouses licensed by the Vermont Department of Agriculture, processing

plants licensed by the department, and retail stores carrying meat products.

The grievants, with the knowledge of the department, used their homes for various work-related purposes. The board found, however, that the great bulk of the work done by grievants was performed on site—that is, at slaughterhouses, processing plants, and retail stores. The amount of work done at home was minimal. Preserving meat and blood samples in their refrigerators, pending transfer to laboratories for analysis, was the only work-related function that could not be done elsewhere.

Prior to 1973 the department provided the meat inspectors with state-owned vehicles. Beginning in July 1973, the state no longer furnished the vehicles. The inspectors then used their own cars from their homes to the various sites of their work. They were paid mileage from their homes, which had been designed "official" or "duty" or "official duty" stations. They were never paid overtime for this travel time between home and the work sites. The sole issue in this case is whether the grievants were entitled to overtime pay for travel time between their homes and assignments for the period January 1, 1973, to November 1, 1976. The following provision governed the payment of overtime for travel, and was in effect throughout this dispute:

It is expected that travel time between work locations shall be conducted during normal working hours. Employees are not eligible for overtime compensation for travel time except where an employee is travelling from work location to work location. The term "work location" for purposes of this section does not include the employee's home or travel to and from conventions, seminars, training courses, study groups and related activities.

Are the meat inspectors correct that they are entitled to overtime pay for the time they spend traveling from their homes to the slaughterhouse and back? See *In re Vermont State Employees' Ass'n.,* 26 W & H Cases 74 (Vermont S.C. 1982).

7. Priscilla C. Brown was employed as a registered pharmacist by Eckerd Drugs, Inc. at one of its drugstores in North Carolina. In accordance with Eckerd's policy, all its pharmacists maintained their own time records, turning in biweekly time sheets indicating the days and hours they had worked during the preceding two weeks. The pharmacists were paid a salary. Corporate policy regarding salaries stated that

Registered pharmacists are guaranteed an agreed upon bi-weekly salary which is not subject to reduction because of changes in the quantity or quality of work performed. The pharmacist must be paid his or her full salary for any week in which he performs any work without regard to the number of days or hours worked, except for deductions for the following:

1. Deductions for absences from work for a day or more for his own personal reasons, other than sickness or accident, and

2. Deductions for absence of a day or more because of sickness or disability, provided these deductions are only made either before the employee has qualified under our established policy of providing compensation for loss of salary occasioned by sickness and disability, or after the employee has exhausted his leave allowance under such policy.

The policy actually put into effect at the Eckerd store in Winston-Salem, where Pharmacist Brown worked required pharmacists to fill in their time sheets with the hours they actually worked. This policy resulted in deductions from certain pharmacists' salaries when they were absent for less than a day for personal reasons. The time sheets were sent to Eckerd's California-based headquarters where the data were fed into a computer that calculated the paychecks. Brown was docked about thirteen times during a two-year period under this system.

Was Pharmacist Brown a professional employee and therefore exempt from the overtime provisions of the FLSA? Was the company's policy on pharmacists' salaries legal under the FLSA? Was the Winston-Salem store's local policy legal? If one or both of those policies was illegal, to what remedy (remedies) are Brown and the pharmacists entitled? See *Brown* v. *Eckerd Drugs, Inc.,* 24 W & H Cases 119 (M.D. North Carolina 1979).

8. A hospital in Washington, D.C., for many years pursued the practice of paying its nurses a salary, but also paying them overtime. All of the nurses were earning salaries above the minimum level required to meet the professional-employee exemption to the FLSA. When the hospital changed its policy and stopped paying the nurses overtime, the nurses sued.

Were the nurses professional employees? If so, can you suggest an argument in support of the nurses' claim for continued overtime compensation? See *Harrison v. Washington Hospital Center,* 86 CCH Labor Cases 33,825 (D.D.C. 1979).

9. The so-called retail or service establishment exception to the FLSA's overtime provision reads:

The provisions of Section 206 . . . and Section 207 of this title shall not apply with respect to . . . any employee employed by any retail or service establishment . . . , if more than 50 per centum of such establishment's annual dollar volume of sales of goods or services is made within the State in which the establishment is located. . . . A "retail or service establishment" shall mean an establishment 75 per centum of whose annual dollar volume of sale of goods or services (or both) is not for resale and is recognized as retail sales or services in the particular industry. . . .

William P. Bringman Company, L.P.A., was a private, for-profit law firm that provided legal services to clients from its law offices in southern Ohio. The firm failed to pay certain nonexempt employees for the overtime they worked.

Should this law firm be exempted from the FLSA by reason of the "retail and service establishment" exception quoted above? Do you need any more facts in order to answer this question? Should all law firms fall under this exemption? See *Donovan* v. *William P. Bringman Co.,* 27 W & H Cases 313 (S.D. Ohio 1985).

10. Olson was employed as a used-car salesman by Superior Pontiac. Superior utilized a multiple method of compensating its sales force. Salesmen were paid daily cash bonuses called SPIFFS for selling designated cars or options. In addition, sales managers would pay cash bonuses to salesmen during their daily sales meetings. Monthly bonuses were paid for volume sales. Superior also paid regular commissions for the sale of all automobiles, with salesmen receiving a percentage of the gross profits on every car they sold.

Superior's salesmen received both weekly and monthly checks. Under this method of compensation, every Thursday salesmen got 70 percent of total commissions. Then, at the end of each month, Superior issued each salesman a settlement check consisting of the 30 percent withheld each week of that month. The purpose of this system was to ensure a fund of money from which Superior could deduct taxes with respect to the various bonuses each salesperson received during the month.

What problems, if any, might Superior's system have encountered with respect to the FLSA? See *Olson* v. *Superior Pontiac-GMC, Inc.,* 765 F.2d 1570, 27 W & H Cases 393 (11th Cir. 1985).

Employee Welfare Programs: Social Security, Workers' Compensation, and Unemployment Compensation

NOT UNTIL THE 1900s, and for a substantial number of American workers not even until the 1930s, did the government provide any assistance to workers affected by unemployment, on-the-job injury, work-related disability, or old age. Until then, Americans (like workers around the world then and even today) relied upon their families, ethnic communities, churches, and social clubs for aid when their incomes were temporarily or permanently disrupted. For instance, Irish coal miners in Pennsylvania in the 1870s might belong to the Ancient Order of Hibernians, a benevolent society with a fund dedicated to assisting the widows and orphans of miners killed in the "pits." Increasingly, too, workers organized and looked to their labor unions for help in times of trouble. But before Congress passed the National Labor Relations Act (NLRA) in 1935, most unions were mere shadows of what they would later become.

Congress did occasionally become involved in the welfare of employees in private industry, even before the ground-breaking legislation of the 1930s. The Railway Labor Act (governing labor relations), which was passed in 1926, and the Federal Employers Liability Act (FELA), which was passed in 1908, predate the NLRA and workers' compensation laws, respectively. The FELA was enacted in recognition of the incredible number of casualties in the railroad industry and of the realities of workers trying to sue their employers in those days. In the early days of the railroad industry, a shocking number of railway workers suffered accidents or were killed at work. Those injured, or the families of those killed, often found attempts at getting recourse from the railway companies an exercise in frustration or futility, or both. The legal realities of going up against the railroad could be intimidating.

Suppose a railroad worker was hit by a railcar that rolled in deadly silence down the track because of a faultily set brake. The injured, perhaps permanently disabled worker might hold the railroad responsible and seek to sue it for money damages. To do so, he would first have to find a lawyer willing to take the case. Having little or no savings, he might find it difficult to obtain an attorney prepared to take on one of the great financial juggernauts of the era. If he did, he faced a daunting set of defenses that the railroad company could raise. The railroad's lawyers most likely would first argue that the hapless employee, by taking the job, had assumed the risk of injury. They would then seek to establish that he somehow had been contributorily negligent, such as by not being alert while in the railyard. Finally, they would invoke the fellow-servant doctrine—that is, they would say that he was not injured by their client, "the railroad," but by a co-worker who had negligently failed to set the brake properly.

As you can see, any worker who recovered what his injuries deserved from the railroad had to have been both very persistent and very lucky. For most workers, or their widows and orphans, the alternative was one of the forms of charity mentioned above, perhaps in combination with some modest form of public dole. But being employed in the key industry of industrialized America, railroad workers were the first able to exert unified pressure to better their circumstances. Theirs was the first major industry to be organized—by several railway brotherhoods, such as the Brotherhood of Railway Clerks. Once organized, they successfully lobbied for passage of the FELA.

Although the FELA still requires an injured railroad worker to file suit in a federal or state court, it substantially reduced the burden of proof placed upon the employee-plaintiff, while depriving the railroad-defendant of some of its most potent defenses. Thus, injured employees generally win their cases under the FELA, which is still in force today.

The FELA not withstanding, England and Germany were well ahead of the United States in enacting social legislation to aid injured and unemployed workers. In England, no less a figure than Winston Churchill worked with David Lloyd George to draft and enact legislation on wages and hours, pensions, and social insurance. In one speech he told the audience, "We want to draw a line below which we will not allow persons to live and labor." The ultimate results of this pledge included a Coal Mines Act establishing an eight-hour workday for miners, a Trade Boards Act setting minimum piecework rates in the sweatshops, a Workman's Compensation Act, and an Old Age Pensions Act.

In Germany, Otto von Bismarck enacted social legislation that made his country the most socially progressive in the world. By 1903 more than 18 million of its workers were protected by accident insurance, 13 million had old-age pensions, and 11 million had health insurance. These social welfare benefits cost the state $100 million—an astronomical sum in those days.

Not until the New Deal era of the 1930s did such legislation become widespread in the United States. The Pennsylvania Superior Court summarized the development of such U.S. laws in a 1946 unemployment compensation decision, *Bliley Electric Company* v. *Unemployment Compensation Board of Review* (45 A.2d 898, 901, 1946):

The statute, almost ten years old, introduced into our law a new concept of social obligation, extended the police power of the State into a virgin field, and created a body of rights and duties unknown to the common law. England was the first common law country to operate a similar system, and its experience began as an experiment in 1911. Its law, revised as trial exposed error, became the basis for the American unemployment compensation system, although in detail there are vast variances between the American and British systems. Wisconsin passed an act in 1932, but it required the enactment of the Social Security Act by Congress on August 14, 1935 to induce other states to adopt the system. All of the states have enacted conforming legislation, and their statutes include the basic requirements laid down by the Act of Congress, but they differ widely and sharply in respect to the details which Congress left open to state legislation.

The pattern of the genesis unemployment benefits identified by the Pennsylvania Superior Court also matches the historical pattern for social security and workers' compensation. Although the roots of these laws can be traced to the second decade of this century (just a bit behind England and Germany), the widespread availability of these important benefits is indebted to President Franklin Roosevelt's New Deal.

All three social welfare programs—social security pensions, workers' compensation, and unemployment compensation—descend from a common history and came into being about the same time. A major distinction between unemployment and workers' compensation versus social security is that the states have primary responsibility for the first two (with some notable exceptions), whereas social security is a federally supervised program applied uniformly across the country. But despite this difference, plus many distinctions between the various states' systems of unemployment or workers' compensation, the common threads, like the common ancestry, make it possible to discuss each of these forms of worker welfare in general terms. Wherever you wind up working in the United States, you will find that state's systems readily recognizable.

This chapter begins with the federal social security program, and then examines workers' compensation and unemployment compensation.

The Social Security and Supplemental Security Acts

Nearly one in every seven Americans—almost thirty-five million people—are recipients of social security benefits. Another four million or so get supplemental security income. This is a remarkably large number of people; yet the graying of the baby boomers means still more beneficiaries in future decades must be supported by the social security funds. This prospect has been a cause of concern and action in recent years.

The social security system was originally entitled "old age and survivor's insurance" (OASI), and the notion that it really was *insurance* was a significant component of Franklin Roosevelt's success in selling the program to the Congress and the country. Yet in reality for its first three decades of existence the OASI was financed from current payroll taxes charged to employers and their employees. Those who looked forward to drawing benefits when they got old paid for the benefits being received by today's pensioners. This was pay-as-you-go, not a real *vested* pension fund or paid-up retirement insurance. But it worked as long as retirees were a modest percentage of the active work force and benefits were low.

As post–World War II baby boomers entered the work force, and especially as employment peaked during the Vietnam War, a surplus actually piled up in the OASI. But during this same time another trend was set in motion that by the mid-1970s would place the OASI's solvency in jeopardy. For years the Social Security Administration career staff aimed toward converting social security from a minimal safety net into an adequate pension. This goal was shared by many congressional liberals and by organized labor. Gradually, these players won their way, not only increasing the typical retiree's benefit and insulating it against inflation, but also expanding the program to cover other needy Americans, such as the permanently disabled.

Meanwhile, the baby boom became a baby bust, while life spans lengthened. Public information from the Census Bureau and the Department of Labor reveals that during the 1970s, 24.1 million young workers entered the labor pool. Only 9 million joined the labor force in the 1980s. The 1990s are predicted to produce only 15.6 million new workers, unless our immigration laws are drastically liberalized. Persons fifty-five and older will constitute a fifth of our population by the turn of the century, and 32.3 percent by 2030. The average American woman produced 3.4 to 3.6 offspring between 1946 and 1964. Today she gives birth to an average 1.8 children. In 1900, people over seventy-four years old made up only 1.2 percent of the population. By 1982, they were 5 percent of the populace. By 2030, their ranks will represent a hefty 10 percent of the country. These figures eloquently illustrate the pressures on the social security system.

These pressures were first felt during Gerald Ford's presidency (1973–1976), hard on the heels of some of the most generous (and short-sighted) social security legislation in the system's history. By 1977 talk of a social security bankruptcy was common, not only in Washington but around the country. Jimmy Carter came into office with the problem on his agenda, and by the time Ronald Reagan took office in 1981, the problem had become critical.

To better understand the system as it is administered and maintained today, we must look at three legislative phases: the original passage of the act, the early 1970s amendments that built in automatic cost-of-living increases and other costly expansions, and the bailout legislation of the early 1980s.

Titles II and VIII of the Social Security Act of 1935

Old-age pensions were near and dear to Franklin Roosevelt well before he was elected president in 1932. Although he was from wealthy and famous New York society stock, his interest in the issue came at least in part from personal experience. In a campaign speech delivered on October 2, 1932, in Detroit, he recounted one such personal perspective on the plight of old people:

> I had been away during the winter time and when I came back I found that a tragedy had occurred. I had had an old farm neighbor, who had been a splendid old fellow—supervisor of his town, highway commissioner of his town, one of the best of our citizens. Before

I left, around Christmastime, I had seen the old man, who was eighty-nine, his old brother, who was eighty-seven, his other brother, who was eighty-five, and his kid sister, who was eighty-three.

When I came back in the spring, I found that in the severe winter that followed there had been a heavy fall of snow and one of the old brothers had fallen down on his way out to the barn to milk the cow and had perished in the snow drift.

The town authorities had come along and had taken the two old men and had put them in the county poorhouse, and they had taken the old lady and had sent her down for want of a better place, to the insane asylum although she was not insane but just old.

As governor of New York, Roosevelt had not gotten very far pushing the notion of old-age pensions. Few other states had done any better. When he took over the Oval Office in 1933, fifteen of forty-eight states had no provisions whatever for aged Americans. The rest paid an average pension of about $16 a month, not enough even in those hard times to pay for one square meal a day. In June 1934, the new president set up the Cabinet Committee on Economic Security with Labor Secretary Frances Perkins, herself a former New York social worker and member of that state's industrial commission, as chairperson.

The committee was pushed along by the efforts of a Californian named Everett Townsend to lobby through Congress his own Townsend Plan for the elderly. The committee also addressed other issues covered in this chapter, such as unemployment compensation, which they decided should be administered by the states. As for social security, they favored federal centralization, since workers might be employed in many places during a career and then ultimately retire somewhere they had never worked. Roosevelt's major contribution to the final scheme, a contribution that proved prophetic, was to insist it be called old-age insurance.

Each contributor was to have her or his own account, even though the fund operated pay-as-you-go and there was no vesting of actual individual contributions. Roosevelt told one colleague that the purpose of that approach was ". . . so those sons of bitches up on the Hill can't ever abandon this system when I'm gone." His idea worked brilliantly. As stated by Harvard's Neustadt and May in *Thinking in Time: The Uses of History for Decision-Makers,* ". . . by 1939 it turned out that the symbols of the thing sufficed—the term, the trappings, the account numbers—never mind the vesting."

The 1970s: Social Security Crisis

The social security crisis began in 1972. The Social Security Act was amended twice that year. In July 1972, social security benefits were increased by Congress 20 percent, effective September 1 of that year. That amendment also introduced automatic cost-of-living increases, tied to the consumer price index, starting in 1975. Then in October 1972 more amendments, effective the following January, were enacted into law; some 3.4 million widows of deceased retirees received enhanced benefits, and all retirees were permitted to earn more income without diminution in their pensions.

A number of factors had combined to cause Congress and President Nixon to permit these very expensive amendments to the thirty-year-old system. OASI funds had piled up into a tidy surplus during the Vietnam War. Nixon wanted to be reelected; signing the social security amendments was only a minor excess of his reelection efforts (as compared to the Watergate scandal that was soon to materialize and eclipse all other issues on the political scene). Presidential politics led lobby opposition, such as from the National Association of Manufacturers, to be muted as well. And so, for perhaps the first time in three decades, social security became an adequate pension, not merely a minimal safety net. But at what price?

Three unexpected trends converged to threaten the fattened fund with fiscal disaster. First, as mentioned above, the birth rate dropped, while life spans of Americans lengthened. Second, inflation began galloping, spurred in part by the first of several successive oil crises. Third came a recession. The term "stagflation," which means persistent inflation together with stagnant consumer demand and relatively high unemployment, entered the economists' lexicon, and by 1977 talk of a social security bankruptcy was common.

Meanwhile, President Carter resisted attempts to reduce pensioners' benefits. When the new president, Ronald Reagan, appeared to endorse some delays in increases in 1981, public opinion lashed back at him with a vengeance.

The 1980s: Recovery?

Reagan's response was to set up a bipartisan commission in the autumn of 1981 to study the problems facing social security. He appointed five members, and the speaker of the house and Senate majority leader each got to appoint five more. Most key players and key interests received some representation on the commission. Six weeks of discussions and negotiations resulted in a commission report. The result was a combination of benefit reductions and delays, and tax increases that have kept the program solvent into the foreseeable future.

Social Security Benefit Programs Today

Retirement Insurance Benefits.   The original and still the main purpose of social security is to provide *partial* replacement of earnings when a worker decides it is time to retire. Although benefits have increased substantially in the last two decades, both in relative and absolute terms, this retirement benefit is still not, and never was, intended to totally replace what that worker was earning prior to retirement. And yet for many Americans over sixty-five, social security is the main, or even the only, source of income. This is true in part because the other major piece of federal legislation dealing with pensions, the Employee Retirement Income Security Act (ERISA), goes a long way toward protecting an employee's accrued pension benefits; but remember from Chapter 17 that it does not require an employer to establish a pension plan for its employees in the first place. And many workers still do not have significant pension plans where they work. Social security is often the only safety net when it is no longer possible to continue working.

Monthly benefits are payable to a retired insured worker from age sixty-two onward. Under some circumstances a spouse and children may also be eligible. For a person to be "fully insured" by social security, he or she must accrue a minimum of forty quarters (that is, ten years) of contributions. These contributions are shared by the employer and the employee, who has no choice but to have the tax taken directly out of each paycheck, until a maximum amount of taxable income (for social security purposes only) has been earned in a calendar year. Once that income level has been reached (approximately $50,000 in 1990), no more social security tax is deducted until the start of the next calendar year.

Being fully insured does not guarantee any particular benefit amount; it only means that some benefit is guaranteed. The average monthly benefit for an individual in 1990 was $566. The average for a married couple, both of whom were fully insured upon retirement, was $966. These averages take into account aged retirees who started receiving benefits years ago, as well as new pensioners, who could receive as much as $975 per month. The average also includes those who retired before sixty-five, which is the age when the maximum available benefit is granted. Those choosing to retire at sixty-two got only 80 percent of the maximum benefit, whereas applicants aged sixty-three and sixty-four were awarded 87 percent and 93 percent of the maximum, respectively.

Benefits can wind up being reduced in yet another way. A retiree applying for social security may be fully insured and age sixty-five, and thus will receive the maximum monthly benefit. But if this retiree continues earning income in excess of $25,000 per year, both this income and the social security benefits themselves will be subject to taxation.

Medicare.   In addition to basic benefits, retired Americans receive a form of health insurance under the social security scheme. Medicare benefits cover a portion of the costs of hospitalization and the medical expenses of insured workers and their spouses age sixty-five and older, as well as younger disabled workers in some circumstances. This insurance is divided into two parts, designated by the federal bureaucracy as A and B.

Part A is hospital insurance for in-patient hospital care, in-patient skilled nursing care, and hospice care. Part B is supplementary medical insurance, which helps defray the costs of doctors' services and other medical expenses not covered by part A.

A worker who applies for social security benefits and is receiving them at age sixty-five is automatically covered under part A. The same is true for someone who has been receiving social security disability benefits (discussed briefly below) for at least twenty-four months. Part B is not entirely free. One-fourth of the premium is paid by the beneficiary, whereas the other three-fourths are covered by the federal government's general revenues. In 1990 the basic monthly premium was $28.60, deducted directly from the insured's social security check.

Disability.   Under the social security scheme, a worker is considered disabled when a severe physical or mental impairment prevents that person from working for a year or more or is expected to result in the victim's death. The disability does not have to be work-related (as is the case for workers' compensation disability, discussed later in this chapter), but it must be total. In other words, if the injured or ailing worker can do some sort of work, though not necessarily the same work as before the disability, then this program probably will not apply. Under some circumstances a disabled worker's spouse, children, or surviving family members are also eligible for benefits.

Just as older workers must accrue forty quarters of credit in order to be fully insured, so too, younger people must earn some social security credits to qualify for disability benefits. For instance, before reaching age twenty-four, a member of the work force would need six credits (six quarters of work subject to social security tax) during the preceding three years. A worker who becomes disabled between ages thirty-one and forty-two must be credited with twenty quarters on his or her account.

After twenty-four months of disability, Medicare is made available, just as in the case of retired Americans. Additionally, the social security system provides services intended to get disabled people back into the work force and off the benefit rolls. Usually, vocational rehabilitation services are provided by state rehabilitation agencies in cooperation with the federal Social Security Administration. The law provides that disability benefits can continue during a nine-month return-to-work trial period. Generally, if the trial is successful, benefits will be continued during a three-month "adjustment period" and then stopped.

Related to this aspect of the social security scheme is supplemental security income, a program financed by general funds from the U.S. Treasury (not social security taxes), and aimed at aiding legally blind, elderly, or partially disabled workers. The law also allows blind workers to earn as much as $780 per month without being considered as holding substantial gainful employment rendering them ineligible for one or both of these federal subsidies.

As noted earlier, although the principal purpose of social security is to provide retirement benefits, the disability coverage is also extremely significant in this country's welfare scheme since most states and many employers fail to provide disability insurance for non-job-related illnesses and injuries. A minority of states (New Jersey, for example) do tax payrolls and paychecks to provide disability coverage. And many companies offer short- and/or long-term disability insurance. But many more do not. Nor does social security comprehensively fill this gap: it applies only after a year of total disability. As such it is less than a complete solution, but it is a safety net that can help keep some individuals off state welfare.

Black Lung Disease.   The federal government has a long history of providing special protection to workers who were in industries that were critical to the economic development of the nation, and who also engaged in particularly dangerous occupations. For instance, as discussed earlier in the chapter, during the first part of this century Congress passed the Federal Employers Liability Act to make it easier for railroad workers to recover against their employers for injuries sustained on and around the trains, where thousands were maimed and injured each year.

Coal miners, too, have often commanded the concern of Congress. This was true in part because a concerted work stoppage by the nation's United Mine Workers could cause the country to freeze in the dark during the long, hard winters of the nineteenth and early twentieth centuries, and shut down factories and railroads at a time when oil was not yet a significant energy source. Furthermore, like railroaders, miners exposed themselves to unusual hazards in order to provide homes, factories, and power plants with fuel. When oil did flood upon the scene after World War II, the mining towns of Pennsylvania and elsewhere suffered particular economic hardship, whereas the bulk of the nation enjoyed the economic benefits of cheap fuel. Particularly hard hit were older miners suffering from silicosis, pneumoconiosis, and other forms of lung disease, known collectively as black lung. Irreparably injured by coal and rock dust before the days when OSHA required wearing respiratory gear, these miners were often too ill to relocate and undergo vocational rehabilitation. Yet they were not yet so disabled by this disease that they qualified under the normal disability tests of social security. Therefore, in 1969 a special program was created by Congress for these workers.

The Federal Coal Mine Health and Safety Act of that year established the black lung benefits program. Some of the benefits under the program are administered by the Social Security Administration and some by the Department of Labor.

Other Federal and State Benefit Programs

Social security programs focus upon working Americans who for one of several reasons—old age, disability, black lung disease—can no longer do their jobs but who have paid into the fund and therefore are entitled to draw benefits from it. But what about people who have never earned such eligibility? As noted earlier, a worker's dependents and survivors can sometimes collect benefits based on that worker's social security account. For others, a variety of other federal and state programs are available.

Food Stamps.   Food stamps are provided by the Department of Agriculture to low-income households to supplement their purchasing ability. Not only the unemployed but also lower-paid workers may qualify for those "coupons," which can be used in most grocery stores and supermarkets, provided they are "spent" on necessities and not on such items as cigarettes and alcoholic beverages. The program is administered by state public assistance (welfare) offices.

Medicaid.   Medicaid is a health service vendor payment program that makes direct payments to providers on behalf of eligible individuals. The program is run by the states with federal financial participation. People who qualify for two other benefit programs, supplemental security income and aid for dependent children, also automatically qualify for Medicaid. In addition to these so-called categorically needy, states are also allowed to elect to cover aged, blind, and disabled individuals, and many states do.

Railroad Retirement.   This program was set up under its own act and with its own board. It is coordinated with the social security system. Payments by employees and covered railroads are at a higher level than social security. The quid pro quo is that retirement can be taken as early as age sixty, and disability benefits are more readily available as well.

Who Must Participate in Social Security?

Most American workers and their employers must pay into the social security system. This has led some religious groups, such as the Amish in Pennsylvania, to object on the basis of their unique religious and social organization. The Amish lead a simple life, mostly on farms and in small communities in southeastern Pennsylvania and other agricultural regions around the country. These insular, close-knit communities care for their own. They neither believe in, nor wish to accept social welfare assistance from outside their sect. Thus they challenged the government's constitutional power to prescribe contributions from them.

UNITED STATES v. LEE

455 U.S. 252 (U.S. Supreme Court, 1982)

BURGER, C. J.

... Appellee, a member of the Old Order Amish, is a farmer and carpenter. From 1970 to 1977, appellee employed several other Amish to work on his farm and in his carpentry shop. He failed to file the quarterly social security tax returns required of employers, withhold social security tax from his employees, or pay the employer's share of social security taxes.

In 1978, the Internal Revenue Service assessed appellee in excess of $27,000 for unpaid employment taxes; he paid $91—the amount owed for the first quarter of 1973—and then sued in the United States District Court for the Western District of Pennsylvania for a refund, claiming that imposition of the social security taxes violated his First Amendment free exercise rights and those of his Amish employees.

The District Court held the statutes requiring appellee to pay social security and unemployment insurance taxes unconstitutional as applied. 497 F. Supp. 180 (1980). The court noted that the Amish believe it sinful not to provide for their own elderly and needy and therefore are religiously opposed to the national social security system. The court also accepted appellee's contention that the Amish religion not only prohibits the acceptance of social security benefits, but also bars all contributions by Amish to the social security system. The District Court observed that in light of their beliefs, Congress has accommodated self-

employed Amish and self-employed members of other religious groups with similar beliefs by providing exemptions from social security taxes. The court's holding was based on both the exemption statute for the self-employed and the First Amendment; appellee and others "who fall within the carefully circumscribed definition provided in 1402(g) are relieved from paying the employer's share of [social security taxes] as it is an unconstitutional infringement upon the free exercise of their religion."

Direct appeal from the judgment of the District Court was taken pursuant to 28 U.S.C. Section 1252.

The exemption provided by Section 1402(g) is available only to self-employed individuals and does not apply to employers or employees. Consequently, appellee and his employees are not within the express provisions of Section 1402(g). Thus any exemption from payment of the employer's share of social security taxes must come from a constitutionally required exemption.

The preliminary inquiry in determining the existence of a constitutionally required exemption is whether the payment of social security taxes and the receipt of benefits interferes with the free exercise rights of the Amish. The Amish believe that there is a religiously based obligation to provide for their fellow members the kind of assistance contemplated by the social security system. Although the Government does not challenge the sincerity of this belief, the Government does contend that payment of social security taxes will not threaten the integrity of the Amish religious belief or observance. It is not within "the judicial function and judicial competence," however, to determine whether appellee or the Government has the proper interpretation of the Amish faith; "[c]ourts are not arbiters of scriptural interpretation." We therefore accept appellee's contention that both payment and receipt of social security benefits are forbidden by the Amish faith. Because the payment of the taxes or receipt of benefits violates Amish religious beliefs, compulsory participation in the social security system interferes with their free exercise rights.

The conclusion that there is a conflict between the Amish faith and the obligations imposed by the social security system is only the beginning, however, and not the end of the inquiry. Not all burdens on religion are unconstitutional. The state may justify a limitation on religious liberty by showing that it is essential to accomplish an overriding governmental interest.

Because the social security system is nationwide, the governmental interest is apparent. The social security system in the United States serves the public interest by providing a comprehensive insurance system with a variety of benefits available to all participants, with costs shared by employers and employees. The social security system is by far the largest domestic governmental program in the United States today, distributing approximately $11 billion monthly to 36 million Americans. The design of the system requires support by mandatory contributions from covered employers and employees. This mandatory participation is indispensable to the fiscal vitality of the social security system. "[W]idespread individual voluntary coverage under social security . . . would undermine the soundness of the social security program." Moreover, a comprehensive national social security system providing for voluntary participation would be almost a contradiction in terms and difficult, if not impossible, to administer. Thus, the Government's interest in assuring mandatory and continuous participation in and contribution to the social security system is very high.

The remaining inquiry is whether accommodating the Amish belief will unduly interfere with fulfillment of the governmental interest. In *Braunfeld* v. *Brown,* (1961), this Court noted that "to make accommodation between the religious action and an exercise of state authority is a particularly delicate task . . . because resolution in favor of the State results in the choice to the individual of either abandoning his religious principle or facing . . . prosecution." The difficulty in attempting to accommodate religious beliefs in the area of taxation is that "we are a cosmopolitan nation made up of people of almost every conceivable religious preference." The Court has long recognized that balance must be struck between the values of the comprehensive social security system, which rests on a complex of actuarial factors, and the consequences of allowing religiously based exemptions. To maintain an organized society that guarantees religious freedom to a great variety of faiths requires that some religious practices yield to the common good. Religious beliefs can be accommodated, but there is a point at which accommodation would "radically restrict the operating latitude of the legislature." It would be difficult to accommodate the comprehensive social security system with myriad exceptions flowing from a wide variety of religious beliefs. The obligation to pay the social security tax initially is not fundamentally different from the obligation to pay income taxes; the difference—in theory at least—is that the social security tax revenues are segregated for use only in furtherance of the statutory program. There is no principled way, however, for purposes of this case, to distinguish between general taxes and those imposed under the Social Security Act. If, for example, a religious adherent believes war is a sin, and if a certain percentage of the federal budget can be identified as devoted to war-related activities, such individuals would have a similarly valid claim to be exempt from paying that percentage of the income tax. The tax system could not function if denominations were allowed to challenge the tax system because tax payments were spent in manner that violates their religious belief. Because the broad public interest in maintaining a sound tax system is of such a high order, religious belief in conflict with the payment of taxes affords no basis for resisting the tax.

Congress has accommodated, to the extent compatible with a comprehensive national program, the practices of those who believe it a violation of their faith to participate in the social security system. In Section 1402(g) Congress granted an exemption, on religious grounds, to self-employed Amish and others. Confining the Section 1402(g) exemption to the self-employed provided for a narrow category which was readily identifiable. Self-employed persons in a religious community having its own "welfare" system are distinguishable from the generality of wage earners employed by others.

Congress and the courts have been sensitive to the needs flowing from the Free Exercise Clause, but every person cannot be shielded from all the burdens incident to exercising every aspect of the right to practice religious beliefs. When followers of a particular sect enter into commercial activity as a matter of choice, the limits they accept on their own conduct as a matter of conscience and faith are not to be superimposed on the statutory schemes which are binding on others in that activity. Granting an exemption from social security taxes to an employer operates to impose the employer's religious faith on the employees.

Congress drew a line in Section 1402(g), exempting the self-employed Amish but not all persons working for an Amish employer. The tax imposed on employers to support the social security system must be uniformly applicable to all, except as Congress provides explicitly otherwise.

Accordingly, the judgment of the District Court is reversed, and the case is remanded for proceedings consistent with this opinion. **Reversed and remanded.**

Workers' Compensation: Limited Liability and Easy Recovery

Workers' compensation, as it has been instituted in virtually every state, is a statutory trade-off. As noted earlier in this chapter, the employer loses several highly successful defenses to the injured employee's claim—assumption of risk, contributory negligence, and the fellow-servant doctrine. In return, employers get immunity from suits by injured employees, with some limited exceptions. (Typically, the exceptions are failure to carry the requisite compensation insurance; intentional, as opposed to accidental, injuries to employees; and those rare circumstances in which the employer, a hospital for example, deals with, and harms, the employee in its capacity as a third-party provider of a service, and not as employer.)

For the worker, typical compensation schemes permit easy access to benefits, relatively simple adjudication of disputed claims, plus the possibility of an additional, perhaps more substantial recovery in a related third-party tort action against, say, the manufacturer of the machine that caused the work-related injury. Employers and insurance carriers often complain about fraudulent claims, usually involving hard-to-disprove back injuries. Perhaps the only possible response to claims of fraud is that any system conceived and run by human beings will be subject to some abuses. The concept of workers' compensation is eminently fair, and in practice it has spared millions of injured workers and their families untold hardship.

Eligibility for Benefits

To be eligible for workers' compensation benefits, an employee's injury must be work-related. This does not mean that an employee who is hurt in an off-the-job accident (such as an automobile accident while driving to a sports event on a Sunday afternoon) is necessarily without any benefits. If the company provides health insurance, this coverage will probably pay the hospital and doctor bills. Many firms have disability insurance, short term and/or long term, in their fringe benefit packages, ensuring some income flow while the injured worker recuperates. But workers' compensation is not a matter of employer choice, but of state law; it is often more generous in amount and/or duration than the employer's disability program (if the company carries one at all).

The issue of work-relatedness has given rise to some interesting litigation. For instance, if the auto accident described above occurred while the employee was commuting to or from the job, it would not be work-related, and therefore would not be covered by workers' compensation insurance. But if the employee were traveling directly from home to a business meeting at which he was delivering a project proposal, if she were making some deliveries for her employer on the way home, or if the accident occurred in the company parking lot, the employee may be covered by workers' compensation. Some states have held that accidents such as these are work-related.

Other cases have involved sports injuries sustained on the company's premises during lunch hour, injuries sustained going to or from the premises for lunch, and many other borderline circumstances. The next case briefly examines a slightly different set of circumstances, in which the employee's underlying physical condition clearly was not caused by any workplace activity, but in which the injury was deemed by the compensation referee to be work-related.

NORTHEASTERN HOSPITAL v. WORKMEN'S COMPENSATION APPEAL BOARD (TURIANO)

578 A.2d 83 (Commonwealth Court of Pennsylvania, 1990)

PALLADINO, J.

Northeastern Hospital (Employer) appeals from an order of the Workmen's Compensation Appeal Board (Board) which affirmed a referee's decision granting Margaret G. Turiano (Claimant) benefits. For the reasons that follow, we affirm.

Claimant filled a claim petition on November 5, 1986, alleging that her work caused her to take an early maternity leave. After completing a mandatory overtime shift which involved heavy lifting, Claimant claims that she sustained premature labor contractions resulting in preterm labor rendering her bedridden for the remainder of her pregnancy. Claimant is seeking compensation from the time she was bedridden until her scheduled maternity leave was to commence. A hearing was held, after which the referee made the following pertinent findings of fact:

> 10. The Referee finds the testimony of Claimant's treating physician, Dr. Hester M. Sonder, M.D., by reports dated July 3, 1986, and October 27, 1986, was competent, credible, convincing and with a reasonable degree of medical certainty when he (sic) opined that Claimant's premature labor was due to excessive standing and long working hours which caused her uterus to become irritable and caused preterm labor which therefore, caused her to take an early leave of absence from work.
>
> 11. The Referee finds the testimony by report of Valerie Bossard, M.D., to be competent, credible, convincing and with a reasonable degree of medical certainty when she opined that Claimant's hospitalization at Northeastern Hospital of Pennsylvania for (sic) June 1, 1986, to June 14, 1986, for preterm labor ruled out medical reasons other than lack of needed bed rest, which was prescribed after discharge.

> 12. The Referee does not find the testimony by report of Paul S. Copit, M.D., to be competent or convincing compared to the testimony of Dr. Sonder and Dr. Bossard.

The referee found that Claimant suffered a work-related injury and ordered compensation from June 6, 1986, to August 1, 1986. Employer appealed to the Board which, without taking additional evidence, affirmed.

On appeal to this court, Employer raises the following issues: (1) whether Claimant's preterm labor condition is a compensable injury; and (2) whether the referee improperly disregarded the medical testimony of Dr. Copit (Copit).

Employer initially argues that Claimant's medical condition did not arise in the course of her employment but was the result of, and was related to, Claimant's voluntary and conscious decision to become pregnant. Therefore, Claimant's medical condition is not an "injury" under Section 301(c)(1) of The Pennsylvania Workmen's Compensation Act, Act of June 2, 1915, which reads as follows:

> (1) The terms "injury" and "personal injury", as used in this act, shall be construed to mean an injury to an employee, regardless of his previous physical condition, arising in the course of his employment and related thereto. . . .

In workmen's compensation cases, the claimant has the burden of proving that an injury arose in the course of employment and was causally connected with the claimant's work. The referee is the ultimate fact-finder where the Board takes no additional evidence, and the findings will not be disturbed when they are supported by substantial, competent evidence. In cases requiring medical testimony, competent evidence means unequivocal testimony.

The referee accepted as credible and competent the testimony of Claimant that she felt and sustained premature labor contractions after working overtime, lifting patients, and going without regular rest breaks. In addition, Claimant offered the testimony of Dr. Hester M. Sonder (Sonder) and Dr. Valerie Bossard (Bossard), establishing that it was the conditions of Claimant's employment which caused the preterm labor. The referee accepted the testimony of Sonder and Bossard as competent and credible, and found that Claimant was injured in the course of her employment. After reviewing the record we conclude that Sonder's and Bossard's testimony was unequivocal and supports the referee's findings.

As to the second issue, Employer argues that the referee improperly disregarded the medical opinion of Copit who testified that nothing in current medical science supports the idea that standing or other vocational physical activity can cause preterm labor. The referee, as fact-finder, is free to accept or reject the testimony of any witness, including a medical witness, in whole or in part. Therefore, it was within the referee's discretion to reject Copit's testimony.

And now, July 23, 1990, the order of the Workmen's Compensation Appeal Board in the above-captioned matter is affirmed.

Workers' Compensation Procedures

If the fifty states were surveyed, not surprisingly at least minor differences would be discovered among all fifty with respect to the procedural aspects of workers' compensation claims (just as states will differ on exactly what constitutes a work-related injury). There are even fairly dramatic procedural differences between some states. Notably, the majority of jurisdictions use a system of compensation referees or Administrative Law Judges (ALJs) to adjudicate claims at the lowest level. But others (the minority) place disputed claims directly into the regular state court system. The discussion that follows will give a rough outline of the "typical" procedures most states follow.

A claim is usually initiated by the injured employee, who reports an accident to the employer (more specifically, to the employee's immediate supervisor, the human resources manager, or someone else designated to process such claims). The employer in turn submits a report of the alleged accident to its insurance carrier. After receiving the report, the carrier will usually require subsequent submission of amplifying information, such as doctor and hospital reports. If the carrier is satisfied with what it sees, it may grant the injured employee benefits. Benefits consist of medical bill payments plus payments in lieu of paychecks, usually at something like one-half to two-thirds of the workers' regular pay.

The carrier may decide that the injury was not work-related, or for some other reason should not be accepted as a valid claim. If so, it will notify the employee accordingly. This notice starts the clock running on a statute of limitations, often two or three years, during which time the employee must contest the denial within the context of the state workers' compensation system. This will probably involve retaining an attorney, since the procedures are simple compared to what occurs in a typical courtroom but are not so simple that claimants can effectively represent themselves. Attorney fees are limited by statute, usually to a maximum of around 20 percent of the claimant's nonmedical (i.e., salary substitution) benefits.

Hearings are held in front of a compensation referee or an ALJ. But these proceedings may be supplemented (and thereby abbreviated) with deposition testimony, particularly from medical experts, such as physicians, who are difficult and expensive to schedule for hearings. A deposition is a formal procedure, usually held in the doctor's office, during which the physician is placed under oath and questioned in turn by the two attorneys representing the claimant and the insurance carrier. If the doctor is the claimant's expert, the claimant's lawyer will conduct a direct examination, after which the carrier's legal counsel will cross-examine. If the physician represents the carrier, then its counsel will go first. Objections, such as to hearsay testimony, will be made on the record, which is transcribed by a court reporter, for later rulings by the referee. Sometimes these depositions are taken on videotape. Whether on tape or in transcript form, such depositions are later submitted to the referee for review and consideration along with the hearing testimony of the claimant, possibly the employer, other witnesses to the accident, and the like.

There is a second context in which such proceedings must take place. Suppose the carrier has agreed to honor the employee's compensation claim. Then, later on, the carrier or the employer contends that the worker is fully recovered and should return to work. The employee and his or her treating physician may disagree, with the result that the worker will refuse to sign off for a final benefit check that acknowledges recovery and readiness to return to work. In some jurisdictions the law allows the carrier to cut off benefits unilaterally, leaving the burden upon the employee to challenge that action, sometimes called a supersedeas. Pennsylvania was such a state until 1984, when a worker named Baksalary and some similarly situated plaintiffs obtained the help of a public service law firm in Philadelphia to challenge such perfunctory actions in federal court. Community Legal Service contended on behalf of Baksalary and friends that such supersedeas procedures were unconstitutional.

BAKSALARY v. STATE WORKMEN'S INSURANCE FUND

579 F. Supp. 218 (U.S.D.C., E.D., Pennsylvania, 1984)

POLLAK, D.J.

Plaintiffs initiated this action in 1976, challenging the constitutionality of certain provisions of the Pennsylvania Workmen's Compensation Act. In particular, plaintiffs allege that the "automatic supersedeas" provision of section 413 of the Act, permits employers and insurers to terminate worker's compensation benefits without according due process of law to those whose benefits are terminated, in violation of the Fourteenth Amendment. The automatic supersedeas terminates benefits without notice to the person receiving benefits. It requires only an employer's or insurer's petition reciting that the benefit recipient has returned to work at the same or higher pay or a petition accompanied by a physician's affidavit averring that the recipient has recovered. Plaintiffs make their due process claim in an ac-

tion under the Civil Rights Act of 1871, 42 U.S.C. Section 1983. . . .

This case involves a challenge to one of the methods by which an employer or insurer obligated to pay benefits under the Pennsylvania Workmen's Compensation Act can cease paying those benefits. Through a set of procedures not pertinent to this action, an individual covered by the Act and injured in the course of his employment can obtain the right to receive weekly benefits payments from his employer. The employer must insure against this obligation. This requirement may be satisfied in one of three ways: (1) the employer may retain a private insurance carrier licensed to provide worker's compensation insurance; (2) the employer may insure through the State Workmen's Insurance Fund, an insurance fund administered by the state; (3) the employer may self-insure. When an employer purchases insurance, the insurer assumes all of the employer's liabilities under the Act and, in effect, stands in the employer's shoes with respect to the employees receiving worker's compensation. Thus, in the ordinary case of an insured employer, the employer has little to do with a compensation matter once the insurer has begun to pay compensation benefits.

When a self-insured employer or an insurer believes that an injured employee who receives compensation benefits has resumed work or recovered his or her health, the employer or insurer will typically seek to terminate the employee's worker's compensation benefits. If the employee does not agree to a termination of his benefits, the employer or insurer files a petition to terminate or modify the compensation with the agency which administers the worker's compensation program, the Bureau of Worker's Compensation. A referee from the Bureau then holds hearings to determine whether grounds for termination or modification exist.

Section 413 of the Act, the subject of this lawsuit, deals with the right to compensation between the time an employer or insurer petitions for termination or modification and the time the referee makes a final determination. Section 413, in pertinent part, provides:

> The filing of a petition to terminate or modify a notice of compensation payable or a compensation agreement or award as provided in this section shall operate as a supersedeas, and shall suspend the payment of compensation fixed in the agreement or by the award, in whole or to such extent as the facts alleged in the petition would, if proved, require only when such petition alleges that the employee has returned to work at his prior or increased earnings or where the petition alleges that the employee has fully recovered and is accompanied by an affidavit of a physician on a form prescribed by the [Bureau of Worker's Compensation] to that effect which is based upon an examination made within fifteen days of the filing of the petition. In any other case, a petition to terminate or modify a compensation agreement or other payment arrangement or award as provided in this section shall not automatically operate as a supersedeas but may be designated as a request for a supersedeas, which may then be granted at the discretion of the referee hearing the case.

Thus, in two sorts of cases an employee receiving benefits can have his benefits terminated pending disposition of his employer's or his employer's insurer's petition to terminate or modify those benefits. The first sort of case is one where the petition alleges that the employee has returned to work at the same or higher wages. The second sort of case is one where the petition alleges that the employee has fully recovered from his disability and the petition is ac-

companied by a doctor's affidavit averring recovery based upon an examination of the employee within the previous fifteen days.

In either of the two automatic supersedeas situations, the filing of the petition suspends the employer's or insurer's obligation forthwith. Before the employer or insurer can successfully file the petition, however, clerical personnel of the Bureau promptly review the petition

> to determine whether [it has] been properly completed and [complies] in form with the requirements of the [Act] and the Bureau's own rules and regulations. If any deficiency as to form is found, the Bureau rejects the petition and returns it, with notice of the nature of any defect, for correction by the party.

This review is addressed to formal issues and involves no consideration of the merits of the petition.

The filing employer or insurer need not serve the employee with a copy of the petition either before or after filing. Instead, the Bureau sends the employee notice of the petition, after filing, at the time (usually no more than five days after receipt of the petition) that the Bureau assigns the matter to a referee.

The employee has no avenue to contest application of the automatic supersedeas other than his defense on the merits of the petition before the referee. Referees typically take one year or more to decide contested cases. Even if he ultimately has his benefits restored retroactively, an employee subject to an automatic supersedeas will find himself without worker's compensation benefits from the time that the Bureau of Worker's Compensation performs its clerical review of his employer's or insurer's petition until the time a referee decides the case. Plaintiffs contend that this constitutes a deprivation of that employee's property interest in his compensation benefits without according the employee due process of law.

We have permitted this action to proceed as both a plaintiffs' and defendants' class action. The plaintiff class includes those as to whom the automatic supersedeas provision has been or may be invoked. The defendant class includes all those who have invoked or may invoke the automatic supersedeas. . . .

This case now has four remaining individual plaintiffs who represent the class. Richard Baksalary injured his left achilles tendon while working for the Midvale-Heppenstall Company. Midvale-Heppenstall had insured with the Pennsylvania Manufacturers' Association Insurance Company ("PMAIC") which paid compensation benefits to Mr. Baksalary from December 27, 1973, until June 12, 1974. On the basis of a June 11 examination by one Dr. Cassidy, PMAIC filed a first petition for termination of Mr. Baksalary's compensation benefits on July 19, 1974, invoking the automatic supersedeas. On August 2, however, PMAIC again began to pay Mr. Baksalary's benefits. Then, on October 25, PMAIC again reversed its field, and stopped paying Mr. Baksalary. On November 22, PMAIC filed a second petition for termination alleging that Mr. Baksalary had recovered as of June 11. PMAIC attached an affidavit of Dr. Cassidy and again invoked the automatic supersedeas. Mr. Baksalary first received notice of the November 22 filing on December 4. Three years later, on December 1, 1977, a referee determined that PMAIC had been on sound ground in discontinuing the payment of benefits to Mr. Baksalary but that it still remained liable for any treatment costs related to Mr. Baksalary's injury, subject to a credit for benefit payments made after June 11, 1974.

Plaintiff William Jones suffered an injury while employed as a truck driver for the Tri-County Hauling Company. American Mutual Liability Insurance Company insured Tri-County against worker's compensation liability. Mr. Jones and American Mutual entered an agreement for payment of compensation benefits beginning on December 5, 1973. American Mutual stopped paying benefits on May 5, 1974, and filed a petition to terminate Mr. Jones' benefits on June 11. Based upon a physician's affidavit that an examination of May 29 showed Mr. Jones' recovery, American Mutual invoked the automatic supersedeas at the time of its June 11 petition. The Bureau of Worker's Compensation mailed notice of Mr. Jones' termination on June 16. Three years later, on August 11, 1977, a referee found that Mr. Jones had not recovered in May of 1974, and ordered American Mutual to pay retroactive benefits to Mr. Jones with interest at ten percent per annum.

Morris Tucker injured his back while packing meat for S. Lotman & Sons, Inc. Bituminous Casualty Corporation insured Lotman. Bituminous and Mr. Tucker agreed that Bituminous owed Mr. Tucker compensation payments beginning November 9, 1973. On July 17, 1974, Bituminous filed a petition to terminate Mr. Tucker's benefits and invoked the automatic supersedeas. Bituminous had not attached a physician's affidavit, but had typewritten on the petition that "J. David Hoffman, M.D. certifies that Morris T. Tucker was able to return to work on July 3, 1974." This apparently sufficed, because Bituminous paid nothing to Mr. Tucker until a referee issued a decision on August 21, 1975, in favor of Mr. Tucker. Bituminous appealed that decision, but the

parties settled on December 19, 1977. During the period of his termination, Mr. Tucker received income from welfare, Social Security Disability Insurance, and his wife's employment.

Charles Samuel had two experiences with the automatic supersedeas provision of Section 413. Samuel worked for the Pennsylvania Liquor Control Board when he hurt his back. The State Workmen's Insurance Fund ("SWIF") insured the Liquor Control Board. . . . "S.W.I.F. is a legislatively created and state-operated insurance carrier from which workers' compensation insurance policies may be purchased by employers to cover all risks of liability under the Act, including employers who have been rejected or cancelled by private insurance carriers."

SWIF began paying compensation to Mr. Samuel as of February 28, 1975. SWIF first terminated these payments on October 7, 1975, on the basis of an examination of Mr. Samuel by Dr. Williams. SWIF petitioned to terminate Mr. Samuel's compensation on October 17 and invoked the automatic supersedeas. The first notice that Mr. Samuel received of the petition was a copy mailed to him by the Bureau on November 7. A referee denied SWIF's petition and awarded retroactive compensation benefits with interest almost eleven months later, on September 20, 1976.

On June 27, 1977, SWIF again filed a petition to terminate Mr. Samuel's benefits. SWIF attached the affidavit of Dr. Stiffel, who had conducted an examination on June 21, and SWIF invoked the automatic supersedeas. A copy of this petition was mailed to Mr. Samuel on July 1. A referee denied SWIF's petition on January 5, 1978, and SWIF appealed. SWIF did not resume payments until the administrative appeal board remanded the case to the referee on April 10, 1978. The referee clarified his January 5, 1978, order on March 19, 1979, to award Mr. Samuel retroactive benefits and ten percent per annum interest.

A claim under Section 1983 alleging a violation of the due process clause of the Fourteenth Amendment requires proof of three elements. First, a Section 1983 claimant must show a deprivation of a constitutionally protected liberty or property interest. Second, the claimant must show that the deprivation was accomplished "under color of state law" and as a result of "state action"; these turn out to mean the same thing. Third, the claimant must show that the method by which the deprivation was effectuated involved a denial of due process—in this case, procedural due process. We proceed to consider each of these elements in turn.

Deprivation

As we discussed in the previous portion of this opinion, Section 413 permits an employer or insurer summarily to suspend worker's compensation payments to an injured employee formerly entitled to those benefits. The employee may protest this suspension and he may obtain a hearing before a referee. The referee may, of course, determine that the employee was no longer entitled to benefits at the time of the petition. However, the referee may find that the employee had a continuing disability or that he had not returned to work. This finding would dictate a decision that the employer or insurer should not have terminated the employee's benefits. In that case, the referee will award the payment of retroactive benefits.... Referees, though, typically take one year or more to decide a case.

We find that when an individual must forego the use of his compensation benefits for as long as one year, even if he receives reimbursement at the end of that period, that individual has undergone the deprivation of a constitutionally protected property interest. During the period of termination, he has lost significant income. He will find this income difficult to replace through borrowing in the market because he has no way of convincing a lender that a referee will eventually award benefits to him; most lenders are likely to assume otherwise. In a similar case involving termination of Social Security Disability Insurance benefits pending a final hearing, the Supreme Court stated that it "has been implicit in our prior decisions ... that the interest of an individual in continued receipt of these benefits is a statutorily created 'property' interest protected by the Fifth Amendment." We see no distinction for this purpose between the federal disability benefits at issue in *Mathews* and the state disability benefits at issue in this case.

State Action

[Discussion omitted.]

... we find that when SWIF acts, the state acts....

Although counsel for the Commonwealth seems to have drawn a distinction between SWIF acting as insurer for a public employer and SWIF acting as insurer for a private employer, our analysis in the preceding subsection leads to the conclusion that SWIF acts for the state whenever it acts. Accordingly, the force of that argument requires us to find that state action exists when SWIF invokes the automatic supersedeas provision of section 413 even when SWIF does so on behalf of a private employer.

We have found state action, then, whenever a public entity insures itself and whenever either a public or private employer uses SWIF to insure. In any of these cases, invocation of the automatic supersedeas by the self-insuring public employer or by the public insurer is "fairly attributable to the state" because the state itself invokes Section 413. We cannot base our conclusion on this ground, however, when a private insurer or employer uses Section 413....

We hold that invocation of Section 413's automatic supersedeas provision by a private insurer or by a private employer involves state action. The Supreme Court has "consistently held that a private party's joint participation with state officials in the seizure of disputed property is sufficient to characterize that party as a 'state actor' for purposes of the Fourteenth Amendment."

In order to invoke the automatic supersedeas, an insurer or employer must file a petition on a form provided by the state. A state agency, the Bureau of Worker's Compensation, must review the petition before the supersedeas may take effect. Although the Bureau does not review the petition's merits, it does review the petition for formal compliance with the Workmen's Compensation Act; the Bureau has a form for returning inadequate petitions. Unless the insurer or employer satisfies the Bureau of the petition's compliance with Section 413, the insurer or employer cannot terminate the employee's benefits. Further, the insurer/employer relies on the Bureau to notify the employee of the termination of benefits.

Section 413's automatic supersedeas procedure requires a filing with the Bureau of Worker's Compensation. This filing is sufficient to constitute "joint participation" and to subject private invocation of the automatic supersedeas to the due process clause.

Due Process

Having decided that benefits terminations under Section 413's automatic supersedeas provision must comply with the Fourteenth Amendment, we now consider whether Section 413 accords plaintiffs sufficient process to constitute due process. We agree with the Supreme Court of Iowa that *Mathews* v. *Eldridge*, 424 U.S. 319 (1976), makes the automatic supersedeas unconstitutional. See *Auxier* v. *Woodward State Hospital-School*, 266 N.W.2d 139 (Iowa 1978), *cert. denied*, 439 U.S. 930 (1979) (holding Iowa version of Section 413 unconstitutional).

In *Mathews*, the Supreme Court held that the Social Security Administration need not provide an evidentiary hearing before terminating an individual's Social Security Disability Insurance benefits. . . . The Court concluded in *Mathews* that disability insurance recipients threatened with a loss of benefits were accorded a sufficient pretermination process, albeit that process was not of a formal evidentiary nature, so that an evidentiary hearing could be postponed until after termination. . . .

The procedures sustained in *Mathews* were perceived by the Court as "provid[ing] the claimant with an effective process for asserting his claim prior to any administrative action. . . ." In marked contrast, Section 413 provides no notice whatsoever until *after* the termination of benefits pending a final hearing.

The foregoing discussion has led us to the conclusion that operation of the automatic supersedeas authorized by Section 413 of the Pennsylvania Workmen's Compensation Act involves conduct reasonably attributable to the state and that Section 413 does not accord worker's compensation recipients due process. Thus, plaintiffs have made out a violation of 42 U.S.C. Section 1983. Plaintiffs are entitled to entry of a judgment declaring the unconstitutionality of the automatic supersedeas provision of Section 413. . . .

Workers' Compensation Preemption by Federal Law

Although workers' compensation has been left primarily to the states to administer, the system does brush up against various federal schemes for compensating workers whom Congress now or at some time in the past considered requiring special protection. Railroad workers have long had recourse to the Federal Employers Liability Act (FELA); sailors come under the Jones Act (46 U.S.C. Section 688); and many other maritime workers ware covered by the Longshoremen's and Harbor Workers' Compensation Act (33 U.S.C. Section 901, *et seq*). U.S. government workers have their own Federal Employees Compensation Act (5 U.S.C. Section 1801). In all cases these acts supersede state workers' compensation laws.

The FELA has given rise to some difficult litigation. Suppose a railroad subsidiary is a trucking company that picks up and delivers goods to the railroad's freight yard, where the subsidiary's drivers are supervised by the railroad yardmaster. Does this make the railroad a joint employer of the driver? If so, can the driver (if injured at the yard) claim workers' compensation benefits against the trucking subsidiary, then turn around and sue the railroad for even more money, such as for pain and suffering, under the FELA? The answer to this question typically turns on the railroad's right to control the driver's activities, as well as the legal relationship between the two companies.

A similar problem can arise when a worker contends that although the employer's liability under state law is limited to paying workers' compensation, separate employer liability exists under a preemptive federal law. In the 1990 case of *Adams Fruit Co., Inc.* v. *Barrett* (494 U.S. 638, 58 U.S.L.W. 4367), the Supreme Court held that workers could bring suit for violations of specific federal legislation despite the fact that they had received benefits under the state workers' compensation law. The court held that the specific federal legislation superseded the exclusivity provisions of the state workers' compensation law.

Unemployment Compensation

Just as social security requires attaining a certain age and contributing over the years to an "account," and workers' compensation requires that the injury occur under working conditions, so eligibility for **unemployment compensation** requires that the "idleness" occur in a specific set of circumstances. Specifically, the employee must be out of work through no fault of his or her own and be available for suitable work, if and when it becomes available.

The concept of fault is an attenuated one; that is, only a high level of fault, termed **willful misconduct,** will serve to disqualify the out-of-work worker from these benefits. Incompetence is considered to be an unfortunate condition, not a basis for affixing guilt, under this branch of employment law. So although an at-will employee, or even one protected by a "good cause" provision in a labor contract, may properly be dismissed for poor performance, that alone will not disqualify him or her from receiving unemployment benefits.

As the concept of "work-related" is the focus of much litigation in the workers' compensation arena, so too is "willful misconduct" an issue of constant debate and redefinition in the unemployment compensation systems of our fifty states. For example, is absenteeism "misconduct?" If it is, when is it "willful"? The employee who is "excessively" (itself a tough term to define) absent or tardy may be lazy, or he or she may have children to get to day care and a bus to catch that is unreliable. In the latter instance, the employee can probably still be discharged, but most likely will not be denied benefits until she or he can find another job.

Even the conduct is clearly willful and wrong, this still may not be enough to disqualify the applicant for unemployment benefits. If, for instance, the misconduct is not readily discernible to the average worker, and the employer failed to promulgate a rule or give a warning for prior infractions, an unemployment referee may be most reluctant to deny benefits.

As with workers' compensation, unemployment compensation litigation usually starts with a terminated worker's application for benefits. Instead of an insurance carrier evaluating the claim, in the unemployment context it is usually evaluated in the first instance by an unemployment office or agency in the area where the worker resides. Regardless of whether the decision is favorable or unfavorable, an appeal is possible. The worker's motive for appealing an unfavorable decision is obvious. But why would an employer challenge the grant of benefits to someone it had let go? The answer is that unemployment benefits are paid for by a tax on the wages of the workers and an equal levy on the employer's total payroll. In most jurisdictions this tax is variable, rising and falling with the particular company's experience in drawing upon the state fund. Consequently, if undeserving discharges are permitted to receive benefits, the employer will experience a gradual increase in these payroll taxes.

The unemployment system is similar to workers' compensation in that challenged decisions go to a referee, and from there can usually be appealed into the state court system, potentially all the way up to a state's supreme court, which typically reviews a few selected cases of special significance each year. Following is a case decided by the mid-level appellate court for the state of Kansas, reviewing a case that had already been passed upon by the state's Employment Security Board of Review (the first step in that state's appellate procedure following the unemployment compensation referee's ruling) and the local trial court.

CITY OF WICHITA v. EMPLOYMENT SECURITY BOARD

13 Kan. App. 2d 729, 779 P.2d 41 (Court of Appeals of Kansas, 1989)

BRAZIL, J.

The City of Wichita (City) appeals a decision by the district court upholding an Employment Security Board of Review (Board) finding that Willie J. Kelly is entitled to unemployment benefits after his employment was terminated.

Kelly was employed by the City as a sewer maintenance worker. After several years of service, his employment was terminated because, according to the City, Kelly drank some beer while at work and had a history of absenteeism. Kelly was initially denied unemployment compensation pursuant to K.S.A. 1988 Supp. 44–706(b) because the examiner found he was discharged for misconduct connected with work. Kelly appealed to the referee.

Kelly and his supervisor Gerald Blain appeared at a hearing before the referee. Blain testified that the City personnel rules prohibit possession or use of alcohol during working hours. Blain testified that he received information that employees had been drinking on the job site. When Blain questioned Kelly about the incident, Kelly admitted sharing a cup of beer with a co-worker while on the job. Blain requested Kelly to sign a statement admitting he had been drinking at work. Kelly testified that he signed the statement because Blain assured him the statement would not be used against him.

The referee concluded that Kelly had one sip of beer from a cup of a co-worker and that the incident could not be considered use of alcohol under the City's rule which states that "[e]mployees may be dismissed for any legitimate business reason, including . . . use, sale, possession or being under the influence of alcohol or drugs during working hours." The referee held Kelly is eligible for benefits.

The City appealed to the Board. The Board adopted the findings of fact and opinion of the referee and affirmed the referee's decision. The City appealed to the district court, which found that the record contains substantial evidence to support the findings of the Board and affirmed the Board's decision.

The scope of review of an administrative proceeding is well known:

> A district court may not, on appeal, substitute its judgment for that of an administrative tribunal, but it restricted to considering whether, as a matter of law, (1) the tribunal acted fraudulently, arbitrarily or capriciously, (2) the administrative order is substantially supported by evidence, and (3) the tribunal's action was within the scope of its authority.
>
> In reviewing a district court's judgment, as above, this court will, in the first instance, for the purpose of determining whether the district court observed the requirements and restrictions placed upon it, make the same review of the administrative tribunal's action as does the district court. . . .

K.S.A. 77-621(c)(4) additionally provides that the court shall grant relief if it determines that the agency erroneously interpreted or applied the law. In *Barnes v. Employment Security Board of Review,* 210 Kan. 664 (1972), the court stated:

> Judicial review of evidentiary matters before the Employment Security Board of Review is made in the light most favorable to the findings of the administrative tribunal.
>
> The findings of the Employment Security Board of Review as to the facts, if supported by evidence and in the absence of fraud, are conclusive and may not be set aside by the district court.
>
> While a court sitting as a Board of Review might have reached a different conclusion on conflicting evidence, or in determining a preponderance of the evidence, it is, nevertheless, bound to uphold the findings of the board if there is relevant evidence before the board to support its findings.

Finally, the claimant is entitled to a liberal interpretation of the law. . . . This Court must determine whether the findings of fact of the Board are supported by substantial competent evidence and whether, in view of the facts, the Board properly interpreted the law.

The board found that Kelly had one sip of beer and that his one sip of beer did not constitute a violation of the employer's rules and, consequently, did not constitute misconduct as defined by K.S.A. 1988 Supp. 44–706(b). The Board concluded Kelly was eligible for benefits. The City argues that the Board improperly interpreted the law in arriving at this decision.

K.S.A. 1988 Supp. 44–706(b) governs the receipt of unemployment benefits. The statute provides that an individual is disqualified from receiving benefits until after the claimant has earned three times the weekly benefit amount in new employment if the individual was discharged for misconduct connected with the work. The statute states:

> (1) For the purposes of this subsection (b), "misconduct" is defined as a violation of a duty or obligation reasonably owed the employer as a condition of employment. In order to sustain a finding that such a duty or obligation has been violated, the facts must show: (A) Willful and intentional action which is substantially adverse to the employer's interests, or (B) carelessness or negligence of such degree or recurrence as to show wrongful intent or evil design. . . .
>
> (2) An individual shall not be disqualified under this subsection (b) if the individual is discharged under the following circumstances: . . .
>
> (B) the individual was making a good-faith effort to do the assigned work but was discharged due to:
>
> (i) inefficiency,
>
> (ii) unsatisfactory performance due to inability, incapacity or lack of training or experience,
>
> (iii) isolated instances of ordinary negligence or inadvertence,
>
> (iv) good-faith errors in judgment or discretion, or
>
> (v) unsatisfactory work or conduct due to circumstances beyond the individual's control.

Substantial evidence exists to support the Board's finding that Kelly had one sip of beer. Kelly testified that he had one sip of beer from someone else's cup. The City argued Kelly drank more beer but did not submit any evidence to substantiate the claim. Accordingly, we conclude that Kelly had one sip of beer and limit our review not to whether Kelly's action constituted a violation of his employer's rules but whether it constituted misconduct under K.S.A. 1988 Supp. 44–706(b), thus disqualifying him from unemployment compensation.

The question of whether a violation of an employer's rule constitutes misconduct has not been decided in Kansas.

Several other states have dealt with this issue. . . . The analysis of the other state courts focuses on whether the employee's action constitutes "misconduct," not whether the employer's rule has been violated.

. . . Here, the City relies on *Washington* v. *Un. Comp. Bd. of Rev.,* 105 Pa. Commw. 215, 523 A.2d 1196 (1987), in which the claimant was discharged for failure to report to duty and possession of intoxicating liquors in violation of the employer's rules. In *Washington,* the court found substantial evidence existed to uphold the Unemployment Compensation Board of Review decision to deny the claimant benefits because he was discharged for willful misconduct.

In this case, the Board awarded Kelly benefits. The district court upheld the decision of the Board and found that having one sip of beer does not constitute misconduct as defined in K.S.A. 1988 Supp. 44–706(b). The facts of this case indicate that Kelly's action was not substantially adverse to the City's interests and did not amount to negligence of such degree as to show wrongful intent or evil design. The facts of this case may more properly be viewed as an isolated instance of ordinary negligence. Substantial evidence exists to support the Board's finding that Kelly is entitled to unemployment compensation.

The City argues that the district court and the Board unreasonably ignored the weight of the evidence. This argument is unsupported by the record.

A review of the hearing transcript indicates that the City was allowed to present evidence pertaining to Kelly's discharge including testimony about his attendance problems and hearsay that Kelly used a city vehicle to purchase beer and gin from a liquor store. The City was given ample opportunity to present its evidence before the referee regarding Kelly's termination.

The City is asking this court to improperly reweigh the evidence presented at the agency hearing, something this court must refrain from doing. The decision of the Board is supported by substantial competent evidence and must accordingly be upheld. **Affirmed.**

Voluntary Quitting

Under normal conditions, an employee cannot quit his job and then apply for unemployment benefits. In other words, when a worker is discontented, she is expected to stick with her current job until she finds another—not quit and collect benefits pending reemployment.

However, in some compelling circumstances the law will allow an employee to leave the employment. In such cases the quit is considered involuntary, because it amounts to a constructive discharge from the job. Some such cases have involved extreme instances of sexual or racial harassment by the employee's immediate supervisor, to the extent that the boards and courts held that no worker should be required to submit to such abuse or risk denial of unemployment compensation. Others have concerned an employee's extreme allergic reaction to substances in the workplace. In all such cases the employee must remain available for alternative jobs that the state employment agency might direct him or her to apply for. (In some instances, such as when an allergy is so severe and general that the employee cannot work at all, workers' compensation might be the more appropriate remedy.)

Two controversial topics today are smoking in the workplace and employer drug testing. As with any significant employment issues, they will infiltrate the unemployment arena and contribute to the evolution of the law, as in the fields of wrongful discharge and job discrimination. The following California case concerned whether an employee who quit his job because of high sensitivity to tobacco smoke could claim unemployment benefits while he looked for a smoke-free workplace to resume employment.

McCROCKLIN v. EMPLOYMENT DEVELOPMENT DEPT. (BUTLER SERVICE GROUP, INC.)

156 Cal. App. 3d 1067 (California Court of Appeals, Third District, 1984)

GILBERT, J.

Robert Earl McCrocklin appeals from a judgment denying his petition for a writ of mandate. The sole issue is whether McCrocklin left his employment "voluntarily without good cause" under Unemployment Insurance Code section 1256. We conclude that he did leave for good cause, and therefore we reverse the judgment.

McCrocklin asserts that his departure was justified because his employer should not have forced him to work in "an inadequately ventilated noisy space reeking of tobacco smoke." The Employment Development Department (EDD), an administrative law judge, the California Unemployment Insurance Appeals Board (CUIAB) and the trial court each disagreed with McCrocklin's assessment of his work situation, thereby snuffing out his claim for unemployment benefits.

Facts

McCrocklin was employed as an engineering writer on an intermittent contract basis by Butler Service Group, Incorporated (Butler) over a period of four years. At the time he

quit his job at Butler, he had been writing a project engineering manual for the company. He worked in a room containing numerous partially enclosed cubicles. McCrocklin's cubicle measured five by six feet and had plywood walls and a glass top. Three of the nine people assigned to work in McCrocklin's area smoked pipes, cigarettes or cigars. The tobacco smoke and noise produced by his coworkers entered the space in McCrocklin's cubicle.

McCrocklin tried unsuccessfully to alleviate the smoke problem in his cubicle by the use of two fans which, McCrocklin testified, only served to put him "in the crossfire of a hurricane." The problem was further aggravated because the area where McCrocklin's cubicle was located was enclosed and unventilated. In addition, the doors to this area were locked at all times due to the confidential nature of the work.

McCrocklin aired his complaints about the ventilation and noise to the management within a week or two after beginning his job. He was promised that the working conditions would soon be ameliorated by the installation of floor to ceiling partitions, an air circulation system, and doors on the cubicles to muffle the sound of other employees' talking and laughing. Despite this promise, the situation remained unchanged. The company denied McCrocklin's request to do his work at home. If this didn't cause smoldering resentment, his having to work on weekends and nights because of the smoke did.

McCrocklin testified that he is not allergic to smoke, although he does find it unpleasant and offensive. He also testified that he occasionally smokes a pipe at home, and that he has smoked cigars in the past. Nonetheless, McCrocklin objected to the carcinogenic effect of breathing smoke produced by other people in an enclosed space. McCrocklin expressed concern that the cigarette smoke would affect his health and that he would be "another guinea pig." He also noted that smoke from certain brands of cigarettes makes his eyes water and his throat raw, and that one of his coworkers used such a brand.

McCrocklin's application for unemployment benefits was denied by the Employment Development Department. The EDD decided that he had quit his job without good cause because there was no showing that the conditions at his workplace resulted in an undue hardship or threat to McCrocklin's health or welfare. He then appealed this determination to an administrative law judge, and a hearing on the matter was conducted which culminated in an affirmation of the EDD's decision. McCrocklin's appeal to the Unemployment Insurance Appeals Board was similarly unsuccessful. Finally, McCrocklin's petition for a writ of mandate pursuant to Code of Civil Procedure section 1094.5 was denied by the court below. Hoping to make a phoenix rise from the ashes of his claim for unemployment benefits, McCrocklin has appealed to this court.

Discussion

The statute controlling McCrocklin's claim for unemployment benefits is section 1256 of the Unemployment Insurance Code, which reads in pertinent part that "[a]n individual is disqualified for unemployment compensation benefits if the director finds that he or she left his or her most recent work voluntarily without good cause. . . ." We must determine whether the administrative agency charged with administering the employment benefits program made a legally supportable interpretation of the legislative meaning in the phrase "'good cause." . . . "Good cause" means a legally sufficient ground or reason for a certain action.

> In general "good cause," as used in an unemployment compensation statute, means such a cause as justifies an employee's voluntarily leaving the ranks of the employed and joining the ranks of the unemployed; the quitting must be for such a cause as would reasonably motivate in a similar situation the average able-bodied and qualified worker to give up his or her employment with its certain wage rewards in order

to enter the ranks of the compensated unemployed." . . . "It has been held that the Legislature intended by the phrase 'good cause' to include some causes which are personal and that it need not necessarily arise out of or be attributable to the employment itself.

The decision of the administrative law judge in this case, which was subsequently adopted by the Unemployment Insurance Board, denied McCrocklin's claim because the absence of competent medical evidence purportedly constrained a finding that he did not have good cause for voluntarily leaving work. Horace Greeley's definition of a cigar as "a fire at one end and a fool at the other" may find support in studies which discuss the deleterious effects of "secondhand" tobacco smoke. There is even legal authority recognizing that exposure to cigarette smoke is a health hazard to nonsmokers. At the hearing, however, McCrocklin failed to present anything other than several hearsay newspaper articles on the subject of smoking. The articles stressed the deleterious effect of cigarette smoke on nonsmokers, and referred to the Surgeon General's Report. While no competent medical evidence was introduced to support a finding that secondhand smoke constituted a health hazard to McCrocklin, the articles nevertheless provided a basis for his reasonable belief that smoke was a health hazard.

By focusing solely on the lack of "competent medical evidence," the EDD, the administrative law judge, the Unemployment Insurance Board and the trial court failed to consider whether McCrocklin was motivated to leave his employment by a reasonable, good faith and honest fear of harm to his health.

In *Rabago* v. *Unemployment Ins. Appeals Bd., supra,* 84 Cal.App.3d 200, the appellant was motivated to quit his job largely because of his fear of potential lead poisoning. The court reviewed several precedent decisions rendered by the Unemployment Insurance Appeals Board and by courts in other jurisdictions. These included one case in which a court found good cause when an employee quit his job because he feared physical injury from doing heavy lifting on the job, although there was no evidence that the employee was advised to quit by a physician. . . . In another case, the CUIAB found that an employee's fear of contracting pneumonia from working in an unheated building constituted good cause for leaving because a reasonable person genuinely desiring to be employed would have done the same to avoid endangering her health. . . .

The *Rabago* court concluded, as we conclude here, that

> . . . a reasonable, good faith and honest fear of harm to one's health or safety from the work environment and conditions of

employment falls within the ambit of good cause as defined by the California cases and comports with the purpose of the Unemployment Insurance Act [citation omitted] and the rule that the courts must liberally construe the act so as to effect all of the relief the Legislature intended to grant [citation omitted]. Further, this result harmonizes with the principle that 'good cause' can include some causes that are personal. . . .

Nonsmokers who must work with smokers should not construe our holding as an invitation to quit their jobs in anticipation that they will automatically receive unemployment benefits. The unrefuted particular facts in this case reflect that McCrocklin's fears were reasonable because of the following: (1) He was working in an enclosed, poorly ventilated room; (2) several of his coworkers in his area smoked; (3) the tobacco smoke could not be excluded from his cubicle; (4) he had a good-faith belief that the smoke had a carcinogenic effect on his health; and (5) breathing smoke from certain brands of cigarettes made his eyes water and his throat raw.

The California Supreme Court recently approved the *Rabago* "reasonable, good faith and honest fear of harm to one's health or safety" test in *Amador* v. *Unemployment Ins. Appeals Board* (1984) 35 Cal.3d 671 [200 Cal.Rptr. 298, 677 P.2d 224]. The court found that the approach contained in *Rabago* "accords with the basic purpose of the code 'to insure a diligent worker against the vicissitudes of enforced unemployment not voluntarily created without good cause.'" (Id., at p. 683) The court concluded that "[i]t can no longer be maintained that a 'diligent' worker is one who blindly follows his or her employer's orders regardless of the potential consequences. The health hazards of the modern work environment—to employees, consumers, and the population at large—are serious and widespread, and the record of employers in controlling those hazards does not inspire such confidence that a reasonable worker can be expected to trust invariably his or her employer's judgment." (Ibid.)

Where the facts in a case are undisputed and opposing inferences may not reasonably be drawn from those facts, the issue of whether or not there is "good cause" is an issue of law. . . . Therefore, in our review of a ruling on a writ of mandate where the probative facts of the case which are not in dispute clearly require a conclusion different from that reached by the trial court, we may disregard its conclusion. . . .

McCrocklin voluntarily left his job because he found working in a smoke-filled environment intolerable, not only because he suffered tangible physical side-effects, but also because he reasonably feared for his health and safety. Our holding is not affected by the trial judge's failure to find that a health hazard existed. "[I]f one reason which constitutes good cause is a substantial motivating factor in causing the employee to quit, the employee is entitled to benefits notwithstanding the existence of one or more other reasons for quitting which would not qualify as good cause." . . . We conclude that McCrocklin reasonably and in good faith feared harm to his health from working in an unventilated room filled with tobacco smoke. Accordingly we hold that he is entitled to unemployment benefits.

McCrocklin could not have anticipated that he would have to breathe tobacco smoke when performing his employment. Working in an enclosed, unventilated smoke-filled room is not an occupational hazard commonly associated with the writing of engineering manuals. Thus we cannot say McCrocklin assumed the risk of breathing smoke-laden air when he accepted employment with Butler Service Group.

The judgment is reversed, with directions to the trial court to issue a writ of mandate ordering the Employment Development Department to pay to McCrocklin the unemployment benefits withheld.

The next case, decided by the Wyoming Supreme Court in 1990, deals with one of the most hotly debated employment topics: drug testing. The federal Drug-Free Workplace Act and the so-called War on Drugs have focused nationwide attention on what is perceived as a major employment problem. Many companies have enlisted in this "war" with great enthusiasm, not necessarily taking into account the impact their drug-testing programs may have on their employees. In the following case, the worker was accused by a co-worker of possibly using marijuana on the job. He was given the choice of submitting to a drug test or quitting his employment.

In analyzing the case, the court seems to be confusing the issues of willful misconduct and voluntary quitting. Nonetheless, its extensive analysis is highly instructive in this sensitive area of the law.

EMPLOYMENT SECURITY COMMISSION OF WYOMING v. WESTERN GAS PROCESSORS, LTD.

786 P.2d 866 (Supreme Court of Wyoming, 1990)

URBIGKIT, J.

This is a misconduct, drug test, employment termination case. Appellant Employment Security Commission of Wyoming (ESC) appeals from a district court reversal of its unemployment compensation benefit determination favoring the employee.

ESC contends the determination was properly based upon findings of fact supported by substantial evidence and upon conclusions of law which are in accordance with law. ESC granted unemployment insurance benefits to employee Donald B. Wilson (Wilson) pursuant to W.S. @ 27-3-311(c) after determining his resignation from employer Western Gas Processors, Ltd. (Western), appellee, was forced and equivalent to discharge. Wilson was allowed unemployment benefits because his discharge was not for misconduct connected with his work because he "did not commit misconduct . . . by simply refusing to submit to an unreasonable demand by his employer." By holding ESC's determinations factually sustainable and justified within proper conclusions of law, we reverse the district court reversal of the agency award.

Facts

Wilson was employed at Western late in 1985 to be a "Field Operations Maintenance" worker (handyman mechanic). When he was hired, there was no corporate policy indicating employees would be subject to any blood or urine tests for illegal drugs or legalized abused intoxicants to ensure the safety of the workplace; nor was there a policy which indicated employees would be subject to such testing when there was a particularized suspicion of improper use. Soon after Wilson began work, his supervisor, Mike Keil, recognized Wilson had difficulty with mathematics and computer usage. In December of 1987, however, Keil noted in a performance report that "Don has a high sense of safety awareness and knowledge. His behavior towards safety and teammates is an asset to Newcastle Plant and the company. He

has a good attitude towards the company and is trying to increase his job knowledge."

On June 17, 1988, the employee began a four-week vacation and was due back on July 15. Two weeks before his return, co-employee Donald Schaff went to Keil to allege Wilson smoked marijuana on the job. This fellow worker reported he had occasionally smelled the scent of marijuana on Wilson, that the co-worker "would get very uptight when he was faced with a problem or a subject that concerned him" and his eyes were sometimes reddish. Schaff was the only fellow employee to make this allegation. The supervisor was aware the relation between these two workers was not friendly. Based on the unilateral and uncorroborated allegation of marijuana use, Keil then notified his supervisor of the Schaff report.

On the first morning back to work following his vacation, Wilson was directed to take a company truck from Newcastle to Gillette (seventy-six miles distance) to pick up a fire extinguisher, get the truck's radio fixed, and meet with Keil at the company's Gillette office at one o'clock. On arriving at the office, the employee was handed a surprise (Dear John) letter signed by his supervisor. The pertinent parts of the letter read:

> I am concerned about the state of your health and require you, as a condition of employment, to submit to a general physical examination, at Company expense, including an eye exam and blood and urine tests, which will involve among other things tests for illegal drugs.
>
> Your physical examination is scheduled for Friday, July 15, 1988, at 2:00 P.M. with Dr. Naramore in Gillette.
>
> Your safety, the safety of others and the safe operation of the gas processing equipment are primary concerns.
>
> According to Company Policy if the blood or urine test results are positive for illegal drugs, you will be discharged immediately. Until the tests results are known (three to five days) you will be on leave with pay and you are not to enter plant property for any reason.
>
> If your blood/urine tests are negative and no other physical impairment is found, you must take immediate action to improve your performance and maintain an improved performance level. We can work together to meet this goal.

With this totally unexpected written notice, Wilson was given three options. He could submit to the physical and return to work in several days if the tests were negative; he could refuse the physical and Western would terminate him on the spot; or he could quit. Wilson did quit and asked if he should call his wife to drive to Gillette to pick him up to which the response was given that he could drive the company truck back the seventy-six miles to Newcastle and finish out the day at work.

On July 25, the ex-employee filed a claim for unemployment benefits. The initial determination by ESC allowed Wilson unemployment benefits and held Western's account chargeable with its proportionate share of benefits which might be paid. The employer protested but the determination was upheld in the redetermination by the Chief of Benefits to ESC who stated "[a]vailable facts indicate that the claimant [Wilson] was to be replaced regardless of the test results." The employer appealed to an appeals examiner. That hearing examiner reversed the redetermination after deciding the employee should be disqualified from benefits because he resigned without good cause connected with his work. That decision was reversed by ESC by determination that Wilson did not commit misconduct when he refused to submit to the drug test because the demand was unreasonable under the circumstance. The appeal by Western to the district court claimed ESC's findings of fact were arbitrary, capricious, and an abuse of discretion because they were not supported by substantial evidence and the conclusions of law were wrong. The district court accepted the appeal contention and ESC now appeals. . . .

Analysis

The issue before this court is narrow. Our review is limited to determining whether ESC's determinations that Wilson was constructively discharged and to allow him unemployment benefits under W.S. 27-3-311(c) because he "did not commit misconduct . . . by simply refusing to submit to an unreasonable demand by his employer" are based on findings of fact supported by substantial evidence and are in accordance with law. Our understanding of ESC's determinations and our standard of review creates a three-fold inquiry. Could ESC determine that Wilson's resignation was equivalent to discharge? Could ESC determine that the demand was unreasonable? Could ESC determine, if the demand was unreasonable, that it was not misconduct connected with work to refuse such a demand?

ESC concluded that the employer's demand to the employee that he yield up a sample of his urine to their corporate physician for analysis or resign on the spot was unreasonable and the resulting resignation constituted a constructive discharge. We find there was sufficient evidence in the record to support the findings of fact necessary to an appropriate conclusion of law that Wilson had been constructively discharged. "Where an employee resigns due to the reasonable belief that his discharge is imminent, his resignation cannot properly be termed 'voluntary'. . . ." Western was quite matter of fact when it admitted Wilson was told his discharge was imminent if he refused to submit immediately to a urine test. We hold that ESC could determine that the resignation was equivalent to discharge.

We also hold ESC could conclude the demand was unreasonable. ESC found the demand unreasonable for three reasons. The request was unreasonable as an "invasion of his [Wilson's] privacy and a violation of other guaranteed constitutional rights." Second, there was no established policy at the time Wilson was hired or later adopted which required, as a condition of the employment, any submission to either random testing for intoxicants or such testing based upon a reasonable and particularized suspicion. Third, the uncorroborated allegations of a hostile co-employee did not form the basis of a reasonable suspicion had such a policy been in place.

> [W]here the conduct or activities for which the claimant is discharged occurred off the working premises and outside the course and scope of employment, the employer must, in order to show that the conduct is work-connected, point to some breach of a rule or regulation that has a reasonable relation to the conduct of the employer's business.

. . . . The rule for on-duty conduct is stated:

> In *Macey* v. *Department of Empl. Sec.,* [110 Wash.2d. 308, 752 P.2d 372 (1988)], we formulated the following three-part test to establish disqualifying misconduct: (1) the employer's rule must be reasonable under the circumstances; (2) the conduct of the employee must be connected with the work; and (3) the conduct of the employee must in fact violate the rule.

The Macey test, however, applies only to on-duty misconduct. . . .

In this case, we lack both an established rule and determinable history for any immediate drug testing practice. The absence of an established employer rule makes application of either the on-duty or off-duty standard difficult here. . . .

While we regard highly the federal constitutional guarantees to privacy as well as the right to privacy in Wyoming, it is not necessary to address the constitutional rights relied upon by ESC to affirm its determinations. Where constitutional difficulties can be avoided legitimately, this court will do so. . . .

We affirm ESC's determination that the demand was unreasonable on more narrow grounds. The demand was unreasonable because there was no corporate policy either existent at the time Wilson was hired or later regularly adopted and adequately circulated which established the submission to either random testing for intoxicants or such testing based upon a reasonable and particularized suspicion to be a general condition for company employment. Nor, had such a policy been in place, are the uncorroborated allegations from a hostile co-employee the basis from which to make a reasonable demand because of a particularized suspicion. The standard of conduct required by the employer must be reasonable before refusal to abide by that standard becomes misconduct.

This conclusion implicitly rejects Western's claim that their handbook inclusion of "[s]erious misconduct of any kind, including being under the influence of alcohol or illegal drugs, fighting . . . , etc. confers implied consent to investigate through drug testing the existence of such drugs in the body" as Western argued. ESC may have eyed the fact that Wilson had signed the Acknowledgment of Receipt of the WGP Company Employee Handbook which stated "[t]he contents of this handbook do not constitute an ex-

press or implied contract of employment." Such a disclaimer works for both parties, not just Western. ESC could rightly disregard Western's argument of implied consent. ESC concluded a unilateral change in the condition of employment was unreasonable and that the uncorroborated allegations from a co-employee with a demonstrated record of hostility toward Wilson cannot form the basis of a reasonable demand. We agree. "[T]here was no condition in the application for employment or the contract of employment to" provide urine samples. This was apparently the first occurrence and there was not even a general company practice. . . .

Accepting ESC's determination that the demand was unreasonable, we review ESC's legal determination that employee misconduct did not occur with refusal of the demand. In *Safety Medical Services, Inc.*, 724 P.2d at 473 and *Roberts* v. *Employment Security Commission of Wyoming*, 745 P.2d at 1355, 1358 (Wyo. 1987), this court addressed employee misconduct. Essential to employee misconduct is a "disregard of . . . standards of behavior which the employer has the right to expect of his employee. . . ." . . . Because Western had no right to expect Wilson to submit to the test, related obviously to his return from vacation, newly created to be a condition of continued employment, there was, under these circumstances, no misconduct at work by test refusal. . . .

QUESTIONS

1. Explain the policy consideration that led the U.S. government to retain federal control of the social security system, while permitting the states to assume primary responsibility for their workers' compensation and unemployment compensation programs.

2. Should government require employers to provide disability insurance for their employees, which would be available whether or not the disability is work-related? If your answer is yes, should this be done at the federal or the state level? Should it be done by means of payroll taxes (like unemployment compensation) or insurance (such as workers' compensation)?

3. Should drug abusers be treated (for purposes of social security, workers' compensation, and unemployment benefits) as wrongdoers who are rendered ineligible or ill persons who should receive such benefits? Is your answer different for any of the three social welfare benefits? If so, what are the underlying policy considerations that cause you to vary your response?

4. What exactly is meant by a work-related injury?

5. What constitutes willful misconduct? How does the worker's mental state figure into the definition?

CASE PROBLEMS

1. The plaintiff was fifty-three years old and employed by the defendant-company for more than twenty-six years when he was fired. Because of the abruptness of the job termination, plus the difficulty he foresaw in finding suitable alternative employment at his age, plaintiff contended that he had suffered emotional distress. Claiming that he was wrongfully discharged, he sued, seeking not only damages for alleged breach of his employment agreement, but additional compensation for his tort (emotional distress) claim.

   The company raised several defenses, including an argument that plaintiff's emotional distress (if proven) was a job-related injury. Therefore, it was covered by the applicable state workers' compensation law, which was the plaintiff's exclusive remedy.

   What arguments can you make supporting the company's position? What counterarguments can the plaintiff's lawyer make? How do you think the court should come out on this issue? See *Mosely* v. *Metropolitan Life Insurance Co.,* 4 BNA IER Cases 1744 (N.D. Cal. 1991), 1991 U.S. Dist. Lexis 11643.

2. The defendant airline was party to a collective bargaining agreement with a union representing its flight attendants. One of the terms of this labor contract required the company to pay workers' compensation to injured attendants flying "overwater" routes in accord with the federal Longshoremen's and Harbor Workers' Compensation Act, the California workers' compensation law, or the Illinois counterpart—"whichever is greater."

   Plaintiff sued under the Racketeer Influenced and Corrupt Organization Act (RICO), charging the airline and several insurance companies with systematically underpaying benefits to her and other flight attendants. The court found that some defendants "all but concede" the underpayments. Yet they defended against the claim on jurisdictional grounds.

   What jurisdictional arguments do you think the defendants made? How should the court rule on these arguments? If the court accepts the defendants' jurisdictional arguments and dismisses the case, is the plaintiff left with a remedy? See *Hubbard* v. *United Airlines,* 741 F.Supp. 195; aff'd by 927 F.2d 1094 (9th Cir. 1991).

3. The plaintiff was employed as a designer by an engineering company that did contract work for the Philadelphia Electric Company at its nuclear power plants. At the time the engineering firm took on this contract, it asked all its employees, as a condition to unescorted access to any "nuke," to sign a form that stated, "I understand that if I refuse to consent to (random drug testing), or if I am not evaluated satisfactorily, that I will be denied access to PECO's premises and precluded from doing subsequent PECO-related work." The plaintiff testified that he refused to sign the form on the ground that, as a designer, he neither had nor required unescorted access to any of the client's nuclear facilities. He continued to work on the PECO contract until he was requested, and refused, to submit to a random drug test. He was then fired.

   Should the Pennsylvania Unemployment Compensation Board grant the plaintiff benefits? Or was he guilty of willful misconduct? See *Moore* v. *Unemployment Compensation Board of Review,* 134 Pa.Cmwlth. 274, 578 A.2d 606 (1990).

4. The employer had two plants, one in Sioux Falls, the other in Sioux City. Employees at both plants were represented by the United Food and Commercial Workers Union. When striking workers from the Sioux City facility set up a picket line at the Sioux Falls plant, the workers there honored the line, in essence engaging in a sympathy strike. During the strike, permanent replacements were hired at the Sioux Falls plant. Once the picket line was pulled, the sympathy strikers offered to return to work unconditionally. However, none were rehired until some two months later.

   Were the Sioux Falls sympathy strikers eligible for unemployment compensation benefits while they were refusing to cross the picket line? Does your answer change if their sympathy strike violated a "no-strike" clause in their collective bargaining agreement with the company?

   Were they eligible for benefits after the picket line was pulled? Does your answer depend upon whether or not they offered to return to work unconditionally?

   How about the striking employees from the Sioux City plant—were they entitled to benefits while on strike? What if the stoppage were a lockout instead of a strike? See *John Morrell & Co.* v. *South Dakota Dept. of Labor,* 460 NW2d 141 (S.D. Supr.Ct. 1990).

5. This problem involves the interaction of two state laws and one important federal law. Hawaii had enacted a plant closing law that, among other things, stated in job losses related to plant closures or relocations, unemployment compensation claimants could collect four weekly wage supplements. Each such supplement would equal the difference between the claimant's average weekly wage and the weekly unemployment benefit from the state compensation fund. This supplement was to come out of the employer's pocket.

When its former employees sued for the supplemental benefit, one Hawaiian company defended the action with the argument that the federal ERISA preempted that portion of the state plant closing act.

Applying what you learned about ERISA from Chapter 17, can you formulate a legal argument the company could use in pursuing this defense? What objection could the employees come back with? How do you think the court came out on the preemption issue? See *Akau* v. *Tel-A-Com Hawaii, Inc.,* U.S. Dist. Lexis 4647; 12 E.B.C. 1378 (Hawaii, 1990).

6. Plaintiffs were employees of a private drug rehabilitation organization. Both were members of the Native American Church. They were fired from their jobs after their employer learned that they had ingested peyote, a hallucinogen used for sacramental purposes in a church ceremony. Subsequent to their job terminations, they were denied unemployment benefits by the Oregon Department of Human Resources, which found that they had been fired for work-related misconduct. They challenged the denial and their case worked its way up to the Supreme Court.

On what legal theories do you think the plaintiffs challenged the department's decision? Should it matter to the case's outcome whether or not possession of peyote is illegal under Oregon state law? How do you think the Supreme Court came out on this case? See *Department of Human Resources of Oregon* v. *Smith,* 494 U.S. 872 (1990).

7. The plaintiff was mentally and functionally incapacitated in an auto accident. Some six months later her husband was appointed her guardian. But it was not until ten years later that he applied on his wife's behalf for disability insurance benefits under the Social Security Act. The act provides, at 42 U.S.C. Section 423(b), that

An individual who would have been entitled to a disability insurance benefit for any month had he filed application therefor before the end of such month shall be entitled to such benefit for such month if such application is filed before the end of the 12th month immediately succeeding such month.

Applying this provision literally to plaintiff's application, to how many months or years of retroactive benefits is the plaintiff entitled? Are there any equitable arguments for deviating from the literal reading of 42 U.S.C. Section 423(b)? Can you think of any broad policy consideration that should be taken into account in deciding the plaintiff's entitlement to retroactive benefits? See *Yeiter* v. *Secretary of Health & Human Services,* 818 F.2d 8 (6th Cir. 1987).

8. In the majority of the fifty states, out-of-work applicants for unemployment compensation typically submit their applications to local unemployment offices, where they are often interviewed personally before a decision on eligibility is rendered. Those who are held to be ineligible are then entitled to pursue an appeal at a hearing held before a referee. Ohio is among the minority of states that do not provide such face-to-face appeals. An unsuccessful unemployment compensation applicant, contending he represented a class, challenged Ohio's system in federal court, arguing that Ohio's procedures offended the federal Constitution.

On what portion(s) of the Constitution could the plaintiff base his challenge to Ohio's unemployment compensation procedures? Did the federal court have jurisdiction to hear this case? If yes, how should the court rule on the substantive issue? See *Kelly* v. *Lopeman,* 680 F. Supp. 1101 (S.D. Ohio 1987).

9. The Social Security Act, at 42 U.S.C. Section 402(x)(1) (Supp. II 1985), terminates disability benefits of imprisoned convicts,

. . . for any month during which such individual is confined in jail, prison, or other penal institution or correctional facility, pursuant to his conviction of an offense which constituted a felony under applicable law, unless such individual is actively and satisfactorily participating in a rehabilitation program which has been specifically approved for such individual by a court of law and, as determined by the Secretary, is expected to result in such individual being able to engage in substantial gainful activity upon release and within a reasonable time.

Can you make an argument that this provision of the act is unconstitutional? Is your argument based on the same or a different portion of the Constitution as is your answer in case problem 8? Is there a jurisdictional problem for the federal court in considering your argument? If so, is it the same or a different jurisdictional problem as the one you may have identified in case problem 8? See *Andujar* v. *Bowen,* 802 F.2d 404 (11th Cir. 1986).

10. Under the relevant provisions of the Social Security Act, a worker receiving old-age or disability benefits can also obtain Child Insurance Benefits for any dependent children. But Congress has carved out an exception with respect to any children who are adopted *after* the worker starts receiving benefits.

What policy considerations do you think were behind congressional passage of this provision? Is it constitutional? If not, who should have standing to challenge it? See *Lindley for Lindley* v. *Sullivan,* 889 F.2d 124 (7th Cir. 1989).

Appendix A

Text of the National Labor Relations Act

49 Stat. 449–57 (1935), as amended by 61 Stat. 136–52 (1947), 65 Stat. 601 (1951), 72 Stat. 945 (1958), 73 Stat. 525–42 (1959), 84 Stat. 930 (1970), 88 Stat. 395–97 (1974), 88 Stat. 1972 (1975), 94 Stat. 347 (1980), 94 Stat. 3452 (1980); 29 U.S.C. Section 169 (Suppl. 1981)

Findings and Policies

Section 1. The denial by some employers of the right of employees to organize and the refusal by some employers to accept the procedure of collective bargaining lead to strikes and other forms of industrial strife or unrest, which have the intent or the necessary effect of burdening or obstructing commerce by (a) impairing the efficiency, safety, or operation of the instrumentalities of commerce; (b) occurring in the current of commerce; (c) materially affecting, restraining, or controlling the flow of raw materials or manufactured or processed goods from or into the channels of commerce, or the prices of such materials or goods in commerce; or (d) causing diminution of employment and wages in such volume as substantially to impair or disrupt the market for goods flowing from or into the channels of commerce.

The inequality of bargaining power between employees who do not possess full freedom of association or actual liberty of contract, and employers who are organized in the corporate or other forms of ownership association substantially burdens and affects the flow of commerce, and tends to aggravate recurrent business depressions by depressing wage rates and the purchasing power of wage earners in industry and by preventing the stabilization of competitive wage rates and working conditions within and between industries.

Experience has proved that protection by law of the right of employees to organize and bargain collectively safeguards commerce from injury, impairment, or interruption, and promotes the flow of commerce by removing certain recognized sources of industrial strife and unrest, by encouraging practices fundamental to the friendly adjustment of industrial disputes arising out of differences as to wages, hours, or other working conditions, and by restoring equality of bargaining power between employers and employees.

Experience has further demonstrated that certain practices by some labor organizations, their officers, and members have the intent or the necessary effect of burdening or obstructing commerce by preventing the free flow of goods in such commerce through strikes and other forms of industrial unrest or through concerted activities which impair the interest of the public in the free flow of such commerce. The elimination of such practices is a necessary condition to the assurance of the rights herein guaranteed.

It is hereby declared to be the policy of the United States to eliminate the causes of certain substantial obstructions to the free flow of commerce and to mitigate and eliminate these obstructions when they have occurred by encouraging the practice and procedure of collective bargaining and by protecting the exercise by workers of full freedom of association, self-organization, and designation of representatives of their own choosing, for the purpose of negotiating the terms and conditions of their employment or other mutual aid or protection.

Definitions

Sec. 2. When used in this Act—

(1) The term "person" includes one or more individuals, labor organizations, partnerships, associations, corporations, legal representatives, trustees, trustees in cases under Title II of the United States Code or receivers.

(2) The term "employer" includes any person acting as an agent of an employer, directly or indirectly, but shall not include the United States or any wholly owned Government corporation, or any Federal Reserve Bank, or any State or political subdivision thereof, or any person subject to the Railway Labor Act, as amended from time to time, or any labor organization (other than when acting as an employer), or anyone acting in the capacity of officer or agent of such labor organization.

(3) The term "employee" shall include any employee, and shall not be limited to the employees of a particular employer, unless the Act explicitly states otherwise, and shall include any individual whose work has ceased as a consequence of, or in connection with, any current labor dispute or because of any unfair labor practice, and who has not obtained any other regular and substantially equivalent employment, but shall not include any individual employed as an agricultural laborer, or in the domestic service of any family or person at his home, or any individual employed by his parent or spouse, or any individual having the status of an independent contractor, or any individual employed as a supervisor, or any individual employed by an employer subject to the Railway Labor Act, as amended from time to time, or by any other person who is not an employer as herein defined.

(4) The term "representatives" includes any individual or labor organization.

(5) The term "labor organization" means any organization of any kind, or any agency or employee representation committee or plan, in which employees participate and which exists for the purpose, in whole or in part, of dealing with employers conserning grievances, labor disputes, wages, rates of pay, hours of employment, or conditions of work.

(6) The term "commerce" means trade, traffic, commerce, transportation, or communication among the several States, or between the District of Columbia or any Territory of the United States and any State or other Territory, or between any foreign country and any State, Territory, or the District of Columbia, or within the District of Columbia or any Territory, or between points in the same State but through any other State or any Territory or the District of Columbia or any foreign country.

(7) The term "affecting commerce" means in commerce, or burdening or obstructing commerce or the free flow of commerce, or having led or tending to lead to a labor dispute burdening or obstructing commerce or the free flow of commerce.

(8) The term "unfair labor practice" means any unfair labor practice listed in section 8.

(9) The term "labor dispute" includes any controversy concerning terms, tenure or conditions of employment, or concerning the association or representation of persons in negotiating, fixing, maintaining, changing, or seeking to arrange terms or conditions of employment, regardless of whether the disputants stand in the proximate relation of employer and employee.

(10) The term "National Labor Relations Board" means the National Labor Relations Board provided for in section 3 of this Act.

(11) The term "supervisor" means any individual having authority, in the interest of the employer, to hire, transfer, suspend, lay off, recall, promote, discharge, assign, reward, or discipline other employees, or responsibly to direct them, or to adjust their grievances, or effectively to recommend such action, if in connection with the foregoing the exercise of such authority is not of a merely routine or clerical nature, but requires the use of independent judgment.

(12) The term "professional employee" means—

(a) any employee engaged in work (i) predominantly intellectual and varied in character as opposed to routine mental, manual, mechanical, or physical work; (ii) involving the consistent exercise of discretion and judgment in its performance; (iii) of such a character that the output produced or the result accomplished cannot be standardized in relation to a given period of time; (iv) requiring knowledge of an advanced type in a field of science or learning customarily acquired by a prolonged course of specialized intellectual instruction and study in an institution of higher learning or a hospital, as distinguished from a general academic education or from an

apprenticeship or from training in the performance of routine mental, manual, or physical processes; or

(b) any employee, who (i) has completed the
courses of specialized intellectual instruction and
study described in clause (iv) or paragraph (a),
and (ii) is performing related work under the supervision of a professional person to qualify himself to become a professional employee as defined in paragraph (a).

(13) In determining whether any person is acting as an
"agent" of another person so as to make such other
person responsible for his acts, the question of
whether the specific acts performed were actually authorized or subsequently ratified shall not be
controlling.

(14) The term "health care institution" shall include any
hospital, convalescent hospital, health maintenance
organization, health clinic, nursing home, extended
care facility, or other institution devoted to the care
of sick, infirm, or aged person.

National Labor Relations Board

Sec. 3.

(a) The National Labor Relations Board (hereinafter
called the "Board") created by this Act prior to its
amendment by the Labor Management Relations Act,
1947, is hereby continued as an agency of the United
States, except that the Board shall consist of five instead of three members, appointed by the President
by and with the advice and consent of the Senate. Of
the two additional members so provided for, one
shall be appointed for a term of five years and the
other for a term of two years. Their successors, and
the successors of the other members, shall be appointed for terms of five years each, excepting that
any individual chosen to fill a vacancy shall be appointed only for the unexpired term of the member
whom he shall succeed. The President shall designate
one member to serve as Chairman of the Board. Any
member of the Board may be removed by the President, upon notice and hearing, for neglect of duty or
malfeasance in office, but for no other cause.

(b) The Board is authorized to delegate to any group of
three or more members any or all the powers which
it may itself exercise. The Board is also authorized to
delegate to its regional directors its power under sec-

tion 9 to determine the unit appropriate for the purpose of collective bargaining, to investigate and provide for hearings, and determine whether a question
of representation exists, and to direct an election or
take a secret ballot under subsection (c) or (e) of
section 9 and certify the results thereof, except that
upon the filing of a request therefor with the Board
by any interested person, the Board may review any
action of a regional director delegated to him under
this paragraph, but such a review shall not, unless
specifically ordered by the Board, operate as a stay of
any action taken by the regional director. A vacancy
in the Board shall not impair the right of the remaining members to exercise all of the powers of the
Board, and three members of the Board shall, at all
times, constitute a quorum of the Board, except that
two members shall constitute a quorum of any group
designated pursuant to the first sentence hereof. The
Board shall have an official seal which shall be judicially noted.

(c) The Board shall at the close of each fiscal year make a
report in writing to Congress and to the President
stating in detail the cases it has heard, the decisions it
has rendered, and an account of all moneys it has
disbursed.

(d) There shall be a General Counsel of the Board who
shall be appointed by the President, by and with the
advice and consent of the Senate, for a term of four
years. The General Counsel of the Board shall exercise general supervision over all attorneys employed
by the Board (other than trial examiners and legal assistants to Board members) and over the officers and
employees in the regional offices. He shall have final
authority, on behalf of the Board, in respect to the investigation of charges and issuance of complaints
under section 10, and in respect of the prosecution
of such complaints before the Board, and shall have
such other duties as the Board may prescribe or as
may be provided by law. In case of a vacancy in the
office of the General Counsel the President is authorized to designate the officer or employee who shall
act as General Counsel during such vacancy, but no
person or persons so designated shall so act (1) for
more than forty days when the Congress is in session
unless a nomination to fill such vacancy shall have
been submitted to the Senate, or (2) after the adjournment *sine die* of the session of the Senate in
which such nomination was submitted.

Sec. 4.

(a) Each member of the Board and the General Counsel of the Board shall receive a salary of $12,000 a year, shall be eligible for reappointment, and shall not engage in any other business, vocation, or employment. The Board shall appoint an executive secretary, and such attorneys, examiners, and regional directors, and such other employees as it may from time to time find necessary for the proper performance of its duties. The Board may not employ any attorneys for the purpose of reviewing transcripts of hearings or preparing drafts of opinions except that any attorney employed for assignment as a legal assistant to any Board member may for such Board member review such transcripts and prepare such drafts. No trial examiner's report shall be reviewed, either before or after its publication, by any person other than a member of the Board or his legal assistant, and no trial examiner shall advise or consult with the Board with respect to exceptions taken to his findings, rulings, or recommendations. The Board may establish or utilize such regional, local, or other agencies, and utilize such voluntary and uncompensated services, as may from time to time be needed. Attorneys appointed under this section may, at the direction of the Board, appear for and represent the Board in any case in court. Nothing in this Act shall be construed to authorize the Board to appoint individuals for the purpose of conciliation or mediation, or for economic analysis.

(b) All of the expenses of the Board, including all necessary traveling and subsistence expenses outside the District of Columbia incurred by the members or employees of the Board under its orders, shall be allowed and paid on the presentation of itemized vouchers therefor approved by the Board or by any individual it designates for that purpose.

Sec. 5. The principal office of the Board shall be in the District of Columbia, but it may meet and exercise any or all of its powers at any other place. The Board may, by one or more of its members or by such agents or agencies as it may designate, prosecute any inquiry necessary to its functions in any part of the United States. A member who participates in such an inquiry shall not be disqualified from subsequently participating in a decision of the Board in the same case.

Sec. 6. The Board shall have authority from time to time to make, amend, and rescind, in the manner prescribed by the Administrative Procedure Act, such rules and regulations as may be necessary to carry out the provisions of this Act.

Rights of Employees

Sec. 7. Employees shall have the right to self-organization, to form, join, or assist labor organizations, to bargain collectively through representatives of their own choosing, and to engage in other concerted activities for the purpose of collective bargaining or other mutual aid or protection, and shall also have the right to refrain from any or all such activities except to the extent that such right may be affected by an agreement requiring membership in a labor organization as a condition of employment as authorized in section 8(a)(3).

Sec. 8.

(a) It shall be an unfair labor practice for an employer—,

    (1) to interfere with, restrain, or coerce employees in the exercise of the rights guaranteed in section 7;

    (2) to dominate or interfere with the formation or administration of any labor organization or contribute financial or other support to it: *Provided,* That subject to rules and regulations made and published by the Board pursuant to section 6, an employer shall not be prohibited from permitting employees to confer with him during working hours without loss of time or pay.

    (3) by discrimination in regard to hire or tenure of employment or any term or condition of employment to encourage or discourage membership in any labor organization: *Provided,* That nothing in this Act, or in any other statute of the United States, shall preclude an employer from making an agreement with a labor organization (not established, maintained, or assisted by any action defined in section 8(a) of this Act as an unfair labor practice) to require as a condition of employment membership therein on or after the thirtieth day following the beginning of such employment or the effective date of such agreement, whichever is the later, (i) if such labor organization is the representative of the employees as provided in section 9(a), in the appropriate collective-bartaining unit covered by such agreement when made, and (ii) unless following an election held as provided in section 9(3) within one year preceding the effective date of such

agreement, the Board shall have certified that at least a majority of the employees eligible to vote in such election have voted to rescind the authority of such labor organization to make such an agreement: *Provided further,* That no employer shall justify any discrimination against any employee for nonmembership in a labor organization (A) if he has reasonable grounds for believing that such membership was not available to the employee on the same terms and conditions generally applicable to other members, or (B) if he has reasonable grounds for believing that membership was denied or terminated for reasons other than the failure of the employee to tender the periodic dues and the initiation fees uniformly required as a condition of acquiring or retaining membership;

(4) to discharge or otherwise discriminate against an employee because he has filed charges or given testimony under this Act;

(5) to refuse to bargain collectively with the representatives of his employees, subject to the provisions of section 9(a).

(b) It shall be an unfair labor practice for a labor organization or its agents—

(1) to restrain or coerce (A) employees in the exercise of the rights guaranteed in section 7: *Provided,* That this paragraph shall not impair the right of a labor organization to prescribe its own rules with respect to the acquisition or retention of membership therein; or (B) an employer in the selection of his representatives for the purpose of collective bargaining or the adjustment of grievances;

(2) to cause or attempt to cause an employer to discriminate against an employee in violation of subsection (a)(3) or to discriminate against an employee with respect to whom membership in such organization has been denied or terminated on some ground other than his failure to tender the periodic dues and the initiation fees uniformly required as a condition of acquiring or retaining membership;

(3) to refuse to bargain collectively with an employer, provided it is the representative of his employees subject to the provisions of section 9(a);

(4) (i) to engage in, or to induce or encourage any individual employed by any person en-

gaged in commerce or in an industry affecting commerce to engage in, a strike or a refusal in the course of his employment to use, manufacture, process, transport, or otherwise handle or work on any goods, articles, materials, or commodities or to perform any services; or (ii) to threaten, coerce, or restrain any person engaged in commerce or in an industry affecting commerce, where in either case an object thereof is:

(A) forcing or requiring any employer or self-employed person to join any labor or employer organization or to enter into any agreement which is prohibited by section 8(e);

(B) forcing or requiring any person to cease using, selling, handling, transporting, or otherwise dealing in the products of any other producer, processor, or manufacturer, or to cease doing business with any other person, or forcing or requiring any other employer to recognize or bargain with a labor organization as the representative of his employees unless such labor organization has been certified as the representative of such employees under the provisions of section 9: *Provided,* That nothing contained in this clause (B) shall be construed to make unlawful, where not otherwise unlawful, any primary strike or primary picketing;

(C) forcing or requiring any employer to recognize or bargain with a particular labor organization as the representative of his employees if another labor organization has been certified as the representative of such employees under the provisions of section 9;

(D) forcing or requiring any employer to assign particular work to employees in a particular labor organization or in a particular trade, craft, or class rather than to employees in another labor organization or in another trade, craft, or class, unless such employer is failing to conform to an order or certification of the Board determining the bargaining representative for employees performing such work:

Provided, That nothing contained in this subsection (b) shall be construed to make unlawful a refusal by any person to enter upon the premises of any employer (other than his own employer), if the employees of such employer are engaged in a strike ratified or approved by a representative of such employees whom such employer is required to recognize under this Act: *Provided further,* That for the purposes of this paragraph (4) only, nothing contained in such paragraph shall be construed to prohibit publicity, other than picketing, for the purpose of truthfully advising the public, including consumers and members of a labor organization, that a product or products are produced by an employer with whom the labor organization has a primary dispute and are distributed by another employer, as long as such publicity does not have an effect of inducing any individual employed by any person other than the primary employer in the course of his employment to refuse to pick up, deliver, or transport any goods, or not to perform any services, at the establishment of the employer engaged in such distribution;

(5) to require of employees covered by an agreement authorized under subsection (a)(3) the payment, as a condition precedent to becoming a member of such organization, of a fee in an amount which the Board finds excessive or discriminatory under all the circumstances. In making such a finding, the Board shall consider, among other relevant factors, the practices and customs of labor organizations in the particular industry, and the wages currently paid to the employees affected;

(6) to cause or attempt to cause an employer to pay or deliver or agree to pay or deliver any money or other thing of value, in the nature of an exaction for services which are not performed or not to be performed; and

(7) to picket or cause to be picketed, or threaten to picket or cause to be picketed, any employer where an object thereof is forcing or requiring an employer to recognize or bargain with a labor organization as the representative of his employees, or forcing or requiring the employees of an employer to accept or select such labor organization as their collective bargaining representative, unless such labor organization is currently certified as the representative of such employees:

(A) where the employer has lawfully recognized in accordance with this Act any other labor organization and a question concerning representation may not appropriately be raised under section 9(c) of this Act,

(B) where within the preceding twelve months a valid election under section 9(c) of this Act has been conducted, or

(C) where such picketing has been conducted without a petition under section 9(c) being filed within a reasonable period of time not to exceed thirty days from the commencement of such picketing: *Provided,* That when such a petition has been filed the Board shall forthwith, without regard to the provisions of section 9(c)(1) or the absence of a showing of a substantial interest on the part of the labor organization, direct an election in such unit as the Board finds to be appropriate and shall certify the results thereof: *Provided further,* That nothing in this subparagraph (C) shall be construed to prohibit any picketing or other publicity for the purpose of truthfully advising the public (including consumers) that an employer does not employ members of, or have a contract with, a labor organization, unless an effect of such picketing is to induce any individual employed by any other person in the course of his employment, not to pick up, deliver or transport any goods or not to perform any services.

Nothing in this paragraph (7) shall be construed to permit any act which would otherwise be an unfair labor practice under this section 8(b).

(c) The expressing of any views, argument, or opinion, or the dissemination thereof, whether in written, printed, graphic, or visual form, shall not constitute or be evidence of an unfair labor practice under any of the provisions of this Act, if such expression contains no threat of reprisal or force or promise of benefit.

(d) For the purposes of this section, to bargain collectively is the performance of the mutual obligation of the employer and the representative of the employees to meet at reasonable times and confer in good faith with respect to wages, hours, and other terms and conditions of employment, or the negotiation of an agreement or any question arising thereunder, and the execution of a written contract incorporating any agreement reached if requested by either party, but such obligation does not compel either party to agree to a proposal or require the making of a concession: *Provided,* That where there is in effect a collective-bargaining contract covering employees in an industry affecting commerce, the duty to bargain collectively shall also mean that no party to such contract shall terminate or modify such contract, unless the party desiring such termination or modification—

(1) serves a written notice upon the party to the contract of the proposed termination or modification sixty days prior to the expiration date thereof, or in the event such contract contains no expiration date, sixty days prior to the time it is proposed to make such termination or modification;

(2) offers to meet and confer with the other party for the purpose of negotiating a new contract or a contract containing the proposed modifications;

(3) notifies the Federal Mediation and Conciliation Service within thirty days after such notice of the existence of a dispute, and simultaneously therewith notifies any State or Territorial agency established to mediate and conciliate disputes within the State or Territory where the dispute occurred, provided no agreement has been reached by that time; and

(4) continues in full force and effect, without resorting to strike or lockout, all the terms and conditions of the existing contract for a period of sixty days after such notice is given or until the expiration date of such contract, whichever occurs later.

The duties imposed upon employers, employees, and labor organizations by paragraphs (2), (3), and (4) shall become inapplicable upon an intervening certification of the Board, under which the labor organization or individual, which is a party to the contract, has been superseded as or ceased to be the representative of the employees subject to the provisions of section 9(a), and the duties so imposed shall not be construed as requiring either party to discuss or agree to any modification of the terms and conditions contained in a contract for a fixed period, if such modification is to become effective before such terms and conditions can be reopened under the provisions of the contract. Any employee who engages in a strike within any notice period specified in this sub-

section, or who engages in any strike with the appropriate period specified in subsection (g) of this section, shall lose his status as an employee of the employer engaged in the particular labor dispute, for the purposes of sections 8, 9, and 10 of this Act, as amended, but such loss of status for such employee shall terminate if and when he is reemployed by such employer. Whenever the collective bargaining involves employees of a health care institution, the provisions of this section 8(d) shall be modified as follows:

(A) The notice of section 8(d)(1) shall be ninety days; the notice of section 8(d)(3) shall be sixty days; and the contract period of section 8(d)(4) shall be ninety days.

(B) Where the bargaining is for an initial agreement following certification or recognition, at least thirty days' notice of the existence of a dispute shall be given by the labor organization to the agencies set forth in section 8(d)(3).

(C) After notice is given to the Federal Mediation and Conciliation Service under either clause (A) or (B) of this sentence, the Service shall promptly communicate with the parties and use its best efforts, by mediation and conciliation, to bring them to agreement. The parties shall participate fully and promptly in such meetings as may be undertaken by the Service for the purpose of aiding in a settlement of the dispute.

(e) it shall be an unfair labor practice for any labor organization and any employer to enter into any contract or agreement, express or implied, whereby such employer ceases or refrains or agrees to cease or refrain from handling, using, selling, transporting or otherwise dealing in any of the products of any other employer, or to cease doing business with any other person, and any contract or agreement entered into heretofore or hereafter containing such an agreement shall be to such extent unenforceable and void: *Provided,* That nothing in this subsection (e) shall apply to an agreement between a labor organization and an employer in the construction industry relating to the contracting or subcontracting of work to be done at the site of the construction, alteration, painting, or repair of a building, structure, or other work: *Provided further,* That for the purposes of this subsection (e) and section 8(b)(4)(B) the terms "any employer," "any person engaged in commerce or in industry affecting commerce," and "any person" when used in relation to the terms "any other producer, processor, or manufacturer," "any other employer," or "any other person" shall not include persons in the relation of a jobber, manufacturer, contractor, or subcontractor working on the goods or premises of the jobber or manufacturer or performing parts of an integrated process of production in the apparel and clothing industry: *Provided further,* That nothing in this Act shall prohibit the enforcement of any agreement which is within the foregoing exception.

(f) It shall not be an unfair labor practice under subsections (a) and (b) of this section for an employer engaged primarily in the building and construction industry to make an agreement covering employees engaged (or who, upon their employment, will be engaged) in the building and construction industry with a labor organization of which building and construction employees are members (not established, maintained, or assisted by any action defined in section 8(a) of this Act as an unfair labor practice) because (1) the majority status of such labor organization has not been established under the provisions of section 9 of this Act prior to the making of such agreement, or (2) such agreement requires as a condition of employment, membership in such labor organization after the seventh day following the beginning of such employment or the effective date of the agreement, whichever is later, or (3) such agreement requires the employer to notify such labor organization of opportunities for employment with such employer, or gives such labor organization an opportunity to refer qualified applicants for such employment, or (4) such agreement specifies minimum training or experience qualifications for employment or provides for priority in opportunities for employment based upon length of service with such employer, in the industry or in the particular geographical area: *Provided,* That nothing in this subsection shall set aside the final proviso to section 8(a)(3) of this Act: *Provided further,* That any agreement which would be invalid, but for clause (1) of thie subsection, shall not be a bar to a petition filed pursuant to section 9(c) or 9(e).

(g) A labor organization before engaging in any strike, picketing, or other concerted refusal to work at any health care institution shall, not less than ten days prior to such action, notify the institution in writing and the Federal Mediation and Counciliation Service of that intention, except that in the case of bargaining

for an initial agreement following certification or recognition the notice required by this subsection shall not be given the expiration of the period specified in clause (B) of the last sentence of section 8(d) of this Act. The notice shall state the date and time that such action will commence. The notice, once given, may be extended by the written agreement of both parties.

Representatives and Elections

Sec. 9.

(a) Representatives designated or selected for the purposes of collective bargaining by the majority of the employees in a unit appropriate for such purposes, shall be the exclusive representatives of all the employees in such unit for the purposes of collective bargaining in respect to rates of pay, wages, hours or employment, or other conditions of employment: *Provided,* That any individual employee or a group of employees shall have the right at any time to present grievances to their employer and to have such grievances adjusted, without the intervention of the bargaining representative, as long as the adjustment is not inconsistent with the terms of a collective-bargaining contract or agreement then in effect: *Provided further,* That the bargaining representative has been given opportunity to be present at such adjustment.

(b) The Board shall decide in each case whether, in order to assure to employees the fullest freedom in exercising the rights guaranteed by this Act, the unit appropriate for the purposes of collective bargaining shall be the employer unit, craft unit, plant unit, or subdivision thereof: *Provided,* That the Board shall not (1) decide that any unit is appropriate for such purposes if such unit includes both professional employees and employees who are not professional employees unless a majority of such professional employees vote for inclusion in such unit; or (2) decide that any craft unit is inappropriate for such purposes on the ground that a different unit has been established by a prior Board determination, unless a majority of the employees in the proposed craft unit votes against separate representation; or (3) decide that any unit is appropriate for such purposes if it includes, together with other employees, any individual employed as a guard to enforce against employees and other persons rules to protect property of the employer or to protect the safety of persons on the employer's premises; but no labor organization shall be certified as the representative of employees in a bargaining unit of guards if such organization admits to membership, or is affiliated directly or indirectly with an organization which admits to membership, employees other than guards.

(c) (1) Wherever a petition shall have been filed, in accordance with such regulations as may be prescribed by the Board—

(A) by an employee or group of employees or any individual or labor organization acting in their behalf alleging that a substantial number of employees (i) wish to be represented for collective bargaining and that their employer declines to recognize their representative as the representative defined in section 9(a), or (ii) assert that the individual or labor organization, which has been certified or is being recognized by their employer as the bargaining representative, is no longer a representative as defined in section 9(a); or

(B) by an employer, alleging that one or more individuals or labor organizations have presented to him a claim to be recognized as the representative defined in section 9(a):

the Board shall investigate such petition and if it has reasonable cause to believe that a question of representation affecting commerce exists shall provide for an appropriate hearing upon due notice. Such hearing may be conducted by an officer or employee of the regional office, who shall not make any recommendations with respect thereto. If the Board finds upon the record of such hearing that such a question of representation exists, it shall direct an election by secret ballot and shall certify the results thereof.

(2) In determining whether or not a question of representation affecting commerce exists, the same regulations and rules of decision shall apply irrespective of the identity of the person filing the petition or the kind of relief sought and in no case shall the Board deny a labor organization a place on the ballot by reason of an order with respect to such labor organization or its predecessor not issued in conformity with section 10(c).

(3) No election shall be directed in any bargaining unit or any subsivision within which, in the pre-

ceding twelve-month period, a valid election shall have been held. Employees engaged in an economic strike who are not entitled to reinstatement shall be eligible to vote under such regulations as the Board shall find are consistent with the purposes and provisions of this Act in any election conducted within twelve months after the commencement of the strike. In any election where none of the choices on the ballot receives a majority, a run-off shall be conducted, the ballot providing for a selection between the two choices receiving the largest and second largest number of valid votes cast in the election.

(4) Nothing in this section shall be construed to prohibit the waiving of hearings by stipulation for the purpose of a consent election in conformity with regulations and rules of decision of the Board.

(5) In determining whether a unit is appropriate for the purposes specified in subsection (b) the extent to which the employees have organized shall not be controlling.

(d) Whenever an order of the Board made pursuant to section 10(c) is based in whole or in part upon facts certified following an investigation pursuant to subsection (c) of this section and there is a petition for the enforcement or review of such order, such certification and the record of such investigation shall be included in the transcript of the entire record required to be filed under section 10(e) or 10(f), and thereupon the decree of the court enforcing, modifying, or setting aside in whole or in part the order of the Board shall be made and entered upon the pleadings, testimony, and proceedings set forth in such transcript.

(e) (1) Upon the filing with the Board, by 30 per centum or more of the employees in a bargaining unit covered by an agreement between their employer and a labor organization made pursuant to section 8(a)(3), of a petition alleging they desire that such authority be rescinded, the Board shall take a secret ballot of the employees in such unit and certify the results thereof to such labor organization and to the employer.

(2) No election shall be conducted pursuant to this subsection in any bargaining unit or any subdivision within which, in the preceding twelve-month period, a valid election shall have been held.

Prevention of Unfair Labor Practices

Sec. 10.

(a) The Board is empowered, as hereinafter provided, to prevent any person from engaging in any unfair labor practice (listed in section 8) affecting commerce. This power shall not be affected by any other means of adjustment or prevention that has been or may be established by agreement, law, or otherwise: *Provided,* That the Board is empowered by agreement with any agency of any State or Territory to cede to such agency jurisdiction over any cases in any industry (other than mining, manufacturing, communications, and transportation except where predominantly local in character) even though such cases may involve labor disputes affecting commerce, unless the provision of the State or Territorial statute applicable to the determination of such cases by such agency is inconsistent with the corresponding provision of this Act or has received a construction inconsistent therewith.

(b) Whenever it is charged that any person has engaged in or is engaging in any such unfair labor practice, the Board, or any agent or agency designated by the Board for such purposes, shall have power to issue and cause to be served upon such person a complaint stating the charges in that respect, and containing a notice of hearing before the Board or a member thereof, or before a designated agent or agency, at a place therein fixed, not less than five days after the serving of said complaint: *Provided,* That no complaint shall issue based upon any unfair labor practice occurring more than six months prior to the filing of the charge with the Board and the service of a copy thereof upon the person against whom such charge is made, unless the person aggrieved thereby was prevented from filing such charge by reason of service in the armed forces, in which event the six-month period shall be computed from the day of his discharge. Any such complaint may be amended by the member, agent, or agency conducting the hearing or the Board in its discretion at any time prior to the issuance of an order based thereon. The person so complained of shall have the right to file an answer to the original or amended complaint and to appear in person or otherwise and give testimony at the place and time fixed in the complaint. In the discretion of the member, agent, or agency conducting the hearing or the Board, any other person may be allowed to intervene in the said proceeding and to present testimony. Any such proceeding shall, so far as practicable, be conducted in accordance with the rules of evidence applicable in the district courts of the United States under the rules of civil procedure for the district courts of the United States, adopted by the Supreme Court of the United States pursuant to the Act of June 19, 1934 (U.S.C., title 28, secs. 723-B, 723-C).

(c) The testimony taken by such member, agent, or agency or the Board shall be reduced to writing and filed with the Board. Thereafter, in its discretion, the Board upon notice may take further testimony or hear argument. If upon the preponderance of the testimony taken the Board shall be of the opinion that any person named in the complaint has engaged in or is engaging in any such unfair labor practice, then the Board shall state its findings of fact and shall issue and cause to be served on such person an order requiring such person to cease and desist from such unfair labor practice, and to take such affirmative action including reinstatement of employees with or without back pay, as will effectuate the policies of this Act: *Provided,* That where an order directs reinstatement of an employee, back pay may be required of the employer or labor organization, as the case may be, responsible for the discrimination suffered by him: *And provided further,* That in determining whether a complaint shall issue alleging a violation of section 8(a)(1) or section 8(a)(2), and in deciding such cases, the same regulations and rules of decision shall apply irrespective of whether or not the labor organization affected is affiliated with a labor organization national or international in scope. Such order may further require such person to make reports from time to time showing the extent to which it has complied with the order. If upon the preponderance of the testimony taken the Board shall not be of the opinion that the person named in the complaint has engaged in or is engaging in any such unfair labor practice, then the Board shall state its findings of fact and shall issue an order dismissing the said complaint. No order of the Board shall require the reinstatement of any individual as an employee who has been suspended or discharged, or the payment to him of any back pay, if such individual was suspended or discharged for cause. In case the evidence is presented before a member of the Board, or before an examiner or examiners thereof, such member, or such examiner or examiners, as the case may be, shall issue and cause to be served on the parties to the proceeding a proposed report, together with a recommended order, which shall be filed with the Board, and if no exceptions are filed within twenty days after service thereof upon such parties, or within such further period as the Board may authorize, such recommended order shall become the order of the Board and become effective as therein prescribed.

(d) Until the record in the case shall have been filed in a court, as hereinafter provided, the Board may at any time, upon reasonable notice and in such manner as it shall deem proper, modify or set aside, in whole or in part, any finding or order made or issued by it.

(e) The Board shall have power to petition any court of appeals of the United States, or if all the courts of appeals to which application may be made are in vacation, any district court of the United States, within any circuit or district, respectively, wherein the unfair labor practice in question occurred or wherein such person resides or transacts business, for the enforcement of such order and for appropriate temporary relief or restraining order, and shall file in the court the record in the proceedings, as provided in section 2112 of title 28, United States Code. Upon the filing of such petition, the court shall cause notice thereof to be served upon such person, and thereupon shall have jurisdiction of the proceeding and of the question determined therein, and shall have power to grant such temporary relief or restraining order as it deems just and proper, and to make and enter a decree enforcing, modifying, and enforcing as so modified, or setting aside in whole or in part the order of the Board. No objection that has not been urged before the Board, its member, agent, or agency, shall be considered by the court, unless the failure or neglect to urge such objection shall be excused because of extraordinary circumstances. The findings of the Board with respect to questions of fact if supported by substantial evidence on the record considered as a whole shall be conclusive. If either party shall apply to the court for leave to adduce additional evidence and shall show to the satisfaction of the court that such additional evidence is material and that there were reasonable grounds for the failure to adduce such evidence in the hearing before the Board, its member, agent, or agency, the court may order such additional evidence to be taken before the Board, its member, agent, or agency, and to be made a part of

the record. The Board may modify its findings as to the facts, or make new findings, by reason of additional evidence so taken and filed, and it shall file such modified or new findings, which findings with respect to question of fact if supported by substantial evidence on the record considered as a whole shall be conclusive, and shall file its recommendations, if any, for the modification or setting aside of its original order. Upon the filing of the record with it the jurisdiction of the court shall be exclusive and its judgment and decree shall be final, except that the court shall be subject to review by the appropriate United States court of appeals if application was made to the district court as hereinabove provided, and by the Supreme Court of the United States upon writ of certiorari or certification as provided in section 1254 of title 28.

(f) Any person aggrieved by a final order of the Board granting or denying in whole or in part the relief sought may obtain a review of such order in any circuit court of appeals of the United States in the circuit wherein the unfair labor practice in question was alleged to have been engaged in or wherein such person resides or transacts business, or in the United States Court of Appeals for the District of Columbia, by filing in such court a written petition praying that the order of the Board be modified or set aside. A copy of such petition shall be forthwith transmitted by the clerk of the court to the Board, and thereupon the aggrieved party shall file in the court the record in the proceeding, certified by the Board, as provided in section 2112 of title 28, United States Code. Upon the filing of such petition, the court shall proceed in the same manner as in the case of an application by the Board under subsection (e) of this section, and shall have the same jurisdiction to grant to the Board such temporary relief or restraining order as it deems just and proper, and in like manner to make and enter a decree enforcing, modifying, and enforcing as so modified, or setting aside in whole or in part the order of the Board; the findings of the Board with respect to questions of fact if supported by substantial evidence on the record considered as a whole shall in like manner be conclusive.

(g) The commencement of proceedings under subsection (e) or (f) of this section shall not, unless specifically ordered by the court, operate as a stay of the Board's order.

(h) When granting appropriate temporary relief or a restraining order, or making and entering a decree enforcing, modifying, and enforcing as so modified, or setting aside in whole or in part an order of the Board, as provided in this section, the jurisdiction of courts sitting in equity shall not be limited by the Act entitled "An Act to amend the Judicial Code and to define and limit the jurisdiction of courts sitting in equity, and for other purposes," approved March 23, 1932 (U.S.C., Supp. VII, title 29, secs. 101–115).

(i) Petitions filed under this Act shall be heard expeditiously, and if possible within ten days after they have been docketed.

(j) The Board shall have power, upon issuance of a complaint as provided in subsection (b) charging that any person has engaged in or is engaging in an unfair labor practice, to petition any district court of the United States (including the District Court of the United States for the District of Columbia), within any district wherein the unfair labor practice in question is alleged to have occurred or wherein such person resides or transacts business, for appropriate temporary relief or restraining order. Upon the filing of any such petition the court shall cause notice thereof to be served upon such person, and thereupon shall have jurisdiction to grant to the Board such temporary relief or restraining order as it deems just and proper.

(k) Whenever it is charged that any person has engaged in an unfair labor practice within the meaning of paragraph (4)(D) of section 8(b), the Board is empowered and directed to hear and determine the dispute out of which such unfair labor practice shall have arisen, unless, within ten days after notice that such charge has been filed, the parties to such dispute submit to the Board satisfactory evidence that they have adjusted, or agreed upon methods for the voluntary adjustment of, the dispute. Upon compliance by the parties to the dispute with the decision of the Board or upon such voluntary adjustment of the dispute, such charge shall be dismissed.

(l) Whenever it is charged that any person has engaged in an unfair labor practice within the meaning of paragraph (4) (A), (B), or (C) of section 8(b), or section 8(e) of section 8(b)(7), the preliminary investigation of such charge shall be made forthwith and given priority over all other cases except cases of like character in the office where it is filed or to which it is referred. If, after such investigation, the officer or regional attorney to whom the matter may be referred has reasonable cause to believe such charge is true and that a complaint should issue, he shall, on behalf of the Board, petition any district court of the United States (including the District Court of the United States for the District of Columbia) within any district where the unfair labor practice in question has occurred, is alleged to have occurred, or wherein such person resides or transacts business, for appropriate injunctive relief pending the final adjudication of the Board with respect to such matter. Upon the filing of any such petition the district court shall have jurisdiction to grant such injunctive relief or temporary restraining order as it deems just and proper, notwithstanding any other provision of law: *Provided further,* That no temporary restraining order shall be issued without notice unless a petition alleges that substantial and irreparable injury to the charging party will be unavoidable and such temporary restraining order shall be effective no longer than five days and will become void at the expiration of such period: *Provided further,* That such officer or regional attorney shall not apply for any restraining order under section 8(b)(7) if a charge against the employer under section 8(a)(2) has been filed and after the preliminary investigation, he has reasonable cause to believe that such charge is true and that a complaint should issue. Upon filing of any such petition the courts shall cause notice thereof to be served upon any person involved in the charge and such person, including the charging party, shall be given an opportunity to appear by counsel and present any relevant testimony: *Provided further,* That for the purposes of this subsection district courts shall be deemed to have jurisdiction of a labor organization (1) in the district in which such organization maintains its principal office, or (2) in any district in which its duly authorized officers or agents are engaged in promoting or protecting the interests of employee members. The service of legal process upon such officer or agent shall constitute service upon the labor organization and make such organization a party to the suit. In situations where such relief is appropriate the procedure specified herein shall apply to charges with respect to section 8(b)(4)(D).

(m) Whenever it is charged that any person has engaged in an unfair labor practice within the meaning of subsection (a)(3) or (b)(2) of section 8, such charge shall be given priority over all other cases except cases of like character in the office where it is filed or to which it is referred and cases given priority under subsection (1).

Investigatory Powers

Sec. 11. For the purpose of all hearings and investigations, which, in the opinion of the Board, are necessary and proper for the exercise of the powers vested in it by section 9 and section 10—

(1) The Board, or its duly authorized agents or agencies, shall at all reasonable times have access to, for the purpose of examination, and the right to copy any evidence of any person being investigated or proceeded against that relates to any matter under investigation or in question. The Board, or any member thereof, shall upon application of any party to such proceedings, forthwith issue to such party subpoenas requiring the attendance and testimony of witnesses or the production of any evidence in such proceeding or investigation requested in such application. Within five days after the service of a subpoena on any person requiring the production of any evidence in his possession or under his control, such person may petition the Board to revoke, and the Board shall revoke, such subpoena if in its opinion the evidence whose production is required does not relate to any matter under investigation, or any matter in question in such proceedings, or if in its opinion such subpoena does not describe with sufficient particularity the evidence whose production is required. Any member of the Board, or any agent or agency designated by the Board for such purposes, may administer oaths and affirmations, examine witnesses, and receive evidence. Such attendance of witnesses and the production of such evidence may be required from any place in the United States or any Territory or possession thereof, at any designated place of hearing.

(2) In case of contumacy or refusal to obey a subpoena issued to any person, any district court of the United States or the United States courts of any Territory or possession, or the District Court of the United States for the District of Columbia, within the jurisdiction of which the inquiry is carried on or within the jurisdiction of which said person guilty of contumacy or refusal to obey is found or resides or transacts business, upon application by the Board shall have jurisdiction to issue to such person an order requiring such person to appear before the Board, its member, agent, or agency, there to produce evidence if so ordered, or there to give testimony touching the matter under investigation or in question; and any failure to obey such order of the court may be punished by said court as a contempt thereof.

(3) Repealed.

(4) Complaints, orders and other process and papers of the Board, its member, agent, or agency, may be served either personally or by registered or certified mail or by telegraph or by leaving a copy thereof at the principal office or place of business of the person required to be served. The verified return by the individual so serving the same setting forth the manner of such service shall be proof of the same, and the return post office receipt or telegraph receipt therefor when registered or certified and mailed or telegraphed as aforesaid shall be proof of service of the same. Witnesses summoned before the Board, its member, agent, or agency, shall be paid the same fees and mileage that are paid witnesses in the courts of the United States, and witnesses whose depositions are taken and the persons taking the same shall severally be entitled to the same fees as are paid for like services in the courts of the United States.

(5) All process of any court to which application may be made under this Act may be served in the judicial district where the defendant or other person required to be served resides or may be found.

(6) The several departments and agencies of the Government, when directed by the President, shall furnish the Board, upon its request, all records, papers, and information in their possession relating to any matter before the Board.

Sec. 12. Any person who shall willfully resist, prevent, impede, or interfere with any member of the Board or any of its agents or agencies in the performance of duties pursuant to this Act shall be punished by a fine of not more than $5,000 or by imprisonment for not more than one year, or both.

Limitations

Sec. 13. Nothing in this Act, except as specifically provided for herein, shall be construed so as either to interfere with or impede or diminish in any way the right to strike, or to affect the limitations or qualifications on that right.

Sec. 14.

(a) Nothing herein shall prohibit any individual employed as a supervisor from becoming or remaining a member of a labor organization, but no employer subject to this Act shall be compelled to deem individuals defined herein as supervisors as employees for the purpose of any law, either national or local, relating to collective bargaining.

(b) Nothing in this Act shall be construed as authorizing the execution or application of agreements requiring membership in a labor organization as a condition of employment in any State or Territory in which such execution or application is prohibited by State or Territorial law.

(c) (1) The Board, in its discretion, may, by rule of decision or by published rules adopted pursuant to the Administrative Procedure Act, decline to assert jurisdiction over any labor dispute involving any class or category of employers, where, in the opinion of the Board, the effect of such labor dispute on commerce is not sufficiently substantial to warrant the exercise of its jurisdiction: *Provided,* That the Board shall not decline to assert jurisdiction over any labor dispute over which it would assert jurisdiction under the standards prevailing upon August 1, 1959.

(2) Nothing in this Act shall be deemed to prevent or bar any agency or the courts of any State or Territory (including the Commonwealth of Puerto Rico, Guam, and the Virgin Islands), from assuming and asserting jurisdiction over labor disputes over which the Board declines, pursuant to paragraph (1) of this subsection, to assert jurisdiction.

Sec. 15. Wherever the application of the provisions of section 272 of chapter 10 of the Act entitled "An Act to establish a uniform system of bankruptcy throughout the United States," approved July 1, 1898, and Acts amendatory thereof and supplementary thereto (U.S.C., title 11, sec. 672), conflicts with the application of the provisions of this Act, this Act shall prevail: *Provided,* That in any situation where the provisions of this Act cannot be validly enforced, the provisions of such other Acts shall remain in full force and effect.

Sec. 16. If any provision of this Act, or the application of such provision to any person or circumstances, shall be held invalid, the remainder of this Act, or the application of such provision to persons or circumstances other than

those as to which it is held invalid, shall not be affected thereby.

Sec. 17. This Act may be cited as the "National Labor Relations Act."

Sec. 18. No petition entertained, no investigation made, no election held, and no certification issued by the National Labor Relations Board, under any of the provisions of section 9 of the National Labor Relations Act, as amended, shall be invalid by reason of the failure of the Congress of Industrial Organizations to have complied with the requirements of section 9(f), (g), or (h) of the aforesaid Act prior to December 22, 1949, or by reason of the failure of the American Federation of Labor to have complied with the provisions of section 9(f), (g), or (h) of the aforesaid Act prior to November 7, 1947: *Provided,* That no liability shall be imposed under any provision of this Act upon any person for failure to honor any election or certificate referred to above, prior to the effective date of this amendment: *Provided, however,* That this proviso shall not have the effect of setting aside or in any way affecting judgments or decrees heretofore entered under section 10(e) or (f) and which have become final.

Individuals with Religious Convictions

Sec. 19. Any employee who is a member of and adheres to established and traditional tenets or teachings of a bona fide religion, body, or sect which has historically held conscientious objections to joining or financially supporting labor organizations shall not be required to join or financially support any labor organization as a condition of employment; except that such employee may be required in a contract between such employees' employer and a labor organization in lieu of periodic dues and initiation fees, to pay sums equal to such dues and initiation fees to a nonreligious nonlabor organization charitable fund exempt from taxation under section 501(c)(3) of title 26 of the Internal Revenue Code, chosen by such employee from a list of at least three such funds, designated in such contract or if the contract fails to designate such funds, then to any such fund chosen by the employee. If such employee who holds conscientious objections pursuant to this section requests the labor organization to use the grievance-arbitration procedure on the employee's behalf, the labor organization is authorized to charge the employee for the reasonable cost of using such procedure.

Appendix B

Text of the Labor Management Relations Act

61 Stat. 136–52 (1947), as amended by 73 Stat. 519ff (1959), 83 Stat. 133 (1969), 87 Stat. 314 (1973), 88 Stat. 396–97 (1974); 29 U.S.C. Sections 141–97 (Supp. 1981)

AN ACT

To amend the National Labor Relations Act, to provide additional facilities for the mediation of labor disputes affecting commerce, to equalize legal responsibilities of labor organizations and employers, and for other purposes.

Be it enacted by the Senate and House of Representatives of the United States of America in Congress assembled.

Short Title and Declaration of Policy

Section 1.

(a) This Act may be cited as the "Labor Management Relations Act, 1947,"

(b) Industrial strife which interferes with the normal flow of commerce and with the full production of articles and commodities for commerce, can be avoided or substantially minimized if employers, employees, and labor organizations each recognize under law one another's legitimate rights in their relations with each other, and above all recognize under law that neither party has any right in its relations with any other to engage in acts or practices which jeopardize the public health, safety, or interest.

It is the purpose and policy of this Act, in order to promote the full flow of commerce, to prescribe the legitimate rights of both employees and employers in their relations affecting commerce, to provide orderly and peaceful procedures for preventing the interference by either with the legitimate rights of the other, to protect the rights of individual employees in their relations with labor organizations whose activities affect commerce, to define and proscribe practices on the part of labor and management which affect commerce and are inimical to the general welfare, and to protect the rights of the public in connection with labor disputes affecting commerce.

TITLE I

Amendments of National Labor Relations Act

Sec. 101. The National Labor Relations Act is hereby amended to read as follows:

(The text of the National Labor Relations Act as amended appears on Appendix A, *supra.*)

Effective Date of Certain Changes

Sec. 102. [Omitted.]
Sec. 103. [Omitted.]
Sec. 104. [Omitted.]

TITLE II

Conciliation of Labor Disputes in Industries Affecting Commerce; National Emergencies

Sec. 201. That it is the policy of the United States that—

(a) sound and stable industrial peace and the advancement of the general welfare, health, and safety of the Nation and of the best interest of employers and employees can most satisfactorily be secured by the settlement of issues between employers and employees through the processes of conference and collective bargaining between employers and the representatives of their employees;

(b) the settlement of issues between employers and employees through collective bargaining may be advanced by making available full and adequate governmental facilities for conciliation, mediation, and voluntary arbitration to aid and encourage employers and the representatives of their employees to reach and maintain agreements concerning rates of pay, hours, and working conditions, and to make all reasonable efforts to settle their differences by mutual agreement reached through conferences and collective bargaining or by such methods as may be provided for in any applicable agreement for the settlement of disputes; and

(c) certain controversies which arise between parties to collective-bargaining agreements may be avoided or minimized by making available full and adequate governmental facilities for furnishing assistance to employers and the representatives of their employees in formulating for inclusion within such agreements provision for adequate notice of any proposed changes in the terms of such agreements, for the final adjustment of grievances or questions regarding the application or interpretation of such agreements, and other provisions designed to prevent the subsequent arising of such controversies.

Sec. 202.

(a) There is hereby created an independent agency to be known as the Federal Mediation and Conciliation Service (herein referred to as the "Service," except that for sixty days after the date of the enactment of this Act such term shall refer to the Conciliation Service of the Department of Labor). The Service shall be under the direction of a Federal Mediation and Conciliation Director (hereinafter referred to as the "Director"), who shall be appointed by the President by and with the advice and consent of the Senate. The Director shall receive compensation at the rate of $12,000 per annum. The Director shall not engage in any other business, vocation, or employment.

(b) The Director is authorized, subject to the civil-service laws, to appoint such clerical and other personnel as may be necessary for the execution of the functions of the Service, and shall fix their compensations in accordance with the Classification Act of

1923, as amended, and may, without regard to the provisions of the civil-service laws and the Classification Act of 1923, as amended, appoint and fix the compensation of such conciliators and mediators as may be necessary to carry out the functions of the Service. The Director is authorized to make such expenditures for supplies, facilities, and services as he deems necessary. Such expenditures shall be allowed and paid upon presentation of itemized vouchers therefor approved by the Director or by any employee designated by him for that purpose.

(c) The principal office of the Service shall be in the District of Columbia, but the Director may establish regional offices convenient to localities in which labor controversies are likely to arise. The Director may by order, subject to revocation at any time, delegate any authority and discretion conferred upon him by this Act to any regional director, or other officer or employee of the Service. The Director may establish suitable procedures for cooperation with State and local mediation agencies. The Director shall make an annual report in writing to Congress at the end of the fiscal year.

(d) All mediation and conciliation functions of the Secretary of Labor or the United States Conciliation Service under section 8 of the Act entitled "An Act to create a Department of Labor," approved March 4, 1913 (U.S.C., title 29, sec. 51), and all functions of the United States Conciliation Service under any other law are hereby transferred to the Federal Mediation and Conciliation Service, together with the personnel and records of the United States Conciliation Service. Such transfer shall take effect upon the sixtieth day after the date of enactment of this Act. Such transfer shall not affect any proceedings pending before the United States Conciliation Service or any certification, order, rule, or regulation theretofore made by it or by the Secretary of Labor. The Director and the Service shall not be subject in any way to the jurisdiction or authority of the Secretary of Labor or any official or division of the Department of Labor.

Functions of the Service

Sec. 203.

(a) It shall be the duty of the Service, in order to prevent or minimize interruptions of the free flow of commerce growing out of labor disputes, to assist parties to labor disputes in industries affecting commerce to settle such disputes, through conciliation and mediation.

(b) The Service may proffer its services in any labor dispute in any industry affecting commerce, either upon its own motion or upon the request of one or more of the parties to the dispute, whenever in its judgment such dispute threatens to cause a substantial interruption of commerce. The Director and the Service are directed to avoid attempting to mediate disputes which would have only a minor effect on interstate commerce if State or other conciliation services are available to the parties. Whenever the Service does proffer its services in any dispute, it shall be the duty of the Service promptly to put itself in communication with the parties and to use its best efforts, by mediation and conciliation, to bring them to agreement.

(c) If the Director is not able to bring the parties to agreement by conciliation within a reasonable time, he shall seek to induce the parties voluntarily to seek other means of settling the dispute without resort to strike, lock-out, or other coercion, including submission to the employees in the bargaining unit of the employer's last offer of settlement for approval or rejection in a secret ballot. The failure or refusal of either party to agree to any procedure suggested by the Director shall not be deemed a violation of any duty or obligation imposed by this Act.

(d) Final adjustment by a method agreed upon by the parties is hereby declared to be the desirable method for settlement of grievance disputes arising over the application or interpretation of an existing collective-bargaining agreement. The Service is directed to make its conciliation and mediation services available in the settlement of such grievance disputes only as a last resort and in exceptional cases.

(e) The Service is authorized and directed to encourage and support the establishment and operation of joint labor management activities conducted by plant, area, and industrywide committees designed to improve labor management relationships, job security and organizational effectiveness, in accordance with the provisions of section 205A.

Sec. 204.

(a) In order to prevent or minimize interruptions of the free flow of commerce growing out of labor disputes, employers and employees and their representatives, in any industry affecting commerce, shall—

(1) exert every reasonable effort to make and main-

tain agreements concerning rates of pay, hours, and working conditions, including provision for adequate notice of any proposed change in the terms of such agreements;

(2) whenever a dispute arises over the terms or application of a collective-bargaining agreement and a conference is requested by a party or prospective party thereto, arrange promptly for such a conference to be held and endeavor in such conference to settle such dispute expeditiously; and

(3) in case such dispute is not settled by conference, participate fully and promptly in such meetings as may be undertaken by the Service under this Act for the purpose of aiding a settlement of the dispute.

Sec. 205.

(a) There is hereby created a National Labor-Management Panel which shall be composed of twelve members appointed by the President, six of whom shall be selected from among persons outstanding in the field of management and six of whom shall be selected from among persons outstanding in the field of labor. Each member shall hold office for a term of three years, except that any member appointed to fill a vacancy occurring prior to the expiration of the term for which his predecessor was appointed shall be appointed for the remainder of such term, and the terms of office of the members first taking office shall expire, as designated by the President at the time of appointment, four at the end of the first year, four at the end of the second year, and four at the end of the third year after the date of appointment. Members of the panel, when serving on business of the panel, shall be paid compensation at the rate of $25 per day, and shall also be entitled to receive an allowance for actual and necessary travel and subsistence expenses while so serving away from their places of residence.

(b) It shall be the duty of the panel, at the request of the Director, to advise in the avoidance of industrial controversies and the manner in which mediation and voluntary adjustment shall be administered, particularly with reference to controversies affecting the general welfare of the country.

Sec. 205A.

(a) (1) The Service is authorized and directed to provide assistance in the establishment and operation of plant, area and industrywide labor management committees which—

  (A) have been organized jointly by employers and labor organizations representing employees in that plant, area, or industry; and

  (B) are established for the purpose of improving labor management relationships, job security, organizational effectiveness, enhancing economic development or involving workers in decisions affecting their jobs including improving communication with respect to subjects of mutual interest and concern.

  (2) The Service is authorized and directed to enter into contracts and to make grants, where necessary or appropriate, to fulfill its responsibilities under this section.

(b) (1) No grant may be made, no contract may be entered into and no other assistance may be provided under the provisions of this section to a plant labor management committee unless the employees in that plant are represented by a labor organization and there is in effect at that plant a collective bargaining agreement.

  (2) No grant may be made, no contract may be entered into and no other assistance may be provided under the provisions of this section to an area or industrywide labor management committee unless its participants include any labor organizations certified or recognized as the representative of the employees of an employer participating in such committee. Nothing in this clause shall prohibit participation in an area or industrywide committee by an employer whose employees are not represented by a labor organization.

  (3) No grant may be made under the provisions of this section to any labor management committee which the Service finds to have as one of its purposes the discouragement of the exercise of rights contained in section 7 of the National Labor Relations Act (29 U.S.C. 157), or the interference with collective bargaining in any plant, or industry.

(c) The Service shall carry out the provisions of this section through an office established for that purpose.

(d) There are authorized to be appropriated to carry out the provisions of this section $10,000,000 for the fiscal year 1979, and such sums as may be necessary thereafter.

(e) Nothing in this section or the amendments made by this section shall affect the terms and conditions of any collective bargaining agreement whether in effect prior to or entered into after the date of enactment of this section.

National Emergencies

Sec. 206. Whenever in the opinion of the President of the United States, a threatened or actual strike or lock-out affecting an entire industry or a substantial part thereof engaged in trade, commerce, transportation, transmission, or communication among the several States or with foreign nations, or engaged in the production of goods for commerce, will, if permitted to occur or to continue, imperil the national health or safety, he may appoint a board of inquiry to inquire into the issues involved in the dispute and to make a written report to him within such time as he shall prescribe. Such report shall include a statement of the facts with respect to the dispute, including each party's statement of its position but shall not contain any recommendations. The President shall file a copy of such report with the Service and shall make its contents available to the public.

Sec. 207.

(a) A board of inquiry shall be composed of a chairman and such other members as the President shall determine, and shall have power to sit and act in any place within the United States and to conduct such hearings either in public or in private, as it may deem necessary or proper, to ascertain the facts with respect to the causes and circumstances of the dispute.

(b) Members of a board of inquiry shall receive compensation at the rate of $50 for each day actually spent by them in the work of the board, together with necessary travel and subsistence expenses.

(c) For the purpose of any hearing or inquiry conducted by any board appointed under this title, the provisions of section 9 and 10 (relating to the attendance of witnesses and the production of books, papers, and documents) of the Federal Trade Commission Act of September 16, 1914, as amended (U.S.C. 19, title 15, secs. 49 and 50, as amended), are hereby made applicable to the powers and duties of such board.

Sec. 208.

(a) Upon receiving a report from a board of inquiry the President may direct the Attorney General to petition any district court of the United States having jurisdiction of the parties to enjoin such strike or lock-out or the continuing thereof, and if the court finds that such threatened or actual strike or lock-out—

(i) affects an entire industry or a substantial part thereof engaged in trade, commerce, transportation, transmission, or communication among the several States or with foreign nations, or engaged in the production of goods for commerce, and

(ii) if permitted to occur or to continue, will imperil the national health or safety, it shall have jurisdiction to enjoin any such strike or lock-out, or the continuing thereof, and to make such other orders as may be appropriate.

(b) In any case, the provisions of the Act of March 23, 1932, entitled "An Act to amend the Judicial Code and to define and limit the jurisdiction of courts sitting in equity, and for other purposes," shall not be applicable.

(c) The order or orders of the court shall be subject to review by the appropriate circuit court of appeals and by the Supreme Court upon writ of certiorari or certification as provided in sections 239 and 240 of the Judicial Code, as amended (U.S.C., title 29, secs. 346 and 347).

Sec. 209.

(a) Whenever a district court has issued an order under section 208 enjoining acts or practices which imperil or threaten to imperil the national health or safety, it shall be the duty of the parties to the labor dispute giving rise to such order to make every effort to adjust and settle their differences, with the assistance of the Service created by this Act. Neither party shall be under any duty to accept, in whole or in part, any proposal of settlement made by the Service.

(b) Upon the issuance of such order, the President shall reconvene the board of inquiry which has previously reported with respect to the dispute. At the end of a sixty-day period (unless the dispute has been settled by that time), the board of inquiry shall report to the President the current position of the parties and the effort which has been made for settlement, and shall include a statement by each party of its position and a statement of the employer's last offer of settlement. The President shall make such report available to the public. The National Labor Relations Board, within the succeeding fifteen days, shall take a secret ballot of the employees of each employer involved in the dispute on the question of whether they wish to accept the final offer of settlement made by their employer as stated by him and shall certify the results thereof to the Attorney General within five days thereafter.

Sec. 210. Upon the certification of the results of such ballot or upon a settlement being reached, whichever happens sooner, the Attorney General shall move the court to discharge the injunction, which motion shall then be granted and the injunction discharged. When such motion is granted, the President shall submit to the Congress a full and comprehensive report of the proceedings, including the findings of the board of inquiry and the ballot taken by the National Labor Relations Board, together with such recommendations as he may see fit to make for consideration and appropriate action.

Compilation of Collective-Bargaining Agreements, Etc.

Sec. 211.

(a) For the guidance and information of interested representatives of employers, employees, and the general public, the Bureau of Labor Statistics of the Department of Labor shall maintain a file of copies of all available collective-bargaining agreements and other available agreements and actions thereunder settling or adjusting labor disputes. Such file shall be open to inspection under appropriate conditions prescribed by the Secretary of Labor, except that no specific information submitted in confidence shall be disclosed.

(b) The Bureau of Labor Statistics in the Department of Labor is authorized to furnish upon request of the Service, or employers, employees, or their representatives, all available data and factual information which may aid in the settlement of any labor dispute, except that no specific information submitted in confidence shall be disclosed.

Exemption of Railway Labor Act

Sec. 212. The provisions of this title shall not be applicable with respect to any matter which is subject to the provisions of the Railway Labor Act, as amended from time to time.

Conciliation of Labor Disputes in the Health Care Industry

Sec. 213.

(a) If, in the opinion of the Director of the Federal Mediation and Conciliation Service a threatened or actual strike or lockout affecting a health care institution will, if permitted to occur or to continue, substantially interrupt the delivery of health care in the locality concerned, the Director may further assist in the resolution of the impasse by establishing within 30 days after the notice to the Federal Mediation and Conciliation Service under clause (A) of the last sentence of section 8(d) (which is required by clause (3) of such section 8(d)), or within 10 days after the notice under clause (B), an impartial Board of Inquiry to investigate the issues involved in the dispute and to make a written report thereon to the parties within fifteen (15) days after the establishment of such a Board. The written report shall contain the findings of fact together with the Board's recommendations for settling the dispute. Each such Board shall be composed of such number of individuals as the Director may deem desirable. No member appointed under this section shall have any interest or involvement in the health care institutions or the employee organizations involved in the dispute.

(b) (1) Members of any board established under this section who are otherwise employed by the Federal Government shall serve without compensation but shall be reimbursed for travel, subsistence, and other necessary expenses incurred by them in carrying out its duties under this section.

(2) Members of any board established under this section who are not subject to paragraph (1) shall receive compensation at a rate prescribed by the Director but not to exceed the daily rate prescribed for GS-18 of the General Schedule under section 5332 of title 5, United States Code, including travel for each day they are engaged in the performance of their duties under this section and shall be entitled to reimbursement for travel, subsistence, and other necessary expenses incurred by them in carrying out their duties under this section.

(c) After the establishment of a board under subsection (a) of this section and for 15 days after any such board has issued its report, no change in the status quo in effect prior to the expiration of the contract in the case of negotiations for a contract renewal, or in effect prior to the time of the impasse in the case of an initial bargaining negotiation, except by agreement, shall be made by the parties to the controversy.

TITLE III

Suits by and against Labor Organizations

Sec. 301.

(a) Suits for violation of contracts between an employer and a labor organization representing employees in an industry affecting commerce as defined in this Act, or between any such labor organizations, may be brought in any district court of the United States having jurisdiction of the parties, without respect to the amount in controversy or without regard to the citizenship of the parties.

(b) Any labor organization which represents employees in an industry affecting commerce as defined in this Act and any employer whose activities affect commerce as defined in this Act shall be bound by the acts of its agents. Any such labor organization may sue or be sued as an entity and in behalf of the employees whom it represents in the courts of the United States. Any money judgment against a labor organization in a district court of the United States shall be enforceable only against the organization as an entity and against its assets, and shall not be enforceable against any individual member or his assets.

(c) For the purposes of actions and procedings by or against labor organizations in the district courts of the United States, district courts shall be deemed to have jurisdiction of a labor organization (1) in the district in which such organization maintains its principal offices, or (2) in any district in which its duly authorized officers or agents are engaged in representing or acting for employee members.

(d) The service of summons, subpoena, or other legal process of any court of the United States upon an officer or agent of a labor organization, in his capacity as such, shall constitute service upon the labor organization.

(e) For the purpose of this section, in determining whether any person is acting as an "agent" of another person so as to make such other person responsible for his acts, the question of whether the specific acts performed were actually authorized or subsequently ratified shall not be controlling.

Restrictions on Payments to Employee Representatives

Sec. 302.

(a) It shall be unlawful for any employer or association of employers or any person who acts as a labor relations expert, adviser, or consultant to an employer or who acts in the interest of an employer to pay, lend, or deliver, or agree to pay, lend, or deliver, any money or other thing of value—

(1) to any representative of any of his employees who are employed in an industry affecting commerce; or

(2) to any labor organization, or any officer or employee thereof, which represents, seeks to represent, or would admit to membership, any of the employees of such employer who are employed in an industry affecting commerce;

(3) to any employee or group or committee of employees of such employer employed in an industry affecting commerce in excess of their normal compensation for the purpose of causing such employee or group or committee directly or indirectly to influence any other employees in the exercise of the right to organize and bargain collectively through representation of their own choosing; or

(4) to any officer or employee of a labor organization engaged in an industry affecting commerce with intent to influence him in respect to any of his actions, decisions, or duties as a representative of employees or as such officer or employee of such labor organization.

(b) (1) It shall be unlawful for any person to request, demand, receive, or accept, or agree to receive or accept, any payment, loan, or delivery of any money or other thing of value prohibited by subsection (a).

(2) It shall be unlawful for any labor organization, or for any person acting as an officer, agent, representative, or employee of such labor organization, to demand or accept from the operator of any motor vehicle (as defined in part II of the Interstate Commerce Act) employed in the transportation of property in commerce, or the employer of any such operator, any money or other thing of value payable to such organization or to an officer, agent, representative or employee thereof as a fee or charge for the unloading, or the connection with the unloading, of the cargo of such vehicle: *Provided,* That nothing in this paragraph shall be construed to make unlawful any payment by an employer to any of his employees as compensation for their services as employees.

(c) The provisions of this section shall not be applicable

(1) in respect to any money or other thing of value payable by an employer to any of his employees whose established duties include acting openly for such employer in matters of labor relations or personnel administration or to any representative of his employees, or to any officer or employee of a labor organization, who is also an employee or former employee of such employer, as compensation for, or by reason of, his service as an employee of such employer; (2) with respect to the payment or delivery of any money or other thing of value in satisfaction of a judgment of any court or a decision or award of an arbitrator or impartial chairman or in compromise, adjustment, settlement, or release of any claim, complaint, grievance or dispute in the absence of fraud or duress; (3) with respect to the sale or purchase of an article or commodity at the prevailing market price in the regular course of business; (4) with respect to money deducted from the wages of employees in payment of membership dues in a labor organization: *Provided,* That the employer has received from each employee, on whose account such deductions are made, a written assignment which shall not be irrevocable for a period of more than one year, or beyond the termination date of the applicable collective agreement, whichever occurs sooner; (5) with respect to money or other thing of value paid to a trust fund established by such representative, for the sole and exclusive benefit of the employees of such employer, and their families and dependents (or of such employees, families, and dependents jointly with the employees of other employers making similar payments, and their families and dependents): *Provided,* That (A) such payments are held in trust for the purpose of paying, either from principal or income or both, for the benefit of employees, their families and dependents, for medical or hospital care, pensions on retirement or death of employees, compensation for injuries or illness resulting from occupational activity or insurance to provide any of the foregoing, or unemployment benefits or life insurance, disability and sickness insurance, or accident insurance; (B) the detailed basis on which such payments are to be made is specified in a written agreement with the employer, and employees and employers are equally represented in the administration of such fund, together with such neutral persons as the representatives of the employers and the representatives of employees may agree upon and in the event the employer and employee groups deadlock on the administration of

such fund and there are no neutral persons empowered to break such deadlock, such agreement provides that the two groups shall agree on an impartial umpire to decide such dispute, or in event of their failure to agree within a reasonable length of time, an impartial umpire to decide such dispute shall, on petition of either group, be appointed by the district court of the United States for the district where the trust fund has its principal office, and shall also contain provisions for an annual audit of the trust fund, a statement of the results of which shall be available for inspection by interested persons at the principal office of the trust fund and at such other places as may be designated in such written agreement; and (C) such payments as are intended to be used for the purpose of providing pensions or annuities for employees are made to a separate trust which provides that the funds held therein cannot be used for any purpose other than paying such pensions or annuities; (6) with respect to money or other thing of value paid by any employer to a trust fund established by such representative for the purpose of pooled vacation, holiday, severance or similar benefits, or defraying costs of apprenticeship or other training program: *Provided,* That the requirements of clause (B) of the proviso to clause (5) of this subsection shall apply to such trust funds; (7) with respect to money or other thing of value paid by any employer to a pooled or individual trust fund established by such representative for the purpose of (A) scholarships for the benefit of employees, their families, and dependents for study at educational institutions, or (B) child care centers for preschool and school age dependents of employees: *Provided,* That no labor organization or employer shall be required to bargain on the establishment of any such trust fund, and refusal to do so shall not constitute an unfair labor practice: *Provided further,* That the requirements of clause (B) of the proviso to clause (5) of this subsection shall apply to such trust funds; (8) with respect to money or any other thing of value paid by any employer to a trust fund established by such representative for the purpose of defraying the costs of legal services for employees, their families, and dependents for counsel or plan of their choice: *Provided,* That the requirements of clause (B) of the proviso to clause (5) of this subsection shall apply to such trust funds: *Provided further,* That no such legal services shall be furnished: (A) to initiate any pro-

ceeding directed (i) against any such employer or its officers or agents except in workman's compensation cases, or (ii) against such labor organization, or its parent or subordinate bodies, or their officers or agents, or (iii) against any other employer or labor organization, or their officers or agents, in any matter arising under the National Labor Relations Act, as amended, or this Act; and (B) in any proceeding where a labor organization would be prohibited from defraying the costs of legal services by the provisions of the Labor-Management Reporting and Disclosure Act of 1959; or (9) with respect to money or other things of value paid by an employer to a plant, area or industrywide labor management committee established for one or more of the purposes set forth in section 5(b) of the Labor Management Cooperation Act of 1978.

(d) Any person who willfully violates any of the provisions of this section shall, upon conviction thereof, be guilty of a misdemeanor and be subject to a fine of not more than $10,000 or to imprisonment for not more than one year, or both.

(e) The district courts of the United States and the United States courts of the Territories and possessions shall have jurisdiction, for cause shown, and subject to the provisions of section 17 (relating to notice to opposite party) of the Act entitled "An Act to supplement existing laws against unlawful restraints and monopolies, and for other purposes," approved October 15, 1914, as amended (U.S.C., title 28, sec. 381), to restrain violations of this section, without regard to the provisions of sections 6 and 20 of such Act of October 15, 1914, as amended (U.S.C., title 15, sec. 17 and title 29, sec. 52), and the provisions of the Act entitled "An Act to amend the Judicial Code to define and limit the jurisdiction of courts sitting in equity, and for other purposes," approved March 23, 1932 (U.S.C., title 29, secs. 101–115).

(f) This section shall not apply to any contract in force on the date of enactment of this Act, until the expiration of such contract, or until July 1, 1948, whichever first occurs.

(g) Compliance with the restrictions contained in subsection (c)(5)(B) upon contributions to trust funds, otherwise lawful, shall not be applicable to contributions to such trust funds established by collective agreement prior to January 1, 1946, nor shall subsection (c)(5)(A) be construed as prohibiting contributions to such trust funds if prior to January 1, 1947, such funds contained provisions for pooled vacation benefits.

Boycotts and Other Unlawful Combinations

Sec. 303.

(a) It shall be unlawful, for the purpose of this section only, in an industry or activity affecting commerce, for any labor organization to engage in any activity or conduct defined as an unfair labor practice in section 8(b)(4) of the National Labor Relations Act, as amended.

(b) Whoever shall be injured in his business or property by reason of any violation of subsection (a) may sue therefore in any district court of the United States subject to the limitations and provisions of section 301 hereof without respect to the amount in controversy, or in any other court having jurisdiction of the parties, and shall recover the damages by him sustained and the cost of the suit.

Restriction on Political Contributions

Sec. 304. Section 313 of the Federal Corrupt Practices Act, 1925 (U.S.C., 1940 edition, title 2, sec. 251; Supp. V, title 50, App., sec. 1509), as amended, is amended to read as follows:

Sec. 313. It is unlawful for any national bank, or any corporation organized by authority of any law of Congress to make a contribution or expenditure in connection with any election to any political office, or in connection with any primary election or political convention or caucus held to select candidates for any political office, or for any corporation whatever, or any labor organization to make a contribution or expenditure in connection with any election at which Presidential and Vice Presidential electors or a Senator or Representative in, or a Delegate or Resident Commissioner to Congress are to be voted for, or in connection with any primary election or political convention or caucus held to select candidates for any of the foregoing offices, or for any candidate, political committee, or other person to accept or receive any contribution prohibited by this section. Every corporation or labor organization which makes any contribution or expenditure in violation of this section shall be fined not more than $5,000; and every officer or director of any corporation, or officer of any labor organization, who consents to any contribution or expenditure by the corporation or labor organization, as the case may be, in violation of this section shall be fined not more than

$1,000 or imprisoned for not more than one year, or both. For the purposes of this section, "labor organization" means any organization of any kind, or any agency or employee representation committee or plan, in which employees participate and which exists for the purpose, in whole or in part, of dealing with employers concerning grievances, labor disputes, wages, rates of pay, hours of employment, or conditions of work.

Strikes by Government Employees

Sec. 305. [Repealed by Ch. 690, 69 Stat. 624, effective August 9, 1955. Sec. 305 made it unlawful for government employees to strike and made strikers subject to immediate discharge, forfeiture of civil-service status, and three-year blacklisting for federal employment.]

TITLE IV

Creation of Joint Committee to Study and Report on Basic Problems Affecting Friendly Labor Relations and Productivity

Sec. 401. There is hereby established a joint congressional committee to be known as the Joint Committee on Labor-Management Relations (hereafter referred to as the committee), and to be composed of seven Members of the Senate Committee on Labor and Public Welfare, to be appointed by the President pro tempore of the Senate, and seven Members of the House of Representatives Committee on Education and Labor, to be appointed by the Speaker of the House of Representatives. A vacancy in membership of the committee, shall not affect the powers of the remaining members to execute the functions of the committee, and shall be filled in the same manner as the original selection. The committee shall select a chairman and a vice chairman from among its members.

Sec. 402. The committee, acting as a whole or by subcommittee shall conduct a thorough study and investigation of the entire field of labor-management relations, including but not limited to—

(1) the means by which permanent friendly cooperation between employers and employees and stability of labor relations may be secured throughout the United States;

(2) the means by which the individual employee may achieve a greater productivity and higher wages, including plans for guaranteed annual wages, incentive profit-sharing and bonus systems;

(3) the internal organization and administration of labor

unions, with special attention to the impact on individuals of collective agreements requiring membership in unions as a condition of employment;

(4) the labor relations policies and practices of employers and associations of employers;

(5) the desirability of welfare funds for the benefit of employees and their relation to the social-security system;

(6) the methods and procedures for best carrying out the collective-bargaining processes, with special attention to the effects of industrywide or regional bargaining upon the national economy;

(7) the administration and operation of existing Federal laws relating to labor relations; and

(8) such other problems and subjects in the field of labor-management relations as the committee deems appropriate.

Sec. 403. The committee shall report to the Senate and the House of Representatives not later than March 15, 1948, the results of its study and investigation, together with such recommendations as to necessary legislation and such other recommendations as it may deem advisable, and shall make its final report not later than January 2, 1949.

Sec. 404. The committee shall have the power, without regard to the civil-service laws and the Classification Act of 1923, as amended, to employ and fix the compensation of such officers, experts, and employees as it deems necessary for the performance of its duties, including consultants who shall receive compensation at a rate not to exceed $35 for each day actually spent by them in the work of the committee, together with their necessary travel and subsistence expenses. The committee is further authorized with the consent of the head of the department or agency concerned, to utilize the services, information, facilities, and personnel of all agencies in the executive branch of the Government and may request the governments of the several States, representatives of business, industry, finance, and labor, and such other persons, agencies, organizations, and instrumentalities as it deems appropriate to attend its hearings and to give and present information, advice, and recommendations.

Sec. 405. The committee, or any subcommittee thereof, is authorized to hold such hearings; to sit and act at such times and places during the sessions, recesses, and adjourned periods of the Eightieth Congress; to require by subpoena or otherwise the attendance of such witnesses and the production of such books, papers, and documents; to administer oaths; to take such testimony; to have such

printing and binding done; and to make such expenditures within the amount appropriated therefor; as it deems advisable. The cost of stenographic services in reporting such hearings shall not be in excess of 25 cents per one hundred words. Subpoenas shall be issued under the signature of the chairman or vice chairman of the committee and shall be served by any person designated by them.

Sec. 406. The members of the committee shall be reimbursed for travel, subsistence, and other necessary expenses incurred by them in the performance of the duties vested in the committee, other than expenses in connection with meetings of the committee held in the District of Columbia during such times as the Congress is in session.

Sec. 407. There is hereby authorized to be appropriated the sum of $150,000, or so much thereof as may be necessary, to carry out the provisions of this title, to be disbursed by the Secretary of the Senate on vouchers signed by the chairman.

TITLE V

Definitions

Sec. 501. When used in this Act—

(1) The term "industry affecting commerce" means any industry or activity in commerce or in which a labor dispute would burden or obstruct commerce or tend to burden or obstruct commerce or the free flow of commerce.

(2) The term "strike" includes any strike or other concerted stoppage of work by employees (including a stoppage by reason of the expiration of a collective-bargaining agreement) and any concerted slow-down or other concerted interruption of operations by employees.

(3) The terms "commerce," "labor disputes," "employer," "employee," "labor organization," "representative," "person," and "supervisor" shall have the same meaning as when used in the National Labor Relations Act as amended by this Act.

Saving Provision

Sec. 502. Nothing in this Act shall be construed to require an individual employee to render labor or service without his consent, nor shall anything in this Act be construed to make the quitting of his labor by an individual employee an illegal act; nor shall any court issue any process to compel the performance by an individual of such labor or service, without his consent; nor shall the quitting of labor by an employee or employees in good faith because of abnormally dangerous conditions for work at the place of employment of such employee or employees be deemed a strike under this Act.

Separability

Sec. 503. If any provision of this Act, or the application of such provision to any person or circumstance, shall be invalid, the remainder of this Act, or the application of such provision to persons or circumstances other than those as to which it is held invalid, shall not be affected thereby.

Text of the Labor-Management Reporting and Disclosure Act of 1959

73 Stat. 519 (1959), as amended, 79 Stat. 888 (1965), 88 Stat. 852 (1974); 29 U.S.C. Sections 401–531 (1970).

SHORT TITLE

Section 1. This Act may be cited as the "Labor-Management Reporting and Disclosure Act of 1959."

Declaration of Findings, Purposes, and Policy

Sec. 2.

(a) The Congress finds that, in the public interest, it continues to be the responsibility of the Federal Government to protect employees' rights to organize, choose their own representatives, bargain collectively, and otherwise engage in concerted activities for their mutual aid or protection; that the relations between employers and labor organizations and the millions of workers they represent have a substantial impact on the commerce of the Nation; and that in order to accomplish the objective of a free flow of commerce it is essential that labor organizations, employers, and their officials adhere to the highest standards of responsibility and ethical conduct in administering the affairs of their organizations, particularly as they affect labor-management relations.

(b) The Congress further finds, from recent investigations in the labor and management fields, that there have been a number of instances of breach of trust, corruption, disregard of the rights of individual employees, and other failures to observe high standards of responsibility and ethical conduct which require further and supplementary legislation that will afford necessary protection of the rights and interests of employees and the public generally as they relate to the activities of labor organizations, employers, labor relations consultants, and their officers and representatives.

(c) The Congress, therefore, further finds and declares that the enactment of this Act is necessary to eliminate or prevent improper practices on the part of labor organizations, employers, labor relations consultants, and their officers and representatives which distort and defeat the policies of the Labor Management Relations Act, 1947, as amended, and the Railway Labor Act, as amended, and have the tendency or necessary effect of burdening or obstructing commerce by (1) impairing the efficiency, safety, or operation of the instrumentalities of commerce; (2) occurring in the current of commerce; (3) materially affecting, restraining, or controlling the flow of raw materials or manufactured or processed goods into or from the channels of commerce, or the prices of such materials or goods in commerce; or (4) causing diminution of employment and wages in such volume as substantially to impair or disrupt the market for goods flowing into or from the channels of commerce.

Definitions

Sec. 3. For the purposes of titles I, II, III, IV, V (except section 505), and VI of this Act—

(a) "Commerce" means trade, traffic, commerce, transportation, transmission, or communication among the several States or between any State and any place outside thereof.

(b) "State" includes any State of the United States, the District of Columbia, Puerto Rico, the Virgin Islands, American Samoa, Guam, Wake Island, the Canal Zone, and Outer Continental Shelf lands defined in the Outer Continental Shelf Lands Act (43 U.S.C. §§ 1331–1343).

(c) "Industry affecting commerce" means any activity, business, or industry in commerce or in which a labor dispute would hinder or obstruct commerce or the free flow of commerce and includes any activity or industry "affecting commerce" within the meaning of the Labor Management Relations Act, 1947, as amended, or the Railway Labor Act, as amended.

(d) "Person" includes one or more individuals, labor organizations, partnerships, associations, corporations, legal representatives, mutual companies, joint-stock companies, trusts, unincorporated organizations, trustees, trustees in bankruptcy, or receivers.

(e) "Employer" means any employer or any group or association of employers engaged in an industry affecting commerce (1) which is, with respect to employees engaged in an industry affecting commerce, an employer within the meaning of any law of the United States relating to the employment of any employees or (2) which may deal with any labor organization concerning grievances, labor disputes, wages, rates of pay, hours of employment, or conditions of work, and includes any person acting directly or indirectly as an employer or as an agent of an employer in relation to an employee but does not include the United States or any corporation wholly owned by the Government of the United States or any State or political subdivision thereof.

(f) "Employee" means any individual employed by an employer, and includes any individual whose work has ceased as a consequence of, or in connection with, any current labor dispute or because of any unfair labor practice or because of exclusion or expulsion from a labor organization in any manner or for any reason inconsistent with the requirements of this Act.

(g) "Labor dispute" includes any controversy concerning terms, tenure, or conditions of employment, or concerning the association or representation of persons in negotiating, fixing, maintaining, changing, or seeking to arrange terms or conditions of employment, regardless of whether the disputants stand in the proximate relation of employer and employee.

(h) "Trusteeship" means any receivership, trusteeship, or other method of supervision or control whereby a labor organization suspends the autonomy otherwise available to a subordinate body under its constitution or bylaws.

(i) "Labor organization" means a labor organization engaged in an industry affecting commerce and includes any organization of any kind, any agency, or employee representation committee, group, association, or plan so engaged in which employees participate and which exists for the purpose, in whole or in part, of dealing with employers concerning grievances, labor disputes, wages, rates of pay, hours, or other terms or conditions of employment, and any conference, general committee, joint or system board, or joint council so engaged which is subordinate to a national or international labor organization, other than a State or local central body.

(j) A labor organization shall be deemed to be engaged in an industry affecting commerce if it—

   (1) is the certified representative of employees under the provisions of the National Labor Relations Act, as amended, or the Railway Labor Act, as amended; or

   (2) although not certified, is a national or international labor organization or a local labor organization recognized or acting as the representative of employees of an employer or employers engaged in an industry affecting commerce; or

   (3) has chartered a local labor organization or subsidiary body which is representing or actively seeking to represent employees of employers within the meaning of paragraph (1) or (2); or

   (4) has been chartered by a labor organization representing or actively seeking to represent employees within the meaning of paragraph (1) or (2) as the local or subordinate body through which such employees may enjoy membership or become affiliated with such labor organization; or

   (5) is a conference, general committee, joint or system board, or joint council, subordinate to a national or international labor organization, which includes a labor organization engaged in an in-

dustry affecting commerce within the meaning of any of the preceding paragraphs of this subsection, other than a State or local central body.

(k) "Secret ballot" means the expression by ballot, voting machine, or otherwise, but in no event by proxy, of a choice with respect to any election or vote taken upon any matter, which is cast in such a manner that the person expressing such choice cannot be identified with the choice expressed.

(l) "Trust in which a labor organization is interested" means a trust or other fund or organization (1) which was created or established by a labor organization, or one or more of the trustees or one or more members of the governing body of which is selected or appointed by a labor organization, and (2) a primary purpose of which is to provide benefits for the members of such labor organization or their beneficiaries.

(m) "Labor relations consultant" means any person who, for compensation, advises or represents an employer, employer organization, or labor organization concerning employee organizing, concerted activities, or collective bargaining activities.

(n) "Officer" means any constitutional officer, any person authorized to perform the functions of president, vice president, secretary, treasurer, or other executive functions of a labor organization, and any member of its executive board or similar governing body.

(o) "Member" or "member in good standing", when used in reference to a labor organization, includes any person who has fulfilled the requirements for membership in such organization, and who neither has voluntarily withdrawn from membership nor has been expelled or suspended from membership after appropriate proceedings consistent with lawful provisions of the constitution and bylaws of such organization.

(p) "Secretary" means the Secretary of Labor.

(q) "Officer, agent, shop steward, or other representative", when used with respect to a labor organization, includes elected officials and key administrative personnel, whether elected or appointed (such as business agents, heads of departments or major units, and organizers who exercise substantial independent authority), but does not include salaried nonsupervisory professional staff, stenographic, and service personnel.

(r) "District court of the United States" means a United States district court and a United States court of any place subject to the jurisdiction of the United States.

TITLE I—BILL OF RIGHTS OF MEMBERS OF LABOR ORGANIZATIONS

Bill of Rights

Sec. 101.

(a) (1) *Equal Rights.*—Every member of a labor organization shall have equal rights and privileges within such organization to nominate candidates, to vote in elections or referendums of the labor organization, to attend membership meetings, and to participate in the deliberations and voting upon the business of such meetings, subject to reasonable rules and regulations in such organization's constitution and bylaws.

(2) *Freedom of Speech and Assembly.*—Every member of any labor organization shall have the right to meet and assemble freely with other members; and to express any views, arguments, or opinions; and to express at meetings of the labor organization his views, upon candidates in an election of the labor organization or upon any business properly before the meeting, subject to the organization's established and reasonable rules pertaining to the conduct of meetings: *Provided,* That nothing herein shall be construed to impair the right of a labor organization to adopt and enforce reasonable rules as to the responsibility of every member toward the organization as an institution and to his refraining from conduct that would interfere with its performance of its legal or contractual obligations.

(3) *Dues, Initiation Fees, and Assessments.*—Except in the case of a federation of national or international labor organizations, the rates of dues and initiation fees payable by members of any labor organization in effect on the date of enactment of this Act shall not be increased, and no general or special assessment shall be levied upon such members, except—

(A) in a case of a local labor organization, (i) by majority vote by secret ballot of the members in good standing voting at a general or special membership meeting, after reasonable notice of the intention to vote upon such question, or (ii) by majority vote of the members in good standing voting in a membership referendum conducted by secret ballot; or

(B) in the case of a labor organization, other than a local labor organization or a federation of national or international labor organizations, (i) by majority vote of the delegates voting at a regular convention, or at a special convention of such labor organization held upon not less than thirty days' written notice to the principal office of each local or constituent labor organization entitled to such notice, or (ii) by majority vote of the members in good standing of such labor organization voting in a membership referendum conducted by secret ballot, or (iii) by majority vote of the members of the executive board or similar governing body of such labor organization, pursuant to express authority contained in the constitution and bylaws of such labor organization: *Provided,* That such action on the part of the executive board or similar governing body shall be effective only until the next regular convention of such labor organization.

(4) *Protection of the Right to Sue.*—No labor organization shall limit the right of any member thereof to institute an action in any court, or in a proceeding before any administrative agency, irrespective of whether or not the labor organization or its officers are named as defendants or respondents in such action or proceeding, or the right of any member of a labor organization to appear as a witness in any judicial, administrative, or legislative proceeding, or to petition any legislature or to communicate with any legislator: *Provided,* That any such member may be required to exhaust reasonable hearing procedures (but not to exceed a four-month lapse of time) within such organization, before instituting legal or administrative proceedings against such organizations or any officer thereof: *And provided further,* That no interested employer or employer association shall directly or indirectly finance, encourage, or participate in, except as a party, any such action, proceeding, appearance, or petition.

(5) *Safeguards Against Improper Disciplinary Action.*—No member of any labor organization may be fined, suspended, expelled, or otherwise disciplined except for nonpayment of dues by such organization or by any officer thereof unless such member has been (A) served with written specific charges; (B) given a reasonable time to prepare his defense; (C) afforded a full and fair hearing.

(b) Any provision of the constitution and by-laws of any labor organization which is inconsistent with the provisions of this section shall be of no force or effect.

Civil Enforcement

Sec. 102. Any person whose rights secured by the provisions of this title have been infringed by any violation of this title may bring a civil action in a district court of the United States for such relief (including injunctions) as may be appropriate. Any such action against a labor organization shall be brought in the district court of the United States for the district where the alleged violation occurred, or where the principal office of such labor organization is located.

Retention of Existing Rights

Sec. 103. Nothing contained in this title shall limit the rights and remedies of any member of a labor organization under any State or Federal law or before any court or other tribunal, or under the constitution and bylaws of any labor organization.

Right to Copies of Collective Bargaining Agreements

Sec. 104. It shall be the duty of the secretary or corresponding principal officer of each labor organization, in the case of a local labor organization, to forward a copy of each collective bargaining agreement made by such labor organization with any employer to any employee who requests such a copy and whose rights as such employee are directly affected by such agreement, and in the case of a labor organization other than a local labor organization, to forward a copy of any such agreement to each constituent unit which has members directly affected by such agreement; and such officer shall maintain at the principal office of the labor organization of which he is an officer copies of any such agreement made or received by such labor organization, which copies shall be available for inspection by any member or by any employee whose rights are affected by such agreement. The provisions of section 210 shall be applicable in the enforcement of this section.

Information as to Act

Sec. 105. Every labor organization shall inform its members concerning the provisions of this Act.

TITLE II—REPORTING BY LABOR ORGANIZATIONS, OFFICERS AND EMPLOYEES OF LABOR ORGANIZATIONS, AND EMPLOYERS

Report of Labor Organizations

Sec. 201.

(a) Every labor organization shall adopt a constitution and bylaws and shall file a copy thereof with the Secretary, together with a report, signed by its president and secretary or corresponding principal officers, containing the following information—

(1) the name of the labor organization, its mailing address, and any other address at which it maintains its principal office or at which it keeps the records referred to in this title;

(2) the name and title of each of its officers;

(3) the initiation fee or fees required from a new or transferred member and fees for work permits required by the reporting labor organization;

(4) the regular dues or fees or other periodic payments required to remain a member of the reporting labor organization; and

(5) detailed statements, or references to specific provisions of documents filed under this subsection which contain such statements, showing the provision made and procedures followed with respect to each of the following: (A) qualifications for or restrictions on membership, (B) levying of assessments, (C) participation in insurance or other benefit plans, (D) authorization for disbursement of funds of the labor organization, (E) audit of financial transactions of the labor organization, (F) the calling of regular and special meetings, (G) the selection of officers and stewards and of any representatives to other bodies composed of labor organizations' representatives, with a specific statement of the manner in which each officer was elected, appointed, or otherwise selected, (H) discipline or removal of officers or agents for breaches of their trust, (I) imposition of fines, suspensions and expulsions of members, including the grounds for such action and any provision made for notice, hearing, judgment on

the evidence, and appeal procedures, (J) authorization for bargaining demands, (K) ratification of contract terms, (L) authorization for strikes, and (M) issuance of work permits. Any change in the information required by this subsection shall be reported to the Secretary at the time the reporting labor organization files with the Secretary the annual financial report required by subsection (b).

(b) Every labor organization shall file annually with the Secretary a financial report signed by its president and treasurer or corresponding principal officers containing the following information in such detail as may be necessary accurately to disclose its financial condition and operations for its preceding fiscal year—

(1) assets and liabilities at the beginning and end of the fiscal year;

(2) receipts of any kind and the sources thereof;

(3) salary, allowances, and other direct or indirect disbursements (including reimbursed expenses) to each officer and also to each employee who, during such fiscal year, received more than $10,000 in the aggregate from such labor organization and any other labor organization affiliated with it or with which it is affiliated, or which is affiliated with the same national or international labor organization;

(4) direct and indirect loans made to any officer, employee, or member, which aggregated more than $250 during the fiscal year, together with a statement of the purpose, security, if any, and arrangements for repayment;

(5) direct and indirect loans to any business enterprise, together with a statement of the purpose, security, if any, and arrangements for repayment; and

(6) other disbursements made by it including the purpose thereof;

all in such categories as the Secretary may prescribe.

(c) Every labor organization required to submit a report under this title shall make available the information required to be contained in such report to all of its members, and every such labor organization and its officers shall be under a duty enforceable at the suit of any member of such organization in any State court of competent jurisdiction or in the district court of the United States for the district in which such labor organization maintains its principal office, to permit such member for just cause to examine any books, records, and accounts necessary to verify such report. The court in such action may, in its discretion, in addition to any judgment awarded to the plaintiff or plaintiffs, allow a reasonable attorney's fee to be paid by the defendant, and costs of the action.

Report of Officers and Employees of Labor Organizations

Sec. 202.

(a) Every officer of a labor organization and every employee of a labor organization (other than an employee performing exclusively clerical or custodial services) shall file with the Secretary a signed report listing and describing for his preceding fiscal year—

  (1) any stock, bond, security, or other interest, legal or equitable, which he or his spouse or minor child directly or indirectly held in, and any income or any other benefit with monetary value (including reimbursed expenses) which he or his spouse or minor child derived directly or indirectly from, an employer whose employees such labor organization represents or is actively seeking to represent, except payments and other benefits received as a bona fide employee of such employer;

  (2) any transaction in which he or his spouse or minor child engaged, directly or indirectly, involving any stock, bond, security, or loan to or from, or other legal or equitable interest in the business of an employer whose employees such labor organization represents or is actively seeking to represent;

  (3) any stock, bond, security, or other interest, legal or equitable, which he or his spouse or minor child directly or indirectly held in, and any income or any other benefit with monetary value (including reimbursed expenses) which he or his spouse or minor child directly or indirectly derived from, any business a substantial part of which consists of buying from, selling or leasing to, or otherwise dealing with, the business of an employer whose employees such labor organization represents or is actively seeking to represent;

  (4) any stock, bond, security, or other interest, legal or equitable, which he or his spouse or minor child directly or indirectly held in, and any income or any other benefit with monetary value

(including reimbursed expenses) which he or his spouse or minor child directly or indirectly derived from, a business any part of which consists of buying from, or selling or leasing directly or indirectly to, or otherwise dealing with such labor organization;

  (5) any direct or indirect business transaction or arrangement between him or his spouse or minor child and any employer whose employees his organization represents or is actively seeking to represent, except work performed and payments and benefits received as a bona fide employee of such employer and except purchases and sales of goods or services in the regular course of business at prices generally available to any employee of such employer; and

  (6) any payment of money or other thing of value (including reimbursed expenses) which he or his spouse or minor child received directly or indirectly from any employer or any person who acts as a labor relations consultant to an employer, except payments of the kinds referred to in section 302(c) of the Labor Management Relations Act, 1947, as amended.

(b) The provisions of paragraphs (1), (2), (3), (4), and (5) of subsection (a) shall not be construed to require any such officer or employee to report his bona fide investments in securities traded on a securities exchange registered as a national securities exchange under the Securities Exchange Act of 1934, in shares in an investment company registered under the Investment Company Act of 1940, or in securities of a public utility holding company registered under the Public Utility Holding Company Act of 1935, or to report any income derived therefrom.

(c) Nothing contained in this section shall be construed to require any officer or employee of a labor organization to file a report under subsection (a) unless he or his spouse or minor child holds or has held an interest, has received income or any other benefit with monetary value or a loan, or has engaged in a transaction described therein.

Report of Employers

Sec. 203.

(a) Every employer who in any fiscal year made—

  (1) any payment or loan, direct or indirect, of

money or other thing of value (including reimbursed expenses), or any promise or agreement therefor, to any labor organization or officer, agent, shop steward, or other representative of a labor organization, or employee of any labor organization, except (A) payments or loans made by any national or State bank, credit union, insurance company, savings and loan association or other credit institution and (B) payments of the kind referred to in section 302(c) of the Labor Management Relations Act, 1947, as amended;

(2) any payment (including reimbursed expenses) to any of his employees, or any group or committee of such employees, for the purpose of causing such employee or group or committee of employees to persuade other employees to exercise or not to exercise, or as the manner of exercising, the right to organize and bargain collectively through representatives of their own choosing unless such payments were contemporaneously or previously disclosed to such other employees;

(3) any expenditure, during the fiscal year, where an object thereof, directly or indirectly, is to interfere with, restrain, or coerce employees in the exercise of the right to organize and bargain collectively through representatives of their own choosing, or is to obtain information concerning the activities of employees or a labor organization in connection with a labor dispute involving such employer, except for use solely in conjunction with an administrative or arbitral proceeding or a criminal or civil judicial proceeding;

(4) any agreement or arrangement with a labor relations consultant or other independent contractor or organization pursuant to which such person undertakes activities where an object thereof, directly or indirectly, is to persuade employees to exercise or not to exercise, or persuade employees as to the manner of exercising, the right to organize and bargain collectively through representatives of their own choosing, or undertakes to supply such employer with information concerning the activities of employees or a labor organization in connection with a labor dispute involving such employer, except information for use solely in conjunction with an administrative or arbitral proceeding or a criminal or civil judicial proceeding; or

(5) any payment (including reimbursed expenses) pursuant to an agreement or arrangement described in subdivision (4);

shall file with the Secretary a report, in a form prescribed by him, signed by its president and treasurer or corresponding principal officers showing in detail the date and amount of each such payment, loan, promise, agreement, or arrangement and the name, address, and position, if any, in any firm or labor organization of the person to whom it was made and a full explanation of the circumstances of all such payments, including the terms of any agreement or understanding pursuant to which they were made.

(b) Every person who pursuant to any agreement or arrangement with an employer undertakes activities where an object thereof is, directly or indirectly—

(1) to persuade employees to exercise or not to exercise, or persuade employees as to the manner of exercising, the right to organize and bargain collectively through representatives of their own choosing; or

(2) to supply an employer with information concerning the activities of employees or a labor organization in connection with a labor dispute involving such employer, except information for use solely in conjunction with an administrative or arbitral proceeding or a criminal or civil judicial proceeding;

shall file within thirty days after entering into such agreement or arrangement a report with the Secretary, signed by its president and treasurer or corresponding principal officers, containing the name under which such person is engaged in doing business and the address of its principal office, and a detailed statement of the terms and conditions of such agreement or arrangement. Every such person shall file annually, with respect to each fiscal year during which payments were made as a result of such an agreement or arrangement, a report with the Secretary, signed by its president and treasurer or corresponding principal officers, containing a statement (A) of its receipts of any kind from employers on account of labor relations advice or services, designating the sources thereof, and (B) of its disbursements of any kind, in connection with such services and the purposes thereof. In each such case such information shall be set forth in such categories as the Secretary may prescribe.

(c) Nothing in this section shall be construed to require any employer or other person to file a report covering the services of such person by reason of his giving or agreeing to give advice to such employer or representing or agreeing to represent such employer before any court, administrative agency, or tribunal of arbitration or engaging or agreeing to engage in collective bargaining on behalf of such employer with respect to wages, hours, or other terms or conditions of employment or the negotiation of an agreement or any question arising thereunder.

(d) Nothing contained in this section shall be construed to require an employer to file a report under subsection (a) unless he has made an expenditure, payment, loan, agreement, or arrangement of the kind described therein. Nothing contained in this section shall be construed to require any other person to file a report under subsection (b) unless he was a party to an agreement or arrangement of the kind described therein.

(e) Nothing contained in this section shall be construed to require any regular officer, supervisor, or employee of an employer to file a report in connection with services rendered to such employer nor shall any employer be required to file a report covering expenditures made to any regular officer, supervisor, or employee of an employer as compensation for service as a regular officer, supervisor, or employee of such employer.

(f) Nothing contained in this section shall be construed as an amendment to, or modification of the rights protected by, section 8(c) of the National Labor Relations Act, as amended.

(g) The term "interfere with, restrain, or coerce" as used in this section means interference, restraint, and coercion which, if done with respect to the exercise of rights guaranteed in section 7 of the National Labor Relations Act, as amended, would, under section 8(a) of such Act, constitute an unfair labor practice.

Attorney-Client Communications Exempted

Sec. 204. Nothing contained in this Act shall be construed to require an attorney who is a member in good standing of the bar of any State, to include in any report required to be filed pursuant to the provisions of this Act any information which was lawfully communicated to such attorney by any of his clients in the course of a legitimate attorney-client relationship.

Reports Made Public Information

Sec. 205.

(a) The contents of the reports and documents filed with the Secretary pursuant to sections 201, 202, 203, and 211 shall be public information, and the Secretary may publish any information and data which he obtains pursuant to the provisions of this title. The Secretary may use the information and data for statistical and research purposes, and compile and publish such studies, analyses, reports, and surveys based thereon as he may deem appropriate.

(b) The Secretary shall by regulation make reasonable provision for the inspection and examination, on the request of any person, of the information and data contained in any report or other document filed with him pursuant to section 201, 202, 203, or 211.

(c) The Secretary shall by regulation provide for the furnishing by the Department of Labor of copies of reports or other documents filed with the Secretary pursuant to this title, upon payment of a charge based upon the cost of the service. The Secretary shall make available without payment of a charge, or require any person to furnish, to such State agency as is designated by law or by the Governor of the State in which such person has his principal place of business or headquarters, upon request of the Governor of such State, copies of any reports and documents filed by such person with the Secretary pursuant to section 201, 202, 203, or 211, or of information and data contained therein. No person shall be required by reason of any law of any State to furnish to any officer or agency of such State any information included in a report filed by such person with the Secretary pursuant to the provisions of this title, if a copy of such report, or of the portion thereof containing such information, is furnished to such officer or agency. All moneys received in payment of such charges fixed by the Secretary pursuant to this subsection shall be deposited in the general fund of the Treasury.

Retention of Records

Sec. 206. Every person required to file any report under this title shall maintain records on the matters required to be reported which will provide in sufficient detail the necessary basic information and data from which the documents filed with the Secretary may be verified, explained or clarified, and checked for accuracy and completeness, and shall include vouchers, worksheets, receipts, and applicable resolutions, and shall keep such records available for examination for a period of not less than five years after the filing of the documents based on the information which they contain.

Effective Date

Sec. 207.

(a) Each labor organization shall file the initial report required under section 201(a) within ninety days after the date on which it first becomes subject to this Act.

(b) Each person required to file a report under section 201(b), 202, 203(a), or the second sentence of 203(b), or section 211 shall file such report within ninety days after the end of each of its fiscal years; except that where such person is subject to section 201(b), 202, 203(a), the second sentence of 203(b), or section 211, as the case may be, for only a portion of such a fiscal year (because the date of enactment of this Act occurs during such person's fiscal year or such person becomes subject to this Act during its fiscal year) such person may consider that portion as the entire fiscal year in making such report.

Rules and Regulations

Sec. 208. The Secretary shall have authority to issue, amend, and rescind rules and regulations prescribing the form and publication of reports required to be filed under this title and such other reasonable rules and regulations (including rules prescribing reports concerning trusts in which a labor organization is interested) as he may find necessary to prevent the circumvention or evasion of such reporting requirements. In exercising his power under this section the Secretary shall prescribe by general rule simplified reports for labor organizations or employers for whom he finds that by virtue of their size a detailed report would be unduly burdensome, but the Secretary may revoke such provision for simplified forms of any labor organization or employer if he determines, after such investigation as he deems proper and due notice and opportunity for a hearing, that the purposes of this section would be served thereby.

Criminal Provisions

Sec. 209.

(a) Any person who willfully violates this title shall be fined not more than $10,000 or imprisoned for not more than one year, or both.

(b) Any person who makes a false statement or representation of a material fact, knowing it to be false, or who knowingly fails to disclose a material fact, in any document, report, or other information required under the provisions of this title shall be fined not more than $10,000 or imprisoned for not more than one year, or both.

(c) Any person who willfully makes a false entry in or willfully conceals, withholds, or destroys any books, records, reports, or statements required to be kept by any provision of this title shall be fined not more than $10,000 or imprisoned for not more than one year, or both.

(d) Each individual required to sign reports under sections 201 and 203 shall be personally responsible for the filing of such reports and for any statement contained therein which he knows to be false.

Civil Enforcement

Sec. 210. Whenever it shall appear that any person has violated or is about to violate any of the provisions of this title, the Secretary may bring a civil action for such relief (including injunctions) as may be appropriate. Any such action may be brought in the district court of the United States where the violation occurred or, at the option of the parties, in the United States District Court for the District of Columbia.

Surety Company Reports

Sec. 211. Each surety company which issues any bond required by this Act or the Welfare and Pension Plans Disclosure Act shall file annually with the Secretary, with respect to each fiscal year during which any such bond was in force, a report, in such form and detail as he may prescribe by regulation, filed by the president and treasurer or corresponding principal officers of the surety company, describing its bond experience under each such Act, including information as to the premiums received, total claims paid, amounts recovered by way of subrogation, administrative and legal expenses and such related data and information as the Secretary shall determine to be necessary in the public interest and to carry out the policy of the Act. Notwithstanding the foregoing, if the Secretary finds that any such specific information cannot be practically ascertained or would be uninformative, the Secretary may modify or waive the requirements for such information.

TITLE III—TRUSTEESHIPS

Reports

Sec. 301.

(a) Every labor organization which has or assumes trusteeship over any subordinate labor organization shall file with the Secretary within thirty days after the date of the enactment of this Act or the imposition of any such trusteeship, and semiannually thereafter, a report, signed by its president and treasurer or corresponding principal officers, as well as by the trustees of such subordinate labor organization, containing the following information: (1) the name and address of the subordinate organization; (2) the date of establishing the trusteeship; (3) a detailed statement of the reason or reasons for establishing or continuing the trusteeship; and (4) the nature and extent of participation by the membership of the subordinate organization in the selection of delegates to represent such organization in regular or special conventions or other policy-determining bodies and in the election of officers of the labor organization which has assumed trusteeship over such subordinate organization. The initial report shall also include a full and complete account of the financial condition of such subordinate organization as of the time trusteeship was assumed over it. During the continuance of a trusteeship the labor organization which has assumed trusteeship over a subordinate labor organization shall file on behalf of the subordinate labor organization the annual financial report required by section 201(b) signed by the president and treasurer or corresponding principal officers of the labor organization which has assumed such trusteeship and the trustees of the subordinate labor organization.

(b) The provisions of sections 201(c), 205, 206, 208, and 210 shall be applicable to reports filed under this title.

(c) Any person who willfully violates this section shall be fined not more than $10,000 or imprisoned for not more than one year, or both.

(d) Any person who makes a false statement or representation of a material fact, knowing it to be false, or who knowingly fails to disclose a material fact, in any report required under the provisions of this section or willfully makes any false entry in or willfully withholds, conceals, or destroys any documents, books, records, reports, or statements upon which such report is based, shall be fined not more than $10,000 or imprisoned for not more than one year, or both.

(e) Each individual required to sign a report under this section shall be personally responsible for the filing of such report and for any statement contained therein which he knows to be false.

Purposes for which a Trusteeship May Be Established

Sec. 302. Trusteeships shall be established and administered by a labor organization over a subordinate body only in accordance with the constitution and bylaws of the organization which has assumed trusteeship over the subordinate body and for the purpose of correcting corruption or financial malpractice, assuring the performance of collective bargaining agreements or other duties of a bargaining representative, restoring democratic procedures, or otherwise carrying out the legitimate objects of such labor organization.

Unlawful Acts Relating to Labor Organization under Trusteeship

Sec. 303.

(a) During any period when a subordinate body of a labor organization is in trusteeship, it shall be unlawful (1) to count the vote of delegates from such body in any convention or election of officers of the labor organization unless the delegates have been chosen by secret ballot in an election in which all the members in good standing of such subordinate body were eligible to participate, or (2) to transfer to such organization any current receipts or other funds of the subordinate body except the normal per capita tax and assessments payable by subordinate bodies not in trusteeship: *Provided,* That nothing herein contained shall prevent the distribution of the assets of a labor organization in accordance with its constitution and bylaws upon the bona fide dissolution thereof.

(b) Any person who willfully violates this section shall be fined not more than $10,000 or imprisoned for not more than one year, or both.

Enforcement

Sec. 304.

(a) Upon the written complaint of any member or subordinate body of a labor organization alleging that such organization has violated the provisions of this title (except section 301) the Secretary shall investigate the complaint and if the Secretary finds probable cause to believe that such violation has occurred and has not been remedied he shall, without disclosing the identity of the complainant, bring a civil action in any district court of the United States having jurisdiction of the labor organization for such relief (including injunctions) as may be appropriate. Any member or subordinate body of a labor organization affected by any violation of this title (except section 301) may bring a civil action in any district court of the United States having jurisdiction of the labor organization for such relief (including injunctions) as may be appropriate.

(b) For the purpose of actions under this section, district courts of the United States shall be deemed to have jurisdiction of a labor organization (1) in the district in which the principal office of such labor organization is located, or (2) in any district in which its duly authorized officers or agents are engaged in conducting the affairs of the trusteeship.

(c) In any proceeding pursuant to this section a trusteeship established by a labor organization in conformity with the procedural requirements of its constitution and bylaws and authorized or ratified after a fair hearing either before the executive board or before such other body as may be provided in accordance with its constitution or bylaws shall be presumed valid for a period of eighteen months from the date of its establishment and shall not be subject to attack during such period except upon clear and convincing proof that the trusteeship was not established or maintained in good faith for a purpose allowable under section 302. After the expiration of eighteen months the trusteeship shall be presumed invalid in any such proceeding and its discontinuance shall be decreed unless the labor organization shall show by clear and convincing proof that the continuation of the trusteeship is necessary for a purpose allowable under section 302. In the latter event the court may dismiss the complaint or retain jurisdiction of the cause on such conditions and for such period as it deems appropriate.

Report to Congress

Sec. 305. The Secretary shall submit to the Congress at the expiration of three years from the date of enactment of this Act a report upon the operation of this title.

Complaint by Secretary

Sec. 306. The rights and remedies provided by this title shall be in addition to any and all other rights and remedies at law or in equity: *Provided,* That upon the filing of a complaint by the Secretary the jurisdiction of the district court over such trusteeship shall be exclusive and the final judgment shall be res judicata.

TITLE IV—ELECTIONS

Terms of Office; Election Procedures

Sec. 401.

(a) Every national or international labor organization, except a federation of national or international labor organizations, shall elect its officers not less often than once every five years either by secret ballot among the members in good standing or at a convention of delegates chosen by secret ballot.

(b) Every local labor organization shall elect its officers not less often than once every three years by secret ballot among the members in good standing.

(c) Every national or international labor organization, except a federation of national or international labor organizations, and every local labor organization, and its officers, shall be under a duty, enforceable at the suit of any bona fide candidate for office in such labor organization in the district court of the United States in which such labor organization maintains its principal office, to comply with all reasonable requests of any candidate to distribute by mail or otherwise at the candidate's expense campaign literature in aid of such person's candidacy to all members in good standing of such labor organization and to refrain from discrimination in favor of or against any candidate with respect to the use of lists of members, and whenever such labor organizations or its officers authorize the distribution by mail or otherwise to members of campaign literature on behalf of any candidate or of the labor organization itself with reference to such election, similar distribution at the request of any other bona fide candidate shall be made by such labor organization and its officers, with equal treatment as to the expense of such distribution. Every bona fide candidate shall have the right, once within 30 days prior to an election of a labor organization in which he is a candidate, to inspect a list containing the names and last known addresses of all members of the labor organization who are subject to a collective bargaining agreement requiring membership therein as a condition of employment, which list shall be maintained and kept at the principal office of such labor organization by a designated official thereof. Adequate safeguards to insure a fair election shall be provided, including the right of any candidate to have an observer at the polls and at the counting of the ballots.

(d) Officers of intermediate bodies, such as general committees, system boards, joint boards, or joint councils, shall be elected not less often than once every four years by secret ballot among the members in good standing or by labor organization officers representative of such members who have been elected by secret ballot.

(e) In any election required by this section which is to be held by secret ballot a reasonable opportunity shall be given for the nomination of candidates and every member in good standing shall be eligible to be a candidate and to hold office (subject to section 504 and to reasonable qualifications uniformly imposed) and shall have the right to vote for or otherwise support the candidate or candidates of his choice, without being subject to penalty, discipline, or improper interference or reprisal of any kind by such organization or any member thereof. Not less than fifteen days prior to the election notice thereof shall be mailed to each member at his last known home address. Each member in good standing shall be entitled to one vote. No member whose dues have been withheld by his employer for payment to such organization pursuant to his voluntary authorization provided for in a collective bargaining agreement, shall be declared ineligible to vote or be a candidate for office in such organization by reason of alleged delay or default in the payment of dues. The votes cast by members of each local labor organization shall be counted, and the results published, separately. The election officials designated in the constitution and bylaws or the secretary, if no other official is designated, shall preserve for one year the ballots and all other records pertaining to the election. The election shall be conducted in accordance with the constitution and bylaws of

such organization insofar as they are not inconsistent with the provisions of this title.

(f) When officers are chosen by a convention of delegates elected by secret ballot, the convention shall be conducted in accordance with the constitution and bylaws of the labor organization insofar as they are not inconsistent with the provisions of this title. The officials designated in the constitution and bylaws or the secretary, if no other is designated, shall preserve for one year the credentials of the delegates and all minutes and other records of the convention pertaining to the election of officers.

(g) No moneys received by any labor organization by way of dues, assessment, or similar levy, and no moneys of an employer shall be contributed or applied to promote the candidacy of any person in an election subject to the provisions of this title. Such moneys of a labor organization may be utilized for notices, factual statements of issues not involving candidates, and other expenses necessary for the holding of an election.

(h) If the Secretary, upon application of any member of a local labor organization, finds after hearing in accordance with the Administrative Procedure Act that the constitution and bylaws of such labor organization do not provide an adequate procedure for the removal of an elected officer guilty of serious misconduct, such officer may be removed, for cause shown and after notice and hearing, by the members in good standing voting in a secret ballot conducted by the officers of such labor organization in accordance with its constitution and bylaws insofar as they are not inconsistent with the provisions of this title.

(i) The Secretary shall promulgate rules and regulations prescribing minimum standards and procedures for determining the adequacy of the removal procedures to which reference is made in subsection (h).

Enforcement

Sec. 402.

(a) A member of a labor organization—

    (1) who has exhausted the remedies available under the constitution and bylaws of such organization and of any parent body or

    (2) who has invoked such available remedies without obtaining a final decision within three calendar months after their invocation,

may file a complaint with the Secretary within one calendar month thereafter alleging the violation of any provision of section 401 (including violation of the constitution and bylaws of the labor organization pertaining to the election and removal of officers). The challenged election shall be presumed valid pending a final decision thereon (as hereinafter provided) and in the interim the affairs of the organization shall be conducted by the officers elected or in such other manner as its constitution and bylaws may provide.

(b) The Secretary shall investigate such complaint and, if he finds probable cause to believe that a violation of this title has occurred and has not been remedied, he shall, within sixty days after the filing of such complaint, bring a civil action against the labor organization as an entity in the district court of the United States in which such labor organization maintains its principal office to set aside the invalid election, if any, and to direct the conduct of an election in hearing and vote upon the removal of officers under the supervision of the Secretary and in accordance with the provisions of this title and such rules and regulations as the Secretary may prescribe. The court shall have power to take such action as it deems proper to preserve the assets of the labor organization.

(c) If, upon a preponderance of the evidence after a trial upon the merits, the court finds—
  (1) that an election has not been held within the time prescribed by section 401, or
  (2) that the violation of section 401 may have affected the outcome of an election
the court shall declare the election, if any, to be void and direct the conduct of a new election under supervision of the Secretary and, so far as lawful and practicable, in conformity with the constitution and bylaws of the labor organization. The Secretary shall promptly certify to the court the names of the persons elected, and the court shall thereupon enter a decree declaring such persons to be the officers of the labor organization. If the proceeding is for the removal of officers pursuant to subsection (h) of section 401, the Secretary shall certify the results of the vote and the court shall enter a decree declaring whether such persons have been removed as officers of the labor organization.

(d) An order directing an election, dismissing a complaint, or designating elected officers of a labor organization shall be appealable in the same manner as

the final judgment in a civil action, but an order directing an election shall not be stayed pending appeal.

Application of Other Laws

Sec. 403. No labor organization shall be required by law to conduct elections of officers with greater frequency or in a different form or manner than is required by its own constitution or bylaws, except as otherwise provided by this title. Existing rights and remedies to enforce the constitution and bylaws of a labor organization with respect to elections prior to the conduct thereof shall not be affected by the provisions of this title. The remedy provided by this title for challenging an election already conducted shall be exclusive.

Effective Date

Sec. 404. The provisions of this title shall become applicable—

(1) ninety days after the date of enactment of this Act in the case of a labor organization whose constitution and bylaws can lawfully be modified or amended by action of its constitutional officers or governing body, or

(2) where such modification can only be made by a constitutional convention of the labor organization, not later than the next constitutional convention of such labor organization after the date of enactment of this Act, or one year after such date, whichever is sooner. If no such convention is held within such one-year period, the executive board or similar governing body empowered to act for such labor organization between conventions is empowered to make such interim constitutional changes as are necessary to carry out the provisions of this title.

TITLE V—SAFEGUARDS FOR LABOR ORGANIZATIONS

Fiduciary Responsibility of Officers of Labor Organizations

Sec. 501.

(a) The officers, agents, shop stewards, and other representatives of a labor organization occupy positions of trust in relation to such organization and its members as a group. It is, therefore, the duty of each such person, taking into account the special problems and functions of a labor organization, to hold its money and property solely for the benefit of the organization and its members and to manage, invest, and expend the same in accordance with its constitution and by-laws and any resolutions of the governing bodies adopted thereunder, to refrain from dealing with such organizations as an adverse party or in behalf of an adverse party in any matter connected with his duties and from holding or acquiring any pecuniary or personal interest which conflicts with the interests of such organization, and to account to the organization for any profit received by him in whatever capacity in connection with transactions conducted by him or under his direction on behalf of the organization. A general exculpatory provision in the constitution and bylaws of such a labor organization or a general exculpatory resolution of a governing body purporting to relieve any such person of liability for breach of the duties declared by this section shall be void as against public policy.

(b) When any officer, agent, shop steward, or representative of any labor organization is alleged to have violated the duties declared in subsection (a) and the labor organization or its governing board or officers refuse or fail to sue or recover damages or secure an accounting or other appropriate relief within a reasonable time after being requested to do so by any member of the labor organization, such member may sue such officer, agent, shop steward, or representative in any district court of the United States or in any State court of competent jurisdiction to recover damages or secure an accounting or other appropriate relief for the benefit of the labor organization. No such proceeding shall be brought except upon leave of the court obtained upon verified application and for good cause shown which application may be made ex parte. The trial judge may allot a reasonable part of the recovery in any action under this subsection to pay the fees of counsel prosecuting the suit at the instance of the member of the labor organization and to compensate such member for any expenses necessarily paid or incurred by him in connection with the litigation.

(c) Any person who embezzles, steals, or unlawfully and willfully abstracts or converts to his own use, or the use of another, any of the moneys, funds, securities, property, or other assets of a labor organization of which he is an officer, or by which he is employed, directly or indirectly, shall be fined not more than

$10,000 or imprisoned for not more than five years, or both.

Bonding

Sec. 502.

(a) Every officer, agent, shop steward, or other representative or employee of any labor organization (other than a labor organization whose property and annual financial receipts do not exceed $5,000 in value), or of a trust in which a labor organization is interested, who handles funds or other property thereof shall be bonded to provide protection against loss by reason of acts of fraud or dishonesty on his part directly or through connivance with others. The bond of each such person shall be fixed at the beginning of the organization's fiscal year and shall be in an amount not less than 10 per centum of the funds handled by him and his predecessor or predecessors, if any, during the preceding fiscal year, but in no case more than $500,000. If the labor organization or the trust in which a labor organization is interested does not have a preceding fiscal year, the amount of the bond shall be, in the case of a local labor organization, not less than $1,000, and in the case of any other labor organization or of a trust in which a labor organization is interested, not less than $10,000. Such bonds shall be individual or schedule in form, and shall have a corporate surety company as surety thereon. Any person who is not covered by such bonds shall not be permitted to receive, handle, disburse, or otherwise exercise custody or control of the funds or other property of a labor organization or of a trust in which a labor organization is interested. No such bond shall be placed through an agent or broker or with a surety company in which any labor organization or any officer, agent, shop steward, or other representative of a labor organization has any direct or indirect interest. Such surety company shall be a corporate surety which holds a grant of authority from the Secretary of the Treasury under the Act of July 30, 1947 (6 U.S.C. 6–13), as an acceptable surety on Federal bonds: *Provided,* That when in the opinion of the Secretary a labor organization has made other bonding arrangements which would provide the protection required by this section at comparable cost or less, he may exempt such labor organization from placing a bond through a surety company holding such grant of authority.

(b) Any person who willfully violates this section shall be fined not more than $10,000 or imprisoned for not more than one year, or both.

Making of Loans; Payment of Fines

Sec. 503.

(a) No labor organization shall make directly or indirectly any loan or loans to any officer or employee of such organization which results in a total indebtedness on the part of such officer or employee to the labor organization in excess of $2,000.

(b) No labor organization or employer shall directly or indirectly pay the fine of any officer or employee convicted of any willful violation of this Act.

(c) Any person who willfully violates this section shall be fined not more than $5,000 or imprisoned for not more than one year, or both.

Prohibition Against Certain Persons Holding Office

Sec. 504.

(a) No person who is or has been a member of the Communist Party or who has been convicted of, or served any part of a prison term resulting from his conviction of, robbery, bribery, extortion, embezzlement, grand larceny, burglary, arson, violation of narcotics laws, murder, rape, assault with intent to kill, assault which inflicts grievous bodily injury, or a violation of title II or III of this Act, or conspiracy to commit any such crimes, shall serve—

(1) as an officer, director, trustee, member of any executive board or similar governing body, business agent, manager, organizer, or other employee (other than as an employee performing exclusively clerical or custodial duties) of any labor organization, or

(2) as a labor relations consultant to a person engaged in an industry or activity affecting commerce, or as an officer, director, agent, or employee (other than as an employee performing exclusively clerical or custodial duties) of any group or association of employers dealing with any labor organization.

during or for five years after the termination of his membership in the Communist Party, or for five years after such conviction or after the end of such imprisonment, unless prior to the end of such five-year period, in the case of a person so convicted or imprisoned, (A) his citizenship rights, having been revoked as a result of such conviction, have been fully restored, or (B) the Board of Parole of the United States Department of Justice determines that such person's service in any capacity referred to in clause (1) or (2) would not be contrary to the purposes of this Act. Prior to making any such determination the Board shall hold an administrative hearing and shall give notice of such proceeding by certified mail to the State, county, and Federal prosecuting officials in the jurisdiction or jurisdictions in which such person was convicted. The Board's determination in any such proceeding shall be final. No labor organization or officer thereof shall knowingly permit any person to assume or hold any office or paid position in violation of this subsection.

(b) Any person who willfully violates this section shall be fined not more than $10,000 or imprisoned for not more than one year, or both.

(c) For the purposes of this section, any person shall be deemed to have been "convicted" and under the disability of "conviction" from the date of the judgment of the trial court or the date of the final sustaining of such judgment on appeal, whichever is the later event, regardless of whether such conviction occurred before or after the date of enactment of this Act.

TITLE VI—MISCELLANEOUS PROVISIONS

Investigations

Sec. 601.

(a) The Secretary shall have power when he believes it necessary in order to determine whether any person has violated or is about to violate any provision of this Act (except title I or amendments made by this Act to other statutes) to make an investigation and in connection therewith he may enter such places and inspect such records and accounts and question such persons as he may deem necessary to enable him to determine the facts relative thereto. The Secretary may report to interested persons or officials concerning the facts required to be shown in any report required by this Act and concerning the reasons for failure or refusal to file such a report or any other matter which he deems to be appropriate as a result of such an investigation.

(b) For the purpose of any investigation provided for in

this Act, the provisions of sections 9 and 10 (relating to the attendance of witnesses and the production of books, papers, and documents) of the Federal Trade Commission Act of September 16, 1914, as amended (15 U.S.C. 49, 50), are hereby made applicable to the jurisdiction, powers, and duties of the Secretary or any officers designated by him.

Extortionate Picketing

Sec. 602.

(a) It shall be unlawful to carry on picketing on or about the premises of any employer for the purpose of, or as part of any conspiracy or in furtherance of any plan or purpose for, the personal profit or enrichment of any individual (except a bona fide increase in wages or other employee benefits) by taking or obtaining any money or other thing of value from such employer against his will or with his consent.

(b) Any person who willfully violates this section shall be fined not more than $10,000 or imprisoned not more than twenty years, or both.

Retention of Rights under Other Federal and State Laws

Sec. 603.

(a) Except as explicitly provided to the contrary, nothing in this Act shall reduce or limit the responsibilities of any labor organization or any officer, agent, shop steward, or other representative of a labor organization, or of any trust in which a labor organization is interested, under any other Federal law or under the laws of any State, and, except as explicitly provided to the contrary, nothing in this Act shall take away any right or bar any remedy to which members of a labor organization are entitled under such other Federal law or law of any State.

(b) Nothing contained in titles I, II, III, IV, V, or VI of this Act shall be construed to supersede or impair or otherwise affect the provisions of the Railway Labor Act, as amended, or any of the obligations, rights, benefits, privileges, or immunities of any carrier, employee, organization, representative, or person subject thereto; nor shall anything contained in said titles (except section 505) of this Act be construed to confer any rights, privileges, immunities, or defenses upon employers, or to impair or otherwise affect the rights of any person under the National Labor Relations Act, as amended.

Effect on State Laws

Sec. 604. Nothing in this Act shall be construed to impair or diminish the authority of any State to enact and enforce general criminal laws with respect to robbery, bribery, extortion, embezzlement, grand larceny, burglary, arson, violation of narcotics laws, murder, rape, assault with intent to kill, or assault which inflicts grievous bodily injury, or conspiracy to commit any of such crimes.

Service of Process

Sec. 605. For the purposes of this Act, service of summons, subpoena, or other legal process of a court of the United States upon an officer or agent of a labor organization in his capacity as such shall constitute service upon the labor organization.

Administrative Procedure Act

Sec. 606. The provisions of the Administrative Procedure Act shall be applicable to the issuance, amendment, or rescission of any rules or regulations, or any adjudication, authorized or required pursuant to the provisions of this Act.

Other Agencies and Departments

Sec. 607. In order to avoid unnecessary expense and duplication of functions among Government agencies, the Secretary may make such arrangements or agreements for cooperation or mutual assistance in the performance of his functions under this Act and the functions of any such agency as he may find to be practicable and consistent with law. The Secretary may utilize the facilities of services of any department, agency, or establishment of the United States or of any State or political subdivision of a State, including the services of any of its employees, with the lawful consent of such department, agency, or establishment; and each department, agency, or establishment of the United States is authorized and directed to cooperate with the Secretary and, to the extent permitted by law, to provide such information and facilities as he may request for his assistance in the performance of his functions under this Act. The Attorney General or his representative shall receive from the Secretary for appropriate action such evidence developed in the performance of his functions under this Act as may be found to warrant consideration for criminal prosecution under the provisions of this Act or other Federal law.

Criminal Contempt

Sec. 608. No person shall be punished for any criminal contempt allegedly committed outside the immediate presence of the court in connection with any civil action prosecuted by the Secretary or any other person in any court of the United States under the provisions of this Act unless the facts constituting such criminal contempt are established by the verdict of the jury in a proceeding in the district court of the United States, which jury shall be chosen and empaneled in the manner prescribed by the law governing trial juries in criminal prosecutions in the district courts of the United States.

Prohibition on Certain Discipline by Labor Organization

Sec. 609. It shall be unlawful for any labor organization, or any officer, agent, shop steward, or other representative of a labor organization, or any employee thereof to fine, suspend, expel, or otherwise discipline any of its members for exercising any right to which he is entitled under the provisions of this Act. The provisions of section 102 shall be applicable in the enforcement of this section.

Deprivation of Rights under Act by Violence

Sec. 610. It shall be unlawful for any person through the use of force or violence, or threat of the use of force or violence, to restrain, coerce, or intimidate, or attempt to restrain, coerce, or intimidate any member of a labor organization for the purpose of interfering with or preventing the exercise of any right to which he is entitled under the provisions of this Act. Any person who willfully violates this section shall be fined not more than $1,000 or imprisoned for not more than one year, or both.

Separability Provisions

Sec. 611. If any provision of this Act, or the application of such provision to any person or circumstances, shall be held invalid, the remainder of this Act or the application of such provision to persons or circumstances other than those as to which it is held invalid, shall not be affected thereby.

Appendix D

Text of the
Civil Rights Act of 1964

42 U.S.C. Section 2000e, as amended by the Civil Rights Act of 1991, P.L. 102–116.

TITLE VII—NONDISCRIMINATION IN EMPLOYMENT

Definitions

Section 701. For the purposes of this subchapter—

(a) The term "person" includes one or more individuals, governments, governmental agencies, political subdivisions, labor unions, partnerships, associations, corporations, legal representatives, mutual companies, joint-stock companies, trusts, unincorporated organizations, trustees, trustees in cases under Title 11, or receivers.

(b) The term "employer" means a person engaged in an industry affecting commerce who has fifteen or more employees for each working day in each of twenty or more calendar weeks in the current or preceding calendar year, and any agent of such a person, but such term does not include (1) the United States, a corporation wholly owned by the Government of the United States, an Indian tribe, or any department or agency of the District of Columbia subject by statute to procedures of the competitive service (as defined in section 2102 of Title 5) or (2) a bona fide private membership club (other than a labor organization) which is exempt from taxation under section 501(c) of Title 26, except that during the first year after March 24, 1972, persons having fewer than twenty-five employees (and their agents) shall not be considered employers.

(c) The term "employment agency" means any person regularly undertaking with or without compensation to procure employees for an employer or to procure for employees opportunities to work for an employer and includes an agent of such a person.

(d) The term "labor organization" means a labor organization engaged in an industry affecting commerce, and any agent of such an organization, and includes any organization of any kind, any agency, or employee representation committee, group, association, or plan so engaged in which employees participate and which exists for the purpose, in whole or in part, of dealing with employers concerning grievances, labor disputes, wages, rates of pay, hours, or other terms or conditions of employment, and any conference, general committee, joint or system board, or joint council so engaged which is subordinate to a national or international labor organization.

(e) A labor organization shall be deemed to be engaged in an industry affecting commerce if (1) it maintains or operates a hiring hall or hiring office which procures employees for an employer or procures for employees opportunities to work for an employer, or (2) the number of its members (or, where it is a labor organization composed of other labor organizations or their representatives, if the aggregate number of the members of such other labor organization) is (A) twenty-five or more during the first year after March 24, 1972, or (B) fifteen or more thereafter, and such labor organization—

(1) is the certified representative of employees under the provisions of the National Labor Relations Act, as amended, or the Railway Labor Act, as amended;

(2) although not certified, is a national or international labor organization or a local labor organization recognized or acting as the representative of employees of an employer or employers engaged in an industry affecting commerce; or

(3) has chartered a local labor organization or subsidiary body which is representing or actively seeking to represent employees of employers within the meaning of paragraph (1) or (2); or

(4) has been chartered by a labor organization representing or actively seeking to represent employees within the meaning of paragraph (1) or (2) has the local or subordinate body through which such employees may enjoy membership or become affiliated with such labor organization; or

(5) is a conference, general committee, joint or system board, or joint council subordinate to a national or international labor organization, which includes a labor organization engaged in an industry affecting commerce within the meaning of any of the preceding paragraphs of this subsection.

(f) the term "employee" means an individual employed by an employer, except that the term "employee" shall not include any person elected to public office in any State or political subdivision of any State by the qualified voters thereof, or any person chosen by such officer to be on such officer's personal staff, or an appointee on the policy making level or an immediate adviser with respect to the exercise of the constitutional or legal powers of the office. The exemption set forth in the preceding sentence shall not include employees subject to the civil service laws of a State government, governmental agency or political subdivision.

With respect to employment in a foreign country, such term includes an individual who is a citizen of the United States.

(g) The term "commerce" means trade, traffic, commerce, transportation, transmission, or communication among the several States; or between a State and any place outside thereof; or within the District of Columbia, or a possession of the United States; or between points in the same State but through a point outside thereof.

(h) The term "industry affecting commerce" means any activity, business, or industry in commerce or in which a labor dispute would hinder or obstruct commerce or the free flow of commerce and includes any activity or industry "affecting commerce" within the meaning of the Labor-Management Reporting and Disclosure Act of 1959, and further includes any governmental industry, business, or activity.

(i) The term "State" includes a State of the United States, the District of Columbia, Puerto Rico, the Virgin Islands, American Samoa, Guam, Wake Island, the Canal Zone, and Outer Continental Shelf lands defined in the Outer Continental Shelf Lands Act.

(j) The term "religion" includes all aspects of religious observance and practice, as well as belief, unless an employer demonstrates that he is unable to reasonably accommodate to an employee's or prospective employee's religious observance or practice without undue hardship on the conduct of the employer's business.

(k) The terms "because of sex" or "on the basis of sex" include, but are not limited to, because of or on the basis of pregnancy, childbirth or related medical conditions; and women affected by pregnancy, childbirth, or related medical conditions shall be treated the same for all employment-related purposes, including receipt of benefits under fringe benefit programs, as other persons not so affected but similar in their ability or inability to work and nothing in section 2000e-2(h) of this title shall be interpreted to permit otherwise. This subsection shall not require an employer to pay for health insurance benefits for abortion, except where the life of the mother would be endangered if the fetus were carried to term, or except where medical complications have arisen from an abortion: Provided, That nothing herein shall preclude an employer from providing abortion benefits or otherwise affect bargaining agreements in regard to abortion.

(l) The term "complaining party" means the Commission, the Attorney General, or a person who may bring an action or proceeding under this title.

(m) The term "demonstrates" means meets the burdens of production and persuasion.

(n) The term "respondent" means an employer, employment agency, labor organization, joint labor-management committee controlling apprenticeship or other training or retraining program, including an on-the-job training program, or Federal entity subject to section 717.

Subchapter Not Applicable to Employment of Aliens Outside State and Individuals for Performance of Activities of Religious Corporations, Associations, Educational Institutions, or Societies

Section 702.

(a) This subchapter shall not apply to an employer with respect to the employment of aliens outside any State, or to a religious corporation, association, educational institution, or society with respect to the employment of individuals of a particular religion to perform work connected with the carrying on by such corporation, association, educational institution, or society of its activities.

(b) It shall not be unlawful under section 703 or 704 for an employer (or a corporation controlled by an employer), labor organization, employment agency, or joint management committee controlling apprenticeship or other training or retraining (including on-the-job training programs) to take any action otherwise prohibited by such section, with respect to an employee in a workplace in a foreign country if compliance with such section would cause such employer (or such corporation), such organization, such agency, or such committee to violate the law of the foreign country in which such workplace is located.

(c) (1) If an employer controls a corporation whose place of incorporation is a foreign country, any practice prohibited by section 703 or 704 engaged in by such corporation shall be presumed to be engaged in by such employer.

(2) Sections 703 and 704 shall not apply with respect to the foreign operations of an employer that is a foreign person not controlled by an American employer.

(3) For purposes of this subsection, the determination of whether an employer controls a corporation shall be based on—

(A) the interrelation of operations;

(B) the common management;

(C) the centralized control of labor relations; and

(D) the common ownership or financial control, of the employer and the corporation.

Unlawful Employment Practices

Section 703.

(a) It shall be an unlawful employment practice for an employer—

(1) to fail or refuse to hire or to discharge any individual, or otherwise to discriminate against any individual with respect to his compensation, terms, conditions, or privileges of employment, because of such individual's race, color, religion, sex, or national origin; or

(2) limit, segregate, or classify his employees or applicants for employment in any way which would deprive or tend to deprive any individual of employment opportunities or otherwise adversely affect his status as an employee, because of such individual's race, color, religion, sex, or national origin.

(b) It shall be an unlawful employment practice for an employment agency to fail or refuse to refer for employment, or otherwise to discriminate against, any individual because of his race, color, religion, sex, or national origin, or to classify or refer for employment any individual on the basis of his race, color, religion, sex, or national origin.

(c) It shall be an unlawful employment practice for a labor organization—

(1) to exclude or to expel from its membership, or otherwise to discriminate against, any individual because of his race, color, religion, sex, or national origin;

(2) to limit, segregate, or classify its membership or applicants for membership or to classify or fail or refuse to refer for employment any individual, in any way which would deprive or tend to deprive any individual of employment opportunities, or would limit such employment opportunities or otherwise adversely affect his status as an employee or as an applicant for employment, because of such individual's race, color, religion, sex, or national origin; or

(3) to cause or attempt to cause an employer to discriminate against an individual in violation of this section.

(d) It shall be an unlawful employment practice for any employer, labor organization, or joint labor-management committee controlling apprenticeship or other training or retraining, including on-the-job training programs to discriminate against any individual because of his race, color, religion, sex, or national origin in admission to, or employment in, any program established to provide apprenticeship or other training.

(e) Notwithstanding any other provision of this subchapter, (1) it shall not be an unlawful employment practice for an employer to hire and employ employees, for an employment agency to classify, or refer for employment any individual, for a labor organization to classify its membership or to classify or refer for employment any individual, or for an employer, labor organization, or joint labor-management committee controlling apprenticeship or other training or retraining programs to admit or employ any individual in any such program, on the basis of his religion, sex, or national origin in those certain instances where religion, sex, or national origin is a bona fide occupational qualification reasonably necessary to the normal operation of that particular business or enterprise, and (2) it shall not be an unlawful employment practice for a school, college, university, or other educational institution or institution of learning to hire and employ employees of a particular religion if such school, college, university, or other educational institution or institution of learning is, in whole or in substantial part, owned, supported, controlled, or managed by a particular religion or by a particular religious corporation, association, or society, or if the curriculum of such school, college, university, or other educational institution or institution of learning is directed toward the propagation of a particular religion.

(f) As used in this subchapter, the phrase "unlawful employment practice" shall not be deemed to include any action or measure taken by an employer, labor organization, joint labor-management committee, or employment agency with respect to an individual who is a member of the Communist Party of the United States or of any other organization required to register as a Communist-action or Communist-front organization by final order of the Subversive Activities Control Board pursuant to the Subversive Activities Control Act of 1950.

(g) Notwithstanding any other provision of this title, it shall not be an unlawful employment practice for an employer to fail or refuse to hire and employ an individual for any position, for an employer to discharge an individual from any position, or for an employ-

ment agency to fail or refuse to refer any individual for employment in any position, or for a labor organization to fail or refuse to refer any individual for employment in any position, if—

(1) the occupancy of such position, or access to the premises in or upon which any part of the duties of such position is performed or is to be performed, is subject to any requirement imposed in the interest of the national security of the United States under any security program in effect pursuant to or administered under any statute of the United States or any Executive order of the President; and

(2) such individual has not fulfilled or has ceased to fulfill that requirement.

(h) Notwithstanding any other provision of this subchapter, it shall not be an unlawful employment practice for an employer to apply different standards of compensation, or different terms, conditions, or privileges of employment pursuant to a bona fide seniority or merit system, or a system which measures earnings by quantity or quality of production or to employees who work in different locations, provided that such differences are not the result of an intention to discriminate because of race, color, religion, sex, or national origin; nor shall it be an unlawful employment practice for an employer to give and to act upon the results of any professionally developed ability test provided that such test, its administration or action upon the results is not designed, intended or used to discriminate because of race, color, religion, sex or national origin. It shall not be an unlawful employment practice under this subchapter for any employer to differentiate upon the basis of sex in determining the amount of the wages or compensation paid or to be paid to employees of such employer if such differentiation is authorized by the provisions of section 206 (d) of Title 29.

(i) Nothing contained in this subchapter shall apply to any business or enterprise on or near an Indian reservation with respect to any publicly announced employment practice of such business or enterprise under which a preferential treatment is given to any individual because he is an Indian living on or near a reservation.

(j) Nothing contained in this subchapter shall be interpreted to require any employer, employment agency, labor organization, or joint labor-management committee subject to this subchapter to grant preferential treatment to any individual or to any group because of the race, color, religion, sex, or national origin of such individual or group on account of an imbalance which may exist with respect to the total number of percentage of persons of any race, color, religion, sex, or national origin employed by any employer, referred or classified for employment by any employment agency or labor organization, admitted to membership or classified by any labor organization, or admitted to, or employed in, any apprenticeship or other training program, in comparison with the total number or percentage of persons of such race, color, religion, sex, or national origin in any community, State, section, or other area, or in the available work force in any community, State, section, or other area.

(k) (1) (A) An unlawful employment practice based on disparate impact is established under this title only if—

(i) a complaining party demonstrates that a respondent uses a particular employment practice that causes a disparate impact on the basis of race, color, religion, sex, or national origin and the respondent fails to demonstrate that the challenged practice is job related for the position in question and consistent with business necessity; or

(ii) the complaining party makes the demonstration described in subparagraph (C) with respect to an alternative employment practice and the respondent refuses to adopt such alternative employment practice.

(B) (i) With respect to demonstrating that a particular employment practice causes a disparate impact as described in subparagraph (A)(i), the complaining party shall demonstrate that each particular challenged employment practice causes a disparate impact, except that if the complaining party can demonstrate to the court that the elements of a respondent's decisionmaking process are not capable of separation for analysis, the decisionmaking process may be analyzed as one employment practice.

(ii) If the respondent demonstrates that a specific employment practice does not cause the disparate impact, the respondent shall not be required to demonstrate that such practice is required by business necessity.

(C) The demonstration referred to by subparagraph (A)(ii) shall be in accordance with the law as it existed on June 4, 1989, with respect to the concept of 'alternative employment practice'.

(2) A demonstration that an employment practice is required by business necessity may not be used as a defense against a claim of intentional discrimination under this title.

(3) Notwithstanding any other provision of this title, a rule barring the employment of an individual who currently and knowingly uses or possesses a controlled substance, as defined in schedules I and II of section 102(6) of the Controlled Substances Act (21 U.S.C. 802(6)), other than the use or possession of a drug taken under the supervision of a licensed health care professional, or any other use or possession authorized by the Controlled Substances Act or any other provision of Federal law, shall be considered an unlawful employment practice under this title only if such rule is adopted or applied with an intent to discriminate because of race, color, religion, sex, or national origin.

(l) It shall be an unlawful employment practice for a respondent, in connection with the selection or referral of applicants or candidates for employment or promotion, to adjust the scores of, use different cutoff scores for, or otherwise alter the results of, employment related tests on the basis of race, color, religion, sex, or national origin.

(m) Except as otherwise provided in this title, an unlawful employment practice is established when the complaining party demonstrates that race, color, religion, sex, or national origin was a motivating factor for any employment practice, even though other factors also motivated the practice.

(n) (1) (A) Notwithstanding any other provision of law, and except as provided in paragraph (2), an employment practice that implements and is within the scope of a litigated or consent judgment or order that resolves a claim of employment discrimination under the Constitution or Federal civil rights laws may not be challenged under the circumstances described in subparagraph (B).

(B) A practice described in subparagraph (A) may not be challenged in a claim under the Constitution or Federal civil rights laws—

 (i) by a person who, prior to the entry of the judgment or order described in subparagraph (A), had—

  (I) actual notice of the proposed judgment or order sufficient to apprise such person that such judgment or order might adversely affect the interests and legal rights of such person and that an opportunity was available to present objections to such judgment or order by a future date certain; and

  (II) a reasonable opportunity to present objections to such judgment or order; or

 (ii) by a person whose interests were adequately represented by another person who had previously challenged the judgment or order on the same legal grounds and with a similar factual situation, unless there has been an intervening change in law or fact.

(2) Nothing in this subsection shall be construed to—

(A) alter the standards for intervention under rule 24 of the Federal Rules of Civil Procedure or apply to the rights of parties who have successfully intervened pursuant to such rule in the proceeding in which the parties intervened;

(B) apply to the rights of parties to the action in which a litigated or consent judgment or order was entered, or of members of a class represented or sought to be represented in such action, or of members of a group on whose behalf relief was sought in such action by the Federal Government;

(C) prevent challenges to a litigated or consent judgment or order on the ground that such judgment or order was obtained through collusion or fraud, or is transparently invalid or was entered by a court lacking subject matter jurisdiction; or

(D) authorize or permit the denial to any person

of the due process of law required by the Constitution.

(3) Any action not precluded under this subsection that challenges an employment consent judgment or order described in paragraph (1) shall be brought in the court, and if possible before the judge, that entered such judgment or order. Nothing in this subsection shall preclude a transfer of such action pursuant to section 1404 of title 28, United States Code.

Other Unlawful Employment Practices

Section 704.

(a) It shall be an unlawful employment practice for an employer to discriminate against any of his employees or applicants for employment, for an employment agency, or joint labor-management committee controlling apprenticeship or other training or retraining, including on-the-job training programs, to discriminate against any individual, or for a labor organization to discriminate against any member thereof or applicant for membership, because he has opposed any practice made an unlawful employment practice by this subchapter, or because he has made a charge, testified, assisted, or participated in any manner in an investigation, proceeding, or hearing under this subchapter.

(b) It shall be an unlawful employment practice for an employer, labor organization, employment agency, or joint labor-management committee controlling apprenticeship or other training or retraining, including on-the-job training programs, to print or publish or cause to be printed or published any notice or advertisement relating to employment by such an employer or membership in or any classification or referral for employment by such a labor organization, or relating to any classification or referral for employment by such an employment agency, or relating to admission to, or employment in, any program established to provide apprenticeship or other training by such a joint labor-management committee, indicating any preference, limitation, specification, or discrimination, based on race, color, religion, sex, or national origin, except that such a notice or advertisement may indicate a preference, limitation, specification, or discrimination based on religion, sex, or national origin when religion, sex, or national origin is a bona fide occupational qualification for employment.

Equal Employment Opportunity Commission

Section 705.

(a) There is hereby created a Commission to be known as the Equal Employment Opportunity Commission, which shall be composed of five members, not more than three of whom shall be members of the same political party. Members of the Commission shall be appointed by the President by and with the advice and consent of the Senate for a term of five years. Any individual chosen to fill a vacancy shall be appointed only for the unexpired term of the member whom he shall succeed, and all members of the Commission shall continue to serve until their successors are appointed and qualified, except that no such member of the Commission shall continue to serve (1) for more than sixty days when the Congress is in session unless a nomination to fill such vacancy shall have been submitted to the Senate, or (2) after the adjournment sine die of the session of the Senate in which such nomination was submitted. The President shall designate one member to serve as Chairman of the Commission, and one member to serve as Vice Chairman. The Chairman shall be responsible on behalf of the Commission for the administrative operations of the Commission, and, except as provided in subsection (b) of this section, shall appoint, in accordance with the provisions of Title 5 governing appointments in the competitive service, such officers, agents, attorneys, administrative law judges, and employees as he deems necessary to assist it in the performance of its functions and to fix their compensation in accordance with the provisions of chapter 51 and subchapter III of chapter 53 of Title 5, relating to classification and General Schedule pay rates: *Provided,* That assignment, removal, and compensation of administrative law judges shall be in accordance with sections 3105, 3344, 5372, and 7521 of Title 5.

(b) (1) There shall be a General Counsel of the Commission appointed by the President, by and with the advice and consent of the Senate, for a term of four years. The General Counsel shall have responsibility for the conduct of litigation as provided in sections 2000e-5 and 2000e-6 of this title. The General Counsel shall have such other duties as the Commission may prescribe or as may be provided by law and shall concur with the Chairman of the Commission on the appointment and supervision of regional attorneys. The General Counsel of the Commission on the effective date of this Act shall continue in such position and perform the functions specified in this subsection until a successor is appointed and qualifies.

(2) Attorneys appointed under this section may, at the direction of the Commission, appear for and represent the Commission in any case in court, provided that the Attorney General shall conduct all litigation to which the Commission is a party in the Supreme Court pursuant to this subchapter.

(c) A vacancy in the Commission shall not impair the right of the remaining members to exercise all the powers of the Commission and three members thereof shall constitute a quorum.

(d) The Commission shall have an official seal which shall be judicially noticed.

(e) The Commission shall at the close of each fiscal year report to the Congress and to the President concerning the action it has taken, and the moneys it has disbursed. It shall make such further reports on the cause of and means of eliminating discrimination and such recommendations for further legislation as may appear desirable.

(f) The principal office of the Commission shall be in or near the District of Columbia, but it may meet or exercise any or all its powers at any other place. The commission may establish such regional or State offices as it deems necessary to accomplish the purpose of this subchapter.

(g) The Commission shall have power—

(1) to cooperate with and, with their consent, utilize regional, State, local, and other agencies, both public and private, and individuals;

(2) to pay to witnesses whose depositions are taken or who are summoned before the Commission or any of its agents the same witness and mileage fees as are paid to witnesses in the courts of the United States;

(3) to furnish to persons subject to this subchapter such technical assistance as they may request to further their compliance with this subchapter or an order issued thereunder;

(4) upon the request of (i) any employer, whose employees, or some of them, or (ii) any labor organization, whose members or some of them, refuse or threaten to refuse to cooperate in

effectuating the provisions of this subchapter, to assist in such effectuation by conciliation or such other remedial action as is provided by this subchapter;

(5) to make such technical studies as are appropriate to effectuate the purposes and policies of this subchapter and to make the results of such studies available to the public;

(6) to intervene in a civil action brought under section 2000e-5 of this title by an aggrieved party against a respondent other than a government, governmental agency or political subdivision.

(h) (1) The Commission shall, in any of its educational or promotional activities, cooperate with other departments and agencies in the performance of such educational and promotional activities.

(2) In exercising its powers under this title, the Commission shall carry out educational and outreach activities (including dissemination of information in languages other than English) targeted to—

(A) individuals who historically have been victims of employment discrimination and have not been equitably served by the Commission; and

(B) individuals on whose behalf the Commission has authority to enforce any other law prohibiting employment discrimination, concerning rights and obligations under this title or such law, as the case may be.

(i) All officers, agents, attorneys, and employees of the Commission shall be subject to the provisions of section 7324 of Title 5, notwithstanding any exemption contained in such section.

(j) (1) The Commission shall establish a Technical Assistance Training Institute, through which the Commission shall provide technical assistance and training regarding the laws and regulations enforced by the Commission.

(2) An employer or other entity covered under this title shall not be excused from compliance with the requirements of this title because of any failure to receive technical assistance under this subsection.

(3) There are authorized to be appropriated to carry out this subsection such sums as may be necessary for fiscal year 1992.

Enforcement Provision

Section 706.

(a) The Commission is empowered, as hereinafter provided, to prevent any person from engaging in any unlawful employment practice as set forth in section 2000e-2 or 2000e-3 of this title.

(b) Whenever a charge is filed by or on behalf of a person claiming to be aggrieved, or by a member of the Commission, alleging that an employer, employment agency, labor organization, or joint labor-management committee controlling apprenticeship or other training or retraining, including on-the-job training programs, has engaged in an unlawful employment practice, the Commission employment practice, the Commission shall serve a notice of the charge (including the date, place and circumstances of the alleged unlawful employment practice) on such employer, employment agency, labor organization, or joint labor-management committee (hereinafter referred to as the 'respondent') within ten days and shall make an investigation thereof. Charges shall be in writing under oath or affirmation and shall contain such information and be in such form as the Commission requires. Charges shall not be made public by the Commission. If the Commission determines after such investigation that there is not reasonable cause to believe that the charge is true, it shall dismiss the charge and promptly notify the person claiming to be aggrieved and the respondent of its action. In determining whether reasonable cause exists, the Commission shall accord substantial weight to final findings and orders made by State or local authorities in proceedings commenced under state or local law pursuant to the requirements of subsections (c) and (d) of this section. If the Commission determines after such investigation that there is reasonable cause to believe that the charge is true, the Commission shall endeavor to eliminate any such alleged unlawful employment practice by informal methods of conference, conciliation, and persuasion. Nothing said or done during and as a part of such informal endeavors may be made public by the Commission, its officers or employees, or used as evidence in a subsequent proceeding without the written consent of the persons concerned. Any person who makes public information in violation of this subsection shall be fined not more than $1,000 or imprisoned for not more than one year, or both. The Commission shall make its determination on reasonable cause as promptly as possible and, so far as practicable, not later than one hundred and twenty days from the filing of the charge or, where applicable under subsection (c) or (d) of this section, from the date upon which the commission is authorized to take action with respect to the charge.

(c) In the case of an alleged unlawful employment practice occurring in a State, or political subdivision of a State, which has a State or local law prohibiting the unlawful employment practice alleged and establishing or authorizing a State or local authority to grant or seek relief from such practice or to institute criminal proceedings with respect thereto upon receiving notice thereof, no charge may be filed under subsection (b) of this section by the person aggrieved before the expiration of sixty days after proceedings have been commenced under the State or local law, unless such proceedings have been earlier terminated, provided that such sixty-day period shall be extended to one hundred and twenty days during the first year after the effective date of such State or local law. If any requirement for the commencement of such proceedings is imposed by a State or local authority other than a requirement of the filing of a written and signed statement of the facts upon which the proceeding is based, the proceeding shall be deemed to have been commenced for the purposes of this subsection at the time such statement is sent by registered mail to the appropriate State or local authority.

(d) In the case of any charge filed by a member of the Commission alleging an unlawful employment practice occurring in a State or political subdivision of a State which has a State or local law prohibiting the practice alleged and establishing or authorizing a State or local authority to grant or seek relief from such practice or to institute criminal proceedings with respect thereto upon receiving notice thereof, the Commission shall, before taking any action with respect to such charge, notify the appropriate State or local officials and, upon request, afford them a reasonable time, but not less than sixty days (provided that such sixty-day period shall be extended to one hundred and twenty days during the first year after the effective day of such State or local law), unless a

shorter period is requested, to act under such State or local law to remedy the practice alleged.

(e) (1) A charge under this section shall be filed within one hundred and eighty days after the alleged unlawful employment practice occurred and notice of the charge (including the date, place and circumstances of the alleged unlawful employment practice) shall be served upon the person against whom such charge is made within ten days thereafter, except that in a case of an unlawful employment practice with respect to which the person aggrieved has initially instituted proceedings with a State or local agency with authority to grant or seek relief from such practice or to institute criminal proceedings with respect thereto upon receiving notice thereof, such charge shall be filed by or on behalf of the person aggrieved within three hundred days after the alleged unlawful employment practice occurred, or within thirty days after receiving notice that the State or local agency has terminated the proceedings under the State or local law, whichever is earlier, and a copy of such charge shall be filed by the Commission with the State or local agency.

(2) For purposes of this section, an unlawful employment practice occurs, with respect to seniority system that has been adopted for an intentionally discriminatory purpose in violation of this title (whether or not that discriminatory purpose is apparent on the face of the seniority provision), when the seniority system is adopted, when an individual becomes subject to the seniority system, or when a person aggrieved is injured by the application of the seniority system or provision of the system.

(f) (1) If within thirty days after a charge is filed with the Commission or within thirty days after expiration of any period of reference under subsection (c) or (d) of this section, the Commission has been unable to secure from the respondent a conciliation agreement acceptable to the commission, the Commission may bring a civil action against any respondent not a government, governmental agency, or political subdivision named in the charge. In the case of a respondent which is a government, governmental agency, or political subdivision, if the Commission has been unable to secure from the respondent a conciliation agreement acceptable to the Commission, the Commission shall take no further action and shall refer the case to the Attorney General who may bring a civil action against such respondent in the appropriate United States district court. The person or persons aggrieved shall have the right to intervene in a civil action brought by the Commission or the Attorney General in a case involving a government, governmental agency, or political subdivision. If a charge filed with the commission pursuant to subsection (b) of this section is dismissed by the Commission, or if within one hundred and eighty days from the filing of such charge or the expiration of any period of reference under subsection (c) or (d) of this section, whichever is later, the Commission has not filed a civil action under this section or the Attorney General has not filed a civil action in a case involving a government, governmental agency, or political subdivision, or the commission has not entered into a conciliation agreement to which the person aggrieved is a party, the Commission, or the Attorney General in a case involving a government, governmental agency, or political subdivision, shall so notify the person aggrieved and within ninety days after the giving of such notice a civil action may be brought against the respondent named in the charge (A) by the person claiming to be aggrieved or (B) if such charge was filed by a member of the Commission, by any person whom the charge alleges was aggrieved by the alleged unlawful employment practice. Upon application by the complainant and in such circumstances as the court may deem just, the court may appoint an attorney for such complainant and may authorize the commencement of the action without the payment of fees, costs, or security. Upon timely application, the court may, in its discretion, permit the Commission or the Attorney General in a case involving a government, governmental agency, or political subdivision, to intervene in such civil action upon certification that the case is of general public importance. Upon request, the court may, in its discretion, stay further proceedings for not more than sixty days pending the termination of State or local proceedings described in subsection (c) or (d)

of this section or further efforts of the Commission to obtain voluntary compliance.

(2) Whenever a charge is filed with the Commission and the Commission concludes on the basis of a preliminary investigation that prompt judicial action is necessary to carry out the purposes of this Act, the Commission, or the Attorney General in a case involving a government, governmental agency, or political subdivision, may bring an action for appropriate temporary or preliminary relief pending final disposition of such charge. Any temporary restraining order or other order granting preliminary or temporary relief shall be issued in accordance with rule 65 of the Federal Rules of Civil Procedure. It shall be the duty of a court having jurisdiction over proceedings under this section to assign cases for hearing at the earliest practicable date and to cause such cases to be in every way expedited.

(3) Each United States district court and each United States court of a place subject to the jurisdiction of the United States shall have jurisdiction of actions brought under this subchapter. Such an action may be brought in any judicial district in the State in which the unlawful employment practice is alleged to have been committed, in the judicial district in which the employment records relevant to such practice are maintained and administered, or in the judicial district in which the aggrieved person would have worked but for the alleged unlawful employment practice, but if the respondent is not found within any such district, such an action may be brought within the judicial district in which the respondent has his principal office. For purposes of sections 1404 and 1406 of Title 28, the judicial district in which the respondent has his principal office shall in all cases be considered a district in which the action might have been brought.

(4) It shall be the duty of the chief judge of the district (or in his absence, the acting chief judge) in which the case is pending immediately to designate a judge in such district to hear and determine the case. In the event that no judge in the district is available to hear and determine the case, the chief judge of the district, or the acting chief judge, as the case may be, shall certify this fact to the chief judge of the circuit (or in his

absence, the acting chief judge) who shall then designate a district or circuit judge of the circuit to hear and determine the case.

(5) It shall be the duty of the judge designated pursuant to this subsection to assign the case for hearing at the earliest practicable date and to cause the case to be in every way expedited. If such judge has not scheduled the case for trial within one hundred and twenty days after issue has been joined, that judge may appoint a master pursuant to rule 53 of the Federal Rules of Civil Procedure.

(g) (1) If the court finds that the respondent has intentionally engaged in or is intentionally engaging in an unlawful employment practice charged in the complaint, the court may enjoin the respondent from engaging in such unlawful employment practice, and order such affirmative action as may be appropriate, which may include, but is not limited to, reinstatement or hiring of employees, with or without back pay (payable by the employer, employment agency, or labor organization, as the case may be, responsible for the unlawful employment practice), or any other equitable relief as the court deems appropriate. Back pay liability shall not accrue from a date more than two years prior to the filing of a charge with the Commission. Interim earnings or amounts earnable with reasonable diligence by the person or persons discriminated against shall operate to reduce the back pay otherwise allowable.

(2) (A) No order of the court shall require the admission or reinstatement of an individual as a member of a union, or the hiring, reinstatement, or promotion of an individual as an employee, or the payment to him of any back pay, if such individual was refused admission, suspended, or expelled, or was refused employment or advancement or was suspended or discharged for any reason other than discrimination on account of race, color, religion, sex, or national origin or in violation of section 2000e-3 (a) of this title.

(B) On a claim in which an individual proves a violation under section 703(m) and a respondent demonstrates that the respondent would have taken the same action in the absence of the impermissible motivating factor, the court—

(i) may grant declaratory relief, injunctive relief (except as provided in clause (ii)), and attorney's fees and costs demonstrated to be directly attributable only to the pursuit of a claim under section 703(m); and

(ii) shall not award damages or issue an order requiring any admission, reinstatement, hiring, promotion, or payment, described in subparagraph (A).

(h) The provisions of sections 101 to 115 of Title 29 shall not apply with respect to civil actions brought under this section.

(i) In any case in which an employer, employment agency, or labor organization fails to comply with an order of a court issued in a civil action brought under this section, the Commission may commence proceedings to compel compliance with such order.

(j) Any civil action brought under this section and any proceedings brought under subsection (i) of this section shall be subject to appeal as provided in sections 1291 and 1292, Title 28.

(k) In any action or proceeding under this subchapter, the court, in its discretion, may allow the prevailing party, other than the Commission or the United States, a reasonable attorney's fee (including expert fees) as part of the costs, and the Commission and the United States shall be liable for costs the same as a private person.

Civil Actions by Attorney General

Section 707.

(a) Whenever the Attorney General has reasonable cause to believe that any person or group of persons is engaged in a pattern or practice of resistance to the full enjoyment of any of the rights secured by this subchapter, and that the pattern or practice is of such a nature and is intended to deny the full exercise of the rights herein described, the Attorney General may bring a civil action in the appropriate district court of the United States by filing with it a complaint (1) signed by him (or in his absence the Acting Attorney General), (2) setting forth facts pertaining to such pattern or practice, and (3) requesting such relief, including an application for a permanent or temporary injunction, restraining order or other order against the person or persons responsible for such pattern or practice, as he deems necessary to insure the full enjoyment of the rights herein described.

(b) The district courts of the United States shall have and shall exercise jurisdiction of proceedings instituted pursuant to this section, and in any such proceeding the Attorney General may file with the clerk of such court a request that a court of three judges be convened to hear and determine the case. Such request by the Attorney General shall be accompanied by a certificate that, in his opinion, the case is of general public importance. A copy of the certificate and request for a three-judge court shall be immediately furnished by such clerk to the chief judge of the circuit (or in his absence, the presiding circuit judge of the circuit) in which the case is pending. Upon receipt of such request it shall be the duty of the chief judge of the circuit or the presiding circuit judge, as the case may be, to designate immediately three judges in such circuit, of whom at least one shall be a circuit judge and another of whom shall be a district judge of the court in which the proceeding was instituted, to hear and determine such case, and it shall be the duty of the judges so designated to assign the case for hearing at the earliest practicable date, to participate in the hearing and determination thereof, and to cause the case to be in every way expedited. An appeal from the final judgment of such court will lie to the Supreme Court.

In the event the Attorney General fails to file such a request in any such proceeding, it shall be the duty of the chief judge of the district (or in his absence, the acting chief judge) in which the case is pending immediately to designate a judge in such district to hear and determine the case. In the event that no judge in the district is available to hear and determine the case, the chief judge of the district, or the acting chief judge, as the case may be, shall certify this fact to the chief judge of the circuit (or in his absence, the acting chief judge) who shall then designate a district or circuit judge of the circuit to hear and determine the case.

It shall be the duty of the judge designated pursuant to this section to assign the case for hearing at the earliest practicable date and to cause the case to be in every way expedited.

(c) Effective two years after March 24, 1972, the functions of the Attorney General under this section shall be transferred to the Commission, together with such personnel, property, records, and unexpended balances of appropriations, allocations, and other funds employed, used, held, available, or to be made available in connection with such functions unless the President submits, and neither House of Congress vetoes, a reorganization plan pursuant to chapter 9 of Title 5, inconsistent with the provisions of this subsection. The Commission shall carry out such functions in accordance with subsections (d) and (e) of this section.

(d) Upon the transfer of functions provided for in subsection (c) of this section, in all suits commenced pursuant to this section prior to the date of such transfer, proceedings shall continue without abatement, all court orders and decrees shall remain in effect, and the Commission shall be substituted as a party for the United States of America, the Attorney General, or the Acting Attorney General, as appropriate.

(e) Subsequent to March 24, 1972, the Commission shall have authority to investigate and act on a charge of a pattern or practice of discrimination, whether filed by or on behalf of a person claiming to be aggrieved or by a member of the Commission. All such actions shall be conducted in accordance with the procedures set forth in section 2000e-5 of this title.

Effect on State Laws

Section 708. Nothing in this subchapter shall be deemed to exempt or relieve any person from any liability, duty, penalty, or punishment provided by any present or future law of any State or political subdivision of a State, other than any such law which purports to require or permit the doing of any act which would be an unlawful employment practice under this subchapter.

Investigations

Section 709.

(a) In connection with any investigation of a charge filed under section 2000e-5 of this title, the Commission or its designated representative shall at all reasonable times have access to, for the purposes of examination, and the right to copy any evidence of any person being investigated or proceeded against that relates to unlawful employment practices covered by this subchapter and is relevant to the charge under investigation.

(b) The Commission may cooperate with State and local agencies charged with the administration of State fair employment practices laws and, with the consent of such agencies, may, for the purpose of carrying out its functions and duties under this subchapter and within the limitation of funds appropriated specifically for such purpose, engage in and contribute to the cost of research and other projects of mutual interest undertaken by such agencies, and utilize the services of such agencies and their employees, and, notwithstanding any other provision of law, pay by advance or reimbursement such agencies and their employees for services rendered to assist the Commission in carrying out this subchapter. In furtherance of such cooperative efforts, the Commission may enter into written agreements with such State or local agencies and such agreements may include provisions under which the Commission shall refrain from processing a charge in any cases or class of cases specified in such agreements or under which the Commission shall relieve any person or class of persons in such State or locality from requirements imposed under this section. The Commission shall rescind any such agreement whenever it determines that the agreement no longer serves the interest of effective enforcement of this subchapter.

(c) Every employer, employment agency, and labor organization subject to this subchapter shall (1) make and keep such records relevant to the determinations of whether unlawful employment practices have been or are being committed, (2) preserve such records for such periods, and (3) make such reports therefrom as the Commission shall prescribe by regulation or order, after public hearing, as reasonable, necessary, or appropriate for the enforcement of this subchapter or the regulations or orders thereunder. The Commission shall, by regulation, require each employer, labor organization, and joint labor-management committee subject to this subchapter which controls an apprenticeship or other training program to maintain such records as are reasonably necessary to carry out the purposes of this subchapter, including, but not limited to, a list of applicants who wish to participate in such program, including the chronological order in which applications were received, and to furnish to the Commission upon request, a detailed description of the manner in which persons are selected to participate in the apprenticeship or other training program. Any employer, employment agency, labor organization, or joint labor-management committee which believes that the application to it of any regulation or order issued under this section would result in undue hardship may apply to the Commission for an exemption from the application of such regulation or order, and, if such application for an exemption is denied, bring a civil action in the United States district court for the district where such records are kept. If the Commission or the court, as the case may be, finds that the application of the regulation or order to the employer, employment agency, or labor organization in question would impose an undue hardship, the Commission or the court, as the case may be, may grant appropriate relief. If any person required to comply with the provisions of this subsection fails or refuses to do so, the United States district court for the district in which such person is found, resides, or transacts business, shall, upon application of the Commission, or the Attorney General in a case involving a government, governmental agency or political subdivision, have jurisdiction to issue to such person an order requiring him to comply.

(d) In prescribing requirements pursuant to subsection (c) of this section, the Commission shall consult with other interested State and Federal agencies and shall endeavor to coordinate its requirements with those adopted by such agencies. The Commission shall furnish upon request and without cost to any State or local agency charged with the administration of a fair employment practice law information obtained pursuant to subsection (c) of this section from any employer, employment agency, labor organization, or joint labor-management committee subject to the jurisdiction of such agency. Such information shall be furnished on condition that it not be made public by the recipient agency prior to the institution of a proceeding under State or local law involving such information. If this condition is violated by a recipient agency, the Commission may decline to honor subsequent requests pursuant to this subsection.

(e) It shall be unlawful for any officer or employee of the Commission to make public in any manner whatever any information obtained by the Commission pursuant to its authority under this section prior to the institution of any proceeding under this subchapter involving such information. Any officer or employee of the Commission who shall make public in any manner whatever any information in violation of this subsection shall be guilty of a misdemeanor and upon conviction thereof, shall be fined not more than $1,000, or imprisoned not more than one year.

Conduct of Hearings and Investigations Pursuant to Section 161 of Title 29

Section 710.

For the purpose of all hearings and investigations conducted by the Commission or its duly authorized agents or agencies, section 161 of Title 29 shall apply.

Posting of Notices; Penalties

Section 711.

(a) Every employer, employment agency, and labor organization, as the case may be, shall post and keep posted in conspicuous places upon its premises where notices to employees, applicants for employment, and members are customarily posted a notice to be prepared or approved by the Commission setting forth excerpts from, or summaries of, the pertinent provisions of this subchapter and information pertinent to the filing of a complaint.

(b) A willful violation of this section shall be punishable by a fine of not more than $100 for each separate offense.

Veterans' Special Rights or Preference

Section 712. Nothing contained in this subchapter shall be construed to repeal or modify any Federal, State, territorial, or local law creating special rights or preference for veterans.

Regulations; Conformity of Regulations with Administrative Procedure Provisions; Reliance on Interpretations and Instructions of Commission

Section 713.

(a) The Commission shall have authority from time to time to issue, amend, or rescind suitable procedural regulations to carry out the provisions of this subchapter. Regulations issued under this section shall be in conformity with the standards and limitations of subchapter II of chapter 5 of Title 5.

(b) In any action or proceeding based on any alleged unlawful employment practice, no person shall be subject to any liability or punishment for or on account of (1) the commission by such person of an unlawful employment practice if he pleads and proves that the act or omission complained of was in good faith, in conformity with, and in reliance on any written interpretation or opinion of the Commission, or (2) the failure of such person to publish and file any information required by any provision of this subchapter if he pleads and proves that he failed to publish and file such information in good faith, in conformity with the instructions of the Commission issued under this subchapter regarding the filing of such information. Such a defense, if established, shall be a bar to the action or proceeding, notwithstanding that (A) after such act or omission, such interpretation or opinion is modified or rescinded or is determined by judicial authority to be invalid or of no legal effect, or (B) after publishing or filing the description and annual reports, such publication or filing is determined by judicial authority not to be in conformity with the requirements of this subchapter.

Application to Personnel of Commission of Sections 111 and 1114 of Title 18; Punishment for Violation of Section 1114 of Title 18

Section 714.

The provisions of sections 111 and 1114, Title 18, shall apply to officers, agents, and employees of the Commission in the performance of their official duties. Notwithstanding the provisions of sections 111 and 1114 of Title 18, whoever in violation of the provisions of section 1114 of such title kills a person while engaged in or on account of the performance of his official functions under this Act shall be punished by imprisonment for any term of years or for life.

Coordination of Efforts and Elimination of Competition among Federal Departments, Agencies, Etc. in Implementation and Enforcement of Equal Employment Opportunity Legislation, Orders, and Policies; Report to President and Congress

Section 715.

The Equal Employment Opportunity Commission shall have the responsibility for developing and implementing agreements, policies, and practices designed to maximize effort, promote efficiency, and eliminate conflict, competition, duplication and inconsistency among the operations, functions and jurisdictions of the various departments, agencies and branches of the Federal Government responsible for the implementation and enforcement of equal employment opportunity legislation, orders, and policies. On or before October 1 of each year, the Equal Employment Opportunity Commission shall transmit to the President and to the Congress a report of its activities, together with such recommendations for legislative or administrative changes as it concludes are desirable to further promote the purposes of this section.

Presidential Conferences; Acquaintance of Leadership with Provisions for Employment Rights and Obligations; Plans for Fair Administration; Membership

Section 716. The President shall, as soon as feasible after July 2, 1964, convene one or more conferences for the purpose of enabling the leaders of groups whose members will be affected by this subchapter to become familiar with the rights afforded and obligations imposed by its provisions, and for the purpose of making plans which will result in the fair and effective administration of this subchapter when all of its provisions become effective. The President shall invite the participation in such conference or conferences of (1) the members of the President's Committee on Equal Employment Opportunity, (2) the members of the Commission on Civil Rights, (3) representatives of State and local agencies engaged in furthering equal employment opportunity, (4) representatives of private agencies engaged in furthering equal employment opportunity, and (5) representatives of employers, labor organizations, and employment agencies who will be subject to this subchapter.

Employment by Federal Government

Section 717.

(a) All personnel actions affecting employees or applicants for employment (except with regard to aliens employed outside the limits of the United States) in military departments as defined in section 102 of Title 5, in executive agencies as defined in section 105 of Title 5 (including employees and applicants for employment who are paid from nonappropriated funds), in the United States Postal Service and the Postal Rate Commission, in those units of the Government of the District of Columbia having positions in the competitive service, and in those units of the legislative and judicial branches of the Federal Government having positions in the competitive service, and in the Library of Congress shall be made free from any discrimination based on race, color, religion, sex, or national origin.

(b) Except as otherwise provided in this subsection, the Equal Employment Opportunity Commission shall have authority to enforce the provisions of subsection (a) of this section through appropriate remedies, including reinstatement or hiring of employees with or without back pay, as will effectuate the policies of this section, and shall issue such rules, regulations, orders and instructions as it deems necessary and appropriate to carry out its responsibilities under this section. The Equal Employment Opportunity Commission shall—

(1) be responsible for the annual review and approval of a national and regional equal employment opportunity plan which each department and agency and each appropriate unit referred to in subsection (a) of this section shall submit in order to maintain an affirmative program of equal employment opportunity for all such employees and applicants for employment;

(2) be responsible for the review and evaluation of the operation of all agency equal employment opportunity programs, periodically obtaining and publishing (on at least a semiannual basis) progress reports from each such department, agency, or unit; and

(3) consult with and solicit the recommendations of interested individuals, groups, and organizations relating to equal employment opportunity. The head of each such department, agency, or unit shall comply with such rules, regulations, orders, and instructions which shall include a provision that an employee or applicant for employment shall be notified of any final action taken on any complaint of discrimination filed by him thereunder. The plan submitted by each department, agency, and unit shall include, but not be limited to—

(1) provision for the establishment of training and education programs designed to provide a maximum opportunity for employees to advance so as to perform at their highest potential; and

(2) a description of the qualifications in terms of training and experience relating to equal employment opportunity for the principal and operating officials of each such department, agency, or unit responsible for carrying out the equal employment opportunity program and of the allocation of personnel and resources proposed by such department, agency, or unit to carry out its equal

employment opportunity program. With respect to employment in the Library of Congress, authorities granted in this subsection to the Equal Employment Opportunity Commission shall be exercised by the Librarian of Congress.

(c) Within 90 days of receipt of notice of final action taken by a department, agency, or unit referred to in subsection (a) of this section, or by the Equal Employment Opportunity Commission upon an appeal from a decision or order of such department, agency, or unit on a complaint of discrimination based on race, color, religion, sex or national origin, brought pursuant to subsection (a) of this section, Executive Order 11478 or any succeeding Executive orders, or after one hundred and eighty days from the filing of the initial charge with the department, agency, or unit or with the Equal Employment Opportunity Commission on appeal from a decision or order of such department, agency, or unit until such time as final action may be taken by a department, agency, or unit, an employee or applicant for employment, if aggrieved by the final disposition of his complaint, or by the failure to take final action on his complaint, may file a civil action as provided in section 2000e-5 of this title, in which civil action the head of the department, agency, or unit, as appropriate, shall be the defendant.

(d) The provisions of section 2000e-5 (f) through (k) of this title, as applicable, shall govern civil actions brought hereunder, and the same interest to compensate for delay in payment shall be available as in cases involving nonpublic parties.

(e) Nothing contained in this Act shall relieve any Government agency or official of its or his primary responsibility to assure nondiscrimination in employment as required by the Constitution and statutes or of its or his responsibilities under Executive Order 11478 relating to equal employment opportunity in the Federal Government.

Procedure for Denial, Withholding, Termination, or Suspension of Government Contract Subsequent to Acceptance by Government of Affirmative Action Plan of Employer; Time of Acceptance of Plan

Section 718.

No Government contract, or portion thereof, with any employer, shall be denied, withheld, terminated, or suspended, by any agency or officer of the United States under any equal employment opportunity law or order, where such employer has an affirmative action plan which has previously been accepted by the Government for the same facility within the past twelve months without first according such employer full hearing and adjudication under the provisions of section 554 of Title 5, and the following pertinent sections: *Provided,* That if such employer has deviated substantially from such previously agreed to affirmative action plan, this section shall not apply: *Provided further,* That for the purposes of this section an affirmative action plan shall be deemed to have been accepted by the Government at the time the appropriate compliance agency has accepted such plan unless within forty-five days thereafter the Office of Federal Contract Compliance has disapproved such plan.

A p p e n d i x E

Text of Title 42 U.S.C. Section 1981

---

42 U.S.C. Section 1981, as amended by the Civil Rights Act of 1991, P.L. 102–166.

Equal Rights under the Law

Section 1981.

(a) All persons within the jurisdiction of the United States shall have the same right in every State and Territory to make and enforce contracts, to sue, be parties, give evidence, and to the full and equal benefit of all laws and proceedings for the security of persons and property as is enjoyed by white citizens, and shall be subject to like punishment, pains, penalties, taxes, licenses, and exactions of every kind, and to no other.

(b) For purposes of this section, the term 'make and enforce contracts' includes the making, performance, modification, and termination of contracts, and the enjoyment of all benefits, privileges, terms, and conditions of the contractual relationship.

(c) The rights protected by this section are protected against impairment by nongovernmental discrimination and impairment under color of State law.

Damages in Cases of Intentional Discrimination in Employment

Section 1981a.

(a) Right of Recovery—

    (1) Civil rights. In an action brought by a complaining party under section 706 or 717 of the Civil Rights Act of 1964 (42 U.S.C. 2000e-5) against a respondent who engaged in unlawful intentional discrimination (not an employment practice that is unlawful because of its disparate impact) prohibited under section 703, 704, or 717 of the Act (42 U.S.C. 2000e-2 or 2000e-3), and provided that the complaining party cannot recover under section 1977 of the Revised Statutes (42 U.S.C. 1981), the complaining party may recover compensatory and punitive damages as allowed in subsection (b), in addition to any relief authorized by section 706(g) of the Civil Rights Act of 1964, from the respondent.

    (2) Disability. In an action brought by a complaining party under the powers, remedies, and procedures set forth in section 706 or 717 of the Civil Rights Act of 1964 (as provided in section 107(a) of the Americans with Disabilities Act of 1990 (42 U.S.C. 12117(a)), and section 505(a)(1) of the Rehabilitation Act of 1973 (29 U.S.C. 794a(a)(1)), respectively) against a respondent who engaged in unlawful intentional discrimination (not an employment practice that is unlawful because of its disparate impact) under section 501 of the Rehabilitation Act of 1973 (29 U.S.C. 791) and the regulations implementing section 501, or who violated the requirements of section 501 of the Act or the regulations implementing section 501 concerning the provision of a reasonable accommodation, or section 102 of the Americans with Disabilities Act of 1990 (42 U.S.C. 12112), or committed a violation of section 102(b)(5) of the Act, against

an individual, the complaining party may recover compensatory and punitive damages as allowed in subsection (b), in addition to any relief authorized by section 706(g) of the Civil Rights Act of 1964, from the respondent.

(3) Reasonable accommodation and good faith effort. In cases where a discriminatory practice involves the provision of a reasonable accommodation pursuant to section 102(b)(5) of the Americans with Disabilities Act of 1990 or regulations implementing section 501 of the Rehabilitation Act of 1973, damages may not be awarded under this section where the covered entity demonstrates good faith efforts, in consultation with the person with the disability who has informed the covered entity that accommodation is needed, to identify and make a reasonable accommodation that would provide such individual with an equally effective opportunity and would not cause an undue hardship on the operation of the business.

(b) Compensatory and Punitive Damages—

(1) Determination of punitive damages. A complaining party may recover punitive damages under this section against a respondent (other than a government, government agency or political subdivision) if the complaining party demonstrates that the respondent engaged in a discriminatory practice or discriminatory practices with malice or with reckless indifference to the federally protected rights of an aggrieved individual.

(2) Exclusions from compensatory damages. Compensatory damages awarded under this section shall not include backpay, interest on backpay, or any other type of relief authorized under section 706(g) of the Civil Rights Act of 1964.

(3) Limitations. The sum of the amount of compensatory damages awarded under this section for future pecuniary losses, emotional pain, suffering, inconvenience, mental anguish, loss of enjoyment of life, and other nonpecuniary losses, and the amount of punitive damages awarded under this section, shall not exceed, for each complaining party—

(A) in the case of a respondent who has more than 14 and fewer than 101 employees in each of 20 or more calendar weeks in the current or preceding calendar year, $50,000;

(B) in the case of a respondent who has more than 100 and fewer than 201 employees in each of 20 or more calendar weeks in the current or preceding calendar year, $100,000; and

(C) in the case of a respondent who has more than 200 and fewer than 501 employees in each of 20 or more calendar weeks in the current or preceding calendar year, $200,000; and

(D) in the case of a respondent who has more than 500 employees in each of 20 or more calendar weeks in the current or preceding calendar year, $300,000.

(4) Construction. Nothing in this section shall be construed to limit the scope of, or the relief available under, section 1977 of the Revised Statutes (42 U.S.C. 1981).

(c) Jury Trial. If a complaining party seeks compensatory or punitive damages under this section—

(1) any party may demand a trial by jury; and

(2) the court shall not inform the jury of the limitations described in subsection (b)(3).

(d) Definitions. As used in this section:

(1) Complaining party. The term 'complaining party' means—

(A) in the case of a person seeking to bring an action under subsection (a)(1), the Equal Employment Opportunity Commission, the Attorney General, or a person who may bring an action or proceeding under title VII of the Civil Rights Act of 1964 (42 U.S.C. 2000e et seq.); or

(B) in the case of a person seeking to bring an action under subsection (a)(2), the Equal Employment Opportunity Commission, the Attorney General, a person who may bring an action or proceeding under section 505(a)(1) of the Rehabilitation Act of 1973 (29 U.S.C. 794a(a)(1)), or a person who may bring an action or proceeding under title I of the Americans with Disabilities Act of 1990 (42 U.S.C. 12101 et seq.).

(2) Discriminatory practice. The term 'discriminatory practice' means the discrimination described in paragraph (1), or the discrimination or the violation described in paragraph (2), of subsection (a).

A p p e n d i x F

Extracts from the Age Discrimination in Employment Act

29 U.S.C. Section 621 et seq., as amended by P.L. 99–592 (1986); P.L. 101–433 (1990); and P.L. 102–166 (1991).

Congressional Statement of Findings and Purpose

Section 621.

(a) The Congress hereby finds and declares that—

  (1) in the face of rising productivity and affluence, older workers find themselves disadvantaged in their efforts to retain employment, and especially to regain employment when displaced from jobs;

  (2) the setting of arbitrary age limits regardless of potential for job performance has become a common practice, and certain otherwise desirable practices may work to the disadvantage of older persons;

  (3) the incidence of unemployment, especially long-term unemployment with resultant deterioration of skill, morale, and employer acceptability is, relative to the younger ages, high among older workers; their numbers are great and growing; and their employment problems grave;

  (4) the existence in industries affecting commerce, of arbitrary discrimination in employment because of age, burdens commerce and the free flow of goods in commerce.

(b) It is therefore the purpose of this chapter to promote employment of older persons based on their ability rather than age; to prohibit arbitrary age discrimination in employment; to help employers and workers find ways of meeting problems arising from the impact of age on employment.

Prohibition of Age Discrimination

Section 623.

(a) It shall be unlawful for an employer—

  (1) to fail or refuse to hire or to discharge any individual or otherwise discriminate against any individual with respect to his compensation, terms, conditions, or privileges of employment, because of such individual's age;

  (2) to limit, segregate, or classify his employees in any way which would deprive or tend to deprive any individual of employment opportunities or otherwise adversely affect his status as an employee, because of such individual's age; or

  (3) to reduce the wage rate of any employee in order to comply with this chapter.

(b) It shall be unlawful for an employment agency to fail or refuse to refer for employment, or otherwise to discriminate against, any individual because of such individual's age, or to classify or refer for employment any individual on the basis of such individual's age.

(c) It shall be unlawful for a labor organization—

  (1) to exclude or to expel from its membership, or otherwise to discriminate against, any individual because of his age;

  (2) to limit, segregate, or classify its membership, or to classify or fail or refuse to refer for employment any individual, in any way which would deprive or tend to deprive any individual of employment opportunities, or would limit such employment opportunities or otherwise adversely

affect his status as an employee or as an applicant for employment because of such individual's age;

(3) to cause or attempt to cause an employer to discriminate against an individual in violation of this section.

(d) It shall be unlawful for an employer to discriminate against any of his employees or applicants for employment, for an employment agency to discriminate against any individual, or for a labor organization to discriminate against any member thereof or applicant for membership, because such individual, member or applicant for membership has opposed any practice made unlawful by this section, or because such individual, member or applicant for membership has made a charge, testified, assisted, or participated in any manner in an investigation, proceeding, or litigation under this chapter.

(e) It shall be unlawful for an employer, labor organization, or employment agency to print or publish, or cause to be printed or published, any notice or advertisement relating to employment by such an employer or membership in or any classification or referral for employment by such a labor organization, or relating to any classification or referral for employment by such an employment agency, indicating any preference, limitation, specification, or discrimination, based on age.

(f) It shall not be unlawful for any employer, employment agency, or labor organization—

(1) to take any action otherwise prohibited under subsections (a), (b), (c), or (e) of this section where age is a bona fide occupational qualification reasonably necessary to the normal operation of the particular business, or where the differentiation is based on reasonable factors other than age;

(2) to take any action otherwise prohibited under subsection (a), (b), (c), or (e) of this section—

(A) to observe the terms of a bona fide seniority system that is not intended to evade the purposes of this Act, except that no such seniority system shall require or permit the involuntary retirement of any individual specified by section 12(a) because of the age of such individual; or

(B) to observe the terms of a bona fide employee benefit plan—

(i) where, for each benefit or benefit package, the actual amount of payment made or cost incurred on behalf of an older worker is no less than that made or incurred on behalf of a younger worker, as permissible under section 1625.10, title 29, Code of Federal Regulations (as in effect on June 22, 1989); or

(ii) that is a voluntary early retirement incentive plan consistent with the relevant purpose or purposes of this Act.

Notwithstanding clause (i) or (ii) of subparagraph (B), no such employee benefit plan or voluntary early retirement incentive plan shall excuse the failure to hire any individual, and no such employee benefit plan shall require or permit the involuntary retirement of any individual specified by section 12(a), because of the age of such individual. An employer, employment agency, or labor organization acting under subparagraph (A), or under clause (i) or (ii) of subparagraph (B), shall have the burden of proving that such actions are lawful in any civil enforcement proceeding brought under this Act; or

(3) to discharge or otherwise discipline an individual for good cause.

[Subsection (g) was repealed.]

(h) Practices of foreign corporations controlled by American employers; foreign persons not controlled by American employers; factors determining control—

(1) If an employer controls a corporation whose place of incorporation is in a foreign country, any practice by such corporation prohibited under this section shall be presumed to be such practice by such employer.

(2) The prohibitions of this section shall not apply where the employer is a foreign person not controlled by an American employer.

(3) For the purpose of this subsection the determination of whether an employer controls a corporation shall be based upon the—

(A) interrelation of operations,

(B) common management,

(C) centralized control of labor relations, and

(D) common ownership or financial control, of the employer and the corporation.

(i) [1] Firefighters and law enforcement officers attaining hiring or retiring age under State or local law on March 3, 1983.

It shall not be unlawful for an employer which is a

State, a political subdivision of a State, an agency or instrumentality of a State or a political subdivision of a State, or an interstate agency to fail or refuse to hire or to discharge any individual because of such individual's age if such action is taken—

(1) with respect to the employment of an individual as a firefighter or as a law enforcement officer and the individual has attained the age of hiring or retirement in effect under applicable State or local law on March 3, 1983, and

(2) pursuant to a bona fide hiring or retirement plan that is not a subterfuge to evade the purposes of this chapter.

(j) Employee pension benefit plans; cessation or reduction of benefit accrual or of allocation to employee account; distribution of benefits after attainment of normal retirement age; compliance; highly compensated employees.

(1) Except as otherwise provided in this subsection, it shall be unlawful for an employer, an employment agency, a labor organization, or any combination thereof to establish or maintain an employee pension benefit plan which requires or permits—

(A) in the case of a defined benefit plan, the cessation of an employee's benefit accrual, or the reduction of the rate of an employee's benefit accrual, because of age, or

(B) in the case of a defined contribution plan, the cessation of allocations to an employee's account, or the reduction of the rate at which amounts are allocated to an employee's account, because of age.

(2) Nothing in this section shall be construed to prohibit an employer, employment agency, or labor organization from observing any provision of an employee pension benefit plan to the extent that such provision imposes (without regard to age) a limitation on the amount of benefits that the plan provides or a limitation on the number of years of service or years of participation which are taken into account for purposes of determining benefit accrual under the plan.

(3) In the case of any employee who, as of the end of any plan year under a defined benefit plan, has

attained normal retirement age under such plan—

(A) if distribution of benefits under such plan with respect to such employee has commenced as of the end of such plan year, then any requirement of this subsection for continued accrual of benefits under such plan, with respect to such employee during such plan year shall be treated as satisfied to the extent of the actuarial equivalent of in-service distribution of benefits, and

(B) if distribution of benefits under such plan with respect to such employee has not commenced as of the end of such year in accordance with section 1056(a)(3) of this title and section 401(a)(14)(C) of title 26, and the payment of benefits under such plan with respect to such employee is not suspended during such plan year pursuant to section 1053(a)(3)(B) of this title or section 411(a)(3)(B) of title 26, then any requirement of this subsection for continued accrual of benefits under such plan with respect to such employee during such plan year shall be treated as satisfied to the extent of any adjustment in the benefit payable under the plan during such plan year attributable to the delay in the distribution of benefits after the attainment of normal retirement age.

The provisions of this paragraph shall apply in accordance with regulations of the Secretary of the Treasury. Such regulations shall provide for the application of the preceding provisions of this paragraph to all employee pension benefit plans subject to this subsection and may provide for the application of such provisions, in the case of any such employee, with respect to any period of time within a plan year.

(4) Compliance with the requirements of this subsection with respect to an employee pension benefit plan shall constitute compliance with the requirements of this section relating to benefit accrual under such plan.

(5) Paragraph (1) shall not apply with respect to any

---

[1] This section is repealed December 31, 1993, Pub. L. No. 99-592, § 3(b), 100 Stat. 3342 (1986).

employee who is a highly compensated employee (within the meaning of section 414(q) of title 26) to the extent provided in regulations prescribed by the Secretary of the Treasury for purposes of precluding discrimination in favor of highly compensated employees within the meaning of subchapter D of chapter 1 of title 26.

(6) A plan shall not be treated as failing to meet the requirements of paragraph (1) solely because the subsidized portion of any early retirement benefit is disregarded in determining benefit accruals.

(7) Any regulations prescribed by the Secretary of the Treasury pursuant to clause (v) of section 411(b)(1)(H) of title 26 and subparagraphs (C) and (D) of section 411(b)(2) of title 26 shall apply with respect to the requirements of this subsection in the same manner and to the same extent as such regulations apply with respect to the requirements of such sections 411(b)(1)(H) and 411(b)(2)

(8) A plan shall not be treated as failing to meet the requirements of this section solely because such plan provides a normal retirement age described in section 1002(24)(B) of this title and section 411(a)(8)(B) of title 26.

(9) For purposes of this subsection—

    (A) The terms "employee pension benefit plan," "defined benefit plan," "defined contribution plan," and "normal retirement age" have the meanings provided such terms in section 1002 of this title.

    (B) The term "compensation" has the meaning provided by section 414(s) of title 26.

(k) A seniority system or employee benefit plan shall comply with this Act regardless of the date of adoption of such system or plan.

(l) [2] Notwithstanding clause (i) or (ii) of subsection (f)(2)(B)—

    (1) It shall not be a violation of subsection (a), (b), (c), or (e) solely because—

        (A) an employee pension benefit plan (as defined in section 3(2) of the Employee Retirement Income Security Act of 1974 (29

U.S.C. 1002(2))) provides for the attainment of a minimum age as a condition of eligibility for normal or early retirement benefits; or

        (B) a defined benefit plan (as defined in section 3(35) of such Act) provides for—

           (i) payments that constitute the subsidized portion of an early retirement benefit; or

           (ii) social security supplements for plan participants that commence before the age and terminate at the age (specified by the plan) when participants are eligible to receive reduced or unreduced old-age insurance benefits under title II of the Social Security Act (42 U.S.C. 401 et seq.), and that do not exceed such old-age insurance benefits.

    (2) (A) It shall not be a violation of subsection (a), (b), (c), or (e) solely because following a contingent event unrelated to age—

           (i) the value of any retiree health benefits received by an individual eligible for an immediate pension;

           (ii) the value of any additional pension benefits that are made available solely as a result of the contingent event unrelated to age and following which the individual is eligible for not less than an immediate and unreduced pension; or

           (iii) the values described in both clauses (i) and (ii);

are deducted from severance pay made available as a result of the contingent event unrelated to age.

        (B) For an individual who receives immediate pension benefits that are actuarially reduced under subparagraph (A)(i), the amount of the deduction available pursuant to subparagraph (A)(i) shall be reduced by the same percentage as the reduction in the pension benefits.

        (C) For purposes of this paragraph, severance pay shall include that portion of supplemen-

---

[2]As amended by the Older Workers Benefit Protection Act, Technical Amendment, Pub. L. 101–521, 104 Stat. 2287 (1990).

tal unemployment compensation benefits (as described in section 501(c)(17) of the Internal Revenue Code of 1986) that—

   (i) constitutes additional benefits of up to 52 weeks;

   (ii) has the primary purpose and effect of continuing benefits until an individual becomes eligible for an immediate and unreduced pension; and

   (iii) is discontinued once the individual becomes eligible for an immediate and unreduced pension.

(D) For purposes of this paragraph and solely in order to make the deduction authorized under this paragraph, the term "retiree health benefits" means benefits provided pursuant to a group health plan covering retirees, for which (determined as of the contingent event unrelated to age)—

   (i) the package of benefits provided by the employer for the retirees who are below age 65 is at least comparable to benefits provided under title XVIII of the Social Security Act (42 U.S.C. 1395 et seq.);

   (ii) the package of benefits provided by the employer for the retirees who are age 65 and above is at least comparable to that offered under a plan that provides a benefit package with one-fourth the value of benefits provided under title XVIII of such Act; or

   (iii) the package of benefits provided by the employer is as described in clauses (i) and (ii).

(E)   (i) If the obligation of the employer to provide retiree health benefits is of limited duration, the value for each individual shall be calculated at a rate of $3,000 per year for benefit year before age 65, and $750 per year for benefit years beginning at age 65 and above.

   (ii) If the obligation of the employer to provide retiree health benefits is of unlimited duration, the value for each individual shall be calculated at a rate of $48,000 for individuals below age 65, and $24,000 for individuals age 65 and above.

   (iii) The values described in clauses (i) and (ii) shall be calculated based on the age of the individual as of the date of the contingent event unrelated to age. The values are effective on the date of enactment of this subsection, and shall be adjusted on an annual basis, with respect to a contingent event that occurs subsequent to the first year after the date of enactment of this subsection, based on the medical component of the Consumer Price Index for all-urban consumers published by the Department of Labor.

   (iv) If an individual is required to pay a premium for retiree health benefits, the value calculated pursuant to this subparagraph shall be reduced by whatever percentage of the overall premium the individual is required to pay.

(F) If an employer that has implemented a deduction pursuant to subparagraph (A) fails to fulfill the obligation described in subparagraph (E), any aggrieved individual may bring an action for specific performance of the obligation described in subparagraph (E). The relief shall be in addition to any other remedies provided under Federal or State law.

(3) It shall not be a violation of subsection (a), (b), (c), or (e) solely because an employer provides a bona fide employee benefit plan or plans under which long-term disability benefits received by an individual are reduced by any pension benefits (other than those attributable to employee contributions)—

(A) paid to the individual that the individual voluntarily elects to receive; or

(B) for which an individual who has attained the later of age 62 or normal retirement age is eligible.

Administration

Section 625. The Commission shall have the power—

(a) to make delegations, to appoint such agents and employees, and to pay for technical assistance on a fee for service basis, as he deems necessary to assist him in the performance of his functions under this chapter;

(b) to cooperate with regional, State, local, and other agencies, and to cooperate with and furnish technical assistance to employers, labor organizations, and employment agencies to aid in effectuating the purposes of this chapter.

Recordkeeping, Investigation, and Enforcement

Section 626.

(a) The Commission shall have the power to make investigations and require the keeping of records necessary or appropriate for the administration of this chapter in accordance with the powers and procedures provided in sections 209 and 211 of this title.

(b) The provisions of this chapter shall be enforced in accordance with the powers, remedies, and procedures provided in sections 211(b), 216 (except for subsection (a) thereof), and 217 of this title, and subsection (c) of this section. Any act prohibited under section 623 of this title shall be deemed to be a prohibited act under section 215 of this title. Amounts owing to a person as a result of a violation of this chapter shall be deemed to be unpaid minimum wages or unpaid overtime compensation for purposes of sections 216 and 217 of this title: *Provided,* That liquidated damages shall be payable only in cases of willful violations of this chapter. In any action brought to enforce this chapter the court shall have jurisdiction to grant such legal or equitable relief as may be appropriate to effectuate the purposes of this chapter, including without limitation judgments compelling employment, reinstatement or promotion, or enforcing the liability for amounts deemed to be unpaid minimum wages or unpaid overtime compensation under this section. Before instituting any action under this section, the Commission shall attempt to eliminate the discriminatory practice or practices alleged, and to effect voluntary compliance with the requirements of this chapter through informal methods of conciliation, conference, and persuasion.

(c) (1) Any person aggrieved may bring a civil action in any court of competent jurisdiction for such legal or equitable relief as will effectuate the purposes of this chapter: *Provided,* That the right of any person to bring such action shall terminate upon the commencement of an action by the Commission to enforce the right of such employee under this chapter.

(2) In an action brought under paragraph (1), a person shall be entitled to a trial by jury of any issue of fact in any such action for recovery of amounts owing as a result of a violation of this chapter, regardless of whether equitable relief is sought by any party in such action.

(d) No civil action may be commenced by an individual under this section until 60 days after a charge alleging unlawful discrimination has been filed with the Commission. Such a charge shall be filed—

(1) within 180 days after the alleged unlawful practice occurred; or

(2) in a case to which section 633(b) of this title applies, within 300 days after the alleged unlawful practice occurred, or within 30 days after receipt by the individual of notice of termination of proceeding under State law, whichever is earlier.

Upon receiving such a charge, the Commission shall promptly notify all persons named in such charge as prospective defendants in the action and shall promptly seek to eliminate any alleged unlawful practice by informal methods of conciliation, conference, and persuasion.

(e) Section 259 of this title shall apply to actions under this chapter. If a charge filed with the Commission under this Act is dismissed or the proceedings of the Commission are otherwise terminated by the Commission, the Commission shall notify the person aggrieved. A civil action may be brought under this section by a person defined in section 11(a) against the respondent named in the charge within 90 days after the date of the receipt of such notice.

(f) (1) An individual may not waive any right or claim under this Act unless the waiver is knowing and voluntary. Except as provided in paragraph (2), a waiver may not be considered knowing and voluntary unless at a minimum—

(A) the waiver is part of an agreement between the individual and the employer that is written in a manner calculated to be understood by such individual, or by the average individual eligible to participate;

(B) the waiver specifically refers to rights or claims arising under this Act;

(C) the individual does not waive rights or

claims that may arise after the date the waiver is executed;

(D) the individual waives rights to claims only in exchange for consideration in addition to anything of value to which the individual already is entitled;

(E) the individual is advised in writing to consult with an attorney prior to executing the agreement;

(F) (i) the individual is given a period of at least 21 days within which to consider the agreement; or

(ii) if a waiver is requested in connection with an exit incentive or other employment termination program offered to a group or class of employees, the individual is given a period of at least 45 days within which to consider the agreement;

(G) the agreement provides that for a period of at least 7 days following the execution of such agreement, the individual may revoke the agreement, and the agreement shall not become effective or enforceable until the revocation period has expired;

(H) if a waiver is requested in connection with an exit incentive or other employment termination program offered to a group or class of employees, the employer (at the commencement of the period specified in subparagraph (F)) informs the individual in writing in a manner calculated to be understood by the average individual eligible to participate, as to—

(i) any class, unit, or group of individuals covered by such program, any eligibility factors for such program, and any time limits applicable to such program; and

(ii) the job titles and ages of all individuals eligible or selected for the program, and the ages of all individuals in the same job classification or organizational unit who are not eligible or selected for the program.

(2) A waiver in settlement of a charge filed with the Equal Employment Opportunity Commission, or an action filed in court by the individual or the individual's representative, alleging age discrimination of a kind prohibited under section 4 or 15 may not be considered knowing and voluntary unless at a minimum—

(A) subparagraphs (A) through (E) of paragraph (1) have been met; and

(B) the individual is given a reasonable period of time within which to consider the settlement agreement.

(3) In any dispute that may arise over whether any of the requirements, conditions, and circumstances set forth in subparagraph (A), (B), (C), (D), (E), (F), (G), or (H) of paragraph (1), or subparagraph (A) or (B) of paragraph (2), have been met, the party asserting the validity of a waiver shall have the burden of proving in a court of competent jurisdiction that a waiver was knowing and voluntary pursuant to paragraph (1) or (2).

(4) No waiver agreement may affect the Commission's rights and responsibilities to enforce this Act. No waiver may be used to justify interfering with the protected right of an employee to file a charge or participate in an investigation or proceeding conducted by the Commission.

Notices to Be Posted

Section 627. Every employer, employment agency, and labor organization shall post and keep posted in conspicuous places upon its premises a notice to be prepared or approved by the Commission setting forth information as the Commission deems appropriate to effectuate the purposes of this chapter.

Rules and Regulations; Exemptions

Section 628. In accordance with the provisions of subchapter II of chapter 5 of Title 5, the Equal Employment Opportunity Commission may issue such rules and regulations as it may consider necessary or appropriate for carrying out this chapter, and may establish such reasonable exemptions to and from any or all provisions of this chapter as it may find necessary and proper in the public interest.

Criminal Penalties

Section 629. Whoever shall forcibly resist, oppose, impede, intimidate or interfere with a duly authorized representative of the Equal Employment Opportunity Commission while it is engaged in the performance of duties under this chapter shall be punished by a fine of not more than $500 or by imprisonment for not more than one year, or by both: *Provided,* however, That no person shall be imprisoned under this section except when there has been a prior conviction hereunder.

Definitions

Section 630. For the purposes of this chapter—

(a) The term "person" means one or more individuals, partnerships, associations, labor organizations, corporations, business trusts, legal representatives, or any organized groups of persons.

(b) The term "employer" means a person engaged in an industry affecting commerce who has twenty or more employees for each working day in each of twenty or more calendar weeks in the current or preceding calendar year: *Provided,* That prior to June 30, 1968, employers having fewer than fifty employees shall not be considered employers. The term also means (1) any agent of such a person, and (2) a State or political subdivision of a State and any agency or instrumentality of a State or a political subdivision of a State, and any interstate agency, but such term does not include the United States, or a corporation wholly owned by the Government of the United States.

(c) The term "employment agency" means any person regularly undertaking with or without compensation to procure employees for an employer and includes an agent of such a person; but shall not include an agency of the United States.

(d) The term "labor organization" means a labor organization engaged in an industry affecting commerce, and any agent of such an organization, and includes any organization of any kind, any agency, or employee representation committee, group, association, or plan so engaged in which employees participate and which exists for the purpose, in whole or in part, of dealing with employers concerning grievances, labor disputes, wages, rates of pay, hours, or other terms or conditions of employment, and any conference, general committee, joint or system board, or joint council so engaged which is subordinate to a national or international labor organization.

(e) A labor organization shall be deemed to be engaged in an industry affecting commerce if (1) it maintains or operates a hiring hall or hiring office which procures employees for an employer or procures for employees opportunities to work for an employer, or (2) the number of its members (or, where it is a labor organization composed of other labor organizations or their representatives, if the aggregate number of the members of such other labor organization) is fifty or more prior to July 1, 1968, or twenty-five or more on or after July 1, 1968, and such labor organization—

  (1) is the certified representative of employees under the provisions of the National Labor Relations Act, as amended, or the Railway Labor Act, as amended; or

  (2) although not certified, is a national or international labor organization or a local labor organization recognized or acting as the representative of employees of an employer or employers engaged in an industry affecting commerce; or

  (3) has chartered a local labor organization or subsidiary body which is representing or actively seeking to represent employees of employers within the meaning of paragraph (1) or (2); or

  (4) has been chartered by a labor organization representing or actively seeking to represent employees within the meaning of paragraph (1) or (2) as the local or subordinate body through which such employees may enjoy membership or become affiliated with such labor organization; or

  (5) is a conference, general committee, joint or system board, or joint council subordinate to a national or international labor organization, which includes a labor organization engaged in an industry affecting commerce within the meaning of any of the preceding paragraphs and this subsection.

(f) The term "employee" means an individual employed by any employer except that the term "employee" shall not include any person elected to public office in any State or political subdivision of any State by the qualified voters thereof, or any person chosen by such officer to be on such officer's personal staff, or an appointee on the policymaking level or an immediate adviser with respect to the exercise of the constitutional or legal powers of the office. The exemption set forth in the preceding sentence shall not include employees subject to the civil service laws of a State government, governmental agency, or political subdivision.

(g) The term, "commerce" means trade, traffic, commerce, transportation, transmission, or communication among the several States; or between a State and any place outside thereof; or within the District of Columbia, or a possession of the United States; or between points in the same State but through a point outside thereof.

(h) The term "industry affecting commerce" means any activity, business, or industry in commerce or in which a labor dispute would hinder or obstruct commerce or the free flow of commerce and includes any activity or industry "affecting commerce" within the meaning of the Labor-Management Reporting and Disclosure Act of 1959.

(i) The term "State" includes a State of the United States, the District of Columbia, Puerto Rico, the Virgin Islands, American Samoa, Guam, Wake Island, the Canal Zone, and Outer Continental Shelf lands defined in the Outer Continental Shelf Lands Act.

(j) The term "firefighter" means an employee, the duties of whose position are primarily to perform work directly connected with the control and extinguishment of fires or the maintenance and use of firefighting apparatus and equipment, including an employee engaged in this activity who is transferred to a supervisory or administrative position.

(k) The term "law enforcement officer" means an employee, the duties of whose position are primarily the investigation, apprehension, or detention of individuals suspected or convicted of offenses against the criminal laws of a State, including an employee engaged in this activity who is transferred to a supervisory or administrative position. For the purpose of this subsection, "detention" includes the duties of employees assigned to guard individuals incarcerated in any penal institution.

(l) The term "compensation, terms, conditions, or privileges of employment" encompasses all employee benefits, including such benefits provided pursuant to a bona fide employee benefit plan.

Age Limits

Section 631.

(a) The prohibitions in this chapter shall be limited to individuals who are at least 40 years of age.

(b) In the case of any personnel action affecting employees or applicants for employment which is subject to the provisions of section 633a of this title, the prohibitions established in section 633a of this title shall be limited to individuals who are at least 40 years of age.

(c) (1) Nothing in this chapter shall be construed to prohibit compulsory retirement of any employee who has attained 65 years of age who, for the 2-year period immediately before retirement, is employed in a bona fide executive or a high policymaking position, if such employee is entitled to an immediate nonforfeitable annual retirement benefit from a pension, profit-sharing, savings, or deferred compensation plan, or any combination of such plans, of the employer of such employee, which equals, in the aggregate, at last $44,000.

(2) In applying the retirement benefit test of paragraph (1) of this subsection, if any such retirement benefit is in a form other than a straight life annuity (with no ancillary benefits), or if employees contribute to any such plan or make rollover contributions, such benefit shall be adjusted in accordance with regulations prescribed by the Secretary, after consultation with the Secretary of the Treasury, so that the benefit is the equivalent of a straight life annuity (with no ancillary benefits) under a plan to which employees do not contribute and under which no rollover contributions are made.

(d) Nothing in this Act shall be construed to prohibit compulsory retirement of any employee who has attained 70 years of age, and who is serving under a contract of unlimited tenure (or similar arrangement providing for unlimited tenure) at an institution of higher education (as defined by section 1141(a) of Title 20).[3]

---

[3] This section is repealed December 31, 1993. Pub. L. 99–592, § 6(b), 100 Stat. 3344 (1986).

Annual Report to Congress

Section 632.

The Equal Employment Opportunity Commission shall submit annually in January a report to the Congress covering its activities for the preceding year and including such information, data, and recommendations for further legislation in connection with the matters covered by this chapter as it may find advisable. Such report shall contain an evaluation and appraisal by the Commission of the effect of the minimum and maximum ages established by this chapter, together with its recommendations to the Congress. In making such evaluation and appraisal, the Commission shall take into consideration any changes which may have occurred in the general age level of the population, the effect of the chapter upon workers not covered by its provisions, and such other factors as it may deem pertinent.

Federal-State Relationship

Section 633.

(a) Nothing in this chapter shall affect the jurisdiction of any agency of any State performing like functions with regard to discriminatory employment practices on account of age except that upon commencement of action under this chapter such action shall supersede any State action.

(b) In the case of an alleged unlawful practice occurring in a State which has a law prohibiting discrimination in employment because of age and establishing or authorizing a State authority to grant or seek relief from such discriminatory practice, no suit may be brought under section 626 of this title before the expiration of sixty days after proceedings have been commenced under the State law, unless such proceedings have been earlier terminated: *Provided,* That such sixty-day period shall be extended to one hundred and twenty days during the first year after the effective date of such State law. If any requirement for the commencement of such proceedings is imposed by a State authority other than a requirement of the filing of a written and signed statement of the facts upon which the proceeding is based, the proceeding shall be deemed to have been commenced for the purposes of this subsection at the time such statement is sent by registered mail to the appropriate State authority.

Nondiscrimination on Account of Age in Federal Government Employment

Section 633a.

(a) All personnel actions affecting employees or applicants for employment who are at least 40 years of age (except personnel actions with regard to aliens employed outside the limits of the United States) in military departments as defined in section 102 of Title 5, in executive agencies as defined in section 105 of Title 5 (including employees and applicants for employment who are paid from nonappropriated funds), in the United States Postal Service and the Postal Rate Commission, in those units in the government of the District of Columbia having positions in the competitive service, and in those units of the legislative and judicial branches of the Federal Government having positions in the competitive service, and in the Library of Congress shall be made free from any discrimination based on age.

(b) Except as otherwise provided in this subsection, the Equal Employment Opportunity Commission is authorized to enforce the provisions of subsection (a) of this section through appropriate remedies, including reinstatement or hiring of employees with or without backpay, as will effectuate the policies of this section. The Civil Service Commission shall issue such rules, regulations, orders, and instructions as it deems necessary and appropriate to carry out its responsibilities under this section. The Equal Employment Opportunity Commission shall—

(1) be responsible for the review and evaluation of the operation of all agency programs designed to carry out the policy of this section, periodically obtaining and publishing (on at least a semiannual basis) progress reports from each department, agency, or unit referred to in subsection (a) of this section;

(2) consult with and solicit the recommendations of interested individuals, groups, and organizations relating to nondiscrimination in employment on account of age; and

(3) provide for the acceptance and processing of complaints of discrimination in Federal employment on account of age.

The head of each such department, agency, or unit shall comply with such rules, regulations, orders, and instructions of the Equal Employment Opportunity

Commission which shall include a provision that an employee or applicant for employment shall be notified of any final action taken on any complaint of discrimination filed by him thereunder. Reasonable exemptions to the provisions of this section may be established by the Commission but only when the Commission has established a maximum age requirement on the basis of a determination that age is a bona fide occupational qualification necessary to the performance of the duties of the position. With respect to employment in the Library of Congress, authorities granted in this subsection to the Equal Employment Opportunity Commission shall be exercised by the Librarian of Congress.

(c) Any person aggrieved may bring a civil action in any Federal district court of competent jurisdiction for such legal or equitable relief as will effectuate the purposes of this chapter.

(d) When the individual has not filed a complaint concerning age discrimination with the Commission, no civil action may be commenced by any individual under this section until the individual has given the Commission not less than thirty days' notice of an intent to file such action. Such notice shall be filed within one hundred and eighty days after the alleged unlawful practice occurred. Upon receiving a notice of intent to sue, the Commission shall promptly notify all persons named therein as prospective defendants in the action and take any appropriate action to assure the elimination of any unlawful practice.

(e) Nothing contained in this section shall relieve any Government agency or official of the responsibility to assure nondiscrimination on account of age in employment as required under any provision of Federal law.

(f) Any personnel action of any department, agency, or other entity referred to in subsection (a) of this section shall not be subject to, or affected by, any provision of this chapter, other than the provisions of section 631(b) of this title and the provisions of this section.

(g) (1) The Equal Employment Opportunity Commission shall undertake a study relating to the effects of the amendments made to this section by the Age Discrimination in Employment Act Amendments of 1978, and the effects of section 631(b) of this title.

(2) The Equal Employment Opportunity Commission shall transmit a report to the President and to the Congress containing the findings of the Commission resulting from the study of the Commission under paragraph (1) of this subsection. Such report shall be transmitted no later than January 1, 1980.

Glossary

Administrative Law Judges (ALJs). Members of a branch of the National Labor Relations Board (NLRB), called the Division of Judges, who are appointed for life and subject to the federal Civil Service Commission rules governing appointment and tenure. They conduct hearings and issue initial decisions on unfair labor practice complaints issued by the regional offices of the general counsel.

affirmative action plans. Arrangements by which an employer agrees to give preference in hiring or promotion of women or minorities. Affirmative action plans are generally set up to remedy prior discrimination in employment.

agency shop. A shop in which employees are not required to join the union but must at least pay the dues and fees required of union members.

ambulatory situs picketing. Picketing that follows the operation of the primary employer, rather than picketing only at a fixed location. For example, a union striking against a ready-mix concrete company would follow the mixer truck and picket near the truck when it was delivering a load of concrete at a construction site.

arbitration. Generally, the final step of the grievance procedure. In arbitration, disputes are settled by a neutral adjudicator chosen by both parties to the dispute.

authorization cards. Signed and dated cards that may simply state that the signatories desire a union certification election to be held; or the cards may state that the signing employee authorizes the union to be his or her bargaining representative.

bargaining unit. The group of employees for which the union seeks to acquire recognition as bargaining agent and to negotiate employment conditions.

bona fide occupational qualification (BFOQ). A particular characteristic about which an employer must demonstrate that business necessity requires an employee to be of a particular religion, sex, or national origin.

captive-audience speeches. Speeches given by representatives of the employer during working hours.

cease and desist order. An order issued by the NLRB when an ALJ finds that an employer or union has been engaging in unfair labor practices.

citation. A written citation issued by an OSHA inspector when an OSHA inspection reveals a violation of an OSHA standard. The citation describes the nature of the violation and may also include a fine.

closed shop. A shop in which all employees must be members of the union as a condition of employment.

closed shop agreements. Agreements by which an employer agrees with a union to hire only members of that union. Closed shop agreements are illegal under the National Labor Relations Act.

codes of fair competition. A collection of laws governing open, equitable, and just competition set up by the National Industrial Recovery Act of 1933.

commerce clause. The clause in the U.S. Constitution that permits Congress to pass laws in areas that affect interstate commerce.

common law. Legal rules and principles created by federal and state courts as opposed to statutory law passed by the legislatures.

common situs picketing. The picketing of an entire construction site by a union that has a dispute with the general contractor.

comparable worth. The principle that employees should receive equal pay for jobs of equal value.

confidential employee. As defined by the NLRB, employees who assist and act in a confidential capacity to persons who formulate, determine, and effectuate management policies in the field of labor relations.

consent election. A union representation election under the auspices of the NLRB, held at the consent of the employer and the interested union without the necessity of a representation hearing and board order.

consumer picketing. Picketing by the union that is directed at consumers, seeking to have them boycott the company with which the union has a dispute.

construct validity. A means of isolating and testing for specific traits or characteristics that are deemed essential for job performance.

content validity. A means of measuring whether the job requirement or test actually evaluates abilities required on the job.

contract bar rule. An NLRB rule that a current collective bargaining agreement between the employer and a union bars a decertification election—that is, a challenge to the incumbent union—for the term of the agreement.

contract compliance program. A Department of Labor program to ensure that employers doing work under government contracts conform to the antidiscrimination policies established by the federal government.

course of employment. A requirement that to be eligible for workers' compensation benefits, an employee must have been injured while serving the employer's business.

craft unit. A unit of employees for purposes of collective bargaining, consisting of all an employer's employees in a single craft or skill classification.

criminal conspiracy. A confederacy between two or more persons formed for the purpose of committing, by their joint efforts, some unlawful or criminal act.

criterion-related validity. Concerned with the statistical correlation between scores received on "paper and pencil" tests and job performance.

decertification. Withdrawal by the NLRB of a union's right to be a bargaining unit's exclusive representative, following a decertification election.

defamation. The communication or publication of an untruth. Written defamation is called libel, and spoken defamation is called slander.

defined benefit plan. A pension plan under which an employer agrees to pay a retired employee a specified amount each month.

defined contribution plan. A pension plan under which an employer agrees to contribute a specified amount into an account for each employee each month.

disability. A portion of regular wages or salary that an injured employee will be eligible to collect while recovering from an on-the-job injury. The amount of benefits depends on whether the disability is partial or total and temporary or permanent.

disparate impact. A situation that occurs when an employer specifies certain requirements for a job that operate to disqualify otherwise capable prospective employees, when those specified requirements do not actually relate to the employee's ability to perform the job (i.e., when neutral job requirements have a discriminatory effect).

disparate treatment. Intentional discrimination in employment, in which an individual is treated differently by the employer because of that individual's race, color, religion, sex, or national origin.

due process of law. The law in its regular course of administration through the courts of justice.

duty of fair representation. A judicially created obligation on the part of the union to fairly represent all employees of the bargaining unit.

economic strike. A strike for economic goals such as higher wages. This term is usually used in contrast to an unfair labor practice strike.

Employee Retirement Income Security Act (ERISA). The federal law governing the management of employee pension and welfare funds.

employerwide unit. A bargaining unit composed of all an employer's employees of a classification or classifications to be represented, at all the company's locations, facilities, or plants.

employment at will. Common law principle that an employee who does not have a contract for a specific period of time can be fired at any time for any reason.

equal protection. The equal protection of the laws of a state that is extended to persons within its jurisdiction, within the meaning of the constitutional requirement, when its courts are open to them on the same conditions as to others, with like rules of evidence and modes of procedure, for the security of their persons and property, the prevention and redress of wrongs, and the enforcement of contracts.

Excelsior list. A list that contains the names and home addresses of all employees eligible to vote in a consent election.

exempt employees. Executive, administrative, and professional employees who are paid a salary and who are not entitled to overtime pay under the Fair Labor Standards Act.

express contract. An employment contract, the terms of which are spelled out in detail by the contracting parties, usually in writing.

Fair Labor Standards Act (FLSA). The federal law governing child labor, minimum wages, and overtime compensation.

feasibility. The standards of safety promulgated by OSHA that must be feasible both technologically and economically. OSHA has the power to impose standards that force employers to adopt the most advanced technology available even though some individual employers may find adopting the standards economically unfeasible.

featherbedding. The practice of getting paid for services not performed or not to be performed.

fiduciary. Any person who exercises discretionary authority or control of a pension or benefit plan or renders authoritative advice with respect to a plan's assets.

Forty-eight hour rule. The NLRB rule that requires a party filing a petition for a certification election to submit evidence of a union demand for recognition, or of employee support for the union, to support the request for an election.

Four-Fifths Rule. A rule that compares the selection rates for the various protected groups under Title VII of the Civil Rights Act of 1964, stating that a disparate impact will be demonstrated when the proportion of applicants from the protected group with the lowest selection rate is less than 80 percent of the selection rate of the group with the highest selection rate.

full faith and credit doctrine. A rule of constitutional law that a judgment of a court of one state will be enforced, upon proper petition, by the courts of all the other states.

grievance. An injury, injustice, or wrong that gives ground for complaint because it is unjust and oppressive.

grievance process. A process set up to deal with complaints under the collective agreement; it is created by the parties to the agreement and can vary widely.

hiring hall. A job referral mechanism whereby employers rely upon unions to refer prospective employees. This practice is common in industries such as trucking, construction, and longshoring.

impasse. A deadlock reached in the course of sincere bargaining; in determining whether an impasse exists, the NLRB considers the number of times the parties have met, the likelihood of progress on the issue, the use of mediation, and so on.

implied contract. An employment contract, the terms of which are inferred from the conduct of the employer and the employee.

independent contractor. One who operates his or her own business and therefore is not an employee when providing services to another. Independent contractors are not covered by the workers' compensation insurance of the companies or persons that buy their services.

in-house union. A union that is organized, dominated, or controlled by the employer.

injunction (labor injunction). A writ issued by a court of equity, restraining the performance of a certain act, used in labor disputes by employers to prevent strikes or boycotts.

intentional infliction of emotional distress. A tort consisting of outrageous conduct that causes the victim severe emotional harm.

interest arbitration. Arbitration used to create a new agreement or to renew an existing one.

just cause. The requirement frequently found in express contracts (especially collective bargaining agreements) that an employee can be fired only for good and sufficient reason, such as willful misconduct.

laboratory conditions. Requirements of the NLRB so that neither side (union or management) engages in conduct that could unduly affect the employees' free choice.

lockout. A cessation of the furnishing of work to employees in an effort to get more desirable terms for the employer from the union.

managerial employees. Employees who formulate and effectuate management policies by expressing and making operative the decisions of their employer. Managerial employees are excluded from NLRB coverage.

mandatory bargaining subjects. Those subjects that "virtually affect the terms and conditions of employment" of the employees in the bargaining unit of a union.

minimum wage. The lowest hourly rate of pay employers are permitted to pay workers covered by the FLSA.

National Institute of Occupational Safety and Health (NIOSH). An agency of the federal government created to conduct research and promote its application to help ensure that workers do not suffer diminished health or reduced life expectancy.

National Industrial Recovery Act (NIRA). An early piece of New Deal legislation that, among other things, created the predecessor to the present NLRB.

National Labor Board. The forerunner of the NLRB. The National Labor Board was created under the National Industrial Recovery Act in 1933, and was abolished in 1934.

National Labor Relations Act. The legislative framework for industrial relations in the private sector. As used in this book, the term National Labor Relations Act includes the Wagner Act of 1935, the Taft-Hartley Act of 1947, and the Landrum-Griffin Act of 1959.

National Labor Relations Board (NLRB). An executive agency of the federal government, set up in 1935 by the National Labor Relations (Wagner) Act. Its purpose is to regulate and enforce provisions of the act, which established the right of labor to organize and bargain collectively with employers.

National Recovery Administration (NRA). A bureau of the federal government set up in 1933 by the National Industrial Recovery Act, to promote employment and recovery from the Depression. The NRA was to coordinate and

codify voluntary agreements among operators in various industries for fair standards of competition in prices, wages, hours of work, and so on, to prevail throughout a particular industry or business.

Norris–La Guardia Act. The federal law that put an end to the use of the federal labor injunction, which had reached epidemic proportions in the 1920s.

Occupational Safety and Health Administration (OSHA). The primary agency created for the enforcement of the Occupational Safety and Health Act. It is an independent agency within the Department of Labor, with authority to promulgate safety standards, inspect work places, and issue citations for safety violations.

Occupational Safety and Health Review Commission (OSHRC). A quasijudicial agency created to adjudicate contested enforcement actions of OSHA.

open season. The sixty-day period prior to the expiration of a collective bargaining agreement when the employees of a rival union can file a petition with the NLRB for an election to test the incumbent union's majority status.

overtime pay. One and one-half times an employee's regular rate of pay for hours in excess of forty worked in a single workweek.

patrolling. Another term for "walking the picket line."

permissive bargaining subjects. Those matters that are not directly related to wages, hours, terms, and conditions of employment.

picketing. The posting of members at all the approaches to the works struck against, for the purpose of observing and reporting the workers going to or coming from the works, and of using such influence as may be in their power to prevent the workers from accepting work there.

pressure tactics. Actions that include picketing, strikes, and boycotts by unions, and lockouts by employers.

prima facie case. Evidence that will suffice until contradicted and overcome by other evidence.

prohibited bargaining subjects. Those proposals that involve violations of the NLRA or other laws, for example, a union attempt to negotiate a closed shop provision.

prohibited transactions. Actions that plan fiduciaries are forbidden to engage in, such as to self-deal with the plan or to invest more than 10 percent of its assets in the securities of a participating employer.

qualified pension plan. A plan that gets preferential tax treatment by satisfying requirements established by the Internal Revenue Service.

Railway Labor Act. Legislation that governs the labor relations of the railroad and airline industries. The Railway Labor Act was passed in 1926.

recognition picketing. The action of picketing an employer for organizational or recognitional purposes when the union is not entitled to recognition under the NLRA.

rights arbitration. A situation in which the dispute involves the interpretation of an existing agreement rather than the creation of a new one.

right-to-work laws. Laws that prohibit union security agreements; where a state has passed such a law, union shop and agency shop agreements are illegal.

runaway shop. The practice of an employer closing shop in one location and opening in another to avoid unionization.

sex-plus discrimination. A situation occurring when an employer places additional requirements upon employees of a certain sex.

sexual harassment. A situation in which employees on the job are subjected to unwelcome sexual remarks, advances, or requests for sexual favors by co-workers or supervisors.

single-plant unit. A bargaining unit limited to the appropriate classification(s) of employees in just one of several of the employer's plants; such a unit is often appropriate when a company's plants are scattered over a broad geographic area.

Social security. Federal income support program started under Franklin Roosevelt's New Deal. Social security programs include retirement benefits and disability income payments.

strike. The act of quitting work by a body of workers for the purpose of coercing their employer to accede to some demand they have made on the employer and that he or she has refused.

super seniority. Preferential treatment given by an employer to union officers and stewards in the event of layoffs or recall of employees.

Twenty-four-hour silent period. A rule that the employer cannot conduct a captive-audience speech before his or her employees during the twenty-four hours immediately preceding a union representation election.

unemployment compensation. Benefits accumulated by the states through a tax imposed on employers and employees and paid to employees who lose their jobs through no fault of their own.

unfair labor practice. Any act that interferes with, restrains, or coerces employees in the exercise of their rights to self-organization; to form, join, or assist labor organizations; to bargain collectively through representatives of their own choosing; and to engage in concerted activities for the purpose of collective bargaining or other mutual aid or protection.

unfair labor practice strike. A work stoppage in protest of the employer's violation of the NLRA; in contrast to economic strikes, those participating in unfair labor practice strikes are entitled to reinstatement, even if the employer hired permanent replacements.

unfunded vested benefits. Pension benefits to which employees have a legal right in the future but for which adequate contributions to the plan have not yet been made.

Uniform Guidelines on Employee Selection Procedures. A series of regulations adopted by the EEOC and other federal agencies that set out the procedure to demonstrate the disparate impact of a job requirement known as the Four-Fifths rule.

union members' "bill of rights." Rights legislated by Congress to guarantee that union internal procedures are fair.

union security agreements. An arrangement in which an employer and a union agree that employees must either join the union or at least pay union dues in order to remain employees.

union shop. A shop in which none but members of a labor union are engaged as workers; a union shop agreement requires that all employees hired by the employer must join the union after a certain period of time, not less than thirty days.

union shop agreement. An agreement between an employer and a union that incorporates a union shop provision requiring employees to join the union within thirty days of their hiring.

union shop clause. A requirement that all present and future members of the bargaining unit become, and remain, union members; they must join the union after thirty days from the date on which they were hired.

vesting. The conveying to an employee pension benefits that become nonforfeitable following a minimum period of employment under the plan although the employee has no present right to collect the benefits.

voluntary recognition. A method of recognition whereby the union, in order to become the exclusive bargaining agent, needs to be designated or selected by a majority of the employees.

Weingarten rights. The rights of a unionized employee to have a union representative present during meetings with representatives of the employer that may result in disciplinary action against the employee.

whipsaw strike. A work stoppage that occurs when the union selectively strikes one firm in the industry; because the firm's competitors are not struck, they can continue to operate and draw business from the struck firm.

willful misconduct. Intentional misbehavior resulting in the discharge of an employee. Such behavior disqualifies the employee from collecting unemployment benefits.

withdrawal liability. The responsibility borne by an employer who has contributed to a multi-employer pension plan and who later seeks to terminate participation in the plan; the withdrawing employer must first pay his or her proportionate share of the plan's unfunded, vested benefits.

workers' compensation. Insurance that almost all American employers are required to carry for the protection of their employees in case of work-related accident or injury. The employee injured on the job is entitled to benefits whether or not the employer is at fault.

workweek. Seven consecutive days, which may commence with any day of the week and on which overtime pay is calculated.

wrongful discharge. The discharge of an employee for a reason that violates some public policy, thereby exposing the employer to tort liability.

yellow dog contract. A contract an employer requires an employee to sign that promises that, as a condition of employment, the employee will not join a union and will be discharged if he or she does join.

Index of Cases

Index of Subjects